Gambero Rosso®
Slow Food Editore

italianwines 2008

ITALIAN WINES 2008

GAMBERO ROSSO®- SLOW FOOD EDITORE

EDITORIAL STAFF FOR THE ORIGINAL EDITION
DANIELE CERNILLI AND GIGI PIUMATTI

SENIOR EDITORS
GIANNI FABRIZIO, TIZIANO GAIA, ELEONORA GUERINI, MARCO SABELLICO

TECHNICAL SUPERVISION
GILBERTO ARRU, DARIO CAPPELLONI, NICOLA FRASSON, GIANCARLO GARIGLIO, FABIO GIAVEDONI, VITTORIO MANGANELLI, RICCARDO VISCARDI, PAOLO ZACCARIA

MEMBERS OF FINAL TASTING PANELS
ALESSANDRO BOCCHETTI, ANTONIO BOCO, GIULIO COLOMBA, PAOLO DE CRISTOFARO, EGIDIO FEDELE DELL'OSTE, GIACOMO MOJOLI, NEREO PEDERZOLLI, LEONARDO ROMANELLI

CONTRIBUTORS
NINO AIELLO, GILBERTO ARRU, STEFANO ASARO, ANTONELLA BAMBA, VITTORIO BARBIERI, ENRICO BATTISTELLA, FRANCESCO BEGHI, ALESSANDRO BOCCHETTI, ANTONIO BOCO, SERGIO BONANNO, MICHELE BRESSAN, PASQUALE BUFFA, PAOLO CAMOZZI, DARIO CAPPELLONI, DIONISIO CASTELLO, DANIELE CERNILLI, ROBERTO CHECCHETTO, GRAZIANO CIPRIANO, GIULIO COLOMBA, PAOLO DE CRISTOFARO, GIANNI FABRIZIO, EGIDIO FEDELE DELL'OSTE, DARIO FERRO, FAUSTO FERRONI, CARLO FIORANI, NICOLA FRASSON, FABIO FUSINA, TIZIANO GAIA, PIETRO GARIBBO, GIANCARLO GARIGLIO, FABIO GIAVEDONI, ELEONORA GUERINI, VITO LACERENZA, MASSIMO LANZA, GIANCARLO LO SICCO, EUGENIO MAILLER, PATRIZIO MASTROCOLA, GIORGIO MELANDRI, GIACOMO MOJOLI, GIOVANNI NORESE, FRANCO PALLINI, DAVIDE PANZIERI, NEREO PEDERZOLLI, ANGELO PERETTI, NICOLA PICCININI, GUIDO PIRAZZOLI, GIGI PIUMATTI, MARIO PLAZIO, FABIO PRACCHIA, FRANCESCO QUERCETTI, PIERPAOLO RASTELLI, LEONARDO ROMANELLI, MARCO SABELLICO, DIEGO SORACCO, MAURIZIO STAGNITTO, HERBERT TASCHLER, RENATO TEDESCO, MASSIMO TOFFOLO, ANDREA VANNELLI, RICCARDO VISCARDI, MASSIMO VOLPARI, PAOLO ZACCARIA

MEMBERS OF REGIONAL TASTING PANELS
ANTONELLA AMODIO, BARBARA ANTOGNINI, ARTEMIO ASSIRI, EMIDIO BACHETTI, SALVATORE BASTA, ALBERTO BETTINI, DENNY BINI, TEODOSIO BUONGIORNO, REMO CAMURANI, GIUSEPPE CARRUS, SERGIO CECCARELLI, ANTONIO CIMINELLI, ENZO CODOGNO, VALENTINA CONGIU, GOFFREDO D'ANDREA, KATHRIN FEHERVARY, PIERO FIORENTINI, NATALE FIORINO, FRANCESCA GAMBERINI, LAURA GIORGI, DARIO LAURENZI, CRISTIANA LAURO, MIRCO MARCONI, MINO MARTUCCI, GIACOMO MAZZAVILLANI, ALESSIA MELI, DANIELE MEREU, ENZO MERZ, FABIO MONGARETTO, VANNI MURARO, UGO ONGARETTO, RENATO ORLANDO, RENATO ORLANDO, ROBERTO PALMIERI, LINA PAOLILLO, LIANO PETROZZI, SIMONE PETROZZI, DANIELA PIRANI, MAX PLETT, RENZO PRIORI, FILIPPO POLIDORI, VALENTINO RAMELLI, MAURIZIO ROSSI, ALESSANDRA RUGGI, BARBARA SCHIFFINI, PAOLO TRIMANI, PAOLO VALDASTRI, VINCENZO VERRASTRO, ALBERTO ZACCONE, MASSIMO ZECCHIN, SIMONE ZOLI

EDITING
DARIO CAPPELLONI, ELEONORA GUERINI, BIANCA MINERDO, VITTORIO MANGANELLI, PAOLO ZACCARIA

EDITORIAL COORDINATOR
GIORGIO ACCASCINA

LAYOUT
SIMONA PICCHIARELLI

TRANSLATIONS COORDINATED AND EDITED BY
GILES WATSON

TRANSLATORS
ANGELA ARNONE, MAUREEN ASHLEY, HELEN DONALD, DAVE HENDERSON, STEPHEN JACKSON, SARAH PONTING, GILES WATSON, AILSA WOOD

PUBLISHER
GAMBERO ROSSO, INC.
PRESIDENT STEFANO BONILLI
636 BROADWAY – SUITE 111 – NEW YORK, NY 10012
TEL. +1-212-253-5653 FAX +1-212-253-8349 – E-MAIL: GAMBEROUSA@AOL.COM

DISTRIBUTION
USA AND CANADA BY ANTIQUE COLLECTORS' CLUB, EASTWORKS, 116 PLEASANT ST # 18 EASTHAMPTON, MA 010207, USA;
UK ANBD AUSTRALIA BY ANTIQUE COLLECTORS' CLUB LTD – SANDY LANE, OLD MARTLESHAM WOODBRIDGE, SUFFOLK IP12 4SD – UNITED KINGDOM
TEL. +44-1394-389950 – FAX +44-1394-389999

ITALIAN WINES 2008
WAS CLOSED ON 20 SEPTEMBER 2007

PRINTED IN ITALY
FOR G. R. H. SPA IN JANUARY 2008
BY PFG GRAFICHE SPA – VIA CANCELLERIA, 62 – 00040 ARICCIA - ROME

3

CONTENTS

THE REGIONS

INDEXES

INTRODUCTION

Here we are again with edition number 21 of Italian wines. We're not sure if this is a record of any kind but it doesn't matter. We do know that in looking back over the history of what is almost unanimously considered to be the most influential publication on Italian wine, we also look back on the crucial moments that have affected the entire sector. The first, in the late 1980s and early 1990s, was piecing back together the image of Italian wine after the catastrophic methanol scandal that slashed more than 40 per cent off Italy's exports. Obviously, this is nothing in comparison with the loss of human life the crime caused but it is indicative of the loss of credibility Italian wine suffered worldwide. But at the same time, new producers were emerging. Often, they were growers who began to release wines made with their own grapes. At last, growers were becoming producers, too, and no longer sold their fruit to agents or buyers, some of whom had been ruined by the methanol scandal. Small growers began to assert themselves in Langhe, led at first by Bartolo Mascarello, who was not a new producer but did put the new movement on its feet. New wineries were springing up in Tuscany as the Supertuscans gained a market foothold for non-DOC wines made from grapes other than sangiovese. Finally, exciting grower-producers were also emerging in Friuli, such as Jermann, Gallo, Gravner and Dorigo. From 1995 to 2000, Italian wine was riding the crest of the wave. Wine had become fashionable and the American and Asian economies were booming. Remember those Asian Tigers? South Korea, Indonesia, Singapore and Japan were becoming seriously interesting markets. Demand for premium wine was soaring and with it prices, which got right out of hand. The trend began at Bordeaux with the 1995 en primeur; Italy and America were quick to follow suit. Tuscany became a promised land as wineries sprang up everywhere. Small producers in Piedmont mushroomed and areas that had previously been considered of secondary importance for premium winemaking suddenly gained prestige. Alto Adige whites, which were still relatively cheap, gained ground and major wineries appeared in the south of Italy, Planeta and Feudi di San Gregorio above all. It was in 2001, before 9/11, that the crisis started. For some months, few took much notice because Italy was now part of Euroland and dramatic price hikes were the order of the day in all sectors. Slowly, people realized that something had changed. The years of plenty were over and this was not just one of those business cycles that economists love. For a couple of years, many producers strove to keep prices high but then the German market collapsed after domestic consumption dropped. Things were little better in the United States and too many bottles were still in the cellar. The wines had been designed for international markets, with occasional excesses in terms of non-traditional grapes and invasive winemaking techniques. Then came the challenging 2003 vintage after an extremely hot, drought-ridden growing year and it was "full astern!" for the ship

INTRODUCTION

of Italian wine. The talk now was of tradition and native vines. Again, there were excesses and risks of a new, traditionalist anti-fashion. But there was also much very positive, utterly endorsable support for organic viticulture, biodynamics and less invasive winemaking procedures. And so we come, very swiftly, to the present day. In tasting many thousands of wines as we compiled each Guide, we have striven to communicate all this for 21 years. We have carried out a wide-ranging examination of the state of affairs in wine, adjusting our organization and approach to a topic that became increasingly complex with each passing year. The team that puts the Guide together each year now has almost 200 members, which is why there are now four senior editors. Gianni Fabrizio and Marco Sabellico have been joined by two younger experts, Eleonora Guerini – the first woman to have such a leading role in an Italian wine guide – and Tiziano Gaia, a long-standing contributor to Slow Food. In other respects, we have stuck to our usual procedure. Work began in May, when the regional tasting committees started to collect samples for evaluation at blind comparative tastings. We tried, wherever possible, to involve protection consortia, chambers of commerce and anyone else who could act as neutral guarantors for the collection of wines and the organization of tasting sessions. Around 70,000 bottles were collected all over Italy for this edition. They had to be sourced, conserved and masked for tasting after being divided into groups of similar wines. Readers can imagine how much work this involved. We also believe that the supervision of this phase by independent institutions is a very positive factor. Such bodies represent all the producers and scrutinize our operations to ensure they are carried out properly, safeguarding the interests of consumers and monitoring what we do, for which we are very grateful. We will thank all of them, in the hope that none are inadvertently omitted: the consortia of Chianti Classico, Brunello and Rosso di Montalcino, Vino Nobile di Montepulciano, Vernaccia di San Gimignano, Chianti Rufina, Morellino di Scansano, Montecucco, Monteregio di Massa Marittima, Franciacorta, Oltrepò Pavese, Valtellina, Soave and Valpolicella, the Enoteca Regionale del Roero, the Enoteca Regionale at Dozza, the Enoteca Regionale at Gattinara, the Istituto Agronomico Mediterraneo at Valenzano, Centro Agroalimentare Umbro at Foligno, the Bolzano Chamber of Commerce, the Avellino Chamber of Commerce, the Trento Chamber of Commerce, the Arezzo Chamber of Commerce, Assivip at Majolati Spontini, Vinea at Offida and the Anteprima group at Lucca. Then there are the Strada del Vino associations of Carmignano and Costa degli Etruschi, and Unioncamere at Matera. Private bodies include the Hotel Gallura at Olbia, the Reserve at Caramanico, the Vineria della Signora in Rosso at Nizza Monferrato, the Enoteca Grapes at Isernia and the Le Due Sorelle restaurant at Messina. If we add those who worked at the consortia to the roughly 130 tasters we deployed, it is obvious that a Guide like this requires

INTRODUCTION

the contribution of at least 250 individuals every year. In short, a whole lot of people. The 30 or so tasting panels, each comprising at least three judges, worked for about two months, tasting around 25,000 wines. Just under 10,000 wines were rejected outright and the rest were awarded scores ranging from zero to Two Glasses. In this first phase, we awarded points out of 100 and selected the roughly 1,500 wines that would go forward to the Three Glass taste-offs. At the end of this huge task, the final awards committee met. Made up of prominent figures on local tasting panels, the committee scrutinized all the wines sent to the finals. Again, all tastings were blind. The judgement here was more drastic: a yes or a no. Each decision was carefully justified. Every wine was discussed and analysed by all the members of the commission, whose votes had equal weight. For this Guide, the following panellists joined Daniele Cernilli, Gigi Piumatti, Gianni Fabrizio, Marco Sabellico, Eleonora and Tiziano Gaia for at least one of the three final taste-offs over a total of 15 days: Vittorio Manganelli, Dario Cappelloni, Nicola Frasson, Giulio Colomba, Giacomo Mojoli, Egidio Fedele dell'Oste, Leonardo Romanelli, Paolo Zaccaria, Fabio Giavedoni, Riccardo Viscardi, Giancarlo Gariglio, Antonio Boco, Paolo De Cristofaro, Alessandro Bocchetti and Nereo Pederzolli. Tastings were held at Città del Gusto in Rome, the Università del Gusto at Pollenzo and the Là di Petros restaurant at Colloredo di Monte Albano. We'll end with one or two notes on the 2008 edition of the Guide. Special awards went to Gaja for Winery of the Year, Mattia Vezzola for Oenologist of the Year, brothers Adriano and Stefano Dezi as Growers of the Year and Saverio Petrilli for Sustainable Viticulture. The top wines were Cavalleri's Franciacorta Collezione Esclusiva '99, our Sparkler of the Year, Dario Raccaro's Collio Tocai '06, the White of the Year, Palari's Faro '05, the Red of the Year, and Passito di Pantelleria Ben Ryé '06 from Donnafugata, our Sweet Wine of the Year. We would also point out the excellent performances by the various Barbaresco '04s and Brunello di Montalcino Riserva '01s, wines that are destined to feature in the cellars of wine lovers and experts for many years to come. Many Amarones from '01 and – unexpectedly – '03 were superb and there were fine showings from the '06 Soave and Verdicchio dei Castelli di Jesi wines. Timorasso dei Colli Tortonesi continues to gain ground thanks to the efforts of producers like Massa and Mariotto as does the other, cooler, south of Italy in zones like Taurasi, Vulture and Etna in particular. Abruzzo showed well with ten Three Glass prizes and Puglia, perhaps for the first time, put on a fine show with a record seven top awards. But the highest number of Three Glass prizes went to Tuscany, just ahead of Piedmont, which paid the price for only moderately good showings by some of its leading wines, Barolo above all. And now enjoy reading the Guide.

Daniele Cernilli and Gigi Piumatti

THREE GLASSES AWARDS 2008

VALLE D'AOSTA

Valle d'Aosta Chardonnay Cuvée Frissonnière		
Les Crêtes Cuvée Bois '05	Les Crêtes	21
Valle d'Aosta Chardonnay		
Élevé en Fût de Chêne '06	Anselmet	18

PIEDMONT

Barbaresco '04	Cantina del Pino	58
Barbaresco '04	Gaja	90
Barbaresco Bric Balin '04	Moccagatta	117
Barbaresco Coparossa '04	Bruno Rocca	143
Barbaresco Currà '04	Sottimano	156
Barbaresco Gallina '04	Oddero	126
Barbaresco Rombone '04	Fiorenzo Nada	123
Barbaresco Ronchi '04	Ronchi	145
Barbaresco S. Stefanetto '04	Piero Busso	54
Barbaresco Sorì Burdin '04	Fontanabianca	88
Barbaresco Sorì Paitin '04	Paitin	128
Barbaresco V. Starderi '04	La Spinetta	157
Barbaresco V. Valeirano '04	La Spinetta	157
Barbaresco Valgrande '04	Ca' del Baio	55
Barbaresco Vign. in Montestefano Ris. '01	Produttori del Barbaresco	36
Barbaresco Vign. Loreto '04	Albino Rocca	142
Barbera d'Alba Ciabot du Re '05	F.lli Revello	140
Barbera d'Alba Sup. '05	Filippo Gallino	91
Barbera d'Asti Bricco dell'Uccellone '05	Braida	48
Barbera d'Asti Pomorosso '05	Coppo	77
Barbera d'Asti Sup. Alfiera '05	Marchesi Alfieri	30
Barbera d'Asti Sup. Nizza Favà '04	Garetto	92
Barbera del M.to Sup. Bricco Battista '04	Giulio Accornero e Figli	28
Barolo Bricco Boschis V. S. Giuseppe Ris. '01	F.lli Cavallotto	66
Barolo Bricco Parussi Ris. '01	Gianfranco Bovio	48
Barolo Brunate '03	Poderi Marcarini	111
Barolo Cannubi Boschis '03	Luciano Sandrone	149
Barolo Enrico VI '03	Monfalletto Cordero di Montezemolo	119
Barolo Fantini Ris. '01	Attilio Ghisolfi	95
Barolo Ginestra V. Casa Maté '03	Elio Grasso	101
Barolo Gran Bussia Ris. '01	Aldo Conterno	74
Barolo Le Coste Mosconi '03	Armando Parusso	128
Barolo Le Gramolere Ris. '01	Giovanni Manzone	110
Barolo Le Rocche del Falletto Ris. '01	Bruno Giacosa	95
Barolo Monfortino Ris. '00	Giacomo Conterno	75
Barolo Percristina '01	Domenico Clerico	71
Barolo Rocche dell'Annunziata Ris. '01	Paolo Scavino	152
Barolo Sarmassa '03	Giacomo Brezza & Figli	49
Barolo V. Gallinotto '03	Mauro Molino	118
Barolo V. Rionda Ris. '01	Vigna Rionda - Massolino	167
Barolo Vigneto Rocche '03	Renato Corino	78
Barolo Villero Ris. '01	Vietti	167
Barolo Voghera Brea Ris. '01	Azelia	35
Boca '03	Le Piane	132
Bramaterra I Porfidi '03	Sella	155
Colli Tortonesi Bianco Costa del Vento '05	Vigneti Massa	169
Colli Tortonesi Bianco Pitasso '05	Claudio Mariotto	113
Gattinara Vign. S. Francesco '03	Antoniolo	32
Ghemme Collis Breclemae '00	Antichi Vigneti di Cantalupo	31
Langhe La Villa '05	Elio Altare - Cascina Nuova	31
Langhe Nebbiolo Costa Russi '04	Gaja	90
Langhe Rosso Bric du Luv '05	Ca' Viola	57
Langhe Rosso Luigi Einaudi '04	Einaudi	84
Monferrato Rosso Rivalta '04	Villa Sparina	171
Monferrato Rosso Sonvico '04	Cascina La Barbatella	37

THREE GLASSES AWARDS 2008

THREE GLASSES AWARDS 2008

VENETO

Amarone della Valpolicella Cl. Calcarole '03	Guerrieri Rizzardi	343
Amarone della Valpolicella '01	Marion	347
Amarone della Valpolicella Case Vecie '03	Brigaldara	324
Amarone della Valpolicella Cl. '03	Allegrini	317
Amarone della Valpolicella Cl. '03	Lorenzo Begali	319
Amarone della Valpolicella Cl. '00	Cav. G. B. Bertani	321
Amarone della Valpolicella Cl. '98	Giuseppe Quintarelli	359
Amarone della Valpolicella Cl. Mazzano '01	Masi	348
Bianco di Custoza Sup. Amedeo '05	Cavalchina	332
Breganze Cabernet Sauvignon Palazzotto '05	Maculan	345
Breganze Cabernet Vign. Due Santi '05	Vigneto Due Santi	374
Capitel Croce '05	Roberto Anselmi	318
Colli Euganei Merlot		
Sassonero Villa Alessi '05	Ca' Lustra	327
Colli Euganei Rosso Calaóne '05	Ca' Orologio	327
Montello e Colli Asolani		
Il Rosso dell'Abazia '04	Serafini & Vidotto	365
Recioto della Valpolicella Cl. Acinatico '04	Stefano Accordini	316
Soave Cl. Calvarino '05	Leonildo Pieropan	357
Soave Cl. La Froscà '06	Gini	342
Soave Cl. Le Bine de Costjola '05	Tamellini	368
Soave Cl. Monte Carbonare '06	Suavia	367
Soave Cl. Monte Fiorentine '06	Ca' Rugate	328
Soave Cl. Monte Grande '06	Prà	358
Soave Cl. Monte Tondo '06	Monte Tondo	351
Soave Cl. Vign. Du Lot '05	Inama	344
Soave Monte Ceriani '05	Tenuta Sant'Antonio	364
Valpolicella Cl. Sup. Caterina Zardini '05	Giuseppe Campagnola	329
Valpolicella Sup. Roccolo Grassi '04	Roccolo Grassi	360

FRIULI VENEZIA GIULIA

Blanc des Rosis '06	Schiopetto	444
Breg Anfora '03	Gravner	418
Capo Martino '05	Jermann	420
COF Bianco Sacrisassi '05	Le Due Terre	413
COF BiancoSesto '06	La Tunella	452
COF Rosso Celtico '04	Moschioni	425
COF Rosso Montsclapade '04	Girolamo Dorigo	412
COF Tocai Friulano V. Storico '06	Adriano Gigante	417
COF Tocai Friulano Zuc di Volpe '06	Volpe Pasini	464
COF Verduzzo Friulano Cràtis '04	Roberto Scubla	445
Collio Bianco Broy '06	Eugenio Collavini	407
Collio Bianco Fosarin '06	Ronco dei Tassi	439
Collio Merlot Graf de La Tour '04	Villa Russiz	461
Collio Pinot Bianco '06	Castello di Spessa	448
Collio Pinot Grigio '06	Branko	399
Collio Sauvignon '06	Oscar Sturm	449
Collio Tocai Friulano '03	La Castellada	405
Collio Tocai Friulano '06	Colle Duga	407
Collio Tocai Friulano '06	Edi Keber	421
Collio Tocai Friulano '06	Doro Princic	433
Collio Tocai Friulano '06	Franco Toros	452
Collio Tocai Friulano Ronco delle Cime '06	Venica & Venica	454
Collio Tocai Friulano Vigna del Rolat '06	Dario Raccaro	434
Fiore di Campo '06	Lis Neris	422
Friuli Grave Merlot Vistorta '05	Vistorta	464
Friuli Isonzo Tocai Friulano '06	Ronco del Gelso	439
Gortmarin '03	Borgo San Daniele	397
Morus Nigra Refosco P. R. '05	Vignai da Duline	458

THREE GLASSES AWARDS 2008

EMILIA ROMAGNA

C. P. Vin Santo Albarola Val di Nure '97	Conte Otto Barattieri di San Pietro	472
Colli di Rimini Cabernet Montepirolo '04	San Patrignano	493
Papiano di Papiano '04	Villa Papiano	501
Sangiovese di Romagna Sup. Michelangiolo Ris. '04	Calonga	475
Sangiovese di Romagna Sup. Pietramora Ris. '04	Fattoria Zerbina	502

TUSCANY

Acciaiolo '04	Castello d'Albola	510
Bolgheri Rosso Sup. Grattamacco '04	Grattamacco	564
Bolgheri Sassicaia '04	Tenuta San Guido	612
Bolgheri Sup. Argentiera '04	Argentiera	512
Bolgheri Sup. Ornellaia '04	Tenuta dell'Ornellaia	586
Brancaia Il Blu '05	Brancaia	526
Brunello di Montalcino Cerretalto '01	Casanova di Neri	536
Brunello di Montalcino Fontelontano Ris. '01	Collemattoni	546
Brunello di Montalcino Phenomena Ris. '01	Sesti - Castello di Argiano	617
Brunello di Montalcino Poggio al Vento Ris. '99	Tenuta Col d'Orcia	545
Brunello di Montalcino Ris. '01	Biondi Santi - Tenuta Il Greppo	522
Brunello di Montalcino Ris. '01	Canalicchio di Sopra	529
Brunello di Montalcino Ris. '01	Donna Olga	553
Brunello di Montalcino Ris. '01	Eredi Fuligni	561
Brunello di Montalcino Ris. '01	Innocenti	567
Brunello di Montalcino Ris. '01	Il Palazzone	587
Brunello di Montalcino Ris. '01	Poggio Antico	595
Brunello di Montalcino Ris. '01	Podere Brizio	593
Brunello di Montalcino Ris. Vigna del Paretaio '01	Talenti	620
Brunello di Montalcino Ugolaia '01	Lisini	571
Brunello di Montalcino V. di Pianrosso Ris. '01	Ciacci Piccolomini D'Aragona	543
Caberlot '04	Podere Il Carnasciale	532
Camalaione '04	Le Cinciole	544
Camartina '04	Querciabella	604
Castello del Terriccio '04	Castello del Terriccio	622
Chianti Cl. Castello di Brolio '04	Barone Ricasoli	518
Chianti Cl. Castello di Fonterutoli '04	Castello di Fonterutoli	557
Chianti Cl. Coltassala Ris. '04	Castello di Volpaia	636
Chianti Cl. Il Margone Ris. '04	Il Molino di Grace	580
Chianti Cl. La Casuccia '04	Castello di Ama	511
Chianti Cl. Poggio ai Frati Ris. '04	Rocca di Castagnoli	607
Chianti Cl. Poggio Rosso Ris. '03	San Felice	611
Chianti Cl. Rancia Ris. '04	Fattoria di Felsina	556
Chianti Cl. Ris. '04	Badia a Coltibuono	513
Chianti Cl. Ris. '04	Livernano	571
Chianti Cl. Ris. '04	La Madonnina - Triacca	574
Chianti Cl. Ris. '04	Rietine	606
Colline Lucchesi Tenuta di Valgiano '04	Tenuta di Valgiano	629
Cortona Il Bosco '04	Tenimenti Luigi D'Alessandro	550
d'Alceo '04	Castello dei Rampolla	604
FSM '04	Castello di Vicchiomaggio	631
Galatrona '05	Fattoria Petrolo	591
I Sodi di San Niccolò '03	Castellare di Castellina	538
Il Decennale '01	Poggio di Sotto	597
Il Pareto '04	Tenute Ambrogio e Giovanni Folonari	557
La Gioia '04	Riecine	605
Le Pergole Torte '04	Montevertine	583
Lupicaia '04	Castello del Terriccio	622
Masseto '04	Tenuta dell'Ornellaia	586
Modus '04	Tenimenti Ruffino	608
Montevertine '04	Montevertine	583

THREE GLASSES AWARDS
2008

Morellino di Scansano Rovente '05	Col di Bacche	544
Nobile di Montepulciano Asinone '04	Poliziano	600
Nobile di Montepulciano Nocio dei Boscarelli '04	Poderi Boscarelli	524
Nobile di Montepulciano Salco Evoluzione '01	Salcheto	609
Oreno '05	Tenuta Sette Ponti	618
Petra Rosso '04	Petra	590
Rocca di Frassinello '05	Rocca di Frassinello	607
Saffredi '04	Fattoria Le Pupille	602
Sant'Antimo Mandrielle '04	Castello Banfi	516
Tignanello '04	Marchesi Antinori	512
Val di Cornia Rosso l'Rennero '05	Gualdo del Re	566
Veneroso '04	Tenuta di Ghizzano	563
Vignamaggio '04	Villa Vignamaggio	635
Vin Santo '95	Avignonesi	513

MARCHE

Conero Sassi Neri Ris. '04	Fattoria Le Terrazze	697
Rosso Piceno Sup. Roggio del Filare '04	Velenosi	699
Solo Sangiovese '05	Fattoria Dezi	678
Verdicchio dei Castelli di Jesi Cl. Le Vaglie '06	Santa Barbara	694
Verdicchio dei Castelli di Jesi Cl. Pietrone Ris. '04	Vallerosa Bonci	699
Verdicchio dei Castelli di Jesi Cl. Plenio Ris. '04	Umani Ronchi	698
Verdicchio dei Castelli di Jesi Cl. Sup. Il Priore '06	Sparapani - Frati Bianchi	695
Verdicchio dei Castelli di Jesi Cl. Sup. Misco '06	Tenuta di Tavignano	697
Verdicchio dei Castelli di Jesi Cl. Villa Bucci Ris. '05	Bucci	669
Verdicchio di Matelica Collestefano '06	Collestefano	674
Vespro '05	Fausti	679

UMBRIA

Calanco '03	Tenuta Le Velette	725
Cervaro della Sala '05	Castello della Sala	721
Merlot '05	Castello delle Regine	720
Montefalco Sagrantino '04	Còlpetrone	711
Montefalco Sagrantino '04	Perticaia	718
Montefalco Sagrantino 25 Anni '04	Arnaldo Caprai	708
Montiano '05	Falesco	713
Torgiano Rosso Vigna Monticchio Ris. '03	Lungarotti	714

LAZIO

Grechetto Latour a Civitella '05	Sergio Mottura	735
Il Vassallo '05	Colle Picchioni - Paola Di Mauro	733

ABRUZZO

Montepulciano d'Abruzzo '02	Valentini	759
Montepulciano d'Abruzzo Colline Teramane Adrano '05	Villa Medoro	761
Montepulciano d'Abruzzo Colline Teramane Neromoro Ris. '03	Bruno Nicodemi	753
Montepulciano d'Abruzzo Colline Teramane Zanna Ris. '03	Dino Illuminati	752
Montepulciano d'Abruzzo San Calisto '05	Valle Reale	760
Montepulciano d'Abruzzo Tonì '04	Luigi Cataldi Madonna	747
Montepulciano d'Abruzzo Villa Gemma '04	Masciarelli	752
Pecorino '05	Luigi Cataldi Madonna	747
Trebbiano d'Abruzzo '04	Valentini	759
Trebbiano d'Abruzzo Castello di Semivicoli '05	Masciarelli	752

MOLISE

Molise Don Luigi '05	Di Majo Norante	767

THREE GLASSES AWARDS 2008

CAMPANIA

Costa d'Amalfi Furore Bianco Fiorduva '06	Cantine Gran Furor Divina Costiera	777
Falerno del Massico Bianco Vigna Caracci '05	Villa Matilde	788
Greco di Tufo '06	Pietracupa	782
Greco di Tufo Cutizzi '06	Feudi di San Gregorio	776
Greco di Tufo Novaserra '06	Mastroberardino	780
Irpinia Serpico '05	Feudi di San Gregorio	776
Montevetrano '05	Montevetrano	781
Taurasi Radici Ris. '01	Mastroberardino	780
Taurasi V. Macchia dei Goti '04	Antonio Caggiano	771
Terra di Lavoro '05	Galardi	777

BASILICATA

Aglianico del Vulture Basilisco '04	Basilisco	798
Aglianico del Vulture Gudarrà '04	Bisceglia	799
Aglianico del Vulture Titolo '05	Elena Fucci	801
Aglianico del Vulture Vign. Serpara '03	Terre degli Svevi	803

PUGLIA

Artas '05	Castello Monaci	816
Castel del Monte Rosso V. Pedale Ris. '04	Torrevento	820
Graticciaia '03	Agricole Vallone	820
Lui '05	Cantina Albea	809
Masseria Maime '05	Tormaresca	819
Primitivo di Manduria Dunico Masseria Pepe '05	Accademia dei Racemi	808
Salice Salentino Rosso Selvarossa Ris. '04	Cantina Due Palme	811

CALABRIA

Gravello '05	Librandi	830
Scavigna Vigna Garrone '04	G.B. Odoardi	831

SICILY

Burdese '05	Planeta	850
Contea di Sclafani Rosso del Conte '04	Tasca d'Almerita	852
Contessa Entellina Milleunanotte '04	Donnafugata	842
Etna Rosso Feudo di Mezzo Quadro delle Rose '05	Tenuta delle Terre Nere	853
Etna Rosso Serra della Contessa '04	Benanti	839
Faro Palari '05	Palari	848
Franchetti '05	Passopisciaro	849
Il Drappo '04	Benanti	839
Litra '04	Abbazia Santa Anastasia	838
Neromàccarj '04	Gulfi	846
Noà '05	Cusumano	842
Passito di Pantelleria Ben Ryé '06	Donnafugata	842
Quater Rosso '05	Firriato	844
Ramione '04	Baglio di Pianetto	838
Sàgana '05	Cusumano	842

SARDINIA

Carignano del Sulcis Sup. Terre Brune '03	Cantina Sociale di Santadi	874
Dettori Rosso '04	Tenute Dettori	867
Radames '01	Antichi Poderi Jerzu	870
Vernaccia di Oristano Antico Gregori	Attilio Contini	866

THE YEAR'S BEST WINE

THE SPARKLER
FRANCIACORTA COLLEZIONE ESCLUSIVA '99 – CAVALLERI

THE WHITE
COLLIO TOCAI FRIULANO '06 – RACCARO

THE RED
FARO '05 – PALARI

THE SWEET
MOSCATO PASSITO DI PANTELLERIA BEN RYÉ '06 – DONNAFUGATA

WINERY OF THE YEAR

GAJA

OENOLOGIST OF THE YEAR

MATTIA VEZZOLA

UP-AND-COMING WINERY

CA' OROLOGIO

BEST PRICED WINE

A. A. PINOT BIANCO PRAESULIS '06 – GUMPHOF

GROWERS OF THE YEAR

ADRIANO AND STEFANO DEZI

AWARD FOR SUSTAINABLE VITICULTURE

SAVERIO PETRILLI

THE STARS

In the Guide's 21-year history, some 90 wineries have earned
Three Glasses at least ten times. Heading the list is Angelo Gaja, who this year brought
his total to 41 and added a fourth Star. That was one very compelling reason for Gaja's
Winery of the Year award. There was a third Star for Maurizio Zanella's Ca' del Bosco,
the king of Franciacorta sparklers. Valentini won a second Star.
This benchmark Abruzzo winery is now in the hands of the legendary Edoardo's heir,
his son Francesco, who shows that he, too, can deliver superb Montepulcianos
and Trebbianos. Eight wineries picked up their first Star: Avignonesi, with yet another
marvellous Vin Santo; Elena Walch, queen of Gewürztraminer; Tenuta Col d'Orcia with
an unimpeachable Poggio al Vento; Le Pupille, a cellar that is driven by the sheer energy
of its owner, Elisabetta Geppetti; Rabajà from Bruno Rocca, a modern Barbaresco maker;
Vietti, the traditional side of Barolo; Elio Grasso, the supreme interpreter of Barolo from
Monforte; and Mastroberardino, one of Italian wine's outstanding cellars. Many more
famous names have eight or nine awards and are homing in on a Star, including Duca
di Salaparuta, Frescobaldi, Sella & Mosca, Castellare di Castellina and many more.

★ ★ ★ ★
41
GAJA (PIEDMONT)

★ ★ ★
32
LA SPINETTA (PIEDMONT)

30
CA' DEL BOSCO (LOMBARDY)

★ ★
26
ALTARE (PIEDMONT)

23
ALLEGRINI (VENETO)
CASTELLO DI FONTERUTOLI (TUSCANY)

22
CASTELLO DI AMA (TUSCANY)

21
FATTORIA DI FELSINA (TUSCANY)

20
VALENTINI (ABRUZZO)

★
19
ANTINORI (TUSCANY)
CLERICO (PIEDMONT)
DORIGO (FRIULI VENEZIA GIULIA)
FEUDI DI SAN GREGORIO (CAMPANIA)
JERMANN (FRIULI VENEZIA GIULIA)
POLIZIANO (TUSCANY)
C. P. SAN MICHELE APPIANO (ALTO ADIGE)
VILLA RUSSIZ (FRIULI VENEZIA GIULIA)

18
CASTELLO DELLA SALA (UMBRIA)
GRAVNER (FRIULI VENEZIA GIULIA)
PLANETA (SICILY)
TENUTA SAN GUIDO (TUSCANY)

17
CASTELLO BANFI (TUSCANY)
BELLAVISTA (LOMBARDY)
GIACOMO CONTERNO (PIEDMONT)
FERRARI (TRENTINO)
MASCIARELLI (ABRUZZO)
VIE DI ROMANS (FRIULI VENEZIA GIULIA)

16
LA BARBATELLA (PIEDMONT)
LIVIO FELLUGA (FRIULI VENEZIA GIULIA)
TENUTA FONTODI (TUSCANY)
TENUTA DELL'ORNELLAIA (TUSCANY)
TENIMENTI RUFFINO (TUSCANY)
PAOLO SCAVINO (PIEDMONT)
SCHIOPETTO (FRIULI VENEZIA GIULIA)

15
CORREGGIA (PIEDMONT)
DAL FORNO (VENETO)

ISOLE E OLENA (TUSCANY)
PIEROPAN (VENETO)
TASCA D'ALMERITA (SICILY)
C. P. TERMENO (ALTO ADIGE)

14
C. P. COLTERENZIO (ALTO ADIGE)
MIANI (FRIULI VENEZIA GIULIA)
QUERCIABELLA (TUSCANY)
ROBERTO VOERZIO (PIEDMONT)

13
ANSELMI (VENETO)
ARGIOLAS (SARDINIA)
CAPRAI (UMBRIA)
CASTELLO DEL TERRICCIO (TUSCANY)
ALDO CONTERNO (PIEDMONT)
CONTERNO FANTINO (PIEDMONT)
BRUNO GIACOSA (PIEDMONT)
MACULAN (VENETO)
NINO NEGRI (LOMBARDY)
BARONE RICASOLI (TUSCANY)
RONCO DEL GELSO (FRIULI VENEZIA GIULIA)

12
MONTEVERTINE (TUSCANY)
MONTEVETRANO (CAMPANIA)
TENUTA SAN LEONARDO (TRENTINO)
C. P. SANTA MADDALENA/CANTINA DI BOLZANO
(ALTO ADIGE)
UBERTI (LOMBARDY)
LE VIGNE DI ZAMÒ (FRIULI VENEZIA GIULIA)

11
BRICCO ASILI BRICCO ROCCHE (PIEDMONT)
CA' VIOLA (PIEDMONT)
C. P. CALDARO (ALTO ADIGE)
CASANOVA DI NERI (TUSCANY)
CHIARLO (PIEDMONT)
LES CRÊTES (VALLE D'AOSTA)
FALESCO (UMBRIA)
FORADORI (TRENTINO)
LA MASSA (TUSCANY)
PRUNOTTO (PIEDMONT)
QUINTARELLI (VENETO)
CASTELLO DEI RAMPOLLA (TUSCANY)
ROCCHE DEI MANZONI (PIEDMONT)
SANDRONE (PIEDMONT)
SERAFINI & VIDOTTO (VENETO)
VENICA & VENICA (FRIULI VENEZIA GIULIA)
FATTORIA ZERBINA (EMILIA ROMAGNA)

10
AVIGNONESI (TUSCANY)
TENUTA COL D'ORCIA (TUSCANY)
GAROFOLI (MARCHE)
ELIO GRASSO (PIEDMONT)
TENUTA J. HOFSTÄTTER (ALTO ADIGE)
LE MACCHIOLE (TUSCANY)
MASTROBERARDINO (CAMPANIA)
LE PUPILLE (TUSCANY)
BRUNO ROCCA (PIEDMONT)
TUA RITA (TUSCANY)
VIETTI (PIEDMONT)
WALCH (ALTO ADIGE)

A GUIDE TO VINTAGES 1971-2004

	BARBARESCO	BRUNELLO DI MONTALCINO	BAROLO	CHIANTI CLASSICO	NOBILE DI MONTEPULCIANO	AMARONE
1971	●●●●	●●●	●●●●●	●●●●●	●●●●	●●●●
1974	●●●●	●●	●●●●	●●●	●●●	●●●●
1975	●●	●●●●●	●●	●●●●	●●●●	●●●
1977	●●	●●●●	●●	●●●●	●●●●	●●●
1978	●●●●●	●●●●	●●●●●	●●●●●	●●●●●	●●●
1979	●●●●	●●●●	●●●●	●●●●	●●●●	●●●●
1980	●●●●	●●●●	●●●●	●●●●	●●	●●●
1981	●●●	●●●	●●●	●●●	●●●	●●●
1982	●●●●●	●●●●●	●●●●●	●●●●	●●●●	●
1983	●●●●	●●●●	●●●●	●●●●	●●●●	●●●●●
1985	●●●●●	●●●●●	●●●●●	●●●●●	●●●●●	●●●●
1986	●●●	●●●	●●●	●●●●	●●●●	●●●
1988	●●●●●	●●●●●	●●●●●	●●●●●	●●●●●	●●●●●
1989	●●●●●	●●	●●●●●	●	●	●●
1990	●●●●●	●●●●●	●●●●●	●●●●●	●●●●●	●●●●●
1991	●●●	●●●	●●●	●●●	●●●	●●
1993	●●●	●●●●	●●●	●●●●	●●●●●	●●●●
1995	●●●●	●●●●●	●●●●	●●●●●	●●●●●	●●●●
1996	●●●●●	●●●	●●●●●	●●●	●●●	●●●
1997	●●●●	●●●●●	●●●●	●●●●●	●●●●●	●●●●●
1998	●●●●	●●●●	●●●●	●●●●	●●●	●●●●
1999	●●●●●	●●●●●	●●●●●	●●●●●	●●●●●	●●●
2000	●●●●	●●●	●●●●	●●●	●●●	●●●●
2001	●●●●●	●●●●●	●●●●●	●●●●●	●●●●●	●●●
2002	●●	●	●	●	●	●●
2003	●●●	●●●	●●●	●●●	●●●	●●●
2004	●●●●●	●●●●●	●●●●●	●●●●●	●●●●●	●●●●

HOW TO USE THE GUIDE

WINERY FIGURES

ANNUAL PRODUCTION
HECTARES UNDER VINE
VITICULTURE METHOD

KEY

○ WHITE WINES
⊙ ROSÉ WINES
● RED WINES

RATINGS

LISTING WITHOUT A GLASS SYMBOL:
A WELL-MADE WINE OF AVERAGE QUALITY IN ITS CATEGORY

♟
ABOVE AVERAGE TO GOOD IN ITS CATEGORY, EQUIVALENT TO 70-79/100

♟♟
VERY GOOD TO EXCELLENT IN ITS CATEGORY, EQUIVALENT TO 80-89/100

♟♟
VERY GOOD TO EXCELLENT WINE SELECTED FOR FINAL TASTINGS

♟♟♟
EXCELLENT WINE IN ITS CATEGORY, EQUIVALENT TO 90-99/100

WINES RATED IN PREVIOUS EDITIONS OF THE GUIDE ARE INDICATED
BY WHITE GLASSES (♟, ♟♟, ♟♟♟), PROVIDED THEY ARE STILL DRINKING AT
THE LEVEL FOR WHICH THE ORIGINAL AWARD WAS MADE

STAR ★

INDICATES WINERIES THAT HAVE WON TEN **THREE GLASS** AWARDS
FOR EACH STAR

PRICE RANGES (1) (2)

1 UP TO $ 4.20 AND UP TO £ 2.45
2 FROM $ 4.21 TO $ 6.00 AND FROM £ 2.46 TO £ 3.50
3 FROM $ 6.01 TO $ 9.00 AND FROM £ 3.51 TO £ 5.25
4 FROM $ 9.01 TO $ 15.60 AND FROM £ 5.26 TO £ 9.10
5 FROM $ 15.61 TO $ 24.00 AND FROM £ 9.11 TO £ 14.00
6 FROM $ 24.01 TO $ 36.00 AND FROM £ 14.01 TO £ 21.00
7 FROM $ 36.01 TO $ 48.00 AND FROM £ 21.01 TO £ 28.00
8 MORE THAN $ 48.01 AND MORE THAN £ 28.01
(1) Approx. retail prices in USA and UK (2) € 1,00 = $ 1.20 = £ 0.70

ASTERISK *
INDICATES ESPECIALLY GOOD VALUE FOR MONEY

NOTE
PRICES INDICATED REFER TO RETAIL AVERAGES. INDICATIONS OF PRICE NEXT
TO WINES ASSIGNED WHITE GLASSES (AWARDS MADE IN PREVIOUS EDITIONS)
TAKE INTO ACCOUNT APPRECIATION OVER TIME WHERE APPROPRIATE

ABBREVIATIONS

A. A.	Alto Adige
C.	Colli
Cl.	Classico
C.S.	Cantina Sociale
Cant.	Cantina
CEV	Colli Etruschi Viterbesi
Cast.	Castello
COF	Colli Orientali del Friuli
Cons.	Consorzio
Coop.Agr.	Cooperativa Agricola
C. B.	Colli Bolognesi
C. P.	Colli Piacentini
Et.	Etichetta
M.	Metodo
M.to	Monferrato
OP	Oltrepò Pavese
P.R.	Peduncolo Rosso
P.	Prosecco
Rif. Agr.	Riforma Agraria
Ris.	Riserva
Sel.	Selezione
Sup.	Superiore
TdF	Terre di Franciacorta
V.	Vigna
Vign.	Vigneto
V. T.	Vendemmia Tardiva

VALLE D'AOSTA

One of life's major challenges is accepting your destiny. In a region where 70 per cent of the wine produced is red, it must be tough to admit that the highest quality comes from the whites. The situation gets even more complicated when you realize that the local cuisine is almost exclusively based on meat dishes, often game, giving strong, mountain flavours. Then there's the fact that practically all the wines are consumed locally, and tourism is the major source of income. Talking with the valley's producers, though, you realize that most are well aware of the potential of their whites. The imbalance stood out even more markedly in our tastings this year because the '05 vintage was not a great one for reds. The harvest was marred by rain, so much so that few wines have reached their usual quality levels. There are two Three Glasses wines this year, neither of them new to the honour. Indeed, Costantino Charrère's Chardonnay picked up its ninth consecutive award, an achievement that puts it ahead of most of Italy's top names. The wine merits all the accolades heaped on it, of course, but so does its producer, a strong-willed man of passion whose skills go beyond winemaking to embrace business expertise, communications and promotion, in which he is active at regional level. But more than anything else, Costantino is a wine man in the purest sense of the word. In paying tribute to him we also pay tribute to all those who have made their mark in the development of high quality winemaking in Italy and other parts of Europe. The other Three Glass prize went to the oak-aged Chardonnay produced by Giorgio Anselmet and his father Renato. The award is starting to become a pleasant habit for this family of small growers from Villeneuve – it's the third in three years – who have the great assets of open-mindedness and willingness to experiment. But the good news doesn't end with top awards. There are other reasons to be proud of what's happening in the region. There are increasing numbers of small producers making their living entirely from winemaking, and Maurizio Fiorano and Michel Vallet just two of them. Long-standing producers – Grosjean is a case in point – are not giving ground. Quite the reverse, for they are back on the attack. There has been a steady build-up of quality at the Cave des Onze Communes under the guidance of president Dino Darensod, which earned it a full profile. The Coopérative de l'Enfer has also recently entered come under the umbrella of Cave du Vin Blanc, adding strength to the role of Morgex and Chambave as the driving force of the co-operative sector. All in all, it's a positive situation for a region that wants to expand its current ambit and open itself up to the market, the public and the future.

Anselmet

FRAZ. LA CRÊTE, 194
11018 VILLENEUVE [AO]
TEL. 3484127121
www.maisonanselmet.vievini.it

L'Atoueyo

LOC. URBAINS, 8
11010 AYMAVILLES [AO]
TEL. 0165902550
www.atoueyo.vievini.it

ANNUAL PRODUCTION 35,000 bottles
HECTARES UNDER VINE 5
VITICULTURE METHOD   Conventional

Despite the plaudits heaped on them recently, Giorgio Anselmet and his father Renato are not resting on their laurels. Indeed, they're redoubling their efforts. At the end of 2007, work will be starting on a new, more spacious cellar since operating in the current one is rather like tightrope walking. They're also working on new vinification techniques for some of the whites, with extended skin maceration for the Pinot Grigio, for example. There is to be no change with the Chardonnay, though, and this year's is again spectacular. All elegance, savoury, and with vanilla and butter notes magnificently melded into its mineral tones, it fully deserves its third consecutive Three Glasses. Le Prisonnier, from super-ripe petit rouge, fumin, mayolet and cornalin, is also excellent, with great impact and well-nuanced fruit. It won Two Glasses, as do the highly concentrated, dense Henri and Arline, the latter softly sweet on both nose and palate without ever falling into the trap of becoming cloying. Stéphanie, from traminer, is distinctive, recalling wild rose and passion fruit. Everything else is invitingly well styled.

ANNUAL PRODUCTION 20,000 bottles
HECTARES UNDER VINE 2
VITICULTURE METHOD   Conventional

L'Atoueyo is one of the newest privately owned wineries in Valle d'Aosta. Despite its youth, the wines are already beginning to show reliably well in our tastings. Actually, it's rare for a bottle to disappoint, prompting us to assert confidently that the wines from Fernanda Saraillon, her husband Guido Jerusel and their son Omar are both high quality and enviably consistent. Again this year, the most distinguished bottle in the range is the complex Fumin, which has a fine nose of leather and wet dog. The Chardonnay, which sees no oak, is nicely deep, with attractive floral hints and a succulent, inviting palate. The Torrette is another wine of great substance. This, and the high quality of its grapes, which create a wine of great typicity that firmly reflects is provenance, again brought it a Two Glass prize. The overall quality of the range is borne out by the inviting character of the less ambitious wines, like the Gamay and the Pinot Noir, which are centred on liveliness and drinkability.

○ Valle d'Aosta Chardonnay Élevé en Fût de Chêne '06	♟♟♟ 6
○ Arline Flétrì '05	♟♟ 6
● Le Prisonnier '05	♟♟ 7
● Valle d'Aosta Pinot Noir '06	♟♟ 5
● Valle d'Aosta Syrah Henri '05	♟♟ 6
● Valle d'Aosta Pinot Gris '06	♟♟ 5
○ Stéphanie '06	♟♟ 4*
● Valle d'Aosta Petit Rouge '06	♟ 4
● Valle d'Aosta Torrette '06	♟ 5
○ Valle d'Aosta Chardonnay Élevé en Fût de Chêne '05	♟♟♟ 6
○ Valle d'Aosta Chardonnay Élevé en Fût de Chêne '04	♟♟♟ 5
● Le Prisonnier '04	♟♟ 6
● Le Prisonnier '03	♟♟ 6

○ Valle d'Aosta Chardonnay '06	♟♟ 4*
● Valle d'Aosta Fumin '05	♟♟ 5
● Valle d'Aosta Torrette '06	♟♟ 4*
● Valle d'Aosta Gamay '06	♟ 4
● Valle d'Aosta Pinot Noir '06	♟ 4
○ Valle d'Aosta Chardonnay '05	♟♟ 4
● Valle d'Aosta Fumin '04	♟♟ 5
○ Valle d'Aosta Chardonnay '04	♟♟ 4
● Valle d'Aosta Fumin '03	♟♟ 5

La Crotta di Vegneron
P.ZZA RONCAS, 2
11023 CHAMBAVE [AO]
TEL. 016646670
www.lacrotta.it

Di Barrò
LOC. CHÂTEAU FEUILLET, 8
11010 SAINT-PIERRE [AO]
TEL. 0165903671
www.vievini.it

ANNUAL PRODUCTION 320,000 bottles
HECTARES UNDER VINE 37
VITICULTURE METHOD Conventional

ANNUAL PRODUCTION 17,000 bottles
HECTARES UNDER VINE 2.5
VITICULTURE METHOD Conventional

There has been an increase in the vineyard area supplying this major co-operative and a corresponding rise in the quality of the wines. All its 130 or so members have played their part in achieving this, supporting president Elio Cornaz and technical director Andrea Costa. This year, it is the Fumin that takes centre stage. It reached the finals, mostly thanks to its distinctive nose, with firm notes of cocoa powder, leather and tobacco that meld into scents of wild red berry fruits. Even though previous releases of the Moscato Passito have been better, the wine is again very attractive, with no hint of cloying and a bitter almond finish. Malvoisie Flètri has good structure. Chambave Supérieur Quatre Vignobles, from petit rouge with a little gamay, pinot noir and fumin, and Nus Superieur Crème, from vien di Nus and petit rouge, are both inviting and full of personality. Best of the dry whites are the highly perfumed, varietal Muscat and the mineral Nus Malvoisie. The other wines tasted are all early drinkers but far from simplistic.

Andrea Barmaz and his wife Elvira Rini are probably the Valle d'Aosta producers who pay most attention to ensuring that their grape cultivation is clean. The fine quality of their fruit has led to wines that, right from their first appearance, have always been full of personality. The wines submitted this year have a stylistic purity, especially on the nose, which they have only rarely achieved in the past. We were bowled over by the Fumin, one of the best in the valley, with its fruity aromas of great finesse and a palate that turns on attractiveness while retaining great complexity. The invigorating, very deep Torrette Supérieur is also first-rate, as is Mayolet, from the indigenous grape of the same name. The Barmaz family have been putting great efforts into this variety since they first started winemaking and it's now producing one of the region's best wines, with nuances of leather and sweet tobacco. The fruity, rounded Chardonnay and the sweet Lo Flapi, which has intense pear aromas, stand proudly beside it.

Wine	Rating
● Valle d'Aosta Fumin Esprit Follet '05	♔♔ 5
● Valle d'Aosta Chambave Sup. Quatre Vignobles '05	♔♔ 4*
● Valle d'Aosta Nus Sup. Crème '05	♔♔ 4*
○ Valle d'Aosta Chambave Moscato Passito '05	♔♔ 6
○ Valle d'Aosta Chambave Muscat '06	♔♔ 4*
○ Valle d'Aosta Nus Malvoisie '06	♔♔ 4*
○ Valle d'Aosta Nus Malvoisie Flètrì '06	♔♔ 6
● Valle d'Aosta Cornalin '06	♔ 4
● Valle d'Aosta Nus Rouge '06	♔ 4
○ Valle d'Aosta Müller Thurgau '06	♔ 4
○ Valle d'Aosta Chambave Moscato Passito '04	♔♔ 6
○ Valle d'Aosta Chambave Moscato Passito '03	♔♔ 6
● Valle d'Aosta Fumin Esprit Follet '04	♔♔ 5

Wine	Rating
○ Lo Flapì '05	♔♔ 6
○ Valle d'Aosta Chardonnay '06	♔♔ 4*
● Valle d'Aosta Fumin '05	♔♔ 5
● Valle d'Aosta Mayolet '06	♔♔ 4*
● Valle d'Aosta Torrette Sup. Clos de Château Feuillet '05	♔♔ 5
● Valle d'Aosta Torrette '06	♔ 4
● Valle d'Aosta Torrette Sup. V. de Torrette '05	♔ 7
● Valle d'Aosta Petit Rouge '06	♔ 4
● Valle d'Aosta Fumin '04	♔♔ 5
● Valle d'Aosta Torrette Sup. V. de Torrette '04	♔♔ 7
● Valle d'Aosta Torrette Sup. Clos de Château Feuillet '04	♔♔ 5
○ Valle d'Aosta Chardonnay '05	♔ 4

Feudo di San Maurizio
FRAZ. MAILLOD, 44
11010 SARRE [AO]
TEL. 3383186831
www.feudo.vievini.it

ANNUAL PRODUCTION 40,000 bottles
HECTARES UNDER VINE 6
VITICULTURE METHOD Conventional

This estate was founded in 1989 by three friends who took on the challenge of producing fine wine in the municipality of Sarre. Just one of the original three remains, Michel Vallet, who cultivates his vines full-time. This is unusual, given the large number of part-time growers in the area, but encouraging. We particularly liked the whites in the range submitted, especially the aromatic ones. Grappillon, from 100 per cent traminer, impressed the tasting panel with its intense varietal aromas, its remarkable complexity on the palate and its outstandingly attractive style. The Müller Thurgau is fresh and easy-drinking without being simplistic. The Chardonnay, too, is attractive, even though the vanilla from the oak and the fruit are not yet perfectly balanced. Two Glasses also went to Mayolet and the sweet Pierrots, the latter made from petit rouge and fumin left to dry on the vine until December. Saro Djablo and Fumin are nice wines but not as good as last year's releases.

F.lli Grosjean
VILLAGGIO OLLIGNAN, 1
11020 QUART [AO]
TEL. 0165775791
www.grosjean.vievini.it

ANNUAL PRODUCTION 70,000 bottles
HECTARES UNDER VINE 7
VITICULTURE METHOD Conventional

The Grosjeans have finally recovered from the problems of the last few years when a mysterious fungus infected their cellars and imparted the unmistakeable smell of rot to their wines. They now again have a full range and, although not everything is perfect, the wines are generally pleasant and characterful. The one that earned most approval was the Fumin, a wine of great length, with tobacco, leather and ripe red berry fruit. Blanc de Dauphin, based on moscato and müller thurgau, is varietal and complex, with aromas of orange peel and wild rose. We preferred last year's Petite Arvine to this year's version, but there was no decline in the heady, deeply perfumed Torrette Vigne Rovetta. The Pinot Noir did not come up to its usual standard but the Pinot Gris, with fresh, inviting acidity, is lovely. The Gamay is an easy drinker.

O Grapillon '06	♥♥	4*
O Valle d'Aosta Chardonnay '06	♥♥	4*
O Valle d'Aosta Müller Thurgau '06	♥♥	4*
● Valle d'Aosta Mayolet '06	♥♥	4*
● Pierrots '05	♥♥	5
● Saro Djablo '05	♥	4
● Valle d'Aosta Fumin '05	♥	5
● Saro Djablo '04	♥♥	4
● Valle d'Aosta Fumin '04	♥♥	4

O Blanc de Dauphin '06	♥♥	4*
O Valle d'Aosta Pinot Gris		
V. Creton '06	♥♥	4*
● Valle d'Aosta Fumin '05	♥♥	5
● Valle d'Aosta Torrette Sup.		
V. Rovetta '06	♥♥	4*
● Valle d'Aosta Gamay '06	♥	4
O Valle d'Aosta Petite Arvine		
V. Rovetta '06	♥	5
● Valle d'Aosta Fumin '04	♥♥	5
● Valle d'Aosta Fumin '03	♥♥	4

★ Les Crêtes
LOC. VILLETOS, 50
11010 AYMAVILLES [AO]
TEL. 0165902274
www.lescretesvins.it

Lo Triolet
LOC. JUNOD, 7
11010 INTROD [AO]
TEL. 016595437
www.lotriolet.vievini.it

ANNUAL PRODUCTION 220,000 bottles
HECTARES UNDER VINE 25
VITICULTURE METHOD Conventional

ANNUAL PRODUCTION 30,000 bottles
HECTARES UNDER VINE 3
VITICULTURE METHOD Conventional

Costantino Charrère's wines, long regarded as simply the best in the Valle d'Aosta, are now also gaining national visibility. And that doesn't just mean the Chardonnay Cuvée Bois, for Costantino comes up with a new gem every year. The latest is a truly memorable version of the Pinot Gris, which has intense minerality and superb fragrance and power, confirming just how well this variety suits the region. But it's the Cuvée Bois that really keeps the Charrère banner aloft. The nose brings grapefruit, aniseed and golden delicious apple aromas to join the characteristic gentle oakiness. The palate, its fruit and oak in good balance, is simply great. All this explains why the wine achieves its ninth consecutive Three Glasses. Our compliments to Costantino. The non-oaked Chardonnay made a fine impression, too, showing succulent with an intense nose. Syrah lovers won't be disappointed by the rounded Coteau La Tour with its fruity aromas and silky tannins. There's more good news from the all cherry and leather Fumin. But everything reflects the estate's well-deserved fame.

After gaining Three Glasses for his Pinot Gris last year, Marco Martin saw no reason to stand still and has continued to experiment. He decided to make a slight change to its vinification method, keeping the must longer on the skins. The result is a wine with an inviting golden-tinged hue. Exuberant, enticing aromas of pear usher in a succulent palate which has acid backbone of great elegance and attractiveness, retaining great freshness. The new MonAtout also scored very highly. Made solely from traminer, a variety which isn't exactly at home in the valley, it nonetheless has the classic, varietal characteristics of roses and lychees. The two oak-aged wines are also well up to speed: the Pinot Gris, with vanilla, pear tart and broom, and Coteau Barrage, from syrah with a little fumin . The rest of the range is reasonable, with Nus Rouge, made from vien di Nus and petit rouge, deserving a special round of applause.

Wine	Rating	Score
○ Valle d'Aosta Chardonnay Cuvée Frissonnière Les Crêtes Cuvée Bois '05	♟♟♟	7
○ Valle d'Aosta Pinot Gris V. Brulant '06	♟	4*
○ Valle d'Aosta Chardonnay Cuvée Frissonnière Les Crêtes '06	♟♟	4*
● Coteau La Tour '05	♟♟	5
○ Les Abeilles '05	♟♟	6
● La Sabla '05	♟♟	4
○ Valle d'Aosta Petite Arvine V. Champorette '06	♟♟	4
● Valle d'Aosta Fumin V. La Tour '05	♟♟	6
● Valle d'Aosta Torrette V. Les Toules '06	♟	4
○ Valle d'Aosta Chardonnay Cuvée Frissonnière Les Crêtes Cuvée Bois '04	♟♟♟	6
○ Valle d'Aosta Chardonnay Cuvée Frissonnière Les Crêtes Cuvée Bois '03	♟♟♟	6
○ Valle d'Aosta Chardonnay Cuvée Frissonnière Les Crêtes Cuvée Bois '02	♟♟♟	6
○ Valle d'Aosta Pinot Gris '06	♟♟	4*
○ Valle d'Aosta Pinot Gris Élevé en Fût de Chêne '06	♟♟	5
○ MonAtout '06	♟♟	4*
● Valle d'Aosta Nus Rouge '06	♟♟	4*
● Valle d'Aosta Coteau Barrage '06	♟♟	5
● Valle d'Aosta Gamay '06	♟	4
● Valle d'Aosta Pinot Noir '06	♟	4
○ Valle d'Aosta Pinot Gris '05	♟♟♟	4
○ Valle d'Aosta Pinot Gris Élevé en Fût de Chêne '05	♟♟	5
○ Valle d'Aosta Pinot Gris Élevé en Fût de Chêne '04	♟♟	5
● Valle d'Aosta Coteau Barrage '05	♟♟	5
● Valle d'Aosta Coteau Barrage '04	♟♟	5
● Coteau Barrage '03	♟♟	5

Cave des Onze Communes

LOC. URBAINS, 14
11010 AYMAVILLES [AO]
TEL. 0165902912
www.caveonzecommunes.it

ANNUAL PRODUCTION 400,000 bottles
HECTARES UNDER VINE N.A.
VITICULTURE METHOD Certified organic

The Cave des Onze Communes is the largest co-operative in the region both in terms of the number of members, which stands at 220, and output. The average quality of the wines has increased considerably in the past few years, mainly thanks to the efforts of president Dino Darensod and skilled winemakers Massimo Bellocchia and Luciano Vada. A large range of wines was submitted, the reds led by the three oak-aged examples, which all gained Two Glasses. The Fumin is intense and full-bodied, with aromas of cherry, tobacco and leather; the full, fruity Pinot Noir has blackcurrant, violet and plum nuances; and the ripe, succulent Torrette Superiore is full of black cherry, pepper and cinnamon. Moving on to the whites, we really enjoyed the fresh, zesty attractiveness of the Petite Arvine, one of the best in the valley. The late-harvest Le Chapìteau is inviting. The main characteristics of other wines are their wonderful drinkability and their value for money, which few in the region can touch.

Cave du Vin Blanc de Morgex et de La Salle

LA RUINE
CHEMIN DES ÎLES, 19
11017 MORGEX [AO]
TEL. 0165800331
www.caveduvinblanc.com

ANNUAL PRODUCTION 170,000 bottles
HECTARES UNDER VINE 20
VITICULTURE METHOD Conventional

There are several changes underway at this co-operative. The most important is the restoration of one of the most spectacular, indeed epic, vineyards in the region, Plagne, which is going to be converted first to organic and then to biodynamic viticulture. There's a major agreement with the Enfer d'Arvier co-operative whereby Morgex's Gianluca Telloli will now be dedicating some of his time to managing the technical side over at Arvier. Moving on to the wines, the two selections, Rayon, with its highly attractive aromas of spring flowers and white-fleshed fruit, and the more lemony, mineral, austere Vini Estremi, both stand out. The sparkling wine that ages five years on its lees wasn't available but the Brut and Extra Brut were. Neither of them currently seems particularly complex but they are very attractive. Chaudelune is most unusual, being aged in different woods. The juicy, easy-drinking Metodo Ancestral, from gamay, made in conjunction with La Crotta, is also atypical.

● Valle d'Aosta Fumin '05	♟♟ 4*
● Valle d'Aosta Torrette Sup. '05	♟♟ 4*
○ Le Chapìteau '05	♟♟ 6
● Valle d'Aosta Pinot Noir '05	♟♟ 4*
○ Valle d'Aosta Petite Arvine '06	♟♟ 4*
○ Valle d'Aosta Pinot Gris '06	♟ 3
● Valle d'Aosta Petit Rouge '06	♟ 4
● Valle d'Aosta Gamay '06	♟ 4
● Valle d'Aosta Torrette Biologico '06	♟ 3
● Valle d'Aosta Fumin '04	♟♟ 4
● Valle d'Aosta Pinot Noir '04	♟♟ 4
○ Valle d'Aosta Petite Arvine '05	♟ 4

○ Valle d'Aosta Blanc de Morgex et de La Salle M. Cl. Extra Brut '05	♟♟ 5
○ Valle d'Aosta Blanc de Morgex et de La Salle Vini Estremi '06	♟♟ 4*
○ Valle d'Aosta Blanc de Morgex et de La Salle Rayon '06	♟♟ 4*
○ Valle d'Aosta Blanc de Morgex et de La Salle '06	♟ 3
○ Valle d'Aosta Blanc de Morgex et de La Salle M. Cl. Brut '05	♟ 4
○ Chaudelune Vin de Glace '04	♟ 5
● Metodo Ancestral '06	♟ 5
○ Valle d'Aosta Blanc de Morgex et de La Salle Rayon '05	♟♟ 4

OTHER WINERIES

Brégy & Gillioz
VIA VERGNOD, 7
11010 SAINT-PIERRE [AO]
TEL. 0041763786668
www.grain-noble.ch

Brégy and Gillioz, from Switzerland, set up this estate in 2001. They make just one wine and it immediately impressed our tasters. It's from petite arvine grapes left to dry on the vine and in the cellar. It has now had a name change, for legal reasons, but in essence remains unaltered in style and quality.

- ○ Référence '05 — 🍷🍷 6
- ○ Podium '04 — 🍷🍷 6
- ○ Podium '03 — 🍷🍷 6

Le Château Feuillet
LOC. CHÂTEAU FEUILLET
11010 SAINT-PIERRE [AO]
TEL. 0165903905
www.chateaufeuillet.vievini.it

Young Maurizio Fiorano again shows his skills as a winemaker with a range of well-made, good quality wines. We especially liked the fruity, spicy Fumin and the enjoyably succulent Torrette. The Petite Arvine is a touch under par. The Chardonnay is fragrant.

- ● Valle d'Aosta Torrette '06 — 🍷🍷 4*
- ● Valle d'Aosta Fumin '05 — 🍷🍷 4*
- ○ Valle d'Aosta Chardonnay '06 — 🍷 4
- ○ Valle d'Aosta Petite Arvine '06 — 🍷 4

Coopérative de l'Enfer
VIA CORRADO GEX, 65
11011 ARVIER [AO]
TEL. 016599238
www.coenfer.it

The major news here is that Enfer is now under the wing of nearby Cave du Vin Blanc, where the technical team, led by Gianluca Telloli, is sure to be making a contribution. Perhaps the change explains the slight quality improvements and the considerable expansion of the range, led by Pinot Gris and Mayolet.

- ● Valle d'Aosta Enfer d'Arvier Clos de Enfer '05 — 🍷🍷 5
- ● Valle d'Aosta Mayolet Vins de Seigneurs '06 — 🍷🍷 4*
- ○ Valle d'Aosta Pinot Gris '06 — 🍷 4

Diego Curtaz
FRAZ. VISERAN, 61
11020 GRESSAN [AO]
TEL. 0165251079
www.diegocurtazvini.it

For years, Diego Curtaz has been made a good Torrette that regularly earns Two Glasses. The fairly complex nose has cherry, blackberry and blackcurrant, and the palate is full and structured, finishing long. Dï Meun, from petit rouge, vuillermin, vien di Nus, cornalin, gamay and mayolet, is enjoyable.

- ● Valle d'Aosta Torrette '06 — 🍷🍷 4*
- ● Dï Meun '06 — 🍷 4

Caves Cooperatives de Donnas
VIA ROMA, 97
11020 DONNAS [AO]
TEL. 0125807096
www.donnasvini.it

Vieilles Vignes is in a different style, and a different quality band, from the other wines submitted by this co-operative. There's red berry fruit, cherry in particular, and plentiful minerality. The basic Donnas is also good.

- ● Valle d'Aosta Donnas '04 — 🍷🍷 4*
- ● Valle d'Aosta Donnas Sup. Vieilles Vignes '03 — 🍷🍷 5

Institut Agricole Régional
RÉGION LA ROCHÈRE, 1A
11100 AOSTA [AO]
TEL. 0165215811
www.iaraosta.it

One function of this leading institute is research into the traditional varieties that have driven viticulture in the valley. There were 23 wines this year, some of them scoring lower than in the past. Nevertheless, we were highly impressed by the Fumin and Petite Arvine.

- ○ Valle d'Aosta Petite Arvine '06 — 🍷🍷 4*
- ● Valle d'Aosta Fumin '05 — 🍷🍷 5
- ● Sang des Salasses '06 — 🍷 5
- ○ Valle d'Aosta Chardonnay '05 — 🍷🍷 4

OTHER WINERIES

Cooperativa La Kiuva
FRAZ. PIED DE VILLE, 42
11020 ARNAD [AO]
TEL. 0125966351
lakiuva@libero.it

Just like last year, the quality of Arnad-Montjovet is better than good but the rest of the range still needs work. The '05 is long, with zip and succulence, and inviting blackberry and cherry fruit. The Chardonnay is fruity and easy drinking with butter and banana dominating the nose.

● Valle d'Aosta		
Arnad-Montjovet Sup. '05	♥♥	4*
○ Valle d'Aosta Chardonnay '06	♥	3

Costantino Praz
FRAZ. TURILLE, 17
11020 JOVENCAN [AO]
TEL. 0165250358
www.vievini.it

Costantino Praz's new wine, a Pinot Gris that we tasted for the first time this year, is quite interesting but there's still plenty of room for improvement. The cherry-and-strawberry Pinot Noir and the tannic, structured Torrette are as inviting as ever. The Gamay is easy drinking.

● Valle d'Aosta Pinot Noir '06	♥♥	4*
● Valle d'Aosta Torrette '06	♥♥	5
● Valle d'Aosta Gamay '06	♥	4
○ Valle d'Aosta Pinot Gris '06	♥	4

Vigneti Rosset
LOC. TORRENT DE MAILLOUD, 4
11020 QUART [AO]
TEL. 016577411

Nicola Rosset is a prominent dealer in the spirits sector. He started producing wine a few years ago and the first results are encouraging. There's a pleasant, fruity Chardonnay, a full-bodied Syrah with hints of wild berries and pepper, and a nicely complex Cornalin that is full on the finish.

● Valle d'Aosta Syrah '06	♥♥	4*
● Valle d'Aosta Cornalin '06	♥	4
○ Valle d'Aosta Chardonnay '06	♥	4

Maison Albert Vevey
FRAZ. VILLAIR
S.DA DEL VILLAIR, 67
11017 MORGEX [AO]
TEL. 0165808930
www.vievini.it

Mario and Mirko Vevey run this tiny, attractive winery tucked away in the mountains. The only wine they produce is Blanc de Morgex et de La Salle and the '06 is savoury and juicy, gaining length from an acidic, but not too tart, palate.

○ Valle d'Aosta Blanc de Morgex		
et de La Salle '06	♥♥	4*

Marziano Vevey
V.LE DEL CONVENTO
11017 MORGEX [AO]
TEL. 0165808931
www.vievini.it

The skilled Marziano Vevey continues to produce very good wines and this year one of them again earned Two Glasses. It's a pale straw with green tinges; the nose is strongly mineral, and has Alpine flowers and chamomile. The palate is refreshingly acidic.

○ Valle d'Aosta Blanc de Morgex		
et de La Salle '06	♥♥	4*

La Vrille
LOC. GRANGEON, 1
11020 VERRAYES [AO]
TEL. 0166543018
www.lavrille-agritourisme.com

Hervé and Luciana Deguillame have created an oasis of peace in the hills above Chambave, opening a farm holiday centre with a small restaurant for guests. Last year, they started vinifying their own grapes and first results are promising, especially for the fragrant Muscat. A dried-grape version will follow.

○ Valle d'Aosta Chambave		
Muscat '06	♥♥	4*
● Valle d'Aosta Cornalin '05	♥	4

PIEDMONT

Piedmont's stamp on the Guide this year stems more from evidence of character than a raft of fine vintages. The wonderful '04 aside, producers have had to tussle with years that were anything but memorable: His Majesty Barolo had to trudge through the blistering heat of 2003, Barbera d'Alba and d'Asti needed to leverage the talent of their makers to emerge decently from an iffy '05, and '06 is merely a promise on the horizon. To get a bit of fat onto the otherwise lean pickings, we had only the Barolo Riservas of long-ago '01. So let us start, for once, by talking about vintages and not provenance. Let us also restate a concept that's as old as the hills: for good or ill, despite having reached the 21st century, and whatever else is boiling in the pot, be it technological progress, investment or producers' experience, there is still going to be year-on-year variation in wine. One vintage, '01, has brought us pearls of great price, pearls that will long be talked about, adding another dimension to the concept of time. And another vintage, '04, is giving us everything you could want from a great wine. Indeed, it was '04 that brought us the lively elegance of the many Barbarescos that we adored – and there are 15 with top honours, the largest number ever – and the richly succulent acidity of the Barberas, and the harmonious fleshiness of the high fliers from Langhe and Monferrato. From a geographical standpoint, we see nebbiolo looking great in all its shapes and forms: Roero, rather than Barbera territory, is becoming again a land of Roero; and in the north, the variety has thrown off its Cinderella's rags and is dancing at the ball dressed as Boca, Ghemme, Gattinara and Bramaterra. If our thoughts then turn to territory it is Alessandria that leaps to mind. After years of a frankly incomprehensible torpor, it is unleashing some of the best whites we've ever tasted, not just superb Timorassos but brilliant Gavis, too. There are also reds of class, including a Barbera, Accornero's Bricco Battista, and a Monferrato Rosso, Villa Sparina's Rivalta, which we hope will be the trigger for the zone to secure a recognizable style and a much higher reputation. We have two further points to raise. The first regards dolcetto, a variety that still doesn't quite know where it stands. Should it be lively or austere, young or aged, oaked or unoaked? The courageous stance of Dogliani producers over the new DOCG is apposite here, and now that the year of tastings is over we shall be eagerly following the development of the more important wines as they come to market. Our second point is a tribute to Angelo Gaja, that most lucid of visionaries and the tireless driving force of an entire category. Without him, the tale unfolding in these pages would probably be very different. May he enjoy his fourth star as it shines over his coronation as Winery of the Year. He deserves it.

Abbona

B.TA SAN LUIGI, 40
12063 DOGLIANI [CN]
TEL. 0173721317
www.abbona.com

ANNUAL PRODUCTION 255,000 bottles
HECTARES UNDER VINE 44
VITICULTURE METHOD Conventional

The Abbona family is an unstoppable war machine. Marziano leads a heavyweight team of family and technicians and has created one of the most comprehensive ranges in the Langhe. Now, having inaugurated his superbly landscaped, beautifully finished, wonderfully spacious new cellars last year, he's working on some new treats for us. I think we can reveal that there will be a classic method sparkler, and that Marziano seems to be pouring all his proverbial enthusiasm into it. In the meantime, we've been digging through his range, to very good effect. Despite unofficial pre-tastings proclaiming a bright future for Dogliani Papà Celso '06, we can't report on it here as under the new DOCG rules it can't be released before the end of 2007. What we did taste was more than satisfactory, especially the two fascinating Barolos, Pressenda and Terlo Ravera, the former all earth and leather, the latter pervasively fruity. Barbera Rinaldi is lovely: fragrant, zesty and elegantly structured. The Nebbiolo is succulent and tannic. Dolcetto San Luigi is a delight, full of youthful fruit. Langhe I Due Ricu '05, a blend of nebbiolo, cabernet and sangiovese, has great character. Cinerino, from viognier, is also excellent.

● Barbera d'Alba Rinaldi '05	🍷🍷	4*
● Barolo Vign. Terlo Ravera '03	🍷🍷	7
● Barolo Pressenda '03	🍷🍷	7
● Nebbiolo d'Alba Bricco Barone '05	🍷🍷	4
● Dolcetto di Dogliani San Luigi '06	🍷🍷	4
○ Cinerino '06	🍷🍷	5
● Langhe Rosso I Due Ricu '05	🍷🍷	5
● Dogliani Papà Celso '05	ΥΥΥ	4
● Dolcetto di Dogliani Papà Celso '04	ΥΥΥ	4
● Dolcetto di Dogliani Papà Celso '00	ΥΥΥ	4
● Barolo Pressenda '00	ΥΥΥ	7
● Barolo Cerviano '01	ΥΥ	7
● Barbera d'Alba Rinaldi '04	ΥΥ	4

Anna Maria Abbona

FRAZ. MONCUCCO, 21
12060 FARIGLIANO [CN]
TEL. 0173797228
www.amabbona.com

ANNUAL PRODUCTION 50,000 bottles
HECTARES UNDER VINE 9
VITICULTURE METHOD Conventional

When Anna Maria Abbona and her husband Franco Schellino decided to give up their jobs in 1989 to return to their family vineyards, many must have thought they were crazy, especially since little of the lustre of Barolo and Barbaresco falls on Farigliano, that part of the Langhe where vines give way to pastureland. Given the altitude, 550 metres, the climate is fairly limiting for viticulture. The only variety that truly seems at ease is dolcetto. And so Anna Maria learnt to maximize what the grape could give: the youngest vines yield an acidulous, easy-drinking Langhe Dolcetto while Sorì dij But, fruity and with good body, represents the Dolcetto di Dogliani denomination to a T. In 2005, the new Dogliani DOCG arrived and the estate was quick to capitalize on it with a superb wine, San Bernardo. This spends 18 months in cask and has the acid-tannin structure and complexity of a higher-level wine. It will also doubtless improve with age. The Nebbiolo is spot-on, too.

● Dogliani San Bernardo '05	🍷🍷	5
● Dolcetto di Dogliani Sorì dij But '06	🍷🍷	4
● Langhe Nebbiolo '05	🍷🍷	4
● Langhe Dolcetto '06	🍷	3
● Dolcetto di Dogliani Maioli '04	ΥΥ	4
● Dolcetto di Dogliani Maioli '05	ΥΥ	4
● Dolcetto di Dogliani Sup. '03	ΥΥ	5
● Dolcetto di Dogliani Sup. '04	ΥΥ	5
● Langhe Rosso Cadò '04	ΥΥ	5
● Langhe Rosso Cadò '03	ΥΥ	5
● Langhe Rosso Cadò '01	ΥΥ	5

F.lli Abrigo
VIA MOGLIA GERLOTTO, 2
12055 DIANO D'ALBA [CN]
TEL. 017369104
www.abrigofratelli.com

ANNUAL PRODUCTION 50,000
HECTARES UNDER VINE 14
VITICULTURE METHOD Natural

If you look through the main entries in last year's Guide you won't find one for the Ernesto and Mariarita Abrigo. But this year here it is, thanks to a solid performance from the majority of their wines. Their potential, and this we've known for a while, is such as to ensure reliably sound wines, and not only with Dolcetto where the siblings are formidable. They submitted three styles this year and all soared well over the Two Glasses threshold. Working upwards, we have a fresh, easy-going but articulate Bric Tumlìn; a clean, fragrant, tannic yet soft Sörì dei Berfi; and a fascinatingly spicy, earthy, savoury, rounded Sörì dei Berfi Vigna Pietrìn. They really have no equal in the zone for stylistic uniformity and overall quality. The other two wines we saw are improving steadily too and would surely have been more impressive had it not been for the vintage. Nevertheless, the acidic Barbera is not without backbone and the powerfully tannic, ripe Nebbiolo holds together well.

Orlando Abrigo
FRAZ. CAPPELLETTO, 5
12050 TREISO [CN]
TEL. 0173630232
www.orlandoabrigo.it

ANNUAL PRODUCTION 75,000 bottles
HECTARES UNDER VINE 15
VITICULTURE METHOD Conventional

This family estate, which will soon have an inviting farm holiday centre nestling among its vineyards, is run by the resourceful Giovanni Abrigo. His property lies right on the edge of the Barbaresco production zone, at the limit of where the vine grows, on high, wind-battered hills. The wines reflect this and unveil unusual aromatics as well as having a vigorous, almost herbaceous tannicity. All three Barbarescos are classy. The most typical of the estate style is the weighty, pervasive, still youthful Vigna Rongallo. Montersino, the second selection, is savoury and spicy. The standard wine is uncomplicatedly rounded. The two Barberas, both '05, come from the township of Trezzo Tinella. Vigna Roreto is fresh and earthy while the selection Mervisano, aged in small oak casks, is more complex and concentrated. There are two well-styled whites from international varieties, Langhe D'Amblè '06, a fresh, fairly balanced, zesty Sauvignon, and the simpler Chardonnay Très '06. The classic Dolcetto and Langhe Nebbiolo are a little edgy.

● Diano d'Alba Bric Tumlìn '06	♟♟ 3*
● Diano d'Alba Sörì dei Berfi V. Pietrìn '06	♟♟ 4*
● Diano d'Alba Sörì dei Berfi '06	♟♟ 3*
● Barbera d'Alba La Galùpa '05	♟ 4
● Nebbiolo d'Alba Tardiss '05	♟ 4
● Diano d'Alba Sörì dei Berfi '05	♟♟ 3
● Diano d'Alba Sörì dei Berfi V. Pietrìn '05	♟♟ 4

● Barbaresco V. Rongallo '04	♟ 6
● Barbaresco '04	♟♟ 6
● Barbaresco V. Montersino '04	♟♟ 6
● Barbera d'Alba Mervisano '05	♟♟ 5
● Barbera d'Alba V. Roreto '05	♟ 4
● Dolcetto d'Alba V. dell'Erto '06	♟ 4
O Langhe Bianco D'Amblè '06	♟ 4
O Langhe Chardonnay Très '06	♟ 4
● Langhe Nebbiolo Settevie '05	♟ 5
● Barbaresco V. Rongallo '00	♟♟ 6
● Barbaresco V. Rongallo '01	♟♟ 6
● Barbaresco V. Rongallo '03	♟♟ 6
● Barbaresco V. Montersino '01	♟♟ 6
● Barbera d'Alba Mervisano '04	♟♟ 5
● Barbaresco V. Montersino '03	♟♟ 6

Giulio Accornero e Figli

CA' CIMA, 1
15049 VIGNALE MONFERRATO [AL]
TEL. 0142933317
www.accornerovini.it

ANNUAL PRODUCTION 100,000 bottles
HECTARES UNDER VINE 20
VITICULTURE METHOD Natural

As usual, all the wines submitted by the Accornero family were excellent, with more than one reaching the finals. Barbera Bricco Battista has not been so exciting for years and earned a new set of Three Glasses. This reflects honourably on the entire family and its artisanal approach. We have no doubt that they will dedicate the award to Massimo, who died prematurely a few years ago. The wine's almost impenetrably deep hue is a treat for the eyes. It has an intense nose full of fruit and balsam introducing a palate that is fragrant, harmonious, cohesive and long. Monferrato Rosso Centenario, from cabernet sauvignon and barbera, is a deep ruby and mingles spiciness with its tertiary aromas from the mostly new French oak barrels used for ageing. Ermanno Accornero's decision to delay submitting Barbera Giulìn '05 until this year was pivotal. The additional bottle age has given it a harmony and balance the wine has never had before. The rest of the range is highly satisfying, from Grignolino Bricco del Bosco, always one of the most successful of its type, to the Freisa, the dessert wine Brigantino and the simple white Fonsìna.

Claudio Alario

VIA SANTA CROCE, 23
12055 DIANO D'ALBA [CN]
TEL. 0173231808
aziendaalario@tiscali.it

ANNUAL PRODUCTION 45,000 bottles
HECTARES UNDER VINE 12
VITICULTURE METHOD Conventional

We know Claudio Alario well. We know all about his summer torments when we send out our requests for tasting samples and we are used to hearing his reply that his bottling schedules do not coincide with our round of tastings. What is there to be done? Not much, to tell the truth. The rhythms of wine production cannot bend to those of wine assessment, or vice versa, so all we can do is to keep our eyes as wide open as possible to the development potential of everything we taste. Producers have to accept the judgements we make calmly and in good faith. Claudio's two Dolcettos are, as ever, quite excellent. Costa Fiore is a juicy, fleshy explosion of red berry fruit, undergrowth and damp earth. Montagrillo instead turns more on savouriness, balanced tannic dryness and length. If they're great now, tasted fresh off the bottling line, just think how they'll be in a few months or years. The other wines, a Barbera of good acidity, a firm Nebbiolo and a rounded Barolo, are all high flyers.

● Barbera del M.to Sup. Bricco Battista '04	♟♟♟	6
● Barbera del M.to Giulìn '05	♟	4*
● Monferrato Rosso Centenario '04	♟♟	6
● Grignolino del M.to Casalese Bricco del Bosco '06	♟♟	4
● Monferrato Freisa La Bernardina '06	♟♟	4
● Casorzo Brigantino '06	♟♟	4
O Monferrato Bianco Fonsìna '06	♟	4
● Barbera d'Asti Bricco Battista '97	♟♟♟	5
● Barbera del M.to Sup. Bricco Battista '99	♟♟♟	6
● Barbera del M.to Sup. Bricco Battista '98	♟♟♟	6
● Barbera del M.to Giulìn '04	♟♟	4

● Diano d'Alba Costa Fiore '06	♟♟	4*
● Diano d'Alba Montagrillo '06	♟♟	4*
● Barbera d'Alba Valletta '05	♟♟	5
● Barolo Riva '03	♟♟	7
● Nebbiolo d'Alba Cascinotto '05	♟♟	5
● Barbera d'Alba Valletta '04	♟♟	5
● Barolo Riva '01	♟♟	7
● Barolo Riva '00	♟♟	7
● Barolo Riva '99	♟♟	7
● Diano d'Alba Costa Fiore '04	♟♟	4
● Diano d'Alba Costa Fiore '05	♟♟	4

F.lli Alessandria
VIA B. VALFRÉ, 59
12060 VERDUNO [CN]
TEL. 0172470113
www.fratellialessandria.it

ANNUAL PRODUCTION 60,000 bottles
HECTARES UNDER VINE 12
VITICULTURE METHOD Conventional

We knew it was going to be difficult to replicate last year's success, when a fabulous '01 release of Barolo San Lorenzo completely dazzled the final tasting commission. But we didn't realize just how difficult: the '03 vintage, with the hottest summer in living memory, made it impossible for any of the estate's leading reds to really scale the peaks. Be careful, though, we're not talking about gross failings, merely details and subtleties that simply took the edge off the wines and certainly didn't cloud the overall picture of a very fine range. The range includes four '03 Barolos. The base-level wine is the one that has been most affected by that summer's heat and doesn't really leap into relief. Moving upwards comes a ripe, tannic Gramolere, a soft, rounded Monvigliero and then the wonderland that is San Lorenzo, seeming only a touch less lively and "out there" than the '01. Next year we'll have the great '04s to taste... With so much nebbiolo to discuss there's little space for the other wines but Barbera Superiore is a real little gem of acidic zest and nose-palate cohesiveness.

Gianfranco Alessandria
LOC. MANZONI, 13
12065 MONFORTE D'ALBA [CN]
TEL. 017378576
www.gianfrancoalessandria.com

ANNUAL PRODUCTION 35,000 bottles
HECTARES UNDER VINE 5.5
VITICULTURE METHOD Conventional

The Alessandria husband-and-wife team runs a good, family-style estate with tons of enthusiasm, clear ideas and rational goals. It all comes through in the wines, which are consistently good. The estate style is extreme cleanliness and great definition in the wines and the use of small oak for ageing is restrained. The two '03 Barolos are well focused and are fully typical of the vintage, yet avoid all cooked or overripe notes. The standard version has a relaxed, open feel. Its nose is graceful and there is yet more grace in the tannins. The San Giovanni selection, while still somewhat closed, has more complexity, with great fullness on the nose and a firmly tannic structure. Barbera Vittoria '05, made from very old vines, is dark, rich, savoury and expansive, in short excellent. The other wines all have great liveliness, balance and drinkability, especially the young Barbera and Dolcetto.

● Barbera d'Alba Sup. La Priora '05	♟ 4*
● Barolo S. Lorenzo '03	♟♟ 7
● Barolo Monvigliero '03	♟♟ 7
● Barolo '03	♟♟ 6
● Verduno Pelaverga '06	♟♟ 4
● Langhe Rosso Luna '05	♟♟ 4
● Barolo Gramolere '03	♟♟ 7
● Barbera d'Alba '06	♟ 4
● Dolcetto d'Alba '06	♟ 4
● Barolo Monvigliero '00	♟♟♟ 7
● Barolo S. Lorenzo '01	♟♟♟ 7
● Barolo S. Lorenzo '97	♟♟♟ 7
● Barolo Monvigliero '95	♟♟♟ 7
● Barolo Monvigliero '01	♟♟ 7
● Barolo Gramolere '01	♟♟ 7
● Barbera d'Alba Sup. La Priora '04	♟♟ 4

● Barbera d'Alba Vittoria '05	♟♟ 6
● Barolo S. Giovanni '03	♟♟ 8
● Barolo '03	♟♟ 7
● Barbera d'Alba '06	♟♟ 4*
● Dolcetto d'Alba '06	♟♟ 4*
● L'Insieme '04	♟♟ 7
● Langhe Nebbiolo '05	♟♟ 5
● Barbera d'Alba Vittoria '96	♟♟♟ 6
● Barbera d'Alba Vittoria '97	♟♟♟ 6
● Barbera d'Alba Vittoria '98	♟♟♟ 6
● Barolo S. Giovanni '00	♟♟♟ 8
● Barolo S. Giovanni '97	♟♟♟ 8
● Barolo S. Giovanni '99	♟♟♟ 8
● Barolo S. Giovanni '98	♟♟♟ 8
● Barolo S. Giovanni '01	♟♟♟ 8
● Barolo '93	♟♟♟ 8

Marchesi Alfieri

P.ZZA ALFIERI, 28
14010 SAN MARTINO ALFIERI [AT]
TEL. 0141976015
www.marchesialfieri.it

ANNUAL PRODUCTION 80,000 bottles
HECTARES UNDER VINE 24
VITICULTURE METHOD Conventional

The Marchesi Alfieri winery is one of the most beautiful and spectacular in the entire Asti Langhe. It's in a real castle. The owners are Emanuela, Antonella and Giovanna San Martino di San Germano, who run it with the assistance of oenologist Mario Olivero. As we have noted for many years now, the average quality of the range is good to say the least, especially on the Barbera front. The nose on Alfiera, aged 15 months in barrique, ranges from crushed flowers to plum before opening to mint and sweet spices. Its palate is warm and structured, and finishes long. This wine of wonderful complexity brought a new Three Glass award to the estate, which has made barbera its trademark. La Tota, with eight months' oak ageing, is also great, full of vigour and wild cherry juiciness. The two Monferratos, San Germano, from 100 per cent pinot nero, and Sostegno, from barbera and pinot nero, are excellent. The Grignolino, with raspberry-like fruitiness and peppery spiciness, is one of the best in its class.

● Barbera d'Asti Sup. Alfiera '05	♉♉♉	6
● Barbera d'Asti La Tota '05	♉♉	4*
● Monferrato Rosso S. Germano '05	♉♉	5
● Monferrato Rosso Sostegno '05	♉♉	4
● Piemonte Grignolino Sansoero '06	♉	4
● Barbera d'Asti Sup. Alfiera '00	♀♀♀	6
● Barbera d'Asti Sup. Alfiera '01	♀♀♀	6
● Barbera d'Asti Sup. Alfiera '99	♀♀♀	6
● Barbera d'Asti Sup. Alfiera '03	♀♀	6
● Barbera d'Asti Sup. Alfiera '04	♀♀	6
● Barbera d'Asti La Tota '99	♀♀	4
● Monferrato Rosso S. Germano '03	♀♀	5
● Monferrato Rosso S. Germano '04	♀♀	5

Giovanni Almondo

VIA SAN ROCCO, 26
12046 MONTÀ [CN]
TEL. 0173975256
www.giovannialmondo.com

ANNUAL PRODUCTION 80,000 bottles
HECTARES UNDER VINE 14
VITICULTURE METHOD Conventional

Domenico Almondo is an affable, knowledgeable winemaker whose approach is methodical and attentive. He imbues his wines with great personality. Domenico's vineyards lie in Montà, just where the Roero starts rising more steeply to crests and sun-drenched hilltops before falling to the flatlands towards Turin. Domenico transforms their grapes into a handful of perfectly calibrated wines. His love of white wines has led him to shape some of the best Arneis we've ever tasted. The fascinating Bricco delle Ciliegie '06 lives up to expectations, all florality, balsam and mineral notes. But yet again this year it's the reds that earned most praise, and yet again they are among those that best reflect their provenance. Roero Bric Valdiana is unusually austere, yet you'd hardly realize it, so smooth is its texture and so silky its tannic weave. It's truly divine. The '05 vintage of the Barbera brings renewed acidity and character. Only rarely in the past has it been so attractive. Even the lesser wines, Roero '05 and Roero Arneis Vigne Sparse '06, showed very well.

● Barbera d'Alba Valbianchera '05	♉♉	5
● Roero Bric Valdiana '05	♉♉	6
○ Roero Arneis Bricco delle Ciliegie '06	♉♉	4*
● Roero '05	♉♉	5
○ Roero Arneis V. Sparse '06	♉	4
● Roero Bric Valdiana '00	♀♀♀	6
● Roero Bric Valdiana '01	♀♀♀	6
● Roero Bric Valdiana '03	♀♀♀	6
● Barbera d'Alba Valbianchera '03	♀♀	5
● Barbera d'Alba Valbianchera '04	♀♀	5
● Roero Bric Valdiana '02	♀♀	6
● Roero Bric Valdiana '04	♀♀	6

★★ Elio Altare - Cascina Nuova

FRAZ. ANNUNZIATA, 51
12064 LA MORRA [CN]
TEL. 017350835
www.elioaltare.com

Antichi Vigneti di Cant

VIA MICHELANGELO BUONA
28074 GHEMME [NO]
TEL. 0163840041
www.cantalupo.net

ANNUAL PRODUCTION 55,000 bottles
HECTARES UNDER VINE 10
VITICULTURE METHOD Natural

ANNUAL PRODUCTION 200,000 bottles
HECTARES UNDER VINE 35
VITICULTURE METHOD Conventional

For a while now, Elio Altare has been talking about retiring. Yet, strangely, whenever we visit him, we still find him out among his vines or bent over a barrique. In effect, we really can't imagine an Elio playing boules or dozing in front of the television, and we're sure that despite having handled 40 vintages, it'll still be a long time before he hangs up his hoe. Meanwhile, his Barolos are back in our tastings. Arborina was particularly admired for its nose full of ripe fruit and its oaky nuances. The Langhe range was stunning, though. Larigi, from barbera, is succulent, balsamic and very long. Arborina is both austere and elegant with violet florality and aniseed and cocoa powder spiciness. La Villa brings nebbiolo and barbera together perfectly to form a savoury wine, full of flavour and graceful tannicity, so much so that it picked up Three Glasses. The highly attractive, more internationally styled L'Insieme, from cabernet sauvignon, nebbiolo, barbera, syrah and petit verdot, also reached the finals. All the others were as good as their fame would suggest.

At last the Arlunno family has won Three Glasses. They have been active in the Ghemme zone since the 17th century, when they were known as Arluno, and grew grapes even then. The family's more recent history starts much later, in the early 1970s, when Alberto's father and uncle started a replanting programme that involved the entire municipality of Ghemme. The estate was officially born in 1977 with the release of the '74 Ghemme. Alberto, who is an oenologist and an agronomist as well as the estate owner, oversees things and the estate now controls almost half the area under vine in the DOCG, including vineyards in the municipality of Romagnano Sesia, as well as Ghemme itself. Overall, the estate's Ghemmes showed well this year. They are from 100 per cent nebbiolo and age for two years in Slavonian oak barrels of various sizes. At times, they can seem hard when young but age softens out their rough edges and allows complexity and class to emerge. Three Glasses went to the aristocratic Collis Breclemae '00, first produced in '79. It's worth noting that for some time now, Alberto has also been producing one of the area's best whites, Carolus, from greco, chardonnay and arneis.

● Langhe La Villa '05	♟♟♟	8
● Langhe Arborina '05	♟♟	8
● Langhe Larigi '05	♟♟	8
● Barolo Vign. Arborina '03	♟♟	8
● L'Insieme '05	♟♟	7
● Barolo '03	♟♟	8
● Dolcetto d'Alba '06	♟♟	4*
● Barbera d'Alba '06	♟♟	4*
● Barolo Vign. Arborina '00	♟♟♟	8
● Barolo Vign. Arborina '01	♟♟♟	8
● Barolo Vign. Arborina '99	♟♟♟	8
● Barolo Vign. Arborina '98	♟♟♟	8
● Langhe Arborina '97	♟♟♟	8
● Langhe Arborina '96	♟♟♟	8
● Langhe Arborina '98	♟♟♟	8
● Langhe Larigi '99	♟♟♟	8
● Langhe Larigi '98	♟♟♟	8
● Langhe La Villa '99	♟♟♟	8

● Ghemme Collis Breclemae '00	♟♟♟	6
● Ghemme Collis Carellae '00	♟♟	6
○ Carolus '06	♟♟	3*
● Ghemme '03	♟♟	5
⊙ Colline Novaresi Il Mimo '06	♟	4
● Colline Novaresi Primigenia '05	♟	3
● Colline Novaresi Villa Horta '05	♟	3
● Ghemme Signore di Bayard '01	♟♟	6
● Ghemme Collis Breclemae '98	♟♟	6
● Ghemme Collis Breclemae '99	♟♟	6
● Ghemme '00	♟♟	5
● Ghemme Collis Carellae '99	♟♟	6

Antico Borgo dei Cavalli

VIA DANTE, 54
28010 CAVALLIRIO [NO]
TEL. 016380115
www.vinibarbaglia.it

ANNUAL PRODUCTION   20,000 bottles
HECTARES UNDER VINE 3
VITICULTURE METHOD   Conventional

Cavallirio is a small village in that part of
northern Piedmont which has recently come
to the fore. Not that the vine is a novelty
here; indeed, it's been around for centuries.
But the area under vine had dropped
drastically, until recently that is, when the
zone gained a new lease of life thanks to
the combination of renewed stimulus in the
long-standing names and a wave of
enthusiasm from new producers. Part of the
credit belongs to the Barbaglia family who
specialize in well-made wines from
indigenous grapes, or at least those that
have put down deep roots in the area, albeit
figurative ones. The estate is small. It's
guided by Sergio, although Silvia, who
recently graduated, is progressively taking
on a greater role. This year, a new wine joins
the range, a fragrant, fresh Croatina of
distinctly high potential. The Boca, now at
its second release, seems to have a clearer
stylistic imprint, suggesting last year's
promise is turning into reality. The Vespolina
is again of high quality, scoring higher than
the Uva Rara for its enticing bite. The
Nebbiolo is vigorous and austere. The
Bianco, from erbaluce, impresses for its
varietal typicity.

Antoniolo

C.SO VALSESIA, 277
13045 GATTINARA [VC]
TEL. 0163833612
antoniolovini@bmm.it

ANNUAL PRODUCTION   60,000 bottles
HECTARES UNDER VINE 15
VITICULTURE METHOD   Conventional

In 1948, after the Second World War, Mario
Antoniolo, who was married to a
descendent of the Nervi family, decided to
set up the estate that still bears his name.
He worked with zeal, bringing prestige to
the crus he had acquired, and in 1977 his
daughter Rosanna started to follow in his
footsteps. She then became the heart of the
estate for the next 25 years. Rosanna
maintained the quality of the wines and
stayed faithful to Gattinara traditions, never
changing track, even at the most difficult
times. Not even the arrival of her children
Lorella and Alberto altered things. The
finesse, rigour and austerity that had
marked out the wines' style continued to
prevail. Alberto has now been supervising
grape-growing and winemaking since 1990,
and has brought the wines even greater
quality. The three Gattinara selections have
a consistently strong zonal character.
Castelle is always the most approachable,
with a softness that sets it apart from the
standard estate style. Osso San Grato is the
most austere, unfolding fully only after some
years. San Francesco forms the ideal mid
way point between these two extremes,
and so won a worthy Three Glasses.

● Boca '03	♟♟ 6
● Colline Novaresi Vespolina Ledi '06	♟♟ 4
○ Colline Novaresi Bianco Lucino '06	♟♟ 4
● Colline Novaresi Croatina Gli Otri '06	♟ 4
● Colline Novaresi Uva Rara Lea '06	♟ 3
● Colline Novaresi Nebbiolo Il Silente '04	♟ 5
● Boca '01	♟♟ 6
● Colline Novaresi Nebbiolo Il Silente '03	♟♟ 5
● Colline Novaresi Vespolina Ledi '05	♟♟ 4

● Gattinara Vign. S. Francesco '03	♟♟♟ 7
● Gattinara Vign. Osso S. Grato '03	♟♟ 7
● Gattinara Vign. Castelle '03	♟♟ 7
● Gattinara '03	♟♟ 6
○ Erbaluce di Caluso '06	♟ 4
● Gattinara Vign. Castelle '00	♟♟♟ 7
● Gattinara Vign. S. Francesco '01	♟♟♟ 6
● Gattinara Vign. Castelle '99	♟♟♟ 7
● Gattinara Vign. Osso S. Grato '01	♟♟♟ 7
● Gattinara Vign. Castelle '01	♟♟ 7
● Gattinara '00	♟♟ 6

Anzivino

C.SO VALSESIA, 162
13045 GATTINARA [VC]
TEL. 0163827172
www.anzivino.net

ANNUAL PRODUCTION 80,000 bottles
HECTARES UNDER VINE 13.5
VITICULTURE METHOD Conventional

Emanuele Anzivino was a Milanese building entrepreneur when, in 1998, he bought several hectares of vineyard in Gattinara's famed Valferana, Castelle and Lucineglio vineyards to satisfy his love of the land. But he didn't want to lose sight of the profitability of his investment so he also set up a delightful farm holiday centre, which is ideal for anyone visiting Valsesia. Emanuele's wines have firm ties with their provenance but avoid being too rough-edged. For ageing, he may use large old botti, 900-litre tonneaux or barriques, depending on the wine and the year. This year, four of the range showed really well. These are two '03 Gattinaras, one standard, the other a longer-oak-aged Riserva; a Bramaterra Riserva '03; and Faticato '04, a Coste della Sesia made from nebbiolo grapes left to dry until November, the style resembling a Valtellina Sforzato. The best of all is the Gattinara Riserva, with just 3,000 bottles made, which has wonderful complexity on the nose and an excellent tannic structure. Finally come two table wines made from blends of indigenous and international grapes.

Araldica Vini Piemontesi

V.LE LAUDANO, 2
14040 CASTEL BOGLIONE [AT]
TEL. 014176311
www.araldicavini.com

ANNUAL PRODUCTION 6,000,000 bottles
HECTARES UNDER VINE 900
VITICULTURE METHOD Conventional

This group is getting seriously to grips with its programme for a high quality line, named Cascinone, which was initiated at the beginning of the century. The leading players are Claudio Manera and Luigi Bertini, who are supported by a loyal, skilled team of winemakers, viticulturists and cellar workers. Recently, alongside the Cascinone wines have been those from the La Battistina estate in Novi Ligure, which has long produced excellent Gavi. The wines tasted this year were faultless, the quality level ranging from good to very good, and all had exemplary cleanliness and definition. The whites are fresh, fruity and most attractive, especially Camillona '05 from sauvignon, which has citrus aromas and a zestily pervasive palate. Arneis Sorilaria has inviting ripe fruit and a slightly sweetish note to the palate. The excellent Gavi La Battistina is full of character and acid backbone but with Bricco Battistina, its youthfulness and oakiness for now still dominates the fruit. Moving on to the reds, Barbera d'Asti D'Annona was not submitted but there was a lovely, well-structured Nebbiolo and a savoury Barbera Rive.

● Gattinara Ris. '03	♈♈	6
● Bramaterra Ris. '03	♈♈	6
● Coste della Sesia Faticato '04	♈♈	7
● Gattinara '03	♈♈	6
● Caplenga	♈	2*
● Nemesi	♈	3*
● Bramaterra '03	♈♈	5
● Bramaterra '02	♈♈	5
● Bramaterra '01	♈♈	5
● Coste della Sesia Faticato '03	♈♈	7
● Il Tarlo '04	♈♈	4
● Gattinara Ris. '01	♈♈	6
● Gattinara '01	♈♈	6

● Langhe Nebbiolo Castellero '05	♈♈	5
● Barbera d'Asti Sup. Rive '05	♈♈	4*
○ Gavi La Battistina '06	♈♈	4*
○ Monferrato Bianco Camillona '06	♈♈	4*
○ Gavi Bricco Battistina '06	♈	4
○ Roero Arneis Sorilaria '06	♈	4
○ Moscato d'Asti Belvedere '06	♈	4
● Brachetto d'Acqui Cavallino '06	♈	4
● Barbera d'Asti Sup. Rive '04	♈♈	4
● Barbera d'Asti Sup. D'Annona '03	♈♈	4
● Barbera d'Asti Sup. Rive '03	♈♈	4
● Monferrato Rosso Luce Monaca '01	♈♈	5
● Monferrato Rosso Luce Monaca '03	♈♈	5

Tenuta dell'Arbiola

LOC. ARBIOLA
REG. SALINE, 67
14050 SAN MARZANO OLIVETO [AT]
TEL. 0141856194
www.arbiola.it

ANNUAL PRODUCTION 120,000 bottles
HECTARES UNDER VINE 20
VITICULTURE METHOD Conventional

Arbiola is one of the Asti wineries that have made most investment in the quality of its wines over the last few years. The credit for this goes to Domenico Terzano and his son Riccardo, who have taken a mere 15 years to build up an estate with fine quality credentials. But recognition must also go to its high-ranking consultants, most notably vineyard manager Federico Curtaz. Moving on to the wines, we start with Barbera Romilda Riserva del Fondatore which is made only in better vintages. The nose swings between cocoa powder and coffee, and between vanilla and roasted hazelnut. The richly textured palate has great drive and an impressive finish. Romilda X is more fruit-led, with cherry and plum, its palate is sweet, really succulent and very long. Monferrato Bianco Arbiola, from chardonnay and sauvignon, is full of nuances of sage, grapefruit and golden delicious apples. The Chardonnay and the fresh Moscato d'Asti each picked up One Glass.

● Barbera d'Asti Sup. Nizza Romilda X '05	🍷🍷	6
● Barbera d'Asti Sup. Nizza Romilda Riserva del Fondatore '01	🍷🍷	7
○ Monferrato Bianco Arbiola '06	🍷🍷	4*
● Barbera d'Asti Carlotta '06	🍷	3
○ Moscato d'Asti Ferlingot '06	🍷	3
○ Piemonte Chardonnay '06	🍷	3
● Barbera d'Asti Sup. Nizza Romilda IX '04	ΥΥ	6
● Barbera d'Asti Sup. Nizza Romilda VIII '03	ΥΥ	6
● Barbera d'Asti Sup. Nizza Romilda VII '01	ΥΥ	6
● Barbera d'Asti Sup. Nizza Romilda VI '00	ΥΥ	6

L'Armangia

FRAZ. SAN GIOVANNI, 122
14053 CANELLI [AT]
TEL. 0141824947
www.armangia.it

ANNUAL PRODUCTION 70,000 bottles
HECTARES UNDER VINE 10
VITICULTURE METHOD Conventional

Ignazio Giovine has been managing his estate since 1993, his diverse range never losing the dynamism and breadth which has always marked it out. This year, that range acquired even more flesh with the new Monferrato Rosso Macchiaferro '05, made from albarossa with ten per cent nebbiolo. It has amazing depth of colour. There is great complexity on the floral, spicy nose with its hints of chestnut and the palate is strongly spicy, its plentiful acidity complemented by good supporting tannin. The whites are appealing, notably the sauvignon-based Monferrato '06, which has a vegetal nose and a long, lively palate. Best of the other reds is Barbera d'Asti Vignali, which scores highly for balance, with the oak being well integrated into the wine's powerful fruitiness. Finally come the sweet wines Mesicaseu, from overripe moscato and chardonnay, and Moscato d'Asti Il Giai.

● Barbera d'Asti Sup. Nizza Titon '04	🍷🍷	4*
● Barbera d'Asti Vignali '04	🍷🍷	6
● Monferrato Rosso Pacifico '04	🍷🍷	4
● Barbera d'Asti Sopra Berruti '06	🍷🍷	3*
● Monferrato Rosso Macchiaferro '05	🍷🍷	3*
○ Piemonte Chardonnay Pratorotondo '06	🍷🍷	3*
○ Mesicaseu '06	🍷	4
○ Monferrato Bianco Enne Enne '06	🍷	2
○ Moscato d'Asti Il Giai '06	🍷	3
○ Piemonte Chardonnay Non '06	🍷	3
● Barbera d'Asti Vignali Castello di Calosso '01	ΥΥ	6
● Barbera d'Asti Vignali Castello di Calosso '00	ΥΥ	6
● Barbera d'Asti Sup. Titon '01	ΥΥ	4
● Barbera d'Asti Sup. Titon '03	ΥΥ	4

Ascheri

VIA PIUMATI, 23
12042 BRA [CN]
TEL. 0172412394
www.ascherivini.it

ANNUAL PRODUCTION 250,000 bottles
HECTARES UNDER VINE 36
VITICULTURE METHOD Conventional

The Ascheri family's wines are truly admirable this year. Visiting the cellars is always a treat for the eyes. It's good to see a working structure that is attractive as well as functional. The Ascheris have invested heavily in their property but there's been a good return, particularly from the visitors and guests at the small hotel and restaurant set around the old enclosed courtyard. Now let's move on to the wines. The family's long experience with grape-growing and winemaking continues to bring dependability throughout the range. There are 36 hectares under vine, in Serralunga, La Morra, Verduno and Bra. From these Matteo, supported by a team of winemakers, produces the classic Langhe names as well as a few less usual, but already highly rated wines. Langhe Bianco Montalupa '05, from viognier, and Langhe Rosso 2003 '03, from syrah, are as fabulous this year as ever. The two '03 Barolos, Vigna dei Pola and Sorano, are quite different from each other but together capture the essence of one of the hottest years on record while still managing to retain freshness and roundness. Everything else is more than satisfactory.

Azelia

FRAZ. GARBELLETTO
VIA ALBA-BAROLO, 53
12060 CASTIGLIONE FALLETTO [CN]
TEL. 017362859

ANNUAL PRODUCTION 52,000 bottles
HECTARES UNDER VINE 12
VITICULTURE METHOD Conventional

This, the winery of the Scavino husband-and-wife team, set below the village of Castiglione Falletto, is a gem. And we're not talking about amazing architecture or breathtaking views, just the superb range of wines they have crafted. They take great care to bring out the identity of each variety and their wines transmit pride in their style, based on elegance and respect for the vine. The emblematic example is the captivating Barolo Voghera Brea Riserva '01, which boasts marked austerity and penetrating richness within a shell of elegance and excellent harmony. It's a great Barolo and carries the winery's image skywards to a comfortable Three Glasses. Then there's a strong array of '03 Barolos, from the broad-cut, classy San Rocco to Bricco Fiasco, highly refined and with finely judged tannins. We welcome the new, long-awaited Barolo Margheria, from vineyards in the Serralunga hills, a lively wine of notable depth, complexity and length. Everything else showed well, especially the basic Barolo whose consolidated, attractive style brings refinement to its varietal personality.

● Barolo Sorano '03	♔♔ 6*
● Barolo V. dei Pola '03	♔♔ 6
● Dolcetto d'Alba S. Rocco '06	♔♔ 4
● Nebbiolo d'Alba Bricco S. Giacomo '05	♔♔ 4
● Verduno Pelaverga Do ut Des '06	♔♔ 4
● Langhe Rosso Montalupa '03	♔♔ 5
O Langhe Bianco Montalupa '05	♔♔ 5
● Barbera d'Alba Fontanelle '06	♔ 4
O Langhe Arneis Cristina Ascheri '06	♔ 4
O Gavi del Comune di Gavi Cristina Ascheri '06	♔ 4
● Dolcetto d'Alba Nirane '06	♔ 4
● Barolo Sorano '00	♔♔♔ 6
● Barolo Sorano Coste & Bricco '00	♔♔ 7
● Barolo Sorano '01	♔♔ 6
● Barolo Sorano Coste & Bricco '01	♔♔ 7

● Barolo Voghera Brea Ris. '01	♔♔♔ 8
● Barolo Bricco Fiasco '03	♔♔ 8
● Barolo S. Rocco '03	♔♔ 8
● Barbera d'Alba Vign. Punta '05	♔♔ 5
● Barolo Margheria '03	♔♔ 8
● Barolo '03	♔♔ 7
● Dolcetto d'Alba Bricco dell'Oriolo '06	♔ 4
● Langhe Nebbiolo '06	♔ 4
● Barolo '91	♔♔♔ 8
● Barolo Bricco Fiasco '01	♔♔♔ 8
● Barolo Bricco Fiasco '93	♔♔♔ 8
● Barolo Bricco Fiasco '96	♔♔♔ 8
● Barolo S. Rocco '99	♔♔♔ 8
● Barolo Bricco Fiasco '95	♔♔♔ 8
● Barolo Voghera Brea Ris. '00	♔♔ 8

Antonio Baldizzone - Cascina Lana

C.SO ACQUI, 187
14049 NIZZA MONFERRATO [AT]
TEL. 0141726734

ANNUAL PRODUCTION 70,000 bottles
HECTARES UNDER VINE 20
VITICULTURE METHOD Conventional

Antonio Baldizzone and his wife Graziana Rizzoli have some of the best vineyards in the Asti zone, with perfect aspect. These give grapes of fabulous quality, and it comes through in the wines. Barbera d'Asti Superiore Nizza again showed very well, gaining Two Glasses. It's a wine of great structure and substance, given a lift by intense aromas of ripe red berry fruit and sweet spices. It was matched by Monferrato Rosso Vën ëd Michen, made from barbera, nebbiolo and cabernet sauvignon. This has a nuanced nose of blackcurrant, plum, bell pepper, thyme, pepper and vanilla, leading to a powerful, long, full-bodied palate. The appealing young Barbera La Cirimela is juicy and lively, with exuberant fruitiness on the nose and immediacy on the palate. Dolcetto La Milana and Moscato d'Asti are both inviting.

Produttori del Barbaresco

VIA TORINO, 54
12050 BARBARESCO [CN]
TEL. 0173635139
www.produttoridelbarbaresco.com

ANNUAL PRODUCTION 420,000 bottles
HECTARES UNDER VINE 100
VITICULTURE METHOD Conventional

The Langhe's mother of all co-operatives doesn't miss a shot. Drawing analogies with others from Alto Adige or other regions has been done to death so we won't waste time on pointless comparisons or meaningless contests. The Produttori are the Produttori. Full stop. Their heritage is their lands, which give wines of marvellously diverse personalities. Even so, they have created a strong spirit of solidarity which translates into a common desire for the highest possible quality and the clearest zonal typicity. This year's range is small since to span the gap until the '04 Barbaresco Riserva selections are ready, the nine '01s are split into two sections, five released last year and four this. It goes without saying that they're all fabulous, so much so that it's hard to choose between the austerity of Montestefano, the silky tannicity of Moccagatta, the intense, earth-and-leather aromas of Montefico and the sumptuous, balanced complexity of Ovello. But Montestefano just pipped the others to the post and collected Three Glasses. Barbaresco '03, which is produced in quantity, retains freshness despite the torrid year. Langhe Nebbiolo '05 is a good everyday drinker and the price is good, too.

● Barbera d'Asti Sup. Nizza '05	♀♀	5
● Barbera d'Asti La Cirimela '06	♀♀	3*
● Monferrato Rosso Vën ëd Michen '05	♀♀	5
● Dolcetto d'Asti La Milana '06	♀	3
O Moscato d'Asti '06	♀	3
● Barbera d'Asti Sup. Nizza '03	♀♀	5
● Barbera d'Asti Sup. Nizza '04	♀♀	5
● Barbera d'Asti Sup. Vën ëd Michen '01	♀♀	5
● Monferrato Rosso Vën ëd Michen '04	♀♀	5

● Barbaresco Vign. in Montestefano Ris. '01	♀♀♀	6
● Barbaresco Vign. in Moccagatta Ris. '01	♀♀	6
● Barbaresco Vign. in Montefico Ris. '01	♀♀	6
● Barbaresco Vign. in Ovello Ris. '01	♀♀	6
● Barbaresco '03	♀♀	5*
● Langhe Nebbiolo '05	♀♀	4*
● Barbaresco Vign. in Montefico Ris. '00	♀♀♀	6
● Barbaresco Vign. in Rio Sordo Ris. '01	♀♀♀	6
● Barbaresco Vign. in Pajé Ris. '01	♀♀♀	6
● Barbaresco '99	♀♀♀	5
● Barbaresco Vign. in Montestefano Ris. '01	♀♀	6

★ Cascina La Barbatella

S.DA ANNUNZIATA, 55
14049 NIZZA MONFERRATO [AT]
TEL. 0141701434
sonvico.barbatella@libero.it

ANNUAL PRODUCTION 22,000 bottles
HECTARES UNDER VINE 4.5
VITICULTURE METHOD Conventional

It's no exaggeration to call this estate a gem. Just enter the courtyard, take a look at the amphitheatre of vines surrounding it or, better, let yourself be caressed by the ever-present soft breeze, and you'll be enraptured. Everything is discreetly small, from the area under vines, fixed at 4.5 hectares, and the output of 22,000 bottles a year to the welcoming, well refurbished farmhouse. Angelo Sonvico has every right to be considered one of the zone's personalities, having tenaciously sought – and achieved – superb quality right from his start in 1982. Credit is certainly also due to his team of professionals, which includes the leading names of Giuliano Noè and Beppe Rattazzo on the winemaking side. The wines speak for themselves so, without too much preamble, let us simply underline the majesty of Monferrato Rosso Sonvico and Barbera d'Asti Superiore Nizza Vigna dell'Angelo, both from the great '04 vintage. The Barbera is elegantly earthy while the Sonvico is a glorious wine, deep, refined and full of character. It holds aloft the reputation of this fine estate and swept up Three Glasses.

Cascina Barisél

REG. SAN GIOVANNI, 30
14053 CANELLI [AT]
TEL. 0141824848
www.barisel.it

ANNUAL PRODUCTION 35,000 bottles
HECTARES UNDER VINE 4
VITICULTURE METHOD Natural

Cascina Barisél is typical of estates in the Piedmont hills, with a large family who all actively participate in running it with one member taking the helm. At Barisél, it's Franco Penna who coordinates the vineyard and cellar work. There are two bits of news this year. Expansion work is under way and a new classic method sparkling wine has been released. This is Enrico Penna Brut '03, made from chardonnay and pinot nero, and it's not only fresh and lively but also very good money. Barbera d'Asti Superiore La Cappelletta '05 was still ageing at the time of our tastings but the standard Barbera Barisél showed excellently with freshness, a good swathe of acidity and sound structure. Moscato d'Asti '06 is in perfect Canelli style, gaining class from scents of sage which marry with the classic varietal aromas. Foravìa, from favorita, now undergoes cold maceration and is well styled, as is Barbera d'Asti Barisél. L'Avìja, a moscato from overripe grapes is, as ever, surprisingly good, and brings the range to a close.

● Monferrato Rosso Sonvico '04	▼▼▼	7
● Barbera d'Asti Sup. Nizza V. dell'Angelo '04	▼▼	6
● Monferrato Rosso Mystère '04	▼▼	6
● Barbera d'Asti La Barbatella '06	▼▼	4*
○ Monferrato Bianco Noè '06	▼▼	4*
● Monferrato Rosso Aldar '06	▼▼	4*
● Barbera d'Asti Sup. Nizza V. dell'Angelo '01	♀♀♀	7
● Monferrato Rosso Mystère '01	♀♀♀	7
● Monferrato Rosso Sonvico '98	♀♀♀	7
● Monferrato Rosso Sonvico '00	♀♀♀	7
● Barbera d'Asti Sup. V. dell'Angelo '98	♀♀♀	7
● Monferrato Rosso Sonvico '03	♀♀♀	7
● Monferrato Rosso Sonvico '97	♀♀♀	7

● Barbera d'Asti Barisél '05	▼▼	4*
○ L'Avìja '05	▼▼	6
○ Moscato d'Asti '06	▼▼	4*
○ Enrico Penna Brut '03	▼▼	4*
○ Monferrato Bianco Foravìa '06	▼	4
● Barbera d'Asti Sup. La Cappelletta '01	♀♀	5
● Barbera d'Asti Sup. La Cappelletta '03	♀♀	5
● Barbera d'Asti Sup. La Cappelletta '04	♀♀	5
○ L'Avìja '03	♀♀	6
○ L'Avìja '04	♀♀	6
○ L'Avìja '01	♀♀	5

Barni

VIA FORTE, 63
13862 BRUSNENGO [BI]
TEL. 015985977

ANNUAL PRODUCTION   20,000 bottles
HECTARES UNDER VINE 6
VITICULTURE METHOD   Conventional

The Barni estate is one of Biella's most
prominent and yet its existence seems to
have spun from a passing infatuation. When
Filippo Barni was still young and working
part-time in his father-in-law's restaurant, he
was overwhelmed by a great love for the
countryside. So he decided to leave his job
and join the wine world. He started to by
vinifying in Gattinara then, in 1994, bought
vineyard land in Brusnengo, in the glorious
amphitheatre that is Mesola, a famous,
south-facing cru. He makes a Bramaterra
and two Coste della Sesia Rossos,
Mesolone and Torrearsa, from these grapes.
But his more innovative wines, Cantagal, a
passito from semi-dried grapes, and
Albaciara, from erbaluce and chardonnay,
come from another vineyard situated in
Brusnengo. Filippo aims for wines of
concentration and fruit, often ageing them in
barriques or tonneaux. With Mesolone out
of the equation this year, the wines that
impressed us the most were Bramaterra
and Cantagal. The former is a powerful,
velvety red that ages 26 months in barrique
whereas Cantagal, from erbaluce grapes
dried for five months, is one of Piedmont's
best dessert wines.

Batasiolo

FRAZ. ANNUNZIATA, 87
12064 LA MORRA [CN]
TEL. 017350130
www.batasiolo.com

ANNUAL PRODUCTION   2,500,000 bottles
HECTARES UNDER VINE 107
VITICULTURE METHOD   Conventional

Batasiolo, long owned by the Dogliani
siblings, is a large property, turning out well
over 2,000,000 bottles, yet there are never
any hiccups in production. But Doglianis
seek to be more than simply one of the
Langhe's few large wineries of note. They
dedicate meticulous attention to every
single bottle and strive to obtain the best
from each wine style. The scrupulous work
of oenologist Giorgio Lavagna also plays an
important part here. Quality is good right
across the board, and the wines from
bought-in grapes stand up well against
those from the property's own. Barolo
Corda della Briccolina has suffered a little
from the hot year and has a rather over-
evolved nose, although there is
compensating tannic dryness on the palate.
Barbaresco '04 is firmly centred on juicy
fruitiness that delivers nice appeal. A great
Dolcetto Bricco di Vergne, a lively Barbera
Sovrana, an opulent Chardonnay Morino
and a subtle Gavi Granée lead the rest of
the range.

● Bramaterra V. Doss Pilun '03	♔♔ 5
○ Cantagal '04	♔♔ 7
● Coste della Sesia Rosso Torrearsa '03	♔♔ 5
○ Albaciara Bianco '06	♔ 5
● Bramaterra V. Doss Pilun '02	♕♕ 5
● Bramaterra V. Doss Pilun '01	♕♕ 5
● Coste della Sesia Rosso Mesolone '01	♕♕ 5
● Coste della Sesia Rosso Mesolone '02	♕♕ 5
● Coste della Sesia Rosso Mesolone '03	♕♕ 5
● Coste della Sesia Rosso Torrearsa '02	♕♕ 5
● Coste della Sesia Rosso Torrearsa '01	♕♕ 5
○ Cantagal '03	♕♕ 7

● Barbaresco '04	♔♔ 6
● Barbera d'Alba Sovrana '06	♔♔ 5
● Barolo Corda della Briccolina '03	♔♔ 8
● Barolo '03	♔♔ 6
● Dolcetto d'Alba Bricco di Vergne '06	♔♔ 4*
○ Langhe Chardonnay Serbato '06	♔♔ 4*
○ Langhe Chardonnay Morino '06	♔♔ 6
○ Gavi del Comune di Gavi Granée '06	♔♔ 4*
○ Dosage Zéro M. Cl. '03	♔ 5
○ Moscato d'Asti Bosc dla Rei '06	♔ 4
○ Roero Arneis '06	♔ 5
○ Langhe Bianco Sunsì '06	♔ 5
● Barolo Corda della Briccolina '90	♕♕♕ 8
● Barolo Corda della Briccolina '89	♕♕♕ 8
● Barolo Corda della Briccolina '88	♕♕♕ 8
● Barolo Bofani '01	♕♕ 8
● Barolo Cerequio '01	♕♕ 8

Luigi Baudana

FRAZ. BAUDANA, 43
12050 SERRALUNGA D'ALBA [CN]
TEL. 0173613354
www.baudanaluigi.com

ANNUAL PRODUCTION 25,000 bottles
HECTARES UNDER VINE 4.5
VITICULTURE METHOD Conventional

Serralunga d'Alba produces great Barolos, as the two made by Luigi Baudana confirm. But we find it even more commendable that this year his best wine is an almost textbook '05 Barbera d'Alba Donatella. The nose has violets, cherries and hints of spice before the palate shows fruity and lively with well-integrated oak. Back with the Barolos, we find Cerretta '03 already has tertiary, spicy aromas and a well-balanced palate while the longer-macerated Baudana '03 is less approachable, with strongly gamey, leathery aromas, but intriguing nonetheless. Dolcetto d'Alba Baudana '05 is both elegant and intense. Langhe Rosso Lorenso '04, which spends a year in oak, is warm, with cocoa powder on the finish, and gains character from the merlot used alongside nebbiolo and barbera. Dolcetto d'Alba '06 is uncomplicatedly well styled. Langhe Chardonnay '06, which sees no oak, has a floral, fruity nose and a long, zesty palate.

Cantine Bava

S.DA MONFERRATO, 2
14023 COCCONATO [AT]
TEL. 0141907083
www.bava.com

ANNUAL PRODUCTION 600,000 bottles
HECTARES UNDER VINE 57
VITICULTURE METHOD Conventional

Cantine Bava was founded in 1911 but only gained strong international visibility in the last 15 years, with the arrival of the fourth generation, Roberto, Giulio and Paolo Bava. Today, there's a sure, business-like touch to the winery's management. Numerous events, such as concerts and art exhibitions, are held, both on-site and further afield, to bring the wines to widespread attention. The marketing is mainly Roberto's concern but Paolo and Giulio have also been busy in the vineyards and cellars, and quality has risen accordingly. The family remains faithful to a policy of not releasing the longer-lived reds too early, hence Barbera Piano Alto '03 was still ageing at the time of our tastings. But we did taste an excellent Barbera Stradivario, the '01, which has a nose of breadth and a velvety palate. Barbera Libera and Monferrato Rosso Cadodo, from nebbiolo with some barbera and merlot, are both as good as ever. The Bavas also have aspirations with sparkling wines and we enjoyed the rich Bianc 'd Bianc and the fruity Rösa, both from the Cocchi line.

Wine	Rating
● Barbera d'Alba Donatella '05	▼▼ 5
● Barolo Baudana '03	▼▼ 7
● Barolo Cerretta Piani '03	▼▼ 7
● Langhe Rosso Lorenso '04	▼▼ 5
● Dolcetto d'Alba Baudana '05	▼▼ 4*
● Dolcetto d'Alba '06	▼ 4
○ Langhe Chardonnay '06	▼ 4
● Barolo Baudana '01	♀♀ 7
● Barolo Baudana '00	♀♀ 7
● Barolo Baudana '99	♀♀ 7
● Barolo Cerretta Piani '01	♀♀ 7
● Barolo Cerretta Piani '00	♀♀ 7
● Barolo Cerretta Piani '99	♀♀ 7

Wine	Rating
● Barbera d'Asti Sup. Stradivario '01	▼▼ 7
● Barbera d'Asti Libera '05	▼▼ 4*
● Monferrato Rosso Vigneti di Cadodo '06	▼▼ 4*
⊙ Alta Langa Brut Rösa Giulio Cocchi '03	▼▼ 6
○ Alta Langa Brut Bianc 'd Bianc Giulio Cocchi '03	▼▼ 6
○ Piemonte Chardonnay Thou Bianc '06	▼ 4
○ Alta Langa Toto Corde Giulio Cocchi '03	♀♀ 5
● Barbera d'Asti Libera '04	♀♀ 4
● Barbera d'Asti Sup. Nizza Piano Alto '01	♀♀ 6

Bel Colle

FRAZ. CASTAGNI, 56
12060 VERDUNO [CN]
TEL. 0172470196
www.belcolle.it

ANNUAL PRODUCTION 150,000 bottles
HECTARES UNDER VINE 5
VITICULTURE METHOD Conventional

This leading winery, situated on the ridge separating Verduno from La Morra, vinifies grapes grown both in the Langhe and in Roero. Its range reads rather like a list of the wine styles of Cuneo province. Having skipped the '02 release of the Barolo Boscato selection, produced from grapes grown near to the Monvigliero vineyard at Verduno, the wine is now back in circulation. It was greatly admired by the tasting panels for its elegant nose of dried flowers, wild rose petals, morello cherry and quinine, introducing its austere palate with well-judged tannicity which grows to a very dense finish. Monvigliero is an elegantly structured wine which reflects the high quality of the grapes used to make it. The succulent, generous Barbera Le Masche is noteworthy, inviting, well-modulated acidity enlivening and increasing its length. It earned Two Glasses, as did Barbaresco Roncaglie, which benefited from an excellent year, and Verduno Pelaverga. Langhe Favorita, Roero Arneis and the Dolcetto are all very decent.

Bera

VIA CASTELLERO, 12
12050 NEVIGLIE [CN]
TEL. 0173630194
www.bera.it

ANNUAL PRODUCTION 120,000 bottles
HECTARES UNDER VINE 20
VITICULTURE METHOD Conventional

This estate first vinified its own grapes over 20 years ago, when Walter returned home, having graduated from the Alba wine school. Since Neviglie is one of the best parts of the Alba zone for moscato production, the family naturally concentrated on this variety. It didn't take long for Bera to become a respected name on the Moscato d'Asti scene and the Su Reimond selection is now one of the most visible in the denomination. Walter's character is phlegmatic and apparently easy-going but in recent years he has been putting great effort into diversifying his range. Now a new Asti Spumante and a new Barbaresco are on their way. For now, the two Moscatos we tasted were glorious. The standard version is all freshness and citrus nuances, both on nose and palate. The fleshier Su Reimond is similarly characterized by citrus. Langhe Sassisto, from barbera, nebbiolo and merlot, is a wine with a great deal of personality.

● Barolo Boscato '03	▼▼ 6
● Barolo Monvigliero '03	▼▼ 6
● Barbaresco Roncaglie '04	▼▼ 6
● Barbera d'Alba Le Masche '05	▼▼ 4*
● Verduno Pelaverga '06	▼▼ 4*
● Dolcetto d'Alba '06	▼ 4
○ Langhe Favorita '06	▼ 4
○ Roero Arneis '06	▼ 4
● Barolo Monvigliero '00	♉ 6
● Barolo Monvigliero '01	♉ 6
● Barolo Monvigliero '99	♉ 6
● Barolo Monvigliero '98	♉ 6
● Barolo Monvigliero '97	♉ 6

○ Moscato d'Asti Su Reimond '06	▼▼ 4*
○ Langhe Chardonnay '06	▼▼ 3*
○ Moscato d'Asti '06	▼▼ 4
● Langhe Sassisto '04	▼▼ 5
○ Bera Brut M. Cl.	▼ 4
● Dolcetto d'Alba '06	▼ 3
● Barbera d'Alba Sup. La Lena '01	♉ 4
● Barbera d'Alba Sup. La Lena '03	♉ 5
● Barbera d'Alba Sup. La Lena '04	♉ 4
● Barbaresco '01	♉ 5
● Barbaresco '00	♉ 7
● Langhe Sassisto '03	♉ 5

Cinzia Bergaglio

VIA GAVI, 29
15060 TASSAROLO [AL]
TEL. 0143342203
la.fornace@virgilio.it

ANNUAL PRODUCTION 20,000 bottles
HECTARES UNDER VINE 7
VITICULTURE METHOD Conventional

The '06 vintage has again seen this estate producing some of the best wines in the Gavi denomination. Their quality further underlines the wisdom of the decision Cinzia and her family made some years ago to stop selling the grapes from their seven hectares of vineyard to other wineries and start vinifying and bottling themselves. The plots are in Rovereto, one of the best localities for Gavi production, right on the border with the similarly good municipality of Tassarolo. Gavi Grifone delle Roveri is a green-tinged, deep straw yellow. The nose has alluring florality and hints of tropical fruit and the palate holds a fine balance between lively acidity and firm body. The other selection, Gavi Fornici, also impressed the tasting panels with its deep, lemony, citrus and balsamic aromas, and the sense of completion, harmony and length on a palate that signs off with a lingering reprise of the notes on the nose.

O Gavi del Comune di Gavi		
Grifone delle Roveri '06	⚆⚆	3*
O Gavi del Comune di Tassarolo		
Fornaci '06	⚆⚆	3*
O Gavi del Comune di Gavi		
Grifone delle Roveri '05	⚇⚇	3
O Gavi del Comune di Tassarolo		
Fornaci '05	⚇⚇	3

Nicola Bergaglio

FRAZ. ROVERETO
LOC. PEDAGGERI, 59
15066 GAVI [AL]
TEL. 0143682195

ANNUAL PRODUCTION 120,000 bottles
HECTARES UNDER VINE 15
VITICULTURE METHOD Conventional

This estate, run by Gianluigi Bergaglio and his family, manages to achieve high quality every year with every wine submitted to our tastings. The Bergaglios have 15 hectares of cortese which they use, as they always have done, to produce just two wines, a standard Gavi and a selection, Minaia. The vines for this cru have excellent aspect and are quite old, which means they yield firm, healthy grapes, bursting with flavour. The Bergaglios then turn that fruit into a deep straw yellow wine with floral, mineral and sometimes balsamic aromas, and an impressively long, fresh palate. Even the typically bitterish finish is satisfying and attractive. The straight Gavi is also a fine wine. Its green-tinged, pale yellow colour introduces a nose of white-fleshed fruit and a supple, cohesive, inviting palate with good acidity.

O Gavi del Comune di Gavi		
Minaia '06	⚆⚆	4*
O Gavi del Comune di Gavi '06	⚆⚆	3*
O Gavi del Comune di Gavi		
Minaia '04	⚇⚇	4
O Gavi del Comune di Gavi		
Minaia '05	⚇⚇	4
O Gavi del Comune di Gavi		
Ciapon '05	⚇⚇	4
O Gavi del Comune di Gavi		
Minaia '03	⚇⚇	4

Bersano

P.zza Dante, 21
14049 Nizza Monferrato [AT]
TEL. 0141720211
www.bersano.it

ANNUAL PRODUCTION 2,600,000 bottles
HECTARES UNDER VINE 240
VITICULTURE METHOD Conventional

Bersano is a large winery whose history
goes back many years. Despite the
considerable quantities handled, the quality
of the wines, particularly those from the
Conti della Cremosina line, is not just high
but also laudably consistent. Let's start with
Monferrato Rosso Pomona, made from
barbera and cabernet sauvignon. The
colour is deep ruby. On the nose there is the
distinct vegetal imprint of cabernet,
softened by intense cherry and strawberry
fruitiness, followed by a vigorous, tannic
palate that shows full and complex,
especially on the finish. The style of Barbera
d'Asti Cremosina, aged nine months in large
old casks, hangs on its austerity although
the finish gives a sound, fragrant fruitiness.
The foremost of the Barbera selections,
Generala, was not available for tasting this
year, but will be back next time. The varietal
Ruché San Pietro is most attractive, as is
Barbera Superiore Nizza, which still needs a
few months in bottle to be at its best.

Guido Berta

LOC. Saline, 53
14050 San Marzano Oliveto [AT]
TEL. 0141856193
bgpm@inwind.it

ANNUAL PRODUCTION 30,000 bottles
HECTARES UNDER VINE 12
VITICULTURE METHOD Natural

Guido Berta belongs to that band of Asti
youngsters who have recently taken over
the running of their parents' estates and
started to tweak quality firmly upwards. At
Berta, the improvement was immediate
and, with Guido's father Giuseppe still giving
valuable advice, each year's samples have
shown gains on what went before. This
year, we tasted an admirable Barbera d'Asti
Superiore Canto di Luna, aged 18 months
in new and one-year-old barriques.
Spiciness and fruit bring elegance to the
nose and the palate is abundantly lively, well
structured and full of intensity. The
succulent, easy-drinking Barbera Le Rondini
is well worth Two Glasses. Grapes for
Chardonnay Le Rondini are picked a little
late. The '05 was not produced but the '06
is inviting. The essence of the other
Chardonnay is its attractiveness. Finally, a
new Moscato showed well.

● Monferrato Rosso Pomona '04	🍷🍷 6
● Barbera d'Asti Sup. Cremosina '05	🍷🍷 6
● Barbera d'Asti Sup. Nizza '04	🍷🍷 5
● Ruché di Castagnole Monferrato S. Pietro '06	🍷🍷 4*
● Barbaresco Mantico '04	🍷 7
● Brachetto d'Acqui Castelgaro '06	🍷 4
○ Moscato d'Asti San Michele '06	🍷 3
● Barbera d'Asti Sup. Generala '97	🍷🍷🍷 7
● Barbera d'Asti Sup. Generala '01	🍷🍷 7
● Barbera d'Asti Sup. Generala '03	🍷🍷 6
● Barbera d'Asti Sup. Generala '04	🍷🍷 6

● Barbera d'Asti Sup. Canto di Luna '04	🍷🍷 4
● Barbera d'Asti Le Rondini '05	🍷🍷 3*
○ Moscato d'Asti '06	🍷🍷 4
○ Piemonte Chardonnay Le Rondini '06	🍷 3
○ Piemonte Chardonnay '06	🍷 4
● Barbera d'Asti Le Rondini '04	🍷🍷 3
● Barbera d'Asti Sup. Canto di Luna '03	🍷🍷 4

Bertelli

VIA SAN CARLO
14055 COSTIGLIOLE D'ASTI [AT]
TEL. 0258314153

ANNUAL PRODUCTION 30,000 bottles
HECTARES UNDER VINE 7
VITICULTURE METHOD Conventional

The Bertelli family has owned this splendid property for generations but now, with Alberto now longer a regular presence on the estate, his sister Elisabetta has called in young Claudio Dacasto to take care of the vines and cellar from day to day while the Bertellis set down production strategy from Milan. This gives primacy to territory focus, which means that the rules are simple: ensure good, sound grapes and the minimum of intervention in the cellars. Our annual visit to the winery always brings surprises but these do not regard the character of the wines, which never deviates from the Costigliole style. Unfortunately, their originality can disconcert the less expert taster. Indeed, producing wines that faithfully reflect each year's weather patterns naturally leads to considerable vintage-to-vintage variation, especially with the whites. Fossaretti '03, from sauvignon, for instance, appears opulent and fat, almost a wine for foie gras or cheese. Mon Mayor, from nebbiolo, and Barbera Montetusa are broad and complex, the former with more austerity. The quality of Barbera Vieilles Vignes '01 brought it to the finals. The Giarone selection, also '01, is minerally and spicy.

● Barbera d'Asti S. Antonio Vieilles Vignes '01	YY (grey)	6
● Barbera d'Asti Giarone '01	**YY**	6
● Barbera d'Asti Montetusa '01	**YY**	6
● Monferrato Rosso Mon Mayor '01	**YY**	6
○ Monferrato Bianco I Fossaretti '03	**YY**	6
○ Piemonte Chardonnay Giarone '04	YY	6
○ Plissé Traminer '03	YY	6
○ Piemonte Chardonnay Giarone '02	YY	6
○ Piemonte Chardonnay Giarone '03	YY	6
○ San Marsan Bianco '03	YY	6
● Barbera d'Asti S. Antonio Vieilles Vignes '00	YY	6
● Barbera d'Asti S. Antonio Vieilles Vignes '99	YY	6
● Monferrato Rosso MB '01	YY	6

Eugenio Bocchino

FRAZ. SANTA MARIA
LOC. SERRA, 2
12064 LA MORRA [CN]
TEL. 0173364226
laperucca@libero.it

ANNUAL PRODUCTION 20,000 bottles
HECTARES UNDER VINE 6
VITICULTURE METHOD Conventional

The philosophy of Eugenio Bocchino and his wife Cinzia can be summed up in two words: dynamism and technique. The continual refinement of winemaking practices and the great care the Bocchinos take in everything they do means theirs continues to be one of the Langhe estates to watch. The main news this year is that the couple have released a new Barolo selection, La Serra '03. They have also started work on a small crop of riesling, the results of which will appear next year, as will our report on Nebbiolo d'Alba La Perucca '04, which wasn't available this time. The nose on La Serra is full of spice, leather, tobacco and scents of violet. Fine-grained tannin on the palate is well sustained by acidity that supports the wine right through to its spicy finish. Barolo Lu '03 is more directed towards violet and ripe plum aromas. Its palate is marked by silky tannins, and there is leather and spice on the finish. The balanced, elegant Barbera d'Alba '05 impressed, as did Langhe Rosso Suo di Giacomo '04, which blends the austerity of nebbiolo with the lively fruit of barbera.

● Barolo La Serra '03	YY (grey)	7
● Barolo Lu '03	**YY**	7
● Barbera d'Alba '05	**YY**	4*
● Langhe Rosso Suo di Giacomo '04	**YY**	6
● Barolo '01	YY	7
● Barolo '00	YY	7
● Langhe Rosso Suo di Giacomo '00	YY	6
● Langhe Rosso Suo di Giacomo '02	YY	5
● Langhe Rosso Suo di Giacomo '03	YY	6
● Nebbiolo d'Alba La Perucca '03	YY	6

Alfiero Boffa

VIA LEISO, 50
14050 SAN MARZANO OLIVETO [AT]
TEL. 0141856115
www.alfieroboffa.com

ANNUAL PRODUCTION 100,000 bottles
HECTARES UNDER VINE 25
VITICULTURE METHOD Conventional

Barbera has become a sort of obsession with Alfiero Boffa, although a nice one. Over the years, he has bought several vineyard plots but before he acquires anything he studies the aspect of the land and the quality of the plants, only investing where the vines are of a certain age so that the grapes will match his exacting requirements. He has recently been joined by his sons Rossano and Simone, who have inherited their father's attachment to the grape. Such dedication to the leading variety around these parts has led to a fine range of wines, led by Barbera d'Asti Muntrivé. This has an opaque ruby colour with purple highlights. There is black cherry, strawberry, cocoa powder and vanilla on the nose and the palate has drive and power, nicely set off by refreshing acidity. Collina della Vedova, Vigna La Riva and Cua Longa are all beautifully made. Vigna More and Monferrato Rosso Velo di Maya, which is produced mainly from barbera, don't quite match last year's versions.

Enzo Boglietti

VIA ROMA, 37
12064 LA MORRA [CN]
TEL. 017350330
www.langhe.net/enzoboglietti

ANNUAL PRODUCTION 70,000 bottles
HECTARES UNDER VINE 20.7
VITICULTURE METHOD Conventional

After the break in production necessitated by the poor '02 vintage, Barolo returns to take pride of place on Enzo and Gianni Boglietti's estate, which has gained in functionality from its new cellars, now in full operation. Four Barolos are produced and all four, including the Barolo Arione '03 from a new vineyard in Serralunga, have a distinct identity, each of which complements the others. Take, for example, the two top scorers. The rounded Barolo Case Nere '03, which has fruit, spice and elegant tannicity, and is already balanced while the austere, serious, complex Barolo Brunate '03, whose palate is so concentrated that it still needs time to become accessible. The same concept applies to the Barberas. Roscaleto '05 is rich, succulent but also elegant. Barbera d'Alba Vigna dei Romani '04, which it just outscored, is pervasive, long and clear-cut. We should also mention the two wines from Vigna Talpone. Fewer than 6,000 bottles are produced but both products are excellent, especially the well-made Langhe Merlot Vigna Talpone '04, which has an ethery, red fruits nose and a seriously good palate with warmth and balance.

● Barbera d'Asti Sup. V. Muntrivé '05	♟♟	5
● Barbera d'Asti Sup. V. Cua Longa '05	♟♟	5
● Barbera d'Asti Sup. Collina della Vedova '04	♟♟	5
● Barbera d'Asti Sup. Nizza Vigna La Riva '04	♟♟	5
● Barbera d'Asti Sup. V. More '05	♟	5
● Monferrato Rosso Velo di Maya '04	♟	5
● Monferrato Rosso Ombra del Ciliegio '05	♟	4
● Barbera d'Asti Sup. Nizza Vigna La Riva '04	♟♟	5
● Barbera d'Asti Sup. Collina della Vedova '03	♟♟	5
● Barbera d'Asti Sup. V. Muntrivé '04	♟♟	5

● Barbera d'Alba Roscaleto '05	♟♟	5
● Barolo Brunate '03	♟♟	8
● Barolo Case Nere '03	♟♟	8
● Langhe Merlot V. Talpone '04	♟♟	6
● Barbera d'Alba V. dei Romani '04	♟♟	7
● Barolo Fossati '03	♟♟	8
● Barolo Arione '03	♟♟	8
● Langhe Rosso Buio '05	♟♟	6
● Langhe Cabernet V. Talpone '04	♟♟	6
● Langhe Nebbiolo '06	♟	5
● Dolcetto d'Alba Tigli Neri '06	♟♟	4*
● Barbera d'Alba '06	♟	4
● Dolcetto d'Alba '06	♟	4
● Barolo Brunate '01	♟♟♟	8
● Barolo Brunate '97	♟♟♟	8
● Barolo Fossati '96	♟♟♟	7
● Barolo Case Nere '99	♟♟♟	8

Bondi

S.DA CAPPELLETTE, 73
15076 OVADA [AL]
TEL. 0143821369
www.bondivini.it

Borgo Maragliano

REG. SAN SEBASTIANO, 2
14050 LOAZZOLO [AT]
TEL. 014487132
www.borgomaragliano.com

ANNUAL PRODUCTION 20,000 bottles
HECTARES UNDER VINE 7
VITICULTURE METHOD Conventional

ANNUAL PRODUCTION 190,000 bottles
HECTARES UNDER VINE 18
VITICULTURE METHOD Conventional

The hills surrounding the village of Ovada are ideal for dolcetto cultivation and Dolcetto di Ovada has one of the highest standings of the numerous Dolcetto denominations in Piedmont. The Bondi family bought Cascina Banaia in 2000 and immediately converted it into a property that could deliver quality with a capital Q. The area, Cappellette, is very well suited to viticulture, the roughly seven hectares of vineyard enjoying good aspect and the dolcetto and barbera vines being of the right age to give fine grapes. Add to this the acknowledged vinifying skills of the Bondis. This year, we particularly admired Dolcetto di Ovada Du'ien. The colour is a deep ruby and the broad, deep nose evokes cherries and black berry fruit, leading to a palate that shows structured, harmonious and very long. But Bondi can also do great things with barbera. The Banaiotta selection works very well and Ruvrin, aged 14 months in small oak, is a weighty, ambitious wine. Monferrato Rosso Le Guie has good style.

We have to admit that Carlo and Silvia Galliano almost left our tasters lost for points of reference. Usually, when we review a winery in this Guide, we start with the wines we consider most important, which means the ones that best reflect its owners' production philosophy. The problem is that Borgo Maragliano seems to have more than one vocation, in the sense that we can't say for sure whether the Galliano family are best at sparkling wines, dried-grape passito wines or cork-bottled Moscatos. All three styles of wines shine. Let's start with the fizz. Both the Rosé and the Brut are wines of outstanding personality, with bready and yeasty aromas, and driving acidity that adds length. The Moscato scores for its unusual fullness and juicy richness, as well as its intense sensations of peach, menthol, citronella and citrus peel. Then we have the late-harvest Loazzolo Vendemmia Tardiva. It's almost amber in hue. The nose is enthralling and the palate is richly sweet yet there's not a hint of cloying. In short, it's a truly fine dessert wine.

● Dolcetto di Ovada Sup. Du'ien '05	♟♟ 4*
● Barbera del M.to Banaiotta '05	♟♟ 5
● Barbera del M.to Ruvrin '04	♟♟ 5
● Monferrato Rosso Le Guie '05	♟ 4
● Barbera del M.to Ruvrin '03	♟♟ 5
● Dolcetto di Ovada Sup. Du'ien '03	♟♟ 4
● Dolcetto di Ovada Sup. Du'ien '04	♟♟ 4

○ Loazzolo	
Borgo Maragliano V. T. '04	♟♟ 6
○ Moscato d'Asti La Caliera '06	♟♟ 3*
⊙ Giovanni Galliano	
Brut Rosé M. Cl. '04	♟♟ 5
○ Giuseppe Galliano Brut M. Cl. '03	♟♟ 5
○ El Calié '06	♟ 3
○ Piemonte Chardonnay	
Crevoglio '06	♟ 3
○ Loazzolo	
Borgo Maragliano V. T. '03	♟♟ 6
○ Loazzolo	
Borgo Maragliano V. T. '01	♟♟ 6

Giacomo Borgogno & Figli

via Gioberti, 1
12060 Barolo [CN]
tel. 017356108
www.borgogno-wine.com

ANNUAL PRODUCTION 100,000 bottles
HECTARES UNDER VINE 14
VITICULTURE METHOD Conventional

This winery is run by Giorgio and Cesare Boschis but their father Franco still often pokes his head between the barrels and vats to keep an eye on what they're doing. The winery has been going for over 250 years but wears its age lightly, with high quality wines emerging vintage after vintage. It's also one of the few wineries with major stocks of old wines, and every year, to the joy of its clients, batches of old Barolo vintages are recorked, relabelled and put on sale. But here tradition is the norm. Maceration on the skins is still long, ageing is in large old Slavonian oak casks and the Barolos are normally released a year after the minimum allowed under DOCG. So we should be seeing the '02s this year, but "should be" is the operative term because they weren't produced. That leaves us the '05 Barbera Superiore and the '05 Langhe Nebbiolo to discuss. The former is lively and has good typicity; the latter has notable power. We should add, though, that the youthful, easy drinking Barbera '06 is a very good wine and the Dolcetto is pleasant, with notable impact on the palate.

● Barbera d'Alba '06	▼▼	4
● Langhe Nebbiolo '05	▼▼	5
● Barbera d'Alba Sup. '05	▼▼	4
● Dolcetto d'Alba '06	▼	4
● Barolo Cl. '98	▽▽▽	8
● Barolo Cl. '99	▽▽	8
● Barolo Cl. '00	▽▽	8
● Barolo Cl. '01	▽▽	8
● Barolo '99	▽▽	7
● Barolo '98	▽▽	8
● Barolo '01	▽▽	8
● Barolo Liste '01	▽▽	8
● Barolo Liste '00	▽▽	8

Boroli

loc. Madonna di Como, 34
12051 Alba [CN]
tel. 0173365477
www.boroli.it

ANNUAL PRODUCTION 170,000 bottles
HECTARES UNDER VINE 32
VITICULTURE METHOD Conventional

Achille Boroli runs this estate, which was founded by his father Silvano, with great competence and every year he announces some major new development. There was the construction of a new cellar on Castiglione Falletto's Villero vineyard, there was the release of a new Barolo Bussia and also of a new Villero Riserva. Now we have the new Barolo Cerequio. It comes from a recently acquired vineyard so the '03 was not shaped by the Borolis but it still scored well. But it's clear that the family is beginning to build up a significant number of Barolo crus, enough to make even the old producers in the area envious. The range is broad and well differentiated. The two Barberas, made with abundant use of new oak, are in a more modern, more extractive style while the Barolos retain a more classic imprint. This year's best selections are the austere '03 Villero, the balsamic, full-bodied Cerequio, also from '03, and the complex '99 Villero Riserva. The standard Barolo is more immediate. Top of the Barberas is Fagiani '04 which has already partially assimilated its oak. The surprise, though, is Dolcetto Madonna di Como which, thanks to its great site and the great vintage, soars to unexpected heights.

● Barolo Villero '03	▼▼	8
● Barolo Cerequio '03	▼▼	8
● Barolo Villero Ris. '99	▼▼	8
● Barolo '03	▼▼	7
● Barbera d'Alba Sup. Fagiani '04	▼▼	6
● Dolcetto d'Alba Madonna di Como '06	▼▼	4*
○ Langhe Chardonnay Bel Amì '06	▼▼	4*
○ Moscato d'Asti Aureum '06	▼▼	4*
● Barbera d'Alba Bricco 4 Fratelli '05	▼	4
● Barolo Villero '00	▽▽▽	8
● Barolo Villero '01	▽▽▽	8
● Barolo Villero '99	▽▽	8
● Barolo Villero '98	▽▽	8
● Barolo Villero Ris. '98	▽▽	8
● Barolo Bussia '01	▽▽	8

Francesco Boschis

FRAZ. SAN MARTINO DI PIANEZZO, 57
12063 DOGLIANI [CN]
TEL. 017370574
www.marcdegrazia.com

ANNUAL PRODUCTION 40,000 bottles
HECTARES UNDER VINE 11
VITICULTURE METHOD Conventional

The Boschis family has been growing grapes for many generations and has been bottling wine for around 40 years. The wines, which are mostly made from indigenous Piedmontese varieties, have a recognizable style that tends to bring out their provenance. This is primarily dolcetto country and the Boschis family, guided by all-important consultant Beppe Caviola, handle the grape with great skill. Two of the leading Dolcetto selections, Vigna dei Prey and Sorì San Martino, were missing from this year's range. Both now come under Dogliani, the zone's new Dolcetto-based DOCG, which precludes their release until the end of 2007, so neither had been bottled at the time of our tastings. Nevertheless, we could, and did, taste Dogliani DOCG Vigna del Ciliegio '05, which had already undergone the additional year's ageing. It's austere, powerful and concentrated, and although it is still searching for final balance it should have a starry future. Barbera Le Masserie and the young, gently fruity Dolcetto Pianezzo are both good. Vigna dei Garisin, from sauvignon, is well styled and inviting.

Luigi Boveri

LOC. MONTALE CELLI
VIA XX SETTEMBRE, 6
15050 COSTA VESCOVATO [AL]
TEL. 0131838165
www.boveriluigi.com

ANNUAL PRODUCTION 60,000 bottles
HECTARES UNDER VINE 15
VITICULTURE METHOD Conventional

Fifteen years have passed since Leopoldo Boveri passed full control of his estate to his son Luigi. Much has changed in that time, but not the humble yet impassioned approach to making and selling wine. He starts from the indisputable premise that quality is everything and so the wines satisfy everyone, from the expert to the simple wine lover. Vignalunga, made from carefully selected barbera grapes and aged with skilful use of oak, is a serious, long-ageing wine of great structure. Boccanera is totally different. It's an easy-drinker and great value for money. Between them comes Poggio delle Amarene, the only Barbera selection in the area to be aged in stainless steel. The strategy of contrasting styles is the same with the whites. There's a Timorasso of great complexity and structure which is usually one of the best in the zone and a fresh, clean, fruity Cortese, Vigna del Prete.

● Dogliani V. del Ciliegio '05	▼▼	4*
● Barbera d'Alba Le Masserie '05	▼▼	5
● Dolcetto di Dogliani Pianezzo '06	▼	4
○ Langhe Bianco V. dei Garisin '06	▼	4
● Dolcetto di Dogliani Sup.		
V. del Ciliegio '04	♈♈	4
● Dolcetto di Dogliani V. dei Prey '05	♈♈	4
● Dolcetto di Dogliani V. dei Prey '04	♈♈	4
● Barbera d'Alba Le Masserie '04	♈♈	5

● Colli Tortonesi Barbera		
Vignalunga '04	▼▼	6
○ Colli Tortonesi Bianco		
Filari di Timorasso '05	▼▼	5
● Colli Tortonesi Barbera		
Boccanera '06	▼▼	3*
● Colli Tortonesi Barbera		
Poggio delle Amarene '05	▼▼	6
○ Colli Tortonesi Cortese		
V. del Prete '06	▼	3
○ Colli Tortonesi Bianco		
Filari di Timorasso '03	♈♈	5
○ Colli Tortonesi Bianco		
Filari di Timorasso '04	♈♈	5
● Colli Tortonesi Barbera		
Vignalunga '03	♈♈	5
● Colli Tortonesi Barbera		
Vignalunga '01	♈♈	5

Gianfranco Bovio

FRAZ. ANNUNZIATA
B.TA CIOTTO, 63
12064 LA MORRA [CN]
TEL. 017350667
www.boviogianfranco.com

ANNUAL PRODUCTION 70,000 bottles
HECTARES UNDER VINE 12
VITICULTURE METHOD Conventional

The winemaking team that Gianfranco Bovio has set up, with Beppe Caviola, Walter Porasso and now also Porasso's son Fabio, ensures high quality across the range but really shines with the Barolo crus. This year, Barolo Bricco Parussi Riserva '01, from a vineyard in Castiglione Falletto, has hit the peaks. It has a glorious, spicy, warm, tertiary nose with morello cherry, cocoa powder, leather and pepper. The highly inviting palate follows through well, and is full and balanced, with silky tannins The well-earned Three Glasses ensure it follows in the footsteps of the legendary '90 Arborina. Barolo Gattera '03 and Barolo Vigna Arborina '03 were also worthy finalists. The Gattera is more complex and austere. Barrique ageing has helped the Arborina towards early balance and a more forward style. Barolo Rocchettevino '03 is also well styled and ready for drinking. The '04 release of Barbera d'Alba Regiaveja brings it back up to its usual quality, with the oak well integrated into the fruit. Then comes Langhe Bianco La Villa '06, one of the best in its class. It brings together chardonnay and sauvignon – in previous years they had been used separately – and sensations range from sage to tropical fruit.

Braida

VIA ROMA, 94
14030 ROCCHETTA TANARO [AT]
TEL. 0141644113
www.braida.it

ANNUAL PRODUCTION 600,000 bottles
HECTARES UNDER VINE 50
VITICULTURE METHOD Conventional

The main news from the Bologna family this year is that they have recently inaugurated a new building, not far from the original one, which will house their offices and bottling line. This will leave more space in the vinification cellar for ageing, in bottle as well as in oak. There's also the news that they have skipped a year with Barbera Ai Suma. It's made by leaving the grapes to overripen on the vine and the weather in '05 made this impossible. The other two Barbera selections are, however, top-notch. Bricco dell'Uccellone has ripe red berry fruitiness plus refined, spicy aromas recalling cocoa powder, liquorice and aniseed. The palate has great succulence and fabulous texture, so much so that the wine gained Three Glasses, confirming the Bolognas in their role as the masters of the variety. Bricco della Bigotta is also superb, with a wild cherry, blackcurrant and blueberry nose, and a refreshing palate depending on balanced acidity and a full structure. Barbera Montebruna is all attractiveness and fills the mouth before coming to a complex, harmonious finish. We round off with two whites, the opulent Il Fiore, from riesling, chardonnay and other local varieties, and the zesty Riesling.

● Barolo Bricco Parussi Ris. '01	♟♟♟	7
● Barolo V. Arborina '03	♟♟	7
● Barolo V. Gattera '03	♟♟	7
● Barbera d'Alba Regiaveja '04	♟♟	5
● Dolcetto d'Alba Dabbene '06	♟♟	4
● Barolo Rocchettevino '03	♟♟	7
○ Langhe Bianco		
V. La Villa '06	♟♟	4
● Barbera d'Alba Il Ciotto '06	♟	4
● Barolo V. Arborina '90	♟♟♟	8
● Barolo V. Arborina '01	♟♟	7
● Barolo V. Arborina '00	♟♟	7
● Barolo V. Gattera '00	♟♟	7
● Barolo V. Gattera '01	♟♟	7
● Barolo Bricco Parussi Ris. '00	♟♟	7

● Barbera d'Asti		
Bricco dell'Uccellone '05	♟♟♟	7
● Barbera d'Asti		
Bricco della Bigotta '05	♟♟	7
● Barbera d'Asti Montebruna '05	♟♟	4
● Monferrato Rosso Il Bacialé '05	♟♟	4
○ Langhe Bianco Il Fiore '06	♟♟	4
○ Langhe Bianco Riesling '06	♟♟	4
● Brachetto d'Acqui '06	♟	4
● Grignolino d'Asti '06	♟	4
● Barbera d'Asti Ai Suma '04	♟♟♟	7
● Barbera d'Asti Ai Suma '89	♟♟♟	7
● Barbera d'Asti		
Bricco dell'Uccellone '03	♟♟♟	7
● Barbera d'Asti		
Bricco dell'Uccellone '01	♟♟♟	7
● Barbera d'Asti		
Bricco dell'Uccellone '98	♟♟♟	7

Brema
VIA POZZOMAGNA, 9
14045 INCISA SCAPACCINO [AT]
TEL. 014174019
vinibrema@inwind.it

ANNUAL PRODUCTION 140,000 bottles
HECTARES UNDER VINE 18
VITICULTURE METHOD Conventional

Alessandra and Ermanno Brema, who run this attractive Nizza estate, put a traditional stamp on their wines. They were the first producers to make Barbera d'Asti a wine of prestige and have become a paradigm of the style. The Bremas are impervious to fashion and happily avoid a high-profile image, so their labels are rarely to be seen in glossy magazines. In return, they have a loyal, affectionate client base. In line with their benchmark status, they submitted a fascinating range of Barberas, all of them reassuringly sound. Their vineyard selection, Bricco della Volpettona, is full of stuffing and shows good balance between its more fruity and more spicy elements. Bricconizza is more immediate, with good, sound fruitiness and plenty of liveliness. Both of them also have subtle vanilla notes from their oak ageing and well-integrated tannins. Ai Cruss, the third Barbera, has a less sharply defined nose but upfront fruit and good acidity. A new wine, Dolcetto d'Asti Montera, has surprisingly good intensity and concentration. The rest of the range also impresses.

Giacomo Brezza & Figli
VIA LOMONDO, 4
12060 BAROLO [CN]
TEL. 0173560921
www.brezza.it

ANNUAL PRODUCTION 80,000 bottles
HECTARES UNDER VINE 16.5
VITICULTURE METHOD Conventional

This is a long-standing, much respected winery. It's run by Enzo Brezza, who brings skill and professionalism to bear on its management. Enzo is predominantly traditionalist in approach but he's not averse to the new, one example being the glass stopper he uses for some wines but not, of course, his Barolos. The range is large, giving us much to discuss. Let's start with the '03 Barolos. The Bricco Sarmass cru, aged in large old casks, is powerful and pervasive but balanced and long. Sarmassa is even better, indeed it took home Three Glasses. The nose is classic, filled with traditional nebbiolo aromas, and shows highly refined. The palate is full and pervasive, flaunting refined elegance plus the softest of tannic weaves. Large old casks were also used for the '05 Nebbiolo, a wine that makes a great impression, but the real revelation was how good the '05 Barbera Cannubi Muscatel is. Aged a year in large new casks, it is full and elegant, with plentiful varietal notes and a long aftertaste. Freisa '06 sees no oak and has an attractively almondy finish. The fresh, easy-drinking Dolcetto '06 also showed well.

● Barbera d'Asti Ai Cruss '06	▼▼ 4*
● Barbera d'Asti Sup. Bricco della Volpettona '05	▼▼ 6
● Barbera d'Asti Sup. Bricconizza '05	▼▼ 6
● Dolcetto d'Asti Montera '06	▼ 4
● Dolcetto d'Asti V. Impagnato '05	▼ 4
● Grignolino d'Asti Le Roche '06	▼ 3
● Brachetto d'Acqui Carlotta '06	▼ 4
● Monferrato Rosso Il Fulvo '05	▼ 5
● Barbera d'Asti Sup. Bricco della Volpettona '04	♀♀ 6
● Barbera d'Asti Sup. Bricco della Volpettona '03	♀♀ 6
● Barbera d'Asti Sup. Bricco della Volpettona '01	♀♀ 6

● Barolo Sarmassa '03	▼▼▼ 7
● Barolo Bricco Sarmassa '03	▼▼ 8
● Nebbiolo d'Alba Santa Rosalia '05	▼▼ 4
● Barbera d'Alba Cannubi Muscatel '05	▼▼ 5
● Barbera d'Alba Santa Rosalia '06	▼ 4
● Dolcetto d'Alba S. Lorenzo '06	▼ 4
● Langhe Freisa Santa Rosalia '06	▼ 4
● Barolo Cannubi '01	♀♀♀ 7
● Barolo Cannubi '96	♀♀♀ 7
● Barolo Cannubi '99	♀♀ 7
● Barolo Bricco Sarmassa '01	♀♀ 8
● Barolo Sarmassa '00	♀♀ 7
● Barolo Sarmassa '01	♀♀ 7

Bric Cenciurio
VIA ROMA, 24
12060 BAROLO [CN]
TEL. 017356317
www.briccenciurio.com

ANNUAL PRODUCTION 45,000 bottles
HECTARES UNDER VINE 13
VITICULTURE METHOD Conventional

This is a family operation, with mother
Fiorella, the two children Alessandro and
Alberto, and uncle Carlo all contributing to
work in vineyards and cellar. The vines are
located in two municipalities, in
Castellinaldo for arneis, and in Barolo for
barbera, nebbiolo, cabernet sauvignon and
brachetto. Beginning with the former, the
arneis-based Vendemmia Tardiva, matured
in 25-hectolitre casks, is truly superlative,
showing structured, soft and elegant.
Equally fine is the steel-fermented standard
'06, with appealing aromatics and good
progression. Nebbiolo '05 shows careful
crafting, with impressive expression and
length. The same goes for Langhe Rosso di
Caialupo '04, which reflects good cabernet
typicity on the nose, superb structure and
development. Barbera Naunda '05 is crisp
and already shows nice balance. As for the
two Barolos, Costa di Rose '03 offers a
complex, intense nose, an imposing,
alcohol-rich palate and a good measure of
elegance. Costa di Rose Riserva '01 has
found harmony, with a generous bouquet
and remarkable length.

Bricco del Cucù
LOC. BRICCO, 10
12060 BASTIA MONDOVÌ [CN]
TEL. 017460153
www.briccocucu.com

ANNUAL PRODUCTION 50,000 bottles
HECTARES UNDER VINE 10
VITICULTURE METHOD Conventional

Bricco del Cucù is the brainchild of Dario
Sciolla. His family has owned lands in these
magnificent hills between Bastia Mondovì
and Roccacigliè for generations but Dario
was the first to bottle the vineyards'
Dolcetto. With farmers' sensitivity to the
rhythms and contours of the land, the family
alternates from working the vineyards to
caring for the hazelnut groves. When he
began here, Sciolla restructured the
woodlands and he has recently planted the
vineyards to international varieties. These
are now in production and they supply fruit
for the long-awaited Langhe Rosso. This
new Diavolisanti, a blend of dolcetto and
merlot, pays homage to the international
style, showing plenty of spice and a velvety
mouthfeel. The same two varieties produce
a second wine, Superboum, which mirrors
its elder sibling, with equally good structure
and more prominent fruit. Dolcetto,
however, is what the Bastia hills produce
best. San Bernardo '05 unleashes enviable
power while the standard '06 does an
effortless job of reflecting the natural fullness
of that vintage.

O Sito dei Fossili V. T. '05	♆♆	6
● Barbera d'Alba Sup. Naunda '05	♆♆	5
● Barolo Costa di Rose '03	♆♆	6
● Barolo Costa di Rose Ris. '01	♆♆	6
● Langhe Nebbiolo '05	♆♆	5
● Langhe Rosso Rosso Di Caialupo '04	♆♆	5
O Roero Arneis Sito dei Fossili '06	♆	4
● Barolo Costa di Rose '01	♀♀	8
● Barolo Costa di Rose '02	♀♀	6
● Barbera d'Alba Sup. Naunda '03	♀♀	5
● Barbera d'Alba Sup. Naunda '04	♀♀	5

● Dolcetto di Dogliani '06	♆♆	3*
O Langhe Bianco '06	♆♆	3*
● Langhe Rosso Superboum '05	♆♆	4
● Langhe Rosso Diavolisanti '04	♆♆	4
● Dolcetto di Dogliani Sup. Bricco S. Bernardo '05	♆♆	4
● Langhe Dolcetto '06	♆	3
● Langhe Dolcetto Vinot '06	♆	3
● Dolcetto di Dogliani '05	♀♀	3
● Dolcetto di Dogliani Sup. Bricco S. Bernardo '04	♀♀	4

Bricco Maiolica
FRAZ. RICCA
VIA BOLANGINO, 7
12055 DIANO D'ALBA [CN]
TEL. 0173612049
www.briccomaiolica.it

ANNUAL PRODUCTION 90,000 bottles
HECTARES UNDER VINE 20
VITICULTURE METHOD Conventional

Beppe Accomo is not only the director of the most prestigious producer in the Diano d'Alba area; he is also the zone's soul and conscience. He stimulates his fellow producers to adopt strategies that will advance the reputation of local wine production. According to Accomo, and we agree with him, Diano has all the qualities that would propel it into the higher ranks of Langhe wines but it needs to find coherent direction for the various styles it presently offers. A tasting of his own Dolcettos may offer an indication. Alongside a classic version, all fruit and freshness, Bricco Maiolica offers a formidable cru, Barbera Vigna Vigia, the product of ceaseless efforts in the vineyard and painstaking attention in the cellar. It is fragrant, very varietal, with eloquent tannins and a taut, harmonious palate, drawing from its terroir firm but juicy acidity, earthiness and balance. We would also mention an austere Nebbiolo and a Langhe Rosso that is all pinot nero, as courageous for its lengthy ageing as it is for the mere concept.

Bricco Mondalino
REG. MONDALINO, 5
15049 VIGNALE MONFERRATO [AL]
TEL. 0142933204
www.briccomondalino.it

ANNUAL PRODUCTION 80,000 bottles
HECTARES UNDER VINE 13
VITICULTURE METHOD Conventional

Mauro Gaudio is one of the most able of Monferrato producers and always succeeds in crafting a fine list of impressive wines. Among Bricco Mondalino's best performers is Barbera Zerolegno, as usual. Preceded by a luminous ruby, it unfurls spicy aromas and then builds a wonderfully balanced, lengthy palate. Barbera Superiore leads off with a garnet-edged ruby and a rich bouquet of smooth spice and vanilla, then introduces vivacious acidity that ensures an overall fine performance. The hot 2003 growing year may have pushed Barbera d'Asti Il Bergantino down a rung for it's slightly disappointing. Both Grignolinos we tasted, the Bricco Mondalino selection and the standard label, share a tendency towards the vegetal, as well as tannins that beg for more time. The structure of the selection, however, certainly gives it the nod over the other version. Malvasia di Casorzo Molignano is more than just good. With acidity and sugar right on target, it's a real pleasure. Monferrato Casalese Cortese is refreshing and well worth uncorking.

● Barbera d'Alba V. Vigia '04	♟♟	5
● Diano d'Alba Sörì		
Bricco Maiolica '06	♟♟	4*
● Dolcetto di Diano d'Alba '06	♟♟	4
● Langhe Rosso Lorié '03	♟♟	6
● Nebbiolo d'Alba Cumot '04	♟♟	5
● Barbera d'Alba '05	♟	4
O Langhe Bianco Rolando '06	♟	4
● Barbera d'Alba V. Vigia '98	♟♟♟	5
● Barbera d'Alba V. Vigia '03	♟♟	5
● Barbera d'Alba V. Vigia '01	♟♟	5
● Barbera d'Alba V. Vigia '00	♟♟	5
● Diano d'Alba Sörì		
Bricco Maiolica '05	♟♟	4
● Diano d'Alba Sörì		
Bricco Maiolica '04	♟♟	4
● Nebbiolo d'Alba Cumot '03	♟♟	5

● Barbera del M.to Sup. '05	♟♟	3*
● Grignolino del M.to Casalese		
Bricco Mondalino '06	♟♟	4
● Barbera del M.to Zerolegno '05	♟♟	4
● Barbera d'Asti Il Bergantino '03	♟	4
● Malvasia di Casorzo d'Asti		
Molignano '06	♟	4
● Grignolino del M.to Casalese '06	♟	4
O Monferrato Casalese Cortese '06	♟	3
● Barbera del M.to Sup. '04	♟♟	3

★ Bricco Rocche - Bricco Asili

VIA MONFORTE, 63
12060 CASTIGLIONE FALLETTO [CN]
TEL. 0173282582
www.ceretto.com

ANNUAL PRODUCTION 60,000 bottles
HECTARES UNDER VINE 18.5
VITICULTURE METHOD Conventional

You can see from quite a distance the plexiglass cube on the edge of the Rocche di Castiglione Falletto ridge. But aficionados of the Ceretto family's Barolo and Barbaresco need no architectural landmarks. They know that the cellar has produced some of the best wines the Langhe has ever produced, for instance Barolo Bricco Rocche '89 or Barbaresco Bricco Asili '78. And almost 30 years later, precious little has changed. The Ceretto brothers are still here at Castiglione Falletto, aided for some years by the next generation, still producing jewels from both Bricco Rocche and from Bricco Asili. We were not able to taste some of the long-standing selections, like Barolo Bricco Rocche, but the great Barolo Brunate was a more than worthy substitute. Gorgeous impressions of tobacco leaf and smooth spices and a warm, velvety palate continue to make this wine a classic of the Barolo DOCG. Prapò, though, is still somewhat closed, as is often the case with Barolos from Serralunga. The two Barbarescos are impressive, with Bernardot particularly fine, and Bricco Asili brims with character and personality.

● Barbaresco Bernardot '04	YY	7
● Barolo Brunate '03	YY	8
● Barbaresco Bricco Asili '04	YY	8
● Barolo Prapò '03	YY	8
● Barbaresco Bricco Asili '85	YYY	8
● Barbaresco Bricco Asili '96	YYY	8
● Barolo Brunate '90	YYY	8
● Barolo Prapò '83	YYY	8
● Barolo Bricco Rocche '89	YYY	8
● Barbaresco Bricco Asili '99	YYY	8
● Barbaresco Bricco Asili '97	YYY	8
● Barbaresco Bricco Asili '89	YYY	8
● Barbaresco Bricco Asili '86	YYY	8
● Barbaresco Bricco Asili '88	YYY	8
● Barbaresco Bricco Asili '03	YY	8

Gian Piero Broglia

TENUTA LA MEIRANA
LOC. LOMELLINA, 22
15066 GAVI [AL]
TEL. 0143642998
www.broglia.eu

ANNUAL PRODUCTION N.A.
HECTARES UNDER VINE 47
VITICULTURE METHOD Conventional

Gian Piero Broglia's property extends over 100 hectares of the verdant, attractive countryside of Gavi. Almost half is planted to vine and cortese of course claims the lion's share. The estate's heart is the intriguing La Meirana villa-farm complex. This is also the name of one of the Gavi selections, so we'll start there. After an especially sparkling straw yellow, a wondrously refreshing nose offers nicely nuanced fragrances of white peach, wisteria blossoms and citrus, which segue into a lengthy, acid-enlivened palate. Even better is Bruno Broglia, which is no surprise, since all of Broglia's winemaking expertise is focused on this selection, starting with the vines. Over half a century old, they give extremely low yields. Sapient cask ageing does the rest. The result is a Gavi of rich, almost distilled, fragrances of wildflowers, honey and gunflint, with a perfect balance of body and acidity that creates a sumptuous palate. Monferrato Rosso is a fine version of dolcetto.

○ Gavi del Comune di Gavi Bruno Broglia '05	YY	5
○ Gavi del Comune di Gavi La Meirana '06	YY	4*
● Monferrato Rosso Le Pernici '06	YY	4*
○ Gavi del Comune di Gavi Bruno Broglia '04	YY	5
○ Gavi del Comune di Gavi Bruno Broglia '03	YY	5
○ Gavi del Comune di Gavi Bruno Broglia '02	YY	5
○ Gavi del Comune di Gavi Bruno Broglia '01	YY	5
○ Gavi del Comune di Gavi Bruno Broglia '00	YY	5
● Monferrato Rosso Le Pernici '05	YY	4
● Monferrato Rosso Bruno Broglia '03	YY	5

Brovia

VIA ALBA-BAROLO, 54
12060 CASTIGLIONE FALLETTO [CN]
TEL. 017362852
www.brovia.net

ANNUAL PRODUCTION 60,000 bottles
HECTARES UNDER VINE 15
VITICULTURE METHOD Conventional

The Brovias are conscientious, traditional growers in the most important Langhe denominations. Their Barolo vineyard selections bring out the absolute best in the nebbiolo grape, which finds an ideal habitat here at Castiglione Falletto. There were no Barolo releases last year so this year our interest was rekindled by an impressive line-up of champions. Ca' Mia, which sees 30 months in oak, offers evolved headiness and hints of violets and then an attack composed of tannins that are never over the line, just smooth and judicious. Rocche dei Brovia, sourced from a venerable vineyard planted in 1966, flaunts a consummate bouquet: spacious, never-ending, filled with liquorice and bottled cherries. Garblèt Sué and Villero are as superlative as ever while the steel-matured Barbera Sorì del Drago stands out for its juicy pulp and succulence. The two Dolcettos are also up on the top rung, where they belong, particularly Solatìo, a thoroughbred in its class.

G. B. Burlotto

VIA VITTORIO EMANUELE, 28
12060 VERDUNO [CN]
TEL. 0172470122
www.burlotto.com

ANNUAL PRODUCTION 60,000 bottles
HECTARES UNDER VINE 12
VITICULTURE METHOD Conventional

History and tradition go hand in hand at G. B. Burlotto, which has been producing wines since the mid 19th century. It currently produces fully 14 wines and tasting reveals a common thread. Although they belong to different categories, they all clearly display their origins in the Langhe terroir. We tasted four Barolos, two of them vineyard selections. The standard label offers a straightforward, delicious accessibility that is compelling while Acclivi, as a blend of vineyards in Verduno, offers an overview of the area, privileging balance over power. The best vineyard in the area yields Monvigliero, a traditional Barolo of great complexity and finesse that gives extraordinarily supple tannins and a long-lingering finish in a class by itself. The iconic Barolo vineyard yields Cannubi, the richest of the four, with a delicious balsamic pungency that informs very expressive tannins. Finally, a classic Nebbiolo, a full-fruited Dolcetto, a spicy Barbera, a peppery Pelaverga and two fine Sauvignon Blancs. Viridis is eminently typical while the cask-aged Dives is richer and more mineral edged.

● Barolo Ca' Mia '03	▼▼	8
● Barolo Rocche dei Brovia '03	▼▼	8
● Barolo Villero '03	▼▼	8
● Barolo '03	▼▼	6
● Barolo Garblèt Sué '03	▼▼	7
● Barbera d'Alba Brea '05	▼▼	5
● Barbera d'Alba Sorì del Drago '05	▼▼	4
● Dolcetto d'Alba Vignavillej '05	▼▼	4
● Dolcetto d'Alba Solatìo '05	▼▼	5
● Barolo Monprivato '90	♈♈♈	8
● Barolo Ca' Mia '00	♈♈♈	8
● Barolo Ca' Mia '96	♈♈♈	8
● Barolo Ca' Mia '01	♈♈	8
● Barolo Villero '01	♈♈	8
● Barolo Villero '00	♈♈	8
● Barolo Rocche dei Brovia '01	♈♈	8

● Barolo Vign. Cannubi '03	▼▼	7
● Barolo Vign. Monvigliero '03	▼▼	7
● Barbera d'Alba Aves '05	▼▼	5
● Langhe Freisa '05	▼▼	4
● Langhe Nebbiolo '05	▼▼	4
● Langhe Mores '04	▼▼	5
● Dolcetto d'Alba '06	▼▼	4
● Barolo Acclivi '03	▼▼	7
○ Langhe Bianco Dives '05	▼▼	4
○ Langhe Bianco Viridis '06	▼▼	4
◉ Rosato Teres '06	▼	4
● Barolo '03	▼	7
● Verduno Pelaverga '06	▼	4
● Barolo Vign. Cannubi '00	♈♈	7
● Barolo Vign. Monvigliero '00	♈♈	7
● Barolo Vign. Cannubi '01	♈♈	7

Piero Busso
VIA ALBESANI, 8
12057 NEIVE [CN]
TEL. 017367156
www.bussopiero.com

ANNUAL PRODUCTION 35,000 bottles
HECTARES UNDER VINE 8
VITICULTURE METHOD Conventional

You always feel warmly welcome when visiting the Busso operation. All the members of the family are calmly but passionately committed to running their winery, a Neive gem. They have created, in a very natural fashion without prejudice or formulas, an equilibrium that enables all of their wines to achieve top quality and convey quite clearly their geographical place of origin. Gallina, which is bottled only in magnum and needs more ageing, was not among the 2004 Barbarescos but Santo Stefanetto not only stands out from its fellows; it took our Three Glasses, encoring the achievement of its previous vintage. A truly sumptuous wine, it melds seamlessly together an elegant aromatic medley ennobled by scents of citrus, smoky oak and pungent earth, superb tannins and a powerful, concentrated palate that still manages to convey true elegance. Borgese is equally stellar, showing equally elegant but more spacious, austere and mineral edged. Mondino is more straightforward and supple, loaded with dense, sweet fruit. All of the other wines are well executed but Barbera Majano '05 is particularly refreshing and delicious.

Ca' Bianca
REG. SPAGNA, 58
15010 ALICE BEL COLLE [AL]
TEL. 0144745420
www.cantinacabianca.it

ANNUAL PRODUCTION 500,000 bottles
HECTARES UNDER VINE 42
VITICULTURE METHOD Conventional

Ca' Bianca is the Gruppo Italiano Vini's presence in Piedmont. A gorgeous estate near Alessandria in the Monferrato hills, the property's winemaking and 42 hectares of estate vineyards are directed by oenologist Marco Galeazzo. This area is particularly propitious for high-quality barbera and almost half of the total vineyard area is justifiably dedicated to that variety. Not one to shut out other favoured Piedmontese sites, Ca' Bianca also operates in the Novi area, with the production of Gavi, and in the Langhe, more precisely in the La Morra zone of Barolo. Barbera d'Asti Chersì, barrique matured for 12 months, shows a dense ruby and delivers rich draughts of pungent wild berry fruit followed by outstanding structure, lengthy progression and a nervy acidity that keeps all the components in balance. Barbera Antè is a delicious treat, with plenty of length, and we were mightily impressed by Teis, which shows as crisp and refreshing as one would wish, glass after glass. Barolo '03 is austere, tannic and impressive, seeming to have shrugged off its hot growing year. Gavi and Dolcetto d'Acqui are both more than worthy efforts.

● Barbaresco S. Stefanetto '04	♟♟♟ 8
● Barbaresco Borgese '04	♟♟ 7
● Barbaresco Mondino '04	♟♟ 6
● Barbera d'Alba V. Majano '05	♟♟ 4
● Langhe Nebbiolo '05	♟♟ 5
● Dolcetto d'Alba V. Majano '06	♟♟ 4*
○ Langhe Bianco '06	♟♟ 4*
● Barbaresco S. Stefanetto '00	♟♟♟ 8
● Barbaresco S. Stefanetto '01	♟♟♟ 8
● Barbaresco S. Stefanetto '03	♟♟♟ 8
● Barbaresco V. Borgese '97	♟♟♟ 7
● Barbaresco Borgese '00	♟♟ 7
● Barbaresco Gallina '01	♟♟ 8
● Barbaresco Borgese '01	♟♟ 7
● Barbaresco Gallina '03	♟♟ 8

● Barbera d'Asti Sup. Chersì '05	♟♟ 5
● Barolo '03	♟♟ 6
● Barbera d'Asti Antè '05	♟♟ 4*
● Barbera d'Asti Teis '06	♟♟ 4*
● Dolcetto d'Acqui '06	♟ 4
○ Gavi '06	♟ 4
● Barbera d'Asti Chersì '01	♟♟ 6
● Barbera d'Asti Sup. Chersì '03	♟♟ 5
● Barbera d'Asti Sup. Chersì '04	♟♟ 5
● Barbera d'Asti Antè '04	♟♟ 4
● Barbera d'Asti Chersì '00	♟♟ 6
● Barbera d'Asti Teis '06	♟ 4

Ca' d' Gal

FRAZ. VALDIVILLA
S.DA VECCHIA DI VALDIVILLA, 1
12058 SANTO STEFANO BELBO [CN]
TEL. 0141847103
www.ca-d-gal.com

ANNUAL PRODUCTION 60,000 bottles
HECTARES UNDER VINE 10
VITICULTURE METHOD Conventional

In just a few years, Alessandro Boido has successfully established one of the most attractive operations in the Moscato production area, specifically in the village of Valdivilla at Santo Stefano Belbo. Not only does his cellar enjoy a fabulous view over his vineyards; he has also opened an osteria, which offers traditional dishes prepared with the best local specialty foods. Guests can also spend the night in well-furnished rooms. The wines that Boido offered us amply justified Ca' d' Gal's reputation for exquisite Moscatos. Vigna Vecchia, which has character enough for medium-term bottle ageing, appears gold yellow and then follows tropical fruit with juicy, succulent fruit. Lumine is remarkable for its lovely suggestions of lime blossom, acacia honey, orange zest and ripe peach. The two house reds are well made, particularly Langhe Rosso Pian del Gaje, an assemblage of freisa, dolcetto and barbera that rests 14 months in new and second-year barriques. One Glass each went to the eminently quaffable Dolcetto d'Alba and to the Asti.

Ca' del Baio

VIA FERRERE, 33
12050 TREISO [CN]
TEL. 0173638219
www.cadelbaio.com

ANNUAL PRODUCTION 100,000 bottles
HECTARES UNDER VINE 20
VITICULTURE METHOD Conventional

We are delighted by the terrific showing from Giulio Grasso. This talented grower has poured his heart and expertise into improving his wines, which are now not just distinctive and reliable but figure in the absolute top ranks in his primary denomination, Barbaresco. The 2004 vintage saw Giulio produce three superlative selections, each with its own well-defined personality. Asili shows powerful, generous, deep and harmonious, with fleshy fruit and character to spare. Marcarini has lengthy development and fairly explodes with fruit, its fine balance and elegance making it already quite likeable. Valgrande, which matures in large botti, lays out the purest of exemplary fruit followed by a palate that is assertive, lean, austere and built for the ages. Three Glasses went to Ca' del Baio for an utterly tempting, admirably distinctive Barbaresco destined for significant evolution. Langhe Nebbiolo, from younger vineyards, is as fine as ever. This elegant, fruity '05 is ready right now for the table. Chardonnay '06 is also enjoyable, presenting deep gold, rich and full in the mouth but crisp and balanced as well. The Moscato is creamy and aromatic with vivacious, lifting acidity.

O Moscato d'Asti V. Vecchia '06	♟♟	5
O Moscato d'Asti Lumine '06	♟♟	4
● Langhe Rosso Pian del Gaje '03	♟♟	4
● Dolcetto d'Alba '05	♟	3
O Asti '06	♟	4
O Moscato d'Asti V. Vecchia '05	♟♟	5
● Langhe Rosso Pian del Gaje '01	♟♟	4

● Barbaresco Valgrande '04	♟♟♟	6
● Barbaresco Asili '04	♟♟	6
● Barbaresco Marcarini '04	♟♟	6
● Langhe Nebbiolo Bric del Baio '05	♟♟	4*
O Langhe Chardonnay Sermine '06	♟♟	5
O Moscato d'Asti '06	♟♟	4*
● Barbaresco Valgrande '99	♟♟♟	6
● Barbaresco Valgrande '03	♟♟	6
● Barbaresco Valgrande '01	♟♟	6
● Barbaresco Valgrande '00	♟♟	6
● Barbaresco Asili '03	♟♟	6
● Barbaresco Asili '01	♟♟	6
● Barbaresco Marcarini '03	♟♟	6

La Ca' Növa
S.DA OVELLO, 4
12050 BARBARESCO [CN]
TEL. 0173635123
lacanova@libero.it

ANNUAL PRODUCTION 50,000 bottles
HECTARES UNDER VINE 13.5
VITICULTURE METHOD Conventional

La Ca' Növa is a classic family-run operation. The three Rocca brothers, joined for some time now by sons Ivano and Marco, still labour in the vines and cellar, practising the style of winemaking traditional in Langhe: meticulous care for the vineyard, careful timing for the harvest, gentle pressing of the clusters, macerations of 15 to 20 days and maturation in large Slavonian oak casks. The 2004 vintage was a great one for nebbiolo and results here confirm it. Both Barbaresco Bric Mentina and Montestefano are outstanding, the former more austere and tannic, the second a touch smoother with good length on the finish. The standard label is almost as fine, showing only a degree less depth. Barbera d'Alba Loreto '05, which spent ten months in large casks, is first-rate, presenting well balanced and enlivened by a tasty vein of acidity throughout. The all-steel Dolcetto '06 is refreshing and accessible, tannins peeking through to render it even more pleasing and energetic.

Ca' Rome' - Romano Marengo
S.DA RABAJÀ, 86/88
12050 BARBARESCO [CN]
TEL. 0173635126
www.carome.com

ANNUAL PRODUCTION 30,000 bottles
HECTARES UNDER VINE 7
VITICULTURE METHOD Conventional

The Marengo family owns this traditional-style cellar and obtains truly remarkable results. Romano has been assisted for some time now by his children Giuseppe and Paola, who continue to follow his approach. And here in Serralunga that means maturations carried out in both small and large oak. With the 2003 vintage, the Barolos are back. Rapet again shows its splendid pedigree, with elegant tannins and an enviable balance of acidity, alcohol and extract. It's a lengthy wine and will no doubt enjoy a lengthy life. Barolo Cerretta, in classic form, is just a step behind with assertive alcohol, a great mouthfeel and a gratifying finale. The winery's two barrique-aged Barbaresco crus performed just as magnificently. Sorì Rio Sordo '04 may pack plenty of muscle but it also has velvety texture plus abundant, pulpy fruit. Maria di Brun '04 is fairly similar, building tremendous depth and an impressive conclusion. Barbera d'Alba La Gamberaja '05 is vivacious, crisp and ready now.

● Barbaresco Bric Mentina '04	♟♟ 5
● Barbaresco Montestefano '04	♟♟ 5
● Barbera d'Alba Loreto '05	♟♟ 4
● Barbaresco '04	♟ 5
● Dolcetto d'Alba '06	♟ 3
● Barbaresco Bric Mentina '01	♟♟♟ 6
● Barbaresco Bric Mentina '02	♟♟ 6
● Barbaresco Bric Mentina '03	♟♟ 6
● Barbaresco Montestefano '02	♟♟ 5
● Barbaresco Montestefano '03	♟♟ 6
● Barbaresco Montestefano '01	♟♟ 6

● Barolo Rapet '03	♟ 7
● Barbaresco Maria di Brun '04	♟♟ 8
● Barbaresco Sorì Rio Sordo '04	♟♟ 7
● Barolo V. Cerretta '03	♟♟ 7
● Barbera d'Alba La Gamberaja '05	♟ 5
● Barolo V. Cerretta '01	♟♟ 7
● Barbaresco Maria di Brun '00	♟♟ 8
● Barbaresco Maria di Brun '01	♟♟ 8
● Barbaresco Maria di Brun '03	♟♟ 8
● Barbaresco Sorì Rio Sordo '00	♟♟ 7
● Barolo V. Cerretta '00	♟♟ 7
● Barolo Rapet '01	♟♟ 7
● Barolo Rapet '00	♟♟ 7
● Barbaresco Sorì Rio Sordo Ris. '01	♟♟ 7
● Barbaresco Sorì Rio Sordo Ris. '00	♟♟ 7
● Barbaresco Sorì Rio Sordo '03	♟♟ 7

Cascina Ca' Rossa
LOC. CASCINA CA' ROSSA, 56
12043 CANALE [CN]
TEL. 017398348
www.cascinacarossa.com

★ Ca' Viola
B.TA SAN LUIGI, 11
12063 DOGLIANI [CN]
TEL. 017370547
www.caviola.com

ANNUAL PRODUCTION 60,000 bottles
HECTARES UNDER VINE 15
VITICULTURE METHOD Conventional

ANNUAL PRODUCTION 50,000 bottles
HECTARES UNDER VINE 11
VITICULTURE METHOD Conventional

Once you start talking to Angelo Ferrio on the subject of winemaking, your first reaction is renewed respect for the cornucopia of emotions in a glass of wine. You are carried along by Ferrio's celebrated and contagious good humour and inspired by the history of a farming complex with an intimate rapport with its surrounding vineyards. Step after step, Cascina Ca' Rossa has become emblematic of an intensely local philosophy, adding another star to the constellation of fine producers in always surprising Roero. Here, sound fruit yields sound wines that are clean, genuine and expressive. The superb Roero Audinaggio '05 upholds that tradition and does so in the very first year of the new DOCG. A seductive nose shows well-distributed complexity that complements the depth and sheer elegance of the mouth while the finish simply enraptures. Roero Mompissano '04's sturdy weight and flawless character portend considerable cellarability and at the moment, its aromatics are rich and satisfying. Barbera d'Alba Mulassa '05 is dense and silky, with a lengthy, spice-edged finish. Plaudits go to the glorious Arneis Merica '06, with its delectable, varietal finale.

To the joy of Beppe Caviola and his wife Simonetta, restoration work has finally ended on their large home next to the cellar and on the office used by this highly respected winemaker for his consultant work in Piedmont and elsewhere in Italy. In addition, three elegantly appointed rooms have been built, which will serve as a future bed and breakfast. As to the wines we tasted, Langhe Nebbiolo Sotto Castello '05 is an impressive new entry, sourced from vineyards in Novello. It summons up cocoa, violets and roses then builds power and richness in the mouth before closing splendidly opulent. Not new, but still one of the best Dolcettos around, Barturot opens with intriguing, rich aromas, then reveals succulent, juicy fruit in the mouth, truly delicious through and through. The barbera and nebbiolo Langhe Rosso Bric du Luv is again stunningly good with everything singing in harmony, with a majestic balance of acidity and tannin. Understandably, another Three Glasses went to Ca' Viola as it took a step towards another Star to go with last year's. We also very much liked Barbera Brichet and the tasty Dolcetto Vilot.

● Barbera d'Alba Mulassa '05	♟♟	6
● Roero Audinaggio '05	♟♟	6
● Roero Mompissano '04	♟♟	6
● Langhe Nebbiolo '06	♟♟	4*
O Roero Arneis Merica '06	♟♟	4*
● Barbera d'Alba '06	♟	4
● Birbét '06	♟	4
● Barbera d'Alba Mulassa '04	♟♟♟	6
● Barbera d'Alba Mulassa '99	♟♟♟	6
● Roero Vigna Audinaggio '96	♟♟♟	6
● Roero Audinaggio '01	♟♟♟	6
● Barbera d'Alba Mulassa '03	♟♟	6
● Roero Audinaggio '04	♟♟	6
● Roero Mompissano '02	♟♟	6
● Roero Mompissano '03	♟♟	6

● Langhe Rosso Bric du Luv '05	♟♟♟	6
● Dolcetto d'Alba Barturot '06	♟♟	5
● Barbera d'Alba Brichet '06	♟♟	5
● Langhe Nebbiolo Sotto Castello '05	♟♟	5
● L'Insieme '04	♟♟	7
● Dolcetto d'Alba Vilot '06	♟♟	4*
● Dolcetto d'Alba Barturot '01	♟♟♟	5
● Dolcetto d'Alba Barturot '05	♟♟♟	5
● Dolcetto d'Alba Barturot '98	♟♟♟	5
● Dolcetto d'Alba Barturot '96	♟♟♟	5
● Langhe Rosso Bric du Luv '03	♟♟♟	6
● Langhe Rosso Bric du Luv '01	♟♟♟	6
● Langhe Rosso Bric du Luv '99	♟♟♟	6
● Langhe Rosso Bric du Luv '98	♟♟♟	6
● Langhe Rosso Bric du Luv '96	♟♟♟	6
● Langhe Rosso Bric du Luv '95	♟♟♟	6

Marco Canato
FRAZ. FONS SALERA
LOC. CA' BALDEA, 18/2
15049 VIGNALE MONFERRATO [AL]
TEL. 0142933653
www.canatovini.it

Cantina del Pino
VIA OVELLO, 31
12050 BARBARESCO [CN]
TEL. 0173635147
www.cantinadelpino.com

ANNUAL PRODUCTION 15,000 bottles
HECTARES UNDER VINE 11
VITICULTURE METHOD Conventional

Once again, Marco Canato's Barbera del Monferrato Superiore La Baldea is the top performer in his line-up. It has great depth of colour, then balance and finesse on the nose, with stellar flavours and savouriness and enjoyable acidity that lifts the finish. Chardonnay Bric di Bric, the winery's iconic white, is barrique-aged for some six months. This '05 shows a gold-tinged straw then lays out a generous array of tropical fruit cosseted with smooth vanilla, and a palate with a silky texture and judicious supporting acidity. With its deep, compelling tonality and opulent aromas, Barbera Superiore Rapet is closing in on Two Glasses, even though this version suffers somewhat from a finish that is not perfectly aligned. Gambaloita is a straightforward but aromatic standard-label Barbera that is drinking beautifully right now. Light ruby in appearance, Grignolino Celio releases nice spice and fruit on the nose and refreshing, tangy acidity. The standard Chardonnay Piasì is well worth trying.

ANNUAL PRODUCTION 35,000 bottles
HECTARES UNDER VINE 7
VITICULTURE METHOD Conventional

Renato Vacca, who owns and manages Cantina del Pino, presented us with wines that were even better than last year's. He is meticulous in both vineyard and cellar, and one of the results is the perfect integration of oak into the overall structure of his wines. Starting with Barbaresco Ovello '03, it is sourced from a vineyard about 70 years old. Opening with considerable finesse, it develops enviable equilibrium and concludes with a lengthy, compelling finish. The fine year certainly helped Barbaresco '04, which is a supreme example of its class. More harmonious and complex than its older brother, it is rich, intriguing, powerful and velvety, plus a string of other adjectives we can sum up in a well-deserved Three Glasses. The other wines not only display excellent overall quality but also offer great value for money. Barbera '05's 18 months in barriques did nothing to blunt its tasty acidity or its varietal fidelity, and it shows great richness in the mouth. Dolcetto '06 is fine, fresh and delicious while Freisa '06 is fun and a vivacious pleaser.

O Piemonte Chardonnay Bric di Bric '05	♀♀ 4*
● Barbera del M.to Sup. La Baldea '05	♀♀ 4*
● Barbera del M.to Gambaloita '06	♀ 3
● Barbera del M.to Sup. Rapet '04	♀ 4
O Piemonte Chardonnay Piasì '06	♀ 3
● Grignolino del M.to Casalese Celio '06	♀ 3
● Barbera del M.to Sup. La Baldea '03	♀♀ 4
● Barbera del M.to Sup. La Baldea '04	♀♀ 4

● Barbaresco '04	♀♀♀ 6*
● Barbaresco Ovello '03	♀♀ 7
● Barbera d'Alba '05	♀♀ 5
● Dolcetto d'Alba '06	♀♀ 4
● Langhe Freisa '06	♀ 4
● Barbaresco '03	♀♀♀ 5
● Barbaresco Ovello '99	♀♀♀ 6
● Barbaresco '02	♀♀ 5
● Barbaresco Ovello '01	♀♀ 6
● Barbaresco Ovello '02	♀♀ 6

Casalone

VIA MARCONI, 100
15040 LU [AL]
TEL. 0131741280
www.casalone.com

ANNUAL PRODUCTION 50,000 bottles
HECTARES UNDER VINE 10
VITICULTURE METHOD Conventional

The Casalone family offered five wines for
tasting this year. Monferrato Rosso Rus,
one of the winery standard-bearers,
comprises barbera, merlot and pinot nero
vinified separately and blended together
some 15 months later. The '05 is in splendid
form, with intense, dark ruby preceding
pungent spice and balsam on the nose that
continue to infuse the very full-flavoured
palate. Overall, the wine is harmonious and
shows excellent progression. Monemvasia,
a vino da tavola from malvasia greca, flaunts
a multi-layered, emphatically aromatic nose.
Three other wines easily earned One Glass
for their remarkable freshness and unalloyed
pleasure. Piemonte Grignolino La Capletta
is a masterpiece of balance while the all-
pinot nero Monferrato Rosso Fandamat
releases youthful, heady draughts of ripe
fruit, although some still young tannins
upset its progression a little on the palate.
We also recommend the late-harvest
Monemvasia, a lovely offering with a
medium-weight body and nicely gauged
acidity.

Cascina Adelaide

VIA AIE SOTTANE, 14
12060 BAROLO [CN]
TEL. 0173560503
www.cascinaadelaide.com

ANNUAL PRODUCTION 45,000 bottles
HECTARES UNDER VINE 7.5
VITICULTURE METHOD Conventional

Cascina Adelaide is relatively young but it is
making progress at a very fast rate.
Businessman Amabile Drocco has been
investing very carefully. He can now count
on vineyards in the best areas of Barolo and
La Morra; a futuristic, new facility that is
extremely well thought-out and harmonizes
with the surrounding countryside; and a
youthful, motivated winemaking staff. The
results are there in the glass. Barolo Preda
'03 is a cleanly delineated modernist wine
with goodish oak showing. Barolo Cannubi
'03 is a step up in character, showing
earthy, floral and soft-contoured, with the
heat from that year blunting its thrust
somewhat. Barolo Riserva Per Elen '01
greatly impressed us with its classic profile.
It's austere, spacious, powerful and deep,
yet ultimately elegant and complex. Barbera
Vigna Preda '05 performed very well, with
its crisp florality and succulent, lively fruit.
Barbera Amabilin '04 is brooding and
concentrated, with good energy and
balance for a fine showing. We also liked
Costa Fiore, a classic Diano d'Alba
Dolcetto.

● Monferrato Rosso Rus '05	▼▼ 4*
○ Monemvasia '06	▼▼ 3*
● Monferrato Rosso Fandamat '04	▼ 4
○ Monemvasia V. T. '05	▼ 5
● Piemonte Grignolino La Capletta '06	▼ 3
● Monferrato Rosso Rus '01	♈♈ 5
● Barbera d'Asti Rubermillo '04	♈♈ 4
● Monferrato Rosso Rus '03	♈♈ 5
● Monferrato Rosso Rus '00	♈♈ 5
● Monferrato Rosso Rus '04	♈♈ 4

● Barolo Per Elen Ris. '01	▼▼ 8
● Barolo Cannubi '03	▼▼ 7
● Barolo Preda '03	▼▼ 8
● Barbera d'Alba Sup. V. Preda '05	▼▼ 5
● Barbera d'Alba Sup. Amabilin '04	▼▼ 5
● Dolcetto di Diano d'Alba Costa Fiore '06	▼▼ 4
● Barolo Cannubi '00	♈♈ 7
● Barolo Cannubi '01	♈♈ 7
● Barolo Preda '01	♈♈ 8
● Barolo Preda '00	♈♈ 8
● Barolo Per Elen Ris. '00	♈♈ 8

Cascina Ballarin

FRAZ. ANNUNZIATA, 115
12064 LA MORRA [CN]
TEL. 017350365
www.cascinaballarin.it

ANNUAL PRODUCTION 40,000 bottles
HECTARES UNDER VINE 7
VITICULTURE METHOD Conventional

Gianni and Giorgio Viberti's operation can always be relied upon for fine quality. With the assistance of spouses and parents, they are building wines of ever more impressive character. The Cascina Ballarin Barolos are all admirable. Bussia '03, from Monforte, went into the national final round, propelled by its floral, already evolved bouquet, balanced palate and judicious oak influence. Equally superlative is Barolo Bricco Rocca '03, from that vineyard in La Morra. Aged in large botti, it is showing elegant, evolved aromas. Barolo I Tre Ciabot '03, matured in a combination of both small and large casks, features a floral bouquet over dried plums. Barbera d'Alba Giuli '05, is sourced from a 50-year-old La Morra vineyard and offers a classy integration of nose and palate while Barbera d'Alba Pilade '05 boasts a fine, straightforward typicity in its fragrances. Well-textured tannins and sound fruit mark both Dolcettos, with Bussia '06 exhibiting the more expansive structure. The two Langhe Rosso blends are satisfying but Langhe Bianco Ballarin '06 is a shade less impressive than in 2005.

Cascina Bongiovanni

FRAZ. UCCELLACCIO
VIA ALBA BAROLO, 4
12060 CASTIGLIONE FALLETTO [CN]
TEL. 0173262184
cascinabongiovanni@libero.it

ANNUAL PRODUCTION 30,000 bottles
HECTARES UNDER VINE 6
VITICULTURE METHOD Conventional

It is always a pleasure to chat with Davide Mozzone, who owns and manages Cascina Bongiovanni. The discussions range wide, and his views on wine are always fascinating, but what counts in the end of course is what goes into the bottle. And here the results speak for themselves. Quite apart from the natural variations in the growing years themselves, Mozzone's wines are consistently admirable. Barolo '03 matures largely in new, small oak and it displays an intriguing nose combining fruit and a pungent earthiness, then opening very full and long on a mouthfilling palate. Equally good is Langhe '05, a partnership of barbera, cabernet sauvignon and nebbiolo that rests in new and used casks. The herbaceous cabernet predominates on the nose but the three varieties fuse together nicely in the mouth, smoothing the tannins and weaving a savoury harmony. Barbera '05, aged in casks of various ages, shows smooth, fresh and floral. Dolcetto di Diano d'Alba '06 is well built and Dolcetto d'Alba '06 delicious. Finally, the house white, Arneis 2006, is fragrant, sturdy and as tasty as you could wish.

● Barolo Bussia '03	8
● Barbera d'Alba Giuli '05	6
● Dolcetto d'Alba Bussia '06	4
● Barolo I Tre Ciabot '03	6
● Langhe Rosso Ballarin '04	5
● Barbera d'Alba Pilade '05	4
● Barolo Bricco Rocca '03	8
● Dolcetto d'Alba Pilade '06	4
● Langhe Rosso Cino '06	3
O Langhe Bianco Ballarin '06	4
● Barolo Bricco Rocca '00	7
● Barolo Bricco Rocca '01	7
● Barolo I Tre Ciabot '00	7
● Barolo Bussia '01	7
● Barolo Bussia '00	7

● Barolo '03	6
● Langhe Rosso Faletto '05	5
● Barbera d'Alba '05	4*
● Dolcetto di Diano d'Alba '06	4
● Dolcetto d'Alba '06	4
O Langhe Arneis '06	4
● Barolo Pernanno '01	7
● Barolo Pernanno '00	7
● Barolo Pernanno '99	7
● Barolo '01	6
● Barolo '02	5

Cascina Bruciata
S.DA RIO SORDO, 46
12050 BARBARESCO [CN]
TEL. 0173638826
cascina.bruciata@tiscali.it

Cascina Castlet
S.DA CASTELLETTO, 6
14055 COSTIGLIOLE D'ASTI [AT]
TEL. 0141966651
www.cascinacastlet.com

ANNUAL PRODUCTION 35,000 bottles
HECTARES UNDER VINE 7
VITICULTURE METHOD Conventional

ANNUAL PRODUCTION 170,000 bottles
HECTARES UNDER VINE 18
VITICULTURE METHOD Natural

Better late than never, Carlo Balbo must have said to himself in 2001. After years of watching his grapes leave for destinations unknown, he finally decided to vinify the fruits of his labours. Assisted by agronomist Federico Curtaz and oenologist Guido Martinetti, and by the painstaking efforts of his own family, Balbo quickly succeeded in reburnishing one of the loveliest and finest quality crus in the entire Barbaresco zone. Carlo's farmer's roots go deep so there was no need to depart from sound, local traditions. He grows the two most classic varieties, nebbiolo and dolcetto, exclusively in the Rio Sordo vineyard and produces just a few wines. This year we preferred, but only by a whisker, the refined, savoury Barbaresco to the more prestigious Rio Sordo, which seems still a bit under the influence of its recent bottling and is suffering a dab too much sweet oak at the moment. The two Dolcettos reflect the splendid 2006 vintage in their bright, crisp fruit and it's hard to choose between the approachable Rio Sordo and the forceful Rian. Langhe Nebbiolo needs more time but its powerful, lengthy progression promises that it will be worth the wait.

The inimitable Mariuccia Borio directs Cascina Castlet, one of Costigliole d'Asti's historic wineries. She radiates energy and an innovative spirit, focusing research and experimentation as well as making wines traditional to the area. We could cite, for example, her work with uvalino, an ancient, almost extinct variety, the setting out of artificial nests for the protection of bird populations and organic control of vineyard pests. Finally, Castlet's new, rational zero-impact cellar, where her Litina and Policalpo Barberas will be spending another year, is up and running. Passing to the wines, we tasted some delicious sweet Moscatos this year. Moscato d'Asti '06 is crisp, intense, fat and rich in the mouth but with no excess. Avié Passito '05 shows floral and honeyed, with all components nicely tucked in, and rolls out a finish that never seems to end. Barbera d'Asti Passum '04 gained top marks. With some upfront notes of ultra-ripe fruit, it's powerful and generous but also releases lovely nuances of chocolate and blossoms. The standard Barberas are fine, with a still version from Asti and a semi-sparkler from Monferrato. Chardonnay A Taj is uncomplicated but very capably executed.

● Barbaresco '04	♥♥ 6
● Barbaresco Rio Sordo '04	♥♥ 6
● Dolcetto d'Alba Rian '06	♥♥ 4*
● Dolcetto d'Alba Vign. Rio Sordo '06	♥♥ 4*
● Langhe Nebbiolo Vign. dell'Usignolo '05	♥ 4
● Barbaresco Rio Sordo '03	♥♥ 6
● Barbaresco Rio Sordo '01	♥♥ 6
● Barbaresco Vign. Balbo '03	♥♥ 6
● Barbaresco Vign. Balbo '01	♥♥ 6

● Barbera d'Asti Sup. Passum '04	♥♥ 5
O Moscato d'Asti '06	♥♥ 4*
O Piemonte Moscato Passito Avié '05	♥♥ 5
O Piemonte Chardonnay A Taj '06	♥ 4
● Barbera d'Asti '06	♥ 4
● Barbera del M.to Goj '06	♥ 4
● Barbera d'Asti Sup. Passum '01	♥♥ 5
● Barbera d'Asti Sup. Passum '03	♥♥ 5
● Monferrato Rosso Policalpo '03	♥♥ 5
● Barbera d'Asti Sup. Litina '03	♥♥ 5
● Monferrato Rosso Policalpo '01	♥♥ 5
● Barbera d'Asti Sup. Litina '04	♥♥ 5
● Monferrato Rosso Policalpo '00	♥♥ 5

Cascina Corte

B.TA VALDIBERTI, 33
12063 DOGLIANI [CN]
TEL. 0172411641
www.cascinacorte.it

ANNUAL PRODUCTION 20,000 bottles
HECTARES UNDER VINE 5.5
VITICULTURE METHOD Certified organic

When Sandro Barosi told us he was leaving his work at Slow Food to go up into the hills and be a farmer, we tried to dissuade him. We reminded him that "the earth is low" and the close-to-the-land, hard-working farmer often doesn't often get his just recompense. Fortunately, he paid little attention and set off on his own road, joined in his adventure by his wife Amalia Battaglio. A few years later, we cheerfully admit that Barosi had been up to the challenge when he provided us with a group of truly fascinating wines. The grapes are grown organically and oenologist Beppe Caviola lends his renowned expertise. Turning to Cascina Corte's wines, Vigna Pirochetta has become a DOCG Dogliani but we'll have to wait a while longer to taste it. In its place, the standard-label Dolcetto di Dogliani does an admirable job. It's a refreshing, scrumptious, ready-to-enjoy crowd pleaser, splendidly varietal and released at a very reasonable price. The Barbera is nicely crisp, with crackling fruit and fragrances of ripe cherry, strawberry and other red berries.

Cascina Fonda

LOC. CASCINA FONDA, 45
12056 MANGO [CN]
TEL. 0173677156
www.cascinafonda.com

ANNUAL PRODUCTION 120,000 bottles
HECTARES UNDER VINE 12
VITICULTURE METHOD Conventional

Almost every year now, brothers Massimo and Franco Barbero pop out a new wine from Cascina Fonda. This year, they offered us a Brut '04, an assemblage of pinot noir and chardonnay. It shows broad fragrances of crusted bread and croissant with a hint of creamy butter, wildflowers and rennet apple. The bead is fairly delicate and judicious acidity allows it to linger. Among the other sparklers, the classic method Asti Driveri is characterized by an elegant, refined bouquet and rich, impressive mousse. The attractive Moscato d'Asti Il Piano boasts delicious sweetness ably kept within bounds by pronounced acidity. We tasted two dry reds. Dolcetto offers plenty of easy-drinking pleasure. This vintage of Barbaresco seems an improvement over the first release from the difficult 2003. We found it complex and multi-faceted, layering its smooth vanilla and cocoa over a tasty base of morello cherry and strawberry.

● Dolcetto di Dogliani '06	♀♀	3*
● Piemonte Barbera '06	♀♀	3*
● Dolcetto di Dogliani '05	♀♀	3
● Dolcetto di Dogliani V. Pirochetta '05	♀♀	4
● Dolcetto di Dogliani V. Pirochetta '04	♀♀	4
● Dolcetto di Dogliani V. Pirochetta '03	♀♀	4

● Barbaresco Bertola '04	♀♀	6
O Asti Driveri M. Cl. '05	♀♀	5
O Brut M. Cl. '04	♀♀	5
O Moscato d'Asti V. Il Piano '06	♀♀	4
O Asti '06	♀	4
● Dolcetto d'Alba Brusalino '06	♀	4

Cascina Garitina
VIA GIANOLA, 20
14040 CASTEL BOGLIONE [AT]
TEL. 0141762162
www.cascinagaritina.it

ANNUAL PRODUCTION 130,000 bottles
HECTARES UNDER VINE 24.5
VITICULTURE METHOD Conventional

Gianluca Morino is a producer with a well thought-out approach, which results in wines that are elegant, accessible and free of over-manipulation. He is also deeply committed to exploiting the full potential of the Nizza subzone. It doesn't seem exaggerated to say that Morino plays a crucial role in his area, which needs strong, new figures but ones who also can work harmoniously with other producers.
Gianluca is concentrating on improving Cascina Garitina, acquiring new vineyards, restructuring the old estate vineyards and broadening the range of wines he produces. We liked the wines we tasted this year. Barbera Neuvsent is particularly impressive, with compellingly rich colour and nose, spacious fruit on the palate, and a finish that is lingering and subtly espresso-edged. There are actually four Barberas, all top-notch. We liked the silky textured, ultra-crisp Caranti '05, the savoury, tangy Bricco Garitta and Vera as well, which is uncomplicated, approachable and lovely. Monferrato Rosso Amis, a partnership of pinot nero, cabernet sauvignon and barbera, scored high for its well-crafted structure and expansive palate. It was one of the finest of the type that we tasted this year.

Cascina La Maddalena
LOC. PIANI DEL PADRONE, 257
15078 ROCCA GRIMALDA [AL]
TEL. 0143876074
www.cascina-maddalena.com

ANNUAL PRODUCTION 25,000 bottles
HECTARES UNDER VINE 5
VITICULTURE METHOD Conventional

Rocca Grimalda is an area in the Ovada DOC dedicated to dolcetto, and one of its finest producers is undoubtedly Cascina La Maddalena, which sources fruit from five hectares of estate vineyards. On the wine front, Monferrato Bricco della Maddalena gives a fairly dark red-purple and fragrances that are clean, heady and youthful, its delicious fruit lingering nicely. The palate has a confident balance between acidity and heft that makes for a vivacious approachability. Barbera Rossa d'Ocra is a very attractive quaffer, showing crisp, rich and long lasting. Among the Dolcettos, Migulle hasn't been bottled yet but Bricco del Bagatto opens deep red, then conveys subtle notes of smooth spice, moist earth and ripe fruit that are nonetheless clean and well delineated. There's decent weight in the mouth and soft texture. The standard version Barbera and Dolcetto are easy drinking and pleasurable.

● Barbera d'Asti Sup. Nizza Neuvsent '04	♟♟ 5
● Barbera d'Asti Bricco Garitta '06	♟♟ 4*
● Barbera d'Asti Sup. Caranti '05	♟♟ 4*
● Monferrato Rosso Amis '03	♟♟ 5
● Barbera d'Asti Vera '06	♟ 4
● Dolcetto d'Asti Caranzano '06	♟ 5
● Brachetto d'Acqui Niades '06	♟ 4
● Barbera d'Asti Sup. Nizza Neuvsent '03	♟♟ 5
● Barbera d'Asti Sup. Nizza Neuvsent '01	♟♟ 5
● Barbera d'Asti Sup. Nizza Neuvsent '00	♟♟ 5
● Barbera d'Asti Sup. Neuvsent '98	♟♟ 5
● Barbera d'Asti Vera '04	♟ 4

● Dolcetto di Ovada Bricco del Bagatto '05	♟♟ 4*
● Monferrato Rosso Bricco della Maddalena '04	♟♟ 5
● Barbera del M.to Rossa d'Ocra '05	♟ 4
● Barbera del M.to '06	♟ 3
● Dolcetto di Ovada '06	♟ 3
● Dolcetto di Ovada Migulle '04	♟♟ 5
● Monferrato Rosso Bricco della Maddalena '03	♟♟ 5

Cascina Roera

FRAZ. BIONZO
VIA BIONZO, 32
14055 COSTIGLIOLE D'ASTI [AT]
TEL. 0141968437

ANNUAL PRODUCTION 20,000 bottles
HECTARES UNDER VINE 4
VITICULTURE METHOD Conventional

Cascina Roera emerged six years ago as the union of two operations led respectively by Carlo Rosso and Piero Nebiolo. The vineyards consist of a section around the winery, in Bionzo, and those near the castle at Costigliole. The estate centres on wines that express the local terroir but produces other styles as well, some of them a little bizarre, with the objective of achieving textural softness and extractive concentration. Barbera Superiore Cardin Selezione '03, for example, is quite heady at 15 per cent alcohol and releases profound impressions of earth and chocolate followed by considerable warmth in the mouth, smooth mouthfeel, and a lengthy finish. That same is true of Chardonnay Le Aie '04 (mentioned by mistake last year instead of the '03). It's rich, exotic, tropical and pungent, so soft it seems sweet and more suited to accompany meats and cheeses than fish. The other Barberas are more immediately accessible but no less attractive for all that. La Roera '05, sourced from the Bionzo vineyards, is well fruited, slightly earthy and rusticated while San Martino '04 is velvety smooth. Freisa is a pleasure, as is Ciapin, a mix of sauvignon, arneis and sémillon.

Renzo Castella Enotecnico

VIA ALBA, 15
12055 DIANO D'ALBA [CN]
TEL. 017369203
renzocastella@virgilio.it

ANNUAL PRODUCTION 28,000 bottles
HECTARES UNDER VINE 10
VITICULTURE METHOD Conventional

Young Renzo Castella, the soul and strong right arm of this small winery in Diano d'Alba, appeared in our Guide for the first time last year. We hoped his wines would repeat their performance this year and in fact the line-up we tasted did just that. His wines, with the single exception of a Barbera d'Alba with over-enthusiastic oak, fairly exude character and distinctiveness and all of them merit Two Glasses. Let's begin with the Dolcetto di Diano d'Alba versions, which were particularly impressive. Vigna della Rivolia boasts fragrant blackberry and redcurrant, then zesty acidity and expressive, well-gauged tannins. Compelling, solid structure does nothing to mar its overall elegance and grace. Vigna Piadvenza may show a tad less concentration on nose and mouth but the general harmony of all its components makes it not a whit less pleasurable. Violets, roses, and tanned leather give great interest to Nebbiolo Vigna Madonnina and its tannins are well under control. Finally, Barbera Vigna Sarcat conserves wonderful fruit but time still needs to tamp down its heady notes of vanilla.

- Barbera d'Asti Sup. S. Martino '04 ▼▼ 4*
- Piemonte Chardonnay
  Le Aie Sel. '04 ▼▼ 4*
- Barbera d'Asti Sup.
  Cardin Sel. '03 ▼▼ 5
- Ciapin Bianco '06 ▼ 3
- Freisa d'Asti '05 ▼ 3
- Barbera d'Asti La Roera '05 ▼ 3
- Barbera d'Asti Sup. S. Martino '03 ▼▼ 4
- Monferrato Rosso V. Piva '03 ▼▼ 4
- Barbera d'Asti Sup. Cardin Sel. '01 ▼▼ 5
- Barbera d'Asti Sup. Cardin '03 ▼▼ 4
- Barbera d'Asti Sup. Cardin '01 ▼▼ 4

- Dolcetto di Diano d'Alba
  V. della Rivolia '06 ▼▼ 3*
- Dolcetto di Diano d'Alba
  V. Piadvenza '06 ▼▼ 3*
- Nebbiolo d'Alba V. Madonnina '05 ▼▼ 4
- Barbera d'Alba V. Sarcat '05 ▼ 3
- Dolcetto di Diano d'Alba
  V. della Rivolia '05 ▼▼ 3

Castellari Bergaglio

FRAZ. ROVERETO, 136
15066 GAVI [AL]
TEL. 0143644000
www.castellaribergaglio.it

ANNUAL PRODUCTION 70,000 bottles
HECTARES UNDER VINE 12
VITICULTURE METHOD Conventional

Rovereto, a large, well-known zone within the municipality of Gavi, is home to many wineries that produce Gavi wines. Castellari Bergaglio is one of the most representative, both for the quality of its offerings and for its deep commitment to the fortunes of the area, which it has relentlessly promoted in many ways over the years. As for this year's wines, the one that we were most excited about was Fornaci, sourced from vineyards planted in an area rich in red-coloured soils. These tend to give to the palate a minerally, sapid edge, which is terrifically appealing, and a vivacious, fresh acidity. Rovereto is equally fine, produced from a vineyard whose vines actually date back to the 1920s. The result is a wine of deep straw yellow, a nose that leans more floral than fruity, and an intriguingly taut, pleasantly bitterish palate. One Glass goes to Gavi Rolona, outstanding for its refreshing, lively mouth.

Castello di Neive

VIA CASTELBORGO, 1
12052 NEIVE [CN]
TEL. 017367171
neive.castello@tin.it

ANNUAL PRODUCTION 150,000 bottles
HECTARES UNDER VINE 26
VITICULTURE METHOD Conventional

In the 19th century, Camillo Benso di Cavour invited the noted French oenologist Oudart to focus his expertise on the production of a dry wine from the nebbiolo grape. Some of his experiments were carried out in the magnificent cellars of Castello di Neive. This striking complex has not lost an iota of its fascination, and a visit to the bottommost cellars, with its ranks of venerable vintages, is a magical moment. The Stupino family has owned the castle since1964, as well as its adjacent vineyards, located in Neive's most renowned crus, Santo Stefano, Gallina, Marcorino and Basarin. Initially, the Stupinos showed little interest in viticulture and the winery's shining past lost lustre. But in less than ten years, the contagious enthusiasm of Italo Stupino and the expertise of Claudio Roggero restored it to its former glory. Barbaresco Santo Stefano '04 expresses almost effortlessly the dynamism and finesse of its terroir. The rest of the line-up is equally outstanding. We mention the two Barberas: Santo Stefano is the more natural while Mattarello is more extracted and tight-wound. Both Dolcettos are well structured and show off the fine qualities of the 2004 growing year.

○ Gavi del Comune di Tassarolo Fornaci '06	🍷🍷 4*
○ Gavi del Comune di Gavi Rolona '06	🍷 4
○ Gavi del Comune di Gavi Rovereto Vignavecchia '06	🍷 4
○ Gavi del Comune di Gavi Pilin '01	🍷🍷 5
○ Gavi del Comune di Gavi Rovereto Vignavecchia '05	🍷🍷 4
○ Gavi del Comune di Tassarolo Fornaci '05	🍷🍷 4

● Barbaresco S. Stefano '04	🍷🍷 6
● Barbera d'Alba Mattarello '05	🍷🍷 5
● Barbera d'Alba S. Stefano '06	🍷🍷 4*
● Langhe Rosso I Cortini '06	🍷🍷 4*
● Dolcetto d'Alba Basarin '06	🍷🍷 4*
○ Piemonte Spumante M. Cl. Castello di Neive '03	🍷🍷 5
○ Castello di Neive Passito '05	🍷 6
○ Langhe Arneis Montebertotto '06	🍷 4
● Dolcetto d'Alba Messoirano '06	🍷 4
● Barbaresco S. Stefano Ris. '01	🍷🍷🍷 8
● Barbaresco S. Stefano Ris. '99	🍷🍷🍷 8
● Barbaresco S. Stefano '01	🍷🍷 6
● Barbaresco S. Stefano '00	🍷🍷 7
● Barbaresco S. Stefano '03	🍷🍷 7

La Caudrina

S.DA BROSIA, 21
12053 CASTIGLIONE TINELLA [CN]
TEL. 0141855126
www.caudrina.it

ANNUAL PRODUCTION 200,000 bottles
HECTARES UNDER VINE 30
VITICULTURE METHOD Conventional

In the Moscato production area, La Caudrina is a leader in wine quality. The new cellar is now functional and it is divided into two completely separate production lines, moscato and barbera. Each of these varieties, in its own distinctive, multi-faceted way, yields fine wines of proven excellence, thanks to the long dedication of Romano Dogliotti and his family. We'll begin with the Moscato d'Astis, both versions of which won terrifically high marks. La Galeisa '06 stands out, sourced from an excellent four-hectare estate vineyard. But not to be overlooked is the somewhat unusual but utterly successful Asti La Selvatica '06. As far as the Barberas are concerned, Superiore Montevenere '04, which receives nine months' maturation in small oak, must be admired for its finesse and concentration. On the other hand, Barbera d'Asti La Solista '05 is well fruited, but less complex.

F.lli Cavallotto

LOC. BRICCO BOSCHIS
S.DA ALBA-MONFORTE
12060 CASTIGLIONE FALLETTO [CN]
TEL. 017362814
www.cavallotto.com

ANNUAL PRODUCTION 100,000 bottles
HECTARES UNDER VINE 23
VITICULTURE METHOD Conventional

The Cavallottos have been growers in the Bricco Boschis cru of Castiglione Falletto for five generations. The winery, directed early on by Gildo and Olivio Cavallotto, was among the first in the Langhe to put Barolo in standard bottles on a regular basis, whereas the custom at that time was to sell it in bulk to merchants. The oldest section of the cellar, dating to 1850, testifies to those customs. The new generation, in the persons of the children of Olivio, Alfio, Giuseppe and Laura, has recently taken over the reins but with no earthshaking changes. The wines are still recognizably traditional, but with an eye to the evolution of style and techniques. The Riserva Barolos, the thoroughbreds closest to the family's heart, receive lengthy maturations in large Slavonian oak botti. It's difficult to choose between Vignolo and Riserva Vigna San Giuseppe, both so close to perfection, but in the end the more classic Vigna San Giuseppe won out and took our Three Glasses without a quibble. From the other wines, all outstanding, we were impressed most by Barolo '03, Barbera Vigna del Cuculo '04 and Langhe Nebbiolo, a pocket Barolo.

O Moscato d'Asti La Galeisa '06	♟♟	3*
O Asti La Selvatica '06	♟♟	4*
● Barbera d'Asti La Solista '05	♟♟	4
● Barbera d'Asti Sup. Montevenere '04	♟♟	5
O Moscato d'Asti Caudrina '06	♟♟	4
O Piemonte Chardonnay Mej '05	♟	4
● Barbera d'Asti La Solista '04	♀♀	4
● Barbera d'Asti Sup. Montevenere '00	♀♀	5
● Barbera d'Asti Sup. Montevenere '99	♀♀	5

● Barolo Bricco Boschis V. S. Giuseppe Ris. '01	♟♟♟	8
● Barolo Vignolo Ris. '01	♟♟	8
● Barolo Bricco Boschis '03	♟♟	7
● Barbera d'Alba V. del Cuculo '04	♟♟	5
● Langhe Nebbiolo '05	♟♟	5
● Dolcetto d'Alba V. Melera '05	♟♟	4
● Langhe Freisa '05	♟♟	4
● Dolcetto d'Alba V. Scot '06	♟	4
● Barolo Bricco Boschis V. S. Giuseppe Ris. '00	♀♀♀	8
● Barolo Bricco Boschis V. S. Giuseppe Ris. '99	♀♀♀	8
● Barolo V. S. Giuseppe Ris. '89	♀♀♀	8
● Barolo Vignolo Ris. '00	♀♀	8
● Barbera d'Alba V. del Cuculo '04	♀♀	5

Cave di Moleto

LOC. MOLETO
REG. MOLETO, 4
15038 OTTIGLIO [AL]
TEL. 0142921468
www.moleto.it

ANNUAL PRODUCTION 110,000 bottles
HECTARES UNDER VINE 27
VITICULTURE METHOD Conventional

Cave di Moleto again presented us with an impressive line-up of wines. Leading the group was the steel-fermented Barbera del Monferrato, with a deep, rich colour and intense aromas, where fresh greens subtly take charge. Rosso Pieve di San Michele, composed of barbera, cabernet sauvignon and merlot, shows a lively, intense ruby red, then varietal aromas ranging from wild red berry fruit to hints of green pepper. The mouth is appealing and still quite fruity, with great length. Grignolino del Monferrato Casalese is enjoyable for its balance and finesse, and the finish shows just a shade of tannin. A dark, almost opaque tonality introduces Barbera Bricco della Prera, complemented by emphatic cinchona and cocoa on the nose, smoothed out nicely by hints of vanilla. Still maturing tannins do slightly hinder complete balance in the mouth. Grassy elements dominate the nose of Mulej '05 and continue through the development and finish. Barbera Procchio is well made.

Ceretto

LOC. SAN CASSIANO, 34
12051 ALBA [CN]
TEL. 0173282582
www.ceretto.com

ANNUAL PRODUCTION 900,000 bottles
HECTARES UNDER VINE 87
VITICULTURE METHOD Conventional

Marcello and Bruno Ceretto were the founders and driving force of the family's group of vineyards and estates, which include La Bernardina Monsordo at Alba, Bricco Rocche at Castiglione Falletto, Bricco Asili at Barbaresco, Arbarei at Albaretto della Torre, Blangé at Castellinaldo and Vignaioli di Santo Stefano at Santo Stefano Belbo. Since the beginning of the century, they have been joined by their four children. Lisa and Alessandro, Marcello's heirs, oversee the administration and production while Roberta and Federico, Bruno's children, take care of public relations and foreign markets. Everything has turned out splendidly, both regarding wine quality and in terms of the high respect the Ceretto name has gained all over the globe. Once again, Arbarei, a riesling from the upper Langhe, emerges as one of the best whites in Langhe and beyond. Minerally nuances enliven an eminently fruity bouquet while a complex, elegant palate is capped by a nervy finish. Monsordo, a four-way blend of cabernet, merlot, syrah and nebbiolo, is impressive, releasing subtle notes of pencil lead, and Nebbiolo Bernardina is appealing and elegant. Barolo Zonchera '03 shows overripe fruit, due probably to the torrid vintage.

● Barbera del M.to '05	♟♟ 3*
● Grignolino del M.to Casalese '06	♟♟ 3*
● Monferrato Rosso Pieve di San Michele '05	♟♟ 5
● Barbera del M.to Bricco della Prera '05	♟ 5
● Monferrato Rosso Mulej '05	♟ 5
● Barbera del M.to Procchio '05	♟ 4
● Barbera del M.to Bricco della Prera '01	♟♟ 5
● Monferrato Rosso Pieve di San Michele '03	♟♟ 5
● Monferrato Rosso Mulej '03	♟♟ 5
● Grignolino del M.to Casalese '05	♟♟ 3

○ Langhe Bianco Arbarei '05	♟♟ 5
● Langhe Rosso Monsordo '04	♟♟ 5
● Barolo Zonchera '03	♟♟ 6
● Nebbiolo d'Alba Bernardina '05	♟♟ 5
● Barbaresco Asij '04	♟ 6
● Dolcetto d'Alba Rossana '06	♟ 4
● Barbera d'Alba Piana '06	♟ 4
○ Langhe Bianco Arbarei '03	♟♟ 5
○ Langhe Bianco Arbarei '04	♟♟ 5
● Langhe Rosso Monsordo '00	♟♟ 6
● Langhe Rosso Monsordo '01	♟♟ 6
● Langhe Rosso Monsordo '02	♟♟ 6
● Langhe Rosso Monsordo '03	♟♟ 6

★ Michele Chiarlo

S.DA NIZZA-CANELLI, 99
14042 CALAMANDRANA [AT]
TEL. 0141769030
www.chiarlo.it

ANNUAL PRODUCTION 950,000 bottles
HECTARES UNDER VINE 100
VITICULTURE METHOD Conventional

Michele Chiarlo is now helped by his sons Alberto and Stefano, the first looking after non-domestic markets and the second as an oenologist. Together, they have built up one of Piedmont's most impressive operations, both in terms of quality and output. Michele has also devoted much effort into developing the local area, with a good example his investments in the La Court art park. The consequences of the unfavourable 2003 year are finally behind them and we were at last able to taste practically the entire line. Only Triumviratum '00 was missing, which we will taste in the '01 version. As always, Barbera La Court was brilliant, brimming with smooth spice and ripe berry and displaying full energy nicely supported by a tangy acidity. Cannubi and Cerequio are both assertive, big-structured Barolos, each with the full, generous character and distinctiveness typical of their crus. Gavi Rovereto makes a fabulous showing, filled with succulent, minerally-edged fruit. Barbera, syrah and cabernet sauvignon go to make up Countacc! Though international in style, there's nothing banal about its superlative quality. All of the other wines are at the expected high performance levels.

Cascina Chicco

VIA VALENTINO, 144
12043 CANALE [CN]
TEL. 0173979411
www.cascinachicco.com

ANNUAL PRODUCTION 230,000 bottles
HECTARES UNDER VINE 28
VITICULTURE METHOD Conventional

Marco and Enrico Faccenda have been achieving enviable quality for quite some time now. Their operation is about to expand, with a new cellar that is a marvel of both architecture and functionality. But their production efforts have never wavered, thanks to the dynamic assistance of their father, Federico. They have always striven to bring out the best of their Roero terroir, with the result that their wines are very well executed and eminently approachable. Full marks go this year to the sturdy Barbera d'Alba Bric Loira '05, which builds amazing depth and breadth, with complexity on the palate and a driven progression of surprising energy. Yet even now it is nicely approachable. On a par is the concentrated Roero Valmaggiore '04, matching abundant tasty fruit on the nose with a finale of flawless sapidity and finesse. this wine is aristocratic to the last drop. Arcàss Passito '05 is rich and harmonious, with a lovely citrus-herbaceous note running throughout its development, thanks to top-quality arneis fruit. Eloquent expression characterizes Roero Montespinato '05 and Roero Arneis while the remaining Cascina Chicco wines are simply masterful, each displaying good typicity and distinctive personality.

● Barbera d'Asti Sup. Nizza La Court '04	♥♥	6
● Barolo Cerequio '03	♥♥	8
● Monferrato Montemareto Countacc! '04	♥♥	6
○ Gavi del Comune di Gavi Rovereto '06	♥♥	4*
● Barolo Brunate '03	♥♥	8
● Barolo Cannubi '03	♥♥	8
● Barbaresco Asili '04	♥♥	7
● Barbera d'Asti Sup. Cipressi della Court '05	♥♥	4
○ Moscato d'Asti Nivole '06	♥♥	3*
● Barbera d'Asti Sup. Nizza La Court '00	♥♥♥	6
● Barbera d'Asti Sup. Nizza La Court '01	♥♥♥	6
● Barbera d'Asti Sup. Nizza La Court '03	♥♥♥	6
● Barolo Cerequio '95	♥♥♥	8
● Barolo Cerequio '96	♥♥♥	8
● Barolo Cerequio '97	♥♥♥	8
● Barolo Cerequio '98	♥♥♥	8

○ Arcàss Passito '05	♥♥	5
● Roero Valmaggiore '04	♥♥	5
● Barbera d'Alba Bric Loira '05	♥♥	5
● Barbera d'Alba Granera Alta '06	♥♥	4
● Roero Montespinato '05	♥♥	4
● Nebbiolo d'Alba Mompissano '05	♥♥	4
○ Roero Arneis Anterisio '06	♥♥	4
○ Langhe Favorita '06	♥	4
○ Arcàss Passito '04	♥♥♥	5
● Nebbiolo d'Alba Mompissano '99	♥♥♥	5
● Barbera d'Alba Bric Loira '97	♥♥♥	5
● Barbera d'Alba Bric Loira '98	♥♥♥	5
● Barbera d'Alba Bric Loira '03	♥♥	5
● Roero Valmaggiore '01	♥♥	5
● Roero Valmaggiore '03	♥♥	5
● Roero Montespinato '03	♥♥	4
● Roero Montespinato '04	♥♥	4

Quinto Chionetti & Figlio

B.TA VALDIBERTI, 44
12063 DOGLIANI [CN]
TEL. 017371179
www.chionettiquinto.com

ANNUAL PRODUCTION 80,000 bottles
HECTARES UNDER VINE 14
VITICULTURE METHOD Conventional

The true spirit of the Langhe hovers about the cellar at number 44, Borgata Valdiberti, in the municipality of Dogliani. Quinto Chionetti's operation is set amidst 14 hectares of estate vines. The Briccolero and San Luigi vineyards yield their two wines, which amount to 80,000 bottles annually. Quinto is on a mission to promote his crus and the exclusive use of steel for vinification with his no-nonsense, unfussy style. Like his very close friend, the great Barolo master Bartolo Mascarello, who recently passed away, Chionetti has kept alive the traditional vision of making wine, regarding it as increasingly important for our own time. Meticulous and wise, he distils his decades of harvests and labour into two unique wines. Briccolero is sinuous, fine textured and silky while San Luigi shows rich fruit, veinings of spice and terroir, and a palate of perfectly balanced harmony. But words can only go so far. Chionetti is the noble art of crafting wine, and to plumb its considerable depths you have to seek it out, there in the Langhe, and let yourself drift off into a legendary dimension of wine.

● Dolcetto di Dogliani Briccolero '06	▼▼	4*
● Dolcetto di Dogliani S. Luigi '06	▼▼	4*
● Dolcetto di Dogliani Briccolero '04	▽▽▽	4
● Dolcetto di Dogliani Briccolero '05	▽▽	4
● Dolcetto di Dogliani Briccolero '03	▽▽	4
● Dolcetto di Dogliani Briccolero '01	▽▽	4
● Dolcetto di Dogliani Briccolero '00	▽▽	4
● Dolcetto di Dogliani S. Luigi '05	▽▽	4
● Dolcetto di Dogliani S. Luigi '04	▽▽	4
● Dolcetto di Dogliani S. Luigi '02	▽▽	4
● Dolcetto di Dogliani S. Luigi '03	▽▽	4
● Dolcetto di Dogliani S. Luigi '01	▽▽	4

Cieck

FRAZ. SAN GRATO
VIA BARDESONO
10011 AGLIÈ [TO]
TEL. 0124330522
www.cieck.it

ANNUAL PRODUCTION 100,000 bottles
HECTARES UNDER VINE 20
VITICULTURE METHOD Conventional

Three new wines. That's the news from Cieck this year. Erbaluce T '04 comes first. It's an experimental wine, produced in collaboration with the department of agriculture at the university of Turin. The harvest continued late, into November, with large cloth screens placed over the pergolas in early August contributing to better grape ripeness and increased polyphenol development. The wine appears gold yellow, with intense fragrances of toastiness and candied fruit. Although warm and heady, and showing good length, it lacks the crispness that would have made it irresistible. The new Nebbiolo '04 is appealing, opening with lovely florality and showing good nose-palate continuity, but the Barbera seemed to us still a bit rustic. All the other wines we tasted were impressive. Passito Alladium '02 stood out, showing richer and with a more traditional cast than in the past, featuring notes of nougat on the nose, a smooth, fat palate and a lighter hand with the oak. The classic method San Giorgio Brut '02, from erbaluce, is classy and pleasurable.

O Caluso Brut S. Giorgio '02	▼▼	4*
O Caluso Brut Calliope '02	▼▼	5
O Caluso Passito Alladium Vign. Runc '02	▼▼	5
O Erbaluce di Caluso T '04	▼▼	4
O Erbaluce di Caluso V. Misobolo '06	▼▼	3*
● Canavese Nebbiolo '04	▼▼	4
● Canavese Barbera '04	▼	4
O Caluso Brut Calliope '01	▽▽	5
O Caluso Brut S. Giorgio '01	▽▽	4
● Canavese Rosso Cieck '03	▽▽	4
● Canavese Rosso Neretto di S. Giorgio '03	▽▽	4
● Canavese Rosso Cieck '01	▽▽	5

F.lli Cigliuti

via Serraboella, 17
12052 Neive [CN]
tel. 0173677185
cigliutirenato@libero.it

ANNUAL PRODUCTION 30,000 bottles
HECTARES UNDER VINE 6.5
VITICULTURE METHOD Conventional

Perched as they are on the splendid Serraboella hill, the Cigliutis always produces wines of surpassing character. The family seems able to coax the best out of every growing year. Their approach is modern and clean, with careful attention paid to the grapes, no excesses and no fancy tricks in the cellar. The star wine, Barbaresco Serraboella '03, reflects this philosophy. It rises above its torrid growing season thanks to nervy acidity while displaying remarkably ample aromas and a good volume of fruit in the mouth. The same fidelity marks out Barbera Serraboella '05, which is pulpy, crisp and velvet textured, as well as absolutely chock-full of fruit and floral impressions. We very much liked Barbera Campass '05, which is a bit darker and more intense overall, with good heft and concentration in the mouth and powerful alcohol. Langhe Briccoserra '04 leans more to the international style. It's a dense, impressively complex nebbiolo and barbera blend but a bit closed in, with the oak contribution evident in the notes of toast and spice on the nose.

● Barbaresco Serraboella '03	TT	7
● Barbera d'Alba Serraboella '05	TT	5
● Barbera d'Alba Campass '05	TT	5
● Langhe Rosso Briccoserra '04	TT	6
● Barbaresco '83	YYY	7
● Barbaresco Serraboella '90	YYY	8
● Barbaresco Serraboella '96	YYY	8
● Barbaresco Serraboella '97	YYY	8
● Barbaresco Serraboella '00	YYY	7
● Barbaresco Serraboella '01	YYY	7
● Barbaresco V. Erte '00	YY	6
● Barbaresco V. Erte '01	YY	6
● Barbaresco V. Erte '03	YY	6
● Langhe Rosso Briccoserra '01	YY	6
● Langhe Rosso Briccoserra '03	YY	6

Tenute Cisa Asinari dei Marchesi di Gresy

s.da della Stazione, 21
12050 Barbaresco [CN]
tel. 0173635222
www.marchesidigresy.com

ANNUAL PRODUCTION 200,000 bottles
HECTARES UNDER VINE 35
VITICULTURE METHOD Conventional

The sight of the magnificent vineyards surrounding this celebrated Langhe cellar is stirring. A careful modernization of the facility has recently been completed. We tasted this year almost all of Tenute Cisa's broad line of superb offerings and they show great class, meticulously marshalled with exemplary sensitivity and straightforwardness by talented oenologist Marco Dotta. Barbaresco Gaiun '03 is an unalloyed delight, with an ultra-appealing bouquet, sturdy body and a relentless, well-balanced finale. Barbaresco Camp Gros '03 is right on top as well, with a taut, compact palate that shows fine integration and complexity. Barbaresco Martinenga '04 is, as always, classic and refined in its expression while Barbera d'Asti Monte Colombo '04 continues steadily along its road to ever greater complexity and finesse. Langhe Virtus '04 is again robust and compelling. Two whites stand out for their flawless expression, the forceful Langhe Sauvignon '06 and the more opulent Villa Giulia '06. Plaudits go to Passito L'Altro Moscato '04 for an enchanting performance. All in all, congratulations are in order for Alberto Di Gresy and his staff for managing to tame such the hot 2003 growing year.

● Barbaresco Camp Gros '03	TT	8
● Barbaresco Gaiun '03	TT	8
● Barbaresco Martinenga '04	TT	8
● Barbera d'Asti Monte Colombo '04	TT	6
● Langhe Rosso Virtus '04	TT	7
○ Piemonte Moscato Passito L'Altro Moscato '04	TT	6
○ Langhe Sauvignon '06	TT	4
○ Langhe Bianco Villa Giulia '06	TT	4
○ Langhe Chardonnay '06	T	4
○ Moscato d'Asti La Serra '06	T	4
● Langhe Nebbiolo Martinenga '06	T	5
● Dolcetto d'Alba Monte Aribaldo '06	T	4
● Barbaresco Camp Gros '00	YYY	8
● Barbaresco Camp Gros '01	YYY	8
● Barbaresco Gaiun '97	YYY	8

★ Domenico Clerico
LOC. MANZONI, 67
12065 MONFORTE D'ALBA [CN]
TEL. 017378171

Elvio Cogno
VIA RAVERA, 2
12060 NOVELLO [CN]
TEL. 0173744006
www.elviocogno.com

ANNUAL PRODUCTION 95,000 bottles
HECTARES UNDER VINE 21
VITICULTURE METHOD Conventional

ANNUAL PRODUCTION 70,000 bottles
HECTARES UNDER VINE 9
VITICULTURE METHOD Conventional

It is hard to say anything new about an artist of wine as great as Domenico Clerico. Although construction of his new cellar makes terrific demands on his time, he is always available and hospitable while keeping up the very high quality of his wines. In our tastings, we seemed to more lightness in the wines, even the Barolos from the hot 2003. Ciabot Mentin Ginestra starts with an interesting openness in the fruit, and a generous array of smooth spices, then releasing nervy acidity that beautifully harmonizes tannic power and alcoholic strength. Pajana is currently more closed in and tight-wound but at the same time smooth, well structured and alluring. Barolo Percristina has again figured in our tastings, this time in the superb '01 vintage, offering a fruit infused with earthy notes and evolved impressions, dense, fine-grained tannins, and a savoury, ultra-supple palate of impressive depth. The alluring fruit of a great harvest, it swept up our Three Glasses. The splendid Arte '05 is a nervy, taut blend of nebbiolo and barbera that shows full flavoured and nicely tannic. Finally, the standard-label offerings are all sound, and reasonably priced, particularly the Dolcetto.

The 17th-century farmhouse of Nadia Cogno and husband Walter Fissore enjoys one of the most splendid views in the Langhe, overlooking the vineyards of Barolo and Monforte, and behind them the hamlet of Novello. Their cellar is surrounded by a large part of their vineyards, which enjoy optimal exposure. This year, we missed Barolo Riserva Elena, one of Elvio Cogno's stars, but we did taste Barolo Ravera. It is of course a child of the hot 2003 but superb nonetheless. Matured in large and small cooperage, it shows judiciously crisp and well balanced on the finish, with tannins well on their way to maturation. Langhe Rosso Montegrilli is a finely structured blend of barbera and nebbiolo that offers richly fruited aromas and a succulent palate of considerable depth. The excellent Barbera Bricco dei Merli is savoury and smooth in the mouth, with fragrant blueberry and redcurrant. Dolcetto Vigna del Mandorlo is delicious and well proportioned. Finally, a word about a unique white made from nascetta, a variety in the Novello area. Relaunched in the mid 1990s by Cogno, it's a wine with solid character, which showcases the variety's slaty minerality and savouriness. It will age as well.

● Barolo Percristina '01	♟♟♟	8
● Barolo Ciabot Mentin Ginestra '03	♟♟	8
● Barolo Pajana '03	♟♟	8
● Langhe Rosso Arte '05	♟♟	6
● Barbera d'Alba Trevigne '05	♟♟	5
● Langhe Dolcetto Visadì '06	♟♟	4*
● Barolo Percristina '95	♟♟♟	8
● Barolo Percristina '96	♟♟♟	8
● Barolo Percristina '97	♟♟♟	8
● Barolo Percristina '98	♟♟♟	8
● Barolo Percristina '99	♟♟♟	8
● Barolo Pajana '95	♟♟♟	8
● Barolo Pajana '90	♟♟♟	8
● Barolo Ciabot Mentin Ginestra '89	♟♟♟	8
● Barolo Ciabot Mentin Ginestra '99	♟♟♟	8
● Barolo Ciabot Mentin Ginestra '01	♟♟♟	8

● Barolo Ravera '03	♟♟	7
○ Langhe Bianco Anas-Cetta '06	♟♟	4*
● Barolo '03	♟♟	6
● Langhe Rosso Montegrilli '05	♟♟	5
● Barbera d'Alba Bricco dei Merli '05	♟♟	5
● Dolcetto d'Alba V. del Mandorlo '06	♟♟	4
● Barolo Ravera '01	♟♟♟	7
● Barolo V. Elena '99	♟♟♟	8
● Barolo V. Elena '01	♟♟♟	8
● Barolo Ravera '00	♟♟	7
● Barolo Ravera '98	♟♟	7
● Barolo Ravera '99	♟♟	7
● Barolo V. Elena '98	♟♟	8
● Barolo V. Elena '97	♟♟	8
○ Langhe Bianco Anas-Cetta '05	♟♟	4

Poderi Colla

LOC. SAN ROCCO SENO D'ELVIO, 82
12051 ALBA [CN]
TEL. 0173290148
www.podericolla.it

ANNUAL PRODUCTION 150,000 bottles
HECTARES UNDER VINE 30
VITICULTURE METHOD Conventional

The Colla brothers, students and heirs of Alfredo Prunotto, own 30 hectares of vineyard, in the Monforte district of Barolo and in Barbaresco and San Rocco Seno d'Elvio near Alba. They favour a traditional approach and their wines display a style that is uncompromising yet clean and sound. Again this year, the Poderi Colla wines exhibited great quality and a well-crafted sense of place. We especially liked Langhe Rosso Bricco del Drago. A blend of 85 per cent dolcetto and the remainder nebbiolo, it opens with elegant fruit before expanding into a sturdy structure and a finale well supported by supple tannins. Barbaresco Roncaglie, though excellent, still shows somewhat closed and needs further time. Barolo Bussia Dardi Le Rose '03 shrugs off a hot year and lays out dense fruit and already mellow tannins. As expected, Barbera Costa Bruna gave us perfumed fruit, a fluid palate and nice length on the finish that tamps down emphatic alcohol. The remainder of the wines do a good job of reflecting the Langhe terroir.

Colle Manora

S.DA BOZZOLE, 4
15044 QUARGNENTO [AL]
TEL. 0131219252
www.collemanora.it

ANNUAL PRODUCTION 70,000 bottles
HECTARES UNDER VINE 20
VITICULTURE METHOD Conventional

Colle Manora is showing every sign of improving, with this year's offerings demonstrating generally impressive quality. At the top of our list is Barbera del Monferrato Manora, with its intense ruby and rich fruit and spice on the nose. In the mouth, the nervy acidity supports a close-knit and sustained progression. To make Rosso Palo Alto, pinot nero, cabernet sauvignon, merlot and barbera are vinified separately then assembled for a wine with kaleidoscopic complexity on the nose and appreciable length and equilibrium on the palate. A blend of cask-aged sauvignon blanc and viognier go to produce the Mila vino da tavola. Pais is a steel-vinified barbera offering intense aromas and nervy acidity. Monferrato Bianco Mimosa always puts on a memorable performance. This time, it paraded intense, intriguingly satisfying aromas, a smooth-textured palate and tasty bolstering acidity. We also recommend Monferrato Rosso Barchetta, a partnership of barbera, merlot and cabernet sauvignon.

● Langhe Rosso Bricco del Drago '04	♈ 5
● Barbaresco Roncaglie '04	♈♈ 7
● Barbera d'Alba Costa Bruna '06	♈♈ 4
● Dolcetto d'Alba Pian Balbo '06	♈♈ 4
○ Langhe Bianco Sanrocco '06	♈♈ 4
● Barolo Bussia Dardi Le Rose '03	♈♈ 7
● Nebbiolo d'Alba '05	♈ 4
● Barolo Bussia Dardi Le Rose '99	♈♈♈ 7
● Barolo Bussia Dardi Le Rose '00	♈♈ 7
● Barolo Bussia Dardi Le Rose '01	♈♈ 7
● Barbaresco Roncaglie '01	♈♈ 7
● Barbaresco Roncaglie '03	♈♈ 7

● Barbera del M.to Manora '04	♈♈ 5
● Barbera del M.to Pais '05	♈♈ 4*
○ Monferrato Bianco Mimosa '05	♈♈ 4*
● Monferrato Rosso Palo Alto '04	♈♈ 5
○ Mila Bianco '05	♈♈ 4
● Monferrato Rosso Barchetta '04	♈ 6
● Barbera del M.to Manora '01	♈♈ 5
● Monferrato Rosso Palo Alto '01	♈♈ 6
● Monferrato Rosso Palo Alto '00	♈♈ 6
● Monferrato Rosso Palo Alto '03	♈♈ 5
● Monferrato Rosso Palo Alto '03	♈ 5

Collina Serragrilli
VIA SERRAGRILLI, 30
12057 NEIVE [CN]
TEL. 0173677010
www.serragrilli.it

ANNUAL PRODUCTION 120,000 bottles
HECTARES UNDER VINE 15
VITICULTURE METHOD Conventional

Nestling high on the Serragrilli hill, this is one of those rare cellars with women in charge, here the three Lequio sisters. Daniela oversees the winemaking operations, with the assistance of Giuliano Noè and Beppe Rattazzo, Rosanna and her husband Piernicola Bruno deal with marketing and Antonella completes the threesome. Their growth and improvement are amazing. Only two years ago, they entered the Guide with a short profile and this year finds them with a wine, Barbaresco Serragrilli, that went all the way to the national final tastings. It's is a fabulous wine, exuding sound, healthy fruit enriched with nuances of tanned leather, and unleashing fine progression and a crisp finish. Barbaresco Basarin carries riper fruit and less oak influence so it's more immediately approachable. Barbera Grillaia is as enjoyable as always, with zesty acidity enlivening dense, tasty fruit. Langhe Grillorosso is an elegant medley of barbera, nebbiolo and cabernet sauvignon while both Dolcetto and Barbera are blessed with opulent palates. The remaining wines all received high marks.

La Colombera
FRAZ. VHO
S.DA COMUNALE PER VHO, 7
15057 TORTONA [AL]
TEL. 0131867795
www.lacolomberavini.it

ANNUAL PRODUCTION 40,000 bottles
HECTARES UNDER VINE 20
VITICULTURE METHOD Conventional

No longer is La Colombera, located at Vho, a surprise of any kind since it has been doing so well for so many years now, not to mention earning high scores in our Guide. The Timorasso is always a gem. After a superb '04, here is an encore with the excellent '05. Earthy mineral and blossoms mingle intriguingly with notes of petrol on the nose while the palate exhibits mouthfeel and nose-palate consistency worthy of a great wine. We liked the cask-aged Barbera Elisa but the other Barbera, Vegia Rampana, dropped below our expectations. Suciaja, made from the nibiò grape, is its usual fine self, and Croatina Arché, here in its second release, is impressive and on its way to being even more so. The cortese-based Bricco Bartolomeo all but conquered Two Glasses and Freisa Colle del Grillo is clean, crisp and totally delicious.

● Barbaresco Serragrilli '04	♟♟	6
● Barbaresco Basarin '03	♟♟	6
● Barbera d'Alba Grillaia '05	♟♟	4*
● Langhe Grillorosso '04	♟♟	4*
● Barbera d'Alba '05	♟	4
● Dolcetto d'Alba '06	♟	4
○ Langhe Grillobianco '05	♟	4
● Barbaresco Basarin '01	♟♟	6
● Barbera d'Alba Grillaia '04	♟♟	4
● Barbaresco Serragrilli '01	♟♟	6
● Barbaresco Serragrilli '03	♟♟	6

○ Colli Tortonesi Timorasso '05	♟♟	5
● Colli Tortonesi Rosso Arché '04	♟♟	4
● Colli Tortonesi Rosso Suciaja '04	♟♟	5
● Piemonte Barbera Elisa '04	♟♟	4
○ Colli Tortonesi Bianco Bricco Bartolomeo '06	♟	3*
● Colli Tortonesi Colle del Grillo '06	♟	3
● Colli Tortonesi Rosso Vegia Rampana '05	♟	4
○ Colli Tortonesi Bianco '04	♟♟	5
● Colli Tortonesi Rosso Suciaja '01	♟♟	5
● Colli Tortonesi Rosso Suciaja '03	♟♟	5
● Piemonte Barbera Elisa '03	♟♟	5
● Colli Tortonesi Rosso Suciaja '02	♟♟	5
● Piemonte Barbera Elisa '00	♟♟	5

Il Colombo - Barone Riccati

VIA DEI SENT, 2
12084 MONDOVÌ [CN]
TEL. 017441607
www.ilcolombo.com

ANNUAL PRODUCTION 15,000 bottles
HECTARES UNDER VINE 3.5
VITICULTURE METHOD Conventional

Il Colombo, located on the road that leads from Bastia to Mondovì, lies in a natural amphitheatre with a view over Mondovì and the mountains that encircle it. Carlo Riccati and his wife Adriana brought this operation critical acclaim, thanks to their superb versions of Dolcetto delle Langhe Monregalesi. Last year, the winery changed hands when it was purchased by the Holms, a Norwegian couple, and it is now directed by Bruno Chionetti and his wife Sabina. Both of them can claim a long, fruitful experience with dolcetto, which they gained when they were at the San Romano di Dogliani winery. As to the wines, the production approach has not changed. Painstaking attention is paid to the vineyards in order to obtain superb fruit. La Chiesetta is sourced from the youngest vineyards, which are east-facing and lower down on the hill. It shows subtle and refreshing, with youthful, heady aromas of sound fruit. Il Colombo, on the other hand, comes from higher up, from a site facing south. It is characterized by solid body, rougher tannins and riper fruit.

★ Aldo Conterno

LOC. BUSSIA, 48
12065 MONFORTE D'ALBA [CN]
TEL. 017378150
www.poderialdoconterno.com

ANNUAL PRODUCTION 120,000 bottles
HECTARES UNDER VINE 25
VITICULTURE METHOD Conventional

In the 20th anniversary edition of our Guide, we nominated Barolo Gran Bussia 1989 as the finest wine ever tasted in the history of this publication. Aldo Conterno has now succeeded, several years later, in producing another magisterial version of his iconic wine. Gran Bussia 2001 picked up incredibly high scores at our final tastings, winning Three Glasses almost without effort. Here is a wine that manages to express to the highest degree what Barolo is all about. Austere and elegant at the same time, it is intense and superlatively built, displaying incredible power supported by wonderful use of oak. A lively ruby in appearance, it gives floral and fruit essences, foregrounding subtle cinchona, vanilla and cocoa that developed over its lengthy, 36-month maturation in large botti. The tannins are glossy and dense; the conclusion of rarely matched power and length. We note the absence of the '03 Barolos but we enjoyed a wonderful version of Favot and the very interesting Barbera Conca Tre Pile. Rosso Quartetto is a foursome of nebbiolo, barbera, merlot and cabernet sauvignon that has its roots deep in the Langhe even though its soul is international.

● Dolcetto delle Langhe Monregalesi Sup. Il Colombo '05	♓♓	4*
● Dolcetto delle Langhe Monregalesi La Chiesetta '06	♓♓	3*
● Dolcetto delle Langhe Monregalesi Il Colombo '97	♔♔♔	4
● Dolcetto delle Langhe Monregalesi Il Colombo '98	♔♔♔	4
● Dolcetto delle Langhe Monregalesi Sup. Il Colombo '03	♔♔	4
● Dolcetto delle Langhe Monregalesi Sup. Il Colombo '04	♔♔	4

● Barolo Gran Bussia Ris. '01	♓♓♓	8
● Langhe Nebbiolo Il Favot '04	♓♓	7
● Barbera d'Alba Conca Tre Pile '04	♓♓	5
● Langhe Rosso Quartetto '04	♓♓	6
● Barolo Bussia Soprana '86	♔♔♔	8
● Barolo Gran Bussia Ris. '82	♔♔♔	8
● Barolo Gran Bussia Ris. '88	♔♔♔	8
● Barolo Gran Bussia Ris. '89	♔♔♔	8
● Barolo Gran Bussia Ris. '90	♔♔♔	8
● Barolo Gran Bussia Ris. '95	♔♔♔	8
● Barolo V. del Colonnello '90	♔♔♔	8
● Barolo V. del Colonnello '90	♔♔♔	8
● Barbera d'Alba Conca Tre Pile '89	♔♔♔	5
● Barbera d'Alba Conca Tre Pile '01	♔♔	5
● Barolo Cicala '01	♔♔	8

★ Conterno Fantino

VIA GINESTRA, 1
12065 MONFORTE D'ALBA [CN]
TEL. 017378204
www.conternofantino.it

ANNUAL PRODUCTION 130,000 bottles
HECTARES UNDER VINE 25
VITICULTURE METHOD Conventional

Guido Fantino and Claudio Conterno have been among the main actors in Barolo's recent history. They started together in 1983 and faced difficult times but established themselves on the market in conditions that were very different from today's. Now those days seem far off but the legacy of energy, enthusiasm, intelligence and tenacity that distinguished the Langhe back then should be safeguarded as an asset as important as the finest vineyards. Like many others, Guido and Claudio acknowledge this heritage and imprint it on their wines through their conscientious work in vineyards and cellar. They submitted an excellent collection this year, even though the challenging 2003 vintage left a bit of a mark in terms of freshness on some labels. But the Langhe Rosso Monprà, from the favourable 2004 vintage, is seductive on the nose, broad and intense on the palate, and shows already well-integrated oak that never masks the elegant, harmonic fruit. The Barolos are fragrant, spicy and tannic, seamlessly melding their alcohol into the overall balance.

★ Giacomo Conterno

LOC. ORNATI, 2
12065 MONFORTE D'ALBA [CN]
TEL. 017378221

ANNUAL PRODUCTION 50,000 bottles
HECTARES UNDER VINE 14
VITICULTURE METHOD   Conventional

Oceans of ink have been spilled over grandfather Giacomo, father Giovanni and son Roberto Conterno. We can safely state, without fear of contradiction, that their wines have written and are still writing the history of one of the most important DOCG zones in our peninsula. For this reason, we will let the wines speak for themselves. Roberto makes them and has inherited his father's strong, fashion-averse character and genuine winemaker's soul. Robert's Monfortino remains a monument to Barolo. After 82 months, or almost seven years, in large barrels, it release a swath of aromatics that runs from ripe blueberries, currants and blackberries to more elegant nuances of as cinnamon, mint and aniseed. This classic Barolo won a commanding Three Glasses. The passage of the years has smoothed out the tannins and the finish is very full with superb structure. Cascina Francia is back after a year's absence and despite the sweltering growing season is in excellent shape. Notes of violet mingle with nuances of thyme, tobacco and leather. Finally, the Barbera is one of the most pleasant traditionally vinified wine of this type. It is fruity, very fragrant, nicely acidic and juicy on the palate.

● Barolo Sorì Ginestra '03	❷❷	8
● Barolo V. del Gris '03	❷❷	8
● Langhe Rosso Monprà '04	❷❷	6
● Barbera d'Alba Vignota '06	❷❷	5
● Langhe Nebbiolo Ginestrino '06	❷❷	5
○ Langhe Chardonnay Bastia '04	❷❷	5
● Dolcetto d'Alba Bricco Bastia '06	❷	4
● Barolo Sorì Ginestra '00	❸❸❸	8
● Barolo Sorì Ginestra '90	❸❸❸	8
● Barolo Sorì Ginestra '91	❸❸❸	8
● Barolo Sorì Ginestra '99	❸❸❸	8
● Barolo Sorì Ginestra '98	❸❸❸	8
● Langhe Rosso Monprà '98	❸❸❸	8
● Langhe Rosso Monprà '97	❸❸❸	8
● Langhe Rosso Monprà '95	❸❸❸	8
● Barolo V. del Gris '96	❸❸❸	8
● Barolo V. del Gris '97	❸❸❸	8
● Barolo V. del Gris '01	❸❸❸	8

● Barolo Monfortino Ris. '00	❸❸❸	8
● Barolo Cascina Francia '03	❷❷	8
● Barbera d'Alba Cascina Francia '05	❷❷	6
● Barolo Cascina Francia '89	❸❸❸	8
● Barolo Cascina Francia '90	❸❸❸	8
● Barolo Cascina Francia '97	❸❸❸	8
● Barolo Cascina Francia '00	❸❸❸	8
● Barolo Cascina Francia '01	❸❸❸	8
● Barolo Monfortino Ris. '85	❸❸❸	8
● Barolo Monfortino Ris. '87	❸❸❸	8
● Barolo Monfortino Ris. '88	❸❸❸	8
● Barolo Monfortino Ris. '90	❸❸❸	8
● Barolo Monfortino Ris. '97	❸❸❸	8
● Barolo Monfortino Ris. '99	❸❸❸	8

Paolo Conterno
VIA GINESTRA, 34
12065 MONFORTE D'ALBA [CN]
TEL. 017378415
www.paoloconterno.com

ANNUAL PRODUCTION 50,000 bottles
HECTARES UNDER VINE 7
VITICULTURE METHOD Conventional

The Conterno estate is a lovely, characteristically Langhe-style family operation with seven hectares under vine concentrated in one of the best zones, the Ginestra cru. Wines from this estate have a balanced, traditional imprint and are probably better suited to enhancing a dinner than tasting on their own. Paolo's son, Giorgio, manages the cellar with consultancy from Beppe Caviola. This year, we were looking forward to the Barolo Ginestra Riserva 2001 but Giorgio decided to let it age another year, so we were happy to fall back, as it were, on the Barolo 2003, which showed itself to be a good interpretation of a difficult vintage. The nose recalls sweet spices, leather and dried flowers. The palate is round, fairly warm but with no excessive alcohol and a fine tannic texture. We liked the two Barberas, a structured, fruity Ginestra and fresh, elegant Bricco Sant'Ambrogio, from a vineyard located in Roddi. The Nebbiolo Bric Ginestra is as good as ever while the Dolcetto has character and pronounced tannins.

Contratto
VIA G. B. GIULIANI, 56
14053 CANELLI [AT]
TEL. 0141823349
www.contratto.it

ANNUAL PRODUCTION 285,000 bottles
HECTARES UNDER VINE 55
VITICULTURE METHOD Conventional

After an enforced absence following an unfavourable growing year, the Contratto Cerequio is back in the race. It is sourced from one of the most celebrated vineyards in the entire Barolo DOCG zone, located in the hollow of La Morra, facing Barolo castle. This Cerequio is so exceptional that, even in a growing season as hot as 2003, it still manages to show elegance in its notes of ripe fruit, well tamed by the oak. The palate is a wonder and unfolds long and harmonious. This truly lovely performance shows off the fruit of the nebbiolo against a smoky background from the ageing oak. The range of wines submitted is in great shape, beginning with the sweet house wine, Contratto, a classic method Asti that is back on sparkling form thanks to a citrus-like note on the nose and a rich, elegant palate. The Brut Giuseppe Contratto Riserva 2003 reveals delicate bubbles, sensations of crusty bread and long-lingering fruit, braced by good acidity. We'll close with the Barberas, cornerstone of winemaking in the province of Asti. The barrique-aged Solus Ad is the more challenging and austere while the standard-label Panta Rei is very pleasant.

● Barbera d'Alba Ginestra '05	♈ 5
● Barolo Ginestra '03	♈ 8
● Barbera d'Alba Bricco Sant'Ambrogio '05	♈ 4
● Langhe Nebbiolo Bric Ginestra '05	♈ 6
● Dolcetto d'Alba Ginestra '06	♈ 4
● Barolo Ginestra '99	♈♈ 8
● Barolo Ginestra Ris. '98	♈♈ 8
● Barolo Ginestra Ris. '99	♈♈ 8
● Barolo Ginestra '00	♈♈ 8
● Barolo Ginestra Ris. '96	♈♈ 8
● Barolo Ginestra Ris. '97	♈♈ 8
● Barolo Ginestra '01	♈♈ 8

○ Asti De Miranda M. Cl. '04	♈ 6
○ Spumante M. Cl. Brut Ris. Giuseppe Contratto '03	♈ 6
● Barolo Cerequio '03	♈ 8
● Barbera d'Asti Solus Ad '05	♈ 7
● Barbera d'Asti Panta Rei '06	♈ 5
○ Asti De Miranda M. Cl. '96	♈♈♈ 6
○ Asti De Miranda M. Cl. '97	♈♈♈ 6
○ Spumante M. Cl. Brut Ris. Giuseppe Contratto '95	♈♈♈ 5
○ Spumante M. Cl. Brut Ris. Giuseppe Contratto '99	♈♈♈ 5
● Barolo Cerequio Tenuta Secolo '97	♈♈♈ 8
● Barolo Cerequio '99	♈♈♈ 8

Coppo

VIA ALBA, 68
14053 CANELLI [AT]
TEL. 0141823146
www.coppo.it

ANNUAL PRODUCTION 420,000 bottles
HECTARES UNDER VINE 56
VITICULTURE METHOD Conventional

Achieving high quality is one thing: confirming the prestige earned during all those years of hard work is another. We can safely say this year that the Coppo siblings from Canelli hit the target. Though several major labels were missing – the Riservas, the Monferrato Mondaccione and Chardonnay Monteriolo, expected next year – the Coppos presented a very respectable range. As ever, plaudits went to the Barbera d'Asti Pomorosso 2005, which shines with elegance, power and complexity. One of the finest wines in its category, it sailed away with Three Glasses. Next in line comes the Monferrato Alterego 2004, a lovely melange of barbera and cabernet with a balsamic nose and powerful, juicy palate supported by smooth tannins. The good Barbera Camp du Rouss 2005 showed powerful and measured with full-flavoured, minerally notes. After 27 years, the Coppo house Barolo returns. A 2003 made with fruit from Castiglione Falletto, it fully expresses the variety and vintage, for good and ill, considering the difficult weather during that particular growing season. The captivating Brut Riserva 2001 unites the force of powerful structure with the finesse of its fruit, braced by fresh acidity.

Giovanni Corino

FRAZ. ANNUNZIATA, 24B
12064 LA MORRA [CN]
TEL. 0173509452

ANNUAL PRODUCTION 50,000 bottles
HECTARES UNDER VINE 16
VITICULTURE METHOD Conventional

Giuliano Corino is part of that group of winemakers from La Morra who for more than 20 years have practised modern-style viticulture, with crop thinning, controlled temperature fermentation and use of barriques, according to the needs of the various wines. This offers an interesting angle on the range submitted for this year's tastings. We'll start with the Barolo 2003, which melds complexity and surprising freshness on the nose with easy, winning drinkability. The Barolo Giachini 2003 charms with its plum and violet bouquet. Powerful tannin on the palate reminds us it is from a scorching growing season while the acidity and freshness are amazing in the finish. The Barolo Arborina 2003 opens with leather that dominates the floral notes. The palate is fresh, complex and tannic before the broad structure dissolves into a long, balsamic finish. Completing this selection is an interesting Langhe Nebbiolo 2006, the elegant standard-label Barbera and a well-typed Dolcetto.

● Barbera d'Asti Pomorosso '05	♀♀♀ 7
● Monferrato Alterego '04	♀♀ 6
● Barbera d'Asti Camp du Rouss '05	♀♀ 4*
○ Gavi La Rocca '06	♀♀ 4
○ Coppo Brut Ris. '01	♀♀ 6
○ Piemonte Chardonnay Costebianche '06	♀ 4
● Barbera d'Asti L'Avvocata '06	♀ 4
● Barolo '03	♀ 7
● Barbera d'Asti Pomorosso '01	♀♀♀ 7
● Barbera d'Asti Pomorosso '04	♀♀♀ 7
● Barbera d'Asti Pomorosso '90	♀♀♀ 5
● Barbera d'Asti Pomorosso '99	♀♀♀ 7
● Barbera d'Asti Pomorosso '03	♀♀♀ 7
● Monferrato Alterego '03	♀♀ 6
● Monferrato Alterego '01	♀♀ 6

● Barolo V. Giachini '03	♀♀ 8
● Barbera d'Alba '06	♀♀ 4
● Barolo '03	♀♀ 7
● Barolo Arborina '03	♀♀ 8
● Dolcetto d'Alba '06	♀ 4
● Langhe Nebbiolo '06	♀ 4
● Barolo Vecchie Vigne '01	♀♀ 8

Renato Corino
B.TA POZZO, 49A
12064 LA MORRA [CN]
TEL. 0173500349

ANNUAL PRODUCTION 30,000 bottles
HECTARES UNDER VINE 6
VITICULTURE METHOD Conventional

We love Renato Corino's lovely winery, which is at last complete and perfectly integrated into the Langhe landscape. Now independent from his brother Giuliano's operation, Renato's estate is up and running thanks to the commitment his family, as is so often the case here. Just a bit more time is needed to finish a small building dedicated to the winery's history. In a small village near the town of La Morra, Renato tends his six hectares under vine planted only to nebbiolo, barbera and dolcetto, all in prime locations, including the two vineyards of Arborina and Rocche. This entry concentrates precisely on these two versions of the 2003 vintage Barolo. The Arborina is stylish and spicy with surprising freshness and elegance, showing appealingly soft with great drinkability. The second offers pleasingly fresh, fruity notes on the nose and soft, silky tannins on the palate, which won it Three well-deserved Glasses. While waiting for the new vintage of the Barolo Vecchie Vigne, we'll console ourselves with the Barbera Pozzo 2004 for leisurely barrique ageing has forged a major wine. The rest of this pleasant range of wines should not be underrated, including a very well-made base Barolo 2003.

Cornarea
VIA VALENTINO, 150
12043 CANALE [CN]
TEL. 017365636

ANNUAL PRODUCTION 75,000 bottles
HECTARES UNDER VINE 14
VITICULTURE METHOD Conventional

There is always a lot of Arneis in the range of wines released by the Bovone family, whose winery has recently been expanded with a magnificent hospitality centre on the summit of the hill that gives its name to the estate. The growth in quality at Cornarea is historically tied to this native white variety from Roero, released in several versions and regularly achieving excellent results. The 2006 vintage of Arneis gives aromas and fragrances that live up to its fame, adding finesse and acidity to our memories of past editions. The late-harvest interpretation – Andrè 2004, a monovarietal arneis-only table wine – wonderfully exploits a memorable harvest, preserving substantial freshness, zest and minerality. Finally, the Passito is at its best, presenting nicely sweet, broad, balanced and elegant. Work on fine-tuning the red wines is going well. This year, we preferred the structured, austerely tannic Roero.

● Barolo Vigneto Rocche '03	♥♥♥	8
● Barolo Vigneto Arborina '03	♥♥	8
● Barbera d'Alba Vigna Pozzo '04	♥	6
● Barolo '03	♥♥	6
● Dolcetto d'Alba '06	♥♥	4*
● Barbera d'Alba '06	♥♥	4*
● Nebbiolo d'Alba '05	♥♥	5
● Barbera d'Alba Vigna Pozzo '03	♀♀	6
● Barolo Vecchie Vigne '01	♀♀	8

○ Tarasco Passito '03	♥	6
○ Roero Arneis '06	♥♥	4*
○ Andrè '04	♥♥	5
● Roero '04	♥♥	4*
● Nebbiolo d'Alba '04	♥	4
○ Tarasco Passito '01	♀♀	6
○ Tarasco Passito '00	♀♀	6
○ Andrè '03	♀♀	5
● Nebbiolo d'Alba '03	♀♀	4
● Roero Sup. '01	♀♀	5
● Roero '03	♀♀	4

★ Matteo Correggia
LOC. CASE SPARSE GARBINETTO, 124
12043 CANALE [CN]
TEL. 0173978009
www.matteocorreggia.com

ANNUAL PRODUCTION 120,000 bottles
HECTARES UNDER VINE 20
VITICULTURE METHOD Natural

The battery of wines from the Correggias gives us a spontaneous feeling of reassurance. Credit goes to Ornella Costa for putting together a top-flight team who assist her watching over each step in the winery's production process from vineyard to cellar. Over the past few years, Ornella's efforts and ambitions have been focused specifically on the vineyards. She is more than ever convinced – and we agree – of the need for a new balance of plant, soil and territory. Her leading reds show that this is the way ahead. The nebbiolo always combines finesse and character, hitting the mark in all its many expressions: Nebbiolo d'Alba La Val dei Preti, Roero and Roero Ròche d'Ampsèj. The last of these is extraordinary in the 2004 vintage and lives up to the expectations of a family that has always produced superb reds. This one has Three Glasses worth of elegance and complexity. The Barbera Marun shows striking harmony of softness and acidity, laying down a benchmark for the type. The Langhe Rosso is now much more than a mere divertissement, having found a precise style themed around elegance. The rest of this magnificent array has plenty of quality and personality.

Giuseppe Cortese
S.DA RABAJÀ, 80
12050 BARBARESCO [CN]
TEL. 0173635131
www.cortesegiuseppe.it

ANNUAL PRODUCTION 50,000 bottles
HECTARES UNDER VINE 8
VITICULTURE METHOD Conventional

Run by Giuseppe and Piercarlo Cortese, this is a winery that knows good wines are made in the vineyard and follows up work there with excellent results in the cellar. Large Slavonian oak is used to age the Barbaresco and Nebbiolo, and 30 per cent new barriques for the Barbera. Now we come to the Barbaresco Rabajà 2004. Old vines and 20 months in oak have given it power and elegance. The nose is rich in aromas that are reprised on the palate. The 2004 version of the Nebbiolo is good. It aged slowly to acquire rich extract and tannins. Underpinned by 16 months in oak, the excellently made Barbera Morassina 2004 is powerful yet at the same time elegant on nose and palate. The unhurried finish is extremely long. The Barbera 2005 saw only stainless steel and preserves the freshness and drinkability typical of the variety. The Dolcetto Trifolera 2006 shows good balance between alcohol and tannins, and good length in the finish. The enjoyable Chardonnay 2006 is also attractive, with taut drinkability.

● Roero Ròche d'Ampsèj '04	♟♟♟	7
● Barbera d'Alba Marun '05	♟♟	6
● Langhe Rosso Le Marne Grigie '04	♟♟	7
● Nebbiolo d'Alba La Val dei Preti '05	♟♟	6
O Langhe Bianco Matteo Correggia '05	♟♟	6
● Anthos Passito '06	♟♟	5
● Barbera d'Alba '05	♟♟	4*
● Roero '05	♟♟	4*
● Anthos '06	♟	4
O Roero Arneis '06	♟	4
● Roero Ròche d'Ampsèj '97	♟♟♟	8
● Roero Ròche d'Ampsèj '98	♟♟♟	8
● Roero Ròche d'Ampsèj '99	♟♟♟	8
● Roero Ròche d'Ampsèj '00	♟♟♟	8
● Roero Ròche d'Ampsèj '01	♟♟♟	8
● Barbera d'Alba Marun '04	♟♟♟	6

● Barbaresco Rabajà '04	♟♟	6
● Barbera d'Alba '05	♟♟	4
● Barbera d'Alba Morassina '04	♟♟	5
● Langhe Nebbiolo '04	♟♟	5
● Dolcetto d'Alba Trifolera '06	♟	4
O Langhe Chardonnay '06	♟	4
● Barbaresco Rabajà Ris. '96	♟♟♟	8
● Barbaresco Rabajà '00	♟♟	6
● Barbaresco Rabajà Ris. '99	♟♟	8
● Barbaresco Rabajà '01	♟♟	6*
● Barbaresco Rabajà '03	♟♟	6
● Barbaresco Rabajà '99	♟♟	6
● Barbaresco Rabajà '98	♟♟	6

Coutandin

B.TA CIABOT, 12
10063 PEROSA ARGENTINA [TO]
TEL. 0121803473
ramie.coutandin@alpimedia.it

ANNUAL PRODUCTION 4,000 bottles
HECTARES UNDER VINE 1.2
VITICULTURE METHOD Conventional

What for Giuliano and Laura Coutandin
began as a hobby, to help them take their
minds off their jobs, has been slowly
transformed by growing passion into a full-
fledged business. Their son Daniele's
interest in viticulture and the time he has
spent on this led the family to set up this
winery. Ramìe is the feather in the cap of the
winery and the Pinerolo DOC zone. At the
confluence of Val Germanasca and Val
Chisone, between the towns of Pomaretto
and Perosa Argentina, the vineyard's dry
stone terraces look as if they are
suspended. In this environment of rare
beauty, more suitable for hillwalkers than
winemakers, the Coutandins lovingly tend
their many tiny plots under vine, planted
between 650 and 860 metres above sea
level. To produce this little big wine,
introduced by Cardinal Richelieu to the
court of Versailles at the end of the 17th
century, much space was given over to the
native avanà, avarengo, neretto (chatus) and
bequet varieties. The resulting wine has
spicy, fruity notes and a fresh, subtle palate.

Cascina Cucco

LOC. CUCCO
VIA MAZZINI, 10
12050 SERRALUNGA D'ALBA [CN]
TEL. 0173613003
www.cascinacucco.com

ANNUAL PRODUCTION 50,000 bottles
HECTARES UNDER VINE 12
VITICULTURE METHOD Conventional

The beautiful estate of the Stroppiana family
is in the capable hands of a large, well-
established team that skilfully manages the
vineyards, cellar and nearby hospitality
centre. Outstanding wines here include the
Barolo Cucco 2003 and Barbera d'Alba
Superiore 2005. The former has a complex
nose with a balsamic hint given by the new
barriques, well-honed tannins and
sweetness. The second makes use of a
good fruit-oak balance and, although
sourced from a newly planted vineyard, has
already acquired a round, mouthfilling body.
The other two Barolos are better than good.
The Cerrati 2003 has an ethery, spicy nose
and decent structure but even better than
this among the estate reds is the Langhe
Rosso Mondo 2005, a lovely blend of
barbera and nebbiolo, which is centred and
balanced on both the nose and palate. The
Dolcetto d'Alba Vughera 2006 and Barbera
d'Alba 2006 are clean and correct while the
Langhe Chardonnay 2006 opens on a rich
nose with good follow-through on the fresh
palate and good length.

● Pinerolese Ramìe '05	🍷🍷 5
● Gagin '06	🍷 4
● Barbichè '03	🍷🍷 4
● Pinerolese Ramìe '03	🍷🍷 5
● Pinerolese Ramìe '04	🍷🍷 5

● Barbera d'Alba Sup. '05	🍷🍷 5
● Barolo V. Cucco '03	🍷🍷 7
● Barolo V. Cerrati '03	🍷🍷 7
● Barolo '03	🍷🍷 7
● Langhe Rosso Mondo '05	🍷🍷 5
○ Langhe Chardonnay '06	🍷🍷 4
● Dolcetto d'Alba Vughera '06	🍷🍷 4
● Barbera d'Alba '06	🍷 4
● Barolo V. Cerrati '99	🍷🍷 7
● Barolo V. Cerrati '00	🍷🍷 7
● Barolo V. Cerrati '01	🍷🍷 7
● Barolo V. Cucco '99	🍷🍷 7
● Barolo V. Cucco '00	🍷🍷 7
● Barolo V. Cucco '01	🍷🍷 7
● Barolo '01	🍷🍷 7
● Barbera d'Alba Sup. '04	🍷🍷 5

Dacapo

S.DA ASTI MARE, 4
14040 AGLIANO TERME [AT]
TEL. 0141964921
www.dacapo.it

ANNUAL PRODUCTION 40,000 bottles
HECTARES UNDER VINE 5
VITICULTURE METHOD Conventional

There is a festival air at this pleasant winery
in the province of Asti. We have in fact
arrived at the tenth anniversary of the date
when two enterprising young men, Paolo
Dania and Dino Riccomagno, set off on this
ambitious project. They started by
purchasing a lovely, rustic farmhouse at
Agliano. After recent restructuring, it now
houses the production facilities for their
unfussy, carefully made estate labels. A
small increase in production is planned for
the future. But they hasten to add that the
winery is designed to be small enough to for
self-management and that's the way it will
stay. It's fairly common point of strength
around here, where low numbers go with
prudent strategies and commitment. Four
wines were presented this year, beginning
with the Ruché, particularly enjoyable
because of its rarity, followed by two
versions of Barbera d'Asti, the Sanbastiàn
2005 and Superiore Nizza Vigna Dacapo
2004. Finally, Monferrato Rosso Tre 2004
expertly balances the aromas and
personalities of its merlot, nebbiolo and
barbera grapes.

Damilano

VIA ROMA, 31
12060 BAROLO [CN]
TEL. 017356265
www.cantinedamilano.it

ANNUAL PRODUCTION 224,000 bottles
HECTARES UNDER VINE 22
VITICULTURE METHOD   Conventional

The long-standing Damilano Barolo estate
has for some years been reclaiming its
former status. Almost all of the
reconstruction work at the estate complex
has been completed, bringing more efficient
use of space for winemaking and ageing
cellars. Among the impressive wines
submitted this year were the Barolos from
the 2003 vintage, which showed good
balance and skilful management of a hot
growing season. The Cannubi confirmed its
breeding with warm, soft, elegant notes of
crushed flowers, cocoa power, light citrus
peel and a well-handled suite of tannins.
Just as good is the Liste, with more
imposing tannic structure and a mineral and
balsam-edged aromatic profile. The line-up
of Barolos ends with the base
Lecinquevigne, which is well crafted, earthy,
caressing and very clean. The other wines
submitted for tasting were decent and well
made, with a special mention going to
Barbera d'Alba La Blu 2005, which shows
fruity on the nose and then full-bodied in the
mouth.

● Monferrato Rosso Tre '04	♀♀ 6
● Barbera d'Asti Sanbastiàn '05	♀♀ 4*
● Barbera d'Asti Sup. Nizza V. Dacapo '04	♀♀ 5
● Ruché di Castagnole M.to Bric Ruché Majoli '06	♀♀ 4*
● Barbera d'Asti Sup. Nizza V. Dacapo '01	♀♀ 5
● Barbera d'Asti Sup. Nizza V. Dacapo '03	♀♀ 5
● Barbera d'Asti Sup. Nizza La Riserva del Fondatore '01	♀♀ 5
● Monferrato Rosso Tre '03	♀♀ 5

● Barolo Cannubi '03	♀♀ 8
● Barolo Liste '03	♀♀ 7
● Barbera d'Alba La Blu '05	♀♀ 5
● Nebbiolo d'Alba '05	♀♀ 4
● Barolo Lecinquevigne '03	♀♀ 7
● Barbera d'Alba '06	♀ 4
O Langhe Arneis '06	♀ 4
● Dolcetto d'Alba '06	♀ 4
● Barolo Cannubi '00	♀♀♀ 8
● Barolo Cannubi '01	♀♀♀ 8
● Barolo Liste '00	♀♀ 8
● Barolo Liste '01	♀♀ 8
● Barolo Cannubi '99	♀♀ 8
● Barolo Liste '99	♀♀ 8
● Barolo Lecinquevigne '02	♀♀ 6
● Barbera d'Alba '06	♀ 4

Sergio Degiorgis
VIA CIRCONVALLAZIONE, 3
12056 MANGO [CN]
TEL. 014189107
www.degiorgis-sergio.com

ANNUAL PRODUCTION   70,000 bottles
HECTARES UNDER VINE 9.5
VITICULTURE METHOD   Conventional

If we were to give an award for the First
Woman of Wine, Patrizia Degiorgis would
be one of the leading contenders for the big
prize. In addition to welcoming wine
connoisseurs, she is always ready and
willing to organize events with her
colleagues from Mango and other
neighbouring municipalities. And as well as
performing this important job of public
relations, she gives her husband Sergio a
helping hand in the day-to-day
management of this wonderful winery. The
range submitted this year was the usual
high quality, two of the wines reaching our
final taste-offs. We are talking here about
the Moscato Sorì del Re and Piemonte
Moscato Passito Essenza. The Moscato
proffers intense aromas of ripe, white-
fleshed fruit like peaches and apricots, lifted
by complex nuances of menthol and lemon
peel. The palate is juicy, full-bodied, fresh
and lingering. The second is aged 18 to 20
months in barrique and mingles the warm
notes of candied fruit with touches of
vanilla, cocoa powder and coffee from the
oak ageing. From the other wines, praise
goes to the Barbera d'Alba 2005 and base
Moscato. The Luna Nuova and Bricco Peso
are fair.

Deltetto
C.SO ALBA, 43
12043 CANALE [CN]
TEL. 0173979383
www.deltetto.com

ANNUAL PRODUCTION   150,000 bottles
HECTARES UNDER VINE 20
VITICULTURE METHOD   Conventional

Tonino Deltetto always gives us an intense
range of wines. This brilliant winery director
knows how to combine the spontaneity of
family management with the precise
organization imposed by market dynamics.
In fact, the total number of bottles and
types of wine produced put Deltetto in a
halfway position between the small estates
and the area's more substantial operations,
making it one of the current benchmarks for
Roero winemaking. The Roero Braja was
missing this year. The 2005 edition will be
back again for the next Guide, fortified by
longer ageing and the new DOCG
denomination. This leaves space for the
many other labels. First in line is a great
Barbera Rocca delle Marasche, fruity, soft
and silky, with a thread of acidity
accompanying the entire palate. It's the
house speciality again this year,
accompanied by a simpler Barbera Bramé
and a convincing and by now sound line-up
of excellent whites, both still and sparkling.

O Moscato d'Asti Sorì del Re '06	♟♟	4*
O Piemonte Moscato Passito		
Essenza '04	♟	5
O Moscato d'Asti '06	♟♟	4
● Barbera d'Alba '05	♟♟	4
● Barbera d'Alba Luna Nuova '06	♟	3
● Dolcetto d'Alba Bricco Peso '06	♟	3
O Essenza '03	♟♟	5
O Moscato d'Asti Sorì del Re '05	♟♟	4
O Moscato d'Asti Sorì del Re '03	♟♟	4
O Moscato d'Asti Sorì del Re '04	♟♟	4

● Barbera d'Alba Sup.		
Rocca delle Marasche '05	♟♟	6
● Barbera d'Alba Sup. Bramé '05	♟♟	4*
O Deltetto Brut	♟♟	5
O Deltetto Extra Brut Ris. '04	♟♟	5
O Roero Arneis S. Michele '06	♟♟	4*
⊙ Deltetto Extra Brut Rosé	♟♟	5
O Bric du Liun '06	♟	5
O Roero Arneis Daivej '06	♟	4
O Langhe Favorita Sarvai '06	♟	4
● Barbera d'Alba Sup.		
Rocca delle Marasche '04	♟♟♟	6
● Roero Braja '04	♟♟	5
O Deltetto Extra Brut Ris. '04	♟♟	5

Luigi Dessilani e Figlio
VIA CESARE BATTISTI, 21
28073 FARA NOVARESE [NO]
TEL. 0321829252
www.dessilani.it

ANNUAL PRODUCTION 250,000 bottles
HECTARES UNDER VINE 40
VITICULTURE METHOD Conventional

Enzio Lucca's overwhelming passion has
now been firmly implanted into the soul of
young Nicola, heir to a long dynasty of
winemakers around Fara, on northern Italy's
winemaking frontier. Dessilani, a name with
an illustrious past, derives from plots of land
given in antiquity to the soldiers of Sulla, the
protagonists of innumerable skirmishes
around here with his arch-enemy, the consul
Marius. The Lucca family took over this
property several decades ago, launching
the dream of the modern estate's founder,
Luigi Dessilani, and producing great wine
from this unique terroir. Today, the challenge
has been won. The wines tasted this year
were absolutely sound, praise going to two
mainstays of the Fara DOC. Caramino, from
80 per cent nebbiolo and 20 per cent
vespolina, performed superbly, showing
deep on the nose, fragrant, juicy, balanced
and long on the palate. The Lochera,
nebbiolo-based with a larger percentage of
vespolina, is austere, very personal, earthy
and full, its tannins revealing no rough
edges. The rest of the Dessilani line-up is
much closer behind than in years past and
includes a fruity Ghemme, a silky Sizzano
and a Nebbiolo to quaff with a will.

Destefanis
VIA MORTIZZO, 8
12050 MONTELUPO ALBESE [CN]
TEL. 0173617189
www.marcodestefanis.com

ANNUAL PRODUCTION 60,000 bottles
HECTARES UNDER VINE 12
VITICULTURE METHOD Conventional

Marco Destefanis's typical Langhe family
estate has for some years now produced
wines that are not just well typed but full of
personality, and very affordable. Clearly, the
area's main variety, dolcetto, is a mainstay
of the Destefani estate. The most important
label, the Vigna Monia Bassa, is unfailingly
impressive, presenting a rich, impenetrable
red and following this with a nose of
remarkable depth and an explosively fruity
note. The structured, powerful palate is
rounded off by a touch of elegance that
extends the extremely attractive
progression. Other stand-out wines are the
Barbera Bricco Galluccio, aged for 11
months in new and once-used barriques,
and the Nebbiolo d'Alba, which proffers
marked but unassertive tannins. The simpler
but very pleasant Dolcetto Bricco Galluccio
has all the typical notes of the variety.
Finally, the Chardonnay and standard-label
Barbera each earned One Glass.

● Fara Caramino '04	¶¶ 6
● Fara Lochera '04	¶¶ 6
● Colline Novaresi Nebbiolo '04	¶¶ 4
● Sizzano '03	¶¶ 5
● Ghemme '03	¶¶ 6
● Fara Caramino '99	¶¶¶ 6
● Fara Caramino '00	¶¶ 6
● Fara Caramino '01	¶¶ 5
● Fara Caramino '03	¶¶ 5
● Ghemme '02	¶¶ 5
● Ghemme '00	¶¶ 6
● Fara Lochera '00	¶¶ 6
● Fara Lochera '03	¶¶ 5

● Dolcetto d'Alba V. Monia Bassa '06	¶¶ 3*
● Barbera d'Alba Bricco Galluccio '05	¶¶ 4
● Dolcetto d'Alba Bricco Galluccio '06	¶¶ 2*
● Nebbiolo d'Alba '05	¶¶ 4
● Barbera d'Alba '06	¶ 3
O Langhe Chardonnay '06	¶ 3
● Dolcetto d'Alba V. Monia Bassa '03	¶¶ 3
● Dolcetto d'Alba V. Monia Bassa '04	¶¶ 3
● Dolcetto d'Alba V. Monia Bassa '05	¶¶ 3
● Nebbiolo d'Alba '05	¶¶ 4

Einaudi
B.TA GOMBE, 31
12063 DOGLIANI [CN]
TEL. 017370191
www.poderieinaudi.com

ANNUAL PRODUCTION 200,000 bottles
HECTARES UNDER VINE 50
VITICULTURE METHOD Conventional

Paola Einaudi, her husband Giorgio Ruffo
and their son Matteo have created a
wonderfully welcoming haven in Dogliani. In
fact, it has few rivals outside the Langhe.
Aside from the beautiful winery, the
headquarters is enhanced by several
tastefully furnished rooms, where you can
enjoy a marvellous view of the vineyards on
their property. This year's news item is the
switch to DOCG of their two showcase
Dolcettos: the rich, full-bodied I Filari 2005,
aged for almost a year in small and medium
sized oak; and the Vigna Tecc 2006 to be
tasted next year. There was also an
excellent performance from the two
Barolos. The Costa Grimaldi, aged 30
months in Slavonian and Allier oak, has
fascinating aromatics that run from dried
flowers to violets and pepper. The Barolo
nei Cannubi, aged 24 months in barrique
and large barrels, has nuances of cocoa
powder, currants, blueberry and golden-leaf
tobacco. Dedicated to the memory of Italian
President Luigi Einaudi, the Langhe Rosso
is a blend of nebbiolo, cabernet sauvignon,
merlot and barbera, and a classic of its
type, showing juicy and long in the fruity
finish. This great wine is back at the top of
its class and earned Three Glasses. The
rest of the range is good.

Erede di Armando Chiappone
LOC. SAN MICHELE, 51
14049 NIZZA MONFERRATO [AT]
TEL. 0141721424
www.eredechiappone.com

ANNUAL PRODUCTION 30,000 bottles
HECTARES UNDER VINE 10
VITICULTURE METHOD Conventional

The affable Daniele Chiappone never stops.
With his parents, Franco and Domenica, he
runs this family operation with a passion
that reaps major successes year after year.
His sister Michela also plays an important
role and contributes when she can. The
results produced for this edition are
admirable, built on extremely careful work in
the vineyards and cellar, all overseen by
Daniele himself. The ten hectares under vine
are all in the municipality of Nizza, some of
them in a single plot around the lovely
village of San Michele where the winery is
located. This more than satisfying range of
starts with the estate and area's most
famous wine, Barbera d'Asti Nizza. We
tasted the Ru 2004, which comes from a
great growing season. A year's ageing in
oak, followed by another in bottle, has
created an elegant result with remarkable
complexity. The Barbera d'Asti Brentura
2005 is a tad easier and fresher. Finally, the
range includes other classics from the zone,
including a successful Freisa d'Asti.

● Langhe Rosso Luigi Einaudi '04	♛♛♛	6
● Barolo nei Cannubi '03	♛	8
● Dogliani I Filari '05	♛♛	5
● Barolo '03	♛♛	7
● Barolo Costa Grimaldi '03	♛♛	8
● Dolcetto di Dogliani '06	♛	4
● Langhe Nebbiolo '05	♛	4
● Piemonte Barbera '05	♛	5
● Barolo nei Cannubi '98	♕♕♕	8
● Barolo nei Cannubi '99	♕♕♕	8
● Barolo nei Cannubi '00	♕♕♕	8
● Barolo Costa Grimaldi '01	♕♕♕	8
● Langhe Rosso Luigi Einaudi '97	♕♕♕	6
● Langhe Rosso Luigi Einaudi '98	♕♕♕	6
● Langhe Rosso Luigi Einaudi '99	♕♕♕	6
● Langhe Rosso Luigi Einaudi '00	♕♕	6
● Langhe Rosso Luigi Einaudi '01	♕♕♕	6
● Dogliani V. Tecc '05	♕♕	4

● Barbera d'Asti Sup. Nizza Ru '04	♛♛	5
● Barbera d'Asti Brentura '05	♛♛	4
● Freisa d'Asti Sanpedra '03	♛♛	3*
● Dolcetto d'Asti Mandola '05	♛♛	4*
O Monferrato Bianco Valbeccara '05	♛	3
● Barbera d'Asti Sup. Nizza Ru '03	♕♕	5
● Barbera d'Asti Sup. Nizza Ru '01	♕♕	5
● Barbera d'Asti Brentura '04	♕♕	4

Tenuta Il Falchetto
FRAZ. CIOMBI
VIA VALLE TINELLA, 16
12058 SANTO STEFANO BELBO [CN]
TEL. 0141840344
www.ilfalchetto.com

ANNUAL PRODUCTION 200,000 bottles
HECTARES UNDER VINE 33.5
VITICULTURE METHOD Conventional

For Moscato lovers, this is a place not to miss. Tenuta Il Falchetto is emerging more and more as one of the finest interpreters of the type, turning out wines that are rich in personality from excellent material. Credit goes to the Forno brothers: agronomists Giorgio and Roberto, house oenologist Adriano and marketing director Fabrizio. The quartet manages a property that this year also includes Tenuta Paradiso, a six-hectare amphitheatre of vineyards at Agliano Terme. Moving on to the wines, Moscato Ciombi tempts with aromas of orange peel, ripe peach and apricot. The palate has a caressing sweetness, supported by confident, refreshing acidity. The Tenuta del Fant is just as good and even more explosive on the nose, where the sensations range from honey to lime blossom. There was another positive performance from Barbera Bricco Paradiso, aged for 14 months in barrique, which proffers sweet spices, wild cherry and pepper. Two Glasses went to the Barbera Pian Scorrone, which sees only steel, and the cosseting Passito. The barbera and cabernet Rosso La Mora is only a step behind.

Alessandro e Gian Natale Fantino
VIA G. SILVANO, 18
12065 MONFORTE D'ALBA [CN]
TEL. 017378253

ANNUAL PRODUCTION 50,000 bottles
HECTARES UNDER VINE 10
VITICULTURE METHOD Conventional

After last year's exploits when our top prize went to their Barolo Riserva 2000, the Fantino brothers doll's house winery in the historic centre of the magnificent village of Monforte has submitted a range that lives up to its reputation. The house champion is in great shape. It's a Riserva aged in large oak barrels for 30 months that has emerged with an austere nose recalling leather, tobacco, dried flowers and violet. The palate is powerful yet juicy, with well-crafted tannins and a full, remarkably long finish. Warmer and even more mature, despite being two years younger, is the Barolo Vigna dei Dardi 2003, which shows aromas of blueberries, currants and wild cherries. The palate unfurls energy and character, concluding with nice fullness. The Barbera is also traditionally themed around notes of cherry, thyme and aromatic herbs. The palate is very much acid-led, a virtue that extends the fascinating progression and suggests a second glass.

O Moscato d'Asti Tenuta del Fant '06	3*
O Moscato d'Asti Ciombi '06	3*
O Piemonte Moscato Passito '04	6
● Barbera d'Asti Sup. Bricco Paradiso '04	4
● Barbera d'Asti Pian Scorrone '06	3*
● Monferrato Rosso La Mora '04	4
● Barbera d'Asti Sup. Bricco Paradiso '03	4
● Barbera d'Asti Sup. La Rossa '03	4
● Monferrato Rosso La Mora '03	4

● Barolo V. dei Dardi Ris. '01	7
● Barbera d'Alba V. dei Dardi '05	4*
● Barolo V. dei Dardi '03	6
● Barolo V. dei Dardi Ris. '00	7
● Barolo V. dei Dardi Ris. '97	7
● Barolo V. dei Dardi Ris. '98	7
● Barolo V. dei Dardi Ris. '99	7
● Barolo V. dei Dardi '97	6
● Barolo V. dei Dardi '98	6
● Barolo V. dei Dardi '99	6

Ferrando
VIA TORINO, 599
10015 IVREA [TO]
TEL. 0125633550
www.ferrandovini.it

Roberto Ferraris
FRAZ. DOGLIANO, 33
14041 AGLIANO TERME [AT]
TEL. 0141954234
az.ferraris@virgilio.it

ANNUAL PRODUCTION 50,000 bottles
HECTARES UNDER VINE 7
VITICULTURE METHOD Conventional

ANNUAL PRODUCTION 35,000 bottles
HECTARES UNDER VINE 9
VITICULTURE METHOD Conventional

The memory is still alive of the Carema Etichetta Nera 2001 that deservedly won Three Glasses in the previous edition of the Guide. It was the first time for a red from Canavese. The 2002 we should have tasted this year was not produced but problems with the growing season seemed not to have affected the very convincing, dried-grape passito Cariola. Big and opulent, it is pleasingly complex on the nose and has a long finish on the palate. The less challenging Solativo 2005, a late-harvest Erbaluce, is fresh and sweet with dried fruit aromas. Both these wines are produced in the Cariole zone on the morainic Serra between Anzasco and Piverone. From recently acquired vineyards in the Borgomasino community come two Erbaluces, Cariola and La Torrazza. The first is balanced and tangy, thanks to particularly strenuous grape selection, while La Torrazza is more direct with touches of acacia honey. Finally, the Ferrando cellar's emblem, Carema, is a the austere, orange-tinted 2003 Nebbiolo with ripe tannins and good harmony.

For 20 years now, Roberto Ferraris has been producing wines from his own vineyards, some in the village of Nobbio and some at Dogliani, but all exclusively from the barbera variety. A new wine has been added to the range this year, Barbera Riserva del Bisavolo, recalling his grandfather's habit of setting aside the best parcels to age in oak either for use later during the year by the family or for the more demanding customers. Aged in 900-litre tonneaux, the 2005 vintage is austere with even more present oak and notes of chocolate and fruit. The La Cricca from the same vintage is stupendous. Grapes from the vines grown in the sunniest section of the vineyard are used to produce this generous, full Barbera with classic aromas of earth and tobacco, an irrepressible, well-rounded, complex palate and sweet, velvety tannins. The Barbera Nobbio 2005 showed excellently. It is sourced from an 80-year-old vineyard still on Vitis rupestris. Elegant and subtle, it manages to deliver compact fullness with perfect harmony of all its components. The basic version from 2005 is simpler but very well typed, juicy and easy-going, not to say available at a sensible price.

O Caluso Passito Vign. Cariola '02	♥♥	6
● Carema Et. Bianca '03	♥♥	5
O Solativo V. T. '05	♥♥	5
● Canavese Rosso La Torrazza '05	♥	4
O Erbaluce di Caluso La Torrazza '06	♥	4
O Erbaluce di Caluso Cariola '06	♥	4
● Carema Et. Nera '01	♥♥♥	6
● Carema Et. Nera '00	♥♥	6
● Carema Et. Nera '98	♥♥	6
● Carema Et. Nera '99	♥♥	6
● Carema Et. Bianca '01	♥♥	5
● Carema Et. Bianca '02	♥♥	5
O Solativo V. T. '04	♥♥	5
O Caluso Passito Vign. Cariola '01	♥♥	6

● Barbera d'Asti Sup. La Cricca '05	♥♥	4*
● Barbera d'Asti Nobbio '05	♥♥	4
● Barbera d'Asti Sup. Riserva del Bisavolo '05	♥♥	4
● Barbera d'Asti '05	♥	3*
● Barbera d'Asti Nobbio '04	♥♥	4
● Barbera d'Asti Sup. La Cricca '01	♥♥	5
● Barbera d'Asti Sup. La Cricca '03	♥♥	5
● Barbera d'Asti Sup. La Cricca '00	♥♥	5
● Barbera d'Asti Nobbio '03	♥♥	4
● Barbera d'Asti Sup. Nobbio '01	♥♥	4
● Barbera d'Asti Sup. La Cricca '04	♥	5

F.lli Ferrero
FRAZ. ANNUNZIATA, 12
12064 LA MORRA [CN]
TEL. 017350691
www.baroloferrero.com

Cascina Ferro
VIA NOSSERIO, 14
14055 COSTIGLIOLE D'ASTI [AT]
TEL. 0141966693

ANNUAL PRODUCTION 30,000 bottles
HECTARES UNDER VINE 3.5
VITICULTURE METHOD Conventional

ANNUAL PRODUCTION 20,000 bottles
HECTARES UNDER VINE 7
VITICULTURE METHOD Conventional

Actor and playwright Eduardo De Fillipo used to say, "Ha da passà 'a nuttata" (a night must pass), referring to any difficult circumstance that forces you to look to tomorrow for hope. The "night" of the 2002 growing year has gone and with the new Guide, we return to review the two flagship products from the Ferrero estate, in other words Barolo Manzoni and Barolo Gattera e Luciani, absent a year ago because they were not produced. Looking back, 2003 wasn't such a bright and shining year, either but the skills of Renato Ferrero and his wife Nina Rasmussen managed to tame that season's uncommon heat. Both Barolos have all their papers in order for pleasure. The Manzoni is fruity and rich in spice with hints of earth and leather. The palate shows well crafted on tones of softness and its finish lingers. The Gattera e Luciani is more austere, presenting intense on the nose with notes of violet and liquorice. The palate is powerful, balancing acid backbone and tannins in a long, harmonious whole. We liked, as always, the 2005 Barbera Goretta. The pulp is juicy, the texture, acid and dense, and the floral notes on the nose return in the finish.

In the municipality of Nosserio near Costigliole d'Asti, not far from Castagnole Lanze, where the earth becomes more clayey and a bit less white, you'll find the country farmhouse of brothers, and former fire fighters, Piero and Maggiorino Ferro, now assisted by young Matteo. The vineyard is located in front of the cellar at an average altitude of 280 metres and includes both slopes, one facing more east to stay cool, planted in about one "giornata", or 3,810 square metres, of chardonnay, and another facing southwest to absorb warmth and power. We only tasted two wines but both are sound. The Chardonnay Realtà 2005 has good concentration, subtle aromas, well-measured oak and lovely freshness. It is sure to improve further in bottle. The exemplary Barbera Superiore Vanet 2004, sourced from a parcel of old vines, shows deep, stylish and earthy. The palate is soft and caressing with tannins as soft as silk. Presented last year, the Barbera Bric and the 2004 Cin, from barbera, freisa and cabernet, confirmed their appeal on retasting.

● Barbera d'Alba Goretta '05	🍷🍷 5
● Barolo Gattera e Luciani '03	🍷🍷 6
● Barolo Manzoni '03	🍷🍷 7
● Barolo Manzoni '03	🍷🍷 7
● Barbera d'Alba Goretta '04	🍷🍷 5
● Barolo Manzoni '99	🍷🍷 7
● Barolo Gattera e Luciani '00	🍷🍷 6
● Barolo Gattera e Luciani '01	🍷🍷 6
● Barolo Manzoni '00	🍷🍷 7
● Barbera d'Alba Goretta '03	🍷🍷 4
● Barolo Gattera e Luciani '99	🍷🍷 6

● Barbera d'Asti Sup. Vanet '04	🍷🍷 6
○ Piemonte Chardonnay Realtà '05	🍷🍷 6
● Barbera d'Asti Sup. Vanet '01	🍷🍷 5
● Barbera d'Asti Bric '03	🍷🍷 4
● Barbera d'Asti Bric '04	🍷🍷 4
● Barbera d'Asti Sup. Vanet '03	🍷🍷 5
● Monferrato Rosso Cin '04	🍷🍷 6
● Monferrato Rosso Cin '03	🍷🍷 5
● Monferrato Rosso Cin '01	🍷🍷 5

Tenuta dei Fiori

FRAZ. RODOTIGLIA
VIA VALCALOSSO, 3
14052 CALOSSO [AT]
TEL. 0141853819
www.tenutadeifiori.com

ANNUAL PRODUCTION 20,000 bottles
HECTARES UNDER VINE 4.5
VITICULTURE METHOD Conventional

The beautiful, secluded valley of Valcalosso welcomes visitors with its rolling, vineyard-covered hills. Here Walter Bosticardo has rebuilt the lovely, family farmhouse and opened an agriturismo facility a few years ago to complement his vineyards. Walter is a fervent supporter of the Colosso zone's winemaking possibilities and has been committed for years to recovering a native variety, gamba di pernice, for he is well aware it has potential and could shape a new identity for the terroir. The Gamba di Pernice 2004 shows off all the prospects for this variety, which traditionally has a special peppery note and fine-grained tannins, which are still a bit hard in this case. We feel this wine needs further time in the cellar to smooth out and give its best. A retasting of the '88 reintroduced us to an incredible red. The two Barberas are good, the fruity and intense Tulipanonero, as well as the Rusticardi, with its peculiar note of menthol. The Monferrato Rosso Cinque File, a blend of barbera and cabernet, shows depth and balance of fruit and spice. Moscato Rairì is velvety.

Fontanabianca

VIA BORDINI, 15
12057 NEIVE [CN]
TEL. 017367195
www.fontanabianca.it

ANNUAL PRODUCTION 60,000 bottles
HECTARES UNDER VINE 14
VITICULTURE METHOD Natural

A visit the Fontanabianca estate is always a pleasure. This small operation located at Bordini near Neive and it is here that Aldo Pola is enjoys the fruits of years of effort and perseverance with Bruno Ferro and the consultancy input from Beppe Caviola in the cellar. Nor should we forget the support of the family, including Aldo's young son Davide, who never misses a chance to help out in the vineyard. As in every edition, the Barbaresco Sorì Burdin is the flagship label, even more so in the 2004 version. This elegant, well-made wine best delivers all the potential of nebbiolo grown in this perfectly suited location. In fact, our tasters had no hesitation in awarding Three Glasses. A bit less striking is the 2004 Barbaresco, sourced from three different vineyards. The Barbera Brunet 2005 acquires lovely structure and character thanks to selection of the best grapes and 15 months ageing in barrique. The other labels in the range – the 2005 Barbera, Dolcetto d'Alba and Langhe Arneis, both from 2006 – are all interesting and share enticing harmony and immediate enjoyability.

● Barbera d'Asti Sup. Rusticardi 1933 Castello di Calosso '04	🍷🍷 6
● Monferrato Rosso Cinque File '04	🍷🍷 5
● Barbera d'Asti Tulipanonero '03	🍷🍷 6
○ Rairì '06	🍷🍷 4
● Gamba di Pernice '04	🍷 4
● Barbera d'Asti Sup. Rusticardi Castello di Calosso '01	🍷🍷 6
● Barbera d'Asti Sup. Rusticardi 1933 Castello di Calosso '03	🍷🍷 6
● Monferrato Rosso Cinque File '03	🍷🍷 5
● Barbera d'Asti Tulipanonero '01	🍷🍷 6
● Monferrato Rosso Cinque File '01	🍷🍷 5

● Barbaresco Sorì Burdin '04	🍷🍷🍷 7
● Barbera d'Alba Brunet '05	🍷🍷 5
● Barbaresco '04	🍷🍷 6
○ Langhe Arneis '06	🍷🍷 4*
● Dolcetto d'Alba Bordini '06	🍷🍷 4*
● Barbera d'Alba '06	🍷🍷 4*
● Barbaresco Sorì Burdin '01	🍷🍷🍷 7
● Barbaresco Sorì Burdin '98	🍷🍷🍷 7
● Barbaresco Sorì Burdin '00	🍷🍷 8
● Barbera d'Alba Brunet '04	🍷🍷 4
● Barbaresco Sorì Burdin '03	🍷🍷 7
● Dolcetto d'Alba Bordini '06	🍷🍷 4

Fontanafredda
VIA ALBA, 15
12050 SERRALUNGA D'ALBA [CN]
TEL. 0173626111
www.fontanafredda.it

Forteto della Luja
REG. CANDELETA, 4
14050 LOAZZOLO [AT]
TEL. 0141831596
www.fortedellaluja.it

ANNUAL PRODUCTION 6,000,000 bottles
HECTARES UNDER VINE 90
VITICULTURE METHOD Conventional

Last year, Fontanafredda was at the centre of rumours about the estate's future. None of these came to anything. Giovanni Minetti's strong, capable hands still hold the reins and the property still belongs to the Monte dei Paschi di Siena bank. Luckily, the rumours didn't distract the amazing team of Minetti, oenologist Drocco and sales director Bruno, who produce the many, excellent labels from this Serralunga winery. What's more, this range lives up fully to Fontanafredda's reputation, despite the fact some of the best labels were absent. There were no Barolo vineyard selections from the unexciting 2002 vintage or the 2000 Barolo Riserva as a result of a carefully considered commercial choice: release is being delayed. We really enjoyed the Barolo Serralunga, a common appellation that will become better known in the future with more favourable vintage years thanks to the Fontanafredda winery's skills. The other champion is Gatinera, a very fine sparkler that gets the Alta Langa DOC zone of to a good start. It's from pinot nero sourced from the highest hills in the Langhe. The rest of the range is sound, above all the Barbaresco Coste Rubìn and the Raimonda and Papagena e Pamina Barberas.

ANNUAL PRODUCTION   60,000 bottles
HECTARES UNDER VINE 8
VITICULTURE METHOD   Conventional

Loazzolo is a world apart. Unlike Langhe or other prized vineyard areas, it still has abundant woodlands. Chestnut, oak and ash still rule these hills. What makes this natural environment unique, particularly the part defined by the course of the river Luja, is the presence of 21 different species of wild orchids. For some years now, the Scaglione family has dedicated various hectares of woodland on their property to the creation of a WWF oasis. The entire family has participated in this important project, from father Giancarlo to children Silvia and Gianni. Their winery, too, is managed on a family basis. The estate champion is Loazzolo Piasa Rischei, a dried-grape passito from moscato brimming with class and elegance, never too sweet and certainly never cloying. The other sweet wine, the fragrant, fruity Brachetto Forteto Pian dei Sogni, is also agreeable. Moscato d'Asti Piasa San Maurizio is well orchestrated, fresh and quaffable. Finally, the pinot nero and barbera Monferrato Rosso Le Grive is slightly below par.

● Barolo Serralunga '03	ŸŸ	6
○ Alta Langa Brut V. Gatinera '03	ŸŸ	5
● Barbaresco Coste Rubìn '04	ŸŸ	6
● Nebbiolo d'Alba Marne Brune '05	ŸŸ	4
● Barbera d'Alba Sup. Papagena e Pamina '04	ŸŸ	4
● Barbera d'Alba Raimonda '05	ŸŸ	3*
○ Moscato d'Asti Moncucco '06	ŸŸ	4
○ Roero Arneis Pradalupo '06	Ÿ	4
● Diano d'Alba La Lepre '06	Ÿ	4
● Barolo Lazzarito V. La Delizia '99	ŸŸŸ	8
● Barolo Lazzarito V. La Delizia '01	ŸŸŸ	8
● Barolo Fontanafredda V. La Rosa '98	ŸŸŸ	8
● Barolo Fontanafredda V. La Rosa '00	ŸŸŸ	8
● Barolo Fontanafredda V. La Rosa '01	ŸŸ	8

● Piemonte Brachetto Forteto Pian dei Sogni '05	ŸŸ	6
○ Loazzolo Piasa Rischei '04	ŸŸ	7
○ Moscato d'Asti Piasa San Maurizio '06	ŸŸ	4
● Monferrato Rosso Le Grive '05	Ÿ	5
○ Loazzolo Piasa Rischei '93	ŸŸŸ	7
○ Loazzolo Piasa Rischei '94	ŸŸŸ	7
○ Loazzolo Piasa Rischei '95	ŸŸŸ	7
○ Loazzolo Piasa Rischei '96	ŸŸŸ	7
○ Loazzolo Piasa Rischei '97	ŸŸŸ	7
○ Loazzolo Piasa Rischei '00	ŸŸ	7
○ Loazzolo Piasa Rischei '01	ŸŸ	7
○ Loazzolo Piasa Rischei '02	ŸŸ	7
○ Loazzolo Piasa Rischei '03	ŸŸ	7

Gabutti – Franco Boasso
B.TA GABUTTI, 3A
12050 SERRALUNGA D'ALBA [CN]
TEL. 0173613165
www.gabuttiboasso.com

★★★★ Gaja
VIA TORINO, 18
12050 BARBARESCO [CN]
TEL. 0173635158
info@gajawines.com

ANNUAL PRODUCTION   30,000 bottles
HECTARES UNDER VINE 5.5
VITICULTURE METHOD   Conventional

ANNUAL PRODUCTION   300,000 bottles
HECTARES UNDER VINE 92
VITICULTURE METHOD   Conventional

There are two major news items from the Franco Boasso estate. The first regards the opening of the I Grappoli agriturismo, a tastefully remodelled country house with four welcoming rooms for tourists. The second is the return to tasting of the two Barolos after the pause imposed by the inauspicious 2002 vintage. Franco's wife Marina and sons Claudio and Ezio lend a helping hand on the estate. Moving on to the wines, we found, as expected, that the two Barolos were outstanding. Gabutti's long ageing – 30 months in large oak barrels – render it particularly complex and rich on the nose, with nuances of tobacco, leather and violets, which precedes a palate of quite remarkable depth. The Serralunga, aged 36 months in 25-hectolitre oak barrels, shows remarkable stuffing with its pleasant fruity aromas and well-crafted tannins. We were very happy with the juicy Dolcetto Meriame and the Grappoli Red, from nebbiolo, barbera and merlot. The chardonnay-only Grappoli White and Barbera 2006 were a step behind.

A further year's bottle ageing has enabled the wines from the Barolo vineyards of Sperss, at Serralunga d'Alba, and Conteisa at La Morra, to come onto the market ready for the corkscrew. Despite the fact they come from the sweltering 2003 growing season, these wines follow in the footsteps of the great selections Angelo Gaja offers connoisseurs worldwide every year. For this edition of the Guide, it was the 2004 labels that hit the heights. This extraordinary vintage produced both excellent quality and good quantity. All the wines tasted deserve unconditional applause. Returning to the highest step on the awards platform is the particularly elegant, classy Barbaresco: the 2003 vintage missed by a nose last year. After years when we became inured to giving awards to muscular wines, it is nice to discover some great bottles that adhere to the most outstanding characteristics of the Barbaresco style. The Costa Russi from the Langhe DOC is a very fine wine. Its brothers, San Lorenzo and Sorì Tildin, are almost as good. Gaja's always sound, international-style house red is Darmagi, from cabernet sauvignon grown at Barbaresco. These fabulous results deserve a special prize, Winery of the Year.

● Barolo Gabutti '03	♈♈	7
● Barolo Serralunga '03	♈♈	6
● Dolcetto d'Alba Meriame '06	♈♈	4*
● Grappoli Red	♈♈	5
● Barbera d'Alba '06	♈	4
O Grappoli White	♈	3
● Barolo Gabutti '00	♈♈	7
● Barolo Serralunga '01	♈♈	7
● Barolo Gabutti '01	♈♈	7
● Barolo Gabutti '98	♈♈	7
● Barolo Gabutti '99	♈♈	7
● Barolo Serralunga '00	♈♈	7

● Barbaresco '04	♈♈♈	8
● Langhe Nebbiolo Costa Russi '04	♈♈♈	8
● Langhe Darmagi '03	♈♈	8
● Langhe Nebbiolo Sperss '03	♈♈	8
● Langhe Nebbiolo Conteisa '03	♈♈	8
● Langhe Nebbiolo Sorì Tildin '04	♈♈	8
● Langhe Nebbiolo Sorì S. Lorenzo '04	♈♈	8
● Barbaresco '01	♈♈♈	8
● Langhe Nebbiolo Costa Russi '03	♈♈♈	8
● Langhe Nebbiolo Sorì S. Lorenzo '03	♈♈♈	8
● Langhe Nebbiolo Sorì Tildin '00	♈♈♈	8
● Langhe Nebbiolo Conteisa '01	♈♈♈	8

Filippo Gallino
FRAZ. VALLE DEL POZZO, 63
12043 CANALE [CN]
TEL. 017398112
www.filippogallino.com

ANNUAL PRODUCTION　70,000 bottles
HECTARES UNDER VINE 13.5
VITICULTURE METHOD　Conventional

Gallino is synonymous the essence of winemaking. There is something immutable, indeed almost ancestral, in the production philosophy of this small, authentic Roero family winery. The passage of time, so insidious elsewhere, has not tarnished its stylistic discipline or its fascinatingly humble approach to its raw material. The secrets are the vineyards: arneis, barbera and nebbiolo vinified into a handful of labels; the character of the wines, which are essential in the sense of austere, dry and free of frills; and the low-profile image and names on the bottles. But what wonderful wines they are! The Roero 2005 and Barbera Superiore 2005 triumphantly tame their sumptuous material, expressing in elegant, stylish features. In particular, the Barbera d'Alba again won Three Glasses this year. This exceptional wine is enduring evidence of how this farming family makes best use of Piedmont's most widely planted variety. Actually, the two top wines are so great they make their respective base wines and the Roero Arneis seem almost small in comparison but in fact they are veritable hymns to the Roero territory.

Gancia
C.SO LIBERTÀ, 66
14053 CANELLI [AT]
TEL. 01418301
www.gancia.it

ANNUAL PRODUCTION　30,000,000 bottles
HECTARES UNDER VINE N.A.
VITICULTURE METHOD　Conventional

The 1850 on the label indicates when this historic estate began operations. Sparkling wines go way back at Canelli. In fact, this small municipality on the river Belbo, in the province of Asti, is Piedmont's most important centre for sparklers. Today, brothers Lamberto and Max and their cousin Edoardo hold the reins. Over the past decade, the Gancia family has invested significantly, acquiring Tenute dei Vallarino and continuing to focus on their traditional skills. Investment led to the creation of the Cantine Gancia line and a makeover at the winery headquarters to enhance functionality. News includes the launch of the Alta Langa project. With other wineries, the Gancias are looking to this to improve their range of sparklers. The 2003 is the first Riserva del Fondatore Carlo Gancia from the Alta Langa DOC to be released. It's a sound classic method wine from pinot nero and chardonnay that reveals characteristic notes of crusty bread on the nose before the palate shows good fruit and confident progression, well supported by acidity. The splendid Asti Camillo Gancia, another classic method sparkler, is concentrated, elegant and stylish in its measured sweetness.

● Barbera d'Alba Sup. '05	♟♟♟	5
● Roero '05	♟	6
● Barbera d'Alba '06	♟♟	4*
● Langhe Nebbiolo '06	♟♟	4*
○ Roero Arneis '06	♟	4
● Barbera d'Alba Sup. '04	♟♟♟	5
● Barbera d'Alba Sup. '97	♟♟♟	5
● Roero Sup. '03	♟♟♟	6
● Roero Sup. '01	♟♟♟	6
● Roero Sup. '99	♟♟♟	6
● Roero Sup. '98	♟♟♟	6
● Roero Sup. '04	♟♟	6
● Roero '05	♟♟	6
● Barbera d'Alba Sup. '03	♟♟	5

○ Asti Camillo Gancia M. Cl. '05	♟♟	6
○ Asti Modonovo '06	♟♟	4
○ Piemonte Brut Carlo Gancia M. Cl.	♟♟	4
○ Alta Langa M. Cl. Brut Carlo Gancia Ris. del Fondatore '03	♟♟	5
○ P. R.osé Blanc Extra Dry	♟	4
⊙ Carlo Gancia M. Cl. Brut Rosé Integral	♟	5
⊙ O. P. Pinot Nero Brut P. Rosé	♟	3

Garetto

S.DA ASTI MARE, 30
14041 AGLIANO TERME [AT]
TEL. 0141954068
www.garetto.it

Gastaldi

VIA ALBESANI, 20
12057 NEIVE [CN]
TEL. 0173677400

ANNUAL PRODUCTION 100,000 bottles
HECTARES UNDER VINE 18
VITICULTURE METHOD Conventional

ANNUAL PRODUCTION 20,000 bottles
HECTARES UNDER VINE 14
VITICULTURE METHOD Conventional

Without a doubt, young Alessandro gets full credit for this estate. His operation is no longer up-and-coming. On the contrary, you could say it is a well-established part of the Asti winemaking landscape. Years ago, he decided to convert the family estate to high quality production and success came quickly. In the vineyards, Alessandro works with a few trusted collaborators on his 18 hectares. The same goes in the cellar where he is always present with support from Enzo, his oenologist. There is a willingness to experiment and above all the steadfast ambition to improve and always give more. The products show this and all proved up to snuff. In fact, there's even a Three Glass winner this time. The champion is the concentrated, fruity and caressing Barbera Superiore Nizza Favà 2004 selection. This thoroughbred Barbera is a wonderful ambassador for its territory. The basic version, Tra Neuit e Dì 2006, is also sound, followed in order of structure and importance by the In Pectore 2005 selection. Whites complete the range and include the pleasant Piemonte Chardonnay Diversamente, oak-aged and still very young.

If getting hold of Dino Gastaldi, even by phone, is difficult, attempting to understand his commercial strategy can be absolutely impossible. At first glance, you could call him a sort of absent-minded professor of wine. That he is one of the most talented winemakers of his day is beyond doubt. Proof is there in his many successes, and he's not even 50, for some of the country's most outstanding restaurateurs are among his adoring fans. It is also true that what stops Dino from presenting his complete range of wines every year is not so much his lack of order as an excess of meticulousness that keeps him striving for perfection. Since perfection is not of this world, in this edition of the Guide, we must content ourselves with the Barbaresco 2003 and the first release of the Barolo Gastaldi, which has 2001 on the label. Both these wines show bags of character. After an initial hint of reduction, the Barbaresco reveals notes of dried flowers and then an austere, tannic palate. The Barolo has an impressive structure and an elegant tannic weave, though it's still a bit marked by oak.

● Barbera d'Asti Sup. Nizza Favà '04	♛♛♛ 5
● Barbera d'Asti Sup. In Pectore '05	♛♛ 4
O Piemonte Chardonnay Diversamente '06	♛♛ 4
● Barbera d'Asti Tra Neuit e Dì '06	♛♛ 3*
O Cortese dell'Alto M.to Le Due Cioche '06	♛ 3
● Barbera d'Asti Sup. Favà '00	♛♛ 5
● Barbera d'Asti Sup. Favà '01	♛♛ 5
● Barbera d'Asti Sup. Favà '03	♛♛ 5
● Barbera d'Asti Sup. In Pectore '04	♛♛ 4

● Barbaresco '03	♛♛ 7
● Barolo '01	♛♛ 8
● Dolcetto d'Alba Sup. Moriolo '90	♛♛♛ 5
● Gastaldi Rosso '88	♛♛♛ 8
● Gastaldi Rosso '89	♛♛♛ 8
O Langhe Bianco Gastaldi '01	♛♛ 6
O Langhe Bianco Gastaldi '02	♛♛ 6
O Langhe Bianco Gastaldi '00	♛♛ 6
● Langhe Rosso Gastaldi '98	♛♛ 7
● Barbaresco '99	♛♛ 7
● Barbaresco '01	♛♛ 7
● Langhe Rosso Castlé '98	♛♛ 7
● Langhe Rosso Castlé '97	♛♛ 7

Piero Gatti

LOC. MONCUCCO, 28
12058 SANTO STEFANO BELBO [CN]
TEL. 0141840918
www.vinigatti.it

ANNUAL PRODUCTION 60,000 bottles
HECTARES UNDER VINE 6.5
VITICULTURE METHOD Conventional

This winery is one of the few Langhe estates run entirely by women. Rita Gatti and her daughter Barbara skilfully manage it with oenological consultancy from the professional Sergio Stella. Their showcase wine could only be Moscato, considering the winery's location in Santo Stefano Belbo, although other varieties are grown and vinified with good results. We'll begin our round-up with the estate champion, the Piemonte Moscato 2006, from grapes grown in various vineyards around the municipality of Santo Stefano. Introduced by stylish perlage and an intense straw-yellow colour, the nose has the grape's varietal aromas of orange peel, wild roses and lightly candied fruit. The full, flavourful palate has a sweetness that is intense but offset by intriguing supporting acidity. The other house dessert wine, Brachetto, is delicate and floral with notes of rose petals and cherries. The interesting Verbeia is a blend of barbera grown at San Martino Alfieri with a touch of freisa from the Turin hills. It shows excellent fruit and sweet, well-crafted tannins. Finally, the elegant Freisa is extremely drinkable.

○ Piemonte Moscato '06	▼▼	4*
● Langhe Freisa '05	▼▼	4*
● Verbeia '05	▼▼	4*
● Piemonte Brachetto '06	▼	4
● Langhe Freisa La Violetta '01	▽▽	4
● Langhe Freisa '05	▽▽	4

Ettore Germano

LOC. CERRETTA, 1
12050 SERRALUNGA D'ALBA [CN]
TEL. 0173613528
www.germanoettore.com

ANNUAL PRODUCTION 55,000 bottles
HECTARES UNDER VINE 13
VITICULTURE METHOD Conventional

Could anyone possibly produce whites at Serralunga, the land of those great, deep, austere Barolos? Well, yes. In addition to top quality reds – not really a surprise given the vine stock available – Sergio produces absolutely impressive, ever-improving whites from chardonnay and riesling grown in the upper Langhe. In particular, this year we are enthusiastic about Hérzu, meaning steep slope. This well-typed, monovarietal Riesling has bright acidity, power and good length. The Chardonnay and Binel, from 40 per cent riesling and 60 per cent chardonnay, are almost as good. But the high-energy Sergio is never still for there are more surprises in store. The effort spent on producing whites has not in any way affected his reds. The Barolo Cerretta from the difficult 2003 shows clear, classic sensations, lovely impact on the palate and sweet tannins. The very good Barbera Vigna della Madre 2005 is powerful, juicy and rich with great fruit and the rest of the range shows high quality, from Balàu, a blend of 50 per cent dolcetto with equal parts of barbera and merlot, to the Dolcetto Pra di Pò. All things considered, this wonderful winery has had a great year.

○ Langhe Bianco Hérzu '05	▼▼	5
● Barbera d'Alba V. della Madre '05	▼▼	5
● Barolo Cerretta '03	▼▼	7
● Barolo Serralunga '03	▼▼	7
● Dolcetto d'Alba Vign. Pra di Pò '06	▼▼	4*
○ Langhe Bianco Binel '05	▼▼	4*
○ Langhe Chardonnay '06	▼▼	4*
● Langhe Rosso Balàu '05	▼▼	5
● Langhe Nebbiolo '05	▼	5
● Dolcetto d'Alba Vign. Lorenzino '06	▼	4
● Barolo Cerretta '01	▽▽▽	7
● Barolo Cerretta '98	▽▽▽	7
● Barolo Cerretta '00	▽▽	7
● Barolo Cerretta '99	▽▽	7
● Barolo Prapò '00	▽▽	7
● Barolo Prapò '01	▽▽	7

La Ghersa
V.LE SAN GIUSEPPE, 19
14050 MOASCA [AT]
TEL. 0141856012
www.laghersa.it

La Ghibellina
FRAZ. MONTEROTONDO, 61
15066 GAVI [AL]
TEL. 0143686257
www.laghibellina.it

ANNUAL PRODUCTION 250,000 bottles
HECTARES UNDER VINE 36
VITICULTURE METHOD Conventional

Like many properties in the area, now distinguished for its quality Barberas and boasting the Nizza subzone, in not so far off times La Ghersa sold its wines in bulk or in demijohns. Only with the arrival of the latest generation at the helm has it been transformed into a winery capable of contending with the best. Today, Massimo Pastura is at the head of this family estate, assisted by oenologist Luca Caramellino. Massimo's vineyards produce above all barbera but he has diversified production that now runs from whites to reds, with rosés along the way, using non-native as well as native varieties. From the Barberas, we enjoyed an easy-drinking, standard-label Piagè and a complex, earthy Camparò 2005, arriving at a powerful, fresh Vignassa that missed out on top honours only by reason of its youth. As usual a step down from the Vignassa is the estate Monferrato Rosso, from barbera, cabernet sauvignon and merlot, which presents lovely notes of pencil lead against a backdrop of oak. The list closes fittingly with a rich Monferrato Bianco from cortese, chardonnay and sauvignon.

ANNUAL PRODUCTION 57,000 bottles
HECTARES UNDER VINE 18
VITICULTURE METHOD Conventional

Alberto and Marina Ghibellini's estate has shown high quality, vintage after vintage, for several years now and the performance at our last tasting was enough to convince us to give this winery more space in these pages. In any case, the winery has all it takes for an ambitious move to top-quality production. La Ghibellina is headquartered at Monterotondo, a sort of "grand cru" of Gavi. The plots, their soil, their ideal positions and the climate, well suited to vines thanks to the influence of winds from the coast, all ensure favourable conditions for viticulture. All the labels tasted this year won Two full Glasses. The Gavi Altius 2005, part aged in oak, offers aromas of elderflower, wisteria and musk preceding a palate that is savoury, full and long. Mainin is, if possible, even more floral and fresh with excellent body. The Monferrato Rosso from barbera also shows great structure and complexity. Acidity and structure complement each other in a wine we appreciated for its sheer appeal and the perfect balance of all its components.

● Barbera d'Asti Sup. Nizza Vignassa '04	▼▼ 6
● Barbera d'Asti Piagè '06	▼▼ 4*
● Monferrato Rosso La Ghersa '04	▼▼ 5
● Barbera d'Asti Sup. Camparò '05	▼▼ 4*
○ Monferrato Bianco Sivoy '06	▼▼ 4*
○ Moscato d'Asti Giorgia '06	▼ 4
⊙ Monferrato Rosato Piagè '06	▼ 3
○ Monferrato Bianco Piagè '06	▼ 3
● Barbera d'Asti Sup. Nizza Vignassa '03	♀♀ 6
● Barbera d'Asti Sup. Nizza Vignassa '01	♀♀ 6
● Barbera d'Asti Sup. Nizza Vignassa '00	♀♀ 6
● Monferrato Rosso La Ghersa '03	♀♀ 5
● Monferrato Rosso La Ghersa '01	♀♀ 5

○ Gavi del Comune di Gavi Altius '05	▼▼ 5
○ Gavi del Comune di Gavi Mainìn '06	▼▼ 4*
● Monferrato Rosso '04	▼▼ 5

Attilio Ghisolfi

LOC. BUSSIA, 27
12065 MONFORTE D'ALBA [CN]
TEL. 017378345
www.ghisolfi.com

★ Bruno Giacosa
VIA XX SETTEMBRE, 52
12057 NEIVE [CN]
TEL. 017367027
www.brunogiacosa.it

ANNUAL PRODUCTION   40,000 bottles
HECTARES UNDER VINE 6.5
VITICULTURE METHOD   Conventional

ANNUAL PRODUCTION   400,000 bottles
HECTARES UNDER VINE 20
VITICULTURE METHOD   Conventional

Gianmarco Ghisolfi's estate is now producing such convincing wines that three out of the seven labels submitted reached our finals with no problems. His winery operates in one of the most famous zones for growing nebbiolo and most of Ghisolfi's production centres on the Barolo, without neglecting various other Langhe wines from the same variety with other grapes. The Barolo Riserva Fantini 2001 and Bricco Visette 2003 showcase all nebbiolo's virtues, underlined by a palate that is full, well structured and extremely long. The Riserva is a real thoroughbred with sensations of wild cherry, wild rose, cocoa powder and leather that won Three Glasses hands down. The Langhe Rosso Alta Bussia 2005 blend should not be missed. Sensations from ripe barbera fruit play on the nose and the austere nebbiolo palate shows pleasant, well-crafted tannins. The Barbera Vigna Lisi 2005 shows oaky on the palate but has very good acidity that refreshes the finish. The rest of the labels are sound, including the intense, well-structured Langhe Carlin and the Pinay, a monovarietal Pinot Nero that's a tad short on the finish.

The story of Bruno Giacosa is the story of the past 50 years of Langhe winemaking. Like few others, he embodies the close ties that unite connoisseurs of nebbiolos from around Alba with the great tradition of long years in wood and large Slavonian oak barrels, picking after the week of All Saints, the tiny bunches of michet or even the lengthy submerged-cap maceration. Unparalleled knowledge of the territory, the result of years walking up and down the rows of Barolo and Barbaresco with his grape broker father, has allowed Bruno in the past to vinify the best grapes in the area. But times have changed and, to adjust to them, Bruno Giacosa has acquired vineyards in his preferred crus: Falletto, Asili and Rabajà. These are the leaders in this edition of the Guide. The incredible terroir at Rocche del Falletto, capable of producing wines that are powerful yet harmonic at the same time, was judged worthy of our Three Glass award. The two white labels, Le Rocche del Falletto and Asili, were managed to overcome the main obstacles of the 2003 vintage, showing very pleasant and at the same time already incredibly ready to drink.

● Barolo Fantini Ris. '01	♈♈♈	8
● Barolo Bricco Visette '03	♈♈	7
● Langhe Rosso Alta Bussia '05	♈♈	5
● Barbera d'Alba V. Lisi '05	♈♈	5
● Langhe Rosso Carlin '05	♈♈	5
● Barolo '03	♈	6
● Langhe Rosso Pinay '05	♈	4
● Barolo Bricco Visette '01	♈♈♈	6
● Langhe Rosso Alta Bussia '00	♈♈♈	6
● Langhe Rosso Alta Bussia '99	♈♈♈	6
● Langhe Rosso Alta Bussia '01	♈♈♈	6
● Barolo Bricco Visette '00	♈♈	7
● Barolo Bricco Visette '99	♈♈	7
● Barolo Fantini Ris. '00	♈♈	7
● Langhe Rosso Alta Bussia '03	♈♈	5
● Langhe Rosso Alta Bussia '04	♈♈	5

● Barolo		
Le Rocche del Falletto Ris. '01	♈♈♈	8
● Barbaresco Asili '03	♈♈	8
● Barolo Le Rocche del Falletto '03	♈♈	8
● Barbera d'Alba Sup. Falletto '05	♈♈	7
O Roero Arneis '06	♈♈	5
● Barbaresco Asili '99	♈♈♈	8
● Barbaresco Santo Stefano '00	♈♈♈	8
● Barolo Falletto '00	♈♈♈	8
● Barolo		
Rocche di Castiglione Falletto '85	♈♈♈	8
● Barolo Falletto '96	♈♈♈	8
● Barolo Falletto Ris. '96	♈♈♈	8
● Barolo Collina Rionda Ris. '82	♈♈♈	8
● Barolo Falletto '01	♈♈♈	8
● Barbaresco Santo Stefano '01	♈♈♈	8
● Barbaresco Asili Ris. '96	♈♈♈	8
● Barbaresco Rabajà Ris. '01	♈♈♈	8

Carlo Giacosa
S.DA OVELLO, 9
12050 BARBARESCO [CN]
TEL. 0173635116
www.carlogiacosa.it

ANNUAL PRODUCTION	40,000 bottles
HECTARES UNDER VINE	5
VITICULTURE METHOD	Conventional

Carlo Giacosa's winery is not one of those that set much store by publicity. But with as little fanfare as ever, it again proves to be one of the best places to buy excellent traditional-style Barbarescos on a budget. Maria Grazia now manages the estate, with her parents Carla and Carlo, and accumulated a fine store of experience. She presents a reliable range crafted around harmonic sensations. The better of the two Barbarescos is Narin, which shows subtler and fuller whereas Montefico still seems a bit closed. Dedicated to grandfather Donato, the 7,000 bottles of Narin is the result of a blend of the most famous vineyard selections: Ovello, Cole and Asili. The two Barberas confirm their excellent quality. Mucin 2006 is more fruit-focused and meatier while Lina 2005 has more spice and power. The Dolcetto Cuchet 2006, with its crisp fruit and dry palate, is a likeably easy drinker. For several years now, the Nebbiolo Maria Grazia has been the winery's best-kept secret. The fresh, fruity nose and dense, savoury tannic texture on the palate have a marvellously Barbaresco-like appeal.

F.lli Giacosa
VIA XX SETTEMBRE, 64
12052 NEIVE [CN]
TEL. 017367013
www.giacosa.it

ANNUAL PRODUCTION	500,000 bottles
HECTARES UNDER VINE	40
VITICULTURE METHOD	Conventional

Under the guidance of family patriarchs Valerio and Renzo, Maurizio and Paolo Giacosa manage an estate that now boasts more than a century of history. Research and innovation are the cornerstones of this winery. This year's installation of more than 100 photovoltaic panels to supply clean energy puts Giacosa at the forefront of winemakers who are sensitive to environmental sustainability. The 2004 vintage sees the definitive farewell of Barbaresco Rio Sordo and a warm welcome to the sumptuous Barbaresco Gian Matè, the loveliest surprise from the range submitted. It is dark on the eye, deep in its earthy, spicy aromas, and broad and lingering in the mouth. Barbaresco Basarin 2004 is also worth mentioning. The Barolo Vigna Mandorlo 2003 embodies all the type's well-known qualities but is a bit spoiled by a difficult vintage. The Barbera Maria Gioana 2004 is at the top of its class, as always. Dolcetto Madonna di Como 2006 shows impressive intensity and complexity, product of a long-awaited vintage year. The array of wines closes with the fragrant Roero Arneis and the well-typed Chardonnay Rorea, both from 2006.

● Barbaresco Narin '04	▼▼ 6
● Barbaresco Montefico '04	▼▼ 6
● Barbera d'Alba Lina '05	▼▼ 4
● Barbera d'Alba Mucin '06	▼▼ 4*
● Langhe Nebbiolo Maria Grazia '06	▼▼ 4
● Dolcetto d'Alba Cuchet '06	▼ 4
● Barbaresco Narin '01	♀♀ 6
● Barbaresco Montefico '00	♀♀ 6
● Barbaresco Montefico '03	♀♀ 6
● Barbaresco Carla '03	♀♀ 6
● Barbaresco Narin '03	♀♀ 6
● Barbaresco Narin '00	♀♀ 6
● Barbaresco Montefico '01	♀♀ 6

● Barbaresco Gian Matè '04	▼▼ 6
● Barbaresco Basarin '04	▼▼ 6
● Dolcetto d'Alba Madonna di Como '06	▼▼ 4
● Barolo V. Mandorlo '03	▼▼ 6
● Barbera d'Alba Maria Gioana '04	▼▼ 5
O Langhe Chardonnay Rorea '06	▼ 4
O Roero Arneis '06	▼ 4
● Barbaresco Basarin '03	♀♀ 6
● Barolo V. Mandorlo '01	♀♀ 6
● Barbaresco Rio Sordo '01	♀♀ 7
● Barolo V. Mandorlo '02	♀♀ 6
● Barolo V. Mandorlo '00	♀♀ 7

Raffaele Gili
LOC. PAUTASSO, 7
12050 CASTELLINALDO [CN]
TEL. 0173639011

ANNUAL PRODUCTION   46,000 bottles
HECTARES UNDER VINE 8
VITICULTURE METHOD   Conventional

This story here began with Raffaele's father, Francesco, from whom Raffaele inherited two passions dear to local hearts at Castellinaldo: the sport of "pallone elastico" and wine. We are in deepest Roero so naturally vineyards dominate the area and it all comes together in the lovely winery and home of Raffaele and his wife Laura, attractively set in the splendid countryside. The vineyards begin behind their house and rise gently across the hill. From the nebbiolo grown in one of these vineyards comes the fruity, tannic and balsamic Roero Bric Angelino, with its good overall balance. The more characteristic Barbera Pautasso has enjoyable, fresh drinkability. Langhe Rosso L'Assemblato comes from a blend of nebbiolo, barbera and cabernet sauvignon characterized by remarkable basic structure, with vegetal notes backed up by powerful alcohol. The two whites from arneis and favorita are simple, nicely typed and made to be drunk young.

Giovanni Battista Gillardi
CASCINA CORSALETTO, 69
12060 FARIGLIANO [CN]
TEL. 017376306
www.gillardi.it

ANNUAL PRODUCTION   35,000 bottles
HECTARES UNDER VINE 7
VITICULTURE METHOD   Conventional

The Gillardis have been winemakers for generations at Farigliano, in the heart of the Dolcetto di Dogliani and Dogliani production zones, both dedicated only to dolcetto. By now, this variety holds no secrets for Giovan Battista and his son Giacomo, whom everyone calls Giacolino. The winery makes two versions of Dolcetto di Dogliani but has decided, at least for now, not to use the DOCG appellation. The two selections, Maestra and Cursalet, are fermented and conditioned in stainless steel vats and differ in origin of their grapes. The base Maestra comes from younger vines. This typical Dolcetto has fruity, heady notes on the nose and a soft, easy-drinking palate. In contrast, Cursalet, an estate vineyard selection, takes its name from the oldest and best-positioned vineyards, located on a special vein of tufa on the Corsaletto farm, which produce a fruity red with lots of beefy extract. Harys, a barrique-aged syrah, and Yeta, from dolcetto with a splash of cabernet, are Giacolino's personal projects. The first is balsamic with a dense tannic texture and still shows the oak. At the moment, Yeta is more expressive but Harys has more character.

● Barbera d'Alba Pautasso '05	♥♥ 4*
● Langhe Rosso L'Assemblato '04	♥♥ 5
● Roero Bric Angelino '04	♥♥ 5
○ Langhe Favorita '06	♥ 3
○ Langhe Arneis '06	♥ 3
● Castellinaldo Barbera d'Alba '01	♀♀ 5
● Roero Bric Angelino '03	♀♀ 5
● Castellinaldo Barbera d'Alba '00	♀♀ 5
● Castellinaldo Barbera d'Alba '04	♀♀ 5
● Nebbiolo d'Alba Sansivé '03	♀♀ 5
● Roero Bric Angelino '01	♀♀ 5
● Nebbiolo d'Alba Sansivé '04	♀♀ 5
● Castellinaldo Barbera d'Alba '03	♀♀ 5

● Dolcetto di Dogliani Cursalet '06	♥♥ 4*
● Langhe Rosso Harys '05	♥♥ 7
● Dolcetto di Dogliani Vign. Maestra '06	♥♥ 4*
● Langhe Rosso Yeta '05	♥♥ 5
● Harys '98	♀♀♀ 7
● Harys '99	♀♀♀ 7
● Harys '04	♀♀ 7
● Harys '03	♀♀ 7
● Dolcetto di Dogliani Cursalet '05	♀♀ 4
● Dolcetto di Dogliani Cursalet '04	♀♀ 4
● Langhe Rosso Yeta '03	♀♀ 5
● Langhe Rosso Yeta '04	♀♀ 5

Cascina Gilli
VIA NEVISSANO, 36
14022 CASTELNUOVO DON BOSCO [AT]
TEL. 0119876984
www.cascinagilli.it

Cascina Giovinale
S.DA SAN NICOLAO, 102
14049 NIZZA MONFERRATO [AT]
TEL. 0141793005
www.cascinagiovinale.com

ANNUAL PRODUCTION 150,000 bottles
HECTARES UNDER VINE 23
VITICULTURE METHOD Conventional

ANNUAL PRODUCTION 25,000 bottles
HECTARES UNDER VINE 7
VITICULTURE METHOD Conventional

Gianni Vergnano confirms his skills at bringing out the best in native Piedmontese varieties such as freisa and bonarda, too often underrated by the general public. But our winemaker has succeeded in the difficult task of creating good products from these varieties in both still and semi-sparkling versions. Supporting Gianni, we find the close-knit, experienced staff of Bruno Tamagnone, Giovanni Matteis, Marco Piovano and Germana Rosa Clot. Two Barberas were submitted this year. The Vigna delle More is rich in character with enjoyable, refreshing acidity and the Sebrì, barrique-conditioned per 15 months, shows spicy yet distinctly fruity. In contrast to earlier editions of the Guide, Freisa Arvelé failed to make Two Glasses because the nose has problems opening up. The semi-sparkling selection, Luna di Maggio, proffers nuances of morello cherry and currants and has juicy tannins. Aged nine months in tonneaux, the Vigna del Forno stands out for its wild berry touches. From the Bonardas, the still Sernù is pleasant and complex while the rest of the range is good quality.

Barbera d'Asti Superiore Anssèma returns to the Guide after a further, enhancing year's bottle age in the cellar. It's a decision that underlines how dedicated they are at this small winery owned by Bruno Ciocca and his wife Anna Solaini, assisted by oenologist Giuliano Noè. Moving on to the tasting, we like the Barbera Anssèma for its intense aromas of ripe currant and morello cherry berry fruit that meld deliciously with spicy nuances of cinnamon, vanilla and cocoa powder from oak conditioning. The palate is deep and juicy with a broad, intriguing finish. Simpler but very agreeable is the Barbera d'Asti 2005, a succulent easy drinker. The Monferrato Trinum, from barbera, dolcetto and cabernet sauvignon, earned Two Glasses for its dense tannic weave, well supported by a freshness that makes the palate complex and satisfying. Finally, the Moscato d'Asti is enjoyable.

● Barbera d'Asti Sebrì '05	♟♟ 4
● Freisa d'Asti Luna di Maggio '06	♟♟ 3*
● Barbera d'Asti V. delle More '05	♟♟ 4
● Freisa d'Asti V. del Forno '05	♟♟ 4
● Malvasia di Castelnuovo Don Bosco '06	♟♟ 4
● Piemonte Bonarda Sernù '05	♟♟ 4
● Dlicà	♟ 5
● Freisa d'Asti Arvelé '06	♟ 6
● Piemonte Bonarda Vivace Moyé '06	♟ 3
● Freisa d'Asti Vivace '06	♟ 3
● Freisa d'Asti Arvelé '04	♟♟ 5

● Barbera d'Asti Sup. Nizza Anssèma '04	♟♟ 5
● Barbera d'Asti '05	♟♟ 4*
● Monferrato Trinum '04	♟♟ 5
O Moscato d'Asti '06	♟ 4
● Barbera d'Asti Sup. Nizza Anssèma '03	♟♟ 5
● Barbera d'Asti Sup. Nizza Anssèma '01	♟♟ 5
● Barbera d'Asti Sup. Nizza Anssèma '00	♟♟ 5
● Monferrato Trinum '03	♟♟ 5

La Giribaldina
REG. SAN VITO, 39
14042 CALAMANDRANA [AT]
TEL. 0141718043
www.giribaldina.com

La Gironda
S.DA BRICCO, 12
14049 NIZZA MONFERRATO [AT]
TEL. 0141701013
www.lagironda.com

ANNUAL PRODUCTION 50,000 bottles
HECTARES UNDER VINE 9
VITICULTURE METHOD   Conventional

Founded in 1995, La Giribaldina has from
the start been managed by Mariagrazia
Macchi and her son Emanuele Colombo.
But the estate team also includes
agronomist Piero Roseo and oenologist
Beppe Caviola. In contrast to the 2007
edition of the Guide, this Calamandrana
winery was missing its most significant
Barbera, Cala delle Mandrie, because the
quartet decided to let it age longer to bring
out all its excellent qualities. From the wines
that were presented for tasting, the Barbera
Vigneti della Val Sarmassa prompted
flattering comments for rich fruity sensations
on the nose, admirably mingled with light
spicy nuances left by a sojourn in 16-
hectolitre oak barrels. The Moscato Passito
is complex and pleasantly sweet, without
being cloying and the fresh, pleasant
Monferrato Bianco Ferro di Cavallo, a
monovarietal Sauvignon fermented
exclusively in stainless steel, shows touches
of sage, tomato leaf and passion fruit on the
nose and then a rich, savoury palate.

ANNUAL PRODUCTION 28,000 bottles
HECTARES UNDER VINE 6
VITICULTURE METHOD   Conventional

La Gironda has vineyards in this historic
zone so superbly suited to producing
Barbera. Here we are actually in Bricco della
Cremosina at Nizza Monferrato, where
Agostino Galandrino several years ago
bought a lovely farm. Now, he manages it
with his daughter Susanna and her husband
Alberto Adamo, with input from oenologist
Beppe Rattazzo and agronomist Piero
Roseo. The excellent Superiore Nizza Le
Nicchie 2004 soared into our finals thanks
to highly complex aromas that range from
ripe berry fruit to more intense sensations,
like coffee, cocoa powder, vanilla, thyme
and leather. The palate has an inviting
mouthfeel with refreshing acidity. La Gena,
which is dynamic and juicy on the palate, as
well as the simple, easy-drinking La Lippa,
earned Two Glasses. A step below these is
the sweet, fragrant Brachetto d'Acqui,
which discloses attractive hints of wild roses
and peach blossom.

● Barbera d'Asti Sup.	
Vign. della Val Sarmassa '05	♈♈ 4*
○ Piemonte Moscato Passito '05	♈♈ 5
○ Monferrato Bianco	
Ferro di Cavallo '06	♈♈ 4
● Barbera d'Asti Monte del Mare '06	♈ 3
● Barbera d'Asti Sup.	
Cala delle Mandrie '03	♟♟ 5
● Barbera d'Asti Sup.	
Cala delle Mandrie '04	♟♟ 5
● Barbera d'Asti Sup.	
Cala delle Mandrie '01	♟♟ 5

● Barbera d'Asti Sup. Nizza	
Le Nicchie '04	♈♈ 5
● Barbera d'Asti La Gena '05	♈♈ 4*
● Barbera d'Asti La Lippa '06	♈♈ 3*
● Brachetto d'Acqui '06	♈ 4
● Barbera d'Asti Sup. Nizza	
Le Nicchie '03	♟♟ 5
● Barbera d'Asti Sup. Nizza	
Le Nicchie '01	♟♟ 5
● Barbera d'Asti Sup. Nizza	
Le Nicchie '00	♟♟ 5
● Barbera d'Asti La Gena '04	♟♟ 4

La Giustiniana

FRAZ. ROVERETO, 5
15066 GAVI [AL]
TEL. 0143682132
www.lagiustiniana.it

ANNUAL PRODUCTION   200,000 bottles
HECTARES UNDER VINE 39
VITICULTURE METHOD   Conventional

Tenuta La Giustiniana is one of the oldest, most beautiful properties in the Gavi area. In fact, Enrico Tomalino and the Lombardini family have a moral obligation to make prestigious wines that do justice to the splendour of the estate. The Gavi Il Nostro Gavi is obtained from rigorous vineyard selections that yield a white with perfectly defined aromas of glycerine, hawthorn, peach blossom and moss. Acidity and body integrate well to give power and character to the palate. We also applaud a superb showing from the Montessora, a Gavi with personality and freshness that is a bit shorter than the above but much better than the Lugarara, whose strength lies in its drinkability. Lovers of La Giustiniana will no doubt have noticed a conspicuous gap or two in the range of wines listed below. The estate crus, Just Bianco from cortese and Just Rosso from nebbiolo and barbera, had not yet been bottled at the time of our tastings. We'll come back to these next year along with the other no-show, the nebbiolo and barbera-based Granciarossa.

Cantina del Glicine

VIA GIULIO CESARE, 1
12052 NEIVE [CN]
TEL. 017367215
www.cantinadelglicine.it

ANNUAL PRODUCTION   40,000 bottles
HECTARES UNDER VINE 5
VITICULTURE METHOD   Conventional

We are very happy to welcome Cantina del Glicine back to the pages of our Guide, this time with a full profile. This jewel of a cellar occupies the rooms of a stunning 17th-century house in the centre of Neive. Their dedication to this building and to the traditional varieties of the zone is a mark of just how serious Adriana Marzi and her husband Roberto Bruno are about winemaking. The bottles presented for tasting impressed us with their stylistic consistency and, in the case of the Barbarescos and the Barbera, the grip and intensity they show on the palate. Of the two Barbarescos on offer, we preferred the Marcorino, which is obtained from a plot on top of a hill. It displays refined fruity sensations and powerful body with tannins that are already evening out. The Curà follows hot on its heels. Obtained from a vineyard that lies along the road from Neive to Barbaresco, it is a more astringent, chewy wine. The barrique-aged Barbera La Sconsolata is also very decent while the version matured without oak is fruity and coherent. We end our notes with a pleasant Dolcetto, a fresh Arneis and an aromatic Moscato d'Asti.

O Gavi del Comune di Gavi	
Il Nostro Gavi '04	♟♟ 5
O Gavi del Comune di Gavi	
Montessora '06	♟♟ 5
O Gavi del Comune di Gavi	
Lugarara '06	♟ 4
O Gavi del Comune di Gavi	
Lugarara '05	♟♟ 4
O Gavi del Comune di Gavi	
Montessora '05	♟♟ 5
● Monferrato Rosso Just '03	♟♟ 5

● Barbaresco Marcorino '04	♟♟ 6
● Barbaresco Curà '04	♟♟ 6
● Barbera d'Alba Sup. La Sconsolata	
Maturata in Barrique '05	♟♟ 5
● Barbera d'Alba La Sconsolata '05	♟♟ 4*
● Dolcetto d'Alba Olmiolo '06	♟ 4
O Moscato d'Asti '06	♟ 4
O Roero Arneis Il Mandolo '06	♟ 4
● Barbaresco Curà '03	♟♟ 6
● Barbaresco Marcorino '03	♟♟ 6

★ Elio Grasso

LOC. GINESTRA, 40
12065 MONFORTE D'ALBA [CN]
TEL. 017378491
www.eliograsso.it

ANNUAL PRODUCTION 70,000 bottles
HECTARES UNDER VINE 14
VITICULTURE METHOD Conventional

After long years of hard work, the lovely Elio Grasso estate now boasts one of Langhe's most evocative ageing areas, a very long, wide tunnel where the prestigious Monforte cellar matures its crus. After a year's sabbatical owing to the challenging weather conditions of 2002, the standard-label Barolos are back. But the Runcot is absent and we will have to wait until 2010 to taste the Riserva, as the 2002 and 2003 will not be released. By way of consolation, we sampled an excellent Casa Maté that matured for 24 months in 25-hectolitre barrels. Balsamic, ethery sensations mingle with hints of ripe red berry fruit on the nose before the alluring, elegant palate unveils fine-grained, velvety tannins. A well-deserved Three Glasses go to this superb interpretation of the growing year. The Gavarini Vigna Chiniera also earned a place in our finals for its nuances of liquorice and roses introducing a full, sweetly tannic entry on the palate. Nor did the elegant basic version of the Barolo and the Barbera Vigna Martina disappoint, the latter juicy with nice acidity that expands across the palate. The Educato Ricco has its usual full nose, the Langhe Nebbiolo is tangy and the Dolcetto dei Grassi full bodied.

Silvio Grasso

FRAZ. ANNUNZIATA
CASCINA LUCIANI, 112
12064 LA MORRA [CN]
TEL. 017350322

ANNUAL PRODUCTION 40,000 bottles
HECTARES UNDER VINE 7
VITICULTURE METHOD Conventional

The Grassos form a united front in which Federico's experience and Marilena's commitment are now complemented by young Silvio's energy. The estate has country traditions but has made significant investments in technology over the years, producing high-quality wines that reflect all the characteristics of the terroir. The Grassos take great pride in their work, and despite the severe limitations of the 2003 vintage, they gave us an outstanding series of Barolos. The Bricco Luciani shows great class, continuity, elegance and consistency with leisurely harmony. The refined Giachini offers exhilarating fruit and develops to reveal fine character. More balsamic and penetrating, the Vigna Plicotti displays graceful complexity and drying tannins, as does the Manzoni, in addition to lingering drinkability. The Pì Vigne is notable for its fullness and expressive generosity and the more classic L'André reveals all the nobility of its large wood maturation in the enveloping richness of the palate. The Barbera d'Alba Fontanile 2004 is an impeccable wine with superb body and freshness, showing soft and full-blooded in its leisurely finish.

● Barolo Ginestra V. Casa Maté '03	♟♟♟ 8
● Barolo Gavarini V. Chiniera '03	♟♟ 8
● Barbera d'Alba V. Martina '04	♟♟ 5
○ Langhe Chardonnay Educato '06	♟♟ 5
● Dolcetto d'Alba dei Grassi '06	♟♟ 4
● Langhe Nebbiolo Gavarini '06	♟ 4
● Barolo Gavarini V. Chiniera '89	♟♟♟ 8
● Barolo Gavarini V. Chiniera '98	♟♟♟ 8
● Barolo Gavarini V. Chiniera '99	♟♟♟ 8
● Barolo Gavarini V. Chiniera '00	♟♟♟ 8
● Barolo Gavarini V. Chiniera '01	♟♟♟ 8
● Barolo Ginestra V. Casa Maté '93	♟♟♟ 8
● Barolo Ginestra V. Casa Maté '90	♟♟♟ 8
● Barolo Runcot '96	♟♟♟ 8
● Barolo Runcot '01	♟♟♟ 8
● Barolo Runcot '98	♟♟♟ 8
● Barolo Runcot '99	♟♟♟ 8
● Barolo Runcot '00	♟♟♟ 8

● Barbera d'Alba Fontanile '04	♟♟ 5
● Barolo Bricco Luciani '03	♟♟ 8
● Barolo Ciabot Manzoni '03	♟♟ 8
● Barolo Giachini '03	♟♟ 7
● Langhe Nebbiolo Peirass '04	♟♟ 5
● Barolo L'André '03	♟♟ 7
● Barolo Pì Vigne '03	♟♟ 6
● Barolo Vigna Plicotti '03	♟♟ 7
● Barolo Bricco Luciani '01	♟♟♟ 8
● Barolo Bricco Luciani '96	♟♟♟ 8
● Barolo Bricco Luciani '95	♟♟♟ 8
● Barolo Bricco Luciani '90	♟♟♟ 8
● Barolo Ciabot Manzoni '00	♟♟ 8
● Barolo Ciabot Manzoni '01	♟♟ 8
● Barolo Pì Vigne '01	♟♟ 6
● Barolo L'André '01	♟♟ 7
● L'Insieme '03	♟♟ 5

Sergio Grimaldi - Ca' du Sindic
LOC. SAN GRATO, 15
12058 SANTO STEFANO BELBO [CN]
TEL. 0141840341
grimaldi.sergio@virgilio.it

ANNUAL PRODUCTION 45,000 bottles
HECTARES UNDER VINE 10
VITICULTURE METHOD Conventional

Work to expand the cellar is finally complete, a project that has kept the able Sergio Grimaldi busy for quite some time. With his wife Angela and son Paolo, Stefano runs this farm estate at Santo Stefano Belbo, the heart of Moscato production. And Ca' du Sindic is one of the most reliable, skilled interpreters of this particular wine type. We'll start our tasting notes with the two labels that have earned this small Langhe estate its well-deserved reputation. They are distinguishable only from the colour of their caps: the gold Oro is a rich, complex wine with nuances of flowers and orange peel and an embracing palate that is sweet but never cloying. The grapes that go to make this selection are cultivated on the slopes of San Maurizio on very steep terrain with excellent exposure. The silver-capped Argento is sourced from the San Grato vines that surround the house. This Moscato has aromas of ripe, white-fleshed peach and apricot fruit and a palate of energy and good length. The Barbera San Grato skipped a the year so we only tasted the basic version, which is fruity and pleasant. We enjoyed the Piemonte Brachetto.

Bruna Grimaldi
VIA RODDINO
12050 SERRALUNGA D'ALBA [CN]
TEL. 0173262094
www.gribaldibruna.it

ANNUAL PRODUCTION 45,000 bottles
HECTARES UNDER VINE 8
VITICULTURE METHOD Conventional

It is no simple matter to run an estate that spans two properties – the vinification facility at Grinzane Cavour and the visitors' centre at Serralunga – plus vineyards scattered across several municipalities in the Langhe and Roero. Yet Franco Fiorino and his wife Bruna Grimaldi take it all in their stride and again the wines they presented for tasting were interesting and agreeable. The Barolo Badarina Vigna Regnola was the judges' pick and made it all the way to our final tastings. This austere selection matures for 24 months in barriques and a further six in the bottle. The nose reveals violets, cherries and wild berries and then entry on the palate is full and firmly structured, with refreshing tannins. The Nebbiolo Briccola and the Barbera Superiore Scassa both have their origins in the municipality of Diano d'Alba. The former is rendered elegant by its generous, enjoyable nose; the second aged for 15 months in new and used 900-litre casks and stands out for its warm fruity, spicy sensations. The Dolcetto d'Alba Vigna San Martino, from grapes sourced at a farm in Grinzane Cavour, and the Langhe Chardonnay Valscura, from plots in Roero's Corneliano d'Alba, are simpler but far from banal.

O Moscato d'Asti Ca' du Sindic Capsula Oro '06	♟♟ 4*
O Moscato d'Asti Ca' du Sindic Capsula Argento '06	♟♟ 4
● Barbera d'Asti '05	♟ 3
● Piemonte Brachetto Ca' du Sindic '06	♟ 3
● Barbera d'Asti San Grato '04	♟♟ 4

● Barolo Badarina V. Regnola '03	♟♟ 6*
● Barbera d'Alba Sup. Scassa '05	♟♟ 4*
● Nebbiolo d'Alba Briccola '04	♟♟ 4*
● Dolcetto d'Alba V. S. Martino '06	♟ 3
O Langhe Chardonnay Valscura '06	♟ 3
● Barbera d'Alba Sup. Scassa '04	♟♟ 4
● Barolo Badarina V. Regnola '01	♟♟ 6
● Nebbiolo d'Alba Briccola '03	♟♟ 4

Giacomo Grimaldi
VIA LUIGI EINAUDI, 8
12060 BAROLO [CN]
TEL. 017335256

La Guardia
PODERE LA GUARDIA, 74
15010 MORSASCO [AL]
TEL. 014473076
www.laguardiavini.it

ANNUAL PRODUCTION 40,000 bottles
HECTARES UNDER VINE 8
VITICULTURE METHOD Conventional

ANNUAL PRODUCTION 150,000 bottles
HECTARES UNDER VINE 70
VITICULTURE METHOD Conventional

Ferruccio Grimaldi has carved out a solid reputation for himself in the Langhe and the wines produced by his estate pay tribute to his passion to bring out the special characteristics of each of his vineyards. Production totals around 40,000 bottles and is growing in terms of both number and overall quality. Next year will see the release of a new Barolo from the Terlo vineyard. Top of the list this year come 5,000 bottles of Barolo Le Coste 2003, an elegant, classy wine with a concentrated palate displaying well-balanced fruit and tannins and a long, intense finish. The other Barolo is also very interesting, presenting austere, with less fruit and fewer tannins in evidence. The Barbera Fornaci gives an impressive performance with fruit and firm structure on the palate lifted by balsamic freshness that spills over into the long finish. We also recommend the excellent Nebbiolo from the Valmaggiore area in Roero, the enjoyable, attractive and tasty Barbera Pistin, and the soft Dolcetto d'Alba with its exuberant personality. Grimaldi is a fine benchmark for those looking to buy quality wines at very reasonable prices.

This estate has appeared in the pages of our Guide since we first started publishing and it continues to perform well across most of the range at every harvest. The Priarone family still aspires to further heights but always from firm roots in tradition and the local territory. Dolcetto is the estate's best-loved variety. Proof comes in the form of its two most successful wines from the Ovada DOC: Villa Delfini and Gamondino. The former discloses notes of wild berries and spice followed by a consistent, dynamic palate whereas Gamondino presents an attractive rich ruby red and tends more to refreshing tones of sweet spice and balsam before unfolding a very convincing palate. The Barbera del Monferrato Ornovo is very pleasant, acidic, edgy and harmonious. Dolcetto and cabernet blend the Monferrato Rosso Innominato also shows well, but the Monferrato Rosso Leone from pinot nero, dolcetto and cabernet is even better. Good, too, are the Cortese La Vigna di Lena and the Chardonnay Villa Delfini.

● Barolo Le Coste '03	♟♟ 7
● Barbera d'Alba Fornaci '05	♟♟ 5
● Barbera d'Alba Pistin '06	♟♟ 4*
● Nebbiolo d'Alba Valmaggiore '05	♟♟ 4*
● Barolo Sotto Castello di Novello '03	♟♟ 6
● Dolcetto d'Alba '06	♟♟ 3*
● Barbera d'Alba Fornaci '03	♟♟ 5
● Barolo Sotto Castello di Novello '01	♟♟ 6
● Barolo Sotto Castello di Novello '00	♟♟ 7
● Barolo Le Coste '99	♟♟ 8
● Barolo Le Coste '00	♟♟ 8
● Barolo Le Coste '01	♟♟ 8
● Barbera d'Alba Fornaci '04	♟♟ 5
● Barbera d'Alba Fornaci '01	♟♟ 6
● Nebbiolo d'Alba Valmaggiore '05	♟♟ 4

● Barbera del M.to Ornovo '05	♟♟ 4
● Dolcetto di Ovada Sup. Villa Delfini '04	♟♟ 4
O Piemonte Chardonnay Villa Delfini '06	♟♟ 4
● Monferrato Rosso Leone '04	♟♟ 4
● Dolcetto di Ovada Sup. Il Gamondino '05	♟♟ 4
O Cortese dell'Alto M.to La Vigna di Lena '06	♟ 4
● Monferrato Rosso Innominato '04	♟ 5
● Dolcetto di Ovada Sup. Villa Delfini '03	♟♟ 4
● Dolcetto di Ovada Sup. Vign. Bricco Riccardo '04	♟♟ 4

Clemente Guasti
C.SO IV NOVEMBRE, 80
14049 NIZZA MONFERRATO [AT]
TEL. 0141721350
www.clemente.guasti.it

Hilberg - Pasquero
VIA BRICCO GATTI, 16
12040 PRIOCCA [CN]
TEL. 0173616197
www.vinipiemonte.com

ANNUAL PRODUCTION 200,000 bottles
HECTARES UNDER VINE 35
VITICULTURE METHOD Conventional

ANNUAL PRODUCTION 20,000 bottles
HECTARES UNDER VINE 5
VITICULTURE METHOD Natural

The Guasti cellar is in rather an unusual location. Today the idea of an estate conjures up images of a property nestling in the green embrace of a rural backdrop. But like many of the commercial estates in the Asti part of Langhe that were designed to handle large volumes, the Guasti cellars lie smack bang in the centre of Nizza Monferrato, on the banks of the Belbo. Managed today by Alessandro and Andrea Guasti, this estate was built with such requirements in mind when it was founded in 1946. The generous spaces house a large number of barrels, almost all of which are made of Slavonian oak in the time-honoured style of the old cellars. It goes without saying that the Guasti brothers' wines are also traditional in style, showing astringent and austere with no concessions to excessive softness, and enhanced by their long sojourn in the barrel. Barbera Barcarato, the only estate wine matured in barrique, for the large part used, displays aromas of cherry and sweet notes of oak. The trio of big Barberas is completed by the rigorous, very characterful Fonda San Nicolao and the more malleable Boschetto Vecchio. The fruity Desideria 2006 offers further proof of the Guastis' skills with Barbera.

A visit to Michelangelo Miclo Pasquero and Annette Hilberg at Bricco Gatti offers a fresh perspective on wine: it's not just about business, winemakers, marketing and trends but first and foremost a question of simplicity, passion and authenticity. Their bottles taste of Piedmont, as Miclo says, and to our minds there is also a hint of Roero, revisited with the consistency of a modern producer dedicated to replicating – in wine – all of the characteristics that the vine offers in its fruit. Metaphors aside, the wines are quite simply exquisite. The Nebbiolo and the Barbera Superiore vie for pole position. The former impresses with its soft austerity and we have ample proof of how well it ages. The Barbera Superiore has rarely shown such fresh, supple supporting acidity. Yet again, we gave the Nebbiolo Three Glasses. The Pedrocha blend is no longer in production and its nebbiolo and barbera grapes have gone to beef up the estate's two big reds. We are thus left with two excellent lesser wines, the Barbera d'Alba and Langhe Nebbiolo, both eminently drinkable and agreeable. Vareij from a blend of brachetto and barbera gives its usual delightful virtuoso performance.

● Barbera d'Asti Sup. Nizza Barcarato '04	♟♟ 6
● Barbera d'Asti Desideria '06	♟♟ 4*
● Barbera d'Asti Sup. Cascina Boschetto Vecchio '04	♟♟ 5
● Barbera d'Asti Sup. Cascina Fonda San Nicolao '04	♟♟ 5
● Barbera d'Asti Sup. '04	♟ 4
● Grignolino d'Asti '06	♟ 4
○ Moscato d'Asti Santa Teresa '06	♟ 4
● Barbera d'Asti Sup. Nizza Barcarato '01	♟♟ 6
● Barbera d'Asti Sup. Cascina Fonda San Nicolao '03	♟♟ 5
● Barbera d'Asti Sup. Nizza Barcarato '03	♟♟ 6
● Barbera d'Asti Sup. Nizza Barcarato '00	♟♟ 6

● Nebbiolo d'Alba '05	♟♟♟ 6
● Barbera d'Alba Sup. '05	♟♟ 6
● Barbera d'Alba '06	♟♟ 4
● Vareij Rosso '06	♟♟ 4
● Langhe Nebbiolo '05	♟♟ 5
● Barbera d'Alba Sup. '97	♟♟♟ 6
● Nebbiolo d'Alba '01	♟♟♟ 6
● Nebbiolo d'Alba '04	♟♟♟ 6
● Nebbiolo d'Alba '03	♟♟♟ 6
● Nebbiolo d'Alba '00	♟♟♟ 6
● Barbera d'Alba Sup. '98	♟♟♟ 6
● Barbera d'Alba Sup. '01	♟♟ 6
● Barbera d'Alba Sup. '03	♟♟ 6
● Barbera d'Alba Sup. '04	♟♟ 6
● Barbera d'Alba Sup. '00	♟♟ 6

Icardi

LOC. SAN LAZZARO
VIA BALBI, 30
12053 CASTIGLIONE TINELLA [CN]
TEL. 0141855159
icardivini@libero.it

ANNUAL PRODUCTION 351,000 bottles
HECTARES UNDER VINE 75
VITICULTURE METHOD   Natural

It's always a pleasure to chat with the
likeable, frank Claudio Icardi, a leading
figure in the wine world. Before you step
into his cellar to taste his vast range of
labels, we suggest you spend some time
with him in his vineyards. The estate's
property includes several plots in the
Langhe and Monferrato, and Claudio's
relationship with them is founded on the
harmony of all of the system's elements.
This extends to the cellar, where
consistency and passion are conveyed to
the wines with the crucial support of Maria
Grazia, Claudio's sister. Given the
impressive vine stock, the estate offers a
broad selection of labels. We'll start our
notes with the Langhe bottles. Top of the list
this year comes the Barbaresco Montubert
2004, an elegant, fruity version of a great
vintage. Produced at Sant'Anna near La
Morra, the Barolo Parej 2003 reflects the
conditions of the growing year but is still
stylish and firmly structured. As well as a
fine range of Barberas, the most impressive
of which is the 2005 Nuj Suj, the Asti wines
also include a fine Monferrato Rosso
Cascina Bricco del Sole 2004, obtained
from a blend of nebbiolo, barbera and
cabernet sauvignon.

Isabella

FRAZ. CORTERANZO
VIA GIANOLI, 64
15020 MURISENGO [AL]
TEL. 0141693000
info@isabellavini.com

ANNUAL PRODUCTION 120,000 bottles
HECTARES UNDER VINE 25.5
VITICULTURE METHOD   Conventional

Now that the sophisticated visitors' centre
next to the cellar is up and running, Gabriele
Calvo has turned his attention to refining his
range of wines. It must have been a difficult
decision to postpone the release of his most
prestigious Barberas, but Gabriele took it.
The Bric Stupui and Truccone selections are
to enjoy an extra year's ageing before being
presented for the Guide. Thus it falls to the
Bricco Montemà Tardivo Tocca to represent
the best of Isabella's production. This
Barbera has a dense red appearance,
pleasant notes of berry fruit on the nose and
good follow-through on a palate sustained
by marked acidity. The still Freisa Bioc
presents an intense ruby red colour, a nose
full of wild berry and aromatic herb aromas,
and a supple palate with a typically tannic,
slightly bitter finish. Rounding off the range
we have the Grignolino Montecastello, a
pale red wine with notes of spice and
undertones of fruit that unfolds agreeable
and balanced on the palate.

● Barbaresco Montubert '04	☐☐ 6
● Monferrato Rosso Cascina Bricco del Sole '04	☐☐ 6
● Barbera d'Asti Nuj Suj '05	☐☐ 5
● Barbera d'Alba Surì di Mù '05	☐☐ 5
● Langhe Rosso Nej '05	☐☐ 5
● Barolo Parej '03	☐☐ 8
● Langhe Nebbiolo Surìsjvan '05	☐☐ 5
○ Monferrato Bianco Pafoj '06	☐☐ 5
○ Moscato d'Asti La Rosa Selvatica '06	☐ 4
● Barbera d'Asti Tabaren '06	☐ 4
● Dolcetto d'Alba Rousori '06	☐ 4
● Barbera d'Asti Nuj Suj '04	☐☐ 6
● Barbaresco Montubert '03	☐☐ 8
● Barolo Parej '01	☐☐ 8
● Monferrato Rosso Cascina Bricco del Sole '03	☐☐ 7

● Barbera del M.to Bric Montemà Tardivo '05	☐☐ 4
● Grignolino del M.to Casalese Montecastello '06	☐☐ 4
● Monferrato Freisa Bioc '05	☐☐ 4
● Barbera d'Asti Bric Stupui '00	☐☐ 6
● Barbera d'Asti Truccone '03	☐☐ 4
● Barbera d'Asti Truccone '04	☐☐ 4
● Barbera d'Asti Bric Stupui '01	☐☐ 5
● Barbera d'Asti Bric Stupui '03	☐☐ 5

Iuli

FRAZ. MONTALDO
VIA CENTRALE, 27
15020 CERRINA MONFERRATO [AL]
TEL. 0142946657
www.iuli.it

ANNUAL PRODUCTION 35,000 bottles
HECTARES UNDER VINE 9
VITICULTURE METHOD Natural

The verdant slopes of Val Cerrina, that picturesque winemaking outpost in Monferrato, continue to send out encouraging signals. Fabrizio Iuli's free spirit is complemented by his sister Cristina and the tight-knit Lerner team of Dan, Gad and Umberta, all of whom offer support and let him develop his ideas. And these are not always easy for an impatient and excitable wine market to accept. How could you describe as anything other than patience-taxing his decision to age his flagship Barbera, the Barabba selection, for an extra year? We shall taste the 2004 edition – perhaps! – in 2008, when Fabrizio believes it will have achieved its peak of maturation. However, our retasting of the 2001 was very rewarding and indicated to both us and him that he has made the right decision. The Barbera Rossore, only a 2005, has also been left to age so we tasted the one remaining Barbera, the virtually newborn Umberta 2006. From the rest of the range, we were offered the Monferrato Malidea to taste again. This soft yet austere blend of nebbiolo and barbera is so graceful it evinces genuine elegance. Finally, Nino, a Pinot Nero, has a pure Monferrato character and an edgy vein that pervades the extremely pleasant palate.

Tenuta La Volta - Cabutto

VIA SAN PIETRO, 13
12060 BAROLO [CN]
TEL. 017356168
www.cabuttolavolta.com

ANNUAL PRODUCTION 90,000 bottles
HECTARES UNDER VINE 36
VITICULTURE METHOD Conventional

Brothers Osvaldo and Bruno Cabutto are the more than worthy heirs to this historic estate, founded in the 1800s. The castle looks out over the splendid panorama of vineyards below, the vinification and ageing areas are clean and modern, and the wines, which are obtained from red varieties and have a rigorously Piedmontese character, are deeply rooted in the territory. The Nebbiolos produced on this estate undergo long macerations and mature in big oak barrels. The end result is typical wines that lend themselves well to long ageing. This year, we tasted an agreeable Barolo La Volta 2003, released in 50,000 bottles, that comes from a hot, dry growing year and shows delicate, fresh aromas with hints of jam and balsamic nuances. The balanced palate displays tannins and body that never hamper the progression. The 4,000 bottles of Barolo Vigna Sarmassa 2001 are exemplary, showing deep and full with well-defined fruit that offers velvety sensations on the palate, thanks to lovely flesh and well-gauged tannins. This is a gem of a Barolo, brimming with tradition, elegance and the essence of nebbiolo, the main variety grown in these beautiful hills.

Wine	Rating
● Barbera del M.to Sup. Umberta '06	ŸŸ 4*
● Monferrato Rosso Nino '05	ŸŸ 5
● Monferrato Rosso Malidea '04	ŸŸ 5
● Barbera del M.to Sup. Barabba '01	ŸŸ 6
● Barbera del M.to Sup. Barabba '03	ŸŸ 6
● Barbera del M.to Rossore '03	ŸŸ 4
● Barbera del M.to Rossore '04	ŸŸ 4
● Barbera del M.to Sup. Umberta '04	ŸŸ 4
● Barbera del M.to Sup. Umberta '03	ŸŸ 4
● Monferrato Rosso Malidea '03	ŸŸ 6

Wine	Rating
● Barolo Ris. del Fondatore V. Sarmassa '01	ŸŸ 8
● Barolo La Volta '03	ŸŸ 7
● Barolo Ris. del Fondatore '99	ŸŸ 8
● Barolo Ris. del Fondatore V. Sarmassa '00	ŸŸ 8
● Barolo Ris. del Fondatore '90	ŸŸ 8
● Barolo Ris. del Fondatore '98	ŸŸ 8
● Barolo Ris. del Fondatore '97	ŸŸ 8
● Barolo V. La Volta '00	ŸŸ 7
● Barolo V. La Volta '99	ŸŸ 7
● Barolo V. La Volta '01	ŸŸ 7
● Barolo Ris. del Fondatore '96	ŸŸ 8

Gianluigi Lano

FRAZ. SAN ROCCO SENO D'ELVIO
S.DA BASSO, 38
12051 ALBA [CN]
TEL. 0173286958
lano.vini@tiscali.it

Ugo Lequio

VIA DEL MOLINO, 10
12057 NEIVE [CN]
TEL. 0173677224
www.ugolequio.it

ANNUAL PRODUCTION 37,000 bottles
HECTARES UNDER VINE 6
VITICULTURE METHOD Conventional

Gianluigi Lano's vineyards and cellar are situated in San Rocco Seno d'Elvio. Administratively speaking, this is Alba territory but in actual fact the small valley of San Rocco lies far from the well-trodden tourist paths and commercial traffic. In this secluded corner of Langhe, Gianluigi Lano has amassed almost 15 years of experience in the vineyard and cellar, earning a solid reputation and acclaim for his policy of producing reasonably priced wines. We are convinced that a tad more style and personality, which will come from more commitment and longer ageing times than the Lanos have been able to dedicate to their wines so far, would take this estate to the highest levels of quality. Again this year, they presented us with a very decent range of wines. The Barbaresco 2004 is good, its only defect being a slight lack of elegance. The attractive line-up of Barberas includes the concentrated Fondo Prà and the more balanced, leisurely Altavilla. The Dolcetto d'Alba Ronchella proffers generous ripe fruit. The Barbera and the basic Dolcetto both have a simple, approachable nose but are exceedingly pleasant, and the rest of the range is very well managed.

ANNUAL PRODUCTION 25,000 bottles
HECTARES UNDER VINE N.A.
VITICULTURE METHOD Conventional

The performance by this estate goes to show just how unconventional Ugo Lequio is. In a year when all Barbaresco producers are proud to show off their 2004 vintages, he has preferred to leave his Gallina to age longer, postponing its release until 2008 when it will have realized its full potential. However, the wines he did present are extremely interesting. The Barbera d'Alba Gallina 2005 stands out for its power, elegance and complexity combined with astonishing drinkability. The Langhe Nebbiolo 2006, which matures in 900-litre casks, exhibits varietal notes enhanced by hints of leather and cinnamon. The palate achieves balance, its flowery aromas integrating perfectly with attractive oaky notes in a liquorice finish. This year the Dolcetto 2005 that we erroneously mentioned last year was on parade and it amazed us with its crisp morello cherry sensations and spicy nuances that emerge on the nose, followed by structural fullness of the palate. The Langhe Arneis 2006 was well up to scratch, showing fresh and flowery with a balsamic finish that makes the palate particularly enjoyable.

● Barbaresco '04	♟♟ 6
● Barbera d'Alba Fondo Prà '05	♟♟ 4*
● Dolcetto d'Alba Ronchella '05	♟♟ 4*
● Barbera d'Alba Altavilla '05	♟♟ 4*
● Barbera d'Alba '05	♟ 3
● Dolcetto d'Alba '06	♟ 3
● Langhe Freisa Vivace '06	♟ 3
O Langhe Favorita '06	♟ 3
● Barbaresco '01	♟♟ 6
● Barbaresco '03	♟♟ 6
● Barbera d'Alba Fondo Prà '04	♟♟ 4
● Barbera d'Alba Fondo Prà '03	♟♟ 5
● Barbera d'Alba Altavilla '04	♟♟ 4
● Barbera d'Alba Altavilla '03	♟♟ 4

● Barbera d'Alba Sup. Gallina '05	♟♟ 4*
● Dolcetto d'Alba '05	♟♟ 4*
● Langhe Nebbiolo '06	♟♟ 5
O Langhe Arneis '06	♟ 4
● Barbaresco Gallina '00	♟♟ 6
● Barbaresco Gallina '01	♟♟ 6
● Barbaresco Gallina Ris. '01	♟♟ 7
● Barbaresco Gallina '03	♟♟ 6
● Barbera d'Alba Gallina '00	♟♟ 4
● Barbera d'Alba Gallina '01	♟♟ 4

Cascina Luisin

S.DA RABAJÀ, 34
12050 BARBARESCO [CN]
TEL. 0173635154
cascinaluisin@tiscali.it

ANNUAL PRODUCTION 30,000 bottles
HECTARES UNDER VINE 7
VITICULTURE METHOD Conventional

Under the guidance of his father, Luigi, Roberto Minuto produces the full gamut of Langhe reds in the traditional manner, which means extremely long macerations and ageing in large barrels. Paradoxically, it was Roberto's basic wines that got the best results. The two 2006 Maggiurs – the Barbera d'Alba and the Nebbiolo d'Alba – and, in particular, the Dolcetto d'Alba Bric Trifüla 2006, with good intensity and backbone, do very well. Although well styled, the Barbaresco Rabajà 2003 and the Barolo Leon 2003 are not at the top of their respective categories although they display reasonable tannic texture on the palate and decent length. The Barbaresco Sorì Paolin 2004, whose release has been postponed until next year, hints at better things to come. The estate's only barrique-aged wine, Barbera d'Alba Asili 2005, is this year's star performer. This little gem made its umpteenth appearance in our finals thanks to generous, juicy fruit, enriched by tertiary notes left by oak-conditioning, and its pleasant balance between alcohol and acidity on the palate.

● Barbera d'Alba Asili '05	▼▼▽	6
● Barbera d'Alba Maggiur '06	▼▼	4*
● Dolcetto d'Alba Bric Trifüla '06	▼▼	4*
● Langhe Nebbiolo Maggiur '06	▼▼	4*
● Barbaresco Rabajà '03	▼	5
● Barolo Leon '03	▼	8
● Barbera d'Alba Asili '00	▽▽▽	6
● Barbera d'Alba Asili '99	▽▽▽	6
● Barbera d'Alba Asili Barrique '97	▽▽▽	6
● Barbera d'Alba Asili '04	▽▽	6
● Barolo Leon '01	▽▽	8
● Barbaresco Rabajà '00	▽▽	7
● Barbaresco Rabajà '01	▽▽	7
● Barbaresco Sorì Paolin '01	▽▽	7
● Barbaresco Sorì Paolin '03	▽▽	7
● Barbaresco Rabajà '99	▽▽	6

Malabaila di Canale

LOC. FRAZ. MADONNA DEI CAVALLI, 19
CASCINA PRADVAJ
12043 CANALE [CN]
TEL. 017398381
www.malabaila.com

ANNUAL PRODUCTION 80,000 bottles
HECTARES UNDER VINE 22
VITICULTURE METHOD Conventional

We are very pleased to award a full profile to an estate that has played a leading role in the history of Roero wine. The cellar belongs to the noble Conti Malabaila di Canale family and was founded when the castle was built in the heart of Roero's main town. The castle has survived intact through the centuries in all of its magnificent splendour. The estate where the harvesting and vinification of the grapes take place is simply stunning. It lies just outside the town at the foot of an amphitheatre of hills planted to vine, in the centre of a valley that is still home to arable land and thickets of trees. Today, the estate has the solid support of a local technician, Alfredo Falletti, who manages the fruit with great skill and oversees its transformation into wines that bear a clear Roero hallmark. We particularly liked the reliable Arneis 2006 for the mineral and acid vein that it displays on nose and palate respectively. The Barbera is a step above, showing full bodied but not heavy, and firmly structured but not woody. In other words, it's balanced and full. Last on our list was the austere, tannic Roero, which has edgy acid grip and a leisurely, harmonious finish of good length.

● Barbera d'Alba Mezzavilla '05	▼▼	4*
● Roero Sup. Castelletto '04	▼▼	5
O Roero Arneis Pradvaj '06	▼▼	4*
O Langhe Favorita '06	▼	3
● Roero Sup. Castelletto '00	▽▽	5
● Roero Sup. Castelletto '01	▽▽	5
● Roero Sup. Bric Volta '04	▽▽	5
● Roero Sup. Castelletto '03	▽▽	5

Malgrà

LOC. BAZZANA
VIA NIZZA, 8
14046 MOMBARUZZO [AT]
TEL. 0141725055
www.malgra.it

ANNUAL PRODUCTION 950,000 bottles
HECTARES UNDER VINE 140
VITICULTURE METHOD Conventional

This year, the house of Mombaruzzo
presented a stand-out range. The estate is
run solidly and with passion by the close-
knit team of Nico Conta, Massimiliano
Diotto, and Ezio and Giorgio Chiarle. The
number of labels presented is large and
quality has never been better. There are
fully four Barberas so all tastes are catered
for. The magnificent 2004 version of the
Mora di Sassi is fruity, full and acid. It's
perfect for those looking for emotion in their
wine. The Gaiana from the same vintage
lacks a whisper of its allure but is still
wonderful. Fornace di Cerreto and Briga
della Mora, from 2005 and 2006
respectively, bring us to the present and
what they lack in weight they make up for
in drinkability. The reds also feature a very
successful Monferrato Treviri from barbera,
dolcetto and cabernet, and an extremely
enjoyable standard-label Nebbiolo from
northern Piedmont. Of the whites on offer,
we liked the Gavi, although the Innuce
remains fragrant after its long ageing. The
Brut is on the threshold of its stylistic prime,
offering aromas of yeast and crusty bread,
and a consistent, harmonious palate.

Malvirà

LOC. CANOVA
VIA CASE SPARSE, 144
12043 CANALE [CN]
TEL. 0173978145
www.malvira.com

ANNUAL PRODUCTION 300,000 bottles
HECTARES UNDER VINE 40
VITICULTURE METHOD Conventional

Roberto and Massimo Damonte's estate
and vineyards, including the beautiful hotel
that is part of the property, dominate the
Canale hills. This year's results confirm the
cellar as a leading light in the Roero wine
world with a range that combines quality
with quantity. As usual, it was the two
Roero Superiores 2004, Mombeltramo and
Trinità, that were vying for top spot. The
former triumphed to take the latest in a
long line of Three Glass trophies for its
elegant nose and sweet, already
characterful palate. Trinità impressed with
its tannins and backbone. It has only just
embarked on a long process of evolution
but is already very good. We noted two fine
performances from the Barbera d'Alba San
Michele 2005, with its intense fruity nose
and balanced palate, and Langhe Bianco
Treuve 2005, which offers sensations of
summer fruit and nicely dosed oak whose
full potential was revealed at our tasting of
previous vintages. The estate presents no
less than five interpretations of Arneis that
show off every facet of the variety, from
minerality and ripe fruit all the way to
Renesium's dried fig aromas. The Favorita
and the sauvignon-based Langhe Bianco
are also very interesting. The other reds
show well.

● Barbera d'Asti Sup. Nizza Mora di Sassi '04	🍷🍷 6
● Barbera d'Asti Sup. Fornace di Cerreto '05	🍷🍷 4*
● Monferrato Rosso Treviri '05	🍷🍷 5
● Barbera d'Asti Sup. Gaiana '04	🍷🍷 4
○ Col dei Ronchi Brut M. Cl. Cuvée Malgrà '03	🍷🍷 5
○ Gavi del Comune di Gavi Poggio Basco '06	🍷🍷 4*
● Barbera d'Asti Briga della Mora '06	🍷 3
● Coste della Sesia Nebbiolo '06	🍷 3
○ Piemonte Chardonnay Innuce '04	🍷 4
● Barbera d'Asti Sup. Nizza Mora di Sassi '03	🍷🍷 6
● Barbera d'Asti Sup. Nizza Mora di Sassi '01	🍷🍷 6

● Roero Sup. Mombeltramo '04	🍷🍷🍷 6
● Roero Sup. Trinità '04	🍷🍷 6
○ Roero Arneis Saglietto '06	🍷🍷 4
● Barbera d'Alba Sup. S. Michele '04	🍷🍷 5
● Barbera d'Alba S. Michele '05	🍷🍷 4
● Langhe Nebbiolo '05	🍷🍷 4
● Langhe Rosso S. Guglielmo '04	🍷🍷 5
○ Langhe Favorita '06	🍷🍷 4
○ Langhe Bianco '06	🍷🍷 4
○ Langhe Bianco Tre Uve '05	🍷🍷 4
○ Roero Arneis Trinità '06	🍷🍷 4
○ Roero Arneis Renesio '06	🍷🍷 4
○ Renesium	🍷🍷 4
● Birbet '06	🍷 3
○ Roero Arneis '06	🍷 4
● Roero Sup. Trinità '03	🍷🍷🍷 6
● Roero Sup. Trinità '01	🍷🍷🍷 6
● Roero Sup. Mombeltramo '00	🍷🍷🍷 6

Giovanni Manzone
VIA CASTELLETTO, 9
12065 MONFORTE D'ALBA [CN]
TEL. 017378114
www.manzonegiovanni.com

ANNUAL PRODUCTION 40,000 bottles
HECTARES UNDER VINE 7.5
VITICULTURE METHOD Conventional

Giovanni Manzone is an authentic wine man, self-effacing and little given to public relations, and it is probably this habit of shying away from the limelight that has prevented him from building a reputation with a wider audience. His wines are so typical that they are almost textbook in style, perfectly embodying the true Langhe spirit. Barolo Le Gramolere Riserva 2001 comes from an exceptional growing year and a vineyard with an excellent position. We loved its ethery notes of violets and cinnamon with undertones of aniseed and pepper. The palate displays austere but measured tannins that never intrude. A magnificent red in the classic nebbiolo style and a wine to enjoy for years to come, it earned Three very full Glasses. The Bricat also made it to our final tastings. Although very mature, it convinced our panel of judges with its fruity nuances led by blueberries and currants, lifted by delicate hints of spice. Le Gramolere and the basic Barolo have excellent texture, as does Barbera Superiore La Serra, whose 18 months in 900-litre casks have given it a lip-smacking palate and good depth. Rosserto from rossese bianco is unusual and the Dolcettos, Langhe Nebbiolo and Barbera 2006 are all pleasant.

Paolo Manzone
LOC. MERIAME, 1
12050 SERRALUNGA D'ALBA [CN]
TEL. 0173613113
www.barolomeriame.com

ANNUAL PRODUCTION 50,000 bottles
HECTARES UNDER VINE 10
VITICULTURE METHOD Conventional

For years, Paolo Manzone acted as consultant oenologist to many of the big wine names in Italy and abroad. In 1999, he decided to restore his own beautiful farmhouse and started to vinify the grapes from his vineyards at Serralunga and Sinio. Two years ago, Paolo and his wife Luisella opened a charming bed and breakfast offering five bedrooms and a spectacular pool. The 2003 vintage was not an easy one, particularly for Nebbiolos, and Paolo's Barolos, especially the base version, suffered the effects of the torrid vintage. The Meriame, however, cruised past the Two Glass mark thanks to mature aromas of red berry fruit and an agreeable, very rewarding entry on the palate. The complex, firmly structured Nebbiolo d'Alba Mirinè is obtained from grapes grown in Sinio. The nose offers fruity sensations of cherry, violet and spice. The simple but exceedingly pleasant Barbera d'Alba Fiorenza impressed with its full, easy-drinking palate. As expected, the Barolo Serralunga needs a few more months to smooth out its still rather boisterous tannins. One Glass went to the Dolcetto d'Alba Magna, aged exclusively in stainless steel.

● Barolo Le Gramolere Ris. '01	￦￦￦	8
● Barolo Bricat '03	￦￦	7
● Barbera d'Alba Sup. La Serra '05	￦￦	5
● Barbera d'Alba '06	￦￦	4
● Barolo Le Gramolere '03	￦￦	7
● Barolo '03	￦￦	6
● Dolcetto d'Alba La Serra '06	￦￦	4
O Rosserto Bianco '05	￦￦	4
● Dolcetto d'Alba Le Ciliegie '06	￦	3
● Langhe Nebbiolo Il Crutin '06	￦	4
● Barolo Le Gramolere Ris. '00	￦￦￦	8
● Barolo Le Gramolere Ris. '99	￦￦￦	8

● Barbera d'Alba Fiorenza '06	￦￦	4*
● Nebbiolo d'Alba Mirinè '05	￦￦	4*
● Barolo Meriame '03	￦￦	7
● Barolo Serralunga '03	￦	6
● Dolcetto d'Alba Magna '06	￦	3
● Barolo Meriame '00	￦￦	7
● Barolo Meriame '01	￦￦	7
● Barolo Meriame '99	￦￦	7
● Barolo Serralunga '01	￦￦	6

Poderi Marcarini

P.ZZA MARTIRI, 2
12064 LA MORRA [CN]
TEL. 017350222
www.marcarini.it

ANNUAL PRODUCTION 110,000 bottles
HECTARES UNDER VINE 17
VITICULTURE METHOD Conventional

After a tough 2006 that required some difficult decisions, Luisa and Manuel Marchetti gave us a full range. We celebrate the return of the Barolos which, despite a challenging growing year, astonished our tasters with their freshness and complexity. We'll start with the Serra 2003 and its plum and violet bouquet followed by a palate balanced between very elegant tannins and the surprising acidity of the balsam-edged finish. The Barolo Brunate 2003 is at the very top of its category and won Three Glasses. It impressed the panel with the power and elegance of its nose, in which notes of violet, rose and eucalyptus emerge laced with a hint of marron glacé. On the palate, silky tannins merge with superb acidity in a long, balsamic finish redolent of cinchona and liquorice. The Roero Arneis 2006, the 2006 Dolcettos – Fontanazza and Boschi di Berri – the Barbera Ciabot Camerano 2005 and the Moscato d'Asti 2006 were all up to snuff. The Langhe Nebbiolo Lasarin 2006 and the Langhe Rosso 2004 are worth investigating. The Nebbiolo has all of the complexities of its grape in a simple, easy-drinking guise and the Ross reveals the aromatics of the barbera, nebbiolo and syrah varieties on its soft, captivating palate.

Marchesi di Barolo

VIA ALBA, 12
12060 BAROLO [CN]
TEL. 0173564400
www.marchesibarolo.com

ANNUAL PRODUCTION 1,500,000 bottles
HECTARES UNDER VINE 120
VITICULTURE METHOD Conventional

This historic Barolo estate, owned by the Abbona and Scarzello families, continues to deliver quality, giving its wines a modern slant but maintaining a strong link with tradition. The range of wines offered for tasting this year features a long list of labels, each of which includes a basic wine flanked by several selections, Barolo being a case in point. All of these products are interesting and some of the selections are very good indeed, easily winning places in our Three Glass finals. Our pick of the 2003 Barolos are the Vigne di Proprietà in Barolo, obtained from a blend of the best fruit in the municipality aged in barriques and put together in a modern style, and the Cannubi, a traditionally elegant DOCG vineyard. The Sarmassa 2003, another historic cru, is excellent, and the basic Coste di Rose is pleasant. The Riserva Grande Annata del Barolo 2001 gave a very interesting performance, exploiting its vintage in full. The rest of the range is very decent and we take our hats off to the barrique-aged Barbera Paiagal 2005 and Dolcetto Madonna di Como 2006.

● Barolo Brunate '03	♟♟♟	8
● Barolo La Serra '03	♟♟	7
● Dolcetto d'Alba Boschi di Berri '06	♟♟	4*
● Barbera d'Alba Ciabot Camerano '05	♟♟	4
● Langhe Nebbiolo Lasarin '06	♟♟	4
● Langhe Rosso '04	♟♟	5
● Dolcetto d'Alba Fontanazza '06	♟	4
O Moscato d'Asti '06	♟	4
O Roero Arneis '06	♟	4
● Barolo Brunate '01	♟♟♟	7
● Barolo Brunate Ris. '85	♟♟♟	7
● Dolcetto d'Alba Boschi di Berri '96	♟♟♟	5
● Barolo Brunate '99	♟♟♟	7
● Barolo Brunate '96	♟♟♟	7
● Barolo La Serra '03	♟♟	7

● Barolo Cannubi '03	♟♟	7
● Barolo Sarmassa '03	♟♟	7
● Barolo Vign. di Proprietà in Barolo '03	♟♟	8
● Barolo Riserva Grande Annata '01	♟♟	8
● Barbaresco Riserva Grande Annata '01	♟♟	8
● Barbaresco Creja '04	♟♟	6
● Dolcetto d'Alba Madonna di Como '06	♟♟	4*
● Barolo Coste di Rose '03	♟♟	6
● Barbera d'Alba Paiagal '05	♟♟	5
O Moscato d'Asti Zagara '06	♟♟	4
● Barbera d'Alba Ruvei '05	♟	4
● Nebbiolo d'Alba Michet '05	♟	4
O Roero Arneis '06	♟	4
O Gavi del Comune di Gavi '06	♟	4
● Barolo Riserva Grande Annata '99	♟♟♟	8

Marchesi Incisa della Rocchetta
VIA ROMA, 66
14030 ROCCHETTA TANARO [AT]
TEL. 0141644647
www.lacortechiusa.it

ANNUAL PRODUCTION 50,000 bottles
HECTARES UNDER VINE 17
VITICULTURE METHOD Conventional

Quality continues to grow at this historic estate in Rocchetta Tanaro. It is expertly run by Barbara Incisa della Rocchetta with the support of her son, Filiberto Massone, and consultant Donato Lanati. Next year will see the release of another Monferrato. We don't know its name as yet but we do know that it has lofty aspirations and that it will be based on a blend of merlot, pinot nero and barbera. Turning to the labels we tasted this year, there was an outstanding performance from the Barbera Sant'Emiliano, which earned it a place on our final tasting table. Concentrated aromas of ripe fruit such as sour cherries and currants meld perfectly with nuances of cocoa powder, tobacco leaf and thyme. Entry on the palate is full and fruity thanks to rich, robust structure. The Barbera Valmorena has magnificent supporting acidity that makes it very fresh and it also offers excellent value for money. The Rollone from barbera and pinot nero shows well, as does the splendid, stunningly spicy Grignolino, which took home Two Glasses. The Marchese Leopoldo was a bit under par but enjoyable nonetheless.

Marenco
P.ZZA VITTORIO EMANUELE, 10
15019 STREVI [AL]
TEL. 0144363133
www.marencovini.com

ANNUAL PRODUCTION 300,000 bottles
HECTARES UNDER VINE 90
VITICULTURE METHOD Conventional

The wines presented by the Marenco family are a true expression of the Strevi terroir. On their 65 hectares the Marencos cultivate the territory's most classic varieties with few concessions to the international palate. The overall level of the labels offered for tasting for this year's edition of the Guide was good. The Barbera d'Asti Bassina's very brilliant, concentrated ruby red announces quite generous, lingering aromas and a big, soft palate whose acidity goes a long way towards lightening the body. The Dolcetto d'Acqui Marchesa also showed well. Notes of red berry fruit, aromatic herbs and sweet spices merge with a taut, juicy, leisurely palate. Moving on to the aromatic wines, the Moscato Scrapona offers varietal hints of yellow-fleshed and citrus fruit. The other wines are more predictable. The Brachetto Pineto displays notes of rose and spice, the Chardonnay Gallet is candid and well styled, and the Carialoso comes vinification of a rare indigenous variety known as caricalasino.

● Barbera d'Asti Sup. Sant'Emiliano '04	?? 5	
● Barbera d'Asti Valmorena '05	?? 4*	
● Grignolino d'Asti '06	?? 4*	
● Monferrato Rosso Rollone '05	?? 4*	
● Monferrato Rosso Marchese Leopoldo '04	? 5	
● Barbera d'Asti Sup. Sant'Emiliano '03	?? 5	
● Barbera d'Asti Sup. Sant'Emiliano '00	?? 5	
● Monferrato Rosso Marchese Leopoldo '03	?? 5	
● Monferrato Rosso Marchese Leopoldo '01	?? 5	

● Barbera d'Asti Bassina '05	?? 4	
● Barbera d'Asti Ciresa '04	?? 6	
O Moscato d'Asti Scrapona '06	?? 4	
O Piemonte Chardonnay Gallet '06	? 4	
O Carialoso '06	? 4	
● Brachetto d'Acqui Pineto '06	? 5	
● Dolcetto d'Acqui Marchesa '06	? 4	
● Barbera d'Asti Ciresa '03	?? 6	
O MuMa '05	?? 4	

Mario Marengo
VIA XX SETTEMBRE, 34
12064 LA MORRA [CN]
TEL. 017350127
marco1964@libero.it

ANNUAL PRODUCTION 18,000 bottles
HECTARES UNDER VINE 3.5
VITICULTURE METHOD   Conventional

Thanks to support from his wife, Eugenia, Marco Marengo runs this lovely estate in La Morra with enormous enthusiasm and a firm hand. His rows are in some of the territory's best vineyards, such as Brunate and Bricco Viole. Marco has plans – at long last! – to build a cellar that will facilitate his work considerably but in the meantime he doesn't seem to have much difficulty with logistics. This year he gave us two very well-made Barolos from 2003, a year that was anything but easy. The Brunate is very successful. Obtained from vines more than 60 years old, it has elegant flowery notes, powerful structure sustained by nice freshness and tannins without a trace of bitterness, flaunting generous aromas on the palate. The Bricco Viole is altogether different but every bit as interesting, presenting balsamic and fruity with juicy tannins. The Nebbiolo d'Alba Valmaggiore from Roero is up to its usual standards, showing good balance and lovely liveliness. Rich in fruity sensations, powerful and still very young, the 2006 Dolcetto is the product of a year that was particularly kind to this variety.

Claudio Mariotto
LOC. VHO
S.DA PER SAREZZANO, 29
15057 TORTONA [AL]
TEL. 0131868500
www.claudiomariotto.it

ANNUAL PRODUCTION 90,000 bottles
HECTARES UNDER VINE 26
VITICULTURE METHOD   Conventional

After the richly deserved result obtained by an outstanding version of Pitasso, Claudio Mariotto did not disappoint us this year. He was back to collect a second Three Glass trophy for an absolutely superb Timorasso 2005 with an exquisitely elegant nose, extraordinary minerality, a big yet refined palate and a never-ending finish. A winner all the way. The second-label Timorasso, Derthona, has little to envy its elder sibling and also won a place at our final tasting table. The Cortese Profilo gave an excellent performance to take a well-earned Two Glasses and the perky Coccalina, another white, also made a good impression. The big event of the year on the red front was the return of Poggio del Rosso to reclaim its rightful position among the ranks of the great Barberas. Last year, a challenging harvest forced it to cede its crown as king of the house reds to Vho, which also showed well in this edition of the Guide. The stainless steel-aged Barbera Territorio is always interesting and the Campo del Gatto from nibiò, a local subvariety of dolcetto, is very successful on its second release. For those who prefer their reds semi-sparkling, the fresh, easy-drinking Martirella is an ideal choice.

● Barolo Brunate '03	🍷🍷	7
● Barolo Bricco Viole '03	🍷🍷	8
● Dolcetto d'Alba '06	🍷🍷	4*
● Nebbiolo d'Alba Valmaggiore '05	🍷🍷	4*
● Barolo Brunate '99	🍷🍷	7
● Barolo Brunate '00	🍷🍷	7
● Barolo Brunate '01	🍷🍷	7
● Barolo Bricco Viole '01	🍷🍷	8
● Barolo Bricco Viole '98	🍷🍷	8
● Nebbiolo d'Alba Valmaggiore '04	🍷🍷	4
● Nebbiolo d'Alba Valmaggiore '03	🍷🍷	4

○ Colli Tortonesi Bianco		
Pitasso '05	🍷🍷🍷	5
○ Colli Tortonesi Bianco		
Derthona '05	🍷🍷	5
● Colli Tortonesi Rosso		
Poggio del Rosso '04	🍷🍷	6
○ Colli Tortonesi Bianco Profilo '06	🍷🍷	4*
● Colli Tortonesi Rosso		
Campo del Gatto '06	🍷🍷	4*
● Colli Tortonesi Rosso Vho '05	🍷🍷	5
● Colli Tortonesi Rosso		
Martirella '06	🍷	4
● Colli Tortonesi Rosso Territorio '06	🍷	4
○ Colli Tortonesi Bianco		
Coccalina '06	🍷	4
○ Colli Tortonesi Bianco		
Pitasso '04	🍷🍷🍷	5

Marsaglia

VIA MADAMA MUSSONE, 2
12050 CASTELLINALDO [CN]
TEL. 0173213048
www.cantinamarsaglia.it

ANNUAL PRODUCTION 70,000 bottles
HECTARES UNDER VINE 15
VITICULTURE METHOD Conventional

Marina Marsaglia's range of wines again proved very good. Marina runs this estate in the territory of Roero with the support of her husband, Emilio, her two children, Monica and Enrico, and oenologist Gianfranco Cordero. The estate's production is vast. Despite its extreme youth, Barbera San Cristoforo exhibits good body and acidity but the Castellinaldo Barbera d'Alba 2004 is an altogether superior affair. Its long sojourn in barriques ensures that the body is very smooth but not overwhelmed by its oak. On the contrary, the oak adds strength and irons out any hint of coarseness to produce a silky, well-rounded, enjoyable wine. The Nebbiolo 2005 is soft and leisurely and the Roero Brich d'America is enhanced by extended maturing and sensations of rain-soaked earth, dried figs, leather and liquorice. As for the two Arneis, the Serramiana is flowery and mineral in tone while the San Servasio is fresh and fruity. Arsicà is a sweet wine obtained exclusively from arneis grapes left on the vine until well into the autumn.

Franco M. Martinetti

VIA SAN FRANCESCO DA PAOLA, 18
10123 TORINO [TO]
TEL. 0118395937
info@francomartinetti.it

ANNUAL PRODUCTION 140,000 bottles
HECTARES UNDER VINE 4.5
VITICULTURE METHOD Conventional

The wines presented by Franco Martinetti and his sons Guido and Michele offer an overview of Piedmont's production. In fact, it's a summary of almost all the sub-Alpine types with the main indigenous varieties of the region well represented. As happened in last year's edition of the Guide, an impressive number of Martinetti labels reached the finals. The Barolo Marasco 2003 overcomes the difficulties of its torrid growing year to unveil great structure and power. It's well rounded and its aromas recall violet and ripe cherry. The two Asti reds, Montruc and Sul Bric, impressed our tasting panel with their rounded profile and appeal, their fruity, vanillaed tones merging superbly and in perfect harmony. The whites also put on an outstanding performance, not least the Minaia with its nose of tropical fruit, grapefruit and pineapple. The Martin is more austere and deep but not intrusive oaky note. We liked the Quarantatre, a headily full spumante. The Georgette is very unusual, giving very intense fruity nuances on the nose.

● Nebbiolo d'Alba San Pietro '05	🍷🍷	4
● Castellinaldo Barbera d'Alba '04	🍷🍷	5
● Roero Sup. Brich d'America '04	🍷🍷	5
O Roero Arneis Serramiana '06	🍷🍷	4*
O Arsicà	🍷	5
O Langhe Arneis San Servasio '06	🍷	4
● Barbera d'Alba S. Cristoforo '06	🍷	4
● Castellinaldo Barbera d'Alba '00	🍷🍷	5
● Roero Sup. Brich d'America '03	🍷🍷	5
● Roero Sup. Brich d'America '02	🍷🍷	5
● Roero Sup. Brich d'America '01	🍷🍷	5
● Castellinaldo Barbera d'Alba '01	🍷🍷	5
● Castellinaldo Barbera d'Alba '03	🍷🍷	5

● Barbera d'Asti Sup. Montruc '05	🍷🍷	6
O Colli Tortonesi Bianco Martin '05	🍷🍷	7
● Monferrato Rosso Sul Bric '05	🍷🍷	6
● Barolo Marasco '03	🍷🍷	8
● Barbera d'Asti Bric dei Banditi '06	🍷🍷	4
● Colli Tortonesi Rosso Lauren '05	🍷🍷	6
O Gavi Minaia '06	🍷🍷	6
O Brut M. Cl. Quarantatre '03	🍷🍷	6
● Colli Tortonesi Rosso Georgette '05	🍷	6
● Barolo Marasco '00	🍷🍷🍷	8
● Barolo Marasco '01	🍷🍷🍷	8
● Barbera d'Asti Sup. Montruc '01	🍷🍷🍷	6
● Barbera d'Asti Sup. Montruc '97	🍷🍷🍷	6
● Barbera d'Asti Sup. Montruc '96	🍷🍷🍷	6
● Monferrato Rosso Sul Bric '00	🍷🍷	6
● Monferrato Rosso Sul Bric '03	🍷🍷	6

Martini & Rossi

LOC. PESSIONE
P.ZZA LUIGI ROSSI, 2
10123 CHIERI [TO]
TEL. 0118108465
www.mymartini.it

ANNUAL PRODUCTION	N.A.
HECTARES UNDER VINE	N.A.
VITICULTURE METHOD	Conventional

In recent years, this big Turin group, owned by Bacardi, has concentrated on redefining Asti Spumante. The headquarters are at Chieri, where all the alcoholic beverages are made, including the famed Martini Vermouth. However, vinification of this unique sweet wine takes place at the production centre in Santo Stefano Belbo, where from mid August the grapes start to pour in from thousands of growers who have always sold their fruit to Martini. Thanks to a major investment in advertising, and the quality of the product itself, Asti is undergoing a renaissance and sales are rocketing. Several millions of bottles of Martini & Rossi's easy-drinking, moderately sweet Spumante are released. The company is also investing in standard cork Moscato d'Asti with promising results. On the dry front, the Oltrepò Pavese Riesling is always a sure bet and the Alta Langa Riserva Montelera Millesimato from pinot nero and chardonnay is beginning to find its own style. The other Brut, the Talento Riserva Montelera obtained from pinot nero and pinot bianco, is not as complex or assertive. We'll round off with an agreeable Prosecco, again from the Sigillo Blu line.

Bartolo Mascarello

VIA ROMA, 15
12060 BAROLO [CN]
TEL. 017356125

ANNUAL PRODUCTION	30,000 bottles
HECTARES UNDER VINE	5
VITICULTURE METHOD	Conventional

Like father, like daughter. Maria Teresa continues to adhere to her famous father's winemaking methods and philosophy. The decisions she makes are life choices and do not just involve the estate. The only way to produce wines that wholly embody a territory is to combine agriculture driven by common sense with close attention to the timing in the vineyard. And this is the spirit in which the Barolo, the Barbera, the Dolcetto and a small amount of Freisa are managed and handled here so that they express their full potential in the great Langhe tradition. The growing year was hot but the 2003 Barolo is back in an interpretation that reflects all the characteristics of the vintage without sacrificing its own personality. Delicacy and elegance are, as ever, the order of the day. Less flowery than usual, the nose offers tangy minerality and a hint of tar that melds with the measured tannins on a palate sustained by generous acidity. The acid tang lingers to enliven a liquorice and cinchona finish. The Barbera Molto is very austere and the Dolcetto is fragrant and tannic.

O Alta Langa Ris. Montelera Brut	
Sigillo Blu '03	♀♀ 6
O Talento Riserva	
Montelera Brut M. Cl.	♀ 5
O Asti Martini	♀ 4
O Moscato d'Asti Sigillo Blu '06	♀ 4
O OP Riesling Brut Sigillo Blu	♀ 4
O Prosecco di Valdobbiadene	
Brut Sigillo Blu	♀ 4
O Alta Langa Ris. Montelera Brut	
Sigillo Blu '02	♀♀ 5

● Barolo '03	♀♀ 8
● Barbera d'Alba	
Vign. S. Lorenzo '05	♀♀ 5
● Dolcetto d'Alba	
Monrobiolo e Ruvè '06	♀♀ 4*
● Langhe Freisa '05	♀♀ 4*
● Barolo '01	♀♀♀ 8
● Barolo '99	♀♀♀ 8
● Barolo '98	♀♀♀ 8
● Barolo '84	♀♀♀ 8
● Barolo '85	♀♀♀ 8
● Barolo '83	♀♀♀ 8
● Barolo '89	♀♀♀ 8
● Barolo '00	♀♀ 8
● Barolo '97	♀♀ 8
● Barolo '96	♀♀ 8

Giuseppe Mascarello e Figlio

S.DA DEL GROSSO, 1
12060 MONCHIERO [CN]
TEL. 0173792126
www.mascarello1881.com

ANNUAL PRODUCTION 45,000 bottles
HECTARES UNDER VINE 12
VITICULTURE METHOD Conventional

It is always a pleasure to visit this historic estate and linger a while listening to the great Mauro Mascarello wax eloquent on the legendary Barolo Pugnane 1971 obtained from the rosé clone, or the Rionda 1979 that was not vinified that year owing to its lack of colour and saw its grapes go to make the Monprivato and the Villero. "No matter how much you think you know about nebbiolo", he says, "it still manages to surprise you...it's a magnificent variety that always has something else to give". Here speaks a man who has weathered many harvests, yet every time he crushes his nebbiolo, he feels a rush of emotion that inspires him to create absolutely superb wines. This year, we were unable to taste the 2003 Barolos, as they fell victim to the hail and drought of a fraught year. However, we were greatly impressed by the Barbera Codana 2004 from a plot on the Monprivato section. Warm and enveloping, full and concentrated, it plays down extract and foregrounds richness of flavour and a velvety texture. The big, earthy Dolcetto Bricco 2005 also showed very well, offering crisp aromas of fruit and a very characterful palate. The Barbera and the Dolcetto Santo Stefano di Perno are more linear.

Tenuta La Meridiana

VIA TANA BASSA, 5
14048 MONTEGROSSO D'ASTI [AT]
TEL. 0141956172
tenutalameridiana@tin.it

ANNUAL PRODUCTION 85,000 bottles
HECTARES UNDER VINE 12
VITICULTURE METHOD Conventional

There's nothing major to report from the house of Giampiero Bianco, one of the most skilled interpreters of Barbera. Giampiero has spoiled us, in the sense that his wines all have a uniform style based on grapes of extremely high quality and discreet use of oak. All that and they're very reasonably priced, too. As we have seen in past editions of the Guide, the wine that collected most plaudits from our judges was Barbera Tra La Terra e Il Cielo. Deep and impenetrable, it offers generous aromas of ripe fruit and sweet spices in which nuances of vanilla, cinchona and black pepper emerge. Entry on the palate is sweet and fulfilling and the finish is juicy. Although it is considered a standard wine, the Barbera Le Gagie is very pleasant indeed with bountiful fruitiness and tempting tanginess. Monferrato Rivaia from nebbiolo, cabernet and barbera is a bit disappointing, tending to yield to the international variety. The Barbera Bricco Sereno, the Vitis and the Passito Sol all give their usual interesting performances. We gave One Glass apiece to Puntet, obtained from chardonnay, cortese and favorita, and La Malaga.

Wine	Rating
● Barbera d'Alba Sup. Codana '04	♟♟ 7
● Dolcetto d'Alba Bricco '05	♟♟ 4*
● Langhe Nebbiolo '04	♟♟ 6
● Barbera d'Alba S. Stefano di Perno '04	♟ 6
● Dolcetto d'Alba S. Stefano di Perno '05	♟ 4
● Barolo Monprivato '01	♟♟♟ 8
● Barolo Monprivato '85	♟♟♟ 8
● Barolo Villero '96	♟♟♟ 8
● Barolo S. Stefano di Perno '98	♟♟♟ 8
● Barolo Monprivato '00	♟♟ 8
● Barolo Monprivato '98	♟♟ 8
● Barolo Villero '01	♟♟ 8
● Barolo S. Stefano di Perno '00	♟♟ 8
● Barolo Monprivato Cà d' Morissio Ris. '97	♟♟ 8

Wine	Rating
● Barbera d'Asti Sup. Nizza Tra La Terra e Il Cielo '04	♟♟ 5
● Barbera d'Asti Sup. Bricco Sereno '05	♟♟ 4*
O Passito Sol '04	♟♟ 6
● Barbera d'Asti Vitis '05	♟♟ 3*
● Barbera d'Asti Le Gagie '05	♟♟ 4*
● La Malaga '06	♟ 4
O Monferrato Bianco Puntet '06	♟ 4
● Monferrato Rosso Rivaia '05	♟ 5
● Monferrato Rosso Rivaia '01	♟♟ 5
● Barbera d'Asti Sup. Tra La Terra e Il Cielo '00	♟♟ 5
● Barbera d'Asti Sup. Nizza Tra La Terra e Il Cielo '03	♟♟ 5
● Monferrato Rosso Rivaia '03	♟♟ 5
● La Malaga '05	♟♟ 4

Moccagatta
S.DA RABAJÀ, 46
12050 BARBARESCO [CN]
TEL. 0173635228

F.lli Molino
LOC. AUSARIO
VIA AUSARIO, 5
12050 TREISO [CN]
TEL. 0173638384
tommy58@libero.it

ANNUAL PRODUCTION 70,000 bottles
HECTARES UNDER VINE 12
VITICULTURE METHOD Conventional

ANNUAL PRODUCTION 70,000 bottles
HECTARES UNDER VINE 12
VITICULTURE METHOD Conventional

A long-standing estate such as the one run by Franco and Sergio Minuto was honour-bound to exploit an excellent year like 2004 to the full. They presented no less than three Barbarescos and we were hard pressed to choose the best. Barbaresco Cole 2004 exhibits superb balance between nose and palate, very elegant character and an almost silky softness that keeps the awesome structure in check. Owing to the partial replanting of the vineyard, a mere 1,100 bottles of the 2004 version are available. The Barbaresco Bric Balin 2004, released in 22,000 bottles, has a concentrated, leisurely nose favouring tertiary aromas and tannins that already show balance in a big yet elegant body. It's a truly outstanding Barbaresco that merits Three Glasses. The Barbaresco Basarin 2004 is not far behind, although it is currently more defined on the palate than the nose. As for the other reds, the 2006 Dolcetto d'Alba is one of the best in its category, showing juicy, clean and harmonious, despite its high alcohol content. Finally, Chardonnay Buschet 2005 lags behind in terms of the balance of its marked oakiness and excessive fruit while the standard Chardonnay 2006 has clear florality and a full, leisurely palate.

The Molino family originally hails from the Asti area and has always had a passionate interest in viticulture and wine. The family nursed a wine dream for years, finally turning it into reality at this beautiful estate in Treiso, which they founded in 1990. Tommaso, Franco and Dario have made rapid progress since then, steadily improving the quality of their wines and stamping them with a distinctive style. This growth has earned them a well-deserved full profile for the impressive level of all the wines we tasted this year. Aged in barriques and large barrels, Barbaresco Teorema displays sound fruit and a faintly spicy nose. The tannins are well-rounded and the palate is very pleasant overall. The Barbaresco Ausario is more austere and shows spicy nuances with undertones of violet, red berry fruit and leather. It's a little rough at the edges but hints at greater things to come. We very much liked the exceptionally harmonious Dolcetto Ausario, in which intense black cherry-led aromas are sustained by remarkable freshness before the finish, buttressed by elegant tannins, makes a stylish farewell.

● Barbaresco Bric Balin '04	♟♟♟	7
● Barbaresco Cole '04	♟♟	7
● Barbaresco Basarin '04	♟♟	7
● Dolcetto d'Alba '06	♟♟	4*
O Langhe Chardonnay Buschet '05	♟♟	5
O Langhe Chardonnay '06	♟♟	4*
● Barbera d'Alba '06	♟	4
● Langhe Nebbiolo '06	♟	5
● Barbaresco Bric Balin '01	♟♟♟	8
● Barbaresco Bric Balin '90	♟♟♟	8
● Barbaresco Cole '97	♟♟♟	8
● Barbaresco Cole '00	♟♟	8
● Barbaresco Cole '01	♟♟	8
● Barbaresco Bric Balin '03	♟♟	8
● Barbaresco Bric Balin '00	♟♟	8
● Barbaresco Bric Balin '99	♟♟	7
● Barbaresco Basarin '00	♟♟	8
● Barbaresco Basarin '01	♟♟	7

● Barbaresco Ausario '04	♟♟	6
● Barbaresco Teorema '04	♟♟	6
● Dolcetto d'Alba Ausario '06	♟♟	4*
● Dolcetto d'Alba Le Quercie '06	♟	3

Mauro Molino

FRAZ. ANNUNZIATA
B.TA GANCIA, 111
12064 LA MORRA [CN]
TEL. 017350814
www.mauromolino.it

ANNUAL PRODUCTION 50,000 bottles
HECTARES UNDER VINE 10
VITICULTURE METHOD Conventional

The first new development to report this year is the current expansion of the cellar, a project in which Mauro Molino is flanked by the enthusiastic Matteo. Starting with the 2007 harvest, this restructuring will facilitate production of the Molinos' classic Langhe wines, which get better with each passing year. We arrived on a bright sunny day in July and let our gaze feast on the emerald vineyards of Annunziata and the village of Gancia. Our tastings confirm that this well-established La Morra estate knows how to interpret a challenging year for Nebbiolos like 2003 in masterly fashion. The three Barolos are spectacular. We start with the house's blue-blooded thoroughbred, Gallinotto. We awarded Three resounding Glasses for its very elegant nose and stylish, fresh-tasting palate. The Vigna Gancia is flowery, subtle and rather deep while the Conca is solid, powerful and full with a lovely sweet finish. The rest of the range is very respectable. Despite its extreme youth the Dolcetto is impeccable and extraordinarily clean, the Barbera and Nebbiolo are lively and well defined, and the firmly structured, fruity Barbera Vigna Gattere is supported by invigorating complexity and acidity.

Monchiero Carbone

VIA SANTO STEFANO ROERO, 2
12043 CANALE [CN]
TEL. 017395568
www.monchierocarbone.com

ANNUAL PRODUCTION 90,000 bottles
HECTARES UNDER VINE 11
VITICULTURE METHOD Conventional

We had a long conversation about wine with Francesco Monchiero, who approaches the subject with calm and rigour. The words of this young Roero producer revealed a clear vision of the territory and of the choices – so far, not easy – that Francesco has had to make as a grower-producer. He is a staunch believer in the potential of Arneis, a white wine obtained from a local variety that is currently enjoying a certain success on the market. For this very reason, effort is needed to maintain its qualitative standards. Here, Monchiero Carbone translates thought into action. If the Re Cit is already fruity, fresh and agreeably acid, the Cecu d'la Biunda selection is complex, deep in its aromas, sustained on the palate, long and harmonious in the finish. Without a doubt, this is one of the best Arneis to come out of 2006. Unfortunately, we haven't left much space for the reds, which is a shame. The cellar presents three outstanding wines, with the two splendid Roero Nebbiolos just ahead of the Barbera. Printi 2004 is the star of the show and earned another Three Glasses for its fantastic character, measured notes of oak and elegance.

● Barolo V. Gallinotto '03	♟♟♟ 8
● Barbera d'Alba V. Gattere '05	♟♟ 6
● Barolo V. Conca '03	♟♟ 8
● Barolo V. Gancia '03	♟♟ 8
● Barbera d'Alba '06	♟♟ 4*
● Dolcetto d'Alba '06	♟♟ 4*
● Langhe Nebbiolo '06	♟♟ 4*
● Barbera d'Alba V. Gattere '96	♟♟♟ 6
● Barbera d'Alba V. Gattere '97	♟♟♟ 6
● Barbera d'Alba V. Gattere '00	♟♟♟ 6
● Barolo V. Gallinotto '01	♟♟♟ 8
● Barolo V. Conca '96	♟♟♟ 8
● Barolo V. Conca '97	♟♟♟ 8
● Barolo V. Conca '00	♟♟♟ 8
● Barolo V. Conca '01	♟♟ 8
● Barolo V. Gancia '01	♟♟ 7

● Roero Printi '04	♟♟♟ 6
● Roero Srü '05	♟♟ 5
O Roero Arneis Cecu d'la Biunda '06	♟♟ 4*
O Langhe Bianco Tamardì '05	♟♟ 4*
O Roero Arneis Re Cit '06	♟♟ 4*
O Piemonte Moscato Passito Sorì di Ruchin '05	♟♟ 5
● Barbera d'Alba MonBirone '05	♟♟ 5
● Roero Printi '00	♟♟♟ 6
● Roero Printi '99	♟♟♟ 6
● Roero Printi '01	♟♟ 6
● Roero Printi '02	♟♟ 6
● Roero Printi '03	♟♟ 6
● Roero Srü '04	♟♟ 5

Monfalletto
Cordero di Montezemolo
FRAZ. ANNUNZIATA, 67
12064 LA MORRA [CN]
TEL. 017350344
www.corderodimontezemolo.com

ANNUAL PRODUCTION	180,000 bottles
HECTARES UNDER VINE	33
VITICULTURE METHOD	Conventional

The news here is that Enrico has sold his land to Elena and Alberto, his brother Gianni's children. This puts the cellar and the vineyards into the hands of one family that will carry on the important historic legacy left by Paolo Cordero di Montezemolo. The ancestral home enjoys a stunning view of the Monfalletto vineyard, dominated by the ancient cedar of Lebanon that is the symbol of the municipality of La Morra. Two of the estate's Barolos appeared in our finals. The Enrico VI bowled us over with its very aristocratic sensations mingling notes of vanilla with hints of pepper, chocolate and ripe red berry fruit. The elegant, well-rounded palate displays tannins that are sweet but never overwhelm. Considering the vintage, this wine is a triumph and we gave it Three very prestigious Glasses. Despite the year, the Bricco Gattera is fresh-tasting, leisurely, juicy and restrainedly fruity. Not quite up to these dizzy standards but still very agreeable are the Barolo Monfalletto with its notes of tobacco, liquorice and cherry, the fruity Barbera d'Alba Funtanì, with its measured notes of oak, and the Langhe Elioro from chardonnay. The Dolcetto d'Alba, Langhe Arneis and Nebbiolo round off this impressive range.

Montaribaldi
FRAZ. TRE STELLE
S.DA NICOLINI ALTO, 12
12050 BARBARESCO [CN]
TEL. 0173638220
www.ilturismo.com/montaribaldi.htm

ANNUAL PRODUCTION	60,000 bottles
HECTARES UNDER VINE	19
VITICULTURE METHOD	Conventional

This solid family estate sees Luciano and Roberto doing a fine job under the guiding hand of their father, Giuseppe, with support from their wives. Montaribaldi's grapes come from some of Langhe's – and Italy's – best zones. As we wait for the new Barbaresco Riserva, this year the well-established Barbaresco Sörì Montaribaldi 2004 shared its crown as best estate wine with Barbera d'Alba dü Gir 2005. The Barbaresco reveals lovely tertiary notes of rhubarb and coffee and perfect tannicity on the palate whereas the Barbera has impressive body and structure as well as great balance thanks to its well-gauged freshness. The two selections also performed well. Barbaresco Palazzina from Neive is clean and still youthfully floral while the Barolo Borzoni from Grinzane currently gives more harmonious fruit on the palate. The range of basic reds is, as usual, very decent. Barbera d'Asti La Consolina 2006 in particular is impeccably clean and fresh. Among the whites, Roero Arneis Capural 2006 stands out for citrus-edged freshness and an agreeable palate.

● Barolo Enrico VI '03	♥♥♥ 8
● Barolo V. Bricco Gattera '03	♥♥ 8
● Barolo Monfalletto '03	♥♥ 6
● Barbera d'Alba Sup. Funtanì '05	♥♥ 6
○ Langhe Chardonnay Elioro '05	♥♥ 5
● Dolcetto d'Alba '06	♥ 4
● Langhe Nebbiolo '06	♥ 5
○ Langhe Arneis '06	♥ 4
● Barolo V. Bricco Gattera '99	♥♥♥ 8
● Barolo V. Enrico VI '96	♥♥♥ 8
● Barolo V. Enrico VI '97	♥♥♥ 8
● Barolo V. Enrico VI '00	♥♥♥ 8
● Barolo V. Enrico VI '01	♥♥ 8
● Barolo V. Bricco Gattera '00	♥♥ 8
● Barolo V. Bricco Gattera '01	♥♥ 8
● Barolo Monfalletto '01	♥♥ 6

● Barbaresco Sörì Montaribaldi '04	♥♥ 6
● Barbera d'Alba dü Gir '05	♥♥ 5
● Barbaresco Palazzina '04	♥♥ 5
● Barbera d'Asti La Consolina '06	♥♥ 3*
● Barolo Borzoni '03	♥♥ 7
● Dolcetto d'Alba Nicolini '06	♥♥ 4*
○ Roero Arneis Capural '06	♥♥ 4*
○ Langhe Chardonnay Stissa d'le Favole '06	♥ 4
○ Moscato d'Asti '06	♥ 4
● Dolcetto d'Alba Vagnona '06	♥ 3
● Langhe Nebbiolo Gambarin '05	♥ 4
● Barbaresco Sörì Montaribaldi '00	♥♥ 6
● Barbaresco Sörì Montaribaldi '03	♥♥ 6
● Barbaresco Sörì Montaribaldi '01	♥♥ 6

Monti

FRAZ. CAMIA
LOC. SAN SEBASTIANO, 39
12065 MONFORTE D'ALBA [CN]
TEL. 017378391
www.paolomonti.com

ANNUAL PRODUCTION 50,000 bottles
HECTARES UNDER VINE 11
VITICULTURE METHOD Conventional

Established in 1996, Paolo Monti's is a fairly young estate and this may be why its owner has departed from Langhe tradition. This year, the wines are notable both for their excellence and the choice of images for their labels, which bear portraits of women by one of the world's greatest contemporary photographers, Norwegian Tom Sandberg. We'll start our review with the Barolo Bussia which, as in previous years, is top of the list thanks to aromas of dried flowers, cinchona, red berry fruit and cocoa powder. The palate exhibits powerful tannins that have to make up for the odd note of roughness but it is very leisurely and has impressive length on nose and palate. It may be the basic version but the other Monti Barolo also shows well with nuances of cherry and strawberry jam that meld to perfection with hints of pepper and vanilla. The Langhe Rosso Dossi Rossi from pure merlot has a concentrated nose full of ripe black berry fruit and cocoa powder aromas. The palate is lively and extremely pleasant with an agreeable finish, proving that there is a lot more to it than just muscle. The easy-drinking Barbera and the Langhe Bianco, a chardonnay and riesling blend, are both good.

● Langhe Rosso Dossi Rossi '04	🍷🍷	6
● Barolo '03	🍷🍷	7
● Barolo Bussia '03	🍷🍷	8
● Barbera d'Alba '05	🍷🍷	6
○ Langhe Bianco L'Aura '06	🍷🍷	6
● Barolo Bussia '99	ΥΥ	8
● Barolo Bussia '00	ΥΥ	8
● Barolo Bussia '01	ΥΥ	8
● Barbera d'Alba '03	ΥΥ	5
● Barbera d'Alba '04	ΥΥ	5
● Langhe Rosso Dossi Rossi '03	ΥΥ	6
● Langhe Rosso Dossi Rossi '01	ΥΥ	6
○ Langhe Bianco L'Aura '05	ΥΥ	6

La Morandina

LOC. MORANDINI, 11
12053 CASTIGLIONE TINELLA [CN]
TEL. 0141855261
www.lamorandina.com

ANNUAL PRODUCTION 100,000 bottles
HECTARES UNDER VINE 25
VITICULTURE METHOD Conventional

The Morando family estate has almost 300 years of history behind it. It is utterly lovely, well kept and organized, and turns out an impressive number of bottles for a family-run affair. The property consists of 25 hectares planted to moscato, barbera and chardonnay plus a plot of nebbiolo at Neive that produces the Barbaresco. Giulio and Paolo put meticulous work into the vineyard and cellar and their wines are excellent. We'll start our notes with the Barbera d'Astis. For this edition of the Guide, the Morandos offered us two standard labels, Cinque Vigne and Zucchetto, and a powerful, solidly built Varmat 2005 that surpasses the others for elegance. The year 2004 is very well reflected in the Barbaresco Bricco Spessa, a balanced, harmonious wine with good ageing potential. The Moscato d'Asti and the celebrated Costa del Sole Passito 2004 obtained from moscato and riesling grapes left to part-dry on the vine are both on their usual spanking form. From syrah, nebbiolo and barbera, the 2004 L'Insieme is powerful and concentrated.

● Barbera d'Asti Varmat '05	🍷🍷	5
○ Moscato d'Asti '06	🍷🍷	4*
○ Costa del Sole Passito '04	🍷🍷	5
○ Langhe Chardonnay '06	🍷🍷	4
● Barbaresco Bricco Spessa '04	🍷🍷	7
● Barbera d'Asti Cinque Vigne '06	🍷🍷	4
● Barbera d'Asti Zucchetto '06	🍷🍷	4
● L'Insieme '04	🍷🍷	8
● Barbera d'Asti Varmat '01	ΥΥ	5
● Barbera d'Asti Varmat '03	ΥΥ	5
● Barbera d'Asti Varmat '04	ΥΥ	6
● Barbaresco Bricco Spessa '03	ΥΥ	8
● L'Insieme '01	ΥΥ	8
○ Costa del Sole Passito '03	ΥΥ	6

Cascina Morassino

S.DA BERNINO, 10
12050 BARBARESCO [CN]
TEL. 0173635149

ANNUAL PRODUCTION 20,000 bottles
HECTARES UNDER VINE 3.5
VITICULTURE METHOD Conventional

The small estate run by Roberto Bianco and his father, Mauro, is the perfect example of how first-class results in terms of overall quality and land-rootedness can be obtained from well-sited vineyards and clean vinification of the fruit, without recourse to cutting-edge technology in the cellar. The Biancos' wines all display distinctive character and clearly defined personality. The Barbaresco Ovello 2004 is a magnificent wine with aristocratic breeding, wonderful fullness, mouthfilling tannic bite and marked minerality – and it still has room to grow. More approachable and soft is the Barbaresco Morassino 2004. It's not as complex but offers lovely fruit and flower varietal definition that expands effortlessly. From the rest of the range, we liked the Nebbiolo 2005, which is a sort of minor-league Barbaresco, and the unusual Vigna del Merlo from merlot, which has grip and tannic weight that derive more from the territory than from the variety.

Stefanino Morra

VIA CASTAGNITO, 50
12050 CASTELLINALDO [CN]
TEL. 0173213489
www.morravini.it

ANNUAL PRODUCTION 65,000 bottles
HECTARES UNDER VINE 10
VITICULTURE METHOD Conventional

Stefanino Morra's is one of the most exciting estates in Roero. This year, the Roero Superiore 2005 was missing from the line-up as it is not yet ready and, unfortunately, Barbera Castlè has yet to make its reappearance as the vineyard is being replanted. We did, however, have the pleasure of retasting the splendid 2001 version that just keeps on getting better. The Roero Srai 2004 went straight through to win a place on our final tasting table and it may well be the best Nebbiolo ever to come out of this estate. The crisp, clean nose reveals crystal-clear notes of red berry fruit, tea leaves and aromatic herbs. The palate follows through well, showing tangy, elegant and well balanced with superbly honed tannins. The dark, imposing Barbera Castellinaldo 2004 is a warm, enfolding wine with a marked presence of oak. It's a bottle worth waiting for. The Barbera 2005 is more easy-drinking and juicy, with notably clean fruit. The Arneis are well-made and interesting, especially the basic 2006, which is excellent value for money.

● Barbaresco Ovello '04	♟♟	7
● Barbaresco Morassino '04	♟♟	6
● Langhe Nebbiolo '05	♟♟	5
● Barbera d'Alba Vignot '05	♟♟	5
● Langhe Rosso V. del Merlo '05	♟♟	5
● Dolcetto d'Alba '06	♟	4
● Barbaresco Ovello '03	♟♟	7
● Barbaresco Ovello '02	♟♟	7
● Barbaresco Ovello '01	♟♟	7
● Barbaresco Ovello '00	♟♟	7
● Barbaresco Ovello '99	♟♟	7
● Barbaresco Morassino '03	♟♟	6
● Barbaresco Morassino '01	♟♟	6
● Barbaresco Morassino '99	♟♟	6

● Roero Srai '04	♟♟	6
● Barbera d'Alba '05	♟♟	4*
● Castellinaldo Barbera d'Alba '04	♟♟	5
○ Roero Arneis '06	♟♟	4*
○ Roero Arneis Vign. S. Pietro '05	♟	4
○ Langhe Favorita '06	♟	4
● Castellinaldo Barbera d'Alba '01	♟♟	5
● Castellinaldo Barbera d'Alba '03	♟♟	5
● Barbera d'Alba Castlè '01	♟♟	5
● Roero Srai '03	♟♟	6
● Roero Srai '01	♟♟	6
● Roero Sup. '04	♟♟	4
● Roero Sup. '03	♟♟	4
● Roero Sup. '01	♟♟	4

F.lli Mossio
VIA MONTÀ, 12
12050 RODELLO [CN]
TEL. 0173617149
www.mossio.com

ANNUAL PRODUCTION 45,000 bottles
HECTARES UNDER VINE 10
VITICULTURE METHOD Conventional

It was only a year ago that Mauro Mossio welcomed us to his beautiful estate: we have warm memories of his friendly smile and hospitality. Mauro was the public face of this family-run cellar with strong country traditions and a well known figure in the wine world. Following his tragic death in an accident at the end of last summer, the family is carrying on the task to which he devoted himself to with such passion and clear-headedness. We wish Valerio, Remo, Claudio and Guido Mossio all the best in this endeavour and are confident that Mauro's spirit will live on in their work. In tribute to this great man, the wines are good, and the Bricco Caramelli and the Piano delli Perdoni Molto are quite lovely. The first is excellent and leads the way for a basic but rigorous range. Quite simply, Bricco Caramelli is the best Dolcetto in its category but we already knew that. The second wine is more elegant and has a fresher fruity, vegetal vein. The Barbera is also very fine, showing acid and solidly built with a long finish. The Nebbiolo is rather austere with impressive backbone and tannins, and the Langhe Rosso is a successful nebbiolo and barbera blend: five labels to lead the estate confidently into a new era.

Mutti
LOC. SAN RUFFINO, 49
15050 SAREZZANO [AL]
TEL. 0131884119

ANNUAL PRODUCTION 55,000 bottles
HECTARES UNDER VINE 15
VITICULTURE METHOD Conventional

The decision to leave San Ruffino to age for an extended period in small barrels has proved to be the right one and this year the Barbera San Ruffino selection is truly outstanding. Powerful and firmly structured, it avoids being muscle-bound. In fact, its key strength lies in its balance. The timorasso-based Castagnoli is first-rate and even though it doesn't have masses of minerality, it still manages to convey fresh, fruity sensations. There's impressive structure and overall it is temptingly drinkable. The estate's other two whites are also spot on. Sauvignon Sull'Aia is notable for its alluring nose and Cortese Noceto for its readiness for the corkscrew. Rivadestra is slightly penalized by vegetal sensations on the nose and didn't quite make the Two Glass mark. The Barbera Boscobarona is less challenging but enjoyable nevertheless and very nicely priced.

● Dolcetto d'Alba Bricco Caramelli '06	♥♥ 4*
● Dolcetto d'Alba Piano delli Perdoni '06	♥♥ 4
● Barbera d'Alba '05	♥♥ 4
● Langhe Nebbiolo '05	♥♥ 5
● Langhe Rosso '05	♥♥ 5
● Dolcetto d'Alba Bricco Caramelli '00	♥♥♥ 4
● Dolcetto d'Alba Bricco Caramelli '05	♥♥ 4
● Dolcetto d'Alba Bricco Caramelli '04	♥♥ 4
● Dolcetto d'Alba Bricco Caramelli '03	♥♥ 4
● Dolcetto d'Alba Bricco Caramelli '02	♥♥ 4

● Colli Tortonesi Rosso S. Ruffino '04	♥♥ 5
○ Colli Tortonesi Bianco Castagnoli '05	♥♥ 5
○ Colli Tortonesi Bianco Sull'Aia '06	♥♥ 4
○ Colli Tortonesi Bianco Noceto '06	♥♥ 3*
● Colli Tortonesi Rosso Boscobarona '06	♥ 3
● Colli Tortonesi Rosso Rivadestra '04	♥ 5
○ Colli Tortonesi Bianco Castagnoli '04	♥♥ 5
● Colli Tortonesi Rosso S. Ruffino '03	♥♥ 5
● Colli Tortonesi Rosso S. Ruffino '01	♥♥ 5

Ada Nada

LOC. ROMBONE
VIA AUSARIO, 12B
12050 TREISO [CN]
TEL. 0173638127
www.adanada.it

ANNUAL PRODUCTION 45,000 bottles
HECTARES UNDER VINE 10
VITICULTURE METHOD Conventional

This very likeable, welcoming family consists of Giancarlo and Ada and their daughters Sara and Annalisa, each with his or her own specific role to play in the vineyard, cellar or agriturismo. The estate's wines are land-rooted, serious and mouthfilling, and come from the vineyards below at Rombone and Valeirano. The very decent Cichin has its origins in the Rombone plots. The 2004 version is still closed, mineral and fruity, with understated tannins and lovely flesh: it promises to develop superbly. The elegant, smooth Valeirano 2004 is more forthright and open with sweet jammy notes while the more challenging Elisa 2003 selection offers very warm, enfolding, almost Mediterranean sensations of dried fruit. The Langhe La Bisbetica 2004, a 50-50 blend of barbera and nebbiolo, also performs very well, full and elegant with sweet, harmonious tannins. We liked the Barbera Salgà 2004. It's slightly salty with rather smoky nuances and a lip-smacking palate. Last but not least comes a very pleasant Dolcetto. The very balanced, well-rounded palate shows just what this often underrated variety is capable of at Treiso.

● Barbaresco Cichin '04	▼▼	7
● Barbaresco Valeirano '04	▼▼	7
● Barbaresco Elisa '03	▼▼	7
● Langhe Rosso La Bisbetica '04	▼▼	6
● Dolcetto d'Alba Autinot '06	▼▼	4
● Barbera d'Alba Salgà '04	▼▼	5
● Barbaresco Cichin '99	▽▽	7
● Barbaresco Cichin '00	▽▽	7
● Barbaresco Cichin '01	▽▽	7
● Barbaresco Cichin '03	▽▽	7
● Barbaresco Elisa '00	▽▽	7
● Barbaresco Valeirano '00	▽▽	7
● Barbaresco Valeirano '01	▽▽	7
● Barbaresco Valeirano '03	▽▽	7

Fiorenzo Nada

LOC. ROMBONE
VIA AUSARIO, 12C
12050 TREISO [CN]
TEL. 0173638254
www.nada.it

ANNUAL PRODUCTION 30,000 bottles
HECTARES UNDER VINE 6.5
VITICULTURE METHOD Conventional

Bruno Nada is passionate about his territory. His enthusiasm comes across in the work he puts in every day. Bruno delves deep into his roots as he creates great wines from the traditional varieties of the zone at his home-cum-cellar nestling among the vineyards of Treiso. The wines are obtained from zones famous for their quality and Bruno manages his vineyards in total harmony with the environment. This is Barbaresco territory and Bruno's Rombone won Three Glasses for its simple complexity, tasty tannins, aromatic notes and the alcohol-rich fruit of the long, classy finish. He did not produce a basic Barbaresco but January will see the release of Barbaresco Vigna Manzola, which will also be available in magnums. The Langhe Seifile is its usual exquisite self. It is obtained from a blend of barbera and nebbiolo that complement each other to create a wine of great overall balance. Two very interesting but less challenging wines complete the range: a dry, flavoursome Barbera and a distinctive Dolcetto whose finish is enhanced by a bitterish hint of almond.

● Barbaresco Rombone '04	▼▼▼	8
● Langhe Rosso Seifile '04	▼▼	8
● Barbera d'Alba '05	▼▼	5
● Dolcetto d'Alba '06	▼▼	4*
● Langhe Rosso Seifile '01	▽▽▽	8
● Langhe Rosso Seifile '96	▽▽▽	8
● Langhe Rosso Seifile '95	▽▽▽	8
● Seifile '93	▽▽▽	8
● Barbaresco Rombone '97	▽▽▽	8
● Barbaresco Rombone '99	▽▽▽	8
● Barbaresco '01	▽▽▽	7
● Langhe Rosso Seifile '03	▽▽	8
● Barbaresco '03	▽▽	7
● Barbaresco Rombone '01	▽▽	8
● Barbaresco Rombone '02	▽▽	8
● Barbaresco Rombone '03	▽▽	8

Cantina dei Produttori Nebbiolo di Carema

VIA NAZIONALE, 32
10010 CAREMA [TO]
TEL. 0125811160
www.saporipiemontesi.it

ANNUAL PRODUCTION 65,000 bottles
HECTARES UNDER VINE N.A.
VITICULTURE METHOD Conventional

The terraces of vines rising up behind Carema form an immense natural amphitheatre that seems to embrace this little Piedmont town on the border with Valle d'Aosta. Wine here speaks of the changing fortunes of the people who live here and their history. The terraces, known as "banche" in the local dialect, are supported by dry stone walls and the earth that fills them was carried up here by shoulder from the valley floor. Stone pathways wind between the tiny plots and properties are highly fragmented and difficult to combine. Indeed, access to some of the vineyards is still only possible via the steep mule tracks. It is no easy task for oenologist-cellarman Manlio Muggianu to coordinate the 45 growers who belong to this cellar but he manages superbly. This year, we were offered two Nebbiolos. Etichetta Nera 2003 already shows good balance but has little complexity on nose and palate. The Riserva 2002 is a more rigorous, flowery wine with soft mineral notes on the nose. The palate shows grip, appealing freshness and confident tannins well tucked in.

Angelo Negro & Figli

FRAZ. SANT'ANNA, 1
12040 MONTEU ROERO [CN]
TEL. 017390252
www.negroangelo.it

ANNUAL PRODUCTION 250,000 bottles
HECTARES UNDER VINE 54
VITICULTURE METHOD Conventional

The estate belonging to the Negro family was faced with a challenge: to live up to the extraordinary results that last year saw their efforts rewarded with a prominent place on the Olympus of Italian wine. We already knew that this was no one-off but actually crowned a long effort to refine the whole range. After tasting this year's offerings, we are even more convinced. The reds are on splendid form: the two Barberas and two Roeros did superbly, the first for their marvellous supporting acidity and the Roeros for a well-handled austerity that makes them extremely enjoyable, as well as very mouthfilling. In more detail, Barbera Bric Bertu and Roero Sudisfà show fabulous elegance while the Nicolon and Prachiosso selections are very successful all round. The Sudisfà even managed to repeat last year's Three Glass win. But if it is true that the quality of a cellar is judged by its basic wines, then the Negro estate is no exception and its lesser labels are absolute gems. The two flowery Arneis, a fine passito and a surprising arneis-based spumante, make this a very attractive range. Last on the list was the Barbaresco. It's not up to the standards of the Roero reds but it's coming along nicely.

● Carema Ris. '02	♟♟ 4
● Carema Et. Nera '03	♟ 4
● Carema Barricato '01	♟♟ 5
● Carema Barricato '00	♟♟ 5
● Carema Barricato '99	♟♟ 5
● Carema Ris. '01	♟♟ 4
● Carema Et. Bianca Ris. '99	♟♟ 4
● Carema Et. Bianca Barricato '98	♟♟ 4
● Carema Et. Nera '01	♟♟ 4

● Roero Sudisfà '04	♟♟♟ 6
● Barbera d'Alba Bric Bertu '05	♟♟ 5
● Roero Prachiosso '04	♟♟ 5
● Barbaresco Basarin '04	♟♟ 6
● Barbera d'Alba Nicolon '05	♟♟ 4
O Roero Arneis Perdaudin '06	♟♟ 4
O Perdaudin Passito '05	♟♟ 6
O Roero Arneis Brut M. Cl. Perdaudin '05	♟ 5
O Roero Arneis Gianat '06	♟ 4
● Roero Sudisfà '03	♟♟♟ 6
● Barbera d'Alba Bric Bertu '03	♟♟ 5
● Roero Sudisfà '01	♟♟ 6
● Roero Sudisfà '00	♟♟ 6
● Barbera d'Alba Bric Bertu '04	♟♟ 5
● Roero Prachiosso '03	♟♟ 5
● Roero Sudisfà '02	♟♟ 6

Nervi

C.SO VERCELLI, 117
13045 GATTINARA [VC]
TEL. 0163833228
www.gattinara-nervi.it

ANNUAL PRODUCTION 100,000 bottles
HECTARES UNDER VINE 33
VITICULTURE METHOD Conventional

We have come to expect great things from Nervi. It presents just one wine at a time – the highly acclaimed Podere dei Ginepri that scored so well last year is not due for release again until 2008 – but the performance is more than enough to compensate for the brevity of the tasting. The Molsino vineyard is a great cru: it rarely disappoints and more often than not its wines display austerity, cleanliness and personality on the palate that are unrivalled. We have full confidence in the estate's new direction. The Bocciolones and the Malgrà "family" of Nico Conta, Massimiliano Diotto, Ezio and Giorgio Chiarle are taking over not just one of the most celebrated names in the territory of Gattinara. They are also inheriting a style and philosophy whose tradition has been passed down through the generations and combining them with a far-seeing modern. As for the 2003 Vigneto Molsino, vineyard selection ensured that only the best fruit was delivered to the cellar, where the skilled hands of the technicians did the rest. Barrels of Slavonian oak caressed the wine, transforming it into a symphony of fruity, earthy aromas, notes of pencil lead and spice, tannic silkiness and harmony. It's quite simply superb.

Andrea Oberto

B.TA SIMANE, 11
12064 LA MORRA [CN]
TEL. 017350104
obertoandrea@libero.it

ANNUAL PRODUCTION 100,000 bottles
HECTARES UNDER VINE 16
VITICULTURE METHOD Conventional

The Oberto family's cellar enjoys a breathtaking view of the Tanaro valley. Who knows, perhaps its position also inspires the Obertos to create such splendid wines. Whatever it is that drives father and son team Andrea and Fabio, it works and they have built a reputation as one of Langhe's better-known estates. The property consists of 16 hectares in the main municipalities of Barolo. Production is unfussy and territory-focused, starting of course with the Barolos. This year's flagship wine comes in three versions and a fourth from the famed Brunate vineyard will swell the ranks next year. The Vigneto Albarella 2003 reflects the torrid growing year but is nevertheless balanced and well made. The 2003 Vigneto Rocche is more complex with a stylish, elegant nose. The excellent Barbera d'Alba Giada is the product of a 2004 that will go down in the annals of the Langhe as one of the great vintages. The Langhe Rosso Fabio 2004 is obtained from a blend of barbera and nebbiolo. The Dolcetto, the Barbera d'Alba and the standard-label Langhe Nebbiolo are all well typed and agreeable.

● Gattinara Vign. Molsino '03	♟♟ 6
● Gattinara Podere dei Ginepri '01	♟♟♟ 6
● Gattinara Vign. Molsino '00	♟♟♟ 6
● Gattinara Vign. Molsino '01	♟♟ 6
● Gattinara Vign. Molsino '99	♟♟ 6

● Barbera d'Alba Giada '04	♟♟ 6
● Barolo V. Rocche '03	♟♟ 8
● Barolo V. Albarella '03	♟♟ 8
● Barolo '03	♟♟ 7
● Barbera d'Alba '06	♟♟ 4*
● Langhe Rosso Fabio '04	♟♟ 6
● Langhe Nebbiolo '06	♟♟ 4*
● Dolcetto d'Alba '06	♟♟ 4*
● Barbera d'Alba Giada '00	♟♟♟ 6
● Barbera d'Alba Giada '97	♟♟♟ 6
● Barbera d'Alba Giada '96	♟♟♟ 6
● Barolo V. Rocche '96	♟♟♟ 8
● Barolo V. Albarella '01	♟♟♟ 8
● Barolo V. Albarella '03	♟♟ 8
● Barolo V. Albarella '99	♟♟ 8
● Barolo V. Albarella '00	♟♟ 8
● Barolo V. Rocche '00	♟♟ 8
● Barolo V. Rocche '01	♟♟ 8

Oddero

FRAZ. SANTA MARIA
VIA TETTI, 28
12064 LA MORRA [CN]
TEL. 017350618
www.oddero.it

ANNUAL PRODUCTION 100,000 bottles
HECTARES UNDER VINE 35
VITICULTURE METHOD Conventional

A eulogy to elegance. That sums up the wines presented by Cristina Oddero and her skilled team. Granted, the legendary Barolo Vigna Rionda is absent from the line-up this year, having fallen victim to the disappointing 2002 growing year but the numerous labels presented are in line with Oddero's style: technically impressive and brimming with personality. The nebbiolo grape takes centre stage in all its many manifestations. The Barolo Mondoca and the Rocche di Castiglione 2003 lead the company of Barolos, the first austere and a tad rustic; the second more yielding, silky and ready to drink. The basic 2003 is less challenging but has lots of character, unlike the Langhe 2006, which is all fruit and drinkability. The Barbaresco 2004 is on dazzling form, showing tannic weight and impeccable balance. We've never seen it this good and it swept off with Three Glasses. It was close-run thing between the Barberas but we preferred the Alba version to the Vinchio selection, which is still well made with nice supporting acidity. The supple Dolcetto, drinking deliciously now, rounds off the range of reds. As for the whites, the Chardonnay is good and the Moscato is soft and flowery.

Tenuta Olim Bauda

REG. PRATA, 50
14045 INCISA SCAPACCINO [AT]
TEL. 014174266
www.tenutaolimbauda.it

ANNUAL PRODUCTION 90,000 bottles
HECTARES UNDER VINE 25
VITICULTURE METHOD Conventional

The Bertolino boys are boys no longer for they have taken their estate to the front rank for excellence. Tenuta Olim Bauda can look down from the heights of the hill on which it sits with justifiable pride in the results achieved to date, ready to take on whatever challenge presents itself with confidence and optimism. Barbera remains, obviously, Gianni, Dino and Diana's prime concern. They present three versions, each differently styled and reflecting its vintage. Barbera is in fact the trio's most successful product. In ascending order of preference we have an inevitably young but very enjoyable standard-label La Villa, which is as upfront as you could wish. Next, the 2005 Le Rocchette 2005 is full, firmly structured and soft. Finally comes the Nizza 2004, as powerful as it is smooth in body, elegance and acidity, with a hint of oak in the finish that promises fullness and cellarability. The rest of the range features a series of well-made whites: a mineral, lip-smacking Gavi; a balanced Chardonnay; and a Moscato that impresses with its nose-palate consistency and measured sweetness.

● Barbaresco Gallina '04	♟♟♟ 7
● Barolo Mondoca di Bussia Soprana '03	♟♟ 8
● Barolo '03	♟♟ 6
● Langhe Nebbiolo '06	♟♟ 4
O Langhe Chardonnay Collaretto '06	♟♟ 4
● Barbera d'Alba '05	♟♟ 4
● Barbera d'Asti Vinchio '05	♟♟ 4
● Barolo Rocche di Castiglione '03	♟♟ 7
● Dolcetto d'Alba '06	♟ 4
O Moscato d'Asti Cascina Fiori '06	♟ 3
● Barolo V. Rionda '00	♟♟♟ 8
● Barolo V. Rionda '01	♟♟♟ 8
● Barolo Mondoca di Bussia Soprana '97	♟♟♟ 8
● Barolo V. Rionda '98	♟♟♟ 8
● Barolo V. Rionda '89	♟♟♟ 8
● Barolo Rocche di Castiglione '01	♟♟ 7

● Barbera d'Asti Sup. Nizza '04	♟♟ 5
● Barbera d'Asti La Villa '06	♟♟ 4
● Barbera d'Asti Sup. Le Rocchette '05	♟♟ 5
O Moscato d'Asti Centive '06	♟♟ 4
O Gavi del Comune di Gavi '06	♟ 4
O Piemonte Chardonnay '05	♟ 5
● Barbera d'Asti Sup. '04	♟♟ 5
● Barbera d'Asti Sup. '03	♟♟ 5
● Barbera d'Asti Sup. '01	♟♟ 5
● Barbera d'Asti Sup. '00	♟♟ 5
● Barbera d'Asti Sup. Nizza '03	♟♟ 5
● Barbera d'Asti Sup. Nizza '01	♟♟ 5

Orsolani

VIA MICHELE CHIESA, 12
10090 SAN GIORGIO CANAVESE [TO]
TEL. 012432386
www.orsolani.it

ANNUAL PRODUCTION 130,000 bottles
HECTARES UNDER VINE 20
VITICULTURE METHOD Conventional

The nymph Albaluce, or "dawnlight", was the love child of the goddess of the dawn and the sun god, had sky-blue eyes, a dewy skin and long, shining hair. She shed a tear that was transformed into the erbaluce grape. Gigi Orsolani, who has dedicated himself heart and soul to cultivating this indigenous Canavese variety, loves to tell visitors this ancient legend. Erbaluce is the variety in his wines, starting with his two metodo classico sparklers. The base of the Gran Riserva 2001 is matured in oak to produce a full wine with impressive structure whereas the Cuvée Tradizione 2003 is stylish and easier to drink. The Sulé 2002, a dried-grape passito, feels the effects of the poor growing year and is less sumptuous than in previous years, but its elegance and appeal remain intact.
The fresh, mineral Erbaluce La Rustia 2006 reveals varietal notes of fruit and aromatic herbs. The orangey Carema Le Tabbie 2003 is austere, intense and marked but well-integrated tannins and aromas that range from flowery notes to liquorice on the nose. The Acini Sparsi is fresher and alcohol-rich with barbera and nebbiolo prevailing over the other local varieties.

Pace

FRAZ. MADONNA DI LORETO
CASCINA PACE, 52
12043 CANALE [CN]
TEL. 0173979544
aziendapace@infinito.it

ANNUAL PRODUCTION 25,000 bottles
HECTARES UNDER VINE 19
VITICULTURE METHOD Conventional

The two Negro brothers are good. After presenting last year a very interesting series of wines, which saw them promoted to full profile status, Dino and Pietro had a hard act to follow. But they more than rose to the challenge with a consistent, clearly identifiable style that is based on good quality fruit managed with care and attention at every step of the production process. They continue to consolidate the range, increasing the amount of wine they bottle and reducing the proportion of grapes that they sell. They have an extensive vineyard holding and their very well-positioned plots are home to the Roero triptych of arneis, barbera and nebbiolo. After a fresh-tasting, agreeable white, we move up a gear to two Barberas that show completely different levels of intensity and concentration – greater in the Superiore, softer in the basic edition – and finally on to the two Roeros. Strange though it may seem, we continue to prefer the younger version to the Superiore, which will become a Riserva from next year. It's a question of taste, or perhaps they've just been better up to now at making the less solidly structured wines.

O Caluso Passito Sulé '02	🍷🍷 6
O Caluso Spumante Cuvée Tradizione Gran Riserva '01	🍷🍷 6
O Erbaluce di Caluso La Rustìa '06	🍷🍷 3*
O Caluso Spumante Brut Cuvée Tradizione '03	🍷🍷 5
● Carema Le Tabbie '03	🍷🍷 5
● Canavese Rosso Acini Sparsi '05	🍷 3
O Caluso Passito Sulé '98	🍷🍷🍷 6
O Caluso Passito Sulé '00	🍷🍷 6
O Erbaluce di Caluso Vignot S. Antonio '04	🍷🍷 5
● Carema Le Tabbie '01	🍷🍷 6

● Barbera d'Alba Sup. '05	🍷🍷 5
● Roero '05	🍷🍷 4*
● Barbera d'Alba '05	🍷🍷 4*
● Langhe Nebbiolo '06	🍷🍷 3*
O Roero Arneis '06	🍷 4
● Roero Sup. '04	🍷 5
● Barbera d'Alba Sup. '04	🍷🍷 4
● Roero '04	🍷🍷 4

Paitin

LOC. BRICCO
VIA SERRA BOELLA, 20
12052 NEIVE [CN]
TEL. 017367343
www.paitin.it

ANNUAL PRODUCTION 60,000 bottles
HECTARES UNDER VINE 17
VITICULTURE METHOD Natural

This family-run estate has won a solid reputation for quality but that doesn't mean the Pasqueros are resting on their laurels. The beautiful new, functional cellar located beside the original one has just been inaugurated and shows that the family continues to aspire to greater things. The Pasqueros are looking to expand production but for the moment we are content to enjoy the wines produced by the competent Giovanni and Silvano, who run the estate with their father, Secondo. After its 2002 sabbatical, the estate's flagship wine is back. Barbaresco Sorì Paitin Vecchie Vigne 2003 is obtained from vineyards planted in 1953.
It is quite excellent and reflects the hot growing year, combining complexity and elegance with a strong tannic element. But the indisputable champ is the elegant, ageworthy Sorì Paitin 2004, from a harvest that will long be remembered. Aromas of ripe black berry fruit meld perfectly with nuances of spice introducing a very stylish palate brimming with nebbiolo elegance. No doubts here. It won Three resounding Glasses. Up next we had two Barberas, the Serra Boella and Campolive, which aged for 18 months in large oak barrels. The rest of the range is well typed and pleasant.

Armando Parusso

LOC. BUSSIA, 55
12065 MONFORTE D'ALBA [CN]
TEL. 017378257
www.parusso.com

ANNUAL PRODUCTION 110,000 bottles
HECTARES UNDER VINE 23
VITICULTURE METHOD Conventional

The Parusso family's passion for wine spans four generations but it has always remained faithful to the same philosophy: the ongoing quest for improvement. Today, Marco and Tiziana are at the helm and manage to consistently turn out modern wines of excellent quality and elegance from their 23 hectares planted to vine. Annual production exceeds 100,000 bottles. We recall the Three Glasses awarded to a memorable Riserva Vecchie Vigne in Mariondino '99 but last year the 2002 Barolos fell foul of the poor growing year. This time, the Parussos offered no fewer than five versions: we were very impressed by the Riserva Vecchie Vigne in Mariondino 2000 and the Bussia 2003. However, to our minds the stand-out in this rich range is Le Coste Mosconi 2003. Austere and modern at the same time, it combines notes of cocoa powder, coffee, vanilla, leather and dried flowers with a very powerful, solidly built palate. We gave it Three full Glasses. The Barbera Superiore Vecchie Vigne Ornati 2004 and the Dolcetto are good. Finally, the two Langhe Biancos are decent as always, notably the 2006 whose varietal sauvignon sensations make it easy and enjoyable to drink. The rest of the range is valid.

● Barbaresco Sorì Paitin '04	♆♆♆	6
● Barbaresco Sorì Paitin Vecchie Vigne '03	♆♆	8
○ Langhe Arneis V. Elisa '06	♆♆	4
● Barbera d'Alba Campolive '05	♆♆	5
● Langhe Paitin '05	♆♆	6
● Nebbiolo d'Alba Ca Veja '05	♆♆	4
● Dolcetto d'Alba Sorì Paitin '06	♆♆	4
● Barbera d'Alba Serra Boella '06	♆♆	4
● Barbaresco Sorì Paitin '95	♆♆♆	7
● Barbaresco Sorì Paitin '97	♆♆♆	7
● Barbaresco Sorì Paitin Vecchie Vigne '01	♆♆♆	8
● Langhe Paitin '97	♆♆♆	6
● Barbaresco Sorì Paitin Vecchie Vigne '99	♆♆♆	8
● Barbaresco Sorì Paitin '01	♆♆	8
● Barbaresco Sorì Paitin '03	♆♆	6

● Barolo Le Coste Mosconi '03	♆♆♆	8
● Barbera d'Alba Sup. Vecchie Vigne Ornati '04	♆♆	6
● Barolo Vecchie Vigne in Mariondino Ris. '00	♆♆	8
● Barolo Bussia '03	♆♆	8
● Barolo '03	♆♆	6
● Barbera d'Alba Ornati '05	♆♆	4
● Barolo Mariondino '03	♆♆	7
● Dolcetto d'Alba Piani Noci '06	♆♆	4
● Langhe Nebbiolo '05	♆♆	5
○ Langhe Bianco '06	♆♆	4
○ Langhe Bianco Bricco Rovella '04	♆	6
● Barolo Bussia V. Munie '96	♆♆♆	8
● Barolo Bussia V. Munie '97	♆♆♆	8
● Barolo Bussia V. Munie '99	♆♆♆	8
● Barolo Vecchie Vigne in Mariondino Ris. '99	♆♆♆	8

Agostino Pavia e Figli

FRAZ. BOLOGNA, 33
14041 AGLIANO TERME [AT]
TEL. 0141954125
mauro.pavia@crasti.it

ANNUAL PRODUCTION 75,000 bottles
HECTARES UNDER VINE 7.5
VITICULTURE METHOD Conventional

This estate has a large production that continues to grow in quality across the entire range of labels. Run by brothers Mauro and Giuseppe Pavia with the invaluable support of their father, Agostino, it is a modern cellar whose wines are deeply rooted in the terroir of Agliano. The products are clean, forthright and typical, some reaching quite superb heights. The Barbera Superiore La Marescialla has long been the stand-out and the round, warm 2004 version reveals balance and elegance, with still prominent oakiness. The Superiore Moliss 2004 is also elegant and flowery with a rather more classic, closed palate. Blina 2005 is an explosive wine with clear fruit and good length, although it still tends to the astringent. From barbera with a little syrah, the very young Monferrato Talin 2004 is rugged and still oaky and will need more time in bottle to unveil its full character. Two well-deserved Glasses also go went the Grignolino for its alluring spicy aromas of pepper and candied peel.

Pecchenino

B.TA VALDIBERTI, 59
12063 DOGLIANI [CN]
TEL. 017370686
www.pecchenino.com

ANNUAL PRODUCTION 90,000 bottles
HECTARES UNDER VINE 24
VITICULTURE METHOD Conventional

Attilio and Orlando Pecchenino are at the forefront of the group of young Dogliani producers responsible for the success enjoyed today by the zone and its key variety, dolcetto. Orlando in particular promotes the concepts of absolute quality, the importance of not being in a hurry and spreading awareness of the potential of the Dogliani terroir, an island unto itself in the world of Langhe world. The Peccheninos' efforts have paid off in the results they have garnered over the years. Dolcetto is, naturally, top dog and is well expressed in the versions of the new DOCG. The Bricco Botti shows that the wine ages brilliantly, softening, smoothing and mellowing into a plush, aroma-rich maturity. The San Luigi is supple and taut, as well as more approachable in terms of price. Sirì d'Jermu was absent, though, as with the advent of the DOCG, it is now released to market in the November following the harvest and had not been bottled at the time of our tastings. In anticipation of the soon-to-be-released Barolo 2004, we enjoyed an austere, tannic Nebbiolo. The Barbera is powerful and elegant with lots of acidity. Vigna Maestro, a white, is a blend of chardonnay, sauvignon and arneis.

● Barbera d'Asti Sup. La Marescialla '04	🍷🍷 5
● Barbera d'Asti Bricco Blina '05	🍷🍷 4
● Barbera d'Asti Sup. Moliss '04	🍷🍷 4
● Grignolino d'Asti '06	🍷🍷 3*
● Monferrato Rosso Talin '04	🍷 5
● Barbera d'Asti La Marescialla '00	🍷🍷 5
● Barbera d'Asti Sup. La Marescialla '01	🍷🍷 5
● Barbera d'Asti Sup. La Marescialla '03	🍷🍷 5
● Barbera d'Asti Sup. Moliss '01	🍷🍷 4
● Barbera d'Asti Sup. Moliss '03	🍷🍷 4
● Barbera d'Asti Blina '03	🍷🍷 4
● Barbera d'Asti Blina '04	🍷🍷 4
● Monferrato Rosso Talin '00	🍷🍷 5

● Dogliani Bricco Botti '05	🍷🍷 5
● Barbera d'Alba Quass '05	🍷🍷 5
● Langhe Nebbiolo V. Botti '05	🍷🍷 5
● Dolcetto di Dogliani S. Luigi '06	🍷🍷 4
○ Langhe V. Maestro '06	🍷 5
● Dolcetto di Dogliani Sirì d'Jermu '03	🍷🍷🍷 5
● Dolcetto di Dogliani Sirì d'Jermu '01	🍷🍷🍷 5
● Dolcetto di Dogliani Sirì d'Jermu '99	🍷🍷🍷 5
● Dolcetto di Dogliani Sirì d'Jermu '98	🍷🍷🍷 5
● Dolcetto di Dogliani Sup. Bricco Botti '04	🍷🍷🍷 5
● Dolcetto di Dogliani S. Luigi '00	🍷🍷🍷 4

Pelissero

VIA FERRERE, 10
12050 TREISO [CN]
TEL. 0173638430
www.pelissero.com

ANNUAL PRODUCTION   250,000 bottles
HECTARES UNDER VINE 35
VITICULTURE METHOD   Conventional

One thing that comes across very clearly on tasting Pelissero wines is the ongoing quest to bring out the full potential of each and every vineyard. The marriage of ancient methods with technological innovation enhances the varietal characteristics of the individual varieties. We were offered three Barbarescos to taste. We'll start with the Vanotu, which displays an elegant, harmonious profile and a palate that already shows balance. The Tulin is powerful and austere with tannins that are still evolving while the Nubiola has class and is the most traditional of the three. In contrast, Long Now is obtained from a blend of nebbiolo and barbera matured for an extended period in small barrels. Its impenetrable appearance is the prelude to powerful structure and a juicy, lip-smacking palate. We liked the two Dolcettos, the intensely fruity Augenta with its impressive structure, and the simply approachable Munfrina. The Barbera Piani is pleasantly fresh, while the Nebbiolo is balanced despite its marked tannic notes. We'll end with a semi-sparking Freisa, refermented in the bottle, and an easy-drinking Favorita.

Cascina Pellerino

LOC. SANT'ANNA, 93
12040 MONTEU ROERO [CN]
TEL. 0173978171
www.cascinapellerino.com

ANNUAL PRODUCTION   100,000 bottles
HECTARES UNDER VINE 8
VITICULTURE METHOD   Conventional

Cascina Pellerino's range of wines has settled down nicely. Cristian Bono is a virtuoso wine man in a Roero that has finally emerged from the shadows to show its qualitative mettle. The partnership he formed recently with Roberto Ghione allows Cristian to devote his time to his true passions – the vineyard and the cellar – without worrying too much about the other equally important aspects of managing a modern estate that now turns out serious numbers. This year, we were not offered the Roero Vicot 2005, as it had been bottled too recently for us to assess it. By way of compensation, we sampled a Leoni 2004 that is fragrant, still very fresh, silky in its tannins and harmonious: in fact, absolutely first-class. The fruity, juicy, acid-rich Barbera Gran Madre is also spot on and the Andrè and Diletta are very impressive companions to the two big reds. Bono is also a very able producer of whites with two Arneis that return to the top of the category. The Favorita is agreeably fruity and the new Brut promises well for the future.

● Barbaresco Nubiola '04	♈♈	6
● Barbaresco Vanotu '04	♈♈	8
● Langhe Rosso Long Now '05	♈♈	6
● Barbaresco Tulin '04	♈♈♈	7
● Barbera d'Alba Piani '06	♈♈	4
● Dolcetto d'Alba Munfrina '06	♈♈	4
● Dolcetto d'Alba Augenta '06	♈♈	4
● Langhe Nebbiolo '06	♈♈	4
● Langhe Freisa '06	♈	2*
○ Langhe Favorita '06	♈	2*
● Barbaresco Vanotu '01	♈♈♈	8
● Barbaresco Vanotu '97	♈♈♈	8
● Barbaresco Vanotu '99	♈♈♈	8
● Barbaresco Vanotu '95	♈♈♈	8
● Barbaresco Tulin '01	♈♈	7
● Barbaresco Vanotu '03	♈♈	8
● Barbaresco Tulin '03	♈♈	7

● Barbera d'Alba Sup. Gran Madre '05	♈♈	5
● Roero Leoni '04	♈♈	6
● Barbera d'Alba Diletta '05	♈♈	4
● Roero Andrè '05	♈♈	4
○ Roero Arneis Boneur '06	♈♈	4
○ Roero Arneis Desiré '06	♈♈	4
○ Langhe Favorita Lorena '06	♈	4
○ Brut M. Cl. Felizia '03	♈	4
● Roero Leoni '01	♈♈	6
● Roero Leoni '03	♈♈	6
● Roero Leoni '00	♈♈	6
● Roero Leoni '02	♈♈	6

Elio Perrone

S.DA SAN MARTINO, 3BIS
12053 CASTIGLIONE TINELLA [CN]
TEL. 0141855803
www.elioperrone.it

Vignaioli Elvio Pertinace

LOC. PERTINACE, 2
12050 TREISO [CN]
TEL. 0173442238
www.pertinace.it

ANNUAL PRODUCTION 140,000 bottles
HECTARES UNDER VINE 12
VITICULTURE METHOD Conventional

ANNUAL PRODUCTION 200,000 bottles
HECTARES UNDER VINE 70
VITICULTURE METHOD Conventional

Stefano Perrone runs this interesting family estate on the Asti side of Langhe with the support of his parents and charming wife, Giuliana. The cellar is well-finished, functional and welcoming. On the list are the classic offerings of the territory, prepared in line with a policy of vinifying local varieties in a traditional manner. Moscato is the chief variety around here and is largely responsible for the fame of this winery so it is only right that we should begin this year's notes with the type. First up we have the complex, firmly structured Clarté 2006. Made with a small proportion of sun-dried grapes, it offers a wonderful expression of Moscato. The Sourgal 2006 is every bit as good. The Perrone range is completed by Barberas, obtained from grapes grown at Isola d'Asti and Costigliole. There are three versions on offer this year, including a very successful new entry, the Tasmorcan 2005 matured in big oak barrels. The Grivò and the Mongovone consolidate their position as the top selections, both showing good ageing potential.

This dynamic co-operative winery at Pertinace has 15 member growers with a total of 70 hectares under vine in some of the finest locations for the production of the zone's traditional wines. The estate releases a wide-ranging series of wines, headed by four Barbarescos, three from single vineyards and a basic version that includes part of the nebbiolo produced by all of the members. The Castellizzano is the cream of the crop, bringing fruit and tannins together to produce an enjoyably moreish wine. The Marcarini has spicy, fruity notes with fine overall elegance while the Nervo is still closed with tannins still to the fore. From the plots at Agliano d'Asti come the grapes that go into Barbera Gratia Plena, a full, solidly built wine slightly prominent alcohol. The Dolcetto selections, from Nervo and Castellizzano, are attractive and cheerfully drinkable. The rest of the range is well managed and offers good value for money.

O Moscato d'Asti Clarté '06	▼▼	4*
● Barbera d'Asti Mongovone '05	▼▼	6
● Barbera d'Asti Grivò '05	▼▼	4
● Barbera d'Asti Tasmorcan '05	▼▼	4
O Moscato d'Asti Sourgal '06	▼▼	4
● Bigarò '06	▼	4
● Barbera d'Asti Mongovone '04	♀♀	6
● Barbera d'Asti Mongovone '00	♀♀	6
● Barbera d'Asti Mongovone '01	♀♀	6
● Barbera d'Asti Grivò '04	♀♀	4

● Barbaresco Vign. Castellizzano '04	▼▼	6
● Barbaresco Marcarini '04	▼▼	6
● Barbaresco Nervo '04	▼▼	6
● Barbaresco '04	▼▼	6
● Barbera d'Asti Gratia Plena '04	▼▼	4
● Dolcetto d'Alba Castellizzano '06	▼▼	4
● Dolcetto d'Alba Vigneto Nervo '06	▼▼	4
● Barbera d'Alba '06	▼	4
● Langhe Rosso Pertinace '04	▼	5
● Langhe Nebbiolo '05	▼	4
● Dolcetto d'Alba '06	▼	4
O Langhe Chardonnay '06	▼	4
O Roero Arneis '06	▼	4
● Barbaresco Nervo '03	♀♀	6
● Barbaresco Nervo '01	♀♀	6
● Barbaresco Marcarini '04	♀♀	6
● Barbaresco Marcarini '00	♀♀	6
● Barbaresco Marcarini '01	♀♀	6

Le Piane

LOC. LE PIANE
28010 BOCA [NO]
TEL. 3483354185
www.bocapiane.com

ANNUAL PRODUCTION 15,000 bottles
HECTARES UNDER VINE 6.5
VITICULTURE METHOD Conventional

Inspired by their great love for the wines of this territory, Christoph Künzli and his partner Alexander Trolf in the mid 1990s acquired half a hectare of the old Campo delle Piane vineyard belonging to Antonio Cerri, a well-known Boca producer. Things have changed a bit since then. The estate has increased its vineyard holding and is now run on his own by Christoph, who is gradually organizing the cellar. The estate has opted to produce wines that reflect the power of the territory without recourse to over-elaborate methods. There is no over-extraction or over-abundance of new oak here, just a few 900-litre casks that are used to temper the fiery nature of the croatina that is the mainstay of the Colline Novaresi Le Piane. The Colline Novaresi La Maggiorina gives more space to the vespolina and uva rara, which are complemented by small doses of croatina and nebbiolo. It's more elegant on the nose and much more subtle on the palate than the Le Piane. But it was the Boca that stunned our judges this year, combining the ripe fruit of the 2003 growing year with the natural minerality of the land. This, the estate's first well-deserved Three Glass winner, is a tribute to Christoph's perseverance.

Fabrizio Pinsoglio

FRAZ. MADONNA DEI CAVALLI, 31BIS
12050 CANALE [CN]
TEL. 0173968401
fabriziopinsoglio@libero.it

ANNUAL PRODUCTION 40,000 bottles
HECTARES UNDER VINE 9
VITICULTURE METHOD Conventional

Fabrizio Pinsoglio is a congenial chap, as well as the very able manager of his estate. He is flanked by his wife, Andreina, and has no doubt been given an extra boost of inspiration by the recent birth of his son, Filippo. In addition to enlarging his family, Fabrizio has transferred operations to the new structure hosting house and cellar just across the road from the old site but far enough to mean a change of municipality from Castellinaldo to Canale. The Roero Arneis Vigneto Malinat 2006 is vinified in stainless steel but stays for three months on the lees and this gives it elegance, structure, delicacy and length on the palate. Fabrizio releases two Barberas: the fresh-tasting, drinkable Vigna Giaconi 2006 and Barbera Bric La Rondolina 2005, which aged for 18 months in barriques, half of which are new. It has emerged with a fascinating swath of aromatics, a powerful, solidly built palate and excellent length in the finish. Last but not least comes a very attractive Roero Superiore 2004. Twenty months in half new small wood and a year in glass result in a generous, tempting nose, good balance and softness, and a leisurely finish.

● Boca '03	▼▼▼	7
● Colline Novaresi La Maggiorina '05	▼▼	3*
● Colline Novaresi Le Piane '05	▼▼	6
● Boca '00	♀♀	5
● Boca '01	♀♀	7
● Boca '99	♀♀	5
● Colline Novaresi Le Piane '01	♀♀	4
● Colline Novaresi Le Piane '03	♀♀	4
● Colline Novaresi Le Piane '04	♀♀	6

● Barbera d'Alba Bric La Rondolina '05	▼▼	5
● Roero Sup. '04	▼▼	5
O Roero Arneis Vign. Malinat '06	▼▼	3*
● Barbera d'Alba Vign. Giaconi '06	♀	4
● Nebbiolo d'Alba '05	♀	4
● Roero Sup. '01	♀♀	5
● Roero Sup. '03	♀♀	5
● Roero '99	♀♀	5
● Barbera d'Alba Bric La Rondolina '04	♀♀	5
● Barbera d'Alba Bric La Rondolina '03	♀♀	5
● Barbera d'Alba Bric La Rondolina '01	♀♀	5
● Barbera d'Alba Bric La Rondolina '00	♀♀	5

Pio Cesare

VIA CESARE BALBO, 6
12051 ALBA [CN]
TEL. 0173440386
www.piocesare.it

ANNUAL PRODUCTION 370,000 bottles
HECTARES UNDER VINE 52
VITICULTURE METHOD Conventional

The noble Pio Cesare estate has its headquarters in the historic centre of Alba and its recently renovated cellars are well worth a visit. Pio Boffa, heir to a family tradition that goes all the way back to 1881, has oriented his production towards quality and his extensive, comprehensive range of wines aspires in this direction. This year, in spite of the torrid 2003 growing year, the estate's two Barbarescos are on fine form: the basic edition is more immediately enjoyable while the Bricco needs a few more months of ageing to bring its awesome raw material into line. The other big wines are also from 2003, this time on the Barolo front. Ornato is succulent and soft but the basic version pays a price with rather rugged tannins. The Barbera d'Alba Fides is very true to its terroir, Serralunga, and shows concentrated and rich. Turning to the whites, the Chardonnay PiodiLei 2005 is, as usual, a marvel of intensity and fullness. L'Altro is not just the other (altro) white but a wonderfully fresh, flowery wine in its own right. The rest of the range is worthy of the reputation of this venerable label.

Pioiero

CASCINA PIOIERO, 1
12040 VEZZA D'ALBA [CN]
TEL. 017365492
www.pioiero.com

ANNUAL PRODUCTION 30,000 bottles
HECTARES UNDER VINE 5.4
VITICULTURE METHOD Conventional

Pioiero's charming farmhouse lies in a tranquil position just beyond the orchard, immersed in the lush vineyards meticulously tended by the talented, experienced Antonio Rabino. His capable wife, Bruna, manages the estate with a steady hand making Pioiero a solid, family-run affair. In other words, it's a small but inspired cellar and one of the brightest stars in the galaxy of Roero's producers. This year, two very impressive wines stood out. The Roero 2005 has generous, attractive aromas, a good follow-through on the palate and elegant balance. Roero Arneis Bric e Val 2006, produced only in the best vintages and ennobled by a few months' ageing in oak, manages to combine substantial body with aromatic appeal. The Arneis 2006 also did well but the Nebbiolo d'Alba 2005 was even better. Both are assertively and authentically varietal. The Langhe Favorita 2006 is alcohol-rich and tempting, with a lip-smacking, easy-drinking finish.

● Barbaresco Il Bricco '03	♀♀	8
● Barbaresco '03	♀♀	8
● Barolo Ornato '03	♀♀	8
● Barolo '03	♀♀	8
● Barbera d'Alba Fides '05	♀♀	6
● Nebbiolo d'Alba '04	♀♀	4
○ Piemonte Chardonnay L'Altro '06	♀♀	4
○ Langhe Chardonnay PiodiLei '05	♀♀	6
● Dolcetto d'Alba '06	♀	4
● Langhe Rosso Il Nebbio '06	♀	4
● Barbaresco Il Bricco '97	♀♀♀	8
● Barolo Ornato '89	♀♀♀	8
● Barolo Ornato '85	♀♀♀	8
● Barbaresco Il Bricco '00	♀♀	8
● Barbaresco Il Bricco '01	♀♀	8
● Barbera d'Alba Fides '04	♀♀	6
● Barolo Ornato '00	♀♀	8
● Barolo Ornato '01	♀♀	8

● Nebbiolo d'Alba '05	♀♀	4*
● Roero '05	♀♀	4*
○ Roero Arneis Bric e Val '06	♀♀	4*
○ Langhe Favorita '06	♀	3
○ Roero Arneis '06	♀	3
● Roero Sup. '01	♀♀	4
● Roero Sup. '03	♀♀	4
● Roero Sup. '04	♀♀	4

E. Pira & Figli
VIA VITTORIO VENETO, 1
12060 BAROLO [CN]
TEL. 017356247
www.pira-chiaraboschis.it

Luigi Pira
VIA XX SETTEMBRE, 9
12050 SERRALUNGA D'ALBA [CN]
TEL. 0173613106

ANNUAL PRODUCTION   19,000 bottles
HECTARES UNDER VINE 3.5
VITICULTURE METHOD   Certified organic

ANNUAL PRODUCTION   50,000 bottles
HECTARES UNDER VINE 10
VITICULTURE METHOD   Conventional

Yet again we were bowled over by the skill, passion, attention to detail and talent shown by Chiara Boschis. Her estate resembles the aisles and nave of a Romanesque church and part of its charm lies in the fact that it combines the very modern with an old part. In the challenging growing year of 2003, Chiara managed to get the best out of the nebbiolo grapes from the harvest and transform them into two very different, very good Barolos. As always, the Cannubi embodies the finesse and elegance of the vineyard and is already approachable thanks to delicate florality. Given time, it will evolve even further. Via Nuova starts off almost rough and closed but gradually opens out to reveal a soul made of structure and solidity, promising to age better than we can expect from that particular growing year. In contrast, the full, fruity 2006 Dolcetto is from a harvest that was very generous with the variety. This is not a wine conceived to be drunk immediately. The Barbera 2005 displays lovely fruit and sustained acidity and a savoury note in the finish that makes it even more drinkable.

After a 2002 so problematical that it forced brothers Giampaolo and Romolo and their father Luigi to withdraw all of their Barolos, they were faced with another challenging vintage in 2003. The prolonged, excessive heat could have jeopardized the fruit's aromas and arrested maturation of the tannins. The Piras had to harvest the grapes much earlier than usual and vinify them with great care to avoid extracting bitter compounds and to preserve the wines' fresh acidity. We are happy to say that the Piras were largely successful in their efforts, even if they did not manage to match the results achieved in 2001. Like the other wines, the Barolo Margheria was produced in a much smaller quantities. It is a typical Serralunga wine with its muscular tannins and a certain alluring rusticity. The very elegant Marenca derives from a vineyard planted in 1990 while the Vigna Rionda has a concentrated nose but needs a bit more time to develop fully. The Barbera is obtained from grapes grown in the municipality of Roddino and is a juicy, extremely drinkable wine, like the Nebbiolo. The Dolcetto is simple and agreeable.

● Barolo Cannubi '03	♟♟ 8
● Barolo Via Nuova '03	♟♟ 8
● Barbera d'Alba '05	♟♟ 5
○ Dolcetto d'Alba '06	♟♟ 4*
● Barolo Ris. '90	♟♟♟ 8
● Barolo '94	♟♟♟ 8
● Barolo Cannubi '00	♟♟♟ 8
● Barolo Cannubi '96	♟♟♟ 8
● Barolo Cannubi '97	♟♟♟ 8
● Barolo Cannubi '01	♟♟ 8
● Barolo Cannubi '99	♟♟ 8
● Barolo Cannubi '98	♟♟ 8
● Barolo Via Nuova '01	♟♟ 8
● Barolo Via Nuova '00	♟♟ 8
● Barolo Via Nuova '99	♟♟ 8

● Barolo V. Rionda '03	♟♟ 8
● Barolo Vign. Marenca '03	♟♟ 8
● Barbera d'Alba Ròche du Tarpùn '05	♟♟ 5
● Barolo Vign. Margheria '03	♟♟ 7
● Langhe Nebbiolo Le Ombre '05	♟♟ 5
● Barolo '03	♟ 7
○ Dolcetto d'Alba '06	♟ 4
● Barolo V. Rionda '00	♟♟♟ 8
● Barolo Vign. Marenca '97	♟♟♟ 8
● Barolo Vign. Marenca '01	♟♟♟ 8
● Barolo Vign. Marenca '00	♟♟ 8
● Barolo Vign. Margheria '01	♟♟ 7
● Barolo V. Rionda '01	♟♟ 8
● Barolo Vign. Marenca '99	♟♟ 8
● Barolo Vign. Margheria '00	♟♟ 7

Castello del Poggio
LOC. POGGIO, 9
14038 PORTACOMARO [AT]
TEL. 0141202543
www.poggio.it

ANNUAL PRODUCTION 700,000 bottles
HECTARES UNDER VINE 180
VITICULTURE METHOD Conventional

Castello del Poggio's production focuses on local varieties, with grignolino and barbera accounting for the lion's share. The Zonin family has 180 hectares planted to vine on the slopes of Portacomaro that they bought around ten years ago. They own one of the biggest wine operations in Italy with headquarters in Gambellara, Veneto. The vineyards form an amphitheatre around the magnificent Valle del Tempio where the remains of an ancient fortress indicate the site of a Templar settlement. To our great regret, the estate's two most prestigious selections were not released this year. The Barbera d'Asti Masaréj has been at a standstill since the 2003 harvest and the Piemonte Barbera Bunéis, the only wine to concede an international note to estate's approach with the use of merlot, is also absent. It meant we had to make do with the second lines that confirm the positive results achieved in recent years. The Grignolino d'Asti is very attractive and shows that the decision to release it after an extra year's ageing was the right one. The Barbera d'Asti 2004 enfolds the palate. Best of the sweet wines is the Moscato, with its aromatic fragrances and a sweet palate that doesn't cloy. The Dolcetto is pleasant.

Paolo Poggio
VIA ROMA, 67
15050 BRIGNANO FRASCATA [AL]
TEL. 0131784929
cantinapoggio@tiscali.it

ANNUAL PRODUCTION 18,000 bottles
HECTARES UNDER VINE 3.1
VITICULTURE METHOD Conventional

There was another fine performance from this small producer. Paolo Poggio makes quality wines while keeping his estate to a size that makes it easy for a family to manage. The products reflect their growing year, for better or for worse, and Paolo simply seeks to interpret the fruit as consistently as he can. In the cellar in particular, he does his best to bring out the qualities of the variety as faithfully as possible without altering its characteristics. Turning to the wines on offer, we are happy to announce one of the best versions of Timorasso Ronchetto we have ever tasted, a perfect balance of structure and aromas. On only its second release, the Croatina Prosone also shows very well. The estate's overall results are even more impressive when you consider that the house champion, Derio, was not presented because it has been left to age for an extra year. The rest of the range merited One full Glass each. And all of these wines are very affordable.

● Grignolino d'Asti '05	♟♟	4
● Barbera d'Asti '04	♟♟	4
● Monferrato Dolcetto '06	♟	4
○ Moscato d'Asti '06	♟	4
● Piemonte Brachetto	♟	
● Piemonte Barbera Bunéis Gianni Zonin Vineyards '00	♟♟	6
● Piemonte Barbera Bunéis Gianni Zonin Vineyards '01	♟♟	6
● Piemonte Barbera Bunéis Gianni Zonin Vineyards '03	♟♟	6
● Barbera d'Asti Masaréj Gianni Zonin Vineyards '03	♟♟	6
● Barbera d'Asti Masaréj Gianni Zonin Vineyards '01	♟♟	6
● Barbera d'Asti Masaréj Gianni Zonin Vineyards '00	♟♟	6

○ Colli Tortonesi Ronchetto '05	♟♟	3*
● Colli Tortonesi Rosso Prosone '05	♟♟	2*
● Colli Tortonesi Barbera Campo La Bà '06	♟	2
● Colli Tortonesi Barbera Teo '06	♟	3
○ Colli Tortonesi Bianco Campogallo '06	♟	4
○ Colli Tortonesi Ronchetto '03	♟♟	3
○ Colli Tortonesi Ronchetto '04	♟♟	3
● Colli Tortonesi Barbera Derio '99	♟♟	4
● Colli Tortonesi Barbera Derio '98	♟♟	4
● Colli Tortonesi Rosso Prosone '04	♟♟	4

Porello

C.SO ALBA, 71
12043 CANALE [CN]
TEL. 0173979324
www.porellovini.it

ANNUAL PRODUCTION 70,000 bottles
HECTARES UNDER VINE 15
VITICULTURE METHOD Conventional

Slowly but surely, a style is emerging in Marco Porello's wines that focuses on cleanliness, fruit and variety.
Contributing to this are vineyard techniques designed to obtain lower yields and rigorous cellar processes. The whites are a case in point, from the agreeable Favorita 2006 to the Roero Arneis Camestrì 2006. The latter is one of the best of its class, a savoury, citrus-like, minerally wine that is also well-rounded and redolent of tropical fruit. Attesting to the quality of the reds are the Roero Torretta 2005 and the Barbera d'Alba Filatura 2005, which went through to our final tastings. The Torretta comes from careful cluster thinning and barrique ageing, displaying lovely elegant aromas on nose and palate lifted by sweet tannins in the long finish. The Barbera has full, complex fruit that has acquired further balance from maturation in barriques. The Barbera d'Alba Mommiano 2006 aged in large barrels is also interesting and pleasantly fresh-tasting while the Nebbiolo d'Alba 2005 is agreeably drinkable and, rightly, does nothing to conceal its assertive tannins.

Ferdinando Principiano

VIA ALBA, 19
12065 MONFORTE D'ALBA [CN]
TEL. 0173787158
www.ferdinandoprincipiano.it

ANNUAL PRODUCTION 30,000 bottles
HECTARES UNDER VINE 7.5
VITICULTURE METHOD Conventional

Ferdinando Principiano's new winemaking philosophy is beginning to take shape. We hesitated before pronouncing judgement as we were wary of drawing hasty conclusions but the results achieved by the Barolo Boscareto 2003 and the Barbera d'Alba La Romualda 2005 encouraged us to take a broader look at the new production process. Ferdinando has eliminated several of the more technological procedures in the cellar and is focusing on natural transformation of healthy, succulent fruit into wine. It's a shame that we examined his wines in the particular years below because they do not always do justice to the efforts made. Despite the tremendous heat of the harvest, the Barolo is absolutely excellent, showing forthright on both nose and soft, round palate. The Barbera is even better, offering clear notes of red berry fruit shot through with lovely acidity. The Sant'Anna di Monforte d'Alba vineyard brings us a Dolcetto of the same name that unfolds fresh, appealing aromatics. The Langhe Nebbiolo and the standard-label Barbera also made a good impression.

Wine	Rating
● Barbera d'Alba Filatura '05	♟♟ 5
● Roero Torretta '05	♟♟ 5
● Barbera d'Alba Mommiano '06	♟♟ 4*
● Nebbiolo d'Alba '05	♟♟ 4*
O Roero Arneis Camestrì '06	♟♟ 4*
O Langhe Favorita '06	♟ 4
● Roero Torretta '04	♟♟♟ 5
● Roero Torretta '03	♟♟ 5
● Roero Torretta '02	♟♟ 5
● Roero Torretta '01	♟♟ 4
● Roero Bric Torretta '00	♟♟ 4
● Barbera d'Alba Filatura '04	♟♟ 5
● Barbera d'Alba Filatura '03	♟♟ 5

Wine	Rating
● Barbera d'Alba La Romualda '05	♟♟ 6
● Barolo Boscareto '03	♟♟ 8
● Dolcetto d'Alba S. Anna '06	♟♟ 4*
● Barbera d'Alba Laura '06	♟ 4
● Langhe Nebbiolo Coste '06	♟ 4
● Barolo Boscareto '93	♟♟♟ 8
● Barolo Boscareto '01	♟♟ 8
● Barolo Boscareto '99	♟♟ 8
● Barolo Boscareto '00	♟♟ 8
● Barbera d'Alba La Romualda '04	♟♟ 6
● Barbera d'Alba La Romualda '03	♟♟ 5

Prinsi
VIA GAIA, 5
12052 NEIVE [CN]
TEL. 017367192
www.prinsi.it

ANNUAL PRODUCTION 60,000 bottles
HECTARES UNDER VINE 14.5
VITICULTURE METHOD Conventional

What a charming family the Lequios are. Paterfamilias Franco is indefatigable on his rounds of vineyard and cellar. He is ably supported by his wife and, above all, his son, Daniele, who has taken the reins of the estate firmly in hand. A project to expand the cellar via an underground tunnel is soon to be launched and we look forward to seeing the results. The range of wines is quite extensive, as the estate aims to present a diverse selection of labels that all offer excellent value for money. The Barbaresco is the estate's flagship product and is present this year in the two Gaia Principe and Gallina selections, both from 2004. The first is easier and exceedingly drinkable while the second is more stylish and elegant with a complexity and depth on the nose that lives up to the reputation of the famous Neive slope. Every bit as mouthfilling is the Langhe Nebbiolo 2004 Vigneto Sandrina after two years in large barrels. It is followed by Calvario 2004, a blend of barbera and nebbiolo and the only wine to age in barriques. The Langhe Chardonnay and the sauvignon-based Camp'd Pietrù Zerosei thrill with their elegance and freshness.

★ Prunotto
REG. SAN CASSIANO, 4G
12051 ALBA [CN]
TEL. 0173280017
www.prunotto.it

ANNUAL PRODUCTION 600,000 bottles
HECTARES UNDER VINE 55
VITICULTURE METHOD Conventional

Established in the early 20th century, Prunotto first made a name for itself thanks to oenologist Alfredo Prunotto, who took it over in 1923. In 1956, the winery passed to the Colla family, who bought it from its founder, before finally being acquired by the great Tuscan house of Antinori, which started marketing Prunotto wines in 1989. In the tradition of previous managements, the current ownership has maintained the professional style, slightly increasing the number of labels presented. The most significant change in philosophy has been acquisitions in some of the vineyards from which the estate selections are obtained: seven hectares in Bussia for Barolo, 27 in Agliano for Barbera d'Asti, five in Bric Turot for Barbaresco and five at Treiso for Moscato. The results show that this is a winery of breeding. The Barolo Bussia 2003 is first-rate with its notes of ripe fruit and elegant, delicately tannic body. The Barbaresco Bric Turot selection is also very successful. An estate can be judged from the quality of its basic wines and Prunotto offers two excellent reds, the Barolo and the Barbaresco. The Barbera Pian Romualdo 2004 is stylish and elegant while the Costamiòle 2003 has mature fruit and structure.

● Barbaresco Gallina '04	🍷🍷 6
● Barbaresco Gaia Principe '04	🍷🍷 6
● Calvario '04	🍷🍷 5
● Langhe Nebbiolo Vign. Sandrina '04	🍷🍷 5
O Camp'd Pietrù Zerosei '06	🍷🍷 5
O Langhe Chardonnay Vign. Tre Fichi '06	🍷🍷 4*
● Dolcetto d'Alba San Cristoforo '06	🍷 4
● Barbaresco Gaia Principe '00	🍷🍷 6
● Barbaresco Gaia Principe '01	🍷🍷 6
● Barbaresco Fausone Ris. '01	🍷🍷 6
● Barbaresco Gallina '00	🍷🍷 6
● Barbaresco Gallina '99	🍷🍷 6

● Barbaresco Bric Turot '03	🍷🍷 8
● Barolo Bussia '03	🍷🍷 8
● Barbera d'Alba Pian Romualdo '04	🍷🍷 6
● Barbaresco '04	🍷🍷 7
● Barolo '03	🍷🍷 7
● Nebbiolo d'Alba Occhetti '04	🍷🍷 5
● Barbera d'Asti Costamiòle '03	🍷🍷 7
● Barbera d'Alba '05	🍷 4
● Monferrato Mompertone '05	🍷 4
● Barbera d'Asti Fiulòt '06	🍷 4
O Moscato d'Asti '06	🍷 4
● Barbera d'Asti Costamiòle '96	🍷🍷🍷 6
● Barbera d'Asti Costamiòle '99	🍷🍷🍷 6
● Barbera d'Asti Costamiòle '97	🍷🍷🍷 6
● Barolo Bussia '01	🍷🍷🍷 8
● Barolo Bussia '98	🍷🍷🍷 8
● Barolo Bussia '99	🍷🍷🍷 8
● Barolo Bussia '96	🍷🍷🍷 8

Carlo Quarello

via Marconi, 3
14020 Cossombrato [AT]
tel. 0141905204
valerio.quarello@libero.it

ANNUAL PRODUCTION 20,000 bottles
HECTARES UNDER VINE 5.5
VITICULTURE METHOD Natural

It was 1963 when Carlo Quarello planted his grignolino vineyard, investing the savings he had accumulated during his years working on cruise ships. It was a courageous decision to return to terra firma and one that was inspired by passion. Over the years, the Monferrato Casalese area has largely lost its winemaking tradition and the once-noble grignolino variety has slipped into oblivion. But fortune favours the bold and Carlo Quarello has become a beacon for the entire area. Today, he is flanked by his son Valerio in the cellar and vineyard and continues his battle to win recognition for the variety, firm in his belief that the austere nobility of its tannins and its fresh, spicy aromas will attract wider consensus. In 2003, Carlo and Valerio increased production by planting plots of nebbiolo and barbera, and this year sees release of the first bottles, which are from the 2006 harvest. The wines are interesting and promise well, and we look forward to seeing their progress in future harvests. But grignolino is still kingpin. The Marcaleone 2006 is a very fine wine, fresh with balanced tannins, notes of spice and woodland flowers, medium body, elegance and character. The Barbera also showed well.

● Grignolino del M.to Casalese Cré Marcaleone '06	TT	4*
● Barbera d'Asti V. Cré '06	TT	4*
● Monferrato Nebbiolo Pionda '06	T	4
● Grignolino del M.to Casalese Cré Marcaleone '05	YY	4
● Grignolino del M.to Casalese Cré Marcaleone '04	YY	4
● Grignolino del M.to Casalese Cré Marcaleone '03	YY	4
● Barbera d'Asti V. Cré '04	YY	4

Renato Ratti

fraz. Annunziata, 7
12064 La Morra [CN]
tel. 017350185
www.renatoratti.com

ANNUAL PRODUCTION 300,000 bottles
HECTARES UNDER VINE 35
VITICULTURE METHOD Conventional

Pietro Ratti, son of the late lamented Renato, has waited a long time to see his new cellar finished. However, it was well worth the wait because the result is a model structure with such graceful lines that, despite its impressive size, it takes nothing away from the charm of the magnificent Annunziata hill. The Barolos are back after a year's sabbatical and two of them went forward to our final tasting table. The Rocche Marcenasco is bursting with violet-led florality, fruity aromas with assertive black cherry and nuances of spice, notably aniseed, black pepper and liquorice. The Conca Marcenasco shows full, solidly built body, elegant tannins and a powerful, embracing finish. Matured in barriques and large barrels of Slavonian oak, the basic version of Marcenasco is also extremely attractive. The Monferrato Rosso Villa Pattono from barbera, nebbiolo, merlot and cabernet sauvignon is nice, offering generous fruit and the typical aromas of its two French varieties. As for the other labels, the Nebbiolo Ochetti and the Monferrato Bianco I Cedri di Villa Pattono, obtained from sauvignon with a dash of chardonnay, are both pleasing.

● Barolo Conca Marcenasco '03	TT	8
● Barolo Rocche Marcenasco '03	TT	8
● Barolo Marcenasco '03	TT	7
O Monferrato Bianco I Cedri di Villa Pattono '06	TT	4*
● Monferrato Rosso Villa Pattono '05	TT	5
● Nebbiolo d'Alba Ochetti '05	TT	5
● Dolcetto d'Alba Colombè '06	TT	4*
● Barbera d'Alba Torriglione '06	T	4
● Barolo Rocche Marcenasco '83	YYY	8
● Barolo Rocche Marcenasco '84	YYY	8
● Barolo Conca Marcenasco '00	YY	8
● Barolo Rocche Marcenasco '99	YY	8
● Barolo Conca Marcenasco '01	YY	8
● Barolo Rocche Marcenasco '00	YY	8
● Barbera d'Alba Torriglione '06	YY	4*
● Barolo Rocche Marcenasco '01	YY	8

Tenuta Castello di Razzano

FRAZ. CASARELLO
LOC. RAZZANO, 2
15021 ALFIANO NATTA [AL]
TEL. 0141922124
www.castellodirazzano.it

ANNUAL PRODUCTION 200,000 bottles
HECTARES UNDER VINE 38
VITICULTURE METHOD Conventional

Over the years, the Olearo family has accustomed us to absolutely spot-on performances, and this year is no exception. Despite the absence of some of its most prestigious wines, which usually score very highly in our Guide, the list presented for tasting was fairly wide-ranging. The Barbera Valentino Caligaris displays sensations of sweet spice, berry fruit and autumn leaf while the acidity on the palate offsets the impressive structure, which is rounded by skilful use of oak. The Barbera d'Asti Superiore Eugenea presents an intense ruby red and offers earthy nuances with tertiary notes left by the oak, developing good acidity on the powerful, balanced palate. The Oro di Razzano is a passito obtained from a blend of 75 per cent sauvignon with moscato. It has a golden yellow colour and a nose rich in notes of honey and apricot. The palate shows a wonderful balance of sugar and acidity. The Grignolino Pianaccio did not quite live up to expectations but it is pleasant and easy to drink nonetheless. The Monferrato Bianco Costa al Sole, a Chardonnay, came close to the Two Glass mark, its tropical fruit nose announcing a fresh-tasting palate with lively, lingering acidity.

Ressia

VIA CANOVA, 28
12052 NEIVE [CN]
TEL. 0173677305
www.ressia.com

ANNUAL PRODUCTION 25,000 bottles
HECTARES UNDER VINE 5
VITICULTURE METHOD Natural

We never tire of extolling the virtues of the Langhe and we are convinced that the environment in which they are conceived and produced plays an important role in making its wines unique. This leads us naturally to Fabrizio Ressia and his beautiful vineyards at Canova in the municipality of Neive. Fabrizio took over the family estate in 1997 and his passion for his work is infectious. In ten years, he has managed to build a fine estate that produces wines of strong character and enviable overall quality. This time, the quality of the wines Fabrizio presented was high enough to earn him a full entry in our Guide. The Barbaresco Canova 2004 is a captivating wine, showing clean if not yet fully expressed on the nose. It gives spicy, gamey aromas, elegant texture and tannins, nice freshness and length. The nebbiolo and barbera Langhe Rosso Resiot also performed well in both of the versions we tasted. The 2004 is more evolved and austere while the 2005 is zestily refreshing. However, what impressed our judges most of all was the level shown by the whole range.

● Barbera d'Asti Sup.	
V. Valentino Caligaris '05	♟♟ 5
● Barbera d'Asti Sup. Eugenea '04	♟♟ 4*
○ Oro di Razzano	♟♟ 5
○ Monferrato Bianco	
Costa al Sole '06	♟ 3
● Grignolino del M.to Casalese	
Pianaccio '06	♟ 3
● Barbera d'Asti Sup.	
V. Valentino Caligaris '04	♟♟ 5
● Barbera d'Asti Sup.	
V. Valentino Caligaris '03	♟♟ 5
● Barbera d'Asti Sup.	
V. del Beneficio '04	♟♟ 5
● Barbera d'Asti Sup. Campasso '04	♟♟ 4
● Barbera d'Asti Sup. Campasso '03	♟♟ 4

● Barbaresco Canova '04	♟♟ 6
● Barbera d'Alba Sup.Canova '05	♟♟ 4*
● Dolcetto d'Alba Sup. Canova '05	♟♟ 4*
● Langhe Rosso Resiot '05	♟♟ 5
● Langhe Rosso Resiot '04	♟♟ 5
● Dolcetto d'Alba Canova '05	♟ 4
● Barbera d'Alba Canova '05	♟ 4

F.lli Revello

FRAZ. ANNUNZIATA, 103
12064 LA MORRA [CN]
TEL. 017350276
www.revellofratelli.it

ANNUAL PRODUCTION 65,000 bottles
HECTARES UNDER VINE 12
VITICULTURE METHOD Natural

There's nothing particular to report from Revello this year, unless you count the return to production of all of the estate's famous vineyard selections after a sabbatical forced by the challenging 2002 vintage. Brothers Carlo and Enzo presented their usual full range of Barolos and we plumped for the Rocche dell'Annunziata ahead of the others for its attractive notes of oak, liquorice, cocoa powder and eucalyptus. The palate shows elegant, well-defined tannins and impressive length in the finish. But Vigna Conca also went to the finals. It starts off rather more closed on the nose but opens out gradually to reveal very generous aromas of fruit and spice with nuances ranging from dry leaves and violets all the way to mint. The palate is powerful and solidly built. The magnificent Barbera Ciabot du Re is back and claimed a Three Glass trophy for the 2005 version. Its refreshing acidity and measured use of oak make it one of the best to come of this DOCG for breadth and mouthfeel with a very long fruity finish. We also noted fine performances from Vigna Giachini and Gattera, as well as the L'Insieme 2004 from nebbiolo, barbera and cabernet sauvignon. The rest of the labels on offer are pleasant.

● Barbera d'Alba Ciabot du Re '05	▼▼▼	6
● Barolo Rocche dell'Annunziata '03	▼▼	8
● Barolo V. Conca '03	▼▼	8
● Barbera d'Alba '06	▼▼	4*
● Barolo V. Gattera '03	▼▼	7
● Barolo V. Giachini '03	▼▼	7
● Barolo '03	▼▼	6
● Langhe L'Insieme '04	▼▼	7
● Dolcetto d'Alba '06	▼	4
● Langhe Nebbiolo '05	▼	5
● Barolo V. Conca '99	▽▽▽	8
● Barolo Rocche dell'Annunziata '97	▽▽▽	8
● Barolo Rocche dell'Annunziata '00	▽▽▽	8
● Barolo Rocche dell'Annunziata '01	▽▽▽	8

Michele Reverdito

B.TA GARASSINI, 74B
12064 LA MORRA [CN]
TEL. 017350336
www.reverdito.it

ANNUAL PRODUCTION 30,000 bottles
HECTARES UNDER VINE 20
VITICULTURE METHOD Conventional

The village of Rivalta at La Morra may not be an oenological heavyweight, like Annunziata or Santa Maria, but it is home to highly talented producer Michele Reverdito. He is a new name in Barolo, having carved out a leading role for himself in one of Italy's noblest DOCGs in the space of just a few short years. Credit also goes to his family, mother Maria, sister Sabrina and father Silvano. Before we get to our review of his wines, we note the absence of Barolo Bricco Cogni, which was not produced in 2002. By way of consolation, we tasted two other labels from the same DOCG: the stylish, elegant Moncucco, with fruity fragrant notes, and the more powerful, muscular Serralunga with tannins clearly in evidence. We also look forward to the release of a Riserva that has been set aside to age for seven years and will be available in 2011. The other wine type this cellar handles well is Barbera, presented in two selections. Butti is full of currant, blueberry and cherry aromatics while the Delia is matured for 12 months in barriques and for a further 12 in large barrels. The Verduno Pelaverga is extremely agreeable, the Langhe Nebbiolo harmonious and the Dolcetto Formica enjoyable.

● Barolo Moncucco '03	▼▼	5*
● Barolo Serralunga '03	▼▼	5*
● Barbera d'Alba Butti '05	▼▼	4*
● Verduno Pelaverga '06	▼▼	3*
● Barbera d'Alba Delia '04	▼▼	3*
● Dolcetto d'Alba Sup. Formica '05	▼	3
● Langhe Nebbiolo Simane '05	▼	4
● Barolo Bricco Cogni '01	▽▽	6
● Barolo Serralunga '02	▽▽	5
● Barolo Moncucco '02	▽▽	5

Carlo Daniele Ricci

VIA MONTALE CELLI, 9
15050 COSTA VESCOVATO [AL]
TEL. 0131838115

ANNUAL PRODUCTION 30,000 bottles
HECTARES UNDER VINE 8
VITICULTURE METHOD Conventional

This year as in past years, the Timorasso Terre del Timorasso outshone the San Leto selection at our tastings, the latter showing excessive vegetal and citrus-like notes while the former has delicious fruit sensations and magnificent balance and softness. Those characteristics won it very high marks from our judges. Of the reds on offer, we were very impressed by the Barbera Castellania. It has an extremely interesting nose redolent of hay and brandied fruit, preceding a palate round, well-integrated aromas and tangible structure. Only its rather youthful, mouth-drying tannins prevent it from achieving even greater things. The Rosso San Martino, obtained from a bend of barbera and nebbiolo, is also very attractive. The Bonarda 'L Matt is its usual agreeable self and requires a few minutes aeration in the glass to bring out its full potential.

Giuseppe Rinaldi

VIA MONFORTE, 3
12060 BAROLO [CN]
TEL. 017356156

ANNUAL PRODUCTION 30,000 bottles
HECTARES UNDER VINE 6.5
VITICULTURE METHOD Natural

It's always a pleasure to chat with Beppe Rinaldi. Conversation quickly jumps from wine to motorbikes or art exhibitions, subjects that may seem worlds apart but that are in fact linked by a single thread which leads us to appreciate all the skill, territoriality, culture and tradition present in his wines. Beppe's Barolos are obtained from two blends created in four prestigious Langhe vineyards and vinified separately according to the most traditional methods before ageing slowly in large wood only. The Brunate-Le Coste is an outstanding Barolo of the first order, showing ethery and stylish with tannins that are in the process of smoothing out. In tribute to its noble Cannubi origins, the Cannubi S. Lorenzo-Ravera has more fruit and faint balsamic notes combined with a firmly structured body. The cellar's other wines are all very interesting and include a Nebbiolo that is not quite as complex as its more aristocratic siblings and a pleasant Barbera that combines freshness with structure. The range is rounded off by a full, fruity Dolcetto and a fragrant wine from ruché grapes grown at Barolo that is well worth tasting.

O Colli Tortonesi Terre del Timorasso '05	♟♟ 4*
● Colli Tortonesi Barbera Castellania '05	♟♟ 5
● Colli Tortonesi Rosso San Martino '05	♟♟ 5
● Piemonte Bonarda 'L Mat '05	♟ 4
O Colli Tortonesi Bianco San Leto '05	♟ 5
O Colli Tortonesi Terre del Timorasso '04	♟♟ 4
O Colli Tortonesi Terre del Timorasso '03	♟♟ 4
O Colli Tortonesi Terre del Timorasso '02	♟♟ 4

● Barolo Brunate-Le Coste '03	♟♟ 7
● Barolo Cannubi S. Lorenzo-Ravera '03	♟♟ 7
● Barbera d'Alba '06	♟♟ 4*
● Dolcetto d'Alba '06	♟♟ 4*
● Langhe Nebbiolo '05	♟♟ 5
● Rosae '06	♟ 4
● Barolo Brunate-Le Coste '01	♟♟♟ 7
● Barolo Brunate-Le Coste '00	♟♟♟ 7
● Barolo Brunate-Le Coste '97	♟♟♟ 7
● Barolo Brunate-Le Coste '99	♟♟ 7
● Barolo Brunate-Le Coste '98	♟♟ 7
● Barolo Brunate-Le Coste '96	♟♟ 7
● Barolo Cannubi S. Lorenzo-Ravera '01	♟♟ 7
● Barolo Cannubi S. Lorenzo-Ravera '00	♟♟ 7

Rizieri

CASCINA RICCHINO
12055 DIANO D'ALBA [CN]
TEL. 0173468540
www.rizieri.com

ANNUAL PRODUCTION 22,000 bottles
HECTARES UNDER VINE 6.5
VITICULTURE METHOD Conventional

Alas, there is no guide that covers all of those multi-purpose structures that offer facilities ranging from visitor centres and restaurants for passing wine lovers. If we were to produce such a tome, Rizieri would come highly recommended: it is a cellar, osteria and inn. If you're after something good to drink or eat or simply somewhere to rest your weary bones, then Rizieri is the place for you. Hats off to Giampiero Piazza, who created the Rizieri project, and to Ivan Milani and Silvio Porzionato, who are largely responsible for visitor reception. Our main concern is, of course, the wines. The estate only produces three labels but they are all high quality. The Dolcetto's nose is shot through with hints of red berry fruit and sweet spices. The palate is lip-smacking, full, round and long. The Barbera shows richness of extraction and acid character. We liked both the nose and palate and note that it gets better with every edition of the Guide. We look forward to great things in the future. The Nebbiolo's initial vegetal, earthy tones open out to reveal a wealth of fruity richness. A velvety palate and silky tannins lead into a finish that echoes the nose's violet and liquorice aromas.

Albino Rocca

S.DA RONCHI, 18
12050 BARBARESCO [CN]
TEL. 0173635145
www.roccaalbino.com

ANNUAL PRODUCTION 90,000 bottles
HECTARES UNDER VINE 15
VITICULTURE METHOD Conventional

There was an excellent performance from Angelo Rocca's estate, which again offered the high level of quality that we have come to expect in recent years. The basic Barbaresco 2004 offers approachable fruit, refreshing acidity and robust tannins. It is a tad closed at present but will develop over time. We move up a gear with the two selections, which are considerably better. The Barbaresco Bric Ronchi 2004 is a dark, concentrated wine with spicy notes that owe much to the small barrels in which it matures. The nose starts out dynamic and full on well-defined fruit and flowers that are faithfully mirrored on the palate. Ample, powerful and deep, it is already drinking superbly but we believe it has even more to offer. The splendid Barbaresco Loreto 2004 has a more austere, classic profile, showing mellow, earthy and mineral. Delicate yet solidly built in the mouth, it entrances with the fullness of its flavour and the sheer elegance that won it Three Glasses. The exquisite Barbera Gepin 2005's bright ruby introduces a restrained nose and a clean, balanced palate with good progression. The extremely drinkable Langhe La Rocca 2006 from cortese is savoury and enjoyable.

● Diano d'Alba Rizieri '06	♟♟	4*
● Barbera d'Alba '05	♟♟	4*
● Nebbiolo d'Alba '05	♟♟	5
● Barbera d'Alba '04	♟♟	5
● Nebbiolo d'Alba '03	♟♟	5
● Nebbiolo d'Alba '04	♟♟	5
● Diano d'Alba Rizieri '05	♟♟	4
● Diano d'Alba Rizieri '04	♟♟	4
● Diano d'Alba Rizieri '03	♟♟	4

● Barbaresco Vign. Loreto '04	♟♟♟	7
● Barbaresco Vign. Brich Ronchi '04	♟♟	7
● Barbera d'Alba Gepin '05	♟♟	5
● Barbaresco '04	♟♟	6
● Dolcetto d'Alba Vignalunga '06	♟♟	4
O Langhe Bianco La Rocca '06	♟♟	5
O Langhe Chardonnay da Bertü '06	♟	4
● Barbaresco Vign. Brich Ronchi '96	♟♟♟	7
● Barbaresco Vign. Brich Ronchi '97	♟♟♟	7
● Barbaresco Vign. Brich Ronchi '00	♟♟♟	7
● Barbaresco Vign. Brich Ronchi '03	♟♟♟	7
● Barbaresco Vign. Loreto '95	♟♟♟	6
● Barbaresco Vign. Loreto '98	♟♟♟	7

★ Bruno Rocca
S.DA RABAJÀ, 60
12050 BARBARESCO [CN]
TEL. 0173635112
www.brunorocca.it

Rocche Costamagna
VIA VITTORIO EMANUELE, 8
12064 LA MORRA [CN]
TEL. 0173509225
www.rocchecostamagna.it

ANNUAL PRODUCTION 60,000 bottles
HECTARES UNDER VINE 15
VITICULTURE METHOD Conventional

ANNUAL PRODUCTION 85,000 bottles
HECTARES UNDER VINE 15
VITICULTURE METHOD Conventional

Rabajà is one of the loveliest, noblest subzones in the DOCG and the home of enviable Barbarescos. For several years now, Rabajà has meant Bruno Rocca to the many fans of this family-run estate. With the eager support of his able sons, Bruno faithfully creates wines that forge a precious link with their terroir in a style based on elegance, balance and drinkability. The Barbaresco Rabajà 2004's expressive excellence announces a harmonious, elegant bouquet, restrained tannins and an austere, leisurely finish with impeccable balance. Barbaresco Coparossa 2004 is another magnificent wine, showing deep and varietal with rich aromatics and discreet supporting tannins. In the debate as to which deserved the higher score, our tasters came down on the side of Coparossa, a superlative red that romped home to Three Glasses. The rest of the range features a delicious Chardonnay Cadet 2006 and a broad, seamless Dolcetto Trifolè with a soft finish. The two Barberas showed well. They're different but have excellent structure and perfectly gauged tannins. There's no 2003 version of the prestigious Barbaresco Maria Adelaide but we have new vigour on the way from three hectares of fine vineyards near Neive.

We have referred to Rocche Costamagna as an urban winery, in that its headquarters lie in the heart of La Morra, a stone's throw from the look-out point that gives an unrivalled view over the entire Barolo area of Langhe. But this edition of the Guide is dedicated to the vineyards, not the cellar. The plots belonging to the Locatelli family are situated in the natural amphitheatre of Rocche dell'Annunziata, in other words in one of the best-known and positions in the entire DOCG. Nature, human endeavour and the expertise of its collaborators – Romana and Caviola in vineyard and cellar, respectively – are the happy combination of elements that make this estate great. This year's performance was truly outstanding. The Barolo Bricco San Francesco has shaken off the worst of 2003's torrid heat and is fragrant, fresh and dynamic as its aromas unfold on nose and palate. In short, this was one of the best showings we have ever seen. The Rocche dell'Annunziata is a whisper less complex and embracing but it's still a fabulous wine and is already drinking well. The two Barberas are both rich in acidity, well-made and enjoyable. We found the Dolcetto Rùbis more attractive than the Murrae.

● Barbaresco Coparossa '04	♀♀♀	8
● Barbaresco Rabajà '04	♀♀	8
● Barbaresco '04	♀♀	7
● Barbera d'Asti '05	♀♀	5
● Barbera d'Alba '05	♀♀	6
● Dolcetto d'Alba V. Trifolè '06	♀♀	4*
O Langhe Chardonnay Cadet '06	♀♀	5
● Barbaresco Maria Adelaide '01	♀♀♀	8
● Barbaresco Rabajà '88	♀♀♀	8
● Barbaresco Rabajà '89	♀♀♀	8
● Barbaresco Rabajà '93	♀♀♀	8
● Barbaresco Rabajà '96	♀♀♀	8
● Barbaresco Rabajà '98	♀♀♀	8
● Barbaresco Rabajà '00	♀♀♀	8
● Barbaresco Rabajà '01	♀♀♀	8
● Barbaresco Coparossa '97	♀♀♀	8
● Barbaresco Coparossa '03	♀♀	8

● Barolo Bricco Francesco Rocche dell'Annunziata '03	♀	7
● Barolo Rocche dell'Annunziata '03	♀♀	7
● Barbera d'Alba Rocche delle Rocche '05	♀♀	4*
● Barbera d'Alba Annunziata '05	♀♀	4*
● Langhe Nebbiolo Roccardo '04	♀♀	4*
● Dolcetto d'Alba Rùbis '06	♀♀	4*
● Dolcetto d'Alba Murrae '06	♀	4
O Langhe Arneis '06	♀	4
● Barolo Bricco Francesco Rocche dell'Annunziata '99	♀♀	7
● Barolo Bricco Francesco Rocche dell'Annunziata '00	♀♀	7
● Barolo Bricco Francesco Rocche dell'Annunziata '01	♀♀	7
● Barolo Rocche dell'Annunziata '00	♀♀	7

★ Podere Rocche dei Manzoni
LOC. MANZONI SOPRANI, 3
12065 MONFORTE D'ALBA [CN]
TEL. 017378421
www.rocchedeimanzoni.it

ANNUAL PRODUCTION 250,000 bottles
HECTARES UNDER VINE 40
VITICULTURE METHOD Conventional

As you take the road up to Monforte, the sight of the magnificent estate belonging to Valentino Migliorini takes your breath away. A magnet for wine lovers, it perfectly represents the high level of quality achieved by a cellar founded on rock-solid principles: uncompromising selection of crus and growing years that reflect the territory and choices in the cellar that complement work in the vineyard. This aristocratic estate is home to Barolo but this year the 2003 selections are absent and several labels have been left to age as they were not deemed ready. It was left to the Barolo Rocche 2003 to keep the flag flying, which it did very well. A lovely range of aromatics and a caressing, consistent palate bode well for the future. The excellent Pinònero 2001 is earthier and more austere on the nose, showing elegant, supple and harmonious in the mouth through to the tannic, spicy finish. We welcome back the Valentino Brut Zero 2000, a refined, leisurely wine with tempting, mature aromas while the Riserva Elena 2003 has the requisite acidulous tanginess. We noted fine performances from L'Angelica 2005 and Barbera Sorito Mosconi, both silky and pleasantly vigorous on the palate.

Flavio Roddolo
FRAZ. BRICCO APPIANI
LOC. SANT'ANNA, 5
12065 MONFORTE D'ALBA [CN]
TEL. 017378535

ANNUAL PRODUCTION 22,500 bottles
HECTARES UNDER VINE 6
VITICULTURE METHOD Natural

Flavio Roddolo is a very unusual producer. In a few, well-chosen words, he shrewdly sums up the methods he employs in the vineyard and the pledge he has made to create completely authentic wines. Flavio is a genuine Langhe wine man and his estate is well worth a visit for anyone wanting to know and appreciate his work. His wines are as unique as they are extraordinary. After a long series of harvests, he is at long last expanding the cellar and the spaces where his beloved bottles rest so that his countryman's sensitivity can better judge when the wine is ready for the corkscrew. The Barolo Ravera 2003 is outstanding, elegant and harmoniously expressive with an austere profile and lingering aromas. The close-knit, cabernet-based Langhe Bricco Appiani lives up to expectations with robust fruity notes in a soft, balanced palate. The Dolcetto d'Alba Superiore 2005 is also well made, showing dense, alcohol-rich, tasty and impressively long. The other labels are full bodied and very drinkable. Overall, the range offers reliable quality and good value for money.

● Barolo Rocche '03	♛♛ 8
● Langhe Rosso Pinònero '01	♛♛ 8
○ Valentino Brut Zero Ris. '00	♛♛ 7
● Barbera d'Alba Sorito Mosconi '04	♛♛ 6
○ Langhe Chardonnay L'Angelica '05	♛♛ 7
○ Valentino Brut Ris. Elena '03	♛♛ 5
● Barolo V. Big 'd Big '99	♛♛♛ 8
● Barolo V. Cappella di S. Stefano '96	♛♛♛ 8
● Barolo V. Cappella di S. Stefano '01	♛♛♛ 8
● Barolo Vigna Big Ris. '90	♛♛♛ 6
● Barolo V. d'la Roul Ris. '90	♛♛♛ 8
● Barolo V. Big Ris. '89	♛♛♛ 8
● Langhe Rosso Quatr Nas '99	♛♛♛ 7
● Langhe Rosso Quatr Nas '96	♛♛♛ 8
○ Valentino Brut Zero Ris. '98	♛♛♛ 7
○ Valentino Brut Zero Ris. '93	♛♛♛ 7

● Barolo Ravera '03	♛♛ 6
● Langhe Rosso Bricco Appiani '04	♛♛ 6
● Barbera d'Alba '04	♛♛ 4*
● Dolcetto d'Alba Sup. '05	♛♛ 4*
● Nebbiolo d'Alba '04	♛♛ 5
● Dolcetto d'Alba '06	♛♛ 3*
● Barolo Ravera '97	♛♛♛ 6
● Barolo Ravera '03	♛♛♛ 6
● Bricco Appiani '99	♛♛♛ 6
● Barolo Ravera '01	♛♛♛ 6
● Barolo Ravera '00	♛♛ 6
● Barolo Ravera '99	♛♛ 6
● Barolo Ravera '02	♛♛ 6
● Barbera d'Alba '03	♛♛ 4
● Langhe Rosso Bricco Appiani '03	♛♛ 6

Ronchi
S.DA RONCHI
12050 BARBARESCO [CN]
TEL. 0173635156
az.ronchi@libero.it

ANNUAL PRODUCTION 20,000 bottles
HECTARES UNDER VINE 5.5
VITICULTURE METHOD Conventional

Helped out by his father, Alfonso, Giancarlo Rocca runs this small family estate in the heart of the cru from which it takes its name. The rows of vines, now grassed over, offer a stunning panorama. As always, it is here that quality has its roots, and in the small, functional cellar Giancarlo limits his own contribution to the minimum. Wine here is made as far as possible by the territory and its traditional varieties. This year, Giancarlo presented us with a superlative 2004, probably his best ever Barbaresco Ronchi. Aged in new barriques for 20 months, it has oak well under control and is distinctive for its fruit and energy, revealing sweet, juicy tannins and a long finish. This absolute gem merited Three resounding Glasses. The basic Barbaresco is also good, just a tad shorter in the finish and a bit more rustic on the nose. We liked the Chardonnay 2005, which conceals impressive alcohol behind enormous freshness and lovely lively fruit, and the classic Barbera, matured in pre-used barriques that have left it bright and full of stuffing. The Dolcetto is clean, powerful and pleasantly drinkable.

Giovanni Rosso
LOC. BAUDANA, 6
12050 SERRALUNGA D'ALBA [CN]
TEL. 0173613142
www.giovannirosso.com

ANNUAL PRODUCTION 20,000 bottles
HECTARES UNDER VINE 9
VITICULTURE METHOD Natural

A visit to this cellar will introduce you to the taciturn Giovanni, the delightful Ester and their flamboyant son, Davide, the life and soul of the Rosso ménage. There are no major developments regarding the wines but we are looking forward to the release of the second Barolo selection next year, La Serra obtained from plots in the upper part of Serralunga. The Rossos have started work to expand their cellar by adding an area for ageing the Barolos to give them space in which to house the big barrels. The use of native yeasts and the absence of filtration are just two of the strong points of this estate, which practises non-invasive agricultural methods. Competent vineyard management in the torrid growing year of 2003 has produced two excellent Barolos that stand out for elegance and freshness. We preferred the more austere, compact Cerretta to the Serralunga. Cerretta has extraordinary body and promises to develop interestingly in the long term. The fruity, fragrant Barbera is very decent and the Dolcetto is pleasant.

● Barbaresco Ronchi '04	▼▼▼ 6
● Barbera d'Alba Terlé '05	▼▼ 4*
● Barbaresco '04	▼▼ 6
○ Langhe Chardonnay '05	▼▼ 4*
● Dolcetto d'Alba Rosario '05	▼ 4
● Langhe Freisa '05	▼ 4
● Barbaresco Ronchi '03	♀♀ 6
● Barbera d'Alba Terlé '04	♀♀ 4
○ Langhe Chardonnay '04	♀♀ 4

● Barolo Cerretta '03	▼▼ 8
● Barolo Serralunga '03	▼▼ 6
● Barbera d'Alba Donna Margherita '05	▼▼ 4*
● Dolcetto d'Alba Le Quattro Vigne '06	▼ 4
● Barolo Cerretta '01	♀♀ 7
● Barolo Cerretta '00	♀♀ 7
● Barolo Serralunga '01	♀♀ 6
● Barolo Serralunga '00	♀♀ 6
● Barbera d'Alba Donna Margherita '01	♀♀ 4
● Barbera d'Alba Donna Margherita '04	♀♀ 4

Rovellotti
INTERNO CASTELLO, 22
28074 GHEMME [NO]
TEL. 0163840393
www.rovellotti.it

F.lli Rovero
LOC. VALDONATA
FRAZ. SAN MARZANOTTO, 218
14100 ASTI [AT]
TEL. 0141592460
www.rovero.it

ANNUAL PRODUCTION 60,000 bottles
HECTARES UNDER VINE 15
VITICULTURE METHOD Conventional

ANNUAL PRODUCTION 80,000 bottles
HECTARES UNDER VINE 20
VITICULTURE METHOD Certified organic

The ancient medieval heart of Ghemme beats to the rhythm of history. Built in the 1300s, this perfectly preserved historic centre offers a glimpse of how people lived and worked in centuries past and stands as a important monument to the customs of yore. This picturesque setting is home to the cellar of the Rovellotti brothers, Antonello and Paolo. The areas where they vinify the grapes cultivated on their 15 hectares of vineyards are to be found in the village's narrow alleyways. Ghemme DOCG is the estate's most important product: this year the two selections that were put on hold last year show that time can do wonders for the austere and highly distinctive wines of upper Piedmont. To our minds, the Riserva came out ever so slightly ahead of Chioso dei Pomi. Its fruit-rich, earthy aromatics are sharper on the nose, the palate is very consistent and the finish is long. In tribute to the estate's vocation for nebbiolo, the Colline Novaresi also showed well. It may be very young but the palate is extremely rewarding and full. The Vespolina, the Uva Rara and the erbaluce-based Bianco are less imposing. All three display strength and individuality in their cleanliness and varietal aromas.

Diversification is the keynote at the estate owned by Claudio, Franco and Michele Rovero. Side by side with a large and varied range of wines is a big distillery business and an agriturismo. Their go-ahead entrepreneurial approach allows them to ride the waves of the market and their decision to go organic when they founded the estate also shows that they have a keen nose for consumer trends. This year, we were particularly impressed by the two Barberas, from the bountiful harvest of 2004. The barrique-aged Rouvè is more firmly structured and enveloping on the palate while the Gustin is more immediately approachable, presenting balance between fruit and acidity. Obtained from a blend of barbera, nebbiolo, merlot and cabernet sauvignon, the Monferrato Rosso Rocca Schiavino is fruity and caressing. The Grignolino La Casalina embodies the characteristics of its wine type in the Asti interpretation, which is all fruit and freshness, less tannic and concentrated than its Casalese cousin. The Monferrato Rosso Lajetto from pinot noir and the Monferrato Bianco Villa Drago from sauvignon are pleasantly accessible.

- Colline Novaresi Nebbiolo Valplazza '06 ▼▼ 4
- Ghemme Costa del Salmino Ris. '01 ▼▼ 6
- Ghemme Chioso dei Pomi '01 ▼▼ 6
- Colline Novaresi Vespolina '06 ▼ 3
- Colline Novaresi Uva Rara '06 ▼ 3
- O Colline Novaresi Bianco Il Criccone '06 ▼ 4
- Ghemme Ris. '98 ♈♈ 6
- Ghemme Ris. '01 ♈♈ 6
- Ghemme Ris. '99 ♈♈ 6

- Barbera d'Asti Sup. Rouvè '04 ▼▼ 5
- Monferrato Rosso Rocca Schiavino '04 ▼▼ 4
- Barbera d'Asti Sup. Vign. Gustin '04 ▼▼ 4
- Grignolino d'Asti Vign. La Casalina '06 ▼▼ 3*
- Monferrato Rosso Lajetto '05 ▼ 4
- O Monferrato Bianco Villa Drago '06 ▼ 3
- Barbera d'Asti Sup. Rouvè '01 ♈♈ 5
- Barbera d'Asti Sup. Rouvè '02 ♈♈ 5
- Barbera d'Asti Sup. Vign. Gustin '03 ♈♈ 4
- Barbera d'Asti Sup. Vign. Gustin '02 ♈♈ 4

Podere Ruggeri Corsini
LOC. BUSSIA CORSINI, 106
12065 MONFORTE D'ALBA [CN]
TEL. 017378625
podereruggericorsini@libero.it

Cascina Salicetti
VIA CASCINA SALICETTI, 2
15050 MONTEGIOCO [AL]
TEL. 0131875192

ANNUAL PRODUCTION 50,000 bottles
HECTARES UNDER VINE 7
VITICULTURE METHOD Conventional

ANNUAL PRODUCTION 25,000 bottles
HECTARES UNDER VINE 16
VITICULTURE METHOD Conventional

The estate belonging to Nicola Argamante and Loredana Addari has achieved a good standard of quality and is earning a name for itself in the Monforte d'Alba wine world. We were very satisfied with the performance of the wines presented this year, a range that is, as usual, diverse and caters to a varied public. The Barolo San Pietro 2003 and the Barbera d'Alba Armujan 2005 won high scores from our judges. The Barolo displays a complex nose with nuances of ripe fruit that regain freshness and soundness on the palate. The second offers sensations of aromatic herbs and spices, notably eucalyptus, mint and vanilla, invigorated by a touch of oak that buttresses the palate. The Barolo Corsini 2003 tends to show the effects of its growing year but makes up for a certain lack of fragrance with an overall impression of excellent body and density. The Langhe Nebbiolo 2005, meanwhile, is all drinkability. The other reds, Dolcetto d'Alba 2006 and Barbera d'Alba 2006, are fresh-tasting, coherent and well made.

We gave a first full profile Anselmo Franzosi, whose management style is reassuringly steady. He carries the mantle of his father, Pietro, who still has a say in the decisions regarding the vineyard and cellar. Anselmo has worked as a consultant for other estates, and this has ensured that his own cellar swiftly achieved high standards of quality. A case in point is the Timorasso Ombra della Luna. It's lip-smacking, mineral, fragrant and infinitely long: in short, an absolute gem of a wine. Nor does the house's second white disappoint. We have already extolled Montarlino in previous editions of the Guide as one of the best cortese-based whites in the territory. Turning to the reds, Morganti outperformed its elder brother, the Punta del Sole. Both are derived from barbera, the Morganti being aged exclusively in stainless steel and impressing with its astonishing freshness and drinkability whereas the cask-conditioned Punta del Sole didn't manage to express itself fully. A few extra months in the bottle should be enough to smooth out the edginess. We had a fine showing, too, from the two Dolcettos, Di Marzi and Rugras – one of the estate's flagship wines – and the agreeable Bonarda Caminari.

● Barbera d'Alba Sup. Armujan '05	♈♈	5
● Barolo Corsini '03	♈♈	6
● Barolo San Pietro '03	♈♈	6
● Langhe Nebbiolo '05	♈♈	4*
● Barbera d'Alba '06	♈	4
○ Dolcetto d'Alba '06	♈	4
● Barolo Corsini '00	♀♀	6
● Barolo Corsini '01	♀♀	6
● Barolo Corsini '02	♀♀	6
● Barbera d'Alba Sup. Armujan '04	♀♀	5
● Langhe Rosso Argamakow '04	♀♀	5
● Langhe Rosso Argamakow '03	♀♀	5

○ Colli Tortonesi Cortese Montarlino '06	♈♈	4
○ Colli Tortonesi Timorasso Ombra della Luna '05	♈♈	4
● Colli Tortonesi Rosso Morganti '05	♈♈	4
● Colli Tortonesi Dolcetto Rugras '05	♈♈	3*
● Colli Tortonesi Rosso Punta del Sole '05	♈	4
● Colli Tortonesi Dolcetto Di Marzi '05	♈	3
● Piemonte Bonarda Caminari '05	♈	3
○ Colli Tortonesi Cortese Montarlino '05	♀♀	4
● Colli Tortonesi Rosso Punta del Sole '04	♀♀	4
● Colli Tortonesi Rosso Morganti '04	♀	4

San Fereolo

LOC. SAN FEREOLO
B.TA VALDIBÀ, 59
12063 DOGLIANI [CN]
TEL. 0173742075
www.sanfereolo.com

ANNUAL PRODUCTION 46,000 bottles
HECTARES UNDER VINE 12
VITICULTURE METHOD Natural

When Nicoletta Bocca decided that her future lay in wine, the aesthetic aspects of the farmhouse and vineyards probably influenced her as much as viticulture. The estate lies near the chapel of San Fereolo on the crest of the hill with the small village of Valdibà in one of the most stunning spots in Langhe. A true artist of wine, Nicoletta manages to imbue her bottles with the rugged personality of the land. She has decided to adopt biodynamic methods and certification is now a mere formality. Valdibà's wines are often rough initially but mature with elegance and these characteristics are present in all their glory in Nicoletta's products. As for the wines themselves, we anxiously await release of the Dogliani 2006. It is part of the new DOCG and as such will not be released until the November following the harvest. Meanwhile, the other house selections are in fine fettle. The Provinciale from nebbiolo is dense in tannic texture while the Austri, obtained from barbera with a small amount of nebbiolo, is balsamic, richly fruity and refreshed by good dose of acidity. Even the Coste di Riavolo from riesling renano recalls a red in its tannins and big structure.

● Langhe Rosso Austri '05	YY (black)	5
○ Langhe Bianco Coste di Riavolo '05	YY (black)	4*
● Langhe Rosso Il Provinciale '05	YY (black)	5
● Dolcetto di Dogliani S. Fereolo '97	YYY	4
● Dolcetto di Dogliani S. Fereolo '99	YYY	4
● Langhe Rosso Austri '03	YYY	5
● Langhe Rosso Brumaio '97	YYY	5
● Langhe Rosso Austri '04	YY	5
● Langhe Rosso Il Provinciale '04	YY	5
● Dogliani '05	YY	4
● Dolcetto di Dogliani Valdibà '04	YY	4

San Romano

B.TA GIACHELLI, 8
12063 DOGLIANI [CN]
TEL. 017376289
www.sanromano.com

ANNUAL PRODUCTION 50,000 bottles
HECTARES UNDER VINE 8
VITICULTURE METHOD Conventional

The estate of San Romano is owned by entrepreneur Giulio Napoli, who over the years has built his cellar into one of the best in the Dogliani area. Last year, we spoke of the dreadful hailstorm that ruined the harvest in September 2005 and compromised the soundness of the wines reviewed in the 2007 edition of the Guide. Happily, the growing year in 2006 was more merciful and the talented San Romano team led by Enrico Durando and supported by consultant Beppe Caviola presented us with two wines of impressive structure and character. The Bricco delle Lepri is readier and enjoyable thanks to its intense notes of cherry-led red berry fruit. The palate is juicy with soft, well-balanced tannins that lead into an agreeably long-lingering finish. The Vigna del Pilone is more austere and rich in flesh, still a tad held back by big structure that we are convinced will come into its own in a few months. It has bags of character, disclosing aromas of cinchona, cocoa powder and black pepper. The palate shows a very pleasant acid vein and closes on a refined note of bitter almond.

● Dolcetto di Dogliani V. del Pilone '06	YY (black)	4*
● Dolcetto di Dogliani Bricco delle Lepri '06	YY (black)	3*
● Dolcetto di Dogliani V. del Pilone '97	YYY	4
● Dolcetto di Dogliani V. del Pilone '99	YYY	4
● Dolcetto di Dogliani V. del Pilone '98	YYY	4
● Dolcetto di Dogliani V. del Pilone '03	YY	4
● Dolcetto di Dogliani V. del Pilone '04	YY	4
● Dolcetto di Dogliani Sup. Dolianum '00	YY	5
● Dolcetto di Dogliani Sup. Dolianum '01	YY	5

Tenuta San Sebastiano
CASCINA SAN SEBASTIANO, 41
15040 LU [AL]
TEL. 0131741353
www.dealessi.it

ANNUAL PRODUCTION 70,000 bottles
HECTARES UNDER VINE 10
VITICULTURE METHOD Conventional

Roberto De Alessi continues to amaze us with his fireworks. Joking apart, the range of wines he offered this year is supremely good, and two of them in particular gave magnificent performances that put them on our final tasting table. The Barbera Superiore Mepari kept up its excellent standards, presenting an impenetrable ruby, a concentrated, complex nose and a powerful palate refreshed by acidity. The Sol-Do's very intense ruby red is the prelude to a cornucopia of aromas that range from fruit to spice. A very confident entry on the palate is followed by echoes of the fruit and impressive aromatic length. A wine at the top of its category, the moscato-based LV Passito displays satisfying nose-palate balance. The fruity nose of the Grignolino is enhanced by flowery nuances and the palate is equally harmonious, offering pleasant drinkability and just the right amount of tannins. We'll end our notes with the standard-label Barbera, a well-made wine with a clean-tasting, refreshing palate.

★ Luciano Sandrone
VIA PUGNANE, 4
12060 BAROLO [CN]
TEL. 0173560023
www.sandroneluciano.com

ANNUAL PRODUCTION 95,000 bottles
HECTARES UNDER VINE 25
VITICULTURE METHOD Conventional

The house of Sandrone has come a long way since 1978, when it picked its first harvest and Luciano decided to adopt an individual approach in the cellar based on innovation, land-rootedness, minimal use of chemicals in the vineyard and an uncompromising quest for quality. His wines embody all of these characteristics and this year the list is back up to five. The Barolo Cannubi Boschis, a real Langhe classic, astonishes with its powerful fruit supported by an embracing, elegant structure and underpinned by silky, magnificently smooth tannins. We had no hesitation in awarding it Three Glasses. Just a heartbeat behind is Barolo Le Vigne, which stands out for an overall freshness that gives it class. A three-hectare block in Roero's Valmaggiore produces the grapes that go into the house Nebbiolo. Its sojourn in untoasted oak allows the terroir full rein and results in a complex, ready wine. The Barbera d'Alba is also superb, its ageing in 900-litre casks imbuing it with spicy notes that enhance both fruit and body. We also applaud the Dolcetto, whose flesh and backbone make for delicious drinking.

Wine	Glasses
● Barbera del M.to Sup. Mepari '05	♥♥ 4*
● Monferrato Rosso Sol-Do '05	♥♥ 4*
● Grignolino del M.to Casalese '06	♥♥ 3*
○ LV Passito '05	♥♥ 4
● Barbera del M.to '06	♥ 3
● Barbera del M.to Mepari '03	♥♥ 4
● Barbera del M.to Mepari '04	♥♥ 4
● Barbera del M.to Mepari '00	♥♥ 4
● Barbera del M.to Mepari '01	♥♥ 4
● Monferrato Rosso Dalera '03	♥♥ 6

Wine	Glasses
● Barolo Cannubi Boschis '03	♥♥♥ 8
● Barolo Le Vigne '03	♥♥ 8
● Barbera d'Alba '05	♥♥ 5
● Nebbiolo d'Alba Valmaggiore '05	♥♥ 6
● Dolcetto d'Alba '06	♥♥ 4*
● Barolo '83	♥♥♥ 8
● Barolo '84	♥♥♥ 8
● Barolo Cannubi Boschis '86	♥♥♥ 8
● Barolo Cannubi Boschis '89	♥♥♥ 8
● Barolo Cannubi Boschis '01	♥♥♥ 8
● Barolo Cannubi Boschis '90	♥♥♥ 8
● Barolo Cannubi Boschis '87	♥♥♥ 8
● Barolo Cannubi Boschis '00	♥♥♥ 8
● Barolo Le Vigne '99	♥♥♥ 8
● Barolo Le Vigne '00	♥♥ 8

Cantine Sant'Agata
REG. MEZZENA, 19
14030 SCURZOLENGO [AT]
TEL. 0141203186
www.santagata.com

Paolo Saracco
VIA CIRCONVALLAZIONE, 6
12053 CASTIGLIONE TINELLA [CN]
TEL. 0141855113
info@paolosaracco.it

ANNUAL PRODUCTION 150,000 bottles
HECTARES UNDER VINE 11
VITICULTURE METHOD Conventional

ANNUAL PRODUCTION 380,000 bottles
HECTARES UNDER VINE 35
VITICULTURE METHOD Conventional

Brothers Franco and Claudio Cavallero are among the most skilled interpreters of the rare native ruché variety. Aside from being capable growers and winemakers, they know how to bring out the best in this grape commercially, so our appreciation is redoubled. The brothers produce a lot of wines. We especially liked the Pro Nobis, which reached our finals thanks to refined notes of violets and wild roses on a distinctly spicy background. The palate is dense, without becoming heavy, and finishes long and complex. The Cavallero brothers also show their skill with Barberas. Cavalé proffers intense notes of cherry preserves mingled with more austere sensations of rain-soaked earth. The enjoyable Altea shows hints of plum and appealing acidity. Monferrato Monterovere, a blend of barbera, nebbiolo and cabernet sauvignon, opens on the nose with luscious waves of blackberry and wild berries. The rest of the array is agreeable, with a special mention for the Grignolino Miravalle.

We visited Paolo Saracco's winery when extensions to the cellar were in full swing but the fact that everybody had a thousand things to finish before the harvest didn't stop them welcoming us with open arms. The Saraccos are moscato makers par excellence in a territory long favourable to this variety. Paolo tends the vineyards, distributed across various plots in the municipality of Castiglione Tinella, and produces very good wines. The bigger cellar will allow the team to organise more efficiently the fermentation equipment, although it will still be within the walls of the family property in the centre of the village. A few international varieties are there, in quantities that are small in comparison to the moscato but large enough to diversify production. The Monferrato Rosso Pinot Nero 2004, Langhe Chardonnay Prasuè 2006 and Monferrato Bianco Riesling 2006 accompany the two classics: the floral, moreish Moscato d'Asti 2006 and Piemonte Moscato d'Autunno 2006, in a class by itself for balance and aromatic intensity.

● Ruché di Castagnole M.to Pro Nobis '06	▼▼ 5
● Barbera d'Asti Sup. Altea '05	▼▼ 4
● Grignolino d'Asti Miravalle '06	▼▼ 4
● Ruché di Castagnole M.to 'Na Vota '06	▼▼ 4
● Monferrato Rosso Monterovere '04	▼▼ 5
● Barbera d'Asti Sup. Cavalé '05	▼▼ 5
● Barbera d'Asti Baby '06	▼ 3
● Ruché di Castagnole M.to Il Cavaliere '06	▼ 4
● Ruché di Castagnole M.to 9.99 '06	▼ 4
● Barbera d'Asti Sup. Cavalé '04	♈♈ 5
● Ruché di Castagnole M.to Pro Nobis '05	♈♈ 5

○ Piemonte Moscato d'Autunno '06	▼▼ 4*
○ Langhe Chardonnay Prasuè '06	▼▼ 4
○ Moscato d'Asti '06	▼▼ 4
○ Monferrato Bianco Riesling '06	▼▼ 4
● Monferrato Rosso Pinot Nero '04	▼▼ 5
○ Piemonte Moscato d'Autunno '04	♈♈ 4
○ Piemonte Moscato d'Autunno '05	♈♈ 4

Roberto Sarotto
VIA RONCONUOVO, 13
12050 NEVIGLIE [CN]
TEL. 0173630228
www.robertosarotto.com

ANNUAL PRODUCTION 150,000 bottles
HECTARES UNDER VINE 50
VITICULTURE METHOD Conventional

The son of growers from Neviglie, Roberto Sarotto was for a long time oenologist at several large estates and co-operative wineries. In consequence, he largely neglected his own property, which sold most of its grapes and did little direct vinification. Less than ten years ago, Roberto tired of wandering and decided to return to Neviglie, settle down and dedicate all his efforts to the family estate. But his keen, ambitious character led him to increase his vine stock by purchasing small farms around southern Piedmont. Today, Roberto has four distinct properties that allow him access to a good part of the region's designated zones. Tenuta Manenti di Gavi, with around ten hectares under vine, enables him to produce two sound whites, Gavi L'Aurora and Gavi di Gavi Bric Sassi, both long-limbed and minerally, with the second more intense and pulpy. We should also mention around 12 hectares in Barolo and Novello, homeland of the two estate Barolos, six hectares in Neive in Gaia Principe and Currà and another 13 hectares that form the winery's original core at Neviglie, where barberas, moscatos, cabernets and nebbiolos rule.

Scagliola
VIA SAN SIRO, 42
14052 CALOSSO [AT]
TEL. 0141853183
scagliola@libero.it

ANNUAL PRODUCTION 135,000 bottles
HECTARES UNDER VINE 22
VITICULTURE METHOD Conventional

Calosso is one of the municipalities with the most vineyards in Italy. It's no surprise, then, that viticulture is still at the heart of the local economy. Excellent producers like the Scagliolas are crucial to safeguarding the territory, protecting it from other activities that, when too invasive, can ruin the integrity of the landscape, in this case the Asti Langhe. The entry into the estate of the new generation represented by Giovanni, who graduated from the wine school in Alba, the acquisition of new vineyards and construction of the cellar show that the Scagliola family intends to continue its march to quality. Again this year, we really enjoyed the Barbera SanSì Selezione, an elegant, long-lingering wine with a rich, varied nose and round, well-structured tannins. The Barbera SanSì and Monferrato Rosso Azörd, from barbera, nebbiolo and cabernet sauvignon, are excellent. The Barbera has lovely ripe fruit and a note of cocoa powder in the finish whereas the other red features a pleasant menthol note. Although the balance and expressivity have still to be refined, it is already very agreeable. The Moscato Volo di Farfalle is good. In fact, it's one of the best in the category.

● Langhe Rosso Enrico I '03	♈♈ 5
● Barbaresco Gaia Principe '03	♈♈ 6
● Barolo Audace Ris. '01	♈♈ 7
● Barbera d'Alba Elena '05	♈♈ 4*
● Barolo Bricco Bergera '03	♈♈ 6
O Langhe Chardonnay Briccomoro '06	♈♈ 4*
O Gavi del Comune di Gavi Bric Sassi '06	♈♈ 4*
O Langhe Arneis Runcneuv '06	♈ 4
O Gavi del Comune di Gavi L'Aurora '06	♈ 4
O Moscato d'Asti Sorì Ciabot '06	♈ 4
● Barbera d'Alba Briccomacchia '05	♈ 4
● Piemonte Brachetto '06	♈ 4
● Barolo Audace Ris. '00	♈♈ 7
● Barolo Audace '00	♈♈ 6
● Barolo Audace '01	♈♈ 6

● Barbera d'Asti Sup. SanSì Sel. '04	♈♈ 7
● Barbera d'Asti Frem '06	♈♈ 4
● Monferrato Rosso Azörd '05	♈♈ 5
O Moscato d'Asti Volo di Farfalle '06	♈♈ 3*
O Piemonte Chardonnay Casot dan Vian '06	♈♈ 3*
● Barbera d'Asti Sup. SanSì '05	♈♈ 5
● Monferrato Dolcetto Busiord '06	♈ 4
O Piemonte Chardonnay '05	♈ 5
● Barbera d'Asti Sup. SanSì Sel. '99	♈♈♈ 7
● Barbera d'Asti Sup. SanSì Sel. '00	♈♈♈ 7
● Barbera d'Asti Sup. SanSì Sel. '01	♈♈♈ 7
● Barbera d'Asti Sup. SanSì '04	♈♈ 5

Giorgio Scarzello e Figli

via Alba, 29
12060 Barolo [CN]
tel. 017356170
www.barolodibarolo.com

ANNUAL PRODUCTION 25,000 bottles
HECTARES UNDER VINE 5.5
VITICULTURE METHOD Conventional

This is a genuine small family estate, managed by the dynamic Federico with the aid of his father Giorgio in the vineyard and his mother looking after the accounts. The vineyard lies in the villages of Sarmassa and Paiagallo at Barolo and Terlo along the road to Novello. At Sarmassa, the Scarzellos own the Merenda farm where, weather permitting, they obtain a delicious selection of Barolo. We were not able to taste it again this year, because it was not bottled in 2003 but the two Barberas from the Paiagallo vineyard scored well. The normal version is fresh and well typed, showing irresistible drinkability, thanks to its savouriness and perfect balance. The Superiore is warmer and velvety, and as balanced and enjoyable as the previous. Released a year late, quite deliberately, the Dolcetto 2005 is floral and earthy with a powerful palate, just like the Nebbiolo 2004, which is subtle and austere with marked acidity.

● Barbera d'Alba Sup. '04	TT	5
● Barbera d'Alba '05	TT	4*
● Langhe Nebbiolo '04	TT	4*
● Dolcetto d'Alba '05	T	4
● Barolo Vigna Merenda '99	YYY	6
● Barolo Vigna Merenda '98	YY	6
● Barolo Vigna Merenda '01	YY	7
● Barolo '01	YY	6
● Barolo '99	YY	6
● Barolo '97	YY	6
● Barolo '96	YY	6

★ Paolo Scavino

fraz. Garbelletto
via Alba-Barolo, 59
12060 Castiglione Falletto [CN]
tel. 017362850
e.scavino@libero.it

ANNUAL PRODUCTION 100,000 bottles
HECTARES UNDER VINE 20
VITICULTURE METHOD Conventional

Enrico Scavino, assisted by his daughter Enrica, manages one of the most interesting winemaking estates in the Langhe. Over the past 20 years, this solid farming family has invested money and effort to build a sound winery with a great reputation. The cellar is spacious, functional and equipped with state-of-the-art technology but still employs more traditional methods. The plots are tended like gardens and scattered across the finest vineyards in the DOCG zone: Cannubi, Rocche dell'Annunziata, Bricco Ambrogio and Fiasco. Barolos with the Scavino label start here and, with the 2003 vintage, all are back in production. Our Three Glasses went to the best of the range, the Rocche dell'Annunziata 2001, which made the most of a favourable vintage year and returned to its former splendour. The rich fruity notes on the nose merge nicely with sensations of tobacco and spice. The imposing palate is complex and caressing, the tannic weave excellent. The Cannubi and Bric dël Fiasc are lovely, the Bricco Ambrogio is good and the Carobric more linear. The range closes with the pleasant, fruity Dolcetto d'Alba and Barbera Affinato in Carati, still seeking better balance.

● Barolo Rocche dell'Annunziata Ris. '01	TTT	8
● Barolo Bric dël Fiasc '03	TT	8
● Barolo Cannubi '03	TT	8
● Barolo Carobric '03	TT	8
● Barolo Bricco Ambrogio '03	TT	8
● Barbera d'Alba Affinato in Carati '04	TT	6
● Dolcetto d'Alba '06	TT	4*
● Barolo Rocche dell'Annunziata Ris. '96	YYY	8
● Barolo Rocche dell'Annunziata Ris. '97	YYY	8
● Barolo Bric dël Fiasc '96	YYY	8
● Barolo Bric dël Fiasc '95	YYY	8
● Barolo Bric del Fiasc '89	YYY	8
● Barolo Bric del Fiasc '85	YYY	8

Sciorio

VIA ASTI-NIZZA, 87
14055 COSTIGLIOLE D'ASTI [AT]
TEL. 0141966610

ANNUAL PRODUCTION 18,000 bottles
HECTARES UNDER VINE 8
VITICULTURE METHOD Conventional

The Piedmontese country house on the
road from Costigliole d'Asti to Nizza
Monferrato has no special features you
would notice. From the outside, it looks
nothing like a winery. But unobtrusiveness is
one of the character traits of Giuseppe and
Mauro, the Gozzellino brothers and the
latest generation at the helm of the family
estate. Even the small, orderly cellar, with
only the most essential equipment, seems
to reflect the Gozzellinos' docile
temperament. But when you taste the
wines, the family theory of oenology
becomes clear. From the single plot that
occupies the amphitheatre-shaped hollow
below the farmhouse, they produce fewer
than 20,000 excellent bottles a year with the
help of oenologist Giorgio Gozzelino. The
range was once packed with vins de garde
but has now been expanded with whites
and standard-label reds. They have even
corrected the tiny blemish of slight over-
oaking, except for the Chardonnay Vigna
Levi. This year, the winery champion is the
Barbera Beneficio 2003, which is almost
chewable yet so elegant. The range closes
with two excellent standard-label wines, the
Barbera and Chardonnay Prasca, and a
pleasant sauvignon-based Monferrato
Bianco, also from 2006.

Franco e Mario Scrimaglio

VIA ALESSANDRIA, 67
14049 NIZZA MONFERRATO [AT]
TEL. 0141721385
www.scrimaglio.it

ANNUAL PRODUCTION 700,000 bottles
HECTARES UNDER VINE 18
VITICULTURE METHOD Conventional

Brothers Giorgio and Francesco Scrimaglio
manage this major Monferrato winery that
excels at producing sound Barbera d'Asti
reds. In addition to the selections, including
the wines reviewed in this entry, the
Scrimaglios offer a broad choice of well-
made, inexpensive, base wines and a series
of labels dedicated to great "Made in Italy"
brands: Fiat, Alfa Romeo, Lancia, Juventus
and Cecchi Records. For this new edition of
the Guide, we tasted eight wines, two
whites and six reds. And it was the reds that
included the most interesting wines from the
estate, beginning with the Barbera d'Asti
Superiore Nizza Acsé. Again this year, it is
among the best in its type. Here we have a
modern wine, concentrated and harmonic
with a finish nicely supported by acidity. The
other Barbera selections were good, the
Crôutin being slightly more convincing than
the Sant'Ippolito. Rocca Nivo, also from
2005, is less challenging with less cohesive
aromatics. Tantra, from cabernet sauvignon
and barbera, is as good as ever. But the
aromas from the two No Cork selections, a
Barbera and a Sauvignon, are more
evanescent. The Futuro 2006 is fruity and
pleasant in its simplicity.

● Barbera d'Asti Sup. Vigna Beneficio '03	🍷🍷 5
● Barbera d'Asti '06	🍷🍷 3*
○ Piemonte Chardonnay Prasca '06	🍷🍷 3*
○ Monferrato Bianco S '06	🍷 3
● Barbera d'Asti Sup. Sciorio '01	🍷🍷 4
● Barbera d'Asti Sup. Sciorio '00	🍷🍷 4
● Barbera d'Asti Sup. Sciorio '03	🍷🍷 4
● Monferrato Rosso Antico Vitigno '01	🍷🍷 5
● Barbera d'Asti Sup. Vigna Beneficio '01	🍷🍷 5

● Barbera d'Asti Sup. Acsé '04	🍷🍷 6
● Barbera d'Asti Sup. Bricco S. Ippolito '05	🍷🍷 5
● Barbera d'Asti Sup. Crôutin '05	🍷🍷 6
● Monferrato Rosso Tantra '05	🍷🍷 6
● Barbera d'Asti Sup. Vign. Rocca Nivo '05	🍷 4
○ Futuro '06	🍷 4
○ Monferrato Bianco No Cork '06	3
● Barbera d'Asti No Cork '06	4
● Barbera d'Asti Sup. Acsé '03	🍷🍷 6
● Barbera d'Asti Sup. Nizza Acsé '01	🍷🍷 6
● Barbera d'Asti Sup. Crôutin '03	🍷🍷 6
● Barbera d'Asti Sup. Crôutin '04	🍷🍷 6
● Monferrato Rosso Tantra '04	🍷🍷 6

Mauro Sebaste

FRAZ. GALLO
VIA GARIBALDI, 222BIS
12051 ALBA [CN]
TEL. 0173262148
www.maurosebaste.it

F.lli Seghesio

LOC. CASTELLETTO, 19
12065 MONFORTE D'ALBA [CN]
TEL. 017378108
az.agricolaseghesio@libero.it

ANNUAL PRODUCTION 140,000 bottles
HECTARES UNDER VINE 18.5
VITICULTURE METHOD Conventional

ANNUAL PRODUCTION 60,000 bottles
HECTARES UNDER VINE 10
VITICULTURE METHOD Conventional

Mauro Sebaste was born to the trade. His mother was Sylla Sebaste, one of the first female winemakers in the Langhe. On leaving the family estate, Mauro built his winery without purchasing any plots. Instead, he established relationships with growers, watching closely over their work in the vineyard, and buys his raw material from them. This year, Mauro presented us with a truly excellent array of Barolos, almost in compensation for the hailstorms that in 2002 deprived us of all his nebbiolo-based wines. The garnet-red Brunate 2003 is elegant on the nose. Spicy notes enhance the fruit on the palate and the finish is fresh with well-integrated oak and soft tannins. The Monvigliero surprised us with its spontaneity, thanks to elegant structure, pleasant spicy notes and nice length. In contrast, the Prapò is more down to earth and the tannins are still edgy, which is typical of its terroir, Serralunga. The Nebbiolo Parigi is concentrated and fruity, perhaps not well typed but very intriguing. The savoury, complex Roero Arneis has • extended lees contact and the Centobricchi Bianco, from sauvignon, is overripe and laced with tropical fruit.

The words "precision" and "passion" summarize the approach of Aldo and Riccardo Seghesio in their vineyards, where every year they strive to achieve the highest quality, using only native varieties for the overwhelming majority of their labels. One of the winery's best weapons is their meticulous work in the vineyards that translates into excellent products. This year, these include the Barolo Vigneto La Villa 2003 and Barbera d'Alba Vigneto della Chiesa 2005. The Barolo redeems its predecessor from the last unfortunate vintage year and throws a nose of good complexity, floral nuances and a sweet palate blessed with extraordinary tannins. The Barbera, on the other hand, is always interesting and has structure that promises excellent cellarability. In a remarkable interpretation of the variety, the Dolcetto d'Alba Vigneto della Chiesa 2006 reveals itself to be a warm, spicy wine with excellent drinkability. Of the remaining two current wines, we prefer the sensations of fruit in the Barbera to the strong tannins in the Nebbiolo. Finally, the Langhe 2005 is a bit mouth drying.

● Barolo Brunate '03	▼▼ 7
● Barolo Monvigliero '03	▼▼ 7
● Barolo Prapò '03	▼▼ 7
● Nebbiolo d'Alba Parigi '05	▼▼ 5
● Langhe Rosso Centobricchi '05	▼▼ 5
● Barbera d'Alba S. Rosalia '06	▼ 4
● Dolcetto d'Alba S. Rosalia '06	▼ 4
○ Roero Arneis '06	▼ 4
○ Langhe Bianco Centobricchi '06	▼ 4
● Barolo Brunate '01	▼▼ 7
● Barolo Brunate '00	▼▼ 7
● Barolo Monvigliero '01	▼▼ 7
● Barolo Prapò '01	▼▼ 7
● Barolo Prapò '00	▼▼ 7
● Barolo Monvigliero '00	▼▼ 7

● Barolo Vign. La Villa '03	▼▼ 7
● Barbera d'Alba Vign. della Chiesa '05	▼▼ 6
● Barbera d'Alba '06	▼▼ 4*
● Langhe Rosso Bouquet '05	▼▼ 6
● Dolcetto d'Alba Vign. della Chiesa '06	▼▼ 4*
● Langhe Nebbiolo '06	▼ 4
● Barbera d'Alba Vign. della Chiesa '00	▼▼▼ 6
● Barolo Vign. La Villa '91	▼▼▼ 7
● Barolo Vign. La Villa '01	▼▼▼ 7
● Barbera d'Alba Vign. della Chiesa '04	▼▼ 6
● Barbera d'Alba Vign. della Chiesa '03	▼▼ 6

Sella

VIA IV NOVEMBRE
13060 LESSONA [BI]
TEL. 01599455
aziendeagricolesella@virgilio.it

ANNUAL PRODUCTION 80,000 bottles
HECTARES UNDER VINE 20
VITICULTURE METHOD Conventional

Tasting the Sella family's wines is like drinking a piece of Italian history. Research done by Gioacchino Sella, the current winery administrator, indicates that the family has occupied this corner of Piedmont since at least 1550. Documents proving the presence of a wine estate owned by the Sellas go back to 1671. At the beginning of the 18th century, the family bottled its first wines, which were presented as gifts to Europe's leading courts. Since that time, the estate has maintained its modest size, around six hectares under vine in Lessona, where the Sella winery practically monopolizes the appellation of the same name, except for the partial acquisition by statesman Quintino Sella toward the end of the 19th century of the first vineyards in Bramaterra. This new label, Bramaterra I Porfidi 2003, brought the winery its second Three Glass award. The selection, aged in ten-hectolitre barrels and barriques, has slipped seamlessly into the range, showing unusually aristocratic elegance and harmony. The Lessona Omaggio a Quintino Sella 2003 and Lessona 2004 are not far behind.

Enrico Serafino

C.SO ASTI, 5
12043 CANALE [CN]
TEL. 0173967111
www.barbero1891.it

ANNUAL PRODUCTION 450,000 bottles
HECTARES UNDER VINE 45
VITICULTURE METHOD Conventional

It would take a huge book to contain on paper the history of this long-standing Piedmont winemaker. We, however, will restrict ourselves to mentioning the important role of Enrico Serafino in the late 19th and early 20th centuries when selling wine was an art and grape growing still had the sepia tones of a silent film. Skipping over the years of decline, we fast forward to the present, where the desire of director Barbero and drive of a beverage colossus like Campari, combined with the skill of first-rate technical staff, have restored lustre to the cellar's production. So we can propose a toast, and what better wine to drink it in than a sparkler, perhaps from the new Alta Langa project? The 2003 edition is floral, juicy and acid-rich with all the potential to become truly great. There's a trilogy of very sound wines from Roero in the fresh Arneis, the elegant Barbera and Roero Pasiunà, which draws character and sweet tannins from its excellent growing year. The Barbaresco 2004 is fragrant and powerful.

● Bramaterra I Porfidi '03	♟♟♟ 6
● Lessona Omaggio a Quintino Sella Ris. '03	♟♟ 7
● Bramaterra '04	♟♟ 5
● Coste della Sesia Rosso Orbello '06	♟♟ 4*
● Lessona '04	♟♟ 5
○ Coste della Sesia Bianco Vignaluce '06	♟ 4
◉ Coste della Sesia Rosato Majoli '06	♟ 3
● Lessona S. Sebastiano allo Zoppo '01	♟♟♟ 6
● Lessona S. Sebastiano allo Zoppo '00	♟♟ 6
● Lessona Omaggio a Quintino Sella Ris. '99	♟♟ 7

● Barbera d'Alba Sup. Parduné '04	♟♟ 4*
● Roero Sup. Pasiunà '04	♟♟ 4*
● Barbaresco '04	♟♟ 6
○ Alta Langa M. Cl. '03	♟♟ 5
○ Roero Arneis '06	♟♟ 4
○ Langhe Chardonnay '06	♟ 3
● Dolcetto d'Alba '06	♟ 3
● Barbera d'Alba Sup. Parduné '03	♟♟ 4
● Roero Sup. '03	♟♟ 4

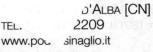

D'ALBA [CN]

TEL.   2209
www.po   sinaglio.it

Sottimano
FRAZ. COTTÀ, 21
12052 NEIVE [CN]
TEL. 0173635186
www.sottimano.it

ANNUAL PRODUCTION 40,000 bottles
HECTARES UNDER VINE 13.5
VITICULTURE METHOD Conventional

ANNUAL PRODUCTION 60,000 bottles
HECTARES UNDER VINE 13
VITICULTURE METHOD Conventional

Look at the chart below and keep in mind the concept that less is more. Brothers Bruno and Silvano Accomo have made it their motto, reducing their range of wines to a minimum and concentrating mostly on classic types from the Diano zone: two versions of Barbera d'Alba, Dolcetto di Diano, in this case also in a base version and a selection, and Nebbiolo d'Alba. We'll begin with the Dolcettos. The classic version is a thoroughly delicious example of a fresh-tasting easy drinker. Clearly more ambitious is the Bric Maiolica, which is austere from the nose and then tannic and round on the palate with a nice, long finish. From the Barberas, the standard label has difficulty unfolding and showing all its potential. Vigna Erta is very fragrant, almost supple in its floral, fruity hints, and braced by meticulous care in the vineyard and a longer stay in the cellar. Finally, the Nebbiolo d'Alba is a bit low-key from an greenish note that has still to be smoothed out but still makes friends because of its precision and ability to reflect on the palate all the fruity, earthy tones on the nose.

The Sottimano family winery is one of the loveliest operations in the Barbaresco DOCG zone. The excellent positions of the vineyards combine with winery management based on a non-invasive, minimum-impact approach, the use of native yeasts, completely natural management of malolactic fermentation, and cautious use of ageing wood specially selected from trusted coopers. Add to this a great vintage like 2004 and the results become truly sensational. Each of the four Barbaresco selections is better than the last, each clean and well defined in its characteristics. The Fausoni is soft, floral, elegant and readiest for the corkscrew. The Currà is dark, minerally, savoury and deep, showing well enough at our tasting to sweep up Three Glasses. The Pajoré is more closed, ripe with fruit and rich in spice. And the last of the quartet, the Cottà, has a ferrous minerality, presenting powerful and full but still quite clenched. The rest of the range is all good, from the rich Barbera Pairolero 2005 to the flavourful Brachetto Secco Maté 2006.

● Barbera d'Alba V. Erta '05	♀♀ 4
● Diano d'Alba Sörì Bric Maiolica '06	♀♀ 4
● Dolcetto di Diano d'Alba '06	♀♀ 3*
● Barbera d'Alba '06	♀ 3
● Nebbiolo d'Alba Giachét '05	♀ 4
● Diano d'Alba Sörì Bric Maiolica '03	♀♀ 4
● Diano d'Alba Sörì Bric Maiolica '05	♀♀ 4
● Barbera d'Alba V. Erta '03	♀♀ 4
● Barbera d'Alba V. Erta '04	♀♀ 4
● Langhe Rosso Sinaij '03	♀♀ 5

● Barbaresco Currà '04	♀♀♀ 7
● Barbaresco Fausoni '04	♀♀ 7
● Barbaresco Pajoré '04	♀♀ 7
● Barbaresco Cottà '04	♀♀ 7
● Barbera d'Alba Pairolero '05	♀♀ 5
● Langhe Nebbiolo '05	♀♀ 5
● Maté '06	♀♀ 4*
● Dolcetto d'Alba Bric del Salto '06	♀♀ 4*
● Barbaresco Cottà '99	♀♀♀ 7
● Barbaresco Cottà '98	♀♀♀ 7
● Barbaresco Pajoré '01	♀♀♀ 7
● Barbaresco Pajoré '00	♀♀♀ 7
● Barbaresco Pajoré '98	♀♀♀ 7
● Barbaresco Fausoni V. del Salto '96	♀♀♀ 7
● Barbaresco Cottà V. Brichet '97	♀♀♀ 7

Luigi Spertino
VIA LEA, 505
14047 MOMBERCELLI [AT]
TEL. 0141959098
www.luigispertino.it

ANNUAL PRODUCTION 40,000 bottles
HECTARES UNDER VINE 6
VITICULTURE METHOD Conventional

Those who have followed the growth in quality over the past few years of this small but significant winery can only be pleased with the great results racked up year after year by Mauro and Luigi Spertino, two wonderful wine men. "Healthy wine in a healthy mind" would be a good Latin motto for these little oenological treasures. The great news is that two beautiful south-facing hectares have been acquired at nearby Bricco di Mombercelli to support the already substantial production of Barbera d'Asti. The 2005 is just fantastic. Deep in colour and earthy on the nose, it shows rich, warm and fruity, with notes that testify to very ripe fruit. From sandy, chalky terroirs, the lovely version of Grignolino 2006 is exemplary with elegant, almost aromatic fragrances of spice and fruit, and dry, well-gauged tannins nicely tucked in. The two sweet liqueur wines, Liberty, from moscato, and the barbera-based Ippocrasso, are distinctive.

★★★ La Spinetta
VIA ANNUNZIATA, 17
14054 CASTAGNOLE DELLE LANZE [AT]
TEL. 0141877396
www.la-spinetta.com

ANNUAL PRODUCTION 450,000 bottles
HECTARES UNDER VINE 100
VITICULTURE METHOD Conventional

The Rivetti brothers presented a monumental line-up includes all the major Langhe types. This time, the excellent Riserve di Barbaresco wines were missing, not having been produced in 2002 because of the adverse weather conditions, but we had the good fortune to taste a remarkable version of Barolo Campè Riserva 2001 that proffers nuances of blueberry, nutmeg and oaky spice. The vigorous palate has a marvellous finish. We were hard pressed to choose the best of the three Barbarescos. The Starderi, from the municipality of Neive, and Valeirano from Treiso are remarkable. The former is compact, almost austere, with rose pepper and cocoa powder sensations mingling with attractive oak. The powerful, rich palate shows assertive yet fine-grained tannins. The Valeirano unfolds with more elegance and smooth tannins, supported by good acidity. These two thoroughbreds romped home to two Three Glass awards. In contrast, the Gallina is just a bit too young. The two Barberas are excellent, like the rest of the range. Despite their fame as extraordinary red wine producers, the Rivettis also make attractive Moscatos. Their leading selection, Bricco Quaglia, is very good.

● Barbera d'Asti '05	⟡⟡ 4*
○ Ottocento Liberty	⟡⟡ 4
● Grignolino d'Asti '06	⟡⟡ 4
● Ippocrasso	⟡⟡ 6
● Barbera d'Asti '04	⟟⟟ 4
● Barbera d'Asti '03	⟟⟟ 4
● Monferrato Rosso La Mandorla '04	⟟⟟ 6
● Monferrato Rosso La Mandorla '01	⟟⟟ 6
○ Lunà Brut M. Cl. '01	⟟⟟ 5

● Barbaresco V. Starderi '04	⟡⟡⟡ 8
● Barbaresco V. Valeirano '04	⟡⟡⟡ 8
● Barbaresco V. Gallina '04	⟡⟡ 8
● Barbera d'Asti Sup. Bionzo '05	⟡⟡ 7
● Monferrato Rosso Pin '05	⟡⟡ 7
● Barolo Campè '03	⟡⟡ 8
● Barolo Campè Ris. '01	⟡⟡ 8
○ Moscato d'Asti Bricco Quaglia '06	⟡⟡ 4
● Barbera d'Alba Vign. Gallina '05	⟡⟡ 7
● Barbera d'Asti Ca' di Pian '05	⟡⟡ 5
○ Langhe Bianco '05	⟡⟡ 6
○ Piemonte Moscato Passito Oro '03	⟡⟡ 7
○ Langhe Chardonnay Lidia '05	⟡⟡ 6
● Barolo Campè della Spinetta '00	⟟⟟⟟ 8
● Barolo Campè della Spinetta '01	⟟⟟⟟ 8
● Barbaresco V. Starderi '01	⟟⟟⟟ 8

Luigi Tacchino

VIA MARTIRI DELLA BENEDICTA, 26
15060 CASTELLETTO D'ORBA [AL]
TEL. 0143830115
www.luigitacchino.it

Michele Taliano

C.SO A. MANZONI, 24
12046 MONTÀ [CN]
TEL. 0173976512
www.talianomichele.com

ANNUAL PRODUCTION 120,000 bottles
HECTARES UNDER VINE 10
VITICULTURE METHOD Conventional

The Tacchino family, the determined Romina in particular, presented a well-assembled range of wines this year. The selections but in particular the standard-label wines made a very good showing. Du Riva was aged unhurriedly in bottle before being submitted to our tastings, which has cost it something in terms of freshness and lightness of approach. Yet this is clearly a serious wine, well able to stand comparison with the best in the region thanks to powerful acidity and extract that drive the long, well-sustained palate. It's accompanied by a range of fine products. We'll start with the Barbera del Monferrato, a standard-label designed to be enjoyed, move on to the fresh, classic Dolcetto with its vibrant aromatics and end with the floral, juicy Gavi. The Cortese Marsenca and Monferrato Rosso Di Fatto, a blend of barbera, dolcetto and cabernet, are little more than well made.

ANNUAL PRODUCTION 60,000 bottles
HECTARES UNDER VINE 12
VITICULTURE METHOD Conventional

The range from the Talianos grows stronger every year. Brothers Alberto and Ezio have developed an estate that, metaphorically speaking, we could call judicious. It's not too small, not too big, designed around the abilities of a small, family team, territory-focused but open to the outside world and keen to find an appropriate style for every wine. The results brought flattering scores for some of the bottles and respect for the others, which are less challenging but no less pleasing. Kudos goes to the Nebbiolos. The Barbaresco and Roero compete for top spot, one by virtue of its sumptuous tannic weave and the other for its quite superb bouquet. The Barberas are only a step behind, with the winning Laboriosa more elegant and powerful than the an enjoyable standard-label version. Other wines include a fragrant Dolcetto and a very fresh-tasting Arneis.

● Dolcetto di Ovada Du Riva '04	❥❥ 4*
● Barbera del M.to '06	❥❥ 3*
O Gavi del Comune di Gavi '06	❥❥ 4
● Dolcetto di Ovada '06	❥❥ 4
O Cortese dell'Alto M.to Marsenca '06	❥ 3
● Monferrato Rosso Di Fatto '03	❥ 5
● Barbera del M.to '05	♀♀ 3
● Barbera del M.to Albarola '04	♀♀ 4
● Dolcetto di Ovada Du Riva '03	♀♀ 4

● Roero Ròche dra Bòssora '04	❥❥ 5
● Barbaresco Ad Altiora '04	❥❥ 6
● Barbera d'Alba A Bon Rendre '06	❥❥ 4
● Barbera d'Alba Laboriosa '04	❥❥ 4
● Langhe Rosso '04	❥❥ 4
● Dolcetto d'Alba Ciabot Vigna '06	❥ 4
● Langhe Nebbiolo Blagheur '06	❥ 4
O Langhe Bianco '04	❥ 4
O Roero Arneis Sernì '06	❥ 4
● Barbaresco Ad Altiora '01	♀♀ 6
● Roero Ròche dra Bòssora '01	♀♀ 5
● Roero Ròche dra Bòssora '03	♀♀ 5
● Barbaresco Ad Altiora '03	♀♀ 6
● Roero Ròche dra Bòssora '00	♀♀ 5
● Barbaresco Ad Altiora '00	♀♀ 6

Castello di Tassarolo

CASINA ALBERINA, 1
15060 TASSAROLO [AL]
TEL. 0143342248
www.castelloditassarolo.it

ANNUAL PRODUCTION 100,000 bottles
HECTARES UNDER VINE 20
VITICULTURE METHOD Natural

Castello di Tassarolo has joined the Guide. This long-established estate in Gavi is managed with skill by Massimiliana Spinola. The wonderful performance this year from all the wines presented brought flattering scores and interest from consumers. The estate began converting to biodynamic agriculture this year and in two or three years, the wines will be certified. For now, we enjoyed the excellent range submitted by the dynamic Massimiliana. A benchmark Gavi in the mid 1990s, Gavi Alborina is back on fine form. It shows a straw yellow with faint streaks of gold, aromas of surprising finesse and recognizable citrus, hedgerow and peach. The palate is warm yet at the same time refreshing thanks to pronounced acidity that smoothes out the compact body. We also liked the other two Gavis. Castello di Tassarolo fills the glass with all the typicity of cortese, expressing pronounced floral and fruity tones. Slightly less intriguing is the S selection, which still earned Two Glasses for its clean palate and enviable freshness.

Terralba

FRAZ. INSELMINA
15050 BERZANO DI TORTONA [AL]
TEL. 013180403

ANNUAL PRODUCTION 50,000 bottles
HECTARES UNDER VINE 15
VITICULTURE METHOD Conventional

Interpreting tasting results from the Terralba estate is not easy. The wines presented by Stefano Daffonchio, who has run the estate for some years now, are always interesting and superbly structured but all require leisurely aeration to give their best. Actually, bottles of the same wine opened a short time apart may give quite different results. This is probably due to the extreme search for imposing structure, which must be supported by perfect corking. As regards the wines themselves, the two Timorassos gave excellent performances. In fact, the Stato is among the best in its type and Derthona is close behind. Deliberately, the estate releases only two whites, both from a timorasso base. From the reds, the Barberas are very good, the Terralba aged in barrique and Identità in stainless steel. The Croatina Montegrande is also very good and is back to its usual levels after skipping a year to enjoy longer maturation in glass.

O Gavi del Comune di Tassarolo Vign. Alborina '05	♟♟ 5
O Gavi del Comune di Tassarolo Castello di Tassarolo '06	♟♟ 4
O Gavi del Comune di Tassarolo S '06	♟♟ 3*
O Gavi del Comune di Tassarolo Castello di Tassarolo '05	♟♟ 4

O Colli Tortonesi Bianco Stato '05	♟♟ 6
O Colli Tortonesi Bianco Derthona '05	♟♟ 5
● Colli Tortonesi Rosso Identità '06	♟♟ 4
● Colli Tortonesi Rosso Vigna di Mezzo '04	♟♟ 5
● Colli Tortonesi Rosso Terralba '04	♟♟ 6
● Colli Tortonesi Rosso Montegrande '04	♟♟ 5
● Colli Tortonesi Rosso La Vetta '05	♟ 5
O Colli Tortonesi Bianco Stato '02	♟♟ 5
O Colli Tortonesi Bianco Stato '04	♟♟ 6
O Colli Tortonesi Bianco Stato '03	♟♟ 5
● Colli Tortonesi Rosso Terralba '03	♟♟ 6

Terre da Vino
VIA BERGESIA, 6
12060 BAROLO [CN]
TEL. 0173564611
www.terredavino.it

Terre del Barolo
VIA ALBA-BAROLO, 5
12060 CASTIGLIONE FALLETTO [CN]
TEL. 0173262053
www.terredelbarolo.com

ANNUAL PRODUCTION 5,300,000 bottles
HECTARES UNDER VINE 4.564
VITICULTURE METHOD Conventional

ANNUAL PRODUCTION 2,500,000 bottles
HECTARES UNDER VINE 610
VITICULTURE METHOD Conventional

This large co-operative winery produces wines in all the designated zones in southern Piedmont. The imposing winery headquarters, built in the mid 1990s in the municipality of Barolo, vinifies and ages wines from the co-operative and private producers that comprise this major operation. The labels reserved for the restaurants are good, with special praise for those wines that are not among the most ambitious selections. Particularly outstanding this year among the wines from the line dedicated to Langhe-born writers Cesare Pavese and Beppe Fenoglio, we have the Barbera d'Asti Superiore La Luna e i Falò 2005 and the Barolo Paesi Tuoi 2003. The former exemplifies this winery's role as a pacesetter in quality and shows elegant, structured and pleasant while the Paesi Tuoi has amazing integrity and finesse. A step up from this is the concentrated Barolo Essenze 2003, which is tannic and graceful in its long-lingering length. Among the major Barberas, the attractively acid-rich Superiore Croere prevails over the Martlet 2005, which is a bit sweet in the finish. The Nebbiolo La Malora 2004 is intense and aristocratic and the white 2006 Tra Donne Sole, from a sauvignon and chardonnay base, is agreeably harmonious.

In 1959, Arnaldo Rivera and a group of partners decided to open a benchmark co-operative winery for all the growers in the Barolo zone. Terre del Barolo was created. Today, there are around 400 member growers and every year 55,000 quintals of grapes are processed for a total production of 38,000 hectolitres in the various types present in the territory. Part of this production is bottled and sold directly by the co-operative, which for the past ten years has had an attractive on-site sales outlet for passing customers and tourists. Over the past few years, the winery's management, led by president Matteo Bosco, has undertaken a major quality project that is now producing excellent results. The key products in the new strategy are the Barolo Riservas, with selections from Diano d'Alba and the various other designated zones in the area. This year, Terre del Barolo presented a new label, the dolcetto-based Dogliani DOCG. Stand-outs among the wines we tasted were the complex, muscular Barolo Riserva Rocche 1999, the dry, fruit-forward Dogliani 2005 and the 2005 Barberas, the Superiore and Valdisera.

● Barbera d'Alba Sup. Croere '05	🍷🍷 5
● Barolo Essenze '03	🍷🍷 7
● Barbera d'Asti Sup. La Luna e i Falò '05	🍷🍷 5
● Barbera d'Asti Sup. Nizza Martlet '05	🍷🍷 5
● Barolo Paesi Tuoi '03	🍷🍷 6
● Langhe Nebbiolo La Malora '04	🍷🍷 5
O Monferrato Bianco Tra Donne Sole '06	🍷🍷 4*
● Barbaresco La Casa in Collina '04	🍷 6
O Gavi del Comune di Gavi Masseria dei Carmelitani '06	🍷 4
O Roero Arneis La Villa '06	🍷 4
O Piemonte Moscato Passito La Bella Estate '05	🍷 5
● Barolo Essenze '01	🍷🍷 7

● Barolo Rocche Ris. '99	🍷🍷 6
● Barbera d'Alba Sup. '05	🍷🍷 3*
● Barbera d'Alba Valdisera '05	🍷🍷 3*
● Diano d'Alba Cascinotto '06	🍷🍷 4
● Dogliani '05	🍷🍷 4
● Barolo '03	🍷 6
● Dolcetto d'Alba Castello '06	🍷 4
● Dolcetto di Diano d'Alba '06	🍷 3
● Verduno Pelaverga '06	🍷 4
● Dolcetto d'Alba '06	🍷 3
● Barolo Castello Ris. '99	🍷🍷 7
● Barolo Rocche Ris. '98	🍷🍷 8
● Barbera d'Alba Sup. '05	🍷🍷 3

Torraccia del Piantavigna

VIA ROMAGNANO, 69A
28074 GHEMME [NO]
TEL. 0163840040
www.torracciadelpiantavigna.it

ANNUAL PRODUCTION 90,000 bottles
HECTARES UNDER VINE 35
VITICULTURE METHOD Conventional

The moment has finally come for Torraccia del Piantavigna to have a full entry in the Guide. With technical help from Beppe Caviola, recent vintages have seen the estate's wines grow in quality. On their arrival in Piedmont, the Francolis created one of the most important distilleries in Italy at Romagnano Sesia. This family business has continued at their new headquarters in Ghemme, surrounded by vineyards in the DOCG zone so Alessandro Francoli's decision to dedicate himself seriously to wine was a difficult one. Today, the estate owns around 35 hectares, five of these in the Ghemme DOCG and almost as many in the Gattinara DOCG. About 25,000 bottles are made from nebbiolo grapes that ripen on the porphyry-rich soil of Gattinara, almost as many as are sourced from the morainic soil of Ghemme, with 90 per cent nebbiolo and ten per cent vespolina. From the 2003 vintage, we preferred the Gattinara because of its greater territorial definition. The less challenging reds from Torraccia del Piantavigna, the Nebbiolo Ramale and the Vespolinas, Maretta and La Mostella, are aged in steel or with brief oaking and offer a pleasant, undemanding introduction to the estate reds.

Giancarlo Travaglini

VIA DELLE VIGNE, 36
13045 GATTINARA [VC]
TEL. 0163833588
www.travaglinigattinara.it

ANNUAL PRODUCTION 250,000 bottles
HECTARES UNDER VINE 42
VITICULTURE METHOD Conventional

The estate that wrote the history of Gattinara area is the work of one lifetime, that of Giancarlo Travaglini, the son, grandson and great-grandson of Gattinara-born growers. In 1958, Giancarlo made a production and life-changing choice when he created the winery to support the family grape-growing business. It would take the committed labour of a generation, the owner's, would be needed to piece together a vineyard holding that includes more than a third of the entire area under vine in the designated zone, in the historic vineyards of Lurghe, Alice and Permolone. Today, Giancarlo's daughter, Cinzia, her mother and her husband are following in his footsteps. Few of the wines see oak but all favour the complexity contributed by the minerally, meaty notes of the terroir to fruit and spice. Unfortunately, Cinzia has not repeated last year's results but then this estate had a transitional vintage and submitted only two wines: the Gattinara 2003, released in more than 150,000 bottles, and the Nebbiolo 2005. Even with the blazing hot 2003 growing season, the Gattinara conserves its signature features of complexity, finesse and length.

● Gattinara '03	♟ 6
● Ghemme '03	♟ 6
● Colline Novaresi Nebbiolo Ramale '04	♟ 5
● Colline Novaresi Vespolina Maretta '06	♟ 4
● Colline Novaresi Vespolina La Mostella '05	♟ 4
● Gattinara '01	♟♟ 6
● Colline Novaresi Nebbiolo Tre Confini '04	♟♟ 4
● Gattinara '00	♟♟ 6
● Ghemme '01	♟♟ 6

● Gattinara '03	♟ 5
● Coste della Sesia Nebbiolo '05	♟ 4*
● Gattinara Ris. '01	♟♟♟ 6
● Gattinara '01	♟♟ 5
● Gattinara '00	♟♟ 5
● Gattinara Ris. '00	♟♟ 6
● Gattinara Ris. '99	♟♟ 6
● Gattinara Ris. '98	♟♟ 6
● Gattinara Ris. '97	♟♟ 6
● Gattinara Tre Vigne '01	♟♟ 6
● Gattinara Tre Vigne '00	♟♟ 6
● Gattinara Tre Vigne '99	♟♟ 6

Traversa - Cascina Bertolotto
VIA PIETRO PORRO, 70
15018 SPIGNO MONFERRATO [AL]
TEL. 014491223

G. D. Vajra
LOC. VERGNE
VIA DELLE VIOLE, 25
12060 BAROLO [CN]
TEL. 017356257
gdvajra@tin.it

ANNUAL PRODUCTION 60,000 bottles
HECTARES UNDER VINE 12
VITICULTURE METHOD   Conventional

At the peak of the Traversa family's
production is Barbera I Cheini, a wine with a
lively colour and intense spicy aromas, in
part contributed by a stay in oak. The palate
is round and full with a lingering finish. The
Monferrato Bianco Il Barigi is created from a
blend of equal parts of cortese and favorita
and the 2006 version surprised us with
complex, intense aromas of tropical fruit,
peach and wisteria. The palate is savoury
and long. La Muïette, a characterful
Dolcetto, came near to a second Glass
thanks to a successful balance of nose and
palate. La Cresta is more rustic and in this
vintage lacks the harmony that has
characterized it in various previous editions.
The dry-vinified Brachetto La Tia is rich in
varietal aromas and has a winning, easy-
drinking style. The Brachetto Il Virginio is
one of the best known dessert wines from
the province of Alessandria and unveils an
unusual swath of thoroughly enjoyable
aromatics.

ANNUAL PRODUCTION 150,000 bottles
HECTARES UNDER VINE 25
VITICULTURE METHOD   Conventional

The Vaira family can shock and surprise. To
enter their winery is to step into a world of
passion, a welcoming spirit and dreams that
have still to come true. These powerful
emotions are created by people like Aldo
and Milena, who make wine above all to
please consumers, with no short cuts or
concessions to the marketplace. This sums
up a philosophy that year after year inspires
a broad range of reliable, premium-quality
labels. The Vairas believe in varieties many
consider secondary, such as freisa and
albarossa. In fact, it is a point of pride and
satisfaction for them. The wines tell the
story of the land and their experience,
beginning with the Barolo Albe 2003, from
an especially hot harvest. The Bricco delle
Viole is as great as ever, showing well-
integrated ripe fruit with nice oak on the
nose. The palate is elegant and almost
austere, with already smooth, chewy
tannins. The rest of the wines are good,
starting with the Riesling 2006, which is
simply a little too young, and on to Freisa
Kyè, a remarkable achievement for this
variety. The Barbera d'Alba Superiore 2005
and Dolcetto Coste & Fossati strode
confidently into the finals.

● Barbera del M.to I Cheini '05	♟♟ 4*
O Monferrato Bianco Il Barigi '06	♟♟ 4*
● Brachetto d'Acqui Il Virginio '06	♟ 4
● Dolcetto d'Acqui La Muïette '05	♟ 4
● La Tia '05	♟ 5
● Dolcetto d'Acqui La Cresta '06	♟ 4
● Barbera del M.to I Cheini '04	♟♟ 4
O Surì di Bertolotto '03	♟♟ 6
● La Tia '03	♟♟ 5

● Barolo Bricco delle Viole '03	♟♟ 8
● Dolcetto d'Alba Coste & Fossati '06	♟♟ 5
O Langhe Bianco '06	♟♟ 5
● Barolo Albe '03	♟♟ 7
● Barbera d'Alba Sup. '05	♟♟ 5
● Langhe Freisa Kyè '05	♟♟ 5
● Dolcetto d'Alba '06	♟ 4
O Moscato d'Asti '06	♟ 4
● Barbera d'Alba Sup. '01	♟♟♟ 5
● Barolo Bricco delle Viole '99	♟♟♟ 8
● Barolo Bricco delle Viole '01	♟♟♟ 8
● Barolo Bricco delle Viole '00	♟♟♟ 8
O Langhe Bianco '02	♟♟♟ 5
O Langhe Bianco '05	♟♟ 5
● Barbera d'Alba Sup. '04	♟♟ 5

Cascina Val del Prete

S.DA SANTUARIO, 2
12040 PRIOCCA [CN]
TEL. 0173616534
valdelprete@tiscali.it

ANNUAL PRODUCTION	40,000 bottles
HECTARES UNDER VINE	11
VITICULTURE METHOD	Natural

We are in the presence of one of the most serious yet successful ranges from the many tasted this year in Roero. Mario Roagna is tireless in his search for quality. After making his mark during those extraordinary years for reds, he has now taken on arneis, "the" white variety in this territory, where Mario absolutely believes in its potential. More care in the vineyard, where Roagna has become over the years a consistent biodynamic grower, and rethinks of winemaking and cellar ageing times are now producing results. This is a white that still has to find its own stylistic stamp but already shows excellent promise. The three main red labels are exquisite and listed in order of preference. The Roero 2004 makes the best of this great vintage year, marrying freshness to softness and a varietal tone to bring home Three Glasses. The Vigna di Lino is even more ready to drink, almost ingratiating in its silky tannins, and a sincere, uncomplicated expression of nebbiolo. The Carolina is a significant Barbera with its fruit, spice and earth bouquet and rich body on the palate. The selection closes with a pleasant, standard-label Barbera.

Tenute dei Vallarino

REG. VALLE ASINARI, 20
14050 SAN MARZANO OLIVETO [AT]
TEL. 0141823048

ANNUAL PRODUCTION	150,000 bottles
HECTARES UNDER VINE	38
VITICULTURE METHOD	Conventional

The Gancias, world-famous sparkler makers, create still wines at Tenute dei Vallarino. Edoardo, Lamberto and Max Gancia have worked hard at this project, begun at the start of the new century, for quality production from estate-owned vineyards. The property is at Monferrato, in Valle Asinari, a fine zone for Barbera production. After the first phase of preparation, the project has now become better defined with the reorganization of the vine stock and presentation of the entire production line. There are many new items with fully 12 labels, four white and eight reds. Among the whites, the interesting La Ciò selection is from bussanello, a variety that was nearly extinct but has been revived by Gancia. The sauvignon-based Pèpero is nicely fragrant and Unisono, from chardonnay, is fruity and rich. The leading red is absent since the 2005 Barbera Nizza Asinari is still maturing so it fell to the Monferrato Dialogo, from cabernet, barbera, nebbiolo and merlot, to defend the winery's honour. The Barbera Filovia is fruity, the Barbera Superiore La Ladra 2005 caressing, the nebbiolo Rispetto tannic, and the syrah Munparlè and merlot Canoro from 2006 pleasant. Finally, the Moscato is excellent.

● Roero '04	▼▼▼	7
● Barbera d'Alba Sup. Carolina '05	▼▼	6
● Barbera d'Alba Serra de' Gatti '06	▼▼	4*
● Nebbiolo d'Alba V. di Lino '05	▼▼	6
○ Roero Arneis Luet '06	▼	4
● Nebbiolo d'Alba V. di Lino '00	♈♈♈	5
● Roero '00	♈♈♈	6
● Roero '01	♈♈♈	7
● Roero '03	♈♈♈	7
● Barbera d'Alba Sup. Carolina '03	♈♈	6
● Nebbiolo d'Alba V. di Lino '03	♈♈	6
● Nebbiolo d'Alba V. di Lino '04	♈♈	6
● Barbera d'Alba Sup. Carolina '04	♈♈	6
● Barbera d'Alba Sup. Carolina '01	♈♈	6

● Monferrato Rosso Dialogo '05	▼▼	6
○ Moscato d'Asti Castello Gancia '06	▼▼	4
● Monferrato Rosso Rispetto '05	▼▼	4
● Barbera d'Asti Filovia '06	▼▼	4
● Barbera d'Asti Sup. La Ladra '05	▼▼	4
● Monferrato Rosso Inter Nos '05	▼▼	4
● Monferrato Rosso Munparlè '06	▼	4
● Monferrato Rosso Canoro '06	▼	4
○ Monferrato Bianco Pèpero '06	▼	4
○ Monferrato Bianco La Ciò '06	▼	4
○ Monferrato Bianco Unisono '06	▼	4
● Barbera d'Asti Sup. Nizza Bricco Asinari '03	♈♈	6
● Barbera d'Asti Sup. Nizza Bricco Asinari '04	♈♈	6

Rino Varaldo

VIA SECONDINE, 2
12050 BARBARESCO [CN]
TEL. 0173635160
varaldo@varaldo.com

ANNUAL PRODUCTION 50,000 bottles
HECTARES UNDER VINE 7
VITICULTURE METHOD Conventional

The Varaldos' Barolo returns to the market with the 2003 vintage, completing the varied selection of wines presented by this winery. The varieties most used are the local nebbiolo, barbera and dolcetto grapes, with a little merlot and cabernet. Brothers Rino and Michele, an oenologist, manage seven hectares under vine, three owned and four rented, and produce nine labels for a total of 50,000 bottles. There are three Barbarescos, two being vineyard selections – Sorì Loreto and Bricco Libero – and one, La Gemma, from a vineyard at Treiso. Sorì Loreto is very good and draws its quality from the 2004 growing season, one of the best in the past few years. Balanced and caressing, it opens on elegant, complex fruity tones. The Bricco Libero is also excellent and adds a pleasant oaky note to the fruit sensations. The rich, powerful La Gemma has stiffish tannins in the finish but the tannins are generous in the Barolo Vigna di Aldo. The Barbera Vigna delle Fate and Fantasia 4.20 are both praiseworthy.

Mauro Veglio

FRAZ. ANNUNZIATA
CASCINA NUOVA, 50
12064 LA MORRA [CN]
TEL. 0173509212
www.mauroveglio.com

ANNUAL PRODUCTION 55,000 bottles
HECTARES UNDER VINE 11
VITICULTURE METHOD Conventional

Following a script we already know and love, here we are again commenting on the excellent range of labels from this lovely winery. The generous sensibility of Daniela and Mauro Veglio is reflected in their wines, which retain their own identity and their close ties to the territory. The desire to interpret and respect the growing season means, for example, knowing how to make a sound, complex Barolo Castelletto 2003, with very personal aromatics. Right behind this is the excellent Barolo Gattera 2003, which shows depth and finesse. The Barolo Arborina 2003 is fuller and caressing whereas the Barolo Rocche 2003 has a powerful tannic crescendo. The Barbera d'Alba Cascina Nuova 2005 shows excellent harmony and elegance, proffering a compendium of typicity, freshness and well-sustained structure. The rest of this impressive line-up also deserves credit for the standard-label Dolcetto and Barbera d'Alba are always sound. We anxiously await the wines from the new family vineyards in Monforte.

● Barbaresco Bricco Libero '04	♀♀ 7
● Barbaresco Sorì Loreto '04	♀♀ 7
● Barbaresco La Gemma '04	♀♀ 7
● Barbera d'Alba V. delle Fate '05	♀♀ 5
● Langhe Rosso Fantasia 4.20 '05	♀♀ 5
● Barolo V. di Aldo '03	♀♀ 8
● Barbera d'Alba '06	♀ 4
● Dolcetto d'Alba '06	♀ 4
● Langhe Nebbiolo '05	♀ 4
● Barbaresco Bricco Libero '97	♀♀♀ 7
● Barbaresco Bricco Libero '01	♀♀♀ 7
● Barbaresco Bricco Libero '03	♀♀♀ 7
● Barbaresco Sorì Loreto '01	♀♀♀ 7
● Barbaresco Sorì Loreto '03	♀♀♀ 7

● Barbera d'Alba	
Cascina Nuova '05	♀♀ 5
● Barolo V. Gattera '03	♀♀ 7
● Barolo Vign. Arborina '03	♀♀ 7
● Barolo Castelletto '03	♀♀ 7
● Barolo V. Rocche '03	♀♀ 7
● Dolcetto d'Alba '06	♀♀ 4*
● Langhe L'Insieme '04	♀♀ 7
● Barbera d'Alba '06	♀ 4
● Langhe Nebbiolo Angelo '05	♀ 6
● Barbera d'Alba	
Cascina Nuova '99	♀♀♀ 5
● Barolo Vign. Arborina '00	♀♀♀ 7
● Barolo Vign. Arborina '01	♀♀♀ 7
● Barolo V. Rocche '96	♀♀♀ 7

Castello di Verduno
VIA UMBERTO I, 9
12060 VERDUNO [CN]
TEL. 0172470284
www.castellodiverduno.com

Eraldo Viberti
FRAZ. SANTA MARIA
B.TA TETTI, 53
12064 LA MORRA [CN]
TEL. 017350308

ANNUAL PRODUCTION 42,000 bottles
HECTARES UNDER VINE 7.5
VITICULTURE METHOD Conventional

ANNUAL PRODUCTION 25,000 bottles
HECTARES UNDER VINE 5
VITICULTURE METHOD Conventional

Tradition, elegance and authenticity are the three distinctive features of wines from Castello di Verduno. Gabriella Burlotto, who also manages the splendid Ca' del Re agriturismo restaurant, and her husband Franco Bianco are helped by a skilled young technician and cellarman, Mario Andrion, and Lorenzo Quarello, in charge of sales and public relations. From the wines, we enjoyed the truly monumental Riserva di Barbaresco Rabajà 1999 with its ripe notes on the nose that recall leather and animal skins and nuances of thyme, rose and violet. The palate shows sweet, perfectly crafted tannins and finishes with great class and enviable length. The Monvigliero stands out as one of the best Barolos made in the particularly difficult 2002 growing season. The Barbera Bricco del Cuculo from the 2005 vintage is released only in 1,000 magnums, to emphasize the importance of a wine that is a delight on both nose and palate. The Basadone is spicy and juicy and the rest of the line-up is extremely well made, with applause going to the base Barbaresco.

The strength and fame of the Langhe comes from a network of producers who have achieved a standard of excellence. Other winemaking areas may attract attention because of a few outstanding winemakers with extremely high quality but there are few other places where the average is this high. This means that it is often difficult to give all the estates the attention they deserve. One such case is Eraldo Viberti, a small producer in terms of bottles produced – just 25,000 – but not in ability or the quality of the wines. The skilled hand of the winemaker is easier to appreciate in difficult or abnormal growing seasons. Eraldo's elegant, approachable 2003 Barolo reflects its territory, La Morra, and shows just how good he is, as did the Barolo from the previous year, the unexciting 2002. The very good Barbera Vigna Clara 2004 enjoys long ageing. Decent acidity supports rich texture resulting in an elegant, balanced wine that stands out for its remarkable length. The Langhe Nebbiolo and Dolcetto d'Alba are also good, the latter marked by attractively youthful acidic grip.

● Barbaresco Rabajà Ris. '99	♟♟ 7
● Barolo Monvigliero '02	♟♟ 7
● Barbaresco '03	♟♟ 5
● Barbera d'Alba Bricco del Cuculo '05	♟♟ 4*
● Verduno Basadone '06	♟♟ 4*
● Dolcetto d'Alba Campot '06	♟ 4
● Barolo Massara '01	♟♟♟ 7
● Barbaresco Rabajà '01	♟♟ 6
● Barbaresco Rabajà Ris. '97	♟♟ 7
● Barbera d'Alba Bricco del Cuculo '05	♟♟ 4
● Barolo Massara '97	♟♟ 7
● Barolo Monvigliero '98	♟♟ 7
● Barbaresco Rabajà '98	♟♟ 6
● Barbaresco Rabajà '97	♟♟ 6
● Barolo Monvigliero '99	♟♟ 6
● Barolo Massara '98	♟♟ 7

● Barbera d'Alba V. Clara '04	♟♟ 6
● Barolo '03	♟♟ 7
● Dolcetto d'Alba '06	♟♟ 3*
● Langhe Nebbiolo '06	♟♟ 4
● Barolo '93	♟♟♟ 7
● Barolo '01	♟♟ 7
● Barolo '00	♟♟ 7
● Barolo '99	♟♟ 7
● Barolo '98	♟♟ 7
● Barbera d'Alba V. Clara '01	♟♟ 6
● Barbera d'Alba V. Clara '00	♟♟ 6
● Barbera d'Alba V. Clara '03	♟♟ 6

Vicara

LOC. MADONNA
CASCINA MADONNA DELLE GRAZIE
15030 ROSIGNANO MONFERRATO [AL]
TEL. 0142488054
www.vicara.it

ANNUAL PRODUCTION 220,000 bottles
HECTARES UNDER VINE 35
VITICULTURE METHOD Certified biodinamic

There are some major absences in the range of wines presented by Domenico Ravizza, head of this important operation in the Casale area. This was to avoid penalizing recently blended or bottled wines that need more cellar time to bring them to readiness. The current Barbera Volpuva has an intense red colour and fruity aromas that alternate with hints of vegetality, preceding a palate that is well sustained and very long. Again this year, the Grignolino del Monferrato Casalese is one of the best in its type. Its slightly pale ruby red heralds a spicy nose enhanced by vegetal notes. The Monferrato Bianco Airales, from a blend of cortese, chardonnay and sauvignon, is a wine with marked varietal characteristics. An intense straw yellow takes you into a palate that echoes the nose and finishes long. Finally, special mention goes to the semi-sparkling Freisa, a classic Monferrato wine.

● Barbera del M.to Volpuva '06	▼▼	4*
● Grignolino del M.to Casalese '06	▼▼	4*
○ Monferrato Bianco Airales '06	▼▼	4*
● Monferrato Freisa '06	▼	4
● Barbera del M.to Sup. Cantico della Crosia '03	▽▽	5
● Barbera del M.to Sup. Cantico della Crosia '04	▽▽	5
● Monferrato Rosso Rubello '03	▽▽	5
● Monferrato Rosso L'Uccelletta '03	▽▽	5
● Monferrato Rosso Rubello '04	▽▽	5
● Barbera del M.to Sup. Vadmò '04	▽▽	4

Vielmin

VIA SAN DAMIANO, 16
12050 CASTELLINALDO [CN]
TEL. 0173213298
ivan.gili@tin.it

ANNUAL PRODUCTION 28,000 bottles
HECTARES UNDER VINE 4.7
VITICULTURE METHOD Conventional

Nine harvests have passed since the first wine was made and bottled by Ivan Gili – Vielmin to his friends – who has a family history in wine that goes back to 1950, when his father's winery sold unbottled wine. Today, with the opening of the lovely, efficient winery in the Roero hills, a die has been cast. Vielmin is no longer a promising youngster from Castellinaldo: he is a fully fledged winemaker and will now lavish even more attention on his grapes and wine production. Two Barberas were presented: Castellinaldo, aged in small oak, and Srëi, which matures in large barrels. The former offers dense texture and sweet fruit while Srëi has a better balance of freshness and alcoholic power. The interesting Arneis, sourced from vineyards in the municipality of Monteu Roero, is dry and fruity with balanced tanginess in the finish. The less convincing Favorita is very slightly sparkling and to close, there is a lean, easygoing Dolcetto that puts fruit to the fore.

● Barbera d'Alba Srëi '05	▼▼	4
● Roero La Rocca '05	▼▼	5
● Castellinaldo Barbera d'Alba '05	▼▼	5
○ Langhe Arneis '06	▼▼	3*
○ Langhe Favorita '06	▼	3
● Langhe Dolcetto '06	▼	3
● Castellinaldo Barbera d'Alba '04	▽▽	5
● Castellinaldo Barbera d'Alba '03	▽▽	5
● Castellinaldo Barbera d'Alba '01	▽▽	5
● Roero La Rocca '01	▽▽	5
● Roero La Rocca '03	▽▽	5
● Roero La Rocca '04	▽▽	5

★ Vietti

P.ZZA VITTORIO VENETO, 5
12060 CASTIGLIONE FALLETTO [CN]
TEL. 017362825
www.vietti.com

ANNUAL PRODUCTION 200,000 bottles
HECTARES UNDER VINE 35
VITICULTURE METHOD Conventional

Welcome to the winery of wonders! Luca Currado and Mario Cordero submitted wines that are more than just impressive: average quality is superb. But let's take things in order with the Barolo Villero, its nose rich in personality with elegant touches of dried flowers, leather, cocoa powder, vanilla and pepper preceding a practically interminable palate. This Riserva shows such an amazing sensory profile that it won a well-deserved Three Glass award at our finals. There are four Barolos from 2003. We were most struck by the Lazzarito, which is appealing thanks to an ethery nose laced with coffee and pepper notes. The elegant, aristocratic Rocche is just as good while the Castiglione and Brunate show less personality. The Asti Barbera, the blackberry, liquorice, and raspberry jam-themed La Crena and its sibling from Alba, Scarrone Vigna Vecchia, with wild cherries, balsamic hints and cocoa powder, both made it to our finals. The Scarrone from Alba and Tre Vigne from Asti were just a step behind. The remarkable Barbaresco Masseria shows strawberry and chocolate with a juicy entry on the long-lingering palate. The Nebbiolo Perbacco is fresh and easy drinking.

Vigna Rionda - Massolino

P.ZZA CAPPELLANO, 8
12050 SERRALUNGA D'ALBA [CN]
TEL. 0173613138
www.massolino.it

ANNUAL PRODUCTION 100,000 bottles
HECTARES UNDER VINE 18
VITICULTURE METHOD Conventional

We have news and confirmation from Massolino. The news regards the purchase of a 1.3-hectare plot at Corda della Briccolina, a renowned vineyard at Serralunga, and the rental of just over a hectare and a half under vine at Castiglione Falletto. Other news is the decision, for the 2003 vintage, to present only a base Barolo that combines grapes from the estate plots in famous vineyards. It is well crafted, with clean floral notes, good suppleness on the palate and a rather juicy finish. But confirmation comes with yet another Three Glass award for the great Vigna Rionda Riserva 2001. A brilliant garnet, it is still a little reticent yet already seductive on the nose with notes of dried rose, cinchona, raspberry and pepper, and balanced, powerful and very long on the palate. It will age very well. From the other wines, we were struck by the Barbera Gisep, in 2004 in one of the best versions ever, which shows fresh and powerful, enhanced by a savoury note in the finish. The base wines are all good, from the powerful Dolcetto to the fragrant Barbera and solid Nebbiolo. The well-crafted Chardonnay 2006, which underwent only minimal malolactic fermentation, is fresh-tasting and spirited.

Wine	Rating	Score
● Barolo Villero Ris. '01	�♟♟♟	8
● Barolo Lazzarito '03	♟♟	8
● Barbera d'Alba Scarrone V. Vecchia '05	♟♟	7
● Barbera d'Asti Sup. Nizza La Crena '04	♟♟	6
● Barbera d'Alba Scarrone '05	♟♟	5
● Barbera d'Asti Tre Vigne '05	♟♟	4
● Barolo Rocche '03	♟♟	8
● Barbaresco Masseria '04	♟♟	7
● Langhe Nebbiolo Perbacco '04	♟♟	5
● Barolo Brunate '03	♟♟	8
● Barolo Castiglione '03	♟♟	7
● Barolo Rocche '01	♟♟♟	8
● Barbera d'Alba Scarrone V. Vecchia '01	♟♟♟	7
● Barbera d'Asti Sup. Nizza La Crena '03	♟♟♟	6

Wine	Rating	Score
● Barolo V. Rionda Ris. '01	♟♟♟	8
● Barbera d'Alba Gisep '04	♟♟	5
● Barolo '03	♟♟	6
● Langhe Nebbiolo '04	♟♟	4*
● Barbera d'Alba '06	♟♟	4*
● Dolcetto d'Alba '06	♟♟	4*
○ Langhe Chardonnay '06	♟	4
○ Moscato d'Asti di Serralunga '06	♟	4
● Barolo Parafada '96	♟♟♟	8
● Barolo V. Rionda Ris. '99	♟♟♟	8
● Barolo V. Rionda Ris. '98	♟♟♟	8
● Barolo Parafada Ris. '90	♟♟♟	8
● Barolo V. Rionda Ris. '90	♟♟♟	8
● Barolo V. Rionda Ris. '97	♟♟♟	8
● Barolo V. Rionda Ris. '96	♟♟♟	8
● Barolo V. Rionda Ris. '00	♟♟	8
● Barolo Margheria '01	♟♟	7

I Vignaioli di Santo Stefano

LOC. MARINI, 26
12058 SANTO STEFANO BELBO [CN]
TEL. 0141840419
www.ceretto.com

ANNUAL PRODUCTION 270,000 bottles
HECTARES UNDER VINE 35
VITICULTURE METHOD Conventional

Here is one of Santo Stefano Belbo's longest established estates, founded more than 30 years ago when the supremacy of industrial producers over small private wineries seemed absolute. The initial members in this wonderful adventure were joined by the Ceretto family who, apart from dedicating time to production, also commercially launched the few labels made at Marini. Predictably, Moscato is king here and is released in three selections. The Moscato d'Asti gives attractive fizz in the glass and a bright yellow colour. The nose unveils all the intriguing notes of the variety, expanding into a bouquet of aromas that run from peach to orange peel. The entry on the palate is sweet and complex, embellished by a marked acidity that refreshes the mouthfeel, with notes of sage, citronella and mint. The Passito starts off with date and tamarind sensations and then veers towards spice, particularly vanilla and cocoa powder.

Il Vignale

LOC. LOMELLINA
VIA GAVI, 130
15067 NOVI LIGURE [AL]
TEL. 014372715
www.ilvignale.it

ANNUAL PRODUCTION 50,000 bottles
HECTARES UNDER VINE 12
VITICULTURE METHOD Conventional

For around a decade, Vignale has been owned by Piero and Vilma Cappelletti who over time have accustomed us to better and better performances. The area under vine includes several hectares carefully managed and supervised by technician Giuseppe Bassi. The Gavi Vilma Cappelletti is one of the DOCG zone's top products but this is nothing new. What we expectantly await is the quality leap that would establish it as one of the region's great whites. The typically floral aromas still have a characteristic finesse, laced with faint balsamic notes. The palate is balanced and assertive acidity adds freshness and appealing drinkability. A step behind in complexity is Vigne Alte, which has fairly intense aromas that recall wisteria and lemon peel before the tangy palate features a slightly bitterish finish. The Rosso di Malì, a fruit-led, ethery, tannic blend of pinot nero and cabernet sauvignon, is very good.

O Asti '06	￥￥ 4*
O Moscato d'Asti '06	￥￥ 4*
O Piemonte Moscato Passito IL '03	￥￥ 5
O Moscato d'Asti '05	￥￥ 4
O Piemonte Moscato Passito IL '02	￥￥ 5
O Asti '05	￥￥ 4

O Gavi Vilma Cappelletti '06	￥￥ 4*
O Gavi Vigne Alte '06	￥￥ 4*
● Monferrato Rosso Rosso di Malì '04	￥￥ 4
O Gavi Vilma Cappelletti '05	￥￥ 4
O Gavi Vilma Cappelletti '04	￥￥ 4
O Gavi Vilma Cappelletti '03	￥￥ 4

Vigne Regali

VIA VITTORIO VENETO, 76
15019 STREVI [AL]
TEL. 0144362600
www.vigneregali.com

Vigneti Massa

P.ZZA G. CAPSONI, 10
15059 MONLEALE [AL]
TEL. 013180302

ANNUAL PRODUCTION 1,900,000 bottles
HECTARES UNDER VINE 75
VITICULTURE METHOD Conventional

ANNUAL PRODUCTION 80,000 bottles
HECTARES UNDER VINE 19.5
VITICULTURE METHOD Conventional

Big-number producer Banfi did things in an appropriately big way when it landed in Piedmont and created an estate with 75 hectares of vineyards. On the one hand, it grows native varieties from the territory and, on the other, attempts to give the product range a modern, international style. The Strevi winery produces many labels. The excellent Barbera Banin is an almost impenetrably dark red with straightforward, nicely intense aromas that range from red berry fruit to sweet spice and rain-soaked earth. The Dolcetto Argusto is also good, showing tannic yet never aggressive and very drinkable. This Dolcetto will improve with bottle ageing. The other Dolcetto, L'Ardì, is still young and will acquire better balance with time. From the aromatic wines, we liked the Brachetto Vigneto La Rosa with its sensations of flower petals and honey. Then there is the Moscato Strevi, flaunting clean, delicate, varietal aromas and a sweet yet never cloying palate. The Gavi is enjoyable for its freshness and easy-drinking style, the Banfi Brut Talento is good and Tener is correct.

Despite the great success of Timorasso, Walter Massa, the creator of this white phenomenon, continues to believe Tortona is a land of great reds and great Barberas in particular. We don't know if he will be happier at our confirmation of the high quality of his two Timorassos or at the return of Bigolla to the ranks of top reds: it's the only red from Tortona to have won a Three Glass award. In the meantime, Walter can enjoy our highest award for Costa del Vento, a fantastic Timorasso selection that shows minerally, zesty, elegant and very long. The rest of the range is less spectacular although perhaps all the more enjoyable for it. The Monleale, another barbera-based red aged in oak, has recently earned better reviews than the Bigolla itself. The Croatina Pertichetta, with warm nuances of coffee and spice, and the Barbera Sentieri, steel aged with clear fruity notes, are champions in their respective categories. In contrast, the Freisa Pietra del Gallo and slightly sparkling white Casareggio, from cortese, are designed for drinkability.

● Barbera d'Asti Vign. Banin '04	♟♟ 5
● Dolcetto d'Acqui Argusto '04	♟♟ 4*
○ Talento Banfi Brut M. Cl.	♟♟ 4*
● Brachetto d'Acqui Vign. La Rosa '06	♟ 4
● Dolcetto d'Acqui L'Ardì '06	♟ 3
○ Moscato d'Asti Strevi '06	♟ 4
○ Tener Brut	♟ 3
○ Gavi Principessa Gavia '06	♟ 3
● Barbera d'Asti Vign. Banin '03	♟♟ 5
● Dolcetto d'Acqui Argusto '03	♟♟ 4
○ Alta Langa Cuvée Aurora '02	♟♟ 5

○ Colli Tortonesi Bianco Costa del Vento '05	♟♟♟ 7
○ Colli Tortonesi Bianco Sterpi '05	♟♟ 7
● Colli Tortonesi Rosso Bigolla '04	♟♟ 7
● Colli Tortonesi Rosso Monleale '04	♟♟ 6
● Colli Tortonesi Rosso Sentieri '06	♟♟ 5
● Colli Tortonesi Rosso Pertichetta '05	♟♟ 5
○ Colli Tortonesi Bianco Derthona '05	♟♟ 6
○ Colli Tortonesi Bianco Casareggio '06	♟ 4
● Colli Tortonesi Freisa Pietra del Gallo '06	♟ 4
● Colli Tortonesi Rosso Bigolla '98	♟♟♟ 7
○ Colli Tortonesi Bianco Sterpi '04	♟♟♟ 7
○ Colli Tortonesi Bianco Costa del Vento '04	♟♟ 7

Villa Fiorita
VIA CASE SPARSE, 2
14034 CASTELLO DI ANNONE [AT]
TEL. 0141401231
www.villafiorita-wines.com

ANNUAL PRODUCTION 80,000 bottles
HECTARES UNDER VINE 12
VITICULTURE METHOD Conventional

This estate is in the hills of Castello d'Annone. The Rondolino family invested here in the early 1980s, rebuilding the lovely country villa and planting to vine the 12 hectares around the cellar. The Rondolinos were among the first in the Asti area to opt for international varieties, establishing interesting and varied vineyards where chardonnay, sauvignon and pinot nero stand alongside the classic grignolino and barbera vines. The two showcase wines were not released to market this year. The Barbera d'Asti Il Giorgione, stopped at the 2003 vintage and the Maniero, from pinot nero and barbera, stopped at 2004. But a nice range of labels was presented in spite of this. Outstanding among the wines tasted was the Monferrato Rosso Nero di Villa Riserva di Famiglia 2005, an oak-aged pinot nero with a deep ruby colour. The nose is shot through with spice and ripe black berry fruit and the elegant palate has well-balanced tannins and acidity. The 2005 Barbera is fruity, the Abaco, from steel-vinified pinot nero, is spicy. Finally, the sauvignon and chardonnay Sovrano is citrus-led.

Villa Giada
REG. CEIROLE, 4
14053 CANELLI [AT]
TEL. 0141831100
www.andreafaccio.it

ANNUAL PRODUCTION 216,500 bottles
HECTARES UNDER VINE 25
VITICULTURE METHOD Conventional

The Faccios have lived in Asti for more than 200 years but it was not until 1990 that Andrea began quality vinification of the fruit from the family vineyards in the municipalities of Agliano, Calosso and Canelli. This apparently short story has nonetheless seen a lot of progress made. This year, the broad range of Barberas is embellished with the selection Superiore Dedicato a Te, obtained from 50-year-old vines and matured for two years in new barriques. The Barbera Bricco Dani 2005 stands out for its violet and leather notes that give complexity to a wine already rich in body. The red PrimoVolo 2004 confirms the unique quality of a wine project conceived with wineries outside the region, La Montecchia in Veneto and Rocca delle Macìe in Tuscany. The Monferrato Rosso Treponti 2005 is amazing in its balanced fusion of nebbiolo and barbera. Mention also goes to the Moscato Ceirole 2006 for soft fizz that elegantly brings together notes of tropical fruit and wild strawberries.

O Monferrato Bianco Sovrano '05	🍷🍷 5
● Barbera d'Asti Sup. '05	🍷🍷 4*
● Monferrato Rosso Nero di Villa Ris. di Famiglia '05	🍷🍷 6
● Monferrato Rosso Abaco '05	🍷🍷 3*
● Grignolino d'Asti Pian delle Querce '05	🍷 3
O Piemonte Chardonnay Le Tavole '06	🍷 4
● Barbera d'Asti Sup. Il Giorgione '03	🍷🍷 5
● Monferrato Rosso Abaco '04	🍷🍷 3
● Monferrato Rosso Maniero '04	🍷🍷 5
● Monferrato Rosso Nero di Villa '04	🍷🍷 6

● Barbera d'Asti Sup. Bricco Dani '05	🍷🍷 5
● Barbera d'Asti Ajan '06	🍷🍷 4*
● Barbera d'Asti Sup. Dedicato a te '03	🍷🍷 8
● Barbera d'Asti Sup. Vign. La Quercia '05	🍷🍷 4*
● Monferrato Rosso Treponti '05	🍷🍷 4*
● PrimoVolo '04	🍷🍷 6
● Barbera d'Asti I Surì '06	🍷 3
O Moscato d'Asti Ceirole '06	🍷 4
O Monferrato Bianco Bricco Mané '05	🍷 4
● Barbera d'Asti Sup. Nizza Bricco Dani '04	🍷🍷 5
● Barbera d'Asti Sup. Bricco Dani '03	🍷🍷 5
● Barbera d'Asti Sup. Bricco Dani '01	🍷🍷 5

Villa Sparina

FRAZ. MONTEROTONDO, 56
15066 GAVI [AL]
TEL. 0143633835
www.villasparina.it

ANNUAL PRODUCTION 480,000 bottles
HECTARES UNDER VINE 56
VITICULTURE METHOD Conventional

Villa Sparina or Villa Beautiful? There are no
better opening words for one of the most
bewitching operations in Gavi. The position
of the estate is beautiful, the main
farmhouse is stupendous and the charming
hospitality centre is dedicated to the
Moccagattas' various reception activities.
And since beauty would be worth little
without good quality products, what about
the wines? Well, wines with the Villa Sparina
label are great. Always at the top of its
category, Gavi Monterotondo gives deep
aromas and a well-balanced, harmonic
palate. The Monferrato Rosso Rivalta is just
as good, its blend of barbera with a little
merlot as mouthfilling and sustained as it is
balanced and ready to drink. This great red
brought Three Glasses back to Gavi for the
Moccagattas. The other wines submitted
also performed well. The base Gavi stands
out for its freshness on the palate. The Extra
Brut from cortese is by now a classic and
Montej Bianco, a blend of international
varieties, is tangy and minerally. The
Barbera Montej is wonderfully upfront and
approachable while Sampò, from barbera
and merlot, is well typed.

Cantina Sociale di Vinchio Vaglio Serra

REGIONE SAN PANCRAZIO, 1
14040 VINCHIO [AT]
TEL. 0141950903
www.vinchio.com

ANNUAL PRODUCTION 1,000,000 bottles
HECTARES UNDER VINE 325
VITICULTURE METHOD Conventional

Over the past few years, Cantina Sociale di
Vinchio Vaglio Serra has accompanied the
rising quality standards of Barbera d'Asti,
starting a school of its own and making
characterful wines linked by shared stylistic
traits. The excellent score for the Insynthesis
selection only confirms this as one of
Piedmont's leading co-operative operations
both in numbers of bottles and for sheer
goodness. Credit for all this goes in part to
the consultancy input from Giuliano Noè
and Mauro Cazzola. Getting back to the top
Barbera d'Asti, it shows an intense ruby red
in the glass, proffering aromas that range
from red berry fruit to echoes of cocoa
powder, vanilla and sweet spice. The palate
has energy and power, with remarkable
length in the finish. The rest of the large
collection of Barberas are all excellent, with
special mentions for the Bricco Laudana
and Vigne Vecchie. The cabernet, merlot
and barbera blend, Monferrato Rosso Tutti
per Uno, is worth uncorking.

● Monferrato Rosso Rivalta '04	♟♟♟ 6
○ Gavi del Comune di Gavi Monterotondo '05	♟♟ 5
● Barbera del M.to Montej '05	♟♟ 4*
● Dolcetto di Ovada Maioli '05	♟♟ 4*
○ Gavi del Comune di Gavi '06	♟♟ 4*
○ Gavi Extra Brut	♟♟ 5
○ Monferrato Bianco Montej '06	♟ 4
● Monferrato Rosso Sampò '04	♟ 4
● Monferrato Rosso Rivalta '99	♟♟♟ 6
● Monferrato Rosso Rivalta '00	♟♟♟ 6
● Barbera del M.to Rivalta '97	♟♟♟ 6
○ Gavi del Comune di Gavi Monterotondo '99	♟♟♟ 5
○ Gavi del Comune di Gavi Monterotondo '04	♟♟ 5
● Monferrato Rosso Rivalta '03	♟♟ 6

● Barbera d'Asti Sup. Sei Vigne Insynthesis '04	♟♟ 7
● Barbera d'Asti Sup. Nizza Bricco Laudana '05	♟♟ 5
● Barbera d'Asti Sup. I Tre Vescovi '05	♟♟ 4*
● Barbera d'Asti Sup. Vigne Vecchie '05	♟♟ 5
● Monferrato Rosso Tutti per Uno '05	♟♟ 5
● Barbera d'Asti '06	♟ 4
● Monferrato Rosso Frusté '06	♟ 5
● Barbera d'Asti Sup. Sei Vigne Insynthesis '01	♟♟♟ 7
● Barbera d'Asti Sup. Sei Vigne Insynthesis '03	♟♟ 7

Gianni Voerzio

S.DA LORETO, 1
12064 LA MORRA [CN]
TEL. 0173509194
voerzio.gianni@tiscali.it

★ Roberto Voerzio

LOC. CERRETO, 1
12064 LA MORRA [CN]
TEL. 0173509196

ANNUAL PRODUCTION 64,000 bottles
HECTARES UNDER VINE 12.5
VITICULTURE METHOD Conventional

Structure, elegance and cleanliness are the mainstays of Gianni Voerzio's production. He regularly achieves these objectives through meticulous work in the vineyard and constant awareness of new winemaking technologies. This year, the range of wines on offer is complete with the return of the Barolo La Serra 2003 – it was absent in the 2002 vintage – which flaunts an intense garnet red introducing complex aromas of plum, cocoa powder and tobacco, and a rich, intense palate. The Langhe Rosso Serrapiù is impressive for its elegance on the nose and balanced acidity that stretches out into a balsam and cinchona finish. The Nebbiolo Ciabot della Luna is an excellent demonstration of the power of nebbiolo, elegantly conditioned in French oak. As ever one of the best wines in the category, the Barbera Ciabot della Luna shows amazing morello cherry and balsamic aromas of eucalyptus that make it extraordinarily drinkable. Closing the range, we have the imposing Dolcetto Rocchettevino, the stylish Freisa Sotto i Bastioni, a fresh Langhe Arneis Bricco Cappellina and the captivating Moscato d'Asti Vigna Sergente, with hints of elderflower and elegant effervescence.

ANNUAL PRODUCTION 35,000 bottles
HECTARES UNDER VINE 17
VITICULTURE METHOD Conventional

Roberto Voerzio's work is characterized by seriousness and the courage of decisions that have made him and his wife Pinuccia two of the most celebrated winemakers in the Langhe and indeed Italy. The decisions we are talking about mostly concern the vineyard, in particular the extremely low yields, which barely top 3,000 kilograms per hectare. As a result, wines from here have great depth, a richness of raw material and extraction that would be difficult to match and, offsetting this, remarkable elegance that recalls the magnificent vineyards that produce the grapes. Moving on to the wines, the 2003 vintage for Barolos was atypical and failed to reach the high points of the growing years that have recently earned the wine laurels and recognition. Roberto managed to get on top of this very hot vintage and created some elegant, powerful wines. The good Sarmassa di Barolo, sold in magnums only, has a nose of ripe fruit and an austere, smooth palate. The sound Cerequio is elegant with oaky notes and the excellent Brunate has depth with aromas of morello cherry and liquorice.

● Barbera d'Alba		
Ciabot della Luna '05	♏♏	5
● Barolo La Serra '03	♏♏	8
● Dolcetto d'Alba Rocchettevino '06	♏♏	4*
● Langhe Freisa Sotti I Bastioni '06	♏♏	4*
● Langhe Nebbiolo		
Ciabot della Luna '05	♏♏	6
● Langhe Rosso Serrapiù '05	♏♏	6
O Moscato d'Asti Vignasergente '06	♏	5
O Roero Arneis		
Bricco Cappellina '06	♏	4
● Barolo La Serra '96	♏♏♏	8
● Barolo La Serra '97	♏♏♏	8
● Barolo La Serra '98	♏♏♏	8
● Barolo La Serra '00	♏♏	8
● Barolo La Serra '01	♏♏	8

● Barolo Brunate '03	♏♏	8
● Barolo Cerequio '03	♏♏	8
● Barolo Sarmassa di Barolo '03	♏♏	8
● Barbera d'Alba Vign.		
Pozzo dell'Annunziata Ris. '96	♏♏♏	8
● Barbera d'Alba Vign.		
Pozzo dell'Annunziata Ris. '99	♏♏♏	8
● Barolo Brunate '89	♏♏♏	6
● Barolo Brunate '90	♏♏♏	8
● Barolo Brunate '93	♏♏♏	8
● Barolo Brunate '96	♏♏♏	8
● Barolo Brunate '98	♏♏♏	8
● Barolo Brunate '99	♏♏♏	8
● Barolo Cerequio '96	♏♏♏	8
● Barolo Cerequio '90	♏♏♏	8
● Barolo Cerequio '91	♏♏♏	8
● Barolo Rocche dell'Annunziata		
Torriglione '00	♏♏♏	8

OTHER WINERIES

Valerio Aloi
VIA PIETRO FISSORE, 6
12046 MONTÀ [CN]
TEL. 0173975604
nico.bono@libero.it

Nicoletta Aloi makes a line of straightforward, terroir-driven wines of excellent overall quality. One is her crisp, approachable Arneis. Up a rung is the succulent, aromatic and nervy Barbera while the Roero exhibits elegant austerity, showing lovely toasty oak and expressive tannins, and length on the finish.

● Roero Bricco Morinaldo '05   ♟♟ 5
● Barbera d'Alba Bricco Valpiana '05 ♟♟ 5
○ Roero Arneis '06   ♟ 4

Osvaldo Barberis
B.TA VALDIBÀ, 42
12063 DOGLIANI [CN]
TEL. 017370054

The young, talented Osvaldo Barberis cultivates eight hectares and specializes in Dolcetto. The excellent San Lorenzo '06 is a pleasure: crisp, easy drinking and reasonably priced. Puncin, now DOCG, wasn't made in this vintage but the fruity, refreshing Barbera Brichat '06 is more than sound.

● Dolcetto di Dogliani
   San Lorenzo '06   ♟♟ 3*
● Piemonte Barbera Brichat '06   ♟ 3
● Dolcetto di Dogliani Puncin '05   ♟♟ 4

Beccaria
VIA GIOVANNI BIANCO, 3
15039 OZZANO MONFERRATO [AL]
TEL. 0142487321
www.beccaria-vini.it

Beccaria has introduced a restyled label. Barbera Superiore Convivium is impressively structured, with fine supporting acidity. Freisa Lilàn '06 shows a wealth of intense fruit on the nose with a hint of grassiness. The well-balanced Grignolino is drinking beautifully while Barbera Evoè is well executed.

● Barbera del M.to Sup. Convivium '05 ♟♟ 4*
● Barbera del M.to Evoè '05   ♟ 4
● Grignolino del M.to Casalese Grignò '06 ♟ 3
● Monferrato Freisa Lilàn '06   ♟ 3

Benotto
VIA SAN CARLO, 52
14055 COSTIGLIOLE D'ASTI [AT]
TEL. 0141966406
benottovini@virgilio.it

The Benotto brothers produce numerous wines in the Piedmontese traditional style at their cellar dating back to 1917. Monferrato Nebieul develops complexity and power, with a long-lingering, rich finale. Barbera d'Asti, a house specialty, is enjoyable and the Dolcetto and the Bonarda are very decent.

● Barbera d'Asti '05   ♟♟ 3*
● Monferrato Rosso Nebieul '04   ♟♟ 5
● Piemonte Bonarda '06   ♟ 4
● Monferrato Dolcetto Plissé '06   ♟ 3

Bianchi
VIA ROMA, 37
28070 SIZZANO [NO]
TEL. 0321810004
www.bianchibiowine.it

Bianchi makes organic wines in the tiny Sizzano DOC, near Novara, but its vineyards stretch into other production zones as well. This year in fact, its two finest wines, both '03s, are from Gattinara. Bianco Luminae is also admirable, as is the delicious Colline Novaresi Nebbiolo.

● Gattinara '03   ♟♟ 5
● Gattinara Vign. Valferana '03   ♟♟ 5
● Colline Novaresi Nebbiolo '05   ♟ 3
○ Colline Novaresi Luminae '06   ♟ 3

Alfonso Boeri
FRAZ. BIONZO
VIA BRICCO QUAGLIA, 10
14055 COSTIGLIOLE D'ASTI [AT]
TEL. 0141968171
www.boerivini.it

The Boeris are grape-growers first and winemakers second and their cellar processes fine-quality fruit. Barbera d'Asti is terrific and quite tasty, as is Moscato Ribota, with intensely fruited fragrances on the nose. The barbera and nebbiolo Barbòlo gained One Glass and do did the approachable Chardonnay.

● Barbera d'Asti Sup. Pörlapà '04   ♟♟ 6
○ Moscato d'Asti Ribota '06   ♟♟ 4
○ Piemonte Chardonnay Beviòn '06   ♟ 4
● Monferrato Rosso Barbòlo '04   ♟ 6

OTHER WINERIES

Borgo Isolabella
VIA CAFFI, 3
14051 LOAZZOLO [AT]
TEL. 014487166
www.borgoisolabella.com

Loazzolo has one of Italy's smallest DOCs, with fine moscato-based offerings. Maria Teresa Isolabella and her husband Lodovico have launched a splendid cellar here. Le Marne is a red blend with fascinating typicity while Moscato offers striking finesse. Equally good are their dry whites.

● Monferrato Le Marne '05	♥♥	4*
○ Monferrato Bianco Solum '06	♥♥	4*
○ Moscato d'Asti Valdiserre '06	♥♥	4*
○ Bianco del Borgo '06	♥	3

Renato Boveri
VIA XXV APRILE, 1
15059 MONLEALE [AL]
TEL. 013180560

We welcome back Renato Boveri, a cellar that has always had good reviews in our Guide. Croatina Costa, a winery star, is impressive but Barbera Sant'Ambrogio seems awkward and needs more time in the bottle. Dolcetto La Cereta is crisply aromatic and a delicious, approachable quaffer.

● Colli Tortonesi Rosso Costa '05	♥♥	5
● Colli Tortonesi Barbera S. Ambrogio '05	♥	4
● Colli Tortonesi Rosso La Cereta '05	♥	4

Cantina del Bricchetto
VIA BRICCHETTO, 4
12057 NEIVE [CN]
TEL. 0173677307
www.cantinadelbricchetto.com

Franco Rocca's Neive-based cellar produces several types of wine. His Barbaresco Albesani '04 is admirable, with notes of stewed fruit and some oak in the mouth, but solidly structured. Oak is a tad too emphatic on the Barbera but Sernì Söri Alessia is a delicious barbera and nebbiolo blend to enjoy now.

● Barbaresco Albesani '04	♥♥	6
● Barbera d'Alba Bricco Sterpone '04	♥	5
● Sernì Söri Alessia '05	♥	5

Francesco Brigatti
VIA OLMI, 31
28019 SUNO [NO]
TEL. 032285037
www.vinibrigatti.it

The Brigattis' wines are excellent overall but space restricts our comments to the two most impressive. The laurels go to Nebbiolo Motfrei '04, sturdy and satisfyingly tannic without any heaviness. The less complicated Rosso Motziflon '04 is more straightforward and accessible but very well crafted.

● Colline Novaresi Nebbiolo V. Motfrei '04	♥♥	4*
● Colline Novaresi Rosso Motziflon '04	♥♥	4*

Renato Buganza
LOC. CASCINA GARBINOTTO, 4
12040 PIOBESI D'ALBA [CN]
TEL. 0173619370
rbuganza@tin.it

Buganza, who entered our Guide three years ago, makes three wines. The Barbera is superb and very enjoyable, showing varietal fidelity on the nose. Roero Bric Paradis '04 is somewhat oak-laden, but intense, and the nicely crisp Arneis exhibits good minerality, broad flavours and a tasty vein of acidity.

● Barbera d'Alba V. Veja '04	♥♥	4*
● Roero Bric Paradis '04	♥♥	5
○ Roero Arneis dla Trifula '06	♥	4

Bussia Soprana
LOC. BUSSIA, 81
12065 MONFORTE D'ALBA [CN]
TEL. 039305182

This winery offers ambitious and simpler wines. We liked Barolo Vigna Colonnello, which opens heady and warm, then builds good structure and complexity in the mouth. Gabutti della Bussia releases cinchona and bottled cherries, though it's a bit short. Langhe Rosso Zenit '03 is full bodied and nicely tannic.

● Barolo Vigna Colonnello '03	♥♥	7
● Langhe Rosso Zenit '03	♥	5
● Barolo Gabutti della Bussia '03	♥	7

OTHER WINERIES

Ca' dei Mandorli
VIA IV NOVEMBRE, 15
14010 CASTEL ROCCHERO [AT]
TEL. 0141760131
www.cadeimandorli.com

Paolo Ricagno and son Stefano cultivate an impressive 180 hectares, from which they produce enjoyable wines, particularly in the dessert category. The outstanding Brachetto Le Donne dei Boschi impressed us, as did the crisp, ultra-aromatic Moscato Dei Giari. One Glass went to the Dolcetto.

● Brachetto d'Acqui	
Le Donne dei Boschi '06	♙♙ 4
○ Moscato d'Asti Dei Giari '06	♙♙ 4
● Dolcetto d'Acqui Il Rujà '06	♙ 4

Cantina Sociale del Canavese
VIA MONTALENGHE, 9
10090 CUCEGLIO [TO]
TEL. 012432034
www.cantinacanavese.it

This co-operative again turned in a fine performance. The coppery-gold Passito Morenico, from erbaluce, releases generous hazelnut-led aromas and its acidity nicely balances the sweetness. Elisa, a sparkling straw yellow, offers florality and good crispness. The Canavese Rosso is well made.

○ Caluso Passito Morenico '02	♙♙ 6
○ Erbaluce di Caluso Elisa '06	♙♙ 3*
● Canavese Rosso '05	♙ 3

La Caplana
VIA CIRCONVALLAZIONE, 4
15060 BOSIO [AL]
TEL. 0143684182
lacaplana@libero.it

Natalino Guido and his family manage La Caplana, whose wines have long exhibited impressive qualities. Gavi Vigna Vecchia is an excellent example, its cortese fruit sourced from vineyards in Zagante and Pilumberto. The standard-label Gavi is also nicely savoury and refreshing, as is the Dolcetto di Ovada.

○ Gavi del Comune di Gavi	
V. Vecchia '06	♙♙ 3*
○ Gavi del Comune di Gavi '06	♙ 4
● Dolcetto di Ovada '06	♙ 3

Carlotta
VIA CONDOVE, 61
10050 BORGONE SUSA [TO]
TEL. 0119646150
rfrancesca@libero.it

The determined Carla Cometto directs this operation at 1,000 metres, and her wines merit respect. Costa Oro is a mix of neretta cuneese, ciliegiolo and barbera in a very personal, fascinating style. The avanà and barbera Rocca del Lupo is fruity and intense while Vigna Combe, from rare local grapes, is complex.

● Valsusa Costa Oro '06	♙♙ 4*
● Valsusa Rocca del Lupo '06	♙♙ 4*
● Valsusa Vigna Combe '06	♙♙ 4*

Tenuta Carretta
LOC. CARRETTA, 2
12040 PIOBESI D'ALBA [CN]
TEL. 0173619119
www.tenutacarretta.it

It's a period of transition for this Roero-based operation. Edoardo Miroglio, the new owner, is carrying out extensive restructuring that affects the production staff, winery equipment and vineyards. As we await more impressive offerings, these wines are pleasing and immediately enjoyable.

○ Roero Arneis V. Canorei '05	♙♙ 5
● Nebbiolo d'Alba '05	♙♙ 4
● Dolcetto d'Alba '06	♙ 4
○ Roero Arneis Cayega '06	4

Carussin
REG. MARIANO, 27
14050 SAN MARZANO OLIVETO [AT]
TEL. 0141831358
www.carussin.it

The Ferro family cultivates 13 hectares organically and is one of the Asti area's most forward-looking operations. The wines display superlative character. That's certainly true of Barbera Asinoi, which has formidably refreshing crispness. Both the Moscato and Lia Vi are delicious.

● Barbera d'Asti Asinoi '06	♙♙ 3*
● Barbera d'Asti Lia Vi '06	♙♙ 3*
○ Moscato d'Asti Filari Corti '06	♙ 3

OTHER WINERIES

La Casaccia
VIA BARBANO DANTE, 10
15034 CELLA MONTE [AL]
TEL. 0142489986

Giovanni Rava's winery earned a well-merited first entry in our Guide. Barbera Superiore Calichè shows elegant fruit and florality followed by a nervy, aromatic palate. Vigna Sant'Anna is only a shade less complex but still outstanding. The Grignolino is exemplary; the Chardonnay extremely well made.

● Barbera d'Asti Sup. Calichè '04	♟♟	5
● Barbera d'Asti V. Sant'Anna '06	♟♟	4*
● Grignolino del M.to Casalese Poggetto '06	♟♟	4*
○ Piemonte Chardonnay Charnò '06	♟	4

Casavecchia
VIA ROMA, 2
12055 DIANO D'ALBA [CN]
TEL. 017369321

The Casavecchia brothers farm 20 hectares and include some of Piedmont's best wine types in their line. Among the wines we liked best were Diano d'Alba and Nebbiolo Piadvenza. Barolo Piantà and Barbera San Quirico are most enjoyable.

● Diano d'Alba Sörì Bruni '06	♟♟	4*
● Nebbiolo d'Alba Piadvenza '05	♟♟	4*
● Barbera d'Alba San Quirico '05	♟	4
● Barolo Piantà '03	♟	6

Cascina Baricchi
VIA TINELLA, 15
12050 NEVIGLIE [CN]
TEL. 0173630141
cascinabaricchi@libero.it

Natale Simonetta continues to do well after introducing the now celebrated ice wine, Solenne, on fine form this year. Also new is a Brut Rosé showing notes of smoke and dried flowers. Rising in quality are Natale's Langhe reds. Barbaresco leads and syrah grapes give Sharà good spice on nose and palate.

● Barbaresco '04	♟♟	6
● Langhe Rosso Sharà '04	♟♟	5
○ Solenne '03	♟♟	8
☺ Visages de Canaille Brut Rosé	♟	6

Cascina Montagnola
S.DA MONTAGNOLA, 1
15058 VIGUZZOLO [AL]
TEL. 0131898558
www.cascinamontagnola.com

The standard-bearer Barbera Rodeo is absent this year but Bianco Risveglio returns with a great performance. From 100 per cent chardonnay, unusual for the Colli Tortonesi, it's as savoury and slaty as you could wish. The croatina Pigmento is a fine effort and Dunin is a crisp, inviting Cortese.

○ Colli Tortonesi Bianco Risveglio '06	♟♟	5
○ Colli Tortonesi Bianco Dunin '06	♟	4
● Colli Tortonesi Rosso Pigmento '06	♟	4

Le Cecche
VIA MOGLIA GERLOTTO, 10
12055 DIANO D'ALBA [CN]
TEL. 017369323
www.lececche.com

Belgian doctor Jan Jules De Bruyne and his wife Paola Invrea purchased this magnificent estate in 2001. Their efforts have resulted in four impressive, enjoyable wines, with the Dolcettos outstanding. The Nebbiolo is delicious and the Barbera shows notes of cask ageing.

● Diano d'Alba '06	♟♟	3*
● Diano d'Alba Sörì Le Cecche '06	♟♟	4*
● Barbera d'Alba '05	♟	4
● Nebbiolo d'Alba Fiammingo '05	♟	4

La Chiara
LOC. VALLEGGE, 24
15066 GAVI [AL]
TEL. 0143642293
www.lachiara.it

La Chiara has appeared many times in our Guide and its superlative Gavis are getting even better. The standard label is excellent, with a floral, quite complex nose and lengthy development. Monferrato Rosso Nabarì, a cabernet, barbera and dolcetto blend, is also very well crafted and balanced.

○ Gavi del Comune di Gavi '06	♟♟	3*
● Monferrato Rosso Nabarì '05	♟♟	4*

OTHER WINERIES

Cocito
LOC. MICCA, 25
12057 NEIVE [CN]
TEL. 017367052
ezio.cocito@tiscali.it

Ezio Cocito has hit the spot with Barbaresco Baluchin Riserva '03, a noble wine that will become even more complex as it evolves in bottle. A fine varietal nose gives a medley of moist earth and pungent scrub and the palate, with a measured oak, is close-knit, aromatic and harmonious in all its elements.

● Barbaresco Baluchin Ris. '03	⟐⟐	8
● Barbaresco Baluchin '02	⟐⟐	8
● Barbaresco Baluchin '01	⟐⟐	8
● Barbaresco Baluchin '03	⟐⟐	8

Clemente Cossetti
VIA GUARDIE, 1
14043 CASTELNUOVO BELBO [AT]
TEL. 0141799803
www.cossetti.it

Cossetti has an annual production of 600,000 bottles and the average quality is fairly high. The wine that we liked the best was La Vigna Vecchi, a deep, austere Barbera with superb overall complexity. The standard-label Barbera is simpler while the Brachetto offers a lovely suite of floral fragrances.

● Barbera d'Asti La Vigna Vecchia '05	⟐	3*
● Barbera d'Asti VentidiMarzo '06	⟐	3
● Brachetto d'Acqui Theo '06	⟐	4

Giovanni Daglio
VIA MONTALE CELLI, 10
15050 COSTA VESCOVATO [AL]
TEL. 0131838262

Giovanni Daglio presented us with an expansive, full-bodied version of Barbera Basinas, with its well-integrated acidity. Nibiò, the local name for dolcetto, is as compelling as usual. The barbera-based Pias and the cortese Vigna del Re are notable for both their quality and their reasonable prices.

● Colli Tortonesi Rosso Nibiò '05	⟐⟐	4*
● Colli Tortonesi Barbera Basinas '04	⟐⟐	4*
● Colli Tortonesi Barbera Pias '0	⟐	3
O Colli Tortonesi Cortese Vigna del Re '06	⟐	3

Vigne Marina Coppi
VIA SANT'ANDREA, 5
15051 CASTELLANIA [AL]
TEL. 3385360111
www.vignemarinacoppi.com

Young Francesco Bellocchio is hard-driving and works long hours in both vineyard and cellar. The wines he presented earned quite high marks, particularly the steel-aged Barbera Castellania. The Favorita, from ultra-ripe fruit, is delicious while Barbera I Grop features luscious aromas of vanilla and espresso.

● Colli Tortonesi Barbera Castellania '05	⟐⟐	4*
● Colli Tortonesi Barbera I Grop '05	⟐⟐	5
O Colli Tortonesi Favorita Marine '06	⟐⟐	5

Costa Olmo
VIA SAN MICHELE, 18
14044 VINCHIO [AT]
TEL. 0141950423
www.costaolmo.com

Paola and Vittorio Limone farm a modest five hectares but they manage to turn out quite distinctive wines. Barbera Superiore won Two Glasses for its superb aromatics and overall complexity. La Madrina was down a rung from past performances but Piemonte Chardonnay is a delicious pleaser.

● Barbera d'Asti Sup. '04	⟐⟐	5
● Barbera d'Asti La Madrina '05	⟐	4*
O Piemonte Chardonnay A Paola '05	⟐	4

Gianni Doglia
FRAZ. ANNUNZIATA, 56
14054 CASTAGNOLE DELLE LANZE [AT]
TEL. 0141878359
wine-doglia@libero.it

Young Gianni Doglia is known for his fine hand with moscato, as our tastings this year confirmed. But we were impressed as well by his all-merlot Monferrato Rosso "!" It's intense and potent, releasing rich fragrances of dried plum and morello cherry.

O Moscato d'Asti '06	⟐⟐	4*
● Monferrato Rosso "!" '04	⟐⟐	5

OTHER WINERIES

Favaro
S.DA CHIUSURE, 1BIS
10010 PIVERONE [TO]
TEL. 012572606
www.cantinafavaro.it

The Favaros' winery is splendidly located on a morainic hill and their Erbaluce wines are sourced from the south-facing Le Chiusure vineyards below the cellar. The first-rate Erbaluce '06 is appealingly complex and refreshing. The Passito is expressive but the other wines are still too cask influenced.

O Caluso Passito Sole d'Inverno '03	▼▼	6
O Erbaluce di Caluso '06	▼▼	4*
O Albaluce V. T. '04	▼	5
O Erbaluce di Caluso 13 Mesi '05	▼	4

Fabio Fidanza
VIA RODOTIGLIA, 55
14052 CALOSSO [AT]
TEL. 0141826921
www.castellodicalosso.it

Fabio Fidanza's Sterlino Castello di Calosso '04 is velvet textured but almost explosive on the palate and impressively lengthy. Barbera d'Asti '05 shows toasty oak as well as tangy acidity. Monferrato Rosso Que Duàn '05 is a complex nebbiolo and cabernet sauvignon blend and an enjoyable quaffer.

● Barbera d'Asti Sterlino Castello di Calosso '04	▼▼	5
● Barbera d'Asti '05	▼▼	3*
● Monferrato Rosso Que Duàn '05	▼	4

Cascina Flino
VIA ABELLONI, 7
12055 DIANO D'ALBA [CN]
TEL. 017369231

The wines from Paolo Monte's Cascina Flino showed well. As usual, Diano d'Alba Vigna Vecchia with its fleshy pulp led the group but the elegant, powerful Nebbiolo was also outstanding. Barolo '03, which it overripe and warm, shows the signs of that difficult year.

● Diano d'Alba V. Vecchia '06	▼▼	4*
● Nebbiolo d'Alba '05	▼▼	4*
● Barolo '03	▼	7

Funtanin
VIA TORINO, 191
12043 CANALE [CN]
TEL. 0173979488

Funtanin produces the Roero classics. In the absence of the top Barberas and Roero Superiore, the most interesting wine was Arneis Pierin di Soc, which has appealing mineral and fruit essences. The standard Arneis and Favorita whites showed well, and Barbera d'Alba '05 is savoury with generous fruit.

O Roero Arneis Pierin di Soc '06	▼▼	4*
O Roero Arneis '06	▼	3
O Langhe Favorita '06	▼	3
● Barbera d'Alba '05	▼	4

Gaggino
S.DA S. EVASIO, 29
15076 OVADA [AL]
TEL. 0143822345
vinigaggino@libero.it

Gabriele Gaggino continues to turn out quality. We found the basic Convivio more refreshing and enjoyable than the Superiore version, its tasty acidity bringing good length and leanness. A luminous, lively red announces the fragrant Barbera La Zarina. Bianco Il Capè's good showing brought it One Glass.

● Dolcetto di Ovada Il Convivio '06	▼▼	3*
● Barbera del M.to La Zarina '06	▼▼	3*
● Dolcetto di Ovada Sup. S. Evasio '05	▼	4
O Monferrato Bianco Il Capè '06	▼	3

Gianni Gagliardo
B.TA SERRA DEI TURCHI, 88
12064 LA MORRA [CN]
TEL. 017350829
www.gagliardo.it

This year, the Gagliardos' reds stood out. Barolo Serre '03's distinctiveness earned high marks. It's quite delicious, showing warm and velvety in the mouth, with tannins well tucked in. Barolo Cannubi is a tad shorter while Batié '05 is nicely tannic yet supple. The very decent Barbera is well made.

● Barolo Serre '03	▼▼	7
● Barolo Cannubi '03	▼▼	8
● Langhe Nebbiolo Batié '05	▼▼	5
● Barbera d'Alba La Matta '05	▼	5

OTHER WINERIES

Produttori del Gavi

VIA CAVALIERI DI VITTORIO VENETO, 45
15066 GAVI [AL]
TEL. 0143642786
cantina.prodgavi@libero.it

This co-operative produces an always reliable line of Gavis. We liked the rich aromas released by Primi Grappoli and its savoury flavours in the mouth. Cascine dell'Aureliana is also excellent with a taut, lean palate and superb depth while La Maddalena displays succulent, minerally fruit.

O Gavi del Comune di Gavi		
La Maddalena '06	¶¶	4*
O Gavi Primi Grappoli '06	¶¶	4*
O Gavi Cascine dell'Aureliana '06	¶¶	4*

La Gioia

LOC. TRIONZO, 43
15078 ROCCA GRIMALDA [AL]
TEL. 0143831966
info@lagioia.net

Alberto Malaspina and his sister Simona run La Gioia, assisted by Attilio Pagli and Federico Curtaz. The vineyards are at Trionzo, renowned for its Dolcetto di Ovada, and La Gioia wines are always admirable. Il Sole Dentro shows rich aromas and smooth mouthfeel while Monferrato Rosso Più Meglio is excellent.

● Monferrato Rosso Più Meglio '04	¶¶	5
● Dolcetto di Ovada		
Il Sole Dentro '05	¶¶	4*

Tenuta Langasco

FRAZ. MADONNA DI COMO, 10
12051 ALBA [CN]
TEL. 0173286972
langasco@ciaoweb.it

Claudio Sacco's wines turned in good performances this year, particularly Nebbiolo Sorì Coppa and Barbera d'Alba Madonna di Como. Both show superb fidelity to their respective varieties and are attractively austere, showing tasty fruit and great length. Just a rung down is the delicious Dolcetto.

● Barbera d'Alba Madonna di Como '05	¶¶	4*
● Nebbiolo d'Alba Sorì Coppa '05	¶¶	4*
● Dolcetto d'Alba		
Madonna di Como V. Miclet '06	¶	3

Castello di Lignano

VIA LIGNANO, 1
15035 FRASSINELLO MONFERRATO [AL]
TEL. 0142925326
www.castellodilignano.com

There have been small winemaking changes: Barbera Valisenda is now a standard version, vinified in steel. We liked the richness on the nose and the finesse and vivacious acidity on the palate. Grignolino shows already evolved aromas and the sauvignon blanc and cortese Grisello is a refreshing easy drinker.

● Barbera del M.to Valisenda '06	¶¶	4*
● Grignolino del M.to Casalese		
V. Tufara '06	¶	4
O Monferrato Bianco Grisello '06	¶	3

La Luna del Rospo

FRAZ. SALERE, 38
14041 AGLIANO TERME [AT]
TEL. 0141954222
www.lalunadelrospo.it

Michael Schaffer and Renate Schütz direct this organic operation and their line-up is again excellent. Barbera d'Asti Bric Rocche '04, with a bouquet of fine, ripe fruit, is generous and seductive. Solo per Laura '04 is a bit less complex but unleashes admirably tasty acidity on the palate.

● Barbera d'Asti Bric Rocche '04	¶¶	4*
● Barbera d'Asti Solo per Laura '04	¶¶	5

Podere Macellio

VIA ROMA, 18
10014 CALUSO [TO]
TEL. 0119833511
www.erbaluce-bianco.it

The Biancos' historic winery is doing very well. Daniele is the talented winemaker and his father Renato is a genuine, wisdom-dispensing grower. The Erbaluce '06 is brightly savoury and shows a pungent herbaceousness. Pas Dosé is dry and fresh, redolent of acacia honey, and the Passito is very typical.

O Caluso Passito '03	¶¶	5
O Erbaluce di Caluso '06	¶¶	3*
O Erbaluce di Caluso		
Spumante M. Cl. Pas Dosé	¶¶	5

OTHER WINERIES

Le Marie
VIA CARDÉ, 5
12032 BARGE [CN]
TEL. 0175345159
raviolobeltramo@tiscali.it

Giorgio Beltramo and Valerio Raviolo revived viticulture in this neglected area and put out great wines. This year, we especially liked the crisp, perfumed Barbera Colombè, as well as Debàrges, a blend of nebbiolo, barbera and local varieties. The Freisa was a lovely surprise and the Bonarda is sound.

● Pinerolese Barbera Colombè '05	♟♟ 4 *
● Pinerolese Debàrges '05	♟♟ 4 *
● Pinerolese Bonarda '06	♟ 3
● Pinerolese Freisa '06	♟ 3

Noceto Michelotti
S.DA BOGLIONA, 15/17
14040 CASTEL BOGLIONE [AT]
TEL. 0141762170
www.nocetomichelotti.com

Again we saw excellent showings for these wines. In fact, Barbera d'Asti '05 competed in the national finals, thanks to its aromatic berry fruit and vivacious acidity. Hardly less fine is Strada del Sole '05, just a tad more astringent. Monferrato Rosso boasts a close-knit, succulent palate.

● Barbera d'Asti '05	♟♟ 4 *
● Barbera d'Asti Strada del Sole '05	♟♟ 4 *
● Monferrato Rosso '05	♟ 4

Franco Mondo
REG. MARIANO, 33
14050 SAN MARZANO OLIVETO [AT]
TEL. 0141834096
francomondo@inwind.it

The Mondo family farms some 13 hectares and consultant Giorgio Berta assists with winemaking. Production is about 60,000 bottles. Barbera Vigna del Salice is again very convincing but Vigna delle Rose seems to have done better in past editions. The Cortese is a well-executed version.

● Barbera d'Asti V. del Salice '05	♟♟ 4 *
● Barbera d'Asti Sup.	
V. delle Rose Sel. '04	♟♟ 5
O Cortese dell'Alto Monferrato '06	♟ 3

Cecilia Monte
VIA SERRACAPELLI, 17
12052 NEIVE [CN]
TEL. 017367454
cecilia.monte@libero.it

Cecilia Monte's winery is one of the more interesting new operations in the Barbaresco area. Serracapelli '04 exudes expansive fragrances of well-ripened cherry and strawberry fruit, and the full, structured palate ends with a bravura finish. Down just a rung is Dolcetto d'Alba Montubert '06.

● Barbaresco Serracapelli '04	♟♟ 6
● Dolcetto d'Alba Montubert '06	♟ 4

Morgassi Superiore
CASE SPARSE SERMORIA, 7
15066 GAVI [AL]
TEL. 0143642007
www.morgassisuperiore.it

The showing of the 2006 vintage demonstrates the reliable quality of the Piacitellis' wines, even though we were able to taste only the standard Gavi. A lovely straw yellow precedes rich fragrances of spring flowers and ripe peach, which continue onto a palate marked by deliciously vibrant acidity.

O Gavi del Comune di Gavi '06	♟♟ 4 *
O Monferrato Bianco	
Timorgasso '04	♟♟ 5

Cantina Sociale di Nizza
VIA ALESSANDRIA, 57
14049 NIZZA MONFERRATO [AT]
TEL. 0141721348
www.nizza.it

This co-operative presented us with two superlative Barberas, each of which received very high marks at our tastings. Magister made a return, repeating good showing in past years, and the same is true of Ceppi Vecchi. Grignolino Reflé is spicy and nicely floral.

● Barbera d'Asti Sup. Magister '05	♟♟ 4 *
● Barbera d'Asti Sup. Ceppi Vecchi '04	♟♟ 4 *
● Grignolino d'Asti Reflé '06	♟ 3

OTHER WINERIES

Pomodolce
VIA IV NOVEMBRE, 7
15050 MONTEMARZINO [AL]
TEL. 0131878135

This organic operation recently acquired some new vineyards. The Timorasso is absolutely first-rate, displaying appealing aromas and fine balance. The Rosso is an impressive blend of barbera and croatina. The croatina-based Fontanino is spacious and delicious, and bears watching in the future.

● Colli Tortonesi Rosso '04	♥♥ 5
○ Colli Tortonesi Bianco Diletto '05	♥♥ 5
● Colli Tortonesi Barbera '06	♥ 4
● Colli Tortonesi Rosso Fontanino '05	♥ 5

La Raia
S.DA MONTEROTONDO, 79
15067 NOVI LIGURE [AL]
TEL. 0143743685
www.la-raia.it

The Rossi Contini family purchased this winery some years ago and converted it to biodynamic farming. A green-tinged straw yellow announces Gavi Pisè, which opens to a complex medley of pear, peach, blossoms and subtle herbs. It has good structure and savouriness. The Gavi is soundly made.

○ Gavi Pisè '06	♥♥ 4
○ Gavi '06	♥ 4

Eraldo Revelli
LOC. PIANBOSCO, 29
12060 FARIGLIANO [CN]
TEL. 0173797154
www.eraldorevelli.com

The Revelli family's wines did superbly, with the 2006 Dolcettos standing out from the long list. Autin Lungh and San Matteo are real pleasures, showing off rich tonalities and well-ripened red berry. Otto Filari is delicious and approachable, and the nebbiolo and dolcetto La Basarisca is well worth a try.

● Dolcetto di Dogliani Autin Lungh '06	♥♥ 4
● Dolcetto di Dogliani S. Matteo '06	♥♥ 4
● Dolcetto di Dogliani Otto Filari '06	♥ 4
● Langhe Rosso La Basarisca '05	♥ 5

Rizzi
VIA RIZZI, 15
12050 TREISO [CN]
TEL. 0173638161
www.cantinarizzi.it

Ernesto Dellapiana, helped by children Jole and Enrico, is pointing his winery in the right direction, steadily achieving better quality, particularly with his Barbarescos. This year all three won Two Glasses, each impressively lean, tannic, powerful and elegant. They all stand out for their superlative style.

● Barbaresco Boito '04	♥♥ 6
● Barbaresco Nervo Fondetta '04	♥♥ 6
● Barbaresco Pajorè Suran '04	♥♥ 6

Daniele Saccoletto
S.S. CASALE-ASTI, 82
15020 SAN GIORGIO MONFERRATO [AL]
TEL. 0142806509
www.saccolettovini.com

Now that his cellar is finished, Daniele Saccoletto can turn all of his time to his wines, which sometimes require difficult decisions in the vineyard. As usual, Grignolino is spicy and approachable. Freisa offers superb varietal berry fruit and crispness on the palate, and Barbera Aurum is well crafted.

● Grignolino del M.to Casalese Vigna in Cornalasca '06	♥♥ 3*
● Barbera del M.to Aurum '04	♥ 5
● Monferrato Freisa V. Fiordaliso '06	♥ 4

Josetta Saffirio
FRAZ. CASTELLETTO, 32
12065 MONFORTE D'ALBA [CN]
TEL. 017378660
www.josettasaffirio.com

This year, all of Sara Vezza's wines tasted were either good or outstanding. Her two lean, austere Barolos exhibit sumptuous structure, with Persiera almost endless on the finish. Barbera d'Alba shows delicious red berry fruit and Langhe Rosso delivers admirably potent tannins.

● Barolo '03	♥♥ 6
● Barolo Persiera '03	♥♥ 7
● Barbera d'Alba '05	♥ 4
● Langhe Rosso Alna Rosso '05	♥ 5

OTHER WINERIES

San Pietro

LOC. SAN PIETRO, 2
15067 TASSAROLO [AL]
TEL. 0143342422
www.tenutasanpietro.it

This decades-old operation debuts in our
Guide after being purchased and made over
by the Alotta family. We tasted two Gavis.
Gorrina, from estate vineyards, lays out long-
lingering floral and citrus notes. Il Mandorlo is
also delicious, showing more on the grassy
side and quite savoury.

O Gavi del Comune di Tassarolo	
Gorrina '05	▼▼ 5
O Gavi del Comune di Tassarolo	
Il Mandorlo '06	▼▼ 4*

Simone Scaletta

LOC. MANZONI, 61
12065 MONFORTE D'ALBA [CN]
TEL. 3484912733
www.viniscaletta.com

The youthful Simone Scaletta is making his first
marks in the wine world with some admirably
distinctive offerings. We found the first-rate
Barolo Chirlet expansive and elegant. The
appealingly fruity Barbera d'Alba Sarsera also
won Two Glasses. Dolcetto Viglioni is crisp,
refreshing and delicious.

● Barbera d'Alba Sarsera '05	▼▼ 4*
● Barolo Chirlet '03	▼▼ 7
● Dolcetto d'Alba Viglioni '06	▼ 4

Schiavenza

VIA MAZZINI, 4A
12050 SERRALUNGA D'ALBA [CN]
TEL. 0173613115
www.schiavenza.com

The Schiavenzas, who own a charming
osteria at Serralunga, presented a group of
imposing Barolos. The traditional Broglio
Riserva '01 is impressively austere. Despite
a challenging year, the two '03s are wines
of great quality, in particular Bricco Cerretta
and Perno.

● Barolo Broglio Ris. '01	▼▼ 6
● Barolo Bricco Cerretta '03	▼▼ 6
● Barolo Perno '03	▼▼ 6
● Barolo Prapò '03	▼ 6

Giacomo Scagliola e Figlio

REG. SANTA LIBERA, 20
14053 CANELLI [AT]
TEL. 0141831146
www.scagliolagiacomo.it

The Scagliola family lived up to its reputation
for alluring Barberas. Of the three versions
tasted, the most impressive was Vigna dei
Mandorli: intense, full-bodied, juicy and with
a nice finish. La Faia, slightly less complex
and extremely crisp, was not far behind.
The basic version is worth One Glass.

● Barbera d'Asti La Faia '04	▼▼ 4*
● Barbera d'Asti V. dei Mandorli '03	▼▼ 4*
● Barbera d'Asti '05	▼ 3

La Scamuzza

CASCINA POMINA, 17
15049 VIGNALE MONFERRATO [AL]
TEL. 0142926214
www.lascamuzza.it

Monferrato Rosso Bricco San Tomaso, a
barbera and cabernet sauvignon blend, is the
La Scamuzza standard-bearer. The nose
ranges from red berry fruit to faint fresh
greens, and expressive tannins underpin the
palate. Baciamisubito is a youthful, delightful
Barbera. The Grignolino has good spiciness.

● Monferrato Rosso	
Bricco San Tomaso '05	▼▼ 5
● Barbera del M.to Baciamisubito '06	▼ 4
● Grignolino del M.to Casalese	
Tumas '06	▼ 4

Giovanni Silva

CASCINE ROGGE, 1B
10011 AGLIÈ [TO]
TEL. 012433356
www.silvavini.com

The Silvas produce a vast array of wines in
the Agliè hills. The two Erbaluces are
excellent. Cryomaceration of the must gives
Dry Ice better fruit expression while Tre
Ciochè offers a more sapid palate. Rosso
Cantagrì, produced from local varieties, has
youthful, heady aromas of lively fruit.

O Erbaluce di Caluso Tre Ciochè '06	▼▼ 3*
O Erbaluce di Caluso Dry Ice '06	▼ 4
● Canavese Rosso Cantagrì '05	▼ 4

OTHER WINERIES

La Smilla
VIA GARIBALDI, 7
15060 BOSIO [AL]
TEL. 0143684245
www.lasmilla.it

This family-run winery has been making wine for generations and the fine showings continue in this edition of our Guide. We liked the estate's vineyard selection, Gavi I Bergi, for its aromas of spring flowers and citrus in the mouth. The basic Gavi and the Dolcetto di Ovada are both well made and enjoyable.

○ Gavi del Comune di Gavi I Bergi '05	🍷🍷 4*
○ Gavi del Comune di Gavi '06	🍷 3
● Dolcetto di Ovada Nsè Pesa '05	🍷 4

Giuseppe Stella
S.DA BOSSOLA, 8
14055 COSTIGLIOLE D'ASTI [AT]
TEL. 0141966142
stellavini@libero.it

The Stellas gave us a great series of Barberas, beginning with Bricco Fubine Il Vino del Maestro, which pours out morello cherry, strawberry, black pepper, vanilla and cocoa. Giaiet also won Two Glasses, showing less power but quite crisp and savoury on the palate. Grignolino Sufragio is fragrantly spicy.

● Barbera d'Asti Bricco Fubine Il Vino del Maestro '05	🍷🍷 5
● Barbera d'Asti Giaiet '05	🍷🍷 4*
● Grignolino d'Asti Vign. Sufragio '06	🍷 3

Castello di Tagliolo
VIA CASTELLO, 1
15070 TAGLIOLO MONFERRATO [AL]
TEL. 014389195
www.castelloditagliolo.com

Oberto Pinelli Gentile and son Luca manage their winery helped by Franco Ferrero. They did not make their Dolcetto La Castagnola in 2002 so we had to fall back on a new offering, La Castagnola 24, from back in 2001. It is somewhat evolved. Dolcetto di Ovada Superiore is more youthful and gratifying.

● Dolcetto di Ovada Sup. '04	🍷🍷 4
● Dolcetto di Ovada La Castagnola 24 '01	🍷 4
○ Bianco Nobile	🍷 3

Tenuta La Tenaglia
S.DA SANTUARIO DI CREA, 5C
15020 SERRALUNGA DI CREA [AL]
TEL. 0142940252
www.latenaglia.com

We return to vintages that brought fame to this winery some years back. Barbera Tenaglia è... shows terrific aromatic richness, which carries over beautifully onto a nicely driven palate. On the same quality rung is Emozioni, a lean but smooth wine. The standard Barbera is crisp and appealing.

● Barbera del M.to Sup. Tenaglia è... '04	🍷🍷 4*
● Barbera d'Asti Emozioni '04	🍷🍷 6
● Barbera d'Asti Bricco Crea '06	🍷 4

Cascina degli Ulivi
S.DA MAZZOLA, 14
15067 NOVI LIGURE [AL]
TEL. 0143744598
www.cascinadegliulivi.it

Stefano Bellotti farms 11 hectares biodynamically. We especially liked his Nibiô, or dolcetto dal raspo rosso, from the Terre Rosse cru. Barbera Mounbé is another fascinating version. The refreshing, delicious Gavi Filagnotti made an extremely felicitous debut.

● Monferrato Dolcetto Nibiô Terre Rosse '05	🍷🍷 4*
● Piemonte Barbera Mounbé '05	🍷 5
○ Gavi del Comune di Tassarolo Filagnotti '06	🍷 4

Castello di Uviglie
LOC. CASTELLO DI UVIGLIE
15030 ROSIGNANO MONFERRATO [AL]
TEL. 0142488132
www.castellodiuviglie.com

Three wines of exceptional character brought Castello di Uviglie into our Guide. Barbera Superiore Le Cave displays multi-faceted aromatics and stunning acidity on the palate. There is more spice on Pico Gonzaga, which has wonderful depth in the mouth. Grignolino San Bastiano is nicely balanced and delicious.

● Barbera del M.to Sup. Le Cave '04	🍷🍷 4*
● Grignolino del M.to Casalese San Bastiano '06	🍷🍷 3*
● Barbera del M.to Sup. Pico Gonzaga '03	🍷🍷 5

OTHER WINERIES

Laura Valditerra
S.DA MONTEROTONDO, 75
15067 NOVI LIGURE [AL]
TEL. 0143321451
laura@valditerra.it

Laura Valditerra's wines are always superlative, including the Gavis, particularly Vigna del Lago. A lovely green-flecked straw, it presents rich, delicate fragrances and nice sapidity. We also liked the refreshing character and balance of the basic Gavi. Monferrato Rosso FiorDesAri is sound.

O Gavi V. del Lago '06	▼▼	4*
● Monferrato Rosso FiorDesAri '05	▼▼	4*
O Gavi '06	▼	4

Valfieri
S.DA LORETO, 5
14055 COSTIGLIOLE D'ASTI [AT]
TEL. 0141966881
www.valfieri.it

The Clerici family does a splendid job with barbera and this year gave us a superlative Barbera d'Asti Superiore. It's full bodied, sturdily structured and pours out fragrant red berry fruit. Monferrato Matot wasn't quite up to its past fine performances but the standard-label Barbera was delightful.

● Barbera d'Asti Sup. '05	▼▼	4*
● Barbera d'Asti '06	▼▼	4*
● Monferrato Rosso Matot '04	▼	5

Cantine Valpane
CASCINA VALPANE, 10/1
15039 OZZANO MONFERRATO [AL]
TEL. 0142486713
www.cantinevalpane.com

Barbera Valpane '03 displays spice and fine, evolved impressions, plus a multi-layered, spacious palate and finish. Rosso Pietro is young but extremely promising, with a dense bouquet, prominent acidity and lengthy progression. Although nose and palate are not perfectly aligned, Perlydia is quite attractive.

● Barbera del M.to Rosso Pietro '06	▼▼	3*
● Barbera del M.to Valpane '03	▼▼	5
● Barbera del M.to Perlydia '04	▼	4

Vecchia Posta
VIA MONTEBELLO, 2
15050 AVOLASCA [AL]
TEL. 0131876254
lavecchiaposta@virgilio.it

Our favourite this year was Rebelot, dialect for a blend, here a mixture of red varieties that includes dolcetto. An impressive purple, it needs a moment before it explodes with fruit fragrances, concluding nicely spicy. The timorasso Il Selvaggio was slightly disappointing but Dolcetto Teraforta is well executed.

● Colli Tortonesi Rosso Rebelot '05	▼▼	3*
O Colli Tortonesi Bianco Il Selvaggio '05	▼	4
● Colli Tortonesi Rosso Teraforta '06	▼	3

Osvaldo Viberti
FRAZ. SANTA MARIA
B.TA SERRA DEI TURCHI, 95
12064 LA MORRA [CN]
TEL. 017350374
www.vibertiosvaldo.it

Osvaldo Viberti produces just over 20,000 bottles a year from his seven hectares of vineyards on the Serra dei Turchi hill. His Barolo, hobbled by a challenging 2003 season, wasn't up its usual self. Barbera d'Alba Mancine and Dolcetto d'Alba Galletto, however, both measured up as excellent offerings.

● Barbera d'Alba Mancine '05	▼▼	5*
● Dolcetto d'Alba Galletto '06	▼▼	3*
● Barolo Serra dei Turchi '03	▼	6

Virna
VIA ALBA, 73
12060 BAROLO [CN]
TEL. 017356120
www.virnabarolo.it

Long expertise and top-quality fruit from estate vineyards make for substantial wines here, with the Barolos standing out. Both the Barolo Cannubi Boschis and the standard Barolo performed splendidly, showing impressively lean, austere and lengthy. Barolo Preda Sarmassa '03 is well made.

● Barolo '03	▼▼	6
● Barolo Cannubi Boschis '03	▼▼	6
● Barolo Preda Sarmassa '03	▼	6

LIGURIA

Liguria has no complaints about the 2006 growing year. Some growers might have handled it more carefully but the overall results are excellent, with old favourites and new entries joining forces to reshape the contours of Ligurian wine. There is a new mindset abroad that focuses on typicity and balanced winemaking, starting in the vineyard and coming to fulfilment in the cellar. Our tastings and winery visits uncovered interesting developments that show how Ligurian wine is alive and kicking, with one or two provisos. Progress is more evident in the western part of the region, which has consolidated and indeed enhanced the qualities of its distinctly original wines, genuine ambassadors for their territory and amply able to rub shoulders with wines from further afield. A careful reading of the figures shows that many estates are making a conscious effort to coax the full potential from the vine types that tradition has bequeathed them by investing in selection. Similar steps have yet to be taken in eastern Liguria, where the wines, especially but not exclusively the Vermentinos, are very competently made but tend to be much of a muchness and rather one-dimensional. What is needed is serious consideration of Liguria's ability to communicate the character of its wines beyond the region's borders. The wines exist, and they are good, but how many people know about them? Wineries should get over their ingrained habit of going it alone and a reliance on their continuing commercial success on the domestic market, which dulls dynamism. They must realize that it is self-defeating not to make the products known in a broader market. But you don't need market studies to see that good-quality wines at the right price from other regions are becoming increasingly entrenched on the wine lists of Liguria's coast and hinterland. Only rarely is the reverse true. Yet Ligurian winemaking is technically impeccable, often also striving for personality in confirmation of the wineries' coming of age, and in some cases stylistic maturity. We shall console ourselves with this year's top prize, which went for the third year in a row to the hard-working professionalism of Riccardo Bruna. It is an award with a subtext and other Ligurian producers should take note. Unsurprisingly, many leading estates, and some just a step behind them, are setting about improving quality. Gratifyingly, results are coming through. Quite a few wines went through to the finals and in some cases could easily have picked up a top prize. That, more than any written comment, speaks volumes for Ligurian wine.

A Maccia

FRAZ. BORGO
VIA UMBERTO I, 54
18020 RANZO [IM]
TEL. 0183318003
www.amaccia.it

ANNUAL PRODUCTION 20,000 bottles
HECTARES UNDER VINE 4
VITICULTURE METHOD Conventional

Reliability is the name of the game here. That's the best way to sum up this cellar based at Ranzo, a village on the borders of the provinces of Imperia and Savona with a long tradition of growing grapes and olives. The wines are meticulously made and bring out the varietal character of the grapes. Even the packaging is eye-catching. Loredana Faraldi is the sort of wine woman who can convey the subtle variations that depend on the growing year. Her wines always have a living spirit. There can be no doubt that this small, family-run winery is doing a good job but Loredana is hoping for even greater things now that her daughter Carlotta has joined the fray. This year, they must be very happy with the Pigato, which unveils fragrant flowers, fruit and minerality that lead into a palate of great finesse. The Rossese is equally tempting and well poised, with a satisfying suite of aromas.

○ Riviera Ligure di Ponente Pigato '06	🍷🍷 4*
● Riviera Ligure di Ponente Rossese '06	🍷 4
○ Riviera Ligure di Ponente Pigato '05	🍷🍷 4

Massimo Alessandri

VIA COSTA PARROCCHIA
18028 RANZO [IM]
TEL. 018253458
www.massimoalessandri.it

ANNUAL PRODUCTION 30,000 bottles
HECTARES UNDER VINE 6
VITICULTURE METHOD Conventional

At the entry to Valle Arroscia, in a special corner of Liguria that you could call a pocket of Pigato, the determined, professional Massimo Alessandri lives out, step by step, his laudable dream of making seriously good wines with a personality of their own and solid links with their territory. We found all those characteristics in the Pigato Vigne Vegie, an assertive wine with balsamic notes, character and delicious freshness. Equally exciting is the Vermentino, a rich, balanced, long-lingering wine while the Pigato Costa de Vigne is a classic of approachable appeal. On the red side of the estate, the syrah and granaccia Ligustico is meaty, ripe and right on song. For such a challenging red, it is delightfully drinkable. The A' Seiana selection – the name means evening – is just as good. The merlot-heavy blend with a dash of cabernet shows even texture, prominent fruit and a soft tannic weave.

● Ligustico '05	🍷🍷 6
● A' Seiana '05	🍷🍷 5
○ Riviera Ligure di Ponente Pigato Vigne Vegie '05	🍷🍷 5
○ Riviera Ligure di Ponente Vermentino Costa de Vigne '06	🍷🍷 4*
○ Riviera Ligure di Ponente Pigato Costa de Vigne '06	🍷 4
● Ligustico '04	🍷🍷 6
○ Riviera Ligure di Ponente Pigato Costa de Vigne '05	🍷🍷 4

Alta Via

LOC. ARCAGNA
18035 DOLCEACQUA [IM]
TEL. 0184488230

ANNUAL PRODUCTION 35,000 bottles
HECTARES UNDER VINE 6
VITICULTURE METHOD Conventional

Savino Formentini and Gianni Arlotti have no family tradition of winemaking but they fell in love with Val Nervia and firmly believe in its potential. Together they created Alta Via and are building it up with discipline and clarity of vision into a genuinely important part of the Ligurian wine scene. Federico Curtaz, a well-known figure on the Italian wine scene, is in charge in the vineyards and cellars. Melding character and balance with innovation and tradition mark out the Alta Via range. One fine example is the carignan and rossese-based Dapprimo, which throws a vibrant nose of ripe red fruits. Soft and full in the mouth, it unveils appealing extract to brace the progression. Also very good is the Rossese, mingling fruit with sweet sensations of spice on its fascinating nose. The palate is warm and meaty. The white Noname, from vermentino grapes with a tiny proportion of viognier, unveils assertive aromatics that range from broom to tropical fruits before the rich-textured, well-balance palate signs off with long-lingering, savoury flourish. Finally, the syrah and rossese Rosarosae flows nicely across the palate.

Laura Aschero

P.ZZA V. EMANUELE, 7
18027 PONTEDASSIO [IM]
TEL. 0183710307
lauraaschero@uno.it

ANNUAL PRODUCTION 60,000 bottles
HECTARES UNDER VINE 2.8
VITICULTURE METHOD Conventional

Marco Rizzo is continuing a centuries-long family tradition of grape growing as he firmly steers the helm of the Lauro Aschero winery, as ever with the help of oenologist Lorenzo Ranò. Grapes come from estate-owned vines at Monte and Posai near Pontedassio but quantities are also bought in from trusted growers mainly in the Albenga and Diano Castello areas. We'll start our review with the Pigato, a peach and apricot-like fruit-led wine with attractive aromas and texture in the mouth as it progresses brightly to an appealing bitterish finale. Just as impressive is the Vermentino, which marries tropical fruit with hints of field herbs. A warm entry on the palate precedes attractive fruit folded in captivating savouriness. The Rossese did well again, showing moderately complex fragrances of red fruits and aromatic herbs before the fresh-tasting palate reveals restrained extract.

● Rossese di Dolceacqua Sup. '06	♟♟	5
● Dapprimo '06	♟♟	4*
○ Noname '06	♟♟	5
☉ Rosarosae '06	♟	4
● Dapprimo '05	♟♟	4
● Rossese di Dolceacqua Sup. '04	♟♟	5
● Rossese di Dolceacqua Sup. '05	♟♟	5
● Skip Intro '04	♟♟	5

○ Riviera Ligure di Ponente Pigato '06	♟♟	4
○ Riviera Ligure di Ponente Vermentino '06	♟♟	4
● Riviera Ligure di Ponente Rossese '06	♟	4
○ Riviera Ligure di Ponente Vermentino '04	♟♟	4
○ Riviera Ligure di Ponente Vermentino '05	♟♟	4
○ Riviera Ligure di Ponente Pigato '03	♟♟	4

Maria Donata Bianchi

VIA DELLE TORRI, 16
18010 DIANO CASTELLO [IM]
TEL. 0183498233

ANNUAL PRODUCTION 35,000 bottles
HECTARES UNDER VINE 4.5
VITICULTURE METHOD Natural

Likeability, professionalism and accessibility are the distinguishing features of Emanuele Trevia, a man who was born to grow grapes and who believes wine is a vehicle for culture and passion, in which quality is a given but always as the outcome of human effort. Emanuele's wines embody this in a style that seeks territory-focused characterization, good concentration and a bond with the past. Environmental sensitivity here means integrated pest management and a ban on chemical fertilizers or weedkillers. This time, we were only able to taste the two clean, stylish, well-integrated base wines as Antico Sfizio will be ready at the end of the year and La Mattana will be released in 2008. The Vermentino has plenty of character, showing a fruit and balsam nose followed by nice progression on the temptingly tangy palate. The Pigato is just as interesting. Its intriguing nose precedes a soft, savoury palate with good balance and a sage-like note leading to an attractive almondy finish.

BioVio

FRAZ. BASTIA
VIA CROCIATA, 24
17031 ALBENGA [SV]
TEL. 018220776
www.biovio.it

ANNUAL PRODUCTION 40,000 bottles
HECTARES UNDER VINE 5
VITICULTURE METHOD Certified organic

Determination pays. Giobatta Aimone Vio knows this well, having decided to make a truly good wine – "bon in da bon", in the local dialect – and actually succeeding. The heart of his project is profoundly traditional but the finesse and freshness derive from modern technology. The Pigato deserves attention for its long, richly evolved aromas and is at the top of the list from this small, environmentally aware winery. Its aim is to make genuine products by growing grapes organically in its vineyards mainly in the Ranzo and Arnasco areas. We seem to go back in time with the fruit-forward, refreshing Vermentino that beautifully mirrors the features of the variety. Meanwhile, the standard-label Pigato is built along the same lines, showing bright, lively acidity and lingering aromas, as is the spicy, savoury Bacilò, from 80-20 rossese di Campochiesa and granaccia.

O Riviera Ligure di Ponente Vermentino '06	🍷🍷 4*
O Riviera Ligure di Ponente Pigato '06	🍷🍷 4*
O Antico Sfizio '04	🍷🍷 4
O Antico Sfizio '05	🍷🍷 4
O Riviera Ligure di Ponente Pigato '05	🍷🍷 4
O Riviera Ligure di Ponente Vermentino '05	🍷🍷 4
● La Mattana '04	🍷🍷 6
● La Mattana '01	🍷🍷 6

O Riviera Ligure di Ponente Pigato Bon in da Bon '06	🍷🍷 5
O Riviera Ligure di Ponente Vermentino Aimone '06	🍷🍷 4*
O Riviera Ligure di Ponente Pigato Marixe '06	🍷 4
● Bacilò '06	🍷 4

Enoteca Bisson

C.SO GIANELLI, 28
16043 CHIAVARI [GE]
TEL. 0185314462
www.bissonvini.it

ANNUAL PRODUCTION 85,000 bottles
HECTARES UNDER VINE 10
VITICULTURE METHOD Conventional

Bisson continues to be one of the most enterprising wineries in eastern Liguria thanks to vineyard management that strives to obtain the absolute maximum from every vintage. Pietro Lugano has always had a preference for local varieties, which he interprets sensitively, bringing out their special characteristics. His range may be a little too extensive but the wines, some of which elicit strong opinions, are invariably distinctive and have their own style. The range, which we have been following for some time, includes savoury fresh Vermentinos with attractive balance. Equally good are the Bianchetta, the Cinque Terre Marea, the soft, fruity Pigato and the Musaico, from 70 per cent dolcetto with 30 per cent barbera, which has finesse and caressing tannins. We were more impressed by the complex nose, warmth and soft texture of the Marea Tardiva, the stylishly harmonious Sciacchetrà, which successfully offsets sweetness with refreshing acidity, and the whistle-clean Makallé Il Granaccia 2006's lovely combination of fruit and minerality.

Bonanni Fellegara

VIA DI LOCA, 189
19017 RIOMAGGIORE [SP]
TEL. 3384063383

ANNUAL PRODUCTION 6,000 bottles
HECTARES UNDER VINE 1
VITICULTURE METHOD Natural

If there is anywhere in the world that can enchant the eyes and soul of the visitor with its sheer beauty, it is the Cinque Terre. And if there is anywhere in the world where viticulture reaches peaks of heroic physical challenge unthinkable elsewhere, that place is again the Cinque Terre. Picture-postcard views, decay, vision, ruin, paradise and perdition are all there in the landscape of a land that links sea and sky. But today, luckily, there are also the resolute small farmers determined not to lose a rural and oenological heritage accumulated over the centuries. Tonino Bonanni, born in Riomaggiore, and Paolo Fellegara, from Crema, farm a few square metres of vines on breath-catchingly steep slopes, vinifying a few thousand bottles in a cellar perched at the top of some dizzying steps. An exceptional guardian angel encourages and watches over them in the person of Elio Altare from La Morra. The Sciacchetrà is a stylishly restrained exercise in sweetness that delights nose and palate while attractive minerality and savouriness are the calling cards of the Cinque Terre. Two pearls from a land of treasure.

● Makallé Il Granaccia '06	❦❦	5
○ Cinque Terre Sciacchetrà '04	❦❦	6
○ Marea Tardiva '06	❦❦	5
○ Cinque Terre Marea '06	❦	4
○ Vermentino Tardiva '06	❦	5
○ Golfo del Tigullio Vermentino Vigna Intrigoso '06	❦	4
○ Golfo del Tigullio Bianchetta Genovese Ü Pastine '06	❦	4
○ Golfo del Tigullio Vermentino Vigna Erta '06	❦	4
○ Pigato '06	❦	4
● Golfo del Tigullio Rosso Il Musaico '06	❦	4
● Makallé '05	❦	5

○ Cinque Terre '05	❦❦	6
○ Cinque Terre Sciacchetrà '05	❦❦	8
○ Cinque Terre Sciacchetrà '04	❦❦	8
○ Cinque Terre '05	❦❦	6
○ Cinque Terre '04	❦❦	6

Bruna

VIA UMBERTO I, 81
18020 RANZO [IM]
TEL. 0183318082
aziendaagricolabruna@libero.it

ANNUAL PRODUCTION 45,000 bottles
HECTARES UNDER VINE 6.2
VITICULTURE METHOD Conventional

Riccardo Bruna is a phenomenon of Ligurian winemaking. You need a plan to make a great wine. You can't overlook anything and you need to know exactly what to do and when to do it. That is precisely the way Pigato U Baccan was created and this edition, too, has found the man and the raw material to acquire that remarkable character made of minerality, exuberant aromatics, elegance and harmony. Three stunning Glasses. The other Pigatos are combine low numbers with high quality, as in fact does the family team that assists Roberto. Le Russeghine is deliciously fruity, savoury, attractively complex and broad while the fresh sensations of the Villa Torrachetta are accompanied by stimulating aromas. Reds receive their fair share of attention: the Rossese is admirably varietal and soft-textured. Finally, our tasters liked the pulp, restrained extract and fruit and balsam progression of the Pulin, from granaccia and syrah with a dollop of barbera.

Calleri

LOC. SALEA D'ALBENGA
REG. FRATTI, 2
17031 ALBENGA [SV]
TEL. 018220085
postmaster@cantinecalleri.com

ANNUAL PRODUCTION 90,000 bottles
HECTARES UNDER VINE N.D.
VITICULTURE METHOD Conventional

Marcello Calleri continues confidently on his way, purchasing fruit from tried and trusted growers and vinifying it with tried and trusted techniques to produce an admirable range. We know how hard it is to maintain premium quality using bought-in grapes but Marcello has always presented us with reliably good, and in some cases very good, wines. Take his Vermentinos. The standard-label version puts the accent on aromas, balance and softness whereas the Muzazzi has more florality and inviting freshness. With their good progression and cleanness, the Pigatos are up to snuff. Saleasco has a nice vein of acidity and a bitterish backdrop that adds allure to the palate while the classic version has greater finesse and breadth on the nose. Finally, Ormeasco is as reliable as ever with its keynote savouriness and soft texture.

○ Riviera Ligure di Ponente Pigato U Baccan '05	♟♟♟ 5
● Rosso Pulin '05	♟♟ 5
○ Riviera Ligure di Ponente Pigato Le Russeghine '06	♟♟ 4*
○ Riviera Ligure di Ponente Pigato Villa Torrachetta '06	♟♟ 4*
● Riviera Ligure di Ponente Rossese '06	♟ 4
○ Riviera Ligure di Ponente Pigato U Baccan '04	♟♟♟ 5
○ Riviera Ligure di Ponente Pigato U Baccan '03	♟♟♟ 5

○ Riviera Ligure di Ponente Pigato Saleasco '06	♟♟ 4*
○ Riviera Ligure di Ponente Pigato '06	♟♟ 4*
○ Riviera Ligure di Ponente Vermentino '06	♟ 4
● Ormeasco di Pornassio '05	♟ 4
○ Riviera Ligure di Ponente Vermentino I Muzazzi '06	♟ 4
○ Riviera Ligure di Ponente Vermentino I Muzazzi '05	♟♟ 4

Giobatta Mandino Cane
VIA ROMA, 21
18035 DOLCEACQUA [IM]
TEL. 0184206120

ANNUAL PRODUCTION 14,000 bottles
HECTARES UNDER VINE 0.5
VITICULTURE METHOD Conventional

We have boundless affectionate esteem for this almost 80-year-old wine man who is inseparable from his work and his land. Mandino Cane is one of those people who make craft wine in the noblest sense of the term and if we add to this that his vineyards are in superb locations, it comes as no surprise that his Rosseses are distinctive as they are impressive. We'll start with the standard Dolceacqua, which is subtle, varietal, fresh-tasting and delicious, and carry on with Vigneto Morghe, one of the best of its type, which bolsters subtle fragrances with firm texture and a savoury palate. We go up a further step with Vigneto Arcagna, a well-gauged medley of softness, full body and elegance that put on one of the finest performances of recent years. Less traditional but equally interesting is the rossese and syrah L'Intruso, a marriage of fruit and spices with sinew and lovely tannic weight.

Cascina Praié
S.DA CASTELLO, 20
17051 ANDORA [SV]
TEL. 019602377
m_viglietti@tin.it

ANNUAL PRODUCTION 40,000 bottles
HECTARES UNDER VINE 7
VITICULTURE METHOD Natural

There have only been six vintages at Cascina Praié, the winery set up by Massimo Viglietti and Anna Maria Corrent, two able agronomists who are partners in work and life, but that hasn't stopped them from making wines of quality and personality in double-quick time. Underlying those results is an approach based on simple, rigorous principles, such as respect for the environment, using natural treatments in the vineyard and adopting cellar procedures that do not alter the wine's character. Whites make up the bulk of production. There are two distinctly good Vermentinos, including a Le Cicale selection that stands out for its swath of mineral and fruit-led aromatics, softness and pulp. The Pigato is also well executed and worth uncorking. The reds flaunt just as assertive a character. Elegant fruit, solid structure and robust tannins are the hallmarks of the granaccia-only Scurbì 2005 and the Ardesia 2005, from 70-30 rossese and cabernet, brings together a fine suite of aromatics with silky texture and good balance.

● Rossese di Dolceacqua Sup.	
Vigneto Arcagna '06	♟♟ 5
● L'Intruso '06	♟♟ 5
● Rossese di Dolceacqua Sup.	
Vigneto Morghe '06	♟♟ 5
● Dolceacqua '06	♟♟ 4*
● Rossese di Dolceacqua Sup.	
Vigneto Arcagna '05	♟♟ 5
● Rossese di Dolceacqua Sup.	
Vigneto Arcagna '04	♟♟ 5
● Rossese di Dolceacqua Sup.	
Vigneto Morghe '05	♟♟ 5
● Rossese di Dolceacqua Sup.	
Vigneto Morghe '04	♟♟ 5

● Ardesia '05	♟♟ 5
● Sciurbì '05	♟♟ 4*
○ Riviera Ligure di Ponente	
Vermentino Le Cicale '05	♟♟ 4*
○ Riviera Ligure di Ponente Pigato	
Il Canneto '06	♟ 4
○ Riviera Ligure di Ponente	
Vermentino Colla Micheri '06	♟ 4
● Ardesia '04	♟♟ 5
● Sciurbì '04	♟♟ 4

Walter De Batté
VIA TRARCANTU, 25
19017 RIOMAGGIORE [SP]
TEL. 0187920127

Durin
VIA ROMA, 2002
17037 ORTOVERO [SV]
TEL. 0182547007
www.durin.it

ANNUAL PRODUCTION 3,500 bottles
HECTARES UNDER VINE 0.9
VITICULTURE METHOD Natural

Walter De Batté is a man with a battle on his hands. We could start and finish the profile of this pioneering Riomaggiore grape grower with the tale of last year's decision not to release a wine. It wasn't a marketing ploy, or indifferent quality, or even a batch of bad corks or problems in the cellar. No, De Batté was unable to produce his Cinque Terre because his grapes were being eaten by the wild boar that skip gracefully through the terraced cliffside vineyards where growers themselves have difficulty keeping their feet. Last year, things went better and we were able this time to enjoy a dry white with quite unique sea salt sensations, crushed fruit and dried flowers. These are wines that will always be controversial but we see them as the successful bottling of essence of Cinque Terre. Even better is the hard-to-find, honey-rich Schiacchetrà, De Batté's flagship wine. Candied peel, white figs, walnutskin and raisins unfold in a textbook sequence of aromas to be echoed on the palate, which finishes long.

ANNUAL PRODUCTION 150,000 bottles
HECTARES UNDER VINE 15.5
VITICULTURE METHOD Conventional

This cellar came into being in the early 1980s when Angelo's son Antonio Basso decided to give up his studies to look after the land that had always belonged to the family. Durin is the entire valley's nickname for this cellar, which over the past few years has earned a reputation among lovers of good Italian wine. The range is produced in a modern, functional cellar and the fruit comes from some of the most exciting vineyards for the local area's classic varieties. Le Braie, Villa, Tenaige and Lunghera are the names of the plots where the Bassos source the pigato, vermentino and lumassina for their whites, and the ormeasco, rossese, granaccia, sangiovese and barbera that go into the reds. We tasted some very encouraging selections this year, starting with the Pigato I S-cianchi, which embodies the cellar philosophy. It's a wine with personality and brings out the typicity of the variety. The palate is savoury and well orchestrated. Equally good was the Vermentino Lunghera. Meanwhile, the reds are doing well with the slender Ormeasco, the typical Pornassio variety, standing up to comparison with the austerely muscular Granaccia.

O Cinque Terre Sciacchetrà '04	♟♟ 8
O Cinque Terre '06	♟♟ 6
O Cinque Terre Sciacchetrà '01	♟♟ 8
O Cinque Terre Sciacchetrà '03	♟♟ 8
O Cinque Terre '04	♟♟ 6

O Riviera Ligure di Ponente Vermentino Lunghera '06	♟♟ 4
O Riviera Ligure di Ponente Pigato I S-cianchi '06	♟♟ 4
● Orneasco di Pornassio Sup. '06	♟♟ 4
● Granaccia '06	♟♟ 4
O Riviera Ligure di Ponente Pigato Vigna Braie '06	♟ 4
● I Matti '05	♟♟ 5
O Riviera Ligure di Ponente Vermentino Lunghera '05	♟♟ 4

Tenuta Giuncheo

LOC. GIUNCHEO
18033 CAMPOROSSO [IM]
TEL. 0184288639
www.tenutagiuncheo.it

ANNUAL PRODUCTION 35,000 bottles
HECTARES UNDER VINE 7
VITICULTURE METHOD Conventional

Results were very satisfying again this year at Tenuta Giuncheo. In this corner of paradise, with its wild woodlands and steep, and sometimes dizzying, hills, the wines embody an innovative spirit that blends successfully with respect for tradition. For that is what Marco Romagnoli, the expert brought in by owner Arnold Schweizer, wants them to do. The Vermentino lives up to its reputation, showing a caressing mouthfeel and an attractive range of fruit-led flavours. We were particularly impressed by the Rossese Pian del Vescovo's captivating flower and balsam aromas introducing a pervasive roundness in the palate's warm progression. The standard Rossese is less complex but still balanced, fruit-forward and faintly tannic. Rossese again, but this time with an equal quantity of syrah, goes into the blend for Lunico, a wine with pressure on the palate, whistle-clean freshness and a lingering finale. Finally, the soft, flowery Rosato is as appealing as ever.

Ottaviano Lambruschi

VIA OLMARELLO, 28
19030 CASTELNUOVO MAGRA [SP]
TEL. 0187674261
ottavianolambruschi@libero.it

ANNUAL PRODUCTION 30,000 bottles
HECTARES UNDER VINE 5
VITICULTURE METHOD Conventional

Clinging to the slopes of deepest Lunigiana are the vineyards of the Lambruschi family, who have been growing grapes well out of the limelight in their disciplined, no-nonsense style for more than half a century. This year Fabio, who has brought his enthusiasm to the winery created by his father Ottaviano, presented a range with a rather exciting red. Maniero, from sangiovese, canaiolo, merlot plus a dash of cabernet, offers attractive red berry fruit and a dry, even palate. On the white side of the list, there are three Vermentinos since Sarticola was not produced. We liked Costa Marina best of the trio. It's minerally, savoury and has intense, well-defined florality. The aromas are reprised on the palate while the sheer length of the finale marked up its score. Drinkability and pleasure are the keynotes of the Alessandro and the standard Vermentino, the latter remarkably refreshing and ideal as an anytime wine.

● Lunico '05	♟♟ 5
● Rossese di Dolceacqua	
Vigneto Pian del Vescovo '05	♟♟ 5
● Rossese di Dolceacqua '06	♟ 4
○ Riviera Ligure di Ponente	
Vermentino '06	♟ 4
☉ Poggio Baraccone '06	♟ 4
● Lunico '04	♟♟ 5
● Rossese di Dolceacqua	
Vigneto Pian del Vescovo '04	♟♟ 5
● Sirius '04	♟♟ 7
● Sirius '03	♟♟ 7
○ Riviera Ligure di Ponente	
Vermentino Eclis '04	♟♟ 5

○ Colli di Luni Vermentino	
Costa Marina '06	♟♟ 4*
● Colli di Luni Rosso Maniero '06	♟ 4
○ Colli di Luni Vermentino '06	♟ 4
○ Colli di Luni Vermentino	
Alessandro '06	♟ 4

La Pietra del Focolare

FRAZ. ISOLA DI ORTONOVO
VIA DOGANA, 209
19034 ORTONOVO [SP]
TEL. 0187662129
www.lapietradelfocolare.it

ANNUAL PRODUCTION 30,000 bottles
HECTARES UNDER VINE 7
VITICULTURE METHOD Conventional

Colli di Luni is a borderland. To the west lies Liguria with La Spezia and the Cinque Terre while to the east is the valley that opens into Tuscany, Carrara and the looming Apuan Alps. It is here that La Pietra del Focolare has been plying its trade for many years, releasing around 30,000 bottles under six labels. Four are selections of Vermentino and two standard reds that mix international and native varieties: sangiovese, merlot and massaretta. Starting with the most approachable, the whites include the refreshingly drinkable Villa Linda and Villa Luce wines while Solarancio and Augusto are more complex, earning flattering scores for their multi-faceted varietal aromatics and an even, well-sustained palate. Truth to tell, the reds are hardly monuments of structure or body but they are well made and give nice supple fruit.

Poggio dei Gorleri

FRAZ. DIANO GORLERI
VIA SAN LEONARDO
18013 DIANO MARINA [IM]
TEL. 0183495207
www.poggiodeigorleri.com

ANNUAL PRODUCTION 45,000 bottles
HECTARES UNDER VINE 4.5
VITICULTURE METHOD Conventional

Giampiero Merano and his sons Matteo and Davide, busy respectively in the vineyards and the commercial side of the business, have made a conscious decision to invest in their enterprise on an ongoing basis. Innovations in cellar and among the rows have brought with them steady improvements in quality, further enhanced by the input of oenologist Beppe Caviola and agronomist Giampiero Romana. Which is why we were unsurprised by this year's results. We'll start with Vermentino Apricus. Crisp and intense on the nose dominated by almond blossom, which is picked up on the palate, it layers this with juicy citrus in an elegant, savoury framework. Next up is Pigato Albium, which unveils a richly complex bouquet. Subtle oaky notes introduce ripe apricot sensations and faint minerality. Ripe, deep raw material on the palate accompanies progression into a long, varietally bitterish finale. There were also good showing from the less challenging Pigato Cycnus and the Vermentino Vigna Sorì and standard version.

Wine	Rating
○ Colli di Luni Vermentino Augusto '06	▼▼ 4*
○ Colli di Luni Vermentino Solarancio '06	▼▼ 5
○ Colli di Luni Vermentino Villa Linda '06	▼ 4
○ Colli di Luni Vermentino Viva Luce '06	▼ 2
● Colli di Luni Rosso Saltamasso '05	▼ 4
● Colli di Luni La Merla dal Becco '05	▼ 5

Wine	Rating
○ Riviera Ligure di Ponente Pigato Albium '06	▼▼ 5
○ Riviera Ligure di Ponente Vermentino Apricus '06	▼▼ 5
○ Riviera Ligure di Ponente Pigato Cycnus '06	▼▼ 4*
○ Riviera Ligure di Ponente Vermentino '06	▼ 4
○ Riviera Ligure di Ponente Vermentino V. Sorì '06	▼ 4
○ Riviera Ligure di Ponente Pigato Cycnus '04	♀♀ 4
○ Riviera Ligure di Ponente Vermentino Apricus '05	♀♀ 5
○ Riviera Ligure di Ponente Pigato Cycnus '05	♀♀ 4
○ Riviera Ligure di Ponente Vermentino Apricus '04	♀♀ 5

La Rocca di San Nicolao

FRAZ. GAZZELLI
VIA DANTE, 10
18027 CHIUSANICO [IM]
TEL. 018352850
www.roccasannicolao.com

ANNUAL PRODUCTION 40,000 bottles
HECTARES UNDER VINE 4
VITICULTURE METHOD Conventional

The cellar and vineyards of La Rocca di San Nicolao are at Gazzelli near Chiusanico, in the hinterland of Imperia, where the winery has set up a spacious tasting area and sales outlet so that visitors can taste the wines and the extra virgin olive oil made at the estate's press. The selections come from the Proxi vineyard at 600 metres above sea level, in a hollow created long ago by a landslip that is protected to the north by the mountain and superbly exposed to sea breezes and sunlight. This year, the two Pigatos did very well, thanks in part to a very favourable growing year. Vigna Proxi releases crisp aromas of yellow-fleshed fruit that herald decent body and admirable fruit in the mouth. In contrast, the standard version privileges citrus on the nose before the well-orchestrated palate unfolds sure-footedly on the palate. Finally, the two Vermentinos may not be particularly complex but their clean pear and apple fruit and firm but not aggressive acidity are enjoyable.

○ Riviera Ligure di Ponente Pigato '06	🍷🍷 4*
○ Riviera Ligure di Ponente Pigato Vigna Proxi '06	🍷🍷 5
○ Riviera Ligure di Ponente Vermentino '06	🍷 4
○ Riviera Ligure di Ponente Vermentino Vigna Proxi '06	🍷 5
○ Riviera Ligure di Ponente Pigato Vigna Proxi '05	🍷🍷 (outline) 5

Le Rocche del Gatto

FRAZ. SALEA
REG. RUATO, 4
17031 ALBENGA [SV]
TEL. 3355223547
www.lerocchedelgatto.it

ANNUAL PRODUCTION 80,000 bottles
HECTARES UNDER VINE 7
VITICULTURE METHOD Conventional

Strong personality and a distinct territorial imprint are the strong suits of wines from Fausto De Andreis, Gigi Crosa di Vergagni and his daughter Clara's winery. Year-to-year consistency has sometimes been lacking in the past, which has penalized the range, but that seems to be a thing of the past. On to the tastings, then, where the pigato-based Spigau Crociata performed well. Intense, inviting ripe yellow-fleshed fruit introduces a warm, juicy palate that signs off in a swath of delicious soft sensations. We also liked the Vermentino, its nicely put together aromas mingling balsam with aromatic herbs. There is plenty of structure, balance and length on the palate. Pigato, the other white, is more slender and less complex, focusing mainly on florality. On the red front, ormeasco-based Macajolo 2005 – the version reviewed last year was the 2004 – puts the accent on red berry fruit sensations while the Rossese highlights sweetness and spice.

○ Riviera Ligure di Ponente Vermentino '06	🍷🍷 4*
○ Spigau Crociata '05	🍷🍷 5
○ Riviera Ligure di Ponente Pigato '06	🍷 4
● Macajolo '05	🍷 4
● Riviera Ligure di Ponente Rossese '06	🍷 4
○ Spigau Crociata '05	🍷🍷 (outline) 5
● Macajolo '04	🍷🍷 (outline) 4

Sancio

via Laiolo, 73
17028 Spotorno [SV]
tel. 019743255
sancioagricola@libero.it

ANNUAL PRODUCTION 40,000 bottles
HECTARES UNDER VINE 3.2
VITICULTURE METHOD Conventional

Not many wine enthusiasts know about Sancio, or at least not as many as the cellar deserves. That could be because the not very outgoing Riccardo is a grower first and foremost, or perhaps it's because only relatively recently has the cellar made a quality leap. Whatever the case, the range does well every year, always managing to take one or two steps forward. Witness the very satisfying and cellarable Pigato Cappellania and the standard version, which has notes of balsam, nice balance and an elegant palate. The reasons for these improvements are obvious: shrewd, chemical-free vineyard management and a revised approach to vinification in a spanking new cellar, from which Riccardo's fruity, fresh-tasting Vermentino has also benefited. Fragrant fruit, attractive depth and a caressing texture are the keynotes of the Rossese, complemented by a warm, soft Granaccia.

○ Riviera Ligure di Ponente Pigato '06	🍷🍷 4*
○ Riviera Ligure di Ponente Pigato Cappellania '06	🍷🍷 5
● Riviera Ligure di Ponente Rossese '06	🍷🍷 4*
● Granaccia Edoardo I '05	🍷 5
○ Riviera Ligure di Ponente Vermentino '06	🍷 4
○ Riviera Ligure di Ponente Pigato Cappellania '05	🍷🍷 5

Terre Bianche

loc. Arcagna
18035 Dolceacqua [IM]
tel. 018431426
www.terrebianche.com

ANNUAL PRODUCTION 55,000 bottles
HECTARES UNDER VINE 8
VITICULTURE METHOD Conventional

A quick glance at the table below will persuade you that this is a premium winery. Despite the reputation for reliability Filippo Rondelli and Franco Laconi have earned, they continue to strive for further improvements while never losing sight of territory and variety-focused typicity. In fact, they are part of a producers' association to safeguard the authenticity of Rossese di Dolceacqua, which is under serious threat. Particularly fine examples of their approach are the elegant, savoury Vermentino, all freshness and fine balance, and the nicely complex, soft-textured Pigato, with its fruit and lingering length, but the pigato and vermentino Arcana Bianco lacks a touch of verve, although it is refreshingly supple. Wine lovers wanting to explore native Ligurian reds would do worse that try the standard-label Terre Bianche Rossese. Its multi-faceted aromatics accompany a dry palate with good depth while stylish fruit and tempting softness are the Bricco Arcagna's calling cards. Finally, Arcano Rosso is as good as ever, if less traditional given the cabernet that joins the rossese in the blend.

● Arcana Rosso '04	🍷🍷 6
● Rossese di Dolceacqua '06	🍷🍷 4*
● Rossese di Dolceacqua Bricco Arcagna '05	🍷🍷 5
○ Riviera Ligure di Ponente Pigato '06	🍷🍷 4*
○ Riviera Ligure di Ponente Vermentino '06	🍷🍷 4*
○ Arcana Bianco '05	🍷 5
○ Arcana Bianco '04	🍷🍷 5
● Arcana Rosso '03	🍷🍷 6
● Arcana Rosso '01	🍷🍷 6
● Rossese di Dolceacqua Bricco Arcagna '01	🍷🍷 5
● Rossese di Dolceacqua Bricco Arcagna '03	🍷🍷 5
● Rossese di Dolceacqua Bricco Arcagna '04	🍷🍷 5

Cascina delle Terre Rosse

VIA MANIE, 3
17024 FINALE LIGURE [SV]
TEL. 019698782

ANNUAL PRODUCTION 32,000 bottles
HECTARES UNDER VINE 5.5
VITICULTURE METHOD Conventional

The bustling beaches and busy traffic of the holiday resort of Finale are only a few steep kilometres from the triumphant vegetation of the Manie tableland. It is in these other-worldly surroundings, in a sun-kissed, tree-girt natural amphitheatre, that Vladimiro Galluzzo has planted his vines. The place is special, work is painstaking and the wines speak for themselves. There are three well-typed Pigatos that range from the elegant substance and fresh flavours of the standard version to the caressing mouthfeel of the Apogeo and the full-bodied roundness of Le Banche. These are the foundations of the white list, which also includes an intriguing Vermentino and the herbaceous L'Acerbina. But we should also make room for the remarkable granaccia, rossese and barbera Solitario, the forerunner of today's western Ligurian reds, which offers subtle spice and fruit, a savoury palate and caressing texture. It's such a good wine that we sent it on to our Three Glass finals. Finally, the Passito made a good impression, combining restrained sweetness with fascinating aromatics.

Il Torchio

VIA PROVINCIALE, 202
19030 CASTELNUOVO MAGRA [SP]
TEL. 0187674075

ANNUAL PRODUCTION 36,000 bottles
HECTARES UNDER VINE 5
VITICULTURE METHOD Conventional

On the borders of Liguria and Tuscany, among hills that are shading into flatlands as they prepare to meet the coast, Il Torchio makes a small, meticulously crafted range of attractively priced wines in the outstanding wine zone of Castelnuovo. Backed by a family tradition of farming that has always included viticulture and olives, Giorgio Tendola has built up a reputation as a serious, reliable wine man who is not afraid to buck the trend. Those who know him admire his volcanic charm, his hospitality, his provocative frankness and his pride in the success of his wines. This time, we come in praise of his Vermentino with its restrained but irresistible fruit, flowers and balsam, balance and delicious flavour. Although less exciting, the vermentino, albarola and trebbianella Di Giorgio is well made, soft-textured and gracious. Rosso Riserva is from merlot and sangiovese with other red varieties. It shows very clean, with crisp aromas and attractive extract, but is also a little thin.

● Solitario '05	♙♙ 6
O Riviera Ligure di Ponente Pigato '06	♙♙ 5
O Riviera Ligure di Ponente Vermentino '06	♙♙ 5
O Apogeo '06	♙♙ 5
O Le Banche '06	♙♙ 5
O L'Acerbina '06	♙♙ 4
O Passito '04	♙ 5
O Riviera Ligure di Ponente Pigato '99	♟♟♟ 5
O Le Banche '05	♟♟ 5
O Apogeo '05	♟♟ 5
O Riviera Ligure di Ponente Pigato '05	♟♟ 5
● Solitario '04	♟♟ 6
● Solitario '03	♟♟ 6

O Colli di Luni Vermentino '06	♙♙ 4*
O Di Giorgio '06	♙ 4
● Colli di Luni Rosso Ris. '04	♙ 5
● Colli di Luni Rosso Ris. '03	♟♟ 5

La Vecchia Cantina
FRAZ. SALEA
VIA CORTA, 3
17031 ALBENGA [SV]
TEL. 0182559881

ANNUAL PRODUCTION 20,000 bottles
HECTARES UNDER VINE 4
VITICULTURE METHOD Conventional

Umberto Calleri's winery is small but perfectly able to provide consistent versions of the classic wine types of the western Ligurian coast. The production philosophy is straightforward. Umberto uses only fruit from his own vines, situated in well-aspected hillside locations at Scuea and Pianboschi in Salea, near Albenga. Winemaking is scrupulously careful and quantity is not a factor in his calculations. This year, the Pigato and the Vermentino provide evidence of the Calleri approach. The Pigato has an intense nose of fruit and balsam that are echoed on the warm, pervasive palate, which signs off with a savoury, faintly bitterish finale. Umberto's Vermentino is almost as good, giving well-defined fragrances of aromatic herbs and Mediterranean scrubland. It follows through well on the palate, which powers on into an admirably long palate. Finally, the cellar's red, Rossese La Scuea, has ripe red fruit followed by a soft, slender palate.

Claudio Vio
FRAZ. CROSA, 16
17032 VENDONE [SV]
TEL. 018276338

ANNUAL PRODUCTION 12,500 bottles
HECTARES UNDER VINE 2
VITICULTURE METHOD Conventional

This small winery has one of the longest traditions in the whole of Pigato territory. The Vio family was enthusiastically growing grapes as long ago as 1920. Faithful to that heritage, current owner Claudio devotes himself to the family business fully aware of the difficulties involved in maintaining the high standards required to carve out a niche in markets where competition gets more intensive by the day. There was a fine performance from the white U Grottu, obtained from a rigorous selection of pigato grapes. Overripe yellow-fleshed fruit fragrances dominate the entry on the nose, giving way to aromatic herbs. The aromatics are nicely reflected on the fruit-rich, yet fresh-tasting and savoury palate. The standard version is less emphatic, giving Mediterranean scrubland and meadow flowers before the palate is perked up by attractive aromatics. Softness and vigorous acidity are the hallmarks of the Vermentino. Finally, the red Runcu Brujau earned a mention.

O Riviera Ligure di Ponente Pigato '06	♟♟ 4*
O Riviera Ligure di Ponente Vermentino '06	♟♟ 4*
● Riviera Ligure di Ponente Rossese La Scuea '06	♟ 4
O Riviera Ligure di Ponente Pigato '05	♟♟ 4

O U Grottu '06	♟♟ 4*
O Riviera Ligure di Ponente Pigato '06	♟ 4
O Riviera Ligure di Ponente Vermentino '06	♟ 4
● Runcu Brujau '06	4

OTHER WINERIES

Anfossi
FRAZ. BASTIA
VIA PACCINI, 39
17031 ALBENGA [SV]
TEL. 018220024
www.aziendaagrariaanfossi.it

It's worth visiting Bastia d'Albenga to see the "paraxo", a lovely crenellated building with a vaulted ceiling that houses the Anfossi cellar. There are two interesting whites from this estate, which is converting to organic production. The fruit-forward Vermentino is savoury and the Pigato has subtle almonds.

○ Riviera Ligure di Ponente Pigato '06	🍷 4
○ Riviera Ligure di Ponente Vermentino '06	🍷 4

Cooperativa Agricoltori della Vallata di Levanto
LOC. GHIARE, 20
19015 LEVANTO [SP]
TEL. 0187800867
www.levanto.com/cooperativa

This small winery has got off to a good start, concentrating on careful vinification with modern techniques to make attractive land-focused wines. Costa di Mattelun, from vermentino, albarola and bosco, is a lovely straw yellow with subtle mineral-nuanced Mediterranean herbs and a juicy, well-balanced palate.

○ Golfo dei Poeti Bianco Lievantù '04	🍷 4
○ Colline di Levanto Costa di Mattelun '06	🍷 4

Alessandro Anfosso
C.SO VERBONE, 175
18036 SOLDANO [IM]
TEL. 3383116590

Alessandro Anfosso makes just two wines and does so well. They are genuine Rosseses with character, authentic flavours and an appetizing palate. Rich fruit and drinkability are the strong suits of the Superiore, which marries fruit and balsam with fresh acidity. Its finesse, roundness and juicy pulp all impress.

● Rossese di Dolceacqua '06	🍷🍷 4*
● Rossese di Dolceacqua Sup. Poggio I Pini '05	🍷🍷 5

Luigi Bianchi Carenzo
VIA I. LANTERO, 19
18013 DIANO SAN PIETRO [IM]
TEL. 0183429072

Luigi Bianchi Carenzo is 70, full of energy and runs an interesting winery with plots at Diano San Pietro and Diano Arentino. We admired the whistle-clean execution of these very valid wines, from the balance and florality of the substantial Vermentino to the attractively long, tangy Pigato.

○ Riviera Ligure di Ponente Pigato '06	🍷🍷 4*
○ Riviera Ligure di Ponente Vermentino '06	🍷🍷 4*

Samuele Heydi Bonanini
VIA DI LOCA, 189
19017 RIOMAGGIORE [SP]
TEL. 3483162470

This recently started cellar turns out a few thousand very decent bottles. Only a few hundred contain Cinque Terre Sciacchetrà, an amber wine with warm aromas of honey and nuts, nice structure and a nicely well-sustained, alcohol-rich palate. The tangy dry version foregrounds vine blossom and almonds.

○ Cinque Terre Sciacchetrà '05	🍷🍷 8
○ Cinque Terre '05	🍷 5
○ Cinque Terre Sciacchetrà '04	🍷 8

Enoteca Andrea Bruzzone
VIA BOLZANETO, 94/96
16162 GENOVA
TEL. 0107455157
www.andreabruzzonevini.it

Andrea Bruzzone is the guardian angel of Val Polcevera wine. Over the years, he has promoted the area by doggedly making wine in daunting conditions. He has enjoyed excellent results, like the headily fruit-forward Pellandrum, a savoury easy drinker, or Assuie, which gives florality with a hint of acerbity.

○ Val Polcevera Vermentino '06	🍷 3
○ Val Polcevera Bianco Assuie '06	🍷 4
● Rosso Pellandrun '05	🍷 4

OTHER WINERIES

Buranco

VIA BURANCO, 72
19016 MONTEROSSO AL MARE [SP]
TEL. 0187817677
www.buranco.info

It's the first vintage for the new owners, the
Grillos, who seem to have inherited the
previous management's experience. The wines
show character. The warm, oak-nuanced
cabernet sauvignon, merlot and syrah Buranco
has a caressing, fruit-led mouthfeel. Both the
dry and dried-grape versions of Cinque Terre
are good.

● Buranco '05	♟♟ 6
○ Cinque Terre '06	♟ 5
○ Cinque Terre Sciacchetrà '05	♟ 8
○ Tra-Dizione '06	♟ 5

Luciano Capellini

VIA MONTELLO, 240B
19017 RIOMAGGIORE [SP]
TEL. 0187920632
www.vinbun.it

Two wines here tell the story of Cinque
Terre. Vino di Buccia is fresh, clean and
assertively aromatic, progressing nicely on
the palate in Mediterranean aromas,
especially dried medlar and apricot fruit and
attractive balsam. The warm, tropical
fragrances of the distinctive Cinque Terre
return on the palate.

○ Vino di Buccia	
Casata dei Beghee '05	♟♟ 6
○ Cinque Terre '06	♟ 6

Il Chioso

LOC. BACCANO
19038 ARCOLA [SP]
TEL. 0187986620

Chioso wines reflect their territory in a rather
traditional style that often fascinates. Take
the two Vermentinos. The standard wine
proffers subtle herbaceousness, fruit and
flowers over delicious acidity whereas the
selection is all softness and fruity pulp. The
Ciliegiolo is a well-made, no-nonsense wine.

○ Colli di Luni Vermentino Stemma '06	♟ 4
○ Colli di Luni Vermentino '06	♟ 4
● Ciliegiolo '06	♟ 4

Colle dei Bardellini

LOC. BARDELLINI
VIA FONTANAROSA, 12
18100 IMPERIA
TEL. 0183291370
www.colledeibardellini.it

This is reliable winery has always released
solidly traditional products in the style of the
western riviera: approachability and drinkability.
We picked out two selections. The Vermentino
combines refreshing tanginess with attractive
fruit and the very nice Pigato has a signature
hint of bitterness.

○ Riviera Ligure di Ponente	
Vermentino V. U Munte '06	♟ 4
○ Riviera Ligure di Ponente Pigato	
V. La Torretta '06	♟ 5

La Colombiera

LOC. MONTECCHIO, 92
19030 CASTELNUOVO MAGRA [SP]
TEL. 0187674265

Piero Ferro's winery is one of the most quality-
focused in Liguria. La Colombiere wines have
personality and reflect their variety. The crisply
defined Vermentino, which marries intense fruit
complexity with tanginess, juicy pulp and good
length, and the soft, full-bodied Celsus
selection are excellent examples.

○ Colli di Luni Vermentino '06	♟♟ 5
○ Colli di Luni Vermentino Celsus '06	♟ 5

La Felce

VIA BOZZI, 36
19034 ORTONOVO [SP]
TEL. 018766789

La Felce is a small winery in the hills of
Ortonovo set up a few years ago by Andrea
Marchesi, a promising wine man who
immediately strove to impress the market.
Andrea releases three wines. We particularly
like the Vermentino, which offers restrained fruit
and forest floor, well-gauged acidity and nice
balance.

○ Colli di Luni Vermentino '06	♟ 4

OTHER WINERIES

Fontanacota
VIA DOLCEDO, 121
18100 IMPERIA
TEL. 0183293456
viniberta@tiscali.it

The Fontanacota vineyard is at Clavi in Val Prino, near a small spring from which the area takes its name. The range includes an elegant, savoury Vermentino and a crisp, flavoursome Pigato with good fruit. Equally interesting are the two Ormeascos, both from a small plot at Pornassio.

● Ormeasco di Pornassio Sup. '05	♥♥ 4*
○ Riviera Ligure di Ponente Vermentino '06	♥♥ 4*
○ Riviera Ligure di Ponente Pigato '06	♥ 4
● Ormeasco di Pornassio '06	♥ 4

Forlini Cappellini
LOC. MANAROLA
VIA RICCOBALDI, 45
19010 RIOMAGGIORE [SP]
TEL. 0187920496
forlinicappellini@libero.it

This winery is emblematic of heroic viticulture. Complex aromas characterize the distinctive sensory profile of these wines. Bottles like the Sciacchetrà show what this territory can produce as the balsam and cakes aromas progress confidently on nose and palate. The refreshing Cinque Terre is redolent of pine resin.

○ Cinque Terre Sciacchetrà Ris. '01	♥♥ 8
○ Cinque Terre '06	♥ 5

Giacomelli
VIA PALVOTRISIA, 134
19030 CASTELNUOVO MAGRA [SP]
TEL. 0187674155

Giacomelli has plots at Ortonovo and Castelnuovo Magra. In charge is Roberto Petacchi, a fine interpreter of local varieties. His deliciously drinkable standard-label Vermentino is fresh-tasting while the Boboli has an attractive breadth of aromatics. Equally good is the balanced, warm Rosso, with nice extract.

● Colli di Luni Rosso '06	♥ 5
○ Colli di Luni Vermentino '06	♥ 5
○ Colli di Luni Vermentino Boboli '06	♥ 5

Il Monticello
VIA GROPPOLO, 7
19038 SARZANA [SP]
TEL. 0187621432
www.ilmonticello.vai.li

On the border with Emilia and Tuscany, where popular traditions and wine influences meet, the Neri siblings make wines, like the elegantly fresh, full-bodied Poggio Paterno, that stand comparison with the longer-lived bottles of neighbouring Tuscany. The fruit-led reds are very drinkable with a warm, dry finish.

● Colli di Luni Rosso Rupestro '06	♥ 4
● Colli di Luni Rosso Poggio dei Magni '04	♥ 4
○ Colli di Luni Vermentino Poggio Paterno '05	♥ 4

Nirasca
FRAZ. NIRASCA
VIA ALPI, 3
18026 PIEVE DI TECO [IM]
TEL. 018336071
www.cascinanirasca.com

Cascina Nirasca is Gabriele Maglio and Marco Temesio's recently founded estate. The wines are well made and precisely styled. Senso, with its fruit and balsam sensations, finesse and weight on the palate, is good and the juicy, long-lingering Ormeasco Superiore is also nice. The Vermentino and Ormeasco are attractive.

● Ormeasco di Pornassio Sup. '05	♥♥ 4*
● Senso '05	♥♥ 5
● Ormeasco di Pornassio '06	♥ 4
○ Riviera Ligure di Ponente Vermentino '06	♥ 4

Antonio Perrino
18035 DOLCEACQUA [IM]
TEL. 0184206267

Antonio Perrino, who signs himself Testalonga on his labels, turns out very good quality wines with one or two stand-outs. The vermentino-only Bianco has complex aromas that follow through on the long, tangy palate but Antonio's best wine again this year was the elegantly poised, varietal, Rossese di Dolceacqua.

○ Bianco Testalonga '06	♥♥ 4*
● Rossese di Dolceacqua '06	♥♥ 5

OTHER WINERIES

Poggi dell'Elmo
CORSO VERBONE, 135
18036 SOLDANO [IM]
TEL. 3384736742

Gianni Guglielmi has a property in one of the best parts of Valle Crosa and he knows what to do with it. His wines are well-tempered and admirably firm-textured. The standard Rossese did well this time, giving a soft, fruity yet vibrant palate while the Superiore is less exciting, if balanced and well defined.

● Rossese di Dolceacqua '06	🍷🍷 4
● Rossese di Dolceacqua Sup. '05	🍷 4

Lorenzo Ramò
VIA S. ANTONIO, 9
18020 PORNASSIO [IM]
TEL. 018333097

Gian Paolo Ramò knows his territory well and is one of the finest interpreters of the dolcetto clone that yields Ormeasco. His 2006 edition is excellent, giving intense ripe cherry aromas and a juicy palate with Ormeasco's attractive bitterish twist in the finish. Sciac-trà is savoury and temptingly drinkable.

● Ormeasco di Pornassio '06	🍷🍷 4*
⊙ Ormeasco di Pornassio Sciac-trà '06	🍷 4

Santa Caterina
VIA SANTA CATERINA, 6
19038 SARZANA [SP]
TEL. 0187629429
akih@libero.it

Organic viticulture and experiments with native and non-native varieties lie behind Andrea Kihlgren's wines. His Vermentinos are dry and fresh. Giuncaro, from tocai, sauvignon blanc and vermentino, mingles softness with minerality and medicinal herbs. Ghiaretolo, from merlot, has loose-knit texture and decent pulp.

○ Colli di Luni Vermentino Poggi Alti '06	🍷 4
● Ghiaretolo '04	🍷 4
○ Colli di Luni Vermentino '06	🍷 4
○ Giuncaro '06	🍷 4

Vis Amoris
LOC. CARAMAGNA
S.DA MOLINO JAVÈ, 23
18100 IMPERIA
TEL. 3483959569
visamoris@libero.it

Vis Amoris is a young estate with modest dimensions and big ambitions. Only one wine was presented but it's seriously good. Rossana Zappa and Roberto Tozzi put their hearts into making Vigna Domè. Intriguingly subtle, full bodied and savoury, it signs off on a note of balsam and bitterness.

○ Riviera Ligure di Ponente Pigato V. Domè '06	🍷🍷 5
○ Riviera Ligure di Ponente Pigato V. Domè '05	🍷🍷 4

LOMBARDY

Lombardy notched up one of its best ever results for this edition of our Guide. The region earned 13 Three Glass awards, including a well-deserved double prize for Ca' del Bosco, which means there were 12 Lombard wineries among the prizes. This fine result does justice to the hundreds of producers in all corners of the region who have committed themselves to high quality. The sheer number of estates involved is revealed by the number reviewed here – 158 in all – making Lombardy one of the biggest regions in our Guide, trailing titans Piedmont and Tuscany and giants Friuli and Veneto. Huge progress has been made in Lombardy over the past decade and one of the areas that best illustrate this achievement is Valtellina, where innovation has not smothered but has instead perfected age-old growing techniques and strengthened the bond with the land. Sfursat is the wine that best exemplifies this, as is testified by the four prizewinners: the '05 from Nino Negri, Valtellina's leading winery, Mamete Prevostini's Albareda '05, Rainoldi's Ca' Rizzieri '02 and Triacca's San Domenico '03. But yet again it was Franciacorta that picked up the lion's share of stemware, with seven Three Glass wines, all classic method cuvées, including the Sparkler of the Year award for Cavalleri di Erbusco's spectacular Franciacorta Collezione Esclusiva Brut '99. Ca' del Bosco notched up an umpteenth double victory with its Franciacorta Dosage Zéro '03 and Satèn '02, placing it among the small elite of wineries that have earned at least 30 Three Glass awards, and overall third place in the rankings for all 21 editions of our Guide. Bellavista presented an unforgettable Franciacorta Extra Brut Vittorio Moretti '01, which earned the extraordinary talented Mattia Vezzola our Oenologist of the Year award. Finally, the rosy picture is completed by Satèn '03 from Gatti, Comarì del Salem '02 from Uberti, and Cabochon '03 from Monte Rossa. Franciacorta may be one of Italy's homes of sparkle but Oltrepò Pavese is equally significant in the sector. The Boatti family from Monsupello won yet another Three Glass award for their OP Pinot Nero Nature, which has become a classic and possibly offers the best value for money of all Italian sparkling wines. This year, Oltrepò went gone further, drawing up a strict production protocol for the new DOCG classic method sparkler. The round-up ends with another of our old favourites, Garda Cabernet Le Zalte '05 from Ruggero Brunori's Cascina La Pertica, which is not only "good to drink" but also "good to think", as it is sourced from biodynamic vineyards. That's the end of the list of prizewinners, but they're followed by a long list of runners-up with excellent wines. Garda, Oltrepò, Franciacorta, Valtellina, Valcalepio and Lugana have all shown that they can aspire to even more prestigious goals.

Marchese Adorno
VIA CORIASSA, 4
27050 RETORBIDO [PV]
TEL. 0383374404
www.marcheseadorno-wines.it

Agnes
VIA CAMPO DEL MONTE, 1
27040 ROVESCALA [PV]
TEL. 038575206
www.fratelliagnes.it

ANNUAL PRODUCTION 150,000 bottles
HECTARES UNDER VINE 80
VITICULTURE METHOD Conventional

The winery owned by Marchese Marcello Cattaneo Adorno has continued its growth, albeit with some inevitable ups and downs. The new cellar has naturally enhanced its great potential. Cliviano '05, a soft, warm Bordeaux blend, has aromas of sun-dried hay, coffee and wild berries with attractive hints of balsam. The deep ruby Barbera Vigna del Re '04 boasts a concentrated nose of spice and red berries and equally intense fruity flesh, although the acidity and tannins require more time in bottle to smooth their edges. Bonarda Frizzante '06 is crisp, fruity and balanced, with well-calibrated tannins and residual sugar. Rugla '04, another Bordeaux blend but more ambitious than Cliviano, has taken a step back after almost reaching our finals last year. This time, despite good structure, depth, spicy aromas and fine-grained tannins, it's penalized by a lack of overall balance and a certain rustic touch. The Pinot Nero '05's youth means it struggles to open up while the Pinot Grigio '06 and the basic Barbera '05 are pleasant and well made.

ANNUAL PRODUCTION 70,000 bottles
HECTARES UNDER VINE 16
VITICULTURE METHOD Conventional

As always, the winery owned by brothers Sergio and Cristiano Agnes is at the forefront of Oltrepò production when it comes to Bonarda, in all its possible forms: still, sparkling, dry, amabile, oaked or unoaked. Poculum '05, aged in barriques, is the only IGT of the five wines presented this year, although it, too, is pure croatina, the bonarda pignolo cultivar. It has a practically impenetrable ruby hue with a fine balsamic nose of sound fruit, faithfully echoed on the compact, rich, chewy palate. Cresta del Ghiffi '06 is the best of the sparkling Bonardas, with wild berry aromas, which shows clean and very soft thanks to velvety tannins and high residual sugar. The drier Bonarda Campo del Monte '06 is succulent and fruity, flaunting plenty of fine-grained tannins. Bonarda Millennium '04 is cask-conditioned. It has good structure and well-calibrated tannins but over-extracted fruit, making it a little syrupy. The still Bonarda Possessione del Console '06 is also nice with aromas of violet and blueberry, good fruity pulp and assertive tannins.

● Cliviano '05	♆♆ 4
● OP Barbera V. del Re '04	♆♆ 6
● OP Bonarda Frizzante '06	♆♆ 4
● OP Barbera '05	♆ 4
● Rugla '04	♆ 6
O OP Pinot Grigio '06	♆ 4
● OP Pinot Nero '05	♆ 5
O Arcolaio '05	♉♉ 4*
● Cliviano '04	♉♉ 4
● OP Bonarda Frizzante '05	♉♉ 4*
● Rugla '03	♉♉ 4
● OP Pinot Nero '04	♉♉ 5
● OP Barbera V. del Re '03	♉♉ 6

● OP Bonarda Campo del Monte '06	♆♆ 3*
● OP Bonarda Cresta del Ghiffi '06	♆♆ 3*
● Rosso Poculum '05	♆♆ 5
● OP Bonarda Millenium '04	♆ 5
● OP Bonarda Possessione del Console '06	♆ 3
● OP Bonarda Campo del Monte '05	♉♉ 3*
● OP Bonarda Cresta del Ghiffi '05	♉♉ 3*
● Rosso Poculum '04	♉♉ 5*
● Rosso Vignazzo '04	♉♉ 4
● Rosso Poculum '03	♉♉ 5
● OP Bonarda Millenium '01	♉♉ 5

Anteo

LOC. CHIESA
27040 ROCCA DE' GIORGI [PV]
TEL. 038599073
www.anteovini.it

ANNUAL PRODUCTION 240,000 bottles
HECTARES UNDER VINE 26
VITICULTURE METHOD Conventional

A benchmark for Oltrepò sparklers, Piero and Antonella Cribellati's estate also stands out for its great range of other wines. Although the recently disgorged Riserva del Poeta '01 will not be released until next year – the 2000 vintage was not produced – the Nature Ecru '02 went through to our finals, where it unveiled attractive fragrances of watermelon, aromatic herbs and wild berries and a crisp, zesty palate with intriguing minerality on the long finish. The Rosé is also very good, characterized by distinct hints of rose and red berries and a soft, appealing palate. Two Glasses also went to the basic Brut. Although simpler, it's nonetheless very pleasant and balanced, testifying to the fact that the winery is capable of producing first-rate classic method sparklers. The same score was also achieved by the exceptionally soft Bonarda Staffolo '06, which has intact, clean fruit and fine-grained tannins, and the aromatic, varietal Moscato di Volpara La Volpe e L'Uva '06. Pinot Nero Coste del Roccolo '06 is pleasantly refreshing. We were less convinced by Ca' dell'Oca '04, a well-made but unexciting Pinot Nero fermented on the skins, or Chardonnay Quattro Marzo '06, which is well typed but fails to charm.

Barone Pizzini

LOC. TIMOLINE
VIA BRESCIA, 3A
25050 CORTE FRANCA [BS]
TEL. 0309848311
www.baronepizzini.it

ANNUAL PRODUCTION 280,000 bottles
HECTARES UNDER VINE 40
VITICULTURE METHOD Certified organic

This estate, managed by Silvano Brescianini with enthusiasm, attention to the environment and focus on wholesomeness of the products, heads a group that also includes Poderi di Ghiaccioforte in Tuscany, Pievalta in Marche and Tenuta del Barco in Puglia. With 40 hectares of organically cultivated vineyards and a new, state-of-the-art cellar, the winery, founded in 1870, offers a carefully crafted range of Franciacortas and territory-dedicated wines. This year, Brescianini has chosen to prolong the ageing of the most important blends. Consequently, in the absence of the vintage Bagnadore, we recommend: the excellent Franciacorta Brut with lively citrus notes and a crisp, supple palate; the Extra Dry with a soft apple and vanilla nose echoed on the palate; and Satèn '03, which displays backbone and pleasant hints of ripe fruit. The Brut and Extra Dry rosés are well typed but less interesting, showing slightly over-evolved. Terre di Franciacorta Bianco '06 is among the best of the vintage while the Rosso '05 is well balanced.

O OP Pinot Nero Brut Cl. Nature Écru '02	♟♟ 5
● OP Bonarda Staffolo '06	♟♟ 4*
O OP Moscato La Volpe e L'Uva '06	♟♟ 4
O OP Pinot Nero Brut Cl.	♟♟ 5
⊙ OP Pinot Nero Brut Cl. Rosé	♟♟ 5
O OP Chardonnay Quattro Marzo '06	♟ 4
● OP Pinot Nero Coste del Roccolo '06	♟ 4
● OP Pinot Nero Ca' dell'Oca '04	♟ 5
O OP Pinot Nero Brut Cl. Anteo Riserva Del Poeta '98	♟♟ 6
O OP Pinot Nero Extra Brut Cl. Anteo Nature Ecru '99	♟♟ 5
O OP Pinot Nero Brut Cl. Riserva del Poeta '99	♟♟ 6
O OP Chardonnay Quattro Marzo '05	♟♟ 4*

O Franciacorta Extra Dry	♟♟ 5
O Franciacorta Brut	♟♟ 5
O TdF Bianco Curtefranca '06	♟♟ 4*
O Franciacorta Satèn '03	♟♟ 6
● TdF Rosso Curtefranca '05	♟ 4
⊙ Franciacorta Rosé Brut	♟ 5
O Franciacorta Extra Brut Bagnadore '02	♟♟ 6
O Franciacorta Satèn '01	♟♟ 6
O Franciacorta Satèn '00	♟♟ 6
O Franciacorta Bagnadore I '99	♟♟ 6
O TdF Bianco Curtefranca '05	♟♟ 4
O Franciacorta Satèn '02	♟♟ 6

Bellaria

FRAZ. MAIRANO
VIA CASTEL DEL LUPO, 28
27045 CASTEGGIO [PV]
TEL. 038383203
www.vinibellaria.it

ANNUAL PRODUCTION 50,000 bottles
HECTARES UNDER VINE 19.5
VITICULTURE METHOD Conventional

The 2003 vintage marks the return of the flagship wines from the estate managed by Paolo Massone: Bricco Sturnèl, from 80 per cent cabernet sauvignon and 20 per cent barbera, and La Macchia, from pure merlot. Although they did not attain the heights of 2001, they did do very well when they reached our finals. Both wines are characterized by a very deep ruby hue and pay the price for the torrid temperatures of the vintage with evolved, overripe fruit, particularly on the nose. The palate is much better. Bricco Sturnèl, which is superior overall, has plenty of flesh and structure, but also freshness and a few sharp edges due to the still maturing fine-grained tannins while La Macchia is softer and jammier. Both require more time in bottle to develop fully. Barbera Olmetto '04 is well made, varietal and fresh tasting with cherry and cocoa aromas and well-calibrated oak. Bonarda La Bria '06 is pleasant, showing just the right amount of tannins, while the attractive golden Chardonnay Costa Soprana '04 still needs time to find the right balance between fruit and oak.

★ Bellavista

VIA BELLAVISTA, 5
25030 ERBUSCO [BS]
TEL. 0307762000
www.terramoretti.it

ANNUAL PRODUCTION 1,000,000 bottles
HECTARES UNDER VINE 184
VITICULTURE METHOD Conventional

It's been a good year, to echo the title of Peter Mayle's charming novel, for two of the Moretti family's estates: Petra in Tuscany, whose Petra '04 won our Three Glass award, and Bellavista, the head of the group, which achieved its umpteenth victory with the extraordinary Extra Brut Vittorio Moretti '01, one of the best wines we tasted this year. The cherry on the cake is our Oenologist of the Year award, which went to Mattia Vezzola, the heart and soul of Bellavista, who has dedicated himself to the estate for decades, becoming emblematic of a viticultural and oenological style that respects the environment, terroir and type of wine produced. The deep, well-structured, flowery Riserva Moretti '01 is flanked by the crisp, elegant, mineral Gran Cuvée Brut '03 and the Gran Cuvée Pas Operé '01, with captivating peach tones and overall complexity. Bianco del Convento dell'Annunciata '04 is full flavoured, mineral and zesty with plenty of fruity pulp. But the entire Bellavista range boasts impressive finesse, elegance and typicity.

● Bricco Sturnèl '03	♆♆	5
● La Macchia '03	♆♆	5
● OP Barbera Olmetto '04	♆♆	4
● OP Bornarda Vivace La Bria '06	♆♆	4*
O OP Chardonnay Costa Soprana '04	♆	5
● Bricco Sturnèl '01	♆♆	5
● La Macchia '00	♆♆	5
● La Macchia '01	♆♆	5
● OP Barbera Olmetto '01	♆♆	4
O OP Chardonnay Costa Soprana '03	♆♆	5
● OP Barbera Olmetto '03	♆♆	4

O Franciacorta Extra Brut Vittorio Moretti '01	♆♆♆	8
O Franciacorta Gran Cuvée Brut '03	♆♆	7
O TdF Bianco Convento dell'Annunciata '04	♆♆	6
O Franciacorta Gran Cuvée Pas Operé '01	♆♆	7
O Franciacorta Cuvée Brut	♆♆	6
O TdF Bianco Uccellanda '04	♆♆	6
O TdF Bianco '06	♆♆	4*
⊙ Franciacorta Rosé Brut Gran Cuvée '03	♆♆	7
⊙ Franciacorta Gran Cuvée Satèn	♆♆	7
O Franciacorta Grand Cuvée Pas Operé '00	♆♆♆	7
O Franciacorta Grand Cuvée Brut '98	♆♆♆	6
O Franciacorta Grand Cuvée Brut '99	♆♆♆	6
O Franciacorta Gran Cuvée Brut '02	♆♆♆	7

Cantina Sociale Bergamasca

VIA BERGAMO, 10
24060 SAN PAOLO D'ARGON [BG]
TEL. 035951098
www.cantinabergamasca.it

ANNUAL PRODUCTION 650,000 bottles
HECTARES UNDER VINE 90
VITICULTURE METHOD Conventional

Cantina Sociale Bergamasca's Valcalepio Moscato Passito Perseo '03 is, as always, frank, well crafted and true to type with a balanced berry fruit nose and well-calibrated tannins. Valcalepio Rosso Akros Riserva '03 shows a bright ruby shading into garnet and boasts typical notes of bell pepper, hay and spices, with good flesh and overall harmony. Valcalepio Rosso Vigna del Conte Riserva '04 is more structured but needs longer bottle ageing to achieve perfect balance, the promise of which earned it Two Glasses. Riserva della Costa '03 has a good nose, fairly fine-grained tannins and reasonable structure. The pleasant, moderately fragrant Manzoni Bianco Sogno is a simple, refreshing white made from pure incrocio Manzoni, a cross of pinot bianco with riesling renano. The two Orologio Valcalepios, Bianco '06 and Rosso '05, are well crafted and true to type, not to say good value for money. Schiava '06, fermented after brief maceration on the skins, is fresh tasting with a fairly deep hue and clear raspberry aromas. Rosso della Bergamasca '06, from merlot, cabernet and franconia, is pleasant while Valcalepio Bianco Leukos '06 is slightly below par.

Guido Berlucchi & C.

LOC. BORGONATO
P.ZZA DURANTI, 4
25040 CORTE FRANCA [BS]
TEL. 030984381
www.berlucchi.it

ANNUAL PRODUCTION 5,000,000 bottles
HECTARES UNDER VINE 580
VITICULTURE METHOD Conventional

Franco Ziliani founded the cellar back in 1961, since when he has been the soul of this leading producer of sparklers and one of the best-loved names in Italian wine worldwide. Gradually, he has handed over the estate to his children, oenologist Arturo, Paolo, who heads the commercial sector, and Cristina, who handles public relations and the Antica Cantina Fratta. The generation handover is bringing results and we note the constant growth in quality of the wines from a cellar that has an annual production of 5,000,000 bottles and controls 500 hectares of vineyards, including 80 that are estate-owned. Although the jewel in the crown is the non-vintage Franciacorta Cuvée Storica Brut, along with the Cellarius Brut and Brut Rosé, both from '03, what surprised us most was the tasting of the basic sparkler Cuvée Imperiale Brut. It has a production run of around 3,500,000 bottles and shows fresh, zesty and packed with fruit, flaunting an extremely attractive, caressing sparkle. As they say in Reims, a winery should be judged on its basic Brut so our compliments go to Guido Berlucchi & C.!

● Valcalepio Rosso Vigna del Conte Ris. '04	♟♟ 5
● Valcalepio Moscato Passito Perseo '03	♟♟ 6
● Valcalepio Rosso Akros Ris. '03	♟♟ 4*
○ Manzoni Bianco Sogno '06	♟ 3
⊙ Schiava '06	♟ 3
○ Valcalepio Bianco Leukos '06	♟ 3
● Rosso '06	♟ 3
○ Valcalepio Bianco Orologio '06	♟ 3
● Valcalepio Rosso della Costa Ris. '03	♟ 6
● Valcalepio Rosso Orologio '05	♟ 3
● Valcalepio Moscato Passito Perseo '01	♟♟ 6
● Valcalepio Moscato Passito Perseo '02	♟♟ 6
● Valcalepio Rosso Akros Ris. '02	♟♟ 4
● Valcalepio Rosso Orologio '04	♟♟ 3*

○ Cellarius Brut '03	♟♟ 6
⊙ Cellarius Brut Rosé '03	♟♟ 6
○ Franciacorta Brut Cuvée Storica	♟♟ 5
○ Gavi V. Il Beneficio '05	♟♟ 5
○ Gavi La Bollina '06	♟♟ 4*
○ Cuvée Imperiale Brut	♟ 5
○ Cuvée Imperiale Brut Extrême	♟ 5
⊙ Cuvée Imperiale Max Rosé	♟ 5
○ TdF Curtefranca '06	♟ 4
○ Cellarius Brut '02	♟♟ 6
⊙ Cellarius Brut Rosé '02	♟♟ 6

F.lli Berlucchi

loc. Borgonato
via Broletto, 2
25040 Corte Franca [BS]
tel. 030984451
www.berlucchifranciacorta.it

ANNUAL PRODUCTION 400,000 bottles
HECTARES UNDER VINE 70
VITICULTURE METHOD Conventional

Pia Donata Berlucchi, president of the Donne del Vino association, has always put enthusiasm and passion into the management of the family estate that she shares with her four brothers. Aided by her daughter Tilli Rizzo and oenologist Cesare Ferrari, Pia releases a range of Franciacortas and still wines that have few rivals in the area, all produced from the family's 70 hectares of vineyards. Satèn '03, for example, is very stylish, with soft overtones of fruit and vanilla supported by fresh acid notes and underscored by a gentle sparkle, ending in a complex and very long mineral finish. The Brut Rosé '03 confirms itself one of the best of its type, with an appealing floral nose and a firm, sinewy, tangy palate. Pas Dosé '03 boasts complexity and charming hints of aromatic herbs while the Brut '03 is dominated by delightful notes of hazelnut, oak and toast, which do not cover the freshness of the fruit. Still wines worthy of mention include Casa delle Colonne, an agreeably deep Bordeaux blend, and the well-made Terre di Franciacorta Bianco '06 and Rosso '05.

○ Franciacorta Satèn '03	🍷🍷	6
● Casa delle Colonne	🍷🍷	8
○ Franciacorta Pas Dosé '03	🍷🍷	6
○ Franciacorta Brut '03	🍷🍷	5
⊙ Franciacorta Rosé Brut '03	🍷🍷	5
○ TdF Bianco '06	🍷	3
● TdF Rosso '05	🍷	3
○ TdF Bianco Dossi delle Querce '04	ΥΥ	4
○ Franciacorta Satèn '02	ΥΥ	6
○ Franciacorta Satèn '01	ΥΥ	6
⊙ Franciacorta Rosé Brut '01	ΥΥ	5
○ Franciacorta Brut '01	ΥΥ	5

Bersi Serlini

loc. Cereto
via Cereto, 7
25050 Provaglio d'Iseo [BS]
tel. 0309823338
www.bersiserlini.it

ANNUAL PRODUCTION 220,000 bottles
HECTARES UNDER VINE 32
VITICULTURE METHOD Conventional

The Bersi Serlini family enthusiastically tends 30 hectares of vineyards on the land once cultivated by Cluniac monks from the nearby monastery of San Pietro in Lamosa. The medieval building at the centre of the estate that formerly housed the cellar is now part of a well-equipped modern structure that produces excellent wines and Franciacortas and features multi-purpose areas. This year, Maddalena Bersi Serlini, her sister Paola and their competent technical staff presented an excellent Extra Brut '02, with a nose of citrus fruit and aromatic herbs and a complex, tangy palate, and a voluptuously elegant Satèn vaunting notes of croissant and white-fleshed fruit jam. The Brut Vintage '02 confirms its thoroughbred status with zestiness and a soft, enfolding, juicy palate. Cuvée n. 4 impressed with its good entry on the palate and soft notes of ripe fruit while the basic Brut is fresh tasting and approachable. The Brut Rosé Rosa Rosae made a good debut, revealing delicate hints of wild berries.

○ Franciacorta Extra Brut '02	🍷🍷	6
○ Franciacorta Brut Vintage '02	🍷🍷	8
○ Franciacorta Satèn	🍷🍷	6
○ Franciacorta Brut Cuvée n. 4	🍷🍷	6
○ Franciacorta Brut	🍷	6
⊙ Franciacorta Brut Rosa Rosae	🍷	6
○ Franciacorta Extra Brut '01	ΥΥ	6
○ Franciacorta Extra Brut '00	ΥΥ	6
○ Franciacorta Brut Vintage '00	ΥΥ	7

Bisi

LOC. CASCINA SAN MICHELE
FRAZ. VILLA MARONE, 70
27040 SAN DAMIANO AL COLLE [PV]
TEL. 038575037
www.aziendagricolabisi.it

ANNUAL PRODUCTION 100,000 bottles
HECTARES UNDER VINE 30
VITICULTURE METHOD Conventional

Claudio Bisi's Barbera Roncolongo is a
regular at our tasting finals, confirming its
status as the very best in Oltrepò year after
year. The '04 vintage also did well with a
broad aromatic spectrum that nicely
integrates spices with tobacco notes and
crisp wild berries before the deep, robust
palate follows through, supported by a
steely vein of acidity. It's already excellent
but is destined to improve further with
ageing. Cabernet Sauvignon Primm '04 has
an impenetrable colour, a balsamic, spicy
nose and good structure. This is another
wine that will improve with cellar time. The
excellent Bonarda Frizzante '06 is soft, well
balanced and fruity and the dried-grape
wine Villa Marone '04 is also very good.
Made with grapes from an old malvasia
vineyard, it shows a beautiful amber colour
with a broad nose of candied fruit, honey,
citrus fruit, aromatic herbs and more
besides, and impressive structure
supported by perfect acidity. We also
awarded Two Glasses to the Riesling '06,
from pure riesling renano, whose floral nose
is just starting to display mineral notes. The
nicely structured Pinot Nero Calonga '04
has attractive aromas but is a little dry on
the fruit.

Ca' dei Frati

FRAZ. LUGANA
VIA FRATI, 22
25019 SIRMIONE [BS]
TEL. 030919468
www.cadeifrati.it

ANNUAL PRODUCTION 677,000 bottles
HECTARES UNDER VINE 68
VITICULTURE METHOD Conventional

The Dal Cero brothers' wines have an
unmistakable profile: fruity depth, exemplary
cleanliness and seductive softness. Year
after year, their elegant bottles confirm the
unique style that has made the estate one
of the undisputed benchmarks for
winemaking in Lake Garda and Lugana in
particular. A perfect example of Ca' dei
Frati's production is Lugana I Frati, whose
'06 vintage is once again highly drinkable,
refreshing, and bursting with apple-like and
floral notes. As usual, Lugana Brolettino put
up an admirable performance. Pratto offers
a new take on trebbiano, placing the accent
on overripeness and an aromatic boost
from sauvignon and chardonnay. The sweet
Tre Filèr impressed us again this year with
its great finesse while the creamy, classic
method Cuvée dei Frati is a charmer and
the Chiaretto is one of the finest on the
shores of Lake Garda. Ronchedone, the
cellar's red, has sweet fruit and caressing
tannins.

● OP Barbera Roncolongo '04	♟♟	5
● OP Bonarda Frizzante '06	♟	3*
● Primm '04	♟♟	5
○ OP Riesling '06	♟♟	3*
○ Bianco Passito Villa Marone '04	♟♟	5
● Calonga '04	♟	5
● OP Barbera Roncolongo '01	♟♟	5
● OP Barbera Roncolongo '03	♟♟	5
● Caionga '03	♟♟	5
● OP Bonarda Frizzante '05	♟♟	3*

○ Lugana I Frati '06	♟♟	4*
○ Cuvée dei Frati Brut '04	♟♟	4
○ Pratto '05	♟♟	4
○ Lugana Brolettino '05	♟♟	4
◉ Riviera del Garda Bresciano I Frati Chiaretto '06	♟♟	4
○ Tre Filer '04	♟♟	5
● Ronchedone '04	♟♟	4
○ Pratto '96	♟♟♟	4
○ Lugana Brolettino Grande Annata '99	♟♟	6
○ Lugana I Frati '05	♟♟	4
○ Lugana I Frati '04	♟♟	4
● Ronchedone Grande Annata '99	♟♟	6
○ Pratto '02	♟♟	5
○ Lugana Brolettino '04	♟♟	4
○ Lugana Brolettino '01	♟♟	4
○ Pratto '03	♟♟	5
● Ronchedone '03	♟♟	4
○ Pratto '04	♟♟	4

★★★ Ca' del Bosco
VIA ALBANO ZANELLA, 13
25030 ERBUSCO [BS]
TEL. 0307766111
www.cadelbosco.it

Ca' di Frara
VIA CASA FERRARI, 1
27040 MORNICO LOSANA [PV]
TEL. 0383892299
www.cadifrara.it

ANNUAL PRODUCTION 1.500,000 bottles
HECTARES UNDER VINE 146
VITICULTURE METHOD Conventional

ANNUAL PRODUCTION 260,000 bottles
HECTARES UNDER VINE 48
VITICULTURE METHOD Conventional

Maurizio Zanella has built a state-of-the-art winery of rare beauty at Erbusco, in the heart of Franciacorta. Here, technology rubs shoulders with works of art. Maurizio produces a selection of Franciacortas and still wines of international renown, made exclusively from the grapes of the estate's 150 hectares of vineyards. The range is very wide and of extraordinarily high quality. Even in the absence of its most prestigious Franciacorta, the Annamaria Clementi selection, which is still ageing, Ca' del Bosco took two Three Glass awards for the unbeatably elegant and invigorating Dosage Zéro '03, which has plenty of backbone and fruit, and the complex, deep, cosseting Satèn '02, a perfectly balanced wine in the crémant style: a blanc de blancs with slightly less carbonation. The list also comprises a series of extraordinary wines, including the lively, opulent Chardonnay '04, which is fresh and well coordinated, the still very young Pinot Nero Pinèro '03, and the Franciacorta Brut '03 with its delicate notes of medicinal herbs. The recently disgorged Franciacorta Brut Cuvée Decennale '96 is a little gem not to be missed.

Year after year, with great tenacity and the unfailing aid of his mother Daniela, father Tullio and brother Matteo, Luca Bellani is constructing one of the most interesting estates in the Oltrepò Pavese. The average quality of the entire list is always very high with peaks of excellence each season. This year, the best performer at our tastings was Riesling Apogeo '06, from late-harvest grapes like the estate's signature Pinot Grigio. While the latter always stands out for its balance, cleanliness, fullness and elegance, the Apogeo is a cut above, thanks to its wonderful fruit and flower aromas, which are echoed on the rich, harmonious palate. The OP Rosso Riserva Il Frater '04 has a slightly different style this time round, showing a balsamic nose and its customary fine-grained tannins, although it leans more towards elegance than weight. Pinot Nero Il Raro Nero '05 is good and true to type; with a touch more finesse, it would have reached our finals. The two IGT wines, Rosso '04, a barbera and pinot nero-heavy blend, and Bianco '06, from chardonnay, riesling, malvasia and other varieties, are both first rate but need more time in bottle.

O Franciacorta Satèn '02	♟♟♟	7
O Franciacorta Dosage Zéro '03	♟♟♟	7
O Franciacorta Brut '03	♟♟	7
O TdF Chardonnay '04	♟♟	8
O Franciacorta Cuvée del Decennale '96	♟♟	8
● Pinèro '03	♟♟	8
● TdF Rosso Curtefranca '04	♟♟	5
O TdF Bianco Curtefranca '06	♟♟	5
O Franciacorta Brut	♟	6
O Franciacorta Cuvée Annamaria Clementi '93	♟♟♟	6
O Franciacorta Dosage Zéro '00	♟♟♟	8
O Franciacorta Cuvée Annamaria Clementi '91	♟♟♟	6
O Franciacorta Cuvée Annamaria Clementi '90	♟♟♟	6
O TdF Chardonnay '02	♟♟♟	8
O Franciacorta Cuvée Annamaria Clementi '96	♟♟♟	8
O Franciacorta Cuvée Annamaria Clementi '98	♟♟♟	8
O Franciacorta Cuvée Annamaria Clementi '99	♟♟♟	8
O Franciacorta Cuvée Annamaria Clementi '97	♟♟♟	8
O Franciacorta Cuvée Annamaria Clementi '95	♟♟♟	8

O OP Riesling Renano Apogeo Raccolta Tardiva '06	♟♟	4*
O Io Bianco '06	♟♟	5
● OP Rosso Il Frater Ris. '04	♟♟	6
● OP Pinot Nero Il Raro Nero '05	♟♟	5
O OP Pinot Grigio Raccolta Tardiva '06	♟♟	4
● Io Rosso '04	♟♟	5
O Io Bianco '02	♟♟	5
O OP Pinot Grigio Raccolta Tardiva '01	♟♟	4
O Io Rosso '03	♟♟	5
O OP Pinot Grigio Raccolta Tardiva '02	♟♟	4
● OP Pinot Nero Il Raro '01	♟♟	5
● OP Rosso Il Frater Ris. '03	♟♟	6
● OP Rosso Il Frater Ris. '01	♟♟	6
O OP Pinot Grigio Raccolta Tardiva '04	♟♟	4
● Cento '03	♟♟	5
O Io Bianco '04	♟♟	5
O OP Riesling Renano Apogeo '05	♟♟	4*
O OP Riesling Renano Apogeo Raccolta Tardiva '04	♟♟	4
O OP Riesling Renano Apogeo '03	♟♟	4

Ca' Lojera
LOC. ROVIZZA
VIA 1886, 19
25019 SIRMIONE [BS]
TEL. 0457551901
www.calojera.com

ANNUAL PRODUCTION 160,000 bottles
HECTARES UNDER VINE 18
VITICULTURE METHOD Conventional

Ambra and Franco Tiraboschi never seem to be in any hurry to bottle and sell their wines. They have always believed in the now widely acknowledged cellarability of Lugana and have consequently chosen to keep several vintages of their whites available to their customers. This is particularly true for Lugana Superiore, which is released only after long ageing: suffice it to say that the most recent vintage on sale is the '04. The juicy, apple-like Superiore '04 di Ca' Lojera is full of the subtle mineral veins typical of trebbiano grown in the clayey soils of Lugana while the basic Lugana '06 is as refreshing, vegetal and appealing as ever. Hints of dried apricot and floral notes characterize the spirited Ravel, from partially dried grapes. Riserva del Lupo '05 probably requires more time in bottle to express itself to the full. This year, the reds put up a good show, with Cabernet and Merlot from the hills on the edge of Lugana. The rosé Monte della Guardia is as reliable as ever and is usually at its best after the winter, almost as though reflecting the estate's unhurried character.

Il Calepino
VIA SURRIPE, 1
24060 CASTELLI CALEPIO [BG]
TEL. 035847178
www.ilcalepino.it

ANNUAL PRODUCTION 220,000 bottles
HECTARES UNDER VINE 15
VITICULTURE METHOD Conventional

Despite presenting a pretty comprehensive range of products, Il Calepino continues to shine for its classic method sparklers. This year, we particularly liked the non-vintage Brut Magnum Cuvée, which is sold only in 1.5-litre bottles. It's straw yellow, with small, vigorous bubbles, prominent but not domineering oak, aromas of cakes, vanilla and toasted hazelnut and good pulp, backbone and depth. Fra' Ambrogio Riserva '01 is also good, with more obvious oak and evolved notes. Although the style is different, the quality is similar, with more than decent richness supported by acidity and a lingering finish. Epias, a sweet Chardonnay with hints of citrus and overripe tropical fruit, is well crafted with good backbone. Kalòs '04, an IGT from cabernet sauvignon, has an overripe style with a nose of wild berry jam featuring notes of spice and pencil lead in the background. Valcalepio Rosso Surìe Riserva '03 flaunts fine aromas with plenty of body and extract but it failed to reach the Two Glass mark, as it's slightly lacking in balance. The Valcalepio Rosso and Bianco and the other sparklers presented are all well made.

O Lugana Sup. '04	🍷🍷 5
O Lugana '06	🍷🍷 4
O Ravel '04	🍷🍷 5
● Garda Cabernet '05	🍷 4
O Lugana Sup. Riserva del Lupo '04	🍷 5
O Garda Chardonnay '04	🍷 4
☉ Monte della Guardia Rosato '06	🍷 3
● Garda Merlot '05	🍷 4
O Lugana Sup. Riserva del Lupo '03	🍷🍷 5
O Lugana '04	🍷🍷 4
O Lugana Sup. '03	🍷🍷 5
O Ravel '03	🍷🍷 5
O Lugana Riserva del Lupo '04	🍷🍷 5
O Lugana Sup. '02	🍷🍷 4
O Lugana '05	🍷🍷 4
O Lugana Sup. '99	🍷🍷 4
O Lugana Sup. '01	🍷🍷 4
O Lugana Sup. Riserva del Lupo '01	🍷🍷 4

O Brut Cl. Ris. Fra Ambrogio '01	🍷🍷 6
O Brut Magnum Cuvée M. Cl.	🍷🍷 8
● Kalòs '04	🍷🍷 7
O Chardonnay Epias	🍷🍷 6
O Brut Cl. Il Calepino '03	🍷 5
● Valcalepio Rosso Surìe Ris. '03	🍷 5
● Valcalepio Rosso '05	🍷 4
O Extra Brut Cl. Il Calepino '02	🍷 5
☉ Brut Cl. Rosé Il Calepino '03	🍷 4
O Valcalepio Bianco '06	🍷 4
O Brut Cl. Il Calepino '02	🍷🍷 4
O Extra Brut Cl. Il Calepino '01	🍷🍷 5

Cantrina

FRAZ. CANTRINA
VIA COLOMBERA, 7
25081 BEDIZZOLE [BS]
TEL. 0306871052
www.cantrina.it

ANNUAL PRODUCTION 20,000 bottles
HECTARES UNDER VINE 5.8
VITICULTURE METHOD Conventional

You need a good helping of single-mindedness to plough your own furrow the way Cantrina does. From the very outset, this small estate, whose first harvests date back to a decade ago, has drawn on Dario Dattoli's farsighted intuition to create first-rate wines that bring out not only the grape variety but above all the character of this tiny district in the deepest hinterland of the Garda zone. Cristina Inganni and Diego Lavo continue this task undaunted, aided by consultant Celestino Gaspari, and their Nepomuceno Merlot has become one of the benchmark reds of the area. The '03 is concentrated and minerally but highly drinkable and the 2004, tasted from the vat, also promises well. Rinè, a blend of sauvignon, sémillon and riesling, is elegantly floral. Eretico defies all attempts at classification: produced from the overripe pinot nero grapes of the torrid summer of 2003, it astonishes and surprises with intriguingly sweet, concentrated wild berries. Zerdì '05, from rebo, has dense fruit and a rustic spiciness.

Caseo

FRAZ. CASEO, 9
27040 CANEVINO [PV]
TEL. 038599937
www.caseowines.com

ANNUAL PRODUCTION 280,000 bottles
HECTARES UNDER VINE 47
VITICULTURE METHOD Conventional

Each year, we point out that this estate fulfils only part of its great potential. Each time, we find good wines and dubious ones, always of different types. One year, we are convinced by the sparklers, the next by the still whites, and so on. This year, our favourite was Malleo '03, a deep, well-made blend of barbera, cabernet and pinot nero, with intact wild berries on the nose and palate, good balance and length. The two Moscatos are also good. Vigna Soleggia '03, from partially dried grapes, is amber with pronounced notes of hazelnut and toast and nice backbone whereas the attractive sparkling La Dote is fresh and clean with hints of citrus fruit and honey. Riesling Le Segrete '06, from pure riesling renano, has good pulp and floral notes with mineral hints that have just started to emerge. Barbera Donna Clarizia '03 boasts bottled black cherries, plenty of oak and good structure. The only reason for its failure to achieve better results is that it's a little short on overall balance. Sauvignon I Crocioni '06 can also be confidently awaited. Bonarda Costa delle More '06 is dark and evolved, giving marked forest floor, while Gioiacaseo and Pinot Nero Rosé, the two classic method sparklers, are both pleasant.

● Nepomuceno '03	♈♈	6
● Eretico '03	♈♈	6
○ Rinè '05	♈♈	4
● Zerdì '05	♈♈	4
● Nepomuceno '01	♈♈	5
● Corteccio '01	♈♈	5
○ Sole di Dario '00	♈♈	6
○ Sole di Dario '03	♈♈	6
○ Sole di Dario '01	♈♈	6
○ Rinè '04	♈♈	4
● Garda Merlot Nepomuceno '99	♈♈	5
○ Rinè '03	♈♈	4
● Garda Merlot Nepomuceno '00	♈♈	6

○ OP Moscato La Dote '06	♈♈	4
○ OP Riesling Renano Le Segrete '06	♈♈	4
○ OP Moscato Passito Soleggia '03	♈♈	6
● Malleo '03	♈♈	6
● OP Barbera Donna Clarizia '03	♈	6
● OP Bonarda Vivace Costa delle More '06	♈	4
⊙ OP Pinot Nero Spumante Cl. Rosé	♈	5
○ OP Sauvignon Blanc I Crocioni '06	♈	4
○ Gioiacaseo Brut '03	♈	5
○ OP Moscato La Dote '04	♈♈	4
○ OP Sauvignon Blanc I Crocioni '04	♈♈	4

Cantina di Casteggio
VIA TORINO, 96
27045 CASTEGGIO [PV]
TEL. 0383806311
www.cantinacasteggio.it

ANNUAL PRODUCTION 2.500,000 bottles
HECTARES UNDER VINE 1.050
VITICULTURE METHOD Conventional

Again, Barbera Console Marcello is Cantina di Casteggio's best wine, this time with the '05 vintage. As usual, it shows an almost impenetrable ruby hue and an intense nose with aromas ranging from ripe wild berries to tobacco, spices and chocolate. On the palate, it's rich, rounded and velvety with the acid backbone typical of the variety, which supports the long finish. Barbera Autari, again from the '05 vintage, has a different style that is less complex and perhaps truer to type but very pleasant, well rounded and balanced. The fresh-tasting Riesling Italico Clefi '06 also performed well, with a nose of flowers, grapefruit, peach and apricot, good fruity pulp and mineral notes on the finish. Although Longobardo '05, an IGT from croatina, barbera, pinot nero and cabernet sauvignon, notched up Two Glasses, it is less convincing than previous vintages because of rather over-extracted fruit and still immature tannins. It's sure to improve in bottle, though. The three Postumio classic method sparklers, all from the '04 vintage, are well made and represent good value for money. Malvasia, Sauvignon and Pinot Grigio '06 are well made and varietal.

CastelFaglia
FRAZ. CALINO
LOC. BOSCHI, 3
25046 CAZZAGO SAN MARTINO [BS]
TEL. 059812411
www.cavicchioli.it

ANNUAL PRODUCTION 250,000 bottles
HECTARES UNDER VINE 20
VITICULTURE METHOD Conventional

The Cavicchioli family from Modena are Lambrusco specialists who arrived in Franciacorta in 1989. Their Cazzago San Martino estate currently produces an impressive 250,000 bottles per year from its own vineyards. House oenologist Sandro Cavicchioli creates an excellent range of wines, which is spearheaded by the Monogram selections. Monogram Brut '98 is complex with a well-coordinated nose and palate giving antique and exotic wood, hazelnut and vanilla aromas combined with a solid structure, sound fruit and good acid backbone. The Satèn Monogram has soft notes of ripe apricot and cakes while the basic Satèn has fresh flowery and citrus sensations on the nose and palate. Another good wine is the Franciacorta Extra Brut, with springtime notes of white-fleshed fruit, while the Brut and Rosé are also pleasant and well made. The two clean, well-styled Prestigio DOCs are good value for money. The Bianco '06 is spirited and fruity and the delicately tannic Rosso '05 discloses notes of blackberry and raspberry.

● OP Barbera Autari '05	▼▼	4
● OP Barbera Console Marcello '05	▼▼	4*
● Il Longobardo '05	▼▼	6
○ OP Riesling Italico Clefi '06	▼▼	3*
○ OP Malvasia '06	▼	3
○ OP Pinot Grigio '06	▼	3
○ OP Sauvignon '06	▼	3
⊙ OP Pinot Nero Brut Postumio Rosè '04	▼	4
○ OP Pinot Nero Brut Postumio '04	▼	4
○ Postumio Brut 100° anniversario	▼	4
● OP Barbera Autari '03	▼▼	3*
● OP Barbera Console Marcello '04	▼▼	4*
● Il Longobardo '02	▼▼	4
● OP Barbera Autari '04	▼▼	3*
● Il Longobardo '04	▼▼	6

○ Franciacorta Brut Monogram '98	▼▼	6
○ Franciacorta Satèn	▼▼	5
○ Franciacorta Satèn Monogram	▼▼	5
○ Franciacorta Extra Brut	▼▼	5
○ Franciacorta Brut	▼	5
⊙ Franciacorta Rosé Brut	▼	5
○ TdF Bianco Prestigio '06	▼	3*
● TdF Rosso Prestigio '05	▼	3*
○ Franciacorta Monogram Brut '99	▼▼	7
○ Franciacorta Monogram Brut '97	▼▼	7

Cavalleri

VIA PROVINCIALE, 96
25030 ERBUSCO [BS]
TEL. 0307760217
www.cavalleri.it

ANNUAL PRODUCTION 250,000 bottles
HECTARES UNDER VINE 43
VITICULTURE METHOD Conventional

It's common knowledge that the Cavalleri family has very deep roots in Franciacorta. Giovanni Cavalleri, the winery's founder, established a profound bond with this territory and invested his energy and creativity in transforming the family estate into one of the finest names in Italian winemaking. Today, the winery is run by his daughter Giulia and an efficient technical staff, who turn out a range of wines of the highest quality. We were very excited by our tasting of the recently disgorged Collezione Esclusiva '99. In fact, this refreshingly lively, elegant Franciacorta has such spectacular complexity and depth that we had to give it our Sparkler of the Year award. You'll be bowled over by the fullness of its splendid spectrum of aromatics, from rockrose to acacia honey, wax and coffee, which culminate in a stunningly long finish. But the whole of the list is outstanding, including wines such as Rosso Tajardino '04, Bianco Rampaneto '05 and the '03 Franciacorta Satèn and Pas Dosé.

Battista Cola

VIA SANT'ANNA, 22
25030 ADRO [BS]
TEL. 0307356195
www.colabattista.it

ANNUAL PRODUCTION 70,000 bottles
HECTARES UNDER VINE 10
VITICULTURE METHOD Conventional

The Cola family manage a classic little wine estate with ten hectares of well-aspected terraced vineyards on the slopes of Monte Alto. Their painstaking attention to production allows them to compete with the big names that have multi-million euro cellars and vineyards in every subzone of the DOCG. This year, we tasted an excellent Satèn that presents soft aromas of ripe damson veined with vegetal and citrus notes preceding a caressing but also solid, refreshingly bright palate. The Brut is equally good, its well-coordinated aromas of ripe apples, pears, vanilla and oak merging nicely with floral nuances. It's fresh, elegant and complex on the palate with plenty of fruit and softness. The Extra Brut is slightly over-evolved and less appealing. Terre di Franciacorta Bianco '06 is good, and came within a hair's breadth of Two Glasses, while the red Tamino '05 boasts pleasantly ripe fruit notes, soft tannins and good overall harmony.

O Franciacorta Collezione Esclusiva Brut '99	♟♟♟	8
O Franciacorta Brut	♟♟	5
O TdF Bianco Rampaneto '05	♟♟	4*
● TdF Rosso Tajardino '04	♟♟	5
O TdF Bianco '06	♟♟	4*
O Franciacorta Pas Dosé '03	♟♟	6
O Franciacorta Satèn '03	♟♟	6
O Franciacorta Collezione Brut '99	♟♟♟	6
O Franciacorta Collezione Esclusiva Brut '97	♟♟	7
⊙ Franciacorta Collezione Rosé '01	♟♟	6
O Franciacorta Satèn '01	♟♟	6
O Franciacorta Pas Dosé '00	♟♟	6
O Franciacorta Collezione Brut '01	♟♟	6
O Franciacorta Pas Dosé '01	♟♟	6
O Franciacorta Satèn '02	♟♟	6
O TdF Bianco Rampaneto '04	♟♟	4
O Franciacorta Pas Dosé '02	♟♟	6
● TdF Rosso Tajardino '03	♟♟	5

O Franciacorta Brut	♟♟	5*
O Franciacorta Satèn	♟♟	6
O Franciacorta Extra Brut	♟	4*
O TdF Bianco '06	♟	4
● TdF Rosso Tamino '05	♟	5
O Franciacorta Brut '02	♟♟	6
O Franciacorta Brut '01	♟♟	6
● TdF Rosso Tamino '03	♟♟	4*

Contadi Castaldi

LOC. FORNACE BIASCA
VIA COLZANO, 32
25030 ADRO [BS]
TEL. 0307450126
www.contadicastaldi.it

ANNUAL PRODUCTION 500,000 bottles
HECTARES UNDER VINE 100
VITICULTURE METHOD Conventional

Founded in the early 1990s, Contadi Castaldi belongs to the Terra Moretti group, like Petra in Tuscany and Bellavista in Franciacorta, to name but two other estates. It is capably and enthusiastically managed by Mario Falcetti, a Trentino oenologist with a past in research. The winery currently produces 500,000 bottles a year of mainly Franciacortas from the grapes of its own 18 hectares of vineyards and the 82 hectares it leases. If there's one wine that is truly representative of the estate, then it's the Satèn, witness the excellent Soul '00, which strolled into our tasting finals. This elegant, full wine is soft, yet has plenty of backbone and complexity with notes of intact fruit and vanilla, firm structure and good length. Satèn '03 is full-bodied and elegant, based on alluring soft notes of apricot and vanilla, and vaunts attractive hints of oak and toast. The fresh, fruity Terre Bianco '06 is attractively full and ranks among the best from the vintage while Terre Rosso '04 boasts a fruity nose, smooth tannins and good body. The other wines are also good.

Tenuta La Costaiola

VIA COSTAIOLA, 25
27054 MONTEBELLO
DELLA BATTAGLIA [PV]
TEL. 038383169
www.lacostaiola.it

ANNUAL PRODUCTION 180,000 bottles
HECTARES UNDER VINE 17
VITICULTURE METHOD Conventional

The quality of the wines presented this year by the estate owned by the Rossetti and Scrivani families is as high as ever. We'll start with Auriga '03, a powerful, meaty Barbera, whose depth is immediately apparent from its intense ruby hue. Aromas of mulberry blossom and black berry fruit lead into a palate whose alcohol is nicely balanced by acidity. All that was missing for admission to our finals was a slightly longer finish. Bonarda Giada '06 is very nicely made and well calibrated, with clear notes of berries and an attractive bright purplish-ruby colour. Once again, the refreshingly clean Haris is one of Oltrepò's best cuve close method sparklers, with aromas of summer fruits and flowers and a fairly long finish. The Pinot Nero Aiole '03 is overripe, spicy and very evolved. It's a good wine but has suffered from the torrid, very dry vintage. Vigna Bricca '05 is no longer an OP Rosso Riserva but an IGT that offers pleasant, fresh drinkability rather than weight and complexity. Croatina Vivace Massona '06 is soft and pleasing, as is Barbera Due Draghi '06, which has attractive ripe cherry aromas.

○ Franciacorta Soul Satèn '00	🍷🍷 7
○ Franciacorta Satèn '03	🍷🍷 6
○ Pinodisé	🍷🍷 5
● TdF Rosso Curtefranca '04	🍷🍷 4*
○ TdF Bianco Curtefranca '06	🍷🍷 4*
○ Franciacorta Brut	🍷 5
⊙ Franciacorta Brut Rosé '03	🍷 6
○ Franciacorta Zéro	🍷 5
○ Franciacorta Satèn '01	🍷🍷 6
○ Franciacorta Soul Satèn '99	🍷🍷 7
○ Franciacorta Satèn '00	🍷🍷 6
○ TdF Bianco Curtefranca '05	🍷🍷 4
○ Franciacorta Satèn '02	🍷🍷 6

● Auriga '03	🍷🍷 5
○ OP Pinot Nero Brut Haris	🍷🍷 4
● OP Bonarda Vivace Giada '06	🍷🍷 3*
● Aiole '03	🍷 5
● Vigna Bricca '05	🍷 4*
● OP Barbera I Due Draghi '05	🍷 4
● Croatina Vivace Massona '06	🍷 3
● Aiole '01	🍷🍷 5
● OP Rosso V. Bricca Ris. '02	🍷🍷 4
● Auriga '01	🍷🍷 5
● Aiole '99	🍷🍷 5

Costaripa

via Costa, 1a
25080 Moniga del Garda [BS]
tel. 0365502010
www.costaripa.it

ANNUAL PRODUCTION 330,000 bottles
HECTARES UNDER VINE 36
VITICULTURE METHOD Conventional

On the Brescian shore of Lake Garda, there is fierce debate about the expressive potential of groppello, the indigenous red grape variety of Valtenesi. Once almost exclusively used for easy-drinking wines, it is now rightly aiming at more ambitious goals while conserving its original characteristics. Imer and Mattia Vezzola wisely choose to age their Maim '04 longer than the previous vintages. The result is impressive, with juicy, satisfying strawberry-led fruit and serious length. Meanwhile, the other groppello reds, Castelline '06 and Campostarne '05, also support the impression that Costaripa is on the right course, marrying stylistic cleanliness with fruity charm. Mazane '06, from marzemino, is deep and distinctive. Further confirmation of Mattia Vezzola's extraordinary talent as a sparkling winemaker comes from the impeccable Costaripa Brut, from chardonnay. The Chiaretto Rosamara is reliable.

● Garda Cl. Groppello Maim '04	TT	5
● Marzemino Le Mazane '06	TT	4
○ Costaripa Brut	TT	5
● Garda Cl. Rosso Campostarne '05	TT	4
● Garda Cl. Groppello Vign. Le Castelline '06	TT	4
⊙ Garda Cl. Chiaretto Rosamara '06	T	4
● Garda Cl. Groppello Maim '00	YY	5
● Garda Cl. Groppello Maim '03	YY	5
● Garda Cl. Rosso Campostarne '02	YY	4*
● Marzemino Le Mazane '05	YY	4
● Garda Cl. Rosso Campostarne '03	YY	4
● Garda Cl. Groppello Vign. Le Castelline '05	YY	4
● Garda Cl. Groppello Maim '01	YY	5

Doria

loc. Casa Tacconi, 3
27040 Montalto Pavese [PV]
tel. 0383870143
www.vinidoria.com

ANNUAL PRODUCTION 140,000 bottles
HECTARES UNDER VINE 30
VITICULTURE METHOD Conventional

This year the Doria family and their master of the cellar Daniele Manini presented a very fine list. Even in the absence of the flagship to send to the finals, which it reached in several past editions of our Guide, almost all the wines effortlessly achieved Two Glasses. We'll start with AD Memorial '04, from nebbiolo, which shows a deep garnet with a complex nose of spice, coffee and bark, followed by notes of wild berries and attractive balsamic hints. On the palate, the fine-grained tannins mesh with good pulp and a long finish. Barbera AD '04, aged in chestnut tonneaux, has its usual intriguing "odd" aromas, which may initially perplex those perceiving them for the first time. Its pulp, cohesion and depth on the palate are very convincing. Riesling Roncobianco '04 is also very good and expresses the characteristic mineral and benzene notes of the variety, accompanied by attractive, crisp fruit and exemplary balance. Bonarda Vivace '06 is well crafted and pleasant while the deep, penetrating OP Rosso Roncorosso '04 appears closed and harsh at first but then opens up to reveal attractive fruity body and a wonderful finish. Brut Querciolo is fairly juicy with an evolved style.

● OP Barbera A.D. '04	TT	5
○ OP Riesling Renano Roncobianco '04	TT	4
● Rosso A.D. Memorial '04	TT	6
● OP Rosso Roncorosso '04	TT	4
● OP Bonarda Vivace '06	TT	4*
○ OP Pinot Nero Brut Querciolo	T	4
● OP Rosso Roncorosso '03	YY	4
● Rosso A.D. '99	YY	6
● Rosso A.D. '98	YY	6
● OP Barbera A.D. '01	YY	4
○ OP Riesling Renano Roncobianco '03	YY	4
○ OP Pinot Nero in bianco Querciolo '04	YY	4
● OP Barbera A.D. '03	YY	4
○ OP Pinot Nero in bianco Querciolo '03	YY	4

Sandro Fay

LOC. SAN GIACOMO DI TEGLIO
VIA PILA CASELLI, 1
23030 TEGLIO [SO]
TEL. 0342786071
elefay@tin.it

ANNUAL PRODUCTION 38,000 bottles
HECTARES UNDER VINE 13
VITICULTURE METHOD Conventional

The tried and tested Fay family team is ever active in research and experimentation, particularly in the vineyard. The fact that the winery did not present its famous Sforzato del Picchio for our tastings is the logical result of this focus and the estate's great respect for the vintages and ageing of its wines. Valgella Carterìa '04 lived up to our expectations. An elegant wine, with a strong personality, it boasts intense, spicy aromas of red berries and dried flowers and is full, juicy and long on the palate. Valgella Ca' Morei '04 flaunts a complex nose, with gamey notes, and a warm, full-bodied palate supported by good acidity. The unusual La Faya '04, from 55 per cent nebbiolo with merlot and syrah, has spicy aromas of pepper and cloves and a full, caressing palate with close-knit tannins and a slightly bitter finish. Sassella Il Glicine '04 is well made and highly drinkable with classic aromas and a fruity palate. The '04 Nebbiolo is nicely crafted but somewhat evanescent.

Ferghettina

VIA SALINE, 11
25030 ADRO [BS]
TEL. 0307451212
www.ferghettina.it

ANNUAL PRODUCTION 300,000 bottles
HECTARES UNDER VINE 100
VITICULTURE METHOD Conventional

The only thing missing to underscore the excellent job that Roberto Gatti's family is doing in this beautiful Franciacorta winery, with a total of 100 hectares of vineyards and a state-of-the-art cellar, is our Three Glass award, which two of its wines came very close to winning this year. They are the complex, delicate Franciacorta Extra Brut '00, with aromas of verbena and thyme and an elegant mineral palate, and the concentrated, vibrant Satèn '03, which also boasts hints of aromatic herbs with a firm and slightly austere character. The Rosé '03 is one of the best of its type, which is enjoying rapid growth in this area. The Ferghettina version focuses on subtlety, revealing attractive florality and hints of red berries. The basic Franciacorta Brut is well balanced and leisurely, in fact it has always been one of the best in the DOCG zone. The list ends with the two excellent Terre di Franciacorta wines: the Bianco '06 and the Rosso '05. Both are well made and true to type, although the white boasts superior structure and elegance.

● Valtellina Sup. Valgella Carterìa '04	♟♟ 5
● La Faya '04	♟♟ 5
● Valtellina Sup. Sassella Il Glicine '04	♟♟ 5
● Valtellina Sup. Valgella Ca' Morèi '04	♟♟ 5
● Nebbiolo '04	♟ 4
● Valtellina Sforzato Ronco del Picchio '02	♟♟♟ 7
● Valtellina Sforzato Ronco del Picchio '03	♟♟ 7
● Valtellina Sforzato Ronco del Picchio '04	♟♟ 7
● Valtellina Sup. Valgella Ca' Morèi '02	♟♟ 6
● Valtellina Sforzato Ronco del Picchio '98	♟♟ 6
● Valtellina Sforzato Ronco del Picchio '99	♟♟ 6
● Valtellina Sforzato Ronco del Picchio '01	♟♟ 6
● Valtellina Sup. Valgella Carteria '03	♟♟ 5
● Valtellina Sup. Sassella Il Glicine '03	♟♟ 5

○ Franciacorta Extra Brut '00	♟♟ 6
○ Franciacorta Satèn '03	♟♟ 6
○ Franciacorta Brut	♟♟ 5*
⊙ Franciacorta Rosé '03	♟♟ 6
○ TdF Bianco '06	♟♟ 4*
● TdF Rosso '05	♟ 4
○ Franciacorta Extra Brut '98	♟♟♟ 6
○ Franciacorta Satèn '99	♟♟♟ 6
○ Franciacorta Satèn '97	♟♟♟ 5*
○ Franciacorta Extra Brut '99	♟♟ 6
○ Franciacorta Satèn '01	♟♟ 6
⊙ Franciacorta Rosé '01	♟♟ 6
⊙ Franciacorta Satèn '02	♟♟ 6
○ TdF Bianco '05	♟♟ 4*

Le Fracce

FRAZ. MAIRANO
VIA CASTEL DEL LUPO, 5
27045 CASTEGGIO [PV]
TEL. 038382526
info@le-fracce.it

ANNUAL PRODUCTION 200,000 bottles
HECTARES UNDER VINE 40
VITICULTURE METHOD Conventional

Oltrepò Pavese Rosso Bohemi '03, the showcase wine of this splendid estate nestling among the hills of Casteggio, is not yet ready for release. In the meantime, Garboso '05, from pure barbera, is the cellar's best wine. Its ruby colour shades into garnet, introducing aromas of spices and wild berries and, above all, attractive, crisp fruity flesh with backbone, balance and a very long finish. The fine OP Riesling Landò '06 is refreshing, clean, varietal and elegant with a floral bouquet. La Rubiosa '06, always one of the best-made Bonardas, flaunts a deep purplish ruby, raspberry, strawberry and blueberry aromas on the nose and a balanced palate with crisp, healthy fruit, soft tannins and good depth. The '05 vintage of Cuvée Bussolera is as good as ever. Produced by the long Charmat method, with ageing for a year on the lees, it has very fine bubbles, a floral nose with hints of wild berries, peach, citrus fruits and cakes, and good length. The elegance of Pinot Grigio Levriere '06 echoes the style of oenologist Roberto Gerbino and would have scored higher if only it had shown a little more body. We were not very convinced by the OP Rosso Cirgà '03, which has good structure, but is evolved and overripe.

Frecciarossa

VIA VIGORELLI, 141
27045 CASTEGGIO [PV]
TEL. 0383804465
www.frecciarossa.com

ANNUAL PRODUCTION 120,000 bottles
HECTARES UNDER VINE 20
VITICULTURE METHOD Conventional

The performance of this historic Casteggio estate was unexceptional this year. Francigeno '04 and Uva Rara '06 were both missing and will be presented next year. As for one of the winery's leading wines, Pinot Nero Giorgio Odero, we were accustomed to more convincing versions, which often reached our finals. The '04 is still rather immature: the wild berries and spices conferred by the oak are not yet well integrated and the tannins need time to develop fully. What we like best at the moment is the long finish, characterized by an attractive hint of liquorice. Still, bottle ageing will make it more harmonious and we awarded it Two Glasses. Bonarda Vivace Dardo '06 is very attractive, with well-calibrated tannins and deep blueberry, gooseberry and forest floor notes. Le Praielle '04 is an IGT whose barbera pedigree is immediately apparent from the bright ruby hue and aromas of cherry and blackberry with spicy undertones. It's fairly soft and balanced but could have scored higher with a little more length. The same is true for the upfront Riesling Gli Orti '06, which shows good backbone but is slightly short. Pinot Nero in Bianco Sillery '06 is very decent.

● Garboso '05	♙♙	4*
● OP Bonarda La Rubiosa '06	♙♙	4*
○ OP Pinot Nero Cuvée Bussolera Extra Brut '05	♙♙	4
○ OP Riesling Landò '06	♙♙	4
○ OP Pinot Grigio Levriere '06	♙	4
● OP Rosso Cirgà '03	♙	5
● Garboso '04	♟♟	4*
● OP Bonarda La Rubiosa '05	♟♟	4
○ OP Riesling Landò '05	♟♟	4
● OP Rosso Cirgà '01	♟♟	5
● OP Rosso Bohemi '99	♟♟	6
○ OP Pinot Nero Cuvée Bussolera Extra Brut '04	♟♟	4

● OP Bonarda Vivace Dardo '06	♙♙	4*
● OP Pinot Nero Giorgio Odero '04	♙♙	5
○ OP Pinot Nero in Bianco Sillery '06	♙	4
○ OP Riesling Renano Gli Orti '06	♙	4*
● OP Rosso Le Praielle '04	♙	4
● OP Pinot Nero Giorgio Odero '00	♟♟	5
● OP Pinot Nero Giorgio Odero '03	♟♟	5
● Francigeno '03	♟♟	5
● OP Rosso Le Praielle '01	♟♟	4
● OP Rosso Le Praielle '02	♟♟	4
● OP Pinot Nero Giorgio Odero '02	♟♟	5

Enrico Gatti

VIA METELLI, 9
25030 ERBUSCO [BS]
TEL. 0307267999
www.enricogatti.it

ANNUAL PRODUCTION 120,000 bottles
HECTARES UNDER VINE 17
VITICULTURE METHOD Conventional

Enrico Gatti's Satèn '03 earned our fourth
consecutive Three Glass award for this
dynamic Erbusco estate owned by Lorenzo
Gatti, his sister Paola and her husband
Enzo Balzarini. The trio have transformed
the little family winery into a gem of an
estate boasting 17 hectares of vineyards
with an annual production figure of just
120,000 very high-quality bottles. Their
Satèn is a potent, concentrated wine with
great structure, which is also elegant, deep
and sensual with opulent fruit and complex
mineral notes. It's flanked by the equally full
Nature, which is spirited, sinewy and
elegant, with hints of hazelnuts and sweet
almonds. The basic Franciacorta Brut has
again shown itself to be a true champion of
value for money. That said, the still wines
that the estate has always offered were not
presented for our tastings and will gradually
be replaced by new Franciacorta blends.
We applaud this brave decision.

Conte Carlo Giorgi di Vistarino

VILLA FORNACE
27040 ROCCA DE' GIORGI [PV]
TEL. 038585117
www.contevistarino.it

ANNUAL PRODUCTION 550,000 bottles
HECTARES UNDER VINE 180
VITICULTURE METHOD Conventional

The makeover of this long-established
estate continues, albeit with some inevitable
ups and downs. This year, our favourites
were the two IGT wines, Sorbe '05 and
Riesling Passito '04. The former, from
croatina, is aged in small casks and has
attractive aromas of wild berries, flowers
and medicinal herbs. Succulent and fruity
on the palate, it presents well-calibrated
tannins and a long finish. The Riesling
Passito is sweet but not cloying, thanks to
good acid backbone. The oak is expertly
gauged and the ripe, fruity palate has
florality and attractive tobacco notes. The
Pinot Nero Pernice '04 has a promising
future, its highly varietal aromas featuring
hints of tar, cassis and coffee while the
generous fine-grained tannins still need time
to develop fully. Bonarda Vivace L'Alcova
'06 is nice, with good fruit. It just missed
Two Glasses because of slightly drying
tannins. Pinot Nero Brut Cuvée della Rocca
is fairly evolved, with almond notes. The
other wines presented are well typed
although we were rather disappointed by
the Riesling 7 Giugno '06, which is lacking
in weight.

O Franciacorta Satèn '03	♥♥♥	6
O Franciacorta Brut	♥♥	5*
O Franciacorta Nature	♥♥	5
O Franciacorta Satèn '01	♀♀♀	5
O Franciacorta Satèn '00	♀♀♀	6
O Franciacorta Satèn '02	♀♀♀	6

● OP Pinot Nero Pernice '04	♥♥	5
O Riesling Passito '04	♥♥	6
● Sorbe '05	♥♥	4
● OP Bonarda L'Alcova '06	♥	3
● OP Pinot Nero Costa del Nero '05	♥	3
● OP Sangue di Giuda Costiolo '06	♥	3
O OP Pinot Nero Cuvée Della Rocca	♥	3
● OP Buttafuoco Monte Selva '05	♥	4*
● OP Pinot Nero Costa del Nero '04	♀♀	3*
● OP Pinot Nero Pernice '03	♀♀	4
● Sorbe '04	♀♀	4

F.lli Giorgi
FRAZ. CAMPONOCE, 39A
27044 CANNETO PAVESE [PV]
TEL. 0385262151
www.giorgi-wines.it

Cantina Sociale La Versa
VIA F. CRISPI, 15
27047 SANTA MARIA DELLA VERSA [PV]
TEL. 0385798411
www.laversa.it

ANNUAL PRODUCTION 1.600,000 bottles
HECTARES UNDER VINE 30
VITICULTURE METHOD Conventional

The first release of Oltrepò Pavese Rosso Clilele, the '05, which Fabiano Giorgi has dedicated to his mother Claudia, his girlfriend Ileana and his sister Eleonora, is interesting and fresh on the nose but overly soft. We think that it would have benefited from less residual sugar. Bonarda Vivace La Brughera '06 has again shown itself to be one of the best of the territory, with fruity aromas and good balance. The dark ruby Buttafuoco Storico Casa del Corno '03 has earthy sensations and overripe fruit, with notes of balsam, blueberries and raspberries. Sangue di Giuda '06 is very well made, giving crisp sensations of strawberries and blackcurrants mingling with florality. The MesDì '05 Chardonnay can point to well-calibrated oak, ripe tropical fruit and good length. Vigalòn '06, an IGT red from the classic Oltrepò blend of barbera, croatina and uva rara, is very pleasant, with soft tannins and attractive clean fruit. Pinot Nero Monteroso '05 is goodish and varietal but the two classic method sparklers, the Rosé and the 1870, although fresh and pleasant, are a little below par with a somewhat abrupt finish. The Extra Dry Rosé Cuvée Eleonor and the Malvasia Frizzante are very decent.

ANNUAL PRODUCTION 6,000,000 bottles
HECTARES UNDER VINE 1.300
VITICULTURE METHOD Conventional

It's not overstating things to say that the entire Oltrepò region should be grateful for the work that Francesco Cervetti has been doing over the past few years. He has restored this long-established co-operative winery to the role its history and potential deserve, making it a benchmark for the entire area. His efforts have been justly rewarded by the presence in our finals of Testarossa Principio '00, an excellent metodo classico Pinot Nero like those produced by the estate 30 years ago. But a further three of its sparklers also achieved high scores: the excellent value Carta Oro, the classic Testarossa '01 and the new Testarossa Rosé '03, all of which are rich, structured, balanced and long, revealing the great potential of metodo classico Pinot Nero in Valle Versa. We were also impressed by the quality of the I Roccoli range, particularly Moscato Passito Lacrimae Vitis '03, Buttafuoco Roccolo delle Viole '04 and Casale del Re '04, a Barbera that needs a little longer in bottle. All the wines in the Terre d'Alteni second line are also excellent value, starting with Barbera Le Piane '05.

● OP Bonarda Vivace La Brughera '06	♟♟	4
○ OP Chardonnay MesDì '05	♟♟	5
● OP Buttafuoco Casa del Corno '03	♟♟	4
● OP Sangue di Giuda Frizzante '06	♟♟	4
● OP Rosso Clilele '05	♟♟	6
○ OP Malvasia Dolce Frizzante '06	♟	4
○ OP Pinot Nero Brut Cl. 1870 '03	♟	6
● OP Pinot Nero Monteroso '05	♟	5
⊙ OP Pinot Nero Gianfranco Giorgi Rosé Pas Dosé '04	♟	5
● Vigalòn '06	♟	3*
● OP Bonarda Vivace La Brughera '05	♟♟	4
○ OP Pinot Nero Brut Cl. Gianfranco Giorgi '03	♟♟	6
● OP Buttafuoco Casa del Corno '02	♟♟	4

○ Cuvée Testarossa Brut Principio '00	♟♟	8
● Casale Del Re '04	♟♟	5
● OP Bonarda Frizzante Ca' Bella '06	♟♟	4
● OP Buttafuoco Roccolo delle Viole '04	♟♟	4
⊙ Spumante Cl. Rosè Brut Testarossa '03	♟♟	5
● OP Sangue di Giuda '06	♟♟	4
○ OP Riesling Roccolo delle Fate '06	♟♟	4
○ OP Pinot Nero Brut Carta Oro	♟♟	4*
○ OP Moscato Passito Lacrimae Vitis '03	♟♟	6
○ Cuvée Testarossa Brut '01	♟♟	5
● OP Barbera Le Piane '05	♟	3
● OP Bonarda Frizzante Donelasco '06	♟	4
○ OP Chardonnay Terre d'Alteni '06	♟	3
● OP Pinot Nero Liutajo Del Re '04	♟	5
○ OP Pinot Grigio Terre D'Alteni '06	♟	3
○ OP Moscato di Volpara '06	♟	4
○ Cuvée Testarossa Principio '99	♟♟	8

Lantieri de Paratico

Loc. Colzano
via Simeone Paratico, 50
25031 Capriolo [BS]
tel. 030736151
www.lantierideparatico.it

ANNUAL PRODUCTION N.D.
HECTARES UNDER VINE 17
VITICULTURE METHOD Conventional

Although the Lantieri de Paratico family is one of the oldest in the area, their estate was set up only in 1970, at the beginning of Franciacorta's legendary rise to fame. The winery is managed by Fabio Lantieri, with the aid of an excellent staff coordinated by consultant oenologist Cesare Ferrari. The cellar uses only the grapes from its own 17 hectares of vineyards, which it transforms into a well-crafted range of wines topped by a selection of Franciacortas. While the vintage Arcadia '03, from a torrid growing season, did not live up to our expectations, the non-vintage Franciacortas provided ample compensation. The Brut has an attractive straw-green hue, a fragrant nose of fruit and flowers and an appealing palate distinguished by delicacy rather than structure. Another excellent offering is the Rosé, with exuberant fresh, cherry notes on the nose and palate, where it shows harmonious and satisfying. Terre di Franciacorta del Vigneto Colzano Bianco '05 and Rosso '04, are well made but the other wines are less interesting.

⊙ Franciacorta Rosé	🍷🍷	5
O TdF Bianco Colzano '05	🍷🍷	5
O Franciacorta Brut	🍷🍷	5
● TdF Rosso Colzano '04	🍷🍷	5
O Franciacorta Satèn	🍷	5
O TdF Bianco '06	🍷	4
O Franciacorta Brut Arcadia '03	🍷	6
O Franciacorta Brut Arcadia '01	YY	6
O Franciacorta Brut Arcadia '02	YY	6
● TdF Rosso Colzano '03	YY	5
O Franciacorta Satèn '00	YY	5

Majolini

Loc. Valle
via Manzoni, 3
25050 Ome [BS]
tel. 0306527378
www.majolini.it

ANNUAL PRODUCTION 160,000 bottles
HECTARES UNDER VINE 20
VITICULTURE METHOD Conventional

The Majolini family has been closely associated with viticulture for centuries. Indeed, a widespread indigenous grape variety of the local vineyards has always been known by the name of "uva majolina". During the 1990s, this family of successful entrepreneurs decided to return to the land and currently manages 20 hectares of vineyards in the municipality of Ome. Credit for the estate's success must go to Ezio Majolini and his nephew Simone, with the invaluable consultancy of oenologist Jean-Pierre Valade. The range, produced in the modern cellar at Ome, is wide and prestigious. Among the many good wines presented this year our favourites were an excellent pair of Franciacortas, which only just missed our highest accolade. They are the satisfying, round, juicy Satèn Ante Omnia '02 and the Franciacorta Pas Dosé Aligi Sassu '03, named after the late artist whose last work was conceived to grace the winery. The wine boasts complex notes of aromatic herbs and is refreshing, piquant and structured. Brut Electo '03 is excellent, with a fresh nose of apples and pears, citrus fruit, butter and cakes and a harmoniously full, caressing palate.

O Franciacorta Aligi Sassu Pas Dosé '03	🍷🍷	8
O Franciacorta Ante Omnia Satèn	🍷🍷	6
O Franciacorta Brut Electo '03	🍷🍷	8
O Ronchello	🍷🍷	5
● TdF Rosso Ruc di Gnoc '04	🍷🍷	5
⊙ Franciacorta Altèra Rosé	🍷	8
O Franciacorta Brut	🍷	7
O Franciacorta Brut Electo '99	YYY	6
O Franciacorta Electo Brut '00	YYY	7
O Franciacorta Electo Brut '97	YYY	6

Le Marchesine

VIA VALLOSA, 31
25050 PASSIRANO [BS]
TEL. 030657005
www.lemarchesine.it

ANNUAL PRODUCTION 320,000 bottles
HECTARES UNDER VINE N.D.
VITICULTURE METHOD Conventional

Giovanni Biatta and his son Loris lavish tender loving care on their fine estate founded in 1985, which owns and leases a total of 27 hectares of vineyards, mainly around Passirano. Average annual production is approximately 220,000 bottles, consisting chiefly of Franciacortas, although an entire range of wines has been created with the assistance of oenologist Jean-Pierre Valade. This year, the Brut Secolo Novo '00 reached our finals, where it distinguished itself with fine apricot-led fruit aromas, depth and elegance. The Brut '00 is equally good, giving floral, buttery hints and an elegant, long, soft palate. Satèn '03 displays appealing fresh citrus notes, delicate softness and subtle aromatic hints while Cabernet Sauvignon Alice '02, Podere Pinot Nero '02 and Terre Bianco '06 also deserved good scores. The other wines are all well up to snuff.

Tenuta Mazzolino

VIA MAZZOLINO, 26
27050 CORVINO SAN QUIRICO [PV]
TEL. 0383876122
www.tenuta-mazzolino.com

ANNUAL PRODUCTION 100,000 bottles
HECTARES UNDER VINE 22
VITICULTURE METHOD Conventional

Pinot Nero Noir '05, the flagship of this handsome estate, achieved a high score for its remarkable trueness to type, expressed in a moderately deep garnet hue, elegant berry fruit aromas with flowery undertones and soft, silky tannins. The overall structure is very good and finishes confidently. It's readier than some previous vintages but will nonetheless improve further with a few more months in bottle. Cabernet Sauvignon Corvino '05 is also highly varietal, flaunting hay and bell pepper followed by coffee, cocoa and spices. There is good body and the finish is long if a little bitter as the tannins have yet to meld in. The Chardonnay Blanc '05 came within a hair's breadth of Two Glasses. It boasts rich, juicy, overripe tropical fruit but is very evolved and almost caramelly. Bonarda Mazzolino '06 is goodish, presenting dark notes of topsoil and autumn leaves accompanied by wild berries and prominent tannins. Mazzolino Brut, a classic method sparkler from pure chardonnay, has citrus and oaky notes from the ageing of 50 per cent of the base cuvée in barriques. The other wines are decent, no-nonsense products.

○ Franciacorta Brut Secolo Novo '00	♟♟ 7
● Cabernet Sauvignon Alice '02	♟♟ 6
○ Franciacorta Brut '00	♟♟ 6
● Il Podere Pinot Nero '02	♟♟ 6
○ Franciacorta Satèn '03	♟♟ 6
○ TdF Bianco Curtefranca '06	♟♟ 4*
● TdF Rosso Curtefranca '05	♟♟ 4*
○ Franciacorta Brut	♟ 5
☉ Franciacorta Brut Rosé '03	♟ 6
○ Franciacorta Extra Brut	♟ 6
● Cabernet Sauvignon Alice '01	♈ 6
● Il Podere Pinot Nero '01	♈ 6

● OP Cabernet Sauvignon Corvino '05	♟♟ 4
○ OP Mazzolino Brut	♟♟ 5
● OP Pinot Nero Noir '05	♟♟ 6
○ Camarà '06	♟ 3*
● Terrazze '06	♟ 3
● OP Bonarda Mazzolino '06	♟ 4
○ OP Chardonnay Blanc '05	♟ 4
● OP Pinot Nero Noir '00	♈ 6
● OP Cabernet Sauvignon Corvino '02	♈ 4
● OP Pinot Nero '02	♈ 6
● Terrazze '05	♈ 3*
● OP Cabernet Sauvignon Corvino '03	♈ 4
● OP Pinot Nero Noir '04	♈ 6

Mirabella

VIA CANTARANE, 2
25050 RODENGO SAIANO [BS]
TEL. 030611197
www.mirabellavini.it

ANNUAL PRODUCTION   500,000 bottles
HECTARES UNDER VINE 60
VITICULTURE METHOD   Conventional

Yet again, Mirabella's Franciacorta Non Dosato was one of the best blends of its type, this time with the '00 vintage, adding further lustre to the estate managed by Francesco Bracchi. One of the best in the DOCG zone for many years, Mirabella currently owns and leases a total area of 60 hectares of vineyards, which yield an annual production of around 500,000 bottles. The Non Dosato has an intense nose of rich fruity notes, aromatic herbs and ripe fruit with elegant tropical hints. On the palate, it's piquant, fresh and well defined, the body is good body and gentle sparkle lingers in the glass. We were also impressed by the soft, fruity Satèn, with its hints of yeast and toast, and the firm, tangy, well-made Brut. Good still wines include the delicate, vanillaed Terre Bianco Palazzina '05 and the Passito Incanto, from chardonnay, with its sweet apricot notes. The estate's other wines are also worth investigating.

Monsupello

VIA SAN LAZZARO, 5
27050 TORRICELLA VERZATE [PV]
TEL. 0383896043
www.monsupello.it

ANNUAL PRODUCTION   280,000 bottles
HECTARES UNDER VINE 50
VITICULTURE METHOD   Conventional

Few estates in Lombardy, and Italy in general, pursue the goal of high-quality production as determinedly as the Boatti family's Monsupello. Just under 50 hectares of vineyards for an annual production figure of 280,000 bottles of excellent wines speak volumes of the care that Carlo Boatti and his son Pierangelo lavish on their darling. The list is very extensive, ranging from serious structured reds, like the deep, soft Rosso del Podere La Borla '03 to thoroughbred whites, including a zesty Chardonnay, a minerally Riesling and a lively, refreshing Sauvignon. But the Boattis' specialities are their metodo classico cuvées. This year, we tasted the elegant Oltrepò Pavese Pinot Nero Brut with its complex notes of red berries and crusty bread, the exceptionally rich, deep Pinot Nero Classese '01, the opulent, layered Oltrepò Pavese Brut Cuvée Ca' del Tava, from pinot nero and chardonnay, and finally the Pinot Nero Nature, which yet again deservedly walked off with our Three Glass award. Bolstered by a zesty swath of acidity, it rolls out wonderfully sound fruit, complex minerality, elegant toastiness, caressing effervescence and truly satisfying length.

O Franciacorta Non Dosato '00	♈♈ 5
O Franciacorta Brut	♈♈ 5*
O T. d F. Bianco Palazzina '05	♈♈ 4*
O Franciacorta Satèn	♈♈ 5
O Passito Incanto '04	♈♈ 6
⊙ Franciacorta Rosé Brut	♈ 5
O Franciacorta Brut Cuvée Demetra	♈ 5
● TdF Rosso Maniero '04	♈♈ 4*
● Nero d'Ombra '01	♈♈ 6
● Nero d'Ombra '00	♈♈ 6
⊙ Franciacorta Brut Rosé '01	♈♈ 4*
⊙ Franciacorta Brut Rosé '00	♈♈ 4

O OP Pinot Nero Cl. Nature	♈♈♈ 5*
O OP Brut Cl. Cuvée Ca' del Tava	♈♈ 7
O OP Pinot Nero Brut Classese '01	♈♈ 5*
● OP Barbera Vivace Magenga '06	♈♈ 4*
● OP Bonarda Vivace Vaiolet '06	♈♈ 4*
● OP Bonarda Calcababio '06	♈♈ 3
O OP Pinot Grigio '06	♈♈ 4*
O OP Chardonnay '06	♈♈ 4*
O OP Sauvignon '06	♈♈ 4*
● OP Rosso Podere La Borla '03	♈♈ 5
● OP Rosso Mosaico Ris. '03	♈♈ 6
O OP Riesling Renano '06	♈♈ 4*
O OP Pinot Nero Brut Cl.	♈♈ 5
O I Germogli Bianchi '06	♈ 4
O I Germogli Rosa '06	♈ 4
O OP Brut Cl. Cuvée Ca' del Tava	♈♈♈ 7
O OP Pinot Nero Cl. Nature	♈♈♈ 5*

Monte Rossa

FRAZ. BORNATO
VIA LUCA MARENZIO, 14
25040 CAZZAGO SAN MARTINO [BS]
TEL. 030725066
www.monterossa.com

ANNUAL PRODUCTION 380,000 bottles
HECTARES UNDER VINE 50
VITICULTURE METHOD Conventional

Emanuele Rabotti has always been involved in the management of Monte Rossa, his family estate. Several years ago, he embarked on a restructuring programme and built a new cellar, giving a further boost to what was already one of the best wineries in the area. He then decided to devote his efforts exclusively to Franciacortas, eliminating all the still wines. Lavishing painstaking attention on every detail, Emanuele has been able to present an exceptionally high-quality range of Franciacortas. Needless to say, the pearl of the collection is Cabochon '03, a superb edition of Monte Rosso's prestige blend. Straw yellow in hue with golden highlights, it proffers delicate bubbles and a complex nose in which white-fleshed fruit mingles with flowers and then tertiary notes of spices, old wood and dried fruit. On the palate, it shows structure and character before the long, cosseting finish with its fruit and more complex mineral sensations is bolstered by good acidity. The other cuvées are up to their usual high standards.

Montelio

VIA D. MAZZA, 1
27050 CODEVILLA [PV]
TEL. 0383373090
montelio.g@virgilio.it

ANNUAL PRODUCTION 130,000 bottles
HECTARES UNDER VINE 27
VITICULTURE METHOD Conventional

This year, the wines of the estate owned by the Brazzola sisters and managed by Mario Maffi put on a good performance. We gave top marks to the red Comprino Mirosa '04, one of the cellar's historic wines, from merlot aged in new barriques. On the nose, there are attractive notes of chocolate and vanilla from the assertive oak, which does not however mask the hints of plum and wild berries. In the mouth, it develops nicely, culminating in a long finish. La Giostra '05, a white from müller thurgau, is also interesting. Golden in hue, with a rich, fruity body, it is attractively refreshing and just needs a little time for the new oak to integrate. The basic Oltrepò Pavese Rosso is in one of its best versions ever, with a deep nose of autumn leaves and berry fruit. It's well defined and succulent, with just the right dose of tannins and a balanced, deliberately very drinkable style. Bonarda Frizzante '06 shows a deep ruby, with clean, healthy fruit and a soft, balanced palate. OP Rosso Riserva Solarolo '03 is overripe, chewy and tannic. The Noblerot '04 dessert wine, from cortese, malvasia and moscato, is good, giving a generous aromatic bouquet of citrus fruit and honey. The other wines of the list are decent.

O Franciacorta Brut Cabochon '03	♟♟♟	7
O Franciacorta P. R. Brut	♟♟	6
O Franciacorta Prima Cuvée Brut	♟♟	5
O Franciacorta Satèn Brut	♟♟	6
☉ Franciacorta Rosé	♟♟	4
O Franciacorta Brut Cabochon '01	♟♟♟	7
O Franciacorta Brut Cabochon '97	♟♟♟	6
O Franciacorta Brut Cabochon '99	♟♟♟	8
O Franciacorta Brut Cabochon '98	♟♟♟	6
O Franciacorta Brut Cabochon '00	♟♟	7

● Comprino Mirosa '04	♟♟	6
O Müller Thurgau La Giostra '05	♟♟	3
● OP Bonarda Frizzante '06	♟♟	3*
● OP Rosso '05	♟♟	3*
O Brut Martinotti La Stroppa	♟	4
O Noblerot '04	♟	5
● OP Rosso Solarolo Ris. '03	♟	5
☉ OP Rosato '06	♟	3
O OP Riesling Italico '06	♟	3*
O OP Cortese '06	♟	3
● Comprino Mirosa '01	♟♟	6
● Comprino Mirosa '03	♟♟	6
O Noblerot '03	♟♟	4
● OP Rosso Solarolo Ris. '00	♟♟	5
● OP Rosso Solarolo Ris. '01	♟♟	5

Montenisa

FRAZ. CALINO
VIA PAOLO VI, 62
25046 CAZZAGO SAN MARTINO [BS]
TEL. 0307750838
www.antinori.it

ANNUAL PRODUCTION N.D.
HECTARES UNDER VINE 60
VITICULTURE METHOD Conventional

In 1999, the Antinori family took over this handsome Franciacorta estate with its 60 hectares of vineyards at Cazzago San Martino, naming it after the mythological Mount Nysa, birthplace of Bacchus. Legend apart, the estate's cuvées are at the top of the DOCG zone's quality ladder. You can appreciate this by tasting Contessa Camilla Maggi '01, which enchanted us with its finesse and complexity. A lustrous greenish straw introduces the tiny bubbles and deep, intense nose that layers elegant notes of toast, oriental spices and slight hints of vanilla over sound fruit. On the palate, it's soft, well rounded, refreshing, elegant and balanced, with a long finish of ripe fruit, coffee and hazelnuts. The Satèn '02, at its debut as a vintage blend, is extremely good, revealing subtle notes of chamomile, ripe fruit and vanilla, while the non-vintage Brut is well made but not stunning.

La Montina

VIA BAIANA, 17
25040 MONTICELLI BRUSATI [BS]
TEL. 030653278
www.lamontina.it

ANNUAL PRODUCTION 450,000 bottles
HECTARES UNDER VINE 48
VITICULTURE METHOD Conventional

La Montina, the beautiful Monticelli winery owned by the Bozza brothers, can point to some impressive figures: almost 50 hectares of vineyards belonging to the estate and under lease for an annual production of around 450,000 bottles of Franciacortas and territory-focused wines. But the most important aspect is the estate's significant progress in quality over the past decade, which has made it one of the best producers in the DOCG zone. Again this year, our favourite was the vintage Franciacorta Brut. The '02 has a bright straw-yellow hue and intense aromas of fruit that mingle with more complex notes of balsam, incense and oak. On the palate, it's structured, elegant and soft, progressing confidently through to a stylish finish laced with yeast and toast. Other excellent offerings include the rounded, vanillaed Satèn and the spirited, fruity basic Brut. The creamy but somewhat light-bodied Extra Brut is only slightly less interesting while the Rosé Demi Sec is uncomplicated and pleasant. On to the still wine front, Chardonnay Rubinia '05 is excellent.

O Franciacorta Brut Contessa Camilla Maggi '01	♟♟ 7
O Franciacorta Satèn '02	♟♟ 7
O Franciacorta Brut	♟ 5
O Franciacorta Brut Contessa Camilla Maggi '00	♟♟ 7

O Franciacorta Brut '02	♟♟ 6
O Franciacorta Satèn	♟♟ 5
O Franciacorta Brut	♟♟ 5
O Rubinia '05	♟♟ 5
O Franciacorta Extra Brut	♟ 5
O TdF Bianco Palanca '06	♟ 3
● TdF Rosso dei Dossi '04	♟ 4
⊙ Franciacorta Rosé Demi Sec	♟ 5
O Franciacorta Extra Brut '01	♟♟ 5
O Franciacorta Extra Brut '02	♟♟ 5
O Franciacorta Brut '01	♟♟ 5
O TdF Bianco Vign. Palanca '05	♟♟ 3*

Monzio Compagnoni

VIA NIGOLINE, 18
25030 ADRO [BS]
TEL. 0307457803
www.monziocompagnoni.com

ANNUAL PRODUCTION 250,000 bottles
HECTARES UNDER VINE 30
VITICULTURE METHOD Conventional

This is an unusual profile that we are
dedicating to Marcello Monzio Compagnoni,
who won our top accolade with his
excellent Franciacorta Extra Brut '03 last
year. The DOCG production protocol
requires a minimum ageing period for
vintage wines that had not been completed
at the time of our tasting. Consequently, we
will have to postpone our assessment of the
'04 vintage until the next edition. This is no
great problem, however, for Marcello also
produces excellent still wines in
Franciacorta and on his Valcalepio estate.
And they are terrific, ranging from the pale,
varietal Pinot Nero Rosso di Nero '03 to the
fruity, leisurely Terre di Franciacorta Ronco
della Seta '06 and Ronco della Seta Rosso
'05, with distinct raspberry notes. From
Valcalepio, we liked the superb, sweet
Moscato di Scanzo Don Quijote '04, with
plenty of fruity pulp, and the Valcalepio
Rosso di Luna '03 with elegant tannins and
ripe blackberry notes. The Valcalepio Bianco
and Rosso Colle della Luna are also
attractive.

Il Mosnel

LOC. CAMIGNONE
VIA BARBOGLIO, 14
25040 PASSIRANO [BS]
TEL. 030653117
www.ilmosnel.com

ANNUAL PRODUCTION 250,000 bottles
HECTARES UNDER VINE 39
VITICULTURE METHOD Conventional

The passing a few months ago of Emanuela
Barboglia, a pioneer of Franciacorta wines
and a charismatic figure, marks the loss of
one of the great characters in the recent
history of this territory. The future of the fine
estate, boasting 65 hectares in Passirano,
including approximately 40 under vine, is
now entirely in the hands of her son Giulio
and daughter Lucia Barzanò, who have
already been running the show for some
years. Giulio and Lucia offer a series of
excellent wines, which lacks only the high
note of a Three Glass award to complete it
but the goal is certainly within their reach. In
the meantime, they presented us with a
distinguished Dosage Zero that is among
the best of its kind, with a flowery nose and
a crisp, firm, elegant palate. Brut Emanuela
Barboglio '03 is complex with good
structure, displaying hints of fruit and
flowers that develop into complex mineral
notes on both the nose and the palate. We
were not completely convinced by the
Satèn of the same vintage, which appears
to have been rather heavily dosed. The
basic Brut and the Rosé Dosage Zero
Parosé '03 are both good while the Sebino
Passito '05 is the best of the still wines.

● Moscato di Scanzo Don Quijote '04	▼▼	6
○ TdF Bianco Ronco della Seta '06	▼▼	4*
● TdF Rosso Ronco della Seta '05	▼▼	4*
● Valcalepio Rosso di Luna '03	▼▼	5
● Rosso di Nero '03	▼▼	5
○ Valcalepio Bianco Colle della Luna '06	▼	3
● Valcalepio Rosso Colle della Luna '05	▼	4
○ Franciacorta Extra Brut '03	▼▼▼	6
● Moscato di Scanzo Don Quijote '03	▼▼	6
○ TdF Bianco della Seta '04	▼▼	5

○ Franciacorta Brut Emanuela Barboglio '03	▼▼	6
○ Franciacorta Dosage Zéro	▼▼	5
○ Sebino Passito '05	▼▼	6
⊙ Franciacorta Pas Dosé Parosé '03	▼▼	6
○ Franciacorta Brut	▼	5
○ TdF Bianco '06	▼	4
○ Franciacorta Satèn '03	▼	6
● TdF Rosso '05	▼	4
○ Franciacorta Brut '00	▼▼	6
○ Franciacorta Satèn '00	▼▼	6
○ Sebino Passito '04	▼▼	6

★ Nino Negri

VIA GHIBELLINI
23030 CHIURO [SO]
TEL. 0342485211
www.ninonegri.it

Pasini - San Giovanni

FRAZ. RAFFA
VIA VIDELLE, 2
25080 PUEGNAGO SUL GARDA [BS]
TEL. 0365651419
www.pasiniproduttori.it

ANNUAL PRODUCTION 830,000 bottles
HECTARES UNDER VINE 36
VITICULTURE METHOD Conventional

ANNUAL PRODUCTION 300,000 bottles
HECTARES UNDER VINE 36
VITICULTURE METHOD Conventional

At Nino Negri, the traditional Sforzato '04, the grandfather of Sforzatos, has outclassed the forerunner of the modern-style wines: the multiple award-winning 5 Stelle. Admittedly, the difference was extremely small but we must say that the '04 bowled us over to sweep up a Three Glass award. Its sober elegance and broad complex nose usher in an exceptionally balanced palate and a deep, refreshing, well-sustained finish. The 5 Stelle still appears a tad muddled, perhaps because it has yet to absorb its oak, but such minor details do not prevent it from unveiling great concentration and opulent fruit. Fracia '04 possesses great finesse, with aromas of blackcurrants and raspberries, and a well-defined palate with supple tannins and an elegant finish. The Mazer and Sassella Le Tense, both from the '04 vintage, are exemplary in their portrayal of the territory. Grumello Sassorosso '04 is fragrant on the nose and vigorous on the palate, with refreshing acidity. Ca' Brione, from sauvignon, chardonnay, incrocio Manzoni and chiavennasca, the local name for nebbiolo, remains the only truly original Valtellina white. It presents a complex, varietal nose and a delicate, balanced palate.

Pasini Produttori has changed its name, reverting to Azienda Agricola Pasini San Giovanni, as it was originally called in 1958, combining the names of the family and the location of the winery. This change has the air of a declaration of intent to focus on the vineyards and the territory. The results of the restyling can be felt right from the basic wines of the excellent 2006 vintage. Garda Classico is a Riesling Renano with an attractive nose of citrus fruit and grass, Groppello is juicy and drinkable, Chiaretto boasts aromas of wild strawberries and Lugana is crisp and flowery. The range features an impressive selection of top-end reds: Cap del Priù '04 and San Gioàn '03 reveal the versatility of groppello, the indigenous grape variety of Valtenesi – Arzane Riserva '04, currently ageing, promises well – while Montezalto has nice weight. The two Ceppo 326 classic method Bruts also performed well, with the Rosé featuring groppello in the base cuvée for the first time.

● Valtellina Sfursat '04	♟♟♟	7
● Valtellina Sfursat 5 Stelle '04	♟♟	8
● Valtellina Sup. Fracia '04	♟♟	8
O Ca' Brione '06	♟♟	5
● Valtellina Sup. Sassella Le Tense '04	♟♟	5
● Valtellina Sup. Mazer '04	♟♟	5
● Valtellina Sup. Grumello Vigna Sassorosso '04	♟♟	5
● Valtellina Sfursat '02	♟♟♟	6
● Valtellina Sfursat 5 Stelle '94	♟♟♟	5
● Valtellina Sfursat 5 Stelle '96	♟♟♟	5
● Valtellina Sfursat 5 Stelle '98	♟♟♟	6
● Valtellina Sfursat 5 Stelle '99	♟♟♟	6
● Valtellina Sfursat 5 Stelle '97	♟♟♟	6
● Valtellina Sfursat 5 Stelle '95	♟♟♟	5
● Valtellina Sfursat 5 Stelle '03	♟♟♟	8
● Valtellina Sfursat 5 Stelle '02	♟♟♟	7
● Valtellina Sfursat '03	♟♟♟	7
● Valtellina Sfursat 5 Stelle '01	♟♟♟	7
● Valtellina Sup. Fracia '02	♟♟	8

● Garda Cabernet Sauvignon Vign. Montezalto '03	♟♟	5
O Garda Cl. Bianco Il Renano '06	♟♟	4
● Garda Cl. Rosso Sup. Cap del Priù '04	♟♟	4
● San Gioan Rosso I Carati '03	♟♟	4
O Ceppo 326 Brut	♟	5
⊙ Garda Cl. Chiaretto Il Chiaretto '06	♟	4
● Garda Cl. Il Groppello '06	♟	4
⊙ Ceppo 326 Rosè Brut '04	♟	5
O Lugana Il Lugana '06	♟	4
● Garda Cabernet Sauvignon Vign. Montezalto '01	♟♟	5
● Garda Cl. Groppello Vign. Arzane Ris. '00	♟♟	4
● Garda Cl. Groppello Vign. Arzane Ris. '01	♟♟	4
O San Gioan Brinat Bianco Dolce '01	♟♟	5
● San Gioan Rosso I Carati '03	♟♟	4
● San Gioan Rosso I Carati '00	♟♟	4
● Garda Cl. Groppello Vign. Arzane Ris. '03	♟♟	4

Cascina La Pertica

LOC. PICEDO
VIA ROSARIO, 44
25080 POLPENAZZE DEL GARDA [BS]
TEL. 0365651471
www.cascinalapertica.it

ANNUAL PRODUCTION 60,000 bottles
HECTARES UNDER VINE 16
VITICULTURE METHOD Certified organic

Le Zalte's trophy collection clearly shows that it is one of the most important Garda reds and Cascina La Pertica's shelves could run out of space to house all our stemware. Made from the grapes – cabernet sauvignon with a touch of merlot from biodynamic vineyards – from a model vineyard planted by Ruggero Brunori and Andrea Salvetti on the gentle hills of Polpenazze, this wine impresses with the concentration and freshness of its fruit and its pleasant drinkability, characteristics of good Garda reds. The 2005 vintage is no exception, and put on another great performance. This year, though, we were astounded by the progress shown by Groppello with the '06 vintage: Il Colombaio combines ripe fruit with intriguingly complex spiciness, paving the way for a very interesting, and in many respects winning, new way forward for the indigenous grape variety of Valtenesi. Groppello also gives structure to another satisfyingly drinkable wine, the Garda Classico Le Sincette '04.

Andrea Picchioni

LOC. CAMPONOCE, 8
27044 CANNETO PAVESE [PV]
TEL. 0385262139
www.picchioniandrea.it

ANNUAL PRODUCTION 60,000 bottles
HECTARES UNDER VINE 8
VITICULTURE METHOD Natural

Andrea Picchioni, with the invaluable aid of his mother Rosa, father Antonio, wife Silvia and 12-year-old daughter Asia, who designs some of the labels, has earned a full profile for his serious work and the improvements in quality on his small estate, whose wines are never ordinary. This year, the highest score went to the complex, structured Buttafuoco Bricco Riva Bianca '03, characterized by seductive balsamic notes and intense aromas of wild berries. Rosso d'Asia '03, a blend with 90 per cent croatina, is also very good. It too has the balsamic hints typical of Val Solinga, where the vineyards are located, and deep, intact ripe fruit, while the tannins of the croatina have yet to develop fully. The other red, Monnalisa '03, is softer, less complex and easier to drink after the addition of 15 per cent merlot to the basic croatina. Bonarda Vivace '06 is one of the best of the vintage, with aromas of black cherry jam, good pulp and fine-grained tannins. Sangue di Giuda is similarly exciting. The basic Buttafuoco, Luogo della Cerasa '06, is well crafted and Soleluna '06 with its attractive coppery highlights is decent.

● Garda Cabernet Le Zalte '05	♥♥♥ 7
● Garda Cl. Groppello Il Colombaio '06	♥♥ 4
● Garda Cl. Rosso Le Sincette '04	♥♥ 5
○ Garda Chardonnay Le Sincette '06	♥ 4
● Il Rosso '05	♥ 4
● Garda Cabernet Le Zalte '01	♥♥♥ 7
● Garda Cabernet Le Zalte '03	♥♥♥ 7
● Garda Cabernet Le Zalte '99	♥♥♥ 7
● Garda Cabernet Le Zalte '04	♥♥♥ 7
● Garda Cabernet Le Zalte '00	♥♥♥ 7
● Garda Cl. Groppello Il Colombaio '05	♥♥ 4

● OP Bonarda Vivace '06	♥♥ 3*
● Rosso d'Asia '03	♥♥ 5
● Monnalisa '03	♥♥ 5
● OP Buttafuoco Bricco Riva Bianca '03	♥♥ 5
● OP Sangue di Giuda '06	♥♥ 3*
● OP Buttafuoco Luogo della Cerasa '06	♥ 4
○ OP Soleluna '06	♥ 4
● OP Bonarda Vivace '05	♀♀ 3
● Rosso d'Asia '01	♀♀ 4
● Rosso d'Asia '00	♀♀ 5

Plozza
VIA SAN GIACOMO, 22
23037 TIRANO [SO]
TEL. 0342701297
www.plozza.com

ANNUAL PRODUCTION 450,000 bottles
HECTARES UNDER VINE 28
VITICULTURE METHOD Conventional

The relentless pursuit of quality continues at this major estate, which is rightly aiming at becoming one of the area's leading wineries. This is the vision of the Zanolari family, who show great sensitivity in interpreting the potential of the territory. All this is exemplified by the range presented, including the uniquely distinctive Numero Uno, from nebbiolo, which is a wine of rare elegance. Made from grapes left to dry for three months, it will benefit from more time in bottle to express its full potential but the nose is striking, it has plenty of elegant tannins and the finish is very long. Passione '02, also from nebbiolo, shows concentrated fruit and a soft palate. The Sforzato Vin da Cà '03 performed very well, showing original balsamic aromas, great balance, compactness and a lingering finish, all at a good price. One of the best Sassellas tasted, Riserva La Scala '03, impressed us with its finesse, warmth and caressing palate. The Inferno '03 is spicy and full bodied with good structure while the Grumello '03 is spot on and true to type.

Mamete Prevostini
VIA LUCCHINETTI, 63
23020 MESE [SO]
TEL. 034341003
www.mameteprevostini.com

ANNUAL PRODUCTION 130,000 bottles
HECTARES UNDER VINE 15
VITICULTURE METHOD Conventional

Our Three Glass award has become a regular fixture for the Sforzato produced by Mamete Prevostini, the oenologist trained by Casimiro Maule who never misses a beat. Yet again this year, Albareda '05 is exceptionally elegant, very typical and varietal but above all it is less impetuous and powerful than its predecessors. Spicy on the nose, it proffers a full, refreshing palate with well-calibrated oak. Corte di Cama '05, from slightly dried nebbiolo grapes, also performed well, showing elegant aromas, close texture and an intense finish that nicely reflects the terroir. Sommarovina '05 has a complex entry on the wild berry-led nose and is long and sturdy on the palate. Sassella '05 is fruity with elegant aromas. It's firm but harmonious on the palate with a leisurely finish. Grumello '05 boasts characteristic hazelnut notes, a rounded, vigorous palate and a lingering finish. Botonero '06 and Santarita '06, both from nebbiolo, are well managed with alcohol-rich nose and fruity palate. Opera '06, a chardonnay, sauvignon and müller thurgau blend, is well executed and has lots of personality.

● Valtellina Numero Uno '03	♟♟ 8
● Valtellina Sforzato Vin da Ca' '03	♟♟ 6
● Valtellina Sup. Sassella La Scala Ris. '03	♟♟ 4
● Passione Barrique '02	♟♟ 7
● Valtellina Sup. Grumello Ris. '03	♟♟ 4
● Valtellina Sup. Inferno Ris. '03	♟♟ 5
● Valtellina Numero Uno '01	♟♟♟ 8
● Passione Barrique '01	♟♟ 7
● Valtellina Sforzato Vin da Ca' '01	♟♟ 6
● Valtellina Sup. La Scala Ris. '01	♟♟ 5
● Valtellina Sup. La Scala Ris. '02	♟♟ 4
● Valtellina Sup. La Scala Ris. '00	♟♟ 5
● Valtellina Sup. Grumello Ris. '02	♟♟ 4
● Valtellina Sforzato Vin da Ca' '02	♟♟ 6

● Valtellina Sforzato Albareda '05	♟♟♟ 7
● Valtellina Sup. Corte di Cama '05	♟♟ 6
● Valtellina Sup. Grumello '05	♟♟ 4
● Valtellina Sup. Sassella Sommarovina '05	♟♟ 5
● Valtellina Sup. Sassella '05	♟♟ 4
● Botonero '06	♟ 3
● Valtellina Santarita '06	♟ 3
○ Opera Bianco '06	♟ 5
● Valtellina Sforzato Albareda '00	♟♟♟ 7
● Valtellina Sforzato Albareda '04	♟♟♟ 7
● Valtellina Sforzato Albareda '03	♟♟♟ 7
● Valtellina Sforzato Albareda '01	♟♟ 7
● Valtellina Sup. Corte di Cama '02	♟♟ 6
● Valtellina Sup. Sassella Sommarovina '04	♟♟ 5
● Valtellina Sup. Corte di Cama '03	♟♟ 6
● Valtellina Sforzato Albareda '02	♟♟ 7

Provenza

VIA DEI COLLI STORICI
25015 DESENZANO DEL GARDA [BS]
TEL. 0309910006
www.provenzacantine.it

ANNUAL PRODUCTION 1,000,000 bottles
HECTARES UNDER VINE 85
VITICULTURE METHOD Conventional

Provenza, the estate established in the 1960s by Walter Contato and now managed by his children Fabio and Patrizia, is one of the wineries that has made the greatest contribution to Lugana's current success on both the home front and internationally. Fabio Contato has lent his name to the leading white, the Lugana Superiore Selezione, whose '05 vintage represents another winning step forward in focusing the fundamental characteristics of trebbiano grown on the clay soil around Lake Garda. It's a wine with firm, crisp fruit and typically bright mineral hints. Lugana Superiore Molin '05 also gives ripe peaches and apricots while Lugana Tenuta Maiolo '06 wins you over with its approachable openness, florality and savouriness. From the reds, the best score went to the other Selezione bearing Fabio Contato's name, the soft, mouthfilling Garda Classico Rosso '04. The Negresco '05 also performed well while the fruity sweetness of the Sol Doré, from partially dried grapes, is extremely pleasant.

Aldo Rainoldi

VIA STELVIO, 128
23030 CHIURO [SO]
TEL. 0342482225
www.rainoldi.com

ANNUAL PRODUCTION 200,000 bottles
HECTARES UNDER VINE 9.6
VITICULTURE METHOD Conventional

Peppino Rainoldi took a wise decision when he decided not to release his Sforzato Cà Rizzieri last year, preferring instead allowed it to age for longer in the cellar to let it open up and develop. His sensitivity has been rewarded with Three Glasses for the excellent '02 vintage of this famous wine. On the nose, crisp, clean aromas of ripe fruit, with hints of balsam and coffee, lead into a full, velvety palate with vibrant acidity and a very long finish. Sfursat '03 has a complex nose, with smoky aromas that mingle with herbaceousness and spicy hints. The palate is austere and sustained, laying on a well-defined encore of red berry jam. Inferno Riserva '03 boasts aromas of autumn leaves with hints of tanned leather and a balanced palate with plenty of soft tannins nicely integrated with the fruit. Crespino '04 has impressive structure, its pervasive nose introducing a lively, round palate supported by good acidity, while the original Grumello '04 parades aromas of plum and notes of dried fruit and a confident, fresh, full-flavoured palate. The well-made Prugnolo '04 has fruity fragrances and a coherent palate with a slightly evanescent finish.

○ Lugana Sup. Sel. Fabio Contato '05	♟♟ 5
⊙ Garda Cl. Chiaretto Tenuta Maiolo '06	♟♟ 4
○ Sol Doré '05	♟♟ 5
○ Lugana Tenuta Maiolo '06	♟♟ 4*
○ Lugana Sup. Molin '05	♟♟ 4
● Garda Cl. Rosso Negresco '05	♟♟ 5
● Garda Cl. Rosso Sel. Fabio Contato '04	♟♟ 6
● Giomè '06	♟ 4
○ Lugana Brut Cl. Ca' Maiol	♟ 5
○ Lugana Brut Sebastian '06	♟ 4
● Garda Cl. Rosso Sel. Fabio Contato '01	♟♟ 7
○ Lugana Sup. Molin '04	♟♟ 5
○ Lugana Sup. Sel. Fabio Contato '03	♟♟ 6
○ Lugana Sup. Sel. Fabio Contato '04	♟♟ 6
○ Lugana Sup. Sel. Fabio Contato '99	♟♟ 6
● Garda Cl. Rosso Negresco '04	♟♟ 5
● Garda Cl. Rosso Sel. Fabio Contato '03	♟♟ 6
○ Sol Doré '04	♟♟ 6
○ Lugana Tenuta Maiolo '05	♟♟ 3

● Valtellina Sfursat Fruttaio Ca' Rizzieri '02	♟♟♟ 7
● Valtellina Sfursat '03	♟♟ 6
● Valtellina Sup. Crespino '04	♟♟ 5
● Valtellina Sup. Inferno Ris. '03	♟♟ 5
● Valtellina Sup. Grumello '04	♟♟ 4
● Valtellina Sup. Prugnolo '04	♟ 4
● Valtellina Sfursat Fruttaio Ca' Rizzieri '00	♟♟♟ 7
● Valtellina Sfursat Fruttaio Ca' Rizzieri '95	♟♟♟ 5
● Valtellina Sfursat Fruttaio Ca' Rizzieri '98	♟♟♟ 6
● Valtellina Sfursat Fruttaio Ca' Rizzieri '97	♟♟♟ 6
● Valtellina Sfursat '02	♟♟ 6
● Valtellina Sfursat Fruttaio Ca' Rizzieri '01	♟♟ 7
● Valtellina Sup. Inferno Ris. '02	♟♟ 5
● Valtellina Sup. Crespino '01	♟♟ 5

Ricci Curbastro

VIA ADRO, 37
25031 CAPRIOLO [BS]
TEL. 030736094
www.riccicurbastro.it

ANNUAL PRODUCTION 260,000 bottles
HECTARES UNDER VINE 30
VITICULTURE METHOD Conventional

The Ricci Curbastro family has been associated with farming for centuries, in both Romagna and Franciacorta, and Riccardo has managed the family estate in Capriolo for the past 20 years. It currently extends over 30 hectares of vineyards and annual production is more than 250,000 bottles. Based on a blend of 50 per cent Chardonnay and 50 per cent Pinot Nero, Riccardo's distinctively styled Extra Brut again reached our tasting finals, this time with the '03 vintage. This deep straw-yellow Franciacorta with rich onion-skin highlights and was only lightly filtered. It has the charm of authentic territory wines, an impression confirmed on the nose, with its red berries and citrus peel, and on the intense, lively palate, where the creamy effervescence is backed up by plenty of structure and sinew. We also liked the excellent Dosaggio Zero Gualberto '01, from mainly pinot noir, which shows firm structure, full flavour and elegant, complex notes of fruit and barley sugar. The estate's other wines are also good.

Tenuta Roveglia

LOC. ROVEGLIA, 1
25010 POZZOLENGO [BS]
TEL. 030918663
www.tenutaroveglia.it

ANNUAL PRODUCTION 200,000 bottles
HECTARES UNDER VINE 56
VITICULTURE METHOD Conventional

The 60 hectares of vineyards belonging to the Zweifel Azzone family's Tenuta Roveglia are almost entirely planted to trebbiano di Lugana, apart from a small area of land dedicated to cabernet sauvignon and merlot. This estate has always demonstrated an explicit vocation for whites, but awareness of the true potential of this little corner of clayey land has only been grasped recently, and the quality of the grapes, entrusted to Paolo Fabiani assisted by consultant oenologist Flavio Prà, is up with the highest standards in the area. This is obviously also the result of radical choices in the vineyard and the latest vintages have yielded a series of wines with strong personality, combining stylistic cleanliness with accurate expression of the terroir. Lugana Superiore Vigna di Catullo '05 has dense fruit with a fresh vegetal vein and restrained hints of medicinal herbs. Filo di Arianna '04, aged in large oak casks, boasts good pulp, florality, spicy hints and subtle mineral overtones. Lugana '06 is approachable and pleasant.

O Franciacorta Extra Brut '03	♟♟ 5*
O Franciacorta Dosaggio	
Zero Gualberto '01	♟♟ 6
O Brolo dei Passoni '05	♟♟ 5
O TdF Bianco V. Bosco Alto '04	♟♟ 4*
● Pinot Nero Sebino '03	♟♟ 5
O Franciacorta Satèn Brut '02	♟♟ 6
O Franciacorta Brut	♟ 5
● TdF Rosso Curtefranca '05	♟ 3
O TdF Bianco Curtefranca '06	♟ 3*
● TdF Rosso Santella del Gröm '04	♟ 4
● Sebino Rosso '05	♟ 3*
O Franciacorta Satèn	♟ 5
● TdF Rosso Santella del Gröm '01	♟♟ 4*
O Brolo dei Passoni '03	♟♟ 5
O Brolo dei Passoni '04	♟♟ 5
● TdF Rosso Santella del Gröm '03	♟♟ 4*

O Lugana Sup. Vigne di Catullo '05	♟♟ 4
O Lugana '06	♟♟ 4
O Lugana Sup. Filo di Arianna '04	♟♟ 5
O Lugana '05	♟♟ 3
O Lugana Sup. Vigna di Catullo '04	♟♟ 4
O Lugana '04	♟♟ 3
O Lugana Sup. Filo di Arianna '02	♟♟ 4

San Cristoforo
VIA VILLANUOVA, 2
25030 ERBUSCO [BS]
TEL. 0307760482
sancristoforo_d@libero.it

ANNUAL PRODUCTION 80,000 bottles
HECTARES UNDER VINE 12
VITICULTURE METHOD Conventional

We've always thought highly of the work of Bruno Dotti and his wife Claudia Cavalleri, who have enthusiastically managed their Erbusco estate since 1992, producing still wines and Franciacortas exclusively from the grapes of their 12 hectares of vineyards. This year marks the debut of the vintage Franciacorta, in the '03 version. Bright straw yellow in hue, it has a creamy mousse and fine perlage. The nose opens with intense tropical, fruity notes that develop into sensations of vanilla and aromatic herbs. On the palate, there is good structure, zestiness, healthy fruit and a caressing effervescence. The Brut is also attractive, although less complex, with an intriguing well-defined flowery nose, fresh vegetal hints, succulent fruit notes and suppleness on the palate. Terre di Franciacorta Bianco '05 is excellent, with fresh notes of peach and full structure. The deep, balanced Terre di Franciacorta Rosso '04 is also good.

Conti Sertoli Salis
P.ZZA SALIS, 3
23037 TIRANO [SO]
TEL. 0342710404
www.sertolisalis.com

ANNUAL PRODUCTION 250,000 bottles
HECTARES UNDER VINE 7
VITICULTURE METHOD Conventional

Sertoli Salis is currently settling down following the changes of recent years, including the replacement of longstanding oenologist Claudio Introini by the well-known consultant Vittorio Fiore. Sforzato Canua '04, with its unmistakable dense aromas of chocolate, red berry jam and spices, earned its regular place in our finals. On the palate, it shows soft and concentrated, with fine-grained tannins and a clear, very long finish. Capo di Terra '04, from slightly dried nebbiolo grapes, is classy and has an original style. The result is a well-balanced, flavoursome wine with intense aromas of ripe fruit and a long finish. We thought that Corte della Meridiana '04, from nebbiolo, had a slightly muddled nose; the palate is round but not overly long. Saloncello '06, from nebbiolo, is fruity, full flavoured and fresh. The crisp, fragrant Torre della Sirena, from pignola and rossola, is decent.

O Franciacorta Brut '03	🍷🍷 6
O Franciacorta Brut	🍷🍷 5
O TdF Bianco '05	🍷🍷 3*
● TdF Rosso '04	🍷 3
● Re Probus '03	🍷🍷 8
O TdF Bianco '03	🍷🍷 4*
● TdF Curtefranca Rosso '03	🍷🍷 4*

● Valtellina Sforzato Canua '04	🍷🍷 7
● Valtellina Sup. Capo di Terra '04	🍷🍷 5
● Il Saloncello '06	🍷 5
● Valtellina Sup. Corte della Meridiana '04	🍷 5
O Torre della Sirena '06	🍷 4
● Valtellina Sforzato Canua '00	🍷🍷🍷 6
● Valtellina Sforzato Canua '97	🍷🍷🍷 6
● Valtellina Sforzato Canua '02	🍷🍷🍷 7
● Valtellina Sforzato Canua '01	🍷🍷🍷 7
● Valtellina Sforzato Canua '99	🍷🍷🍷 6
● Valtellina Sforzato Canua '03	🍷🍷 7
● Valtellina Sup. Corte della Meridiana '00	🍷🍷 5
● Valtellina Sup. Capo di Terra '02	🍷🍷 5
● Valtellina Sup. Capo di Terra '03	🍷🍷 5

Lo Sparviere
VIA COSTA, 2
25040 MONTICELLI BRUSATI [BS]
TEL. 030652382
www.losparviere.com

ANNUAL PRODUCTION 120,000 bottles
HECTARES UNDER VINE 30
VITICULTURE METHOD Conventional

Heir to one of Europe's oldest industrial families, Ugo Gussalli Beretta owns a fine estate of 150 hectares, including 30 under vine at Monticelli Brusati, managed by his wife Monique Poncelet. Lo Sparviere produces a select range of still wines and Franciacortas, spearheaded by the Franciacorta Extra Brut '01, a very fresh vintage sparkler, with a complex nose of crusty bread, ripe fruit, flowers, oak and roasted coffee beans. On the palate, it's elegant and well defined, unfolding dynamic, zesty, deep and full. Less heavyweight, but very pleasant is the Brut '03, which has good backbone and notes of citrus fruit and toast, while the Rosé Brut, from pinot nero, is also attractive, if slightly lightweight. Although we weren't totally convinced by the Satèn, whose aromas lack definition, we did like the complex, structured Terre di Franciacorta Rosso del Vigneto Sergnana '03.

Travaglino
LOC. TRAVAGLINO, 6A
27040 CALVIGNANO [PV]
TEL. 0383872222
www.travaglino.it

ANNUAL PRODUCTION 250,000 bottles
HECTARES UNDER VINE 80
VITICULTURE METHOD Conventional

Fabrizio Marzi's Riesling Campo della Fojada has always been one of the best in Oltrepò. This is excellent wine country, where the vines grow on white soil that gives it an unmistakable bouquet of aromatic herbs with hints chamomile-led flowers and minerals. On the palate, it's full and juicy, supported by a good vein of acidity that carries it on to a lingering finish. Pinot Nero Brut Classese '03 is well executed and the oak well handled. Brilliant in hue, it throws a full nose of bread-like notes, toasted hazelnuts and citrus fruit, tiny bubbles and remarkable structure. The full, opulent Chardonnay Campo della Mojetta '04 is interesting with nicely restrained oak and a nose of ripe banana and spring flowers. Rosé Monteceresino, a classic method sparkler, has an attractive, almost coppery colour, delicate, continuous perlage, smoky notes and good fruity pulp. Pinot Nero Pernero '06 is vinified without oak. It's uncomplicated, varietal and enjoyable, showing silky tannins. Barbera Campo dei Ciliegi '05 and Cabernet Campo della Calastrega '04 are equally varietal, crisp and precise. Finally, the evolved Pinot Nero Brut Grand Cuvée has an attractive golden colour, full flavour and good body.

O Franciacorta Extra Brut '01	♟♟ 6
O Franciacorta Brut '03	♟♟ 5
● TdF Rosso Il Sergnana '03	♟♟ 4*
O Franciacorta Satèn	♟ 5
⊙ Franciacorta Rosé Brut	♟ 6
O Franciacorta Extra Brut '98	♟♟ 5*
O Franciacorta Extra Brut '00	♟♟ 5
O Franciacorta Extra Brut '99	♟♟ 5

O OP Chardonnay	
Campo della Mojetta '04	♟♟ 4
O OP Pinot Nero Brut Classese '03	♟♟ 5
O OP Riesling	
Campo della Fojada '06	♟♟ 4
● OP Barbera Campo dei Ciliegi '05	♟ 4
● OP Cabernet Sauvignon	
Campo della Calastrega '04	♟ 4
⊙ OP Pinot Nero Brut Rosé	
Monteceresino	♟ 5
● OP Pinot Nero Pernero '06	♟ 4*
O OP Pinot Nero Grand Cuvée	♟ 5
O OP Riesling	
Campo della Fojada '04	♟♟ 4
O OP Pinot Nero Brut Classese '01	♟♟ 5
O OP Riesling	
Campo della Fojada '05	♟♟ 4

Triacca

VIA NAZIONALE, 121
23030 VILLA DI TIRANO [SO]
TEL. 0342701352
www.triacca.com

ANNUAL PRODUCTION 700,000 bottles
HECTARES UNDER VINE 47
VITICULTURE METHOD Conventional

Sforzato San Domenico '03 performed admirably, showing how patience pays and how, once again, longer ageing produces a finer wine. Three Glasses, then, for this elegant, true-to-type, concentrated and complex red. The rounded aromas offer fruit and flower sensations with a Mediterranean feel. On the palate, it shows full and balanced, with the various components in perfect harmony. Prestigio '03 is very good, giving concentrated, crisp fruity aromas and notes of medicinal herbs. Assertive, flavoursome and cosseting on the palate, it signs off with a long finale. Riserva La Gatta '02 is a classic example of a territory-driven wine. The rich, fruity nose is followed by a full palate with close-knit tannins and a lingering finish. Casa La Gatta '04 has fruit fragrances laced with vegetal hints, a balanced palate and a leisurely finish carried by good acidity. The juicy, flavoursome Sassella '04 has aromas of flowers and red berries and holds together well in the fresh finish.

★ Uberti

LOC. SALEM
VIA E. FERMI, 2
25030 ERBUSCO [BS]
TEL. 0307267476
www.ubertivini.it

ANNUAL PRODUCTION 160,000 bottles
HECTARES UNDER VINE 24
VITICULTURE METHOD Conventional

Over the past decade and a half, Agostino and Eleonora Uberti's blends have offered us infinite emotions. Franciacortas of great character and complexity, they are made to stand the test of time and crafted from the grapes of the estate's handsome vineyards, which are tended with the same care lavished on every detail in the cellar. The successful husband-and-wife team was joined several years ago by their oenologist daughter Silvia, who has gained important experience abroad and shares not only her parents' profession but also their genuine passion for sparkling wines. Again this year, the excellent list is headed by Comarì del Salem, whose '02 vintage proves itself one of the best cuvées in Italy, managing to combine incredible body, elegance and complexity with truly enticing drinkability. This year also marks the debut of a new Franciacorta, the Nondosato Sublimis '01, whose strengths lie in its acid backbone, complex mineral tones and rich structure. The quality of the entire range is laudably high.

● Valtellina Sforzato San Domenico '03	♟♟♟ 7
● Valtellina Sup. La Gatta Ris. '02	♟♟ 6
● Valtellina Sup. Prestigio '03	♟♟ 7
● Valtellina Sup. Sassella '04	♟♟ 5
● Valtellina Sup. Casa La Gatta '04	♟ 5
● Valtellina Prestigio Millennium '97	♟♟♟ 5
● Valtellina Sforzato San Domenico '01	♟♟♟ 7
● Valtellina Sforzato '00	♟♟♟ 7
● Valtellina Sforzato '99	♟♟♟ 6
● Valtellina Sforzato San Domenico '02	♟♟ 7
● Valtellina Sup. Prestigio '01	♟♟ 7
● Valtellina Sup. La Gatta Ris. '00	♟♟ 5
● Valtellina Sup. La Gatta Ris. '01	♟♟ 6
● Valtellina Sup. Sassella '03	♟♟ 5
● Valtellina Sup. Prestigio '02	♟♟ 7

○ Franciacorta Extra Brut Comarì del Salem '02	♟♟♟ 7
○ Franciacorta Non Dosato Sublimis '01	♟♟ 7
○ Franciacorta Brut Francesco I	♟♟ 5
○ Franciacorta Satèn Magnificentia	♟♟ 6
○ Franciacorta Extra Brut Francesco I	♟♟ 5
☉ Franciacorta Rosé Francesco I	♟ 5
● TdF Curtefranca Rosso '05	♟ 4
○ TdF Bianco Curtefranca '06	♟ 4
○ Franciacorta Extra Brut Comarì del Salem '01	♟♟♟ 7
○ Franciacorta Extra Brut Comarì del Salem '98	♟♟♟ 7
○ Franciacorta Extra Brut Comarì del Salem '95	♟♟♟ 6
○ Franciacorta Brut Comarì del Salem '00	♟♟♟ 7
○ Franciacorta Brut Comarì del Salem '93	♟♟♟ 6

Vanzini

Fraz. Barbaleone, 7
27040 San Damiano al Colle [PV]
Tel. 038575019
www.vanzini-wine.com

ANNUAL PRODUCTION 800,000 bottles
HECTARES UNDER VINE 17
VITICULTURE METHOD Conventional

The Vanzini brothers' Bonarda Frizzante '06 is always a safe bet. Its deep ruby hue introduces clean, well-defined aromas of blackberry, blueberry and raspberry, attractive crisp, healthy fruit, balanced tannins and residual sugar, before bowing out with a lingering finish. The same is true for the Sangue di Giuda '06, which shows impenetrable colour and a fruity, fragrant nose. On the palate, it's harmonious and sweet but not cloying, thanks to good acidity, and the tannins are velvety. Barbera '06 has hints of ripe morello cherry, good structure and backbone and a well-sustained finish. Pinot Nero Rosé Extra Dry is a sparkler produced by the Charmat method, with an onion-skin hue and a fine, persistent bubbles accompanied by attractive development, clear notes of red berries, pulp and backbone. Another good Vanzini wine is Oltrepò Pavese Rosso Barbaleone '03, which was highly promising when we tasted it from the vat. It has suffered from the dry vintage, though, and shows slightly overripe fruit with roughish tannins. Moscato Spumante is well made, with fragrances of tropical and citrus fruit, while the Pinot Nero Extra Dry, a Charmat method sparkler, is refreshing and pleasant.

Vercesi del Castellazzo

Via Aureliano, 36
27040 Montù Beccaria [PV]
Tel. 038560067
vercesidelcastellazzo@libero.it

ANNUAL PRODUCTION 80,000 bottles
HECTARES UNDER VINE 15
VITICULTURE METHOD Conventional

The estate owned by the Vercesi family focuses mainly on reds. This year, it did not present its two most representative wines, the still Bonarda Fatila and Rosso Castellazzo, whose 2003 vintage reached our finals last year. Consequently, it was Barbera Clà '05 that stole the limelight. Showing deep ruby with a purplish rim, it discloses hints of morello cherry, violet, coffee and spices with a seductive balsamic vein. On the palate, there is very attractive fruit, a nice balance of alcohol and acidity and good depth. OP Rosso Pezzalunga '06 is very well crafted. Vinified exclusively in steel, its most appealing features are its crisp wild berry notes and pleasant drinkability. Vespolino '06 is an IGT red obtained from 100 per cent vespolina, an indigenous variety that yields clean well-defined wild berries and highly distinctive spicy notes. We were pleasantly surprised by the soft, easy-drinking Baccarossa '06, from 50 per cent barbera with merlot and vespolina, at a price of just three and a half euros at the cellar door. But Pinot Nero Luogo dei Monti '04 disappointed, showing very evolved and overripe. Bonarda Luogo della Milla '06 and Pinot Nero in Bianco Gugiarolo '06 are not bad.

● OP Barbera '06	🍷🍷 3*
● OP Bonarda Frizzante '06	🍷🍷 3*
☉ OP Pinot Nero Rosé Extra Dry	🍷🍷 4*
● OP Sangue di Giuda '06	🍷🍷 4*
● OP Barbaleone '03	🍷 5
○ OP Pinot Nero Extra Dry	🍷 4
○ OP Moscato Spumante Charmat '06	🍷 4
● OP Barbaleone '01	🍷🍷 5
● OP Sangue di Giuda '05	🍷🍷 4*
● OP Bonarda Frizzante '05	🍷🍷 4*
● OP Sangue di Giuda '04	🍷🍷 4

● OP Barbera Clà '05	🍷🍷 4
● OP Rosso Pezzalunga '06	🍷🍷 3*
● Vespolino '06	🍷🍷 3*
● Bacca Rossa '06	🍷 2*
● OP Bonarda Luogo della Milla '06	🍷 3
○ OP Pinot Nero in Bianco Gugiarolo '06	🍷 3
● OP Pinot Nero Luogo dei Monti '04	🍷 4
● OP Barbera Clà '04	🍷🍷 4
○ OP Pinot Nero in Bianco Gugiarolo '05	🍷🍷 3*

Bruno Verdi
VIA VERGOMBERRA, 5
27044 CANNETO PAVESE [PV]
TEL. 038588023
www.verdibruno.it

ANNUAL PRODUCTION 100,000 bottles
HECTARES UNDER VINE 9
VITICULTURE METHOD Conventional

It's no accident that OP Rosso Cavariola Riserva has reached our finals for the third year running. Paolo Verdi's gem has long been one of the best Oltrepò reds and can point to outstanding consistency of quality and coherency of style for this area. The '04 stands out for its deep ruby hue and hallmark balsamic aromas. Next come spicy notes derived from good-quality oak and berry fruit, which are faithfully echoed on the palate, where the tannins display their usual silky texture, well balanced by acidity, alcohol and structure in a harmonious and very long whole. The true-to-type Barbera Campo del Marrone '05 is very good, showing softness but without eschewing acidity. Brut Classico Vergomberra '04 is spirited and lively, with tiny bubbles, aromas of cakes, hazelnuts and wild berries and a swath of acidity reminiscent of a pas dosé. The two dessert wines, Moscato di Volpara and Sangue di Giuda '06, are very well executed and perfectly true to type. Pinot Nero '05 is consistent, well defined and varietal while Pinot Grigio, Buttafuoco and Bonarda '06 are correct and pleasant.

Giuseppe Vezzoli
VIA COSTA SOPRA, 22
25030 ERBUSCO [BS]
TEL. 0307267579
eveniogv@libero.it

ANNUAL PRODUCTION 130,000 bottles
HECTARES UNDER VINE 40
VITICULTURE METHOD Conventional

Giuseppe Vezzoli took the helm of the family estate a few years ago, giving it an extraordinary boost. In a short space of time, he has expanded the estate's original five hectares with a further 35 under lease, bringing production – which obviously focuses on Franciacortas – to around 130,000 bottles a year. The results are first rate, thanks to Giuseppe's passion, excellent raw materials and the invaluable advice of consultant oenologist Cesare Ferrari. This year, Giuseppe presented only Franciacortas at our tastings. Our favourite was the intense, full-flavoured Brut '03, which gives attractive aromas of yeast and toast, plenty of backbone and the typical delicate aromatic notes that often characterize Erbusco blancs de blancs. Brut Nefertiti '01 shows pleasantly complex notes of coffee, peach jam and oak while the good Rosé is soft and fruity, although not as impressive as the version we tasted last year. The Satèn and undosed Nefertiti Dizeta '01 are both good.

● OP Rosso Cavariola Ris. '04	♀♀	5
● OP Barbera Campo del Marrone '05	♀♀	4
○ OP Moscato Volpara '06	♀♀	3*
● OP Sangue di Giuda Dolce Paradiso '06	♀♀	3*
○ OP Brut Cl. Vergomberra '04	♀♀	5
● OP Pinot Nero '05	♀♀	4
● OP Bonarda Vivace Possessione di Vergomberra '06	♀	3
○ OP Pinot Grigio '06	♀	3*
● OP Buttafuoco '06	♀	3
● OP Rosso Cavariola Ris. '02	♀♀	5
● OP Rosso Cavariola Ris. '03	♀♀	5
● OP Barbera Campo del Marrone '04	♀♀	4
● OP Pinot Nero '04	♀♀	4
○ OP Brut Cl. Vergomberra '03	♀♀	5
● OP Rosso Cavariola Ris. '01	♀♀	5
● OP Sangue di Giuda Dolce Paradiso '05	♀♀	3*
● OP Bonarda Vivace Possessione di Vergombera '05	♀♀	3*
● OP Barbera Campo del Marrone '01	♀♀	4

○ Franciacorta Brut '03	♀♀	6
○ Franciacorta Brut Nefertiti '01	♀♀	7
⊙ Franciacorta Rosé	♀♀	6
○ Franciacorta Extra Brut Nefertiti Dizeta '01	♀	7
○ Franciacorta Satèn	♀	6
○ Franciacorta Brut '01	♀♀	6
○ Franciacorta Brut Nefertiti '00	♀♀	7
○ Franciacorta Brut '02	♀♀	6
○ Franciacorta Satèn '01	♀♀	6

Villa
VIA VILLA, 12
25040 MONTICELLI BRUSATI [BS]
TEL. 030652329
www.villa-franciacorta.it

ANNUAL PRODUCTION 310,000 bottles
HECTARES UNDER VINE 37
VITICULTURE METHOD Conventional

Paolo Bianchi's estate, located at the foot of the Madonna della Rosa hills in Monticelli Brusati, is one of the most interesting in the DOCG zone. It includes a perfectly restored former farming settlement that now houses modern cellar equipment, surrounded by well-tended vineyards, including some on the terraced slopes. With the advantage of an exceptionally skilled technical staff, it has all everything needed to be a top winery: witness the awards that it has collected over the years. This time, we liked the impeccable Brut Cuvette '02, with its fresh vein of acidity and vanilla notes, and were impressed by the very delicate Brut Selezione '01, which offers ripe fruit, attractive oak and mineral sensations. Other excellent wines include the firm, vigorous Brut '03, the complex, convincing Rosé Demi Sec '03 and the fresh, mouthfilling Satèn from the same vintage. The Satèn Selezione '01 is perhaps slightly over-evolved while the red Querqus '03, from merlot, and Terre di Franciacorta Bianco Pian della Villa '05, are both very good.

Villa Crespia
VIA VALLI, 11
25030 ADRO [BS]
TEL. 0307451051
www.fratellimuratori.com

ANNUAL PRODUCTION 400,000 bottles
HECTARES UNDER VINE 60
VITICULTURE METHOD Conventional

Year after year, the wines from Villa Crespia acquire body and complexity, confirming the soundness of the work carried out several years ago by oenologist and researcher Francesco Iacono. The estate is one of the islands in the Muratori archipelago, which comprises estates on Ischia, in Sannio and in Maremma as well as in Franciacorta, where it has 60 hectares planted to vine. One of the cornerstones of his system is single-vineyard vinification, which aims to enhance the characteristics of each individual selection. This year, our favourite was Dosaggio Zero Cisiolo '02, from pinot nero, which presents an attractive coppery hue, red berries on the nose with oaky and mineral notes, firm structure and good acid backbone on the palate. Satèn Cesonato, with apricot notes, and the spirited, zesty Brut Novalia, are also very convincing. Rosé Brolese is good, with attractive fruit, while Brut Miolo and Dosaggio Zero Numerozero are interesting.

O Franciacorta Brut '03	❢❢ 5
O Franciacorta Satèn '03	❢❢ 6
● Querqus '03	❢❢ 6
O TdF Bianco Pian della Villa '05	❢❢ 4
O Franciacorta Brut Sel. '01	❢❢ 7
O Franciacorta Cuvette Brut '02	❢❢ 6
⊙ Franciacorta Rosé Demi Sec '03	❢❢ 6
O Franciacorta Cuvette Diamant Pas Dosé '02	❢ 6
● TdF Rosso Gradoni '04	❢ 5
O Franciacorta Satèn Sel. '01	❢ 8
O TdF Bianco '05	❢ 4
O Franciacorta Brut '01	❢❢ 5*
O TdF Bianco Pian della Villa '04	❢❢ 4
● TdF Rosso Gradoni '03	❢❢ 5

O Franciacorta Dosaggio Zero Cisiolo '02	❢❢ 5
O Franciacorta Satèn Brut Cesonato	❢❢ 7
⊙ Franciacorta Rosé Extra Brut Brolese '03	❢❢ 8
O Franciacorta Brut Novalia	❢❢ 6
O Franciacorta Brut Miolo	❢ 5
O Franciacorta Numerozero	❢ 5
⊙ Franciacorta Brolese Rosé Extra Brut '02	❢❢ 8

OTHER WINERIES

Al Rocol
VIA PROVINCIALE, 79
25050 OME [BS]
TEL. 0306852542
www.alrocol.com

Gianluigi Vimercati, the skilled heir to ancient viticultural traditions, makes excellent still wines and Franciacortas on his fine estate in Ome. The refreshing, zesty Ca' del Luf '03 is captivating, with rich fruit, as is the Satèn, which boasts attractive notes of vanilla and flowers.

O Franciacorta Brut Ca' del Luf '03	▼▼	6
O Franciacorta Satèn '03	▼▼	5

Riccardo Albani
LOC. CASONA
S.DA SAN BIAGIO, 46
27045 CASTEGGIO [PV]
TEL. 038383622
www.vinialbani.it

Albani's golden Riesling '05 is full, fat and very evolved, with a distinctive style, accentuated mineral notes and a long palate. Bonarda Vivace '06 has fruity pulp and well-calibrated tannins but falls short on the nose, which is lacking in definition. The Barbera '05 still needs to find the right balance.

O OP Riesling Renano '05	▼▼	4*
● OP Barbera '05	▼	4
● OP Bonarda Vivace '06	▼	4

Tenuta degli Angeli
FRAZ. SANTO STEFANO
VIA FARA, 2
24060 CAROBBIO DEGLI ANGELI [BG]
TEL. 035687130
www.tenutadegliangeli.it

The distinctive Valcalepio Moscato Passito di Carobbio degli Angeli '04 is very sweet, giving cinnamon and honey. Valcalepio Bianco Triplok '05 has an interesting nose with aromatic herbs, citrus notes and crisp ripe fruit while Spumante Classico Brut Degli Angeli '01 is uncomplicated and well made.

O Valcalepio Bianco Triplok '05	▼▼	4
● Valcalepio Moscato Passito di Carobbio degli Angeli '04	▼▼	7
O Spumante Brut Cl. degli Angeli '01	▼	5

Antica Tesa
LOC. MATTINA
VIA MERANO, 28
25080 BOTTICINO [BS]
TEL. 0302691500

The estate owned by the Noventa family has handled the '04 vintage very well and offers three good Botticinos from different vineyards. Vigna del Gobbio is excellent, showing soft, full and juicy, as is the firm, lingering, blackberry-led Pià della Tesa. Vigna degli Ulivi is lighter but also very nice.

● Botticino Vigna del Gobbio '04	▼▼	6
● Botticino Pià della Tesa '04	▼▼	5
● Botticino Vigna degli Ulivi '04	▼	4

Avanzi
VIA TREVISAGO, 19
25080 MANERBA DEL GARDA [BS]
TEL. 0365551013
www.avanzi.net

The opening of the new winery building has given fresh impetus to the Avanzi family's production. The flagship red is still Cabernet Vigna Bragagna, packed with overripe fruit. Both the Luganas are nice, with the Superiore '05 showing particularly well. Garda Classico Chiaretto '06 has an alluring nose.

● Garda Cabernet Sauvignon V. Bragagna '03	▼▼	5
O Lugana Sup. Sirmione '05	▼▼	4
⊙ Garda Cl. Chiaretto Il Vino di una Notte '06	▼	4
O Lugana di Sirmione V. Bragagna '06	▼	4

Paolo Bagnasco
FRAZ. LOGLIO DI SANTA MARIA DELLA VERSA
27047 SANTA MARIA DELLA VERSA [PV]
TEL. 0385262329
www.cantinabagnasco.it

Paolo Bagnasco released two still Bonardas from the 2003 vintage. We slightly preferred Vigna Casapaglia, whose hallmarks are fragrant fruity aromas and fine mature tannins. Vigna del Sole is also good but falls down slightly on the finish. The Sangue di Giuda '06 is all no-nonsense fruit.

● OP Bonarda V. Casapaglia '03	▼▼	3*
● OP Bonarda V. del Sole '03	▼	4
● OP Sangue di Giuda '06	▼	3

OTHER WINERIES

Barboglio De Gaioncelli
FRAZ. COLOMBARO
VIA NAZARIO SAURO
25040 CORTE FRANCA [BS]
TEL. 0309826831
www.barbogliodegaioncelli.it

Guido Costa's fine estate, with 15 hectares of fine vineyards in Corte Franca, makes consistently good wines. We liked the excellent Dosage Zero Claro '02, which is dense and sinewy, giving smoke and minerals, and the firmly structured, soft, juicy Extra Dry that reveals white-fleshed fruit.

O Franciacorta Extra Dry	♟♟	4*
O Franciacorta Dosage Zero Claro '02	♟♟	6

F.lli Bettini
LOC. SAN GIACOMO
VIA NAZIONALE, 4A
23036 TEGLIO [SO]
TEL. 0342786068
bettvini@tin.it

Sforzato '04's traditional nose precedes a warm, caressing palate whose close-knit tannins lead into a long finish. The classy Sassella Reale '04 has complex, fruit aromas and a flavoursome, well-sustained palate. Vigna La Cornella '04 shows elegant fruit and a juicy palate with a long, full finish.

● Valtellina Sfursat '04	♟♟	7
● Valtellina Sup. Sassella Reale '04	♟♟	5
● Valtellina Sup. Valgella V. La Cornella '04	♟	5

Conti Bettoni Cazzago
VIA MARCONI, 6
25046 CAZZAGO SAN MARTINO [BS]
TEL. 0307750875
www.contibettonicazzago.it

Agronomist Vincenzo Bettoni Cazzago runs his Cazzago San Martino estate with enthusiasm. Brut Tetellus '03 is excellent, with complex overtones of smouldering logs and a harmonious, full palate, as is the non-vintage Satèn Brut, which gives soft, opulent notes of ripe fruit and vanilla.

O Franciacorta Brut Tetellus '03	♟♟	5
O Franciacorta Brut Satèn	♟♟	4*
O Franciacorta Brut Tetellus '00	♟♟	6

Bonomi - Tenuta Castellino
VIA SAN PIETRO, 46
25030 COCCAGLIO [BS]
TEL. 0307721015
www.tenutabonomi.it

The Bonomi family owns this handsome estate with 16 hectares of vineyards at the foot of Mount Orfano. Our favourites were the good Franciacorta Satèn, with attractive aromas of hawthorn and acacia blossom and a caressingly soft palate, and the richly structured red Cordelio '04, with distinct blackberry.

O Franciacorta Satèn	♟♟	4*
● TdF Rosso Curtefranca Cordelio '04	♟♟	5
● TdF Rosso Curtefranca Cordelio '03	♟♟	6

La Boscaiola
VIA RICCAFANA, 19
25033 COLOGNE [BS]
TEL. 0307156386
www.laboscaiola.com

Giuliana Cenci produces a well-crafted range of still wines and Franciacortas on her Cologne estate. This year we were impressed by the white Giuliana '05, a bright straw-green wine with a rich nose of ripe white-fleshed fruit laced with delicate vegetal notes. The Brut was less captivating than last time.

O TdF Bianco Giuliana '05	♟♟	4*
O Franciacorta Brut	♟	5

Boschi
VIA ISEO, 76
25030 ERBUSCO [BS]
TEL. 03077245
www.agricolaboschi.it

Franco Timoteo Metelli offers a wide range of Franciacortas and territory-dedicated wines. This year, we liked the two Rosés, a Brut and a Demi Sec. The former has a brilliant pale pink hue, intense fresh aromas and good structure, while the latter offers prominent ripe fruit and cherry jam.

☉ Franciacorta Rosé Brut	♟♟	5
☉ Franciacorta Rosé Demi Sec	♟	5

OTHER WINERIES

Tenuta Il Bosco
LOC. IL BOSCO
27049 ZENEVREDO [PV]
TEL. 0385245326
www.ilbosco.com

Bonarda Vivace '06 is among the best in Oltrepò, with sound red berries and elegant tannins. Poggio Pelato '04 is varietal and well balanced, just needing a little more depth to wine another Glass. The two Philèo cuve close sparklers are pleasant and fresh, although we preferred the Rosé's good fruit.

● OP Bonarda Vivace '06 — ꝟꝟ 3*
○ OP Pinot Nero Brut Philèo — ꝟ 4
● OP Pinot Nero Poggio Pelato '04 — ꝟ 4
⊙ Extra Dry Phileo Rosè — ꝟ 4

Bosio
LOC. TIMOLINE
VIA MARIO GATTI
25040 CORTE FRANCA [BS]
TEL. 030984398
www.bosiofranciacorta.it

Agronomist Cesare Bosio has also turned his hand to winemaking on the family's 30-hectare estate. We liked the soft, flavoursome Satèn, with aromas of ripe apricot and flowers, and the Extra Brut Boschedòr '03, which is impressively fresh and cleanly styled.

○ Franciacorta Satèn — ꝟꝟ 5
○ Franciacorta Extra Brut Boschedòr '03 — ꝟꝟ 5

Bredasole
LOC. BREDASOLE
VIA SAN PIETRO, 44
25030 PARATICO [BS]
TEL. 035910407
www.bredasole.it

The Ferrari brothers and consultant oenologist Corrado Cugnasco make still wines and Franciacortas from the estate's 16 hectares of vineyards. We liked the Franciacorta Satèn, with a rich tropical fruit and vanilla nose and soft, zesty palate. The Pas Dosé is goodish and well made, but slightly over-evolved.

○ Franciacorta Satèn — ꝟꝟ 5
○ Franciacorta Pas Dosé — ꝟ 5

Luciano Brega
FRAZ. BERGAMASCO, 7
27040 MONTÙ BECCARIA [PV]
TEL. 038560237

The garnet-ruby Bonarda Casapaia '05 has a deep, intense nose with crisp blackberry and earthier hints. On the palate, it has ripe fruit, plenty of fine-grained tannins, well-calibrated oak and a long finish with after-aromas of liquorice. Bonarda Vivace '06 is pleasant and well made, giving violets.

● OP Bonarda Casapaia '05 — ꝟꝟ 3*
● OP Bonarda Vivace '06 — ꝟ 3

Cantina Sociale di Broni
VIA SANSALUTO, 81
27043 BRONI [PV]
TEL. 038551505
cantinasocialebroni@tin.it

We liked the balanced, fragrant Sangue di Giuda Bronis '06. Bonarda Frizzante Bronis Selezione '06 is well made, with clean, well-defined fruit and fine-grained tannins. Wild berries and gamey sensations characterize the nose of the soft Buttafuoco Bronis '04. The fruity OP Rosso Bronis '02 is decent.

● OP Bonarda Bronis Sel. '06 — ꝟꝟ 3*
● OP Sangue di Giuda Bronis '06 — ꝟꝟ 1*
● OP Buttafuoco Bronis '04 — ꝟ 2
● OP Rosso Bronis '02 — ꝟ 3

La Brugherata
FRAZ. ROSCIATE
VIA G. MEDOLAGO, 47
24020 SCANZOROSCIATE [BG]
TEL. 035655202
www.labrugherata.it

The '03 vintage of Valcalepio Rosso Doglio Riserva is as good as ever, with notes of spices and ripe hay and marked tannins. Cabernet Priore '04 is highly varietal but has a slightly short finish. The Valcalepio Vescovado Rosso '05 and Bianco '06 are pleasant, upfront and well made.

● Valcalepio Rosso Doglio Ris. '03 — ꝟꝟ 5
● Priore '04 — ꝟ 5
○ Valcalepio Bianco Vescovado '06 — ꝟ 4
● Valcalepio Rosso Vescovado '05 — ꝟ 4

OTHER WINERIES

Ca' del Gè
FRAZ. CA' DEL GÈ, 3
27040 MONTALTO PAVESE [PV]
TEL. 0383870179
www.cadelge.it

Riesling Italico '06 is straw yellow with golden highlights, offering delicate flowery fragrances, good tropical fruit, backbone and great length. The enjoyable, cherry-led Barbera '06 is uncomplicated while Bonarda Frizzante '06 is very soft with intact fruit.

● OP Barbera '06	🍷🍷	2*
○ OP Riesling '06	🍷🍷	2*
● O. P. Bonarda Frizzante '06	🍷	2

Ca' del Santo
LOC. CAMPOLUNGO, 4
27040 MONTALTO PAVESE [PV]
TEL. 0383870545
www.cadelsanto.it

Sangue di Giuda Trepoderi '06 is well defined with nice fruit while Pinot Nero Il Nero '04 has spice and wild berries followed by fine-grained tannins. Bonarda Vivace Grand Cuvée '06 tempts with crisp fruit and the 50 + 50 '05, from pinot nero and cabernet sauvignon, unveils smoky hints and overripe fruit.

● OP Sangue di Giuda Trepoderi '06	🍷🍷	3
● OP Bonarda Vivace Grand Cuvée '06	🍷	4
● 50 + 50 '05	🍷	4
● Pinot Nero Il Nero '04	🍷	4

Ca' Montebello
LOC. MONTEBELLO, 10
27040 CIGOGNOLA [PV]
TEL. 038585182
www.camontebello.it

The Scarani family's Bonarda Frizzante '06 is soft, fragrant and fruity, with raspberry and cherry top notes. Pinot Nero '06 is fresh and uncomplicated with varietal notes, while Sangue di Giuda '06 boasts a good balance of tannins and sugar.

● OP Bonarda Frizzante '06	🍷🍷	3*
● OP Sangue di Giuda '06	🍷	3
● Pinot Nero '06	🍷	3

Ca' Tessitori
VIA MATTEOTTI, 15
27043 BRONI [PV]
TEL. 038551495
catessitori@linterfree.it

Luigi Giorgi's Bonarda Frizzante '06 has good fruit and prominent tannins. The OP Rosso Borghesa '06 is uncomplicated and enjoyable while the IGT Chardonnay '06 has attractive aromas of tropical fruit but disappointing structure on the palate. The classic method spumante has been more expressive in the past.

● OP Rosso Borghesa '06	🍷	4
○ Chardonnay '06	🍷	4
● OP Bonarda Frizzante '06	🍷	4

Calvi
FRAZ. VIGALONE, 13
27044 CANNETO PAVESE [PV]
TEL. 038560034
www.andreacalvi.it

Andrea Calvi's Bonarda Vivace '06 opens up nicely after a little aeration to reveal good fruit and ripe tannins. The Chardonnay Spirit '04 has a golden hue and good fruit and structure but is marred by rather intrusive oak. Rui '02, a barbera, cabernet sauvignon and merlot blend, has vegetal and spicy notes.

○ OP Chardonnay Spirit '04	🍷	4
● OP Bonarda Vivace '06	🍷	3
● Rui '02	🍷	4

Caminella
VIA DANTE ALIGHIERI, 13
24069 CENATE SOTTO [BG]
TEL. 035941828
www.caminella.it

The estate's good table wines include Ricco il Goccio di Sole, from part-dried moscato di Scanzo grapes; the poised, fruity Luna Rossa, from cabernet, merlot and pinot nero; and the full-bodied Verde Luna, from chardonnay, sauvignon blanc and pinot bianco. Valcalepio Rosso Ripa di Luna '05 is uncomplicated.

● Luna Rossa '05	🍷🍷	5
● Goccio di Sole '05	🍷🍷	6
● Valcalepio Rosso Ripa di Luna '05	🍷	4
○ Verde Luna Bianco '04	🍷	4

OTHER WINERIES

Carlozadra
VIA GANDOSSI, 13
24064 GRUMELLO DEL MONTE [BG]
TEL. 035830244

We awarded Two Glasses to Carlozadra
Extra Dry Liberty for its fine bubbles, clear
tropical fruit, flowers and cakes, softness
and verve. Nature '01, which was known as
Nondosato until last year, has evolved notes
and marked toastiness. We also gave Two
Glasses to the elegant Brut '02.

O Carlozadra Extra Dry Liberty	♙♙	5
O Carlozadra Brut Cl. Nature '01	♙	6
O Carlozadra Brut Cl. '02	♙♙	5

Cascina Gnocco
FRAZ. LOSANA, 20
27040 MORNICO LOSANA [PV]
TEL. 0383892280
www.cascinagnocco.it

OP Rosso Riserva Donna Cecilia '03 is
balanced, giving wild berries, smooth
tannins and good body. The unusual,
intriguing Orione '05, from the vinification of
indigenous Mornico grapes, is aged in 900-
litre casks and will be better understood
with more time in bottle. Riesling Ambrogina
'06 is refreshing.

● OP Rosso Donna Cecilia Ris. '03	♙♙	5
O OP Riesling Italico Ambrogina '06	♙	4
● Orione '05	♙	8

Cascina San Pietro
FRAZ. CALINO DI CAZZAGO SAN MARTINO
VIA SAN PIETRO, 30
25040 CAZZAGO SAN MARTINO [BS]
TEL. 035912448
www.cascinaspietro.it

Giuseppe Pecis makes a well-crafted range
of still wines and Franciacortas on his fine
estate. This year, we liked the Extra Brut
Tere' dei Trici '03, which has good body on
the mineral and toast-laced nose and
palate. The Satèn is balanced and opulent,
with a profusion of sweet, vanilla notes.

O Franciacorta Extra Brut Tere' dei Trici '03	♙♙	5
O Franciacorta Satèn	♙♙	5*

Tenimenti Castelrotto - Torti
FRAZ. CASTELROTTO, 6
27047 MONTECALVO VERSIGGIA [PV]
TEL. 0385951000
www.tortiwinepinotnero.com

Bonarda Vivace Brioso '05 has sound fruit,
interesting earthy notes and well-calibrated
tannins. The varietal Pinot Nero '03 flaunts
well-gauged oak but the torrid '03 growing
year has made it very evolved and overripe,
stripping it of some finesse. The sparkling
Brut Casaleggio is simple and appealing.

● OP Bonarda Vivace Brioso '05	♙♙	4
● OP Pinot Nero '03	♙	5
O OP Brut Casaleggio '06	♙	5

Castelveder
VIA BELVEDERE, 4
25040 MONTICELLI BRUSATI [BS]
TEL. 030652308
www.castelveder.it

Renato and Elena Alberti produce around
100,000 bottles of excellent still wines and
Franciacortas each year from their 12
hectares under vine. We liked the elegant,
evolved Brut '01 for its backbone, structure
and complexity in the mouth and the
attractive Satèn for its soft attack and good
body.

O Franciacorta Brut '01	♙♙	5
O Franciacorta Satèn	♙	5
O Franciacorta Brut '00	♙♙	5

Caven Camuna
VIA CAVEN, 1
23036 TEGLIO [SO]
TEL. 0342484330
www.cavencamuna.it

Ripe black berries with hints of fruit preserve
and oriental spices pervade the intense
nose of Sforzato Messere '02. The palate is
rounded, unveiling perfectly integrated
tannins and a long-lingering finish.

● Valtellina Sforzato Messere '02	♙♙	7

OTHER WINERIES

Le Chiusure

FRAZ. PORTESE
VIA BOSCHETTE, 2
25010 SAN FELICE DEL BENACO [BS]
TEL. 0365626243
www.lechiusure.net

Alessandro Luzzago's programme to enhance quality while focusing on the classic grapes of the Brescian shore of Lake Garda is going well. Malborghetto, from rebo, merlot and barbera; Campei, from barbera, marzemino and sangiovese; and Groppello are all very drinkable, with bags of fruit and personality.

- ● Garda Cl. Groppello '05 — 🍷🍷 4
- ● Mal Borghetto '04 — 🍷🍷 5
- ● Campei '04 — 🍷 4

Castello di Cigognola

P.ZZA CASTELLO, 1
27040 CIGOGNOLA [PV]
TEL. 038585601
infocastellodicigognola@securfin.com

Gianmarco and Letizia Moratti's Barbera has again shown itself to be a wine of substance. Like the '03, the '04 also presents a deep ruby, the nose dominated by tertiary aromas of coffee and sweet spices from expertly calibrated oak, while the complex palate is structured, fruity and balanced.

- ● OP Barbera '04 — 🍷🍷 6
- ● OP Barbera '03 — 🍷🍷 6

Il Cipresso

VIA CERRI, 2
24020 SCANZOROSCIATE [BG]
TEL. 0354597005
www.ilcipresso.info

As always, the balanced, upfront Serafino '04 is one of the best Moscato di Scanzos, with good typicity and length. Valcalepio Rosso Bartolomeo Riserva '04 is intense and harmonious while Valcalepio Rosso Dionisio '05 is simpler yet elegant and Valcalepio Bianco Melardo '06 convinces on the nose.

- ● Moscato di Scanzo Serafino '04 — 🍷🍷 7
- ● Valcalepio Rosso Bartolomeo Ris. '04 — 🍷🍷 5
- ○ Valcalepio Bianco Melardo '06 — 🍷 4
- ● Valcalepio Rosso Dionisio '05 — 🍷 4

Cantine Colli a Lago

LOC. SAN MARTINO DELLA BATTAGLIA
LOC. SELVA CAPUZZA
25010 DESENZANO DEL GARDA [BS]
TEL. 0309910381
www.selvacapuzza.it

Of all the many, very reliable wines made by the Formentini family, we liked Madèr '05, a Garda Classico Superiore, and the excellent Lugana Superiore '05, from grapes sourced from the Selva Capuzza estate. The rare, florality-led San Martino della Battaglia and the very fruity Chiaretto are also intriguing.

- ● Garda Cl. Sup. Rosso Madèr '05 — 🍷🍷 4
- ○ Lugana Sup. Selva Capuzza '05 — 🍷🍷 5
- ⊙ Garda Cl. Chiaretto Selva Capuzza '06 — 🍷 4
- ○ San Martino della Battaglia Campo del Soglio '06 — 🍷 4

Comincioli

LOC. CASTELLO
VIA ROMA, 10
25080 PUEGNAGO SUL GARDA [BS]
TEL. 0365651141
www.comincioli.it

A great experimenter with the grape and olive cultivars of Valtenesi, Gianfranco Comincioli has decided to produce two Chiarettos from different vintages, with results that are always interesting. The elegant, spirited Perlì is a white from Valtenesi erbamàt and trebbiano while Gropèl '04 is a powerful red.

- ○ Perlì '06 — 🍷🍷 4
- ⊙ Riviera del Garda Bresciano Chiaretto Vintage '05 — 🍷🍷 4
- ● Riviera del Garda Bresciano Gropèl '04 — 🍷🍷 5
- ⊙ Riviera del Garda Bresciano Chiaretto '06 — 🍷 4

Cornaleto

VIA CORNALETTO, 2
25030 ADRO [BS]
TEL. 0307450507
www.cornaleto.it

The 1992 vintage yielded exceptional grapes on the estate belonging to the Lancini family, which boasts 18 well-aspected hectares on Monte Alto at Adro. It's still possible to purchase the Dosage Zero '92, which shows full, complex, deep and mineral. The non-vintage Brut is correct and well made, as usual.

- ○ Franciacorta Brut — 🍷🍷 4
- ○ Franciacorta Dosage Zero '92 — 🍷🍷 6

OTHER WINERIES

Le Corne
LOC. CORNE
LOC. CORNE, 4
24064 GRUMELLO DEL MONTE [BG]
TEL. 035830215
www.lecorne.it

Valcalepio Rosso Torre Dolia '05 has attractive fruit and flower aromas laced with balsam, sound fruit and good balance while the well-structured Riserva Messernero '03 has more overripe notes and marked spice. Valcalepio Bianco Messerbianco '05, aged in oak casks, and Torre Dolia '06 are well executed.

● Valcalepio Rosso Messernero Ris. '03	♟♟	5
● Valcalepio Rosso Torre Dolia '05	♟♟	4*
○ Valcalepio Bianco Messerbianco '05	♟	4
○ Valcalepio Bianco Torre Dolia '06	♟	3

La Costa
FRAZ. COSTA
VIA CURONE, 15
22050 PEREGO [LC]
TEL. 0395312218
www.la-costa.it

Solesta '05, from chardonnay and riesling renano, did well again this year, unveiling a complex, ripe nose and elegant, balanced palate. San Giobbe '05, from pinot nero, is well styled with spicy fragrances. Serìz '05 is a merlot, cabernet and syrah blend with good fruit on the nose and poised in the mouth.

● Serìz '05	♟	5
○ Solesta '05	♟♟	4
● San Giobbe '05	♟	5

Delai
VIA MORO, 1
25080 PUEGNAGO SUL GARDA [BS]
TEL. 0365555527

The rich fruit and spices of the '04 vintage of Sergio Delai's Fronsaga confirms the progress made by this interesting Garda red, from barbera with groppello and sangiovese. The Groppello is long and satisfyingly drinkable. Both the Sovenigo, from marzemino, and the Chiaretto will improve with age.

● Fronsaga '04	♟♟	5
● Garda Bresciano Groppello Mogrì '06	♟♟	4
● Sovenigo '05	♟	5
⊙ Garda Bresciano Chiaretto '06	♟	4

Lorenzo Faccoli & Figli
VIA CAVA, 7
25030 COCCAGLIO [BS]
TEL. 0307722761
az.faccoli@libero.it

The Faccoli brothers lovingly tend vineyards at Coccaglio, from which they produce well-crafted Franciacortas. This time, we liked the Rosé Brut for its appealing rose, cherry and strawberry nose and soft, elegant palate, as well as the austere Dosage Zero '02, with its vein of acidity and caressing fizz.

⊙ Franciacorta Rosé Brut	♟	5
○ Franciacorta Dosage Zero '02	♟♟	5

Fiamberti
VIA CHIESA, 17
27044 CANNETO PAVESE [PV]
TEL. 038588019
www.fiambertivini.it

Riesling Vigna Croce di Montevenedoso '06 has good backbone and the zesty classic method Fiamberti is well executed. Bonarda Frizzante Vigna Bricco della Sacca '06 is fragrant and true to type. Finally, Buttafuoco Storico Vigna Solenga '03 gives balsam and wild berries, although the finish is slightly short.

● OP Bonarda Frizzante Bricco della Sacca '06	♟♟	4*
○ OP Brut Cl. Fiamberti	♟♟	5
○ OP Riesling Italico V. Croce Montevenedoso '06	♟♟	3*
● OP Buttafuoco Storico V. Solenga '03	♟	5

Fondazione Fojanini
VIA VALERIANA, 32
23100 SONDRIO [SO]
TEL. 0342512654

Sforzato '01 has complex aromas of dried fruit and a rich, round palate with well-integrated tannins and a long finish. Sassella '02 has good character and robust body, well sustained by fresh acidity, and the elegant Sassella Le Barberine '01 has a varietal nose and a complex, dynamic palate.

● Valtellina Sup. Sassella Le Barberine Ris. '01	♟♟	
● Valtellina Sup. Sforzato '01	♟♟	
● Valtellina Sup. Sassella '02	♟	

OTHER WINERIES

Fortesi
FRAZ. CA' NOVA, 4
27040 ROVESCALA [PV]
TEL. 038575093
www.fortesi.com

Elena Franco and Filippo Fortin's Bonarda Vivace '06 has an attractive impenetrable hue and aromas of violet and wild berries. Uva Rara '06 is pleasant and well typed with hints of spices. Ombre Rosse '03 is a very rustic still Bonarda, sporting abundant, roughish tannins and evolved notes.

● OP Bonarda Vivace '06	♀♀ 4
● Uva Rara '06	♀♀ 4
● OP Bonarda Ombre Rosse '03	5

Antica Cantina Fratta
VIA FONTANA, 11
25040 MONTICELLI BRUSATI [BS]
TEL. 030652068
www.anticafratta.it

Cristina Ziliani puts great effort into this estate, which has always made Franciacortas. All three wines we tasted are excellent, from the elegant Brut '03 to the delightful Satèn and the excellent firm-bodied, blackberry-led Terre Rosso, sourced from the old Tenuta Ragnoli vineyard at Erbusco.

O Franciacorta Satèn	♀♀ 6
● TdF Rosso Ragnoli '05	♀♀ 5
O Franciacorta Brut '03	♀♀ 5

Fattoria Gambero
FRAZ. CASE NUOVE
27045 SANTA MARIA
DELLA VERSA [PV]
TEL. 038579268
www.fattoriailgambero.it

Vittorio Ferrario's Bonarda Frizzante Alborada '06 is fragrant and fruity while Pinot Nero Tinterosse '05 and Teston '06, a Cabernet Sauvignon vinified without oak, are pleasingly fresh and varietal. Pinot Nero Brut Cl. Principe d'Onore '04, debuting this year, has ripe fruit but an over-tart finish.

● OP Bonarda Frizzante Alborada '06	♀♀ 3
● OP Pinot Nero Tinterosse '05	♀ 4
O OP Pinot Nero Brut Principe d'Onore '04	♀ 4
● Teston '06	♀ 4*

Gatta
VIA SAN ROCCO, 33
25064 GUSSAGO [BS]
TEL. 0302772950
www.paginegialle.it/agricolagatta

Mario Gatta is a name destined for greater things in our Guide as the quality of his wines is constantly improving. This year, he amazed us with a very fresh, full, complex Arcano Brut '94, which reached our finals. The well-made Franciacorta Brut shows crisp fruit, firm structure and a supple palate.

O Franciacorta Brut Arcano '94	♀♀ 7
O Franciacorta Brut	♀♀ 4*

Castello di Grumello
VIA FOSSE, 11
24064 GRUMELLO DEL MONTE [BG]
TEL. 0354420817
www.castellodigrumello.it

Valcalepio Rosso Riserva Colle Calvario '03 is harmonious and well crafted with crisp fruit, good structure and a fairly long finish. The wild berry-themed Valcalepio Moscato Nero Passito '00 is clean tasting and warm while Valcalepio Bianco '06 is simple but rather attractively fruity.

● Valcalepio Moscato Nero Passito '00	♀♀ 6
● Valcalepio Rosso Colle del Calvario Ris. '03	♀♀ 6
O Valcalepio Bianco '06	♀ 3

La Guarda
FRAZ. CASTREZZONE
VIA ZANARDELLI, 49
25080 MUSCOLINE [BS]
TEL. 0365372948
www.laguarda.com

Gigi Negri is in no hurry. He waits for his wines to reach maturity before releasing them. This year, he presented Marzemino '02 and Barbera '04, two highly drinkable, affordable reds of character. Chiaretto '06 is among the best of its vintage from Lake Garda. As ever, the Groppello is frank and agreeable.

⊙ Garda Cl. Chiaretto '06	♀♀ 4*
● Garda Barbera '04	♀♀ 4*
● Garda Marzemino '02	♀ 4*
● Garda Cl. Groppello '06	♀ 3*

OTHER WINERIES

Isimbarda

LOC. CASTELLO
CASCINA ISIMBARDA
27046 SANTA GIULETTA [PV]
TEL. 0383899256
www.tenutaisimbarda.com

Riesling Vigna Martina '06 boasts golden highlights, mineral-laced flowery aromas, good pulp, backbone and balance. OP Rosso Montezavo Riserva '04 has hints of spices and wild berries but not quite enough depth for a second Glass. The semi-sparkling varietal Barbera and Bonarda '06 are nice if undemanding.

O OP Riesling Renano Vigna Martina '06	🍷🍷 4
● OP Bonarda Vivace '06	🍷 4
● OP Rosso Montezavo Ris. '04	🍷 5
● OP Barbera Vivace '06	🍷 3

Leali di Monteacuto

FRAZ. MONTEACUTO
VIA DOSSO, 4
25080 PUEGNAGO SUL GARDA [BS]
TEL. 0365651291

Antonio Leali's red Simut deserves the excellent reputation it enjoys on the Lombardy shore of Lake Garda. The '04 vintage of this groppello and marzemino blend gives impressively rich fruit and caressing softness. Groppello '05 displays fruit and spices while the Riesling '06 is appealing.

● Garda Bresciano Groppello '05	🍷🍷 4
● Simut '04	🍷🍷 5
O Garda Riesling '06	🍷 4

Lurani Cernuschi

VIA CONVENTO, 3
24031 ALMENNO SAN SALVATORE [BG]
TEL. 035642576
www.luranicernuschi.it

The interesting Opis '06, from incrocio Manzoni, has a good fruity nose and a well-sustained palate and finish. Valcalepio Rosso '04 is well made, balanced and long, giving wild berries and spices. The good Cabernet Sauvignon Umbriana '04 is firm with full body. Valcalepio Bianco '06 is nice and refreshing.

O Opis '06	🍷🍷 3*
● Valcalepio Rosso '04	🍷🍷 3*
● Umbriana '04	🍷 3
O Valcalepio Bianco '06	🍷 3

Castello di Luzzano

LOC. LUZZANO, 5
27040 ROVESCALA [PV]
TEL. 0523863277
www.castelloluzzano.it

The bright ruby Barbera Oreste '05 is very convincing with its red berry fruit and good supporting acidity. Bonarda Carlino '06 has wild berries and violets, good pulp and youthful tannins. The refreshing, varietal Pinot Nero Umore Nero '06 is very drinkable.

● OP Barbera Oreste '05	🍷🍷 4
● OP Bonarda Carlino '06	🍷 4
● OP Pinot Nero Umore Nero '06	🍷 4*

Martilde

FRAZ. CROCE, 4A1
27040 ROVESCALA [PV]
TEL. 0385756280
www.martilde.it

Martilde's wines are improving fast. The structure and balance of Barbera La Strega, la Gazza e il Pioppo '04 won it a place in our finals. Bonarda Ghiro Rosso d'Inverno '04 has ripe, healthy fruit and the dry Malvasia Piume '06 is fresh, with thyme and lavender, while Bonarda Vivace Gianna '06 has good pulp.

● OP Barbera La Strega, la Gazza e il Pioppo '04	🍷🍷 5
● OP Bonarda Ghiro Rosso d'Inverno '04	🍷🍷 5
O OP Malvasia Piume '06	🍷🍷 4
● OP Bonarda Vivace Gianna '06	🍷 3

Medolago Albani

VIA REDONA, 12
24069 TRESCORE BALNEARIO [BG]
TEL. 035942022
www.medolagoalbani.it

Valcalepio Rosso Riserva I Due Lauri is good, as usual. The '03 has more pulp than the '02 and a very appealing spicy nose. Cabernet Sauvignon Villa Redona '03 is pleasant and full flavoured with good overall balance. The uncomplicated, refreshing Valcalepio Bianco has tropical fruit fragrances.

● Valcalepio I Due Lauri Ris. '03	🍷🍷 4
O Valcalepio Bianco '06	🍷 3
● Villa Redona '03	🍷 4

OTHER WINERIES

Cantine di Mezzaluna
LOC. CASA TACCONI, 13
27040 MONTALTO PAVESE [PV]
TEL. 0383870282
www.cantinedimezzaluna.it

This year marks the debut of this Montalto Pavese estate in our Guide. Pinot Nero '05 won Two Glasses for its self-assured, consistent style. Vigna Rugà '05 is a Bordeaux blend with hints of bracken and bell peppers with notes of autumn leaves and good fruity body. Bonarda '06 is a little short on balance.

● OP Pinot Nero '05	♆♆	4
● Vigan Rugà '05	♆	4
● OP Bonarda '06	♆	3

Montagna
VIA CAIROLI, 67
27043 BRONI [PV]
TEL. 038551028
www.cantinemontagna.it

Cabernet Sauvignon Viti di Luna '01 is frank on the nose and soft in the mouth. The clean, fruity Bonarda Frizzante Sopralerighe '06 offers soft tannins. The copper-tinged Pinot Nero Brut Martinotti Sopralerighe has good backbone, and the honey and orange blossom Moscato Frizzante Viti di Luna '06 is typical.

● OP Cabernet Sauvignon Viti di Luna '01	♆♆	3*
● OP Bonarda Frizzante Sopralerighe '06	♆♆	3*
○ OP Pinot Nero Brut Martinotti Sopralerighe		♆ 3
○ OP Moscato Frizzante Viti di Luna '06	♆	2

Marchesi di Montalto
LOC. COSTA GALLOTTI
27040 MONTALTO PAVESE [PV]
TEL. 3394982856
www.marchesidimontalto.it

Riesling Italico Monsaltus '04, from botrytized grapes, is always surprisingly good, showing full and oily with deep minerality. The drinkable Barbera Cascina Bellaria '04 is varietal and fairly simple. Strangely, OP Rosso Riserva Re Rosso '03 is less dense than the '02. Bonarda Vivace '06 is a rustic, meaty wine.

○ OP Riesling Italico Monsaltus '04	♆♆	4
● OP Bonarda Vivace Cascina Francone '06	♆	3
● OP Barbera Cascina Bellaria '04	♆	4
● OP Re Rosso Ris. '03	♆	5

Monte Cicogna
VIA DELLE VIGNE, 6
25080 MONIGA DEL GARDA [BS]
TEL. 0365503200
www.montecicogna.it

The Materossi family's winery is housed in an old farmstead just outside Moniga, overlooking Lake Garda. It produces wines that reflect the territory in a convincing and rustically traditional style. Groppello Beana is a good example, with fruity, earthy and spicy notes.

● Garda Cl. Rosso Groppello Beana '05	♆	4
○ Garda Cl. Bianco Il Torrione '05	♆	4
○ Lugana S. Caterina '06	♆	4
● Garda Cl. Rosso Sup. Rubinere '04	♆	4

Tenuta Monte Delma
LOC. VALENZANO
25050 PASSIRANO [BS]
TEL. 0306546161
www.montedelma.it

Piero Berardi enthusiastically manages the family estate, which has been busy growing grapes for the past 80 years. Both the Franciacortas we tasted were very good. The juicy, fruity Brut is fresh and well balanced, while the Satèn has opulent fruit and flowers that develop vanilla notes and a supple palate.

○ Franciacorta Brut	♆♆	5
○ Franciacorta Satèn	♆♆	5

Montenato Griffini
VIA SPARANO, 13/14
27049 BOSNASCO [PV]
TEL. 0385272904
www.montenatogriffini.it

Barbara Faravelli Santambrogio's estate is one of the few in Oltrepò to release still Bonarda only. The plentiful tannins seem to suggest longer bottle ageing. Of the two '04 wines, we prefer the Etichetta Nera, aged in small oak, which is more harmonious and mature: the other version is a little rough.

● OP Bonarda Puntofermo Etichetta Nera '04	♆♆	4
● OP Bonarda Puntofermo Etichetta Bianca '04	♆	3

OTHER WINERIES

Monterucco
VALLE CIMA, 38
27040 CIGOGNOLA [PV]
TEL. 038585151
www.monterucco.it

The Valenti family's Bonarda Frizzante Vigna Il Modello '06 gives violet and raspberry notes, fine-grained tannins and perceptible residual sugar. Valentina '06 is a dry Malvasia IGT with close-focused aromas of flower and peach tea and an alluring fruity texture.

● OP Bonarda Frizzante V. Il Modello '06	♀	3
○ Valentina '06	♀	3

Nettare dei Santi
VIA CAPRA, 17
20078 SAN COLOMBANO AL LAMBRO [MI]
TEL. 0371200523
www.nettaredeisanti.it

San Colombano Mombrione Riserva '04 has distinct notes of toast and good flesh. Passito di Verdea '03 is zesty with attractive citrus while the husky-style Podere Roverone '06, from barbera, croatina, uva rara, cabernet and merlot, is soft and simple. The sparkling Domm is restrained and rather evolved.

○ Passito di Verdea '03	♀	4
● Podere Roverone '06	♀	2
○ Spumante Brut Cl. Domm	♀	4
● San Colombano Mombrione Ris. '04	♀	4

Olivini
LOC. SAN MARTINO DELLA BATTAGLIA
DEMESSE VECCHIE, 2
25015 DESENZANO DEL GARDA [BS]
TEL. 0309910268
www.olivini.net

Despite being relative newcomers to the Garda wine scene, the Olivinis have earned respect for their classically styled wines obtained from trebbiano di Lugana and merlot. Demesse Vecchie sports fruit and minerality while Notte a San Martino has rich pulp. The Lugana and the classic Brut are both nice.

○ Lugana Sup. Demesse Vecchie '04	♀♀	4
● Notte a San Martino '04	♀♀	5
○ Lugana Brut '04	♀	4
○ Lugana '06	♀	3

Olmo Antico
VIA MARCONI, 8
27040 BORGO PRIOLO [PV]
TEL. 0383872672
www.olmoantico.it

Paolo Baggini's interesting balsam-laced Barbera '04 is robust. His spirited Riesling Olmo Bianco '06 displays a very distinctive upfront style. Croatina 14 Ottobre '06 has attractive healthy fruit while Merlot Giorgio Quinto '04 requires further bottle age to achieve balance.

● Barbera '04	♀♀	5
○ Olmo Bianco '06	♀♀	4
● Croatina 14 Ottobre '06	♀	4
● Giorgio Quinto '04	♀	6

Panigada - Banino
VIA DELLA VITTORIA, 13
20078 SAN COLOMBANO AL LAMBRO [MI]
TEL. 037189103
vinobanino@hotmail.com

Bianco Passito Aureum '04, from malvasia, is interesting, with a nose of cannolo cakes and candied peel, a chewy palate and appealing acidity that offsets the sweetness. San Colombano Banino '05 is somewhat rustic while Vigna La Merla Riserva '03 is again very good.

● Passito Aureum '04	♀♀	6
● San Colombano Banino '05	♀	3
● San Colombano V. La Merla Ris. '03	♀♀	5

Tenuta Pegazzera
LOC. PEGAZZERA
VIA VIGORELLI
27045 CASTEGGIO [PV]
TEL. 0383804646
www.pegazzera.it

The pleasant Riesling Italico Brut has an intriguingly rich bouquet. We liked Orgoglio '04, from almost pure merlot, with its alluring chewy fruit. Cabernet Sauvignon Ligna '04, is balanced and highly varietal, only just missing a second Glass. Pinot Nero Petrae '04 is very evolved.

○ OP Riesling Italico Brut	♀♀	3
● Orgoglio '04	♀♀	5
● OP Cabernet Sauvignon Ligna '04	♀	4
● OP Pinot Nero Petrae '04	♀	4

OTHER WINERIES

Percivalle
VIA TORCHI, 9
27040 BORGO PRIOLO [PV]
TEL. 0383871175
www.percivalle.com

Paolo Percivalle's Barbera Costa del Sole '03 is beefy but still has some rough edges. The compact, fruity Bonarda Frizzante Amanti '06 is better. La Cura '04 is a Bordeaux blend whose oak should integrate with time in bottle. Triade '06, from chardonnay, riesling and pinot nero, flaunts an attractive nose.

● OP Bonarda Frizzante Amanti '06	♟♟ 3*
● OP Barbera Costa del Sole '03	♟ 4
○ Triade '06	♟ 3
● La Cura '04	♟ 4

Piccolo Bacco dei Quaroni
FRAZ. COSTAMONTEFEDELE
27040 MONTÙ BECCARIA [PV]
TEL. 038560521
www.piccolobaccodeiquaroni.it

The nice Barbera Gustavo '05 is very flavoursome and fruity. Pinot Nero Vigneto La Fiocca '04 gives blackcurrants, pepper and cloves and lots of fine-grained tannins. Both the Bonarda Vivace Mons Acutus '06 and the Buttafuoco Vigneto Ca' Padroni '03 have succulent but rather aggressive tannins.

● OP Barbera Gustavo '05	♟♟ 2*
● OP Pinot Nero Vign. La Fiocca '04	♟♟ 4*
● OP Bonarda Vivace Mons Acutus '06	♟ 3*
● OP Buttafuoco Vign. Ca' Padroni '03	♟ 4

Pietrasanta
VIA SFORZA, 55/57
20078 SAN COLOMBANO AL LAMBRO [MI]
TEL. 0371897540
carlopietrasanta@mìvlombardia.com

San Colombano Podere Costa Regina Riserva '03 has a wild berry nose and an appealingly spicy palate with fine-grained tannins. Unfortunately, it lacks depth, which stopped it from scoring higher. The Pinot Nero '04 is varietal and fairly rustic in style while Rosso della Costa has marked tertiary notes.

● Pinot Nero '04	♟ 4
● Rosso della Costa '04	♟ 4
● San Colombano Podere Costa Regina Ris. '03	♟ 5

Podere della Cavaga
VIA GAFFORELLI, 1
24060 FORESTO SPARSO [BG]
TEL. 035930939
www.vinicavaga.it

The well-structured Valcalepio Rosso Foresto Riserva '03 gives notes of bell pepper, ripe hay and spices and is surprisingly fresh for a '03. We liked the slightly overripe aromas of the Valcalepio Rosso Foresto '04, which is a bit short on the finish. The Valcalepio Bianco Adamante '06 is taut on the palate.

● Valcalepio Rosso Foresto Ris. '03	♟♟ 6
○ Valcalepio Bianco Adamante '06	♟ 3
● Valcalepio Rosso Foresto '04	♟ 4

Quadra
VIA SANT'EUSEBIO, 1
25033 COLOGNE [BS]
TEL. 0307157314
www.quadrafranciacorta.it

The Ghezzi family has many business interests in Italy and Argentina. Quadra is a young estate, founded in 2003, which has already attracted attention with wines such as its attractive Satèn, with aromatic herbs and citrus fruits introducing a fresh, supple palate, and the nicely balanced, fresh Brut.

○ Franciacorta Satèn	♟♟ 5
○ Franciacorta Brut	♟ 5

Quaquarini
LOC. MONTEVENEROSO
VIA CASA ZAMBIANCHI, 26
27044 CANNETO PAVESE [PV]
TEL. 038560152
www.quaquarinifrancesco.it

Both the Bonarda Frizzante '06 and the Sangue di Giuda '06 are crisp, fragrant and well made, with crunchy fruit and an alluringly impenetrable ruby hue. The very evolved Buttafuoco Storico Vigna Pregana '01 has good fruity pulp. The Brut Classese '01 is pleasant, but less complex than previous vintages.

● OP Sangue di Giuda '06	♟♟ 3*
● OP Bonarda Frizzante '06	♟♟ 3*
○ OP Brut Classese '01	♟ 4
● OP Buttafuoco Storico V. Pregana '01	♟ 6

OTHER WINERIES

Riccafana
VIA FACCHETTI, 91
25033 COLOGNE [BS]
TEL. 0307156797
www.riccafana.com

While last year saw the triumph of the Fratus Rosé, this time it's the Satèn. The soft, elegant Fratus '03 is excellent, vaunting complex hints of toast and oak with a very attractive background and a well-defined, juicy palate with lingering apricot notes. The Rosé Demi Sec is good.

O Franciacorta Satèn	🍷🍷	4*
O Franciacorta Satèn Fratus '03	🍷🍷	5
⊙ Franciacorta Rosé Demi Sec	🍷	5

Ricchi
VIA FESTONI, 13D
46040 MONZAMBANO [MN]
TEL. 0376800238
www.cantinaricchi.it

The Chardonnay Meridiano '06 has alluring aromas of melon and tropical fruit, while the Cabernet Ribò '04 is varietal with good weight. This year, Passito Le Cime, from moscato and garganega, was below par, with toastiness too prominent. Cornalino, a Bordeaux blend, is a nice, uncomplicated food wine.

O Garda Chardonnay Meridiano '06	🍷🍷	4*
● Garda Cabernet Ribò '04	🍷	4
O Passito Le Cime	🍷	5
● Cormalino Rosso	🍷	2

Ronco Calino
FRAZ. TORBIATO - LOC. QUATTRO CAMINI
VIA FENICE, 45
25030 ADRO [BS]
TEL. 0307451073
www.roncocalino.it

Paolo Radici makes excellent still wines and Franciacortas on his handsome Adro estate. The best of these is the solidly traditional Brut '01, which has notes of yeast and toast and a firm palate, although the basic Brut is almost as captivating, proffering crisp fruit and then good balance and softness.

O Franciacorta Brut '01	🍷🍷	6
O Franciacorta Brut	🍷🍷	5
O TdF Bianco '06	🍷🍷	4*

Ruiz de Cardenas
LOC. MAIRANO
VIA MOLLIE, 35
27045 CASTEGGIO [PV]
TEL. 038382301
www.ruizdecardenas.it

The elegant Galanta Brut Classico Reserve '01 progresses well with roasted hazelnut aromas and nice body. Of the two Pinot Nero '03 selections, we preferred Brumano, which has better integrated oak and more depth and balance than Vigna Miraggi. Pinot Nero Vigna Le Moine '04 is pleasant and varietal.

● OP Pinot Nero Brumano '03	🍷🍷	5
O Galanta Brut Cl. Reserve '01	🍷🍷	5
● OP Pinot Nero Vigna Miraggi '03	🍷	5
● OP Pinot Nero Vigna La Moine '04	🍷	3

Tenuta San Francesco
VIA SCAZZOLINO, 55
27040 ROVESCALA [PV]
TEL. 029085141
info@alziati.it

Annibale Alziati sent us two '05 Bonardas. We liked the still version, which has sound, crisp wild berry fruit. The slightly sparkling Bonarda has an interesting nose but over-assertive tannins. While the succulent, fruity Barbera San Francesco '03 gives carefully gauged oak, the finish is rather edgy.

● OP Bonarda San Francesco '05	🍷🍷	3*
● OP Barbera San Francesco '05	🍷	3
● OP Bonarda Vivace San Francesco '05	🍷	3

San Michele
VIA GARIBALDI, 48-50
25020 CAPRIANO DEL COLLE [BS]
TEL. 0309747329
www.vinisanmichele.it

Although the Capriano del Colle area has historically been red wine country but today it is the whites that are attracting most attention. San Michele's aromatic Montecorso, an IGT Montenetto, and the spirited Capriano Bianco, based on trebbiano, confirm this trend. The Rosso Riserva is good.

O Capriano del Colle Bianco '06	🍷🍷	4
O Montecorso '06	🍷🍷	4
● Capriano del Colle Rosso '05	🍷	4
● Capriano del Colle Rosso Ris. '04	🍷	5

OTHER WINERIES

Tenuta Scarpa Colombi
VIA GROPPALLO, 26
27049 BOSNASCO [PV]
TEL. 0385272081
www.colombiwines.com

Marubbio '05, a still Bonarda, is beefy, compact and balanced. The Chardonnay Brut Teresco is fairly simple and well made, with crisp hints of tropical fruit and flowers. Pinot Nero Ariolo '05 is not very complex and still developing while the Pinot Nero Brut is fresh and uncomplicated.

● OP Bonarda Marubbio '05	🍷🍷 4
● OP Pinot Nero Ariolo '05	🍷 4
○ Spumante Brut Teresco	🍷 4
○ OP Pinot Nero Brut	🍷 4

Scuropasso
FRAZ. SCORZOLETTA, 40/42
27043 PIETRA DE' GIORGI [PV]
TEL. 038585143
www.scuropasso.it

Fabio Marazzi's Pinot Nero Brut Classico Roccapietra '02 shows evolved but crisp, clean aromas of tropical and citrus fruits. The appeal of Bonarda Vivace Palatinus '06 lies in its rich fruit, good balance and softness. Sangue di Giuda '06 is fresh and pleasant, with an attractive nose of wild berries.

● OP Bonarda Vivace Palatinus '06	🍷🍷 3*
○ OP Pinot Nero Brut Cl. Roccapietra '02	🍷🍷 5
● OP Sangue di Giuda '06	🍷 2

Vincenzo Tallarini
VIA FONTANILE, 7/9
24060 GANDOSSO [BG]
TEL. 035834003
www.tallarini.com

Satiro '03 has good fruity pulp and marked toast. Valcalepio Rosso Riserva San Giovannino '03 offers blackberries, blueberries, bell peppers and ripe hay, accompanied by good pulp and fine-grained tannins. Moscato di Scanzo '03 is still looking for balance and Valcalepio Rosso Arlecchino '04 is uncomplicated.

● Satiro '03	🍷🍷 6
● Valcalepio Rosso San Giovannino Ris. '03	🍷🍷 5
● Moscato di Scanzo '03	🍷 7
● Valcalepio Rosso Arlecchino '04	🍷 4

Togni Rebaioli
FRAZ. ERBANNO
VIA ROSSINI, 19
25047 DARFO BOARIO TERME [BS]
TEL. 0364529706

There's just one drawback with Enrico Togni's wines: they have not had time to age properly. Still, you can sympathize with wanting to release an IGT – Valcamonica, created in 2003 – as soon as possible. Otherwise, these are robust, fruity mountain reds with lots of character.

● Lambrù '05	🍷🍷 4
● Millesettecentotre '05	🍷🍷 4
● Merlot Rebaioli Cav. Enrico '05	🍷 5

La Tordela
VIA TORRICELLI, 1
24060 TORRE DE' ROVERI [BG]
TEL. 035580172
www.latordela.it

Torre de' Roveri's intense, deep Valcalepio Rosso Riserva Campo Roccoli Vecchi '03 is the best of its type, with good balance, a very satisfying spicy nose and a long finish. The pleasant Merlot '04 is simple, varietal and well made while the Valcalepio Rosso '04 has overripe notes and nice density.

● Valcalepio Rosso Campo Roccoli Vecchi Ris. '03	🍷🍷 6
● Merlot '04	🍷 2
● Valcalepio Rosso '04	🍷 3
● Valcalepio Moscato Passito di Torre de' Roveri '03	🍷🍷 7

La Torre
FRAZ. MOCASINA DI CALVAGESE
25080 CALVAGESE DELLA RIVIERA [BS]
TEL. 030601034
www.pasini-latorre.com

Attilio Pasini's estate in the wilds of the Garda hinterland creates wines of impressive personality. The best are Cabernet Castagneto '03, with plenty of overripe fruit, and a Chardonnay Brut metodo classico of great personality and charming creaminess. The rest of the list is reliable.

○ Garda Chardonnay Brut La Torre	🍷🍷 5
● Garda Cabernet Sauvignon Castagneto '03	🍷🍷 5
○ Garda Cl. Bianco Rossetto '06	🍷 3
● Garda Cl. Rosso Sup. Rosso del Cuntì '02	🍷 4

OTHER WINERIES

Torrevilla
VIA EMILIA, 4
27050 TORRAZZA COSTE [PV]
TEL. 038377003
www.torrevilla.it

Rosso del Centenario is a table wine from barbera, croatina, cabernet and pinot nero, with nice notes of spice and balsam and a velvety palate. Cortese La Genisia Garlà '06 is well executed with good backbone. The better of the two metodo classicos is La Genisia Brut Cl. '03, as the Classese is over-evolved.

○ OP La Genisia Garlà '06	▼▼	4*
● 100 Vendemmie Rosso del Centenario	▼▼	5
○ Brut Cl. La Genisia '03	▼	4
○ OP Brut Classese	▼	4

Pietro Torti
FRAZ. CASTELROTTO, 9
27047 MONTECALVO VERSIGGIA [PV]
TEL. 038599763
www.pietrotorti.it

The quality of Sandro Torti's wines is always good. Bonarda '06 is very soft and fragrant, while Fagù '06 is a fruity Chardonnay with unusual Sauvignon Blanc-like notes. The first release of the Pinot Nero Brut is an agreeable, well-made sparkler and the Riesling Italico '06 also came close to Two Glasses.

○ Fagù '06	▼▼	4*
● OP Bonarda Vivace '06	▼▼	3*
○ OP Pinot Nero Brut '04	▼	5
○ OP Riesling Italico '06	▼	3

Cantina Sociale Val San Martino
VIA BERGAMO, 1195
24030 PONTIDA [BG]
TEL. 035795035
www.cantinavalsanmartino.com

Valcalepio Rosso Riserva '03 has attractive, fruity pulp and varietal notes of green peppers, blackberries and hay. The white Riera '06, from incrocio Manzoni and riesling renano, has good structure and a nice apple-like nose lifted by flowers, citrus and a hint of balsam. Schiava '06 is a fresh, fruity rosé.

○ Riera Bianco '05	▼▼	3
● Valcalepio Rosso Ris. '03	▼▼	5
◉ Schiava '06	▼	2

Vigna Dorata
FRAZ. CALINO
VIA SALA, 80
25046 CAZZAGO SAN MARTINO [BS]
TEL. 0307254275
www.vignadorata.it

Luciana Mingotti's Calino estate makes elegant Franciacortas and still wines, as exemplified by the Brut, with its complex notes of ripe fruit, aromatic herbs and vanilla, and the pleasant lively Rosé, a medley of raspberry and wild strawberry. The Runcat '04 DOC is also good and has excellent structure.

○ Franciacorta Brut	▼▼	6
● TdF Rosso Runcat '04	▼▼	4*
◉ Franciacorta Rosè	▼▼	6

Chiara Ziliani
VIA FRANCIACORTA, 7
25050 PROVAGLIO D'ISEO [BS]
TEL. 030981661
www.cantinazilianichiara.it

Chiara Ziliani's wines and Franciacortas are always interesting and are sourced exclusively from the estate's 12 hectares of vineyards. This time, our favourite was the rich, juicy Satèn, which offers soft fruit, vanilla and flowers on nose and palate. The Brut and the Conte di Provaglio red are interesting.

○ Franciacorta Satèn	▼▼	5
○ Franciacorta Brut	▼	5
● TdF Rosso Conte di Provaglio '05	▼	4

Emilio Zuliani
VIA TITO SPERI, 28
25080 PADENGHE SUL GARDA [BS]
TEL. 0309907026
www.vinizuliani.it

The '03 Groppello Balosse and Riserva mark the turning point in the Zuliani family's production of the wine. The Balosse, sourced from a vineyard of the same name next to a peat bog, is elegant and complex, while the Riserva is rustic and traditional. The lusty Superiore did well and the Chiaretto is nice.

● Garda Cl. Balosse '03	▼▼	5
● Garda Donna Lucia Rosso Sup. '03	▼▼	4
◉ Garda Cl. Chiaretto Rosso Chiaro '06	▼	4
● Garda Groppello Ris. '03	▼	4

TRENTINO

Things here could have gone better but also worse. Trentino viticulture and winemaking not only have problems asserting their worth but are also in a slow, and unfortunately steady, spiral towards standardization. Thanks to impeccable organization from Trentino authorities, the chamber of commerce and various promotion groups, we tasted a flood of wines. All of them were well made and in line with local traditions but few had the qualities necessary to reach our final taste-offs. A few thoroughbreds failed to make the roll call. Unfortunate growing seasons even forced us to do without Granato by Elisabetta Foradori, as well as the Riserva Giulio Ferrari and some Trentodocs – written that way in a new promotional campaign – as well as a few late-harvest wines. The sparklers showed absolutely top quality, as well as certain white blends and traditional Bordeaux-style reds, so we awarded Three Glasses to wines that are by now hardly news. But two newcomers were as unexpected as they were appealing, the Teroldego Riserva from Cantina Rotaliana at Mezzolombardo and the sparklers from Nicola Balter. A well-deserved award went to the Rotaliana Teroldego for of its all-round excellence, despite being released in considerable numbers – almost 100,000 bottles! – at a very attractive price. Otherwise, sparklers, or rather Trentodocs, swept the board. An endorsement went to the Altemasi Graal from Cavit, Abate Nero also encored its prize-winning performance while the coveted Three Glasses went to the Ferrari Perlé – more quality in quantity – and there was praise aplenty for the Riserva '01 by Nicola Balter, a maker of red wines who for the past few vintages has been a leading exponent of the sparkling revolution in this corner of the Dolomites. The endorsements included the San Leonardo from Marchesi Guerrieri Gonzaga, who patiently left the 2003 to age and become an exceptionally fine wine. Finally, the excellent white Olivar is back on the scene from the Cesconi family, perhaps the best winemakers and growers in the Dolomites. So things were not that bad but they really could, and should, get better. We expected more from certain estates: La Vis, Pojer & Sandri, Pravis, Vallarom, Rosi and Castel Noarna, to name just a few. We hope something changes. The 2007 harvest began as early as 2 August and produced good bases for sparkling wines. Trentodoc will be pleased. We trust those many, great producers of other Trentino wines will be equally happy, the ones who do so much with a myriad vineyards strung along terraces where vines have grown for centuries. In many cases, these growers, winemakers and traders never meet to thrash things out, preventing the Made in Trentino label from making the leap in quality and visibility that everyone would like to see.

Abate Nero

FRAZ. GARDOLO
SPONDA TRENTINA, 45
38014 TRENTO [TN]
TEL. 0461246566
www.abatenero.it

ANNUAL PRODUCTION 65,000 bottles
HECTARES UNDER VINE 65
VITICULTURE METHOD Conventional

Abate Nero encored last year's success and
won another Three Glass award with a
distinctive Cuvée dell'Abate Riserva '02.
Chardonnay, pinot nero and a substantial
percentage of pinot bianco give sparklers
created by Luciano Lunelli character and
great elegance with stylish citrus-like notes,
acid backbone and a rich, tangy finish. This
Trentino winery was born out of an
association created largely by Luciano
Lunelli when he still worked as manager of a
well-known Rotaliano winery, with help from
Eugenio de Castel Terlago and other trusted
collaborators. The cellar selects grapes from
growers in the hills around Lavis, towards
Valle di Cembra, grapes specifically grown
for sparkling wines according to precise
growing criteria established by regulations
from the Trento DOC spumante classico
institute. The bunches are later crushed in
the winery facilities located on the left bank
of the Avisio river. Abate Nero releases
around 70,000 bottles of Trento DOC in four
types. Apart from the Riserva, there are
Brut, Extra Brut and Extra Dry wines, all
approachable, high-quality sparklers with
affordable price tags.

Nicola Balter

VIA VALLUNGA II, 24
38068 ROVERETO [TN]
TEL. 0464430101
www.balter.it

ANNUAL PRODUCTION 62,500 bottles
HECTARES UNDER VINE 10
VITICULTURE METHOD Conventional

For years, Nicola Balter has dedicatedly
worked his splendid hillside estate above
Rovereto among the pines of what is called
the "town wood". Around ten or so well-
tended hectares were initially planted to
varieties intended for still red wines and
were later joined by chardonnay and pinot
nero for the production of sparklers. In a
short time, Nicola Balter went from a red
wine maker to one of the most enthusiastic
sparkling wine producers in Trentino. And it
was his Riserva 2001 sparkler that won our
Three Glasses. A creamy, perfectly crafted
spumante with minerality, aromatic herbs
and cakes, good depth and backbone, and
a fresh, tangy finish with elegant length. The
other house wines are just as convincing:
the powerful cabernet, merlot and lagrein
blend, Barbanico, a prize-winner a few
years ago, the tempting Clarae, from
sauvignon, chardonnay and traminer, the
Trento Brut and the affordable, easy-
drinking Lagrein-Merlot.

O Trento Brut Cuvée dell'Abate Ris. '02	♈♈♈ 6
O Trento Abate Nero Brut '04	♈♈ 5
O Trento Abate Nero Extra Brut '04	♈♈ 5
O Trento Abate Nero Extra Dry '04	♈ 5
O Trento Brut Cuvée dell'Abate Ris. '01	♉♉♉ 6
O Trento Abate Nero Brut '03	♉♉ 5
O Trento Abate Nero Extra Brut '03	♉♉ 5

O Trento Balter Ris. '01	♈♈♈ 6
● Barbanico '04	♈♈ 5
O Clarae '06	♈♈ 4*
O Balter Brut	♈♈ 4*
● Cabernet Sauvignon '05	♈♈ 4*
● Lagrein-Merlot '06	♈ 4
O Sauvignon '06	♈ 4
● Barbanico '00	♉♉ 5
O Trento Brut Ris. '00	♉♉ 6
● Barbanico '03	♉♉ 5
● Barbanico '01	♉♉ 5
O Clarae '04	♉♉ 4

Bellaveder
LOC. MASO BELVEDERE
38010 FAEDO [TN]
TEL. 0461650171
www.bellaveder.it

Bolognani
VIA STAZIONE, 19
38015 LAVIS [TN]
TEL. 0461246354
www.bolognani.com

ANNUAL PRODUCTION 30,000 bottles
HECTARES UNDER VINE 7.4
VITICULTURE METHOD Conventional

ANNUAL PRODUCTION 70,000 bottles
HECTARES UNDER VINE 4.4
VITICULTURE METHOD Conventional

After a quiet debut, now comes confirmation. In just a few harvests, Maso Bellaveder has managed to make its mark, giving its wines character, cosseting the vineyards and masterfully bringing out the special profile of grapes from the Faedo subzone in a limited production of fewer than 30,000 bottles. Maso Belvedere is located on the first hill in Faedo, right above the agricultural institute, from where it dominates the entire valley of the Campo Rotaliano, with the mountains of Val di Non and Sole in the background. Tranquillo Lucchetta has transformed the buildings into a multi-purpose structure with a wine bar-cum-restaurant and a cellar carved beneath the vineyards. The range of wines contains two reds, two whites and a dried-grape passito from traminer, a variety selected on the basis of the soil type and exposure. The wines are well made with their own rather interesting style, especially the Rosso Bellaveder, a merlot-led blend with added teroldego and lagrein. It's among the best reds in the region, presenting intense with rich, juicy fruit, well-integrated tannins and remarkable length.

Expert cellarmen, the Bolognanis have carried on the family wine merchant's business established by their father Nilo in the 1950s. But some years ago, Diego and his siblings created their own estate and cultivate vineyards they purchased near Trento. The label's showcase wines come specifically from their own vines, watched over from grape to glass. Few other Trentino wineries boast such up-to-date winemaking technology, capable of successfully vinifying large parcels of grapes selected in Valle di Cembra and along the Adige River. The Bolognanis are betting on the Gabàn, a wine named after one of the oldest human settlements in the Adige valley and the Alps. This major red from a Bordeaux blend has a solid, deep, minerally, framework and great personality that again took it all the way to our finals, where it just missed Three Glasses.

● Rosso Bellaveder '05	⟡⟡ 4*
○ Trentino Chardonnay '06	⟡⟡ 4*
● Trentino Lagrein '05	⟡ 5
○ Traminer Aromatico Passito '06	⟡ 6
○ Trentino Traminer '06	⟡ 4
● Rosso Bellaveder '04	⟡⟡ 4
○ Trentino Chardonnay '05	⟡⟡ 4

● Gabàn '04	⟡⟡ 6
● Teroldego Armilo '05	⟡ 4
○ Trentino Müller Thurgau '06	⟡ 3
○ Trentino Traminer Aromatico Sanròc '05	⟡ 4
● Gabàn '00	⟡⟡ 6
● Gabàn '01	⟡⟡ 6
● Gabàn '03	⟡⟡ 6
● Teroldego Armilo '00	⟡⟡ 5
● Teroldego Armilo '01	⟡⟡ 4*
● Teroldego Armilo '03	⟡⟡ 4
● Teroldego Armilo '04	⟡⟡ 4
● Teroldego Armilo '02	⟡⟡ 4

Borgo dei Posseri

loc. Pozzo Basso, 1
38061 Ala [TN]
tel. 0464671899
www.borgodeiposseri.com

ANNUAL PRODUCTION 45,000 bottles
HECTARES UNDER VINE 18
VITICULTURE METHOD Conventional

The Pilati-Mainenti family has won its wine wager at Borgo dei Posseri. This young couple, Margherita and Martin, have in a few years as owners and managers transformed pasture and woodland into a property particularly well suited to vines. They have rebuilt the existing structures, constructed the cellar and started vinifying grapes, initially only müller thurgau, then slowly moving on to sauvignon, chardonnay and merlot. Every wine comes from just one variety and a single vineyard. For the time being, the couple only produce a few thousand bottles but they have ambitious plans to expand the area under vine and plant new varieties while respecting the landscape of this mountain slope. This will enhance the special nature of their estate as well as publicize this little-known corner of Trentino with its mix of vineyards and woodlands. The best wine this year was the Sauvignon Furiel '06, which is varietal, zesty, intense and fresh with good texture.

O Sauvignon Furiel '06	🍷🍷 5
O Chardonnay Malusel '06	🍷 5
O Müller Thurgau Quaron '06	🍷 4
● Merlot Rocol '04	🍷🍷 4
O Müller Thurgau Quaron '05	🍷🍷 4*

Conti Bossi Fedrigotti

via Unione, 43
38068 Rovereto [TN]
tel. 0464439250
www.bossifedrigotti.com

ANNUAL PRODUCTION 180,000 bottles
HECTARES UNDER VINE 35
VITICULTURE METHOD Conventional

Since spring 2007, this historic estate winery has been managed by Masi Agricola, the dynamic operation from Sant'Ambrogio, Valpolicella, owned by Sandro Boscaini, one of the world's great wine entrepreneurs. The Bossi Fedrigotti siblings have kept their property intact and manage the land but everything else, from vinification – still in the lovely cellar in Rovereto – to marketing, will be handled by the staff in Verona. The Bossi Fedrigottis took the unexpected decision to create a synergy between the two operations, which are not physically very distant and are connected by the river Adige, a long history and a shared production philosophy. The wines in the Guide are still those vinified at the family winery, managed by Maria Josè Bossi Fedrigotti, and include all the Dolomite IGTs, from Teroldego to Fojaneghe, the latter a blend created in the 1960s by Leonello Letrari, winery cellarman at the time, and the flagship wine of the Bossi Fedrigottis. The most convincing product this year is the easy-drinking Teroldego '06, a well-typed, full, fruit-forward bottle with moreish appeal.

● Teroldego '06	🍷🍷 4*
● Fojaneghe Rosso '05	🍷 5
● Trecento '05	🍷 4
● Trentino Marzemino '06	🍷 4
● Fojaneghe Rosso '04	🍷🍷 5
● Trecento '04	🍷🍷 4
● Trentino Marzemino '05	🍷🍷 4
● Trecento '03	🍷🍷 4

Cavit

VIA PONTE DI RAVINA, 31
38040 TRENTO [TN]
TEL. 0461381711
www.cavit.it

ANNUAL PRODUCTION 75,000,000 bottles
HECTARES UNDER VINE 5,700
VITICULTURE METHOD Conventional

Here comes another endorsement for the many, invariably good, Cavit wines at our tastings. A wholehearted vote of confidence goes to the 2000 edition of the Riserva Graal, an intriguing sparkler with a fine mousse, a broad range of aromatics, including candied fruit and rennet apples, elegance and minerality with remarkable structure and a long finish. The Vino Santo Arèle is also appealing and balanced, as are many, many other solid, well-crafted wines. From metodo classico sparklers to wines from native varieties, a Marzemino with unusual power and a fragrant Schiava, all these wines show class perhaps unmatched by any other co-operative of this size. Cavit is an umbrella for a dozen co-operative wineries and sells almost 100,000,000 bottles a year. The managerial abilities of Giacinto Giacomini and the professionalism of his extraordinary staff have again put Cavit at the top of the co-operative league table.

Cesarini Sforza

FRAZ. RAVINA
VIA STELLA, 9
38040 TRENTO [TN]
TEL. 0461382200
www.cesarinisforza.com

ANNUAL PRODUCTION 1,400,000 bottles
HECTARES UNDER VINE N.D.
VITICULTURE METHOD Conventional

Established in the 1970s, Cesarini Sforza was one of the first brands on the Italian sparkling wine landscape. A dynamic, constantly evolving winery, Cesarini Sforza was acquired by Gruppo La Vis and the renowned wine distribution company, Fratelli Rinaldi. Winery staff and production strategies have been completely rethought. The first results from this new direction are distinctly good, starting with the Tridentum '04, a Trento DOC spumante classico from 80 per cent chardonnay with a dash of pinot nero. The complex, caressing bouquet shows hints of white-fleshed fruit followed by notes of toasted bread and coffee. The palate is zesty, structured and soft with remarkable balance, shades of gingerbread marking the long finish. The Rosé is also good, and in fact among the best on the Trentino sparkling wine scene, with fresh wild berry aromas and hints of vanilla. The fresh, tangy palate shows outstanding red berry fruit.

O Trento Brut Altemasi Graal Ris. '00	�

6 |
O Trentino Vino Santo Arèle '97	8
O Cuvée Maso Torresella '04	5
● Teroldego Rotaliano Bottega Vinai '05	4
● Trentino Marzemino dei Ziresi Farfossi Sup. '05	4
O Trentino Sup. Maso Toresella '04	5
● Trentino Rosso Quattro Vicariati '04	5
O Trento Altemasi Brut Millesimato '00	5
O Trentino Nosiola Bottega de' Vinai '06	4
O Trentino Müller Thurgau Bottega de' Vinai '06	4
⊙ Trentino Moscato Rosa Amula '05	5
● Trentino Pinot Nero Bottega de' Vinai '05	4
O Trentino Schiava Gentile Bottega de' Vinai '06	4
O Trentino Sauvignon Bottega de' Vinai '06	4

O Trento Tridentum '04	5
O Cuvée Brut Ris.	4
⊙ Trento Rosé Cuvée Brut	5
O Trento Tridentum '02	5
O Trento Brut '99	4
O Trento Brut '00	4
O Trento Brut '01	5

Cesconi

FRAZ. PRESSANO
VIA MARCONI, 39
38015 LAVIS [TN]
TEL. 0461240355
cesconi@cr-surfing.net

ANNUAL PRODUCTION 130,000 bottles
HECTARES UNDER VINE 19
VITICULTURE METHOD Conventional

A model winemaking family, skilled at working the vines and even more competent in vinifying their harvests, the Cesconis confirm their status as leading players in the good drinking stakes in Trentino and beyond. The Olivar '05 is an exciting white from a skilful blend of chardonnay, pinot bianco, pinot grigio and a small percentage of sauvignon. It presents intense and concentrated with good backbone and freshness, despite robust alcohol. At last, it has again won our Three Glass award. Also in the finals was the Traminer Aromatico '05, which is presented mature, in other words at least 18 months after vinification, like all the Cesconi whites. The reds, too, are good, beginning with the Rosso del Pivier '04, a complex monovarietal Merlot with remarkable structure. Finally, a special mention goes to the fragrant Prabi, from the location of the vineyard near Arco, an easy-drinking white at a reasonable price.

Concilio

ZONA INDUSTRIALE, 2
38060 VOLANO [TN]
TEL. 0464411000
www.concilio.it

ANNUAL PRODUCTION 8,000,000 bottles
HECTARES UNDER VINE 520
VITICULTURE METHOD Conventional

This solid winemaking company managed by Giorgio Flessati makes great wines. The range of 14 products submitted to our tasting again shows how quantity and quality can be combined, at competitive prices. Despite the more than 8,000,000 bottles produced, Concilio has never stopped carefully selecting the wines it offers its customers. These selections begin even before the harvest, out among the vines, to ensure perfectly ripe grapes. Credit for this approach goes to the managerial staff of this renowned Trentino wine house, named after the celebrated Council of Trent in the mid-16th century. We should mention the well-made, varietal Chardonnay '06 with its good structure, the juicy, well-typed Pinot Grigio Maso Guà '06 and the Merlot '05 from the Vigneti delle Meridiane line, an intense, caressing product made at a completely independent winery with a cellar at Casteller, the vine-covered hill south of Trento.

Wine	Rating
O Olivar '05	♈♈♈ 5
● Rosso del Pivier '04	♈♈ 6
O Traminer Aromatico '05	♈♈ 5
O Chardonnay '05	♈♈ 5
O Nosiola '05	♈♈ 4
O Prabi Bianco '05	♈♈ 4
O Pinot Grigio '05	♈♈ 5
● Rosso Cesconi '04	♈♈ 5
☉ Trentino Lagrein Rosato '06	♈ 3
O Olivar '01	♈♈♈ 5
O Olivar '02	♈♈ 5
● Rosso del Pivier '03	♈♈ 6
O Olivar '03	♈♈ 5
O Chardonnay '04	♈♈ 5
O Olivar '04	♈♈ 5

Wine	Rating
● Teroldego Rotaliano Braide Sel. '05	♈♈ 4
O Trentino Chardonnay '06	♈♈ 4
O Trentino Pinot Grigio Maso Guà Sel. '06	♈♈ 4
● Trentino Merlot Vigneti delle Meridiane '05	♈♈ 4
☉ Clarius Rosè Brut	♈ 3
O Trentino Müller Thurgau Lagaria '06	♈ 3
O Tenatius	♈ 4
● Trentino Marzemino Mozart Sel. '05	♈ 4
O Trentino Müller Thurgau '06	♈ 4
● Trentino Rosso Mori Vecio '03	♈ 4
● Teroldego Rotaliano Braide '03	♈♈ 4
● Trentino Rosso Mori Vecio '01	♈♈ 5
● Teroldego Rotaliano Braide '02	♈♈ 5
O Trentino Chardonnay '05	♈♈ 4

Cantina d'Isera

VIA AL PONTE, 1
38060 ISERA [TN]
TEL. 0464433795
www.cantinaisera.it

ANNUAL PRODUCTION 650,000 bottles
HECTARES UNDER VINE 230
VITICULTURE METHOD Conventional

Cantina d'Isera has just celebrated its first century but it doesn't show its age. This may be the most dynamic, innovative co-operative winery in Trentino in terms of management and its strategy of combining quality, profitability for its members and promotion of local varieties, especially marzemino. Manager Fausto Campestrini is a young oenologist who already has substantial experience. The cellar has recently been made over and the co-operative plans to enhance the standing of its wines, in particular showing that quality wines can be made here from white grapes, belying the notion that Vallagarina is home to Marzemino alone. Sentieri is a Bordeaux blend, showing clear, clean and slightly vegetal with good body and freshness. The classic Marzemino confirms its fresh-tasting suppleness and appeal. The Müller Thurgau is getting better. It's sourced from grapes grown on the steep slopes around Isera and high altitude terraces, where the grape finds its best expression.

● Trentino Rosso Sentieri '03	🍷🍷 4
● Teroldego '06	🍷 3
● Trentino Marzemino '06	🍷 3
○ Trentino Müller Thurgau '06	🍷 3
⊙ Valdadige Schiava Costa Felisa '06	🍷 2
● 907 '03	🍷 5
● Trentino Rebo '05	🍷 4
● Trentino Merlot '05	🍷 3
○ Trentino Chardonnay '06	🍷 3
● Trentino Cabernet '05	🍷 3
● Trentino Rosso Sentieri '01	🍷🍷 4

Marco Donati

VIA CESARE BATTISTI, 41
38016 MEZZOCORONA [TN]
TEL. 0461604141
donatimarcovini@libero.it

ANNUAL PRODUCTION 100,000 bottles
HECTARES UNDER VINE 20
VITICULTURE METHOD Conventional

Calling Marco Donati tireless would be an understatement. Marco is one of the most dynamic winemakers in Trentino, always at the head of the queue at events promoting wine culture. Obviously, he is also busy working his vineyards near the winery, a remodelled 15th century structure, and his olive groves towards Lake Garda that produce a fine extravirgin olive oil. The estate offers a broad range of wines, although the Teroldego remains Marco's pride and joy. Vinified in two versions, the more ambitious is dedicated to the Sangue del Drago, the dragon's blood of an ancient legend regarding the birth of wine. The other style is easy-going and designed for more immediate consumption. This year, however, both editions were merely decent. Certainly the 2005 growing season was not favourable for this variety in this zone and prevented the Sangue del Drago from giving its usual performance. In contrast, the well-crafted Nosiola '06 is good, presenting minerally with almondy, savoury notes and a clean, well-typed style. It's still young but already very attractive.

○ Trentino Nosiola '06	🍷🍷 4
● Teroldego Rotaliano Sangue del Drago '05	🍷 6
○ Trentino Müller Thurgau Albeggio '06	🍷 4
○ Trentino Riesling Stellato '06	🍷 4
● Teroldego Rotaliano Bagolari '06	🍷 4
● Trentino Marzemino '06	🍷 4
○ Trentino Riesling Stellato '06	🍷 4
● Teroldego Rotaliano Sangue del Drago '03	🍷🍷 6
● Teroldego Rotaliano Sangue del Drago '04	🍷🍷 6

F.lli Dorigati
VIA DANTE, 5
38016 MEZZOCORONA [TN]
TEL. 0461605313
www.dorigati.it

Endrizzi
LOC. MASETTO, 2
38016 SAN MICHELE ALL'ADIGE [TN]
TEL. 0461650129
www.endrizzi.it

ANNUAL PRODUCTION 100,000 bottles
HECTARES UNDER VINE 5.5
VITICULTURE METHOD Conventional

ANNUAL PRODUCTION 500,000 bottles
HECTARES UNDER VINE 40
VITICULTURE METHOD Conventional

The Dorigatis have the temperament of real cellarmen but are also expert winemakers and top sparkling wine producers. The family dynasty is firmly rooted in the history of wine on the Piana Rotaliana, the mountain hollow in the Dolomites that is particularly well suited for the teroldego variety, considered by Trentino residents their leading native variety. Dorigatis have been making wine for five generations and continue to concentrate on the house variety, teroldego of course, without neglecting other varieties, some grown on their plots and some selected from trusted growers. The cellar has all the charm of an artisanal facility, constructed in the family home located in the town centre, where once every house had its own wine cellar and grapes were the only crop it was possible to harvest. Dorigati wines are frank and sincere, with special care being focused on the Methius spumante, always one of the top sparklers in Trentino. The 2001 vintage may be slightly less convincing than on other occasions – perhaps it needs more cellar time – but it can still compete with the best.

Word play on the dialect pronunciation of the family name created the title of the winery founded by the Endricis, who in the local parlance are the Endrizzis. Initially involved in buying grapes, for some years now this winery has used mostly grapes from its own vineyards or trusted growers adjacent to the recently remodelled headquarters. The vineyards around the cellar, in the direction of Faedo and Castel Monreale, show how the entire production is marked by respect for the environment so as to bring out the best in the grapes, and the wines, with no extreme winemaking procedures. Results are increasingly encouraging with each passing harvest. These wines have their own precise style, which in some cases is quite captivating, based more on elegance than power or immediacy. Teroldego Maso Camorz Riserva '04 went into our finals for its intense mineral and elderflower aromas, not to mention a juicy, savoury palate of great length. Other excellent wines are the Masetto Bianco '05, a blend of chardonnay, pinot bianco, riesling and sauvignon that is minerally and savoury, with thrust on the palate, and the intense, juicy Masetto Nero '04, sweet and elegant although the tannins are still prominent.

O Trento Methius Brut Ris. '01	♟♟	7
● Teroldego Rotaliano '05	♟♟	4
● Trentino Cabernet '05	♟	4
O Trentino Pinot Grigio '06	♟	4
● Trentino Rebo '05	♟	4
⊙ Trentino Lagrein Kretzer '06	♟	4
O Trento Methius Brut. Ris. '98	♟♟♟	7
O Trento Methius Brut Ris. '00	♟♟♟	7

● Teroldego Rotaliano Maso Camorz Ris. '04	♟♟	4
O Trento Endrizzi Brut Ris. '02	♟♟	5
● Masetto Nero '04	♟♟	5
O Masetto Dulcis '05	♟♟	5
O Masetto Bianco '05	♟♟	4
● Gran Masetto '04	♟	6
O Trentino Müller Thurgau '06	♟	4
O Trentino Chardonnay '06	♟	4
O Masetto Dulcis '04	♟♟	5

★ Ferrari
VIA PONTE DI RAVINA, 15
38100 TRENTO [TN]
TEL. 0461972311
www.ferrarispumante.it

ANNUAL PRODUCTION	4,800,000 bottles
HECTARES UNDER VINE	120
VITICULTURE METHOD	Conventional

Congratulations first of all. For the first time, the Lunelli brother's Ferrari has managed to win our Three Glass award with the Perlé 2002, a top spumante not just for quality but also quantity. Almost half a million bottles are turned out every year. Praise goes to the Lunellis' perseverance. The youngest generation of this bubbly family now works full time at the winery, doing everything possible to safeguard its reputation and these authentically Trentino sparklers. Courageously, the Riserva del Fondatorel Giulio Ferrari 1998 was not produced. The reason was the hailstorm that compromised ripening of the grapes at Maso Pianizza so there is no Giulio '98. But there was a great performance from the elegant '02 Perlé, which showed minerally and creamy with a long, caressing and very pleasing finish. The other four sparklers – the Rosé, the two Maximums and the traditional Brut, of which this year almost three and a half million bottles were released – were also good. Yet more reasons for festive toasts.

★ Foradori
VIA DAMIANO CHIESA, 1
38017 MEZZOLOMBARDO [TN]
TEL. 0461601046
www.elisabettaforadori.com

ANNUAL PRODUCTION	200,000 bottles
HECTARES UNDER VINE	25
VITICULTURE METHOD	Certified biodynamic

Only someone who has profound respect for nature, love for the vine and awareness of wine's ability to evolve over time would decide to skip a year. That is what happened here and you will not see an '05 Granato in the table below. In some ways, this choice was hard; in others, necessary. Elisabetta Foradori has worked to biodynamic tenets for four years and is now close to certification. She did not consider the 2005 harvest up to the usual standards and so decided not to produce it, after a series of tests that began when the bunches of teroldego were still on the plant and continued after fermentation. Only two wines remained to carry the banner of this splendid winery. The Foradori '05, a monovarietal Teroldego, is a wine with great charm, frequently unjustly considered the little brother of Elisabetta's muscular Granato. Although still quite young, it shows notes of coffee, good texture and remarkable fullness. From sauvignon and incrocio Manzoni, the always sound, complex Myrto '05 is still slightly marked by oak but shows remarkable acid backbone, freshness, minerality and elegance. In other words, it's a white you can enjoy either still young or in a few years' time.

O Trento Brut Perlé '02	♥♥♥ 6		O Myrto '05	♥♥ 5	
O Trento Brut	♥♥ 6		● Foradori '05	♥♥ 5	
O Trento Brut Maximum	♥♥ 5		● Granato '00	♥♥♥ 7	
O Trento Maximum Demi Sec	♥♥ 6		● Granato '04	♥♥♥ 7	
O Trento Giulio Ferrari '95	♥♥♥ 8		● Granato '93	♥♥♥ 5	
O Giulio Ferrari '88	♥♥♥ 8		● Granato '99	♥♥♥ 5	
O Giulio Ferrari '90	♥♥♥ 8		● Granato '96	♥♥♥ 5	
O Giulio Ferrari '92	♥♥♥ 8		● Granato '91	♥♥♥ 5	
O Giulio Ferrari '91	♥♥♥ 8		● Granato '03	♥♥♥ 7	
O Giulio Ferrari '89	♥♥♥ 8		● Granato '01	♥♥♥ 7	
O Giulio Ferrari '94	♥♥♥ 8		● Granato '02	♥♥♥ 7	
O Trento Giulio Ferrari '96	♥♥♥ 8		O Myrto '03	♥♥ 5	
O Trento Giulio Ferrari '97	♥♥♥ 8		O Myrto '04	♥♥ 5	
O Giulio Ferrari '93	♥♥♥ 8				
O Trento Brut Perlé '01	♥♥ 6				

Gaierhof

VIA IV NOVEMBRE, 51
38030 ROVERÈ DELLA LUNA [TN]
TEL. 0461658514
www.gaierhof.com www.masopoli.com

ANNUAL PRODUCTION 550,000 bottles
HECTARES UNDER VINE 130
VITICULTURE METHOD Conventional

We ask Luigi Togn to excuse us if we combine in one entry wines from two separate estates, Gaierhof and Maso Poli. It is just a matter of space. In the meantime, the Togn family, on the border between Trentino and Alto Adige, continues to expand Vinicola Gaierhof, their business as wine merchants, while in the hills of Pressano above Lavis, the Maso Poli estate's production is increasingly impressive. Large quantities come from the main winery but their are also significant numbers from Maso, which can call on the unique location of the hillside vineyards, a choice zone for chardonnay and the other white grapes that go into Sorni, a blend of nosiola, müller thurgau and chardonnay. The fresh, fruity 2006 version is excellent, with good acid grip. The two Teroldego Rotalianos from Gaierhof are very nice. The 2005 has gentian root aromas and shows fruity and clear with a long, minerally finish on the palate. The Riserva '03 is fragrant, still tannic with remarkable structure and texture, and notes of bottled cherries. The rest of the range is good.

Grigoletti

VIA GARIBALDI, 12
38060 NOMI [TN]
TEL. 0464834215
www.grigoletti.com

ANNUAL PRODUCTION 60,000 bottles
HECTARES UNDER VINE 7
VITICULTURE METHOD Conventional

In Trentino, the right bank of the river Adige between Trento and Rovereto has been planted to merlot for more than a century. Grape farmers gambled on merlot first for the high yields the variety guaranteed practically every autumn. Later, they continued to believe in the variety because it was capable of creating interesting wines with appeal. Producers viewed it as the only red that could replace Marzemino. It is no coincidence that the Italian Merlot Exhibition has been held in Aldeno for the past ten years or so. At Nomi, the Grigolettis tend a few hectares planted mainly to merlot. They make two versions and also use these grapes to give character to their other reds. They even leave merlot, along with other varieties, to part-dry until the winter to make a dessert wine, Maso Federico. The excellent Antica Vigna di Nomi '05 is soft, complex, fruity and long while the good Carestel '06 is fresher, supple and vegetal. The Pinot Grigio '06 is also quite nice, showing well typed and minerally with good texture. The other wines are upfront and spontaneous, bearing the typical imprint of winemakers on the right bank of the Adige, who have earned the name "merlotists".

O Sorni Maso Poli '06	♟♟ 4
● Teroldego Rotaliano Ris. '03	♟♟ 6
● Teroldego Rotaliano '05	♟♟ 4
● Syrah '06	♟ 4
O Trentino Sauvignon '06	♟ 4
O Trentino Sup. Muller Thurgau dei 700 '06	♟ 5
● Trentino Sup. Pinot Nero Maso Poli '04	♟ 5
O Trentino Traminer Aromatico '06	♟ 4
O Trentino Pinot Grigio '06	♟ 4
● Syrah '05	♟♟ 4
● Teroldego Rotaliano Sup. '03	♟♟ 4
● Teroldego Rotaliano '04	♟♟ 4

● Trentino Merlot Antica Vigna di Nomi '05	♟♟ 5
● Maso Federico Passito Rosso '02	♟♟ 5
● Trentino Merlot Carestel '06	♟♟ 4
O Trentino Pinot Grigio '06	♟♟ 4
● Gonzalier '04	♟ 5
O Trentino Chardonnay L'Opera '06	♟ 4
● Trentino Marzemino '06	♟ 4
O San Martin V.T. '05	♟ 5
● Trentino Merlot Antica Vigna di Nomi '04	♟♟ 5
● Trentino Merlot Antica Vigna di Nomi '03	♟♟ 5

La Vis/Valle di Cembra
VIA DEL CARMINE, 7
38015 LAVIS [TN]
TEL. 0461440111
www.la-vis.com

ANNUAL PRODUCTION 5,500,000 bottles
HECTARES UNDER VINE 1.350
VITICULTURE METHOD Conventional

La Vis needs no introductions. This is one of the best-known co-operative wineries on the market with operations in Tuscany, in Chianti and the Morellino area, and Sicily, as well as recent acquisitions in Trentino. This commercial expansion marches in step with improvement in quality. We'll start by mentioning wines that are veritable portraits of Trentino, such as those harvested in the upper Valle di Cembra, an excellent zone for Müller Thurgau and certain Pinot Nero selections. Then come the classics from Lavis, first of all Chardonnay then the various white and red blends. All the wines submitted for tasting were worthy of the La Vis label and there were some excellent performances. First on our list was the white Ritratto blend from chardonnay, pinot grigio and riesling, an intense wine with aromas of acacia honey. The palate is juicy and minerally with a long, consistent finish. Following this comes an elegant Merlot and an equally good selection of Müller Thurgau Vigna delle Forche, a benchmark for the type that presents impressively fragrant, intense and deep.

Letrari
VIA MONTE BALDO, 13/15
38068 ROVERETO [TN]
TEL. 0464480200
www.letrari.it

ANNUAL PRODUCTION 150,000 bottles
HECTARES UNDER VINE 23
VITICULTURE METHOD Conventional

Lucia Letrari, daughter of Nello, has steered the family estate through several harvests now, helped by her brother Paolo Emilio and with her father's valuable input. Wines from the 2006 harvest were bottled as late as possible to achieve optimum maturity. Although some varieties paid a price of an indifferent growing season, other types and vintages are among the best in their categories. The Riserva '99 spumante is one such. Dedicated to the winery's founding in 1976, it was disgorged in spring 2007. This classic Brut from chardonnay and pinot nero shows caressing aromas of aromatic herbs and honey, silky structure, complexity and a verve that plays off minerality and acid freshness. The other two classic sparklers are equally sound, as is the Pinot Grigio, the rare Moscato Rosa and the Bordeaux blend Ballistarius, from the dozen or so wines presented.

O Ritratto Bianco '06	♀♀ 5	
O Trentino Chardonnay Ritratti '06	♀♀ 4	
O Trentino Müller Thurgau V. delle Forche '06	♀♀ 4	
O Trentino Müller Thurgau Maso Roncador '06	♀♀ 4	
O Trentino Müller Thurgau Dos Caslìr '06	♀♀ 4*	
● Trentino Pinot Nero Vigna di Saoisent '05	♀ 4*	
O Trentino Sorni Bianco '06	♀ 4	
● Trentino Merlot Ritratti '05	♀ 4	
● Trentino Pinot Nero Ritratti '05	♀ 4	
● Ritratto Rosso '03	♀♀♀ 5	
O Ritratto Bianco '05	♀♀ 5	
● Ritratto Rosso '04	♀♀ 5	
● Trentino Cabernet Sauvignon Ritratti '03	♀♀ 4	
● Trentino Cabernet Sauvignon Ritratti '04	♀♀ 4	

O Trento Riserva del Fondatore 976 '99	♀♀ 7	
● Ballistarius '03	♀♀ 6	
● Trentino Moscato Rosa '04	♀♀ 4	
O Trento Brut Ris. '02	♀♀ 6	
O Trentino Pinot Grigio '06	♀♀ 4	
O Trento Brut '04	♀♀ 5	
⊙ Aes '06	♀ 4	
● Enantio '03	♀ 5	
O Trentino Chardonnay '06	♀ 3	
● Trentino Maso Lodron '03	♀ 4	
● Trentino Marzemino '06	♀ 4	
● Trentino Cabernet Sauvignon '03	♀ 5	
O Trento Riserva del Fondatore '98	♀♀ 6	
● Trentino Maso Lodron '02	♀♀ 4	
O Trento Brut Ris. '01	♀♀ 6	

Longariva
FRAZ. BORGO SACCO
VIA R. ZANDONAI, 6
38068 ROVERETO [TN]
TEL. 0464437200
www.longariva.it

ANNUAL PRODUCTION 100,000 bottles
HECTARES UNDER VINE 22
VITICULTURE METHOD Natural

This increasingly influential winery makes bottles of character and excellent versatility. Marco Manica and his wife Rosanna tend their vineyards like gardens, cultivating a series of small vineyards set into the slopes of the mountains surrounding Rovereto, on the side facing Lake Garda. Overall production runs to 100,000 bottles. Most of these wines are from white varieties, although that emblematic grape from Vallagarina, marzemino, is never missing. Always attentive to the natural balance of the vineyard, these winemakers aim to contain the energy of the vines to harvest rich, concentrated grapes. The reds are seriously good. All are from 2003, from the Merlot Tovi to the Cabernet Quartella Riserva, to the winery's must-drink wine, the elegant Bordeaux blend Tre Cesure Riserva, with its sweet tannins, balance and depth. The decent Pinot Nero Zinzèle Riserva has all-round depth, a persuasive appeal and good alcohol. The whites are deep in colour, tangy and very pleasant, ranging from standard labels, such as the Pinot Bianco Pergole, and those from the 2005 vintage, like the Sauvignon Cascari.

Maso Furli
LOC. FURLI
VIA FURLI, 32
38015 LAVIS [TN]
TEL. 0461240667
masofurli@libero.it

ANNUAL PRODUCTION 15,000 bottles
HECTARES UNDER VINE 4
VITICULTURE METHOD Conventional

Marco Zanoni and his family tend a postage-stamp property embedded among the houses on the edge of Lavis. But this winery is as small in size as it is professional and innovative in its management, and in turning grapes into wine. In fact, Marco Zanoni, together with other winemaker friends, has created vinification techniques that call for the crushing and first fermentation of the must to be protected from oxidation to create truly fragrant wines. As usual, the Bordeaux blend Rosso Furli '04 is very good and only produced in a few thousand units. It is intense, rich and dense with outstanding notes of pencil lead, sweet tannins and great body. In other words, this is a high quality wine that only the most experienced winemakers can produce. The only two whites submitted to our tastings were below expectations. The Chardonnay '05, always one of the most distinctive from Trentino, is deep and full in its colour and sensory profile. The Incrocio Manzoni '05 is an almost experimental small-batch wine that still needs to be fine-tuned.

● Trentino Cabernet Quartella Ris. '03	♈♈	4
● Trentino Merlot Tovi '03	♈♈	4
● Trentino Rosso Tre Cesure Ris. '03	♈♈	5
○ Trentino Chardonnay Praistel Sel. '05	♈	5
○ Trentino Pinot Grigio Graminé '06	♈	5
● Trentino Sauvignon Cascari '05	♈	4
● Trentino Pinot Nero Zinzèle Ris. '03	♈	7
○ Trentino Pinot Bianco Pergole '06	♈	5
● Trentino Marzemino '06	♈	4
○ Trentino Pinot Grigio Graminé '06		5
○ Trentino Pinot Bianco Pergole '05	♈♈	5
○ Trentino Sauvignon Cascari '04	♈♈	4
● Trentino Merlot Tovi '01	♈♈	4
● Trentino Merlot Tovi '02	♈♈	4

● Maso Furli Rosso '04	♈♈	5
○ Trentino Chardonnay '05	♈	5
○ Incrocio Manzoni '05		5
● Maso Furli Rosso '03	♈♈	5
● Maso Furli Rosso '01	♈♈	5
● Maso Furli Rosso '02	♈♈	5
○ Trentino Chardonnay '04	♈♈	5

Maso Martis
LOC. MARTIGNANO
VIA DELL'ALBERA, 52
38100 TRENTO [TN]
TEL. 0461821057
www.masomartis.it

ANNUAL PRODUCTION 60,000 bottles
HECTARES UNDER VINE 12
VITICULTURE METHOD Conventional

Antonio Stelzer and his wife Roberta
Giuriali's estate in the foothills of Calisio has
some of the best locations around Trento.
Often, the cellar turns out wines and
sparklers with an aromatic tone deliberately
veined with sweetness and vanilla, notes
that come through on both nose and palate.
Family management gives special attention
to chardonnay and pinot nero, varieties
destined to go into the Trento wines that are
increasingly in demand by the market. From
70 per cent pinot nero with some
chardonnay, the good Riserva '01 shows
broad, complex aromas with notes of
toasted bread and mineral shades followed
by a palate that offers good structure with
notes of white-fleshed fruit and butter. Also
good is the Brut Rosé, from pinot nero with
five per cent chardonnay, the full palate
showing ripe black berry fruit. There is no
lack of still wines, from the varietal, very
characterful Moscato Rosa, which is among
the best in its type this year, to the
Chardonnay.

MezzaCorona
VIA DEL TEROLDEGO, 1
38016 MEZZOCORONA [TN]
TEL. 0461616399
www.mezzacorona.it

ANNUAL PRODUCTION 30,000,000 bottles
HECTARES UNDER VINE 3.500
VITICULTURE METHOD Conventional

With more than 30,000,000 bottles and
affiliated wineries throughout Italy, this co-
operative colossus continues to expand and
improve the quality of its wines. Most of
course are designed for the international
market, released in large numbers and very
competitively priced. The headquarters at
Mezzocorona, a facility occupying 12
hectares, releases showcase Trentino wines
like the Rotari spumante classico and
obviously the Teroldego Rotaliano, as well
as the more traditional Pinot Grigio. We
tasted ten or so wines, all very well made
and so well crafted you'd think they came
from a small winery. Flavio Rotari '01 is a
blanc de blancs with a complex nose
showing citrus notes with shades of honey
and cakes that took it into our finals. The
palate is balanced, soft and minerally with a
fresh, consistent finish. Also excellent are
the Rotari Rosé, from 75 per cent pinot nero
and chardonnay, which shows aromas of
berry fruit and baking, and a dry, full-bodied,
fresh palate with a coffee finish, and the
intense, clean, fruity Rotari Riserva '02.

● Moscato Rosa '06	♈ 6
○ Sole d'Autunno '06	♈ 6
○ Trentino Chardonnay '06	♈ 4
○ Trento Brut Ris. '01	♈ 6
⊙ Trento Rosé Brut	♈ 5
● Moscato Rosa '04	♈♈ 5
○ Trentino Chardonnay L'Incanto '04	♈♈ 4
⊙ Trento Brut Rosé '03	♈♈ 6
○ Trento Brut Ris. '00	♈♈ 6

○ Trento Rotari Flavio '01	♈ 7
○ Trento Rotari Brut Ris. '02	♈♈ 5
⊙ Trento Rosé Rotari Brut	♈♈ 5
● Teroldego Rotaliano Nòs Ris. '03	♈ 6
● Trentino Marzemino Castel Firmian '06	♈ 4
○ Trento Rotari Cuvée 28	♈ 5
○ Trentino Pinot Grigio Ris. '05	♈ 5
○ Trentino Müller Thurgau Castel Firmian '06	♈ 4
● Trentino Lagrein Castel Firmian '05	♈ 4
○ Trento Rotari Brut Ris. '01	♈♈ 5

Casata Monfort

VIA CARLO SETTE, 21
38015 LAVIS [TN]
TEL. 0461246353
www.cantinemonfort.it

ANNUAL PRODUCTION	150,000 bottles
HECTARES UNDER VINE	40
VITICULTURE METHOD	Conventional

Lorenzo Simoni actually deserves two entries. Not just because his wines are good but also because he has purchased Maso Cantanghel, that glorious small winery at Civezzano. The whole range of wines from this label was convincing, starting with the most authentically traditional. These are obtained from estate-grown fruit, selecting grapes from old varieties cultivated in marginal areas by growers involved in a project to recover grape varieties from Trentino's rural heritage. Wanderbara, vernaza, portoghesa, and sanct Lorenz are just a few of the types, planted in Valsugana, Val di Cembra and obviously not far from Maso Cantanghel. The seriously complex Blanc de Sers '06, a blend of six varieties including vernaza and wanderbara, shows floral touches and a rich, mineral-laced aromatic palate. The Trento Brut Casata Monfort is fresh and tangy with notes of hawthorn and minerality and a long, supple finish. The Pinot Nero Maso Cantanghel is decent with pleasant cherry sensations.

Castel Noarna

FRAZ. NOARNA DI NOGAREDO
VIA CASTELNUOVO, 19
38060 NOGAREDO [TN]
TEL. 0464413295
www.castelnoarna.com

ANNUAL PRODUCTION	35,000 bottles
HECTARES UNDER VINE	7
VITICULTURE METHOD	Conventional

Marco Zani's wines have never done so well. We were utterly convinced by all the bottles we tasted and sent the Salvanèl and Bianco di Castelnuovo on to the finals. With the experimentation of the past few years now over, the harvest of fully ripe grapes from the slope overlooking Rovereto, the vines below the castle walls, and careful vinification have made Castel Noarna wines first-class ambassadors for their territory. The Zani family is known as restaurateurs and hoteliers in Rovereto, and for some time now also as agricultural entrepreneurs. Marco Zani tends the vineyards himself, controlling every phase of production from harvest to distribution. The wines that Marco's efforts produce exhibit remarkable charm and cellarability, having spent a year in bottle before release and showing every prospect of further improvement over time.

O Blanc de Sers '06	♟♟ 4
O Trento Brut Monfort	♟♟ 5
☉ Monfort Rosa '06	♟ 5
● Trentino Pinot Nero Maso Cantanghel '04	♟ 5
● Teroldego Rotaliano '06	♟ 4
● Trentino Lagrein '04	♟ 4
● Trentino Pinot Nero '05	♟ 5
O Blanc de Sers '05	♟♟ 4

O Bianco di Castelnuovo '05	♟♟ 5
O Salvanèl '05	♟♟ 4
● Mercuria Rosso '04	♟♟ 5
● Romeo '04	♟♟ 6
O Nosiola '05	♟ 4
O Bianco di Castelnuovo '04	♟♟ 5
● Romeo '03	♟♟ 6

Pisoni

FRAZ. PERGOLESE DI LASINO
LOC. SARCHE
VIA SAN SIRO, 7A
38070 LASINO [TN]
TEL. 0461564106
www.pisoni.net

ANNUAL PRODUCTION 40,000 bottles
HECTARES UNDER VINE 16
VITICULTURE METHOD Natural

The Pisonis are one of the oldest families in the world of Trentino wine. In 1852, they obtained the first certification for vinifying and selling wine in the area between Castel Madruzzo and Castel Toblino, precisely where the cellar and distillery are headquartered today. Each of the three family groups is in charge of a different area: sparkling wine production – the Pisonis were among the first sparkling wine producers in Trentino; grape growing and winemaking at the vinification cellar; and finally distilling. A few years ago, the cellar was remodelled and biodynamic methods have been adopted. As a result, the wines are growing in quality, especially blends like the chardonnay, pinot bianco and sauvignon, San Siro '06, which shows fresh, floral, full and juicy, and the '04 Rebo, the best version in Trentino from its vintage. We also liked the Vino Santo, a family treat. Several magnificent past vintages are now available, such as the marvellous 1983, with its great minerality and dried fig notes, offset by attractively refreshing acidity.

Pojer & Sandri

LOC. MOLINI, 4
38010 FAEDO [TN]
TEL. 0461650342
www.pojeresandri.it

ANNUAL PRODUCTION 250,000 bottles
HECTARES UNDER VINE 25
VITICULTURE METHOD Conventional

For more than 30 years, Mario Pojer and Fiorentino Sandri have led the troop of Trentino winemakers who believe in experimentation and absolute dedication to their work, ever ready to rethink their approach and tackle new production challenges. Now they are experimenting in the cellar with vinification methods, from crushing in an oxygen-free environment to washing the grapes to eliminate potential residue from the few necessary chemical treatments in the vineyards. Meanwhile, they are expanding the estate in upper Valle di Cembra and producing a fortified wine, Merlino, that is the perfect way to round off a meal. Pojer & Sandri may be a cauldron of ideas and an experimental laboratory, yet work in the vineyards is marked by tradition. There was no Three Glass award but three wines did make it to our finals. Faye Bianco '02, from chardonnay and pinot bianco, is as characterful as ever, showing floral, fresh, very balanced and elegant on the palate with a long finish that reveals good acid grip. The sparklers were equally excellent. The Rosé has a fine perlage, aromas of spice and red berry fruit and a balanced, fresh, floral palate. The Cuvée '00/'01 is rich, full and creamy with bracing acidity.

○ Trentino Vino Santo '83	🍷🍷 6
○ Trentino Bianco San Siro '06	🍷🍷 4
● Trentino Rebo '04	🍷🍷 5
● Sarica Rosso '04	🍷 5
● Pinot Nero '04	🍷 4
○ Trentino Nosiola '06	🍷 4
○ Trento Brut '03	🍷 4

○ Bianco Faye '02	🍷🍷 5
○ Spumante Cuvée '00/'01	🍷🍷 6
⊙ Brut Rosé	🍷🍷 4
○ Essenzia '05	🍷🍷 6
○ Sauvignon '06	🍷🍷 5
○ Trentino Traminer Aromatico '06	🍷🍷 5
● Rosso Faye '04	🍷🍷 6
○ Müller Thurgau Palai '06	🍷🍷 4
○ Nosiola '06	🍷🍷 4
● Pinot Nero '06	🍷 5
⊙ Vin dei Molini Rosato '06	🍷 4
● Pinot Nero Rodel Pianezzi Ris. '03	🍷 5
○ Bianco Faye '01	🍷🍷🍷 5
● Rosso Faye '00	🍷🍷🍷 6
● Rosso Faye '93	🍷🍷🍷 5
● Rosso Faye '94	🍷🍷🍷 5
● Rosso Faye '03	🍷🍷 6
○ Nosiola '05	🍷🍷 4

Pravis

LOC. LE BIOLCHE, 1
38076 LASINO [TN]
TEL. 0461564305
www.pravis.it

ANNUAL PRODUCTION 200,000 bottles
HECTARES UNDER VINE 32
VITICULTURE METHOD Conventional

At Pravis, the painstaking work continues of vinifying grapes from many tiny plots, spread throughout the Valle dei Laghi from Trento and Lake Garda to the Brenta Dolomites. Each plot is planted to a different variety where the white grapes are overripened to obtain characterful wines like the Stravino di Stravino, a complex blend of riesling, incrocio Manzoni, chardonnay, sauvignon and kerner. This intense wine has citrus aromas, a caressing bouquet, savouriness and ripe concentration, its notes of candied fruit and figs leading to a vibrant finish accompanied by good acid grip that ensures cellar potential. Equally rich and complex is Ora, a white from nosiola grapes left to part-dry on racks then vinified and aged in acacia barrels. Polìn, a Pinot Grigio selection, is always flavourful with distinctive coppery highlights. Two red wines are outstanding: Madruzzo, from pinot nero, and Rebo from a local variety created in the 1950s by Rebo Rigotti, a researcher born here in the Valle dei Laghi.

O Pinot Grigio Polin '06	🍷🍷 4*
O Stravino di Stravino '04	🍷🍷 5
O L'Ora '05	🍷🍷 5
O Nosiola Le Frate '06	🍷🍷 5
● Madruzzo '04	🍷 5
● Rebo Rigotti '05	🍷 4
O Sauvignon Atesino Teramara '06	🍷 5
O Müller Thurgau St. Thomà '06	🍷 4
O Stravino di Stravino '03	🍷🍷 6
O L'Ora '04	🍷🍷 5
O Nosiola Le Frate '05	🍷🍷 5

Eugenio Rosi

VIA TAVERNELLE, 3B
38060 VOLANO [TN]
TEL. 0464461375
www.vignaioli.trentino.it

ANNUAL PRODUCTION 18,000 bottles
HECTARES UNDER VINE 5.5
VITICULTURE METHOD Certified organic

Eugenio Rosi is perhaps one of the Italian winemakers who produce the fewest bottles – he doesn't even reach 20,000 a year – yet at the same time he is one of the most influential oenologists and a born experimenter. He made a lifestyle choice, preferring to dedicate himself to his estate rather than place his experience and as a wine technician at the service of large wineries. He was the first in Trentino to study techniques to part-dry grapes and convert his small plots to biodynamic growing methods. A committed maker of red wines, he produces around 8,000 bottles of Esegesi, a juicy, balsamic Bordeaux blend with tannins well tucked in and lovely length, and releases the same number of bottles of Poiema, from marzemino, with notes of ripe blackberry and liquorice, shades of aromatic herbs, and a deliciously moreish finish. Dòron is a Marzemino from overripe grapes left to part dry on racks. This tireless winemaker shuns the limelight although many seek him out, imitate him and above all, like us, praise his wines.

● Trentino Rosso Esegesi '03	🍷🍷 5
● Dòron '04	🍷🍷 6
● Trentino Marzemino Poiema Ris. '05	🍷🍷 5
● Dòron '00	🍷🍷 6
● Trentino Rosso Esegesi '02	🍷🍷 5
● Dòron '01	🍷🍷 6
● Trentino Marzemino Poiema '04	🍷🍷 5
● Trentino Marzemino Poiema '03	🍷🍷 5
● Dòron '03	🍷🍷 6
● Dòron '02	🍷🍷 6
● Trentino Rosso Esegesi '01	🍷🍷 5
● Trentino Rosso Esegesi '00	🍷🍷 5

Cantina Rotaliana

VIA TRENTO, 65B
38017 MEZZOLOMBARDO [TN]
TEL. 0461601010
www.cantinarotaliana.it

ANNUAL PRODUCTION 1,000,000 bottles
HECTARES UNDER VINE 340
VITICULTURE METHOD Conventional

Cantina Rotaliana is back on our Three Glass list but not for its most eagerly awaited wine, Clesurae, although that also went through to our finals. It was the Riserva 2004 that won the prize. This fantastic Teroldego is minerally, elegant, dynamic, taut and fresh yet at the same time full-bodied and concentrated, a mature body and a lingering finish. In other words, it's a wine that deserves the prize because it is supremely well made, a fine example of a Teroldego Rotaliano that is readily available and fairly priced. But things went differently for Clesurae, the winery's flagship Teroldego. It pays the price of an unfavourable vintage and an excess of oak. Praise goes to the Riserva and the other good wines from the Cantina del Teroldego, another name for this co-operative managed by skilled oenologist Leonardo Pilati. The '06 Teroldego, Etichetta Rossa, and the rest are all very well-made wines.

★ Tenuta San Leonardo

FRAZ. BORGHETTO ALL'ADIGE
LOC. SAN LEONARDO
38060 AVIO [TN]
TEL. 0464689004
www.sanleonardo.it

ANNUAL PRODUCTION 145,000 bottles
HECTARES UNDER VINE 21
VITICULTURE METHOD Conventional

Passion for viticulture, absolute dedication to the values of the land and the identity of a single valley all drive Marchese Carlo Guerrieri Gonzaga and his son Anselmo to produce wine. Here are two wines in perfect tune with one another, San Leonardo and Villa Gresti. Both are in a class of their own, and both are cosseted with the same care, but both are different in composition. Above all, they are distinct in style, although both respect the progress of the seasons, their vinification, ageing and maturation varying according to the growing year. The 2003 Villa Gresti was presented last year. Now it is San Leonardo's turn and the same vintage has yielded the same grace. In some ways, this San Leonardo is unusual in its fresh, youthful aromatic profile, with plenty of the ripe fruity tones typical of Campi Sarni at Borghetto. Yet this is also a more immediate, agile wine with subtle acid backbone and great delicacy. Several vertical tastings starting from 1983 hint that this long-lived wine will give more that a little satisfaction to those who can wait a few more years.

● Teroldego Rotaliano Ris. '04	￥￥￥ 4
● Teroldego Rotaliano Clesurae '05	￥￥ 6
● Teroldego Rotaliano Etichetta Rossa '06	￥￥ 3
● Thamè Rosso '05	￥ 5
○ Trentino Pinot Bianco '06	￥ 3
● Groppello di Revò '06	￥ 5
○ Trentino Pinot Grigio '06	￥ 3
● Trentino Merlot '06	￥ 3
○ Thamè Bianco '06	￥ 5
● Trentino Cabernet '06	￥ 3
○ Trentino Moscato Giallo '06	￥ 4
● Trentino Lagrein '06	￥ 3
● Teroldego Rotaliano Clesurae '04	￥￥ 6
● Teroldego Rotaliano Ris. '03	￥￥ 4

● San Leonardo '03	￥￥￥ 8
● San Leonardo '00	￥￥￥ 8
● San Leonardo '90	￥￥￥ 5
● San Leonardo '94	￥￥￥ 5
● San Leonardo '96	￥￥￥ 5
● San Leonardo '99	￥￥￥ 8
● San Leonardo '97	￥￥￥ 5
● Villa Gresti '03	￥￥￥ 7
● San Leonardo '95	￥￥￥ 5
● San Leonardo '93	￥￥￥ 5
● San Leonardo '01	￥￥￥ 8
● San Leonardo '88	￥￥￥ 5
● Villa Gresti '00	￥￥ 7
● Villa Gresti '01	￥￥ 7
● Merlot '03	￥￥ 4

Istituto Agrario Provinciale San Michele all'Adige

VIA EDMONDO MACH, 1
38010 SAN MICHELE ALL'ADIGE [TN]
TEL. 0461615252
www.ismaa.it

ANNUAL PRODUCTION 250,000 bottles
HECTARES UNDER VINE 60
VITICULTURE METHOD Conventional

Founded under the Hapsburgs more than 130 years ago to promote progress in agriculture and particularly viticulture and winemaking in Trentino, this institute has for some time been a reference point for winemakers, oenologists and university researchers from Italy and abroad. R&D, experimentation and practical oenology have put San Michele at the cutting edge of study of the vine genome in the effort to understand the plant and improve growing and grapes without detracting from typicity. One of the best oenologists in Trentino, Enrico Paternoster, manages the school's winery. The special cuvées are still ageing in the historic cellar but all the wines are beautifully conceived. Even the standard-label products are utterly reliable. In particular, the '06 Pinot Bianco, with white peach aromas, is juicy and minerally with a complex, dynamic finish. Other good wines include the long, well-typed Riesling, the fragrant Müller Thurgau, a fresh, balanced white with typical almondy notes in the finish, and the dense, compact Rosso Castel San Michele, a red of good texture and concentration.

Arcangelo Sandri

VIA VANEGGE, 4
38010 FAEDO [TN]
TEL. 0461650935
sand_arca@libero.it

ANNUAL PRODUCTION 20,000 bottles
HECTARES UNDER VINE 3
VITICULTURE METHOD Conventional

After completing university studies in oenology, young Nadia and Sonia enthusiastically manage the family estate, aided by their father. Arcangelo Sandri is a winemaker who for years has contributed to bringing out the best of the special qualities in wines from Faedo. The two Sandri hectares of vineyards are planted to four different varieties and tended with care to yield a few thousand bottles of typically Faedo wines, separately vinified in small selections of carefully tended grapes. Unfortunately, the 2006 growing season was not an easy one and did not yield grapes of the usual quality in the hill country towards Valle di Cembra. Wines from the Sandri sisters pay the price and show excessive oak. The decent Müller Thurgau Cosler is fragrant and completely in line with tradition, as is the Lagrein Capòr '04. We sincerely expected something more from both the Chardonnay and Traminer but never mind. The wines are good just as they are.

O Trentino Pinot Bianco '06	♀♀ 4
O Trentino Bianco Castel San Michele '05	♀♀ 5
O Trentino Riesling '06	♀♀ 4
● Trentino Rosso Castel San Michele '05	♀♀ 5
● Trentino Rosso Monastero '05	♀♀ 6
O Trentino Müller Thurgau '06	♀♀ 4
O Trentino Chardonnay '06	♀ 4
O Trentino Moscato Giallo '06	♀ 4
O Trentino Pinot Grigio '06	♀ 4
● Trentino Rosso Monastero '03	♀♀ 6
● Trentino Rosso Monastero '04	♀♀ 6
O Trentino Pinot Bianco '05	♀♀ 4
● Trentino Rosso Castel San Michele '04	♀♀ 5

O Trentino Chardonnay I Canopi '06	♀ 4
O Trentino Müller Thurgau Cosler '06	♀ 4
● Trentino Lagrein Capòr '04	♀ 5
O Trentino Traminer Razer '06	♀ 4
● Trentino Lagrein Capòr '03	♀♀ 5
O Trentino Chardonnay I Canopi '05	♀♀ 4

de Tarczal

FRAZ. MARANO D'ISERA
VIA G. B. MIORI, 4
38060 ISERA [TN]
TEL. 0464409134
www.detarczal.com

ANNUAL PRODUCTION   120,000 bottles
HECTARES UNDER VINE 17
VITICULTURE METHOD   Conventional

Country gentleman and passionate
winemaker Ruggero de Tarczal eschews
attempts to amaze us with new sensations.
His reliable wines have the force of tradition
and comply with his estate's production
philosophy and the progress of the
seasons. Despite the last two growing
years, which were far from ideal for him or
many other winemakers in the Dolomites,
he has had no lack of positive reviews.
Some of the credit for this goes to
uncompromising vineyard management that
puts the vines first. The most interesting
product this year was the Trentino Cabernet
Sauvignon '03, which has varietal
grassiness and a rich, mature palate. From
the rest of the range, the Marzemino d'Isera
'05 is well made, the Chardonnay '06, fruity
and pleasant and the Pinot Bianco '06,
fresh, supple and marked by floral notes.

Toblino

LOC. SARCHE
VIA LONGA, 1
38070 CALAVINO [TN]
TEL. 0461564168
www.toblino.it

ANNUAL PRODUCTION   280,000 bottles
HECTARES UNDER VINE 650
VITICULTURE METHOD   Conventional

Cantina di Toblino vinifies grapes from the
Valle dei Laghi, almost 10,000,000
kilograms of various varieties coming from
its 600 member growers. This co-operative
winery, part of the Cavit group, specializes
in wines from nosiola, a native variety that it
interprets in various types of wine. Toblino is
the leading producer of Vino Santo,
released only after years of ageing and
conditioning, such as the Tradizione '97
with its signature oxidized notes. For a few
harvests, the cellar has also produced Ora
which, in the 2004 version, is rich and
generously structured. The '06 Nosiola is
also good, showing fresh and easy drinking.
Winery president Carlo Filiberto Bleggi is
such a committed innovator he has started
up a project for the production of late
harvest wines, and begun remodelling the
winery facilities, while continuing to improve
the range of wines on offer. We close with
Trento Brut Antares '01, a fresh wine with
aromas of white-fleshed fruit and freshly
baked cakes introducing a full, well-
balanced palate.

● Trentino Cabernet Sauvignon '03	♛♛ 4*
○ Trentino Chardonnay '06	♛ 4
● Trentino Marzemino d'Isera Sup. '05	♛ 4
○ Trentino Pinot Bianco '06	♛ 4
○ Trentino Pinot Bianco '05	♛♛ 4

○ Trentino Vino Santo Tradizione '97	♛♛ 6
○ Trento Brut Antàres '01	♛♛ 4
○ L'Ora '04	♛♛ 5
● Teroldego '04	♛ 3
○ Trentino Nosiola '06	♛ 3
○ Trentino Traminer '06	♛ 4
☉ Trentino Lagrein Kretzer '06	♛ 3
● Trentino Rebo '05	♛ 3
○ Trentino Müller Thurgau '06	♛ 3

Vallarom

FRAZ. MASI, 21
38063 AVIO [TN]
TEL. 0464684297
www.vallarom.it

ANNUAL PRODUCTION 45,000 bottles
HECTARES UNDER VINE 8
VITICULTURE METHOD Conventional

The name Vallarom goes back to the early years of the second millennium, and even then was linked to farming alluvial plots along the river Adige. It evokes the labours of the earliest winemakers in the area. Filippo Scienza and his wife Barbara conduct the family business with consultancy from his illustrious relatives: his Uncle Attilio is a leading vine scholar. The couple are keen to experiment with new growing techniques so they can harvest according to the balance of nature. But the Scienzas also rightly wanted to personalize their range and set up a project to make genuinely territory-focused wines. They have experimented with lambrusco a foglia frastagliata, marzemino, moscato giallo trentino and other native varieties but have not neglected international varieties. Their wines are vinified with skill and craftsmanship, as befits winemakers who are enthusiastic about their work and welcome comparisons with other wines. The pleasant, interesting Chardonnay '06 is fresh and well structured and the Syrah '05 is nicely varietal.

Vilàr

VIA CAVOLAVILLA, 35
38060 VILLA LAGARINA [TN]
TEL. 0464409028
luigispagnolli@vilar.it

ANNUAL PRODUCTION 20,000 bottles
HECTARES UNDER VINE 4.5
VITICULTURE METHOD Conventional

If you are looking for an authentic Trentino winemaker, you have found him. Luigi Spagnolli is a tiller of the soil with a passion for vines. He graduated in oenology and has worked for years at the family estate but for a few harvests now has operated on his own in vineyards on the valley floor, others in the hills towards Rovereto and still others among the hillside castles and villages of Vallagarina. His production is limited to fewer than 20,000 bottles a year but is influential nonetheless. Gigi Spagnolli is tenacious, willing to accept criticism and comparisons with other winemakers, and has a vine stock that includes traditional and international varieties. From a blend of cabernet, merlot, teroldego and lagrein he makes Morela '04, an increasingly convincing wine with great structure, excellent length and a long finish. It's very pleasant if still rather young. The Cabernet Sauvignon '04 is good, although its excessive vegĕtal tones should be corrected. Completing the range are the uncomplicated, varietal '06 Marzemino, the Traminer Aromatico '06 and the Nosiola '06 from vineyards high in the hills, a minerally, savoury, perkily fresh-tasting offering.

● Syrah '05	♈♈ 6
○ Chardonnay '06	♈♈ 5
● Cabernet Sauvignon '05	♈ 4
● Campi Sarni Rosso '04	♈ 5
○ Enantio '06	♈ 4
○ Moscato Giallo '06	♈ 4
○ Vadum Caesaris '06	♈ 4
● Pinot Nero '05	♈ 5
● Trentino Marzemino '06	♈ 4
● Merlot '06	♈ 4
● Syrah '04	♈♈ 6
● Syrah '03	♈♈ 6
○ Vadum Caesaris '05	♈♈ 4

● Cabernet Sauvignon '04	♈♈ 4
● Morela '04	♈♈ 6
○ Nosiola '06	♈ 4
● Trentino Marzemino '06	♈ 4
○ Traminer Aromatico '06	♈ 5
● Morela '03	♈♈ 6
● Cabernet Sauvignon '03	♈♈ 4
● Morela '02	♈♈ 6
● Trentino Marzemino '05	♈♈ 4

Villa Corniole
FRAZ. VERLA
VIA AL GREC', 23
38030 GIOVO [TN]
TEL. 0461695067
www.villacorniole.com

Vivallis
VIA VALENTINI, 37
38060 CALLIANO [TN]
TEL. 0464834113
www.vivallis.it

ANNUAL PRODUCTION 90,000 bottles
HECTARES UNDER VINE 14
VITICULTURE METHOD Conventional

ANNUAL PRODUCTION 1,000,000 bottles
HECTARES UNDER VINE 730
VITICULTURE METHOD Conventional

Porphyry from the Valle di Cembra is used in the construction industry but it's also a mineral that influences vines. Because this stone is refractory and distributed across various plots, it can warm terraced vineyards at high altitudes. Quarries are clearly not attractive to the eye but they are an important source of economic development for the valley. The Pellegrinis are building contractors and actually carved their new cellar out of the porphyry. They have been producing wines for a few years now with consultancy input from expert oenologist Walter Weber. Some of the vineyards stand on porphyry near the cellar and others are located on the valley floor in the area between Mezzolombardo and Mezzocorona, which ideal for Teroldego. Villa Corniole confirmed that it is a reliable exponent of the variety with a juicy Teroldego Rotaliano '05 that shows ripe tannins and prominent minerality. But there is also Cimbro, the Pellegrini blend of teroldego, lagrein and merlot, which is broad and intense on a nose of wild berries and tobacco, then long on the acidity-underpinned palate. The white wines are simpler but clean and pleasant.

After a change of name and logo a few harvests ago, Vivallis' adjustment phase is now behind it. The leading winery of the SAV group, the Vallagarina growers' association, is now more visible but also can compete with greater impact, thanks to first-class technical staff managed by Mauro Baldessari and Flavio Cristoforetti. Some time ago, Vivallis started a detailed zoning programme to be able to cultivate only the varieties most suited to the various soil types and produce single-vineyard selections. Marzemino has found a welcoming home here but other varieties, such as nosiola and müller thurgau, give interesting results in the Vallagarina hills. The wide range of wines is well crafted and great value for money. Marzemino Vigna dei Ziresi is very good and in the 2005 vintage again showed itself to be one of the best, and perhaps the best, of its type, presenting varietal with remarkable structure and attractive notes of aromatic herbs. The Marzemino d'Isera gives ripe blackberry and cinchona, followed by a full, dense palate with a long Mediterranean herb finish.

● Cimbro '05	▽▽	4*
● Teroldego Rotaliano '05	▽▽	4
○ Trentino Chardonnay '06	▽	4
○ Trentino Pinot Grigio '06	▽	4
○ Trentino Müller Thurgau '06	▽	4
● Teroldego Rotaliano '03	▽▽	4
○ Trentino Müller Thurgau '05	▽▽	4
● Teroldego Rotaliano '04	▽▽	4

● Trentino Marzemino di Isera Sup. '05	▽▽	4*
● Trentino Marzemino Vigna dei Ziresi Sup. '05	▽▽	5
○ Trentino Bianco Vigna Pra' dei Fanti '04	▽	4
● Trentino Merlot V. Borgosacco '05	▽	4
○ Trentino Müller Thurgau Vigna Servìs '06	▽	4
○ Trentino Pinot Grigio Vigna Reselé '06	▽	5
○ Trentino Sup. Bianco Aura '06	▽	4
○ Trentino Traminer Vigna San Biagio '06	▽	4
○ Trentino Nosiola Vigna Vallunga '06	▽	4
○ Trentino Moscato Giallo Vigna Giere '06	▽	5
● Trentino Marzemino Vigna Fornas '05	▽	4
● Trentino Cabernet Sauvignon Vigna Carbonera '05	▽	4
● Trentino Lagrein Vigna Costa '05	▽	4
● Trentino Marzemino di Isera Sup. '04	▽▽	4

Conti Wallenburg

LOC. MARTIGNANO
VIA BASSANO, 3
38100 TRENTO [TN]
TEL. 045913399
www.vinimontresor.it

ANNUAL PRODUCTION 150,000 bottles
HECTARES UNDER VINE 6
VITICULTURE METHOD Conventional

The opening of the new tunnel on the Trento ring road has cut down the traffic passing in front of this attractive country estate, rebuilt by the Montresors, a long-established winemaking and growing family from Verona. They set up here in order to have a few prized Trentino wines on their extensive list, restructuring the farm and building a new cellar and agriturismo facilities. Above all, the surrounding vineyards have been recovered. They are in effect hanging gardens that safeguard the Trento hill from further real estate speculation. After the first harvests from the past few years, Conti Wallenburg wines are already showing a certain authority. Whether because of the cellar staff's skill or the oenological consultants or the outstanding vineyard terrain in the area, Riserva degli Ambasciatori, a Teroldego selected from the vineyards on the Piana Rotaliana, is among the best tasted this year. It flaunts a solid, deep palate, sweet, elegant tannins and lovely texture. The Brut Corte Imperiale is also good, with full, appealing aromas, hints of citrus and an agreeably fruit-forward palate. The other wines are flavourful and improving all the time.

Roberto Zeni

FRAZ. GRUMO
VIA STRETTA, 2
38010 SAN MICHELE ALL'ADIGE [TN]
TEL. 0461650456
www.zeni.tn.it

ANNUAL PRODUCTION 189,000 bottles
HECTARES UNDER VINE 20
VITICULTURE METHOD Conventional

Roberto Zeni is president of the Trentino winemakers' association, now celebrating its 20th anniversary. This outstanding personality on the Trentino winemaking scene has for years fought to safeguard small producers. Many of these, including Roberto, his brother Andrea and the family's younger generation, grow grapes that go into varietal wines with a firmly rooted sense of place. At their cellar on the banks of the river Adige, the Zenis vinify several varieties, from teroldego to nosiola and moscato rosa, and have expanded the distillery to make elegant grappas. In addition, they are focusing on selections of grapes to make sparkling wines. The most convincing product this year is actually a sparkler, Zeni Brut Riserva '95, from 90 per cent chardonnay with a dash of pinot nero, which ages on the yeasts at least ten years to develop its tiny, delicate bubbles. The complex aromas range from white-fleshed fruit to lavender and aromatic herbs. The dense, structured palate has a long, minerally and oaky finish. The three sound versions of Teroldego include one traditional, a Riserva and, unusually, a passito from part-dried grapes. The whites are flavourful and well made, in particular the Sortì '06, from a cuvée of pinot bianco, riesling and sauvignon.

● Teroldego Rotaliano Ris. degli Ambasciatori '04	♟♟ 5
○ Trento Corte Imperiale Brut	♟♟ 5
● Marquardo '05	♟ 6
● Marquardo '04	♟ 6
☉ Cuvée Costantinopoli Rosé	♟ 5
○ Traminer Aromatico '06	♟ 4
● Marquardo '03	♟♟ 6

○ Trento Zeni Brut Ris. '95	♟♟ 6
● Ororosso '06	♟♟ 6
○ Sortì '06	♟♟ 5
● Teroldego Rotaliano Pini '03	♟ 7
● Teroldego Rotaliano Vign. Le Albere '05	♟ 4
☉ Trentino Moscato Rosa '06	♟ 5
○ Trentino Sauvignon Vigneto Ronchi '06	♟ 4
○ Trentino Nosiola Maso Nero '06	♟ 4
○ Sortì '05	♟♟ 5
● Teroldego Rotaliano Vign. Le Albere '04	♟♟ 4
● Trentino Moscato Rosa '05	♟♟ 7

OTHER WINERIES

Augusto Zadra
VIA IV NOVEMBRE, 15
38028 REVÒ [TN]
TEL. 3402976388
www.elzeremia.it

Augusto Zadra is the winemaker who saved Groppello di Revò from extinction. He makes just a few thousand bottles with grapes from ungrafted vines grown on the steep slope of Revò. There are two versions of Groppello, one from old vine stock and the other from renewed vineyards.

● Groppello di Revò El Zeremia '03	🍷 5
● Groppello di Revò '05	🍷 4

Cantina Sociale di Avio
VIA DANTE, 14
38063 AVIO [TN]
TEL. 0464684008
www.viticoltoriinavio.it

The structure of this co-operative winery has been completely reorganized to improve the handling and vinifying of grapes from its new vineyards. Although it only produces a few thousand bottles now, it will soon be ready to re-establish its wines' status and expand its market.

O Trentino Pinot Grigio '06	🍷 3
O Trentino Sup. V. T. '05	🍷 4

Barone de Cles
VIA G. MAZZINI, 18
38017 MEZZOLOMBARDO [TN]
TEL. 0461601081
www.baronedecles.it

The noble Cles dynasty was already cultivating vines here in the 14th century. The flagship wine is the Teroldego, grown at Maso Scari, a cru in the hollow between Noce and Adige. For some years now, the estate has been busy replanting its vineyards to recover all the appeal of the prestigious Cles wines.

● Teroldego Rotaliano Maso Scari '04	🍷🍷 5
● Trentino Lagrein '05	🍷 4
● Rosso del Cardinale '04	🍷 4

Riccardo Battistotti
VIA 3 NOVEMBRE, 21
38060 NOMI [TN]
TEL. 0464834145
www.battistotti.com

Among those who select the best grapes at Nomi are the Battistottis, who have also been tending their own vineyards for some years. They produce the classic range of Vallagarina wines and a special small batch fermentation of an intense, nicely textured Moscato Rosa.

● Trentino Moscato Rosa '05	🍷🍷 6
● Trentino Marzemino '06	🍷 4
● Trentino Marzemino Verdini '05	🍷 4
O Trentino Müller Thurgau '06	🍷 4

Bongiovanni
LOC. SABBIONARA
VIA SANT' ANTONIO, 28
38063 AVIO [TN]
TEL. 0464684388
www.aziendagricolaabongiovanni.com

Bongiovanni is a typical country estate producing just a few thousand bottles every year. Only four wines are made from estate-grown grapes, with special care and attention given to lambrusco a foglia frastagliata, the Terra dei Forti Enantio, among the best from the vintage, and the Marzemino.

● Trentino Enantio Terra dei Forti '05	🍷🍷 4*
● Trentino Marzemino '06	🍷 4
O Trentino Pinot Grigio '06	🍷 4
O Trentino Chardonnay '06	🍷 4

Campo Maseri
VIA ROTALIANA, 27A
38017 MEZZOLOMBARDO [TN]
TEL. 0461601486
www.villadevarda.com

The winemaking estate of Luigi Dolzan, committed wine entrepreneur and discerning judge of wines, presents a dozen well-made, good-value products. Particularly well crafted is the Teroldego, presented in two versions alongside traditional Trentino whites like Chardonnay and Pinot Grigio.

● Teroldego Rotaliano Ris. '04	🍷🍷 5
● Teroldego Rotaliano '05	🍷 4
O Trentino Chardonnay '06	🍷 4
O Trentino Pinot Grigio '06	🍷 4

OTHER WINERIES

Cipriano Fedrizzi
VIA 4 NOVEMBRE, 1
38017 MEZZOLOMBARDO [TN]
TEL. 0461602328

Small yet influential, this estate works to improve the quality of its Teroldego and Lagrein. The limited output includes a few thousand bottles with Teroldego as the star, particularly the Due Vigneti selection, a savoury, long-lived wine penalized only by the small quantities produced.

● Teroldego Rotaliano Due Vigneti '05	▼▼ 5
● Teroldego Rotaliano '05	▼ 4
● Trentino Lagrein '05	▼ 4

Renzo Gorga
VIA DEL PARCO, 58
38064 FOLGARIA [TN]
TEL. 0464721161
www.vinigorga.com

Renzo Gorga's winery is one of the highest in Italy, located in Folgaria at 1,187 metres above sea level. Grapes grown in Vallagarina are vinified up here almost on the ski slopes, on the high plain facing Lavarone. An ever more discerning winemaker, Renzo Gorga turns out frank, characterful wines.

○ Pinot Grigio '06	▼ 4
● Trentino Marzemino V. Paradaia '05	▼ 4
● Trentino Marzemino '06	▼ 3
● Trentino Cabernet Sauvignon '04	▼ 5

Lunelli
VIA PONTE DI RAVINA, 15
38100 TRENTO [TN]
TEL. 0461972311
www.ferrarispumante.it

The Lunellis cultivate almost exclusively white varieties at this Trento estate. But this year, they only presented Maso Montalto, a monovarietal Pinot Nero that Mauro Lunelli makes for the pleasure of testing his skills on this fascinating variety. This very drinkable wine shows amazing concentration.

● Trentino Pinot Nero Maso Montalto '04	▼▼ 6
● Trentino Pinot Nero Maso Montalto '03	♀▼ 6

Madonna delle Vittorie
VIA LINFANO, 81
38062 ARCO [TN]
TEL. 0464505432
www.madonnadellevittorie.it

From vineyards on the Trentino side of the Garda lakeshore, Madonna delle Vittorie produces a series of classic Trentino wines and a few blends. The Trento Millesimato sparkler is always sound. Several white wines are very attractive, especially the Sommolago blend and a fragrant Teroldego.

○ Trento Brut '04	▼▼ 4
○ Trentino Riesling '06	▼ 4
● Teroldego Rotaliano '05	▼ 3
○ Sommolago '06	▼ 4

Mori - Colli Zugna
VIA DEL GARDA, 35
38065 MORI [TN]
TEL. 0464918154
www.cantinamoricollizugna.it

The Mori-Colli Zugna co-operative is a Cavit group operation that has an independent line, Vigna del Gelso. As in other co-operatives, the 600 member growers have learned to produce less but better. The Teroldego, with intense blackberry fruit and a forthright palate, and the varietal Chardonnay are good.

● Trentino Rosso Rossoreale '04	▼▼ 4
● Terodelgo V. del Gelso '05	▼ 4
○ Trentino Chardonnay V. del Gelso '06	▼ 3

Diego e Francesco Moser
LOC. GARDOLO DI MEZZO
38040 TRENTO [TN]
TEL. 0461990786
www.cantinemoser.com

Cycling champion Francesco Moser has been tending vineyards and managing his lovely winery for some years. The wines have grown in number and quantity – almost 100,000 bottles – and quality has kept pace. The forthright Lagrein Dea Mater and nice clean Müller Thurgau are both interesting.

○ Chardonnay '06	▼ 4
○ Müller Thurgau '06	▼ 4
○ Moscato Giallo '06	▼ 5
● Lagrein Dea Mater '06	▼ 5

OTHER WINERIES

Cantina Sociale di Nomi
VIA ROMA, 1
38060 NOMI [TN]
TEL. 0464834195
www.athesiavini.it

Cantina di Nomi's is increasingly respectful of tradition. The Marzemino, which is juicy, rich in pulp and body, and the varietal, very convincing Merlot are the outstanding wines from this long-established co-operative. The whites are also reliably good.

● Trentino Marzemino Antichi Portali Le Fornas '05	� 4*
● Trentino Merlot Le Campagne '05	♟♟ 4
○ Trentino Müller Thurgau Antichi Portali Nambiol '06	♟ 4

Giovanni Poli
LOC. SANTA MASSENZA
VIA VEZZANO S. MASSENZA, 37
38070 VEZZANO [TN]
TEL. 0461864119
www.poligiovanni.it

Giovanni and Graziano Poli are master distillers, although they keep a close eye on their lakeside vineyards at Santa Massenza. Here, the nosiola variety has many characterful interpretations, including Vino Santo. The two reds, Rebo and Cabernet Fuggè, are flavourful and simple.

● Trentino Cabernet Fuggè '03	♟ 4
○ Trentino Vino Santo Emblemi d'Amor '01	♟ 6
○ Trentino Nosiola Goccia d'Oro '06	♟ 4
● Rebo '05	♟ 4

Redondèl
VIA ROMA, 28
38017 MEZZOLOMBARDO [TN]
TEL. 0461601618
info@redondel.it

Producing less than 15,000 bottles, all from teroldego, Paolo Zanini is one of the upcoming interpreters of the variety. He grows and ferments it separately with careful vineyard selection. He presents a more immediate base version and the fuller-bodied, more cellarable Mezum.

● Teroldego Rotaliano Mezum '05	♟ 5
● Teroldego Rotaliano '05	♟ 4
● Teroldego Rotaliano Il Dannato '02	♟♟ 6

Cantina Riva del Garda
VIA LUTTI, 10
38066 RIVA DEL GARDA [TN]
TEL. 0464522133
www.agririva.it

This versatile co-operative winery has a brand new operations centre. The dozen wines produced are characterized by their frank character and accessible prices. There's a good wine from teroldego called, in honour of the zone, Rivaldego and a fresh, fragrant Trento Cuvée Ponale.

○ Trento Cuvée Ponale	♟♟ 4
● Rivaldego '06	♟ 4
● Trentino Merlot Créa '04	♟♟ 4

Alessandro Secchi
FRAZ. SERRAVALLE DI ALA
LOC. COLERI, 10
38061 ALA [TN]
TEL. 0464696647
www.secchivini.it

There's a bigger range of wines from this small but progressive estate, competently managed by Alessandro Secchi's family. Here in lower Vallagarina, the climate is so mild that they make excellent extravirgin olive oil. The good Merlot is well typed, varietal and round.

● Trentino Merlot '05	♟♟ 5
● Realgar '06	♟ 4
○ Berillo d'Oro '06	♟ 4
● Trentino Pinot Nero '05	♟ 4

Armando Simoncelli
VIA NAVICELLO, 7
38068 ROVERETO [TN]
TEL. 0464432373

This long-established Vallagarina winemaker is one of the most sincere interpreters of Marzemino and more. On his lovely estate, he also makes a classic spumante, vinifies white varieties and produces an interesting Bordeaux-type red, the elegantly long, deep Navesèl, and many other wines at fair prices.

● Trentino Rosso Navesèl '04	♟♟ 5
○ Trentino Pinot Bianco '06	♟ 4
● Trentino Rosso Navesèl '03	♟♟ 5

OTHER WINERIES

Spagnolli
VIA G. B. ROSINA, 4A
38060 ISERA [TN]
TEL. 0464409054
www.vinispagnolli.it

The Spagnollis from Isera guarantee
authenticity in production and honesty in
business. A family committed to vinifying
grapes harvested in Vallagarina, some from
their estate and the rest from contributing
growers, they create a dozen or so reliable,
characterful wines, above all Marzemino.

● Trentino Marzemino '06	♥	4
○ Trentino Moscato Giallo '06	♥	4
○ Trentino Nosiola '06	♥	4
● Trentino Marzemino Don Giovanni '05	♥	5

De Vescovi Ulzbach
P.ZZA GARIBALDI, 12
38016 MEZZOCORONA [TN]
TEL. 0461605648
www.devescoviulzbach.it

Growers since 1708, this operation has
been bottling for only a couple of seasons.
But the results are excellent. The two
interpretations of Teroldego are opulent and
full of character. Young Giulio De Vescovi
continues to forge ahead and is only held by
such the cellar's limited output.

● Teroldego Rotaliano Vigilius Ris. '04	♥♥	6
● Teroldego Rotaliano '05	♥♥	4
● Teroldego Rotaliano '04	♀♀	5
● Teroldego Rotaliano Vigilius Ris. '03	♀♀	6

Villa Piccola
LOC. VILLA PICCOLA, 4
38010 FAEDO [TN]
TEL. 0461650420

Walter Rossi is a winemaker who has been
replanting his hillside vineyards for years.
The first harvests from the new plantings are
encouraging, especially the juicy, elegantly
well crafted Pinot Nero selection, Silbrarii.
The Traminer and Chardonnay are also
good.

● Pinot Nero Silbrarii '05	♥♥	5
○ Traminer Silbrarii '06	♥	4
○ Chardonnay Argentarie '06	♥	4

Luigi Zanini
VIA DE GASPERI, 42
38017 MEZZOLOMBARDO [TN]
TEL. 0461601496
www.zaniniluigi.com

With his cellar in the heart of the village,
Oscar Zanini is one of the small-scale,
dynamic Campo Rotaliano producers
committed to bringing out the best in their
Teroldegos, like the rich, fruity Le Cervare
'05. In addition to the Teroldegos, the two
wines from chardonnay are also good.

● Teroldego Rotaliano Le Cervare '05	♥♥	5
○ Gocce di Sole '04	♥	6
● Teroldego Rotaliano '06	♥	3
○ Trentino Chardonnay '06	♥	4

ALTO ADIGE

Despite Alto Adige's low oenological numbers – 356,000 hectolitres amounts to only 0.7 per cent of Italy's production – the region stands out for quality. It won 22 Three Glass awards this year. But we feel the most significant fact is the number of wines it sent to our finals – more than 160 – putting Alto Adige in the first rank of Italian winemaking. This has never happened before. It is not just that the number of wineries has increased and entries in the Guide have gone from 85 to 92. The number of finalists shows well-established maturity that involves all the grower-producers in the province of Bolzano. We should also add the wines are acquiring greater personality and the various production zones are taking specific identities. For example, we no longer refer to generic Alto Adige Gewürztraminers but can point to those from Termeno, Caldaro, Valle Isarco and so on, each with its own distinguishing characteristics. This is true to a certain extent for all wine types and for us represents the greatest success for Alto Adige's producers. This year, we want to underline the much anticipated explosion of a wine we have said for years is the trump card of white wine producers in Alto Adige: Pinot Bianco. In addition to winning three Three Glass awards, it has shown, among other things, a potential that has yet to be completely explored. Valle Isarco and Valle Venosta made a strong showing, cornering the market on prizes in spite of the smallish production numbers. On the other hand, with some major exceptions, 2006 proved not to be a great year for aromatic wines, such as Gewürztraminer and Sauvignon, yet it was excellent for Riesling and even exceptional for Schiava. In general, there was a drop in the alcohol content of white wines, leading to fresher, more balanced products. We firmly believe this is the way forward. The Pinot Neros from the 2004 and 2005 vintages are rather good. Tastings overall were the most encouraging of the past ten years, although there were no Three Glass prizes, perhaps because of a certain prejudice that says good Pinot Neros can only come from Burgundy. There were excellent reviews for Lagrein, a wine that has by now convinced even the most sceptical, and Cabernet Sauvignon, which can look any other wine in the eye with the Lafoa '03 from Colterenzio. Alto Adige has also established itself as the region for some the best Italian sweet wines. In terms of estates, Produttori di San Michele Appiano celebrates its first century by winning two Three Glass awards, a difficult achievement also managed by Elena Walch. Gumphof's Markus Prackwieser, with his Pinot Bianco Praesulis '06, wins the prize for Best Priced Wine, again showing how Alto Adige is a promised land for good-value wines.

Abbazia di Novacella
FRAZ. NOVACELLA
VIA DELL'ABBAZIA, 1
39040 VARNA/VAHRN [BZ]
TEL. 0472836189
www.abbazianovacella.it

ANNUAL PRODUCTION 500,000 bottles
HECTARES UNDER VINE 70
VITICULTURE METHOD Conventional

Standing out in Valle Isarco is getting more and more difficult but Abbazia di Novacella sailed effortlessly to Three Glasses with Sylvaner Praepositus '06 and strung together a ribbon of impeccable wines with high or very high scores. The impression from the outside is one of a perfectly oiled machine that leaves nothing to chance and is constantly on the lookout for further improvements. The results are there for everyone to see in wines with great character. The fashionable term "terroir" is not an empty word at Abbazia di Novacella. Credit goes to the winning duo of estate director Urban von Klebelsberg and the talented, almost too modest, oenologist, Celestino Lucin. The Three Glass winner this year convinced us with its usual character but the '06 version has gained something in depth and elegance. However, we should mention the great qualities of three wines from the basic line. The Veltliner, Pinot Grigio and Sylvaner cruised into our finals, an unmistakeable sign of reliability with few equals among Italy's producers.

Cantina Produttori Andriano
VIA DELLA CHIESA, 2
39010 ANDRIANO/ANDRIAN [BZ]
TEL. 0471510137
www.andrianer-kellerei.it

ANNUAL PRODUCTION 300,000 bottles
HECTARES UNDER VINE 85
VITICULTURE METHOD Certified biodynamic

Apart from being the oldest co-operative winery in Alto Adige, founded and built back in 1893, Cantina Produttori di Andriano, in its welcoming winemaking centre in Val d'Adige, is also the largest organic wine producer in Alto Adige. For years, it has offered us a broad range of always reliable wines from the Tor di Lupo line as well as the Sonnengut selections. In first place this year, we find the solid Lagrein Tor di Lupo '05, aged two years in large barrels and barriques. In this version, this dense, austere red is enhanced by a clear minerality and, although still quite young, it already expresses significant complexity. These outstanding results are the work of Albert Sinn, the oenologist in charge of the cellar for more than 20 years, and young manager Hansjörg Hafner, who has also established a laudable pricing policy. We should again mention the line of organic wines here, for years a benchmark of dependability in the sector.

O A. A. Valle Isarco Sylvaner Praepositus '06 ♆♆♆ 5	● A. A. Lagrein Scuro Tor di Lupo '05 ♆♆ 6
O A. A. Sauvignon Praepositus '06 ♆♆ 5	● A. A. Merlot Sonnengut Ris. '04 ♆♆ 5
O A. A. Valle Isarco Pinot Grigio '06 ♆♆ 4*	● A. A. Merlot Tor di Lupo '04 ♆♆ 6
O A. A. Valle Isarco Veltliner '06 ♆♆ 4*	● A. A. Schiava
O A. A. Valle Isarco Sylvaner '06 ♆♆ 4*	Sonnengut Justiner '06 ♆♆ 4*
● A. A. Lagrein Praepositus Ris. '04 ♆♆ 6	O A. A. Terlano Sauvignon
● A. A. Moscato Rosa Praepositus '06 ♆♆ 6	Tor di Lupo '06 ♆♆ 4
● A. A. Pinot Nero Praepositus Ris. '04 ♆♆ 6	O A. A. Terlano Pinot Bianco
O A. A. Valle Isarco Kerner '06 ♆♆ 4*	Sonnengut '06 ♆♆ 4
O A. A. Valle Isarco Kerner Praepositus '06 ♆♆ 5	● A. A. Cabernet Tor di Lupo '04 ♆ 6
O A. A. Valle Isarco Gewürztraminer Praepositus '06 ♆♆ 5	● A. A. Lagrein Ris. Sel. Sonnengut '04 ♆ 5
O A. A. Valle Isarco Müller Thurgau '06 ♆♆ 4*	● A. A. Cabernet Tor di Lupo '00 ♆♆♆ 5
O A. A. Valle Isarco Gewürztraminer '06 ♆♆ 4*	● A. A. Lagrein Scuro
● A. A. Lagrein Praepositus Ris. '00 ♆♆♆ 6	Tor di Lupo '00 ♆♆♆ 5
O A. A. Valle Isarco Sylvaner Praepositus '05 ♆♆♆ 4*	● A. A. Cabernet Tor di Lupo '01 ♆♆ 6
O A. A. Valle Isarco Kerner Praepositus '04 ♆♆♆ 5	O A. A. Gewürztraminer
O A. A. Valle Isarco Kerner Praepositus '03 ♆♆♆ 5	Sel. Tor di Lupo '04 ♆♆ 6
O A. A. Valle Isarco Kerner Praepositus '05 ♆♆♆ 5*	● A. A. Lagrein Ris. Sel. Sonnengut '03 ♆♆ 5

Baron Widmann

ENDERGASSE, 3
39040 CORTACCIA/KURTATSCH [BZ]
TEL. 0471880092
www.baron-widmann.it

ANNUAL PRODUCTION 35,000 bottles
HECTARES UNDER VINE 15
VITICULTURE METHOD Conventional

Andreas Widmann is a man of great discretion and courtesy who shows character and clear conviction in his growing and winemaking choices. Andreas' wines reflect this style, elegant, even refined, and discreet, so they risk passing unobserved in a world, even in winemaking, where excess and arrogance win out all too frequently. We like Baron Widmann's wine because they are restrained. Just taste the refined Sauvignon '06 with its fresh, linear development and none of those vegetal excesses that sometimes make the wine type disagreeable. The same goes for Rot '05, a blend of cabernet sauvignon, franc and merlot that shows soft and deep, with engaging drinkability and aristocratic style. But all the wines produced at this splendid, ancient Cortaccia wine house are made in an understated style, including the Weiss, Moscato Giallo and delicious Schiava, all from 2006. We will have to wait to taste the definitive version of the interesting experiment with petite marsanne.

● A. A. Cabernet-Merlot Rot '05	🍷🍷	5
○ A. A. Weiss '06	🍷🍷	4*
○ A. A. Moscato Giallo '06	🍷🍷	4*
● A. A. Schiava '06	🍷🍷	3*
○ A. A. Sauvignon '06	🍷🍷	4*
● A. A. Cabernet-Merlot Auhof '97	YYY	5
● A. A. Cabernet-Merlot Rot '04	YY	5
○ A. A. Weiss '05	YY	4*
○ A. A. Gewürztraminer '05	YY	4
○ A. A. Sauvignon '05	YY	4

Josef Brigl

LOC. SAN MICHELE
VIA MADONNA DEL RIPOSO, 3
39057 APPIANO/EPPAN [BZ]
TEL. 0471662419
www.brigl.com

ANNUAL PRODUCTION 2,000,000 bottles
HECTARES UNDER VINE 50
VITICULTURE METHOD Conventional

Ignaz and Josef Brigl own of one of the oldest winemaking estates in Alto Adige and one of the best vineyards in the entire province. Great tradition is in the air you breathe here, where the earliest records of this estate go back to the 14th century. But the Brigls also show the ability to adapt to the needs of an ever more difficult market. We fell, however, that this extremely significant potential has not been fully exploited over the past few years. So it was with great pleasure this time that we noticed positive signs across the entire range of a renewal in character and stylistic definition, perhaps also indicating that estate management felt the need to intervene. The wines are interesting, from the most typical types, such as the Lagrein Brighlhof '04, or the '06 Santa Maddalena Rielerhof, which went on to our finals, the two 2004 Pinot Neros, Brighlhof and Kreuzbichler, and the fragrant, varietal Pinot Bianco Haselhof '06. We await results over the next few years, convinced this estate is capable of making further advances along the road to absolute quality.

● A. A. Santa Maddalena Rielerhof '06	🍷🍷	4*
○ A. A. Gewürztraminer Windegg '06	🍷🍷	4
● A. A. Pinot Nero Kreuzbichler '04	🍷🍷	5
○ A. A. Sauvignon '06	🍷🍷	4
● Keil '06	🍷🍷	4*
○ A. A. Terlano Drei König Hof '06	🍷🍷	4*
● A. A. Schiava Grigia Kaltenburg '06	🍷🍷	4*
● A. A. Pinot Nero Briglhof Ris. '04	🍷🍷	5
○ A. A. Pinot Bianco Haselhof '06	🍷🍷	4*
● A. A. Lagrein Scuro Briglhof '04	🍷🍷	5
● A. A. Merlot Windegg Ris. '04	🍷🍷	4
○ A. A. Gewürztraminer Windegg '05	YY	4
● A. A. Lagrein Scuro Briglhof '03	YY	5
○ A. A. Sauvignon '05	YY	4*

Cantina Produttori Burggräfler
VIA PALADE, 64
39020 MARLENGO/MARLING [BZ]
TEL. 0473447137
www.burggraefler.it

ANNUAL PRODUCTION 1,200,000 bottles
HECTARES UNDER VINE 143
VITICULTURE METHOD Conventional

Hansjörg Donà has been Kellermeister for 20 years at this reliable Merano-area co-operative winery that has always produced well-made, well-priced wines, although they sometimes lack the touch of personality that would give quality a fillip. Encouragingly, we noted a certain general advance in this sense across the whole range of wines this time. This opinion is backed up by the fact that in a growing year like 2006, not the best for the type, the cellar may have released its best Gewürztraminer of the past few years. The MerVin '06 is concentrated yet fresh, dynamic and minerally, with good development and a truly endless finish. This is among the best from the vintage and only a step away from our top prize. This real gem is flanked by a series of excellent wines: the Meranese Schickenburg '06, Moscato Giallo Passito Schickenburg '05, Pinot Bianco Privat '06 and Cabernet-Lagrein Mervin '04 are all commendable.

★ Cantina di Caldaro
VIA CANTINE, 12
39052 CALDARO/KALTERN [BZ]
TEL. 0471963149
www.kellereikaltern.com

ANNUAL PRODUCTION 1,500,000 bottles
HECTARES UNDER VINE 290
VITICULTURE METHOD Conventional

This historic winery in Caldaro earns two mentions, both positive. The first is the Three Glass award won by the Moscato Giallo Passito Serenade '04. The second is confirmation for the Lago di Caldaro Solos '06, certified biodynamic by Demeter. Serenade confirmed its class again in the 2004 version, showing warmer and more Mediterranean than the previous edition that won our prize for Sweet Wine of the Year, but with a fresher, leaner silhouette that loses nothing in complexity, harmony – quite the reverse – and depth. We were particularly struck by the balsamic vein that accompanies every phase of tasting and the clear supporting acidity. Estate oenologist Helmuth Zozin has been working for years on the conversion to biodynamic production of a significant number of hectares. This first result is this very spicy Lago di Caldaro, which shows elegant, minerally and unhurriedly drinkable. The rest of the range is at its usual high level. Special mention goes to the Castel Giovanelli line. Congratulations to the 410 member growers of this co-operative and their wonderful director, Armin Dissertori.

○ A. A. Gewürztraminer MerVin '06	5
● A. A. Lagrein-Cabernet MerVin '04	6
○ A. A. Pinot Bianco Privat '06	4*
● A. A. Meranese Algunder Rosengarten '06	4*
● A. A. Meranese Schickenburg '06	4*
○ A. A. Sauvignon MerVin '06	5
○ A. A. Moscato Giallo Schickenburg '06	4*
● A. A. Merlot-Lagrein Privat '05	5
● A. A. Merlot MerVin '04	6
○ A. A. Chardonnay Privat '06	4
○ A. A. Pinot Bianco Privat '05	4
○ A. A. Gewürztraminer Privat '04	4

○ A. A. Moscato Giallo Passito Serenade '04	6
● A. A. Lago di Caldaro Scelto Pfarrhof '06	4*
○ A. A. Chardonnay Castel Giovanelli '05	6
○ A. A. Sauvignon Castel Giovanelli '05	6
● A. A. Cabernet Sauvignon Pfarrhof Ris. '05	6
○ A. A. Gewürztraminer Campaner '06	5
○ A. A. Chardonnay Wadleith '06	4*
● A. A. Lagrein Spigel '05	5
● A. A. Lago di Caldaro Solos '06	4*
○ A. A. Pinot Bianco Vial '06	4*
○ A. A. Sauvignon Premstaler '06	4
● A. A. Pinot Nero Saltner '05	5
○ A. A. Gewürztraminer Campaner '96	3
○ A. A. Moscato Giallo Passito Serenade '95	6
○ A. A. Moscato Giallo Passito Serenade '99	6
○ A. A. Sauvignon Castel Giovanelli '02	6
○ A. A. Moscato Giallo Passito Serenade '03	6

★ Cantina Produttori Colterenzio

LOC. CORNAIANO/GIRLAN
S.DA DEL VINO, 8
39057 APPIANO/EPPAN [BZ]
TEL. 0471664246
www.colterenzio.it

ANNUAL PRODUCTION 1,600,000 bottles
HECTARES UNDER VINE 315
VITICULTURE METHOD   Conventional

For those who know a little about winemaking developments in Alto Adige, the Three Glass award won by the '03 Cabernet Sauvignon Lafòa was one of the easiest to predict in the last decade after the its impressive pre-release showings. Character, concentration and power married to elegance and definition are the backbone of this red, firmly established at the top of its wine type. The tannins are smooth and refined and the unstoppable development is supported by flawlessly balanced acidity. But this operation, managed by Luis Reifer, presents an entire array of wines with impressive quality, beginning with the best version ever of Pinot Bianco Acclivis Cornell '05 that has at last found the right touch of oak, and on to the classic Chardonnay Formigar Cornell '05, the Sauvignon Lafòa '06 and Pinot Nero Villa Nigra Cornell '04. But in addition to these champions, the overall quality of this production should be underlined, beginning with the base line, a gold mine for good drinking at the right price.

Cantina Produttori Cornaiano

LOC. CORNAIANO/GIRLAN
VIA SAN MARTINO, 24
39050 APPIANO/EPPAN [BZ]
TEL. 0471662403
www.girlan.it

ANNUAL PRODUCTION 1,150,000 bottles
HECTARES UNDER VINE 205
VITICULTURE METHOD   Conventional

The arrival of Gherard Kofler at the court of this long-established Appiano winery has produced radical, positive improvements across the entire broad range of wines produced. The five labels that reached our finals are only the classic tip of the iceberg in a sea of high and very high scores for products with great personality across the board. It all goes to demonstrate the careful labour in the vineyard by member growers, well managed by the winery's technical staff. Particularly well-made wines include the taut, vibrant Pinot Bianco Plattenriegl '06, the elegant, mineral Gewürztraminer SelectArt '06, and the well-defined, stylish Chardonnay and Sauvignon SelectArt '06. The Schiava deserves special mention, or rather, the Super Schiava Gschleier '06. Complex aromas of spice and tobacco usher in a fresh, minerally, almost earthy palate with a deep, vibrant finish. Not far from this in terms of quality, produced since 1962, is the historic Schiava Fass N.9 from the same vintage. It's less austere than the Gschleier but just as complex and pleasant. The list of the convincing wines could continue well beyond our available space, which should tell you something.

● A. A. Cabernet Sauvignon Lafòa '03	▼▼▼	8
○ A. A. Chardonnay Cornell Formigar '05	▼▼	5
○ A. A. Sauvignon Lafoa '06	▼▼	6
● A. A. Merlot Siebeneich Ris. '04	▼▼	5
○ A. A. Pinot Bianco Cornell Acclivis '05	▼▼	5
○ A. A. Chardonnay Altkirch '06	▼▼	4*
○ A. A. Pinot Grigio '06	▼▼	4*
○ A. A. Sauvignon Prail '06	▼▼	4
● A. A. Pinot Nero Cornell Villa Nigra '04	▼▼	6
○ A. A. Pinot Grigio Puiten '06	▼▼	4
○ A. A. Pinot Bianco Weisshaus '06	▼▼	4*
○ A. A. Pinot Bianco '06	▼▼	4*
● A. A. Lagrein Mantsch Ris. '04	▼▼	5
○ A. A. Gewürztraminer Cornell Atisis '06	▼▼	5
○ A. A. Gewürztraminer Passito Cornell Canthus '05	▼▼	6
● A. A. Lagrein Cornell Sigis Mundus '03	▼▼	6
● A. A. Cabernet Sauvignon Lafoa '00	▼▼▼	8
● A. A. Cabernet Sauvignon Lafoa '01	▼▼▼	8

○ A. A. Chardonnay SelectArt Flora '05	▼▼	4*
○ A. A. Gewürztraminer SelectArt Flora '06	▼▼	5
○ A. A. Sauvignon SelectArt Flora '06	▼▼	5
● A. A. Schiava Gschleier SelectArt Flora '06	▼▼	4*
○ A. A. Pinot Bianco Plattenriegl '06	▼▼	4*
○ A. A. Chardonnay '06	▼▼	4*
● A. A. Pinot Nero Patricia '05	▼▼	4
○ A. A. Bianco '06	▼▼	4*
● A. A. Schiava Fass N. 9 '06	▼▼	4*
○ A. A. Sauvignon Indra '06	▼▼	4*
○ A. A. Müller Thurgau Valzer '06	▼▼	4*
○ A. A. Moscato Giallo Pasithea Oro '05	▼▼	6
● A. A. Moscato Rosa Passito Pasithea Rosa '05	▼▼	6
● A. A. Moscato Rosa Passito Pasithea Rosa '04	▼▼	6
○ A. A. Pinot Bianco Plattenriegl '05	▼▼	4*
○ A. A. Sauvignon SelectArt Flora '05	▼▼	5

Cantina Produttori Cortaccia

STRADA DEL VINO, 23
39040 CORTACCIA/KURTATSCH [BZ]
TEL. 0471880115
www.kellerei-kurtatsch.it

★ Elena Walch

VIA A. HOFER, 1
39040 TERMENO/TRAMIN [BZ]
TEL. 0471860172
www.elenawalch.com

ANNUAL PRODUCTION 900,000 bottles
HECTARES UNDER VINE 210
VITICULTURE METHOD Conventional

ANNUAL PRODUCTION 350,000 bottles
HECTARES UNDER VINE 30
VITICULTURE METHOD Conventional

Cantina Produttori di Cortaccia, the long-established winery in the lower Adige valley managed by the influential Arnold Terzer, issues blue-chip wines. Around 200 member growers produce grapes from all the classic Alto Adige varieties. The wines are technically flawless and over the past few years have been losing a certain heaviness that had held them back, acquiring more elegance in its place. First place laurels this year go to the Bianco Freienfeld V.T. '06, a table wine from 70 per cent moscato giallo and the rest gewürztraminer with especially convincing fullness and elegance. The Chardonnay Falsenhof '06 has fresh, floral aromas and offers supple liveliness on the palate through to a deep, dynamic finish, all this at better than good value for money. But one look at the list of wines on this page below will give you some idea of the quality across the entire range of production.

Winning two Three Glass awards for the second consecutive year is no easy feat. But to win with the same wines, the Gewürztraminer Kastelaz '06 and Lagrein Castel Ringberg '04, demonstrates a maturity in production that has few equals among the wine estates of Alto Adige and indeed further afield. This is due to the energetic Elena Walch and her well-organized, efficient team, as well as the extraordinary cru that is the Kastelaz vineyard. It is on this extraordinary hill with its dizzyingly steep slopes that grapes for the Kastelaz Gewürztraminer are grown. Clear exotic aromas mingle mango and lychees that usher in a concentrated palate with a lean profile. The acidity is simply perfect, still austere, with a determinedly dry, full-flavoured finish. Praise also goes to the Lagrein '04, born outside the zone yet still a real classic because of the accolades it has won. Notes of spice and mineral lead to a meaty palate, full yet stylish. The tannins are sweet and finish echoes the nose with notes of pencil lead and smoky shades. The rest of the range is impressive to say the least.

○ A. A. Chardonnay Felsenhof '06	♀♀ 4*
○ Bianco Freienfeld V. T. '05	♀♀ 6
● A. A. Cabernet-Merlot Soma '05	♀♀ 5
○ A. A. Gewürztraminer Brenntal '06	♀♀ 6
● A. A. Merlot Brenntal '04	♀♀ 6
○ A. A. Müller Thurgau Hofstatt '06	♀♀ 4
○ A. A. Sauvignon Fohrhof '06	♀♀ 4
● A. A. Schiava Grigia Sonntaler '06	♀♀ 4*
○ A. A. Bianco Freienfeld '05	♀ 5
● A. A. Cabernet Kirchhügel '05	♀ 5
○ A. A. Pinot Bianco Hoftatt '06	♀ 4
● A. A. Cabernet Freienfeld '97	♀♀♀ 6
● A. A. Lagrein Scuro Fohrhof '00	♀♀♀ 5
● A. A. Merlot Brenntal '97	♀♀♀ 5
○ A. A. Gewürztraminer Brenntal '00	♀♀♀ 6
○ A. A. Gewürztraminer Brenntal '02	♀♀♀ 6
○ A. A. Bianco Freienfeld '04	♀♀ 5

○ A. A. Gewürztraminer Kastelaz '06	♀♀♀ 6
● A. A. Lagrein Castel Ringberg Ris. '04	♀♀♀ 6
○ A. A. Bianco Beyond the Clouds '05	♀♀ 7
○ A. A. Cashmere Passito '05	♀♀ 7
● A. A. Merlot Kastelaz Ris. '03	♀♀ 7
● A. A. Cabernet Sauvignon Castel Ringberg Ris. '04	♀♀ 7
○ A. A. Chardonnay Cardellino '06	♀♀ 5
○ A. A. Pinot Grigio Castel Ringberg '06	♀♀ 5
○ A. A. Pinot Bianco Kastelaz '06	♀ 5
⊙ Rosé 20/26 '06	♀ 4
● Kermesse '04	♀ 7
○ A. A. Bianco Beyond the Clouds '02	♀♀♀ 6
○ A. A. Gewürztraminer Kastelaz '04	♀♀♀ 6
○ A. A. Gewürztraminer Kastelaz '00	♀♀♀ 5
● A. A. Lagrein Castel Ringberg Ris. '03	♀♀♀ 6
○ A. A. Gewürztraminer Kastelaz '05	♀♀♀ 6

Graf Enzenberg Tenuta Manincor

San Giuseppe al Lago, 4
39052 Caldaro/Kaltern [BZ]
tel. 0471960230
www.manincor.com

ANNUAL PRODUCTION 200,000 bottles
HECTARES UNDER VINE 48
VITICULTURE METHOD Natural

An estate with a history that goes back to 1608, and a winery founded in 1996, are the core of the noble Enzenberg family's Tenuta Manincor, located in one of the most beautiful areas of Alto Adige just above Lake Caldaro. Over the past few years, talk here has focused on the new cellar, an architectural gem built underneath the vineyards in perfect harmony with nature. But the winery's future will be even more affected by another profound change. Since the beginning of 2006, all 45 hectares of vineyards will be managed in compliance with biodynamic principles. The wines, however, still have to find their definitive personality. Over the past few years, we have felt they were frequently a bit too concentrated and the use of oak was a bit too prominent. Now they seem to be experiencing a phase of change. More elegance, more character and above all more drinkability are the hallmarks of the new vintages. The particularly outstanding red Cassiano '04, a complex cuvée of merlot, cabernet franc, petit verdot and syrah, is spicy with notes of fruit and autumn leaves. The palate is full and structured with well-ripened tannins and a long-lingering finish.

● Cassiano '04	TT	6*
● A. A. Pinot Nero Mason '05	TT	6
● Castel Campan '03	TT	8
● Reserve del Conte '05	TT	4
○ Reserve della Contessa '05	TT	4
○ Sophie '05	TT	5
○ Le Petit de Manincor '05	TT	6
● A. A. Pinot Nero Mason di Mason '03	TT	8
○ A. A. Moscato Giallo '06	TT	4
● A. A. Lago di Caldaro Cl. Sup. '06	T	4
⊙ La Rose de Manincor '06	T	4
● A. A. Lagrein '05	T	6
● A. A. Cabernet Sauvignon Cassiano '97	YYY	5

Erbhof Unterganzner Josephus Mayr

fraz. Cardano
via Campiglio, 15
39053 Bolzano/Bozen
tel. 0471365582
mayr.unterganzner@dnet.it

ANNUAL PRODUCTION 60,000 bottles
HECTARES UNDER VINE 8.5
VITICULTURE METHOD Conventional

Josephus Mayr has not won a Three Glass award in three years because, right or wrong, we felt his wines were excessive and not always balanced. A man of rare courtesy but with a rather prickly character, Josephus did not exactly take this well. This year, we were the first to rejoice that Unterganzner had won our top prize with an impeccable version of Lamarein from lagrein grapes, a portion of them part-dried. We are even happier because we feel the whole range presented by Josephus has rediscovered its earlier brilliance. These wines have unmistakable character, concentrated yet vibrant and balanced, starting with his most extreme wine, Lamarein '05. Intense spicy and smoky aromas lead into a palate that is impressive in its solidity yet perked up by acidity that makes it juicy and enjoyable. The liquorice finish underlines a very deep close still slightly marked by the oak. But the Lagrein Riserva '04 every bit as good. Austere in the Unterganzner style, it reveals overwhelming progression on the palate. The surprise is a magnificent Chardonnay '06 – yes, that's '06. Welcome back, Josephus.

● Lamarein '05	TTT	7
○ A. A. Chardonnay '06	TT	4*
● A. A. Lagrein Scuro Ris. '04	TT	5
● A. A. Santa Maddalena Cl. '05	TT	4*
● A. A. Cabernet Ris. '04	TT	6
⊙ A. A. Lagrein Rosato '06	TT	4
● A. A. Santa Maddalena '06	TT	4*
● A. A. Lagrein Scuro Ris. '00	YYY	5
● A. A. Lagrein Scuro Ris. '01	YYY	5
● A. A. Lagrein Scuro Ris. '99	YYY	5
● A. A. Lagrein Scuro Ris. '98	YYY	5
● A. A. Lagrein Scuro Ris. '97	YYY	5
● A. A. Cabernet Ris. '02	YY	5
● A. A. Lagrein Scuro Ris. '03	YY	5
● Composition Reif '01	YY	6
● Lamarein '04	YY	7
● Lamarein '03	YY	7

Cantina Sociale Erste & Neue
VIA DELLE CANTINE, 5/10
39052 CALDARO/KALTERN [BZ]
TEL. 0471963122
www.erste-neue.it

Falkenstein - Franz Pratzner
VIA CASTELLO, 15
39025 NATURNO/NATURNS [BZ]
TEL. 0473666054
www.falkenstein.bz

ANNUAL PRODUCTION 1,000,000 bottles
HECTARES UNDER VINE 320
VITICULTURE METHOD Conventional

ANNUAL PRODUCTION 45,000 bottles
HECTARES UNDER VINE 7
VITICULTURE METHOD Natural

Much has changed at Prima & Nuova in Caldaro, with 520 members one of the most important co-operative wineries in Alto Adige. The new management – president Manfred Schullian, oenologist Gerhard Sanin and sales manager Hannes Durnalder – has submitted a new range of wines distinguished by their style and typicity. These wines come from one of the best zones in the territory and five of them qualified for the Three Glass finals this year: the Pinot Bianco Stern '06, which shows fruity, elegant, typical and classical; the Lago di Caldaro Scelto Puntay '06, one of the most characteristic versions of this great indigenous variety; the dried-grape passito Anthos '04, a cuvée from moscato giallo, gewürztraminer and sauvignon that presents complex and balanced with an appealingly refined freshness; and finally Sauvignon Puntay '06, a wine that more than deserved Three Glasses for its straw-yellow colour, intensity on the nose with aromas of elderflower and tomato leaf, savouriness and lingering length in the mouth. The new management at Prima & Nuova is promising.

Four wines made it to our finals – Riesling, Pinot Bianco, Gewürztraminer and Sauvignon – all of them among the best in their respective categories. Does this mean anything? Clearly, Franz Pratzner from Naturns is a very talented winemaker but that alone is not enough. We are well aware that the term "terroir" has been used and abused over the past few years so much it has become annoying. But when you taste the wines from Falkenstein, how can you avoid talking about the terroir of Val Venosta? Wines that are this austere and light, with these smoky, almost peaty, shades, can only be made here. In spite of its almost embarrassing youth, the Riesling '06 already shows complex notes of gunflint, damson and this smoky vein that is Val Venosta's trademark. The palate has almost violent yet aristocratic minerality. The progression is austere yet confident. The acidity is almost cutting but supported by juicy fruit with a finish that has far away echoes. Needless to say it won Three Glasses with the effortless ease of a one-of-a-kind wine. The rest of the range is simply great.

O A. A. Sauvignon Puntay '06	♟♟♟	5
O A. A. Anthos Bianco Passito '04	♟♟	6
● A. A. Lago di Caldaro Scelto Puntay '06	♟♟	4*
O A. A. Pinot Bianco Puntay '06	♟♟	4*
O A. A. Sauvignon Stern '06	♟	5
O A. A. Gewürztraminer Puntay '06	♟♟	5
O A. A. Sauvignon '06	♟♟	4*
● A. A. Lagrein Puntay Ris. '04	♟♟	5
● A. A. Lago di Caldaro Scelto Leuchtenburg '06	♟♟	4*
● A. A. Cabernet-Merlot Feld '05	♟	5
O A. A. Moscato Giallo Secco Barleit '06	♟	4
O A. A. Pinot Bianco Prunar '06	♟	4
● A. A. Cabernet Puntay '97	♟♟♟	5
O A. A. Gewürztraminer Puntay '97	♟♟♟	5
O A. A. Gewürztraminer Puntay '01	♟♟♟	5
O A. A. Anthos Bianco Passito '03	♟♟	6
● A. A. Lagrein Puntay Ris. '03	♟♟	5
O A. A. Pinot Bianco Prunar '05	♟♟	4*

O A. A. Valle Venosta Riesling '06	♟♟♟	6
O A. A. Valle Venosta Gewürztraminer '06	♟♟	5
O A. A. Valle Venosta Sauvignon '06	♟♟	5
O A. A. Valle Venosta Pinot Bianco '06	♟♟	5
● A. A. Valle Venosta Pinot Nero '05	♟♟	6
O A. A. Valle Venosta Riesling '98	♟♟♟	5
O A. A. Valle Venosta Riesling '00	♟♟♟	5
O A. A. Valle Venosta Riesling '05	♟♟♟	6
O A. A. Valle Venosta Pinot Bianco '04	♟♟	5
O A. A. Valle Venosta Pinot Bianco '05	♟♟	5
O A. A. Valle Venosta Pinot Bianco '03	♟♟	5
O A. A. Valle Venosta Riesling '03	♟♟	6
O A. A. Valle Venosta Sauvignon '05	♟♟	5
O A. A. Valle Venosta Sauvignon '04	♟♟	5
O A. A. Valle Venosta Riesling '04	♟♟	5
O A. A. Valle Venosta Riesling '02	♟♟	6
● A. A. Valle Venosta Pinot Nero '04	♟♟	6

Garlider - Christian Kerchbaumer

FRAZ. VELTURNO/FELDTHURNS
VIA UNTRUM, 20
39040 BOLZANO/BOZEN
TEL. 0472847296
www.garlider.2-ec.com

ANNUAL PRODUCTION 14,000 bottles
HECTARES UNDER VINE 3.5
VITICULTURE METHOD Natural

Boyish Christian Kerschbaumer is a true winemaker who works near Chiusa, in the southern part of Valle Isarco. His care in the vineyard is almost maniacal and his interest in nature has led him to progressively convert to organic production methods. But Christian also likes to experiment in the cellar and so, sometimes, there are no selected yeasts and no malolactic. These wines have great personality and a sense of place, showing concentrated and big with substantial alcohol, characteristics our winemaker manages to keep perfectly under control, infusing them with elegance and harmony. This is confirmed by the Sylvaner '06, a stylish, sun-ripe wine with vibrant, deep development. Just as good is the estate's showcase wine and the one we expect to give exciting results in the near future, the Veltliner that comes from Christian's highest vineyards at around 650 metres above sea level. The 2006 version shows power and concentration kept in check by vibrant acidity. Only its extreme youth kept it from reaching a higher score. There will be other chances to taste it.

Glögglhof - Franz Gojer

FRAZ. SANTA MADDALENA
VIA RIVELLONE, 1
39100 BOLZANO/BOZEN
TEL. 0471978775
www.gojer.it

ANNUAL PRODUCTION 40,000 bottles
HECTARES UNDER VINE 4.3
VITICULTURE METHOD Conventional

Franz Gojer, head of the historic Glögglhof estate located in the Santa Maddalena Classico subzone, is a character. With his jovial, smiling face and direct, down-to-earth way of introducing himself, he is an ambassador for Santa Maddalena and Lagrein, the most typical wines from this zone. He has been bottling them since 1982 and again this year took us on a trip through the Bolzano winemaking tradition, beginning with his two Santa Maddalenas, the Classico and the Rondell selection, both from 2006. In the first, intense aromas of ripe blackberry and smoke open the way to a fragrant, juicy, taut palate. The second adds confident mineral notes and a more solid, austere structure. The Lagrein Riserva '05 is as usual one of the reference points for this type of wine. One third aged in new barriques, it has typical spice and aromatic herb aromas, showing fragrant and fresh on the palate with well-integrated oak and a nice long finish. The standard-label Lagrein is pleasant and drinkable.

○ A. A. Valle Isarco Müller Thurgau '06	▼▼ 4*
○ A. A. Valle Isarco Veltliner '06	▼▼ 5*
○ A. A. Valle Isarco Sylvaner '06	▼▼ 4*
● A. A. Pinot Nero '05	▼▼ 5*
○ A. A. Valle Isarco Gewürztraminer '06	▼▼ 5*
○ A. A. Valle Isarco Pinot Grigio '06	▼▼ 4
○ A. A. Valle Isarco Veltliner '05	♀♀♀ 4*
○ A. A. Valle Isarco Sylvaner '04	♀♀ 4*
○ A. A. Valle Isarco Sylvaner '05	♀♀ 4*
○ A. A. Valle Isarco Veltliner '04	♀♀ 4*
● A. A. Pinot Nero '04	♀♀ 5
○ A. A. Valle Isarco Müller Thurgau '05	♀♀ 4
○ A. A. Valle Isarco Pinot Grigio '05	♀♀ 4
○ A. A. Valle Isarco Gewürztraminer '05	♀♀ 5

● A. A. Lagrein Scuro Ris. '05	▼▼ 5
● A. A. Merlot Spitz '05	▼▼ 5
● A. A. Santa Maddalena Rondell '06	▼▼ 4*
● A. A. Santa Maddalena Cl. '06	▼▼ 4*
● A. A. Lagrein '06	▼ 4
● A. A. Lagrein Scuro Ris. '03	♀♀ 5
● A. A. Lagrein Scuro Ris. '99	♀♀ 4
● A. A. Lagrein Scuro Ris. '04	♀♀ 5
● A. A. Lagrein '05	♀♀ 4*
● A. A. Merlot Spitz '04	♀♀ 5
● A. A. Santa Maddalena Rondell '05	♀♀ 4*

Griesbauerhof - Georg Mumelter
VIA RENCIO, 66
39100 BOLZANO/BOZEN
TEL. 0471973090
www.tirolensisarsvini.it

Cantina Gries/Cantina di Bolzano
FRAZ. GRIES
P.ZZA GRIES, 2
39100 BOLZANO/BOZEN
TEL. 0471270909
www.kellereibozen.com

ANNUAL PRODUCTION 25,000 bottles
HECTARES UNDER VINE 3.3
VITICULTURE METHOD Conventional

ANNUAL PRODUCTION 1,100,000 bottles
HECTARES UNDER VINE 170
VITICULTURE METHOD Conventional

Georg Mumelter is the archetype of an Alto Adige grower-producer. Timid and reserved yet hardworking, Georg has a lot of love for his land and wines, made in the heart of Bolzano's wine zone. Although production is limited, these are all typical, well-made wines with great character and perfect examples of their types. We'll start with the magnificent Lagrein Riserva '04, among the best from the vintage. Concentrated and caressing, it unveils tannins that are close-knit and smooth, progressing with balance and typicity into a long, well-defined finish. It is still very young but should express itself better after a few months in bottle. Not far behind is the Cabernet Sauvignon Riserva '04, which opens with deep aromas of cinchona and morello cherry. The palate is dense and minerally yet balanced and elegant, lifted by lovely notes of leather and tobacco in the finish. Simply delicious – but this is just confirmation – is the Santa Maddalena Classico '06. It's appealing and well made, tantalizingly drinkable and a paragon for the type.

Cantina Gries has always been famous for its splendid reds, especially Lagrein but also Cabernet and Merlot, and has a strong tradition in Moscato Giallo Passito. This serves as an introduction to the real surprise, which may not be all that unexpected after all. The Three Glass award went to the Pinot Bianco Collection Dellago '06. This powerful, concentrated white offers aromas of white peach and lucerne. The palate is dense, slightly salty and supported by clean acidity. In the mouth, it shows off its muscles but they are well-proportioned and harmonious. This is the eighth harvest for this wine and Stefan Filippi has cared for it, year after year, like a child, watching it grow and improve, identifying the best plots on the estate's vast vine stock. So it's a success that has nothing to do with coincidence. On the other hand, we were a bit perplexed by the red wines, which are good but not extraordinary like those usually turned out by Cantina Gries. In fact, they have won more than one Three Glass prize. While waiting for recovery next year, we'll raise a nice glass of Pinot Bianco.

● A. A. Cabernet Sauvignon '04	♟♟ 5
● A. A. Lagrein Scuro Ris. '04	♟♟ 5
● A. A. Lagrein '05	♟♟ 4*
● A. A. Santa Maddalena Cl. '06	♟♟ 3*
☉ A. A. Lagrein Rosato '06	♟ 4
● A. A. Lagrein Scuro Ris. '99	♟♟♟ 5
● A. A. Cabernet Sauvignon '01	♟♟ 5
● A. A. Lagrein Scuro Ris. '01	♟♟ 5
● A. A. Lagrein Scuro Ris. '00	♟♟ 5
● A. A. Cabernet Sauvignon '03	♟♟ 5
● Isarcus '04	♟♟ 4*
● A. A. Lagrein Scuro Ris. '02	♟♟ 5

○ A. A. Pinot Bianco Collection Dellago '06	♟♟♟ 4*
● A. A. Lagrein Grieser '06	♟♟ 4*
○ A. A. Moscato Giallo Vinalia '05	♟♟ 7
● A. A. Moscato Rosa Rosis '06	♟♟ 6
● A. A. Lagrein Grieser Baron Carl Eyrl '05	♟♟ 4
● A. A. Lagrein Grieser Prestige Line Ris. '05	♟♟ 6
● A. A. Lagrein Merlot Mauritius '05	♟♟ 6
● A. A. Cabernet Collection Otto Graf Huyn Ris. '05	♟ 4
● A. A. Merlot Prestige Line Siebeneich Ris. '05	♟ 6
● A. A. Lagrein Scuro Grieser Prestige Line Ris. '00	♟♟♟ 6
○ A. A. Moscato Giallo Vinalia '03	♟♟♟ 6
○ A. A. Moscato Giallo Vinalia '99	♟♟♟ 5

Gummerhof - R. Malojer

VIA WEGGESTEIN, 36
39100 BOLZANO/BOZEN
TEL. 0471972885
www.malojer.it

ANNUAL PRODUCTION 100,000 bottles
HECTARES UNDER VINE 6
VITICULTURE METHOD Conventional

Once isolated in a sea of vineyards north of Bolzano, Gummerhof boasts an ancient history. First mentioned in documents dating from 1480, the winery today is managed by Elisabeth, Urban and Alfred Malojer, who use the most modern growing and winemaking techniques to create a range of high quality products. Wines submitted for tasting this year were excellent and we are happy to say they won back for the estate its full Guide profile. First of all, the Lagrein Riserva '04 is one of the best from this vintage, giving a juicy, dense red with ripe, mouthfilling tannins, well supported by lively acidity, all held together in an elegant ensemble. This estate's reliability in dealing with this difficult type is confirmed in the Lagrein Gries '05, aged exclusively in large casks. Despite less imposing structure than previous editions, it shows sweet tannins and a convincing, harmonious finish. This is a return in grand style.

Gumphof - Markus Prackwieser

LOC. NOVALE DI PRESULE, 8
39050 FIÈ ALLO SCILIAR
VÖLS AM SCHLERN [BZ]
TEL. 0471601190
www.gumphof.it

ANNUAL PRODUCTION 35,000 bottles
HECTARES UNDER VINE 4.5
VITICULTURE METHOD Conventional

A great Pinot Bianco Praesulis '06 won Three Glasses in an especially favourable vintage year for this type, one that Markus Prackwieser coaxed to perfection. His Pinot Bianco already shows well-defined aromas of damson and hedgerow. The palate is straining at the bit with energy and grip, clear notes of gunflint and a juicy, elegant progression that leads to a gutsy, harmonious finish. We feel it is important to add here that the price of this wine, like all Gumphof products, is more than honest, so much so it won our award for Best Priced Wine. Markus is one of those producers who are always looking for new inspiration and so here are the first vintages of Gewürztraminer and Pinot Nero after trips to Irpinia to learn about different winemaking operations. The fruit of all this effort, and a perfect terroir like that in Fiè allo Sciliar, are vibrant, minerally wines with outstanding personality. The same holds true for the Sauvignon Praesulis, for years now one of the best of its type, as well as the standard-label Schiava '06, a sure-fire winner in the enjoyability stakes. For the Pinot Nero, we will wait for the vineyards to mature. If the wines are this good already, they can only get better.

● A. A. Lagrein Scuro Ris. '04	⬜⬜	5
● A. A. Cabernet-Lagrein Bautzanum Ris. '04	⬜⬜	5
● A. A. Lagrein Scuro Gummerhof zu Gries '05	⬜⬜	4*
○ A. A. Pinot Bianco '06	⬜⬜	4*
○ A. A. Sauvignon Gur zur Sand Classic '06	⬜⬜	4*
● A. A. Cabernet Ris. '04	⬜	5
● A. A. Merlot Ris. '04	⬜	5
● A. A. Cabernet-Lagrein Bautzanum Ris. '03	⬜⬜	5
● A. A. Cabernet Ris. '01	⬜⬜	5
● A. A. Lagrein Scuro Ris. '02	⬜⬜	5
● A. A. Lagrein Scuro Ris. '03	⬜⬜	5

○ A. A. Pinot Bianco Praesulis '06	⬜⬜⬜	4*
○ A. A. Sauvignon Praesulis '06	⬜⬜	4*
● A. A. Schiava '06	⬜⬜	3*
○ A. A. Gewürztraminer Praesulis '06	⬜⬜	5
● A. A. Pinot Nero '05	⬜⬜	5
○ A. A. Pinot Bianco '06	⬜⬜	4*
○ A. A. Sauvignon Praesulis '04	⬜⬜⬜	5*
○ A. A. Pinot Bianco Praesulis '04	⬜⬜	4*
○ A. A. Sauvignon Praesulis '05	⬜⬜	5
○ A. A. Sauvignon Praesulis '02	⬜⬜	4
○ A. A. Gewürztraminer Praesulis '05	⬜⬜	5
○ A. A. Pinot Bianco Praesulis '05	⬜⬜	4*

Franz Haas

VIA VILLA, 6
39040 MONTAGNA/MONTAN [BZ]
TEL. 0471812280
www.franz-haas.it

ANNUAL PRODUCTION 250,000 bottles
HECTARES UNDER VINE 35
VITICULTURE METHOD Conventional

The Haas Manna did the double, picking up another Three Glass award for a great 2005 version. In fact, we found it even better than the 2004. From a blend of 50 per cent riesling, 20 per cent gewürztraminer and chardonnay, and the rest sauvignon, it has already complex aromas of tropical fruit and aromatic herbs. The palate is meaty and taut, with a delicate almondy vein, and progresses elegantly to a deep, spirited finish. This aristocratic wine is still young but has a long life ahead, predictably, in light of the results of a recent vertical tasting of ten vintages. Franziscus Haas and Luisa Manna have something to celebrate already but to do so, they may have to wait until work on the new winery, which is dragging on, has been completed. Considering Franz's skill and passion for this variety, the two Pinot Neros could not be anything but excellent. The Schweizer '04 and base '05 are very good, the latter a real Alto Adige Pinot Nero. Fresh and floral, it has a supple development with a perky mineral vein. The Schweizer of course shows greater class, sweet tannins and a vibrant acidity but is really still too young.

Haderburg

FRAZ. BUCHOLZ
LOC. POCHI, 30
39040 SALORNO/SALURN [BZ]
TEL. 0471889097
www.haderburg.it

ANNUAL PRODUCTION 80,000 bottles
HECTARES UNDER VINE 12
VITICULTURE METHOD Certified biodynamic

As you cross the regional border into Alto Adige from the south, above Salorno, the ruins of the castle of Salorno Haderburg rise over the rocky slopes. The castle has lent its name to this winery located at Pochi di Salorno, 400 metres above sea level. The heart of the estate is Hausmannhof, where Luis Ochsenreiter makes his range of still and sparkling wines. There are some great sparklers – the Haderburg Brut, Haderburg Pas Dosé and Hausmannhof Riserva – whites, like the Hausmannhof Chardonnay and Gewürztraminer Blaspichl sourced from vineyards located at Termeno, the celebrated Hausmannhof and Hausmannhof Riserva Pinot Neros and the Merlot-Cabernet Erah, a wine of grip, structure and character, whose last vintage, the '03, swept into the Three Glass finals. This estate's latest acquisition is Obermairlhof, located above Chiusa in Valle Isarco, with almost three hectares of vineyards between 620 and 700 metres above sea level. This is where classic Valle Isarco whites originate: a well-typed, elegant Sylvaner; a fresh, minerally Riesling; and an interesting Gewürztraminer.

O Manna '05	♔♔♔	5
● A. A. Moscato Rosa '05	♔♔	6
● A. A. Pinot Nero '05	♔♔	5
● A. A. Pinot Nero Schweizer '04	♔♔	6
O A. A. Pinot Bianco '06	♔♔	4*
O A. A. Gewürztraminer '06	♔♔	5
● A. A. Merlot '03	♔♔	5
O A. A. Pinot Grigio '06	♔♔	4
O A. A. Müller Thurgau '06	♔♔	4*
● A. A. Moscato Rosa Schweizer '00	♔♔♔	5
● A. A. Pinot Nero Schweizer '02	♔♔♔	6
O Manna '04	♔♔♔	5
● A. A. Pinot Nero Schweizer '01	♔♔♔	6
● A. A. Moscato Rosa Schweizer '99	♔♔♔	5
O Manna '02	♔♔	5
O A. A. Pinot Bianco '05	♔♔	4
● A. A. Pinot Nero Schweizer '01	♔♔	6

O A. A. Cl. Brut Hausmannhof Ris. '96	♔♔	7
● A. A. Erah '03	♔♔	6
O A. A. Cl. Brut Pas Dosé '02	♔♔	5
● A. A. Pinot Nero Hausmannhof Ris. '04	♔♔	6
O A. A. Valle Isarco Riesling Obermairlhof '06	♔♔	5
O A. A. Valle Isarco Sylvaner Obermairlhof '06	♔♔	4*
O A. A. Valle Isarco Gewürztraminer Obermairlhof '06	♔♔	5
● A. A. Pinot Nero Hausmannhof '05	♔♔	5
O A. A. Chardonnay Hausmannhof '06	♔	4
O A. A. Spumante Brut	♔	5
O A. A. Gewürztraminer Blaspichl '06	♔	5
O A. A. Valle Isarco Sylvaner Obermairlhof '05	♔♔♔	4*
● A. A. Pinot Nero Hausmannhof Ris. '03	♔♔	6

Hoandlhof - Manfred Nössing

FRAZ. KRANEBIH
VIA DEI VIGNETI, 66
39042 BRESSANONE/BRIXEN [BZ]
TEL. 0472832672
www.manninoessing.com

ANNUAL PRODUCTION 17,000 bottles
HECTARES UNDER VINE 4.3
VITICULTURE METHOD Conventional

A person like Manni Nössing offers so many points for discussion that we could write at least five Guide profiles every year. For example, we could speak of the finally finished cellar and residence, the definitive shift to stainless steel-only fermentation and ageing, the plans for new structures on high ground, and Manni's fraught relationship with wine guides – we arm ourselves with patience – or we could discuss the man himself. His appearances at the Three Glass awards ceremony creates a certain embarrassment among some of his more formal colleagues. But no, let's talk instead about the '06 Kerner, the best ever from Hoandlhof. We feel this variety has its limits but what Manni has managed to draw from it this year amazed even the most sceptical. It's a very concentrated white – 25 grams dry extract and eight grams residual sugar – but the palate shows fantastic drinkability, assertively expressive complexity and an overwhelming finish, in the Manni Nössing style. The Sylvaner '06 is very good but we are ready to bet that the Veltliner will be the next Three Glass winner. Any takers?

★ Tenuta J. Hofstätter

P.ZZA MUNICIPIO, 7
39040 TERMENO/TRAMIN [BZ]
TEL. 0471860161
www.hofstatter.com

ANNUAL PRODUCTION 720,000 bottles
HECTARES UNDER VINE 53.5
VITICULTURE METHOD Conventional

Four wines in the finals, and another seven with high scores, would be a more than satisfying result for any estate not owned by Martin Foradori. This wine globetrotter will be angry, though, because he is a real professional. It is not Martin's way to be content because he knows if you do not work to constantly improve the quality of your products, you won't well wine. We were most convinced this year by a delightful 2004 version of the Pinot Nero Vigna S. Urbano. The already complex aromas of tobacco and red berry fruit, held together by a delicate smoky note, introduce a meaty, sensual, caressing structure. The progression is aristocratic and finishes taut and dynamic. The Gewürztraminer Kolbenhof '06 is just a bit too warm but we loved the fragrant standard version. The real surprise was De Vite '06, from 60 per cent pinot bianco, 30 per cent müller thurgau and the rest sauvignon, a floral, minerally and almost salty wine with a complex finish. And the price is equally attractive.

○ A. A. Valle Isarco Kerner '06	♟♟♟	4*
○ A. A. Valle Isarco Sylvaner '06	♟♟	4*
○ A. A. Valle Isarco Veltliner '06	♟♟	4*
○ A. A. Valle Isarco Kerner '02	♟♟♟	4
○ A. A. Valle Isarco Kerner '03	♟♟♟	4*
○ A. A. Valle Isarco Kerner '05	♟♟♟	4*
○ A. A. Valle Isarco Sylvaner '04	♟♟♟	4*
○ A. A. Valle Isarco Gewürztraminer '01	♟♟	4*
○ A. A. Valle Isarco Gewürztraminer '03	♟♟	4*
○ A. A. Valle Isarco Veltliner '05	♟♟	4*
○ A. A. Valle Isarco Sylvaner '05	♟♟	4*
○ A. A. Valle Isarco Sylvaner '02	♟♟	4
○ A. A. Valle Isarco Kerner '04	♟♟	4*

○ A. A. Gewürztraminer Kolbenhof '06	♟♟	6
○ De Vite '06	♟♟	4*
● A. A. Pinot Nero Barthenau V. S. Urbano '04	♟♟	8
○ A. A. Gewürztraminer '06	♟♟	4*
● A. A. Barthenau V. S. Michele '06	♟♟	5
○ A. A. Gewürztraminer Joseph V. T. '05	♟♟	6
○ A. A. Pinot Bianco '06	♟♟	4
● Yngram '04	♟♟	7
● A. A. Pinot Nero Ris. '04	♟♟	6
● A. A. Lagrein Scuro Steinraffler '04	♟♟	6
● A. A. Lagrein '06	♟	4
○ A. A. Gewürztraminer Kolbenhof '01	♟♟♟	6
● A. A. Pinot Nero S. Urbano '95	♟♟♟	7
○ A. A. Gewürztraminer Kolbenhof '04	♟♟♟	5
○ A. A. Gewürztraminer Kolbenhof '99	♟♟♟	4
○ A. A. Gewürztraminer Kolbenhof '98	♟♟♟	4
○ A. A. Gewürztraminer Kolbenhof '03	♟♟♟	5

Köfererhof - Günther Kershbaumer

FRAZ. NOVACELLA
VIA PUSTERIA, 3
39040 VARNA/VAHRN [BZ]
TEL. 0472836649
info@koefererhof.it

ANNUAL PRODUCTION 48,000 bottles
HECTARES UNDER VINE 5.5
VITICULTURE METHOD Conventional

The four wines in our finals last year were not enough to win a first Three Glass award. So this year, young Günther Kershbaumer, nicknamed Il Bisonte (The Bison), by his fellow trenchermen, had to improve. He landed five wines in the finals and finally netted the coveted Three Glasses with the old vineyard selection of Sylvaner R '06. Though still young, it shows complex aromas of benzene and white-fleshed fruit. The palate has an almost violent impact and unique character but there is well-sustained, balanced progression and impressive depth. It's a Sylvaner with a very personal yet absolutely convincing style. This small estate's vineyards are the northernmost in Italy, lying above the 47th parallel north, right on the edge of grape country south of the Alps. A wine we love very much, and one that gives a clear idea of Köfererhof's potential, is the '06 Riesling. Although still too young, it shows off a whole range of aromatic herbs seasoned with a unique smoky note. The meaty, confident palate shows bright acidity and overwhelming dynamism. We are ready to bet that in a couple of years it will have few equals.

Tenuta Kornell

LOC. SETTEQUERCE
VIA BOLZANO, 23
39018 TERLANO/TERLAN [BZ]
TEL. 0471917507
www.kornell.it

ANNUAL PRODUCTION 60,000 bottles
HECTARES UNDER VINE 15
VITICULTURE METHOD Conventional

Wines from the Kornell estate in Settequerce near Terlano, first released in the 2001 vintage, are no longer a novelty. The image is carefully groomed and above all the products are excellent. This splendid family property has plots on loose-packed clayey, sandy and porphyry-rich soil, a Mediterranean climate and vines planted between 1985 and 2005. Owner Florian Brigl is a man with a passion for winemaking and the proof is in his wines. Six wines are currently produced, three of these being released as Staves, the name of the farmland around the estate since the 13th century. The wines produced are no-frills, natural offering. Concentrated yet not to the point of caricature, they are modern yet respectful of the grape varieties used. Again this year, the wine we liked most was the Cabernet Sauvignon Staves '04, a red with an aristocratic bearing, ripe, sweet tannins and a taut, dynamic finish. We also mention the Sauvignon Cosmas '06, the best ever version from this estate.

Wine	Rating
O A. A. Valle Isarco Sylvaner R '06	♙♙♙ 5
O A. A. Valle Isarco Kerner '06	♙♙ 5
O A. A. Valle Isarco Sylvaner '06	♙♙ 4*
O A. A. Valle Isarco Riesling '06	♙♙ 5
O A. A. Valle Isarco Pinot Grigio '06	♙♙ 4*
O A. A. Valle Isarco Gewürztraminer '06	♙♙ 5
O A. A. Valle Isarco Müller Thurgau '06	♙♙ 4*
O A. A. Valle Isarco Gewürztraminer '05	♈♈ 5
O A. A. Valle Isarco Kerner '05	♈♈ 5
O A. A. Valle Isarco Sylvaner '05	♈♈ 4*
O A. A. Valle Isarco Riesling '05	♈♈ 5
O A. A. Valle Isarco Riesling '04	♈♈ 5
O A. A. Valle Isarco Liebelei Passito '03	♈♈ 6
O A. A. Valle Isarco Müller Thurgau '05	♈♈ 4*
O A. A. Valle Isarco Pinot Grigio '05	♈♈ 4*

Wine	Rating
● A. A. Cabernet Sauvignon Staves '04	♙♙ 6
● A. A. Lagrein Greif '05	♙♙ 4*
O A. A. Terlaner Savignon Cosmas '06	♙♙ 4*
● A. A. Zeder '05	♙♙ 4*
● A. A. Merlot-Cabernet Sauvignon Cuvée Staves '04	♙♙ 5
● A. A. Merlot Staves '04	♙♙ 6
● A. A. Cabernet Sauvignon Staves '02	♈♈ 6
● A. A. Merlot-Cabernet Sauvignon Staves '03	♈♈ 6
● A. A. Merlot Staves '03	♈♈ 6
● A. A. Cabernet Sauvignon Staves '03	♈♈ 6
● A. A. Lagrein Greif '04	♈♈ 4*
● A. A. Merlot Staves '02	♈♈ 6
● A. A. Merlot-Cabernet Sauvignon Cuvée Staves '02	♈ 5

Tenuta Kränzl - Graf Franz Pfeil

VIA PALADE, 1
39010 CERMES/TSCHERMS [BZ]
TEL. 0473564549
www.labyrinth.bz

ANNUAL PRODUCTION 35,000 bottles
HECTARES UNDER VINE 6
VITICULTURE METHOD Certified biodynamic

There is a lot of talk about a globalized market, the standardization of taste and so forth. Franz Pfeil's Weingut Kränzl is a safe haven for anyone who wants to get away from all that. This very special winemaker and cellarman has created a sort of ecological oasis near Tscherms, along the valley that connects Bolzano and Merano. Strictly organic since 1985, Pfeil has fashioned an extraordinary garden labyrinth on his estate as testimony to his confident commitment to the defence of nature. His wines perfectly reflect this philosophy. These are anything but technological, to use a term that is becoming irritating. No, Kränzl wines are natural and above all they are wines that Franz Pfeil likes. From this year's offerings, the Baslan Reserve '05, a monovarietal Schiava, still seems to be one of the estate's most representative products. Spicy and floral with characteristic almondy notes, it presents a dense, velvety palate with a long finish characterized by an outstanding mineral vein. The Gewürztraminer Passito Dorado '04 is concentrated and sweet but braced by good acidity.

Kuenhof - Peter Pliger

LOC. MARA, 110
39042 BRESSANONE/BRIXEN [BZ]
TEL. 0472850546
pliger.kuenhof@rolmail.net

ANNUAL PRODUCTION 20,000 bottles
HECTARES UNDER VINE 5.5
VITICULTURE METHOD Natural

What more can you say about Peter Pliger and his wines that would not demean the man's unique contribution? We would like to emphasize the term "man", and not "character", because Peter is real, just as his wines are real. We could say all four of his wines sailed through to our finals, the first time this has happened, and that the Sylvaner '06 – the best ever made at Kuenhof, at least until the next one – won Three Glasses. It's a wine as subtle and deep as a cut from a katana sword but maybe we should also have awarded them to the Riesling Kaiton '06, and perhaps the Veltliner. But we feel that Peter and his family would like it better if we wrote about his current labours, which are titanic for a small producer like Peter. Two hundred metres above his farm, he is restoring plots abandoned for decades and planting new terraced vineyards to riesling, supported by 500 metres of traditional Valle Isarco stone walls. As for Peter and Brigitte's wines, we can only add they come ever closer to sheer poetry.

○ A. A. Gewürztraminer Passito Dorado '04	♛♛ 6
● A. A. Meranese Hügel Baslan Ris. '05	♛♛ 4*
○ A. A. Pinot Bianco Helios '06	♛♛ 5
● A. A. Pinot Nero Ris. '04	♛♛♛ 5
● A. A. Cabernet Sauvignon-Merlot Sagittarius '04	♛ 6
○ A. A. Dorado '02	♛♛ 6
○ A. A. Pinot Bianco Helios '02	♛♛ 5
● A. A. Meranese Hügel Baslan Ris. '04	♛♛ 4
● A. A. Cabernet Sauvignon-Merlot Sagittarius '01	♛♛ 6
○ A. A. Gewürztraminer Passito Dorado '03	♛♛ 6
○ A. A. Pinot Bianco Helios '04	♛♛ 5
● A. A. Pinot Nero Ris. '02	♛♛ 5

○ A. A. Valle Isarco Sylvaner '06	♛♛♛ 4*
○ A. A. Valle Isarco Gewürztraminer '06	♛♛ 4*
○ A. A. Valle Isarco Riesling Kaiton '06	♛♛ 4*
○ A. A. Valle Isarco Veltliner '06	♛♛ 4*
○ A. A. Valle Isarco Riesling Kaiton '05	♛♛♛ 4*
○ A. A. Valle Isarco Sylvaner '03	♛♛♛ 4*
○ Kaiton '99	♛♛♛ 4
○ Kaiton '01	♛♛♛ 4
○ A. A. Valle Isarco Sylvaner V.T. '04	♛♛♛ 4*
○ A. A. Valle Isarco Sylvaner '02	♛♛♛ 4*
○ A. A. Valle Isarco Riesling Kaiton '04	♛♛ 4*
○ A. A. Valle Isarco Veltliner '04	♛♛ 4*
○ A. A. Valle Isarco Sylvaner '05	♛♛ 4*

Cantina Laimburg
LOC. LAIMBURG, 6
39040 VADENA/PFATTEN [BZ]
TEL. 0471969700
www.laimburg.bz.it

Loacker Schwarhof
LOC. SANTA GIUSTINA, 3
39100 BOLZANO/BOZEN
TEL. 0471365125
www.loacker.net

ANNUAL PRODUCTION 180,000 bottles
HECTARES UNDER VINE 45
VITICULTURE METHOD Conventional

ANNUAL PRODUCTION 60,000 bottles
HECTARES UNDER VINE 7
VITICULTURE METHOD Certified biodynamic

The experimental agricultural and forestry centre in Laimburg has been turning out high quality technicians for decades. An efficient winery operation connected to this professional training school, with its renowned clonal research activities, vinifies grapes sourced from various vineyards in the best terrains in Alto Adige, with different soil types at different altitudes. Two lines are produced here. The "vini del podere", traditional standard-label wines, and the more characterful "selezione maniero" wines, mostly aged in small oak barrels, with names taken from the Ladin legends of the Dolomites. We were most convinced this year by the Pinot Nero Selyèt Riserva '04, which shows already complex red berry fruit and floral aromas. The palate tempts with silky tannins, a solid yet lean profile and deep, confident finish. The Pinot Bianco '06 is mineral, taut and juicy. As usual, the Laimburg classic, Lagrein Riserva Barbagòl '04, is very convincing. The rest of the production shows its usual reliability.

The Schwarhof estate has existed since 1334 and is in the Santa Maddalena production zone. Red wines come from Schwarhof and nearby Kohlerhof while white grapes come from the Kalter Keller vineyard in Valle Isarco. Since 1979, Rainer and Hayo Loacker's production philosophy has focused on the strict application of organic agricultural principals in their vineyards and winery, a difficult task with naturally fluctuating results. We must say that in the past few years their hard work has rewarded them with constant quality and steady reliability. How could we not appreciate the Pinot Nero Norital '05, with its velvety nose and supple palate sustained by a lively acidity and a distinctly mineral finish, or the fragrant, juicy Merlot Iwain '05 with its distinct note of cinchona? From the whites, the Sauvignon Blanc Tasnim '06 is particularly pleasing. But the whole range of Loacker wines is aimed at palates seeking natural products with outstanding personality.

● A. A. Pinot Nero Selyèt Ris. '04	ҰҰ	5
● A. A. Lagrein Scuro Barbagòl Ris. '04	ҰҰ	6
● A. A. Merlot '04	ҰҰ	4
○ A. A. Sauvignon Oyèll '06	ҰҰ	5
○ A. A. Pinot Bianco '06	ҰҰ	4*
○ A. A. Sauvignon Passito Saphir '04	Ұ	8
● A. A. Lagrein Scuro Barbagòl Ris. '00	ҰҰҰ	6
● A. A. Lagrein Scuro Barbagòl Ris. '01	ҰҰ	6
● A. A. Lagrein Scuro Barbagòl Ris. '03	ҰҰ	6
● A. A. Lagrein Scuro Ris. '98	ҰҰ	6
○ A. A. Pinot Bianco '05	ҰҰ	4*
○ A. A. Sauvignon Oyèll '02	ҰҰ	4*
○ A. A. Sauvignon Passito Saphir '03	ҰҰ	8
● A. A. Pinot Nero Selyèt Ris. '01	ҰҰ	5
○ A. A. Gewürztraminer Elyònd '05	ҰҰ	5
○ A. A. Sauvignon Passito Saphir '02	ҰҰ	8

● A. A. Cabernet Lagrein Kastlet '04	ҰҰ	5
● A. A. Merlot Ywain '05	ҰҰ	5
○ A. A. Valle Isarco Sylvaner Ysac '06	ҰҰ	4*
○ A. A. Sauvignon Blanc Tasnim '06	ҰҰ	5
● A. A. Santa Maddalena Cl. Morit '06	ҰҰ	4
● A. A. Pinot Nero Norital '05	ҰҰ	5
○ A. A. Chardonnay Ateyon '05	ҰҰ	5
○ A. A. Moscato Giallo V.T. Chrysanta '06	Ұ	5
○ A. A. Valle Isarco Gewürztraminer Atagis '06	Ұ	5
● A. A. Merlot Ywain '04	ҰҰҰ	5*
○ A. A. Moscato Giallo V.T. Chrysanta '06	ҰҰҰ	5*
○ A. A. Valle Isarco Gewürztraminer Atagis '02	ҰҰ	5
○ A. A. Valle Isarco Sylvaner Ysac '04	ҰҰ	4
● A. A. Cabernet Lagrein Kastlet '03	ҰҰ	5
● A. A. Pinot Nero Norital '04	ҰҰ	5

H. Lun

VIA VILLA, 22/24
39044 EGNA/NEUMARKT [BZ]
TEL. 0471813256
www.lun.it

ANNUAL PRODUCTION 300,000 bottles
HECTARES UNDER VINE 30
VITICULTURE METHOD Conventional

In Alto Adige's long winemaking tradition, the Lun winery is one of the oldest, at the forefront for more than 160 years. After losing its lustre for a few years, it has delighted us by making a comeback with technically impeccable wines – nothing new there – but with the pinch more personality that takes them across the line between a well-made wine and a good one. Signs of this renaissance were evident last year but this time Lun let rip with a truly convincing series of wines, two of which went into our Three Glass finals. Our compliments go to the Gewürztraminer Sandbichler V.T. '05 with its complex aromas of dried apricot and botrytis. The very concentrated palate, with 230 grams of sugar, shows notes of dates and sage and ten grams of vibrant acidity that refreshes the lingering balsamic finish. A classy Lagrein, the Riserva Albertus '04 has typical aromas. The palate is marvellous, showing tough, close-knit texture in combination with sweet tannins, almost earthy minerality, well-balanced acidity and a deep, complex finish. The date with Three Glasses has merely been postponed.

Cantina Vini Merano

LOC. MAIA BASSA
VIA SAN MARCO, 11
39012 MERANO/MERAN [BZ]
TEL. 0473235544
www.meranerkellerei.com

ANNUAL PRODUCTION 400,000 bottles
HECTARES UNDER VINE 139
VITICULTURE METHOD Conventional

We begin the entry for this small co-operative winery near Merano with a reprimand for the great Kellermeister, Stefan Kapfinger, who did not submit for our tasting two splendid Schiavas we particularly like, the Valle Venosta Sonnenberg and the St. Valentin from Merano. Having said this, the wines submitted were as sound as usual beginning with the Valle Venosta Pinot Bianco Sonneberg '06, which is an object lesson in terroir. Delicate in its white peach and gunflint aromas, it progresses stylish and dynamic in the mouth with an only apparently lean finish. Among the convincing wines from the Graf Von Meran line, special mention goes to the Gewürztraminer '06, for years one of the very best, and the Sauvignon and Pinot Bianco, both from '06 with a touch of elegance and harmony in common. But since man does not live by white alone, there's a Cabernet Graf Von Meran Riserva '04 that presents austere yet fresh and vibrant with a juicy, minerally finish. In other words, the labels change but luckily not the quality of the wines.

○ A. A. Gewürztraminer Sandbichler V. T. '05	♈ 7
● A. A. Lagrein Scuro Albertus Ris. '04	♈ 5
○ A. A. Bianco Sandbichler '06	♈ 4
○ A. A. Riesling '06	♈ 4*
○ A. A. Chardonnay '06	♈ 4*
○ A. A. Sauvignon Sandbichler '06	♈ 5
○ A. A. Sauvignon '06	♈ 4
● A. A. Santa Maddalena '06	♈ 3*
○ A. A. Gewürztraminer Sandbichler '06	♈ 5
○ A. A. Bianco Sandbichler '05	♆ 4
● A. A. Lagrein Scuro Albertus Ris. '02	♆ 5
○ A. A. Sauvignon '05	♆ 4

○ A. A. Val Venosta Pinot Bianco Sonnenberg '06	♈ 4*
● A. A. Cabernet Sauvignon Graf Von Meran Ris. '04	♈ 5
○ A. A. Gewürztraminer Amadeus V. T. '05	♈ 6
● A. A. Lagrein Segen Ris. '04	♈ 5
● A. A. Merlot Freiherr Ris. '04	♈ 6
⊙ Mitterberg Rosalie '06	♈ 3*
● A. A. Val Venosta Pinot Nero Sonnenberg '05	♈ 4*
○ A. A. Sauvignon Graf Von Meran '06	♈ 5
○ A. A. Sauvignon '06	♈ 4*
○ A. A. Pinot Bianco Graf Von Meran '06	♈ 4*
○ A. A. Moscato Giallo Passito Sissi Graf von Meran '04	♈ 6
● A. A. Meraner Eines Fürsten Traum '06	♈ 4*
○ A. A. Gewürztraminer Graf Von Meran '06	♈ 5
○ A. A. Gewürztraminer Graf Von Meran '05	♆ 5*
○ A. A. Sauvignon Graf Von Meran '05	♆ 5

Cantina Convento Muri-Gries

P.ZZA GRIES, 21
39100 BOLZANO/BOZEN
TEL. 0471282287
www.muri-gries.com

ANNUAL PRODUCTION 450,000 bottles
HECTARES UNDER VINE 30
VITICULTURE METHOD Conventional

We had another well-deserved endorsement for Muri Gries and its Lagrein Abtei Riserva '04, for several years now one of the very best Alto Adige Lagreins. This is in part thanks to the research into the variety, unique in the region, carried out behind the venerable walls of this monastery. In fact, no other winery has dedicated such passion and commitment to the objective of "maintaining and enhancing the characteristics of this type, its native flavour, rustic elegance and identity", as Christian Werth puts it. The Muri Gries Kellermeister is now one of the best interpreters of this native grape in both the vineyard, where more than 20 subvarieties of Lagrein are under observation, and the cellar, managed by Walter Bernard. The various Lagreins are excellent, from the traditional Kretzer-Rosé to the classic Lagrein right up to the grand Riserva Abtei Muri. In the '04 vintage, the last of these, our Three Glass winner, is introduced by rich, intense aromas of berries, cherries and blackcurrants tinged with chocolate. The rich, round palate shows a leaner than usual structure with caressing tannins, full flavour and a lingering farewell.

Cantina Nals Margreid

VIA HEILIGENBERG, 2
39010 NALLES/NALS [BZ]
TEL. 0471678626
www.kellerei.it

ANNUAL PRODUCTION 800,000 bottles
HECTARES UNDER VINE 150
VITICULTURE METHOD Conventional

When a winery manages to send eight wines into the finals, words are almost superfluous. The facts speak for themselves. We would just like to mention the truly extraordinary efforts by the managerial staff of this small co-operative winery, which processes grapes from the three distinct communities of Nalles, Niclara and Magré, the first in the subzone of Terlano, northwest of Bolzano, the other two lying to the south of Cortaccia. The dynamic manager and distinguished gourmet, Gottfried Pollinger, and the young man with clear ideas, Kellermeister Harald Schraffl – congratulations on his recent marriage! – are more than just a guarantee for the future. Naturally, we cannot tell you about all eight finalists so we'll restrict ourselves to mentioning the Pinot Bianco Sirmian '06, which won a marvellous Three Glass award for a spectrum of aromatics of rare typicity, with florality, sage and even a hint of grapefruit. The fresh, succulent palate shows great dynamism, like a genuine Alto Adige Pinot Bianco. In what little space remains, we'll mention the Gewürztraminer Baron Salvadori '06, one of the very best wines of its type, and the fantastic Galea '06 from old vines.

Wine	Rating
● A. A. Lagrein Abtei Ris. '04	▼▼▼ 5
○ A. A. Bianco Abtei Muri '05	▼▼ 4*
● A. A. Santa Maddalena '06	▼▼ 3*
☉ A. A. Lagrein Rosato '06	▼▼ 4*
● A. A. Lagrein '06	▼ 4
○ A. A. Pinot Grigio '06	▼ 4
● A. A. Lagrein Abtei Ris. '00	♈♈♈ 5
● A. A. Lagrein Abtei Ris. '96	♈♈♈ 5
● A. A. Lagrein Abtei Ris. '99	♈♈♈ 5
● A. A. Lagrein Abtei Ris. '02	♈♈♈ 5
● A. A. Lagrein Abtei Ris. '03	♈♈♈ 5
● A. A. Lagrein Abtei Ris. '98	♈♈♈ 5
● A. A. Lagrein Abtei Ris. '97	♈♈♈ 5
● A. A. Lagrein Abtei Ris. '01	♈♈♈ 5

Wine	Rating
○ A. A. Pinot Bianco Sirmian '06	▼▼▼ 4*
● A. A. Cabernet Sauvignon Baron Salvadori Ris. '04	▼▼ 6
● A. A. Merlot-Cabernet Anticus Baron Salvadori Ris. '04	▼▼ 6
● A. A. Schiava Galea '06	▼▼ 4*
○ A. A. Moscato Giallo Passito Baronesse '05	▼▼ 6
● A. A. Lagrein Baron Salvadori Ris. '04	▼▼ 5
○ A. A. Chardonnay Baron Salvadori '05	▼▼ 5
○ A. A. Gewürztraminer Baron Salvadori '06	▼▼ 5
☉ A. A. Lagrein Rosato '06	▼▼ 3*
○ A. A. Sauvignon Mantele '06	▼▼ 5
○ A. A. Pinot Bianco Penon '06	▼▼ 4*
○ A. A. Pinot Grigio Punggl '06	▼▼ 4*
● A. A. Merlot Baron Salvadori Ris. '03	▼▼ 6
○ A. A. Chardonnay Baron Salvadori '00	♈♈♈ 5
○ A. A. Moscato Giallo Passito Baronesse '03	♈♈ 6
● A. A. Schiava Galea '05	♈♈ 4*

Josef Niedermayr
LOC. CORNAIANO/GIRLAN
VIA CASA DI GESÙ, 15
39050 APPIANO/EPPAN [BZ]
TEL. 0471662451
www.niedermayr.it

ANNUAL PRODUCTION 350,000 bottles
HECTARES UNDER VINE 40
VITICULTURE METHOD Conventional

The best products submitted this year by Josef Niedermayr, one of the great authorities in the wine world of Alto Adige, included more than just sweet wines. Sure, the Aureus '05 is always top of the class and could be called anything except dry. Nevertheless, this dried-grape passito white, from 60 per cent sauvignon and 30 per cent chardonnay with a pinch of gewürztraminer, is accompanied by some other fairly significant wines. The Aureus is now a classic and it is difficult not to be charmed by its delicately botrytic aromas and sweet yet never cloying flavour, well supported by generous acidity. Confirming what we said earlier, the Lagrein Riserva '05 is among the best of its type, a concentrated red with near unrivalled elegance. The fresh palate finishes on minerals and spice, buoyed by round, mellow tannins. The two '06 Sauvignons are particularly outstanding. The Allure shows a very distinctive note of nettles and Naun has exuberant minerality. The rest of the list comprises wines that are technically impeccable and rather well typed.

Niklaserhof - Josef Sölva
LOC. SAN NICOLÒ
VIA DELLE FONTANE, 31A
39052 CALDARO/KALTERN [BZ]
TEL. 0471963432
www.niklaserhof.it

ANNUAL PRODUCTION 50,000 bottles
HECTARES UNDER VINE 5.5
VITICULTURE METHOD Conventional

Josef Sölva from the Niklas winery at Caldaro makes great whites and has always believed in pinot bianco, an oft-underrated variety. The whites submitted this year from his estate are excellent, two reaching the Three Glass finals. Fermented in oak barrels with long lees contact, the Pinot Bianco Klaser R '05 opens on pleasant, inviting notes of ripe fruit and follows this with a structured, harmonious palate. From a cuvée of Pinot bianco and Sauvignon aged for a year in oak casks, the complex Bianco Mondevinum '05 has intense fruity notes on both the nose and palate. In other words, two lovely wines come from this small family estate that, as Josef Sölva says, strives to vitalize wine with a personal style and love for the product. The Pinot Bianco '06 is fresh, savoury and salty. The Sauvignon '06 is elegantly aromatic. The Kerner '06 is special and finally, the Lago di Caldaro Scelto '06 and Lagrein-Cabernet Klaser Riserva '04 are both good.

○ A. A. Aureus '05	♟ 7
● A. A. Lagrein Aus Gries Ris. '05	♟♟ 6
● A. A. Pinot Nero Ris. '04	♟♟ 6
○ A. A. Sauvignon Allure '06	♟♟ 5
○ A. A. Sauvignon Lage Naun '06	♟♟ 5
● Euforius '05	♟♟ 6
● A. A. Lagrein Gries Blacedelle '06	♟♟ 5
● A. A. Schiava Ascherhof '06	♟♟ 4
○ A. A. Gewürztraminer Lage Doss '06	♟♟ 6
○ A. A. Terlano Hof zu Pramol '06	♟ 4
○ A. A. Aureus '99	♟♟♟ 6
○ A. A. Aureus '03	♟♟ 7
○ A. A. Sauvignon Lage Naun '04	♟♟ 5
○ A. A. Sauvignon Allure '04	♟♟ 5
○ A. A. Aureus '04	♟♟ 7
○ A. A. Gewürztraminer Lage Doss '05	♟♟ 6

○ A. A. Bianco Mondevinum '05	♟♟ 5
○ A. A. Pinot Bianco Klaser R '05	♟♟ 4*
○ A. A. Pinot Bianco '06	♟♟ 4*
○ A. A. Sauvignon '06	♟♟ 4*
○ A. A. Kerner '06	♟ 4
● A. A. Lago di Caldaro Scelto Cl. '06	♟ 3
● A. A. Lagrein-Cabernet Klaser Ris. '04	♟ 5
○ A. A. Kerner '05	♟♟ 4*
○ A. A. Bianco Mondevinum '04	♟♟ 5
○ A. A. Pinot Bianco Klaser '04	♟♟ 4
○ A. A. Pinot Bianco '05	♟♟ 4*
○ A. A. Bianco Mondevinum '03	♟♟ 5
○ A. A. Pinot Bianco Klaser '02	♟♟ 4
○ A. A. Sauvignon '05	♟♟ 4
○ A. A. Pinot Bianco Klaser '05	♟♟ 4

Nusserhof - Heinrich Mayr

via Mayr Nusser, 72
39100 Bolzano/Bozen
tel. 0471978388

ANNUAL PRODUCTION 15,000 bottles
HECTARES UNDER VINE 2.5
VITICULTURE METHOD Certified biodynamic

The Hazelnut Farm, as Nusserhof would be in English, strides into the main section of the Guide. For years now, we have been keeping an eye on this small, certified organic estate to the north of Bolzano. The reason for all this attention is simple. It's a small clos – the estate is completely surrounded by a long wall – that produces wines of great character, uses traditional production methods and has a very personal style. Although not always perfect, the wines are never boring. All this is down to that personable producer, Heirich Mayr, who is also a good musician and great wine taster. His showcase wine is naturally Lagrein, a wine that is very different from the many versions of the type that we find a bit tame. From 30-year old vines and aged in large barrels, the Lagrein Riserva '04 has stylish, complex aromas with smoky notes that quickly give way to blackcurrant, blueberry and musk. The explosion of fruit and spice on the palate manages to deliver drinkability, despite the assertive structure, thanks to a balance of acidity and tannins on the one hand, and alcohol and fruit softness on the other. Tyroldego, from teroldego grapes, is more than just interesting.

● A. A. Lagrein Scuro Ris. '04	🍷🍷 4*
⊙ A. A. Lagrein Rosato '06	🍷🍷 3*
● Tyroldego	🍷🍷 4*
○ A. A. Blaterle '06	🍷🍷 3*
● A. A. Lagrein Scuro Ris. '01	🍷🍷 4*
● A. A. Lagrein Scuro Ris. '02	🍷🍷 4*
○ A. A. Blaterle '05	🍷🍷 3*
○ A. A. Blaterle '05	🍷🍷 3*

Pacherhof - Andreas Huber

fraz. Novacella
v.lo Pacher, 1
39040 Varna/Vahrn [BZ]
tel. 0472835717
www.pacherhof.com

ANNUAL PRODUCTION 50,000 bottles
HECTARES UNDER VINE 6.5
VITICULTURE METHOD Natural

The Pacherhof vineyards are among the oldest and most southerly in Valle Isarco. These sand and gravel limestone plots, exposed to the south and southwest at around 700 metres above sea level, yield lively, aromatic wines, with plenty of elegance and backbone after fermentation in stainless steel and large barrels. Add to this the confident stamp of young Andreas Huber. We found only one defect with the Sylvaner Alte Reben '06. Its extreme youth at the moment of our tasting kept this splendid wine from expressing all its extraordinary character and dynamism. The same goes for the Kerner, a complex wine with superb fullness and depth as well as penetration. The same consideration applies to the Riesling '06. It's a great pity since it shows rare finesse with caressing notes of medicinal herbs and an austere, stony palate. The splendid Müller Thurgau was the only wine ready for the corkscrew and it's much more than a simple Müller Thurgau. It's a pity but one thing is certain: Andreas will have plenty of opportunity to make good.

○ A. A. Valle Isarco Riesling '06	🍷🍷 5
○ A. A. Valle Isarco Sylvaner Alte Reben '06	🍷🍷 5
○ A. A. Valle Isarco Kerner '06	🍷🍷 5
○ A. A. Valle Isarco Sylvaner '06	🍷🍷 5
○ A. A. Valle Isarco Müller Thurgau '06	🍷🍷 4
○ A. A. Valle Isarco Riesling '04	🍷🍷🍷 5*
○ A. A. Valle Isarco Sylvaner Alte Reben '05	🍷🍷🍷 5
○ A. A. Valle Isarco Kerner '04	🍷🍷 4*
○ A. A. Valle Isarco Müller Thurgau '05	🍷🍷 4*
○ A. A. Valle Isarco Sylvaner Alte Reben '04	🍷🍷 5
○ A. A. Valle Isarco Riesling '05	🍷🍷 5
○ A. A. Valle Isarco Kerner '05	🍷🍷 4*

Pfannenstielhof - Johannes Pfeifer

VIA PFANNESTIEL, 9
39100 BOLZANO/BOZEN
TEL. 0471970884
www.pfannenstielhof.it

ANNUAL PRODUCTION 38,000 bottles
HECTARES UNDER VINE 4
VITICULTURE METHOD Conventional

Johannes Pfeifer is a true winemaker. Based in the Bolzano area, he is careful and a hard worker, passionate about wine, committed to constant improvement, frank, hospitable and to round it all off a nice guy. We must say his wines are very like him. They are authentic, sincere, technically well made and a perfect marriage of tradition and modernity. We'll begin with one of the best '06 Santa Maddalenas we tasted. It's so good it reached the Three Glass finals, which is rather unusual for this type. But this wine is exceptional, showing typical, juicy and pleasantly drinkable yet with a certain complexity. As usual, the Lagrein Riserva '04 is still young yet already expresses uncommon grip on the palate and a character that portends a future for this wine that will be exciting to say the least. Actually, it would be no bad thing to consider postponing its release. For a few years now, Pfannenstielhof has also been working to produce a Pinot Nero. The '04 version has started taking on a fairly defined personality of finesse and freshness on the palate.

● A. A. Santa Maddalena Cl. '06	♟♟	3*
● A. A. Lagrein Scuro '06	♟♟	4*
● A. A. Pinot Nero '04	♟♟	5
● A. A. Lagrein Scuro Ris. '04	♟♟	5
● A. A. Lagrein Scuro Ris. '00	♟♟	5
● A. A. Lagrein Scuro Ris. '99	♟♟	5
● A. A. Lagrein Scuro '05	♟♟	4*
● A. A. Pinot Nero '02	♟♟	5
● A. A. Lagrein Scuro Ris. '03	♟♟	5
● A. A. Santa Maddalena Cl. '05	♟♟	3*

Tenuta Ritterhof

S.DA DEL VINO, 1
39052 CALDARO/KALTERN [BZ]
TEL. 0471963298
www.ritterhof.it

ANNUAL PRODUCTION 290,000 bottles
HECTARES UNDER VINE 7.5
VITICULTURE METHOD Conventional

The Ritterhof estate, owned by the Roner family of the renowned distillery in Termeno, has managed in just few years to become one of the most important wineries in the area. Over the last few years, oenologist Hannes Bernard and manager Ludwig Kaneppele have always submitted a better than merely good range of wines. Two of these, the Pinot Bianco '06 and Lagrein Manus Riserva '04, made it to the finals this year. One of the best in its category from the region, the Pinot Bianco Ritterhof shows fresh fruit on the nose and a zesty, salty, elegantly fresh palate. The Lagrein Manus Riserva '04 has great complexity and character, presenting full, structured and juicy. But our compliments also go to all the other labels. The whites include a Müller Thurgau with great class, an elegant, aromatic Sauvignon and two Geürztraminers, the Crescendo and Ritterhof, that have great potential. The Schiava Putzleiten and Pinot Nero Crescendo are very fruity, fresh and inviting. The Cabernet-Merlot Crescendo has sweet tannins and good length.

● A. A. Lagrein Manus Ris. '04	♟♟	6
○ A. A. Pinot Bianco '06	♟♟	4*
● A. A. Cabernet Merlot Crescendo Ris. '04	♟♟	5
● A. A. Lagrein Crescendo Ris. '04	♟♟	5
● A. A. Pinot Nero Crescendo '05	♟♟	6
○ A. A. Müller Thurgau '06	♟♟	4
● A. A. Schiava Putzleitn '06	♟♟	4
○ A. A. Sauvignon '06	♟♟	4
○ A. A. Gewürztraminer '06	♟♟	4*
○ A. A. Gewürztraminer Crescendo '06	♟	5
○ A. A. Pinot Grigio Crescendo '06	♟	5
● Perlhof Crescendo '06	♟	5
● A. A. Lagrein Manus Ris. '03	♟♟	5
○ A. A. Pinot Grigio '05	♟♟	4*
○ A. A. Sauvignon '05	♟♟	4*
● A. A. Cabernet Merlot Crescendo Ris. '03	♟♟	5

Hans Rottensteiner

VIA SARENTINO, 1A
39100 BOLZANO/BOZEN
TEL. 0471282015
www.rottensteiner-weine.com

Castel Sallegg

V.LO DI SOTTO, 15
39052 CALDARO/KALTERN [BZ]
TEL. 0471963132
www.castelsallegg.it

ANNUAL PRODUCTION 400,000 bottles
HECTARES UNDER VINE 10
VITICULTURE METHOD Natural

ANNUAL PRODUCTION 120,000 bottles
HECTARES UNDER VINE 31
VITICULTURE METHOD Conventional

Northwest of Bolzano, at the entrance to Val Sarentino, you'll find Toni and Hannes Rottensteiner's historic estate, one of the most reliable wineries in the entire province of Bolzano. Excellent technique and great personality characterize Rottensteiner wines with the Lagrein in first place as far as the 2008 Guide is concerned. In a modern style but with absolutely balanced use of new oak, the Lagrein Grieser Riserva Select '04 is a juicy red with sweet, smooth tannins and no-nonsense progression on a palate livened up by a forthright mineral vein. It's a great Lagrein. Just as good is the '03 vintage of the same wine. Laudably, its release to market was delayed for a year and it shows more powerful structure than its younger brother, veined with clear, deep spice. By now a classic, the Santa Maddalena Premstallerhof is as excellent as ever and, favoured by the positive 2006 growing season, is particularly fragrant and pleasantly drinkable. Finally, the distinctive Gewürztraminer Cancenai V.T. '06 is concentrated and long on the palate.

A new wind blows through the old walls of Castel Sallegg in Caldaro. Over the past few years, there has been less talk of this winery, once the cradle of the prized moscato rosa and, with its vineyards in the best plots in the territory, a stronghold of wines from the Lago di Caldaro DOC. The new, young oenologist, Matthias Hauser, has many changes planned, from the creation of a new line to more emphasis on quality. We wish him much success because this winery has enormous potential. This year, Castel Sallegg surprised us with its Merlot, always a strong point in their production. The Merlot Riserva '03 shows notes of red berries and plums the a pleasant, full palate with structure and sweet tannins. The first vintage of the new Merlot Nussleiten '03 is a wine with great structure and powerful, giving full flavour and length. Other good wines this year include the well-structured Pinot Grigio '06, which is deep and complex yet also well supported by acidity, and the fresh, lean, minerally Gewürztraminer '06.

● A. A. Lagrein Grieser Select Ris. '04	♔♔ 5
○ A. A. Gewürztraminer Cancenai '05	♔♔ 4*
● Prem '06	♔♔ 4
● A. A. Santa Maddalena Cl. Premstallerhof '06	♔♔ 4*
○ A. A. Gewürztraminer Passito Cresta '05	♔♔ 6
○ A. A. Müller Thurgau '06	♔♔ 4*
● A. A. Lagrein Grieser Select Ris. '03	♔♔ 5
☉ A. A. Lagrein Kretzer '06	♔ 4*
● A. A. Pinot Nero Mazzon Select Ris. '04	♔ 5
○ A. A. Pinot Bianco Carnol '06	♔ 4
● A. A. Lagrein Ris. '02	♕♕♕ 4*
○ A. A. Gewürztraminer Cancenai '02	♕♕ 5
○ A. A. Gewürztraminer Passito Cresta '04	♕♕ 6
● Prem '04	♕♕ 4

● A. A. Merlot Ris. '03	♔♔ 5
● A. A. Merlot Nussleiten Ris. '03	♔♔ 7
○ A. A. Gewürztraminer '06	♔♔ 4*
○ A. A. Pinot Grigio '06	♔♔ 4*
● A. A. Lagrein Ris. '03	♔ 5
○ A. A. Pinot Bianco '06	♔ 4
● A. A. Merlot Ris. '02	♕♕ 5
○ A. A. Pinot Bianco '05	♕♕ 4
○ A. A. Pinot Bianco '04	♕♕ 4
○ A. A. Pinot Grigio '05	♕♕ 4*

★ Cantina Produttori San Michele Appiano

VIA CIRCONVALLAZIONE, 17/19
39057 APPIANO/EPPAN [BZ]
TEL. 0471664466
www.stmichael.it

ANNUAL PRODUCTION 1,900,000 bottles
HECTARES UNDER VINE 362
VITICULTURE METHOD Conventional

Evidently, Hans Terzer wanted to throw a big celebration for the 100th anniversary of San Michele Appiano and his own 30 years of association with the winery while sorting out a little problem that was bothering him. He may have gone over the top. Eight wines in the finals, two Three Glass awards and an endless series of products with very high scores summarize this year's impressive performance. It would be hard to do better. Given the space available, we'll mention only that the Bianco Passito Comtess '05, from 70 per cent gewürztraminer and equal parts riesling and sauvignon, is well up this year's list of the best sweet wines. After a complex nose of citrus and saffron, the palate is dense yet flaunts a splendid acidity to refresh the full, harmonious body where the saffron returns almost explosively in a finish that seems never-ending. All these fantastic wines risk overshadowing another Three Glass award – actually the 13th – for the Sauvignon St. Valentin. In an unimpressive vintage for the type like 2006, this wine shows its usual superlative quality with an elegance that has now become its trademark. For the other wines, just look at the chart below.

Cantina Sociale San Paolo

LOC. SAN PAOLO
VIA CASTEL GUARDIA, 21
39050 APPIANO/EPPAN [BZ]
TEL. 0471662183
www.cantinasanpaolo.com

ANNUAL PRODUCTION 1,000,000 bottles
HECTARES UNDER VINE 195
VITICULTURE METHOD Conventional

The acquisition of the Kössler estate by this major co-operative winery is now complete, so you will also find Kössler products in the chart below. Founded in 1907, Cantina di San Paolo produces the classic wines from the zone. Although always sound, its bottles sometimes they suffer from a lack of personality. The Lagrein DiVinus '04 particularly convinced us with its caressing tobacco and spice aromas. The lean, stylish palate shows nice smooth tannins and upfront yet well-balanced acidity. The finish is long and complex. One of the estate warhorses is also excellent. The Pinot Grigio Eggleiten Exclusiv '06 is characterized by clear aromas of elderflower and williams pear before the round, harmonious palate closes with a long, dynamic finish. From Kössler, a special mention goes to the full, juicy Cuvée St. Pauls '04, a red from cabernet and merlot, and the Spumante Praeclarus Noblesse '98.

O A. A. Bianco Passito Comtess '05 ♟♟♟ 6	● A. A. Lagrein Scuro DiVinus Ris. '04 ♟♟ 6
O A. A. Sauvignon St. Valentin '06 ♟♟♟ 5	O A. A. Pinot Grigio
O A. A. Chardonnay St. Valentin '05 ♟♟ 5	Exclusiv Egg Leiten '06 ♟♟ 4*
● A. A. Lagrein St. Valentin '04 ♟♟ 6	● A. A. Merlot DiVinus Ris. '04 ♟♟ 5
● A. A. Cabernet St. Valentin '04 ♟♟ 6	O A. A. Pinot Bianco Passion '06 ♟♟ 5
O A. A. Hunrt Johr Jubiläumswein '06 ♟♟ 6	O A. A. Talento Praeclarus Noblesse '98 ♟♟ 6
● A. A. Schiava Pagis '06 ♟♟ 4*	● A. A. Cuvée St. Pauls '04 ♟♟ 4
O A. A. Pinot Bianco Schulthauser '06 ♟♟ 4*	● A. A. Merlot Tschidererhof '05 ♟♟ 4*
● A. A. Cabernet Ris. '04 ♟♟ 5	O A. A. Schiava Passion '06 ♟♟ 4
● A. A. Merlot St. Valentin '04 ♟♟ 6	O A. A. Sauvignon Passion '06 ♟♟ 5
O A. A. Gewürztraminer St. Valentin '06 ♟♟ 5	O A. A. Sauvignon Exclusiv Gfilhof '06 ♟♟ 4
O A. A. Pinot Bianco St. Valentin '05 ♟♟ 5	O A. A. Gewürztraminer Passion '06 ♟ 5
● A. A. Merlot Ris. '04 ♟♟ 5*	O A. A. Pinot Bianco Spiegelleiten '06 ♟ 4
● A. A. Pinot Nero Ris. '04 ♟♟ 5	O A. A. Talento Praeclarus Brut ♟ 5
● A. A. Pinot Nero St. Valentin '04 ♟♟ 6	O A. A. Pinot Grigio Glockleiten '06 ♟ 4
O A. A. Pinot Grigio St. Valentin '05 ♟♟ 5	● A. A. Merlot Exclusiv Huberfeld '04 ♟ 4
O A. A. Chardonnay Merol '06 ♟♟ 4*	O A. A. Pinot Bianco Exclusiv Plötzner '06 ♟ 4
O A. A. Sauvignon Lahn '06 ♟♟ 4*	● A. A. Lagrein Scuro DiVinus Ris. '02 ♟♟ 6

★ **Cantina Produttori**
Santa Maddalena/Cantina di Bolzano
VIA BRENNERO, 15
39100 BOLZANO/BOZEN
TEL. 0471270909
www.cantinabolzano.com

Peter Sölva & Söhne
VIA DELL'ORO, 33
39052 CALDARO/KALTERN [BZ]
TEL. 0471964650
www.soelva.com

ANNUAL PRODUCTION 1,200,000 bottles
HECTARES UNDER VINE 130
VITICULTURE METHOD Conventional

A Three Glass prize for the Lagrein Riserva Taber '05 may not really be news but the fact it has won it nine times in the past 11 years might well be. This is indicative of a Taber plan behind this wine, a plan that started in one of the most beautiful vineyards in the province and has grown year after year with constant improvements until it achieved its current form: a wine with rare intensity, character and elegance that is now synonymous with Lagrein. The 2005 version, a fresh, more austere and indeed tighter vintage than others, shows pulp yet great freshness and definition. The tannins have by now acquired a finesse that is difficult to surpass. We should add that it is also a long-lived wine and a recent vertical tasting disproved any rumours to the contrary. Just taste the splendid '95. Stefan Filippi has also given us the delicious Santa Maddalena '06, in the base and Huck am Bach versions, and a surprising Gewürztraminer '06 that landed in our finals. And there's the usual series of other impeccable wines.

ANNUAL PRODUCTION 75,000 bottles
HECTARES UNDER VINE 11
VITICULTURE METHOD Conventional

Wines from the Peter Sölva & Söhne estate did really well this year. Although good for the past few years, this time they shifted into a higher gear of elegance, typicity, character and structure. Young oenologist Christian Belutti and dynamic owner Stefan Sölva have shown they are capable of skilfully managing the enormous potential on their hands. With two wines in the finals, the results are more than satisfying. The Terlano Pinot Bianco De Silva '06 shows intensely fruity, savoury, concentrated and elegant with great length, just like the Amistar Rosso '04, a powerful cuvée of Bordeaux blends. From the De Silva line, we also liked the Sauvignon '06, Lagrein Rosé '06, Lago di Caldaro Scelto Peterleiten '06 and Merlot '04. For the Sölvas, the old family name De Silva is "synonymous with the selection of grapes and care for the vineyards in keeping with a long family tradition", and Amistar is a "philosophy born in the vineyard that finishes with pleasure in the glass". Congratulations to this estate, one of the oldest operations in Caldaro.

● A. A. Lagrein Scuro Taber Ris. '05	♟♟♟	6
○ A. A. Gewürztramier '06	♟♟	4*
● A. A. Santa Maddalena Cl. Huck am Bach '06	♟♟	4*
○ A. A. Chardonnay Kleinstein '06	♟♟	4*
○ A. A. Valle Isarco Müller Thurgau '06	♟♟	4*
○ A. A. Sauvignon Mock '06	♟♟	4
● A. A. Santa Maddalena Cl. '06	♟♟	3*
○ A. A. Gewürztramier Kleinstein '06	♟♟	5
● A. A. Lagrein Scuro Perl '05	♟♟	4
● A. A. Pinot Nero Ris. '05	♟	5
● A. A. Lagrein Scuro Taber Ris. '01	♟♟♟	6
● A. A. Lagrein Scuro Taber Ris. '02	♟♟♟	7
● A. A. Lagrein Scuro Taber Ris. '03	♟♟♟	6
● A. A. Lagrein Scuro Taber Ris. '04	♟♟♟	6

○ A. A. Sauvignon Desilvas '06	♟♟	5
● Amistar Rosso '04	♟♟	6
○ A. A. Terlano Pinot Bianco Desilvas '06	♟♟	5
● A. A. Lago di Caldaro Scelto Cl. Sup. Desilvas Peterleiten '06	♟♟	4*
⊙ A. A. Lagrein Rosato Desilvas '06	♟♟	4
● A. A. Merlot Desilvas Ris. '04	♟♟	5
● Amistar Edizione A '04	♟♟	7
● A. A. Cabernet Franc Amistar '04	♟♟	6
● A. A. Lagrein Scuro Desilvas '06	♟	5
● A. A. Lagrein Scuro Desilvas '05	♟♟	4
○ A. A. Sauvignon Desilvas '05	♟♟	5
● Amistar Rosso '03	♟♟	6
● Amistar Edizione S '02	♟♟	7
● Amistar Rosso '02	♟♟	6

Stroblhof

LOC. SAN MICHELE
VIA PIGANÒ, 25
39057 APPIANO/EPPAN [BZ]
TEL. 0471662250
www.stroblhof.it

ANNUAL PRODUCTION 30,000 bottles
HECTARES UNDER VINE 3.7
VITICULTURE METHOD Conventional

As far back as the 19th century, Stroblhof
had already begun to produce its own wine,
Schiava and Pinot Bianco Strahler, the two
varieties typical to this zone. Thirty years
ago, the first vines of gewürztraminer and
pinot nero were planted and it was the latter
variety that made this small estate famous.
After a critical period, sisters Rosmarie and
Christine Hanny, with Andreas Nicolussi-
Leck, Rosmarie's husband and manager of
the estate and winery since 1995, today
oversee a growing winery that also enjoys
consultancy from a certain Hans Terzer.
Here once again is the outstanding Pinot
Nero in two versions, the Riserva and
Pigeno '04 selection. In particular, the
elegant Riserva shows very fine-grained
tannins and a long, minerally finish, making
it perhaps the best Pinot Nero of the
vintage. But our heroes were a step away
from triumph with the Pinot Bianco Strahler
'06 for its aromas of sage and
Mediterranean herbs, as well as hawthorn
and white peach. The palate is lean and
spirited with a deep, fragrant finish. All in all,
a splendid wine.

Taschlerhof - Peter Wachtler

LOC. MARA, 107
39042 BRESSANONE/BRIXEN [BZ]
TEL. 0472851091
www.taschlerhof.com

ANNUAL PRODUCTION 19,000 bottles
HECTARES UNDER VINE 3.9
VITICULTURE METHOD Natural

We are very happy for this small estate at
Mara/Mahr, a small village south of
Bressanone, and Peter Wachtler, one of the
producers who has contributed to the
success of Valle Isarco wines. The finally
finished new cellar and newly planted
vineyards have given further momentum to
his family estate. The vineyards are in the
woods at about 550 metres above sea level
with southwest exposure. The wines are
very typical and show great character, with
slightly less forced acidity compared to
other producers from the zone but with the
typical minerality of Valle Isarco whites. If we
wanted to give young Peter any advice, it
would be to search for further improvement
in the character of his wines. Although well
made and the result of strict grape
selection, we are convinced they do not fully
exploit their potential. Having said this, the
Sylvaner Lahner '06 and Kerner '06 are
both very good while offering a glimpse of
something even greater. We are convinced
major surprises are on the way from
Taschlerhof in the next few years.

O A. A. Pinot Bianco Strahler '06	♟♟ 4*
● A. A. Pinot Nero Pigeno '04	♟♟ 5
● A. A. Pinot Nero Ris. '04	♟♟ 6
O A. A. Gewürztraminer Pigeno '06	♟♟ 5
O A. A. Sauvignon Nico '06	♟♟ 5
O A. A. Chardonnay Schwarzhaus '06	♟ 4
● A. A. Pinot Nero Ris. '02	♟♟ 6
O A. A. Pinot Bianco Strahler '03	♟♟ 4*
O A. A. Pinot Bianco Strahler '04	♟♟ 4
O A. A. Pinot Bianco Strahler '05	♟♟ 4
O A. A. Sauvignon Nico '05	♟♟ 5
● A. A. Pinot Nero Ris. '03	♟♟ 6
● A. A. Pinot Nero Pigeno '02	♟♟ 5

O A. A. Valle Isarco Gewürztraminer '06	♟♟ 5
O A. A. Valle Isarco Sylvaner '06	♟♟ 4*
O A. A. Valle Isarco Sylvaner Lahner '06	♟♟ 5
O A. A. Valle Isarco Kerner '06	♟♟ 5
O A. A. Valle Isarco Kerner '05	♟♟ 4*
O A. A. Valle Isarco Sylvaner Lahner '05	♟♟ 5*
O A. A. Valle Isarco Gewürztraminer '05	♟♟ 5
O A. A. Valle Isarco Sylvaner '05	♟♟ 4*
O A. A. Valle Isarco Sylvaner '02	♟♟ 4

Cantina Terlano

VIA COLLI D'ARGENTO, 7
39018 TERLANO/TERLAN [BZ]
TEL. 0471257135
www.cantina-terlano.com

ANNUAL PRODUCTION 1,000,000 bottles
HECTARES UNDER VINE 140
VITICULTURE METHOD Conventional

The Terlano gang strikes again this year, winning Three Glasses with a great Sauvignon Quarz '05, a distinctively Terlano wine. The austere nose with aromas of gunflint and even smoky notes introduces a solid, minerally, spirited palate with unstoppable progression. The only limit is its extreme youth that still partially blocks its great potential. Alongside this champion, we find the particularly fresh and elegant Chardonnay '95, the savoury, fleshy Sauvignon Winkl '06 and the Pinot Bianco Riserva Vorberg '04, as usual still a bit reticent though with odd slightly mature notes. We also mention what is perhaps one of the best Gewürztraminer Lunares ever produced and a Terlano Nova Domus Riserva '03, at last with less invasive wood than usual. If we really want to find the fly in the ointment in the production of this benchmark co-operative winery, we could point out the good-value wines from the base line, in particular the Terlano and Pinot Bianco '06, which are good but we are used to even better.

★ Cantina Termeno

S.DA DEL VINO, 144
39040 TERMENO/TRAMIN [BZ]
TEL. 0471860126
www.tramin-wine.it

ANNUAL PRODUCTION 1,400,000 bottles
HECTARES UNDER VINE 220
VITICULTURE METHOD Conventional

The confidence with which Willi Stürz tackles a difficult variety like gewürztraminer is impressive. This is even more true in a growing year like 2006, which was far from ideal, particularly in terms of aromatics. The position of the vineyards, in the zone above Termeno called Söll, is wonderful for soil and site climate. Even so the Nussbaumer '06 continues to astonish us. It probably will not reach the heights of the '05 but its ability to combine power and elegance, concentration and freshness, complexity and pleasant drinkability have become the hallmarks of the wine. The Three Glass award is almost inevitable. The late-harvested Gewürztraminer Terminum '05 has impeccable balance. Just to underline Willi's respect for this variety, we tasted the delicious standard-label '06. The particularly elegant Sauvignon Montan '06 ages exclusively in stainless steel, acquiring great finesse. Then there is the usual Pinot Grigio Unterebner '06, the Lagrein Urban '05 and the white Stoan '06, from 60 per cent chardonnay with the rest sauvignon, pinot bianco and gewürztraminer.

Wine	Rating
○ A. A. Terlano Sauvignon Quarz '05	♟♟♟ 6
○ A. A. Terlano Chardonnay '95	♟♟ 8
○ A. A. Terlano Sauvignon Winkl '06	♟♟ 4*
○ A. A. Terlano Pinot Bianco Vorberg Ris. '04	♟♟ 4*
○ A. A. Chardonnay Cl. '06	♟♟ 4*
○ A. A. Terlano Chardonnay Kreuth '05	♟♟ 4
○ A. A. Terlano Müller Thurgau '06	♟♟ 4*
○ A. A. Terlano Pinot Bianco Cl. '06	♟♟ 4*
○ A. A. Terlano Nova Domus Ris. '04	♟♟ 6
○ A. A. Terlano Cl. '06	♟♟ 4*
● A. A. Lagrein Porphyr Ris. '04	♟♟ 6
○ A. A. Gewürztraminer Lunare '05	♟♟ 6
● A. A. Lagrein Porphyr '02	♟♟♟ 8
○ A. A. Terlano '91	♟♟♟ 8
○ A. A. Terlano Chardonnay '94	♟♟♟ 8
○ A. A. Terlano Pinot Bianco Vorberg Ris. '02	♟♟♟ 4*
○ A. A. Terlano Pinot Bianco Vorberg '01	♟♟♟ 4*
○ A. A. Pinot Grigio '06	♟♟ 4*

Wine	Rating
○ A. A. Gewürztraminer Nussbaumer '06	♟♟♟ 5
○ A. A. Gewürztraminer Passito Terminum '05	♟♟ 8
○ A. A. Pinot Grigio Unterebner '06	♟♟ 5
○ A. A. Sauvignon Montan '06	♟♟ 5
○ A. A. Stoan '06	♟♟ 5
● A. A. Lagrein Urban '05	♟♟ 6
○ A. A. Gewürztraminer '06	♟♟ 4*
● A. A. Pinot Nero Ris. '04	♟♟ 6
○ T Bianco '06	♟♟ 3*
● A. A. Schiava Freisinger '06	♟♟ 4*
○ A. A. Pinot Bianco '06	♟♟ 4*
○ A. A. Gewürztraminer Roan V. T. '05	♟♟ 6
○ A. A. Gewürztraminer Nussbaumer '04	♟♟♟ 5
● A. A. Lagrein Scuro Urban '02	♟♟♟ 6
○ A. A. Gewürztraminer Nussbaumer '05	♟♟♟ 5

Thurnhof - Andreas Berger

LOC. ASLAGO
VIA CASTEL FLAVON, 7
39100 BOLZANO/BOZEN
TEL. 0471288460
www.thurnhof.com

ANNUAL PRODUCTION 20,000 bottles
HECTARES UNDER VINE 3.5
VITICULTURE METHOD Conventional

Over the past few years, we have teased young Andreas Berger about his passion for his work. We felt at times this led him to overdo things, asking more from his lovingly tended grapes than they were capable of giving. This year, his wines seem to be acquiring greater balance. Thurnhof is a small estate with a few years behind it, actually all the way back to 1175. It's located in the area around Bolzano-Aslago, a warm, sunny zone, with particularly high temperatures that guarantee complete ripening of red grapes. The benchmark wine at Thurnhof is naturally Lagrein and the Riserva '04 convinced us to send it to our finals. This red is still a bit austere but already has typicity and assertive character with great minerality and tannins that are prominent buy balanced by confident fruit and spice. The Santa Maddalena '06 and robust Cabernet Sauvignon Riserva '04 are both excellent.

Tiefenbrunner

FRAZ. NICLARA
VIA CASTELLO, 4
39040 CORTACCIA/KURTATSCH [BZ]
TEL. 0471880122
www.tiefenbrunner.com

ANNUAL PRODUCTION 700,000 bottles
HECTARES UNDER VINE 20.5
VITICULTURE METHOD Conventional

The Tiefenbrunner name is well known, even to those who are not in the business, because it was one of the first estates to take awareness of Alto Adige wines beyond the borders of the province of Bolzano. Credit goes to Herbert Tiefenbrunner, an enterprising entrepreneur and charismatic personality in Alto Adige. Over the past few years, his son Christof has been discreetly, as is his character, taking over the reins of the winery. We must say Tiefebrunner wines are getting more and more like Christof. These wines are elegant, even delicate, painted more in light and shade than gaudy colours. Perhaps precisely for this reason, when tasted together with more concentrated, full-bodied wines, they can tend to be overshadowed. Our advice is to depend on wines like the Sauvignon Kirchleiten, the white Cuvée Anna, from equal parts of pinot bianco and grigio, and the fine Müller Thurgau Feldmarschall, all from 2006. Outstanding reds from the Linticlarus line include the Cabernet Sauvignon, Lagrein Riserva and Pinot Nero Riserva, all from 2004. We should also mention the very commendable pricing policy.

● A. A. Lagrein Scuro Ris. '04	♟ 5
● A. A. Cabernet Sauvignon Ris. '04	♟♟ 5
● A. A. Lagrein Scuro Merlau '06	♟♟ 4*
● A. A. Santa Maddalena '06	♟♟ 4*
● A. A. Cabernet Merlot Wienegg '04	♟♟ 6
○ A. A. Moscato Giallo '06	♟ 4
○ A. A. Moscato Giallo Passito Passaurum '05	♟ 6
● A. A. Lagrein Scuro '99	♟♟♟ 4*
● A. A. Cabernet Sauvignon Ris. '99	♟♟ 5
● A. A. Lagrein Scuro Merlau '05	♟♟ 4*
● A. A. Lagrein Scuro Ris. '02	♟♟ 5
● A. A. Cabernet Sauvignon Ris. '03	♟♟ 5
● A. A. Lagrein Scuro Ris. '03	♟♟ 5
● A. A. Cabernet Merlot Wienegg '01	♟♟ 6

● A. A. Cabernet Sauvignon Linticlarus Ris. '04	♟♟ 6
○ Feldmarschall von Fenner zu Fennberg '06	♟♟ 5
○ A. A. Sauvignon Kirchleiten '06	♟♟ 4*
○ A. A. Cuvée Anna Castel Turmhof '06	♟♟ 4*
○ A. A. Chardonnay Castel Turmhof '06	♟♟ 4
● A. A. Schiava Grigia Castel Turmhof '06	♟♟ 4*
● A. A. Pinot Nero Linticlarus Ris. '04	♟♟ 5
● A. A. Lagrein Linticlarus Ris. '04	♟♟ 5
○ A. A. Gewürztraminer '06	♟♟ 4*
○ A. A. Gewürztraminer Castel Turmhof '06	♟♟ 5
○ A. A. Chardonnay Linticlarus '05	♟♟ 5
● A. A. Lagrein Castel Turmhof '05	♟ 4
○ Feldmarschall von Fenner zu Fennberg '05	♟♟♟ 5
○ A. A. Cuvée Anna Castel Turmhof '05	♟♟ 4*
● A. A. Lagrein Linticlarus Ris. '02	♟♟ 5
● A. A. Cabernet Sauvignon Linticlarus Ris. '03	♟♟ 6

Untermoserhof - Georg Ramoser

VIA SANTA MADDALENA, 36
39100 BOLZANO/BOZEN
TEL. 0471975481
untermoserhof@rolmail.net

ANNUAL PRODUCTION 40,000 bottles
HECTARES UNDER VINE 4.5
VITICULTURE METHOD Conventional

Georg Ramoser is a serious, passionate producer whose immense efforts in the vineyard are all aimed at a drastic reduction in yields and maintaining the typicity of his wines while giving them a distinctly modern spin. The Santa Maddalena Classico zone, on the outskirts of Bolzano, is famous for its reds. These wines are a bit closed and difficult in their youth but have great potential for ageing and growth over time. With real character and great intensity, the Lagrein Riserva '04, more than 30 percent of which aged in new 700-litre barrels instead of the classic barriques, presents an impenetrable colour and comprehensively expresses the typical aromas of this variety. The concentrated palate has silky, close-knit tannins and closes with a complex finish that unfolds nicely. The Santa Maddalena is fragrant and juicy, unsurprisingly the product of a favourable year like 2006. The standard-label Lagrein is fresh and quaffable, with lively minerality. We look forward to the release of the Lagrein Riserva '05, which has been extremely promising since our first tastings.

Tenuta Unterortl - Castel Juval

FRAZ. JUVAL, 1B
39020 CASTELBELLO CIARDES
KASTELBELL TSCHARS [BZ]
TEL. 0473667580
www.unterortl.it

ANNUAL PRODUCTION 30,000 bottles
HECTARES UNDER VINE 4
VITICULTURE METHOD Conventional

"The essence of terroir" could be the motto of Tenuta Uterortl at Castelbello Ciardes, under the skilful management of Martin and Gisela Aurich. The estate is located 20 kilometres west of Merano in lower Val Venosta, on the hill of Castel Juval owned by Reinhold Messner, who also owns Uterortl. The vineyards are at significant altitudes of between 600 and 850 metres above sea level, with slopes that reach 45 per cent. We can assure you anyone with a fear of heights may not enjoy a visit here, despite the breathtaking beauty of the site. Martin was the first in Alto Adige to release a Riesling two years after the harvest. That turned out to be a good decision because the Windbichel '05 selection, from a small vineyard just above the cellar, won Three resounding Glasses. It proffers a complex damson and gunflint bouquet. The palate is edgy with those famous smoky notes – and just for the record, the wine sees only stainless steel – and an overwhelming progression that gives a new dimension to the term minerality. Along the same lines is the '06 Riesling. It's a bit more subtle but with just the same energy. Other news here is that the cellar is now using screw caps.

● A. A. Lagrein Scuro '06	♟♟	4*
● A. A. Lagrein Scuro Ris. '04	♟♟	5
● A. A. Santa Maddalena Cl. '06	♟♟	4*
● A. A. Merlot Ris. '04	♟♟	5
● A. A. Lagrein Scuro Ris. '03	♟♟♟	5*
● A. A. Lagrein Scuro Ris. '97	♟♟♟	5
● A. A. Lagrein Scuro Ris. '01	♟♟	5
● A. A. Lagrein Scuro '05	♟♟	4*
● A. A. Santa Maddalena Cl. '05	♟♟	4*
● A. A. Merlot Ris. '03	♟♟	5
● A. A. Merlot Ris. '02	♟♟	5
● A. A. Lagrein Scuro Ris. '02	♟♟	5

○ A. A. Valle Venosta		
Riesling Windbichel '05	♟♟♟	5
○ A. A. Valle Venosta Riesling '06	♟♟	5*
○ A. A. Valle Venosta		
Pinot Bianco '06	♟♟	4*
● A. A. Valle Venosta Pinot Nero '05	♟♟	5
● Juval Gneis '06	♟	4
○ A. A. Valle Venosta Riesling '00	♟♟♟	4
○ A. A. Valle Venosta Riesling '03	♟♟♟	5*
○ A. A. Valle Venosta Riesling '04	♟♟♟	5*
○ A. A. Valle Venosta Riesling '01	♟♟	4*
○ A. A. Valle Venosta Riesling '05	♟♟	5*
○ A. A. Valle Venosta Riesling '02	♟♟	5
○ A. A. Valle Venosta Pinot Bianco '04	♟♟	4*
○ A. A. Valle Venosta Pinot Bianco '05	♟♟	4*
○ A. A. Valle Venosta		
Riesling Windbichel '04	♟♟	5
● A. A. Valle Venosta Pinot Nero '04	♟♟	5

Cantina Produttori Valle Isarco
VIA COSTE, 50
39043 CHIUSA/KLAUSEN [BZ]
TEL. 0472847553
www.cantinavalleisarco.it

Vivaldi - Arunda
VIA PAESE, 53
39010 MELTINA/MÖLTEN [BZ]
TEL. 0471668033
www.arundavivaldi.it

ANNUAL PRODUCTION 700,000 bottles
HECTARES UNDER VINE 130
VITICULTURE METHOD Conventional

ANNUAL PRODUCTION 75,000 bottles
HECTARES UNDER VINE N.A.
VITICULTURE METHOD Conventional

Kellermeister Thomas Dorfmann is a man of few words but plenty of action. He lived up to his reputation again this time by giving us an impressively good series of wines. There was no Three Glass prize but Thomas came close with his Riesling Aristos '06, which shows concentrated, austere and mineral, with great dynamism. Only the slightly bitterish finish stopped it winning our top prize. The three other wines in our finals were just as good: Veltliner, Sylvaner and a surprising Gewürztraminer, all 2006, and all from the Aristos line. These are wines with great character, a tad austere in their youth perhaps, as is the estate style, but from scrupulously tended vineyards and made with an eye to quality. We should add that special something called Valle Isarco, which Thomas knows exactly how to interpret. It should also be remembered that the estate is rightly famous for its basic wines, which have always been very good and sold at affordable prices in a zone where, with one or two commendable exceptions, price tags have been over-ambitious for some time.

Joseph Reiterer is one of the most enthusiastic specialists in the sector and for years has been a benchmark for makers of sparkling wine in Alto Adige. In tandem with his wife Marianna, he manages this winery located in Meltina at 1,200 metres above sea level, which makes it one of the highest sparkling wineries in Europe, if not the world. Arunda, or Vivaldi, depending whether the product is for the German or Italian-speaking market, produces many cuvées with an increasingly high percentage of chardonnay where they are actual blanc de blancs. Long periods on the lees give these sparklers their distinctive finesse and subtle elegance. The ever-excellent Extra Brut Cuvée Marianna shows classic florality and crusty bread aromas. The savoury palate expands crisply into an elegant finish. The Extra Brut Riserva '03, a cuvée of chardonnay and pinot nero, is also interesting. It offers a delicate nose featuring fruity, floral notes and minerally nuances. The lean, stylish palate finishes long and clear.

○ A. A. Valle Isarco Gewürztraminer Aristos '06	♟♟	5
○ A. A. Valle Isarco Sylvaner Aristos '06	♟♟	4*
○ A. A. Valle Isarco Veltliner Aristos '06	♟♟	4*
○ A. A. Valle Isarco Riesling Aristos '06	♟♟	4*
○ A. A. Sauvignon Aristos '06	♟♟	4
○ A. A. Valle Isarco Kerner Aristos '06	♟♟	4*
○ A. A. Valle Isarco Müller Thurgau Aristos '06	♟♟	4*
○ A. A. Valle Isarco Kerner Passito Nectaris '05	♟♟	7
○ A. A. Valle Isarco Sylvaner '06	♟♟	3*
○ A. A. Valle Isarco Pinot Grigio Aristos '06	♟♟	4*
● A. A. Valle Isarco Klausener Laitacher '06	♟♟	4*
○ A. A. Valle Isarco Gewürztraminer Passito Nectaris '05	♟♟	7
○ A. A. Valle Isarco Kerner '06	♟♟	4*
○ A. A. Valle Isarco Kerner Aristos '05	♟♟♟	4*
○ A. A. Valle Isarco Veltliner Aristos '03	♟♟♟	4*
○ A. A. Valle Isarco Gewürztraminer Aristos '05	♟♟	5

○ A. A. Spumante Extra Brut Cuvée Marianna	♟♟	6
○ A. A. Spumante Extra Brut Arunda Ris. '03	♟♟	6
⊙ A. A. Brut Rosé Arunda	♟♟	5
○ A. A. Spumante Blanc de Blancs Arunda	♟	6
○ A. A. Spumante Extra Brut Arunda Ris. '98	♟♟	6
○ A. A. Spumante Brut Vivaldi '99	♟♟	4

Tenuta Waldgries
Christian Plattner

LOC. SANTA GIUSTINA, 2
39100 BOLZANO/BOZEN
TEL. 0471323603
www.waldgries.it

Peter Zemmer

S.DA DEL VINO, 24
39040 CORTINA/KURTINIG [BZ]
TEL. 0471817143
www.zemmer.com

ANNUAL PRODUCTION 50,000 bottles
HECTARES UNDER VINE 5
VITICULTURE METHOD Natural

We remain firmly convinced young Christian Plattner is one of the greatest interpreters of Alto Adige's most famous red wine, Lagrein. We say this for various reasons, starting with the fact his wines have rare character, good stylistic definition and above all a rooted sense of place. Christian's splendid, old farm is located on the hill of Santa Maddalena and he manages the vineyards with skill and attention, meticulously focusing on natural techniques. The only problem we feel should be mentioned, one that kept Waldgries from winning Three Glasses this year, is that the showcase Lagreins are released too soon and are still too marked by new oak. This is a pity since the structure and character that show in wines like the Lagrein Riserva '05 or Lagrein Mirell '04 are unique and would be perfect with less intrusive oak. After this affectionate tug of the ear, we underline that the Santa Maddalena '06 is, as always, one of the best from the vintage. Christian also knows how to make good whites. His Sauvignon '06 is simply splendid.

ANNUAL PRODUCTION 600,000 bottles
HECTARES UNDER VINE 65
VITICULTURE METHOD Conventional

Standards of quality at Helmuth and Günther Zemmer's estate have been better than just good for several years now. In a region like Alto Adige, where competition is tough, it is not always easy to hold onto a position at the top. This is even more the case in our Guide where the space stays the same while the number of wineries grows every year. In particular, this estate's interpretation of Chardonnay is regularly among the best in the region. This year, however, the wine that convinced us most was the splendid Lagrein Riserva '05, made from grapes grown at Ora. An intense bouquet precedes a palate that surprises with the integrity of its fruit, accompanied by sweet tannins and well-gauged acidity. The finish is fragrant and complex. This austere Lagrein shows a balanced use of oak but there is still room for improvement. The convincing Chardonnay '06 is minerally and gutsy. We should mention that prices are reasonable, something that is increasingly rare even in Alto Adige.

● A. A. Lagrein Scuro Ris. '05	ŢŢ	6
○ A. A. Sauvignon '06	ŢŢ	4*
● A. A. Santa Maddalena Cl. '06	ŢŢ	4*
● A. A. Moscato Rosa '05	ŢŢ	6
● A. A. Lagrein '06	ŢŢ	4
● A. A. Lagrein Scuro Mirell '04	ŢŢ	7
● A. A. Cabernet Sauvignon '99	ŢŢŢ	6
● A. A. Lagrein Scuro Mirell '01	ŢŢŢ	7
● A. A. Lagrein Scuro Mirell '02	ŢŢ	7
● A. A. Lagrein Scuro Ris. '01	ŢŢ	6
● A. A. Santa Maddalena Cl. '05	ŢŢ	4*
● A. A. Lagrein Scuro Ris. '03	ŢŢ	6
● A. A. Lagrein Scuro Mirell '03	ŢŢ	7
● A. A. Cabernet Sauvignon Laurenz '04	ŢŢ	6
● A. A. Lagrein Scuro Ris. '04	ŢŢ	6

● A. A. Lagrein Reserve '05	ŢŢ	4*
○ A. A. Chardonnay '06	ŢŢ	4*
○ A. A. Pinot Bianco La Lot '06	ŢŢ	4*
○ A. A. Pinot Grigio '06	ŢŢ	4*
○ Cortinie Bianco '06	ŢŢ	4
● Cortinie Rosso '05	ŢŢ	5
● A. A. Lagrein Reserve '03	ŢŢ	5
○ A. A. Pinot Bianco La Lot '05	ŢŢ	4*
● Cortinie Rosso '02	ŢŢ	5
○ A. A. Pinot Grigio '05	ŢŢ	4

OTHER WINERIES

Baron Di Pauli

VIA CANTINE, 12
39052 CALDARO/KALTERN [BZ]
TEL. 0471963696
www.barondipauli.com

This gem of a winery is now ready for promotion to a full entry. The results are there for all to see: three out of four wines in the finals is a compelling calling card. We also have no doubt that Helmut Zozin is heading down the right road.

● A. A. Arzio Merlot Cabernet '05	🍷🍷 7
○ Enosi '06	🍷🍷 5
● A. A. Kalkofen Kalterersee Cl. Sup. '06	🍷🍷 4*
○ A. A. Gewürztraminer Exilissi '05	🍷🍷 7

Bessererhof - Otmar Mair

NOVALE DI PRESULE, 10
39050 FIÈ ALLO SCILIAR/VÖLS AM SCHLERN [BZ]
TEL. 0471601011
www.bessererhof.it

Otmar Mair's estate at Novale di Presule made a good showing, having entered the Guide last year with 30,000 bottles from ten hectares under vine. Kudos this year goes to a delicious Schiava Fhelt '06 and a minerally, vibrantly juicy Pinot Bianco '06.

○ A. A. Pinot Bianco '06	🍷🍷 4*
● A. A. Schiava Fehlt '06	🍷🍷 3*
○ A. A. Moscato Bianco '06	🍷 4
● Zweigelt Roan '04	🍷 5

Braunbach

LOC. SETTEQUERCE
VIA PADRE ROMEDIUS, 5
39018 TERLANO/TERLAN [BZ]
TEL. 0471910184
www.braunbach.it

Surrounded by well-tended vines, Maso Braunbach is located on the slopes of San Genesio in the heart of the classic Santa Maddalena zone. Our tasting results ran hot and cold. The best products include the Lagrein Calldiv '05 and Spumante Brut '03.

● A. A. Lagrein Scuro Calldiv '05	🍷🍷 4
○ A. A. Spumante Von Braunbach Brut '03	🍷🍷 5
○ A. A. Gewürztraminer Calldiv '06	🍷 4

Brunnenhof - Kurt Rottensteiner

LOC. MAZZON
VIA DEGLI ALPINI, 5
39044 EGNA/NEUMARKT [BZ]
TEL. 0471820687
www.brunnenhof-mazzon.it

Our money is on this estate. A serious, meticulous producer, Kurt Rottensteiner works his small estate – only five hectares for 20,000 bottles – near Mazzon. His Pinot Nero Riserva '05 is one of the best of the vintage. The Gewürztraminer '06 shows surprising character but is still too young.

● A. A. Pinot Nero Ris. '05	🍷🍷 6
○ A. A. Gewürztraminer '06	🍷🍷 5

Castelfeder

VIA PORTICI, 11
39044 EGNA/NEUMARKT [BZ]
TEL. 0471820420
www.castelfeder.it

This dependable Egna estate, which turns out some 400,000 bottles a year, made a more than interesting debut. The wines submitted were technically impeccable with a special mention for the Pinot Nero Burgum Novum Riserva '04 and the particularly elegant, varietal Pinot Bianco '06.

● A. A. Cabernet Burgum Novum Ris. '04	🍷🍷 5
● A. A. Lagrein Burgum Novum Ris. '03	🍷🍷 5
● A. A. Pinot Nero Burgum Novum Ris. '04	🍷🍷 6
○ A. A. Pinot Bianco '06	🍷🍷 4*

Ebnerhof - Johannes Plattner

FRAZ. CARDANO - LOC. RENON
LASTE BASSE, 21
39053 BOLZANO/BOZEN
TEL. 0471365120
www.ebnerhof.it

Wines from the small Plattner organic estate are gaining cult status. Johannes makes products that are well typed and forthright and at the same time technically well made. The Santa Maddalena is as sumptuous as ever and the Sauvignon delicious. Both are from 2006 and sold at old-fashioned prices.

● A. A. Santa Maddalena '06	🍷🍷 4*
○ A. A. Sauvignon '06	🍷🍷 4*
● Merleum '04	🍷🍷 6

OTHER WINERIES

Egger-Ramer
VIA GUNCINA, 5
39100 BOLZANO/BOZEN
TEL. 0471280541
www.egger-ramer.com

Only reasons of space keep the Egger brothers' lovely estate from entering the main section of the Guide. But these wines' quality is constantly improving and two of them deservedly reached our finals. Praise goes to the Lagrein Tenuta Kristan Riserva '04 for its typicity and harmony.

- ● A. A. Lagrein Gries Tenuta Kristan Ris. '04 🍷🍷 5
- ● A. A. Santa Maddalena Cl. Reiseggerhof '06 🍷🍷 4*
- ○ A. A. Valle Isarco Müller Thurgau '06 🍷🍷 4*
- ● A. A. Lagrein Scuro Gries Kristan '06 🍷 4

Gottardi
LOC. MAZZON
VIA DEGLI ALPINI, 17
39044 EGNA/NEUMARKT [BZ]
TEL. 0471812773
www.gottardi-mazzon.com

Nine hectares and around 50,000 bottles are the numbers from an estate venerated by connoisseurs of Alto Adige Pinot Nero. Sadly, these great wines are almost unobtainable even in Bolzano. The Riserva '03 shows surprising freshness and the basic '05 is supremely drinkable.

- ● A. A. Pinot Nero Ris. '03 🍷🍷 7
- ● A. A. Pinot Nero '05 🍷🍷 6

Istituto Tecnico Agrario Ora
VIA DEL CASTELLO, 10
39040 ORA/AUER [BZ]
TEL. 0471810538
www.ofl-auer.it

Affiliated to the provincial agricultural institute in Ora/Auer, this small, organic estate produces around 20,000 bottles a year. The range of wines this time is convincing for technical correctness and typicity, beginning with the Chardonnay '06 and Merlot '05.

- ○ A. A. Chardonnay '06 🍷🍷 4
- ● A. A. Lagrein Ris. Bioland '04 🍷🍷 4
- ● A. A. Merlot '05 🍷🍷 4*
- ○ A. A. Chardonnay Passito Aurum '05 🍷 6

Kettmeir
VIA DELLE CANTINE, 4
39052 CALDARO/KALTERN [BZ]
TEL. 0471963135
www.kettmeir.com

Owned by the Marzotto/Santa Margherita group, Kettmeir at Caldaro is one of the best – and best-known – wineries in Alto Adige. The remarkable range of wines submitted this year features an estate classic, the Pinot Nero Maso Reiner '04, alongside a splendid Pinot Bianco '06.

- ○ A. A. Müller Thurgau '06 🍷🍷 4
- ○ A. A. Sauvignon '06 🍷🍷 4
- ● A. A. Pinot Nero Maso Reiner '04 🍷🍷 5*
- ○ A. A. Pinot Bianco '06 🍷🍷 4*

Tenuta Klosterhof
Oskar Andergassen
LOC. CLAVENZ, 40
39052 CALDARO/KALTERN [BZ]
TEL. 0471961046
ww.garni-klosterhof.com

Klosterhof is back with a bang. Its great Pinot Nero Panigl '04 won a spot at our finals. As if this were not enough, a whole series of excellent wines came from this small Caldaro winery with little more than two hectares under vine yielding around 20,000 bottles each year.

- ● A. A. Pinot Nero Panigl '04 🍷🍷 6
- ● A. A. Pinot Nero Ris. '04 🍷🍷 6
- ○ A. A. Moscato Giallo '06 🍷 4

Köfelgut - Martin Pohl
RIONE AI TRE CANTI, 12
39020 CASTELBELLO CIARDES
KASTELBELL TSCHARS [BZ]
TEL. 0473624634
info@koefelgut.com

Valle Venosta is becoming a destination for connoisseurs of out of the ordinary wines. Köfelgut is reliable even though they produce very few bottles. The Pinot Bianco and Riesling '06 should not be missed and the Gewürztraminer '06 has rare dynamism. Martin Pohl's wines are never boring.

- ○ A. A. Valle Venosta Gewürztraminer '06 🍷🍷 5
- ○ A. A. Valle Venosta Pinot Bianco '06 🍷🍷 4*
- ○ A. A. Valle Venosta Riesling '06 🍷🍷 4*

OTHER WINERIES

Kupelwieser
S.DA DEL VINO, 24
39040 CORTINA/KURTINIG [BZ]
TEL. 0471809240
www.kupelwieser.it

This Cortina estate is a guarantee of quality, with ten hectares under vine and an annual production of around 80,000 bottles sold at fair prices. Outstanding wines include a fragrant Chardonnay '06 and the usual Lagrein Intenditore '05, the estate's long-standing warhorse.

○ A. A. Chardonnay '06	♥♥ 4*
○ A. A. Pinot Bianco '06	♥♥ 4*
● A. A. Lagrein Intenditore '05	♥♥ 5
○ A. A. Pinot Grigio '06	♥ 4

Hartmann Lentsch
VIA NAZIONALE, 71
39051 BRONZOLO/BRANZOOL [BZ]
TEL. 0471596017
weingut_lentsch@dnet.it

This reliable estate in Bassa Atesina confirmed last year's great performance. Kudos goes to a solid Cabernet Riserva '03 that showed concentrated and powerful but with supporting freshness and clear depth. The Moscato Giallo Muskatell '06 is one of the best of its type.

○ A. A. Moscato Giallo Muskatell '06	♥♥ 4*
● A. A. Cabernet Ris. '03	♥♥ 4*
● A. A. Lagrein Morus '03	♥ 5
● A. A. Merlot Ris. '03	♥ 4

Lieselehof - Werner Morandell
VIA KARDATSCH, 6
39052 CALDARO/KALTERN [BZ]
TEL. 0471965060
www.lieselehof.com

The small Liesele estate at Caldaro turns out roughly 10,000 good bottles from two hectares, organically managed by Werner Morandell. Werner plants with rare varieties at high altitudes and the nice Sweet Claire passito is from the rare bronner grape. The whole range has character and typicity.

● A. A. Lago di Caldaro Amadeus '06	♥♥ 4*
● Maximilian '04	♥♥ 5
○ Sweet Claire '05	♥♥ 6
○ Julian '06	♥ 5

K. Martini & Sohn
LOC. CORNAIANO/GIRLAN
VIA LAMM, 28
39050 APPIANO/EPPAN [BZ]
TEL. 0471663156
www.martini-sohn.it

Karl Martini and his son Gabriel always produce good wines, releasing around 350,000 bottles a year from 30 rented and owned hectares. The Sauvignon Palladium '06, Lagrein Cabernet Coldirus '05 and Pinot Bianco Palladium '06 are particularly interesting. They just lack a little personality.

○ A. A. Pinot Bianco Palladium '06	♥♥ 4*
● A. A. Lago di Caldaro Cl. Felton '06	♥♥ 3*
○ A. A. Sauvignon Palladium '06	♥♥ 4*
⊙ A. A. Lagrein Cabernet Coldirus Palladium '05	♥♥ 4

Messnerhof - Bernhard Pichler
LOC. SAN PIETRO, 7
39100 BOLZANO/BOZEN
TEL. 0471977162
www.messnerhof.net

Likeable Bernard Pichler has a very small estate, but we feel his wines are improving from year to year. Classic wines from the Bolzano zone are in the spotlight here. The fragrant Lagrein Riserva '05 is still too young and the Santa Maddalena '06 is nice and juicy.

● A. A. Lagrein Ris. '05	♥♥ 4
● A. A. Santa Maddalena '06	♥♥ 4*
● Belleus '05	♥♥ 5

Milla - Gert Pomella
VIA MILLA, 3
39040 CORTACCIA/KURTATSCH [BZ]
TEL. 0471880676
gert.pomella@aadon.it

With three hectares of vineyard and production of around 22,000 bottles a year, this Cortaccia estate produces only one wine, Milla Laiten '04, from 55 per cent cabernet franc, ten per cent cabernet sauvignon and the rest merlot. It's fresh, juicy and has plenty of thrust.

● A. A. Merlot Cabernet Milla Laiten '04	♥♥ 5

OTHER WINERIES

Ignaz Niedrist
LOC. CORNAIANO/GIRLAN
VIA RONCO, 5
39050 APPIANO/EPPAN [BZ]
TEL. 0471664494
ignazniedrist@rdmail.net

Ignaz Niedrist is one of the most serious, reliable producers in the entire province of Bolzano and one who looks for balance and elegance in his wines. Truth to tell, we find them a bit too simple this year. They're well enough made but we expect a bit more personality from someone like Ignaz.

● A. A. Lagrein Berger Gei '05	🍷🍷 5
● A. A. Pinot Nero '05	🍷🍷 5
○ A. A. Terlano Sauvignon '06	🍷🍷 5
○ Bianco '06	🍷🍷 4

Obermoser - H. & T. Rottensteiner
FRAZ. RENCIO
VIA SANTA MADDALENA, 35
39100 BOLZANO/BOZEN
TEL. 0471973549
www.obermoser.it

Heinrich Rottensteiner and his son Thomas have had a bit of an interim growing year at their estate. These wines come from the Santa Maddalena Classico zone. The product of the same name from the '06 vintage stood out for its uncommon minerality and pressure.

● A. A. Santa Maddalena Cl. '06	🍷🍷 4*
● A. A. Lagrein '06	🍷 4
● A. A. Lagrein Grafenleiten Ris. '05	🍷 5

Oberrautner - Anton Schmid
FRAZ. GRIES
VIA M. PACHER, 3
39100 BOLZANO/BOZEN
TEL. 0471281440
www.schmid.bz

Schmid Oberrautner is a classic, family-run, Alto Adige estate in Gries on the edge of Bolzano. Andreas Schmid works alongside his son Florian. These are straightforward, well-made wines at good prices, starting with the nice, zesty Pinot Bianco '06 and the robust Lagrein Riserva Oro '04.

○ A. A. Pinot Bianco '06	🍷🍷 4*
● A. A. Lagrein Scuro Grieser Oro Ris. '04	🍷🍷 5
● A. A. Pinot Nero '05	🍷🍷 5
● A. A. Santa Maddalena Steinbauer '06	🍷 3

Tenuta Pfitscherhof Klaus Pfitscher
VIA GLENO, 9
39040 MONTAGNA/MONTAN [BZ]
TEL. 0471819773
www.pfitscher.it

Our compliments go to Klaus Pfitscher for his best performance ever. In fact, he's in the Other Wineries section merely for reasons of space. The delicious Pinor Nero Matan '04 showed well in our finals. But then every bottle from his small production is better than just good.

● A. A. Pinot Nero Matan '04	🍷🍷 5
● Cortazo '04	🍷🍷 5
● A. A. Lagrein Kotznloater '05	🍷🍷 5
● A. A. Pinot Nero '05	🍷🍷 5

Thomas Pichler
VIA DELLE VIGNE, 4
39052 CALDARO/KALTERN [BZ]
TEL. 0471963094
pichler.thomas@dnet.it

This tiny estate at Caldaro has less than a hectare of vineyard and only produces around 7,000 bottles. But what great wines! From the Chardonnay Untermazzon '06 to the Lago di Caldaro '06 and Lagrein Sand Riserva '05, all are well typed and technically impeccable.

● A. A. Lagrein Sand Ris. '05	🍷🍷 5
○ A. A. Chardonnay Untermazzon '06	🍷🍷 4*
● A. A. Lago di Caldaro Aruum '06	🍷🍷 4*

Pralatenhof - Roland Rohregger
PIANIZZA DI SOTTO, 15/A
39052 CALDARO/KALTERN [BZ]
TEL. 0471962541
www.paelatenhof.it

This small but experienced winery is managed by talented Roland Rohregger and produces 15,000 bottles from 2.5 hectares under vine at Pianizza di Sotto, a village near Caldaro. The Pinot Grigio '06 is excellent and deservedly made it to the finals for its great typicity and elegance.

○ A. A. Pinot Grigio '06	🍷🍷 4*
● A. A. Lago Di Caldaro '06	🍷🍷 3*

OTHER WINERIES

Castello Rametz
LOC. MAIA ALTA
VIA LABERS, 4
39012 MERANO/MERAN [BZ]
TEL. 0473211011
www.rametz.com

Stanislaus Schmid's estate at Merano put on an even more convincing performance than last year's, a sign that the owner has decided to make changes in estate management. Particularly well made wines include the fresh yet solidly built Chardonnay and the Riesling, both from the 2006 vintage.

O A. A. Chardonnay '06	🍷🍷 4*
O A. A. Riesling '06	🍷🍷 4
● A. A. Pinot Nero '04	🍷🍷 6
O Cèsuret '04	🍷 6

Röckhof - Konrad Augschöll
VIA SAN VALENTINO, 9
39040 VILLANDRO/VILLANDERS [BZ]
TEL. 0472847130

Konrad Augschöll's long-established Röckhof estate near Villandres in Valle Isarco generally submits one of the most interesting Müller Thurgaus from all Alto Adige. It did so again this time but added the surprise of an elegant, concentrated Riesling '06 in perfect Valle Isarco style.

O A. A. Valle Isarco Müller Thurgau '06	🍷🍷 4
O A. A. Valle Isarco Riesling '06	🍷🍷 4*
O Caruess '06	🍷 4

Castello Schwanburg
VIA SCHWANBURG, 16
39010 NALLES/NALS [BZ]
TEL. 0471678622
www.schwanburg.com

It is with great regret we find ourselves forced to demoted this historic estate to the Other Wineries section. Over the past few years, we have noticed a certain lack of clarity in the cellar's wines. The range this year includes some sound products but we expect the best from an estate like this.

● A. A. Lagrein Scuro Ris. '04	🍷🍷 5
O A. A. Pinot Bianco Pitzon '06	🍷🍷 4*
● A. A. Santa Maddalena Lunhof '06	🍷🍷 4*
● A. A. Merlot - Cabernet Sauvigon Geierberg '04	🍷🍷 6

Sebastian Stocker
VIA CHIESA, 62
39018 TERLANO/TERLAN [BZ]
TEL. 0471256032

Sebastian Stocker is a cult figure in Alto Adige. This passionate maker of sparkling wines produces a small – too small – amount of spumante classico. His Extra Brut Riserva '00, from chardonnay, sauvignon and pinot bianco, has intense, elegant aromas, showing structure and harmony on the palate.

O A. A. Spumante Stocker Extra Brut Ris. '00	🍷🍷 6

Strasserhof - Hannes Baumgartner
FRAZ. NOVACELLA
UNTERRAIN, 8
39040 VARNA/VAHRN [BZ]
TEL. 0472830804
www.strasserhof.info

One of the oldest estates in Valle Isarco, with the most northerly vineyards in the province of Bolzano, Strasserhof is also one of the most exciting. Young Hannes Baumgartner submitted a series of really impressive wines, beginning with the classic Kerner and Sylvaner from the 2006 vintage.

O A. A. Valle Isarco Kerner '06	🍷🍷 4*
O A. A. Valle Isarco Sylvaner '06	🍷🍷 4*
O A. A. Valle Isarco Müller Thurgau '06	🍷🍷 4
O A. A. Valle Isarco Gewürztraminer '06	🍷 4

Karl Vonklausner
VIA CASTELLANO, 30/A
39042 BRESSANONE/BRIXEN [BZ]
TEL. 0472833700
www.vonklausner.it

Christian Vonklausner's small estate in Valle Isarco has two hectares under vine on the northern outskirts of Bressanone and makes its entry into the Guide thanks to a series of wines that are at last convincing. The Sylvaner and Kerner, both from the 2006 vintage, were particularly intriguing.

O A.A. Sylvaner '06	🍷🍷 4*
O A.A. Kerner '06	🍷🍷 4*
O A.A. Müller Thurgau '06	🍷🍷 4*

OTHER WINERIES

Wilhelm Walch
VIA A. HOFER, 1
39040 TERMENO/TRAMIN [BZ]
TEL. 0471860103
www.walch.it

Wines from the Walch estate, managed by Elena Walch's husband, at Termeno are bankers. The 600,000 bottles produced are also sold at extremely competitive prices. Among the best are the Schiava Grigia Plattensteig '06, a real delight, and the Pinot Grigio Marat '06.

● A. A. Cabernet-Merlot Jeras '04	🍷🍷 5
● A. A. Schiava Plattensteig '06	🍷🍷 4*
○ A. A. Pinot Grigio Marat '06	🍷🍷 4*
○ A. A. Gewürztraminer '06	🍷 4

Alois Warasin
LOC. CORNAIANO/GIRLAN
VIA COLTERENZIO, 1
39047 APPIANO/EPPAN [BZ]
TEL. 0471662462
weine.a.warasin@rolmail.net

With four hectares and 10,000 bottles produced, this small estate at Cornaiano showed even further improvement. Among the best from the 2006 vintage, the Sauvignon is complex with citrus-like notes and a broad, minerally palate. There are also other extremely sound wines.

○ A.A. Sauvignon '06	🍷🍷 3*
● A.A. Pinot Nero '04	🍷🍷 4
○ A.A. Pinot Bianco '06	🍷 3*

Josef Weger
LOC. CORNAIANO
VIA CASA DEL GESÙ, 17
39050 APPIANO/EPPAN [BZ]
TEL. 0471662416
www.wegerhof.it

The historic, 80,000-bottle Weger estate at Cornaiano enters the Guide with a series of convincing wines. The best is the dried-grape passito Rodon Maso delle Rose '06, from gewürztraminer, sauvignon, pinot bianco and grigio, which made it to our finals. The rest of the range is more than reliable.

○ Rodon '06	🍷🍷 6
● A. A. Pinot Nero '05	🍷🍷 4*
● Joanni '03	🍷🍷 5
● A. A. Lagrein '05	🍷 4

Zohlhof Josef Michael Unterfrauner
ZOHLHOF, 60
39040 VELTURNO/FELDTHUNRNS [BZ]
TEL. 0472847400
www.zoehlhof.it

Josef Michael Unterfrauner manages less than two hectares of organically managed vineyards in Valle Isarco. The more convincing of the two wines submitted, the Gewürztraminer '06, shows confident aromas of elderflower, aromatic herbs and even liquorice, and then a concentrated, almost salty palate.

○ A.A. Gewürztraminer '06	🍷🍷 4*

VENETO

If we had to summarize Veneto winemaking in a word, we would probably choose "maturity". But it has not come about overnight. No, maturity is the destination of a journey that began a long time ago, when the producers in this fertile region were still debating whether to pursue higher quality or continue making simple wines to satisfy the insatiable demand of the home market. The solution was a compromise that was barely profitable until about ten years ago but has now made Veneto one of Italy's most forward-looking wine regions. The key was the pursuit of quality without neglecting aspects like lightness and drinkability. Today's excellent haul of Three Glass awards is just the tip of the iceberg for underneath the surface are numerous top quality wines that combine territory with tradition, native grapes with international varieties and oak with stainless steel, spicing the offering with good value for money. There many new developments this year, both among the Three Glass wineries and concerning the trends across the region. Soave is still making progress, hot on the heels of Valpolicella thanks to an excellent vintage and ongoing improvements in agricultural and winery management. These are the factors that have at last brought Monte Tondo and Tenuta Sant'Antonio into the limelight: the latter is no stranger to our award but this is the first time it has won with a Soave, a memorable version of the Monte Ceriani. Cavalchina turned in another excellent performance while in eastern Veneto we must mention the rise of the Colli Euganei, a zone that has new entries in the Guide, in the finals and among the Three Glass winners, particularly the affirmation of Ca' Orologio, which was also nominated Up-and-Coming Winery of the Year, and first-time winner Ca' Lustra with a great Merlot. Along the foothills, the lion's share goes, as usual, to Maculan, Due Santi and Serafini & Vidotto. All these wineries work with international grape varieties but still beautifully express their respective terroirs. Lastly, Valpolicella is still queen of the region with ten awards. Hereabouts, Amarone reacted much better than other wine types to the difficult 2003 vintage, thanks to flavour profiles that comfortably tuck in the edginess of the extract. Lining up with the big names for the first time are the Campedelli family, whose Amarone earned Marion its first Three Glasses, Guerrieri Rizzardi with another fine performance, the return of Accordini, and Brigaldara and Masi showing evidence of seriously good estate management. There was a particularly fine performance from Bertani's Amarone and we also note the reliability of Allegrini, which has been delivering quality for many years, and Begali, a Three Glass winner for its Amarone Classico.

Stefano Accordini

FRAZ. PEDEMONTE
VIA ALBERTO BOLLA, 9
37020 SAN PIETRO IN CARIANO [VR]
TEL. 04537029
www.accordinistefano.it

ANNUAL PRODUCTION   40,000 bottles
HECTARES UNDER VINE   11
VITICULTURE METHOD   Conventional

Accordini's place on the Valpolicella winemaking scene is becoming increasingly well defined. The fact that his son Giacomo has begun working in the winery, mainly in the vineyards, and the fine quality of the grapes from the newer vineyards at about 400 metres above sea level in Mazzurega and Cavalo, enable Tiziano to focus on production. The results are absolutely outstanding, as is demonstrated by the Three Glasses awarded to the Recioto Acinatico, which is powerful, sweet, very modern in style and elegantly sophisticated. The two Amarones were also extremely impressive. The Fornetto 2001 is profound, richly extracted and slow to unfold while the Acinatico 2003 has fresh florality and minerally aromas that introduce a generally approachable palate. Passo, a local variation on Bordeaux blending, is has weight, generosity and depth whereas the Valpolicella Ripasso is more traditional in style but supremely drinkable.

Adami

FRAZ. COLBERTALDO
VIA ROVEDE, 27
31020 VIDOR [TV]
TEL. 0423982110
www.adamispumanti.it

ANNUAL PRODUCTION   520,000 bottles
HECTARES UNDER VINE   N.A.
VITICULTURE METHOD   Conventional

Wines from Adami are a benchmark for the whole area. Their reliable high quality leaves no room for surprises. This absolute dependability is rooted in total harmony with the land and profound technical knowledge that avoids altering the nature of the prosecco grape and instead brings out its true nature. As usual, the Dry Giardino is one of the best versions of the type we tasted. The generous, fruity swath of aromas is outstandingly delicate and clean, ushering in a succulent palate with fine, creamy fizz. The usual fruity aromas are accompanied by floral sensations in the Cartizze before the palate shows taut progression with nicely integrated sweetness. The Brut Bosco di Gica and Extra Dry dei Casel are not far behind previous pair, which are the cellar's prestige products, both giving the same generous, sophisticated aromas and an equally rich palate.

● Recioto della Valpolicella Cl. Acinatico '04	♟♟♟ 7
● Amarone della Valpolicella Cl. Acinatico '03	♟♟ 8
● Amarone della Valpolicella Cl. Vign. Il Fornetto '01	♟♟ 8
● Passo Rosso '05	♟♟ 6
● Valpolicella Cl. Sup. Ripasso Acinatico '05	♟♟ 5
● Valpolicella Cl. '06	♟ 4
● Amarone della Valpolicella Cl. Vign. Il Fornetto '95	♟♟♟ 8
● Amarone della Valpolicella Cl. Vign. Il Fornetto '93	♟♟♟ 8
● Recioto della Valpolicella Cl. Acinatico '00	♟♟♟ 7
● Amarone della Valpolicella Vign. Il Fornetto '00	♟♟ 8

○ P. di Valdobbiadene Dry Vign. Giardino '06	♟♟ 4*
○ P. di Valdobbiadene Bosco di Gica Brut	♟♟ 4
○ P. di Valdobbiadene Extra Dry dei Casel	♟♟ 4
○ Cartizze Dry	♟♟ 5
○ P. di Valdobbiadene Tranquillo Giardino '06	♟ 4
○ Waldaz Brut Ris.	♟ 4

★★ Allegrini
VIA GIARE, 5
37022 FUMANE [VR]
TEL. 0456832011
www.allegrini.it

Andreola Orsola
LOC. COL SAN MARTINO
VIA CAL LONGA, 52
31010 FARRA DI SOLIGO [TV]
TEL. 0438989379
www.andreolaorsola.it

ANNUAL PRODUCTION 800,000 bottles
HECTARES UNDER VINE 70
VITICULTURE METHOD Conventional

ANNUAL PRODUCTION 350,000 bottles
HECTARES UNDER VINE 20
VITICULTURE METHOD Conventional

The strength of the successful Allegrini lies in its extensive vine stock, with plots in prestigious vineyards like Grola, Poja and Palazzo della Torre. But where would mankind be without ambition and new challenges? So there's an exciting new coming onstream at Cavarena and we'll be tasting its fruits in a few years' time. Meanwhile, this year's curiosity is a white, the bright, gutsy Soave 2006. Having skipped the 2002 vintage, the 2003 Amarone is back on superb form and walked away with Three Glasses for its quite outstanding balance, rare indeed in such a hot growing year. Fines herbes and floral aromas accompany the progression on the palate, which shows great finesse and tannins well tucked in. La Poja 2003 is up to its usual standard, showing ripe, sunny, tight knit and alluring. The Recioto is less approachable than usual, only unbending after several minutes in the glass. Do not be deceived by the poise of the fruit. That initial reticence soon becomes depth, opening into a stylish, silky finish. Lastly, congratulations for the sumptuous La Grola.

The products of Prosecco estates are sometimes limited to a range of sparkling wines which differ only in their residual sugar. But this lovely winery has a much more, and perhaps even excessively, well-stocked range of whites and reds, sparkling, semi-sparkling and still. On tasting, however, the wines are all strikingly well made and very fine expressions of their grapes and wine types. The lion's share, of course, goes to Valdobbiadene's signature grape, vinified here in three versions: a vibrant, mature Dry Millesimato, a floral and exuberantly drinkable Extra Dry and the fragrantly firm-structured Brut. Only just below this trio are Valbone, a light, dry traditional-style red, the uncomplicated, moreish standard-label Cabernet Franc and the Verdiso, a fruity, gutsy white. The Prosecco Passito Pensieri is soft and mouthfilling while the Prosecco Tranquillo and Cartizze are well typed.

● Amarone della Valpolicella Cl. '03	♟♟♟ 8
● Recioto della Valpolicella Cl. Giovanni Allegrini '04	♟♟ 7
● La Poja '03	♟♟ 8
● Palazzo della Torre '04	♟♟ 5
● La Grola '04	♟♟ 5
● Valpolicella Cl. '06	♟♟ 4*
○ Soave '06	♟♟ 4*
● La Poja '01	♟♟♟ 8
● Amarone della Valpolicella Cl. '01	♟♟♟ 8
● Amarone della Valpolicella Cl. '00	♟♟♟ 8
● Amarone della Valpolicella Cl. '98	♟♟♟ 8
● Amarone della Valpolicella Cl. '97	♟♟♟ 8
● Amarone della Valpolicella Cl. '96	♟♟♟ 8
● Amarone della Valpolicella Cl. '95	♟♟♟ 8
● Amarone della Valpolicella Cl. '93	♟♟♟ 8
● Recioto della Valpolicella Cl. Giovanni Allegrini '00	♟♟♟ 6

○ P. di Valdobbiadene Brut Vign. Dirupo	♟♟ 4
○ P. di Valdobbiadene Dry Mill. '06	♟♟ 4
○ P. di Valdobbiadene Extra Dry Vign. Dirupo	♟♟ 4
○ P. di Valdobbiadene Tranquillo Romit	♟ 3
○ P. Passito Pensieri '04	♟ 6
○ Verdiso '06	♟ 3
● Cabernet Franc '06	♟ 3
● Valbone Rosso '04	♟ 4
○ P. di Valdobbiadene Frizzante	4
○ Verdiso Frizzante	4
○ Cartizze	5

★ Roberto Anselmi
VIA SAN CARLO, 46
37032 MONTEFORTE D'ALPONE [VR]
TEL. 0457611488
www.robertoanselmi.com

ANNUAL PRODUCTION 600,000 bottles
HECTARES UNDER VINE 70
VITICULTURE METHOD Conventional

Roberto Anselmi's wines reflect his
character: direct and dynamic yet complex,
as befits a man of such personality. With his
initiatives and ideas that often buck the
trend, Roberto has always striven to make
contribution to the development and
promotion of the local area and the
garganega grape, trying to find the best
interpretation of the fruit in his wines harvest
after harvest. As often happens, the leading
wine, Capitel Croce 2005, still has simple,
youthful aromas that will lead to more
complex sensations after ageing in bottle.
The palate is truly impressive, showing
stylish, dynamic and very subtle. It's an
excellent example of how the garganega
grape can gain appeal and complexity from
its encounter with oak. This wonderful wine
strolled off with Three Glasses. The Capitel
Foscarino 2006 opens slowly, revealing ripe,
almost sweet fruit, nicely offset by
surefooted, gutsy progression. The
seamlessly characterful San Vincenzo 2006
is excellent value for money.

Balestri Valda
VIA MONTI, 44
37038 SOAVE [VR]
TEL. 0457675393
www.vinibalestrivalda.com

ANNUAL PRODUCTION 45,000 bottles
HECTARES UNDER VINE 13
VITICULTURE METHOD Conventional

Following its debut appearance in the Guide
last year, this recently founded winery
consolidated its position. Although Guido
Rizzotto comes from a family connected to
the wine sector – his father was a well-
known local sparkling wine producer – he
has only been seriously growing grapes and
making wine for a few years, with
enthusiastic, invaluable assistance from his
daughter Laura. The results were not long in
coming, thanks to determination, technical
skill and a good dozen or so hectares of
hillside vineyards, all close to the winery. The
Soave Classico, a blend of garganega and
trebbiano di Soave fermented in stainless
steel vats, has a captivatingly rustic
personality, depth and complexity.
Lunalonga, fermented and aged in
barriques, lacks a little finesse but has a
strikingly supple, dynamic palate. Sengialta
is well typed with an attractive floral
fragrance.

O Capitel Croce '05	▼▼▼ 5
O Capitel Foscarino '06	▼▼ 4*
O San Vincenzo '06	▼▼ 4*
O Capitel Croce '04	♀♀♀ 5
O Capitel Croce '03	♀♀♀ 5
O Capitel Croce '02	♀♀♀ 5
O Capitel Croce '01	♀♀♀ 5
O Capitel Croce '00	♀♀♀ 5
O Capitel Croce '99	♀♀♀ 5
O I Capitelli '04	♀♀ 6
O Capitel Foscarino '05	♀♀ 4*
O Capitel Foscarino '04	♀♀ 4
O I Capitelli '03	♀♀ 7
O I Capitelli '02	♀♀ 7

O Soave Cl. '06	▼▼ 4
O Soave Cl. Lunalonga '05	▼▼ 4
O Soave Cl. Sengialta '06	▼ 4
● Scaligio '04	▼ 5
O Soave Cl. '05	♀♀ 3

Lorenzo Begali

VIA CENGIA, 10
37020 SAN PIETRO IN CARIANO [VR]
TEL. 0457725148
www.begaliwine.it

ANNUAL PRODUCTION 60,000 bottles
HECTARES UNDER VINE 8
VITICULTURE METHOD Conventional

The origins of the Begali winery date back to 1943. The first wines were made in 1986 and since 1995 all the wine has been bottled. Today, Lorenzo and his wife Adriana run the operation with their children Giordano and Tiliana. The vineyards are situated in the village of Cengia, at the foot of the Castelrotto hill. The winery's activity is built on the local corvina, corvinone and rondinella grapes, with small but valuable contributions from international varieties. We should say straight away that the long-awaited release of the 2004 Recioto is extraordinary, showing dark, dense, balsamic, floral and generous, a fine expression of Valpolicella's noblest scion. Despite the hot year, the Amarone 2003 is distinctly fresh-tasting and remarkably drinkable, with spices, red berries and good extract that earned it Three Glasses. The Valpolicella Ripasso La Cengia is excellent: a subtle, vibrant wine with hints of raspberries, redcurrants and cherries. The Tigiolo, from corvina, cabernet sauvignon, rondinella and merlot, is very good while the delicious, youthful Valpolicella is exemplary.

Cecilia Beretta

LOC. SAN FELICE EXTRA
VIA BELVEDERE, 135
37131 VERONA
TEL. 0458432101
www.ceciliaberetta.it

ANNUAL PRODUCTION 200,000 bottles
HECTARES UNDER VINE 89
VITICULTURE METHOD Conventional

With almost 90 hectares under vine in the best production zones, competent and motivated staff in the vineyards and cellar and the backing of a very traditional, ambitious family like the Pasquas, results could only be of the calibre that Cecilia Beretta presents every year. In fact recently, the range has grown and the average quality of the wines has improved, making this a benchmark winery for Valpolicella. The flagship bottle is still the now-classic Amarone Terre di Cariano, which is clearly defined and generous on the nose with good texture and length on the palate. The Amarone from the wider area is also very interesting, with simpler but equally satisfying aromas. Of the two Valpolicellas, we preferred the Terre di Cariano, with its taut, sound palate, while the Ripasso is an excellent interpretation of tradition. The uncomplicated but beautifully made Soave performed well and lastly the Recioto and Picàie Bianco were both enjoyable.

● Amarone della Valpolicella Cl. '03	❏❏❏ 7
● Recioto della Valpolicella Cl. '04	❏❏ 7
● Tigiolo '04	❏❏ 6
● Valpolicella Cl. Sup. Ripasso Vign. La Cengia '05	❏❏ 5
● Valpolicella Cl. '06	❏❏ 3*
● Amarone della Valpolicella Cl. Vign. Monte Ca' Bianca '01	❏❏❏ 8
● Amarone della Valpolicella Cl. Vign. Monte Ca' Bianca '00	❏❏❏ 8
● Amarone della Valpolicella Cl. Vign. Monte Ca' Bianca '99	❏❏❏ 8
● Amarone della Valpolicella Cl. Vign. Monte Ca' Bianca '97	❏❏❏ 8
● Recioto della Valpolicella Cl. '00	❏❏❏ 7
● Amarone della Valpolicella Cl. '01	❏❏ 8
● Amarone della Valpolicella Cl. Vign. Monte Ca' Bianca '98	❏❏ 8

● Amarone della Valpolicella Cl. Terre di Cariano '03	❏❏ 8
● Amarone della Valpolicella '03	❏❏ 7
○ Soave Cl. Brognoligo '06	❏❏ 4
● Valpolicella Cl. Sup. Terre di Cariano '04	❏❏ 4*
● Valpolicella Sup. Ripasso '04	❏❏ 4
○ Picàie Bianco '05	❏ 4
○ Recioto di Soave Case Vecie '04	❏ 6
● Amarone della Valpolicella Cl. Terre di Cariano '99	❏❏❏ 7
● Amarone della Valpolicella Cl. Terre di Cariano '01	❏❏ 8
● Valpolicella Cl. Sup. Terre di Cariano '03	❏❏ 4
● Amarone della Valpolicella Cl. Terre di Cariano '00	❏❏ 7

Desiderio Bisol & Figli

FRAZ. SANTO STEFANO
VIA FOLLO, 33
31049 VALDOBBIADENE [TV]
TEL. 0423900138
www.bisol.it

ANNUAL PRODUCTION 650,000 bottles
HECTARES UNDER VINE 65
VITICULTURE METHOD Natural

Bisol confirmed its status as a prestigious winery able to combine the traditional with the contemporary while marrying the contribution of the young to winery and marketing with the experience of the older generations. This talent for integration applies equally well to the production phases directly managed by Bisol, from cultivation of the vineyards, which are particularly extensive in comparison with the average for other local operations, to winery and sparkling winemaking activities. The range of products is well thought-out and made to the usual high standard, starting with the Vigneti del Fol, with its sophisticated aromas of flowers and pear and apple fruit and generous, creamy palate. The Cartizze is subtle, delicate and stylish. Also excellent are the Talento Brut Riserva, with generous fruity aromas and a taut, vibrant palate, and the Duca di Dolle, which combines complexity and style with a balance in the mouth.

F.lli Bolla

P.ZZA CITTADELLA, 3
37122 VERONA
TEL. 0458090911
www.bolla.it

ANNUAL PRODUCTION 15,000,000 bottles
HECTARES UNDER VINE 350
VITICULTURE METHOD Conventional

Much has changed at Bolla, and quickly. While last year's Guide was being printed, the Gruppo Italiano Vini bought the property and this Piazza Cittadella winery is now one of the stars in the Calmasino group's firmament. The new commercial plan has inevitably slowed down presentation of the wines and this year we were unable to taste the more ambitious products. Giampaolo Vaona still runs the winery and the renovation work begun a few years ago still continues. The Amarone 2004 is very good, offering a modern, well-defined expression of ripe, juicy, healthy fruit with huge structure on a palate supported by acidity and adequate tannins. If you consider that hundreds of thousands of bottles are produced of this wine alone, this is an outstanding result. The cool 2005 growing year has endowed Soave Le Maddalene with slender body and light aromas while the Tufaie is uncomplicated and refreshingly drinkable.

O P. di Valdobbiadene Extra Dry	
Vigneti del Fol '06	▼ 5
O P. di Valdobbiadene Dry	
Garney '05	▼▼ 5
O Cartizze '06	▼▼ 6
O P. di Valdobbiadene Brut	
Crede '06	▼▼ 4
O Duca di Dolle Prosecco Passito	▼▼ 7
O P. di Valdobbiadene Dry Salis '06	▼▼ 4
O Talento Brut Ris. '00	▼▼ 6
O P. di Valdobbiadene Brut Jeio '06	▼ 4
O Talento Eliseo Bisol	
Cuvée del Fondatore '00	▼ 7
O P. di Valdobbiadene Extra Dry	
Colmei Jeio '06	▼ 4
O P. di Valdobbiadene	
Tranquillo Molera '06	▼ 4

● Amarone della Valpolicella Cl. '04	▼▼ 7
● Cabernet Sauvignon Creso '01	▼ 6
O Soave Cl. Tufaie '06	▼ 4
● Valpolicella Cl. Sup.	
Le Pojane '04	▼ 5
O Soave Cl. Sup. Le Maddalene '05	▼ 4
● Amarone della Valpolicella Cl.	
Capo di Torbe '03	▼▼ 8
● Valpolicella Cl. Sup.	
Capo di Torbe '03	▼▼ 5
● Amarone della Valpolicella Cl.	
Le Origini '03	▼▼ 7
● Amarone della Valpolicella Cl. '03	▼▼ 7
● Valpolicella Cl. Sup. Capo di Torbe '01	▼▼ 5
● Amarone della Valpolicella Cl.	
Capo di Torbe '01	▼▼ 8
● Amarone della Valpolicella Cl.	
Le Origini '01	▼▼ 8

Cav. G. B. Bertani

VIA ASIAGO, 1
37023 GREZZANA [VR]
TEL. 0458658444
www.bertani.net

La Biancara

FRAZ. SORIO
C.DA BIANCARA, 14
36053 GAMBELLARA [VI]
TEL. 0444444244
www.biancaravini.it

ANNUAL PRODUCTION 2,000,000 bottles
HECTARES UNDER VINE 180
VITICULTURE METHOD Conventional

ANNUAL PRODUCTION 50,000 bottles
HECTARES UNDER VINE 12
VITICULTURE METHOD Natural

Bertani has been part of Valpolicella history since 1857 and has its own distinctively traditional style. It is the very essence of wine, brimming with the finesse, elegance and drinkability that distinguish great wines whatever their provenance. We had proof of this when we tried the fantastically fresh-tasting, appetizing, luscious Recioto 1940 and a Secco Bertani 1953 which is still in excellent shape. They open wonderfully slowly, almost on tiptoe, offering vividly moving, ever-changing sensations. This marvellous overture introduces today's wines with a magical thread of continuity. After six years' ageing in large barrels, the Amarone 2000 has a complex, multi-faceted bouquet of subtle spice and generous fruit. An enthusiastic Three Glasses. Right behind it is the Amarone Valpantena 2003. The Recioto 2005 aged in cherry wood barrels is a wonderful expression of this winery's style but the best of the Valpolicellas is the Ognisanti while an honourable mention goes to the 400,000 bottles of Secco Bertani 2004. The Cabernet Sauvignon Albion is very good. But Bertani is not just about red wines: there are some beautifully made whites, like the delicious, harmonious Soave Sereole.

We can only acknowledge Angiolino Maule's commendable passion and commitment. He is always in the front line defending typicality and the terroir. Nor has he been slow in adopting radical alternative agricultural methods like biodynamic farming. Angiolino's thirst for authenticity has often led him to courageous experimentation, sometimes with very exciting results. All this serves to explain the great esteem in which Angiolino is held, and to focus as accurately as possible the current production situation. Our tasters noted his characterful, spontaneous wines but opinion was divided over some liberties that tend to compromise their finesse. It has to be said that some wines – Pico above all – may regain the lustre of better days through further ageing. Sassaia is very well made and the beautifully drinkable Recioto is excellent while the late-harvested Taibane is rather unapproachable at the moment. From the reds, we liked the minerally Tocai Rosso and the enjoyably rounded Merlot.

● Amarone della Valpolicella Cl. '00	♟♟♟	8
○ Soave Sereole '06	♟♟	4
● Valpolicella Cl. Sup. Vigneto Ognisanti '04	♟♟	5
● Albion Cabernet Sauvignon '04	♟♟	6
● Recioto della Valpolicella Valpantena '05	♟♟	5
● Amarone della Valpolicella Valpantena Villa Arvedi '03	♟♟	7
● Valpolicella Valpantena Secco Bertani '04	♟♟	4
● Valpolicella Cl. Sup. Ripasso '04	♟♟	5*
○ Le Lave '05	♟	4
● Valpolicella Cl. Villa Novare '06	♟	4
● Amarone della Valpolicella Cl. '99	♟♟♟	8
● Amarone della Valpolicella Cl. '98	♟♟♟	8
● Amarone della Valpolicella Cl. '97	♟♟♟	8
● Amarone della Valpolicella Cl. '85	♟♟♟	8

○ Sassaia '06	♟♟	4*
○ Recioto di Gambellara '03	♟♟	6
● Canà Rosso '05	♟♟	4
● Merlot '04	♟♟	5
● Tocai Rosso '05	♟	5
● Masieri Rosso '06	♟	4
○ Masieri Bianco '06	♟	3
○ Taibane V. T. '00	♟	7
○ Pico '02	♟♟♟	4
○ Pico '04	♟♟	5
○ Sassaia '05	♟♟	4
○ Pico '03	♟♟	4
○ Sassaia '04	♟♟	4
○ Sassaia '03	♟♟	4

Borin Vini & Vigne

FRAZ. MONTICELLI
VIA DEI COLLI, 5
35043 MONSELICE [PD]
TEL. 042974384
www.viniborin.it

ANNUAL PRODUCTION 140,000 bottles
HECTARES UNDER VINE 33
VITICULTURE METHOD Conventional

After many years of dedication to making scrupulously reliable wines sold at fair prices from a wide, well-balanced range, here is the big bang: a new wine now stands head and shoulders above the rest, ready to leap to supreme quality. Zuan, made mainly from cabernet with some merlot, is not a DOC wine but it is still deeply connected to the Colli Euganei, expressing the warmth and light of the area with enthralling, alluring aromas and a firm, harmonious, very long palate. In the presence of a wine like this, the growth of the rest of the range risks going almost unnoticed but the Cabernet Vigna Costa 2005, for example, has never been so impressive. Moving on, you'll find Fiore di Gaia, a dry, tangy and very supple Moscato, and Sette Chiesette, a charmingly balsamic dried-grape wine. The classic Borin family wines are also on good form, the two Riservas, Mons Silicis 2004 and Rocca Chiara 2005, expressing the sunny nature of the territory. Last up was the deep, harmonious Corte Borin, an impressive Manzoni Bianco.

F.lli Bortolin Spumanti

FRAZ. SANTO STEFANO
VIA MENEGAZZI, 5
31049 VALDOBBIADENE [TV]
TEL. 0423900135
www.bortolin.com

ANNUAL PRODUCTION 350,000 bottles
HECTARES UNDER VINE 20
VITICULTURE METHOD Conventional

Valeriano Bortolin's family has deep roots in the world of Prosecco and Valdobbiadene with a strong, ancient tradition and unswerving devotion to quality. Today, Valeriano's children, Andrea, Claudia and Diego, work alongside him with renewed commitment to the same objective: flawlessly made Prosecco. The 350,000 bottles produced annually are almost all sparkling wines made from prosecco grapes and are split across a selection of labels to cater for all possible demands. The most striking wine this year was Rù, an Extra Dry with fruity aromas and a tangy, sophisticated palate. The Brut is only a whisker less imposing, thanks to its varietal aromas of apples and pear fruit on the nose followed by a dry, uncomplicated and very enjoyable palate. The other Extra Dry is also good while the Cartizze is generous and alluringly sweet. The Colli di Conegliano Bianco has fresh aromas and a light palate.

● Zuan '04	♏♏ 6
● Colli Euganei Cabernet Sauvignon V. Costa '05	♏♏ 4*
O Corte Borin '06	♏♏ 5
O Fiore di Gaia '06	♏♏ 5
● Colli Euganei Cabernet Sauvignon Mons Silicis Ris. '04	♏♏ 6
● Colli Euganei Merlot Rocca Chiara Ris. '05	♏♏ 6
O Colli Euganei Fior d'Arancio Passito Sette Chiesette '03	♏♏ 6
O Colli Euganei Chardonnay Vigna Bianca '05	♏ 4
O Colli Euganei Pinot Bianco Monte Archino '06	♏ 4
● Colli Euganei Merlot V. del Foscolo '05	♏ 4

O P. di Valdobbiadene Brut '06	♏♏ 4
O P. di Valdobbiadene Extra Dry '06	♏♏ 4
O P. di Valdobbiadene Extra Dry Rù '06	♏♏ 4
O Cartizze '06	♏ 5
O P. di Valdobbiadene Dry '06	♏ 4
O Vigneto del Convento Extra Brut	♏ 4
O Colli di Conegliano Bianco '06	♏ 4

Bortolomiol

VIA GARIBALDI, 142
31049 VALDOBBIADENE [TV]
TEL. 0423974911
www.bortolomiol.com

Bosco del Merlo

VIA POSTUMIA, 14
30020 ANNONE VENETO [VE]
TEL. 0422768167
www.boscodelmerlo.it

ANNUAL PRODUCTION 2,200,000 bottles
HECTARES UNDER VINE 5
VITICULTURE METHOD Conventional

The Valdobbiadene and Prosecco wine area owes much to this estate and its founder Giuliano, who powered the initial drive to enhanced quality and visibility for a wine that is now admired and enjoyed worldwide. Quality is founded on grapes, of course, but also on technical details in the cellar and – why not? – image and this Valdobbiadene winery has always been careful to give place due emphasis on these factors in its production. From the many sparkling wines presented, one now-classic bottle stands out: the Extra Dry Banda Rossa, a beautifully made Prosecco with elegantly creamy mousse. The Senior is just as sweet with fruity, floral aromas on the nose and a more convincingly gutsy palate, with acidity to the fore. Cartizze and Maior are both softer on the palate, with prevalently mature, cake-like aromas. In contrast, the two Bruts exploit their low residual sugar to highlight the integrity of their aromas.

ANNUAL PRODUCTION 430,000 bottles
HECTARES UNDER VINE 128
VITICULTURE METHOD Conventional

The passion, commitment and dedication that brothers and sister team Lucia, Carlo and Roberto Paladin have poured into boosting the quality of their wide range of products, while maintaining strong links to the terroir, has been rewarded this year by excellent results. Let's start with a spectacular version of the Ruber Capitae, a merlot-heavy Bordeaux blend with bags of personality. Wild berries alternate with stylish fines herbes on the nose before the nicely balanced palate shows broad and sophisticated, with juicy fruit and mature, silky tannins. The Refosco Roggio dei Roveri is an excellent example of how a modern style can keep its links with tradition. This very drinkable wine layers elegantly subtle floral sensations over the juicily healthy, intriguing fruit. The rest of the products are all excellent, from the powerful Vineargenti, a blend of cabernet sauvignon and malbec, to the vibrant, floral Tocai Juti, the profound Merlot Campo Camino and the balsamic Sauvignon Turranio.

○ P. di Valdobbiadene Extra Dry Sel. Banda Rossa '06	♟♟	4
○ P. di Valdobbiadene Extra Dry Senior	♟♟	4
○ Cartizze	♟	6
○ P. di Valdobbiadene Tranquillo Canto Fermo '06	♟	4
○ P. di Valdobbiadene Frizzante Il Ponteggio	♟	4
○ P. di Valdobbiadene Dry Maior	♟	4
○ P. di Valdobbiadene Brut Motus Vitae mill. '05	♟	5
○ P. di Conegliano Valdobbiadene Tranquillo Canto Fermo '06	♟	4
○ P. di Valdobbiadene Brut Prior	♟	4

● Lison-Pramaggiore Refosco P. R. Roggio dei Roveri '04	♟♟	6
● 360 Ruber Capitae Rosso '04	♟♟	5
● Lison-Pramaggiore Merlot Campo Camino '04	♟♟	4
● Vineargenti '01	♟♟	6
○ Lison-Pramaggiore Cl. Tocai Juti '05	♟♟	4
○ Lison-Pramaggiore Sauvignon Turranio '06	♟♟	4
○ Lison-Pramaggiore Pinot Grigio '06	♟	4
○ Verduzzo Soandre '05	♟	4
○ Priné '05	♟	5
● Lison-Pramaggiore Refosco P. R. Roggio dei Roveri '03	♟♟	6
● 360 Ruber Capitae '03	♟♟	5

Brigaldara

FRAZ. SAN FLORIANO
VIA BRIGALDARA, 20
37020 SAN PIETRO IN CARIANO [VR]
TEL. 0457701055
www.valpolicella.it/brigaldara

ANNUAL PRODUCTION 200,000 bottles
HECTARES UNDER VINE 45
VITICULTURE METHOD Conventional

Stefano Cesari's production philosophy is based on the sincerity and cleanliness of his wines. All procedures in the vineyard and cellar are directed towards fulfilling this objective, from the meticulous cosseting of the grapes to the respect shown for their varietal characteristics and the avoidance of intrusive winemaking techniques. In consequence, Brigaldara wines are distinctively natural and simple but not predictable for they have plenty of finesse and lean, understated profile. The Amarone Case Vecie 2003 suffered from the hot growing year, showing marked alcohol and boisterous tannins as well as attractive grip and skilful, balanced handling of the substantial raw material. Its sheer elegance puts it in a class of its own and it deservedly picked up our highest accolade, Three Glasses. The Recioto 2004, in contrast, benefited from a cooler year emerging delicate, with well-controlled sugar and alcohol. Vegro, a Valpolicella made using the ripasso technique of adding unpressed Amarone skins to the fermented wine, has serious stuffing and is the most rustic bottle in the range. The Valpolicella 2005 is nicely made.

Sorelle Bronca

FRAZ. COLBERTALDO
VIA MARTIRI, 20
31020 VIDOR [TV]
TEL. 0423987201
www.sorellebronca.com

ANNUAL PRODUCTION 250,000 bottles
HECTARES UNDER VINE 20
VITICULTURE METHOD Certified organic

Antonella and Ersiliana Bronca's winery is hardly typical of its area. Although the range focuses on Prosecco, the care, passion and enthusiasm reserved for still wines put it on another level. The decision to dedicate the most suitable vineyard to each wine shows a knowledge and working style that is quite different from the approach normally associated with Prosecco. Ser Bele, a Bordeaux blend that impresses at first sip, gave a great performance. The aromas may still be very youthful but it already enthrals with masterly handling of the texture and the finesse of the palate. The interesting Manzoni Bianco, released in magnums only, is vinified with maceration on the skins. Its aromatics are mature and mineral-edged while the palate is dry and full-bodied. The sparkling wines are very well made and Particella 68 is particularly outstanding for its generous, sunny aromas and dense, fizzy texture on the palate. The Brut and Extra Dry are uncomplicated and highly enjoyable.

● Amarone della Valpolicella		
Case Vecie '03	♚♚♚	8
● Recioto della Valpolicella Cl. '04	♚♚	7
● Valpolicella Cl. '05	♚♚	4
● Valpolicella Cl. Sup. Ripasso		
Il Vegro '03	♚♚	5
○ Passito Bianco '03	♚♚	6
⊙ Dindarella '06	♚	4
● Amarone della Valpolicella		
Case Vecie '00	♚♚♚	7
● Amarone della Valpolicella Cl. '99	♚♚♚	7
● Amarone della Valpolicella Cl. '98	♚♚♚	7
● Amarone della Valpolicella Cl. '97	♚♚♚	7
● Amarone della Valpolicella		
Case Vecie '01	♚♚	7
● Amarone della Valpolicella		
Case Vecie '99	♚♚	7
● Recioto della Valpolicella Cl. '03	♚♚	7

● Colli di Conegliano Rosso		
Ser Bele '04	♚♚	6
○ P. di Valdobbiadene Brut '06	♚♚	4*
○ P. di Valdobbiadene Extra Dry		
Particella 68 '06	♚♚	4*
○ P. di Valdobbiadene Extra Dry '06	♚♚	4*
○ Manzoni Bianco '04	♚♚	8
○ Colli di Conegliano Bianco		
Delico '05	♚	4
● Colli di Conegliano Rosso		
Ser Bele '03	♚♚	6
● Colli di Conegliano Rosso		
Ser Bele '02	♚♚	6
● Colli di Conegliano Rosso		
Ser Bele '01	♚♚	6
● Colli di Conegliano Rosso		
Ser Bele '00	♚♚	6

Luigi Brunelli
VIA CARIANO, 10
37029 SAN PIETRO IN CARIANO [VR]
TEL. 0457701118
www.brunelliwine.com

Buglioni
FRAZ. CORRUBIO
VIA CAMPAGNOLE, 55
37029 SAN PIETRO IN CARIANO [VR]
TEL. 0456760681
www.buglioni.it

ANNUAL PRODUCTION 90,000 bottles
HECTARES UNDER VINE 9.5
VITICULTURE METHOD Conventional

ANNUAL PRODUCTION 70,000 bottles
HECTARES UNDER VINE 16
VITICULTURE METHOD Conventional

In historic Corte Cariano, the third generation of Brunellis to dedicate their lives to winemaking is taking its first steps: Alberto, who will soon graduate from university, his eyes shining with enthusiasm is rolling up his sleeves. He does have help from his father Luigi, who describes himself as a passionate winemaker and poet, and his practical-minded mother Luciana. It was she who supervised renovation work on the building used for the shop and tasting room, with flats and bedrooms upstairs, in the vineyards of the peaceful, ancient Corte. The corvina-based Corte Cariano 2005 is undemanding while the Campo Praesel has an impressively soft palate and very ripe fruit. Pa' Riondo, a ripasso-technique Valpolicella, is appetizing on the nose with generous fruit and fines herbes, followed by satisfyingly balanced softness on the palate. Despite its good texture, the 2003 Amarone seems immature and the tannins are still looking for balance. The garganega-based Passito Re Sol is sun-ripe, balsamic and pleasantly harmonious.

A little in the background with respect to other wineries and a little difficult to define, the Buglioni family's winery turns out reliable products with a good level of quality. The vineyards are located in various areas, making it possible to for them to carry out targeted selection of the grapes according to the type of wine to be produced. The 2005 growing year enabled Mariano and his father Alfredo to make a luscious Recioto, with intense jam and bitter chocolate on the nose and a palate that brims with flavour, held in check by well-honed tannins. The two Valpolicella Superiores are very interesting, although we preferred the Il Bugiardo for its more complex aromas and savoury, well-textured palate. Il Ruffiano, as the name suggests, is more ingratiatingly approachable but we were not all that impressed by the Amarone, which seems to have suffered from the excessively warm vintage. Finally, the standard-label Valpolicella put on an excellent performance and was only a whisker away from a second Glass.

● Amarone della Valpolicella Cl. '03	♟♟ 7
● Valpolicella Cl. Sup. Ripasso Pa' Riondo '05	♟♟ 4*
● Valpolicella Cl. Sup. Campo Praesel '05	♟♟ 4*
● Valpolicella Cl. '06	♟ 4
● Corte Cariano Rosso '05	♟ 4
O Passito Re Sol '04	♟ 6
O Carianum Bianco'06	♟ 4
● Amarone della Valpolicella Cl. Campo del Titari '96	♟♟♟ 8
● Amarone della Valpolicella Cl. Campo del Titari '97	♟♟♟ 8
● Amarone della Valpolicella Cl. Campo del Titari '01	♟♟ 8

● Valpolicella Cl. Sup. Ripasso Il Bugiardo '04	♟♟ 5
● Recioto della Valpolicella Cl. Il Recioto '05	♟♟ 6
● Amarone della Valpolicella Cl. L'Amarone '03	♟ 7
● Valpolicella Cl. Sup. Il Ruffiano '05	♟ 4
● Valpolicella Cl. Il Valpolicella '06	♟ 4
● Amarone della Valpolicella Cl. L'Amarone '01	♟♟ 7
● Valpolicella Cl. Sup. Ripasso Il Bugiardo '03	♟♟ 5
● Valpolicella Cl. Sup. Il Ruffiano '04	♟♟ 4
● Recioto della Valpolicella Cl. '03	♟♟ 6

Tommaso Bussola

LOC. SAN PERETTO
VIA MOLINO TURRI, 30
37024 NEGRAR [VR]
TEL. 0457501740
www.bussolavini.com

ANNUAL PRODUCTION 80,000 bottles
HECTARES UNDER VINE 9.5
VITICULTURE METHOD Conventional

Even a skilled producer like Tommaso
Bussola has to surrender to unpredictable
weather so this year there were rather fewer
wines than usual. Although it may be a
shame to taste so few wines from San
Peretto, we must acknowledge this
producer's professionalism in not producing
an Amarone TB for 2002 while reckoning it
was too soon to release the 2003 and
2004. Of course, the two magnificent
Reciotos helped us survive these absences
and once again the wines earned our
praises. The wonderful thing about Recioto,
Valpolicella's traditional wine, is that it is
possible to make – and taste – two equally
fine wines that are nonetheless very
different. The 2005 is clearly defined with an
explosion of fruit jam and Alpine herbs,
showing alluringly soft and subtly tannic on
the palate. TB, on the other hand, is much
warmer and more complex, with plenty of
appeal on the concentrated but well-
balanced palate with its very long-lingering
finish.

Ca' La Bionda

FRAZ. VALGATARA
LOC. BIONDA, 4
37020 MARANO DI VALPOLICELLA [VR]
TEL. 0456801198
www.calabionda.it

ANNUAL PRODUCTION 110,000 bottles
HECTARES UNDER VINE 29
VITICULTURE METHOD Natural

Alessandro and Nicola Castellani run the
winery founded by their father Pietro with
increasingly impressive results. From the
beginning, our heroes decided to focus on
high quality vineyard management using the
most natural methods possible, just as in
the cellar they limit human intervention in
their pursuit of wine that is not only good
but also reflects its terroir and climate. The
two 2003 Amarones did very well. The basic
version is generous, approachable and
fresh-tasting despite its massive structure
whereas Ravazzol is deeper and edgier with
an austere, minerally palate. The two very
interesting Valpolicellas are made entirely
from fresh grapes without the usual local
ripasso technique. We preferred Casal
Vegri, sourced from a vineyard entirely given
over to the wine type, for its complex
aromas and rigorous, edgy style. The
Ravazzol has simpler, more approachable
aromas and a savoury, extremely
harmonious palate.

● Recioto della Valpolicella Cl. '05	♟♟	7
● Recioto della Valpolicella Cl. TB '03	♟♟	8
● Recioto della Valpolicella Cl. BG '03	♟♟♟	7
● Recioto della Valpolicella Cl. TB '99	♟♟♟	8
● Recioto della Valpolicella Cl. TB '97	♟♟♟	8
● Recioto della Valpolicella Cl. TB '98	♟♟♟	8
● Recioto della Valpolicella Cl. TB '95	♟♟♟	8
● Recioto della Valpolicella Cl. TB '01	♟♟	8
● Amarone della Valpolicella Cl. TB Vign. Alto '00	♟♟	8

● Amarone della Valpolicella Cl. Vign. di Ravazzol '03	♟♟	7
● Valpolicella Cl. Sup. Campo Casal Vegri '04	♟♟	5
● Amarone della Valpolicella Cl. '03	♟♟	6
● Valpolicella Cl. Sup. Vign. di Ravazzol '05	♟	4
● Amarone Cl. Vign. di Ravazzol Ris. Pietro Castellani '01	♟♟	8
● Recioto della Valpolicella Cl. Vign. Le Tordare '04	♟♟	6
● Valpolicella Cl. Sup. Campo Casal Vegri '03	♟♟	5
● Amarone Cl. Vign. di Ravazzol Ris. Pietro Castellani '00	♟♟	8
● Amarone della Valpolicella Cl. Vign. di Ravazzol '00	♟♟	7
● Amarone della Valpolicella Cl. '00	♟♟	6

Ca' Lustra
LOC. FAEDO
VIA SAN PIETRO, 50
35030 CINTO EUGANEO [PD]
TEL. 042994128
www.calustra.it

Ca' Orologio
VIA CA' OROLOGIO, 7A
35030 BAONE [PD]
TEL. 042950099
www.caorologio.com

ANNUAL PRODUCTION	190,000 bottles
HECTARES UNDER VINE	35
VITICULTURE METHOD	Conventional

ANNUAL PRODUCTION	20,000 bottles
HECTARES UNDER VINE	12
VITICULTURE METHOD	Certified organic

Ca' Lustra, masterfully run by the indefatigable Franco Zanovello and Ivano Giacomin, who share a thorough knowledge of the local area, has shown extraordinary ability in turning out a flawless range of characterful wines every year. From the Villa Alessi selection come two memorable reds, Merlot Sassonero 2005 and Girapoggio 2004, a 60-40 blend of cabernet sauvignon and cabernet franc. The former is sophisticated and stylish with minerally aromas and fines herbes on the nose and a nicely lingering, savoury palate. This marvellous wine earned Ca' Lustra Three Glasses in tribute to the steady quality maintained by this Colli Euganei winery. The powerful, characterful Girapoggio has all the attributes of the cabernet grape with a mineral edge from its Euganei terroir. The Fior d'Arancio Passito also made a very good impression, showing incredible aromatics that make it ideal for those who love strong sensations. From the rest of the range, we'd like to mention the cabernet sauvignon, franc and merlot Rosso Nativo, which undergoes extended maceration; the mature, broad and mouthfilling Moscato Secco 'A Cengia, a classic of its type; and the good Manzoni Bianco Pedevenda. All the other wines are enjoyable.

The Ca' Orologio winery is situated in the lovely Baone in a charming villa with accommodation and a view of the enchanting surrounding landscape. It's a setting that inspired the determined Mariagioia Rosellini to make her presence felt here very rapidly, albeit discreetly and courteously, in a busy area with lots of potential. Last year's Three Glasses were a just reward for her intense hard work and they spurred Mariagioia on to renew her efforts across the range. Although the Relógio 2005, from carmenère with a dash of cabernet sauvignon, was not presented, the other wines have kept the flag flying. The Colli Euganei Rosso Calaóne, from merlot, cabernet and a little barbera, is a wonderful piece of work and impressed us with ripe fruit aromas nicely offset by oakiness. The palate is powerful and well structured with ripe fruit to compensate the tannins and smooth down the hint of oak that betrays the wine's youth. It won Three well-deserved Glasses to go with our prize for the year's Up-and-Coming Winery. The white Salaróla, from mainly tocai and moscato, is delicious and the Barbera Lunisóle is excellent.

● Colli Euganei Merlot Sassonero Villa Alessi '05	???	5
● Colli Euganei Cabernet Girapoggio Villa Alessi '04	??	5
○ Colli Euganei Fior d'Arancio Passito Villa Alessi '05	??	5
● Colli Euganei Merlot '05	??	3*
○ Moscato Secco 'A Cengia Villa Alessi '06	??	4
○ Sauvignon Olivetani Villa Alessi '06	??	4
○ Manzoni Bianco Pedevenda Villa Alessi '06	??	4
● Colli Euganei Rosso Nativo Villa Alessi '05	??	5
● Colli Euganei Cabernet '05	?	4
○ Colli Euganei Pinot Bianco '06	?	3

● Colli Euganei Rosso Calaóne '05	???	5
● Lunisóle '05	??	5
○ Salaróla '06	??	4*
● Relógio '04	???	5
● Colli Euganei Rosso Calaóne '04	??	4
● Colli Euganei Rosso Calaóne '03	??	5
● Relógio '03	??	5

Ca' Rugate

VIA PERGOLA, 72
37030 MONTECCHIA DI CROSARA [VR]
TEL. 0456176328
www.carugate.it

ANNUAL PRODUCTION 400,000 bottles
HECTARES UNDER VINE 45
VITICULTURE METHOD Conventional

Ca' Rugate has its heart in Soave and its head in Valpolicella. Although they do not neglect their vocation as white winemakers, the Tessaris are acquiring skill and confidence with reds and are now among the finest practitioners of the art. The fruit is very high quality and in the cellar intervention is limited to the bare necessities. Garganega is the star of the whites but in the next few years it will be joined by trebbiano di Soave, with its gracefully fresh, aromatics. The San Michele is an excellent basic wine and the Monte Alto is soft and sensual, with better absorbed oak than we have seen in the past. The Bucciato has an intoxicating nose with aromas of tropical fruit and spice, followed by a big, dry palate. The great Monte Fiorentine is quite youthfully fresh and minerally, promising to become very complex but already impressive thanks to its confident palate. So impressive, in fact, that it again won Three Glasses. From the reds, we picked out the gamey, enjoyably complex Campo Lavei and the splendid Amarone, which is soft, savoury and fresh-tasting with a long finish.

Cambrago

FRAZ. SAN ZENO
VIA CAMBRAGO, 7
37030 COLOGNOLA AI COLLI [VR]
TEL. 0457650745
casavini4@casavinicolacambrago.191.it

ANNUAL PRODUCTION 90,000 bottles
HECTARES UNDER VINE 14
VITICULTURE METHOD Conventional

As the Colognola ai Colli valley belongs to both the Soave and Valpolicella designated zones, the wineries usually work with both types. But Cambrago prefers to focus all its attention on Soaves, with results that are more than good. Steady commitment to work in the vineyard and in the cellar, with significant contributions from consultant Flavio Prà, Cambrago's wines are becoming a benchmark for enthusiasts thanks to dependably flawless quality, vintage after vintage. The Recioto is excellent with its intriguing aromas of liquorice, candied citrus peel and dried flowers, well-balanced sweetness and very long finish. Of the two Soaves presented, we liked the aromatic finesse and gutsy palate of the Cerceni while the Vigne Maiores reveals the more rustic nature of the garganega grape with simplicity and supple progression on the palate.

O Soave Cl. Monte Fiorentine '06	♟♟♟	4*
O Soave Cl. Monte Alto '05	♟♟	4*
O Bucciato '05	♟♟	4*
● Amarone della Valpolicella '03	♟♟	7
● Valpolicella Sup. Campo Lavei '05	♟♟	5
● Recioto della Valpolicella L'Eremita '05	♟♟	6
O Soave Cl. San Michele '06	♟♟	3
O Recioto di Soave La Perlara '05	♟♟	5
● Valpolicella Rio Albo '06	♟	3
O Soave Cl. Monte Fiorentine '05	♛♛♛	4
O Soave Cl. Monte Fiorentine '04	♛♛♛	4
O Soave Cl. Sup. Monte Alto '00	♛♛♛	4
O Soave Cl. Sup. Bucciato '99	♛♛♛	4
O Soave Cl. Sup. Monte Alto '96	♛♛♛	4
● Amarone della Valpolicella '01	♛♛	7

O Soave Cl. I Cerceni '06	♟♟	3*
O Recioto di Soave I Cerceni '04	♟♟	5
O Soave Vigne Maiores '06	♟	2*
O Soave Cl. I Cerceni '05	♛♛	4
O Recioto di Soave I Cerceni '03	♛♛	6

Giuseppe Campagnola

LOC. VALGATARA
VIA AGNELLA, 9
37020 MARANO DI VALPOLICELLA [VR]
TEL. 0457703900
www.campagnola.com

ANNUAL PRODUCTION 4,800,000 bottles
HECTARES UNDER VINE 75
VITICULTURE METHOD Conventional

Giuseppe Campagnola never misses the mark. The leading wines in his substantial range are always among the best to be found in Valpolicella. This is due to the technical ability of his winery staff as well as long-standing close relationship with the land and with his neighbours. Almost all the grapes come from the Marano valley, which is also where his family is comes from. This is perhaps the area of Valpolicella that expresses best the grape's subtle, vibrant aromas with a slim, never intrusive structure, even when the grapes are partially dried. Just taste the two house champions, Amarone and Valpolicella Caterina Zardini. Both proffer an approachable, generous range of aromas and convincingly subtle, supple palates. This year, we liked the Valpolicella very much. It's a deeply sound wine with huge potential, which more than earned its Three Glasses. The Soave Monte Foscarino is also very.good, showing fruity and stylish, like the basic Amarone and the generous Recioto Casotto del Merlo.

● Valpolicella Cl. Sup. Caterina Zardini '05	🍷🍷🍷	4*
● Amarone della Valpolicella Cl. Caterina Zardini '03	🍷🍷	7
● Amarone della Valpolicella Cl. '04	🍷🍷	6
● Recioto della Valpolicella Cl. Casotto del Merlo '05	🍷🍷	5
○ Soave Cl. Vign. Monte Foscarino Le Bine '06	🍷🍷	3*
● Valpolicella Cl. Sup. Ripasso Vign. di Purano Le Bine '05	🍷	4
● Amarone della Valpolicella Cl. Caterina Zardini '01	YYY	7
● Amarone della Valpolicella Cl. Caterina Zardini '99	YYY	7
● Amarone della Valpolicella Cl. Caterina Zardini '00	YY	7

Canevel Spumanti

LOC. SACCOL
VIA ROCCAT E FERRARI, 17
31049 VALDOBBIADENE [TV]
TEL. 0423975940
www.canevel.it

ANNUAL PRODUCTION 600,000 bottles
HECTARES UNDER VINE 12
VITICULTURE METHOD Conventional

Valdobbiadene's vineyards make it one of the most beautiful landscapes in Italy. Steep, vine-clad slopes plummet to the valley floor in an environment where machines can do little to relieve the patient, back-breaking labour of the grower. This is another reason why wineries here often do not have extensive vine stock of their own but rely on growers to supplement the harvest, offering them support and supervision throughout the years. The winery's task is then to make the best possible use of the fruit it receives, using technology and experience, as is the case with Canevel. The range presented includes all the wine types covered by the designated areas production specifications and prices are fair. The two Prosecco Extra Drys gave an excellent performance. The basic version is joyously varietal and juicy on the palate while the Millesimato is even more so, showing sophisticated floral aromas with pear and apple fruit, and a taut palate with more structure. Finally, the Cartizze is rounded and tropical while the fragrant Demi Sec deserves a special mention.

○ P. di Conegliano Valdobbiadene Il Millesimato Extra Dry '06	🍷🍷	4
○ Cartizze	🍷🍷	5
○ P. di Valdobbiadene Extra Dry	🍷🍷	4
○ P. di Conegliano Valdobbiadene Brut	🍷	4
○ P. di Valdobbiadene Demi Sec	🍷	4
○ P. di Valdobbiadene Tranquillo	🍷	4

Giordano Emo Capodilista

VIA VILLA RITA
35030 BAONE [PD]
TEL. 049637294
www.classica.it

ANNUAL PRODUCTION 14,000 bottles
HECTARES UNDER VINE 10
VITICULTURE METHOD Conventional

The extraordinary Colli Euganei zone is an area of volcanic hills that encapsulates the sunny Mediterranean soul of this part of Veneto. Its cool, high slopes contribute fresh, complex aromas. Within this area, Baone perhaps represents the peak of this perfect combination, so much so that a group of local producers, naturally including the explosive Giordano Emo Capodilista, is working to bring the territory into the spotlight. The cool, damp weather of 2005 brought with it subtle, sophisticated aromas, and in the case of the Cabernet Ireneo, endowing those aromas with considerable breadth. The palate opens out beautifully revealing elegance and silky tannins. Donna Daria is at the other end of the sensory scale, giving profound aromas of mineral and candied citrus fruit, spices and fresh flowers, and pronounced sweetness on a palate generously supported by vibrant acidity through to a thrillingly long finish.

● Colli Euganei Cabernet Sauvignon Ireneo '05	🍷🍷 6
○ Colli Euganei Fior d'Arancio Passito Donna Daria '05	🍷🍷 6
● Colli Euganei Cabernet Sauvignon Ireneo '04	YY 6
○ Colli Euganei Fior d'Arancio Passito Donna Daria '04	YY 6
● Colli Euganei Cabernet Sauvignon Ireneo '03	YY 6
● Colli Euganei Cabernet Sauvignon Ireneo '02	YY 6
○ Colli Euganei Fior d'Arancio Passito Donna Daria '02	YY 6
● Colli Euganei Cabernet Sauvignon Ireneo '01	YY 6
○ Colli Euganei Fior d'Arancio Passito Donna Daria '01	YY 6

La Cappuccina

FRAZ. COSTALUNGA
VIA SAN BRIZIO, 125
37032 MONTEFORTE D'ALPONE [VR]
TEL. 0456175036
www.lacappuccina.it

ANNUAL PRODUCTION 195,000 bottles
HECTARES UNDER VINE 30
VITICULTURE METHOD Certified organic

The Tessari family – Pietro, Sisto and their sister Elena – have moved into their new winery, which is unfussy, functional and above all spacious. Producing both red and white wines had created considerable problems of storage for barrels and bottles in the old premises. The most interesting results come from Campo Buri, a blend of carmenère and slightly dried oseleta. Its ripe fruit aromas with their hints of raisining are followed by minerality and aromatic herbs. The wine is even more impressive on the palate where its massive, solid structure also manages to be supple and fresh-tasting. The Arzimo is just a step down. This garganega-based dried-grape wine takes its cue from tertiary notes and well-gauged sweetness. The more ambitious Soaves are not as impressive as usual. Fontégo is uncomplicated and enjoyably drinkable while the San Brizio presents mature aromas but overly soft sensations. The simpler Soave, Sauvignon and Madégo are all reliably good.

○ Arzìmo Passito '05	🍷🍷 5
● Campo Buri '04	🍷🍷 5
● Carmenos Passito '05	🍷 5
● Madégo '06	🍷 4
○ Sauvignon '06	🍷 4
○ Soave Fontégo '06	🍷 4
○ Soave San Brizio '05	🍷 4
○ Soave '06	🍷 3
● Campo Buri '02	YY 5
○ Soave Fontégo '05	YY 4
○ Soave Fontégo '04	YY 4
○ Soave Fontégo '03	YY 4
○ Soave San Brizio '04	YY 4
○ Soave San Brizio '03	YY 4
○ Soave San Brizio '02	YY 4

Casa Roma

VIA ORMELLE, 19
31020 SAN POLO DI PIAVE [TV]
TEL. 0422855339
www.casaroma.com

ANNUAL PRODUCTION 200,000 bottles
HECTARES UNDER VINE 28
VITICULTURE METHOD Conventional

Raboso, raboso and even more raboso. That, in a nutshell, is how we might sum up Adriano and Gigi Peruzzetto's winery. The two cousins are as dissimilar in appearance as they are in character but both are determined to take Piave winemaking to the top with its oldest and most intractable child, the raboso grape. This determination can be seen not only in the effort they lavish on producing the wine but also in their resistance to the temptation to fashion an serious red from other grapes. Their only wine with really serious ambitions is Raboso: the others are there to cater for customers looking for a good-value, enjoyable bottle. The 2003 harvest gave the Raboso ripe, vibrantly fruity aromas and its varietal vegetal sensations seem to be softer and better absorbed. Acidity and tannin lend the palate finesse and long-lingering flavour. From the whites, we would point out the San Dordi and the Vinegia, from marzemina bianca, which has aromas of Mediterranean scrubland and a tangy, taut palate.

Michele Castellani

FRAZ. VALGATARA
VIA GRANDA, 1
37020 MARANO DI VALPOLICELLA [VR]
TEL. 0457701253
www.castellanimichele.it

ANNUAL PRODUCTION 300,000 bottles
HECTARES UNDER VINE 48
VITICULTURE METHOD Conventional

Sergio Castellani never stops for a moment. He's always organizing his vineyards, purchasing new ones or rebuilding his winery. In recent years, he has even built a little lodge with a swimming pool. Sergio epitomizes an area that has continued to move forward, despite the recession of recent years, investing in his main business of wine but also restructuring buildings that had never been renovated. The wines are released in two lines: Ca' del Pipa and I Castei. In both cases, the most impressive bottles were the Reciotos, proof of Sergio's skill with this traditional wine that symbolizes the heritage of Valpolicella. The Recioto Monte Fasenara I Castei has enfolding aromas of stewed fruit and a palate that of almost explosive sweetness firmly held in place by rigorous, densely woven tannins. The Ca' del Pipa is more austere but marked by oakiness while the two Amarones are rich in structure and juicy fruit.

● Piave Raboso '03	♟♟ 5
○ San Dordi '06	♟♟ 4
○ Vinegia '06	♟ 3
○ Sauvignon '06	♟ 3
○ Manzoni Bianco '06	♟ 3
● Cabernet Franc '06	♟ 3
● Raboso Passito Callarghe '04	♟ 6
● Piave Merlot '06	♟ 3
● Piave Raboso '02	♟♟ 5
● Piave Raboso '01	♟♟ 5
● Piave Raboso '00	♟♟ 5
● Piave Raboso '99	♟♟ 5

● Recioto della Valpolicella Cl. Le Vigne Ca' del Pipa '04	♟♟ 7
● Recioto della Valpolicella Cl. Monte Fasenara I Castei '05	♟♟ 7
● Amarone della Valpolicella Cl. Campo Casalin I Castei '03	♟♟ 7
● Amarone della Valpolicella Cl. Le Vigne Ca' del Pipa '03	♟♟ 7
● Valpolicella Cl. Sup. Ripasso Costamaran I Castei '04	♟ 5
● Valpolicella Cl. Sup. Ripasso Costamaran I Castei '05	♟ 5
● Valpolicella Cl. Campo del Biotto I Castei '06	♟ 3
● Recioto della Valpolicella Cl. Le Vigne Ca' del Pipa '99	♟♟♟ 7
● Amarone della Valpolicella Cl. Campo Casalin I Castei '01	♟♟ 8

Cantina del Castello

CORTE PITTORA, 5
37038 SOAVE [VR]
TEL. 0457680093
www.cantinacastello.it

ANNUAL PRODUCTION 130,000 bottles
HECTARES UNDER VINE 13
VITICULTURE METHOD Conventional

Arturo Stocchetti loves to talk about the long tradition behind the wines of Cantina del Castello, which were among the first to be bottled in this area. These are wines imbued with a sort of classicism, each with its own precise identity and raison d'être that goes far beyond trends. The vineyards are managed with scrupulous care and special attention is paid to the landscaping and aesthetic impact. While the clean, moreish Soave Castello is a perfect introduction to the range, the Pressoni is once again austere and crystal-clear. Fresh-tasting, floral, healthy and tangy, it is a wine of light rather than texture and will be even better in a couple of years' time. The Carniga, Arturo's tribute to old-style Soaves, undergoes long ageing on the yeasts, emerging luscious and buttery with a sensation of warmth softened by fresh minerality. The Acini Soavi matured in large barrels and shows very good balance of structure and finesse. No dried-grape wines were made from the 2005 harvest.

○ Soave Cl. Pressoni '06	▼▼	4*
○ Soave Cl. Acini Soavi '05	▼▼	5
○ Soave Cl. Carniga '05	▼	5
○ Soave Cl. Castello '06	▼	4
○ Soave Cl. Sup. Monte Pressoni '01	▽▽▽	4
○ Soave Cl. Carniga '04	▽▽	4
○ Soave Cl. Pressoni '05	▽▽	4
○ Soave Cl. Acini Soavi '04	▽▽	5
○ Soave Cl. Pressoni '04	▽▽	4
○ Soave Cl. Pressoni '03	▽▽	4

Cavalchina

FRAZ. CUSTOZA
LOC. CAVALCHINA
VIA SOMMACAMPAGNA, 7
37066 SOMMACAMPAGNA [VR]
TEL. 045516002
www.cavalchina.com

ANNUAL PRODUCTION 500,000 bottles
HECTARES UNDER VINE 75
VITICULTURE METHOD Conventional

After last year's excellent results, Luciano and Franco Piona show just how valid the strategy that won Three Glasses for their Bianco di Custoza actually is. Every year, the pair present a broad, well-formulated range of wines that reveal a general improvement in quality. Low yields and separate vinifications to bring out the best in each variety have resulted in an enthralling Custoza Superiore Amedeo 2005 with floral, apple and pear fruit aromas that shows subtle and stylish yet firm and sumptuous. As did the previous vintage, the 2005 went home with Three Glasses. The Garganega Paroni 2005 from Monzambano property impressed. Making the best of a very good year, it flaunts rich, mouthfilling structure on a taut, vibrant palate. Turning to the reds, the Merlot Faial is complex, powerful, savoury and nicely harmonious while the Cabernet Falcone, which will age comfortably, is all elegance and sophistication. The Corvina and Sauvignon Valbruna are wines of character.

○ Bianco di Custoza Sup. Amedeo '05	▼▼▼	4*
○ Garda Garganega Paroni La Prendina '05	▼▼	4*
● Garda Merlot Faial La Prendina '04	▼▼	6
● Garda Cabernet Sauvignon Vign. Il Falcone La Prendina '04	▼▼	5
○ Bianco di Custoza '06	▼▼	4
○ Garda Sauvignon Valbruna La Prendina '05	▼▼	4
⊙ Feniletto La Prendina '06	▼▼	4
● Garda Corvina La Prendina '05	▼▼	4
● Bardolino Sup. S. Lucia Cavalchina '05	▼	4
● Garda Merlot La Prendina '06	▼	3
○ Bianco di Custoza Sup. Amedeo '04	▽▽▽	4

Domenico Cavazza & F.lli

C.DA SELVA, 22
36054 MONTEBELLO VICENTINO [VI]
TEL. 0444649166
www.cavazzawine.com

ANNUAL PRODUCTION 1,000,000 bottles
HECTARES UNDER VINE 150
VITICULTURE METHOD Conventional

The Cavazza brothers' winery has for many years divided its attentions between its native land of Gambellara and Colli Berici a few kilometres away, a particularly well-suited area for growing red varieties. Here the winery made investments long ago and can now call on extensive, beautifully organized vineyards. But the most important news comes from Gambellara, where years of hard work have at last yielded prestigious results in the form of Creari, a Gambellara which was already striking in the 2005 version. The next vintage breezed though to our final tastings with generous aromas ranging from flowers to apple and pear fruit with very subtle minerally hints, and a tangy palate with succulent grip. The Berici wines also performed very well indeed, starting with Fornetto, a light but deliciously drinkable red, followed by the rich, fruity Merlot Cicogna, and lastly the charming Dulcis Cicogna. The whole range is fairly priced.

Giorgio Cecchetto

FRAZ. TEZZE DI PIAVE
VIA PIAVE, 67
31020 VAZZOLA [TV]
TEL. 043828598
www.rabosopiave.com

ANNUAL PRODUCTION 220,000 bottles
HECTARES UNDER VINE 39
VITICULTURE METHOD Conventional

Giorgio Cecchetto's story is inextricably interwoven with his land and its leading grape, raboso, a difficult variety to tame but which can show loads of ruggedly assertive and sometimes edgy character. Most of the winery's effort goes into promoting this wine and no other ambitious wines are made that might steal the raboso's thunder. The one exception is merlot, which although not a native variety has been grown along the Piave river for over a century. Sante has fresh fruit aromas and a good, supple, long-lasting body. The Raboso from the hot year of 2003 has vibrant fruit aromas with vegetal hints and a taut palate whose biting acidity endows the palate with freshness and a certain restlessness. The rest of the range focuses on standard-label white and red wines with good varietal expression and slender body.

O Gambellara Cl.	
Creari Capitel S. Libera '06	♥♥ 4*
● Colli Berici Cabernet	
Costiera Capitel S. Libera '05	♥♥ 4
● Fornetto Capitel S. Libera '05	♥♥ 4
O Dulcis Cicogna '05	♥♥ 5
● Colli Berici Merlot Cicogna '05	♥♥ 5
● Colli Berici Tocai Rosso	
Concerto '05	♥ 5
O Gambellara Cl. La Bocara '06	♥ 4
● Syrhae Cicogna '05	♥ 5
● Colli Berici Merlot Cicogna '04	♀♀ 5
● Colli Berici Tocai Rosso '03	♀♀ 5
● Colli Berici Merlot Cicogna '03	♀♀ 5
● Colli Berici Cabernet Cicogna '03	♀♀ 5

● Piave Raboso '03	♥♥ 5
● Piave Merlot Sante '05	♥♥ 4
● Cabernet Franc '06	♥ 3
O Incrocio Manzoni 6.0.13 '06	♥ 3
● Piave Cabernet Sauvignon '06	♥ 3
O Piave Pinot Grigio '06	3
● Piave Raboso Gelsaia '03	♀♀ 6
● Piave Merlot Sante '03	♀♀ 5

Italo Cescon

FRAZ. RONCADELLE
P.ZZA DEI CADUTI, 3
31024 ORMELLE [TV]
TEL. 0422851033
www.cesconitalo.it

ANNUAL PRODUCTION 800,000 bottles
HECTARES UNDER VINE 95
VITICULTURE METHOD Conventional

This traditional winery from the Piave area is enthusiastically managed by the founder's children – Domenico, Gloria and Graziella – who are committed to improving the standards of their wines and above all, imbuing them with distinctive personalities. The decision to enlarge the estate by purchasing new vineyards reflects this commitment. The Amaranto 72, a blend of separately vinified cabernet sauvignon, merlot, cabernet franc and marzemino, greets the nose with very appealing ripe fruit aromas that contrast with stylish floral hints and taut, supple progression on the palate. Raboso La Cesura is an excellent modern interpretation of an old wine type that puts the accent on ripe fruit and proffers a powerful, close-knit palate with good structure. The Cabernet Riserva is also generously broad, revealing all the aristocratic qualities of its grape on a moderately well-structured palate. The Chardonnay La Cesura is full bodied, beautifully made and rich with tropical fruit aromas.

Coffele

VIA ROMA, 5
37038 SOAVE [VR]
TEL. 0457680007
www.coffele.it

ANNUAL PRODUCTION 120,000 bottles
HECTARES UNDER VINE 27
VITICULTURE METHOD Conventional

The road rises slowly up from Soave round hairpin bends to Castelcerino, one of the designated zone's best-placed crus at an altitude of 350 metres. Here you will find Alberto and Chiara Coffele, two of the new generation of producers of Veneto's leading white. Their vineyards stand here in this extraordinary terroir, where the black, limestone-rich soil is complemented by sun and wind, creating ideal conditions for producing great wines. Alberto's concept of winemaking hinges on elegance and easy drinking, which means fresh fruit, florality and minerally aromas. All this comes out marvellously well in the generously rounded Ca' Visco 2006, a deep, seriously good blend of garganega and trebbiano di Soave. Alzari, a monovarietal Garganega aged in large wooden barrels, is every bit as impressive, showing lustrous vibrancy and style. The Coffeles' basic Soave is a typical interpretation of the garganega grape that offers peaches and almonds, as well as unmissable value for money. The wonderful sweet Recioto Le Sponde is quite excellent.

● Amaranto 72 '04	▼▼ 6
● Piave Cabernet La Cesura Ris. '04	▼▼ 5
● Piave Raboso La Cesura Ris. '03	▼▼ 5
○ Piave Chardonnay La Cesura '06	▼▼ 4*
○ Manzoni Bianco La Cesura '06	▼ 4
○ Piave Pinot Grigio La Cesura '06	▼ 4
○ Müller Thurgau La Cesura '06	▼ 4
○ P. di Valdobbiadene Extra Dry	▼ 4
○ Italo 06 '05	▼ 5
● Piave Merlot La Cesura Ris. '04	▼ 5
● Piave Raboso La Cesura Ris. '02	▼▼ 5
● Piave Cabernet La Cesura Ris. '02	▼▼ 4
● Piave Cabernet La Cesura Ris. '03	▼▼ 5

○ Recioto di Soave Cl. Le Sponde '05	▼ 6
○ Soave Cl. Alzari '05	▼▼ 5
○ Soave Cl. Ca' Visco '06	▼▼ 4*
○ Soave Cl. '06	▼▼ 4*
○ Soave Cl. Ca' Visco '05	▼▼▼ 4
○ Soave Cl. Ca' Visco '04	▼▼▼ 4
○ Soave Cl. Ca' Visco '03	▼▼▼ 4
○ Recioto di Soave Cl. Le Sponde '04	▼▼ 6
○ Recioto di Soave Cl. Le Sponde '03	▼▼ 6
○ Soave Cl. Alzari '04	▼▼ 5
○ Soave Cl. Alzari '03	▼▼ 5

Col Vetoraz

FRAZ. SANTO STEFANO
S.DA DELLE TRESIESE, 1
31040 VALDOBBIADENE [TV]
TEL. 0423975291
www.colvetoraz.it

ANNUAL PRODUCTION 800,000 bottles
HECTARES UNDER VINE 12
VITICULTURE METHOD Conventional

Every time we finish our round of tastings, we can't help noticing that this lovely Valdobbiadene winery is always right on target. It could be the delightful location, the opportunity to select the best lots of fruit, or the very appealing style but winemaker Loris Dall'Acqua, the heart of the winery, always manages to bring aromatic finesse and taut, juicy lightness out of the prosecco grape to make captivatingly elegant wines. The range is limited, enabling all the winery staff to focus their attention on the selections ageing in the vats. It would be hard to say which is the most impressive wine, since they are all impeccably good and utterly faithful to their respective types. The Extra Dry is joyous and sunny, the Brut assertive, the Cartizze full bodied and mature and the Millesimato exquisite, with sophisticated floral and citrus aromas and a delicate, creamy palate.

Conte Collalto

VIA 24 MAGGIO, 1
31058 SUSEGANA [TV]
TEL. 0438738241
www.collalto.it

ANNUAL PRODUCTION 800,000 bottles
HECTARES UNDER VINE 135
VITICULTURE METHOD Conventional

This large Susegana-based winery continues its broad-ranging project to renew all areas of the business, much of the cellar to livestock farming, on one of Veneto's most attractive and best-preserved historic villages on a beautifully kept estate that we recommend visiting. The wines, too, are taking great strides forward. In the absence of the estate champion, Torrai, we consoled ourselves with a lavish version of Rambaldo VIII, a Bordeaux blend in a modern key with a well-defined nose and very elegant palate. The two Proseccos made an equally excellent impression. The Brut is varietally aromatic on the nose with a compact, gutsy palate whereas the Extra Dry, with its higher residual sugar, has a sun-ripe, approachable palate. Also good are the Wildbacher, named after the Austrian grape that has long since acclimatized here, and the tangy, subtly aromatic Colli di Conegliano Bianco Schenella I.

○ P. di Valdobbiadene	
Dry Millesimato '06	🍷🍷 4
○ Cartizze	🍷🍷 6
○ P. di Valdobbiadene Brut	🍷🍷 4
○ P. di Valdobbiadene Extra Dry	🍷🍷 4

○ Colli di Conegliano Bianco	
Schenella I '06	🍷🍷 4*
○ P. di Conegliano Brut	
San Salvatore	🍷🍷 4*
○ P. di Conegliano Extra Dry	🍷🍷 4*
● Wildbacher '05	🍷🍷 4*
● Rambaldo VIII '03	🍷🍷 5
○ P. di Conegliano Tranquillo '06	🍷 3
○ Verdiso '06	🍷 3
○ Manzoni Bianco '06	🍷 3
● Incrocio Manzoni 2.15 '05	🍷 4
● Piave Cabernet '05	🍷 3
● Piave Cabernet Torrai Ris. '00	🍷🍷 5
● Rambaldo VIII '02	🍷🍷 5
● Piave Cabernet Torrai Ris. '99	🍷🍷 5

Le Colture
FRAZ. SANTO STEFANO
VIA FOLLO, 5
31049 VALDOBBIADENE [TV]
TEL. 0423900192
www.lecolture.it

ANNUAL PRODUCTION 520,000 bottles
HECTARES UNDER VINE 50
VITICULTURE METHOD Conventional

A glance at the figures above the profile will
show that Cesare and Renato Ruggeri's
winery differs from most Prosecco
producers in the range and style of the
wines produced, as well as in their
relationship with the land and vineyards. In
an area where most wineries buy in their
grapes, Le Colture has a substantial
vineyard holding and can so maintain
almost total control of the production
process. This is not just a Prosecco
operation for production of reds is also
coming up to speed at the Montello estate,
which has a very pleasant reception
building. But the most satisfying results still
come from the Valdobbiadene area.
Cartizze and Cruner continue to act as
influential ambassadors for the prosecco
grape and the local area. The former has
uncomplicated, but vibrant, very clearly
defined, aromas and an impressively firm
palate whereas the Cruner is more complex
and sophisticated on both nose and palate.
Finally, Rosso Orsere fell just short of Two
Glasses.

O Cartizze	♟	5
O P. di Valdobbiadene Dry Cruner	♟♟	4*
O P. di Valdobbiadene Brut Fagher	♟	4
O P. di Valdobbiadene Extra Dry Pianer '06	♟	4
● Rosso Orsere '03	♟	4
O P. di Valdobbiadene Tranquillo Masaré '06	♟	4
O P. di Valdobbiadene Frizzante Mas	♟	4
● Colli di Conegliano Rosso Salera '03	♟	5

Corte Gardoni
LOC. GARDONI, 5
37067 VALEGGIO SUL MINCIO [VR]
TEL. 0457950382
www.cortegardoni.it

ANNUAL PRODUCTION 200,000 bottles
HECTARES UNDER VINE 25
VITICULTURE METHOD Conventional

We have to admit that Gianni Piccoli has
always stayed true to a light, elegant
winemaking style that offers grip on the
palate, even when the market has been
pushing for chewy, over-concentrated
wines. Corte Gardoni has never lost sight of
its mission to offer quality and easy-drinking
pleasure. Today, the market tide is gradually
turning, Gianni's wines are now
extraordinarily contemporary, and he can
savour his revenge. Thanks in part to
several favourable years, the wines
presented this year are very good indeed.
Let's begin with Bardolino Le Fontane,
which shows a gutsy quality we had not
seen for a while backing up an enjoyably
taut, succulent palate with intense fruit. The
new Custoza Mael is excellent, showing
cheerful generosity in the mouth while the
Custoza 2006 is fragrant and racy on the
palate. When we sampled the reds, we
noted the Rosso di Corte was displaying its
usual class. This Bordeaux blend tips its hat
at France rather than California. Finally, our
tasters had a word of praise for the
intriguingly flavoursome Chiaretto.

⊙ Bardolino Chiaretto '06	♟♟	3*
O Bianco di Custoza Mael '06	♟♟	4
O Bianco di Custoza Passito Fenili '05	♟♟	6
● Rosso di Corte '04	♟♟	5
● Bardolino Le Fontane '06	♟♟	3*
● Bardolino Sup. '05	♟♟	4
● Becco Rosso '05	♟	4
● Garda Merlot Vallidium '04	♟	5
O Garda Chardonnay Vallidium '06	♟	4
O Nichesole Vallidium '06	♟	4
O Bianco di Custoza '06	♟	3
● Bardolino Sup. '04	♟♟	4
● Bardolino Sup. '03	♟♟	4
● Bardolino Sup. '02	♟♟	4

Corte Rugolin
FRAZ. VALGATARA
LOC. RUGOLIN
37020 MARANO DI VALPOLICELLA [VR]
TEL. 0457702153
www.corterugolin.it

ANNUAL PRODUCTION	60,000 bottles
HECTARES UNDER VINE	11
VITICULTURE METHOD	Conventional

Elena and Federico Coati have opted to postpone release of their Amarone Monte Danieli, which they consider not yet ready for the corkscrew, but the Amarone Crosara de le Strie helped us get over the disappointment. It's from the same vintage but less richly extracted and so it is already mature and drinking beautifully. As we did last year, we thought the Valpolicella Superiore was the most impressive bottle with its sound, incredibly fresh fruit aromas backing a taut but supple, dry palate with creamy tannins. The Amarone gives crisp, well-defined fruit streaked through with minerality and medicinal herbs that are nicely reflected on the savoury, harmonious palate. Lastly, there's an honourable mention for the standard-label Valpolicella, a wine type the cellar is particularly skilful at handling. Fruit melding with aromas of pepper and flowers that lead into a supple, relaxed palate make this wine an ideal companion at the dinner table.

Corte Sant'Alda
LOC. FIOI
VIA CAPOVILLA, 28
37030 MEZZANE DI SOTTO [VR]
TEL. 0458880006
www.cortesantalda.it

ANNUAL PRODUCTION	82,000 bottles
HECTARES UNDER VINE	16.8
VITICULTURE METHOD	Certified organic

Marinella Camerani has plenty of character and sensitivity. Over time, she and Cesar Roman have come to realize that the real personality of a wine derives from attentive growers who respect the environment and shrewd work in the cellar to bring out the best in the grape during its evolution into wine without forcing that development. The 20003 Amarone comes from a very dry year with little temperature variation and shows characteristically vibrant fruit alongside spicy and minerally aromas. The huge palate is an exemplary mix of strength and elegance. The Valpolicella Superiore Mithas is equally impressive and very appealing. Ripe, healthy fruit reveals itself slowly amid subtle hints of aromatic herbs and wonderful minerally sensations. The rest of the range is also excellent, from the very impressive yet simple, harmonious Soave to the succulent Valpolicella Cà Fiui.

● Valpolicella Cl. Sup. Ripasso '04	▼▼ 5
● Amarone della Valpolicella Cl. Crosara de le Strie '03	▼▼ 6
● Valpolicella Cl. '06	▼▼ 3*
● Valpolicella Cl. Sup. Ripasso '03	♡♡ 5
● Amarone della Valpolicella Cl. Monte Danieli '01	♡♡ 7
● Amarone della Valpolicella Cl. Monte Danieli '00	♡♡ 7
● Amarone della Valpolicella Cl. Monte Danieli '99	♡♡ 7
● Amarone della Valpolicella Cl. Monte Danieli '98	♡♡ 7
● Amarone della Valpolicella Cl. Monte Danieli '97	♡♡ 7

● Amarone della Valpolicella '03	▼▼ 8
● Valpolicella Sup. Mithas '03	▼▼ 7
○ Soave V. di Mezzane '06	▼▼ 4*
● Valpolicella Sup. '04	▼▼ 6
● Valpolicella Cà Fiui '06	▼▼ 4*
● Valpolicella Sup. '03	♡♡♡ 6
● Amarone della Valpolicella '00	♡♡♡ 8
● Amarone della Valpolicella '98	♡♡♡ 8
● Amarone della Valpolicella '95	♡♡♡ 8
● Amarone della Valpolicella '90	♡♡♡ 8
● Amarone della Valpolicella Mithas '95	♡♡♡ 8
● Amarone della Valpolicella Mithas '00	♡♡ 8
● Valpolicella Sup. Mithas '01	♡♡ 6
● Valpolicella Sup. Mithas '00	♡♡ 6

★ Romano Dal Forno

FRAZ. CELLORE
LOC. LODOLETTA, 1
37030 ILLASI [VR]
TEL. 0457834923
www.dalforno.net

ANNUAL PRODUCTION 45,000 bottles
HECTARES UNDER VINE 25
VITICULTURE METHOD Conventional

Romano Dal Forno's bottles never fail to astonish for quality, which is always very high indeed, interpretation of the vintage, and handling of the designated zone's wine types. Were it not so depressing, we might even raise a smile at the legislation that creates a Passito Rosso, since this wine was not recognized as Recioto della Valpolicella. But the inadequacy of the production protocols makes it possible for DOC or DOCG wines of dubious quality to be sold in discount supermarkets while at the same time preventing one of the greatest Reciotos to be identified as such. This wine is guaranteed a long lifespan by its generous fruit, alluring sweetness and enormous body. Unlike many other producers, Dal Forno produced Amarone even in the unfavourable 2002 growing year and has offered us a wine that shuns extremes, preserving the typical Dal Forno style that combines concentration with opulence. The Valpolicella is built on the same lines but is still marked by oak.

Luigino Dal Maso

LOC. SELVA
C.DA SELVA, 62
36054 MONTEBELLO VICENTINO [VI]
TEL. 0444649104
www.dalmasovini.com

ANNUAL PRODUCTION 500,000 bottles
HECTARES UNDER VINE 30
VITICULTURE METHOD Conventional

Driven by Nicola Dal Maso's endless energy, this Montebello winery forges firmly ahead in the right direction. The garganega-based whites made at Gambellara get more exciting by the year: the extremely enjoyable basic Ca' Fischele; the contemporary but not excessive Riva del Molino, which is well-structured with aromas of almonds and citrus, and the alluring Recioto Riva dei Perari. And there's more good news from the Colli Berici. Here, the now-mature vineyards are delivering series of reds with good personality. The aromas of the Terra dei Rovi, made from cabernet sauvignon, carmenère and merlot, embrace balsam and flowers while the palate is fresh, powerful and spontaneous. Colpizzarda is at the heart of a concerted effort to bring out all the potential of the tocai rosso grape in Colli Berici. Close-knit texture, streaked with a minerally note, refresh a particularly subtle, long-lingering palate.

Wine	Rating
● Valpolicella Sup. Vign. di Monte Lodoletta '03	▼▼ 8
● Amarone della Valpolicella Vign. di Monte Lodoletta '02	▼▼ 8
● Vigna Seré Passito '03	▼▼ 8
● Amarone della Valpolicella Vign. di Monte Lodoletta '01	▼▼▼ 8
● Amarone della Valpolicella Vign. di Monte Lodoletta '00	▼▼▼ 8
● Amarone della Valpolicella Vign. di Monte Lodoletta '99	▼▼▼ 8
● Amarone della Valpolicella Vign. di Monte Lodoletta '98	▼▼▼ 8
● Amarone della Valpolicella Vign. di Monte Lodoletta '97	▼▼▼ 8
● Amarone della Valpolicella Vign. di Monte Lodoletta '96	▼▼▼ 8

Wine	Rating
● Colli Berici Tocai Rosso Colpizzarda '05	▼▼ 5
● Terra dei Rovi Rosso '05	▼▼ 6
● Colli Berici Cabernet Casara Roveri '04	▼▼ 5
O Recioto di Gambellara Cl. Riva dei Perari '05	▼▼ 5
O Gambellara Cl. Riva del Molino '06	▼▼ 4*
● Colli Berici Cabernet Montebelvedere '05	▼▼ 4*
● Colli Berici Merlot Casara Roveri '04	▼▼ 5
O Gambellara Cl. Ca' Fischele '06	▼ 3
● Colli Berici Tocai Rosso Colpizzarda '04	▽▽ 4
● Terra dei Rovi Rosso '04	▽▽ 6
● Terra dei Rovi Rosso '03	▽▽ 6

De Stefani

VIA CADORNA, 92
30020 FOSSALTA DI PIAVE [VE]
TEL. 042167502
www.de-stefani.it

ANNUAL PRODUCTION 300,000 bottles
HECTARES UNDER VINE 40
VITICULTURE METHOD Conventional

Although all the wines here have been demoted to the status of IGTs, the profile of the winery owned by Alessandro De Stefani and his father Tiziano follows the pattern typical of wineries along the river Piave. There's a decent area under vine and a broad range of wines catering for all tastes. The three winery complexes, at Fossalta, Monastier and Refrontolo, make wines with very different aspirations. Yet again, the most impressive bottle was the rich, mouthfillingly soft Olmera, an original blend of tocai and sauvignon. Hot on its heels was Terre Nobili, a blend of cabernet sauvignon, merlot and refosco. This red unveils well-developed, vibrant aromas and a rounded, mature palate. Only just behind the leading pair is Vitalys, which combines the freshness of the chardonnay grape with the rich texture of tocai, resulting in a dense but not daunting white. The other bottles on the list are reliably good but there are apecial mentions for the Brut Tombola di Pin and the Refosco Kreda.

F.lli Degani

FRAZ. VALGATARA
VIA TOBELE, 3A
37020 MARANO DI VALPOLICELLA [VR]
TEL. 0457701850
aldo.degani@tin.it

ANNUAL PRODUCTION 30,000 bottles
HECTARES UNDER VINE 4
VITICULTURE METHOD Conventional

The Degani brothers grew up in an atmosphere where the winery was an extension of the home. Very little has changed since then but the cellar has decided to rent a warehouse further down the valley in the near future. This will become the shipping office, making more working space available at Valgatara. The Degani family could soon be making use of four more hectares in the Classico zone at Fumane. When restructuring and replanting work is complete, we will see a gradual increase in the quantity of wine produced, starting with the 2008 vintage. The Classico Superiore Cicilio, made with the ripasso technique, has a generous fruity nose with hints of chocolate but is still seeking harmony on the palate. Despite its youth, the Amarone 2004 shows depth and concentration that augur well for cellarability. The Recioto La Rosta 2005 has good, well-integrated texture and balance while the Amarone La Rosta is redolent of herbs and minerality with a taut, dry palate that falls off a little in the finish.

● Terre Nobili Rosso '05	♥♥ 6
O Olmera '06	♥♥ 6
O Vitalys '06	♥♥ 4
O Chardonnay '06	♥ 4
O P. Spumante Extra Dry Metodo Zero	♥ 4
O Tombola di Pin M. Cl. Brut '01	♥ 7
O Pinot Grigio '06	♥ 5
O Passito Passut '04	♥ 7
● Colli di Conegliano Refrontolo Passito '04	♥ 7
● Soler '04	♥ 5
● Merlot '05	♥ 5
● Refosco P. R. Kreda '05	♥ 6
O Olmera Le Ronche '05	♀♀ 5
O Olmera Le Ronche '04	♀♀ 5

● Amarone della Valpolicella Cl. '04	♥♥ 5
● Amarone della Valpolicella Cl. La Rosta '04	♥♥ 6
● Valpolicella Cl. Sup. Cicilio Ripasso '04	♥♥ 4*
● Recioto della Valpolicella Cl. La Rosta '05	♥♥ 5
● Recioto della Valpolicella Cl. '05	♥ 5
● Amarone della Valpolicella Cl. '03	♀♀ 5
● Amarone della Valpolicella Cl. '01	♀♀ 6
● Recioto della Valpolicella Cl. La Rosta '03	♀♀ 5
● Recioto della Valpolicella Cl. La Rosta '02	♀♀ 6

Fasoli

FRAZ. SAN ZENO
VIA C. BATTISTI, 49
37030 COLOGNOLA AI COLLI [VR]
TEL. 0457650741
www.fasoligino.com

ANNUAL PRODUCTION 150,000 bottles
HECTARES UNDER VINE 18
VITICULTURE METHOD Certified organic

The winery owned by the Fasoli brothers, Amadio and Natalino, is rather unusual in several ways. Located in an area where the two leading Veronese designated areas, Soave and Valpolicella, jostle for vineyard space, it is a cellar with a deep-rooted passion for dried-grape white and red wines, organically managed vineyards and the Fasolis' decision to plant international grape varieties. The results are very good indeed on the white and red fronts. From the whites we particularly liked two garganega-based wines, the fresh, lean, no-nonsense Soave Borgoletto and Liber, a monovarietal, oak-tinged garganega with good structure and grip. Turning to the reds, we were unable to taste the Amarone, which was not presented, so we focused our attention on two Merlots. The rounded, robustly structured Calle has Mediterranean scrubland aromas and minerally hints on the nose and the Orgno reveals even greater depth and richness of extract. The Recioto San Zeno is also good.

Il Filò delle Vigne

VIA TERRALBA, 14
35030 BAONE [PD]
TEL. 042956243
www.ilfilodellevigne.it

ANNUAL PRODUCTION 40,000 bottles
HECTARES UNDER VINE 18
VITICULTURE METHOD Conventional

Do not be deceived by the lack of coloured glasses below. In some ways, these wines are even more impressive than the Three Glasses that just escaped this Baone cellar last year. The difference is in the vintages presented. A professional winery, run by Nicolò Voltan and Carlo Giordani with the assistance of Andrea Boaretti and cellar manager Matteo Zanaica, Il Filò delle Vigne produced the best possible interpretation of everything the hot summer of 2003 had to offer. Borgo delle Casette is well-rounded with explosive ripe fruit aromas and a soft, mouthfilling palate where rugged tannins keep the wine's rich palate in line. Vigna Cecilia di Baone is fresher, since it aged exclusively in concrete-lined vats. It offers mature aromas although the palate is slimmer and more savoury. Luna del Parco is less well rounded after the damp autumn weather in 2005 but it is subtle on both nose and palate. The two dry whites are interesting. Vigna delle Acacie is fresh and well defined whereas Calto delle Fate is more structured and challenging.

○ Liber Bianco '04	▼▼	5
○ Soave Borgoletto '06	▼▼	4*
● Merlot Calle '05	▼▼	6
● Merlot Orgno '05	▼▼	7
● Pinot Nero Sande '03	▼	6
○ Recioto di Soave S. Zeno '04	▼	6
○ Soave Pieve Vecchia '05		5
○ Soave Borgoletto '05	▼▼	4
○ Recioto di Soave S. Zeno '03	▼▼	6
○ Recioto di Soave S. Zeno '02	▼▼	6
● Merlot Calle '04	▼▼	6
● Merlot Calle '03	▼▼	6

● Colli Euganei Cabernet Borgo delle Casette Ris. '03	▼▼	5
● Colli Euganei Cabernet Vigna Cecilia di Baone Ris. '03	▼▼	5
○ Colli Euganei Fior d'Arancio Luna del Parco '05	▼▼	6
○ Colli Euganei Pinot Bianco Vigna delle Acacie '06	▼	4
○ Il Calto delle Fate '05	▼	5
○ Colli Euganei Fior d'Arancio Luna del Parco '04	▼▼	6
● Colli Euganei Cabernet Borgo delle Casette Ris. '02	▼▼	5
● Colli Euganei Cabernet Borgo delle Casette Ris. '01	▼▼	5
● Colli Euganei Cabernet Borgo delle Casette Ris. '00	▼▼	5

Silvano Follador

FRAZ. SANTO STEFANO
LOC. FOLLO
VIA CALLONGA, 11
31040 VALDOBBIADENE [TV]
TEL. 0423900295
www.silvanofollador.it

ANNUAL PRODUCTION 45,000 bottles
HECTARES UNDER VINE 4
VITICULTURE METHOD   Natural

A few years ago brother and sister Silvano and Alberta Follador inherited this very small farm and threw themselves into this adventure with passion and enthusiasm from the first, demonstrating a desire to follow alternative, unusual directions for the Prosecco zone, primarily biodynamic farming. The young pair seem particularly enamoured of this system lately, which aims to restrict human and technical interference with the wines as much as possible. It is an interesting approach to apply, particularly to a land and a wine like Prosecco, whose sparkling version is heavily reliant on technology. The results are encouraging although up until now they have not moved too far away from conventional procedures, especially in the cellar. Both the Cartizze and the Brut, which will probably be the only wine produced here in the future, walk away with Two Glasses, having impressed us with their clearly defined aromas and harmonious flavour.

Le Fraghe

LOC. COLOMBARA, 3
37010 CAVAION VERONESE [VR]
TEL. 0457236832
www.fraghe.it

ANNUAL PRODUCTION 90,000 bottles
HECTARES UNDER VINE 28
VITICULTURE METHOD   Conventional

The term benchmark usually refers to assessing the results of a financial product or a business procedure. If we were to look for a benchmark Bardolino for the traditional area, we would probably end up choosing from the products of Matilde Poggi, who for many years has presented us with flawless Bardolinos that combine satisfyingly lean palates with thoroughly respectable complexity on the nose. The Bardolino 2006 has both floral and earthy aromas, entering on the palate with compelling fruit roundness and then managing to remain supple and fragrant. As usual, the light sprinkling of spice so typical of corvina grapes grown on Lake Garda emerges over time. The savoury rosé version of Bardolino, Chiaretto Ròdo, has berry fruit aromas. The Garganega Camporengo is as ever a successful interpretation of the hilly terroir between Garda and Valdadige. Finally, the 2004 version of the winery's lovely Cabernet, Quaiare, will be released later on as ageing has been extended.

O Cartizze	♟♟ 5
O P. di Valdobbiadene Brut	♟♟ 4

● Bardolino '06	♟♟ 3*
☉ Bardolino Chiaretto Ròdon '06	♟ 3
O Garganega Camporengo '06	♟ 3
● Quaiare Cabernet '03	♟♟ 4
● Quaiare Cabernet '01	♟♟ 5
● Quaiare Cabernet '00	♟♟ 5
● Quaiare Cabernet '98	♟♟ 5
● Quaiare Cabernet '97	♟♟ 5
● Quaiare Cabernet '96	♟♟ 5

Tenute Galtarossa
VIA ANDREA MONGA, 9
37029 SAN PIETRO IN CARIANO [VR]
TEL. 0456838307
www.tenutegaltarossa.com

Gini
VIA MATTEOTTI, 42
37032 MONTEFORTE D'ALPONE [VR]
TEL. 0457611908
www.ginivini.com

ANNUAL PRODUCTION 50,000 bottles
HECTARES UNDER VINE 80
VITICULTURE METHOD Conventional

ANNUAL PRODUCTION 200,000 bottles
HECTARES UNDER VINE 30
VITICULTURE METHOD Conventional

Valpolicella is not just hills and valleys. Much of the vine stock is situated on the plains and wineries usually use the grapes for the production of plain beverage wines. Since he embarked on his venture, Giacomo Galtarossa has always energetically demonstrated that with careful vineyard management and skilful cellar work, it is possible to obtain high profile results from the plains where human effort may even be more crucial than in the big name crus. Giacomo only presented us with one wine, since the Valpolicella and the red Massabò are still resting in the cellar, and that one wine was the Amarone from the promising 2004 vintage. Despite its early release, the wine already shows dry, crisp fruit freshness although the oak is still a little over-assertive. The considerable pulp is very successfully handled on the wine's beautifully balanced palate.

One of the things that make wine a cultural icon as well as a drink is that it cannot be invented from one day to the next. You need land in good wine country, a good quality grape, hard work and lots of time, all the time required by the vine to put down deep roots, and by the grower to find a way of bringing together all these variables. None of these things are missing at the winery belonging to Sandro and Claudio Gini, who have always been two of the most meticulous producers in the Soave area. The vine stock is almost a century old, and in some cases even older, and brings us two exceptional interpretations of the great Verona white. The first is the tropical yet mineral-edged Salvarenza, with its excellent structure and grip. But it was the second, La Froscà, one of the creamiest, most stylish versions of the wine type that picked up Three resounding Glasses. Finally, the Soave Classico has strikingly harmonious flavours while the Sorai and Maciete Fumé are Verona interpretations of two international grapes.

● Amarone della Valpolicella Cl. '04	♟♟ 7
● Amarone della Valpolicella Cl. '03	♟♟ 7
● Amarone della Valpolicella Cl. '01	♟♟ 7
● Amarone della Valpolicella Cl. '00	♟♟ 7
● Valpolicella Cl. Sup. Corte Colombara '04	♟♟ 5
● Valpolicella Cl. Sup. Corte Colombara '03	♟♟ 5
● Valpolicella Cl. Sup. Corte Colombara '02	♟♟ 5

O Soave Cl. La Froscà '06	♟♟♟ 5
O Soave Cl. Contrada Salvarenza Vecchie Vigne '05	♟♟ 5
O Soave Cl. '06	♟♟ 4*
O Chardonnay Sorai '05	♟♟ 5
O Sauvignon Maciete Fumé '06	♟ 5
O Soave Cl. La Froscà '05	♟♟♟ 5
O Soave Cl. Sup. Contrada Salvarenza Vecchie Vigne '00	♟♟♟ 6
O Soave Cl. Sup. Contrada Salvarenza Vecchie Vigne '98	♟♟♟ 5
O Soave Cl. Sup. La Froscà '97	♟♟♟ 5
O Soave Cl. Sup. La Froscà '99	♟♟♟ 5
O Soave Cl. Contrada Salvarenza Vecchie Vigne '04	♟♟ 5

Gregoletto

FRAZ. PREMAOR
VIA SAN MARTINO, 83
31050 MIANE [TV]
TEL. 0438970463
www.gregoletto.com

ANNUAL PRODUCTION 200,000 bottles
HECTARES UNDER VINE 15
VITICULTURE METHOD Conventional

It's hard to do justice to Guerrieri Rizzardi, a history-soaked winery with a high profile and vine stock in all the most important DOC zones around Verona, not to mention an increasingly impressive range. So after last year's excellent performance, which saw Three Glasses going to Amarone Villa Rizzardi, we are delighted to have enjoyed Tacchetto, a Bardolino with extraordinary grip and finesse. The subtle, varied aromas are echoed on a palate that combines full body with grip, lightness and savouriness, rounding off with a long finish. In short, it's a hymn to wines made for drinking, not just tasting. The Soave Costeggiola is back on the fine form of a few years ago while the Valpolicella Poiega shows complex aromas and integrity on the palate. Finally, the two Amarones are both still very young. Villa Rizzardi has red berries and spices on the nose with a powerful, warm palate while Calcarole is more closed, although it also has superb texture and a shining future ahead. It was thanks to these prospects that it earned its richly deserved Three Glasses.

Guerrieri Rizzardi

VIA VERDI, 4
37011 BARDOLINO [VR]
TEL. 0457210028
www.guerrieri-rizzardi.it

ANNUAL PRODUCTION 600,000 bottles
HECTARES UNDER VINE 100
VITICULTURE METHOD Conventional

Stefano Inama's wines are always a guarantee of quality. Although production is neatly divided between Colli Berici and Soave, which means very different grapes and land, the results are invariably good and show an admirable uniformity of style. And the Inama style is based on rich extract, grip and freshness, qualities that are not always easy to find in wines. This year, we particularly enjoyed the whites, which have drawn the very best from favourable harvests. Vin Soave is excellent and placed at the bottom of the range only in terms of numbers and price. It is actually a very fine quality wine with a perfectly harmonious, succulently tangy palate. The rounded, juicy Foscarino is also very good but the most thrilling of all is Du Lot, a generous, mineral-edged, fruity white with a tangy, long-lingering palate. Its supreme quality earned Stefano Inama Three resounding Glasses. The sumptuous Oracolo is very good and the debut version of Carmenère Più shows promise.

● Colli di Conegliano Rosso '03	♀♀ 6
● Merlot '05	♀♀ 3*
○ Colli di Conegliano Bianco Albio '06	♀♀ 4
○ Prosecco Frizzante '06	♀♀ 3*
○ P. di Conegliano Extra Dry	♀♀ 4
○ P. di Conegliano Valdobbiadene Tranquillo '06	♀♀ 3*
○ Manzoni Bianco '06	♀♀ 4
○ Pinot Bianco '06	♀♀ 4
○ Chardonnay '06	♀ 3
○ Verdiso Frizzante '06	♀ 3
● Cabernet '05	♀ 3
○ Colli di Conegliano Bianco Albio '05	♀♀ 3

● Amarone della Valpolicella Cl. Calcarole '03	♀♀♀ 8
● Amarone della Valpolicella Cl. Villa Rizzardi '03	♀♀ 7
● Bardolino Cl. Sup. Munus '05	♀♀ 5
● Bardolino Cl. Tacchetto '06	♀♀ 4
● Valpolicella Cl. Sup. Ripasso Poiega '05	♀♀ 4
⊙ Rosa Rosae '06	♀♀ 4
○ Soave Cl. Costeggiola '06	♀♀ 4
○ Soave Cl. '06	♀ 3
○ Valdadige Chardonnay Vignaunica '06	♀ 4
● Valpolicella Cl. '06	♀ 3
● Amarone della Valpolicella Cl. Villa Rizzardi '01	♀♀♀ 7
● Amarone della Valpolicella Cl. Calcarole '00	♀♀ 8

Inama

LOC. BIACCHE, 50
37047 SAN BONIFACIO [VR]
TEL. 0456104343
www.inamaaziendaagricola.it

ANNUAL PRODUCTION 300,000 bottles
HECTARES UNDER VINE 45
VITICULTURE METHOD Conventional

Stefano Inama's wines are always a guarantee of quality. Although production is neatly divided between Colli Berici and Soave, which means very different grapes and land, the results are invariably good and show an admirable uniformity of style. And the Inama style is based on rich extract, grip and freshness, qualities that are not always easy to find in wines. This year, we particularly enjoyed the whites, which have drawn the very best from favourable harvests. Vin Soave is excellent and placed at the bottom of the range only in terms of numbers and price. It is actually a very fine quality wine with a perfectly harmonious, succulently tangy palate. The rounded, juicy Foscarino is also very good but the most thrilling of all is Du Lot, a generous, mineral-edged, fruity white with a tangy, long-lingering palate. Its supreme quality earned Stefano Inama Three resounding Glasses. The sumptuous Oracolo is very good and the debut version of Carmenère Più shows promise.

Castello di Lispida

VIA IV NOVEMBRE, 4
35043 MONSELICE [PD]
TEL. 0429780530
www.lispida.com

ANNUAL PRODUCTION 18,000 bottles
HECTARES UNDER VINE 8
VITICULTURE METHOD Natural

The concept of natural farming, developed by Japanese farmer Masanobu Fūkuoka, is the inspiration for Alessandro Sgaravatti's work at Castello di Lispida in the Colli Euganei. It's rather like going back to basics, to recover land that has been mauled and exploited by human greed in order to bring out the character of territory and vine, allowing the wine to evolve in respectful silence. Having visited the very cradle of viticulture in the Caucasus, Alessandro has now been experimenting with earthenware jars for some years. His Amphora, a white from tocai grapes that undergo very long maceration on the skins, is now famous. We recommend opening the bottle early and then pouring the wine into a large glass to allow it to breathe and dispel the slightly muzzy sensations. The more impressive Terralba 2003, made mainly from tocai, is floral, fruity and enjoyably drinkable. The Montelispida, a monovarietal Merlot, has aromas of violets and a succulent, lingering palate. The merlot-heavy Terraforte is sumptuous with a flavoursome hint of cherries. Finally, the new H is a sparkler and well worth tasting.

O Soave Cl. Vign. Du Lot '05	♟♟♟	5
O Soave Cl. Vign. di Foscarino '05	♟♟	5
O Soave Cl. Vin Soave '06	♟♟	4
● Oracolo '03	♟♟	8
● Carmenère Più '05	♟	6
O Soave Cl. Vign. Du Lot '01	♟♟♟	5
O Soave Cl. Vign. Du Lot '00	♟♟♟	5
O Soave Cl. Vign. Du Lot '99	♟♟♟	5
O Soave Cl. Vign. Du Lot '96	♟♟♟	5
O Soave Cl. Vign. Du Lot '03	♟♟	5
O Soave Cl. Vign. Du Lot '02	♟♟	5
O Soave Cl. Vign. di Foscarino '04	♟♟	5

● Montelispida '02	♟♟	6
O Terralba '03	♟♟	6
O Amphora '05	♟	7
O H Brut '06	♟	5
● Terraforte '02	♟	6
● Montelispida '01	♟♟	6
● Terraforte '01	♟♟	6
O Amphora '04	♟♟	7

Conte Loredan Gasparini

FRAZ. VENEGAZZÙ
VIA MARTIGNAGO ALTO, 23
31040 VOLPAGO DEL MONTELLO [TV]
TEL. 0423870024
www.venegazzu.com

ANNUAL PRODUCTION 280,000 bottles
HECTARES UNDER VINE 80
VITICULTURE METHOD Natural

The return of Lorenzo Palla to work in the winery with his father Giancarlo has triggered enthusiasm and renewed commitment. The already very interesting results from recent years have developed further and we don't just mean the winery's two standard-bearers; we're also talking about the basic products, which provide an image of the winery's solidity. The house champ is again Capo di Stato, a Bordeaux blend. Its aromas are still very youthful, and almost heady, but the palate is where this wine really impresses with substantial texture flawlessly handled and supported by fresh acidity and fine-grained tannins. The Venegazzù della Casa is just a step behind and is already harmonious, again performing better on the palate, where it shows savoury and good texture. The Falconera is very good. Its simple, fruity nose and character in the mouth offer dry, vigorous drinking. The Manzoni Bianco and Prosecco Brut came close to a second Glass.

★ Maculan

VIA CASTELLETTO, 3
36042 BREGANZE [VI]
TEL. 0445873733
www.maculan.net

ANNUAL PRODUCTION 850,000 bottles
HECTARES UNDER VINE 39
VITICULTURE METHOD Conventional

Many years have passed since Fausto Maculan asserted himself as one of the leaders of the Italian wine renaissance. Now that certain vineyard and cellar procedures are taken for granted, it is good to remember that a few years back only a few producers were pushing for quality. The Maculan range gets bigger every year and both the reds and the sweet wines are very reliable. Experimentation continues in the cellar to avoid premature oxidation of the must in the whites and preserve their freshness. Vespaiolo 2006 has benefited from this, with its combination of cleanness and fresh aromas. Among the reds, we noted the huge structure of Fratta and Crosara, supported by California-style use of new oak, and certainly recommend them to lovers of this type. The more stylish, long-limbed Cabernet Palazzotto, however, is a better expression of the potential of Breganze. With its finesse and wonderfully healthy fruit, it won another Three Glass prize to go with the one from last year's Guide. On the sweet wine front, we had a special mention for Torcolato, as ever a winery champion of finesse and concentration.

● Capo di Stato '04	♀♀ 6
● Falconera Rosso '05	♀♀ 4
● Venegazzù della Casa '04	♀♀ 5
○ Montello e Colli Asolani Prosecco Brut	♀ 4
○ Manzoni Bianco '06	♀ 4
● Capo di Stato '03	♀♀ 6
● Venegazzù della Casa '03	♀♀ 5
● Capo di Stato '02	♀♀ 6
● Venegazzù della Casa '02	♀♀ 5
● Capo di Stato '00	♀♀ 6

● Breganze Cabernet Sauvignon Palazzotto '05	♀♀♀ 5
● Fratta '05	♀♀ 8
○ Breganze Torcolato '05	♀♀ 7
○ Acininobili '03	♀♀ 8
● Breganze Rosso Crosara '05	♀♀ 8
● Brentino '05	♀♀ 4
● Madoro Passito '05	♀♀ 7
● Breganze Cabernet '05	♀ 4
● Speaia '05	♀ 4
○ Breganze Vespaiolo '06	♀ 3
○ Pino & Toi '06	♀ 3
○ Ferrata '06	♀ 5
○ Dindarello '06	♀ 5
○ Breganze di Breganze '06	♀ 4
● Breganze Cabernet Sauvignon Palazzotto '04	♀♀ 5
● Fratta '01	♀♀♀ 8

Manara

FRAZ. SAN FLORIANO
VIA DON CESARE BIASI, 53
37020 SAN PIETRO IN CARIANO [VR]
TEL. 0457701086
www.manaravini.it

ANNUAL PRODUCTION 75,000 bottles
HECTARES UNDER VINE 11
VITICULTURE METHOD Conventional

The Manara brothers are a marvellously coherent example of how winemaking tradition and innovation can coexist in harmony. The various growing years are interpreted pragmatically and enthusiastically in the vineyards while the cellar procedures are carried out with no preconceived ideas, respecting the identity of the territory and the vintage. Special praise goes to the Valpolicella Le Morete, a successful attempt to achieve rich concentration and personality without neglecting tradition. This is a very drinkable, spontaneously elegant wine, thanks also to a light hand during vinification. The more impressive Amarone was the Classico, which is mature and traditional without excess. The Postera is tighter but also richer, and will be worth coming back to in a few years. Guido Manara, from 70 per cent cabernet sauvignon with some merlot and croatina, is rich in texture but still struggling to absorb the oak. The Recioto Moronalto is very fresh-tasting while El Rocolo has juicier fruit and nicely judged sweetness.

Le Mandolare

LOC. BROGNOLIGO
VIA FONTANA NUOVA, 1
37030 MONTEFORTE D'ALPONE [VR]
TEL. 0456175083
www.cantinalemandolare.com

ANNUAL PRODUCTION 60,000 bottles
HECTARES UNDER VINE 25
VITICULTURE METHOD Conventional

As always with great wines, the strength of Soave comes from many different factors, each of which contributes in its own way to the final result. These include varied territory, good soil composition of laval basalt and limestone, and a very hardy grape variety that is not especially rich in aromas but sensitive to growing conditions and able to express every shade of variation. Finally, there is the grape's versatility, like that of clay waiting to be shaped in the hands of a skilled producer. It is thanks to this that Renzo Rodighiero and his wife Germana produce three dry wines and one sweet, representing four aspects of Soave and the garganega grape. Monte Sella is the finest expression of this grape, showing rich but supple on its taut, mouthwatering palate. Il Roccolo, on the other hand, reveals the variety's simplicity and healthy rustic character while Corte Menini shows its more yielding and accessible side. Lastly, the Recioto highlights the sunny Mediterranean nature of the territory.

● Amarone della Valpolicella Cl. '03	▼▼	6
● Guido Manara '04	▼▼	6
● Amarone della Valpolicella Cl. Postera '03	▼▼	6
● Recioto della Valpolicella Cl. El Rocolo '04	▼▼	5
● Recioto della Valpolicella Cl. Moronalto '05	▼▼	5
● Valpolicella Cl. Sup. Le Morete Ripasso '04	▼▼	4*
○ Strinà Passito '04	▼	5
● Valpolicella Cl. Sup. '04	▼	3
● Amarone della Valpolicella Cl. '00	♀♀♀	6
● Amarone della Valpolicella Cl. '01	♀♀	6
● Amarone della Valpolicella Cl. '02	♀♀	6
● Guido Manara '03	♀♀	6

○ Soave Cl. Sup. Monte Sella '05	▼▼	4*
○ Recioto di Soave Cl. Le Schiavette '05	▼▼	5
○ Soave Cl. Il Roccolo '06	▼▼	3*
○ Soave Cl. Corte Menini '06	▼	3
○ Soave Cl. Sup. Monte Sella '04	♀♀	4
○ Recioto di Soave Cl. Le Schiavette '04	♀♀	5
○ Recioto di Soave Cl. Le Schiavette '03	♀♀	5

Marcato

VIA PRANDI, 10
37030 RONCÀ [VR]
TEL. 0457460070
www.marcatovini.it

ANNUAL PRODUCTION 420,000 bottles
HECTARES UNDER VINE 98
VITICULTURE METHOD Conventional

Marcato has its main centre at Roncà, on the outer limits of the Soave Classico zone but production covers three designated zones with very different products and ambitions. Vineyards in the province of Verona produce three dry wines and a dried-grape wine: we particularly liked Recioto di Soave Il Duello for its lively tropical aromas, rounded body and nicely integrated sweetness. The property at Lessinia, in contrast, brings us two sparkling wines and another dried-grape product, all made from durello grapes. The biting acidity of this variety endows the wines with personality: the Charmat version is the most approachable and uncomplicated, whereas the Passito is generous, mature and complex, and the Metodo Classico has mature aromas on the nose accompanying a taut, sophisticated palate. The third estate is in the Colli Berici, now emerging as one of Veneto's most interesting areas. The excellent Pianalto is a Cabernet Riserva with richly expressive aromas and a long, savoury palate. The Merlot Asinara and Cabernet La Giareta are simpler but equally well made.

Marion

LOC. MARCELLISE
VIA BORGO, 1
37036 SAN MARTINO BUON ALBERGO [VR]
TEL. 0458740021
www.marionvini.it

ANNUAL PRODUCTION 30,000 bottles
HECTARES UNDER VINE 14
VITICULTURE METHOD Conventional

Marion is on its unstoppable way up. Every year, the whole range of wines tasted is flawless and in some cases reaches the very peak of quality. Congratulations to Stefano Campedelli and his wife Nicoletta: we hope they will continue along their chosen path. The Amarone 2001 has a modern oak-tinged profile with nicely concentrated fruit. Toasted oak aromas alternate on the generous, complex nose with ripe red berries, florality and minerally sensations while the considerable texture is deftly handled on the balanced palate. This extraordinary Amarone brought the family's hard work Three well-deserved Glasses. The Valpolicella Superiore 2003 is equally impressive, in some ways reprising the features of the previous wine but differing in its much lighter, suppler flavour. Stefano and Nicoletta's Teroldego is curious as ever, showing mature and mouthfilling with clear hints of red berries and chocolate, and an approachable palate.

● Colli Berici Cabernet Pianalto Ris. '02	▼▼ 7
O Lessini Durello Brut M. Cl. '02	▼▼ 4
O Lessini Durello Passito '03	▼▼ 5
O Recioto di Soave Il Duello '04	▼▼ 5
O Soave Colli Scaligeri I Prandi '06	▼ 4
O Soave Cl. Tenute Barche '06	▼ 4
O Soave Cl. Sup. Il Tirso '05	▼ 4
O Lessini Durello Brut	▼ 3
O Col Creo '05	▼ 4
● Colli Berici Merlot Vign. Asinara La Giareta '03	▼ 4
● Colli Berici Cabernet La Giareta '05	▼ 4
● Colli Berici Cabernet Pianalto Ris. '01	♀♀ 7
O Lessini Durello Passito '02	♀♀ 5

● Amarone della Valpolicella '01	▼▼▼ 8
● Valpolicella Sup. '03	▼▼ 6
● Teroldego '03	▼▼ 6
● Amarone della Valpolicella '00	♀♀ 8
● Amarone della Valpolicella '99	♀♀ 8
● Teroldego '02	♀♀ 6
● Teroldego '01	♀♀ 6
● Valpolicella Sup. '02	♀♀ 6
● Valpolicella Sup. '01	♀♀ 6

Masari

LOC. MAGLIO DI SOPRA
VIA MASETTO, 18
36078 VALDAGNO [VI]
TEL. 0445410780
www.masari.it

ANNUAL PRODUCTION 25,000 bottles
HECTARES UNDER VINE N.A.
VITICULTURE METHOD Natural

There have been far-reaching changes in the Agno valley, which has become a major industrial centre. Wine has always been produced here but without any great ambitions. So credit must go to Massimo Dal Lago and Arianna Tessari for their determination and insight in making significantly good wines here, successfully reflecting the local terroir. The reds, blended from cabernet sauvignon and merlot, draw character and personality from long macerations and judicious use of wood. The San Martino is more approachable and enjoyable, with clearly defined fruit and a captivating palate, whereas the Masari is more profound, its floral and fruity aromas accompanied by prominent gamey notes right up to the long vibrant finish. The uncomplicated Agnobianco, obtained from garganega and durella, is mineral-edged and fresh-tasting while the original Passito Doro shows unusual balance, its sweetness refreshed by the acidity of the durella grape, while botrytis and minerality enhance its complexity.

Masi

FRAZ. GARGAGNAGO
VIA MONTELEONE, 2
37020 SANT'AMBROGIO
DI VALPOLICELLA [VR]
TEL. 0456832500
www.masi.it

ANNUAL PRODUCTION 3,500,000 bottles
HECTARES UNDER VINE N.A.
VITICULTURE METHOD Conventional

When you are writing about a winery like Sandro Boscaini's Masi, which has been riding the crest of the wave for several decades, it is hard not become repetitive. It is always interesting to notice how Masi copes with new challenges and new markets without losing its bearings, staying firmly rooted in a classic, traditional style. Let's begin our review of the well-stocked range of wines presented with the Amarone Mazzano 2001, a perfect example of this modern yet traditional approach. The complex aromas range from dried fruit to freshly mown grass, lifted by minerality and forest floor, before it explodes onto the palate, where it progresses wonderfully with plenty of body. We gave this wonderful wine Three Glasses. The Costasera suffers a little from having been released too early but it has concentration and texture to spare, while the Vaio Armaron has been made over in a more contemporary key without losing any of its distinctive personality. Lastly, we had an honourable mention for Brolo di Campofiorin, which has never had such depth.

O Doro Passito Bianco '04		6
● Masari '05		6
● San Martino '06		4*
O Agnobianco '06		4*
O Doro Passito Bianco '03		5
O Doro Passito Bianco '02		5
O Doro Passito Bianco '01		5
● Masari '04		6
● Masari '03		6
● Masari '02		6

● Amarone della Valpolicella Cl. Mazzano '01		8
● Amarone della Valpolicella Cl. Costasera '04		6
● Il Brolo di Campofiorin '04		5
● Amarone della Valpolicella Cl. Vaio Armaron '03		8
● Campofiorin '04		4
● Valpolicella Cl. Sup. Anniversario 650 Anni Serego Alighieri '03		5
O Possessioni Bianco Serègo Alighieri '06		4
O Masianco '06		4
● Amarone della Valpolicella Cl. Campolongo di Torbe '00		8
● Amarone della Valpolicella Cl. Campolongo di Torbe '93		6

Roberto Mazzi

LOC. SAN PERETTO
VIA CROSETTA, 8
37024 NEGRAR [VR]
TEL. 0457502072
www.robertomazzi.it

ANNUAL PRODUCTION 60,000 bottles
HECTARES UNDER VINE 8
VITICULTURE METHOD Conventional

Now that building work on the cellar is complete, the winery has focused its attention on the new Amarone. In line with the Mazzi style, the new wine is not a super-selection designed to entice critics, clients and wads of cash. In fact, it is sourced from a new vineyard, Castel, whose character is in Antonio and Stefano's view sufficiently different from Punta di Villa to warrant a separate label. It put on an excellent performance dominated by approachable, delicious fruit before the rounded palate, which remains perfectly light and supple. Even more impressive is the Valpolicella Poiega, which has taken full advantage of the splendid 2004 growing year to offer a broad swath of aromatics followed by a firm, very elegant palate with a long, very clearly defined finish. The Valpolicella Superiore is almost as good, with simpler, more approachable fruit on the nose and a more characterful, savoury, emphatically well-orchestrated palate that opens out beautifully.

● Valpolicella Cl. Sup. Vign. Poiega '04	🍷🍷	5
● Amarone della Valpolicella Cl. Castel '03	🍷🍷	8
● Valpolicella Cl. Sup. '05	🍷🍷	4*
● Amarone della Valpolicella Cl. Punta di Villa '03	YY	8
● Valpolicella Cl. Sup. Vign. Poiega '03	YY	5
● Recioto della Valpolicella Cl. Le Calcarole '03	YY	6
● Amarone della Valpolicella Cl. Punta di Villa '01	YY	7
● Valpolicella Cl. Sup. Vign. Poiega '02	YY	4
● Amarone della Valpolicella Cl. Punta di Villa '00	YY	7

Firmino Miotti

VIA BROGLIATI CONTRO, 53
36042 BREGANZE [VI]
TEL. 0445873006
www.firminomiotti.it

ANNUAL PRODUCTION 25,000 bottles
HECTARES UNDER VINE 5
VITICULTURE METHOD Conventional

Firmino Miotti is an icon in Breganza. Veneto traditions and culture find fertile ground at this winery, combining with vines and barrels to bring forth sincere, authentic wines. The energetic Franca does not appear burdened by her inheritance. She is quietly, determinedly infusing the wines with new sensitivity, and in consequence they are more mature and better finished. Vespaiolo comes from a native grape that has characteristically high acidity balanced by well-proportioned alcohol content. Those interested in local varieties will find a few little gems here, like the semi-sparkling Pedevendo, the champagne of long ago, and Groppello, a red wine with powerful extract. The Valletta is in its completion phase and requires more time to find the balance it needs. Breganze Rosso is very spontaneous, stylish and well made with beautiful echoes of its terroir thanks to restrained extract. The soft Le Colombare 2006 is a blend of tocai, pinot bianco, vespaiolo and riesling while the Torcolato is, as ever, one of the best of its type.

○ Breganze Torcolato '04	🍷🍷🍷	7
● Rosso Valletta '04	🍷🍷🍷	6
● Breganze Rosso '05	🍷🍷	4
○ Breganze Vespaiolo '06	🍷🍷	3*
○ Le Colombare '06	🍷🍷	3*
○ Pedevendo '06	🍷	3
○ Breganze Pinot Bianco '06	🍷	3
● Breganze Cabernet '05	🍷	4
● Groppello '06	🍷	4
● Rosso Valletta '03	YY	6
● Rosso Valletta '02	YY	6
● Rosso Valletta '01	YY	6
● Rosso Valletta '00	YY	6
○ Breganze Torcolato '03	YY	7
○ Breganze Torcolato '02	YY	7
○ Breganze Torcolato '01	YY	7
○ Le Colombare '05	YY	3

Ornella Molon Traverso

FRAZ. CAMPO DI PIETRA
VIA RISORGIMENTO, 40
31040 SALGAREDA [TV]
TEL. 0422804807
www.ornellamolon.it

ANNUAL PRODUCTION 350,000 bottles
HECTARES UNDER VINE 42
VITICULTURE METHOD Conventional

The Piave area is difficult to interpret. On one hand, its vocation for wine has been well known for over a century but on the other, local wineries have often concentrated on producing well typed but unambitious wines. In this context, the efforts of Ornella Molon and Giancarlo Traverso have stood out from the beginning. Every year, they present a range of wines that beautifully interprets the area's vocation for everyday wines alongside a selection of high profile wines, the Ornella line. Rosso di Villa, a monovarietal Merlot, gave an excellent performance, embodying the local territory with a wink at the rest of the world. The aromas are distinctively mature and pervasive, although the oak is still a little over-insistent. The more traditional Vite Rossa is a classic Bordeaux blend with complex aromas and a light savoury palate. Staying with the reds, the Cabernet is firm while from the whites, we picked out the succulent Traminer and broad, mature Chardonnay.

Monte Fasolo

LOC. FAEDO
VIA MONTE FASOLO, 2
35030 CINTO EUGANEO [PD]
TEL. 0429634030
www.montefasolo.com

ANNUAL PRODUCTION 200,000 bottles
HECTARES UNDER VINE 72
VITICULTURE METHOD Conventional

We were looking forward with interest to tasting the wines from Fattoria Monte Fasolo to see how the new products compared to last year's fine performance. In the event, the results were well up to snuff and the winery's leading red, Cabernet Le Tavole, did very well indeed even in a less than exciting growing year like 2005. Even more important, this wine is land-rooted and reflects the weather conditions of the vintage. We see the sunny nature of the Colli Euganei transformed here into subtle sensations of aromatic herbs and wild berries on the nose, followed by a slender but tense, stylish palate. The two wines representing the entry level of the quality wines are from the same vintage year and gave an excellent performance. Rusta is a fragrant red with a refreshing, gutsy palate and the white Milante reflects its aromatic grapes in a fragrant, tangy tasting experience. The two sparkling wines are well typed, especially the Fior d'Arancio.

● Piave Cabernet Ornella '04	♥♥ 5
● Vite Rossa Ornella '03	♥♥ 5
● Piave Merlot Rosso di Villa '04	♥♥ 6
O Piave Chardonnay Ornella '06	♥♥ 4
O Traminer Ornella '06	♥♥ 4
O Bianco di Ornella '06	♥ 5
O Sauvignon Ornella '06	♥ 4
O Vite Bianca Ornella '05	♥ 5
● Piave Raboso Ornella '03	♥ 5
● Piave Merlot Ornella '04	♥ 5
● Piave Merlot Rosso di Villa '03	♀♀ 6
● Piave Merlot Rosso di Villa '02	♀♀ 6
● Piave Merlot Rosso di Villa '01	♀♀ 6
● Piave Merlot Rosso di Villa '00	♀♀ 6
● Piave Merlot Rosso di Villa '99	♀♀ 6

● Colli Euganei Cabernet Podere Le Tavole '05	♥♥ 4
● Colli Euganei Rosso Rusta '05	♥♥ 3*
O Milante '05	♥♥ 4
O Colli Euganei Fior d'Arancio Spumante Dolce '06	♥♥ 4
O Colli Euganei Bianco Brut	♥ 4
● Colli Euganei Cabernet Podere Le Tavole '04	♀♀ 4
● Colli Euganei Rosso Rusta '04	♀♀ 3

Monte Tondo
LOC. MONTE TONDO
VIA S. LORENZO, 89
37038 SOAVE [VR]
TEL. 0457680347
www.montetondo.it

ANNUAL PRODUCTION 160,000 bottles
HECTARES UNDER VINE 27
VITICULTURE METHOD Conventional

Soave is difficult wine country. On this steep, rugged land, viticulture has only slowly taken root as the stubborn perseverance of growers has kept the vines alive. Gino Magnabosco is the perfect incarnation of the strong-willed farmer who never gives up, works untiringly and has plenty of experience. There is a vision of the future behind his straightforward spontaneity. All that effort and passion are not wasted. Fortunately, the rewards come in high quality wines that Gino often releases at very reasonable prices. While we expected great things from the leading wine, Foscarin Slavinus, we actually received even more from the Monte Tondo, a Soave rich in the fragrance of the land that shows freshly floral and vegetal with a tangy, gutsy palate. In contrast, its elder brother is more poised on nose and palate, sophisticated and stylishly put together. Thanks to this Monte Tondo, Three Glasses finally went to Magnabosco's winery after many close calls in recent years. From the vineyards on the plain comes a Soave Mito as enjoyable as it is uncomplicated and every inch the perfect everyday wine.

La Montecchia
VIA MONTECCHIA, 16
35030 SELVAZZANO DENTRO [PD]
TEL. 049637294
www.lamontecchia.it

ANNUAL PRODUCTION 110,000 bottles
HECTARES UNDER VINE 23
VITICULTURE METHOD Conventional

Situated to the north of the zone, almost marking entry into the Colli Euganei for those coming from Padua or Vicenza, the Capodilista family winery defends the territory with its well-rooted winemaking traditions. Credit for this goes prevalently to Giordano Emo Capodilista. Since he began working at the winery, he has striven to promote the entire designated area as well as Montecchia itself. The leading red, Villa Capodilista, is a Bordeaux blend with distinctive natural elegance. Almost congenitally averse to fashionable concentration, it is faithful to its style, showing tense, long and characterful. A worthy second wine is Ca' Emo, which is approachable and accessible, while the Godimondo is a monovarietal Carmenère with a generous, firm mouthfeel. The Fior d'Arancio Spumante is exquisitely and fragrantly exuberant while the Merlot attracts attention with its assertively sweet, warmly pervasive ripe fruit. The Pinot Bianco and Forzatè, from 100 per cent raboso, are dependable and forthright.

O Soave Cl. Monte Tondo '06	♟♟♟ 4*
O Soave Cl. Sup. Foscarin Slavinus '04	♟♟ 5
● Amarone della Valpolicella '02	♟♟ 6
● Cabernet Sauvignon Giunone '04	♟ 4
O Soave Mito	♟ 2*
O Recioto di Soave '03	♟ 5
O Soave Cl. Casette Foscarin '04	♟♟ 4
O Soave Cl. Sup. Foscarin Slavinus '03	♟♟ 5
O Soave Cl. Casette Foscarin '03	♟♟ 4
O Soave Cl. Sup. Foscarin Slavinus '02	♟♟ 5
O Soave Cl. Sup. Vign. in Casette Foscarin '01	♟♟ 4

O Colli Euganei Moscato Fior d'Arancio Spumante '06	♟♟ 4
● Colli Euganei Rosso Villa Capodilista '04	♟♟ 6
● Colli Euganei Rosso Ca' Emo '05	♟♟ 3*
● Godimondo '06	♟♟ 4
● Colli Euganei Merlot '04	♟ 4
● Forzatè Raboso '05	♟ 4
O Colli Euganei Pinot Bianco '06	♟ 3
O Colli Euganei Moscato Fior d'Arancio Passito '03	♟♟ 6
● Colli Euganei Rosso Villa Capodilista '03	♟♟ 6
● Colli Euganei Rosso Villa Capodilista '01	♟♟ 6
● Colli Euganei Rosso Villa Capodilista '00	♟♟ 6

Cantina Sociale di Monteforte d'Alpone
VIA XX SETTEMBRE, 24
37032 MONTEFORTE D'ALPONE [VR]
TEL. 0457610110
www.cantinadimonteforte.it

Montegrande
VIA TORRE, 2
35030 ROVOLON [PD]
TEL. 049 5226276
www.vinimontegrande.it

ANNUAL PRODUCTION   300,000 bottles
HECTARES UNDER VINE 1,500
VITICULTURE METHOD   Conventional

ANNUAL PRODUCTION   250,000 bottles
HECTARES UNDER VINE 23
VITICULTURE METHOD   Conventional

It is hard to talk about a co-operative winery in an area where over 90 per cent of the land is controlled by co-operatives. The great risk is to see them as welfare structures. But when you taste Gaetano Tobin's wines, you realize that above all else this winery vinifies its members' grapes with the utmost care. It should also be said that despite the extensive vine stock available, the production range of Cantina di Monteforte is relatively small, which makes strict selection of the best batches possible before bottling. The excellent Soave Vigneti di Castellaro is generous, well rounded and juicy, with beautiful balance and length. Just a step behind is Clivus, which is simpler and more yielding on the palate. The Recioto di Soave is tropical, mature and has marked dried grape characteristics. Finally, the Amarone Re Teodorico also performed well.

For years, the Colli Euganei area has been moving forward quietly, almost as if it did not wish to be part of the renaissance of Italian winemaking, preferring to stay with the local market and profiting from the nearby spa to sell all its products. But at last, wineries like this one owned by the Cristofanon family, who have emerged with determination on the quality winemaking scene, are stepping out of their agricultural box. The range of wines is extensive with interesting products at really reasonable prices. There are three ambitious wines from the Colli Euganei DOC, a Cabernet, a merlot-based Rosso and a Passito, demonstrating deep-rooted links with the local area. The Cabernet, Sereo, is medium bodied and very harmonious with approachable varietal aromas. The second and most impressive of the three is Vigna delle Roche, with its exquisitely Veneto-style peppery and subtly grassy aromas alongside the fruit and a slender, succulently drinkable palate. Lastly the Fior d'Arancio Passito is sun-ripe and alluring.

O Recioto di Soave Cl.	
Il Sigillo I Vini del Chiostro '04	▼▼ 5
O Soave Cl. Clivus '06	▼▼ 3*
O Soave Cl. Sup.	
Vign. di Castellaro '05	▼▼ 4
● Amarone della Valpolicella	
Re Teodorico '04	▼▼ 6
● Recioto della Valpolicella	
I Vini del Chiostro '04	▼ 5
O Lessini Durello Brut M. Cl.	▼ 4
O Soave Cl. I Vini del Chiostro '06	▼ 3
O Soave Cl. Clivus '05	▼▼ 3
O Soave Cl. Sup.	
Vign. di Castellaro '04	▼▼ 4

O Colli Euganei	
Fior d'Arancio Passito '04	▼▼ 4*
● Colli Euganei Cabernet	
Sereo '04	▼▼ 4*
● Colli Euganei Rosso	
V. delle Roche '05	▼▼ 4*
● Colli Euganei Cabernet '06	▼ 2
O Colli Euganei Bianco '06	▼ 2
O Castearo '06	▼ 2
O Colli Euganei Fior d'Arancio	
Passito '03	▼▼ 4
● Colli Euganei Rosso	
V. delle Roche '04	▼▼ 4

Giacomo Montresor

via Ca' di Cozzi, 16
37124 Verona
tel. 045913399
www.vinimontresor.it

ANNUAL PRODUCTION 3,500,000 bottles
HECTARES UNDER VINE 152
VITICULTURE METHOD Conventional

The Montresor family winery shows that you don't have to be small to make quality wine. Quantity and quality can, in fact, coexist. Of course, it's not easy but with such a large vineyard holding anything is possible. From the wines presented this year, we particularly enjoyed the Valpolicella Castelliere delle Guaite, with its striking aromas of stewed fruit and cocoa powder lifted by slowly released spice. The palate is very full bodied but still remains supple and enjoyably drinkable. The Sauvignon Sansaia is equally good, showing impressively appealing and stylish with a delicate but generous nose. The grapes were not able to ripen perfectly in the very warm 2003 growing year so both the Amarone Castelliere delle Guaite and the Capitel della Crosara have good concentration but rather austere, drying extract. The Recioto Re Teodorico is succulent and mouthfilling while the Custoza Monte Fiera is generous and harmonious.

● Valpolicella Cl. Primo Ripasso Castelliere delle Guaite '04	▼▼	6
○ Bianco di Custoza Vign. Monte Fiera '06	▼▼	5
○ Sauvignon Sansaia '06	▼▼	5
○ Lugana Gran Guardia '06	▼	5
● Amarone della Valpolicella Cl. Capitel della Crosara '03	▼	8
● Recioto della Valpolicella Re Teodorico '04	▼	6
● Amarone della Valpolicella Cl. Castelliere delle Guaite '03	▼	8
● Amarone della Valpolicella Cl. Castelliere delle Guaite '01	▽▽	8
● Amarone della Valpolicella Cl. Castelliere delle Guaite '00	▽▽	8
● Amarone della Valpolicella Cl. Castelliere delle Guaite '99	▽▽	8

Mosole

fraz. Corbolone
via Annone Veneto, 60
30029 Santo Stino di Livenza [VE]
tel. 0421310404
www.mosole.com

ANNUAL PRODUCTION 220,000 bottles
HECTARES UNDER VINE 28.5
VITICULTURE METHOD Conventional

The significant clay content of the soil in the Lison-Pramaggiore DOC zone promises great Merlots, although until recently it was hard to find bottles that supported this theory. Production focused on light, moreish current-vintage wines. Today, it is safe to say that this area's leading variety is merlot, thanks in large measure to Lucio Mosole and his Merlot Ad Nonam. At last, a profoundly Veneto wine, the true child of this land snatched from the sea, forcefully asserts its quality in clear, vibrant aromas of fruit, spices and flowers, and a firm, creamy, lingering palate. The other top wines are also well worth a glance, though: the Cabernet Hora Sexta, a generous, beautifully balanced red; the gutsy, salty Tocai Eleo; and the intensely fragrant, drinkable Eleo Rosso. The rest of the range includes simple but fragrantly harmonious standard-label wines.

● Lison-Pramaggiore Merlot Ad Nonam '04	▼▼	5
● Lison-Pramaggiore Cabernet Hora Sexta '04	▼▼	4
● Lison-Pramaggiore Rosso Eleo '05	▼▼	4
○ Lison-Pramaggiore Tocai Eleo '06	▼▼	4
● Lison-Pramaggiore Cabernet '06	▼	3
○ Hora Sexta '05	▼	4
● Lison-Pramaggiore Refosco P. R. '06	▼	3
○ Lison-Pramaggiore Sauvignon '06	▼	3
○ Lison-Pramaggiore Chardonnay '06	▼	3
○ Pinot Grigio '06		3

Il Mottolo
LOC. LE CONTARINE
VIA COMEZZARE
35030 BAONE [PD]
TEL. 049632185

ANNUAL PRODUCTION 15,000 bottles
HECTARES UNDER VINE 5
VITICULTURE METHOD Conventional

The term "Il Mottolo" describes the limestone contours typical of the Colli Euganei where the land, first and foremost, vineyards, and the quality of work carried out in them are the foundations on which Sergio Fortin and Roberto Dalla Libera have built their winery. It is still a very young business – only in its third year of bottling – but this is its second appearance in the Guide. Sergio and Roberto both come from other sectors but are in love with wine, so they rely on the invaluable collaboration of a leading local winemaker, Franco Zanovello, and vineyard manager Filippo Giannone. The vineyards are mainly situated in the municipal area of Baone, with a small part in Arquà, and there are four wines, three reds and a white. The leading wine is Serro, a well-textured Colli Euganei Rosso that offers great value for money. The Cabernet and Merlot are dense and typical while the white Le Contarine, based mainly on moscato fior d'arancio, stands out as deliciously aromatic.

Musella
VIA FERRAZZETTE, 2
37036 SAN MARTINO
BUON ALBERGO [VR]
TEL. 045973385
www.musella.it

ANNUAL PRODUCTION 120,000 bottles
HECTARES UNDER VINE 31
VITICULTURE METHOD Conventional

Anyone lucky enough to see the Musella winery from above will agree that it is breathtaking. This estate of 220 unspoilt hectares is just a few kilometres from Verona and only the few buildings, which blend perfectly into the landscape, betray the presence of man. And then there are the vineyards, chiselled into the heart of the woodlands that cover most of the area and positioned for the best possible aspects and weather conditions. The rest takes place in the cellar where the huge respect shown for the grapes brings very prestigious bottles. One such is the Amarone 2003 from the Palazzina vineyard: vibrant aromas lead into a full body and excellent texture with a long, sophisticated finish. The Valpolicella Ripasso echoes this style, albeit on a different level and with contrasting concentration, but it is equally complex and harmonious. The Monte del Drago, an original blend of corvina and cabernet, and the succulent Valpolicella Vigne Nuove both put on an excellent performance.

O Le Contarine '06	♟♟ 3*
● Colli Euganei Cabernet V. Marè '05	♟♟ 3*
● Colli Euganei Merlot Comezzara '05	♟♟ 3*
● Colli Euganei Rosso Serro '05	♟♟ 4*
● Colli Euganei Rosso Serro '04	♟♟ 4
● Colli Euganei Merlot Comezzara '04	♟♟ 3

● Amarone della Valpolicella '03	♟♟ 7
● Valpolicella Sup. Ripasso '04	♟♟ 4*
● Monte del Drago Rosso '03	♟♟ 6
● Valpolicella Sup. Vigne Nuove '05	♟♟ 4
● Recioto della Valpolicella '04	♟♟ 6
O Bianco del Drago '04	♟ 4
● Amarone della Valpolicella Senza Titolo '00	♟♟ 8
● Amarone della Valpolicella '01	♟♟ 7
● Amarone della Valpolicella '00	♟♟ 7
● Amarone della Valpolicella '99	♟♟ 7
● Monte del Drago Rosso '02	♟♟ 6
● Monte del Drago Rosso '01	♟♟ 6
● Valpolicella Sup. Ripasso '03	♟♟ 6

Angelo Nicolis e Figli
VIA VILLA GIRARDI, 29
37029 SAN PIETRO IN CARIANO [VR]
TEL. 0457701261
www.vininicolis.com

ANNUAL PRODUCTION 180,000 bottles
HECTARES UNDER VINE 42
VITICULTURE METHOD Conventional

At the Nicolis winery, the sensation is one of solid continuity and tradition, fed by the energy the brothers invest in all phases of production. Since 2007, the hectares under vine have increased. At Maso, six of the 20 are now fully productive and there are more medium and large barrels in the cellar, where available space for vinification and racking has been increased. The new underground area will also provide a tasting room looking onto the cellar and barrels. These positive developments are perceptible in the wines, which are all characterized by vibrant fruit perked up by freshness and underpinned by structure. The standard-label Valpolicella is fresh-tasting and uncomplicated while the Superiore Seccal has huge potential and will settle down with a little more cellar time. Testal, from corvina with small additions of cabernet and merlot, is tense and refreshing, with a generous nose and palate, while the Amarone performs better in the mouth, which has lots of body and appealing finesse.

Nino Franco
VIA GARIBALDI, 147
31049 VALDOBBIADENE [TV]
TEL. 0423972051
www.ninofranco.it

ANNUAL PRODUCTION 1,000,000 bottles
HECTARES UNDER VINE 2.5
VITICULTURE METHOD Conventional

There's a breath of fresh air at Franco. Daughter Silvia has now permanently joined the winery staff, bringing her youthful breeziness, to work alongside Primo and his wife Annalisa in the running of one of Prosecco's most prestigious wineries. The excellent harvest of 2006 produced the most incredible "faìve" (sparks) ever. Faìve is also the name of the Rosé, made mainly from merlot, which opens our review of the wines with its red berries, aromatic herbs and a very enjoyable hint of tannins. Prosecco finds its finest expression again in the very subtle, stylish Primo Franco, the winery flagship. The generous, alluring Cartizze lives up to expectations with its complex aromas. Rive di San Floriano is brilliant, vibrant and rich in fruit aromas and Rustico is exemplary, released in 750,000 thoroughly respectable bottles. The Prosecco Tranquillo Sassi Bianchi, which originates from the vineyard at Grave di Stecca, is one of the best of its type, with aromas of spring flowers and fresh fruit.

● Amarone della Valpolicella Cl. '03	♼♼ 7
● Testal '03	♼♼ 5
● Valpolicella Cl. Sup. Seccal '04	♼♼ 5
● Valpolicella Cl. '06	♼ 4
● Valpolicella Cl. Sup. '05	♼ 4
● Amarone della Valpolicella Cl. Ambrosan '98	♼♼♼ 8
● Amarone della Valpolicella Cl. Ambrosan '93	♼♼♼ 8
● Amarone della Valpolicella Cl. Ambrosan '01	♼♼ 8
● Amarone della Valpolicella Cl. '01	♼♼ 7
● Amarone della Valpolicella Cl. Ambrosan '00	♼♼ 8
● Amarone della Valpolicella Cl. '00	♼♼ 7
● Amarone della Valpolicella Cl. '98	♼♼ 7

O P. di Valdobbiadene Brut Rive di S. Floriano '06	♼ 4 *
O P. di Valdobbiadene Dry Primo Franco '06	♼♼ 5
O Cartizze	♼♼ 5
O P. di Valdobbiadene Brut	♼♼ 4
O P. di Valdobbiadene Brut Rustico	♼ 4
O P. di Valdobbiadene Tranquillo Sassi Bianchi '06	♼ 4
⊙ Brut Rosé Faìve '06	♼ 4
O P. di Valdobbiadene Dry Primo Franco '05	♼♼ 4

Novaia

VIA NOVAIA, 1
37020 MARANO DI VALPOLICELLA [VR]
TEL. 0457755129
www.novaia.it

ANNUAL PRODUCTION 30,000 bottles
HECTARES UNDER VINE 7
VITICULTURE METHOD Conventional

Valpolicella is not just open valleys beautifully exposed to sunlight. There are also hidden recesses, small clearings that open up suddenly before the visitor's eyes, where the woods seem to dissolve to make way for vineyards. Novaia's vines are in the Marano valley, surrounded by spontaneous flora and cultivated with great care and respect by the Vaona brothers, who have replanted over the years and almost completely abandoned the traditional Verona pergola training system. Our tour continues to the cellar, of course, where the Amarone Le Balze is still maturing slowly. Amarone Corte Vaona gave a good performance with traditional overripe, mineral-edged aromas and dense, powerful structure on the palate. The taut, juicy Recioto Le Novaje is lighter, despite its considerable sweetness. The Valpolicella I Cantoni is captivating with well put together aromas and a savoury palate while an honourable mention goes to the Valpolicella Classico 2005.

Ottella

FRAZ. S. BENEDETTO DI LUGANA
LOC. OTTELLA
37019 PESCHIERA DEL GARDA [VR]
TEL. 0457551950
www.ottella.it

ANNUAL PRODUCTION 200,000 bottles
HECTARES UNDER VINE 30
VITICULTURE METHOD Conventional

The farmstead, which can be glimpsed on the old coat of arms with the eight small heads from which the winery takes its name, is close to little lake Frassino. This wet zone in the clayey Lugana area is of great natural interest and lies a stone's throw from Lake Garda. It's ideal terroir for trebbiano di Lugana, a grape which develops fruity, almost aromatic sensations if properly cared for, and these are nicely interpreted by Francesco and Michele Montresor and their father Lodovico. All three Lugana bottles are good: Le Creete 2006 has edgy vegetal sensations that should veer over time towards varietal minerally hints; the Molceo 2005 is very clearly fruity; and the Lugana 2006 is more approachably drinkable. Prima Luce gave a lovely performance as usual. This stylish dried-grape wine is also based on trebbiano grapes. Yet again there was impressive juicy fruit came from the Campo Sireso, made from merlot – which has long since acclimatized here – with corvina veronese and cabernet. The Ottella rosé and red are both appealingly moreish.

● Amarone della Valpolicella Cl. Corte Vaona '03	▼▼ 6*
● Recioto della Valpolicella Cl. Le Novaje '04	▼▼ 5
● Valpolicella Cl. Sup. I Cantoni '04	▼▼ 4
● Valpolicella Cl. '05	▼ 3
● Valpolicella Cl. Sup. Ripasso '04	▼ 4
● Amarone della Valpolicella Cl. Le Balze '01	♈♈ 8
● Amarone della Valpolicella Cl. Le Balze '00	♈♈ 8
● Amarone della Valpolicella Cl. Le Balze '99	♈♈ 8
● Amarone della Valpolicella Cl. Le Balze '98	♈♈ 8
● Valpolicella Cl. Sup. I Cantoni '03	♈♈ 4

● Campo Sireso '05	▼▼ 5
○ Lugana '06	▼▼ 4*
○ Prima Luce Passito '05	▼▼ 6
○ Lugana Le Creete '06	▼▼ 4*
○ Lugana Sup. Molceo '05	▼▼ 5
⊙ Roses Roses '06	▼ 4
● Rosso Ottella '06	▼ 4
● Campo Sireso '04	♈♈ 5
● Campo Sireso '03	♈♈ 5
○ Lugana Le Creete '05	♈♈ 4
○ Lugana Sup. Molceo '04	♈♈ 5
○ Prima Luce Passito '02	♈♈ 6
○ Prima Luce Passito '01	♈♈ 6

★ Leonildo Pieropan
VIA CAMUZZONI, 3
37038 SOAVE [VR]
TEL. 0456190171
www.pieropan.it

Piovene Porto Godi
FRAZ. TOARA
VIA VILLA, 14
36020 VILLAGA [VI]
TEL. 0444885142
www.piovene.com

ANNUAL PRODUCTION 350,000 bottles
HECTARES UNDER VINE 45
VITICULTURE METHOD Conventional

Nino Pieropan is one of the great gentlemen of wine in Soave and in Italy. His wines are amazingly consistent in quality. The tasting of two of his old vintages was an exciting educational experience that confirms the development potential of local whites. Even the simple basic Soave 2006, mature and fresh thanks to that year's weather, is a textbook example of grace, approachability and mouthfeel. The Calvarino, made from garganega and trebbiano, is true to its proverbial finesse: the flavours expand into an austere but promising profile, where the minerally components from the soil give the wine a typical salty note echoed in the wonderful, lustrous finish. In fact, it is so lustrous that it walked away with Three Glasses. As no dried-grape wines were produced in 2005, more effort went into La Rocca, which is soft and velvety with a gutsy finish streaked through with nicely gauged acidity. The marked concentration hints at a radiant future for this wine. New arrival Ghes, a fragrant sparkling rosé made from corvina grapes in memory of Pieropan's friend, Cesare Franceschetti, has not yet been released.

ANNUAL PRODUCTION 80,000 bottles
HECTARES UNDER VINE 32
VITICULTURE METHOD Conventional

Tommaso Piovene runs this long-established estate with great skill and credit is due for his efforts in recent years to steer the winery in the direction of fine quality wines. Tommaso is also responsible for promoting a heritage shared with the whole area, Tocai Rosso, of which he makes two quite distinct types, Riveselle and Thovara. The former undergoes brief maceration and traditionally tends to be very pleasant and drinkable. Thovara is distinctly more ambitious, coming from selected grapes picked when very ripe. It ages in small oak barrels which endow it with a hitherto unknown richness and complexity. This year, we liked the broad swath of subtle aromatics with their floral, fruity and spicy hints and the generous yet leanish palate. Also worth mentioning are the Merlot Fra i Broli and the cask-conditioned Sauvignon Campigie, both of which earned Two Glasses, and the enjoyable Pinot Bianco Polveriera.

○ Soave Cl. Calvarino '05	♟♟♟	5
○ Soave Cl. La Rocca '05	♟♟	6
○ Soave Cl. '06	♟♟	4*
○ Recioto di Soave Le Colombare '03	♟♟	6
○ Soave Cl. Calvarino '04	♟♟♟	5
○ Soave Cl. Calvarino '03	♟♟♟	5
○ Soave Cl. Calvarino '02	♟♟♟	5
○ Soave Cl. Sup. Calvarino '98	♟♟♟	5
○ Soave Cl. La Rocca '02	♟♟♟	6
○ Soave Cl. Sup. La Rocca '00	♟♟♟	6
○ Soave Cl. Sup. La Rocca '99	♟♟♟	6
○ Soave Cl. Sup. La Rocca '98	♟♟♟	6
○ Soave Cl. Sup. La Rocca '96	♟♟♟	6
○ Soave Cl. Sup. La Rocca '95	♟♟♟	6
○ Passito della Rocca '93	♟♟♟	6
○ Passito della Rocca '95	♟♟♟	6

● Colli Berici Tocai Rosso Thovara '04	♟♟	6
● Colli Berici Merlot Fra i Broli '04	♟♟	6
○ Sauvignon Campigie '06	♟♟	5
○ Colli Berici Pinot Bianco Polveriera '06	♟♟	4
○ Colli Berici Sauvignon Vigneto Fostine '06	♟	4
● Colli Berici Tocai Rosso Vigneto Riveselle '06	♟	3
● Polveriera Rosso '06	♟	4
● Colli Berici Tocai Rosso Thovara '03	♟♟	6
● Colli Berici Cabernet Vign. Pozzare '03	♟♟	5
● Colli Berici Merlot Fra i Broli '03	♟♟	5
○ Colli Berici Pinot Bianco Polveriera '05	♟♟	4

Umberto Portinari

FRAZ. BROGNOLIGO
VIA SANTO STEFANO, 2
37032 MONTEFORTE D'ALPONE [VR]
TEL. 0456175087
portinarivini@libero.it

ANNUAL PRODUCTION 30,000 bottles
HECTARES UNDER VINE 4
VITICULTURE METHOD Conventional

Umberto Portinari's winery is at the peak of the local quality pyramid but it has maintained a family dimension of warm-heartedness, sacrifice and endless hard work. Even today, not all the wine is bottled, showing that product selection is severe and that behind these bottles lie decisions which are not always easy to communicate to the market but which reflect a professional approach to problem-solving. We only tasted two wines, with very different results not only in terms of Glasses but also in style. The Santo Stefano is aged in oak and released after extended ageing. The 2003 growing year did not endow it with the freshness required by such a richly textured wine, so it is massive and sumptuous with a soft, mouthfilling palate. The Ronchetto, on the other hand, is the very essence of freshness, not only in its varietal aromas of apple and pear fruit and flowers but also for its very slow development in bottle. The palate is solidly structured and supported by succulent acidity.

Prà

VIA DELLA FONTANA, 31
37032 MONTEFORTE D'ALPONE [VR]
TEL. 0457612125
grazianopra@libero.it

ANNUAL PRODUCTION 220,000
HECTARES UNDER VINE 20
VITICULTURE METHOD Conventional

The way Graziano Prà makes Soave shows the area's potential. The winery's three selections are sourced from hillside vineyards on volcanic and clayey soil, and are in three different styles, each in its own way reflecting the grape and the vintage year. The second version of the Staforte has already found its personality, presenting generous and powerful with considerable structure and a broad, tangy, gutsy palate that improves with bottle ageing. The stylish, generous, mature Monte Grande is a year younger and now a classic of the DOC zone. The usual fruity sweetness lifted by light hints of citrus and spice is offset by a finely balanced palate and it walked away with Three stylish Glasses. Finally, the oak-aged Colle Sant'Antonio is soft and mature with broad, generously varietal aromas and a distinctively rounded flavour. The succulent basic Soave and the vibrant, tropical Recioto are both good wines.

O Soave Cl. Ronchetto '06	♟♟ 4*	
O Soave Santo Stefano '03	♟ 5	
O Soave Sup. V. Albare Doppia Maturazione Ragionata '97	♟♟♟ 4	
O Soave Albare Doppia Maturazione Ragionata '05	♟♟ 4	
O Soave Cl. Ronchetto '05	♟♟ 4	
O Soave Albare Doppia Maturazione Ragionata '04	♟♟ 4	
O Soave Cl. Ronchetto '04	♟♟ 4	
O Soave V. Albare Doppia Maturazione Ragionata '02	♟♟ 4	

O Soave Cl. Monte Grande '06	♟♟♟ 5	
O Soave Cl. Staforte '05	♟♟ 5	
O Soave Cl. '06	♟♟ 4*	
O Recioto di Soave Le Fontane '05	♟♟ 6	
O Soave Cl. Colle S. Antonio '05	♟♟ 5	
O Soave Cl. Monte Grande '05	♟♟♟ 5	
O Soave Cl. Monte Grande '04	♟♟♟ 5	
O Soave Cl. Monte Grande '03	♟♟♟ 5	
O Soave Cl. Monte Grande '02	♟♟♟ 5	
O Soave Cl. Sup. Monte Grande '00	♟♟♟ 5	
O Soave Cl. Staforte '04	♟♟ 4	
O Soave Cl. Colle S. Antonio '04	♟♟ 5	
O Soave Cl. Colle S. Antonio '02	♟♟ 5	
O Soave Cl. '05	♟♟ 4	

★ Giuseppe Quintarelli

VIA CERÈ, 1
37024 NEGRAR [VR]
TEL. 0457500016
giuseppe.quintarelli@tin.it

ANNUAL PRODUCTION 60,000 bottles
HECTARES UNDER VINE 12
VITICULTURE METHOD Conventional

The Quintarelli family, led by the great Giuseppe, sends a strong message of continuity for the legendary Valpolicella area. The wines do the rest, as demonstrated by our retasting of the unique, inimitable Valpolicella 1999, to which we awarded Three Glasses last year. Ageing has endowed it with immeasurable appeal and a velvety texture that all wine lovers should savour. Returning to the present and the wines tasted for this year's edition of the Guide, the Amarone '98 is a real gem, an inimitable classic Amarone. Poetry, intensity and depth find their full expression here in an explosion of cherry fruit and harmony that will continue to echo for years. This is an example and lesson in style that all producers and consumers should explore and earned Three very well-deserved Glasses. But Quintarelli is not just about special Amarones and Valpolicellas for there are also more normal wines in this range, Primo Fiore, from cabernet, corvina and a little merlot, and the garganega-heavy Bianco Secco.

Le Ragose

FRAZ. ARBIZZANO
VIA LE RAGOSE, 1
37024 NEGRAR [VR]
TEL. 0457513241
www.leragose.com

ANNUAL PRODUCTION 150,000 bottles
HECTARES UNDER VINE 19
VITICULTURE METHOD Conventional

From Le Ragose, Arnaldo Galli and his children watch the city's buildings gradually advancing towards the precious slopes of their vineyards and the traditional Valpolicella zone. The Galli family is still a benchmark for its position and the ethical line Marta and Arnaldo adopted years ago in order to revive the winery and keep tradition alive in their Amarone and Valpolicella production. Le Ragose wines interpret and adapt tradition to every single vintage year. They are not outstanding for strength but they do offer the subtle sensations contributed by the lands and the grapes. The Amarone is a good representative of the winery's classic style with its very rich nose, followed by seductive, impressive softness and complexity. The 2003 growing year overwhelmed the Valpolicella with almost excessively full aromas, although the broad silky palate recalls the usual Le Ragose style. The Recioto is very richly extracted thanks to exemplary drying of the grapes and the nose and palate present the full range of fruit, jam and aromatic herbs, all supported by huge structure.

● Amarone della Valpolicella Cl. '98	￥￥￥ 8
● Primo Fiore '04	￥￥ 6
○ Bianco Secco '06	￥￥ 5
● Amarone della Valpolicella Cl. '97	￥￥￥ 8
● Amarone della Valpolicella Cl. '86	￥￥￥ 8
● Amarone della Valpolicella Cl. '84	￥￥￥ 8
● Amarone della Valpolicella Cl. Ris. '83	￥￥￥ 8
● Amarone della Valpolicella Cl. Sup. Ris. '85	￥￥￥ 6
● Amarone della Valpolicella Cl. Sup. Monte Cà Paletta '93	￥￥￥ 8
● Recioto della Valpolicella Cl. '95	￥￥￥ 8
● Rosso del Bepi '96	￥￥￥ 8
● Valpolicella Cl. Sup. '99	￥￥￥ 8

● Amarone della Valpolicella Marta Galli '01	￥￥ 8
● Recioto della Valpolicella Cl. '05	￥￥ 6
● Valpolicella Cl. Sup. Marta Galli '03	￥￥ 6
● Amarone della Valpolicella Cl. '86	￥￥￥ 8
● Amarone della Valpolicella Cl. '88	￥￥￥ 8
● Amarone della Valpolicella Cl. '02	￥￥ 8
● Amarone della Valpolicella '01	￥￥ 8
● Amarone della Valpolicella '99	￥￥ 8
● Amarone della Valpolicella '98	￥￥ 8
● Valpolicella Cl. Sup. Le Sassine '03	￥￥ 4

Roccolo Grassi

VIA SAN GIOVANNI DI DIO, 19
37030 MEZZANE DI SOTTO [VR]
TEL. 0458880089
roccolograssi@libero.it

ANNUAL PRODUCTION 38,000 bottles
HECTARES UNDER VINE 13.5
VITICULTURE METHOD Conventional

The estate's winemaking activity is
organized by Marco and Francesca Sartori,
who have a very clear idea of how to best
represent the area they live and work in,
following the vocation of each vineyard and
growing year while constantly improving
their care of the vines. Fortunately, the
winery lacks any burning ambition to grow
in size so all the Sartoris' efforts are focused
on the vineyards and the wines in the cellar.
Low, balanced yields endow the Valpolicella
Superiore with fine-grained tannins,
charming depth on the nose and palate and
wonderful ageing potential. This is an
extraordinarily polished, iron-rich Valpolicella
with so much fruit that it picked up Three
Glasses. Every bit as good is the profound,
mature and mouthfilling Amarone, with
texture and austerity on the palate. The
Soave La Broia is also very impressive and
harmonious, with a characteristically
excellent mix of wine, oak and personality.
All the wines reflect the character of this
pleasant Mezzane valley with their finesse,
and it is a quality that appeals to increasing
numbers of enthusiasts today.

Vigna Roda

LOC. CORTELÀ
VIA MONTE VERSA, 1569
35030 VÒ [PD]
TEL. 0499940228
www.vignaroda.com

ANNUAL PRODUCTION 40,000 bottles
HECTARES UNDER VINE 17
VITICULTURE METHOD Conventional

This winery owned by Gianni Strazzacappa
has earned its place on the list of cellars to
have emerged in recent years in the Colli
Euganei regional park. Gianni has converted
the estate founded by his father into a new
business with clear quality objectives, and
at considerable sacrifice. His policy is one of
small steps, which may not make for huge
performances but on the other hand it
means that every gain is stable. The leading
wine is Scarlatto, a blend of mainly merlot
with some cabernet, aged in small wooden
barrels, which presents vibrant and rich in
fruit and minerally aromas that are echoed
on the tense, subtly harmonious palate. The
three basic steel-vinified reds, a Merlot, a
Cabernet and another red, are all
interesting, showing nicely concentrated
with generous flavour. Lastly, the Fior
d'Arancio Passito is warm, tropical and
aromatic, with nicely balanced sweetness.
The two dry whites, a Chardonnay and a
Colli Euganei Bianco, are fresh and well
typed.

● Valpolicella Sup.		
Roccolo Grassi '04	♟♟♟	6
● Amarone della Valpolicella		
Roccolo Grassi '03	♟♟	8
○ Soave Sup. La Broia '05	♟♟	4*
● Amarone della Valpolicella		
Roccolo Grassi '00	♟♟♟	8
● Amarone della Valpolicella		
Roccolo Grassi '99	♟♟♟	8
● Amarone della Valpolicella		
Roccolo Grassi '01	♟♟	8
● Amarone della Valpolicella		
Roccolo Grassi '98	♟♟	8
● Recioto della Valpolicella		
Roccolo Grassi '03	♟♟	6
● Valpolicella Sup.		
Roccolo Grassi '03	♟♟	6

● Colli Euganei Cabernet '06	♟♟	3*
● Colli Euganei Rosso Scarlatto '05	♟♟	4
○ Colli Euganei Fior d'Arancio		
Passito '04	♟♟	5
○ Colli Euganei Bianco '06	♟	3
○ Colli Euganei Chardonnay		
Cà Zamira '06	♟	3
● Colli Euganei Rosso '06	♟	3
● Colli Euganei Merlot '06	♟	3
● Colli Euganei Scarlatto '04	♟♟	4
● Colli Euganei Rosso Scarlatto '03	♟♟	4

Roeno
VIA MAMA, 5
37020 BRENTINO BELLUNO [VR]
TEL. 0457230110
www.cantinaroeno.com

ANNUAL PRODUCTION   80,000 bottles
HECTARES UNDER VINE 25
VITICULTURE METHOD   Conventional

Valdadige is a difficult land, cramped and
windswept, where orchards and buildings
jostle for the little available space and vines
have to fight tooth and nail to keep the
best-aspected sites. Of course, when a
family has wine and viticulture in its DNA,
everything becomes easier and the results
are sure to follow. The Fugatti brothers have
given new impetus to the winery founded by
their father, developing vineyards and
projects that offer a cross-section of this
excellent land. The Cristina is on fine form.
It's a sweet wine of remarkable calibre made
from late-harvested trebbiano with smaller
proportions of sauvignon, pinot grigio and
chardonnay. Alternating on the nose are
aromas of candied citrus, flowers and
liquorice, preceding well-gauged sweetness
on a long palate braced by very nice acid
grip. The rich, juicily harmonious red
Enantio, made from foja tonda, is also
excellent. The rest of the range focuses on
fresh, fragrantly drinkable wines, with the
Pinot Grigio standing out.

Ruggeri & C.
VIA PRÀ FONTANA
31049 VALDOBBIADENE [TV]
TEL. 04239092
www.ruggeri.it

ANNUAL PRODUCTION   900,000 bottles
HECTARES UNDER VINE 9
VITICULTURE METHOD   Conventional

Anyone who thinks prosecco-based
sparklers are all the same, and that only
technology makes the difference, should
taste Ruggeri's wines. The numbers are
those of a big winery but Paolo Bisol and
his staff dedicate artisanal passion and care
to the production process. Just try the two
most original selections: Vecchie Viti, on its
second release, and Giustino B., which is
now over ten years old. The former is made,
as the name suggests, from vines almost a
century old scattered around the vineyards
of various growers. This wine expresses the
deepest soul of the local area, with simple,
clearly defined aromas, a very well-
structured palate for its type and a dry,
tangy mouthfeel. Giustino B. represents the
typical lightness, finesse and class of the
variety and shows vibrantly fragrant with
subtle fizz throughout the progression of the
wine. The Cartizze, Giall'Oro, Santo Stefano
and Quartese are flawlessly made bottles
which will satisfy even the most
discriminating tasters.

O Cristina V. T. '04	▼▼ 5
● Valdadige Terra dei Forti Enantio '06	▼▼ 4
● Teroldego I Dossi '06	▼ 4
O Valdadige Pinot Grigio '06	▼ 4
O Valdadige Terra dei Forti Pinot Grigio '06	▼ 4
O Müller Thurgau Le Giarre '06	▼ 4
O Valdadige Chardonnay Le Fratte '06	▼ 3
O Cristina V. T. '03	♈♈ 5

O P. di Valdobbiadene Extra Dry Giustino B. '06	▼▼ 5
O P. di Valdobbiadene Brut Vecchie Viti '06	▼▼ 5
O P. di Valdobbiadene Dry S. Stefano	▼▼ 4*
O P. di Valdobbiadene Brut Quartese	▼▼ 5
O Cartizze	▼▼ 5
O P. di Valdobbiadene Extra Dry Giall'Oro	▼ 4
O Pinot Grigio Vign. Cornuda '06	▼ 4
O P. di Valdobbiadene Brut Vecchie Viti '05	♈♈ 5
O P. di Valdobbiadene Extra Dry Giustino B. '05	♈♈ 5

Le Salette

VIA PIO BRUGNOLI, 11C
37022 FUMANE [VR]
TEL. 0457701027
www.lesalette.it

ANNUAL PRODUCTION 180,000 bottles
HECTARES UNDER VINE 35
VITICULTURE METHOD Conventional

In winemaking, expertise is vital and experience can be acquired in the field but what makes a difference is passion. Franco and Monica Scamperle's wines beautifully express the passion of these two producers. The Fumane valley provided the stones for the construction of the Arena in Verona and for thousands of years it has also been the home of prestigious vineyards. Le Salette's very enjoyable Valpolicella I Progni 2004 enters the palate with vegetal aromas, followed by succulent fruit and adequate length. The Amarone La Marega 2003 calmly reveals its qualities on a solid, harmonious palate while the Amarone Pergole Vece seems to have suffered from the hot weather, although it is as satisfying as ever. The Recioto Pergole Vece is excellent, with great balance and a complex nose, and could improve with age to show the valley's vocation for dried-grape wines. The other Recioto, Le Traversagne, is light and fluent while the Ca' Carnocchio, which is no longer released as a DOC wine, was very impressive.

La Sansonina

LOC. SANSONINA
37019 PESCHIERA DEL GARDA [VR]
TEL. 0457551905
www.sansonina.it

ANNUAL PRODUCTION 13,000 bottles
HECTARES UNDER VINE 12
VITICULTURE METHOD Conventional

Carla Prospero's solitary adventure in the morainic southern part of the Lake Garda area, in its tenth year now since the first vintage of 1997, is a mixture of old and new. Attempting to make a great red merlot-based wine among the trebbiano vineyards of Lugana, an area with a wealth of native white varieties, might have looked like a gamble were it not for the fact that locals had long since pinpointed the French variety as the only plausible alternative to the dominant white grapes. The idea was already there, even though few were applying it. La Sansonina, named after the ancient farm that is now being beautifully restored, grafted onto this traditional intuition a rigorously modern approach to running a vineyard and vinification. The results up until now have always been dependably good and the 2004 vintage provides timely confirmation. Its rich, deep colour introduces a caressingly mouthfilling palate brimming with juicy fruit.

● Recioto della Valpolicella Cl. Pergole Vece '04	🍷🍷 6
● Amarone della Valpolicella Cl. La Marega '03	🍷🍷 6
● Amarone della Valpolicella Cl. Pergole Vece '03	🍷🍷 8
● Valpolicella Cl. Sup. Ripasso I Progni '04	🍷🍷 4*
● Ca' Carnocchio '04	🍷🍷 5
● Recioto della Valpolicella Cl. Le Traversagne '04	🍷 6
● Amarone della Valpolicella Cl. Pergole Vece '95	🍷🍷🍷 8
● Recioto della Valpolicella Cl. Pergole Vece '03	🍷🍷 6

● Sansonina '04	🍷🍷 7
● Sansonina '03	🍷🍷 7
● Sansonina '01	🍷🍷 7
● Sansonina '00	🍷🍷 7
● Sansonina '97	🍷🍷 7
● Sansonina '98	🍷🍷 7

Santa Margherita

VIA ITA MARZOTTO, 8
30025 FOSSALTA DI PORTOGRUARO [VE]
TEL. 0421246111
www.santamargherita.com

ANNUAL PRODUCTION   12,500,000 bottles
HECTARES UNDER VINE 23
VITICULTURE METHOD   Conventional

An old TV commercial used to promise that it wouldn't astonish with special effects but instead convince with the quality of the product it recommended. Santa Margherita applies this very philosophy to its wines, focusing on substance instead of aiming for very high quality in restricted numbers. The range of wines is well stocked, reliable and good value for money. All this, of course, is achieved without skimping on quality and renewal, as was made clear last year. The Malbech is again profound and slow to yield up its aromas, showing strikingly well-orchestrated and firmly structured. Alongside it is the new Refosco, following in its footsteps both in label design and in quality. The aromas are fresher and more youthful while the palate is unexpectedly gutsy. The winery's traditional Merlot Versato came close to a second Glass and the other products are all well typed and beautifully balanced.

Santa Sofia

FRAZ. PEDEMONTE
VIA CA' DEDÉ, 61
37020 SAN PIETRO IN CARIANO [VR]
TEL. 0457701074
www.santasofia.com

ANNUAL PRODUCTION   550,000 bottles
HECTARES UNDER VINE 35
VITICULTURE METHOD   Conventional

We were saying last year that Santa Sofia had changed gear and we must congratulate the Begnoni family for restoring sheen and drive to the whole range in just a few years. They have not yet earned a top accolade but all the wines seem to be focused and beautifully made. We tasted a lot of wines and many of them were rather good. Let's begin with the splendid version of Gioé, the Amarone selection made only in exceptional growing years and a faithful guardian of the tradition of grape drying and lightness of flavour. Next up was the 2003 Amarone, which is more modern and gutsier, and then came the Recioto della Valpolicella, with its penetrating aromas and well-balanced sweetness. The Valpolicella Montegradella is more traditional in style and, like the Amarone Gioé, is a point of contact between past and present. The Ripasso is in a similar vein, although this wine seems to strive for a modern, soft flavour. Finally, we gave honourable mentions to the Merlot Corvina and the Soave Montefoscarino.

● Malbech '05	♟♟ 4*
● Refosco '05	♟♟ 4*
● Versato '05	♟ 4
O A. A. Pinot Grigio Impronta del Fondatore '06	♟ 4
O Trentino Chardonnay '06	♟ 3
O Valdadige Pinot Grigio '06	♟ 4
O P. di Valdobbiadene Extra Dry	♟ 4
O P. di Valdobbiadene Brut	♟ 4
O Luna dei Feldi '06	♟ 4
O Cartizze	♟ 5
● Malbech '04	♟♟ 5
● Versato '04	♟♟ 4

● Amarone della Valpolicella Cl. '03	♟♟ 7
● Amarone della Valpolicella Cl. Gioé '00	♟♟ 8
● Valpolicella Cl. Sup. Montegradella '04	♟♟ 5
● Recioto della Valpolicella Cl. '03	♟♟ 6
● Predaia '02	♟ 5
● Merlot Corvina '05	♟ 3
● Valpolicella Sup. Ripasso '05	♟ 5
● Valpolicella Cl. '05	♟ 4
⊙ Bardolino Chiaretto Cl. '06	♟ 3
O Soave Cl. Montefoscarino '06	♟ 3
O Lugana '06	♟ 3
O Custoza Montemagrin '06	3
● Amarone della Valpolicella Cl. '01	♟♟ 7
● Amarone della Valpolicella Cl. '00	♟♟ 7
● Amarone della Valpolicella Cl. Gioé '98	♟♟ 8

Tenuta Sant'Antonio

FRAZ. SAN BRICCIO
VIA MONTI GARBI
37030 MEZZANE DI SOTTO [VR]
TEL. 0457650383
www.tenutasantantonio.it

ANNUAL PRODUCTION 378,000 bottles
HECTARES UNDER VINE 50
VITICULTURE METHOD Conventional

Not content with the extraordinary results achieved by their reds, the Castagnedi brothers have turned to their range of whites, taking great strides forward in Soave, too. After all, the genes inherited from their parents, co-founders of the Cologonola ai Colli co-operative winery, had to make their presence felt sooner or later. That's why we tasted a great Soave Monte Ceriani 2005, an intensely tropical, mineral-edged wine with a firm, well-structured palate with plenty of grip. It was a cracking debut and earned the Castagnedis Three Glasses. On the red front, we recorded the usual fine performance from the Amarone Campo dei Gigli, which exploited the hot growing year to produce an even more strikingly full and mature profile. The same year and the same touch were there for the Recioto Argille Bianche, whose exuberant sweetness is reined in by dense tannic texture. The Valpolicella La Bandina shows flawless quality and is ever closer in style to the Amarone while Monti Garbi is more complex and traditional. Finally, there was an excellent performance from the Amarone Antonio Castagnedi.

Santi

VIA UNGHERIA, 33
37031 ILLASI [VR]
TEL. 0456520077
www.carlosanti.it

ANNUAL PRODUCTION 2,000,000 bottles
HECTARES UNDER VINE 70
VITICULTURE METHOD Conventional

The one particular aspect of Santi that we like to point out is how this large winery, owned by the even larger Gruppo Italiano Vini, produces an excellent Amarone, a wine that never seems to have a bad year, and has also renewed its efforts in Valpolicella. With the official arrival of the Ripasso, Valpolicella has enjoyed a boost that means it can now compete on an equal footing with the nobler Amarone. For about five years, Solane has been one of the champions of this category thanks to a broad swath of stylish aromatics and, above all, a delicate palate. Its best features are its finesse and a tension in the mouth that set it apart from the Amarone. The very good Soave Monteforte easily won a second Glass, proving that it is a classic of the DOC zone. An excellent performance also came from the Amarone Proemio, with its vibrant aromas and a subtle, progressive, stylish palate. This wine is still youthful but will improve with appropriate bottle ageing. Lastly, the Lugana Melibeo and Bardolino Ca' Bordenis are dependably good.

O Soave Monte Ceriani '05	♟♟♟ 4*
● Amarone della Valpolicella Campo dei Gigli '03	♟♟ 8
● Valpolicella Sup. La Bandina '04	♟♟ 5
● Recioto della Valpolicella Argille Bianche '03	♟♟ 6
● Amarone della Valpolicella Sel. Antonio Castagnedi '04	♟♟ 7
● Valpolicella Sup. Ripasso Monti Garbi '04	♟♟ 4
● Valpolicella Sup. La Bandina '01	♟♟♟ 6
● Amarone della Valpolicella Campo dei Gigli '99	♟♟♟ 8
● Amarone della Valpolicella Campo dei Gigli '98	♟♟♟ 8
● Amarone della Valpolicella Campo dei Gigli '97	♟♟♟ 8

● Valpolicella Cl. Sup. Solane Ripasso '05	♟♟ 4*
● Amarone della Valpolicella Proemio '04	♟♟ 7
O Soave Cl. Vigneti di Monteforte '06	♟♟ 4
O Lugana Melibeo '06	♟ 4
● Amarone della Valpolicella '04	♟♟ 6
● Bardolino Cl. Vigneto Ca' Bordenis '06	♟ 4
● Valpolicella Cl. Le Caleselle '06	♟ 3
● Amarone della Valpolicella Proemio '03	♟♟♟ 7
● Amarone della Valpolicella Proemio '00	♟♟♟ 7
● Amarone della Valpolicella Proemio '01	♟♟ 7

Casa Vinicola Sartori

FRAZ. SANTA MARIA
VIA CASETTE, 2
37024 NEGRAR [VR]
TEL. 0456028011
www.sartorinet.com

ANNUAL PRODUCTION 15,000,000 bottles
HECTARES UNDER VINE 40
VITICULTURE METHOD Conventional

The working relationship here with Franco Bernabei continues and that's not all. The distinct improvement that concerned the more ambitious Sartori bottles is slowly extending to the whole range, which is increasingly balanced and impressive. Proof of this can be found by uncorking the Regolo, which has joined the Valpolicella Superiore designation and behaves like a faithful, contemporary exponent of tradition. The rich minerally aromas and red berries on the nose precede a firm palate with good grip. The excellent Amarone Corte Brà is an example of the delicate, balanced expression possible from this type, just like the Valpolicella Montegradella, with its fresh, supple palate. Freshness is also the main feature of the monovarietal Corvina and the standard-label Valpolicella. Rounding off the range are the wines from the I Saltari estate. The powerful, generous Amarone puts the accent on red berry fruit and spice while the Valpolicella has characteristic complex aromas and a dry, austere palate.

★ Serafini & Vidotto

VIA CARRER, 8/12
31040 NERVESA DELLA BATTAGLIA [TV]
TEL. 0422773281
serafinievidotto@serafinievidotto.com

ANNUAL PRODUCTION 100,000 bottles
HECTARES UNDER VINE 21
VITICULTURE METHOD Conventional

Francesco Serafini's exuberant nature is continually leading him into new projects, prompting him to put his skills to the test himself and consolidate his winemaking vision. But that's the way it has been since the adventure began, for Francesco and Antonello have always tried to create wines whose strength is expressing the typical features of the area, freshness and elegance above all, while respecting their own concept of how a wine should be. The excellent Phigaia is a good example, showing unusual finesse with clearly defined, generous aromas reflected on the tense, succulent palate, beautifully backed up by acidity. The sophisticated Rosso dell'Abazia, made from cabernet sauvignon, franc and merlot, makes a huge impact and is astonishingly successful at mixing acidity, softness and tannin into a disarmingly simple whole. It amazed us again in the 2004 version, and won Three very elegant Glasses. The Pinot Nero is subtle and impressive. The Raboso, created almost for fun as an interesting experiment, is rugged yet appealing at the same time. The rest of the wines in the range are all good.

● Amarone della Valpolicella		
Le Vigne di Turano I Saltari '03	♟♟	8
● Amarone della Valpolicella Cl.		
Reius '03	♟♟	7
● Amarone della Valpolicella Cl.		
Corte Brà '01	♟♟	7
● Valpolicella Sup.		
Le Vigne di Turano I Saltari '04	♟♟	6
● Valpolicella Sup.		
Ripasso Regolo '03	♟♟	4
● Valpolicella Cl. Sup.		
Vign. di Montegradella '05	♟♟	4
● Valpolicella Cl. '06	♟	3
● Corvina '06	♟	4
○ Lugana La Musina '06	♟	4
○ Soave Cl. Vign. di Sella '06	♟	4
● Amarone della Valpolicella		
Le Vigne di Turano I Saltari '01	♟♟	8

● Montello e Colli Asolani		
Il Rosso dell'Abazia '04	♟♟♟	6
● Montello e Colli Asolani		
Phigaia '04	♟♟	4*
● Raboso '05	♟♟	5
● Pinot Nero '04	♟♟	7
○ Bollicine di Prosecco	♟♟	4
○ Il Bianco '06	♟♟	4
⊙ Bollicine Rosé	♟	4
● Montello e Colli Asolani		
Il Rosso dell'Abazia '03	♟♟♟	6
● Il Rosso dell'Abazia '02	♟♟♟	7
● Il Rosso dell'Abazia '01	♟♟♟	7
● Il Rosso dell'Abazia '00	♟♟♟	7
● Il Rosso dell'Abazia '95	♟♟♟	7
● Il Rosso dell'Abazia '96	♟♟♟	7
● Il Rosso dell'Abazia '98	♟♟♟	7
● Il Rosso dell'Abazia '97	♟♟♟	7

Cantina di Soave

V.LE VITTORIA, 100
37038 SOAVE [VR]
TEL. 0456139811
www.cantinasoave.it

ANNUAL PRODUCTION N.A.
HECTARES UNDER VINE 4,200
VITICULTURE METHOD Conventional

We are by now used to seeing thoroughly respectable performances from the Cantina di Soave but it is always pleasant to note that progress continues year by year, and is particularly intense in the case of white wines. Credit goes to the whole technical team but an important part is also played by the determination to shine of all 1,500 member growers. Not everyone is fortunate enough to have the opportunity of selecting grapes from over 4,000 hectares of vineyards and full advantage should be taken of this good fortune, as the Cantina does here at Soave. The excellent Recioto Mida mingles tropical fruit with hints of oak alongside luxurious sweetness while the Soave Castelcerino expresses the more austere, nobler side of the garganega grape. Turning to the reds, we again enjoyed the Amarone with its rounded, yet nicely supple flavour and the Ripasso 2004, with clearly defined fruity aromas and a savoury palate. The Valpolicella Superiore came close to a second Glass.

F.lli Speri

FRAZ. PEDEMONTE
VIA FONTANA, 14
37020 SAN PIETRO IN CARIANO [VR]
TEL. 0457701154
www.speri.com

ANNUAL PRODUCTION 350,000 bottles
HECTARES UNDER VINE 60
VITICULTURE METHOD Certified organic

The underlying philosophy of the Speri family, now in its fifth generation, is to produce wines with a precise identity that the consumer can recognize and come back to over the years. The project is based on a close bond with tradition and a capacity for renewal in proportion to the changing times. All this is accomplished while focusing on promoting the traditional Valpolicella grapes, above all corvina and corvinone, and comes to its natural conclusion in a range of light, drinkable wines. Having skipped the unfavourable 2002 vintage, the Amarone from the drought-ridden 2003 year is magnificent, showing very stylish, subtle, velvety and mineral-edged. The Recioto La Roggia is again excellent. Youthful and heady with hints of blackberry and cherry jam, it flaunts a lovely drinkable palate with a long finish. This version of the Valpolicella Sant'Urbano shows exemplary sophistication. The Ripasso, making its debut, gave a worthy account of itself while the young Valpolicella also has typical hints of spices and cherries.

● Amarone della Valpolicella Rocca Sveva '03	♟♟ 7
● Valpolicella Sup. Ripasso Rocca Sveva '04	♟♟ 5
○ Recioto di Soave Cl. Mida Rocca Sveva '04	♟♟ 6
○ Soave Cl. Sup. Castelcerino Rocca Sveva '05	♟♟ 4*
○ Garda Chardonnay Rocca Sveva '06	♟ 4
○ Équipe 5 Brut '03	♟ 5
○ Soave Cl. Rocca Sveva '06	♟ 4
● Garda Cabernet Sauvignon Rocca Sveva '04	♟ 4
● Valpolicella Sup. Rocca Sveva '04	♟ 4

● Amarone della Valpolicella Cl. Vign. Monte Sant'Urbano '03	♟ 8
● Valpolicella Cl. Sup. Sant'Urbano '04	♟♟ 5
● Recioto della Valpolicella Cl. La Roggia '04	♟ 7
● Valpolicella Cl. Sup. Ripasso '05	♟♟ 5
● Valpolicella Cl. '06	♟ 4
● Amarone della Valpolicella Cl. Vign. Monte Sant'Urbano '01	♟♟♟ 8
● Amarone della Valpolicella Cl. Vign. Monte Sant'Urbano '00	♟♟♟ 8
● Amarone della Valpolicella Cl. Vign. Monte Sant'Urbano '97	♟♟♟ 8
● Amarone della Valpolicella Cl. Vign. Monte Sant'Urbano '90	♟♟♟ 6
● Amarone della Valpolicella Cl. Vign. Monte Sant'Urbano '95	♟♟♟ 8

I Stefanini

VIA CROSARA, 21
37032 MONTEFORTE D'ALPONE [VR]
TEL. 0456175249
tessari.francesco@genie.it

ANNUAL PRODUCTION 40,000
HECTARES UNDER VINE 20
VITICULTURE METHOD Conventional

After years of increasing appreciation for Soave from critics and market alike, albeit always for the same big names, we are delighted to mark the Guide debut of this new winery, which makes just three wines, all aged in stainless steel. Owner Francesco Tessari founded the winery in 2003 knowing he could count on the support of his father Giuseppe and uncle Valentino, who own the land. The flat plains area of Monteforte Stefano is the source of the fruit for Il Selese, a Soave that has all the joyous huskiness of the garganega grape with floral and vegetal aromas and a taut, gutsy palate. In contrast, the two selections come from Monte Tenda, and are named after the two tenant farmers who looked after them for so many years – di Fice and de Toni. Fruit for the former comes from three very high terraces and the wine is generous, tangy and fruity. Grapes for de Toni are grown lower down the hillside and the wine shows unusual finesse that emerges in floral and smoky aromas over hints of apple and pear fruit that are beautifully reflected on the firm palate with its long exciting finish.

Suavia

FRAZ. FITTÀ DI SOAVE
VIA CENTRO, 14
37038 SOAVE [VR]
TEL. 0457675089
www.suavia.it

ANNUAL PRODUCTION 100,000 bottles
HECTARES UNDER VINE 12
VITICULTURE METHOD Conventional

The good fortune enjoyed by the Soave area and its wine is due to wineries like this one, owned by the Tessari family. The Tessaris believed in the territory in less glowing times when the wine was considered very ordinary. Now, they are worldwide ambassadors for this small but great DOC zone. Today Arianna, Meri, Valentina and Alessandra share the workload under the watchful eye of their father Giovanni and mother Rosetta, who are always ready to offer help and experience. Suavia's vineyards are not just measured in hectares for altitude, site climate, the age of the vines and human skills are all factors that bring to life some of Italy's best white wines. Carbonare expresses the almost brutal, minerally nature of this land with the irresistible panache of a film star. It swaggered off with Three Glasses. Le Rive is finer and more sophisticated, ennobled by the oak, while the Soave Classico is a summary of everything this type can offer. The Recioto Acinatium is excellent as usual.

O Soave Cl. Monte de Toni '06	♟♟ 3*
O Soave Il Selese '06	♟♟ 3*
O Soave Cl. Monte di Fice '05	♟ 3
O Soave Il Selese '05	♟♟ 3

O Soave Cl. Monte Carbonare '06	♟♟♟ 4*
O Soave Cl. Le Rive '05	♟♟ 5
O Recioto di Soave Acinatium '04	♟♟ 6
O Soave Cl. '06	♟♟ 4
O Soave Cl. Monte Carbonare '05	♟♟♟ 4
O Soave Cl. Monte Carbonare '04	♟♟♟ 4
O Soave Cl. Monte Carbonare '02	♟♟♟ 4
O Soave Cl. Le Rive '02	♟♟♟ 5
O Soave Cl. Sup. Le Rive '00	♟♟♟ 5
O Soave Cl. Sup. Le Rive '98	♟♟♟ 5
O Soave Cl. Monte Carbonare '03	♟♟ 4
O Recioto di Soave Acinatium '03	♟♟ 6
O Recioto di Soave Acinatium '02	♟♟ 6

Tamellini

VIA TAMELLINI, 4
37038 SOAVE [VR]
TEL. 0457675328
piofrancesco.tamellini@tin.it

ANNUAL PRODUCTION 160,000 bottles
HECTARES UNDER VINE 17
VITICULTURE METHOD Conventional

In just over five years, Gaetano and
Piofrancesco Tamellini's winery has become
a benchmark for Soave thanks to the high
quality of all the wines and to the brothers'
ability to stamp them with the Tamellini
style, which is by no means a foregone
conclusion. A small part of the credit also
goes to the ability of the garganega grape
to highlight differences but the remaining
responsibility is in the hands of the winery,
its scrupulous work in the vineyards and
the care taken in the cellar. The Soave Le
Bine has changed its name to Le Bine de
Costjola but the essence of the wine
remains the same: rich, fruity, minerally
aromas followed by a very firm, taut palate
with great concentration and succulence.
All these factors earned it Three Glasses.
The simpler, more accessible Soave 2006
presents the same style on a smaller scale
while the explosive Recioto Vigna Marogne
shows excellent intensity, concentration
and sweetness in an unforgettable wine.

Giovanna Tantini

LOC. OLIOSI
VIA GOITO, 10
37014 CASTELNUOVO DEL GARDA [VR]
TEL. 0457575070
www.giovannatantini.it

ANNUAL PRODUCTION 20,000 bottles
HECTARES UNDER VINE 11.5
VITICULTURE METHOD Conventional

The 2006 harvest was only Giovanna
Tantini's fourth at Oliosi, in the morainic hills
inland from Lake Garda. In this short space
of time, however, Giovanna has been able
to carve herself an important niche in the
Lake Garda winemaking sector. She has
done this with a style based from the
beginning on innovation, both in the
vineyard, which has been redesigned with
the help of Federico Curtaz, and in styling
the wines, with Attilio Pagli in charge. The
Bardolino is a perfect example of the
winery's approach, performing – rather
unusually – better after its second year,
when fruit and tannin have achieved an ideal
balance, thanks to a sprinkling of the
appetizing spice typical of the local corvina
grape. The Ettore is the result of a complex
project to highlight the personality of the
corvina veronese grape through shoot
cutting and partial drying in wooden cases.
Small percentages of cabernet and merlot
are added to the blend.

O Soave Cl. Le Bine de Costjola '05	4*
O Recioto di Soave V. Marogne '03	6
O Soave '06	4
O Soave Cl. Le Bine '04	4
O Soave Cl. Le Bine '03	5
O Soave Cl. Le Bine '02	5
O Soave '05	4
O Recioto di Soave V. Marogne '02	6
O Recioto di Soave V. Marogne '01	5
O Recioto di Soave V. Marogne '00	5
O Recioto di Soave V. Marogne '99	5

● Ettore '05	7
● Bardolino '06	4*
☉ Bardolino Chiaretto '06	4
● Bardolino '04	4
● Ettore '03	5
● Bardolino '05	4

F.lli Tedeschi

FRAZ. PEDEMONTE
VIA G. VERDI, 4
37029 SAN PIETRO IN CARIANO [VR]
TEL. 0457701487
www.tedeschiwines.com

ANNUAL PRODUCTION   500,000 bottles
HECTARES UNDER VINE 25
VITICULTURE METHOD   Conventional

Few Valpolicella wineries can claim the solid foundations, tradition and continuity of the establishment where the Tedeschi family has been active for decades. Antonietta, Sabrina and Riccardo supervise all stages of production and marketing, although their parents are always around to make their reassuringly expert presence felt. The 2003 vintage year was generally below par throughout Italy but in Valpolicella it enhanced the soft, rounded sensations of the fruit, which demonstrated excellent potential. The Tedeschis did not miss this opportunity to produce both of the more ambitious Amarone selections, Capitel Monte Olmi and La Fabriseria. The former has very concentrated fruit with light minerally hints on the nose and a powerful, very lingering palate. Fabriseria is even richer in extract and slow to yield up its aromas but its wonderful raw material cannot fail to work to its advantage. The current Valpolicella is excellent, in fact one of the best around as usual, while the Nicalò and San Rocco are very complex but require more time to find harmony.

Viticoltori Tommasi

FRAZ. PEDEMONTE
VIA RONCHETTO, 2
37020 SAN PIETRO IN CARIANO [VR]
TEL. 0457701266
www.tommasiwine.it

ANNUAL PRODUCTION   900,000 bottles
HECTARES UNDER VINE 165
VITICULTURE METHOD   Conventional

Tommasi wines are ever more impressive, maintaining a contemporary quality and style without abandoning their deeply imprinted traditional and classic features. The increasingly large vineyard holding makes it possible to monitor the plants perfectly, thus improving the quality of the grapes, which are handled appropriately in the cellar. From the well-stocked range of wines we particularly liked the Amarone Monte Masua for its mix of traditional and modern features. Austere in its presentation of generous aromas, including fines herbes and cocoa powder, dried fruit and minerally hints, it then opens out softly and sumptuously on the palate. Just a step behind is the Crearo della Conca d'Oro, a red that combines the fruity sweetness of the corvina grape and the peppery spice of cabernet franc while the rich Recioto Fiorato has nicely judged sweetness. The Valpolicella Ripasso and Rafael are flawlessly made and the Lugana San Martino and current Valpolicella are very enjoyable.

- Amarone della Valpolicella Cl.
  Capitel Monte Olmi '03   ♟♟ 8
- Amarone della Valpolicella Cl.
  La Fabriseria '03   ♟♟ 8
- Valpolicella Cl. Lucchine '06   ♟♟ 3*
- Valpolicella Cl. Sup.
  Capitel dei Nicalò '05   ♟♟ 4
- Valpolicella Sup.
  Capitel San Rocco Ripasso '05   ♟♟ 4
- Amarone della Valpolicella Cl.
  Capitel Monte Olmi '01   ♟♟♟ 8
- Amarone della Valpolicella Cl.
  Capitel Monte Olmi '99   ♟♟♟ 8
- Amarone della Valpolicella Cl.
  Capitel Monte Olmi '95   ♟♟♟ 8
- Amarone della Valpolicella Cl.
  Capitel Monte Olmi '97   ♟♟♟ 8
- Amarone della Valpolicella Cl. '03   ♟♟ 6

- Amarone della Valpolicella Cl.
  Monte Masua Il Sestante '03   ♟♟ 8
- Crearo della Conca d'Oro '05   ♟♟ 5
- Recioto della Valpolicella Cl.
  Fiorato '05   ♟♟ 6
- Valpolicella Cl. Sup.
  Vign. Rafael '05   ♟♟ 5
- Valpolicella Cl. Sup. Ripasso '05   ♟♟ 5
- Valpolicella '06   ♟ 4
- O Lugana Vign. San Martino
  Il Sestante '06   ♟ 4
- Amarone della Valpolicella Cl. '03   ♟♟ 7
- Amarone della Valpolicella Cl.
  Ca' Florian '03   ♟♟ 8
- Amarone della Valpolicella Cl.
  Monte Masua Il Sestante '01   ♟♟ 8
- Crearo della Conca d'Oro '04   ♟♟ 5

Trabucchi

LOC. MONTE TENDA
37031 ILLASI [VR]
TEL. 0457833233
www.trabucchivini.it

Cantina Sociale della Valpantena

FRAZ. QUINTO
VIA COLONIA ORFANI DI GUERRA, 5B
37034 VERONA
TEL. 045550032
www.cantinavalpantena.it

ANNUAL PRODUCTION 70,000 bottles
HECTARES UNDER VINE 19
VITICULTURE METHOD Certified organic

ANNUAL PRODUCTION 7,000,000 bottles
HECTARES UNDER VINE N.A.
VITICULTURE METHOD Conventional

Although success only came last year with its first Three Glass award, this lovely winery has made top quality wines for some time. In 2007, the bottles tasted made it through to our finals, or walked away with at least Two Glasses. While the Valpolicella Terre di San Colombano led the field last year, this time there are two champions, both made from partially dried grapes, Amarone and Recioto. The former is striking in style, with fresh fruity, floral aromas followed by a distinctively supple and light palate where even the warmth of the 2003 growing year has failed to leave its mark. The more explosive, heady Recioto Cereolo has vibrant aromas of jam and Mediterranean scrubland, with alluring, nicely blended sweetness. Lastly, we come to the two Valpolicellas. The San Colombano is succulent and refreshing while the Terre del Cereolo is denser and reveals a little more depth.

The Cantina della Valpantena owes a great deal of its success to the work of Luca Degani, who has perfectly interpreted the magic moment Valpolicella is currently enjoying. The commitment of the member growers in the vineyards has been renewed, the cellar techniques perfected and, above all, the classic wine types have been interpreted in a contemporary key and promoted with effective marketing techniques. As usual, we were presented with a large number of wines that yielded more than satisfactory results. Let's start with the two sweet Recioto della Valpolicella wines, with their different styles. Tesauro has a modern, progressive palate but is not entirely convincing on the nose while the simpler 2005 hits the target with its spontaneous, approachable character. It's the same story with the Amarones. The 2004 is fruity and rounded while the Torre del Falasco seems to need more time to find full harmony. The Valpolicella Torre del Falasco is very good, showing depth and complexity on the nose and then an impressively austere palate.

● Amarone della Valpolicella '03	♈♈ 8
● Recioto della Valpolicella Cereolo '04	♈♈ 8
● Valpolicella Sup. Terre del Cereolo '03	♈♈ 5
● Valpolicella Sup. Terre di S. Colombano '04	♈♈ 5
● Valpolicella Sup. Terre di S. Colombano '03	♈♈♈ 5
● Amarone della Valpolicella '02	♈♈ 8
● Amarone della Valpolicella '01	♈♈ 8
● Amarone della Valpolicella '00	♈♈ 8
● Amarone della Valpolicella '99	♈♈ 7
● Amarone della Valpolicella '98	♈♈ 8
● Recioto della Valpolicella '04	♈♈ 8
● Recioto della Valpolicella '03	♈♈ 7

● Amarone della Valpolicella Valpantena '04	♈♈ 6
● Recioto della Valpolicella Valpantena '05	♈♈ 6
● Valpolicella Sup. Ripasso Torre del Falasco '05	♈♈ 4*
● Valpolicella Sup. Torre del Falasco '05	♈♈ 4*
● Amarone della Valpolicella Torre del Falasco '03	♈ 7
● Corvina Falasco '06	♈ 2
● Valpantena Sup. '05	♈ 4
● Valpantena Ritocco '05	♈ 4
● Recioto della Valpolicella Tesauro '04	♈ 6
○ Chardonnay Baroncino '06	♈ 3
● Amarone della Valpolicella Valpantena '03	♈♈ 5

Cantina Sociale Valpolicella
VIA CA' SALGARI, 2
37024 NEGRAR [VR]
TEL. 0456014300
www.cantinanegrar.it

ANNUAL PRODUCTION 7,500,000 bottles
HECTARES UNDER VINE 500
VITICULTURE METHOD Conventional

At last, here is a co-operative winery that has begun to look at Valpolicella as something more than Amarone's younger brother, producing a characterful, traditional, ambitious wine. We cannot help but admire this productive effort since we have been pointing out for many years that Valpolicella Superiore should play a more significant role. Our convictions are strengthened as we see them reflected in the objectives and plans of the winery run by Daniele Accordini. Named Verjago after the old name for Negrar, the key wine is the child of its local area above all, also deriving from brief partial drying of the grapes, which endows the wine with juicier fruit and more rounded body. The strong suit is of course acidity. Three Amarones were presented: the sumptuous Manara; the edgier, more spirited Classico; and the Jago, which is very richly extracted and still seeking harmony. The Recioto is an explosively fruity, joyous wine that is strikingly successful in keeping its very marked sweetness under control.

Massimino Venturini
FRAZ. SAN FLORIANO
VIA SEMONTE, 20
37020 SAN PIETRO IN CARIANO [VR]
TEL. 0457701331
www.viniventurini.com

ANNUAL PRODUCTION 90,000 bottles
HECTARES UNDER VINE 12
VITICULTURE METHOD Conventional

If only 90,000 bottles are produced from 12 hectares of vineyards, in an area that never seems to suffer a crisis, it must mean that the estate is not prepared to compromise on quality. This is how Daniele and Marco Venturini work, with passion and care, making high profile wines at a fair price without some of the restlessness that plagues some of their peers. The results are clear for all to see thanks to two Amarones and a Recioto, all of which are memorable, impressive and outstandingly classy wines in the traditional style. Le Brugnine, a Recioto, avoids the trap of a sugary, concentrated style. In fact, the palate is well backed up by acidity that also perks up the subtle, floral aromas. It is hard to choose between the two Amarones. Campomasua is powerful, soft without being sweet, mouthfilling and mature whereas the 2003, on the other hand, is edgier and more austere on the palate. The two Valpolicella selections are also both good, preserving a veiled ruggedness while remaining very enjoyably drinkable. This is a fine range of wines from a classic country winery.

● Valpolicella Cl. Sup. Verjago Domini Veneti '04	♟♟ 5
● Amarone della Valpolicella Cl. Domini Veneti '03	♟♟ 6*
● Amarone della Valpolicella Cl. Manara '00	♟♟ 8
● Recioto della Valpolicella Cl. Domini Veneti '05	♟♟ 5
● Amarone della Valpolicella Cl. Vign. di Jago Domini Veneti '03	♟♟ 7
○ Soave Cl. Vign. di Ca' de Napa Domini Veneti '06	♟ 4
● Valpolicella Cl. Sup. Vign. di Torbe Domini Veneti '04	♟ 4
● Amarone della Valpolicella Cl. Vign. di Jago Domini Veneti '01	♟♟ 7
● Recioto della Valpolicella Cl. Domini Veneti '05	♟♟ 5

● Amarone della Valpolicella Cl. '03	♟♟ 6*
● Amarone della Valpolicella Cl. Campomasua '01	♟♟ 7
● Recioto della Valpolicella Cl. Le Brugnine '03	♟♟ 6
● Valpolicella Cl. '06	♟ 3
● Valpolicella Cl. Sup. '05	♟ 4
● Recioto della Valpolicella Cl. Le Brugnine '97	♟♟♟ 6
● Amarone della Valpolicella Cl. '01	♟♟ 6
● Amarone della Valpolicella Cl. '00	♟♟ 7
● Amarone della Valpolicella Cl. '99	♟♟ 7
● Amarone della Valpolicella Cl. Campomasua '00	♟♟ 7
● Recioto della Valpolicella Cl. Le Brugnine '01	♟♟ 6

Agostino Vicentini

FRAZ. SAN ZENO
VIA C. BATTISTI, 62C
37030 COLOGNOLA AI COLLI [VR]
TEL. 0457650539
vicentiniagostino@libero.it

ANNUAL PRODUCTION 60,000 bottles
HECTARES UNDER VINE 14
VITICULTURE METHOD Conventional

Agostino Vicentini and his wife Teresa own a winery that has transformed its farming activity over the last ten years from a focus on fruit-growing to wine production, and the results are very interesting. Their deep-rooted relationship with the land and its fruits gives these wines plenty of character. They may be a little rugged but they are frank and authentic, as well as very reasonably priced all down the line. The family's work is diversified, mainly focusing on Soave even if there are plenty of Valpolicellas since the vineyards are located in both DOC zones. From these many interesting wines, we liked the Soave Il Casale for its mature, appetizing aromas and rounded palate with good grip. The slim-bodied Soave Terrelunghe is just a step behind. Turning to the reds, we were impressed by the healthily rugged Valpolicella Superiore. The tropical, appealing Recioto di Soave is also very good, showing sweet and light at the same time.

Vignale di Cecilia

LOC. FORNACI
VIA CROCI, 14
35030 BAONE [PD]
TEL. 042951420
www.vignaledicecilia.it

ANNUAL PRODUCTION 18,000 bottles
HECTARES UNDER VINE 8
VITICULTURE METHOD Conventional

Now that the cellar extensions are finished, Paolo Brunello can at last dedicate body and soul to his vineyards. To tell the truth, the vineyards have always been the crucial element but only this year has the winery been able to tackle significant expansion and the first result is a new white wine, Benavides, an original blend of garganega and moscato. The new plantings are in a splendid, beautifully aspected position where volcanic soil gives the wines an aromatic, mineral-edged sensation strongly characteristic of the local area. This is very noticeable in the red Covolo, which is aged entirely in concrete vats. This forthright, dynamic wine shows very ripe red berries on the nose followed by interesting hints of aromatic herbs and a taut palate. The Passacaglia is more concentrated and profound, presenting spices and a minerally streak along with the varietal aromas. And that Benavides is savoury and satisfyingly drinkable.

O Recioto di Soave '06	ΨΨ 6
O Soave Vign. Terrelunghe '06	ΨΨ 3*
O Soave Sup. Il Casale '06	ΨΨ 5
● Valpolicella Sup. '04	ΨΨ 4
● Valpolicella Sup. Idea Bacco '04	Ψ 5
● Valpolicella Vign. Boccascalucce '05	Ψ 3
O Recioto di Soave '04	ΨΨ 6
O Soave Vign. Terrelunghe '05	ΨΨ 3
O Soave Vign. Terrelunghe '04	ΨΨ 3

● Colli Euganei Rosso Passacaglia '04	ΨΨ 5
● Colli Euganei Rosso Covolo '05	ΨΨ 4
O Benavides '06	ΨΨ 3*
O Folia '03	ΨΨ 5
● Colli Euganei Rosso Passacaglia '03	ΨΨ 5
● Colli Euganei Rosso Passacaglia '02	ΨΨ 5
● Colli Euganei Rosso Passacaglia '01	ΨΨ 5

Vignalta

FRAZ. LUVIGLIANO
VIA DEI VESCOVI, 5
35038 TORREGLIA [PD]
TEL. 0499933105
www.vignalta.it

ANNUAL PRODUCTION 250,000 bottles
HECTARES UNDER VINE 55
VITICULTURE METHOD Conventional

In recent years, Vignalta has been experiencing its own little revolution with the arrival or departure of staff and partners. But Vignalta is still there, at the peak of Colli Euganei winemaking, its strength based on vineyards in the most favourable areas and cellar procedures that fully exploit the wonderful fruit. Lucio Gomiero and Graziano Cardin present a range of high profile wines, among which the Gemola and Alpianae are outstanding. These two wines are very different but both are faithful to their local area and respective wine types. Gemola is a merlot-heavy blend with some cabernet franc that flaunts sophisticated aromas and a firm palate with silky, fine-grained tannins. Alpianae opens with aromas of candied citrus fruit, spices and flowers before the noticeable sweetness on the palate is perfectly countered by acidity. The Agno Casto, from pinot bianco, the moscato secco-based Sirio and Rosso Riserva, from merlot and cabernet, form a solid, dependable base while Agno Tinto, made from syrah with some local varieties, and the merlot and cabernet Rosso Venda provide a worthy alternative to the nobler bottles.

Le Vigne di San Pietro

VIA S. PIETRO, 23
37066 SOMMACAMPAGNA [VR]
TEL. 045510016
www.levignedisanpietro.it

ANNUAL PRODUCTION 70,000 bottles
HECTARES UNDER VINE 10
VITICULTURE METHOD Conventional

The arrival as an investor in this winery of Giovanni Boscaini, who represents a famous Verona wine business, has brought Carlo Nerozzi about ten hectares of vineyards in Valpolicella, to be added to a similar holding in the Garda area. While we will have to wait for the 2007 vintage to taste the Verona products, we are amply consoled by the results from the area inland from Lake Garda. These confident wines offer an excellent interpretation of the morainic hillside terroir, under the supervision of consultant winemaker Federico Giotto. The two leading reds are I Balconi Rossi 2004, named after the vineyard which grows mainly corvina veronese with a small amount of cabernet and merlot, and Refolà 2003. Both are captivating for their fruit-forward intensity, grip and no-nonsense style. The CorDeRosa, a rosé made from corvina grapes, is absolutely enjoyable while Centopercento, a monovarietal Corvina, and Custoza are both impeccable.

● Colli Euganei Rosso Gemola '04	♙♙ 6
○ Colli Euganei Fior d'Arancio Passito Alpianae '05	♙♙ 5
○ Sirio '06	♙♙ 4
○ Colli Euganei Moscato '06	♙♙ 4
○ Colli Euganei Pinot Bianco Agno Casto '06	♙♙ 5
○ Colli Euganei Pinot Bianco '06	♙♙ 4*
● Agno Tinto '05	♙♙ 6
● Colli Euganei Rosso Ris. '04	♙♙ 4*
● Colli Euganei Rosso Venda '05	♙ 4
● Colli Euganei Rosso Gemola '01	♟♟♟ 6
● Colli Euganei Rosso Gemola '00	♟♟♟ 6
● Colli Euganei Rosso Gemola '95	♟♟♟ 6
● Colli Euganei Rosso Gemola '98	♟♟♟ 6
● Colli Euganei Rosso Gemola '03	♟♟ 6
○ Colli Euganei Fior d'Arancio Passito Alpianae '04	♟♟ 5

● I Balconi Rossi '04	♙♙ 6
● Refolà Cabernet Sauvignon '03	♙♙ 7
● Centopercento '05	♙♙ 3*
☉ CorDeRosa '06	♙♙ 4*
○ Custoza '06	♙♙ 4*
○ Sud '95	♟♟♟ 7
○ Sanpietro '04	♟♟ 4
● I Balconi Rossi '03	♟♟ 6
● Refolà Cabernet Sauvignon '01	♟♟ 7
● Refolà Cabernet Sauvignon '00	♟♟ 7

Vigneto Due Santi
V.LE ASIAGO, 174
36061 BASSANO DEL GRAPPA [VI]
TEL. 0424502074
vignetoduesanti@virgilio.it

Villa Bellini
LOC. CASTELROTTO DI NEGARINE
VIA DEI FRACCAROLI, 6
37020 SAN PIETRO IN CARIANO [VR]
TEL. 0457725630
www.villabellini.com

ANNUAL PRODUCTION 100,000 bottles
HECTARES UNDER VINE 18
VITICULTURE METHOD Conventional

ANNUAL PRODUCTION 10,000 bottles
HECTARES UNDER VINE 3
VITICULTURE METHOD Certified organic

Adriano and Stefano Zonta have redesigned the family winery, founded in 1965 and renovated in 1988. From the very beginning, the idea was to find a distinctive interpretation of the local area through careful study of the soil and grapes. This has yielded enjoyable wines that are ready to drink as soon as they are released but also capable of revealing further grace over time. Now that the vines have matured, the wines have in turn become more complete and mouthfilling, as is shown by the success they have enjoyed in this edition of the Guide. The excellent 2006 vintage gave us densely textured whites with a perfect mix of structure and acidity. The Breganze Bianco, from tocai grapes, is powerful, spicy, tangy and heady with alcohol. The Malvasia is floral, aromatic and iodine-edged while the Sauvignon is fragrant, soft and captivating. Turning to the reds, we liked the simple but far from ordinary Cabernet, which is fruity, floral, rounded and satisfyingly drinkable. The Merlot is always dependable while the Cabernet Vigneto Due Santi is very well judged, firm and still very youthful with good ageing prospects. It is still the Zonta's house champion and we gave it the coveted Three Glasses.

When you chat with Cecilia Trucchi as you stroll in her small garden-like vineyard around Villa Bellini, you not only grasp an overall sensation of order and harmony but above all, the calm determination of someone who is living out her own choices. What many producers might consider a bonus is, for Cecilia, one of the essential components of her decision to make wine. Other crucial elements are the organic farming of her vineyard with its new bush-trained vines and the decision to focus on the two wine types she considers pivotal to the area and her own winery, Valpolicella and Recioto. The Taso 2004 is a Superiore made from partially dried grapes and shows very elegant with a gutsy but supple palate. The Recioto is very dense with interesting balsamic hints and minerality followed by a stylish, succulent palate.

● Breganze Cabernet Vign. Due Santi '05	🍷🍷🍷 5
● Breganze Rosso '05	🍷🍷 4*
● Breganze Cabernet '05	🍷🍷 4*
O Breganze Bianco Rivana '06	🍷🍷 4*
O Malvasia Campo di Fiori '06	🍷🍷 4*
O Breganze Sauvignon Vign. Due Santi '06	🍷🍷 4*
O Prosecco Extra Dry '06	🍷 4
● Breganze Cabernet Vign. Due Santi '04	🍷🍷🍷 5
● Breganze Cabernet Vign. Due Santi '03	🍷🍷🍷 5*
● Breganze Cabernet Vign. Due Santi '00	🍷🍷🍷 5
● Breganze Cabernet Vign. Due Santi '02	🍷🍷 5

● Recioto della Valpolicella Cl. Uva Passa '04	🍷🍷 7
● Valpolicella Cl. Sup. Il Taso '04	🍷🍷 5
● Amarone della Valpolicella Cl. '01	🍷🍷 7
● Amarone della Valpolicella Cl. '00	🍷🍷 7
● Amarone della Valpolicella Cl. '99	🍷🍷 7
● Valpolicella Cl. Sup. Il Taso '03	🍷🍷 5
● Valpolicella Cl. Sup. Il Taso '02	🍷🍷 4
● Valpolicella Cl. Sup. Il Taso '01	🍷🍷 4

Villa Monteleone
FRAZ. GARGAGNAGO
VIA MONTELEONE, 12
37020 SANT'AMBROGIO
DI VALPOLICELLA [VR]
TEL. 0457704974
www.villamonteleone.com

ANNUAL PRODUCTION 35,000 bottles
HECTARES UNDER VINE 7
VITICULTURE METHOD Conventional

Lucia Duran is working with a passion to create a range of wines that upholds the winemaking style her husband Professor Raimondi believed in. Central to this style is the objective of achieving elegance and finesse rather than robust concentration while maintaining each wine's personality in perfect harmony with the local area. In recent years, Lucia has been assisted by promising young consultant Federico Giotto, which reflects the spirit of this winery. The Amarone Campo San Paolo is astonishingly elegant and extraordinarily drinkable, with aromas that develop gradually, alternating lightly fruity sensations with mineral and balsamic hints. The tense, subtle palate progresses very nicely. The Amarone Classico 2003 shows the effects of the hot growing year but is enjoyably rich and complex with a slightly dense tannic weave. The Valpolicella Campo San Vito, made using the ripasso technique of adding unpressed Amarone skins to the fermented wine, is succulent with toasted oak on the nose.

Villa Spinosa
LOC. JAGO
37024 NEGRAR [VR]
TEL. 0457500093
www.villaspinosa.it

ANNUAL PRODUCTION 35,000 bottles
HECTARES UNDER VINE 18
VITICULTURE METHOD Conventional

For 20 or so years, Enrico Cascella has been pursuing his own dream of wines that are far removed from fashion against the splendid backdrop of Villa Spinosa, the old proprietor's residence in the vineyards climbing up the hills near Jago. The cornerstone of Enrico's winemaking philosophy is the promotion of the local area with one eye on tradition, without losing sight of the importance of the human element. The wines reflect this vision, with unassertive aromas that focus on finesse. The Amarone is unquestionably the best example: the nose expresses strong hints of balsam, fines herbes and bottled fruit before the palate presents tense and savoury, light yet lingering, profound and well orchestrated. The Valpolicella Superiore Jago is made in a traditional style with overripe, bitterish sensations. The aromas are rounded off and enhanced by attractive minerally, gamey hints before the palate reveals good texture.

- Amarone della Valpolicella Cl. '03 ♟♟ 8
- Amarone della Valpolicella Cl. Campo S. Paolo '01 ♟♟ 8
- Valpolicella Cl. Sup. Campo S. Vito '04 ♟♟ 5
- Valpolicella Cl. Campo S. Lena '06 ♟ 4
- Valpolicella Cl. Sup. Campo S. Vito '03 ♟♟ 5
- Amarone della Valpolicella Cl. '01 ♟♟ 8
- Amarone della Valpolicella Cl. '00 ♟♟ 8

- Amarone della Valpolicella Cl. '00 ♟♟ 7
- Valpolicella Cl. Sup. Jago '03 ♟♟ 5
- Amarone della Valpolicella Cl. '99 ♟♟ 7
- Amarone della Valpolicella Cl. '98 ♟♟ 8

Vigneti Villabella

FRAZ. CALMASINO
LOC. CANOVA, 2
37011 BARDOLINO [VR]
TEL. 0457236448
www.vignetivillabella.com

ANNUAL PRODUCTION 500,000 bottles
HECTARES UNDER VINE 220
VITICULTURE METHOD Certified organic

Villabella has found its home – and what a home! – at Villa Cordevigo. This will gradually become the winery's nerve centre but the decision has been made and the renovations on the Villa are in full swing. The building will include offices, a tasting room and a cellar that blend into the surroundings, fully respecting the beautiful local landscape. It's a huge investment for a huge job undertaken with strength and determination by the owner families and all the staff. The wines presented this year are well up to speed with previous vintages, even with the absence of the Amarone Fracastoro. The Villa Cordevigo is a very nicely extracted red with a dry, creamy palate and just a hint of edgy oak on the nose. The Valpolicella Ripasso shows good handling of texture and should reveal greater finesse in the finish as it develops further. The whites are always enjoyable but our expectations focus on the upcoming edition of Villa Cordevigo Bianco, from garganega and sauvignon, which will see the light of day in 2008.

● Amarone della Valpolicella Cl. '03	🍷🍷	6
● Villa Cordevigo Rosso '03	🍷🍷	6
● Valpolicella Cl. Sup. Ripasso '04	🍷🍷	4
○ Soave Cl. La Torretta '06	🍷🍷	4*
○ Bianco di Custoza Fiordaliso '06	🍷	3
○ Lugana Ca' del Lago '06	🍷	4
○ Pinot Grigio V. di Pesina '06	🍷	4
● Bardolino Cl. V. Morlongo '05	🍷	4
● Montemazzano Rosso '04	🍷	4
● Valpolicella Cl. I Roccoli '06		4
● Amarone della Valpolicella Cl. '01	🥂🥂	6
● Amarone della Valpolicella Cl. Fracastoro '01	🥂🥂	7
● Villa Cordevigo Rosso '01	🥂🥂	6

Viviani

LOC. MAZZANO
VIA MAZZANO, 8
37020 NEGRAR [VR]
TEL. 0457500286
www.cantinaviviani.com

ANNUAL PRODUCTION 70,000 bottles
HECTARES UNDER VINE 10
VITICULTURE METHOD Conventional

Claudio Viviani is a bundle of energy, attentive to the smallest details and gifted with the right amount of self-doubt deriving from awareness of the huge responsibility in his hands. He has to vinify the grapes from excellent wine country at Mazzano, in the upper Negrar valley. The results are already clear from tasting the current Valpolicella with its exuberant floral freshness. Continuing with Viviani's more ambitious wines, the Valpolicella Campo Morar is ready for the corkscrew now. It has very richly extracted, ripe, healthy fruit as well as minerally sensations followed by a dense, creamy palate. The Tulipano Nero brims with maturity, the fruity aromas giving way to varietal notes of crushed flowers and earth that are echoed on the palate with its long, succulent finish. The Recioto is sumptuous, sweet and beautifully harmonious.

● Amarone della Valpolicella Cl. Tulipano Nero '00	🍷🍷	8
● Recioto della Valpolicella Cl. '04	🍷🍷	7
● Valpolicella Cl. Sup. Campo Morar '04	🍷🍷	6
● Valpolicella Cl. '06	🍷	4
● Amarone della Valpolicella Cl. Casa dei Bepi '01	🥂🥂🥂	8
● Amarone della Valpolicella Cl. Casa dei Bepi '00	🥂🥂🥂	8
● Amarone della Valpolicella Cl. Casa dei Bepi '98	🥂🥂🥂	8
● Amarone della Valpolicella Cl. Casa dei Bepi '97	🥂🥂🥂	8
● Amarone della Valpolicella Cl. Tulipano Nero '97	🥂🥂🥂	8
● Valpolicella Cl. Sup. Campo Morar '01	🥂🥂🥂	6

Zenato

FRAZ. S. BENEDETTO DI LUGANA
VIA S. BENEDETTO, 8
37019 PESCHIERA DEL GARDA [VR]
TEL. 0457550300
www.zenato.it

ANNUAL PRODUCTION 1,200,000 bottles
HECTARES UNDER VINE 70
VITICULTURE METHOD Conventional

In one of the winery's leaflets it says: "a family's passion brings together two terroirs". We must admit that the Zenato family treats the Lugana and Valpolicella zones as if they were two children, allowing each to follow its own ambitions and successes, confident that the education they have received at home will see them through. And these wines have come a long way. Almost 50 years after it was founded, Zenato is still firmly in the hands of Sergio, who now has his children Alberto and Nadia working with him. The twin souls of the winery have given birth to two great wines: the Amarone, from the hot 2003 growing year, is astonishingly elegant and assertively fresh, while the Lugana Massoni has never been so impressive. Generous aromas on the nose are followed by a taut, austere palate. We have no space to mention all the beautifully made wines presented but we would like to point out a new wine, Cresasso, a wonderfully dense, well-orchestrated monovarietal Corvina. The other wines are all good, including the enjoyable Lugana Sergio Zenato and the well-structured Valpolicella Ripassa. The basic wines are more than just well typed.

F.lli Zeni

VIA COSTABELLA, 9
37011 BARDOLINO [VR]
TEL. 0457210022
www.zeni.it

ANNUAL PRODUCTION 800,000 bottles
HECTARES UNDER VINE 25
VITICULTURE METHOD Conventional

Fausto Zeni and his sisters Elena and Federica have taken up the reins of the family winery, reacting with extraordinary ability to the sudden loss of their father Nino, for many years one of the leading lights of Lake Garda winemaking. Now that the building work on the new cellar is finished and the wine museum inside the winery has been enlarged, the three youngsters are thinking of restyling the products in the well-formulated range they source from the estate's vineyards at Bardolino and through shrewd purchases from tried and tested growers in the other parts of the province of Verona. Their local-style bottles tend to be jolly, approachably drinkable fun wines although the Bardolino Superiore, from grapes harvested when overripe, veers towards fruity sweetness. The Costalago is an enjoyable experimental red originating from the brief drying of corvinone, cabernet and merlot. Outstanding among the wines not produced in the Garda area are the Soave Marogne and the basic Amarone.

● Amarone della Valpolicella Cl. '03	ΨΨ 6
○ Lugana Vign. Massoni Santa Cristina '06	ΨΨ 4*
● Cresasso '04	ΨΨ 6
● Valpolicella Sup. Ripassa '04	ΨΨ 5
● Valpolicella Cl. Sup. '04	ΨΨ 4
○ Lugana Sergio Zenato '05	ΨΨ 5
○ Lugana S. Benedetto '06	Ψ 4
○ Rigoletto Passito Santa Cristina '05	Ψ 5
● Amarone della Valpolicella Cl. Sergio Zenato '95	ΨΨΨ 8
● Amarone della Valpolicella Cl. Sergio Zenato '00	ΨΨΨ 8
● Amarone della Valpolicella Cl. Sergio Zenato Ris. '98	ΨΨΨ 8
● Amarone della Valpolicella Cl. Ris. Sergio Zenato '95	ΨΨΨ 8
● Amarone della Valpolicella Cl. '97	ΨΨΨ 6

○ Soave Cl. Marogne '05	ΨΨ 4*
● Amarone della Valpolicella Cl. '04	ΨΨ 6
● Costalago Rosso '05	ΨΨ 5
● Bardolino Cl. Sup. '06	ΨΨ 4*
● Amarone della Valpolicella Cl. Barrique '03	Ψ 7
● Recioto della Valpolicella Cl. '05	Ψ 5
● Merlar Rosso '05	Ψ 6
⊙ Bardolino Chiaretto Cl. Vigne Alte '06	Ψ 3
⊙ Bardolino Cl. '06	Ψ 2
○ Soave Cl. Vigne Alte '06	Ψ 3
○ Lugana V. Alte '06	Ψ 3
● Amarone della Valpolicella Cl. '03	ΨΨ 6
● Bardolino Cl. Sup. '04	ΨΨ 4

Zonin

VIA BORGOLECCO, 9
36053 GAMBELLARA [VI]
TEL. 0444640111
www.zonin.it

ANNUAL PRODUCTION   23,000,000 bottles
HECTARES UNDER VINE 1,800
VITICULTURE METHOD   Conventional

The numbers here are terrifyingly
impressive. Zonin has 1,800 hectares
scattered over seven Italian regions for a
total production of 23,000,000 bottles.
Despite its strongly Italian, or even
international, image, the heart and brains of
this Gambellara-based winery remain in
Veneto, firmly in the hands of the Zonin
family, who have put together a thoroughly
respectable technical staff led by Franco
Giacosa. Only four wines were presented
but they nicely represent the Zonin universe.
First up was an approachably expressive
Amarone, with prevalent aromas of ripe fruit
and cocoa powder and a soft, sunny palate
thanks to the alcohol and residual sugar.
The interesting Ripasso is more complex
and profound on the nose and shows
strikingly austere and harmonious. Then
come the two whites. One of them, Il
Giangio, is the missing link between the
modern winery and the culture of its inland
area. It's a vibrant, floral Gambellara with a
slender, freshly drinkable palate. Finally, the
Prosecco Special Cuvée is very pleasant.

Zymè

VIA CA' DEL PIPA, 1
37029 SAN PIETRO IN CARIANO [VR]
TEL. 0457701108
www.zyme.it

ANNUAL PRODUCTION   20,000 bottles
HECTARES UNDER VINE 9
VITICULTURE METHOD   Conventional

A small revolution has taken place at Zymè
which has reduced the partnership to just
Celestino Gaspari and Francesco Parisi. But
more importantly, a change has taken place
in operative terms since all the external
work on the winery has been completed.
Now, Celestino and Francesco can dedicate
their time exclusively to the increasingly
impressive and seriously good Zymè
products, which are also released in
significant numbers. There is a new white,
called Il Bianco From Black to White, as an
unequivocal indication of how this wine is
obtained through the mutation of the black
rondinella berry into a white grape. Its
distinctive features are vibrant aromas and a
very savoury palate. The Harlequin is
powerful, closed and eminently cellarable
while the Kairos is more approachable and
captivating. Lastly, the Oseleta Oz gets
more focused and harmonious with each
passing year.

● Amarone della Valpolicella '04	▼▼	6
● Valpolicella Sup. Ripasso '04	▼▼	4*
○ Gambellara Cl.		
Podere Il Giangio '06	▼	3
○ Prosecco Brut Special Cuvée		3
● Amarone della Valpolicella '03	♀♀	6
● Amarone della Valpolicella '00	♀♀	6
○ Recioto di Gambellara		
Podere il Giangio Aristòs '03	♀♀	6

● Kairos '04	▼▼	8
● Harlequin '01	▼▼	8
● Oseleta Oz '04	▼▼	6
○ Il Bianco From Black to White '06	▼	4
● Kairos '03	♀♀	8
● Oseleta Oz '03	♀♀	6

OTHER WINERIES

Ida Agnoletti
LOC. SELVA DEL MONTELLO
VIA SACCARDO, 55
31040 VOLPAGO DEL MONTELLO [TV]
TEL. 0423620947

Ida Agnoletti has very clear ideas about quality and tenaciously pursues this objective for her more ambitious and her simpler wines. The Merlot, for example, shuns accessible softness for gutsy, well-structured simplicity. Seneca is richer and complex with rich aromatic herbs on the nose.

● Seneca '04	▼▼ 4*
● Montello e Colli Asolani Merlot '05	▼ 3
● Seneca '03	♈♈ 4

Aleandri
VIA CALLALTA, 52
31045 MOTTA DI LIVENZA [TV]
TEL. 0422765571
www.tenutealeandri.it

Aleandri comprises four different wineries, two in Friuli and two in Veneto, Aleandri at Lison-Pramaggiore and Ca' Vittoria at Conegliano. Both wineries produce beautifully made wines. The Prosecco Millesimato has uncomplicated, varietal aromas followed by a creamy, nicely orchestrated palate.

○ Prosecco di V. Dry Millesimato Ca' Vittoria '06	▼▼ 4
● Lison-Pramaggiore Merlot Aleandri '06	▼ 3

Antolini
VIA PROGNOL, 22
37020 MARANO DI VALPOLICELLA [VR]
TEL. 0457755351
www.antolinivini.it

The Antolini siblings' winery in the Valpolicella DOC zone is small. From the start, they decided not to follow fashion but to give the wines a clearly defined style, favouring edgy acidity over softness. The result is perceptible on their Amarone, which is supple and light in the mouth.

● Amarone della Valpolicella Cl. '04	▼▼ 7
● Recioto della Valpolicella Cl. '05	▼ 6
● Valpolicella Cl. Sup. Ripasso '05	▼ 5
● Valpolicella Cl. '05	▼ 3

Astoria Vini
VIA CREVADA, 44
31020 REFRONTOLO [TV]
TEL. 04236699
www.astoria.it

The Polegato family winery is back in the Guide thanks to a balanced range of dependably good products. As well as a good selection of still wines, there's a fine line-up of prosecco-based sparklers. The excellent Cartizze has very clear varietal aromas and the Casa di Vittorino is just a step behind.

○ Cartizze '05	▼▼ 5
○ P. di Valdobbiadene Dry Casa di Vittorino	▼ 4

Barollo
VIA BELLUDI, 30
35123 PADOVA [PD]
TEL. 049650813
www.barollo.com

The Barollo brothers are recovering an area long neglected by winemakers, the plain between Venice and Treviso. The excellent Merlot has very concentrated fruit echoed by hints of spice on the well-rounded palate. The Frater Rosso is refreshingly drinkable and the Bianco is savoury and succulent.

● Piave Merlot '04	▼▼ 5
○ Frater Bianco '06	▼ 4
● Frater Rosso '06	▼ 4
○ Piave Chardonnay '05	▼ 5

Cantina Beato Bartolomeo da Breganze
VIA ROMA, 100
36042 BREGANZE [VI]
TEL. 0445873112
www.cantinabreganze.it

Founded over 50 years ago, the Cantina di Breganze now has over 1,000 members cultivating 70 per cent of the DOC zone. Results are excellent, thanks to the hard work of the winery staff. The outstanding Kilò is a complex, dry, robust Cabernet. The Vespaiolo brings a new dimension to the wine type.

● Breganze Cabernet Kilò Ris. '03	▼▼ 5
○ Breganze Vespaiolo Sup. Savardo '06	▼▼ 4*
○ Breganze Bianco Sup. Savardo '06	▼ 4

OTHER WINERIES

Le Bertole
VIA EUROPA, 20
31049 VALDOBBIADENE [TV]
TEL. 0423975332
www.lebertole.com

We applaud the increasingly impressive range of sparklers from Le Bertole, whose wide range of wines are always focused and value for money. We liked the Dry Supreme for its floral aromas and apple and pear fruit. The Extra Dry is husky but very impressive on the palate.

O P. di Valdobbiadene Dry Supreme	♟♟	4*
O P. di Valdobbiadene Extra Dry	♟♟	3*
O P. di Valdobbiadene Brut	♟	4
O Cartizze	♟	5

Carlo Boscaini
VIA SENGIA
37010 SANT'AMBROGIO
DI VALPOLICELLA [VR]
TEL. 0457731412
www.boscainicarlo.it

This is a sound range of wines from Carlo and Mario Boscaini of Sant'Ambrogio, who focus on the classic Valpolicella types. The Amarone is on fine form, showing richly extracted and well-orchestrated on the palate. The Valpolicella Ca' Bussin is interesting while La Preosa is richer with more structure.

● Amarone della Valpolicella Cl. San Giorgio '03	♟♟	6
● Valpolicella Cl. Ca' Bussin '05	♟	3
● Valpolicella Cl. Sup. La Preosa '04	♟	4

Le Carline
VIA CARLINE, 24
30020 PRAMAGGIORE [VE]
TEL. 0421799741
www.lecarline.com

Daniele Piccinin is a scrupulous producer committed to his winery and also to promoting the local DOC zone, Lison-Pramaggiore. The very wide range of wines is sourced from organically farmed vineyards. Dogale, from part-dried verduzzo, is alluring and the Refosco fresh-tasting and fragrant.

● Lison-Pramaggiore Refosco P. R. '05	♟♟	3*
O Dogale Passito	♟♟	5
O Lison-Pramaggiore Lison '06	♟	3

Case Paolin
VIA MADONNA MERCEDE, 53
31040 VOLPAGO DEL MONTELLO [TV]
TEL. 0423871433
www.casepaolin.it

Montello is becoming one of the most exciting parts of eastern Veneto, as Venegazzù showed a few decades ago. The Pozzobons gave us a Bordeaux blend from overripe grapes, which has rich aromas of jam and cocoa powder. The Manzoni Bianco is good and the Cabernet Sauvignon approachable.

● Montello e Colli Asolani Sup. San Carlo '04	♟♟	5
● Cabernet Sauvignon '05	♟	3
O Manzoni Bianco Santi Angeli '06	♟	4

Gerardo Cesari
LOC. SORSEI, 3
37010 CAVAION VERONESE [VR]
TEL. 0456260928
www.cesari-spa.it

The cutting edge of this large winery's production is Valpolicella and its wines. The wide, well-balanced range of bottles should meet all demands, including those of price. Valpolicella Busan is interesting, rich and mature with warm alcohol sensations. The Amarone is firm and the Ripasso Mara soft.

● Valpolicella Cl. Sup. Ripasso Bosan '04	♟♟	4*
● Valpolicella Sup. Ripasso Mara '04	♟	4
● Amarone della Valpolicella Cl. '04	♟	6

Colle Mattara
FRAZ. CARBONARA DI ROVOLON
VIA G. VERDI, 80
35030 ROVOLON [PD]
TEL. 0495227094

Filippo Livian's vineyards are excellently aspected on the west-facing slope of the Colli Euganei. The range is small but the wines are forthright. The Rosso is an interesting merlot-heavy blend with striking aromas of ripe fruit and aromatic herbs. The Fior d'Arancio is also excellent.

● Colli Euganei Rosso '03	♟♟	4*
O Colli Euganei Fior d'Arancio Passito '03	♟♟	5
● Colli Euganei Cabernet '06	♟	3

OTHER WINERIES

Corte Aleardi
FRAZ. GARGAGNAGO
VIA GIARE, 15
37020 SANT'AMBROGIO DI VALPOLICELLA [VR]
TEL. 0457701379

As well as large, internationally known wineries, Valpolicella also boasts many smaller, less famous names that release equally fine wines. One such estate is Corte Aleardi, active for many years. Its two exciting Valpolicellas are the complex Bure Alto and the huskier, more traditional, Montepalà

- Valpolicella Cl. Sup.
  Ripasso Bure Alto '03 ΥΥ 5
- Valpolicella Cl. Sup. Montepalà '02 Υ 5

Corteforte
VIA OSAN, 45
37022 FUMANE [VR]
TEL. 0456839104
www.corteforte.com

Corteforte is situated in the Fumane valley, in the Valpolicella Classico zone, and in recent years it has been concentrating on quality. Despite the small numbers of bottles, the range of wines is extensive. The Amarone Vigneti di Osan is very mature and exuberant while the red Concentus is more compact.

- Concentus '04 ΥΥ 7
- Amarone della Valpolicella Cl.
  Vign. di Osan '00 ΥΥ 8
- Recioto della Valpolicella Cl. '04 Υ 7

La Costa di Romagnano
LOC. LA COSTA
37034 GREZZANA [VR]
TEL. 0458650111
www.agricosta.it

Unfortunately, we only tasted one wine from this young Grezzana winery, which is why it has a short profile this year. Despite the unfavourable 2002 growing year, the Recioto della Valpolicella shows strikingly healthy fruit and a generous palate with well-orchestrated sweetness, extract and complex aromas.

- Recioto della Valpolicella
  Vign. Calandra di Romagnano '02 ΥΥ 5
- Amarone della Valpolicella
  Vign. Calandra di Romagnano '02 ΥΥ 6

Casa Coste Piane
FRAZ. SANTO STEFANO
VIA COSTE PIANE, 2
31040 VALDOBBIADENE [TV]
TEL. 0423900219

Before the Charmat method was adopted, Prosecco Spumante was made by spontaneous second fermentation in bottle but it never achieved the vivacious sparkle of classic method wines. Prosecco is still the leading Follador product, showing delicately sparkling and extraordinarily savoury.

- O P. di Valdobbiadene Frizzante Sur Lie ΥΥ 3*
- O P. di Valdobbiadene Extra Dry
  San Venanzio Υ 4
- O P. di Valdobbiadene Tranquillo Υ 3

Costozza
FRAZ. COSTOZZA
P.ZZA DA SCHIO, 4
36023 LONGARE [VI]
TEL. 0444555099

We are delighted at the road being taken by Costozza. The decision to postpone release of their wines to give them more bottle ageing time is laudable. Meanwhile, we have been able to assess development of the 2004 wines, which is proceeding steadily with finesse the keynote.

- Rosso Costozza '04 ΥΥ 5
- Rosso Costozza '03 ΥΥ 5
- Colli Berici Cabernet '04 ΥΥ 4
- Colli Berici Cabernet '03 ΥΥ 5

Valentina Cubi
LOC. CASTERNA, 60
37022 FUMANE [VR]
TEL. 0457701806
www.valentinacubi.it

In Valpolicella, wineries with a distinguished tradition are being joined by a growing number of good, more recently founded estates. At Cubi, the prevailing style pursues very mature aromas enhancing the almost decadent charm of the wines. A fine example is Amarone Morar, with its very ripe fruit aromas.

- Amarone della Valpolicella Cl. Morar '03 ΥΥ 7
- Valpolicella Cl. Iperico '05 Υ 3
- Amarone della Valpolicella Cl. Morar '01 ΥΥ 7

OTHER WINERIES

De Faveri
Fraz. Bosco
Via Sartori, 21
31020 Vidor [TV]
Tel. 0423987673

Often the most interesting sparkling Proseccos are the one that rely on residual sugar. At De Faveri, the opposite applies, with a high-profile production of Bruts. The type owes its fine quality to the grapes and the skill of the producer. The basic Brut and the Selezione Nera are both well typed.

O P. di Valdobbiadene Brut	🍷🍷 4
O P. di Valdobbiadene Brut Sel. Nera	🍷🍷 4
O Cartizze	🍷 5
O P. di Valdobbiadene Dry	🍷 4

F.lli Fabiano
Via Verona, 6
37060 Sona [VR]
Tel. 0456081111
www.fabiano.it

Fabiano's modernization goes on, not so much in the cellar, where the technology is respectable, as in the production philosophy, with increasingly well-typed wines. The house champ is Vajo, a rich, juicy Bordeaux blend with a dollop of part-dried corvina. The Valpolicella Negraro is making progress.

● Vajo '05	🍷🍷 5
● Valpolicella Cl. Sup. Ripasso Negraro '05	🍷 4
O Lugana Argillaia '06	🍷 4

Giovanni Fattori
Via S. Pertini, 21d
37032 Monteforte d'Alpone [VR]
Tel. 0457460041
www.fattoriandgraney.it

We like the wines from this lovely winery, where Soave meets international varieties like sauvignon and pinot grigio. The Sauvignon Motto Piane is on fine form with apple and pear fruit and florality. The first Roncha, an interesting blend of traditional and international grapes, has freshness and grip.

O Sauvignon Motto Piane '06	🍷🍷 4
O Soave Cl. '06	🍷 3
O Soave Cl. Motto Piane '06	🍷 4
O Roncha '06	🍷 4

Filippi
Loc. Castelcerino
Via Libertà, 55
37038 Soave [VR]
Tel. 0457675005

In Soave, as elsewhere, we are watching an increasing number of wineries that combine maximum respect for the land and with minimal intervention during vinification. Filippi is one such, and the results are good. The mature, fruity Recioto Calprea and the husky but firmer Soave Castelcerino provide proof.

O Recioto di Soave Calprea '05	🍷🍷 6
O Soave Colli Scaligeri Castelcerino '06	🍷🍷 4*
O Recioto di Soave Calprea '04	🍷🍷 5

Marchesi Fumanelli
Fraz. San Floriano
Loc. Squarano
37029 San Pietro in Cariano [VR]
Tel. 0457704875

Valpolicella has wide valleys, like Fumane and Negrar, but also gentle slopes like those around San Floriano, the home of Marchesi Fumanelli. From the wines presented, we liked Squarano, a complex Valpolicella of depth that has a strikingly subtle palate.

● Valpolicella Cl. Sup. Squarano '03	🍷🍷 5
● Valpolicella Cl. '06	🍷 3
O Flora '06	🍷 3
O Terso Bianco '04	🍷 5

Fattoria Garbole
Via Fracanzana, 6
37039 Tregnago [VR]
Tel. 0457809020
www.fattoriagarbole.it

Fattoria Garbole is one of Valpolicella's small, new wineries, working outside the DOC zone but producing traditional wines. We very much like the Amarone for its very contemporary nose and balance on the palate. This firm, powerful wine cannot fail to improve with appropriate cellar time.

● Amarone della Valpolicella '03	🍷🍷 7
● Valpolicella Sup. '04	🍷 5

OTHER WINERIES

La Giaretta

FRAZ. VALGATARA
VIA DEL PLATANO, 12
37020 MARANO DI VALPOLICELLA [VR]
TEL. 0457701791

Valpolicella is where modernity and tradition meet, exchanging styles and sensations to produce a wide-ranging, multi-faceted panorama. This is mirrored in the sensations of Francesco Vaona's extensive range of wines. The rich Valpolicella I Quadretti has modern aromas and flavour.

- Valpolicella Cl. Sup. I Quadretti '04 ▼▼ 5
- Valpolicella Cl. Sup. '04 ▼ 4
- Amarone della Valpolicella Cl. '03 ▼ 6

Grotta del Ninfeo

VIA BOSCHETTO, 6
37030 LAVAGNO [VR]
TEL. 0458980154
www.grottadelninfeo.it

The part of Valpolicella east of Verona is called Classica but the vocation and tradition for wine are the same, as is shown by the wines of the Fraccaroli family winery at Lavagno. The Amarone, from the hot year of 2003, has a mature, fruity nose. A step behind is the Ripasso, with more traditional aromas.

- Amarone della Valpolicella '03 ▼▼ 6
- Valpolicella Sup. Ripasso '04 ▼ 4
- Valpolicella Sup. Ripasso '03 ▼▼ 5
- Valpolicella Sup. '03 ▼▼ 5

Latium

VIA GIARA, 34
37031 ILLASI [VR]
TEL. 3929048995
www.latiummorini.it

The Morini family wines did well, earning more than flattering approval on their debut in the Guide. We liked the Amarone, which is profound, minerally and characterful. The rich Valpolicella Campo Prognai is still young, but full of potential, and the Soave is fresh-tasting.

- Amarone della Valpolicella
  Campo Leon '03 ▼▼ 7
- Valpolicella Sup. Campo Prognai '04 ▼▼ 5
- Soave Campo Le Calle '06 ▼ 4

Lenotti

VIA S. CRISTINA, 1
37011 BARDOLINO [VR]
TEL. 0457210484
www.lenotti.com

This large operation has been working in several sectors for years, including Garda-type wines and some often interesting forays into Valpolicella. The latter area gives Amarone Di Carlo, a powerful red with complex aromas. The tropical Soave Capocolle shows nicely integrated oak and Bardolino Le Olle is soft.

- Soave Cl. Capocolle '06 ▼▼ 4
- Amarone della Valpolicella Cl.
  Di Carlo '01 ▼▼ 8
- Bardolino Cl. Sup. Le Olle '05 ▼ 4

Giuseppe Lonardi

VIA DELLE POSTE, 2
37020 MARANO DI VALPOLICELLA [VR]
TEL. 0457755154
www.lonardivini.it

Up in Marano di Valpolicella, Giuseppe Lonardi divides his time between his restaurant and his winery, with good results in both. The cool climate of the upper Marano valley made it possible to produce a classy Amarone even in the hot year of 2003. The rustic Ripasso offers good quality.

- Amarone della Valpolicella Cl. '03 ▼▼ 8
- Valpolicella Cl. Sup. Ripasso '05 ▼▼ 6
- Privilegia Rosso '04 ▼ 7
- Valpolicella Cl. '06 ▼ 4

Masottina

LOC. CASTELLO ROGANZUOLO
VIA BRADOLINI, 54
31020 SAN FIOR [TV]
TEL. 0438400775

Masottina is a large winery in the Treviso area which offers a very wide selection of wines for all requirements. The very good Merlot Vigneto Ai Palazzi is a generous, fragrant wine with a captivatingly delicate palate that signs off with a juicy finish.

- Piave Merlot Ai Palazzi Ris. '04 ▼▼ 5
- Cartizze ▼ 6
- P. di Conegliano Extra Dry ▼ 3
- Piave Chardonnay ai Palazzi '06 ▼ 4

OTHER WINERIES

Merotto
LOC. COL SAN MARTINO
VIA SCANDOLERA, 21
31010 FARRA DI SOLIGO [TV]
TEL. 0438989000

Graziano Merotto lavishes passion and skill on his prosecco-based spumantes, as do all the wineries from Valdobbiadene to Conegliano Veneto. The Cartizze gave an impressive performance, showing sound, floral and very approachable on the palate. The Brut Barreta and La Primavera di Barbara are dependably good.

O Cartizze	♥♥	6
O P. di Valdobbiadene Brut Barreta	♥	4
O P. di Valdobbiadene Dry La Primavera di Barbara	♥	4

Monte del Frà
STRADA PER CUSTOZA, 35
37066 SOMMACAMPAGNA [VR]
TEL. 045510490
www.montedelfra.it

The Bonomo family is turning its attention to Valpolicella, where the purchase of new vineyards will mean a further rise in production. From this area comes the most impressive wine, a Valpolicella with aromas of raisins and medicinal herbs and a temptingly taut, juicy palate.

● Valpolicella Cl. Sup. Ripasso '03	♥♥	5
O Bianco di Custoza '06	♥	3
● Bardolino '06	♥	3
● Valpolicella Cl. '06	♥	3

Montecariano
VIA VALENA, 3
37029 SAN PIETRO IN CARIANO [VR]
TEL. 0456838335
www.montecariano.it

Montecariano is at San Pietro in Cariano, under the Valpolicella Classica hills. Production is still limited in quantity but high in quality, as we saw at this year's tastings. The Amarone has a lively nose and is still edgy on the palate while the Puntara is a robustly expressive Cabernet Sauvignon.

● Puntara Cabernet Sauvignon '03	♥♥	5
● Amarone della Valpolicella Cl. '03	♥♥	7
● Valpolicella Cl. '05	♥	3
● Valpolicella Cl. Sup. Ripasso '03	♥	5

Marco Mosconi
VIA PARADISO, 5
37031 ILLASI [VR]
TEL. 0457834000
mosconimarco@tiscali.it

To get an idea of how lively an area is, take a look at the small growers emerging so the diminutive Mosconi winery attracted our attention. Only two wines are made but the Soave Località Paradiso is a perfect expression of the terroir with its firm body and juicy palate. The Soave 2006 is simpler.

O Soave Località Paradiso '06	♥♥	4
O Soave '06	♥	4

Walter Nardin
LOC. RONCADELLE
VIA FONTANE, 5
31024 ORMELLE [TV]
TEL. 0422851622

This winery works in two DOC zones of eastern Veneto, Piave and Lison-Pramaggiore. The range of wines is wide but focused on quality and the wines offer good value for money. We recommend the Rosso della Ghiaia, from merlot, cabernet and raboso, and the Rosso del Nane, from refosco.

● Rosso della Ghiaia '03	♥♥	4*
● Lison-Pramaggiore Cabernet Franc '06	♥	3
● Piave Merlot Rosso del Nane '05	♥	4

Paladin
VIA POSTUMIA, 12
30020 ANNONE VENETO [VE]
TEL. 0422768167
www.paladin.it

The Paladin cellar's products centre on wines with a precise sense of place and reflect their origin in Lison-Pramaggiore, on the Adriatic coast. We were particularly impressed by two of the wines, a complex, well-structured Malbech and the fresh, forthright Refosco. We also liked the Traminer.

● Lison-Pramaggiore Refosco P. R. '06	♥♥	4*
● Malbech Gli Aceri '03	♥♥	5
O Traminer '06	♥	4

OTHER WINERIES

Vigneti e Cantine Pasqua
LOC. SAN FELICE EXTRA
VIA BELVEDERE, 135
37131 VERONA
TEL. 0458432111
www.pasqua.it

Now in the new San Felice premises, with production and administration under one roof, the Pasqua brothers' large operation is even more firmly established in Valpolicella, where the more ambitious products come from. Amarone Villa Borghetti is rich and spicy and the Valpolicella is fresh-tasting.

● Valpolicella Sup. Ripasso
  Villa Borghetti '05   ♛♛ 5
● Amarone della Valpolicella Cl.
  Villa Borghetti '03   ♛♛ 7

Perlage
VIA CAL DEL MUNER, 1
31020 FARRA DI SOLIGO [TV]
TEL. 0438900203
www.perlagewines.com

Prosecco makes more use of technology than the rest of Veneto, as this wine requires technical support to achieve creaminess and finesse. That makes it even more striking to find an organic winery with better than good results. The very interesting Brut Canah is mature and well-structured on the palate.

○ P. di Valdobbiadene Brut Canah   ♛♛ 4*
○ P. di Valdobbiadene Extra Dry
  Col di Manza   ♛ 4

Le Pignole
VIA MEUCCI, 87
36040 BRENDOLA [VI]
TEL. 0444405440
www.lepignole.com

Colli Berici is a favourable but little exploited wine area. Wineries like Gianna Bortolamai and Paolo Padrin's Le Pignole are trying to establish it. Although not DOC-registered, the vines are in the Colli Berici zone. Cabernet franc and carmenère grapes are used for the Soastene, a peppery, beautifully balanced red.

● Soastene '05   ♛♛ 4*
● Torengo '05   ♛ 6
○ Sisara '06   ♛ 3
○ Solarente '06   ♛ 3

Albino Piona
FRAZ. CUSTOZA
VIA BELLAVISTA, 48
37060 SOMMACAMPAGNA [VR]
TEL. 045516055

The new winery is complete and the Piona family has moved production there, improving the organization of winemaking procedures. The Bardolino performed beautifully, combining fresh fruit and spice with a taut, very enjoyable palate. The Chiaretto is very nice as a food wine.

● Bardolino '06   ♛♛ 3
● Azobé '04   ♛ 5
● Merlot Campo Massimo '05   ♛ 4
☉ Bardolino Chiaretto '06   ♛ 3

Giorgio Poggi
VIA POGGI, 7
37010 AFFI [VR]
TEL. 0457236222
www.cantinepoggi.com

As well as the classic Garda DOC products, the Poggi family also makes a small quantity of wine in neighbouring Valpolicella. The Moretto, a fragrant Valpolicella with ripe fruit and herbs, is an excellent example. The Bardolino Campi Regi is good, as is the fresher, leaner Bardolino Classico.

● Valpolicella Cl. Sup. Il Moretto '02   ♛♛ 4
● Bardolino Sup. Campi Regi '05   ♛ 4
○ Garda Le Tortone '05   ♛ 4
● Bardolino Cl. '06   ♛ 3

Luigino e Marco Provolo
VIA SAN CASSIANO, 2
37030 MEZZANE DI SOTTO [VR]
TEL. 0458880106
www.viniprovolo.com

For years the Mezzane valley, just east of Valpolicella Classica, has been one of the most interesting subzones, with wineries like Provolo making a limited range of high-quality wines. Take Campotorbian, for instance, a deep, firmly structured red. The Amarone has generous alcoholic warmth.

● Valpolicella Sup. Ripasso
  Campotorbian '03   ♛♛ 6
● Valpolicella Sup. Gino '04   ♛♛ 5
● Amarone della Valpolicella '03   ♛ 7

OTHER WINERIES

Tenuta S. Anna

LOC. LONCON
VIA MONS. P. L. ZOVATTO, 71
30020 ANNONE VENETO [VE]
TEL. 0422864511

The improved quality of this large Generali insurance group-owned operation has been driven by the basic wines. The whole line is now richer and better defined, with good results especially among the traditional varieties. The Refosco is heady with floral hints, the Tocai is tangy and the Merlot chewy.

● Lison-Pramaggiore Refosco P. R. '06	▼▼ 4
● Lison-Pramaggiore Merlot '06	▼ 3
○ Lison-Pramaggiore Tocai Cl. '06	▼ 4

Santa Eurosia

FRAZ. SAN PIETRO DI BARBOZZA
VIA DELLA CIMA, 8
31040 VALDOBBIADENE [TV]
TEL. 0423973236

Prosecco di Valdobbiadene is one of the best-known sparklers in the world, in part because of the dedication of its producers. Ranges usually hinge on three wines with different levels of residual sugar. The excellent Cartizze has a creamy, elegant palate, as does the Brut, for which the winery has a knack.

○ Cartizze	▼▼ 5
○ P. di Valdobbiadene Brut	▼▼ 4*
○ P. di Valdobbiadene Extra Dry	▼ 4

Tenuta Solar

VIA DANTE, 125
37032 MONTEFORTE D'ALPONE [VR]
TEL. 0456100550

Although quantities are still quite small, Tenuta Solar offers a wide selection of wines, all with an excellent standard of quality. The house champion is the El Re, a vibrant Recioto di Soave expressing floral and candied citrus aromas with distinctive, perfectly balanced sweetness.

○ Recioto di Soave Cl. El Re '05	▼▼ 5
○ Soave Cl. La Posta '06	▼ 4
○ Soave Cl. Sup. Le Caselle '05	▼ 4
○ Soave Cl. Le Barcole '06	▼ 4

David Sterza

LOC. CASTERNA
VIA CASTERNA, 37
37022 FUMANE [VR]
TEL. 0457704201

Casterna is a little village near the more famous town of Fumane. This small winery's products are emerging for their good quality and territory focus. The Amarone shows no ill effects from the heat of 2003 and has a firm, dynamic palate. The well-typed Ripasso has ripe fruit and a sturdy palate.

● Valpolicella Cl. Sup. Ripasso '05	▼▼ 5
● Amarone della Valpolicella Cl. '03	▼▼ 7
● Recioto della Valpolicella Cl. '04	▼ 6
● Amarone della Valpolicella Cl. '03	♀♀ 7

Sutto

VIA SAN LORENZETTO, 9
31040 SALGAREDA [TV]
TEL. 0422744063
www.sutto.it

The Piave DOC zone covers a very extensive area from the hills to the sea, but the most interesting parts are those with rich clay soil where the merlot grape is at home. And Sutto's Merlot impressed us with its harmonious aromas and subtle yet dense flavour profile.

● Piave Merlot Ris. '04	▼▼ 5
● Piave Raboso '04	▼ 6
○ Sauvignon '06	▼ 3
○ Manzoni Bianco '06	▼ 5

Tanorè

SAN PIETRO DI BARBOZZA
VIA MONT DI CARTIZZE, 3
31040 VALDOBBIADENE [TV]
TEL. 0423975770

Nestling in one of the most attractive parts of the whole Valdobbiadene zone, Tanorè is a dependably good winery. We loved the Cartizze, made with grapes from the top vineyard in this part of Veneto, which has traditional apple and pear aromas. The Brut has simpler aromas but a gutsy palate with good grip.

○ P. di Valdobbiadene Brut	▼▼ 4*
○ Cartizze	▼▼ 5
○ P. di Valdobbiadene Tranquillo	▼ 4

OTHER WINERIES

Le Tende
FRAZ. COLÀ
VIA TENDE, 35
37010 LAZISE [VR]
TEL. 0457590748

Three DOC zones share the Veneto side of Lake Garda, all focused on native grapes with more recent input from international varieties. The very interesting Bardolino is heady with floral hints, the Merlò is pleasant and approachable, the Custoza light though not predictable and the Chiaretto savoury.

● Bardolino Cl. '06	♥♥ 3*
⊙ Bardolino Chiaretto Cl. '06	♥ 3
○ Bianco di Custoza '06	♥ 3
● Garda Merlot Merlò '06	♥ 4

Tenuta Teracrea
LOC. LISON
VIA ATTIGLIANA, 61
30026 PORTOGRUARO [VE]
TEL. 0421287041

Antonio Bigai's wines may not be monsters of elegance but they always impress, especially the buttery, characterful Lison, with its rich salty, iodine notes, and the Malvasia, which is subtler but equally gutsy. Finally, A Mi Manera is released in red and white versions. We just preferred the red.

● A Mi Manera Rosso '06	♥♥ 4
○ Lison-Pramaggiore Lison Cl. '06	♥♥ 3
○ A Mi Manera Bianco '06	♥ 4
○ Malvasia '06	♥ 3

Tezza
LOC. POIANO DI VALPANTENA
VIA MAIOLI, 4
37142 VERONA [VR]
TEL. 045550267

Although the address shows Verona as the head office of this winery, the cellar and other activities are all in the vineyard-smothered district of Poiano. Production focuses on traditional wines and the generous Amarone Brolo delle Giare is outstanding for its clear notes of raisined grapes.

● Amarone della Valpolicella	
Valpantena Brolo delle Giare '02	♥♥ 7
● Recioto della Valpolicella	
Valpantena Brolo delle Giare '03	♥ 5

La Tordera
VIA ALNÈ BOSCO, 23
31020 VIDOR [TV]
TEL. 0423985362
www.latordera.it

Vidor is a short way from the Prosecco winemaking centre of Valdobbiadene, in an area swarming with cellars that make the most popular spumante in Italy and, perhaps, the world. La Tordera's wines are excellent. The tangy, gutsy Brut is rich in apple and pear fruit, and the Cartizze Dry is creamy and floral.

○ P. di Valdobbiadene Brut	♥♥ 4*
○ Cartizze Dry	♥♥ 5
○ P. di Valdobbiadene Extra Dry	♥ 4
○ P. di Valdobbiadene Dry Cru	♥ 4

Cantina Produttori di Valdobbiadene
FRAZ. SAN GIOVANNI
VIA SAN GIOVANNI, 45
31030 VALDOBBIADENE [TV]
TEL. 0423982070

The wines produced by this large Valdobbiadene cellar are dependably good. In particular, we liked the Val d'Oca line, which offers wines well able to hold their own against more famous labels. The excellent Millesimato is a Spumante Dry with cakey aromas. The Uvaggio Storico has a gutsier flavour.

○ P. di Valdobbiadene Extra Dry	
Uvaggio Storico Val d'Oca	♥♥ 5
○ P. di Valdobbiadene Dry	
Millesimato Val d'Oca '06	♥♥ 4

Luigi Valetti
LOC. CALMASINO DI BARDOLINO
VIA PRAGRANDE, 8
37010 BARDOLINO [VR]
TEL. 0457235075

The Valetti family's wines are a benchmark for the Bardolino DOC. The products have adapted to the market demand for greater concentration while maintaining their characteristically light, supple palate. The best exponent of this typical style is the Superiore.

● Bardolino Cl. Sup. '05	♥♥ 3*
● Bardolino Cl. '06	♥ 2
○ Bianco di Custoza '06	♥ 2
⊙ Bardolino Cl. Chiaretto '06	♥ 2

OTHER WINERIES

Villa di Maser
VIA CORNUDA, 1
31010 MASER [TV]
TEL. 0423923003
www.villadimaser.it

Villa di Maser is in the Asolo area, on the gently rolling hills below the Pre-Alps. The Cabernet is an interesting red that eschews huge extract, preferring to express generous, complex aromas. The Merlot 2003 follows the same style.

● Cabernet '03   ▼▼ 4*
● Merlot '03   ▼ 4

Villa Giona
LOC. CENGIA
VIA CENGIA, 8
37029 SAN PIETRO IN CARIANO [VR]
TEL. 0456855011

Valpolicella is not just about raisining or ripasso. It's also an area where the grapes can ripen perfectly without requiring special procedures to achieve greater concentration. Villa Giona is a red wine made according to this style, taking full advantage of perfectly ripe merlot, cabernet and syrah grapes.

● Villa Giona '04   ▼▼ 7
● Villa Giona '03   ▼▼ 7
● Villa Giona '01   ▼▼ 7
● Villa Giona '00   ▼▼ 7

Villa Sandi
VIA ERIZZO, 112
31035 CROCETTA DEL MONTELLO [TV]
TEL. 0423665033
www.villasandi.it

Situated at Crocetta, north of Montello, Villa Sandi focuses on still wines. In the absence of the house champ, Corpore, made with the help of Renzo Cotarella, we consoled ourselves with an excellent Marinali Rosso with a taut, succulent palate. Avitus, made from Manzoni bianco, is interesting.

● Marinali Rosso '05   ▼▼ 5
○ Avitus '05   ▼▼ 5
○ Opere Trevigiane Brut Ris. '01   ▼▼ 6
○ Cartizze   ▼ 5

Viticoltori Riuniti dei Colli Euganei
VIA G. MARCONI, 314
35030 VÒ [PD]
TEL. 0499940011
info@virice.it

An area can be judged by its wines but the best gauge is the co-operative winery. This one is more impressive every year, starting with the basic wines. The excellent Notte di Galileo is a red with generous aromas and a rich, mouthfilling palate. The Cabernet Palazzo del Principe is also very good.

● Colli Euganei Cabernet Sauvignon
    Palazzo del Principe '03   ▼▼ 4*
● Colli Euganei Rosso
    Notte di Galileo Ris. '03   ▼▼ 4*

Martino Zanetti
VIA CHISINI, 79
31053 PIEVE DI SOLIGO [TV]
TEL. 0438841608
casebianche@online.it

Martino Zanetti, who is very active in the food sector, makes very good wines at his Treviso estate. The products are split into two lines, Case Bianche and Col Sandago. The latter includes the more ambitious wines, like Camoi, a complex and profound Bordeaux blend with a gutsy, vibrantly acidic palate.

● Camoi Col Sandago '04   ▼▼ 5
○ P. di Conegliano Valdobbiadene
    Extra Dry Case Bianche   ▼ 4
● Wildbacher Col Sandago '04   ▼ 6

Pietro Zardini
VIA DON P. FANTONI, 3
37020 SAN PIETRO IN CARIANO [VR]
TEL. 0456800589
www.pietrozardini.it

Pietro Zardini is a small winery but the owner's accumulated experience as a consultant has produced a rapid increase in quality in just a few years. The Amarone is very impressive. Slow to yield its aromas, it is dry and gutsy on the palate while the Lugana has ripe fruit aromas and a harmonious palate.

● Amarone della Valpolicella Cl. '03   ▼▼ 7
○ Lugana '06   ▼▼ 4
● Recioto della Valpolicella Cl. '03   ▼ 6
● Valpolicella Cl. '05   ▼ 4

FRIULI VENEZIA GIULIA

Early 2006 in Friuli was characterized by fairly low temperatures and the right alternation of rainfall and dry weather to delay flowering slightly. From late May to late July, temperatures were much higher although lower than in summer 2003. Patchy rain across the region encouraged ripening and yields appeared to be much lower than in the previous growing year. On 12 August or thereabouts, a short period of heavy rain began, ending at just the right moment to enable the grapes to complete their ripening in the best possible way, especially for the whites. Day-night temperature fluctuations were considerable, a necessary condition if aromas are to be safeguarded. Subsequently, the weather settled down and stayed favourable, enabling the harvest to take place without anxiety. For the first time in many years, growers could select the best moment to pick their grapes. Final quantities were below average, not just in terms of fruit harvested but also in the must-to-fruit ratio. It was inevitable that wines would be concentrated and alcoholic but what was surprising was their high level of acidity. We look forward to observing how the wines from the 2006 harvest will evolve over time since growers in Friuli are agreed that it was a uniquely favourable vintage. All this has not, however, been reflected in the number of Three Glass awards to the region's wines because impressive structure was not always accompanied by the elegance that has been Friuli's hallmark, particularly for the signature whites. As usual in recent years, the variety that garnered most awards was tocai friulano, a name that can appear on labels up to the 2006 vintage. As we write these notes, the regional authority is exploring ways forward and the name Friulano, used for the 2007 vintage, has been registered across the EU. Apart from sauvignon, another variety that is climbing the heights of quality is malvasia, which is vinified in a dry style in Friuli. It yields some of the most aroma-rich and well-structure wines in the region. But Dario Raccaro's Tocai Friulano Vigna del Rolat 2006 stands head and shoulders above the rest and the Guide awarded it the title of White of the Year. Silvio Jermann made a welcome return to the top category while Gianfranco Gallo, Vie di Romans and Livio Felluga missed out, to mention three wineries that interrupted a long series of Three Glass vintages. Newcomers include brothers Massimo and Marco Zorzettig's La Tunella with Biancosesto, the tiny Vignai da Duline cellar, owned by Lorenzo and Federica Mocchiutti, for the Refosco dal Peduncolo Rosso Morus Nigra, and Davide and Michele Moschioni's Moschioni estate for the Rosso Celtico blend. The other winners are hardly news, having been firmly entrenched at the top for years.

Alberice

VIA BOSCO ROMAGNO, 4
33040 CORNO DI ROSAZZO [UD]
TEL. 0422765571
www.tenutealeandri.it

ANNUAL PRODUCTION 210,000 bottles
HECTARES UNDER VINE 25
VITICULTURE METHOD Conventional

When Tenute Aleandri took over this property at Bosco Romagno, the declared aim was to revamp the winery and aim for quality. It is a project shared by many other producers but in this case, the declaration was followed by concrete action, including the collaboration of outstanding consultants like Marco Simonit and Gianni Menotti, and the introduction of new vinification techniques, such as barrique ageing for the reds. The results were surprisingly good and astonishingly swift to materialize. This year, Alberice sent two wines – the Malvasia and Sauvignon – to our final tastings. The varietal Malvasia is fresh and at the same time intense while the Sauvignon offers assertive varietal aromas lifted by smokiness. As for the rest of the range, the Pinot Grigio's gunflint and pear aromatics are very varietal, the Schioppettino is spicy, the Refosco unveils distinct peaty notes and the Tocai is all elegance and minerality. Finally, we liked the spice, candied citrus peel, hay and chocolate medley of the Cabernet Franc.

O COF Malvasia '06	♟♟	4*
O COF Sauvignon '06	♟♟	4*
● COF Cabernet Franc '05	♟♟	4
● COF Schioppettino '05	♟♟	4
O COF Pinot Grigio '06	♟♟	4
O COF Tocai Friulano '06	♟♟	4
● COF Refosco P. R. '05	♟♟	4
● COF Cabernet Sauvignon '05	♟	4
O COF Chardonnay '06	♟	4
● COF Merlot '05	♟	4
● COF Merlot '05	♟♟	4
● COF Rosso Tango '03	♟♟	5

Altran

LOC. CORTONA, 19
33050 RUDA [UD]
TEL. 0431970356

ANNUAL PRODUCTION 30,000 bottles
HECTARES UNDER VINE 26
VITICULTURE METHOD Conventional

Altran is the surname of the brothers who in 1964 set up this extensive farm, where they also established an agriturismo facility that is now a highly regarded restaurant. It was taken over in 1998 and is now rented and managed by Luciano Pinat and Guido Lanzellotti. The farm has specialized and Marco Diamante now looks after the 26 hectares under vine. Large-scale replanting is producing increasingly encouraging results and one wine in particular stands out, Traminer Aromatico, a type that has found a very congenial home in the Friuli Aquileia DOC zone. It is a real shame that production is limited for the time being to 2,500 bottles, obtained from old vines. Upfront on nose and palate, it has an intriguing saltiness that lingers satisfyingly. The Pinot Bianco is another excellent product. Elegant, complex and fresh-tasting, it signs off with an alluring finish. Agreeable and persuasive, the Tocai Friulano unveils a fine suite of aromatics. Finally, we would point out that Altran is expanding production with admirable caution and releases its wines at prices that offer exceptional value for money.

O Friuli Aquileia Pinot Bianco '06	♟♟	3*
O Friuli Aquileia Traminer Aromatico '06	♟♟	3*
O Friuli Aquileia Tocai Friulano '06	♟	3
● Friuli Aquileia Refosco P. R. '05	♟	3
O Friuli Aquileia Chardonnay '06		3
● Cabernet Sauvignon '03	♟♟	3
O Friuli Aquileia Pinot Bianco '03	♟♟	3

Tenuta di Angoris
LOC. ANGORIS, 7
34071 CORMONS [GO]
TEL. 048160923
www.angoris.com

ANNUAL PRODUCTION 850,000 bottles
HECTARES UNDER VINE 130
VITICULTURE METHOD Conventional

For those with a background in industry, it is always hard to digest the timescale of agriculture even after years of experience in the sector. We are talking about Luciano Locatelli, the dynamic entrepreneur who in 1968 purchased the several hundred hectares of Tenuta di Angoris. Only some of the estate was planted to vine but most supplied feed for the farm's livestock. The big change took place a few years ago when Luciano summoned his daughter Claudia to join him. After a fairly lengthy apprenticeship, she took charge. Claudia left livestock farming to one side and focused on quality winemaking, calling in top-rank professionals. First, Marco Simonit arrived to take the vineyards in hand and later on Riccardo Cotarella was engaged for winemaking. Meanwhile the young, locally trained wine technician, Alessandro Del Zovo, is honing his skills. Today, Massimo Locatelli has joined his sister and several excellent wines are emerging from the cellar, starting with a Colli Orientali del Friuli Sauvignon that can stand comparison with Friuli's finest. The hills also provide a lovely, full-bodied Collio DOC Tocai Friulano with good weight on the palate. All in all, the range is a very pleasant surprise.

Antonutti
FRAZ. COLLOREDO DI PRATO
VIA D'ANTONI, 21
33037 PASIAN DI PRATO [UD]
TEL. 0432662001
www.antonuttivini.it

ANNUAL PRODUCTION 600,000 bottles
HECTARES UNDER VINE 17
VITICULTURE METHOD Conventional

It has been more than 80 years since the Antonutti estate opened for business at Colloredo di Prato, a village not far from Udine. Adriana Antonutti and her husband Lino are not people to look to the past. They and their children gave the estate a thorough makeover and are now beginning to reap the benefits and this year their wines are seriously good. Best of all are the Pinot Grigio and the Sauvignon Poggio Alto. Fresh fruit laced with elegant dried flowers introduce the Pinot Grigio, which expands convincingly on the palate, showing pear-like aromas and generous minerality. The Sauvignon from the Poggio Alto line is part-matured in barrique and stands out for the elegance of its citrus, peach and elderflower aromas and an intriguingly fragrant palate offers finesse and honey-scented hints that meld with the fruity structure. The rest of the range is reassuringly varietal and the Tocai has a distinctive note of pennyroyal.

Wine	Rating
O COF Sauvignon Vôs da Vigne '06	♥♥ 4*
O Collio Tocai Friulano Vôs da Vigne '06	♥♥ 4*
O COF Bianco Spìule '05	♥♥ 5
O Collio Pinot Grigio Vôs da Vigne '06	♥♥ 4
● COF Refosco P. R. Vôs da Vigne '05	♥ 4
O COF Ribolla Gialla Vôs da Vigne '06	♥ 4
O Friuli Isonzo Sauvignon Villa Angoris '06	♥ 4
O COF Chardonnay Vôs da Vigne '06	♥ 4
O Friuli Isonzo Pinot Bianco Villa Angoris '06	♥ 4

Wine	Rating
O Friuli Grave Pinot Grigio '06	♥♥ 3*
O Friuli Grave Sauvignon Blanc Poggio Alto '06	♥♥ 4*
O Friuli Grave Chardonnay '06	♥ 3
O Friuli Grave Tocai Friulano '06	♥ 3
O Friuli Grave Sauvignon '06	♥ 3
O Friuli Grave Chardonnay Poggio Alto '05	♥ 4
● Friuli Grave Merlot '05	♥ 3
O Friuli Grave Pinot Grigio Poggio Alto '05	♥ 4
O Friuli Grave Traminer Poggio Alto '06	♥ 4
● Friuli Grave Refosco P. R. '04	♥ 3
● Friuli Grave Pinot Nero '06	3

Ascevi - Luwa

LOC. UCLANZI, 24
34070 SAN FLORIANO DEL COLLIO [GO]
TEL. 0481884140
www.asceviluwa.it

Conti Attems

FRAZ. LUCINICO
VIA GIULIO CESARE, 36A
34170 GORIZIA
TEL. 0481393619
www.attems.it

ANNUAL PRODUCTION   200,000 bottles
HECTARES UNDER VINE 30
VITICULTURE METHOD   Conventional

ANNUAL PRODUCTION   350,000 bottles
HECTARES UNDER VINE 50
VITICULTURE METHOD   Conventional

The Pintar family has been in charge of the Ascevi estate since 1972. The winery's name derives from that of the vineyard at Asci and Luwa, added to the original name in the early 1990s, comes from Luana and Walter, Mariano and Loredana Pintar's two children. The cellar is right on the border with Slovenia and vinifies fruit from the 30 hectares at Asci and Uclanzi but the Pintars aim to expand output when three and a half hectares of recently purchased vines come onstream. Two separate lines are released, Ascevi and Luwa di Ascevi. They are sourced from two separate, differently aspected vineyards on marl and sandstone soil of Eocene origin. Sauvignon, this time Ronco dei Sassi 2006, is again the best Ascevi wine. After a nose of seriously intense peach and sage, the nicely weighted palate echoes these aromas to finish full, elegant and lingering.

It was 1106 when the bishop of Salzburg made a gift of land to Corrado Attems, marking the start of the Conti Attems thousand-year history in Friuli. The family's most famous scion is undoubtedly Conte Douglas. He inherited the estate in 1935 and after the war, modernized the vineyards and consolidated the family's holdings. In the mid 1960s, he founded the Consorzio Collio, whose president he would remain until 1999. In the following year, he decided to broaden the family horizons by forging an alliance with one of Italy's great wine dynasties, the Tuscany-based Marchesi de' Frescobaldi. The estate's headquarters are at Lucinico in the municipality of Gorizia. Attems is a borderland winery whose vineyard lie along the frontier with Slovenia and between the rivers Judrio and Isonzo. Our favourite this time was Cicinis 2005, a blend of sauvignon, tocai and pinot bianco that greets the nose with sweet fruit and confectioner's cream. It is complex and almost oily on the palate, where marked acidity also comes through.

○ Collio Pinot Grigio Ascevi '06	♀♀ 4*
○ Collio Sauvignon Ronco dei Sassi Ascevi '06	♀♀ 5
○ Collio Chardonnay Luwa '06	♀ 4
○ Ribolla Gialla Ronco de Vigna Vecia Ascevi '06	♀ 4
○ Collio Sauvignon Ascevi '98	♀♀♀ 4
○ Collio Sauvignon Ascevi '00	♀♀ 4
○ Collio Sauvignon Ascevi '05	♀♀ 5

○ Collio Bianco Cicinis '05	♀♀ 5
● Collio Merlot '04	♀ 4
○ Chardonnay '06	♀ 4
○ Ribolla Gialla '06	♀ 4
● Refosco P. R. '05	♀ 4
○ Collio Pinot Grigio '06	♀ 4
○ Collio Sauvignon '06	♀ 4
○ Collio Pinot Bianco '06	♀ 4
○ Collio Tocai Friulano '06	♀ 4
● Collio Merlot '02	♀♀ 4
● Collio Merlot '03	♀♀ 4

Bastianich
VIA CASALI OTTELIO, 7
33040 PREMARIACCO [UD]
TEL. 0432700943
www.bastianich.com

ANNUAL PRODUCTION 110,000 bottles
HECTARES UNDER VINE 28
VITICULTURE METHOD Conventional

Bastianich is a famous name on the eastern seaboard of the United States, where Lidia is a well-known presenter of cookery programmes on several networks and with her son Giuseppe, aka Joe, has opened a chain of successful restaurants in Manhattan, New Jersey, Kansas City and Las Vegas. The family is originally from Istria and has purchased vineyards in Friuli, where Valter Scarbolo and Denis Lepore manage their investment. Currently, there are 28 hectares under vine and the cellar, which is a maximum of seven or eight kilometres from the vineyards, is supervised by Andrea Brunisso. Emilio Del Medico and Maurizio Castelli consult. In short, the team is utterly dependable and after every vintage releases wines designed for the American market that we very much like, too. Top of the range again is Vespa Bianco, from chardonnay, sauvignon and one tenth picolit aged in wood that is still to the fore. Merlot, refosco and cabernet go into Vespa Rosso 2004, a complex wine with plenty of structure, while the nose of the 2003 Calabrone reveals partial raisining of its merlot, refosco, cabernet franc and pignolo fruit.

Tenuta Beltrame
FRAZ. PRIVANO
LOC. ANTONINI, 4
33050 BAGNARIA ARSA [UD]
TEL. 0432923670
www.tenutabeltrame.it

ANNUAL PRODUCTION 100,000 bottles
HECTARES UNDER VINE 25
VITICULTURE METHOD Conventional

The enterprising Cristian Beltrame has made his estate a beacon for the Aquileia DOC zones. Over the past years, he has carried out major work on the estate and restructured the vineyards so that today, he is making premium-quality wines from vines about 15 years old that are now coming to maturity. As is shown by its history and the results below, Tenuta Beltrame is a red wine estate. With the exception of the Rebus blend, Cristian and his consultant oenologist Golino release their reds to market without ageing in small wood. The aim is to conserve the aromas of the fruit. That is why their products are textbook stuff, particularly the Cabernet Franc and the Merlot. Despite not being the easiest variety to grow in Friuli, the Cabernet Sauvignon flaunts robust extract and balsamic notes. The first release of the Bordeaux blend Rebus unveils encouraging fragrances of blackberry tart and camphor. What about the whites? They're all well typed with the Sauvignon standing out for finesse and a savoury finish.

O Vespa Bianco '05	♟ 5
● Vespa Rosso '04	♟♟ 6
● Calabrone '03	♟♟ 8
O COF Tocai Friulano '06	♟♟ 4*
⊙ Rosato '06	♟ 4
O COF Tocai Friulano Plus '02	♟♟♟ 5
O Vespa Bianco '00	♟♟♟ 5
O Vespa Bianco '01	♟♟♟ 5
O Vespa Bianco '99	♟♟♟ 5
O Vespa Bianco '03	♟♟♟ 5
O Vespa Bianco '04	♟♟♟ 5

● Friuli Aquileia Cabernet Franc '05	♟♟ 4
● Rebus '04	♟♟ 4
O Friuli Aquileia Sauvignon '06	♟♟ 4
● Friuli Aquileia Merlot '05	♟♟ 4
● Friuli Aquileia Cabernet Sauvignon '05	♟♟ 4
O Friuli Aquileia Chardonnay '06	♟ 4
O Friuli Aquileia Pinot Bianco '06	♟ 4
O Friuli Aquileia Tocai Friulano '06	♟ 4
● Friuli Aquileia Refosco P. R. '05	♟ 4
O Friuli Aquileia Pinot Grigio '06	♟ 4
O Friuli Aquileia Chardonnay Pribus '05	♟ 4
● Friuli Aquileia Cabernet Sauvignon Ris. '03	♟♟ 4
● Friuli Aquileia Merlot Ris. '03	♟♟ 4

Anna Berra

VIA RAMANDOLO, 29
33045 NIMIS [UD]
TEL. 0432790296
www.annaberra.it

ANNUAL PRODUCTION 25,000 bottles
HECTARES UNDER VINE 8
VITICULTURE METHOD Conventional

Ivan Monai provided us with a pleasant surprise last year when the fine performance of his wines earned his cellar a Guide profile. To show just how good he is, Ivan again sent us a Ramandolo Anno Domini that we in turn sent on to the Three Glass finals for the second year in a row. The grapes are loft-dried and the resulting must ferments in barrique, where it stays for 18 months. After six months in bottle, it is released to market. Intense yet elegant and free of excess, it has poise on nose and palate, where the sweetness never cloys as it offers up notes of caramel-covered figs, peach tea and candied citrus peel. But the cellar is more than just Ramandolo and this year we enjoyed a really good Refosco. Traditionally, the variety is at its peak in the hills of Nimis and this example is distinctly warm and fruit-forward, showing hints of liqueur cherries and blackberry tart. The aromas are reprised on the well-sustained palate, which has plenty of intriguingly bright thrust. Finally, the 2003 Merlot has decent progression in the mouth.

Bidoli

FRAZ. ARCANO SUPERIORE
VIA FORNACE, 19
33030 RIVE D'ARCANO [UD]
TEL. 0432810796
www.bidolivini.com

ANNUAL PRODUCTION 1,000,000 bottles
HECTARES UNDER VINE N.A.
VITICULTURE METHOD Conventional

This winery was founded in 1924 and has always been run by the Bidoli family, first by grandfather Alessandro, then by Titta, the father, and now by brother and sister Margherita and Arrigo. The Bidolis buy in all the grapes they vinify in their spacious cellar, created out of a former brickworks, the "fornâs dai fradis", or siblings' brickworks from which one of the labels takes its name. We can only admire the dependably high quality of some Bidoli wines over the years, including the Merlot Briccolo and the Pinot Bianco and Sauvignon from the Fornas dai Fradis line. It is not easy to achieve such reliability using bought-in grapes and it speaks volumes for the Bidolis' serious approach to their task. We liked the Merlot for its extract and warm notes of chocolate and cherry jam. The Pinot Bianco's virtues include a varietal typicity that proffers elegant apple and spring flowers while the Sauvignon has intense, almost pungent aromas of bell pepper and elderflower. We would also mention the Cabernet Briccolo, which has attractive balsam sensations.

O Ramandolo Anno Domini '03	♟♟	6
● COF Refosco P. R. Ris. '03	♟♟	5
● COF Merlot Ris. '03	♟	5
O Ramandolo Anno Domini '02	♟♟	6
O COF Picolit Ris. '02	♟♟	6
O Ramandolo Anno Domini '01	♟♟	4
O COF Picolit Ris. '03	♟♟	6

● Friuli Grave Cabernet Briccolo '05	♟♟	4
● Friuli Grave Merlot Briccolo '05	♟♟	4
O Friuli Grave Pinot Bianco Fornas dai Fradis '06	♟♟	3*
O Friuli Grave Sauvignon Fornas dai Fradis '06	♟♟	3*
O Friuli Grave Chardonnay '06	♟	2
O Friuli Grave Pinot Grigio Fornas dai Fradis '06	♟	3
O Friuli Grave Traminer Aromatico Fornas dai Fradis '06	♟	3

Tenuta di Blasig
VIA ROMA, 63
34077 RONCHI DEI LEGIONARI [GO]
TEL. 0481475480
www.tenutadiblasig.it

ANNUAL PRODUCTION 60,000 bottles
HECTARES UNDER VINE 16
VITICULTURE METHOD Conventional

Elisabetta Bortolotto Sarcinelli, assisted in cellar and vineyard by Enrica Orlandino and by Valentina Casula for distribution, is still in the throes of comprehensive restructuring that may be having some impact on quality from vintage to vintage. This year, the Gli Affreschi label, released only in better years, is back on the shelves. And it was Rosso Gli Affreschi that made the biggest impression at our tastings. A Bordeaux blend aged for a year in new and once-used French barriques, it has a deep hue still brimming with anthocyanins that heralds a long, austere palate with a wealth of fruit and extract. The characteristically sinewy but nicely cherry, pepper and chocolate- themed Refosco is equally good. The Malvasia, Pinot Grigio, Tocai and the two Merlots are more than just well typed. It's a pity, though, that the dried-grape Le Lule with its slightly cloying baked apples has yet to fulfil its promise.

La Boatina
VIA CORONA, 62
34071 CORMONS [GO]
TEL. 048160445
www.paliwines.com

ANNUAL PRODUCTION 120,000 bottles
HECTARES UNDER VINE 72
VITICULTURE METHOD Conventional

La Boatina's vine stock comprises 32 hectares in the Collio DOC zone and 40 or so in Isonzo. After launching the Pali Wines brand, which includes this winery and the nearby Castello di Spessa property, owner Loretto Pali aims to release his Collio production as Castello di Spessa and keep La Boatina for Friuli Isonzo DOC wines. Investments in new plantings are now producing results, thanks in part to input from agronomist Marco Simonit. In the cellar, Domenico Lovat's partnership with consultant Gianni Menotti transforms the excellent grapes into wines that get more exciting every year. The only Collio wine we are reviewing here is a very nice Picol Maggiore, a Bordeaux blend that neatly sums up the warm 2003 growing year. The splendid Ribolla Gialla has fresh williams pears, the Tocai stands out for savouriness and elegance, and the Pinot Bianco offers lime blossom and apple.

- ● Friuli Isonzo Rive di Giare
  Refosco P. R. '05   🍷🍷 4*
- ● Rosso Gli Affreschi '03   🍷🍷 5
- ○ Friuli Isonzo Malvasia '06   🍷 4
- ● Friuli Isonzo Merlot '05   🍷 4
- ● Friuli Isonzo Merlot Gli Affreschi '04   🍷 5
- ○ Friuli Isonzo Pinot Grigio '06   🍷 4
- ○ Friuli Isonzo Tocai Friulano '06   🍷 4
- ○ Le Lule '05   5
- ● Friuli Isonzo Rive di Giare
  Refosco P. R. '04   🍷🍷 4
- ○ Le Lule '03   🍷🍷 5

- ● Collio Rosso Picol Maggiore '03   🍷🍷 5
- ○ Friuli Isonzo Pinot Bianco '06   🍷🍷 4*
- ○ Friuli Isonzo Tocai Friulano '06   🍷🍷 4*
- ○ Ribolla Gialla '06   🍷🍷 4*
- ○ Friuli Isonzo Chardonnay '06   🍷 4
- ○ Friuli Isonzo Pinot Grigio '06   🍷 4
- ○ Friuli Isonzo Verduzzo Pérle '05   🍷 6
- ○ Friuli Isonzo Sauvignon '06   🍷 4
- ● Friuli Isonzo
  Cabernet Sauvignon '05   🍷 4
- ● Friuli Isonzo Cabernet Franc '06   🍷 4
- ○ Friuli Isonzo Pinot Grigio '06   🍷 4
- ○ Friuli Isonzo Sauvignon '06   🍷 4

Borgo Conventi

S.DA DELLA COLOMBARA, 13
34070 FARRA D'ISONZO [GO]
TEL. 0481888004
www.borgoconventi.it

ANNUAL PRODUCTION 350,000 bottles
HECTARES UNDER VINE 50
VITICULTURE METHOD Conventional

Since 2001, this long-established Friulian winery has belonged to the Tuscany-based Ruffino group. At first, the new owners devoted their energies to reorganizing the estate but in recent vintages, there have been distinct signs of improvements in production. The first wines to show evidence of the changes were the ones from the Collio and this time the Isonzo DOC bottles bearing the I Fiori del Borgo label have also improved considerably. The efforts of Paolo Corso and his team are probably beginning to pay off. On the Collio front, we like the velvet-smooth progression on the palate of the Merlot, the sunny tropical fruit of the Chardonnay and the finesse of the very varietal Pinot Grigio. Those Isonzo improvements are testified by the Pinot Grigio, with its attractive crusty bread and gunflint, and a Chardonnay that impresses with its apple, banana and almond milk aromatics.

Borgo del Tiglio

FRAZ. BRAZZANO
VIA SAN GIORGIO, 71
34070 CORMONS [GO]
TEL. 048162166

ANNUAL PRODUCTION 35,000 bottles
HECTARES UNDER VINE 8.5
VITICULTURE METHOD Conventional

To get an idea of Borgo del Tiglio wines and their creator, Nicola Manferrari, you just have to look at the cellar. On the outside, it's a traditional farmhouse near the church at Brazzano. There is nothing to hint at what you find inside and beneath it, where modern technology and winemaking techniques – there are French barriques everywhere – reign supreme. In the middle is a guide to tell the winery's story and remind visitors that most of the work is done in the vineyard, as it was in the past. Meticulous research and detailed studies lie behind the choice of planting patterns, varieties and vineyard management options. The end result is a very personal range, forward-looking yet with solid roots in the past and a distinct sensory profile. Aromatics are fruit-led, milky and vanillaed while palates are rich and fatty but not cloying, thanks to well-gauged acidity. These are wines that provoke strong reactions and need cellar time to give their best. Lovers of the genre will appreciated this year's Studio di Bianco, the Chardonnay Selezione with its dark label and the Tocai.

O Collio Chardonnay '06	♟♟ 4
● Collio Merlot '04	♟♟ 4
O Collio Pinot Grigio '06	♟♟ 4
O Collio Sauvignon Colle Blanchis '06	♟♟ 5
O Friuli Isonzo Chardonnay '06	♟♟ 4
O Friuli Isonzo Pinot Grigio '06	♟♟ 4
O Collio Ribolla Gialla '06	♟ 4
O Collio Sauvignon '06	♟ 4
O Friuli Isonzo Sauvignon '06	♟ 4
O Friuli Isonzo Tocai Friulano '06	♟ 4
● Friuli Isonzo Refosco P. R. '06	♟ 4
O Collio Tocai Friulano '06	♟ 4

O Collio Chardonnay Sel. '05	♟♟ 7
O Collio Tocai Friulano '05	♟♟ 6
O Collio Studio di Bianco '05	♟♟ 7
O Collio Chardonnay '05	♟♟ 6
O Collio Bianco '05	♟♟ 6
O Collio Bianco Ronco della Chiesa '01	♟♟♟ 7
O Collio Tocai Friulano Ronco della Chiesa '90	♟♟♟ 6
O Collio Bianco Ronco della Chiesa '02	♟♟♟ 7
O Collio Chardonnay '00	♟♟♟ 5
O Collio Chardonnay Sel. '99	♟♟♟ 6
O Collio Malvasia Sel. '99	♟♟ 6
● Collio Rosso della Centa '96	♟♟ 6
● Collio Rosso '00	♟♟ 7
O Collio Chardonnay '04	♟♟ 6
O Collio Bianco '02	♟♟ 6

Borgo delle Oche
VIA BORGO ALPI, 5
33098 VALVASONE [PN]
TEL. 0434899398
www.borgodelleoche.it

ANNUAL PRODUCTION 25,000 bottles
HECTARES UNDER VINE 7
VITICULTURE METHOD Conventional

United at work as in life, Luisa Menini and Nicola Pittini have managed in the few short years since 2004 to give their small cellar in the medieval village of Valvasone a character and style that sets them apart from other products of the Grave DOC zone. Very ripe fruit and prolonged fermentation make these wines complex and characterful. And improvement is continuous across the range, showing that this is a cellar to bank on. Particularly striking is Luisa and Nicola's happy touch when they are vinifying Traminer. This year, the dry version and the dried-grape Bianco Alba went through to our Three Glass finals. The former tempts with elegantly understated ginger, wild rose and tropical fruit whereas Bianco Alba stands out for its candied citrus peel, dried rose and apricot aromatics. Svual, the Bordeaux blend, is seriously good, complementing spiciness with cherry tart. Finally, the well-structured Pinot Grigio is attractively rich palate while the Refosco lacks only a little body to aspire to higher things.

Borgo San Daniele
VIA SAN DANIELE, 16
34071 CORMONS [GO]
TEL. 048160552
www.borgosandaniele.it

ANNUAL PRODUCTION 60,000 bottles
HECTARES UNDER VINE 18
VITICULTURE METHOD Conventional

The Mauri siblings don't rest on their laurels. They are constantly in search of new techniques that respect tradition and are environmentally sustainable. Year after year, they show that they are serious, reliable winemakers. Considering how young they are, we look forward to the Mauris becoming increasingly important for Friuli's oenological future. This year, they presented the 2006 versions of their Pinot Grigio and Arbis Blanc, their Tocai Friulano from 2005, the Arbis Ros from 2004 and the 2003 Gortmarin: this is a cellar that aims to differentiate its wines and offer consumers a wide range of vintages to choose from. Gortmarin is a blended red produced only in vintages when quality parameters are particularly favourable. In fact, the wine has only been made in 1994, 1997, 2001 and 2003. Complex and intense aromas of ripe red berry fruit, spices, balsam and torrefaction hint at a great red to be echoed on a well-structured, full-bodied palate with rich depth and seamless progression. It's a textbook red wine and amply justified our Three Glass award. A quick glance at the results below will confirm that the rest of the range is equally impressive.

O Bianco Alba '06	♀♀	5
O Traminer Aromatico '06	♀♀	4*
O Pinot Grigio '06	♀♀	4
● Rosso Svual '04	♀♀	5
O Bianco Lupi Terrae '05	♀	4
● Refosco P. R. '05	♀	4
O Chardonnay '05	♀	4
O Bianco Alba '05	♀♀	5
O Bianco Alba '04	♀♀	5
O Traminer Aromatico '05	♀♀	4*
O Traminer Aromatico '05	♀♀	4*

● Gortmarin '03	♀♀♀	5
● Arbis Ros '04	♀♀	6
O Arbis Blanc '06	♀♀	5
O Friuli Isonzo Tocai Friulano '05	♀♀	5
O Friuli Isonzo Pinot Grigio '06	♀♀	5
O Arbis Blanc '05	♀♀♀	5
O Friuli Isonzo Arbis Blanc '02	♀♀♀	5
O Friuli Isonzo Pinot Grigio '04	♀♀♀	5
O Arbis Blanc '06	♀♀♀	5
O Friuli Isonzo Pinot Grigio '99	♀♀♀	5
O Friuli Isonzo Tocai Friulano '97	♀♀♀	5
O Friuli Isonzo Tocai Friulano '03	♀♀♀	5

Borgo Savaian

VIA SAVAIAN, 36
34071 CORMONS [GO]
TEL. 048160725
stefano.bastiani@libero.it

ANNUAL PRODUCTION 40,000 bottles
HECTARES UNDER VINE 12
VITICULTURE METHOD Conventional

Now that Stefano Bastiani has made over his cellar, he can concentrate on improving a range this is already very good indeed. The estate is on the slopes of Monte Quarin with vineyards in the Collio and Isonzo DOC zones. Soil types range from the classic marly "ponca" of the Collio to the gravelly terrain of the Isonzo flatlands. With this range of growing environments, Stefano manages to maintain consistent quality with peaks for a number of his wines. We are referring in particular to his Pinot Bianco, Pinot Grigio and Merlot Tolrem. The Pinot Bianco tempts with its apple pip nuances and rich body. The Pinot Grigio has a particularly fine palate, lifted by bright citrus notes. After a year in barrique, the Merlot Tolrem is richly spiced and creamy. Also excellent are the soft, elegant Sauvignon, the baked apple and candied citrus peel Verduzzo with its pleasingly fresh palate, and the very balsamic Cabernet Franc, which has distinct hints of white pepper.

Cav. Emiro Bortolusso

VIA OLTREGORGO, 10
33050 CARLINO [UD]
TEL. 043167596
www.bortolusso.it

ANNUAL PRODUCTION 120,000 bottles
HECTARES UNDER VINE 35
VITICULTURE METHOD Conventional

Brother and sister Clara and Sergio Bortolusso's winery is in a lovely lagoon setting with fish pools where their father Emiro once farmed sea bass and gilthead bream for the family table. The Friuli Annia DOC zone is practically on the coast – its highest elevation is three metres above sea level – which explains why the local wines have a slightly salty note. The Bortolussos are the territory's leaders for quality and their white wines in particular are excellent value for money. With input from consultant Luigino De Giuseppe, the cellar has again released a truly elegant, fresh-tasting Pinot Bianco with great structure and lingering length on the palate. The Sauvignon is very varietal, its elderflower and tomato leaf nose preceding a white peach and grapefruit-themed palate. Delicious pear pervades the nose and palate of the Tocai Friulano. Finally, the Verduzzo Friulano's excellence is no longer a surprise. It's not often you find one this good outside the Colli Orientali del Friuli.

● Collio Merlot Tolrem '04	▼▼	5
○ Collio Sauvignon '06	▼▼	4
○ Friuli Isonzo Verduzzo Friulano '05	▼▼	4
○ Collio Pinot Grigio '06	▼▼	4
○ Collio Pinot Bianco '06	▼▼	4
● Collio Merlot '05	▼	4
● Friuli Isonzo Cabernet Franc '05	▼	4
○ Collio Tocai Friulano '06	▼	4
○ Collio Chardonnay '06	▼	4
○ Friuli Isonzo Traminer Aromatico '06	▼	4

○ Friuli Annia Pinot Bianco '06	▼▼	3*
○ Friuli Annia Sauvignon '06	▼▼	3*
○ Friuli Annia Malvasia '06	▼	3
○ Friuli Annia Pinot Grigio '06	▼	3
○ Friuli Annia Tocai Friulano '06	▼	3
○ Friuli Annia Verduzzo Friulano '06	▼	4
● Friuli Annia Refosco P. R. '06	▼	3
● Friuli Annia Merlot '06		3

Rosa Bosco

VIA ROMA, 5
33040 MOIMACCO [UD]
TEL. 0432722461
info@rosabosco.it

ANNUAL PRODUCTION 14,000 bottles
HECTARES UNDER VINE N.A.
VITICULTURE METHOD Conventional

The management plan adopted by Rosetta and her young team seems to be working out nicely. All of the grapes used for the wines are bought in but the vines are looked after by Rosetta herself. She has many years' experience in viticulture and knows what she wants from them. This year, there was no Merlot. It's a wine that stays in 225-litre barrels for two years and needs a very long time in bottle. The cellar is in the capable hands of Rosetta's son, Alessio, who gave us some exciting news. In the middle of August, he completed the tirage of the first Rosa Bosco spumante. It's a classic method wine, of course. Release is scheduled for December 2008 but the precise date will be decided according to how the wine evolves. Friuli produces some of Italy's finest whites so sparkling wines could be a product for the future. Rosetta's Sauvignon Blanc 2006 is redolent of confectioner's cream, yeasted cake, croissant and peach that tell you this is an excellent wine. The palate follows through well, progressing attractively over a faint hint of vanilla.

O COF Sauvignon Blanc '06	🍷🍷	6
O COF Sauvignon Blanc '02	YYY	6
O COF Sauvignon Blanc '05	YY	6
O COF Sauvignon Blanc '03	YY	6
O COF Sauvignon Blanc '04	YY	6
● COF Rosso Il Boscorosso '04	YY	7
● COF Rosso Il Boscorosso '01	YY	7
● COF Rosso Il Boscorosso '02	YY	7
● COF Rosso Il Boscorosso '03	YY	7

Branko

LOC. ZEGLA, 20
34071 CORMONS [GO]
TEL. 0481639826

ANNUAL PRODUCTION 30,000 bottles
HECTARES UNDER VINE 6
VITICULTURE METHOD Conventional

Some time ago, Igor Erzetic was one of Cormons' up and coming wine men but in the past three or four years he has left that behind him. His consistently fine bottles are wines to bank, regardless of the vagaries of the growing year. This is all down to the meticulous care Igor lavishes on his six or seven hectares under vine, which enable him to bring to the cellar fruit that is well nigh perfect. Igor's father, Branko, still works in the vineyard while Igor puts into practice in the cellar the professional skills he has acquired by working at various local wineries. Four wines in our Three Glass finals out of five presented is a fabulous result, deserving more than mere applause. The Pinot Grigio is its usual complex, elegant self thanks to impeccably handled brief conditioning in large wood. The rich, warm palate has great breadth of fruit and an irresistibly tempting finish. It's a Pinot Grigio for the record books, repeating the exploit of last year's Guide. Fruit and structure are the calling cards of all the wines that Igor released this year, which is undoubtedly the best yet for the Branko label.

O Collio Pinot Grigio '06	🍷🍷🍷	5
O Collio Chardonnay '06	🍷🍷	5
O Collio Sauvignon '06	🍷🍷	5
O Collio Tocai Friulano '06	🍷🍷	5
● Red Branko '04	🍷	5
O Collio Pinot Grigio '05	YYY	5
O Collio Sauvignon '05	YY	5
O Collio Pinot Grigio '04	YY	5
O Collio Chardonnay '02	YY	5
O Collio Chardonnay '06	YY	5

Livio e Claudio Buiatti
VIA LIPPE, 25
33042 BUTTRIO [UD]
TEL. 0432674317
www.buiattivini.it

ANNUAL PRODUCTION 30,000 bottles
HECTARES UNDER VINE 8
VITICULTURE METHOD Conventional

Claudio Buiatti and his wife Viviana run their small winery in the hills at "in Mont e Poianis" near Buttrio with enthusiasm and tangibly good results. The area is an outstandingly good one for viticulture. There is evidence that Buiattis were growing grapes around Buttrio as long ago as the early 20th century. The winery is small but quality oriented. The vineyards are planted to modern patterns, pruning is thorough and the rows are grassed over. All this contributes to the results that the Buiattis achieve, which are excellent. We picked out the Tocai for its varietal sensations mingling with warm tropical fruit. Equally good is the Sauvignon, a touch green on the nose but very soft in the mouth. We also liked the Momon Ros Bordeaux blend, which spends almost two years in wood of various sizes. The nose is dominated by rich chocolate and ripe briary fruit, lifted by more elegant nuances of tobacco and mint. The full palate is just as convincing and flaunts a fine suite of tannins. Another high scorer was the distinctly varietal Pinot Bianco.

Valentino Butussi
VIA PRÀ DI CORTE, 1
33040 CORNO DI ROSAZZO [UD]
TEL. 0432759194
www.butussi.it

ANNUAL PRODUCTION 90,000 bottles
HECTARES UNDER VINE 16
VITICULTURE METHOD Conventional

The Butussi family is part of winemaking history in the hills at Corno di Rosazzo. In the early 20th century, Valentino Butussi started the winery. It was subsequently improved by his son Angelo, who today runs the estate on the sandstone marl at Prà di Corte with his wife Pierina and their four children, all of whom are involved in the business in one capacity or another. The cellar is typically Friulian in that it releases a large number of labels and quality is high. We would point out the tropical fruit in the Pinot Grigio, the attractive mingling of balsam and fruit sensations in the Refosco, the full-bodied Tocai, the freshness of the Chardonnay, the varietal character of the Cabernet Franc and the distinct nectarine, pineapple and citron of the Sauvignon. There is a special mention for the Picolit, made with grapes from vines ranging from ten to 40 years of age, which is particularly alluring for its impressive honey and citrus aromas. The two blends, Bianco and Rosso di Corte, are well made, although they lack the complexity that would have taken them on to higher things.

● COF Rosso Momon Ros Ris. '04	▼▼ 5
○ COF Sauvignon '06	▼▼ 4*
○ COF Tocai Friulano '06	▼▼ 4*
● COF Cabernet '05	▼ 4
○ COF Pinot Grigio '06	▼ 4
○ COF Pinot Bianco '06	▼ 4
● COF Refosco P. R. '05	▼ 4
○ COF Picolit '05	▼ 6
○ COF Verduzzo Friulano '04	4
● COF Merlot '05	4
● COF Refosco P. R. '04	♈♈ 4
● COF Rosso Momon Ros Ris. '03	♈♈ 5
● COF Merlot '04	♈♈ 4

● COF Cabernet Franc '06	▼▼ 4
○ COF Sauvignon '06	▼▼ 4
● Friuli Grave Refosco P. R. '06	▼▼ 4
○ COF Tocai Friulano '06	▼▼ 4
○ COF Chardonnay '06	▼▼ 4
○ COF Picolit '05	▼▼ 7
○ COF Pinot Grigio '06	▼▼ 4
○ COF Bianco di Corte '05	▼ 4
○ Friuli Grave Pinot Bianco '06	▼ 4
● Friuli Grave Merlot '06	▼ 4
● COF Rosso di Corte '05	▼ 5
● COF Cabernet Sauvignon '05	▼ 4
○ COF Verduzzo Friulano '05	▼ 4
○ COF Ribolla Gialla '06	4

Maurizio Buzzinelli
LOC. PRADIS, 20
34071 CORMONS [GO]
TEL. 048160902
www.buzzinelli.com

Ca' Bolani
VIA CA' BOLANI, 2
33052 CERVIGNANO DEL FRIULI [UD]
TEL. 043132670 - 043130904
www.cabolani.it

ANNUAL PRODUCTION 100,000 bottles
HECTARES UNDER VINE 24
VITICULTURE METHOD Conventional

ANNUAL PRODUCTION 1,200,000 bottles
HECTARES UNDER VINE 550
VITICULTURE METHOD Conventional

Maurizio Buzzinelli's winery has 16 hillside hectares, some of them leased, in a zone where the average estate has ten, as well as eight on the flatlands of the Isonzo DOC zone. Last year, work on restructuring and extending the cellar was completed so Maurizio can devote all his energies to the 100,000 bottles he turns out each year. His wife Marzia looks after most of the public relations work, as well as their small son Jacopo. For several years, Maurizio has been bottling a standard line and the Ronc dal Luis wines he obtains from selected fruit. The latter two, a Chardonnay and a Tocai Friulano, are aged in large wood but the results do not perhaps justify the extra effort, especially in comparison to the wines vinified in steel only. We are sure that the Ronc dal Luis wines will yield better results in future as Maurizio hones his techniques and that they will lose the confectioner's cream and vanilla notes left by the oak. The fruity, fatty Tocai Friulano has great structure and is only a whisker less savoury than the selection. It's also fresher-tasting.

The Ca' Bolani winery embraces three separate estates, Ca' Bolani, Molin di Ponte and Ca' Vescovo, for a total of 900 hectares, of which 550 are under vine. It would take several dozen Collio wineries to cover the same area! Ca' Bolani is a major factor in Friulian winemaking and is certainly the Zonin group property that is closest to owner Gianni's heart. The decision to purchase Ca' Bolani was taken in the early 1970s and it was the first investment of its kind the group made outside the Veneto region. Ca' Bolani's technical staff comprises Roberto Marcolini, Marco Fornasin and Catia Zorat, coordinated by Piedmont-born Marco Rabino. The 2006 Chardonnay earned Two Glasses for its sensations on the nose of banana, sweet fruit and discernible lime blossom, echoed on a palate of tropical fruit, apples and pears braced by well-gauged acidity.

O Collio Tocai Friulano '06	🍷🍷	4
O Collio Tocai Friulano Ronc dal Luis '06	🍷🍷	4
O Collio Chardonnay Ronc dal Luis '06	🍷	4
O Collio Chardonnay '06	🍷	4
O Collio Pinot Grigio '06	🍷	4
O Collio Ribolla Gialla '06		3

O Friuli Aquileia Chardonnay '06	🍷🍷	4
O Friuli Aquileia Sauvignon Tamànis Gianni Zonin Vineyards '06	🍷	4
O Friuli Aquileia Tocai Friulano '06	🍷	4
O Friuli Aquileia Sauvignon '06	🍷	4
O Friuli Pinot Bianco '06	🍷	4
● Friuli Aquileia Refosco P. R. Alturio '04	🍷	5
● Friuli Aquileia Cabernet Franc '05	🍷	4

Ca' Ronesca

LOC. LONZANO
CASALI ZORUTTI, 2
34070 DOLEGNA DEL COLLIO [GO]
TEL. 048160034
www.caronesca.it

ANNUAL PRODUCTION 200,000 bottles
HECTARES UNDER VINE 56
VITICULTURE METHOD Conventional

Veneto-based entrepreneur Davide Alcide
Setten acquired Ca' Ronesco last year and
is now getting to grips with the world of
wine. His first moves are encouraging for
the wines are more than decent. It shows
how right he was to put his faith in the long-
standing estate oenologist, Franco Dalla
Rosa. This year, there's also a new line,
released as The Fabolous Four. It's a
selection from a vintage – the exceptionally
favourable 2006 – that produced
outstanding fruit. We liked the Pinot Grigio
from this line for its varietal character, drive
and attractive softness. Even better was the
Sauvignon, which went through to our
Three Glass finals. It's a wine that manages
to balance green bell pepper and tomato
leaf with softer peach notes and balsam.
Nice, too, is the tangy, minerally base Pinot
Grigio, the Chardonnay, which has bright
citrus and sweet almonds, and the classic
florality of the temptingly fresh Ribolla
Gialla. Bianco Marnà confirmed its premium status
with a palate of white chocolate and banana
sensations.

Ca' Tullio & Sdricca di Manzano

VIA BELIGNA, 41
33051 AQUILEIA [UD]
TEL. 0431919700
www.catullio.it

ANNUAL PRODUCTION 450,000 bottles
HECTARES UNDER VINE 78
VITICULTURE METHOD Conventional

As is often the case in larger wineries, there
is the odd inconsistency in the labels of
this cellar, which Paolo Calligaris runs
superbly well. Commercial considerations
have probably led to the expansion of the
range but great care is needed to avoid
confusion among the various lines,
especially for wines sourced in the hill
country. The cellar vinifies grapes from
about 80 hectares, some in the Friuli
Aquileia DOC zone and some in the Colli
Orientali del Friuli, making a total of 450,000
bottles a year. The cellars are just south of
the town of Aquileia in two lovely buildings
created by restructuring former tobacco
drying houses. The cellar team is led by
oenologists Francesco Visintin and Roberta
Bassi, hospitality is in the hands of Patrizia
Sepulcri and the marketing manager is
Gianni Cantarutti. We particularly like two
wines this year, the remarkably complex
Verduzzo Friulano 2006 from the Sdricca
vineyard, which offers candied citrus peel,
baked apple and liqueur apricots, and the
Traminer, obtained by grafting the legendary
vines from Viola that once made this variety
famous in the flatlands of Friuli.

O Collio Sauvignon '06	▼▼ 4*
O Collio Bianco Marnà '05	▼▼ 5
O Collio Chardonnay '06	▼▼ 4
O Collio Pinot Grigio '06	▼▼ 4
O Collio Pinot Grigio The Fabolous Four '06	▼▼ 5
O Collio Ribolla Gialla '06	▼▼ 4
O Collio Ribolla Gialla The Fabolous Four '06	▼ 5
● Collio Pinot Nero The Fabolous Four '06	▼ 5
O Collio Tocai Friulano The Fabolous Four '06	▼ 5
● Collio Cabernet Franc Podere San Giacomo '01	▼▼ 6
O Collio Chardonnay '06	♀ 4

O COF Verduzzo Friulano Sdricca '06	▼▼ 6
O Traminer Viola '06	▼▼ 5
O COF Ribolla Gialla Sdricca '06	▼ 4
● Friuli Aquileia Refosco P. R. '06	▼ 4
O Friuli Aquileia Traminer Aromatico '06	▼ 4
● Friuli Aquileia Rosso Il Patriarca d'Aquileia '05	▼ 4
O COF Tocai Friulano Sdricca '06	▼ 4
● COF Pignolo Sdricca '05	4

Paolo Caccese

LOC. PRADIS, 6
34071 CORMONS [GO]
TEL. 048161062
www.paolocaccese.com

ANNUAL PRODUCTION 35,000 bottles
HECTARES UNDER VINE 6
VITICULTURE METHOD Conventional

The growing year did its part but it was above all Paolo Caccese's hard work and professionalism that produced the very heartening results from the range this time. You can't help liking Paolo, not least because he's one of those people who obstinately refuse to have anything to do with email communications. A few months ago, he took over the chairmanship of the Consorzio Collio, an acknowledgement of his intelligence and shrewdness on the part of his colleagues. This time round, Paolo's Malvasia has come up trumps on all fronts. The wine is elegant and mouthfilling, with hints of lime blossom and lavender. But Pradis is above all a Pinot Bianco vineyard and the Caccese version is as excellent as always, hinting at golden delicious apples over citrus fruit and almost soft in texture thanks to its robust alcohol. The Tocai Friulano expands on the palate in fresh fruit sensations, signing off with a long, alcohol-rich finish. We also liked the well-made Traminer Aromatico.

Alfieri Cantarutti

VIA RONCHI, 9
33048 SAN GIOVANNI AL NATISONE [UD]
TEL. 0432756317
www.cantaruttialfieri.it

ANNUAL PRODUCTION 130,000 bottles
HECTARES UNDER VINE 54
VITICULTURE METHOD Conventional

This winery began its life about 30 years ago, when Alfiero Cantarutti acquired a magnificent Ronco with a small farmhouse in the hills just outside Rosazzo. Over the years, the estate has gradually expanded to its present-day 50 hectares under vine. The cellar's proficiency is evidenced in the range of vinification methods employed, a sign of the courage and technical skill of the winemakers. We'll start our round-up with the classic, and excellent, Bianco Canto blend of tocai, pinot bianco and sauvignon, a fresh-tasting wine attractively redolent of tomato leaf, banana and delicious apple. Next up is Tocai The Spirit of Ghost, an example of extreme winemaking for a very original product that gives petits fours, peach tea and dried flowers. Finally, we come to the sparklers. There's a successful classic method, Epilogo di Cantalfieri, a blanc de noir from pinot nero that we enjoyed for its hazelnut, honey and intense minerality. Also attractive is the distinctive creamy texture of the Tocai.

O Collio Malvasia '06	▼▼ 4*
O Collio Tocai Friulano '06	▼▼ 4
O Collio Pinot Bianco '06	▼▼ 4*
● Collio Cabernet Franc '05	▼ 4
● Collio Merlot '05	▼ 4
O Collio Müller Thurgau '06	▼ 4
O Collio Pinot Grigio '06	▼ 4
O Collio Sauvignon '06	▼ 4
O Collio Traminer Aromatico '06	▼ 4

O COF Bianco Canto '06	▼▼ 4
O Epilogo di Cantalfieri '04	▼▼ 5
O COF Tocai Friulano The Spirit of Ghost '04	▼▼ 8
O COF Ribolla Gialla '06	▼ 4
O COF Tocai Friulano '06	▼ 4
● COF Merlot Ronco San Michele '03	7
⊙ Prologo di Cantalfieri '04	5

Canus
VIA GRAMOGLIANO, 21
33040 CORNO DI ROSAZZO [UD]
TEL. 0432759427
www.canus.it

ANNUAL PRODUCTION 35,000 bottles
HECTARES UNDER VINE 11
VITICULTURE METHOD Conventional

Canus, which strides confidently into the
Guide this year, was purchased in 2004 by
Ugo Rossetto, a successful Pordenone-
based furnishings entrepreneur who
handed management over to his children,
design expert Dario and Lara, an
accountant. The enthusiastic duo called in
a vinegrower who knows the area well,
Renato Cozzarolo, and agronomist Carlo
Peratoner. The estate's name is the Latin
for the family's nickname, Grisòn, meaning
grey or greying. Meticulous, modern
vineyard management, cellar techniques
that respect local tradition and make
cautious use of wood, a lack of pretension
in the market and attractive, highly original
labels are some of the factors that have
contributed to the quality and success of
Canus wines. The elegant Tocai Friulano
gives very ripe fruit, progressing well on the
palate, and is the cellar's top wine.
Harmony is the keynote of the Pinot Grigio
and the Sauvignon whereas the strong suit
of Jasmine, from part cask-conditioned
chardonnay, sauvignon, pinot grigio and
tocai friulano, is complexity.

Il Carpino
LOC. SOVENZA, 14A
34070 SAN FLORIANO DEL COLLIO [GO]
TEL. 0481884097
www.ilcarpino.com

ANNUAL PRODUCTION 70,000 bottles
HECTARES UNDER VINE 15
VITICULTURE METHOD Conventional

Anna and Franco Sosol run their winery with
firm hand and clear head. Several years
ago, the made the strategic decision to
release as Il Carpino the reds and whites
that age in wood and keep Vigna Runc for
their bright fresh wines that are vinified and
aged in steel. We know that it's always risky
to release oak-aged whites. They demand
skill with wood and raw material that is of
sufficient quality to withstand the impact of
the oak. Over the years, Franco Sosol has
acquired those skills: his wines are original,
excellent and in some cases outstanding.
One such is the Malvasia, which beautifully
fuses the fatty, balsamic contribution of the
oak with fresh flowers and citrus. The
Bianco is equally good. This blend of
sauvignon, ribolla gialla and chardonnay
gives creamy sensations and a long,
lingering finish where tea and sweet spice
peek through. The merlot-only Rubrum is
original in every respect from its intense ripe
fruit to the velvet-smooth progression on the
palate while the Bordeaux blend Rosso has
stylish violet-like sensations.

O COF Tocai Friulano '06	♟♟ 4*
O COF Bianco Jasmine '06	♟♟ 4
O COF Pinot Grigio '06	♟♟ 4
O COF Sauvignon '06	♟♟ 4
O COF Chardonnay '06	♟ 4
O COF Ribolla Gialla '06	♟ 4

O Bianco Carpino '04	♟♟ 5
O Collio Malvasia Il Carpino '04	♟♟ 6
O Collio Chardonnay Il Carpino '04	♟♟ 5
O Collio Sauvignon Il Carpino '04	♟♟ 5
● Rubrum Il Carpino '03	♟♟ 8
O Ribolla Gialla Il Carpino '04	♟♟ 5
● Rosso Carpino '04	♟♟ 6
O Bianco V. Runc '06	♟ 4
O Collio Ribolla Gialla V. Runc '06	♟ 4
O Collio Sauvignon V. Runc '06	♟ 4
● Rubrum Il Carpino '99	♟♟♟ 8
O Bianco Carpino '03	♟♟ 5

Casa Zuliani
VIA GRADISCA, 23
34070 FARRA D'ISONZO [GO]
TEL. 0481888506
www.casazuliani.com

ANNUAL PRODUCTION 120,000 bottles
HECTARES UNDER VINE 17
VITICULTURE METHOD Conventional

In 1923, Zuliano Zuliani purchased a lovely villa and estate from the Austrian Winter family. Today, Bruna Zuliani lives there and the vineyards now extend over 17 hectares. Her grandson Federico Frumento took over a few years ago, transmitting his enthusiasm to Claudio Tomadin, who was and is the estate manager. The choice of Gianni Menotti as consultant winemaker explains the leap forward in quality that the estate has made in very short order. All in all, we perhaps should have expected this year's low-key performance, even though Casa Zuliani remains one of the region's leading cellars. Sauvignon Winter is again at the top of the list, showing varietal tomato leaf, sage and elderflower then a complex, citrus-led palate with great length: a textbook Friulian Sauvignon. Freshness and elegance are the keynotes of the Chardonnay Winter while the Tocai Friulano has rich fruit in the mouth, signing off with marvellous appeal. The Malvasia is a step behind the 2005 edition but still offers all the character of the variety, hinting at violets and minerality on the palate.

La Castellada
FRAZ. OSLAVIA, 1
34170 GORIZIA
TEL. 048133670

ANNUAL PRODUCTION 23,000 bottles
HECTARES UNDER VINE 9
VITICULTURE METHOD Natural

The winery that Nicolò Bensa runs with his son is not particularly long-standing but it is looked on as a historic cellar that winemakers in Oslavia have to take measure themselves against. As a benchmark operation, La Castellada is an acknowledged leader of the movement to reinterpret wine that gained new stimulus at Oslavia. There have been changes of mind – a marked return to single-variety wines – but care has been taken to avoid extremes. Open-vat fermentation, increasingly prolonged skin contact, wood ageing, vat maturation and bottling without filtration make for warm wines that are free of rough edges and rich in extract, released many years after the vintage: whites come out more after than three years and reds are bottle-aged for over six. The best wine this time was the impressive Tocai, whose complex plum, wisteria and sage aromas precede a weighty, savoury palate that echoes the nose and leaves you with a lingering balsamic goodbye. This marvellous white justly received Three Glasses. Finally, both the Bianco and the Ribolla are outstanding but the Rosso isn't at its best.

O Collio Malvasia '06	▼▼	4*
O Winter Sauvignon '06	▼▼	5
O Winter Chardonnay '05	▼▼	5
O Collio Tocai Friulano '06	▼▼	4*
O Collio Chardonnay '06	▼	4
O Friuli Isonzo Pinot Grigio '06	▼	4
O Collio Sauvignon '06	▼	4
O Collio Pinot Grigio '06	▼	4
O Collio Pinot Bianco '06	▼	4
● Collio Merlot '05		4
● Winter Rosso '03	♉♉	5
O Winter Sauvignon '05	♉♉	5
O Winter Chardonnay '04	♉♉	5

O Collio Tocai Friulano '03	▼▼▼	6
O Collio Bianco della Castellada '03	▼▼	6
O Collio Ribolla Gialla '03	▼▼	6
O Collio Chardonnay '03	▼	6
O Collio Sauvignon '03	▼	6
● Collio Rosso della Castellada '00	▼	8
O Collio Bianco della Castellada '98	♉♉♉	6
● Collio Rosso della Castellada '99	♉♉♉	8
O Collio Bianco della Castellada '99	♉♉♉	6
O Collio Tocai Friulano '02	♉♉	6

Castelvecchio

VIA CASTELNUOVO, 2
34078 SAGRADO [GO]
TEL. 048199742
www.castelvecchio.com

ANNUAL PRODUCTION 250,000 bottles
HECTARES UNDER VINE 40
VITICULTURE METHOD Conventional

Castelvecchio is the most influential wine estate in the northern Carso, a DOC zone whose limestone-based geological configuration means it has low fertility and poor water retention. It is separated from the Collio DOC by the broad Isonzo valley, which also brings cold north-easterly winds. Viticulture is challenging and human intervention has made it economically viable by flanking it with other activities. There have, for example, been major replantings of olive groves. But wine, and red wine in particular, is still the estate's main product with the accent on native varieties, refosco and terrano, that may have had some of the rough edges removed but retain their territorial character. This year, there is an exception to prove the rule. It's the tangy, long-lingering Malvasia Istriana with its attractively understated aromatics. It is followed by another, more predictable, surprise in the complex, firm-textured Merlot 2003, redolent of liquorice and ripe cherries. And there is further confirmation from Sagrado Rosso, a cabernet given territory focus by a small proportion of terrano. All the other wines are well up to expectations.

Marco Cecchini

LOC. CASALI DE LUCA
VIA COLOMBANI
33040 FAEDIS [UD]
TEL. 0432720563
www.cecchinimarco.com

ANNUAL PRODUCTION 40,000 bottles
HECTARES UNDER VINE 10
VITICULTURE METHOD Conventional

Marco Cecchini sent us a limited range of his wines as he is well aware that his reds need more time in glass. Meanwhile his partner, oenology graduate Sonia Dell'Oste, has returned from Burgundy and this has confirmed Marco in his ambitions, one of which is to continue experimenting with riesling, a variety of whose potential he is convinced. Currently, the estate has ten or so hectares under vine, almost all of them in hillside locations. Gibil Crespan is in charge of vineyard management. Consulting for Sonia in the cellar is the Terra&Vino team, led by Alessio Dorigo. Tovè remains Marco's best wine. It's a white from 95 per cent tocai friulano with a little verduzzo that treats the nose to confectioner's cream before expanding into apricot and citrus fruit in the mouth, ending on sensations of softness. The Pinot Grigio Bellagioia comes from a vineyard of the same name, combining freshness with breadth and admirable alcoholic structure. Finally, Verlit is a moderately sweet wine with baked apple and almond paste aromas and bright acidity.

○ Carso Malvasia Istriana '06	♥♥	4*
● Carso Merlot '03	♥♥	6
● Sagrado Rosso '03	♥♥	6
● Carso Cabernet Sauvignon '04	♥	5
● Carso Cabernet Franc '04	♥	5
● Carso Refosco P. R. '04	♥	5
○ Carso Traminer Aromatico '06	♥	4
● Carso Cabernet Sauvignon '03	♀♀	5
● Carso Terrano '05	♀♀	4
● Sagrado Rosso '02	♀♀	6

○ COF Bianco Tovè '06	♥♥	4*
○ Pinot Grigio Bellagioia '06	♥♥	4*
○ COF Verduzzo Friulano Verlit '05	♥	6
○ COF Bianco Tovè '02	♀♀	4
○ COF Bianco Tovè '05	♀♀	4
○ COF Verduzzo Friulano Verlit '02	♀♀	6
○ COF Verduzzo Friulano Verlit '03	♀♀	6

Eugenio Collavini

LOC. GRAMOGLIANO
VIA DELLA RIBOLLA GIALLA, 2
33040 CORNO DI ROSAZZO [UD]
TEL. 0432753222
www.collavini.it

ANNUAL PRODUCTION 1,500,000 bottles
HECTARES UNDER VINE 173
VITICULTURE METHOD Conventional

We are no longer surprised at the range of wines from Manlio Collavini. His estate is a significantly large one, comprising 173 estate-owned and contracted hectares and turning out a million and a half bottles a year. Yet Manlio is utterly convinced that the only way forward is quality so while he concentrates more and more attention on his standard-label products, he is also refining his selections. Rigorous bunch selection and cellar techniques like part-drying, freezing and reverse osmosis enable the winery to concentrate the natural elements of the must if necessary. Working with Manlio are his wife, Anna, their sons Luigi and Giovanni and oenologist Walter Bergnach in the cellar. Yet again, the tocai, chardonnay and sauvignon Broy is the cellar's top wine, brilliantly combining elegance and fruit richness. It's a hugely complex white that effortlessly picked up Three Glasses. After-aromas of grapefruit and pineapple put the finishing touches to a Sauvignon Blanc Fumât – "smoked" in Friulian – that fills the nostrils with intense elderflower syrup fragrances. Finally, the refosco and pignolo Forresco has seriously good structure.

Colle Duga

LOC. ZEGLA, 10
34071 CORMONS [GO]
TEL. 048161177

ANNUAL PRODUCTION 35,000 bottles
HECTARES UNDER VINE 7.5
VITICULTURE METHOD Conventional

Although last year, Damian Princic's appearance on the list of Three Glass winners might have been something of a surprise but this time, informed consumers have already placed their orders for his Tocai Friulano, a superb wine again this time. As things stand, you'll have to search the wine shops and restaurants to find it. Nevertheless, a generous 12,000 units went into bottle. It may not be a huge quantity but this is certainly not a garage wine. Intense and warm on the pear-led nose, it has a warm, rich palate with a twist of almond in the finish that adds charm, despite the robust alcohol. No wonder it repeated last year's Three Glass triumph. But there's more. Many admirers like the peach and grapefruit of Damian's Sauvignon or the liquorice-laced Collio Bianco, from sauvignon, tocai and chardonnay, or the red fruits tart of his Merlot. Never mind that the Pinot Grigio and Chardonnay are not quite as good. Damian's friendship with oenologist Giorgio Bertossi generates these lovely wines from fruit that his father Luciano helps to grow. Keep an eye on this small cellar.

O Collio Bianco Broy '06	♟♟♟	5
O Collio Sauvignon Blanc Fumât '06	♟♟	4*
● COF Rosso Forresco '03	♟♟	6
O COF Ribolla Gialla Turian '06	♟♟	5
● COF Schioppettino Turian '03	♟♟	6
O COF Picolit '03	♟♟	8
O Collio Pinot Grigio Canlungo '06	♟	4
O Collio Bianco Broy '03	♟♟♟	5
O Collio Bianco Broy '04	♟♟♟	5
O Collio Bianco Broy '05	♟♟	5
● Collio Merlot dal Pic '01	♟♟	6
● Collio Merlot dal Pic '03	♟♟	6

O Collio Tocai Friulano '06	♟♟♟	4*
O Collio Bianco '06	♟♟	5
O Collio Sauvignon '06	♟♟	4
● Collio Merlot '05	♟♟	5
O Collio Chardonnay '06	♟	4
O Collio Pinot Grigio '06	♟	4
O Collio Tocai Friulano '05	♟♟♟	4
O Collio Tocai Friulano '04	♟♟	4
O Collio Bianco '05	♟♟	4
O Collio Pinot Grigio '05	♟♟	4
O Collio Chardonnay '05	♟♟	4
O Collio Sauvignon '05	♟♟	4
● Collio Merlot '03	♟♟	4
● Collio Merlot '04	♟♟	4

Colmello di Grotta

LOC. VILLANOVA
VIA GORIZIA, 133
34070 FARRA D'ISONZO [GO]
TEL. 0481888445
www.colmello.it

ANNUAL PRODUCTION 100,000 bottles
HECTARES UNDER VINE 17
VITICULTURE METHOD Conventional

In past editions, we have noted that
Francesca Bortolotto's estate in two
excellent DOC zones like Collio and Friuli
Isonzo has been unable to make the quality
leap of which it looks capable, despite the
consultancy input of a very fine oenologist,
Fabio Coser. It could be a coincidence but
this year Francesca presented us with a
surprisingly good Merlot. It stands head and
shoulders above the rest of the range and,
even more astonishingly, comes from a
vintage that was less than generous with
red grapes. We sincerely hope that this
improvement will spread to the rest of the
estate's list, where the Isonzo DOC
Cabernet Sauvignon is looking very
promising indeed. We would also like to
mention the very attractive Collio Tocai
Friulano and Ribolla Gialla.

Gianpaolo Colutta

VIA ORSARIA, 32A
33044 MANZANO [UD]
TEL. 0432510654
www.coluttagianpaolo.com

ANNUAL PRODUCTION 150,000 bottles
HECTARES UNDER VINE 30
VITICULTURE METHOD Conventional

In charge of this winery are Gianpaolo
Colutta and his daughter Elisabetta, who
looks after all things technical. Great
attention is focused on all stages of
production but particular care is taken of the
vineyards, which have been replanted at
higher densities and grassed over, and in
the recently expanded barrel cellar, which
lends longevity and structure to the wines.
Father and daughter are both enamoured of
native varieties and it is no coincidence that
one such wine, Schioppettino, is at the top
of their list, along with Rosso Frassinolo, a
Bordeaux blend with a dash of tazzelenghe.
We liked the Schioppetino's warm,
blackberry tart fragrances and its
progression on the palate, which has
attractive weight and echoes the nose
deliciously. Rosso Frassinolo ages for a year
in small wood and then stays in steel for
three more. Its very balsamic aromas
emerge against a background of cherries
and dried roses before the palate unveils
lashings of fruit. Finally, we would mention
again that the Pinot Grigio is an attractive
wine that just needs a little more length to
earn a second Glass.

● Friuli Isonzo Merlot '04	♟♟	4*
● Friuli Isonzo Cabernet Sauvignon '04	♟♟	4
○ Collio Tocai Friulano '06	♟	4
○ Collio Pinot Grigio '06	♟	4
○ Friuli Isonzo Chardonnay '06	♟	4
○ Friuli Isonzo Sauvignon '06	♟	4
○ Friuli Isonzo Pinot Grigio '06	♟	4
○ Collio Ribolla Gialla '06	♟	4
○ Collio Sauvignon '06	♟	4
● Rondon Rosso '03	♟	6
○ Collio Chardonnay '06		4
● Friuli Isonzo Cabernet Sauvignon '03	♟♟	4

● COF Rosso Frassinolo '03	♟♟	6
● COF Schioppettino '06	♟♟	6
● COF Refosco P. R. '05	♟	5
● COF Merlot '06	♟	4
● COF Pinot Nero '06	♟	5
● COF Tazzelenghe '03	♟	7
○ COF Pinot Bianco '06	♟	4
○ COF Pinot Grigio '06	♟	4
○ COF Ribolla Gialla '06	♟	5
○ COF Verduzzo Friulano '06		5

Giorgio Colutta

via Orsaria, 32
33044 Manzano [UD]
tel. 0432740315
www.colutta.it

ANNUAL PRODUCTION 130,000 bottles
HECTARES UNDER VINE 24
VITICULTURE METHOD Conventional

Giorgio Colutta's passion and commitment are exemplary. He is a tireless worker, never satisfied with what he has achieved and always on the lookout for new challenges. The vine stock grows every year and there are now 24 hectares, a quarter of which have been replanted and have at last come onstream. Antonio Maggio looks after them. The cellar now functions with enviable smoothness since the new vinification and storage extensions were completed. Queen of the cellars is still the ever-dependable Clizia Zambiasi, who arrived in Friuli from Trentino. The estate includes some superb agriturismo accommodation in the 18th-century residence. On its third release, the Pignolo is beginning to look good. Concentrated, with nicely handled extract, it is a wine to lay down. The Sauvignon is strikingly elegant and intense while we preferred the standard version of the Tocai Friulano since the Selezione Giorgio Colutta is a tad over-oaked. The reds from 2005 all bear the scars of a difficult growing year that was particularly trying just before the harvest.

● COF Pignolo '03	🍷🍷	7
○ COF Tocai Friulano '06	🍷🍷	4*
○ COF Sauvignon '06	🍷🍷	4*
○ COF Pinot Grigio '06	🍷	4
● COF Schioppettino '05	🍷	5
○ COF Ribolla Gialla '06	🍷	5
○ COF Tocai Friulano Sel. Giorgio Colutta '06	🍷	5
○ COF Verduzzo Friulano '05	🍷	6
● COF Cabernet '05		4
○ COF Chardonnay '06		4

Paolino Comelli

fraz. Colloredo di Soffumbergo
via Case Colloredo, 8
33040 Faedis [UD]
tel. 0432711226
www.comelli.it

ANNUAL PRODUCTION 50,000 bottles
HECTARES UNDER VINE 12.5
VITICULTURE METHOD Conventional

There can be no doubt that notary Pierluigi – "Pigi" to his friends – Comelli has a fully fledged business up and running in the unwelcoming hills at Faedis. His vision now embraces a splendid vineyard, a modern, well fitted out cellar, elegant agriturismo facilities created by making over various ancient houses in the area and, further down the slopes, a kiosk where you can taste the estate's wines. None of this has distracted Pigi from his principal activity, winemaking. Average quality standards are good and when it comes to Tocai, they ascend into excellence. The Comelli Tocai is impressively varietal, giving complex crusty bread and almond-led aromas in a delightful overall elegance that adds allure. On its first outing, the antique rose, distinctly mineral Pinot Grigio Amplius hit the spot and no mistake. Elegant and rich, the Chardonnay is as good as ever while there are also two fine reds, the Cabernet Sauvignon and Rosso Soffumbergo. The former is more firmly structured than most Friulian Cabernet Sauvignons and Rosso Soffumbergo is a blend of native and international grapes – refosco, pignolo, merlot and cabernet – emerging richly textured and with a ripe tannic weave.

○ COF Tocai Friulano '06	🍷🍷	4*
● COF Cabernet Sauvignon '05	🍷🍷	4
○ COF Chardonnay '06	🍷🍷	4
○ COF Pinot Grigio Amplius '06	🍷🍷	4
● COF Rosso Soffumbergo '04	🍷🍷	5
○ COF Bianco Locum Nostrum '04	🍷	4
● COF Merlot '05	🍷	4
○ COF Sauvignon '06	🍷	4
● COF Rosso Soffumbergo '03	🍷🍷	5

Dario Coos

LOC. RAMANDOLO
VIA RAMANDOLO, 5
33045 NIMIS [UD]
TEL. 0432790320
www.dariocoos.it

ANNUAL PRODUCTION 35,000 bottles
HECTARES UNDER VINE 7
VITICULTURE METHOD Conventional

Officially, Dario Coos's winery opened in 1986 but Dario is in fact the fifth generation of his family to produce wine. Dario is very territory-conscious and for several years was a champion of the name given around here to the grapes of verduzzo dorato or giallo, a variant that yields Ramandolo wine. Once the territory that could use the name had been redefined, the long trek started towards the goal of DOCG status, which today has finally become part of local oenology. For years, Dario Coos's wines have been at the top of the local quality tree, invariably going on to the Three Glass finals. He makes several products from ramandolo fruit, of which the leading wine is Romandus from part-dried, barrique-fermented grapes. Elegant and intense, it has hallmark caramel-covered apple and dried fig fragrances, layering these with sweet pipe tobacco on the palate. It's a genuinely fine sweet wine. Longhino is steel vinified and Vindos has some sauvignon grapes in the blend.

Conte D'Attimis-Maniago

VIA SOTTOMONTE, 21
33042 BUTTRIO [UD]
TEL. 0432674027
www.contedattimismaniago.it

ANNUAL PRODUCTION 400,000 bottles
HECTARES UNDER VINE 85
VITICULTURE METHOD Conventional

To look back over the history of the Conte D'Attimis-Maniago estate is to survey a significant slice of Friuli's winemaking past. It was 1585 when a noble wedding brought with it the present-day winery at Buttrio and the importance of the cellar's production in the 18th century is well documented. Finally, modern winemaking got under way in 1930 as the wine was finally sold in some of the first bottles seen in the region. But this substantial heritage weighs lightly on the modern estate, which this year presented us with an excellent range that has two distinct peaks, the traditional Malvasia and the Tazzelenghe. Both went through to our final tastings. We liked the Malvasia's complex apricots, peaches, confectioner's cream and tobacco as well as its full-bodied palate. Tazzelenghe is a rugged native variety that in this version tempts with subtle blackberry tart, milk chocolate and liqueur cherry notes. We also enjoyed the Sauvignon's contrast of vegetal and fruit aromas while the Verduzzo Tore delle Signore is fresh and far from cloying. Finally, Rosso Vignaricco is earthy and intriguingly spicy.

O Ramandolo Romandus '04	♟♟	6
O Ramandolo Il Longhino '04	♟♟	5
O Vindos '06	♟	4
O COF Picolit '05	♟	7
O Ramandolo '00	♟♟	5
O Ramandolo Romandus '02	♟♟	6
O COF Picolit '03	♟♟	7
O Ramandolo '02	♟♟	8
O Ramandolo Il Longhino '03	♟♟	5
O Ramandolo '03	♟♟	5
O Ramandolo '01	♟♟	6

O COF Malvasia '06	♟♟	4*
● COF Tazzelenghe '03	♟♟	6
O COF Bianco Ronco Broilo '04	♟♟	6
● COF Merlot '05	♟♟	4
● COF Rosso Vignaricco '03	♟♟	5
O COF Verduzzo Friulano Tore delle Signore '06	♟♟	4
O COF Sauvignon '06	♟♟	4
O COF Tocai Friulano '06	♟♟	4
O Ribula Brut	♟	5

Di Lenardo

FRAZ. ONTAGNANO
P.ZZA BATTISTI, 1
33050 GONARS [UD]
TEL. 0432928633
www.dilenardo.it

ANNUAL PRODUCTION	600,000 bottles
HECTARES UNDER VINE	45
VITICULTURE METHOD	Conventional

The Di Lenardo family acquired this estate in 1878. The main building was once a posthouse where travellers on the nearby Strada Napoleonica called in for refreshment and to change their horses. Later, it was converted into a farm and today it is one of the Grave DOC zone's leading wine estates. Max Di Lenardo is a can-do entrepreneur who in a very few years has built up a business network that spans the globe. Most of his wines are sold in the United States, the United Kingdom and various parts of Europe. Step by step, he is also advancing into the Far East. In fact, some 80 per cent of the 600,000 bottles released each year are sold outside Italy. Our hero has opted not to work with a single oenologist on a permanent basis, preferring to call in Italy's finest wine technicians to optimize work in his cellar. The Tocai Friulano Toh! has only moderately varietal with its aromatic and tropical fruit notes preceding a complex palate of impressive breadth and persistence.

Carlo Di Pradis

LOC. PRADIS, 22BIS
34071 CORMONS [GO]
TEL. 048162272
www.carlodipradis.it

ANNUAL PRODUCTION	80,000 bottles
HECTARES UNDER VINE	15
VITICULTURE METHOD	Conventional

Boris and David Buzzinelli are reliable, extremely hard-working grape growers who have named their estate after their father Carlo and the place where they have built their new cellar. When he was in charge, Carlo opted for quality and now follows his sons' progress with pride. The seven hectares around the cellar at Pradis are in the Collio DOC and a further eight, on the flatlands at Cormons, are in the Isonzo zone while output hovers around 80,000 bottles a year. Results this year reveal excellent quality but we were hoping for something even better, given the very favourable growing year. Our favourite is the Collio Pinot Grigio with its elegant fruit on the nose, assertive front palate and fine progression that shows, structure, richness, warmth and well-gauged acidity, signing off with a cornucopia of fruit. Distinct pear-like aromas emerge in the warm bouquet of the Tocai Friulano, a wine of excellent structure and remarkable length.

O Chardonnay Father's Eyes '06	🍷🍷	4
● Merlot Just Me '05	🍷🍷	5
O Friuli Grave Tocai Friulano Toh! '06	🍷🍷	4
O Friuli Grave Pinot Bianco '06	🍷🍷	3*
● Friuli Grave Cabernet '06	🍷	3
O Friuli Grave Sauvignon Blanc '06	🍷	3
O Friuli Grave Pinot Grigio '06	🍷	3
● Ronco Nolè Rosso '05	🍷	4
O Verduzzo Pass the Cookies '06	🍷	4
O Friuli Grave Chardonnay '06	🍷	3

O Collio Tocai Friulano '06	🍷🍷	4
O Collio Pinot Grigio '06	🍷🍷	4
O Collio Bianco Pradis '05	🍷	4
O Friuli Isonzo Sauvignon BorDavi '06	🍷	4
O Friuli Isonzo Chardonnay BorDavi '06	🍷	4
● Friuli Isonzo Merlot BorDavi '04		4
O Collio Sauvignon '06		4
O Friuli Isonzo Pinot Grigio BorDavi '06		4
O Collio Tocai Friulano '05	🍷🍷	4
O Collio Tocai Friulano Scusse '04	🍷🍷	4

★ Girolamo Dorigo

LOC. VICINALE
VIA DEL POZZO, 5
33042 BUTTRIO [UD]
TEL. 0432674268
www.montsclapade.com

ANNUAL PRODUCTION 180,000 bottles
HECTARES UNDER VINE 35
VITICULTURE METHOD Conventional

Born in 1934, Girolamo Dorigo has to some extent withdrawn from the day-to-day management of the cellar and vineyards but since he enjoys enviably robust health, he finds it hard to stay out of the front line. In contrast, his son Alessio at a certain point in his life decided to devote all his energies to the family estate, and also to consult for various other wineries, as readers will note from the relevant profiles. For several years, the Dorigos' policy has been to focus production on outstanding value for money, releasing new products that the market has taken to its heart. One such is the excellent Traminer, of which only 3,000 bottles are available for now. The Pignolo 2004 was slightly disappointing but the Montsclapade from the same vintage was every bit as good as we hoped. A 60-40 blend of cabernet sauvignon and merlot aged in wood for two years, it flaunts complexity and fine structure with hints of red fruit jam, wood and extract that are managed with flawless skill. It's a superb red and thoroughly deserved its Three Glasses. Sauvignon Ronc di Juri is at last firing on all cylinders, its vanilla no more than a backdrop for a vibrantly good wine.

Mauro Drius

VIA FILANDA, 100
34071 CORMONS [GO]
TEL. 048160998
drius.mauro@adriacom.it

ANNUAL PRODUCTION 70,000 bottles
HECTARES UNDER VINE 11.5
VITICULTURE METHOD Conventional

Mauro Drius runs this cellar with his father Sergio, showing all the tenacity and prudence that derive from a long tradition of working the land. There are no flights of fancy and no sudden changes of tack. Energies here are focused on the biological equilibrium of the vineyards and the relentless improvement of the wines released to market. Mauro's wines are the blue chips of the oenological stock market, offering low risk, steady growth and occasionally some very pleasant surprises. We were impressed again this year by the quality of the wines from the two Drius hectares in the Collio zone. The very varietal, wellstructured Tocai and Sauvignon are impeccably drinkable and the Sauvignon in particular is stylishly elegant, despite the weight of its considerable alcohol. The Isonzo version of the Tocai is also outstanding, as is Vignis di Sìris, a blend of tocai, sauvignon and pinot bianco, but the star from the DOC is the Pinot Grigio, one of the best examples from 2006. There may not be a superstar in the range but this year, the average quality of Drius wines is among the best in the region.

● COF Rosso Montsclapade '04	▼▼▼	7
○ COF Sauvignon Vign. Ronc di Juri '06	▼▼	6
● COF Pignolo di Buttrio '04	▼▼	8
○ COF Sauvignon '06	▼▼	4*
○ Dorigo Cuvée Brut M. Cl.	▼▼	5
○ COF Traminer '06	▼▼	4*
● COF Refosco P. R. '04	▼▼	4
○ COF Chardonnay '06	▼	6
○ COF Pinot Grigio '06	▼	4
● COF Refosco '06	▼	4
● COF Pignolo di Buttrio '01	▼▼▼	8
● COF Pignolo di Buttrio '02	▼▼▼	8
● COF Rosso Montsclapade '01	▼▼▼	7
● COF Pignolo di Buttrio '03	▼▼▼	8

○ Collio Sauvignon '06	▼▼	4*
○ Friuli Isonzo Pinot Grigio '06	▼▼	4*
○ Collio Tocai Friulano '06	▼▼	4*
○ Friuli Isonzo Bianco Vignis di Sìris '05	▼▼	4
○ Friuli Isonzo Tocai Friulano '06	▼▼	4
○ Friuli Isonzo Malvasia '06	▼	4
○ Friuli Isonzo Pinot Bianco '06	▼	4
● Friuli Isonzo Merlot '04	▼	4
● Friuli Isonzo Cabernet '04		4
○ Collio Tocai Friulano '02	▼▼▼	4
○ Friuli Isonzo Bianco Vignis di Sìris '02	▼▼▼	4
○ Collio Tocai Friulano '05	▼▼▼	4
○ Friuli Isonzo Pinot Bianco '00	▼▼▼	4
○ Collio Sauvignon '05	▼▼	4

Le Due Terre

VIA ROMA, 68B
33040 PREPOTTO [UD]
TEL. 0432713189

ANNUAL PRODUCTION 20,000 bottles
HECTARES UNDER VINE 5
VITICULTURE METHOD Natural

You don't change a winning team. Flavio and Silvana Basilicata seem to have found their niche, making just four wines, all exceptional. Flavio's unassuming description of his winery transports us into a cellar with human dimensions, where the impact on the environment is minimal and there is respect for the necessary bond that links winemaking to the territory and the rhythms of nature. In the vineyard, Flavio uses only sulphur and copper which, in addition to a very small amount of sulphur dioxide, are the only chemicals to intrude into the winemaking process. Yeasts are native and fermentations spontaneous. There is no racking, filtering is carried out with a light touch, bottling follows the phases of the moon and all the wines stay in the cellar for two years before release to market. Sacrisassi Bianco 2005 is a blend of tocai friulano and ribolla gialla. Very intense and aromatic on the nose, it proffers crisp sensations of ripe fruit but minerality and sheer elegance are the strong suits of this wine. Thanks to its impressive personality, Sacrisassi Bianco picked up Three Glasses. Also interesting, if still youngish, is the refosco and schioppettino Sacrisassi Rosso.

○ COF Bianco Sacrisassi '05	TTT	6
● COF Merlot '05	TT	7
● COF Pinot Nero '05	TT	6
● COF Rosso Sacrisassi '05	TT	7
● COF Merlot '00	YYY	7
● COF Rosso Sacrisassi '98	YYY	7
● COF Rosso Sacrisassi '97	YYY	7
● COF Merlot '03	YYY	6
● COF Merlot '02	YYY	7
○ COF Bianco Sacrisassi '02	YY	6
● COF Rosso Sacrisassi '04	YY	7
● COF Merlot '04	YY	7
○ COF Bianco Sacrisassi '03	YY	6
○ COF Bianco Sacrisassi '04	YY	6

Dario e Luciano Ermacora

FRAZ. IPPLIS
VIA SOLZAREDO, 9
33040 PREMARIACCO [UD]
TEL. 0432716250
www.ermacora.com

ANNUAL PRODUCTION 160,000 bottles
HECTARES UNDER VINE 25
VITICULTURE METHOD Conventional

With each passing year, Dario and Luciano Ermacora consolidate their position at the top of Friulian winemaking. Family history helps for it is more than 80 years since Ermacoras started tending their well-ordered farm on the hill at Ipplis. Dario and Luciano have introduced a modern approach to the winery, rigorous management of vineyards and cellar, not to say attention to detail in the wines, which stand out for the perfection of their style and their faithfulness to the variety with which they are made. There were no top awards this time but the overall performance of the range is excellent, especially in the classic Pinot Bianco and Pignolo wines and the fresh, brilliantly typed Pinot Grigio. The Pinot Bianco has strikingly rich, intense aromatics that range from crusty bread to green apples, russet pears and almonds. The expansive, savoury palate nicely echoes the aromas of the nose. In the Pignolo it is sensations of red fruit jam and cinchona that stand out, making this a remarkably smooth wine. Not far behind is the fragrant, sun-drenched Tocai, the distinctly fruity Sauvignon and a Picolit that discloses subtle fragrances and an elegant palate.

● COF Pignolo '03	TT	6
○ COF Pinot Bianco '06	TT	4*
○ COF Pinot Grigio '06	TT	4*
○ COF Picolit '05	TT	7
○ COF Sauvignon '06	TT	4
○ COF Tocai Friulano '06	TT	4
● COF Refosco P. R. '05	T	4
○ COF Verduzzo Friulano '06	T	4
● COF Pignolo '00	YYY	5
○ COF Pinot Bianco '05	YY	4*
● COF Pignolo '02	YY	6
● COF Pignolo '01	YY	6
○ COF Pinot Grigio '05	YY	4*
● COF Refosco P. R. '04	YY	4

Fantinel

FRAZ. TAURIANO
VIA TESIS, 8
33097 SPILIMBERGO [PN]
TEL. 0427591511
www.fantinel.com

ANNUAL PRODUCTION   4,000,000 bottles
HECTARES UNDER VINE 250
VITICULTURE METHOD   Conventional

The Fantinel story is well known. Eminent Friulian restaurateur and hotel keeper Mario decided to make his own wines as long ago as 1969. He may not have foreseen that Fantinel would acquire over the years a vine stock of 250 hectares and produce a number of bottles that put it firmly in the front rank of Italian winemaking. Quantity is one distinguishing feature of the Fantinel operation but the group's philosophy is still centred on quality, respect for tradition and ceaseless efforts to maintain and refine the sensory profiles of the wines released. The Fantinel vine stock is split over the Collio DOC zone, where part of the Sant'Helena line is sourced, the Colli Orientali and the Grave, which contribute to the Sant'Helena and Borgo Tesis wines. The Collio Tocai and Sauvignon came away from our tastings with Two Glasses each. The intense Tocai shows breadth, fullness and complexity backed up by nice acidity whereas the varietal Sauvignon unveils peach and sage that return satisfyingly in the mouth.

★ Livio Felluga

FRAZ. BRAZZANO
VIA RISORGIMENTO, 1
34071 CORMONS [GO]
TEL. 048160203
www.liviofelluga.it

ANNUAL PRODUCTION   800,000 bottles
HECTARES UNDER VINE 155
VITICULTURE METHOD   Conventional

We like to mention initiatives that link wine with culture and we do so here as we leaf through the elegant volume published to celebrate the half century of the celebrated map label that makes Livio Felluga bottles so instantly recognizable. It is a journey around maps, seen from the perspectives of writers, academics and international celebrities. The initiative is entirely in harmony with the Felluga style, which combines intelligence, elegance and thoughtfulness for the consumer. But on to the wines. This year, the cellar opted not to release Terre Alte but it is an absence that is amply compensated by other wines of excellence. Shàrjs, from chardonnay and ribolla, has come on marvellously with its refined sensations of wisteria and sweet spice as well as its delicious fruit. A successful melding of soft pineapple, apricot and orange aromas with fresher minerally sensations are the hallmark of the Pinot Grigio. Sossò, from refosco, merlot and pignolo, is warm, velvety and attractively structured. Finally, we enjoyed the toasted almonds of the Picolit, which signs off with a pleasingly fresh finale.

O Collio Tocai Friulano Sant'Helena '06	▼▼	5
O Collio Sauvignon Sant'Helena '06	▼▼	5
● Friuli Grave Cabernet Sauvignon Sant'Helena '04	▼	5
● Friuli Grave Merlot Borgo Tesis '05	▼	4
O Friuli Grave Chardonnay Borgo Tesis '06	▼	4
O Ribolla Gialla Vigneti Sant'Helena '06	▼	4
● Friuli Grave Refosco P. R. Sant'Helena '04	▼	5
O Collio Pinot Grigio Sant'Helena '06		5
● Friuli Grave Merlot Borgo Tesis '00	♟♟	4
● Friuli Grave Merlot Borgo Tesis '04	♟♟	4
● Friuli Grave Merlot Borgo Tesis '03	♟♟	4

O COF Picolit Ris. Rosazzo '04	▼▼	8
O Shàrjs '06	▼▼	4*
O COF Pinot Grigio '06	▼▼	5
● COF Rosazzo Sossò Ris. '03	▼▼	7
● COF Refosco P. R. '05	▼▼	5
● Vertigo '05	▼▼	4
O COF Tocai Friulano '06	▼▼	5
O Collio Sauvignon '06	▼▼	4
● COF Refosco P. R. '99	♟♟♟	7
O COF Rosazzo Bianco Terre Alte '99	♟♟♟	5
O COF Rosazzo Bianco Terre Alte '02	♟♟♟	6
O COF Rosazzo Bianco Terre Alte '04	♟♟♟	7
O COF Rosazzo Bianco Terre Alte '01	♟♟♟	6
● COF Rosazzo Sossò Ris. '01	♟♟♟	7

Marco Felluga
VIA GORIZIA, 121
34070 GRADISCA D'ISONZO [GO]
TEL. 048199164
www.marcofelluga.it

Fiegl
FRAZ. OSLAVIA
LOC. LENZUOLO BIANCO, 1
34070 GORIZIA
TEL. 0481547103
www.fieglvini.com

ANNUAL PRODUCTION 650,000 bottles
HECTARES UNDER VINE 120
VITICULTURE METHOD Conventional

We could fairly say that this is the big numbers property in Marco Felluga's group. But that doesn't mean that the 650,000 bottles released are not excellent. All are made in the image of the family's flagship Russiz Superiore, a product of seriously good skills and attention to detail by a technical team with great depth of experience. This profile also includes wines from the Felluga estate in Chianti Classico, the San Nicolò a Pisignano winery whose bottles are making their Guide debut this year. It was Sorripa, of the two wines we tasted, that had more structure and complexity. From the Friulian range, we liked the freshness of Bianco Molamatta, a blend of tocai, ribolla and pinot bianco, the soft fruit of Pinot Grigio Mongris, the fragrant sage, tobacco and apricot of the Sauvignon and the rich, sunny ripeness of the Tocai. The Bordeaux blend Rosso Carantan impressed with its assertive jam and cinchona aromas. Rounding off is the tempting, extremely varietal Moscato Rosa, the perfect wine for lovers of the type.

ANNUAL PRODUCTION 140,000 bottles
HECTARES UNDER VINE 26
VITICULTURE METHOD Conventional

What a fine family the Fiegls are! The various brothers and other relatives make a perfect team. Their estate is in truly outstanding wine country at Oslavia, a subzone that is the jewel in the crown of the Collio Goriziano, and the winery has ancient roots, dating from 1782. Today, Ales, Josko and Rado are in charge with help from Martin and Silvana. These Oslavia guys turn out about 140,000 bottles a year from 26 hectares under vine. In early August, they also inaugurated a permanent exhibition of finds from the Great War that came to light when they were excavating for the new plantings that the Fiegls will be tending with their usual care. This means it will be possible to visit the estate, taste the wines and find out about the epoch-making events that went on here in Oslavia and on Monte Sabotino from 1915 to 1918. Back on the wine front, we were astounded by the deliciously warm, appealingly varietal Malvasia 2006 with its well-defined aromas of ripe fruit and spring flowers. Its full palate is laced with mineral sensations that bind it indissolubly to the territory.

● Carantan '03	▼▼	6
● Sorripa S. Nicolò a Pisignano '03	▼▼	5
○ Collio Pinot Grigio Mongris '06	▼▼	4
○ Collio Sauvignon '06	▼▼	4
☉ Moscato Rosa '04	▼▼	5
○ Collio Tocai Friulano '06	▼▼	4
○ Collio Bianco Molamatta '06	▼▼	5
○ Collio Chardonnay '06	▼	4
● La Poggiona S. Nicolò a Pisignano '03	▼	4
● Refosco P. R. Ronco dei Moreri '05	▼	4
● Castello di Buttrio Pignolo '03	♀♀	6

○ Collio Malvasia '06	▼▼	4*
● Collio Merlot Leopold '02	▼▼	4
○ Collio Ribolla Gialla '06	▼▼	4
○ Collio Chardonnay '06	▼▼	4
○ Collio Tocai Friulano '06	▼▼	4
○ Collio Pinot Grigio '06	▼▼	4
○ Collio Cuvée Blanc Leopold '05	▼	5
● Rosso Cuvée Rouge Leopold '02	▼	6
○ Collio Sauvignon '06	▼	4
○ Collio Pinot Bianco '06	▼	4
○ Collio Leopold Cuvée Blanc '02	♀♀	4
● Rosso Cuvée Rouge Leopold '01	♀♀	6

Foffani

FRAZ. CLAUIANO
P.ZZA GIULIA, 13
33050 TRIVIGNANO UDINESE [UD]
TEL. 0432999584
www.foffani.it

ANNUAL PRODUCTION 80,000 bottles
HECTARES UNDER VINE 10
VITICULTURE METHOD Conventional

Criticism is sometimes resented but in other cases it is a spur to action. Foffani, which dropped out of the Guide last year, may have taken the second option because the winery has bounced right back into our selection of premium-quality estates in Friuli and the improvement is evident. The Foffani cellar is at Clauiano, one of Italy's loveliest villages, and deserves a visit for the elegantly refined agriturismo facilities and the original permanent exhibition on the colours of wine. The beauty of the location probably helped the cellar to bring back up to speed a good range led by a Pinot Grigio and a Merlot Riserva. Fresh citrus aromas pervade the Pinot Grigio while the Merlot, which ages for two years in large wood, acquiring attractive balsamic nuances that knit well with the fragrances of blackberry tart, chocolate and coffee. We would also point out the freshness and of the Sauvignon and the almond-led varietal character of the Tocai.

Forchir

FRAZ. PROVESANO
VIA CIASUTIS, 1B
33095 SAN GIORGIO DELLA RICHINVELDA [PN]
TEL. 042796037
www.forchir.it

ANNUAL PRODUCTION 1,000,000 bottles
HECTARES UNDER VINE 226
VITICULTURE METHOD Natural

Forchir is more than a century old but doesn't show its age, as the energy of its owners – the theatrical Gianfranco Bianchini and the more measured Enzo Deana – the freshness and technical polish of its wines and the modern winemaking facilities all show. Managing more than 200 hectares on three sites and maintaining quality across the range – all the wines presented were much more than well made – with good value for money is no easy task. It shows that Forchir is a serious winery. The best of this year's wines are Pinot Bianco Campo dei Gelsi, the classic Tocai that Forchir releases as Friulano and the Cabernet Franc. The first of the trio is the result of mass selection and ages in large wood, emerging with its melon and white plum aromas laced with subtle vanilla. What we liked about the Tocai was the sweet tropical fruit and varietal sensations of almonds and yeasts while the Cabernet Franc wooed our tasters with balsamic nuances and a lovely citrus-led finish. Sauvignon L'Altro, which stands out for its vibrant freshness, is also worth uncorking.

● Friuli Aquileia Merlot Ris. '03	♀♀ 6
○ Friuli Aquileia Pinot Grigio Sup. '06	♀♀ 4*
● Friuli Aquileia Merlot '05	♀ 5
○ Friuli Aquileia Sauvignon Sup. '06	♀ 4
○ Friuli Aquileia Tocai Friulano Sup. '06	♀ 4
● Friuli Aquileia Cabernet Sauvignon '04	5
● Friuli Aquileia Refosco P. R. '05	5
○ Friuli Aquileia Chardonnay Sup. '06	4

● Friuli Grave Cabernet Franc Braidate '06	♀♀ 4*
○ Friuli Grave Pinot Bianco Campo dei Gelsi '06	♀♀ 4*
○ Friuli Grave Friulano Lusor '06	♀♀ 4*
○ Friuli Grave Sauvignon L'Altro '06	♀ 4
○ Friuli Grave Traminer Aromatico '06	♀ 3
○ Bianco Un Blanc '06	♀ 4
● Friuli Grave Merlot '06	♀ 4
● Friuli Grave Refosco P. R. '06	♀ 4
● Friuli Grave Refoscone '05	♀ 5
● Rosso Un Neri '06	♀ 4
○ Friuli Grave Pinot Bianco Campo dei Gelsi '05	♀♀ 4
○ Friuli Grave Sauvignon '05	♀♀ 3
○ Friuli Grave Pinot Grigio '05	♀♀ 3
● Friuli Grave Refoscone '03	♀♀ 5

Conti Formentini

via Oslavia, 5
34070 San Floriano del Collio [GO]
tel. 0481884131
www.contiformentini.it

ANNUAL PRODUCTION 320,000 bottles
HECTARES UNDER VINE 75
VITICULTURE METHOD Conventional

Conti Formentini has a heritage of history that has made it a leading actor on the territory's wine stage for centuries. And when we say territory, we are talking about an area that extends from what is now Hungary to Alto Adige, Styria, Slovenia and Friuli. In recent years, a document came to light that rekindled controversy over the origin of the name Tocai for it says that in 1632 the noblewoman Aurora Formentini took to her Hungarian husband Adam Batthyany as part of her dowry 300 "toccai" vines. Today, the estate is part of Gruppo Italiano Vini but its history goes back officially to 1520. Members of religious orders, including the Abbess Rylint, have left their mark on the property, expanding viticulture considerably. The cellar is managed by Marco Del Piccolo, who has consultancy input from Piedmont-based Marco Monchiero and its most outstanding wine is dedicated to the abbess. Rylint, obtained from chardonnay, pinot grigio and sauvignon, layers confectioner's cream and banana fragrances with apple and apricot on the palate, which is elegant, rich and tangily attractive.

○ Collio Bianco Rylint '06	🍷🍷	4*
○ Collio Chardonnay Torre di Tramontana '05	🍷	5
○ Collio Pinot Grigio '06	🍷	4
● Collio Rosso Tajut '05	🍷	4
○ Collio Bianco Rylint '05	YY	4

Adriano Gigante

via Rocca Bernarda, 3
33040 Corno di Rosazzo [UD]
tel. 0432755835
www.adrianogigante.it

ANNUAL PRODUCTION 60,000 bottles
HECTARES UNDER VINE 13
VITICULTURE METHOD Conventional

What's the best way to celebrate a winery's 50th anniversary? Well, a Three Glass award is not a bad option. It has been 50 vintages since grandfather Ferruccio started the Gigante cellar and it was far-sighted Ferruccio who saw the potential of the long-established tocai vineyard that today gives Adriano, Giuliana and Ariedo the selection they call Tocai Vigneto Storico. This is a wine that has notched up its fourth top award and perfectly marries almost cream-like richness with fresh pennyroyal and apple pip sensations. Assertively full bodied on the palate, it delights the taste buds with trademark varietal almond notes. The Sauvignon and Pignolo are equally impressive. Freshness and finesse are the Sauvignon's calling cards as it melds wisteria, elderflower and green apples whereas the Pignolo is firmly fruit-forward with complex leather and talcum powder notes. The long Gigante list of premium wines goes on and we would point out the rich spicy Schioppettino, the austere Cabernet Franc, the soft fruit of the refosco, schioppettino and merlot-based Rosso Giudizio, the very varietal Pinot Grigio, the full-bodied Tocai and the sweet but not cloying Picolit.

○ COF Tocai Friulano V. Storico '06	🍷🍷🍷	5
○ COF Sauvignon '06	🍷🍷	4*
● COF Pignolo '03	🍷🍷	6
● COF Cabernet Franc '05	🍷🍷	4
● COF Rosso Giudizio '05	🍷🍷	5
● COF Schioppettino '05	🍷🍷	5
○ COF Pinot Grigio '06	🍷🍷	4
○ COF Tocai Friulano '06	🍷🍷	4
○ COF Picolit '04	🍷🍷	7
○ COF Verduzzo Friulano '05	🍷🍷	4
○ COF Chardonnay '06	🍷	4
○ COF Ribolla Gialla '06	🍷	4
○ COF Tocai Friulano Storico '00	YYY	5
○ COF Tocai Friulano V. Storico '03	YYY	5
○ COF Tocai Friulano V. Storico '05	YYY	5
○ COF Tocai Friulano V. Storico '04	YY	5
○ COF Sauvignon '05	YY	4
● COF Merlot Ris. '03	YY	6

Gradis'ciutta

LOC. GIASBANA, 10
34070 SAN FLORIANO DEL COLLIO [GO]
TEL. 0481390237
robigradis@libero.it

ANNUAL PRODUCTION 60,000 bottles
HECTARES UNDER VINE 17
VITICULTURE METHOD Conventional

We were right last year when we said that Gradis'ciutta's lack of stellar wines was due to building work on the new cellar. Now that Robert Princic has big new spaces to work in, the stars are out again. Robert may be young but he has very clear ideas and plenty of ability. In the short term, he aims to reduce the number of wines released and concentrate on his white blend, the true expression of the territory. Just now, we can again enjoy an excellent, elegantly refined Ribolla Gialla redolent of flowers, rennet apples and faraway hints of confectioner's cream. The palate is bright and fresh-tasting with perceptions of crusty bread. Equally good is the generously extracted Pinot Grigio that shows good progression on a peach, damson and spring flower-themed palate. We also liked the Chardonnay, which echoes on the palate its nose of fresh bananas and pear drops. The Tocai is very fruity and the Sauvignon unveils distinct aromas of melon and grapefruit. Finally, there's a good Cabernet Franc with varietal nuances of blackberry tart and rosemary.

★ Gravner

FRAZ. OSLAVIA
LOC. LENZUOLO BIANCO, 9
34070 GORIZIA
TEL. 048130882
www.gravner.it

ANNUAL PRODUCTION 39,000 bottles
HECTARES UNDER VINE 18
VITICULTURE METHOD Natural

It's no easy matter to write about Josko, not least because to express the emotions his wines excite you would have to be a poet, a musician or a painter. We shall restrict ourselves to a couple of observations. Josko is a leader who tenaciously, knowledgeably, defends his decisions but is willing to discuss them. Like all leaders, he has something different, if not exactly new, to say and on the wine scene there are those who support him and those who disagree. Josko's new ideas come not from the top of his head but are the conscious result of reflection on the devastating impact humanity has on the natural environment. Believing in your own decisions also means believing your way ahead is sustainable from all points of view. After all, a maggoty apple may be organic but it won't be much of a commercial success. In consequence, there are parameters of balance, cleanness and elegance that have to be respected but often aren't. In Josko's case, the results are intellectually absorbing and sensorially intriguing, especially regarding his whites, or pseudowhites. Try them and find out how much of a poet, musician or painter you are.

○ Collio Pinot Grigio '06	♟♟	4*
○ Collio Ribolla Gialla '06	♟♟	4*
○ Collio Chardonnay '06	♟♟	4
○ Collio Tocai Friulano '06	♟♟	4
○ Collio Sauvignon '06	♟♟	4
● Collio Cabernet Franc '05	♟♟	4
○ Bratinis '05	♟	4
● Collio Rosso dei Princic '04	♟	5
○ Collio Bianco del Tùzz Ris. '04	♟♟	4
○ Collio Ribolla Gialla '05	♟♟	4
○ Collio Sauvignon '05	♟♟	4
○ Collio Pinot Grigio '05	♟♟	4
● Collio Rosso dei Princic '03	♟♟	5

○ Breg Anfora '03	♟♟♟	8
○ Ribolla Anfora '03	♟♟	8
● Rosso Gravner '02	♟♟	8
● Rujno '97	♟	8
○ Breg Anfora '02	♟♟♟	8
○ Breg '00	♟♟♟	8
○ Breg '99	♟♟♟	8
○ Breg '98	♟♟♟	8
○ Chardonnay '87	♟♟♟	5
○ Sauvignon '93	♟♟♟	5
○ Ribolla Anfora '02	♟♟♟	8
○ Ribolla Anfora '01	♟♟♟	8

Iole Grillo
FRAZIONE ALBANA, 60
33040 PREPOTTO [UD]
TEL. 0432713201
www.vinigrillo.it

Marcello e Marino Humar
LOC. VALERISCE, 2
34070 SAN FLORIANO DEL COLLIO [GO]
TEL. 0481884094
www.humar.it

ANNUAL PRODUCTION 35,000 bottles
HECTARES UNDER VINE 7.5
VITICULTURE METHOD Conventional

Anna Muzzolini has gradually put together a team of collaborators who have enabled the quality of Grillo wines to make an appreciable step forward. For two years, wine technician Giuseppe Tosoratti has been working at the cellar, backed up by consultancy input from Ramon Persello. Equally crucial have been the contributions of Anna's husband Andrea Bianchini and her very competent mother Iole Grillo. Their working environment in the ancient winery buildings is further enhanced by the view over the vineyards. This year, the Sauvignon attracted our attention. Its Two full Glasses were earned by green pepper and bell pepper fragrances that stand out against a subtle fruit base. The assertive entry on the palate opens with green notes that give way to softer, spicy sensations. The very spicy Refosco is on top form and the Bordeaux blend Rosso Guardafuoco proffers hints of plum jam and plenty of verve. Varietal aromas are the hallmark of the Tocai, whose palate is attractively soft and redolent of alluring sugared almonds.

ANNUAL PRODUCTION 100,000 bottles
HECTARES UNDER VINE 30
VITICULTURE METHOD Conventional

After starting life as a mixed-crop farm, the estate of brothers Marcello and Marino Humar converted to viticulture in the 1950s and bottling began in 1960. Now Loreta, Stefano and his wife Daria, cousin Dario and his wife Natascia continue the work of the earlier generation while adding the touch of modernity and innovation that lifts the overall image of the range. Output is a mixed bag of excellent wines and less than marvellous bottles like the Pinot Nero and the Verduzzo, which are well made but still need to find their feet. On the other hand, the estate is in superb wine country, the green hills of San Floriano, one of the Collio's finest vineyards. From the excellent wines, we would pick out the minerally Tocai with its pears and ripe oranges. Also very good is the tempting Pinot Grigio, which holds up well in the mouth right through to a long, savoury finish. Finally, the bright, fresh Ribolla Gialla offers a swath of pleasing fruit sensations.

O COF Sauvignon '06	♈♈	4*
● COF Refosco P. R. '05	♈♈	4
● COF Rosso Guardafuoco '04	♈♈	5
O COF Tocai Friulano '06	♈♈	4
O COF Bianco Santa Justina '05	♈	4
● COF Cabernet Franc '05	♈	4
● COF Schioppettino '05	♈	5
O COF Pinot Grigio '06	♈	4
● COF Merlot '03	♈♈	5

O Collio Pinot Grigio '06	♈♈	4*
O Collio Ribolla Gialla '06	♈♈	4*
O Collio Tocai Friulano '06	♈♈	4*
O Collio Chardonnay '06	♈	4
O Collio Sauvignon '06	♈	4
● Collio Pinot Nero '05		4
O Verduzzo '05		5

Jacùss

FRAZ. MONTINA
V.LE KENNEDY, 35A
33040 TORREANO [UD]
TEL. 0432715147
www.jacuss.com

ANNUAL PRODUCTION 50,000 bottles
HECTARES UNDER VINE 10
VITICULTURE METHOD Conventional

We are always in awe when we read the
evaluations after our tastings of the wines
from this small cellar run by brothers Andrea
and Sandro Jacuzzi. We know how
challenging the pair's task is as they tend
their plots scattered across the hills at
Montina and struggle to make wine in a
cramped vinification cellar. But every time,
we note with satisfaction that they make
steady progress. This time, we recorded a
distinct improvement in the reds, which
often used to have one or two tannin-
inspired rough edges. We were particularly
surprised by Rosso Lindi Uà, a blend of
merlot, cabernet sauvignon and refosco.
Talcum powder, cinchona, currant tart and
chocolate all come through on the nose
before the warm palate reveals its structure.
The Pinot Bianco is as good as ever,
offering apples and minerality, the
Sauvignon is all citrus and the very intense
Picolit flaunts honey and candied citrus
peel. Fresh tropical fruit and flowers are the
Tocai's best points while the Refosco
earned One very full Glass. All it lacks is a
touch of concentration on the palate.

★ Jermann

FRAZ. RUTTARS
LOC. TRUSSIO, 11
34070 DOLEGNA DEL COLLIO [GO]
TEL. 0481888080
www.jermann.it

ANNUAL PRODUCTION 280,000 bottles
HECTARES UNDER VINE 43
VITICULTURE METHOD Conventional

In recent years, Silvio Jermann's wines have
been missing out on Three Glasses. Work
on the new cellar at Ruttars was absorbing
all the energy and attention of the great
Friulian wine man with roots in Slovenia. But
the cellar is rational, spectacular and nature-
friendly. Every detail is filled with meaning
that may not always be obvious. Only the
story that has unfolded in time, space and
Silvio's mind holds the key. This year, there
were Three Glasses for Capo Martino,
named for the vineyard at Ruttars, or
"Rotârs" as Silvio spells it, but then he has
been signing himself "Sylvio" for a while. It's
a fabulous wine that crowns a project born
in 1991, when Silvio purchased the
vineyard. Made exclusively from local
varieties – tocai, ribolla, malvasia and picolit
– it is incredibly elegant and harmonious,
proffering a symphony of fruit and flowers to
sign off with incomparable length. Subtle
and balanced, the Vintage Tunina, from
sauvignon, chardonnay, malvasia, ribolla
and picolit, is only a step behind. This year,
Silvio and his son Angelo also made a
magnificent Vinnae from ribolla, tocai and
riesling, a summary of the winemaking
history of Slovenia, Friuli and Austria to
which Silvio feels he belongs.

O COF Picolit '04	♟♟ 7
O COF Pinot Bianco '06	♟♟ 4*
O COF Tocai Friulano '06	♟♟ 4*
O COF Sauvignon '06	♟♟ 4*
● COF Rosso Lindi Uà '03	♟♟ 4*
● COF Cabernet Sauvignon '04	♟ 4
● COF Refosco P. R. '04	♟ 4
● COF Schioppettino Fucs e Flamis '05	♟ 4
● Tazzelenghe '03	♟ 4
O COF Sauvignon '05	♟♟ 4

O Capo Martino '05	♟♟♟ 7
O Vinnae '06	♟♟ 5
O Vintage Tunina '05	♟♟ 8
O Sauvignon '06	♟♟ 5
O W... Dreams... '05	♟♟ 7
O Müller Thurgau '06	♟♟ 5
● Blau&Blau '05	♟♟ 7
● Pignacolusse '04	♟♟ 6
O Capo Martino '97	♟♟♟ 7
O Capo Martino '93	♟♟♟ 5
O Vintage Tunina '00	♟♟♟ 7
O Vintage Tunina '99	♟♟♟ 7
O Vintage Tunina '97	♟♟♟ 6
O Vintage Tunina '01	♟♟♟ 8
● Pignacolusse '00	♟♟♟ 6

Kante

FRAZ. S. PELAGIO
LOC. PREPOTTO, 1A
34011 DUINO AURISINA [TS]
TEL. 040200255
kante.edi@libero.it

ANNUAL PRODUCTION 35,000 bottles
HECTARES UNDER VINE 12
VITICULTURE METHOD Natural

Edi Kante is one of a kind. Artistic and stubborn by nature, he has a superb cellar carved from the Carso rock in a territory where running a self-supporting winery is a big challenge. Edi believes in the potential of his land and has proved his point by making memorable versions of international wines like Sauvignon and Chardonnay but he also sees a future for native grapes, even though malvasia, vitovska and terrano can yield disappointingly rough wines if handled incorrectly. But Edi stands out like a beacon, focusing on the minerality and savouriness of his wines to give them a sense of place. In comparison with his past peaks of glory, results from recent vintages have been low-key for Edi has been reviewing his winemaking processes, getting his new cellar in shape and bringing new vineyards on stream. Now, however, he is back at the top. All his wines this year, released in one-litre bottles, sailed past the Two Glass mark and two came within a hair's breath of our top award. We should point out that all are from the unexciting 2004 vintage.

Edi Keber

LOC. ZEGLA, 17
34071 CORMONS [GO]
TEL. 048161184

ANNUAL PRODUCTION 60,000 bottles
HECTARES UNDER VINE 10
VITICULTURE METHOD Natural

No praise is too much for Edi Keber and his wife Silvana. Courteous, welcoming, intelligent and modest, they have recovered and promoted a family tradition thanks in part to Edi's courageous decision ten years ago to release just three or four wines. We are also impressed by their son Kristjan, who has been an enthusiastic helper in vineyard and cellar since he was a little boy. Now that Kristjan has a diploma from the oenology school at Cividale under his belt, he has decided to continue his studies while still devoting time to the estate. In the past, we have noted reduction on the nose of Edi's Tocai that meant it needed time to breathe, the balance of the latest vintage is quite impeccable. The intense fruit is wonderfully elegant and the warm, salt-tinged palate reveals close-knit but agile texture and enviable length. The Three Glass award was never in doubt. Edi's Collio Bianco 2006, from tocai, malvasia and ribolla with a touch of pinot bianco and pinot grigio, is an essay in elegance and body. A little more work is needed on the Collio 2003, a traditional white from tocai, ribolla and malvasia aged for a year in large wood and bottled without filtration.

Wine		Rating
O Carso Chardonnay '04	₮₮	6
O Carso Sauvignon '04	₮₮	6
O Carso Vitovska '04	₮₮	6
O Carso Malvasia '04	₮₮	6
O Carso Sauvignon '91	₮₮₮	6
O Carso Sauvignon '92	₮₮₮	6
O Chardonnay '90	₮₮₮	6
O Chardonnay '94	₮₮₮	6
O Carso Chardonnay '02	₮₮	6
O Carso Chardonnay '03	₮₮	6
O Carso Sauvignon '01	₮₮	6
O Carso Sauvignon '03	₮₮	6
O Carso Malvasia '03	₮₮	6
O Carso Vitovska '03	₮₮	6

Wine		Rating
O Collio Tocai Friulano '06	₮₮₮	5
O Collio Bianco '06	₮₮	5
O Collio Collio Bianco '03	₮	5
● Collio Collio Rosso '06	₮	5
O Collio Bianco '02	₮₮₮	4
O Collio Tocai Friulano '03	₮₮₮	4
O Collio Tocai Friulano '97	₮₮₮	4
O Collio Tocai Friulano '99	₮₮₮	4
O Collio Tocai Friulano '95	₮₮₮	4
O Collio Tocai Friulano '05	₮₮₮	5
O Collio Bianco '04	₮₮₮	5
O Collio Tocai Friulano '01	₮₮₮	4
O Collio Tocai Friulano '04	₮₮	5
O Collio Bianco '05	₮₮	5

Lis Neris
VIA GAVINANA, 5
34070 SAN LORENZO ISONTINO [GO]
TEL. 048180105
www.lisneris.it

ANNUAL PRODUCTION 350,000 bottles
HECTARES UNDER VINE 54
VITICULTURE METHOD Conventional

When a grower is awarded Three Glasses, it's always a happy moment. For Alvaro Pecorari, to have won the prize for his Fiore di Campo is even more significant. This is a wine from Alvaro's standard line, not one of the selections and riservas that have made his international reputation. It shows that Alvaro's talents can shine through even in wines that are apparently uncomplicated. We say "apparently" because the steel-vinified, tocai-only Fiore di Campo is a wine of subtle shades and nuances. It unveils its armoury little by little, deploying minerality and citrus sensations to finish on varietal sweet almonds. Balanced on the palate, which reprises the nose, it is assertive on entry and full-bodied through to the finish. Lis, from pinot grigio, chardonnay and sauvignon, is up to its usual high standards, showing soft in texture with a long, vanillaed finish, Pinot Grigio Gris has barley sugar, white-fleshed fruit and pennyroyal notes and the velvety Sauvignon Picol is very balsamic. Finally, there is a rich bouquet of candied citrus peel, dried apricots and caramel-covered figs on the traditionally elegant, well-rounded Tal Lùc.

Livon
FRAZ. DOLEGNANO
VIA MONTAREZZA, 33
33048 SAN GIOVANNI AL NATISONE [UD]
TEL. 0432757173
www.livon.it

ANNUAL PRODUCTION 625,000 bottles
HECTARES UNDER VINE 105
VITICULTURE METHOD Conventional

It was another low-key vintage for this leading Friulian cellar. We do not know why some of Livon's standard-bearers have stumbled the way they have but something went wrong in 2005 in particular. It's a shame, even though this big-numbers winery might be able to look on a few tens of thousands of less successful bottles as a minor mishap. We should remember that Livon has more than 100 hectares in Friuli's hill country, including nine at Tenuta RoncAlto. But there were two extremely fine reds on show in the Merlot TiareMate 2005 and the classic TiareBlù from the same vintage. TiareMate does not let its boisterous extract overshadow lovely concentration and structure that lifts the complexity of its fruit sensations. TiareBlù, from the vineyard of the same name at Ruttars, is a 90-10 blend of merlot and cabernet sauvignon that gives pleasing liquorice over a beautifully balanced backdrop of red fruits preserves. Finally, the very dry, fresh-tasting, firm-textured Ribolla Gialla RoncAlto is back on form.

O Fiore di Campo '06	♟♟♟	4*
O Lis '05	♟♟	6
O Pinot Grigio Gris '05	♟♟	5
O Sauvignon Picol '05	♟♟	4*
O Tal Lùc '05	♟♟	7
O Confini '05	♟♟	6
O Pinot Grigio '06	♟♟	4
O Chardonnay Jurosa '05	♟♟	5
O Sauvignon '06	♟	4
O Chardonnay '06		4
O Pinot Grigio Gris '04	♟♟♟	5
O Lis '03	♟♟♟	6
O Tal Lùc '02	♟♟♟	7
O Friuli Isonzo Pinot Grigio Gris '01	♟♟♟	5
O Friuli Isonzo Chardonnay Jurosa '00	♟♟♟	5

● Collio Merlot TiareMate '05	♟♟	5
O Collio Ribolla Gialla RoncAlto '06	♟♟	5
● TiareBlù '05	♟♟	5
● COF Refosco P. R. Riul '05	♟	4
O Collio Tocai Friulano Ronc di Zorz '06	♟	5
O Collio Sauvignon Valbuins '06	♟	5
O Collio Pinot Grigio Braide Grande '06	♟	5
O Collio Bianco Solarco '06	♟	5
● Collio Cabernet Sauvignon RoncAlto '05		6
O Braide Alte '00	♟♟♟	6
● TiareBlù '00	♟♟♟	6
O Braide Alte Grand Cru '98	♟♟♟	6
● TiareBlù '03	♟♟	6

Tenuta Luisa

FRAZ. CORONA
VIA CORMONS, 19
34070 MARIANO DEL FRIULI [GO]
TEL. 048169680
www.viniluisa.com

ANNUAL PRODUCTION 300,000 bottles
HECTARES UNDER VINE 70
VITICULTURE METHOD Conventional

In the heart of the Isonzo DOC zone at Corona, a location that has every right to be considered a subzone, Eddi and Nella Luisa have built up a lovely winery, now run by the competent Michele and Davide. The family is lovely, too, for everyone is involved in the overall plan, adding value that owes much to the enthusiasm with which it is pursued. All this harmony is of course reflected in the wines, especially those from the Luisa line, which we particularly liked at our tastings. This year, three wines vie for first place. The tried and trusted Tocai gives citrus, plum, acacia blossom and sage, signing off with stylishly long length, the commercially underrated Pinot Bianco has elegance, florality and alluringly close-knit yet well-typed freshness, and the surprising Sauvignon offers peach, apricot, tomato leaf, characteristic grip and consistency. We would also give the Pinot Grigio a special mention.

○ Friuli Isonzo Pinot Bianco '06	🍷🍷	4*
○ Friuli Isonzo Sauvignon '06	🍷🍷	4*
○ Friuli Isonzo Tocai Friulano '06	🍷🍷	4*
○ Friuli Isonzo Pinot Grigio '06	🍷🍷	4
● Friuli Isonzo Cabernet Franc '06	🍷	4
○ Friuli Isonzo Chardonnay '06	🍷	4
● Rôl '02	🍷	5
● Friuli Isonzo Cabernet Franc I Ferretti '03	🍷	5
● Friuli Isonzo Cabernet Sauvignon I Ferretti '02		5
○ Friuli Isonzo Tocai Friulano '03	YYY	4
○ Friuli Isonzo Tocai Friulano '05	YY	4
● Friuli Isonzo Cabernet Franc '06	YY	4
○ Friuli Isonzo Tocai Friulano '04	YY	4

Magnàs

VIA CORONA, 47
34071 CORMONS [GO]
TEL. 048160991
www.magnas.it

ANNUAL PRODUCTION 25,000 bottles
HECTARES UNDER VINE 10
VITICULTURE METHOD Conventional

The family of Luciano Visintin, aka Magnàs, set up this winery in the 1970s. Since then, the likeable Luciano and his dependable wife Sonia have made progress, expanding the vine stock, which today covers about ten hectares, and gradually cutting down their dairy farming commitments: not that this stops Luciano from making delectable cheeses every day with the milk from his few cows. For the past few years, the estate has included lovely agriturismo facilities, where guests can savour Sonia's special recipes. In cellar and vineyard, the couple's son Andrea is playing an increasingly important role and is now in charge of winemaking operations. Needless to say, Luciano is always on hand with a quiet suggestion or comment. Yet again, we savoured a superb Sauvignon offering elderflower and pineapple aromas followed by a complex palate of tropical fruit, grapefruit and peach, saltiness and nice length. Pears and apples grace the nose of the Pinot Grigio while the rich, doughy palate reveals good alcohol and length. Fruit-led richness is the hallmark of the Tocai and the Chardonnay shares the overall personality of the entire Magnàs range, which is never aggressive.

○ Friuli Isonzo Pinot Grigio '06	🍷🍷	4*
○ Friuli Isonzo Sauvignon '06	🍷🍷	4*
○ Friuli Isonzo Tocai Friulano '06	🍷🍷	4*
○ Friuli Isonzo Chardonnay '06	🍷	4
○ Friuli Isonzo Pinot Grigio '05	YY	4

Valerio Marinig

VIA BROLO, 41
33040 PREPOTTO [UD]
TEL. 0432713012
www.marinig.it

ANNUAL PRODUCTION 25,000 bottles
HECTARES UNDER VINE 8
VITICULTURE METHOD Conventional

Valerio Marinig's wines are always reliable and sold and distinctly consumer-friendly prices. That is also true of the range we tasted this year. But first let's talk about the winery. The eight hectares under vine are in the valley of the river Judrio, which further upstream separates Slovenia from Italy and at Prepotto marks the border of the Collio and Colli Orientali del Friuli DOC zones. Years ago, the cellar was a single large space but at last Valerio has appropriate facilities for his winemaking, including a very attractive barrel cellar. Valerio's father Sergio is always supportive, especially when it comes to working among the vines, and his mother Marisa is an excellent cook whose delicious nibbles keep visitors and customers happy. Once again, Sauvignon is one of Valerio's best wines and this time earned Two full Glasses for its tomato leaf and elderflower nose, followed by a rich, well-sustained palate of lingering peach and pineapple. The Pinot Bianco is a fine wine while the other whites and the Cabernet are all very well made.

Masut da Rive

VIA MANZONI, 82
34070 MARIANO DEL FRIULI [GO]
TEL. 048169200
www.masutdarive.com

ANNUAL PRODUCTION 100,000 bottles
HECTARES UNDER VINE 20
VITICULTURE METHOD Conventional

When people at Mariano talk about Masut da Rive, they mean Silvano Gallo and his very competent sons Marco and Fabrizio. Outside the town, the name is synonymous with excellent white and red wines. The estate's vines stand on gravelly terrain that lend freshness to the whites but it also contains a layer of iron-rich soil that imbues the reds with structure and cellarability. It is only right that two whites, the Pinot Bianco and the Sauvignon, and a red, the Cabernet Sauvignon, lead the Masut da Rive range this year. The varietal Pinot Bianco has generous fresh citrus and almonds preceding a palate of complexity and elegance whereas the Sauvignon marries subtle elderflower and white peach to fragrant, well-balanced progression on the palate. The Cabernet Sauvignon is one of the best in Friuli. Wave on wave of red fruit, mint, chocolate and leather tempt the nose and return in the mouth. Fresh tropical fruit characterizes the Tocai and the Vigna Candida selection flaunts a distinct minerally note. Last on our list is a fine, spicily rich Cabernet Franc with varietal nuances of hay.

O COF Sauvignon '06	♀♀ 4*
O COF Pinot Bianco '06	♀♀ 4
O COF Tocai Friulano '06	♀ 4
O COF Chardonnay '06	♀ 4
● COF Cabernet Franc '05	♀ 4
● COF Merlot '05	4

O Friuli Isonzo Pinot Bianco '06	♀♀ 4*
O Friuli Isonzo Rive Alte Sauvignon '06	♀♀ 4*
● Friuli Isonzo Cabernet Sauvignon '05	♀♀ 4*
● Friuli Isonzo Cabernet Franc '05	♀♀ 4
O Friuli Isonzo Tocai Friulano Vigna Candida '06	♀♀ 4
O Friuli Isonzo Rive Alte Tocai Friulano '06	♀♀ 4
O Friuli Isonzo Rive Alte Chardonnay '06	♀ 4
O Friuli Isonzo Rive Alte Pinot Grigio '06	♀ 4
● Friuli Isonzo Rive Alte Merlot '05	♀ 4
● Friuli Isonzo Rive Alte Merlot '04	♀♀ 4
● Friuli Isonzo Rosso Semidis '03	♀♀ 5

Davino Meroi

VIA STRETTA, 7B
33042 BUTTRIO [UD]
TEL. 0432674025
parco.meroi@virgilio.it

ANNUAL PRODUCTION 20,000 bottles
HECTARES UNDER VINE 14
VITICULTURE METHOD Conventional

The outgoing Paolo Meroi's cellar is almost directly beneath the church tower at Buttrio, where for two decades Paolo has been successfully combining winemaking with a flourishing restaurant. His new objective is to replant all his old vineyards at the substantial density of 6,000 vines per hectare and switch from Casarsa training to Guyot. Today, the Meroi estate has 14 hectares under vine but there are plans to expand this to about 22 over the next ten years. Paolo has always had Enzo Pontoni to help him out and their collaboration produces warm, complex wines that manage to express power and elegance at the same time. All flaunt wonderful concentration that lets subtle fruit notes peek through. Take the Dominin 2003, for example. Dense, with hints of red fruits and faint spiciness, it has a richly complex, confident front palate. The Tocai Friulano 2006 is full-bodied and intense, its very well-gauged acidity accompanying a savoury finish laced with ripe citrus.

Moschioni

LOC. GAGLIANO
VIA DORIA, 30
33043 CIVIDALE DEL FRIULI [UD]
TEL. 0432730210
vinimoschioni@libero.it

ANNUAL PRODUCTION 35,000 bottles
HECTARES UNDER VINE 13
VITICULTURE METHOD Natural

It's been 20 years since Michele Moschioni started working in the family winery, first in tandem with his father, Davide, and then taking over management responsibilities. Unlike most growers in Friuli, Michele restricts his white vine stock to picolit, concentrating almost all his production on red varieties, native above all but also international. The 13 hectares under vine never yield more than 40 quintals of fruit each, the vineyards are farmed organically, grapes are dried off and lightly raisined before crushing, natural yeasts are used for fermentation and the wine is bottled without filtration. This time, the merlot and cabernet sauvignon-based Rosso Celtico is even better than before. Higher than average yields of 60 quintals per hectare have given the structure elegance and a hint of geranium in the alluring aromatics refines the substantial warm red fruit without cramping the wine's austere complexity. Never before have we seen such complexity or elegance in Moschioni reds and that was why we awarded the wine its first Three Glasses. Cinchona, plums and assertive tannins are the hallmarks of the upfront, full-bodied Pignolo, a truly excellent wine.

● COF Rosso Dominin '03	♥♥ 8
○ COF Tocai Friulano '06	♥♥ 6
● COF Merlot Ros di Buri '05	♥♥ 6
● COF Rosso Nestri '04	♥♥ 4
○ COF Picolit '05	♥♥ 7
○ COF Verduzzo Friulano '05	♥♥ 6
○ COF Sauvignon '05	♥♥ 7
○ COF Chardonnay '05	♥ 7
○ COF Chardonnay '03	♀♀ 7
○ COF Chardonnay '04	♀♀ 7
○ COF Tocai Friulano '03	♀♀ 6
○ COF Tocai Friulano '04	♀♀ 6
● COF Rosso Dominin '01	♀♀ 8
● COF Rosso Dominin '02	♀♀ 8

● COF Rosso Celtico '04	♥♥♥ 6
● COF Pignolo '04	♥♥ 8
● COF Refosco P. R. '04	♥♥ 5
● COF Rosso Reâl '04	♥♥ 6
● COF Schioppettino '04	♥ 7
● COF Rosso Celtico '01	♀♀ 6
● COF Rosso Celtico '02	♀♀ 6
● COF Rosso Celtico Non Filtrato '03	♀♀ 6
● COF Pignolo '01	♀♀ 8
● COF Pignolo '02	♀♀ 8
● COF Pignolo Non Filtrato '03	♀♀ 8
● COF Schioppettino Non Filtrato '03	♀♀ 6
● COF Reâl Non Filtrato '03	♀♀ 6

Mulino delle Tolle

FRAZ. SEVEGLIANO
VIA MULINO DELLE TOLLE, 15
33050 BAGNARIA ARSA [UD]
TEL. 0432928113
www.mulinodelletolle.it

ANNUAL PRODUCTION 100,000 bottles
HECTARES UNDER VINE 22
VITICULTURE METHOD Conventional

Cousins Giorgio and Eliseo Bertossi keep a
sure hand on their estate, which includes
lovely agriturismo facilities as well as a
winery on the road to Grado. Work on a
modern cellar has now been completed,
which should raise the quality bar even
higher. Giorgio is the winery's oenologist
and everyone knows how good he is but to
manage year after year to turn out a top-
quality range, regularly hitting the mark with
the same wine types, is no easy task. His
Malvasia and Bianco Palmade are again
excellent this time and are joined by a Tocai
that is remarkably weighty and rich in the
mouth, disclosing distinct almonds and
nectarines. Invitingly, the Malvasia's
aromatics include dried flowers, orange peel
and pears. Entry on the palate is full and
well sustained through to a finish of dried
flowers and melons. Bianco Palmade is a
blend of malvasia, chardonnay and
sauvignon that shows rich and creamy with
all sorts of nuances that find complete
harmony on the palate before the long finale
closes with confectioner's cream and fresh
citrus. And only a step or two behind is the
fresh-tasting, vigorous Sauvignon.

Muzic

LOC. BIVIO, 4
34070 SAN FLORIANO DEL COLLIO [GO]
TEL. 0481884201
www.cantinamuzic.it

ANNUAL PRODUCTION 90,000 bottles
HECTARES UNDER VINE 15
VITICULTURE METHOD Conventional

Giovanni Muzic is known as Ivan to his
friends. Gradually, he and his wife Orietta
are climbing up the Friulian quality ladder.
Truth to tell, the Muzic family has a tradition
of winemaking as solid as the foundations
of the delightful 16th-century underground
cellar where Ivan welcomes friends and
visitors. Contributing to the fine quality of
Muzic wines are the local climate and soil at
San Floriano, one of the Friulian Collio's
special subzones. And since we are in the
Collio, three whites top the Muzic list after
our tastings. Bric is a blend of malvasia,
ribolla and tocai that opens slowly to win
you over with its complex banana and
pineapples notes, and a creamy-textured
finish. Equally impressive is the Sauvignon
Vigna Pàjze, an assertive wine with pungent
bell pepper tempered by peach-like
sensations and refreshing minerality in the
finish. Finally, there had to be a Ribolla
Gialla, one of local growers' favourite
varieties. Ivan's version is varietal, fresh-
tasting and subtly elegant overall.

O Friuli Aquileia Malvasia '06	▼▼	3*
O Friuli Aquileia Bianco Palmade '06	▼▼	4
O Friuli Aquileia Tocai Friulano '06	▼▼	3*
● Friuli Aquileia Cabernet Franc '06	▼	3
O Friuli Aquileia Sauvignon '06	▼	4
● Friuli Aquileia Refosco P. R. '06	▼	4
O Friuli Aquileia Malvasia '05	▼▼	3
● Friuli Aquileia Rosso Sabellius '01	▼▼	4
● Friuli Aquileia Rosso Sabellius '03	▼▼	4

O Collio Bianco Bric '06	▼▼	4*
O Collio Sauvignon V. Pàjze '06	▼▼	4*
O Collio Ribolla Gialla '06	▼▼	4*
O Collio Chardonnay '06	▼	4
O Collio Tocai Friulano '06	▼	4
● Friuli Isonzo Merlot '05	▼	4
● Friuli Isonzo Cabernet Franc '05	▼	4
O Collio Pinot Grigio '06	▼	4

Pierpaolo Pecorari
VIA TOMMASEO, 36C
34070 SAN LORENZO ISONTINO [GO]
TEL. 0481808775
www.pierpaolopecorari.it

Perusini
LOC. GRAMOGLIANO
VIA TORRIONE, 13
33040 CORNO DI ROSAZZO [UD]
TEL. 0432675018
www.perusini.com

ANNUAL PRODUCTION 160,000 bottles
HECTARES UNDER VINE 32
VITICULTURE METHOD Certified organic

ANNUAL PRODUCTION 50,000 bottles
HECTARES UNDER VINE 12
VITICULTURE METHOD Conventional

This estate is in the upper part of the Isonzo flatlands, where the influence of the Adriatic, cool winds from central Europe and shallow, well-drained alluvial soil create an outstanding environment for growing grapes. The list of wines is long and the labels are not always easy to read. Several types are made. The fresh, easy-drinking young base wines are vinified in steel and identified by variety name only. Altis is the label on three more challenging, structured whites, vinified with skin contact and aged on the lees, and the oak-aged wines, for which the vine name is accompanied by a brand name. From the first category, we picked out the Pinot Grigio, Sauvignon and Malvasia for their classic styling and a fresh note that nicely offsets the alcohol. The Altis wines did not quite live up to their ambitions and only the Pinot Grigio stood out from the pack. From the more ambitious products, we noted the complex, lingering sensations, especially on the palate, of the Kolaus and Soris.

Teresa Perusini runs an estate of considerable complexity with the effective support of her husband, Giacomo De Pace. The 60 estate-owned hectares is partly planted to vine but much has been left as woodland. A number of farmhouses have been completely converted and made over to Teresa's tastes. We should note, too, that Resi, as she is known to one and all, is an art historian. There's also a delightful restaurant, Il Postiglione, to complete the estate's hospitality resources. But visitors' curiosity will be aroused by the truncated pyramid tower whose upper floors now serves as the estate's offices and whose basement is the barrique cellar. Designed by the University of Venice, it complements the noble lines of the main residence. In the vineyards, Pierpaolo Sirch is in charge while the Terra&Vini group looks after the cellar. Again, it was the Pinot Grigio that we liked. The 2006 edition is redolent of yellow apples over fresh fruit salad. Its broad, well-orchestrated palate starts out well, progresses seamlessly and lingers endlessly. Meanwhile on the red front, we noted that the wines are a little slow to evolve.

O Chardonnay Soris '05	♟♟	6
O Pinot Grigio '06	♟♟	4
O Sauvignon '06	♟♟	4
O Sauvignon Kolaus '05	♟♟	6
O Malvasia '06	♟♟	4
● Merlot '05	♟	4
O Sauvignon Altis '05	♟	5
O Pinot Grigio Altis '05	♟	5
O Merlot Baolar '04	♟	6
O Pinot Bianco Altis '05		5
● Refosco P. R. '05		4
O Pinot Bianco Altis '04	♟♟	5
O Pinot Grigio Altis '04	♟♟	5

O COF Pinot Grigio '06	♟♟	4
O COF Ribolla Gialla '06	♟	4
O COF Riesling '06	♟	4
● COF Merlot Etichetta Nera '05	♟	5
● COF Cabernet Sauvignon '05		5
● COF Rosso del Postiglione '05		5
O COF Sauvignon '06		4
O COF Chardonnay '06		4
● COF Merlot '05		5
O COF Pinot Grigio '04	♟♟	4
O COF Pinot Grigio '05	♟♟	4

Petrucco

VIA MORPURGO, 12
33042 BUTTRIO [UD]
TEL. 0432674387
www.vinipetrucco.it

Petrussa

VIA ALBANA, 49
33040 PREPOTTO [UD]
TEL. 0432713192
www.petrussa.it

ANNUAL PRODUCTION 100,000 bottles
HECTARES UNDER VINE 25
VITICULTURE METHOD Conventional

ANNUAL PRODUCTION 60,000 bottles
HECTARES UNDER VINE 10
VITICULTURE METHOD Conventional

The passion that husband and wife team Paolo and Lina Petrucco devote to their winemaking is rewarded by a return to a full profile after a year in the Guide's Other Wineries section. Paolo, who is an engineer, told us frankly he was unhappy with the results of his range and explained what he was going to do about it, putting agronomist Marco Simonit in charge of vineyard management and appointing Gianni Menotti as consultant winemaker. Both are contributing to the experience of the estate's own oenologist, Flavio Cabas, and results are already coming through, not so much in the wines themselves as in the winery's general organization and planning. Two wines stand out, and they were crafted by Flavio, the Picolit 2005 and the Pignolo 2003. Both are truly iconic, as the former is a native sweet wine and the latter an equally autochthonous red. The Picolit tempts the nose with figs and dried apricots, its palate showing sweet and doughy in texture with just the right note of acidity, good complexity and fine length. On the nose, the Picolit gives blackberries and plums while the assertive extract is nicely gauged.

Parsimony and tenacity have been the secrets of brothers Paolo and Gianni Petrussa as they expanded their vine stock to the present eight hectares, which they flank with a couple more they rent. They have also extended the cellar little by little, enabling them to tackle their vinification and storage problems, using force of ingenuity where technology was lacking. But the brothers nurse hopes of increasing production and have drafted a plan that effectively doubles the cellar's floor area. The Petrussas are equally skilled at vinifying white, red or sweet wines but this time round, the Verduzzo that they release as Pensiero 2004 isn't up to its usual standards while their version of Prepotto's signature wine, Schioppettino, is marvellous. Blueberry and currant fragrances are echoed on the intense yet charmingly elegant palate. The Cabernet hints at black cherries and sweet peppers while the Tocai Friulano and Sauvignon are intense and beautifully proportioned.

○ COF Picolit '05	♟♟	7
● COF Pignolo Ronco del Balbo '03	♟♟	6
○ COF Pinot Grigio '06	♟	4
● COF Refosco P. R. Ronco del Balbo '05	♟	4
○ COF Ribolla Gialla '06	♟	4
○ COF Tocai Friulano '06	♟	4
○ COF Chardonnay '06		4
○ COF Sauvignon '06		4

● COF Cabernet '06	♟♟	4*
● COF Schioppettino '04	♟♟	6
○ COF Sauvignon '06	♟♟	4*
○ COF Tocai Friulano '06	♟♟	4*
○ COF Pinot Bianco '06	♟	4
○ Pensiero '04	♟	6
○ COF Chardonnay '05	♟	5
● COF Merlot '06		4

Roberto Picèch

LOC. PRADIS, 11
34071 CORMONS [GO]
TEL. 048160347
www.picech.it

ANNUAL PRODUCTION 28,000 bottles
HECTARES UNDER VINE 7
VITICULTURE METHOD Conventional

Roberto Picèch has some of his father Egidio's traits, which has led to his inheriting the nickname Ribel. An immensely sociable man, Roberto can also be very determined in following a path that particularly in the past led to the release of wines that clashed with accepted wisdom. As is so often the case, a dedicated group of admirers grew up around those very wines. We should say straight away that Roberto seems to have calmed down, partly because early in the year he acquired a new daughter with a sunny disposition, Athena. His new responsibilities as a father, and the completion of structuring work in the cellar, have added focus to Roberto's winemaking. His seven hectares under vine have produced a complex, salty Bianco Jelka. Its rich fruit reveals no trace of the ten months it spent in wood but it does foreground extract from the eight to ten days' contact with the skins of its ribolla, malvasia and tocai grapes. We also enjoyed the elegant intensity of the Pinot Bianc, despite its robust alcohol. The Malvasia and Tocai are textbook stuff.

Tenuta Pinni

VIA SANT'OSVALDO, 3
33096 SAN MARTINO AL TAGLIAMENTO [PN]
TEL. 0434899464
www.tenutapinni.com

ANNUAL PRODUCTION 40,000 bottles
HECTARES UNDER VINE 13.8
VITICULTURE METHOD Conventional

The youthful enthusiasm of brothers Francesco and Roberto Pinni is tempered by professional skill that enables them to run their cellar, now ten years old, with determination, insight and an eye on the future. This year, they presented us with a fine series of wines from their lovely 16th-century villa in an ancient flatlands village near Spilimbergo. Early on, the cellar attracted attention for its reds but in recent vintages, it has made all-round improvements that have brought the whites up to a very high standard indeed. We could only take our hats off at the firm structure and fruit-led softness of the Tocai, not to mention the elegant bell pepper and citrus fragrances of a Sauvignon that signs off with a long savoury finale. But those excellent reds are still being made. We liked the poise and marked varietal character of the Refosco as well as its pepper and clove spice, and ripe plum-led fruit.

O Collio Bianco Jelka '05	🍷🍷 5
O Collio Malvasia '06	🍷🍷 5
O Collio Pinot Bianco '06	🍷🍷 5
O Collio Tocai Friulano '06	🍷🍷 5
● Collio Rosso Ris. '04	🍷 6
O Collio Bianco Jelka '99	🍷🍷🍷 4
O Collio Bianco Jelka '00	🍷🍷 4
O Collio Bianco Jelka '03	🍷🍷 5
O Collio Bianco Jelka '04	🍷🍷 5
● Collio Rosso Ris. '01	🍷🍷 6
● Collio Rosso '02	🍷🍷 4
● Collio Rosso '03	🍷🍷 4

O Friuli Grave Tocai Friulano '06	🍷🍷 4*
O Sauvignon '06	🍷🍷 4*
● Refosco P. R. '05	🍷🍷 4*
● Cabernet Franc '05	🍷 4
● Cabernet Sauvignon '05	🍷 4
O Chardonnay '06	🍷 4
O Pinot Grigio '06	🍷 4
● Friuli Grave Rosso '00	🍷🍷 5
● Friuli Grave Rosso '02	🍷🍷 5
● Friuli Grave Rosso della Tenuta '03	🍷🍷 5
O Ucelut '01	🍷🍷 5
O Ucelut '00	🍷🍷 5

Vigneti Pittaro
LOC. ZOMPICCHIA
VIA UDINE, 67
33033 CODROIPO [UD]
TEL. 0432904726
www.vignetipittaro.com

ANNUAL PRODUCTION 500,000 bottles
HECTARES UNDER VINE 90
VITICULTURE METHOD Conventional

Piero Pittaro has long been a beacon on the Friulian wine scene, partly because he has served the world association of oenologists in prominent roles and has also headed the regional authority's wine service. He is also one of the few producers of sparkling wines in Friuli to use the classic method and his sparklers are both appealing and solidly structured, like this 1999 Brut Etichetta Oro selection. At the Pittaro winery is a museum of wine-related glass with spectacular collections of glasses, bottles and other containers as well as fascinating reconstructions of wine spaces of the past. The cellar manager is the outstanding oenologist Stefano, who is also the regional head of the Federdoc association. It is interesting to note that Pittaro uses glass stoppers for young-drinking wines instead of the traditional cork. Piero is the only major producer of Manzoni Bianco, a cross of pinot bianco and riesling renano, and the wine gives intense peach and pear before the citrus-laced palate progresses with attractive complexity. Varietal notes dominate the Traminer Aromatico while the riesling, chardonnay and sauvignon Bianco has room for improvement.

Plozner
FRAZ. BARBEANO
VIA DELLE PRESE, 19
33097 SPILIMBERGO [PN]
TEL. 04272902
www.plozner.it

ANNUAL PRODUCTION 500,000 bottles
HECTARES UNDER VINE 55
VITICULTURE METHOD Conventional

The Plozner winery's steady growth in recent years has been remarkable. A glance at the results below might make you think it was located in Friuli's hill country and not on the gravel-rich alluvial flatlands of Spilimbergo. In line with the old adage that you should aim high but keep you feet on the ground, the cellar releases a premium line from clonal selection that has further boosted quality. We are happy to point out the clean elegance of Bianco Moscabianca, from 40-year-old tocai clones, the successful marriage of green tomato leaf notes with softer peach-like sensations in the Sauvignon Quattroperuno Uno, the rich fruit of the Merlot Peeecora Nera and the full minerality of the Pinot Grigio Malpelo. Often, premium labels detract from the quality of standard lines but Plozner bucks that trend, too, as you can tell from the traditional Sauvignon with its bell pepper and citrus, the very varietal Pinot Grigio and the fresh-tasting, pineapple-led Chardonnay.

O Manzoni '06	♟♟ 4
O Friuli Grave Traminer Aromatico '06	♟♟ 4
O Friuli Grave Bianco '05	♟ 4
O Friuli Grave Chardonnay Mousqué '06	♟ 4
O Friuli Grave Sauvignon '06	♟ 4
O Pittaro Brut Etichetta Oro '99	♟ 6
● Moscato Rosa Valzer in Rosa '06	♟ 4

O Bianco Moscabianca '06	♟♟ 4
O Friuli Grave Pinot Grigio '06	♟♟ 4
O Friuli Grave Sauvignon '06	♟♟ 4
O Pinot Grigio Malpelo '06	♟♟ 4
O Friuli Grave Chardonnay '06	♟♟ 3*
O Sauvignon Quattroperuno Uno '06	♟♟ 4
● Merlot Peeecora Nera '05	♟♟ 4
O Friuli Grave Tocai Friulano '06	♟ 3
● Friuli Grave Merlot '05	♟ 3
● Refosco P. R. Bastiano '06	4
O Sauvignon Quattroperuno Uno '05	♟♟ 4
O Bianco Moscabianca '05	♟♟ 4
O Pinot Grigio Malpelo '05	♟♟ 4

Damijan Podversic
VIA BRIGATA PAVIA, 61
34170 GORIZIA
TEL. 048178217
damijan.go@virgilio.it

ANNUAL PRODUCTION 24,000 bottles
HECTARES UNDER VINE 10
VITICULTURE METHOD   Natural

Three wines vinified in truncated cone-shaped oak vats with more than 60 days' skin contact, no temperature control and no selected yeasts or enzymes before ageing for about two years in 20-30 hectolitre barrels and going into bottle without fining or filtration are Damijan Podversic's impressive calling cards. The sediment in the bottle is to be welcomed because it helps to conserve the wine. These three are wines that should not be served too cold as this would emphasize the extract. There's a chardonnay, tocai and malvasia-based Bianco, a territory-focused monovarietal, Ribolla, and a Rosso from merlot and cabernet sauvignon in which, despite what critics sometimes claim, the varietal characteristics are clearly distinguishable. Take him or leave him, Damijan is not a man to compromise and the growing year also played its part. We were very impressed this time by Kaplja, which is showing itself long-lived, and particularly by Prelit, where plum, blackcurrant cordial and tobacco accompany a warm, complex palate with good length and texture. Only the Ribolla failed to live up to expectations. There is a hint of asperity and a bitter note on the back palate that detract from a good profile overall.

Aldo Polencic
LOC. PLESSIVA, 13
34071 CORMONS [GO]
TEL. 048161027
aldopolencic@virgilio.it

ANNUAL PRODUCTION   20,000 bottles
HECTARES UNDER VINE 7
VITICULTURE METHOD   Conventional

Over the past two years, Aldo Polencic, who runs this winery with his father Ferdinando, has been busy extending the cellar and reorganizing his work spaces. Despite this, average quality of Aldo's wines has remained high and in fact his Tocai Friulano Bianco degli Ulivi went through to the Three Glass finals. The words "degli Ulivi" on the label should distinguish the wines that go into 500-litre oak barrels but they are absent from the label of the Pinot Grigio, which is part-aged in wood. Aldo takes advantage of occasional consultancy input from his sister Marinka, an expert oenologist who works in Tuscany, and his wines are noteworthy for their substantial structure, rich mouthfeel and robust alcohol. In a nutshell, these are wines to match with hearty fare, not for anytime drinking. That is certainly the case with the alcohol and glycerine-rich Tocai Friulano Bianco degli Ulivi, a salty, long-lingering wine redolent of pears and peaches. Elegance is not the strong suit of Aldo's Pinot Bianco, an intense, full-bodied wine and the same can be said of his Pinot Grigio.

● Rosso Prelit '04	🍷🍷 6
○ Kaplja '04	🍷🍷 6
○ Ribolla Gialla '04	🍷 6
○ Ribolla Gialla '03	🍷🍷 6
○ Kaplja '03	🍷🍷 6
○ Collio Bianco '00	🍷🍷 5

○ Collio Tocai Friulano Bianco degli Ulivi '06	🍷🍷 6
○ Collio Pinot Bianco degli Ulivi '06	🍷🍷 6
○ Collio Pinot Grigio '06	🍷🍷 5
○ Collio Tocai Friulano '00	🍷🍷🍷 4
○ Collio Tocai Friulano '03	🍷🍷 4
○ Collio Pinot Bianco degli Ulivi '05	🍷🍷 6
○ Collio Tocai Friulano Unico '05	🍷🍷 6
○ Collio Tocai Friulano '05	🍷🍷 6
○ Collio Pinot Grigio '05	🍷🍷 5

Isidoro Polencic

LOC. PLESSIVA, 12
34071 CORMONS [GO]
TEL. 048160655
www.polencic.com

Flavio Pontoni

VIA PERUZZI, 8
33042 BUTTRIO [UD]
TEL. 0432674352
www.pontoni.it

ANNUAL PRODUCTION 120,000 bottles
HECTARES UNDER VINE 25
VITICULTURE METHOD Conventional

ANNUAL PRODUCTION 30,000 bottles
HECTARES UNDER VINE 5
VITICULTURE METHOD Conventional

Isidoro Polencic's estate is a comprehensive summary of Collio winemaking for our hero has plots in several parts of the DOC zone with differing soil types and site climates. If we add to this the experience of his father Doro and the enthusiastic contribution of youngsters Alex, Elisabetta and Michele, who acts as technical manager, it is easy to see why the estate is so successful. For now, we can enjoy yet another excellent vintage with three wines that reached our finals. The Pinot Bianco is subtle and delicately mineral. The Pinot Grigio, a Polencic classic, proffers very intense fruit that melds with subtle yeast sensations and the Tocai Fisc, from a vineyard in an exceptionally good location, is a wonderful medley of fresh pennyroyal and wild herbs with richer notes of peaches and almond milk. There is distinct tropical fruit in the Chardonnay and the tempting Bianco is unashamedly fresh-tasting. We liked the palate of the Sauvignon, which mingles sage and bell pepper with white-fleshed fruit. Finally, the Tocai is fragrant with orange peel and hazelnut cream aromas.

Flavio Pontoni's estate can now look back on just over a century of history. Grapes were first grown here in 1904 by Flavio's grandfather Luigi, his father Giuseppe carried on the tradition and now it is Flavio's turn. His four hectares under vine plus one that is leased mean that he can only bottle about 30,000 units in an average year. The cellar is small and vinification takes place under the watchful eye of Giovanni Munisso. Like many other small growers in Buttrio, Flavio has four rooms – the Braidès agriturismo – for farmstays to pad out the family budget. This time, we thought his Pinot Grigio was excellent, showing as broad swath of aromatics and a fresh, warm palate that progresses elegantly against an appealing backdrop of confectioner's cream. The Malvasia reveals the variety's trademark green apples and lavender. The Sauvignon is intense on nose and palate but also slightly held in check by rather inelegantly assertive aromatics. Finally, the Chardonnay is fresh-tasting yet distinctly yeasty, with aromatic nuances on the back palate.

O Collio Pinot Bianco '06	🍷🍷 4*
O Collio Tocai Friulano Fisc '06	🍷🍷 5
O Collio Pinot Grigio '06	🍷🍷 4*
O Collio Bianco '06	🍷🍷 4
O Collio Tocai Friulano '06	🍷🍷 4
O Collio Chardonnay '06	🍷🍷 4
O Collio Sauvignon '06	🍷🍷 4
O Collio Ribolla Gialla '06	🍷 4
O Collio Pinot Grigio '98	🍷🍷🍷 4
O Collio Tocai Friulano '04	🍷🍷🍷 4
O Collio Tocai Friulano '05	🍷🍷 4
O Collio Pinot Grigio '04	🍷🍷 4
O Collio Pinot Grigio '05	🍷🍷 4
● Oblin Ros '01	🍷🍷 6
● Oblin Ros '03	🍷🍷 6

O COF Pinot Grigio '06	🍷🍷 4*
O COF Chardonnay '06	🍷 4
O COF Malvasia Istriana '06	🍷 4
O COF Sauvignon '06	🍷 4
O COF Tocai Friulano '06	🍷 3
O COF Verduzzo Friulano '06	🍷 4
O COF Chardonnay '05	🍷🍷 3
O COF Malvasia Istriana '05	🍷🍷 3

Primosic

FRAZ. OSLAVIA
LOC. MADONNINA DI OSLAVIA, 3
34170 GORIZIA
TEL. 0481535153
www.primosic.com

ANNUAL PRODUCTION 200,000 bottles
HECTARES UNDER VINE 31
VITICULTURE METHOD Conventional

In the past three years, Primosic sent first two then three wines to our finals, proof that quality at the winery is exceptionally high. It is justly a source of pride for Silvestro Primosic, whose first bottles date from 1956 and who in 1967 was the first to release wines with Collio on the label. Today, the estate is run by his sons Marko and Boris but Silvestro is always on hand with a wise word of advice. Marko is a very competent young grower who has an important role in the Consorzio Collio. In fact, he is one of the minds behind the consortium, thanks to his knowledge of world markets. The estate has 26 hectares in the hill country and five on the Isonzo flatlands, grapes from the latter going, with purchased fruit, into the Palmade line, whose biggest seller is Pinot Grigio. The Ribolla Gialla Riserva gets better with each passing year, revealing remarkable breadth on the harmonious palate along with satisfying structure and length. Chardonnay Gmajne is reminiscent of the great wines of Burgundy with its carefully gauged use of wood and rich, creamy texture. The Tocai, too, is astonishingly rich, giving pear, tea and citrus-led aromatics.

Doro Princic

LOC. PRADIS, 5
34071 CORMONS [GO]
TEL. 048160723
doroprincic@virgilio.it

ANNUAL PRODUCTION 60,000 bottles
HECTARES UNDER VINE 10
VITICULTURE METHOD Conventional

What can we say about a cellar whose humblest white jostled for a place in the Three Glass finals? Add the sheer "simpatia" that Sandro Princic and his wife Grazia dispense to one and all and you will understand our enthusiasm. Sandro is the son of the legendary Doro, who passed away a few years ago and whose modest property was the benchmark for premium wines when few wineries focused on quality. Towards the end, Doro no longer even needed to taste a wine: he could tell you how good it was by sniffing the glass. Sandro does not restrict himself to sniffing wines but he won't let you buy any of his until you have tasted most of the range. Luckily, it's not a big list comprising only five whites and two reds. They say that wines resemble their makers. In most cases, this is not true but Sandro is an exception if we consider the generous opulence of his wines' structure, aromatics and appealing drinkability, despite substantial alcohol. Sandro's Tocai has all these characteristics. Sometimes, it even outperforms his signature Pinot Bianco and on this occasion it swept up Three Glasses. But don't miss Sandro's Malvasia, one of the most varietal versions around, or his warm Sauvignon.

O Collio Chardonnay Gmajne '05	⧉ 6
O Collio Tocai Friulano Belvedere '06	⧉ 5
O Collio Ribolla di Oslavia Ris. '05	⧉ 6
O Collio Sauvignon Gmajne '06	⧉ 6
O Ribolla Gialla '06	⧉ 5
O Collio Pinot Grigio Murno '06	⧉ 5
O Collio Bianco Klin Ris. '03	⧉ 6
O Collio Chardonnay Gmajne '03	⧉ 5
O Collio Sauvignon Gmajne '05	⧉ 5
O Collio Chardonnay Gmajne '04	⧉ 5
O Collio Bianco Klin Ris. '01	⧉ 5
O Collio Ribolla Gialla di Oslavia '04	⧉ 5

O Collio Tocai Friulano '06	⧉ 5
O Collio Malvasia '06	⧉ 5
O Collio Pinot Bianco '06	⧉ 5
O Collio Sauvignon '06	⧉ 5
O Collio Pinot Grigio '06	⧉ 5
O Collio Pinot Bianco '95	⧉ 5
O Collio Pinot Bianco '02	⧉ 5
O Collio Pinot Bianco '04	⧉ 5
O Collio Pinot Bianco '05	⧉ 5
O Collio Tocai Friulano '93	⧉ 5
O Collio Tocai Friulano '05	⧉ 5
O Collio Tocai Friulano '04	⧉ 5
O Collio Malvasia '05	⧉ 5
O Collio Pinot Grigio '05	⧉ 5
O Collio Sauvignon '05	⧉ 5

Dario Raccaro

VIA SAN GIOVANNI, 87
34071 CORMONS [GO]
TEL. 048161425

ANNUAL PRODUCTION 25,000 bottles
HECTARES UNDER VINE 4.5
VITICULTURE METHOD Conventional

For many years, Dario Raccaro has looked on his Tocai Friulano as the best version there is, although we have not always agreed. But this time we were more inclined to assent, from our first tastings of the various vats in which this stellar wine was maturing. It is a wine we could justly call legendary, in the sense that the origin of the Rolat vines is shrouded in mystery. It is known that the first rooted cuttings were planted in the early 20th century. That much is history but legend at Cormons would have it that they came directly from Hungary, something that scientific research has been unable to prove. Whatever the case, subsequent plants were propagated from those original vines, which today provide the fruit for Dario Raccaro's stunning Tocai Friulano. Vinified and aged exclusively in steel, it is elegant, intense, full bodied, warm, savoury, rich, mouthfilling and very, very long. Three Glasses and White of the Year. But what about Dario's Collio Bianco, from tocai, sauvignon and pinot grigio? Incredibly broad on nose and palate, it expands seamlessly in the mouth, the aromas lingering seductively. Finally, the alcohol and glycerine-rich Malvasia leaves a sensation of softness.

O Collio Tocai Friulano Vigna del Rolat '06	TTT	5
O Collio Bianco '06	TT	5
O Collio Malvasia '06	TT	5
O Collio Bianco '02	YYY	4
O Collio Bianco '03	YYY	5
O Collio Tocai Friulano '01	YYY	4
O Collio Tocai Friulano '05	YYY	5
O Collio Tocai Friulano '04	YYY	5
O Collio Tocai Friulano '00	YYY	4
O Collio Bianco '04	YY	5
O Collio Malvasia '05	YY	5
O Collio Malvasia '04	YY	5
O Collio Tocai Friulano '03	YY	5
O Collio Tocai Friulano '02	YY	5

Teresa Raiz

VIA DELLA ROGGIA, 22
33040 POVOLETTO [UD]
TEL. 0432679556
www.teresaraiz.it

ANNUAL PRODUCTION 140,000 bottles
HECTARES UNDER VINE 20
VITICULTURE METHOD Conventional

Paolo Tosolini holds an oenology qualification from the Conegliano Veneto wine school. In 1971, he founded this winery, which he named after his grandmother, the woman who instilled in him a love of wine. Patiently, he has built up the vine stock to 13 hectares at the cellar and a further seven a few kilometres away. The vineyards have been almost completely replanted with the collaboration of the French nurseryman Pépinières Guillaume, taking the vine density from 1,200 to the present 5,000 plants per hectare. The fruit is first quality and Paolo achieves high volume production through careful purchases in the area. For some time, the Terra&Vini team has been consulting. The most successful wine on the list is the Pinot Grigio, much of which goes for export. But the Teresa Raiz product that we like best is still the elegant Ribolla Gialla, an intense fruit and flower-led wine with good structure and sinew. We also thought the Tocai Friulano was impressive. It opens slowly but expands on the palate into a truly delicious finish.

O COF Ribolla Gialla '06	TT	4*
O COF Tocai Friulano '06	TT	4*
O Chardonnay Le Marsure '06	T	4
O Pinot Grigio Le Marsure '06	T	4
O Sauvignon Le Marsure '06	T	4
O COF Pinot Grigio '06	T	4
● COF Rosso Decano Rosso '04	T	6
● Merlot Le Marsure '05		4
O COF Pinot Grigio '05	YY	4
O COF Ribolla Gialla '04	YY	4
O COF Ribolla Gialla '03	YY	5
O Pinot Grigio Le Marsure '04	YY	3*

Rocca Bernarda

FRAZ. IPPLIS
VIA ROCCA BERNARDA, 27
33040 PREMARIACCO [UD]
TEL. 0432716914
www.roccabernarda.com

ANNUAL PRODUCTION 200,000 bottles
HECTARES UNDER VINE 55
VITICULTURE METHOD Conventional

You breathe in history on a visit to this lovely winery dominated by the recently restored 17th-century Rocca. From the Valvason-Maniago family, the first owners, to the Sovereign Order of Malta to which it currently belongs, some 500 years have passed. But if you were expecting a backward-looking cellar reluctant to change, you would be wrong. This year, the range prepared by Paolo Dolce and Piedmont-born technician Marco Monchiero, which is universally known for an excellent Picolit, took us by surprise with a fine line-up of '06 wines. The Tocai seamlessly fuses citron with orange and lemon-like sensations and hints of yeasts. The Pinot Grigio is fragrant, showing subtle acacia blossom and biscuits. "Fresh-tasting" is the adjective for the Chardonnay with its vibrant notes of orange, banana and pineapple while the Sauvignon suggests "well rounded". The Ribolla Gialla may not be particularly varietal with its marked fruit perceptions but it is attractive. But let's go back to the Picolit. It's back on top form both for its alluring mosaic of dried apricot, citrus fruits, figs and vanilla and for its elegantly restrained, balanced progression in the mouth.

Paolo Rodaro

LOC. SPESSA
VIA CORMONS, 60
33040 CIVIDALE DEL FRIULI [UD]
TEL. 0432716066
paolorodaro@yahoo.it

ANNUAL PRODUCTION 200,000 bottles
HECTARES UNDER VINE 40
VITICULTURE METHOD Conventional

We visited Paolo Rodaro's winery when the harvest was in full swing and we were struck by the thousands of cases he had ready for the grapes that would go into his Romain wines. As well as being the label for products made with fruit grown near Bosco Romagno, it also indicates his way of interpreting refosco, schioppettino, pignolo and merlot, leaving the fruit to dry for a whole month in plastic cases before crushing. According to Paolo, this overripening is not intended to make the wines more concentrated. He wants the grapes to ripen to a degree that cannot be achieved by leaving them on the vine. The 2006 Rodaro Chardonnay's intense, complex ripe fruit is reprised on the palate, which is fat, substantial and very long. Finally, the Pignolo Romain 2004 has moderately intense red fruit followed by an assertive, well-defined palate whose beautifully handled extract lifts the finale.

O COF Picolit '05	♟♟ 8
O COF Pinot Grigio '06	♟♟ 4*
O COF Tocai Friulano '06	♟♟ 4*
O COF Chardonnay '06	♟♟ 4
O COF Ribolla Gialla '06	♟♟ 4
O COF Sauvignon '06	♟♟ 4
O COF Bianco Vineis '06	♟ 4
● COF Refosco P. R. '06	♟ 4
● COF Merlot Centis '01	♟♟ 6
● COF Merlot Centis '03	♟♟ 5
● COF Merlot Centis '02	♟♟ 6

O COF Chardonnay '06	♟♟ 4
O COF Picolit '05	♟♟ 7
O Ronc '05	♟♟ 4
O COF Sauvignon '06	♟♟ 4
● COF Pignolo Romain '04	♟♟ 6
● COF Schioppettino Romain '05	♟♟ 6
● COF Merlot Romain '04	♟ 6
O COF Ribolla Gialla '06	♟ 4
O COF Tocai Friulano '06	♟ 4
O COF Verduzzo Friulano '06	♟ 4
● COF Refosco P. R. Romain '03	♟♟♟ 6
O Ronc '00	♟♟♟ 4
O COF Sauvignon Bosc Romain '96	♟♟♟ 5
O COF Picolit '02	♟♟ 7
O COF Picolit '04	♟♟ 7
O COF Picolit '03	♟♟ 7

Roncada

LOC. RONCADA, 5
34071 CORMONS [GO]
TEL. 048161394
www.roncada.34x.com

ANNUAL PRODUCTION 100,000 bottles
HECTARES UNDER VINE 24
VITICULTURE METHOD Conventional

The first evidence of viticulture at the Roncada estate dates from 1882. Subsequently, the property was acquired by the Wegenast family from Heilbron, who introduced several vine types from their homeland, including müller thurgau and franconia. In the 1940s, the Germanic element was reinforced when the noble Winmdisch-Graez family moved in. Finally, the estate was acquired by the current owners, the Mattioni family. The Roncada wines we like best are the classics from the Collio, especially the Pinot Bianco, Pinot Grigio and Tocai. Subtle spring flower and almond sensations characterize the Pinot Bianco while the Pinot Grigio is deliciously refreshing in the mouth. The Tocai has marked florality laced with tempting pears, peaches and apples. But what about those German bottles? Well, the subtly floral Müller Thurgau is rather attractive but the varietal Franconia, a typically rough-edged red, got no more than a mention in dispatches.

O Collio Pinot Bianco '06	🍷🍷	5
O Collio Pinot Grigio '06	🍷🍷	5
O Collio Tocai Friulano '06	🍷🍷	4
O Collio Chardonnay '06	🍷	4
● Collio Merlot '05	🍷	5
O Collio Müller Thurgau '06	🍷	5
O Collio Sauvignon '06		4
● Collio Cabernet Franc '05		4
● Franconia '05		5
● Collio Cabernet Sauvignon '05		5
O Collio Pinot Bianco '05	YY	4

La Roncaia

FRAZ. CERGNEU
VIA VERDI, 26
33045 NIMIS [UD]
TEL. 0432790280
www.laroncaia.com

ANNUAL PRODUCTION 40,000 bottles
HECTARES UNDER VINE 22
VITICULTURE METHOD Conventional

Since the purchase in 1999, the Fantinel group has looked on La Roncaia as a key property for promoting territory-focused varieties. Marco Fantinel looks after La Roncaia on behalf of the family and he pulled off the coup of the century when he signed up consultant Tibor Gal, the Hungarian oenologist who created the Ornellaia estate's wines. Sadly, Tibor passed away tragically in February 2006 but his legacy in the cellar, where he trained the young technicians, lives on and it was evident in the wines we tasted. Fruit comes from 22 hectares of vineyards and other small growers in the area. There are six and a half spectacular hillside hectares planted to picolit, making it the largest vineyard in the region dedicated to this emblematic variety. Grapes for Refosco Gheppio are part-dried for three weeks and the wine ages in small wood for a couple of years. It emerges complex, well-structure and redolent of varietal spiciness. Bianco Eclisse is a 90-10 blend of sauvignon and picolit. Dry and refreshing, it gives very appealing sensations of citrus. Finally, the Ramandolo melds varietal baked apples with oak-derived bananas.

O COF Bianco Eclisse '06	🍷🍷	5
● COF Refosco Gheppio '01	🍷🍷	6
O COF Tocai Friulano '06	🍷	5
O Ramandolo '04	🍷	6
O COF Picolit '04		6
O COF Picolit '01	YY	8
● COF Merlot '02	YY	4
O COF Bianco Eclisse '02	YY	5
O COF Bianco Eclisse '05	YY	5

Il Roncat - Giovanni Dri

LOC. RAMANDOLO
VIA PESCIA, 7
33045 NIMIS [UD]
TEL. 0432790260
www.drironcat.com

ANNUAL PRODUCTION 50,000 bottles
HECTARES UNDER VINE 10
VITICULTURE METHOD Conventional

Giovanni Dri is a long-standing grower to whom goes the distinction of being the first to launch a wine from a local variant of verduzzo friulano. His cellar is mainly fitted out for hospitality and technology is kept to a bare minimum in order to bring out the full character of the grapes. Making reds is no easy task in an area exposed to cold wines and hail but Giovanni perseveres, although results are not always gratifying. Il Roncat, from half refosco grapes and then decreasing proportions of schioppettino, cabernet sauvignon and merlot, is Giovanni's best red. But his sweet whites, which are typical of the subzone, are another matter altogether, starting with a decidedly delicious Picolit nuanced with lingering sultana perceptions. Giovanni's Ramandolo, a DOCG wine, also has sultanas, beautifully set off by green apple sensations. Those sultanas are reprised on the substantial palate, which signs off with depth, freshness and savouriness.

Ronchi di Manzano

VIA ORSARIA, 42
33044 MANZANO [UD]
TEL. 0432740718
www.ronchidimanzano.com

ANNUAL PRODUCTION 300,000 bottles
HECTARES UNDER VINE 55
VITICULTURE METHOD Conventional

Roberta Borghese has expanded her cellar to give her barrel stock more room for she aims to release wines that are judiciously aged in wood of various sizes. Space was found by excavating the hill behind the cellar in order not to impact on the vine and olive tree-dotted countryside. Roberta's estate comprises 55 hectares in three properties, Ronc di Subule, Ronc di Scossai and Ronco di Rosazzo, each more ravishingly beautiful than the last. The vines are tended with meticulous care by Raiko while the cellar is monitored by the oenologist Boris with technicians Ivan and Aldo. The range is diversified, which means that the main label is flanked by Vigne della Rocca wines and the production that is sold unbottled. All told, output is around 300,000 units a year. We thought the Tocai Friulano was particularly good, its almondy twist coming through on nose and palate. The Chardonnay gives yeasts and golden delicious apples whereas the Sauvignon tempts the nose with elderflower and sages followed by citrus and yellow peach on the palate. Finally, the Rosazzo Bianco is outstandingly complex and well balanced.

○ COF Picolit '05	♟♟ 8
○ Ramandolo '06	♟♟ 5
● COF Refosco '05	♟ 5
● COF Rosso Il Roncat '03	♟ 6
● COF Cabernet '05	4
○ COF Picolit '04	♟♟ 8
○ COF Picolit '03	♟♟ 8
○ Ramandolo Uve Decembrine '04	♟♟ 7
○ Ramandolo Uve Decembrine '03	♟♟ 7

○ COF Chardonnay '06	♟♟ 4
○ COF Tocai Friulano Sup. '06	♟♟ 4
○ COF Sauvignon '06	♟♟ 4
○ COF Rosazzo Bianco '06	♟♟ 4
● Le Zuccule '01	♟ 6
● COF Cabernet Sauvignon '05	♟ 4
○ COF Pinot Grigio '06	♟ 4
● COF Merlot '05	4
○ COF Verduzzo Friulano '05	4
● COF Refosco P. R. '05	4
○ COF Rosazzo Bianco '05	♟♟ 4
○ COF Chardonnay '05	♟♟ 4

Ronco Blanchis

VIA BLANCHIS, 70
34070 MOSSA [GO]
TEL. 0423870024
www.venegazzu.com

ANNUAL PRODUCTION   25,000 bottles
HECTARES UNDER VINE 10
VITICULTURE METHOD   Natural

In 2001, Giancarlo Palla decided to purchase this winery on the Blanchis hill in Friuli's Collio DOC zone, having already made a name for himself as the owner of the Loredan Gasparin estate in the Veneto. Giancarlo immediately set about focusing on quality, engaging first-rate technicians like agronomists Marco Simonit and Pierpaolo Sirch and oenologist Gianni Menotti. With back-up of that calibre, excellence was sure to follow and, in fact, this year we celebrate his debut in the Guide with a full profile. Restricting the range to just four whites is a shrewd move that many of the region's wineries would do well to emulate. All four are supremely well typed, exquisitely expressing their varieties as well as the standards of quality Giancarlo has now achieved. The Chardonnay is very tangy and fresh, the citron and elderflower Sauvignon is alluring on the nose and assertive on the palate while the Tocai gives nectarine-led fruit laced with sage. Finally, the Pinot Grigio is a textbook example of gunflint and pear varietal character.

Ronco dei Pini

VIA RONCHI, 93
33040 PREPOTTO [UD]
TEL. 0432713239
www.roncodeipini.it

ANNUAL PRODUCTION   120,000 bottles
HECTARES UNDER VINE 14.5
VITICULTURE METHOD   Conventional

Giuseppe and Claudio Novello's wine adventure has completed its first decade. Actually, the Novellos had been involved in wine since 1968, when Vito Novello bought his first plots. The reins then passed to his children, who split up and formed two separate wineries. Ronco dei Pini vinifies grapes from four estate-owned hectares in the Colli Orientali and ten rented in the Collio, as well as a fair quantity of bought-in fruit. The vineyards are looked after by Daniele Stramare and oenologist Renato De Doni is in charge in the cellar. Our notes confirm the overall reliability of Ronco dei Pini wines, some 120,000 bottles of which are released each year. The Sauvignon is the stand-out with its elegantly restrained aromatics and intense, grapefruit-themed palate. Verduzzo Riccovino lost marks for the volatile acidity that many believe is essential if a sweet wine is not to become cloying. We liked its varietal baked apple and toasted hazelnut aromas, which are reprised on the palate.

O Collio Chardonnay '06	¶¶ 4*
O Collio Pinot Grigio '06	¶¶ 4*
O Collio Sauvignon '06	¶¶ 4*
O Collio Tocai Friulano '06	¶¶ 4*

O Collio Sauvignon '06	¶¶ 4
● COF Cabernet '05	¶ 5
● COF Merlot '05	¶ 5
O Collio Pinot Grigio '06	¶ 4
O COF Tocai Friulano '06	¶ 4
O Verduzzo Friulano Riccovino '06	¶ 6
O COF Pinot Bianco '06	¶ 4
● Limes Rosso '05	6
O Collio Chardonnay '06	4
O Verduzzo Friulano Riccovino '04	¶¶ 5
O Verduzzo Friulano Riccovino '05	¶¶ 6

Ronco dei Tassi
LOC. MONTE, 38
34071 CORMONS [GO]
TEL. 048160155
www.roncodeitassi.it

★ ## Ronco del Gelso
VIA ISONZO, 117
34071 CORMONS [GO]
TEL. 048161310
www.roncodelgelso.com

ANNUAL PRODUCTION   76,000 bottles
HECTARES UNDER VINE 12
VITICULTURE METHOD   Conventional

This year's Three Glass award for Bianco Fosarin is the seventh for Ronco dei Tassi. Even though they may be getting used to the feeling, we are sure that Fabio Coser and his family will be very happy. The prize confirms that the constancy and quality of their work, and their policy of releasing poised, elegant wines continues to attract admirers and enthusiasts. Even for an expert wine man like Fabio, awards like this corroborate past decisions and reinforce a commitment to quality. Bianco Fosarin is a blend of tocai, malvasia and pinot bianco. Consistent and successful in the market, it offers stylish sensations of tropical fruit, flowers and peach. A velvet-smooth, triumphantly balanced palate progresses seamlessly to a finish of fresh bananas. We instantly picked up box hedge aromas in the Sauvignon, mingling with grapefruit and elderflower. The Pinot Grigio is remarkably savoury, melding this nicely into the soft structure. Chocolate, dried roses and cinchona are the keynotes of the stylish Rosso Cjarandon. The Tocai is as varietal as the aromatic herbs, rue, thyme and lemon zest-laced Malvasia is vibrant.

ANNUAL PRODUCTION   150,000 bottles
HECTARES UNDER VINE 22
VITICULTURE METHOD   Conventional

This is Giorgo Badin's year. In a vintage when the very hot weather shattered many high hopes, only the most skilful growers and winemakers managed to maintain sensory profiles, elegance and seamless continuity on the palate. Special mentions go to two wines that came within an ace of our top award and which represent the return to favour of two varieties that recent fashions have unjustly neglected. One is Malvasia, back on the list now that the vine stock has been replanted, and the other is Pinot Bianco. Both are whistle clean, the Malvasia giving lavender and the Pinot Bianco crusty bread, plum, spring flowers and pear, and both are compact, well sustained and extremely drinkable. But it is the Tocai that stands head and shoulders above the rest. Here is a wine that embodies all Giorgio's oenological touchstones, from elegance to poise, close-knit texture, persistence and bright freshness nicely offset by softness and appealing drinkability. Three Glasses. The same attributes are found throughout the range, particularly in the classic Bianco Latimis, Sauvignon and Pinot Grigio.

O Collio Bianco Fosarin '06	♛♛♛ 4*
O Collio Pinot Grigio '06	♛♛ 4*
O Collio Sauvignon '06	♛♛ 4*
O Collio Malvasia '06	♛♛ 4
O Collio Tocai Friulano '06	♛♛ 4
● Collio Rosso Cjarandon '04	♛♛ 5
O Collio Picolit '05	♛ 6
O Collio Bianco Fosarin '04	♛♛♛ 4
O Collio Bianco Fosarin '96	♛♛♛ 4
O Collio Sauvignon '05	♛♛♛ 4
O Collio Sauvignon '98	♛♛♛ 4
● Collio Rosso Cjarandon '01	♛♛♛ 5
● Collio Rosso Cjarandon '00	♛♛♛ 5
● Collio Rosso Cjarandon '03	♛♛ 5

O Friuli Isonzo Tocai Friulano '06	♛♛♛ 4*
O Friuli Isonzo Malvasia '06	♛♛ 4*
O Friuli Isonzo Pinot Bianco '06	♛♛ 4*
O Friuli Isonzo Bianco Latimis '06	♛♛ 4
O Friuli Isonzo Sauvignon '06	♛♛ 4
O Friuli Isonzo Chardonnay '06	♛♛ 5
O Friuli Isonzo Pinot Grigio Sot lis Rivis '06	♛♛ 5
● Friuli Isonzo Cabernet Franc '06	♛ 4
O Friuli Isonzo Riesling '06	♛ 4
● Friuli Isonzo Merlot '01	♛♛♛ 5
O Friuli Isonzo Rive Alte Tocai Friulano '05	♛♛♛ 4
O Friuli Isonzo Rive Alte Tocai Friulano '04	♛♛♛ 4
O Friuli Isonzo Tocai Friulano '03	♛♛♛ 4
O Friuli Isonzo Tocai Friulano '01	♛♛♛ 4
O Friuli Isonzo Tocai Friulano '97	♛♛♛ 4

Ronco delle Betulle

LOC. ROSAZZO
VIA ABATE COLONNA, 24
33044 MANZANO [UD]
TEL. 0432740547
www.roncodellebetulle.it

ANNUAL PRODUCTION 60,000 bottles
HECTARES UNDER VINE 13.75
VITICULTURE METHOD Conventional

Wine women in Friuli are claiming the space they undoubtedly deserve. Ivana Adami is a particularly determined example of the genre, having run her beautiful estate for about 20 years. Ronco delle Betulle has about 13 hectares under vine, enabling Ivana to release 60,000 or so bottles each year. Located next to the abbey at Rosazzo, it is a winery that maintains high quality standards year after year. In fact, the Ronco delle Betulle Pignolo was one of the best we tasted. Its coffee-led aromatics are complex and intense before the palate shows rich and clean after a quite stunning entry. There were Two well-deserved Glasses for this native Friulian red of which Ivana is a great champion. The Narciso Rosso 2003 is very exciting. The ruby hue introduces a warm, intense nose with a rich, nicely structured bouquet of delightful complexity. Assertive on entry, the palate signs off with an elegant, long-lingering finish. The Tocai Friulano 2006 has a varietal nose and a powerful, fruit-forward palate with substance, richness and impressive length.

Ronco di Prepotto

VIA BROLO, 45
33040 PREPOTTO [UD]
TEL. 0432281118
www.roncodiprepotto.com

ANNUAL PRODUCTION 30,000 bottles
HECTARES UNDER VINE 10
VITICULTURE METHOD Conventional

This winery, owned by Giampaolo Macorig who runs it with his father Annibale, can look back on more than a century of history. The man who started the estate was Giuseppe Macorig, who handed over to Gino, who was succeeded by Annibale and then Giampaolo. Vineyard management is almost entirely organic. This is the realm of Annibale, who looks after the grassed-over rows whose canopies are only 80 centimetres off the ground. Success in recent years has encouraged the Macorigs to extend their vine stock and there are now ten hectares, to which they have added a couple more that are rented. They also buy in grapes from small-scale local growers whom Annibale and Giampaolo supervise closely. In the cellar, respected oenologist Emilio Del Medico consults and the Altrimenti agency has created some very attractive labels. Bianco Lavinia, from tocai, malvasia and riesling renano, is briefly aged in oak, emerging seamlessly full bodied, harmonious and broad. Rosso Zeus comes from schioppettino, refosco and merlot. It's concentrated, well structured and the tannins are finely honed.

● COF Rosazzo Rosso Narciso '03	♟♟	6
○ COF Tocai Friulano '06	♟♟	4*
○ COF Ribolla Gialla '06	♟♟	4
○ COF Sauvignon '06	♟♟	4
● COF Rosazzo Pignolo '04	♟♟	7
● COF Cabernet Franc '05	♟	5
○ COF Rosazzo Bianco Vanessa '05	♟	5
○ COF Pinot Grigio '06	♟	4
● Narciso Rosso '94	♟♟♟	6
● COF Rosazzo Rosso Narciso '00	♟♟	6
● COF Rosazzo Rosso Narciso '01	♟♟	6
● COF Cabernet Franc '04	♟♟	5
● Franconia '04	♟♟	5

● COF Rosso Zeus '04	♟♟	6
○ COF Bianco Lavinia '04	♟♟	6
○ COF Tocai Friulano '06	♟	4
○ COF Bianco Lavinia '03	♟♟	6
● COF Rosso Zeus '03	♟♟	6
○ COF Tocai Friulano Vigneti dei Monti Sacri '05	♟♟	4

Roncùs

VIA MAZZINI, 26
34070 CAPRIVA DEL FRIULI [GO]
TEL. 0481809349
www.roncus.it

ANNUAL PRODUCTION 40,000 bottles
HECTARES UNDER VINE 12
VITICULTURE METHOD Conventional

Determinedly, Marco Perco continues on his personal path towards wine that ever more faithfully reflects its territory. We are at Capriva, in the heart of Collio wine country, planting patterns are carefully designed and extreme, innovative techniques are the order of the day in the cellar. What are the results? Well, the wines are highly distinctive, bright with minerality, velvety softness and a hint of balsam. Not for the first time, the Bianco Vecchie Vigne was the pick of the crop. It's a territory-focused blend of malvasia, tocai and ribolla that needs time to reveal its secrets. It opens slowly, releasing balsam-like sensations with white-fleshed fruits tart and vanilla. Solid structure on the palate is laced with peach, almond and sweet tobacco. Varietal pennyroyal in the Tocai melds nicely with tropical fruit while the Sauvignon marries spice and camphor with rounder perceptions of ripe tomato. We would also mention the Pinot Bianco, a wine whose subtle dried flowers and sweet spice are sure to evolve well.

Russiz Superiore

VIA RUSSIZ, 7
34070 CAPRIVA DEL FRIULI [GO]
TEL. 048199164
www.marcofelluga.it

ANNUAL PRODUCTION 200,000 bottles
HECTARES UNDER VINE 60
VITICULTURE METHOD Conventional

The Fellugas have been part of the world of wine for more than a century. Originally from Istria, the family has viticulture written in its genes. More recently, Marco Felluga has infused science and innovation into the winery, which is outstanding for its modern approach and eagerness to explore. Now Roberto, the fifth generation of Felluga winemakers, has the task of carrying on a journey that is firmly focused on higher things. This year, there was no Three Glass winner but quality in depth was obvious across the range. We'll start with the invitingly sun-ripe Tocai, which deliciously sets vanilla off against notes of citrus. The Sauvignon offers a velvety mouthfeel and a tangy finish. Bianco Col Disôre, for pinot bianco, tocai, sauvignon and ribolla gialla, is a richly faceted wine with sensations that range from smokiness to peanut butter, banana, acacia blossom and oranges, wonderfully perked up on the palate by refreshing acidity. We would also point out the complex Merlot, the fresh violets of the Cabernet Franc, the tropical fruits of the Pinot Grigio, the structure of the Rosso Riserva and the subtly restrained Pinot Bianco.

O Collio Bianco Vecchie Vigne '04	♟♟	6
O Sauvignon '05	♟♟	5
O Collio Tocai Friulano '05	♟♟	5
O Pinot Bianco '05	♟	5
O Collio Bianco '05	♟	5
● Val di Miez '04	♟	6
O Roncùs Bianco Vecchie Vigne '01	♟♟♟	6
O Collio Bianco Vecchie Vigne '02	♟♟	6
O Collio Bianco Vecchie Vigne '03	♟♟	6
O Pinot Bianco '04	♟♟	5
O Collio Tocai Friulano '04	♟♟	5

O Collio Bianco Col Disôre '05	♟♟	6
O Collio Tocai Friulano '06	♟♟	5
O Collio Sauvignon '06	♟♟	5
O Collio Pinot Bianco '06	♟♟	5
O Collio Pinot Grigio '06	♟♟	5
● Collio Cabernet Franc '04	♟♟	5
● Collio Merlot '04	♟♟	5
● Collio Rosso Riserva degli Orzoni '03	♟♟	8
O Collio Bianco Russiz Disôre '00	♟♟♟	5
O Collio Bianco Russiz Disôre '01	♟♟♟	6
O Collio Sauvignon '98	♟♟♟	5
O Collio Sauvignon '04	♟♟♟	6
O Collio Sauvignon '05	♟♟♟	5
O Collio Tocai Friulano '99	♟♟♟	5
● Collio Rosso Ris. degli Orzoni '93	♟♟♟	6
● Collio Rosso Riserva degli Orzoni '94	♟♟♟	7

Russolo
VIA SAN ROCCO, 58A
33080 SAN QUIRINO [PN]
TEL. 0434919577
www.russolo.it

ANNUAL PRODUCTION 150,000 bottles
HECTARES UNDER VINE 16
VITICULTURE METHOD Conventional

After three generations of making wine, the Russolo family has recently been improving its quality and this year went on to the Three Glass finals with Mussignaz, from müller thurgau only. The house style is a mix of fresh fragrances accompanied by distinct fruit softness, setting Russolo wines apart from other Grave DOC products. It's all down to the site climate. The gravelly soil near the mountains ensures day-night temperature variations and stable temperatures for the vine root system. But we were talking about that Mussignaz, a wine that has been impressive for some years. Rose and peach sensations greet the nose and progression in the mouth is velvety before the refreshing finale offers a reprise of the initial aromas. Other wines we liked were the elegant blended red Borgo di Peuma, the varietal Pinot Nero Grifo Nero, the fresh tropical Bianco Doi Raps, a white blend, and the attractive fruit and spice of the Cabernet.

San Simone
LOC. RONDOVER
VIA PRATA, 30
33080 PORCIA [PN]
TEL. 0434578633
www.sansimone.it

ANNUAL PRODUCTION 900,000 bottles
HECTARES UNDER VINE 50
VITICULTURE METHOD Conventional

Family winery is a term that is often abused but at San Simone it fits to a T. Brisottos have been growing grapes for four generations and now, after the unexpected loss of her husband Gino, Liviana has taken over while her children Anna, Antonio and Chiara are all involved in various roles. The wines are the classics of the lower Pordenone flatlands; the whites are fresh and varietal while the reds are more structured, taking advantage of the rich, clayey soils of the area. That sums up this year's wines. The Sauvignon, with its fresh-tasting, dynamic palate, and the very varietal, spicy and robustly extracted Cabernet Franc Sugano lead an admirable list from which no wine dipped below a One Glass score. Other wines to look out for are the Chardonnay, which gives intense banana and pineapple, and the gamey, balsam Refosco Re Sugano, which is bound to improve even further when ageing has evened out and smoothed off its tannins.

O Müller Thurgau Mussignaz '06	♟♟	4*
● Cabernet Ris. '02	♟♟	4
● Pinot Nero Grifo Nero '04	♟♟	5
● Refosco P. R. Ris. '04	♟♟	4
● Borgo di Peuma '03	♟♟	5
O Chardonnay Ronco Calaj '06	♟♟	4
O Doi Raps '05	♟♟	4
O Malvasia Istriana '06	♟	4
O Pinot Grigio Ronco Calaj '06	♟	4
☉ Moscato Rosa Prato delle Rose '06	♟	4
● Refosco P. R. I Legni '03	♟♟	4
● Pinot Nero Grifo Nero '03	♟♟	5
O Doi Raps '04	♟♟	4
O Müller Thurgau Mussignaz '05	♟♟	4

● Friuli Grave Cabernet Franc Sugano '05	♟♟	4*
O Friuli Grave Sauvignon '06	♟♟	3*
● Friuli Grave Cabernet Sauvignon Nexus '04	♟	4
● Friuli Grave Merlot Evante '05	♟	6
O Friuli Grave Chardonnay '06	♟	3
O Friuli Grave Pinot Grigio '06	♟	3
● Bris Rosso '06	♟	3
O Friuli Grave Tocai Friulano '06	♟	3
● Friuli Grave Refosco P. R. Re Sugano '05	♟	4
● Friuli Grave Merlot Evante '03	♟♟	6
● Friuli Grave Merlot Evante '04	♟♟	6

Sant'Elena

VIA GASPARINI, 1
34072 GRADISCA D'ISONZO [GO]
TEL. 048192388
sant.elena@libero.it

Scarbolo

FRAZ. LAUZACCO
V.LE GRADO, 4
33050 PAVIA DI UDINE [UD]
TEL. 0432675612
www.scarbolo.com

ANNUAL PRODUCTION   130,000 bottles
HECTARES UNDER VINE 30
VITICULTURE METHOD   Conventional

ANNUAL PRODUCTION   150,000 bottles
HECTARES UNDER VINE 25
VITICULTURE METHOD   Conventional

Dominic Nocerino's winery makes bottles for the international market. They are accessible to all palates but quality is always a priority. This means discreet use of low temperatures, selected yeasts, blends, cask conditioning, ageing on the lees and malolactic fermentation to produce wines that may not be outstandingly individual but are invariably well made, clean and appealing. Currently, there seems to be a return to differentiating the range with more single-variety wines on offer. Particularly interesting this time were the Pinot Grigio, one of the most reliable Sant'Elena wines, and the Sauvignon, a new product and one that takes full advantage of an excellent growing year for the variety. From the rest of the list, the Bordeaux blend Rosso Tato, the Cabernet Sauvignon and the Bianco JN, from chardonnay and sauvignon fruit, all confirm the house style.

Valter Scarbolo appears to have realized that you can't combine quantity with quality unless you have complete control over the entire production process. In the past, Valter used to supplement his output with a significant quantity of locally purchased fruit but since last year, he has been vinifying only estate-grown grapes. His estate comprises 25 densely planted hectares that enable our hero to release 150,000 bottles a year. Much of the output is consumed at Valter's restaurant on the road from Udine to Grado. The change in policy produced an immediate leap in quality, thanks in part to a fine growing year. With consultancy input from Maurizio Castelli and Emilio Del Medico, the Scarbolo cellar presented us with wines that impressed right from our first tastings in the spring. The Tocai Friulano is a stand-out. Green apples and peaches precede intense fruity sensations on a palate bolstered by good alcohol and graced with remarkable length. Valter's Terrano is very varietal and equally good. Bianco del Viotto, from wood-fermented tocai, sauvignon and chardonnay aged in steel, is fresh-tasting and creamy.

O Pinot Grigio '06	⚲⚲ 5
O Sauvignon '06	⚲⚲ 5
● Cabernet Sauvignon '04	⚲ 5
O Bianco JN '05	⚲ 5
● Merlot '04	⚲ 5
● Tato Rosso '04	⚲ 6
● Merlot Ros di Rol '04	⚲ 7
O Bianco JN '04	⚱⚱ 5
O Pinot Grigio '04	⚱⚱ 5
O Pinot Grigio '05	⚱⚱ 5
● Merlot '03	⚱⚱ 5
● Tato Rosso '04	⚱⚱ 6

O Friuli Grave Bianco del Viotto '04	⚲⚲ 5
O Friuli Grave Sauvignon '06	⚲⚲ 3*
O Friuli Grave Tocai Friulano '06	⚲⚲ 3*
O Friuli Grave Pinot Grigio '06	⚲ 3
O Friuli Grave Chardonnay '06	⚲ 3

★ Schiopetto

VIA PALAZZO ARCIVESCOVILE, 1
34070 CAPRIVA DEL FRIULI [GO]
TEL. 048180332
www.schiopetto.it

ANNUAL PRODUCTION 189,100 bottles
HECTARES UNDER VINE 30
VITICULTURE METHOD Conventional

When we looked over the results of Schiopetto wines at our tastings, we reflected that at last the cellar has returned to its former glory. After an understandable period of bewilderment following the death of that great winemaker, Mario Schiopetto, his children have taken the winery back to the elevated status that it habitually earned in the past. Maria Angela is in charge of administration, Carlo looks after sales and twin Giorgio has always been a passionate worker in vineyard and cellar. Together, they have inherited the legacy, and image, that Mario left. Marco Simonit in the vineyards and Donato Lanati in the cellar provide superior consultancy input. But let's enjoy these fantastic wines, starting with the superb Blanc des Rosis from tocai, pinot grigio, sauvignon, malvasia and ribolla grapes, an impeccably broad, complex essay in sheer elegance. In fact, it strolled off with Three Glasses. Elegance is the trait d'union of Schiopetto wines, emerging in the varietal Sauvignon with its subtle hints of tomato leaf. Finally, the Mario Schiopetto Bianco, from Colli Orientali chardonnay and tocai from the Collio, is a wine for the cellar, if you can resist the temptation of uncorking it now.

La Sclusa

LOC. SPESSA
VIA STRADA DI S. ANNA, 7/2
33043 CIVIDALE DEL FRIULI [UD]
TEL. 0432716259
www.lasclusa.it

ANNUAL PRODUCTION 150,000 bottles
HECTARES UNDER VINE 35
VITICULTURE METHOD Conventional

It was grandfather Giobatta, known to one and all as Tita Tramuntin, who built the first cellar when he was still a tenant farmer. His son Gino later extended it and improved efficiency. For several years, Gino has been assisted by his sons Germano and Luciano, who have always been particularly attentive to quality. There are now 35 hectares of vineyards yielding a total of 150,000 bottles a year. In the past two editions, the cellar has earned promotion from the Other Wineries and this year has a full profile, coming within an ace of Three Glasses with an outstandingly clean, varietal Picolit. It could well be the most genuine example of the wine type, which too often suffers from poorly handled cask conditioning. The La Sclusa version is all elegance on nose and palate, its sweetness nicely restrained and its aromatics ranging from apple to almond paste, dried figs and sultanas. Uncork a bottle of Picolit Vigna del Torrione 2005 and see for yourself. The Sauvignon's elderflower fragrances accompany complex structure, saltiness and juicy pulp. The Tocai, too, is substantial, the Ribolla Gialla is refreshing and harmonious while the Pinot Grigio has well-defined fruit.

O Blanc des Rosis '06	♟♟♟	5
O Collio Sauvignon '06	♟♟	5
O Collio Pinot Bianco '06	♟♟	5
O Collio Tocai Friulano '06	♟♟	5
O Mario Schiopetto Bianco '06	♟♟	6
● Rivarossa '05	♟♟	5
● Poderi dei Blumeri Rosso '04	♟♟	6
O Collio Pinot Grigio '06	♟	5
O Collio Pinot Bianco '00	♟♟♟	5
O Collio Pinot Bianco Amrità '97	♟♟♟	6
O Collio Pinot Bianco Amrità '96	♟♟♟	5
O Mario Schiopetto Bianco '03	♟♟♟	6
O Mario Schiopetto Bianco '02	♟♟♟	6
O Collio Sauvignon '97	♟♟♟	5
O Collio Tocai Friulano '00	♟♟♟	5
O Collio Tocai Friulano '95	♟♟♟	5
O Collio Tocai Friulano '94	♟♟♟	5
O Collio Tocai Friulano '93	♟♟♟	5

O COF Picolit V. del Torrione '05	♟	7
O COF Pinot Grigio '06	♟♟	4
O COF Ribolla Gialla '06	♟♟	4
O COF Tocai Friulano '06	♟♟	4
O COF Sauvignon '06	♟♟	4
● COF Merlot '06	♟	4
O COF Pinot Grigio '05	♟♟	4

Roberto Scubla

FRAZ. IPPLIS
VIA ROCCA BERNARDA, 22
33040 PREMARIACCO [UD]
TEL. 0432716258
www.scubla.com

ANNUAL PRODUCTION 60,000 bottles
HECTARES UNDER VINE 11.5
VITICULTURE METHOD Conventional

A huge mulberry tree more than 100 years old stands guard at the entrance to the Scubla winery. In the early 20th century, silkworm farming was widespread in Friuli Venezia Giulia, which is why you still find mulberry trees along the rows of vines, beside farm tracks, over ditches and around farmhouses. The silkworms would be placed in lofts on wooden racks, which suggested the idea of drying verduzzo grapes on the same racks that once held the silkworms. Cràtis is in fact the Friulian word for racks. Piled high in a northeast-facing loft, they are ventilated by the bora gales in November and December, which soon reduces their yield to 15 litres of must per quintal. Verduzzo Friulano Cràtis has a sweet, concentrated nose of citrus, dried fruit and marmalade that return on the palate, where the fruit is backed up by the grape's trademark extract. This great sweet wine amply deserved Three Glasses. Pomèdes and Speziale are Roberto Scubla's two extremely interesting blends. Pomèdes has distinct pear and apple, good weight in the mouth and faint hints of vanilla while Speziale reveals tropical and citrus-like fragrances that take you through to a very elegant finale.

Renzo Sgubin

VIA FAET, 15/1
34071 CORMONS [GO]
TEL. 0481630297
renzo.sgubin@tiscali.it

ANNUAL PRODUCTION 30,000 bottles
HECTARES UNDER VINE 10
VITICULTURE METHOD Conventional

Renzo Sgubin belongs to a very close family. The patriarch is his father, Bruno, aka Bruno da Mont, since he was born on Mount Quarin, a stone's throw from where in 1970 he bought the estate he had farmed as a tenant. His brother Sergio devotes most of his attention to his earth-moving business and vies with Paolo Rizzi for the title of "crafter of vineyards". But Friuli's viticulturists can only benefit from this good-humoured rivalry. It is true that Renzo Sgubin's vineyards are a delight to the eye. The ten hectares of perfect rows are tended with meticulous care. Expansion and restructuring of the cellar, where steel predominates, dates from 1999. Renzo's marketing policies are very cautious and he bottles only some of the wine he could actually sell. He doesn't want to be left with unsold bottles in his storage areas. Some of the wines are very big hitters, especially the Tocai Friulano, which has a complex, intense nose and a firm, well-sustained palate. There are sensations of sage, tomato leaf and bell pepper on the nose of the Sauvignon, which adds grapefruit in the mouth. The Pinot Grigio is stylish and intense.

O COF Verduzzo Friulano Cràtis '04	TTT 6
O COF Bianco Pomèdes '05	TT 5
O COF Bianco Speziale '06	TT 4*
● COF Merlot '05	TT 5
O COF Pinot Bianco '06	TT 4
O COF Tocai Friulano '06	TT 4
● COF Rosso Scuro '04	TT 5*
● COF Cabernet Sauvignon '05	T 5
O COF Sauvignon '06	T 4
O COF Bianco Pomèdes '04	TTT 5
O COF Bianco Pomèdes '99	TTT 5
O COF Bianco Pomèdes '98	TTT 5
O COF Verduzzo Friulano Graticcio '99	TTT 6
O COF Sauvignon '05	TT 4
O COF Verduzzo Friulano Cràtis '02	TT 6
O COF Verduzzo Friulano Cràtis '03	TT 6
O COF Tocai Friulano '05	TT 4

O Friuli Isonzo Pinot Grigio '06	TT 4*
O Friuli Isonzo Tocai Friulano '06	TT 4*
O Friuli Isonzo Sauvignon '06	TT 4*
O Friuli Isonzo Chardonnay '06	T 4
● Collio Merlot '05	4

Simon di Brazzan

FRAZ. BRAZZANO
VIA SAN ROCCO, 17
34070 CORMONS [GO]
TEL. 048161182
www.simondibrazzan.com

ANNUAL PRODUCTION 35,000 bottles
HECTARES UNDER VINE 7
VITICULTURE METHOD Conventional

There's plenty of experience here, and great raw material, while owner Daniele Drus is skilled but results are slow to come, perhaps because the cellar is still seeking a way forward. There's nothing new to report, as the tocai-based Blanc di Simon confirms with its inviting personality. It lacks the extra something that would make it a champion but it is warm, deep, long, soft and caressingly pervasive. The Malvasia has a touch too much alcohol and the aromatics are a tad bitterish but honey and apple on the palate ensure the palate is pleasing. Classic pear-like notes characterize the copper-tinged Pinot Grigio, which progresses purposefully with distinct minerality. Equally classic is the Sauvignon, its bell peppers and elderflower braced by acid bite. For the last two wines, more weight and less sweetness would have earned much higher marks from our tasters.

Giordano Sirch

VIA FORNALIS, 277
33043 CIVIDALE DEL FRIULI [UD]
TEL. 0432709835
www.sirchwine.com

ANNUAL PRODUCTION 50,000 bottles
HECTARES UNDER VINE 11
VITICULTURE METHOD Conventional

Giordano Sirch's estate extends over 11 hectares of vineyard in a coolish area between Cividale and Prepotto that is considered more suitable for making whites than reds. Giordano's son Luca runs the ship but he can call on some outstanding helpers. In the vineyard, he gets a hand from his brother Pierpaolo, the co-founder of the Preparatori d'Uva (fruitmakers) company that manages the vine stock of various prestigious wineries up and down Italy, not to mention Priorato in Spain. The Terra&Vini group of technicians led by Alessio Dorigo is on hand for vinification but they will tell you that the fruit that arrives in the vat cellar is so good all they have to do is avoid errors. The most frequent adjective on our tasting notes is elegant, sometimes for the nose, sometimes for the palate and sometimes for both. The Sauvignon and Pinot Grigio earned Two full Glasses apiece for their rich fruit, the former citrus-led and the other fruit salad-like with tropical hints. The Tocai Friulano is rich and full bodied.

O Blanc di Simon '06	⬤⬤	5
O Malvasia '06	⬤	5
O Pinot Grigio '06	⬤	5
O Sauvignon '06	⬤	5
● Cabernet Franc '06		5
O Pinot Grigio '05	⬤⬤	4

O COF Pinot Grigio '06	⬤⬤	4*
O COF Sauvignon '06	⬤⬤	4*
O COF Ribolla Gialla '06	⬤⬤	4
O COF Tocai Friulano '06	⬤⬤	4
O COF Tocai Friulano Mis Mas '06	⬤	3
O COF Refosco '06		4
O COF Sauvignon '05	⬤⬤	4
O COF Pinot Grigio '05	⬤⬤	4
O COF Tocai Friulano '05	⬤⬤	4

Skerk

FRAZ. S. PELAGIO
LOC. PREPOTTO, 20
34011 DUINO AURISINA [TS]
TEL. 040200156
www.skerk.com

ANNUAL PRODUCTION 15,000 bottles
HECTARES UNDER VINE 6
VITICULTURE METHOD Natural

Sandi Skerk got involved in wine without any prior preparation except the experience acquired by working alongside his father, Boris. For the past few years, he has been the driving force in this small cellar with its six hectares of Carso vineyards, which means vines that cling to the rocks, fighting a daily battle against erosion. It's a unique environment where only some varieties manage to acclimatize. That explains the prevalence of native vine types, like vitovska, malvasia and terrano, a local subvariety of refosco. Sandi's lack of any specialization is one reason why he is so keen on research and experimenting, opening new prospects for the wines of this small cellar. We have no need to emphasize the care with which the vines are tended. Nor do we need to point out that the wines are not filtered, as it states prominently on the labels. Do not be surprised, then, if these wines are slightly hazy. The main things are complex, yet not overblown, structure of the wines, the respect for the varietal nature of local wine types and the original interpretation of the international Sauvignon grape.

Edi Skok

LOC. GIASBANA, 15
34070 SAN FLORIANO DEL COLLIO [GO]
TEL. 0481390280
www.skok.it

ANNUAL PRODUCTION 35,000 bottles
HECTARES UNDER VINE 12
VITICULTURE METHOD Conventional

Edi Skok and his sister Orietta are two very likeable wine people who tend 12 hectares under vine that the family has owned since 1968. Visitors are generally surprised to see the main residence, built in the 16th century by the counts of Salzburg. It passed through various noble hands to the barons Teuffenbach, who finally sold it to the local farming family, the Skoks. Today, the residence is a tasting room and social space while winemaking takes place elsewhere. Only part of the wine goes into bottle, which means that the Skoks release about 35,000 units each year. The Bianco Pe Ar takes its name from the first syllables of the head of the household, Pepi, and uncle Armando, while the wine comes from chardonnay, part-aged in barrique for almost a year, pinot grigio and sauvignon. Oak is so beautifully handled that it is undetectable on the fresh, elegant wine with its close-knit, complex structure. The appealing Tocai Friulano Zabura is named after its vineyard of provenance. Freshness and fruit stand out in both the Pinot Grigio and the Sauvignon.

O Carso Malvasia Non Filtrato '05	🍷🍷 5
O Carso Sauvignon Non Filtrato '05	🍷🍷 5
O Carso Vitovska Non Filtrato '05	🍷🍷 5
● Carso Terrano Non Filtrato '05	🍷 5
O Carso Malvasia Non Filtrato '04	♈ 4
O Carso Sauvignon Non Filtrato '04	♈ 4
O Carso Vitovska Non Filtrato '05	♈ 4

O Collio Bianco Pe Ar '05	🍷🍷 4*
O Collio Sauvignon '06	🍷🍷 4*
O Collio Tocai Friulano Zabura '06	🍷🍷 4*
O Collio Pinot Grigio '06	🍷🍷 4*
O Collio Chardonnay '06	🍷 4
● Collio Merlot '05	🍷 4
O Collio Pinot Grigio '04	♈ 4
O Collio Pinot Grigio '05	♈ 4

Leonardo Specogna

via Rocca Bernarda, 4
33040 Corno di Rosazzo [UD]
tel. 0432755840
www.specogna.it

ANNUAL PRODUCTION 100,000 bottles
HECTARES UNDER VINE 19
VITICULTURE METHOD Conventional

Graziano and Gianni Specogna suffered a heavy blow when their father Leonardo passed away. The cause was a tragic accident in the very vineyard that Leonardo had first tended in 1963. But the two brothers and the young grandchildren set to work with admirable determination. Soon, they were again releasing a premium-quality range that must be the best from the cellar in recent years. Outstandingly good are the Tocai and Merlot Oltre. The Tocai has reined in the vegetal notes that used to be a keynote and is now more elegant, giving white melon, fresh roses and apricot. Spice is the distinguishing feature of the Merlot Oltre, which melds it with fruity softness and signs off with a long cinchona and balsam finish. In the Chardonnay, we were struck by the upfront banana, mango, pineapple and sweet tobacco sensations that round out the wine marvellously. The Sauvignon, too, has a new tack, showing delicately refined peach and wisteria. Finally, the Pinot Grigio is a one-off both for its blush hues and the red fruits aromas on the nose.

● COF Merlot Oltre '03	🍷🍷	6
○ COF Tocai Friulano '06	🍷🍷	4*
○ COF Chardonnay '05	🍷🍷	4
○ COF Sauvignon '06	🍷🍷	4
○ Pinot Grigio '06	🍷🍷	4
● COF Merlot '05	🍷	4
● COF Refosco P. R. '05	🍷	4
○ COF Verduzzo Friulano '06	🍷	4
● COF Pignolo '04	🍷	5
● COF Cabernet Franc '06		4

Castello di Spessa

via Spessa, 1
34070 Capriva del Friuli [GO]
tel. 0481639914
www.paliwines.com

ANNUAL PRODUCTION 80,000 bottles
HECTARES UNDER VINE 30
VITICULTURE METHOD Conventional

Castello di Spessa is part of Pali Wines, the wine and spirits label belonging to Loretto Pali, the go-getting businessman who is increasingly involved in wine. The spectacularly beautiful castle has ancient cellars and stands next to a popular golf course, not to mention hotel and restaurant facilities. To achieve the superb results that the cellar can boast this year, Loretto relies on Domenico Lovat, the estate's long-standing oenologist, consultant winemaker Gianni Menotti and in the vineyard Marco Simonit. There are about 30 hectares under vine in a natural amphitheatre that produces the finest wines in Capriva. The Sauvignons are again excellent, the standard-label dominated by elderflower and the Segrè selection, picked in three passes, is nuanced with grapefruit, yellow peaches and white peaches. The Tocai Friulano has fantastic structure and the palate drives on and on but the Pinot Bianco is the star, picking up Three Glasses at our finals. Its stunningly rich fruit never jeopardizes the aristocratic elegance. Finally, the oak-aged Pinot Bianco di Santarosa is a wine with a great future, as it has already demonstrated in the past.

○ Collio Pinot Bianco '06	🍷🍷🍷	5
○ Collio Sauvignon '06	🍷🍷	5
○ Collio Tocai Friulano '06	🍷🍷	5
○ Collio Sauvignon Segrè '06	🍷🍷	6
○ Collio Pinot Bianco di Santarosa '04	🍷🍷	6
○ Collio Pinot Grigio '06	🍷🍷	5
○ Collio Ribolla Gialla '06	🍷🍷	5
● Collio Merlot Torriani '03	🍷🍷	6
● Collio Pinot Nero Casanova '04	🍷	6
○ Collio Tocai Friulano '05	YYY	5
○ Collio Sauvignon Segrè '03	YYY	6
○ Collio Sauvignon Segrè '02	YYY	6
○ Collio Pinot Bianco '01	YYY	4
○ Collio Pinot Bianco '97	YYY	4

Oscar Sturm

LOC. ZEGLA, 1
34071 CORMONS [GO]
TEL. 048160720
www.sturm.it

ANNUAL PRODUCTION 60,000 bottles
HECTARES UNDER VINE 10
VITICULTURE METHOD Conventional

The Sturm family's roots can be traced back to Andritz, on the outskirts of Graz in Austria, but during the 19th century, they moved to the Cormons area and integrated with the Slovene-speaking community. For many years, the winery's guiding light was Oscar Sturm but recently his son Patrick has taken over in the cellar while elder brother Denis, who has a degree from the Bocconi university in Milan, is always ready to help out. A couple of years ago, the Sturms finished restructuring the cellar, also creating a generously sized tasting room where the many private customers who visit the estate are entertained. It was a close-run thing to find the best wine on the list and our Three Glass winner. This time, it was the cellar's historic Sauvignon that scored highest, giving pervasive but elegantly restrained elderflower and tomato in a harmonious ensemble. But we also loved the williams pear notes of the Tocai Friulano and the wealth of fruit in the Bianco Andritz, from sauvignon and pinot grigio.

O Collio Sauvignon '06	♟♟♟	4*
O Collio Bianco Andritz '06	♟♟	5
O Collio Tocai Friulano '06	♟♟	4
O Chardonnay Andritz '06	♟♟	4
O Collio Pinot Grigio '06	♟	4
O Collio Tocai Friulano '05	♟♟♟	4
O Collio Sauvignon '05	♟♟	4
O Collio Sauvignon '04	♟♟	4
O Collio Pinot Grigio '05	♟♟	4
O Collio Pinot Grigio '04	♟♟	4

Subida di Monte

LOC. MONTE, 9
34071 CORMONS [GO]
TEL. 048161011
www.subidadimonte.it

ANNUAL PRODUCTION 60,000 bottles
HECTARES UNDER VINE 10
VITICULTURE METHOD Conventional

Cristian and Andrea Antonutti are coming on nicely. Their youthful enthusiasm is now tempered by the experience they have acquired over the years. Part of the vine stock has been replanted to modern patterns, no longer do they use chemicals in the vineyards and in the cellar the wines age slowly on the lees to achieve their own special sensory profiles and quality. The Antonuttis have concentrated on a limited number of labels, which are released only when they have matured to the full. That's why the Bianco Valeas Vincas, which has made such a good impression in the past, will come out later on when the time is right. What are the results like? Excellent for the whites? The Pinot Grigio is clean and elegant while the Tocai gives lovely dried flower sensations with acacia honey and the varietal note of almonds. We would mention the attractive contrast of peach-like flavours and savouriness in the Sauvignon. And the reds? There still a little way to go. The youthful alcohol of the Cabernet Franc is appealing but the Merlot is no more than well made.

O Collio Sauvignon '06	♟♟	4
O Collio Pinot Grigio '06	♟♟	4
O Collio Tocai Friulano '06	♟♟	4
● Collio Cabernet Franc '05	♟	4
● Collio Merlot '05		4
O Collio Tocai Friulano '05	♟♟	4
● Collio Rosso Poncaia '00	♟♟	5
● Collio Rosso Poncaia '03	♟♟	5

Matijaz Tercic
LOC. BUKUJE, 9
34070 SAN FLORIANO DEL COLLIO [GO]
TEL. 0481884193
tercic@tiscalinet.it

Franco Terpin
LOC. VALERISCE, 6A
34070 SAN FLORIANO DEL COLLIO [GO]
TEL. 0481884215
francoterpin@virgilio.it

ANNUAL PRODUCTION   30,000 bottles
HECTARES UNDER VINE 11.5
VITICULTURE METHOD   Conventional

ANNUAL PRODUCTION   15,000 bottles
HECTARES UNDER VINE 10
VITICULTURE METHOD   Conventional

Often, reorganization is held up as an excuse for a brief or lengthier blip in wine quality. But Matijaz has restructured his vine stock and then the cellar while his wines just keep getting better. This is a significant signal for it means the winery is one to bank on. There was further confirmation from this year's range. Again, they mark an improvement even though the two flagship products, Merlot and Planta, were not released and will come out next year. Vino degli Orti, a 50-50 blend of tocai and malvasia, enjoyed a great growing year for both varieties and exhibits all the weight on the palate and intensity of aroma that are written in the genes of the two grapes. The Pinot Bianco was just as good, showing classic elegance, peach, summer flowers and croissant aromas, and a fresh-tasting, nicely poised palate. Also on top form was the Pinot Grigio, its long-lingering fruit complementing a distinct minerality. We also enjoyed the Sauvignon, whose agreeable vegetality is veined with tarragon, whereas the Ribolla needs fine-tuning. Oenophiles will note that the label says that it contains ten per cent of the rare glera variety.

"Franco Terpin's wines are like the man himself for their structure, assertiveness, style and rigour, as well as their solarity of manner and originality of style. These are ambitious wines. They evoke stories. They make you dream". This passage, taken from the winery's brochure, mirrors the philosophy of a first-rate wine man. Long macerations, ambient yeasts and unfiltered wines are some of the choices Franco Terpin has made for his wines and reflect the originality of his personality. But the wines are more than just original: they are extremely good. Bianco Stamas, from sauvignon, pinot grigio and chardonnay, is a wine we could call muscular yet elegant. The assertive nose gives peach tea, vanilla and gunflint, finishing stylishly on notes of bananas and flowers. Rosso Sialis is a Bordeaux blend that stands out for spice, hay, camphor and rain-soaked earth sensations, before the palate unveils its admirable texture and timbre. The very coppery Pinot Grigio Sialis is very special thanks to intriguing red fruit and pear drop nuances while the Tocai Friulano is a successful marriage of balsam and tropical fruit.

O Collio Pinot Bianco '06	♟♟	4
O Collio Pinot Grigio '06	♟♟	4
O Vino degli Orti '06	♟♟	4
O Collio Chardonnay '06	♟	4
O Collio Sauvignon '06	♟	4
O Collio Ribolla Gialla '06	♟	5
● Collio Merlot Seme '03	♟♟	6
O Collio Pinot Bianco '05	♟♟	4
O Vino degli Orti '05	♟♟	4

O Collio Bianco Stamas '04	♟♟	5
● Rosso Sialis '03	♟♟	6
O Pinot Grigio Sialis '04	♟♟	6
O Collio Tocai Friulano '04	♟♟	5
O Bianco Sialis '04	♟♟	6
O Collio Bianco '01	♟♟	5
O Collio Bianco '02	♟♟	5
O Collio Bianco Stamas '03	♟♟	5

Terre di Ger

FRAZ. FRATTINA
S.DA DELLA MEDUNA
33076 PRAVISDOMINI [PN]
TEL. 0434644452
www.terrediger.it

ANNUAL PRODUCTION   120,000 bottles
HECTARES UNDER VINE 48
VITICULTURE METHOD   Conventional

For years, Gianni Spinazzè has been lavishing his energies on this estate, which began operations in 1986 and whose name is an acronym from Gianni, Edda and their son Robert. It was Robert who decided in 1999 to devote himself full time to the cellar and aim for quality, which is why we enjoyed such great results this year. But before we talk about the wines, here is some information about the property. About 40 hectares are planted to vine and another ten have just been planted, with Pierpaolo Sirch supervising. The cellar works harmoniously with the Terra&Vini team's Alessio Dorigo, whose thoughtful advice enables it to get the best out of the lovely fruit that comes solely from estate-owned vines. The Sauvignon is wonderful, progressing delightfully on the palate, which discloses tomato leaf and white peach sensations. There is a distinct difference in the aromatics, but not the quality, of the Chardonnay 2006 and the Oro 2005 selection, whose cask conditioning is evident. Finally, the Pinot Grigio is salty and temptingly tropical.

Toblâr

LOC. RAMANDOLO, 17
33045 NIMIS [UD]
TEL. 0432755840
www.specogna.it

ANNUAL PRODUCTION   90,000 bottles
HECTARES UNDER VINE N.A.
VITICULTURE METHOD   Conventional

Graziano Specogna's sons have set up Toblâr – it means barn in Friulian – a cellar that vinifies fruit bought in from trusted local growers. We know how hard it is to work like this, which is why we are so impressed by the reliably good quality of the products released. After all, the cellar is driven by the enthusiasm and judgement of two young winemakers. Like any father who sees his lessons bearing fruit, Graziano must be very proud of how well Andrea and Cristian are progressing. Actually, we should say how excellently, given the dependably high quality of Sauvignonas, which has a characteristically intense nose of tomato leaf and apricot delicately laced with subtle smokiness. All this is echoed on the rich palate, which layers sage-like notes over the other aromas. Gris is also in the Specogna family style. Almost rosé in hue, it tempts with red fruit and dried flowers. Toblâr is based at Nimis so the range also has to include a fine, honeyed Ramandolo with balsam notes and long, candied citrus peel finale.

O Sauvignon Blanc '06	▼▼	3*
O Friuli Grave Chardonnay '06	▼▼	3*
O Friuli Grave Chardonnay Capsula Oro '05	▼▼	4
O Friuli Grave Pinot Grigio '06	▼▼	3*
● Refosco '05	▼	4
● Friuli Grave Cabernet Franc '05	▼	3
● Friuli Grave Merlot '05		3
O Limine '05	▼▼	4

O Sauvignonas '06	▼▼	4*
O Ramandolo '04	▼▼	4
O Gris '06	▼▼	4
● Cabernet Franc Uve Rosse '06	▼	5
O Sauvignonas '05	▼▼	4

Franco Toros

LOC. NOVALI, 12
34071 CORMONS [GO]
TEL. 048161327
www.vinitoros.com

ANNUAL PRODUCTION 70,000 bottles
HECTARES UNDER VINE 10
VITICULTURE METHOD Conventional

This year's news is that Franco's 25-year-old daughter Eva is working full time at the winery, looking after administration and sales. This can only be to the good for it lets Franco concentrate on the vineyards and winemaking he loves so much. There are no particular problems here but once you reach the top, expectations are inevitably high. So let's enjoy Franco's entry in the competition for the best Tocai in Cormons, which probably also means the best in the region. The Toros entry this year in fine fettle. Intense pear, apple, hawthorn and bitter honey sensations accompany a rich, warm palate that expands into an essay in depth and power. Three very stylish Glasses. There were good performances from the Toros stable's other two thoroughbreds. The Pinot Bianco needs to breathe a little before it finds its feet but then it explodes onto the palate, warmer and creamier than usual, hinting at yeasts and ripe medlars, whereas the Merlot proffers blackberries, plums and chocolate with a full, close-knit palate that progresses seamlessly and echoes the nose. As for the rest of the range, they're also excellent, especially the Sauvignon.

La Tunella

FRAZ. IPPLIS
VIA DEL COLLIO, 14
33040 PREMARIACCO [UD]
TEL. 0432716030
www.latunella.it

ANNUAL PRODUCTION 450,000 bottles
HECTARES UNDER VINE 80
VITICULTURE METHOD Conventional

Every year, the Three Glass awards excite speculation. Critics and ordinary wine enthusiasts draw up their own list of winners long before our finals, on the basis of advance tastings in the spring or casual visits to wineries. This year, BiancoSesto from Massimo and Marco Zorzettig and their mother Gabriella was so convincing right from the first tastings that it was an evens bet for our top prize early on. And win it did, bringing Three Glasses to this lovely winery for the very first time. Last time, the tocai friulano and ribolla gialla-based BiancoSesto nearly hit the jackpot and this year it finally won. Fermented in 30-hectolitre Slavonian oak barrels, it aged in stainless steel vats that preserved the freshness of the aromas. On the nose, spring flowers and honey meld with pears, apples and citrus before the rich, fresh-tasting palate adds peach, apricot and banana, to sign off with a long finish. Tocai and ribolla gialla come together again in the excellent Campo Marzio, which fermented and aged in small wood, and reveal a milkiness that is veiled by the rich fruit. Finally, a special word of praise for oenologist Luigino Zamparo, whose modesty and skill few can match.

O Collio Tocai Friulano '06	♈♈♈	5
● Collio Merlot '04	♈♈	8
O Collio Pinot Bianco '06	♈♈	5
O Collio Chardonnay '06	♈♈	5
O Collio Pinot Grigio '06	♈♈	5
O Collio Sauvignon '06	♈♈	5
● Collio Merlot Sel. '97	♈♈♈	6
O Collio Pinot Bianco '05	♈♈♈	5
O Collio Pinot Bianco '03	♈♈♈	5
O Collio Pinot Bianco '01	♈♈♈	4
O Collio Pinot Bianco '00	♈♈♈	4
O Collio Tocai Friulano '04	♈♈♈	5
O Collio Tocai Friulano '03	♈♈♈	5
O Collio Tocai Friulano '02	♈♈♈	5

O COF BiancoSesto '06	♈♈♈	4*
O COF Bianco Campo Marzio '05	♈♈	5
O COF Picolit '05	♈♈	7
O COF Bianco Rjgialla Selènze '06	♈♈	4
● COF Rosso L'Arcione '03	♈♈	5
O COF Pinot Grigio '06	♈	4
O Noans '05	♈	6
O COF Sauvignon '06	♈	4
O COF Tocai Friulano Selènze '06	♈	4
● COF Schioppettino Selènze '04	♈	5
O COF BiancoSesto '05	♈♈	4
O COF Picolit '04	♈♈	7
● COF Schioppettino Selènze '03	♈♈	4

Valchiarò

FRAZ. TOGLIANO
VIA DEI LAGHI, 4C
33040 TORREANO [UD]
TEL. 0432715502
www.valchiaro.it

ANNUAL PRODUCTION 40,000 bottles
HECTARES UNDER VINE 12
VITICULTURE METHOD Conventional

It's been 16 years since six friends from different backgrounds decided to bring their plots and enthusiasms together in one dynamic wine estate. At first, it was a hobby but over the years, involvement has grown and with it the size of the team. There have been one or two changes of personnel but what remains is the original drive, which now focuses on quality. We need only mention the consultant winemaker, Gianni Menotti, and point to the very functional new cellar. With all this going for it, we were not surprised to see the Verduzzo going through to our final Three Glass tastings this year, thanks to varietal notes of baked apple, candied citrus peel and caramel-covered figs as well as rich concentration in the mouth. We also liked the vibrantly fresh-tasting florality of the Pinot Grigio. Tocai Nexus offers varietal sensations that hinge on almonds and crusty bread. Intensity and complexity on the nose are the Merlot's strong suits, enhanced by balsam and sweeter chocolate nuances. We were also struck by the palate of the Picolit, particularly its long candied peel finale.

Valpanera

VIA TRIESTE, 5A
33059 VILLA VICENTINA [UD]
TEL. 0431970395
www.valpanera.it

ANNUAL PRODUCTION 300,000 bottles
HECTARES UNDER VINE 50
VITICULTURE METHOD Conventional

This Friulian flatlands winery was once strongly focused on the native refosco dal peduncolo rosso variety, with which it had carried out experiments with various vinification techniques. Giampietro Dal Vecchio, who is in love with refosco, and his oenologist Luca Marcolini continue to be fascinated by, and deeply involved with, the grape but again this year they make it clear that the cellar can reach equally high peaks with other products. Take Rosso Alma, for instance. It's a blend of half refosco with cabernet sauvignon and merlot that spends two years in small and large wood. What emerges is a red with heady aromas of cinchona, talcum powder, berry jam and subtle hints of camphor. The palate echoes these satisfyingly with attractively soft texture. From the rest of the range, we would mention the ripe fruit of the Refosco Superiore and the vibrant freshness of Bianco, a blend of sauvignon, chardonnay and tocai friulano.

O COF Verduzzo Friulano '05	♟♟	4*
O COF Picolit '04	♟♟	6
O COF Pinot Grigio '06	♟♟	4
● COF Merlot Vigna del Miches '03	♟♟	4
O COF Tocai Friulano Nexus '06	♟♟	4
O COF Sauvignon '06	♟	4
O COF Tocai Friulano '06	♟	4
O COF Tocai Friulano Nexus '03	♟♟	4
O COF Verduzzo Friulano '03	♟♟	4
O COF Verduzzo Friulano '04	♟♟	4
O COF Tocai Friulano Nexus '04	♟♟	4

● Friuli Aquileia Rosso Alma '03	♟♟	5
● Friuli Aquileia Cabernet Sauvignon '05	♟	3
● Friuli Aquileia Refosco P. R. '05	♟	3
● Friuli Aquileia Refosco P. R. Sup. '04	♟	4
● Rosso di Valpanera '05	♟	3
O Friuli Aquileia Bianco '06	♟	4
O Friuli Aquileia Verduzzo Friulano '06	♟	4
O Friuli Aquileia Chardonnay '06	♟	4
● Friuli Aquileia Refosco P. R. Ris. '03	♟♟	5

★ Venica & Venica
LOC. CERÒ, 8
34070 DOLEGNA DEL COLLIO [GO]
TEL. 048161264
www.venica.it

La Viarte
VIA NOVACUZZO, 51
33040 PREPOTTO [UD]
TEL. 0432759458
www.laviarte.it

ANNUAL PRODUCTION 230,000 bottles
HECTARES UNDER VINE 33.5
VITICULTURE METHOD Conventional

We make several visits each year to the lovely winery owned by brothers Gianni and Giorgio Venica, which was founded in 1936 by their grandfather Daniele. Our excuse is that we are keeping an eye on the development of the wines but the setting is beautiful and the estate complements viticulture with superb agriturismo facilities. That's why we were in no doubt that the 2008 edition of the Guide would include a Three Glass Venica wine. We were less certain about which wine it would be. There were plenty of candidates since the Venicas had taken full advantage of an exceptional growing year. The Venica team also includes: Ornella, the cellar's image; Gianpaolo, its future; Sirch and Simonit, who ensure that first-quality fruit is available with their pruning skills; and Renato Geremini, who supplied the technology for the cellar, which has been thoroughly made over. It was Tocai Friulano Ronco delle Cime that won Three Glasses, combining supreme elegance, intensity, appeal, substance and generous fruit with perfectly gauged alcohol. Close behind come an outstanding Malvasia, the classic Sauvignon Ronco delle Mele, the Pinot Bianco and the Pinot Grigio Jesera, all truly excellent.

ANNUAL PRODUCTION 100,000 bottles
HECTARES UNDER VINE 26
VITICULTURE METHOD Conventional

In 1973, Giuseppe Ceschin purchased 35 hectares in the hills of the Colli Orientali to devote his energies to the dream that had brought him to Friuli in 1960: wine. La Viarte, which means springtime in Friulian, stands atop a hill between Ruttars and Prepotto in one of the loveliest locations in the area, where it enjoys a stunning panoramic view. Heading the team is Giulio who today tends 26 hectares planted to vine with his parents Giuseppe and Carla, producing around 100,000 bottles a year. In 2003, Giulio's passion for local red varieties tempted him to purchase five more hectares where he grows pignolo, refosco and schioppettino. The new plantings are certain to enhance the quantity and quality of the range. In the longer term, it is Giulio's intention to grow exclusively native varieties. In fact, it was a blend of two native types that we like best this time. Siùm, meaning dream, is an elegant dried-grape wine from picolit and verduzzo. Almond milk, custard and dried apricots on the nose introduce a sweet but not heavy palate of harmony, richness and elegance taking you through to a textbook finish.

○ Collio Tocai Friulano Ronco delle Cime '06	▼▼▼ 5
○ Collio Malvasia '06	▼▼ 5
○ Collio Pinot Grigio Jesera '06	▼▼ 5
○ Collio Sauvignon Ronco delle Mele '06	▼▼ 6
○ Collio Pinot Bianco '06	▼▼ 5
○ Collio Ribolla Gialla '06	▼▼ 5
● Collio Merlot '05	▼ 4
● Refosco P. R. Bottaz '04	▼ 6
○ Collio Sauvignon Ronco delle Mele '05	♉♉♉ 5
○ Collio Tocai Friulano Ronco delle Cime '02	♉♉♉ 6
○ Collio Tocai Friulano Ronco delle Cime '00	♉♉♉ 5

○ Siùm '04	▼▼ 6
○ COF Sauvignon '06	▼▼ 5
○ COF Tocai Friulano '06	▼▼ 4
● COF Schioppettino '04	▼▼ 5
○ COF Bianco Liende '05	▼ 5
○ COF Pinot Grigio '06	▼ 4
○ COF Ribolla Gialla '06	▼ 4
● COF Refosco P.R. '04	▼ 5
● COF Rosso Roi Ris. '03	▼ 6
● COF Tazzelenghe '03	▼ 5
○ COF Sauvignon '05	♉♉ 4
○ Siùm '02	♉♉ 6
○ Siùm '03	♉♉ 6
● COF Merlot '03	♉♉ 5
● COF Schioppettino '02	♉♉ 5
● COF Schioppettino '03	♉♉ 5

Alessandro Vicentini Orgnani
FRAZ. VALERIANO
VIA SOTTOPLOVIA, 4A
33094 PINZANO AL TAGLIAMENTO [PN]
TEL. 0432950107
www.vicentiniorgnani.com

ANNUAL PRODUCTION 60,000 bottles
HECTARES UNDER VINE 19
VITICULTURE METHOD Conventional

Alessandro Vicentini Orgnani's winery is in the green hills at Valeriano, at the foot of the Carnic Pre-Alps. The vineyards have been replanted to modern criteria and stand in orderly rows around the delightful cellar, which includes elegant tasting areas and a stunning pergola with marvellous views over the entire estate and surrounding hill country. What about the wines? This year, there was a clear improvement all down the list but we are hoping for even more, particularly from the reds for which in our opinion the territory is especially well suited. The Pinot Grigio is as good as we have come to expect, giving intense varietal gunflint and williams pears fragrances before the broad, rich-textured palate unfolds into a refreshingly savoury finish. The Tocai is very fruity and the Chardonnay Braide Cjase intrigues with distinct varietal banana-like sensations and fresher apple fruit. Best of the reds, we thought, was the Merlot, which gives distinct plum jam and coffee.

Gestioni Agricole Vidussi
VIA SPESSA, 18
34071 CAPRIVA DEL FRIULI [GO]
TEL. 048180072
www.vinimontresor.it

ANNUAL PRODUCTION 400,000 bottles
HECTARES UNDER VINE 32
VITICULTURE METHOD Conventional

The Verona-based Montresor family decided to lease the Vidussi estate with its 25 hectares of vineyard in the Collio and seven in the neighbouring Colli Orientali del Friuli DOC zone. The Vidussi property boasts vines in outstandingly good locations both in terms of soil type and of site aspect, which means the fruit is exceptionally good. Luigino De Giuseppe is the cellar's long-standing oenologist, and also consults for many other wineries in the Guide. As in the past, he again succeeded this time in exploiting to the full the growing year with a wonderful Pinot Bianco. We can never stress too much that the depression at Capriva, and its extension at Pradis near Cormons, are the spiritual home of the pinot bianco vine. This version encapsulates all the classic sensory perceptions of the grape, in other words elegance and complexity. Even when the fruit fragrances are very assertive, and backed up by generous alcohol, the wine never loses its appeal. The rest of the range is excellent but the fragrant, fruit-forward Malvasia stands out.

○ Friuli Grave Pinot Grigio '06	♟♟ 3*
● Friuli Grave Merlot '05	♟ 4
● Cabernet Franc '06	♟ 3
○ Friuli Grave Chardonnay Braide Cjase '06	♟ 4
○ Friuli Grave Sauvignon '06	♟ 3
○ Friuli Grave Tocai Friulano '06	♟ 3
● Friuli Grave Cabernet Sauvignon '05	3
○ Friuli Grave Pinot Grigio '05	♟♟ 3
○ Ucelut '01	♟♟ 7
○ Ucelut '03	♟♟ 7
● Friuli Grave Merlot '03	♟♟ 4

○ Collio Pinot Bianco '06	♟♟ 4*
○ Collio Malvasia '06	♟♟ 4
○ Collio Sauvignon '06	♟♟ 4
○ Collio Chardonnay '06	♟ 4
○ Collio Tocai Friulano Croce Alta '06	♟ 4
● Ribolla Nera o Schioppettino '06	♟ 5
○ Collio Pinot Grigio '06	4
○ Collio Traminer Aromatico '06	4
○ Collio Ribolla Gialla '06	4
○ Collio Tocai Friulano Croce Alta '04	♟♟ 4
○ Collio Sauvignon '05	♟♟ 4

★ Vie di Romans
LOC. VIE DI ROMANS, 1
34070 MARIANO DEL FRIULI [GO]
TEL. 048169600
www.viediromans.it

ANNUAL PRODUCTION 230,000 bottles
HECTARES UNDER VINE 44
VITICULTURE METHOD Conventional

You may disagree with some points but you have to respect commitment to experimentation and ideas for their intrinsic value. This is all the truer when the experimenter has tried and tested competence in the subject matter. And we have the utmost respect for Gianfranco Gallo and his efforts, which focus on ripe fruit to make wines that will endure over the years. For the record, Gianfranco says his whites can be laid down for up to 15 years and are at their best seven to ten years after the harvest. His approach is consistent across the range. Late harvests are followed by low temperature skin contact, settling, selected yeasts, prolonged ageing on the lees and an equivalent period in bottles. Malolactic fermentation is almost always complete. When it comes to tasting, however, time and prudence are of paramount importance to assess the results of this philosophy. For the time being, the stars of the range are the usual labels, with the newer bottles in the role of commendable supporting actors.

Vigna del Lauro
LOC. MONTE, 38
34071 CORMONS [GO]
TEL. 048160155
www.roncodeitassi.it

ANNUAL PRODUCTION 42,000 bottles
HECTARES UNDER VINE 6
VITICULTURE METHOD Conventional

Quality in a winery is the ability to maintain the value of products over time. The consumer will take this as a reassuring sign of reliability, particularly if the price tag on the bottle is affordable. Vigna del Lauro wines meet both those criteria. Take, for example, the excellent quality of the Ribolla Gialla, which we sent on to the Three Glass finals for the second year in a row. The highly skilled Fabio Coser and German importer Eberhard Spangenberg are in charge here and again uncorked for us a very fragrant wine with a lovely medley of oranges, dried flowers and minerality that derives from their very mature vines. The Sauvignon is also back on form, showing a lovely contrast of the variety's trademark greener notes and soft, fruit-led sensations. Subtle florality marks out the Tocai, which layers this with peaches and white damsons. Like all Fabio's wines, the Merlot offers finesse in tandem with a fair helping of varietal character.

O Friuli Isonzo Bianco Flors di Uis '05	♥♥ 5
O Friuli Isonzo Sauvignon Piere '05	♥♥ 5
O Friuli Isonzo Sauvignon Vieris '05	♥♥ 6
O Friuli Isonzo Chardonnay Vie di Romans '05	♥♥ 5
O Dut'Un '04	♥♥ 7
O Friuli Isonzo Tocai Friulano Dolee '05	♥♥ 5
O Friuli Isonzo Malvasia Istriana Dis Cumieris '05	♥♥ 5
O Friuli Isonzo Pinot Grigio Dessimis '05	♥♥ 5
O Friuli Isonzo Chardonnay Ciampagnis Vieris '05	♥♥ 5
O Friuli Isonzo Rive Alte Sauvignon Vieris '04	♥♥♥ 6
O Dut'Un '02	♥♥♥ 7

O Collio Ribolla Gialla '06	♥♥ 4*
O Collio Sauvignon '06	♥♥ 4
O Collio Tocai Friulano '06	♥♥ 4
● Friuli Isonzo Merlot '04	♥♥ 4
O Collio Pinot Grigio '06	♥ 4
O Friuli Isonzo Chardonnay '06	♥ 4
O Collio Sauvignon '99	♥♥♥ 4
O Collio Ribolla Gialla '05	♥♥ 4

Vigna Petrussa

FRAZIONE ALBANA, 47
33040 PREPOTTO [UD]
TEL. 0432713021
www.vignapetrussa.it

ANNUAL PRODUCTION 25,000 bottles
HECTARES UNDER VINE 6.5
VITICULTURE METHOD Conventional

Vigna Petrussa's label carries a Lombard helmet, which we like to associate with the tenacity and perseverance shown by owner Hilde Petrussa, a woman who is, as it were, reborn. After spending most of her life in an office, Hilde rediscovered the country life on the seven hectares under vine in her native town, which seems to have transformed this likeable lady and her husband Renato. Their daughter Francesca is a London-based architect and it was she who drew up the plans for the attractive cellar and efficient, modern tasting room. Good taste and attention to detail in the furnishings complement equally close attention to the vineyards. Quality at Vigna Petrussa has come on immensely since successful Friulian oenologist Emilio Del Medico started to consult in the cellar. The 2004 Schioppettino that we are reviewing this year is not the one that appeared in last year's Guide. In fact, it was vinified in compliance with the regulations for the anxiously awaited Schioppettino di Prepotto subzone. That means 24 months' ageing in barrique and at least six in glass to make a wine with serious structure.

Vigna Traverso

VIA RONCHI, 73
33040 PREPOTTO [UD]
TEL. 0422804807
www.molon.it

ANNUAL PRODUCTION 60,000 bottles
HECTARES UNDER VINE 22
VITICULTURE METHOD Conventional

Stefano Traverso manages this attractive estate for his family, which purchased it in 1998 and subsequently extended the vine stock with further acquisitions in the Prepotto area. The vineyards needed to be thoroughly overhauled and in some cases, the Traversos recovered plots whose bare outline was all that was left on the once-terraced hillslopes. At that stage, the input of Pierpaolo Sirch from the Preparatori d'Uva team was crucial. He and Stefano's father Giancarlo carefully sought the most appropriate vines for the available terrain. Equally important is the relationship with Terra&Vini, the Friulian group that supports the estate's oenologist, Simone Casazza. Traverso, by the way, includes the Veneto-based Ornella Molon winery. Early releases tended towards an opulence that is easier to achieve here than on the Veneto flatlands but today the range is subtler, evidencing greater aromatic balance. The best of the range this time was the Merlot Sottocastello 2004 with its notes of warm fruits and forest floor. Schioppettino and Cabernet Franc are outstanding while the Tocai and Sauvignon are always just right.

● COF Schioppettino '04	♟♟ 5
○ COF Picolit '04	♟♟ 6
○ COF Tocai Friulano '06	♟♟ 4*
○ Richenza '05	♟♟ 5
○ COF Sauvignon '06	♟ 4
○ COF Tocai Friulano '02	♟♟ 4

● COF Merlot Sottocastello '04	♟♟ 6
● COF Cabernet Franc '05	♟♟ 4
● COF Schioppettino '05	♟♟ 5
○ COF Tocai Friulano '06	♟♟ 4
○ COF Sauvignon '06	♟♟ 4
○ COF Bianco Sottocastello '06	♟ 5
○ COF Ribolla Gialla '06	♟ 4
○ COF Pinot Grigio '06	♟ 4
● COF Merlot '05	♟ 4
● COF Refosco P. R. '05	4
○ COF Pinot Grigio '05	♟♟ 5
○ COF Tocai Friulano '05	♟♟ 4
● COF Refosco P. R. '02	♟♟ 5
● COF Rosso Sottocastello '04	♟♟ 7
● COF Rosso Sottocastello '01	♟♟ 5

Vignai da Duline

LOC. VILLANOVA
VIA IV NOVEMBRE, 136
33048 SAN GIOVANNI AL NATISONE [UD]
TEL. 0432758115
www.vignaidaduline.com

★ Le Vigne di Zamò

LOC. ROSAZZO
VIA ABATE CORRADO, 4
33044 MANZANO [UD]
TEL. 0432759693
www.levignedizamo.com

ANNUAL PRODUCTION 18,000 bottles	ANNUAL PRODUCTION 250,000 bottles
HECTARES UNDER VINE 7	HECTARES UNDER VINE 67
VITICULTURE METHOD Certified organic	VITICULTURE METHOD Natural

It is with great pleasure that we hail the first Three Glass award for this old-fashioned, indeed almost artisanal, estate, belonging to partners at work and in life Lorenzo Mocchiutti and Federica Magrini. The cellar is small but its ideas are profound and deeply bound up with the territory. The wines reflect the personalities of their makers. As Lorenzo says, "they convey the memory the grape has of the territory where it took shape". Morus Nigra is a single-variety Refosco that we enjoyed for the complexity of its spice, liqueur cherry and earthy fragrances. Warm and full bodied on the palate, it delivers hints of tar and a long pepper and hay finale. A Riserva version of the wine will be released in 2009 under the name Rosso di Sofia, in honour of the couple's young daughter. We'll be back to talk about that. For now, we'll carry on with a Pinot Grigio that combines full-bodied fruit aromas with refreshing mineral and apple. Sun-ripe tropical fruit is the Tocai's calling card while the Chardonnay offers yeasty and cream-like sensations. Finally, the merlot and cabernet franc Rosso Viburnum is dark and austere but shows great depth and robust extract.

Brothers Pierluigi and Silvano Zamò want to find a balance between commercial demands and quality that eschews compromise. Their stated aim is to enhance the value of their standard-label wines while continuing to release superb selections. The way ahead is to increase the quantity of estate-grown fruit available, which they have done by purchasing the six hectares of the former Querciabella farm next to their own vineyards. The Zamos' determination translates into refusing to release major labels in minor vintages, such as 2002 and 2005. Again this time, there was no Three Glass wine but the winery is still one of Friuli's very best. For the past few years, the estate has pinned many of its hopes on Tocai Vigne Cinquant'Anni, a wine that differs from the classic Friulian version in that it is cask-conditioned but above all has immense structure, thanks to the venerable age of the vines. The Pinot Bianco Tullio Zamò is an exceptional wine, to be uncorked at least five years after the harvest and the Ronco delle Acacie 2005, from chardonnay, tocai, pinot bianco and picolit, is another wine for the cellar.

● Morus Nigra Refosco P. R. '05	♟♟♟	6
○ COF Pinot Grigio '06	♟♟	4*
○ COF Chardonnay '05	♟♟	5
● COF Rosso Viburnum '05	♟♟	5
○ Friuli Grave Tocai Friulano '06	♟♟	4
○ COF Bianco Morus Alba '05	♟	5
○ COF Chardonnay '03	♟♟	5
○ COF Chardonnay '04	♟♟	5
● Morus Nigra Refosco P. R. '04	♟♟	6
● COF Rosso Viburnum '04	♟♟	5

○ COF Rosazzo Bianco Ronco delle Acacie '05	♟♟	6
○ COF Tocai Friulano V. Cinquant'Anni '05	♟♟	6
○ COF Pinot Bianco Tullio Zamò '05	♟♟	5
○ COF Pinot Grigio '06	♟♟	5
○ COF Bianco Zamò '06	♟♟	4*
○ COF Tocai Friulano '06	♟♟	5
● COF Refosco P. R. Re Fosco '04	♟	6
○ COF Sauvignon V. Cinquant'Anni '05	♟	5
○ COF Sauvignon '06	♟	5
○ COF Tocai Friulano V. Cinquant'Anni '00	♟♟♟	5
○ COF Tocai Friulano V. Cinquant'Anni '99	♟♟♟	5
● COF Rosazzo Pignolo '01	♟♟♟	8

Vigne Fantin Noda'r
LOC. ORSARIA
VIA CASALI OTTELIO, 4
33170 PREMARIACCO [UD]
TEL. 043428735
www.fantinnodar.it

ANNUAL PRODUCTION 60,000 bottles
HECTARES UNDER VINE 22
VITICULTURE METHOD Conventional

In 1991, Attilio Pignat from Pordenone bought the 20 hectares of vineyard with their farmhouse and cellar in the hills that separate Buttrio from Premariacco, one of Friuli's very finest wine zones. He quickly realized that to improve quality he would have to replant at a higher density of 5,000 vines per hectare, which he did in 1993 and 1994. A few years later, Fantin Noda'r presented us with a range of wines that opened the doors of the Guide. Since 2002, the winery has been a Guide fixture and this year, one bottle went through to our finals. Credit must surely go to the oenologist, Francesco Spitaleri, and vineyard manager Stefano Bortolussi, who have been working with Dr Pignat for years. The nose of the Sauvignon is intense and complex yet elegant, with elderflower syrup notes peeking through the fig leaf and tomato leaf. All are echoed faithfully on the palate, which layers them with pleasing pineapple in a rich, warm and very persistent progression. Elegance is also the hallmark of the broad Tocai Friulano, which gives pears and almonds.

Villa De Puppi
VIA ROMA, 5
33040 MOIMACCO [UD]
TEL. 0432722461
www.depuppi.it

ANNUAL PRODUCTION 50,000 bottles
HECTARES UNDER VINE 30
VITICULTURE METHOD Conventional

Luigi De Puppi is one of Italy's best-known industrial and financial consultants. He also has a wine estate extending over 30 hectares, two thirds of it around the cellar itself, where Luigi's son Valfredo is directing makeover and expansion operations. The consultants are some of the finest in Friuli, starting with master fruitmakers Marco Simonit and Pierpaolo Sirch. The grapes they prepare are then vinified by Marco Pecchiari and Alessio Dorigo. With that sort of support, it is easy to see why the winery has made such strides after effectively setting up only in 2004. We should also mention Caterina, Valfredo's sister and enthusiastic helper. The wine we liked from our first tastings was the Sauvignon. Concentrated and redolent of elderflower and bell pepper, it is juicy, tangy, broad and lingering. Taj Blanc is a tocai friulano-only white with impressive structure for a flatlands product and glycerine richness that might make it seem soft on the palate. Elegance is a distinguishing characteristic of Villa De Puppi wines and the creamy, fresh-tasting Chardonnay is no exception.

O COF Sauvignon '06	♟♟	4*
O COF Tocai Friulano '06	♟♟	4
O COF Ribolla Gialla '06	♟	4
O COF Sauvignon '05	♟♟	4

O Sauvignon '06	♟♟	4*
O Chardonnay '06	♟♟	4
O Taj Blanc '06	♟♟	4
● Merlot '04		4

Villa Frattina
FRAZ. GHIRANO
VIA PALAZZETTO, 68
33080 PRATA DI PORDENONE [PN]
TEL. 0434605911
www.villafrattina.it

ANNUAL PRODUCTION 450,000 bottles
HECTARES UNDER VINE 50
VITICULTURE METHOD Conventional

Villa Frattina has been acquired by Averna
to supplement the products distributed in
Italy and abroad. Under various labels, the
giant group's vast range includes hazelnut
chocolates, nougat, pralines and so on as
well as the celebrated amaro digestive.
There are 50 hectares straddling the
provinces of Pordenone, Treviso and Venice
while oenologist Ivan Molaro has the job of
winemaking. Some years ago, Averna
engaged the services of Donato Lanati, the
Piedmont-based university teacher who has
state-of-the-art analysis and consultancy
facilities. Villa Frattina is the name of the
splendid 16th-century manor house that
today goes onto the label of the cellar's Brut
sparkling wine only. All the others are
released as Frattina. Our tasters loved the
Tocai Italico for its tobacco, candied orange
peel and pear aromas, beautifully structured
palate and good length. Bianco di Gale,
from chardonnay and pinot grigio,
progresses seamlessly in the mouth. Finally,
the merlot, refosco and cabernet franc
Robbio is more convincing on the nose than
on the palate.

Villa Martina
FRAZ. BRAZZANO
LOC. CÀ DELLE VALLADE, 3B
34071 CORMONS [GO]
TEL. 048160733
www.villamartina.it

ANNUAL PRODUCTION 80,000 bottles
HECTARES UNDER VINE 10
VITICULTURE METHOD Conventional

Villa Martina made a sure-footed entry to
the Guide this year. It has ten hectares at
Brazzano, an excellent subzone in the Collio
Friulano. Mario Sfiligoi and his wife Luciana
started up in the late 1960s "with empty
pockets but clear ideas", as Mario likes to
say. Now, their three daughters all
contribute to the running of the family
estate. Michela looks after sales and
administration, Patrizia is the cellar
technician and young Martina, after whom
the winery was named, takes care of
production. It's very much a women's
winery, then, and the wines themselves are
fresh-tasting and elegant, as well as very
good value for money. The stand-outs are a
Pinot Grigio with spring flower and rennet
apple fragrances introducing a savoury
palate, a varietally spicy but, unlike many
versions, not aggressive Cabernet Franc
and a very complex, full-bodied Refosco
with very attractive extract.

O Lison-Pramaggiore	
Tocai Italico '06	▼▼ 4*
O Lison-Pramaggiore	
Pinot Grigio '06	▼ 4
O Lison-Pramaggiore Sauvignon '06	▼ 4
O Bianco di Gale '06	▼ 5
● Robbio '04	▼ 5
● Lison-Pramaggiore	
Cabernet Sauvignon '06	4
O Lison-Pramaggiore	
Pinot Grigio '05	▼▼ 4

● Cabernet Franc '05	▼▼ 4*
● Friuli Isonzo Refosco P. R. '06	▼▼ 4*
O Collio Pinot Grigio '06	▼▼ 4*
O Collio Tocai Friulano '06	▼▼ 4*
● Collio Cabernet Franc '04	▼ 4
● Collio Merlot '05	▼ 4
O Collio Sauvignon '06	▼ 4

Villa Ronche

LOC. VISTORTA
VIA VISTORTA, 82
33077 SACILE [PN]
TEL. 043471135
www.villaronche.it

ANNUAL PRODUCTION 300,000 bottles
HECTARES UNDER VINE 36
VITICULTURE METHOD Conventional

The estate at Villa Ronche is managed by Brandino Brandolini d'Adda and his staff, with wine technician Alec Ongaro in charge of vinification. The 150 hectares of countryside, 36 of which are under vine, supply fruit for 300,000 bottles a year. Most of the vine stock is next to the stunningly beautiful villa at Cordignano, just over the regional border in Veneto. Winemaking facilities are in one of the villa's barchessa outbuildings where you will find traditional tools, such as the cement vats that so many producers are slowly rediscovering. The cellar has created a surprising wine, Treanni, which appears bearing the Conte Brandolini d'Adda label, which from next year should replace the la Villa Ronche. Treanni, produced with consultancy input from two French oenologists, George Pauli and Samuel Tinon, is vinified in a rather unusual fashion. The wines, in this case from the 2003, 2004 and 2005 vintages, are from cabernet franc, refosco and merlot. Wines from the current vintage stay in steel for a year, the previous year's wines spend a year in pre-used barriques and the others pass two years in Slavonian oak barrels. The final product is magnificent.

● Treanni Rosso	🍷🍷	4*
○ Friuli Grave Pinot Grigio '06	🍷🍷	4*
○ Friuli Grave Sauvignon '06	🍷🍷	4*
○ Friuli Grave Tocai Friulano '06	🍷	3
○ Friuli Grave Traminer Aromatico '06	🍷	4
○ Friuli Grave Chardonnay '06		3
○ Friuli Grave Tocai Friulano '05	🍷🍷	3

★ Villa Russiz

VIA RUSSIZ, 6
34070 CAPRIVA DEL FRIULI [GO]
TEL. 048180047
www.villarussiz.it

ANNUAL PRODUCTION 180,000 bottles
HECTARES UNDER VINE 35
VITICULTURE METHOD Conventional

This influential winery, part of the Adele Cerruti charity, gives the lie to claims that public management of assets has to be passive. The institute has 94 hectares, 35 planted to vine, and generates profits that are reinvested in the estate and in supporting children from needy families. The chariman is the dynamic Silvano Stefanutti, who is always pressing for new initiatives that inspire the estate manager, the outstanding oenologist Gianni Menotti. One of the estate's advertising brochures talks about passion, commitment, fervour and tradition. Anyone who knows Gianni will know that these concepts sum him up to perfection. It all comes together in a range of wines from which it is always hard to pick which one will win a Three Glass. Merlot Graf de La Tour is every inch a champion, superb now but capable of maturing successfully in the cellar for at least 15 years and with a hint of grassiness that is instantly reminiscent of Bordeaux. This wonderful red was our choice for Three Glasses. But what about the Malvasia? Or the Tocai Friulano, the Sauvignon de La Tour, the Pinot Grigio or the standard-label Sauvignon? Or the Pinot Bianco or the Chardonnay, all hard on the Merlot's heels?

● Collio Merlot Graf de La Tour '04	🍷🍷🍷	7
○ Collio Malvasia '06	🍷🍷	5
○ Collio Pinot Grigio '06	🍷🍷	5
○ Collio Tocai Friulano '06	🍷🍷	5
○ Collio Sauvignon '06	🍷🍷	5
○ Collio Sauvignon de La Tour '06	🍷🍷	6
○ Collio Chardonnay Gräfin de La Tour '05	🍷🍷	6
○ Collio Pinot Bianco '06	🍷🍷	5
○ Collio Riesling '06	🍷🍷	5
○ Collio Ribolla Gialla '06	🍷🍷	5
● Collio Merlot '05	🍷	5
● Collio Cabernet Sauvignon '05	🍷	5
○ Collio Sauvignon de La Tour '05	🍷🍷🍷	6
○ Collio Sauvignon de La Tour '02	🍷🍷🍷	6
○ Collio Tocai Friulano '04	🍷🍷🍷	5
● Collio Merlot Graf de La Tour '02	🍷🍷🍷	7
● Collio Merlot Graf de La Tour '99	🍷🍷🍷	7

Tenuta Villanova

LOC. VILLANOVA
VIA CONTESSA BERETTA, 29
34072 FARRA D'ISONZO [GO]
TEL. 0481889311
www.tenutavillanova.com

ANNUAL PRODUCTION 400,000 bottles
HECTARES UNDER VINE 100
VITICULTURE METHOD Conventional

Tenuta Villanova, which dates back to 1499, is a beautiful, welcoming estate. Its geologically interesting location features Collio-type "islands" of chalk and clay alternating with calcified sand that rise out of the Isonzo "sea" where gravel and alluvial sand is covered by a thin, fertile layer tinged brownish by ferrous iron. Villanova's list of wines is long and includes selections, the Collio range and the Isonzo line, itself split into a standard label and Masi di Villanova, the property identified from the 1499 document in the Chapter of Aquileia. The classiest and most characterful of the Masi wines is the Malvasia while in the Collio, it is the year of Friulano, formerly known as Tocai, which is still slightly green and gives sage, bananas, almond paste, and the classic pear notes, elegant bouquet and fresh-tasting drinkability of the Pinot Grigio. From the selections, we liked the surprisingly good Sauvignon with its peach, elderflower and mint – all it needs is a tad more length – and the quaffable pinot nero-based Brut, which is fresh, flavoursome and fruity.

Vinài dell'Abbàte

LOC. ROSAZZO
P.ZZA ABBAZIA, 15
33044 MANZANO [UD]
TEL. 0432759429
www.tenutealeandri.it

ANNUAL PRODUCTION 120,000 bottles
HECTARES UNDER VINE 12
VITICULTURE METHOD Conventional

After various changes of administration, this splendid estate owned by the Archiepiscopal Curia of Udine was handed over to the Tenuta Aleandri group, which owns various other wineries in Friuli and Veneto. Not for the first time, we would point out that hiring consultants of the calibre of Marco Simonit and Pierpaolo Sirch in the vineyards and Gianni Menotti in the cellar ensures rapid growth in quality. The cellar's origins are lost in the mists of time but it is known that monks built a cellar here in the late 13th century to press the grapes and olives grown in the area. The oil disappeared in 1929, when frost killed off the olive trees, but today the estate again has more than 800, planted in the 1980s and 1990s. It was here that an obscure parish priest, Fr Nadalutti, kept the last remaining vines of pignolo, which the canny Girolamo Dorigo set about saving from extinction, at the suggestion of Gino Veronelli. You can tell that Gianni Menotti made the superb Sauvignon, a wine with supremely vigorous progression. We look forward to even more stunning wines in the coming years.

O Collio Pinot Grigio '06	♟♟ 4
O Villanova Brut	♟♟ 5
O Friuli Isonzo Malvasia Saccoline '06	♟♟ 4
O Collio Friulano '06	♟♟ 4
O Collio Sauvignon Ronco Cucco '06	♟♟ 5
O Collio Chardonnay Ronco Cucco '06	♟ 5
O Friuli Isonzo Chardonnay '06	♟ 4
O Collio Ribolla Gialla '06	♟ 4
O Friuli Isonzo Sauvignon '06	♟ 4
O Collio Picolit Ronco Cucco '05	6

O COF Sauvignon '06	♟♟ 4*
O COF Chardonnay '06	♟♟ 4
● Broili Ros	♟♟ 4
● COF Cabernet Sauvignon Ronco dei Domenicani '01	♟ 5
O COF Ribolla Gialla '06	♟ 5
● COF Merlot Ronco dei Benedettini '01	♟ 5
● COF Pignolo Ris. '00	♟♟ 7
O COF Picolit '03	♟♟ 6
O COF Sauvignon '05	♟♟ 4

Franco Visintin

VIA ROMA, 37
34072 GRADISCA D'ISONZO [GO]
TEL. 048199974

ANNUAL PRODUCTION 40,000 bottles
HECTARES UNDER VINE 6
VITICULTURE METHOD Conventional

This is not one of the wineries that the media spotlight falls on with any regularity but that probably doesn't bother the likeable Franco Visintin very much. In reality, the cellar looks for its future to its circle of loyal customers and admirers, and the network of local relationships that it has built up over the years in Gradisca d'Isonzo, a place that is halfway between town and city, countryside and factory developments, and Italy and central Europe. What Franco offers all his customers is reliable quality, fair prices and generous hospitality. This time, we thought the Tocai and the Malvasia were a cut above the rest. It was a particularly fine vintage for both varieties, although in some wines alcohol makes its presence felt. At Visintin, however, fresh sensations, suppleness and depth of fruit in the Tocai, and the bouquet of the Malvasia, enhance drinkability appreciably. Other wines to go for are the Bordeaux blend Stàngja Rosso and the Chardonnay but the rest of the range is impeccably managed.

Andrea Visintini

VIA GRAMOGLIANO, 27
33040 CORNO DI ROSAZZO [UD]
TEL. 0432755813
www.vinivisintini.com

ANNUAL PRODUCTION 130,000 bottles
HECTARES UNDER VINE 28
VITICULTURE METHOD Conventional

We should mention straight away that this is a cellar deserving our admiration both for the people who run it and for its extremely consumer-friendly pricing. Started in 1973 by Andrea Visintin, the cellar has passed gradually to his children Oliviero and twins Palmira and Cinzia. There are 28 hectares under vine, almost all near the cellar, including the Collio DOC vineyard. The estate landmark is the tower dating from 1560. Recently restored, it was in turn built on the site of a Roman watchtower. Since the tower is a listed building, it hampered the expansion of the cellar until the Visintins opted for facilities that are completely underground and meet their requirements without altering the landscape. Intense and upfront, the mightily impressive Sauvignon unveils a savoury palate that proffers yellow peach and ripe pineapple. A step behind is the Bianco, from tocai, picolit and pinot bianco, further proof that dry-vinified picolit can give blended wine an extra edge. Finally, the Merlot Riserva Torion is a delightful surprise.

O Friuli Isonzo Tocai Friulano '06	▼▼ 3*
O Friuli Isonzo Chardonnay '06	▼ 3
O Friuli Isonzo Malvasia '06	▼ 3
● Stàngja Rosso '04	▼ 4
● Friuli Isonzo Cabernet Franc '05	4
● Friuli Isonzo Merlot '05	3
● Stàngja Rosso '00	▼▼ 4
● Stàngja Rosso '01	▼▼ 4
● Stàngja Rosso '03	▼▼ 4

O COF Sauvignon '06	▼▼ 4*
O COF Bianco '06	▼▼ 4
O COF Pinot Bianco '06	▼▼ 4
O Collio Malvasia '06	▼▼ 4
O COF Tocai Friulano '06	▼▼ 4
● COF Merlot Ris. Torion '04	▼▼ 4
● COF Merlot '05	▼ 4
O COF Pinot Grigio '06	▼ 4
O COF Ribolla Gialla '06	▼ 4
O COF Tocai Friulano '05	▼▼ 3
O Collio Malvasia '04	▼▼ 4
O Collio Malvasia '05	▼▼ 4

Vistorta

VIA VISTORTA, 82
33077 SACILE [PN]
TEL. 043471135
www.vistorta.it

ANNUAL PRODUCTION 77,000 bottles
HECTARES UNDER VINE 40
VITICULTURE METHOD Natural

Brandino Brandolini manages this estate, which originally extended over the entire village of Vistorta, with an enthusiasm that seems to intensify with each passing year. His meticulous care over details is symbolized by the superb parkland surrounding the main residence. Its huge barchessa outbuildings are used for storing wines from previous vintages and an eye-catching display of medium-sized barrels. Brandino's education was acquired in the United States and France, the country that has also given him two consultants – and friends – in George Pauli and Samuel Tinon. The 40 or so hectares planted to merlot clones selected in France are managed by Marco Simonit, whose expert work among the rows further enhances the quality of the fruit that arrives in the cellar. Alec Ongaro prepares the blends of the part of the wine that will go into Vistorta's prestigious bottles. We'll try to sum up this outstanding wine in Brandino's own words: "A modern, elegant, long-lived wine of freshness and drinkability, with moderate alcohol and a modest price tag". You will find all these qualities in the 2005 edition, a great red and an object lesson in elegance that deservedly won Three Glasses.

Volpe Pasini

FRAZ. TOGLIANO
VIA CIVIDALE, 16
33040 TORREANO [UD]
TEL. 0432715151
www.volpepasini.net

ANNUAL PRODUCTION 330,000 bottles
HECTARES UNDER VINE 52
VITICULTURE METHOD Conventional

Volpe Pasini is an estate in constant expansion, both in vine stock and in numbers of bottles released. Owner Emilio Rotolo is adamant that the future belongs to wineries that can present their products in a worldwide market. His aim is to reach an output of 1,000,000 bottles a year. That goal looks a long way off but it is not beyond the bounds of possibility, given Emilio's determination. This year, there was a major change in the cellar as consultant Riccardo Cotarella took his leave, to be replaced by Alessio Dorigo's Friuli-based Terra&Vini group. This time, Volpe Pasini picked up Three Glasses for a superb Tocai Friulano Zuc di Volpe, a fresh yet warm wine with an intriguing nose of peach-laced pear in an elegant, long-lingering whole. Merlot Focus and Sauvignon Zuc di Volpe are estate classics and they, too, did well. For the past couple of years, the Pinot Grigio Zuc di Volpe has been outperforming the Ipso selection, where the oak is a little too evident.

● Friuli Grave Merlot Vistorta '05	▼▼▼	5
● Friuli Grave Merlot Vistorta '04	♈♈♈	5
● Friuli Grave Merlot Vistorta '03	♈♈♈	5
● Friuli Grave Merlot Vistorta '02	♈♈	5
● Friuli Grave Merlot Vistorta '00	♈♈	5
● Friuli Grave Merlot Vistorta '99	♈♈	5
● Friuli Grave Merlot Vistorta '98	♈♈	5
● Friuli Grave Merlot Vistorta '97	♈♈	5

○ COF Tocai Friulano Zuc di Volpe '05	▼▼▼	5
○ COF Sauvignon Zuc di Volpe '06	▼▼	5
● COF Merlot Focus '05	▼▼	6
○ COF Pinot Bianco Zuc di Volpe '06	▼▼	5
○ COF Pinot Grigio Zuc di Volpe '06	▼▼	5
● COF Refosco P. R. Zuc di Volpe '05	▼▼	5
○ COF Pinot Grigio Grivò '06	▼	4
○ COF Sauvignon '06	▼	4
○ COF Pinot Grigio Ipso '05	▼	4
○ COF Ribolla Gialla Zuc di Volpe '06	▼	4
○ COF Sauvignon Zuc di Volpe '05	♈♈♈	5
○ COF Sauvignon Zuc di Volpe '04	♈♈♈	5
● COF Refosco P. R. Zuc di Volpe '01	♈♈♈	5
● COF Merlot Focus Zuc di Volpe '99	♈♈♈	5
○ COF Pinot Grigio Zuc di Volpe '05	♈♈	4

Francesco Vosca

FRAZ. BRAZZANO
VIA SOTTOMONTE, 19
34070 CORMONS [GO]
TEL. 048162135
voscafrancesco@libero.it

ANNUAL PRODUCTION 15,000 bottles
HECTARES UNDER VINE 6
VITICULTURE METHOD Conventional

Francesco Vosca is something of an old-time winemaker, given his absolutely unfussy approach to his vineyards and postage stamp-sized cellar. He does all the work himself, which makes it difficult for him to produce wine and visit potential customers at the same time. Francesco also only bottles as much wine as he thinks he can sell, keeping in the vat some products he thinks could become outstanding. The vine stock comprises six hectares, just under half in the Collio DOC zone and the rest on the Isonzo flatlands. In the hill country, his tocai, malvasia and pinot grigio vines are double arch-trained, known locally as "alla cappuccina" training, while in the Isonzo DOC he grows sauvignon and chardonnay. Most of the work among the rows is done by Francesco himself but at harvest time, the whole of the family lends a hand. Thanks in part to advice from Luigino De Giuseppe and Mauro Mauri, Francesco has produced an excellent, very varietal Malvasia redolent of lavender, violets and pears. Equally fine is the lingering, savoury Tocai Friulano with its pear and hazelnut sensations.

Zidarich

FRAZ. S. PELAGIO
LOC. PREPOTTO, 23
34011 DUINO AURISINA [TS]
TEL. 040201223
www.zidarich.it

ANNUAL PRODUCTION 18,000 bottles
HECTARES UNDER VINE 6
VITICULTURE METHOD Natural

In Carso's wine country, perhaps because of shared cultural roots or more likely because both aim to defend an infertile land that struggles to regenerate itself, many estates are adopting techniques that resemble those used in Oslavia, in the Collio Goriziano. Skin contact, natural yeasts, careful use of wood, no filtration, no temperature control and no stabilization are the order of the day. But Carso winemakers do not simply copy Oslavia. Leading exponents, at least, imbue the process with their own personality and the distinctive mark of the Carso terroir. That means savouriness that verges on saltiness, vibrant acidity and aromas over extract. In the case of Zidarich, everything is tempered by a desire not to spring surprises on the consumer. Here, the wines project a constancy of purpose that is expressed in weight on the palate, balance, cleanness and varietal character. You will find this in all the wines from this year's range, including the Prulke blend of sauvignon, vitovska and malvasia.

O Collio Malvasia '06	🍷🍷 4*
O Collio Tocai Friulano '06	🍷🍷 4*
O Collio Pinot Grigio '06	🍷 4
O Friuli Isonzo Sauvignon '06	🍷 4
O Friuli Isonzo Chardonnay '06	🍷 4
O Collio Bianco Frut Blanc '05	4
O Collio Malvasia '04	🍷🍷 4
O Collio Malvasia '05	🍷🍷 4
O Friuli Isonzo Sauvignon '04	🍷🍷 4
O Collio Tocai Friulano '05	🍷🍷 4
O Collio Tocai Friulano '04	🍷🍷 4
O Collio Pinot Grigio '05	🍷🍷 4

O Carso Malvasia '05	🍷🍷 6
O Prulke '05	🍷🍷 6
O Carso Vitovska '05	🍷🍷 6
● Carso Terrano '05	🍷🍷 6
O Prulke '02	🍷🍷 6
O Prulke '04	🍷🍷 6
O Carso Vitovska '04	🍷🍷 6
O Prulke '03	🍷🍷 6

Zof

FRAZ. SANT'ANDRAT DEL JUDRIO
VIA GIOVANNI XXIII, 32A
33040 CORNO DI ROSAZZO [UD]
TEL. 0432759673
www.zof.it

ANNUAL PRODUCTION 90,000 bottles
HECTARES UNDER VINE 13
VITICULTURE METHOD Conventional

Daniele Zof represents the current generation of a family with roots in Austria and Prussia that settled in this part of Friuli more than a century ago, although it was only a couple of decades ago that they adopted viticulture as their main source of income. It was Daniele's father Alberto who started but Daniele effected the sea change that put quality at the top of the list of priorities. We should say straight away that he has been successful, thanks in part to own efforts and in part to the crucial collaboration of Donato Lanati, whom he met at university and who has been consulting now for several years. Today, Daniele has found his professional feet and releases a range of consistently well-made products. His Ribolla Gialla is again one of the best around but we would encourage you to try his oak-aged chardonnay and sauvignon Bianco Sonata, which has now reined in the contribution of the wood. Finally, the 2003 version of the cabernet sauvignon, merlot and schioppettino-based Va' Pensiero is very good indeed.

Zuani

LOC. GIASBANA, 12
34070 SAN FLORIANO DEL COLLIO [GO]
TEL. 0481391432
www.zuanivini.it

ANNUAL PRODUCTION 40,000 bottles
HECTARES UNDER VINE 10
VITICULTURE METHOD Conventional

Go-getting wine woman Patrizia Felluga continues to expand the vine stock of her estate. She is the daughter of Marco Felluga, one of the fathers of modern Friulian winemaking but Patrizia has followed her own star. This year, she has 14 hectares under vine, of which ten are currently in production. As she gradually, radically, replants the vines, Patrizia has adopted management techniques that enable her to bring first-quality grapes to the cellar. Plantings patterns are high-density and yields per vine are low. In addition, the cellar itself has been made over so that it blends in better with the landscape. Patrizia's son Antonio is now very much part of the team while daughter Caterina contributes when she has time off from her studies. Winemaking concentrates on just two wines: a selection, Zuani, which is cask conditioned and released to market in its second year; and Zuani Vigne, sourced from the recently purchased vineyards and vinified in steel. The tempting, youthful Zuani is complex, concentrated and citrus-led whereas the Vigne stands out for freshness, a savoury note and its wealth of fruit.

O COF Bianco Sonata '05	♥♥	5
O COF Ribolla Gialla '06	♥♥	4*
● COF Cabernet Franc '05	♥	4
O COF Sauvignon '06	♥	4
O COF Tocai Friulano '06	♥	4
● Rosso Va' Pensiero '03	♥	5
O COF Pinot Grigio '06	♥	4
O COF Picolit '04	♥	6
● COF Merlot '05		4
O COF Verduzzo Friulano '05		4
O COF Ribolla Gialla '05	♀♀	4
O COF Ribolla Gialla '04	♀♀	4

O Collio Bianco Zuani '05	♥♥	6
O Collio Bianco Zuani Vigne '06	♥♥	5
O Collio Bianco Zuani '04	♀♀	5
O Collio Bianco Zuani '03	♀♀	5
O Collio Bianco Zuani '02	♀♀	5
O Collio Bianco Zuani '01	♀♀	5
O Collio Bianco Zuani Vigne '03	♀♀	4
O Collio Bianco Zuani Vigne '04	♀♀	5

OTHER WINERIES

Blason
VIA ROMA, 32
34072 GRADISCA D'ISONZO [GO]
TEL. 048192414
www.vinidocisonzo.it

Giovanni Blason's wines reflect their growing year and this time the range was more impressive than it was on our last visit. Tocai Friulano is the cellar's strong suit in a well typed, warm, savoury version plenty of elegance. A hint of acidity thins the Pinot Grigio but the fresh Cabernet Franc is attractive.

O Friuli Isonzo Tocai Friulano '06	♥♥	4*
O Friuli Isonzo Pinot Grigio '06	♥	4
● Friuli Isonzo Cabernet Franc '06	♥	4

Alfredo Bracco
FRAZ. BRAZZANO
VIA XXIV MAGGIO, 28
34070 CORMONS [GO]
TEL. 048160002
www.braccovini.it

Oenologist Elisabetta Bracco's small cellar makes its Guide debut. Friulian by heritage and French by training, Elisabetta brings these two elements together in the tocai and sauvignon Bianco Bracco. Tocai Ultimo is an intense wine from 60-year-old vines and the Pinot Bianco is bright and savoury.

O Friuli Isonzo Bianco Bracco '06	♥♥	4*
O Friuli Isonzo Pinot Bianco '06	♥	4
O Friuli Isonzo Tocai Friulano Ultimo '06	♥	4

Brojli - Franco Clementin
VIA G. GALILEI, 5
33050 TERZO D'AQUILEIA [UD]
TEL. 043132642
www.fattoriaclementin.it

The place name Brojli is from the Celtic Brògilos, meaning small plots of land. Franco Clementin estate comprises six or so "brojli" in the municipalities of Terzo d'Aquileia and Aquileia. The soil is the clay and sand of the Aquileia DOC while Franco's Pinot Bianco 2006 is a wine of rare length and elegance.

O Friuli Aquileia Pinot Bianco '06	♥♥	3*
O Chardonnay '06	♥	3
● Friuli Aquileia Refosco '06	♥	3

Cadibon
VIA CASALI GALLO, 1
33040 CORNO DI ROSAZZO [UD]
TEL. 0432759316
www.cadibon.com

Despite the handover from Gianni and Ameris Bon to their children Luca and Francesca, the cellar continues to feature in the top half of the quality ranking. None of the wines earned a second Glass but there were spikes in the Tocai Friulano, although it is thinned by too much acidity, and the Verduzzo Friulano.

O COF Ribolla Gialla '06	♥	4
● COF Refosco P. R. '06	♥	4
O COF Tocai Friulano '06	♥	4
O COF Verduzzo Friulano '06	♥	4

Ca' Madresca
VIA LOMBARDIA, 5
33080 FIUME VENETO [PN]
TEL. 0434560013
adriano_test@libero.it

Adriano Teston is an expert oenologist who launched his family winery in January 2003. He has no vine stock, buying in his fruit from suppliers whose vineyard management he supervises. Adriano is in the Guide this year thanks to his single-variety Chardonnay, Nibbio, and an interesting Sauvignon Reys.

O Collio Sauvignon Reys '06	♥♥	4*
O Nibbio '06	♥♥	3*
● Collio Cabernet Sauvignon Reys '05	♥	4

Ca' Selva
S.DA DI SEQUALS, 11A
33090 SEQUALS [PN]
TEL. 0421274704
www.caselva.it

Ca' Selva has 34 hectares of specialized vineyards in a zone so little inclined to high yields that it is called "i magredi", meaning "the lean lands". Admirably, it has long been practising rigorously organic viticulture. This year's top wine was the Refosco, followed by the Tocai and Pinot Grigio.

● Refosco P. R. Jevade '05	♥♥	3*
O Friuli Grave Tocai Friulano Sclavon '06	♥	3
O Pinot Grigio Gardisane '06	♥	4

OTHER WINERIES

Castello di Buttrio
VIA MORPURGO, 9
33042 BUTTRIO [UD]
TEL. 0432673015
www.castellodibuttrio.it

Alessandra Felluga steps forward into the front rank of Friulian wine with the cellar she is now running on her own. Marco Felluga's youngest daughter releases just two wines, both excellent. Her Tocai Friulano is complex and slightly salty while her acidity-rich Chardonnay is ideal for laying down.

○ COF Tocai Friulano '06	♟	6
○ Chardonnay '06	♟	6

Castello di Rubbia
SAN MICHELE DEL CARSO
34070 SAVOGNA D'ISONZO [GO]
TEL. 0481882681
www.castellodirubbia.it

Natasa Cernic grows only native varieties with the help of oenologist Marco Pecchiari and Marco Simonit in the vineyard. Her new cellar, in the Carso rock, is stunning. The fatty Malvasia has wonderful spring flowers, williams pears and enough alcohol to seem soft on the back palate. Her Terrano is very varietal.

○ Malvasia '06	♟	5
● Terrano '05	♟	5
○ Bianco della Bora '05		5

Colli di Poianis
VIA POIANIS, 34A
33040 PREPOTTO [UD]
TEL. 0432713185
www.collidipoianis.com

In 1999, Danilo and Gabriele Marinig made their father Paolino's dream come true and started their own winery. The 11 hectares are in a subzone best known for Schioppettino, the top Marinig wine thanks to varietal black cherry and raspberries. Equally fine is the Sauvignon, which tempts the nose with nice elderflower.

○ COF Sauvignon '06	♟♟	4*
● COF Schioppettino '06	♟♟	5
● COF Rosso Ronco della Poiana '05	♟	5
○ COF Tocai Friulano '06	♟	4

Cantina Produttori di Cormòns
VIA VINO DELLA PACE, 31
34071 CORMONS [GO]
TEL. 048160579
www.cormons.com

Missing from last year's Guide, this is one of the region's most influential wine enterprises. The huge range embraces several DOC zones but our favourite was the fresh, fruit-forward Colli Orientali del Friuli Ribolla Gialla. The savoury, substantial Collio Tocai Friulano Rinascimento also impressed.

○ COF Ribolla Gialla '06	♟♟	4
○ Collio Tocai Friulano Rinascimento '06	♟	4
○ Collio Pinot Grigio '06	♟	4
○ Friuli Isonzo Pinot Grigio Rosänder '06	♟	4

Do Ville
VIA MITRAGLIERI, 2
34077 RONCHI DEI LEGIONARI [GO]
TEL. 0481775561
www.doville.it

Brothers Paolo and Gianni Bonora vinify with both estate-grown and bought-in fruit. Ars Vivendi is their range of fresh wines for immediate consumption whereas Do Ville wines are made for the cellar. The '06 Malvasia is fresh, flowery, attractively varietal and savoury.

○ Malvasia Ars Vivendi '06	♟♟	3*
● Merlot Do Ville '04	♟	5
● Cabernet Sauvignon Do Ville '04	♟	5

Draga
LOC. SCEDINA, 8
34070 SAN FLORIANO DEL COLLIO [GO]
TEL. 0481884182
www.draga.it

This winery, founded in the 1970s, is back in the Guide after thorough-going refurbishment by Milan Miklus, who vinifies the grapes from nine hectares at Draga and Breg. The range is a rollercoaster in terms of quality but there are three stand-outs: Bianco di Collina, Ribolla Gialla and Tocai.

○ Collio Bianco Bianco di Collina '06	♟♟	4*
○ Collio Ribolla Gialla '06	♟♟	5
○ Collio Tocai Friulano '06	♟♟	4
○ Collio Pinot Grigio '06		4

OTHER WINERIES

Albano Guerra
LOC. MONTINA
V.LE KENNEDY, 39A
33040 TORREANO [UD]
TEL. 0432715077

Nine hectares under vine give Dario Guerra an annual output of 50,000 bottles. Dario enters the Guide with some intriguing wines. The white Passiòn, from pinot grigio, tocai, sauvignon, verduzzo and picolit, is a fresh, tangy product with apple and citrus notes. The Picolit and Tocai Friulano almost won a second Glass.

○ COF Bianco Passiòn '06	♥♥	4*
○ COF Picolit '05	♥	6
○ COF Sauvignon '06	♥	4
○ COF Tocai Friulano '06	♥	4

Thomas Kitzmüller
FRAZ. BRAZZANO
VIA XXIV MAGGIO, 56
34070 CORMONS [GO]
TEL. 048160853
thomas.kitzmuller@virgilio.it

Welcome back to Thomas Kitzmüller, who has four hectares at Brazzano, where Collio meets the Isonzo DOC. He releases 17,000 bottles and some wine in demijohns. The Tocais from Collio and Isonzo – the Corte Marie line – are seriously good. The Collio version is soft while the Isonzo Tocai is salty and citrus-like.

○ Friuli Isonzo Tocai Friulano Corte Marie '06	♥♥	3*
○ Collio Tocai Friulano '06	♥♥	4
● Friuli Isonzo Rosso '05	♥	4

Albino Kurtin
LOC. NOVALI, 9
34071 CORMONS [GO]
TEL. 048160685

After a few years' exile, the Kurtin winery is back in the Guide thanks to a sterling performance. Albino Kurtin's estate covers about ten hectares and releases 60,000 bottles a year. His best bottles are Sauvignon, Pinot Grigio, Tocai Friulano and Opera Prima, a blend of pinot bianco, ribolla gialla and chardonnay.

○ Collio Pinot Grigio '06	♥♥	3*
○ Collio Sauvignon '06	♥♥	3*
○ Bianco Opera Prima '06	♥	4
○ Collio Tocai Friulano '06	♥	3

Giulio Manzocco
VIA C. BATTISTI, 61
34071 CORMONS [GO]
TEL. 048160590
www.vinimanzocco.com

The first vines here were planted in 1930, when grandfather Amedeo returned from Australia and bought land at Cormons. On the borders of the Collio and Isonzo DOC zones, this family cellar is run today by Dario Manzocco. His Pinot Grigio has classic pear, apple and ripe fruit aromas that are echoed on the palate.

○ Collio Pinot Grigio '06	♥♥	4
○ Collio Pinot Bianco '06	♥	4
● Friuli Isonzo Cabernet Franc '05	♥	4
○ Collio Tocai Friulano '06	♥	4

Midolini
VIA DELLE FORNACI, 1
33044 MANZANO [UD]
TEL. 0432754555
www.midolini.com

After two years' absence, Gloria Midolini's cellar is back in the Guide. There are 35 hectares of vineyards and the same again currently being planted. Uvaggio Bianco, from chardonnay, tocai and sauvignon, gives well-defined pear and apple. Ronco dell'Angelica, from tocai only, flaunts elegant fruit.

○ COF Bianco Rosacroce Uvaggio Bianco '06	♥♥	5
○ COF Pinot Grigio Rosacroce '06	♥	5
○ COF Bianco Rosacroce Ronco dell'Angelica '06	♥	5

Pighin
FRAZ. RISANO
V.LE GRADO, 1
33050 PAVIA DI UDINE [UD]
TEL. 0432675444
www.pighin.com

It has to be a blip if Fernando Pighin's influential family winery isn't punching its weight this time. Still, we are happy to see that the tocai, sauvignon and pinot bianco Bianco Terre di Risano with its varietal bell pepper is doing well. The Pighin Pinot Grigio Grave and Sauvignon Collio are as reliable as ever.

○ Friuli Grave Bianco Terre di Risano '06	♥♥	3*
○ Friuli Grave Pinot Grigio '06	♥	4
○ Collio Sauvignon '06	♥	4

OTHER WINERIES

Ronco dei Folo

VIA DI NOVACUZZO, 46
33040 PREPOTTO [UD]
TEL. 055859811
www.tenutefolonari.com

Ronco dei Folo, owned by Tenute Ambrogio and Giovanni Folonari, is a bigger winery than most in Friuli with its 38 hectares. The strong suit is whites and best of all is the tangy, intensely fragrant Tocai Friulano which has a savoury, alcohol-rich palate and good depth.

O COF Tocai Friulano '06		4
O COF Sauvignon '06		4
O COF Pinot Grigio '06		4
● COF Schioppettino '05		4

Ronco del Gnemiz

VIA RONCHI, 5
33048 SAN GIOVANNI AL NATISONE [UD]
TEL. 0432756238
roncodelgnemiz@libero.it

Serena Palazzolo looks to be specializing in reds, at least they performed distinctly better than her whites at our tastings. The Bordeaux blend Rosso offers satisfying complexity with hints of overripe fruit and softer tannins than the Merlot.

● COF Merlot Sol '03		7
● COF Rosso del Gnemiz '03		7
O Bianco San Zuan '06		5

Rubini

LOC. SPESSA
VIA CASE RUBINI, 4
33043 CIVIDALE DEL FRIULI [UD]
TEL. 0432716161
www.villarubini.net

This long-established winery at Spessa, near Cividale, confirmed its status. Set in excellent wine country around a beautiful ancient stately home, Rubini presented a balsamic Merlot with liqueur cherry and cinchona aromas, a very decent crusty bread Tocai and a flowery Chardonnay.

● COF Merlot '05		4
O COF Chardonnay '06		4
O COF Tocai Friulano		
What's in a name '06		4

Torre Rosazza

FRAZ. OLEIS
LOC. POGGIOBELLO, 12
33044 MANZANO [UD]
TEL. 0422864511
www.borgomagredo.it

It wasn't the best of years for this Genagricola-owned estate whose 95 hectares in a single block yield two lines, 200,000 units of Poggiobello wines and 350,000 of Torre Rosazza. The products are very well made but we hoped for more from wines like Ribolla Gialla or Cabernet Sauvignon. The Picolit is the stand-out.

O COF Picolit '04		6
O COF Ribolla Gialla '06		4
● COF Cabernet Sauvignon '05		4
O COF Tocai Friulano '06		4

Villa Vitas

LOC. STRASSOLDO
VIA SAN MARCO, 5
33050 CERVIGNANO DEL FRIULI [UD]
TEL. 043193083
www.vitas.it

This family winery is trying to shake off the flatlands stereotype with consultants Andrea Pittana and Francesco Spitaleri. Its best wine is the merlot, cabernet and refosco-based Rosso, which has well-crafted fruit. Attractive melon and yeasty notes lift the Chardonnay while the Sauvignon is rustic and sinewy.

O Friuli Aquileia Chardonnay '06		4
O Friuli Aquileia Sauvignon Blanc '06		4
● Friuli Aquileia Rosso		
Vign. Romano '03		5

Vodopivec

LOC. COLLUDROZZA, 4
34010 SGONICO [TS]
TEL. 040229181
www.vodopivec.it

Paolo and Valter Vodopivec took the bold decision to make only two wines from a single variety, vitovska. Their bush-trained stock is planted at 10,000 vines per hectare, skin contact goes on for two weeks and the wines age in 30-hectolitre Slavonian oak barrels for 30 months. The wine is unfiltered and emerges amber.

O Vitovska '04		7
O Vitovska Solo '04		8

EMILIA ROMAGNA

A snapshot of the current situation in Emilia Romagna shows light and shade. Each area, in fact almost each province, seems to lead its own separate life, with a production philosophy and marketing strategy not shared by its neighbours. The Colli Piacentini has earned esteem for producing outstanding whites and reds but the latter are not earning the recognition they deserve, largely because the diverse styles in which Gutturnio is being produced end up bewildering consumers. But there is no tarnish on the glorious tradition of producing superb meditation wines, either by semi-drying the aromatic malvasia di Candia or by utilizing the more sophisticated Vin Santo process. Barattieri's capture of Three Glasses with its sumptuous Albarola Val di Nure constitutes the affirmation of a tradition that should be recovered and exercised with renewed energy. The Lambrusco category, concentrated in the provinces of Parma, Reggio Emilia and Modena, is traversing a period of enthusiasm, as is shown by the large number of fine versions and even more by the fact that most of the producers are large-scale enterprises, convinced that quality is the only road to market presence, even in the niche world of sparkling reds. In contrast, no new developments are visible in the Colli Bolognesi. The usual hard core of producers is doing well but overall the area is experiencing problems getting up to speed. What is needed is a collaborative effort among all involved that would lead to a more clear-cut identity for the area's wines. Recent divisions among members of the DOC consortium can only make things worse. Finally, we come to Romagna, or rather the Romagnas, reflecting the numerous dichotomies within this part-region. There is the Romagna of the large co-operatives and the one of the small growers who have left them; there is the handful of long-time operations and the large numbers of just-emerging quality producers. One Romagna strives after quality while another still follows the post-war policy of quantity. There is a Romagna centred on Sangiovese di Romagna; a second capable of crafting red wines of great character and distinction, witness the likes of Michelangiolo di Calonga, Papiano di Papiano di Villa Papiano, Pietramora di Fattoria Zerbina and Montepirolo di San Patrignano; and a third Romagna bottles wines that are decent but unremarkable, often designed to highlight superfluous tannic extraction or cask-driven sweetness, a consumer preference well past its sell-by date. At this juncture, the only real obstacle that seems to be hindering the perceptible drive towards excellence over the last few years is time. The vineyards, most of them planted only fairly recently, need time to reach full maturity. Time is needed so that young producers can develop and improve their repertoire of knowledge and experience.

Baraccone

LOC. CA' DEI MORTI, 1
29028 PONTE DELL'OLIO [PC]
TEL. 0523877147
www.baraccone.it

Conte Otto Barattieri di San Pietro

VIA DEI TIGLI, 100
29020 VIGOLZONE [PC]
TEL. 0523875111
ottobarattieri@libero.it

ANNUAL PRODUCTION 22,000 bottles
HECTARES UNDER VINE 7.5
VITICULTURE METHOD Conventional

Andreana Burgazzi's modest winemaking enterprise is located in the Val Nure, part of a larger area whose outstanding viticultural conditions enable capable producers to offer wines of magnificent depth and complexity. This is precisely the case with Ronco Alto, sourced from a venerable vineyard lying at 400 metres' elevation, and one of the best Gutturnio Riservas to emerge from the 2004 vintage. The nose is complex and nicely layered but the wine really shines on the palate, unleashing a dynamic, self-confident progression powering through to a majestic finish that seems to march on forever. Colombaia '05 is a Gutturnio Superiore that also impressed us with succulent, well-ripened fruit expanding nicely on a palate that is tight knit but lively, thanks to fine tannins. Among the light sparklers, we can recommend the Gutturnio '06, which follows a splendid '05 and has to be one of the best in its class. Plump, succulent fruit liberally suffuses nose and palate, and it unfurls an expansive, lengthy development that contributes to the wine's exuberant suppleness.

ANNUAL PRODUCTION 120,000 bottles
HECTARES UNDER VINE 38
VITICULTURE METHOD Conventional

Massimiliana Barattieri and her brother Alberico run a family winery that produces one of Italy's most highly praised Vin Santos. It took Three Glasses for the first time with the '96 vintage and has come back for an encore with the '97. Produced with a mother, or yeast complex, that dates back to 1823, this is a wine with few peers. It does not undergo filtration so its antique gold appearance is slightly cloudy. The bouquet offers notes of crisp menthol that enliven a cornucopia of honey, dried figs, sweet pipe tobacco and zabaglione. Those sensations are magnified on a palate that is rich and hedonistic, remarkably dense yet nimble and well balanced, concluding with a veritable peacock's tail of aromas, the hallmark and privilege of every great meditation wine. The winery classics include Sauvignon Frizzante, which in the '06 version is nicely mature and seems to have rediscovered its brio and distinction. Although one might quibble a bit at the nose, Gutturnio Traversini '06 displays an energy and brightness of fruit that make it sheer quaffing pleasure.

● C. P. Gutturnio Ronco Alto Ris. '04	♥♥ 4*
● C. P. Gutturnio Frizzante '06	♥ 3*
● C. P. Gutturnio Sup. Colombaia '05	♥♥ 4

○ C. P. Vin Santo Albarola	
Val di Nure '97	♥♥♥ 6
○ C. P. Sauvignon Frizzante '06	♥ 3
● C. P. Gutturnio Traversini '06	♥ 3
○ C. P. Vin Santo Albarola	
Val di Nure '96	♥♥♥ 6
○ C. P. Vin Santo Albarola	
Val di Nure '95	♥♥ 6
● Il Faggio '03	♥♥ 6

Francesco Bellei

VIA PER MODENA, 80
41030 BOMPORTO [MO]
TEL. 059812449
www.francescobellei.it

ANNUAL PRODUCTION 70,000 bottles
HECTARES UNDER VINE 5
VITICULTURE METHOD Conventional

The relationship between Christian Bellei
and the Cavicchioli family of San Prospero
has been growing ever more creative and
entrepreneurial. The Cavicchiolis have been
partners in the enterprise for some years
now, managing the marketing side, which
leaves Christian a freer hand with
production. It means he can pour even
more of his energies into his beloved bottle
refermentation project, a sparkling wine
technique taught him by his father Beppe.
Christian has acquired such expertise that
his modest operation at Bomporto now
produces only wines of this style. The
hillside vineyards planted to chardonnay
and pinot nero go into his Brut Extra
Cuvée, a superlative non-vintage sparkler
whose overall evolved characteristics
fetchingly exalt its appealing fragrance and
crispness. The elegant, full-bodied Brut
Rosso is as successful as always,
produced from lambrusco di Sorbara
grapes grown on the plains. The same
variety yields Rifermentazione Ancestrale,
unusual in that it is not disgorged and
therefore remains somewhat cloudy. It
exhibits a delicate citrus impression and is
firm and assertive on the palate.

Stefano Berti

LOC. RAVALDINO IN MONTE
VIA LA SCAGNA, 18
47100 FORLÌ
TEL. 0543488074
www.stefanoberti.com

ANNUAL PRODUCTION 30,000 bottles
HECTARES UNDER VINE 8
VITICULTURE METHOD Natural

Stefano Berti's winery is located in the first
hills that rise south of Forlì, on the border of
the Predappio area, where traditionally
Romagna's best sangiovese-based wines
are made. His operation is modest in size
and everything is on Stefano's shoulders.
He works both vineyard and cellars, and
makes every decision, large and small. To
understand his approach, you just have to
access his website and read his blog. There
he is, ready to share what he is thinking and
doing with anyone who wants to chat or
simply find out about his production
philosophy. A brimming Two Glasses go to
Calisto '05, a striking Sangiovese. If it
seems a tad evolved and ultra-ripe on the
nose, there's no lack of elegance in the
mouth, where lively acidity keeps full, dense
fruit just this side of excess. The lengthy
finale, though, is slightly drying. The winery's
second-tier Sangiovese, Ravaldo '06, is
quite a different animal: pulpy, charged and
crisp to a fault. It boasts imposing weight
and tight contours, with dense tannins that
a few more years will round off nicely.

● Brut Rosso Extra Cuvée '04		🍷🍷 4
○ Brut Extra Cuvée		🍷🍷 5
● Lambrusco Rifermentazione Ancestrale '06		🍷 4
● Brut Rosso Extra Cuvée '03		🍷🍷 4
☉ Brut Rosé Extra Cuvée '98		🍷🍷 6
○ Brut Cuvée Speciale '99		🍷🍷 5
○ Brut Cuvée Speciale '97		🍷🍷 5

● Sangiovese di Romagna Sup. Calisto '05		🍷🍷 5
● Sangiovese di Romagna Sup. Ravaldo '06		🍷🍷 4*
● Sangiovese di Romagna Sup. Calisto '01		🍷🍷🍷 5
● Sangiovese di Romagna Sup. Calisto '04		🍷🍷 5
● Sangiovese di Romagna Sup. Calisto '03		🍷🍷 5
● Sangiovese di Romagna Sup. Calisto '00		🍷🍷 5
● Sangiovese di Romagna Sup. Ravaldo '05		🍷🍷 4

Raffaella Alessandra Bissoni

LOC. CASTICCIANO
VIA COLECCHIO, 280
47032 BERTINORO [FC]
TEL. 0543460382
www.vinibissoni.com

ANNUAL PRODUCTION	13,000 bottles
HECTARES UNDER VINE	4.5
VITICULTURE METHOD	Natural

Raffaella Bissoni cultivates four hectares in one of Romagna's most favoured enclaves, the limestone-rich terrains around Bertinoro. She's the one that does the cultivation too, with a commitment that is truly inspiring. Raffaella will work long hours among the vines to spare them from chemical products and machines, and her work in the cellar manifests the same total respect for nature. Some may smile, but the example set by small producers such as Bissoni, usually at the cost of incredible efforts, stands as a real heritage that we will understand over time. Sangiovese Riserva '04 is an elegant offering with textbook varietal character, releasing crisp fruit that seems almost floral. The palate develops full and smooth, and the lengthy finish is quite elegant, although perhaps just a touch dry. We found Albana Passito '04 impressive, too. With an appealing amber, it tends to an intriguing complex of spices, particularly thyme and rosemary, which continue to infuse the mouth. The palate is fat and sweet but well within bounds.

Tenuta Bonzara

VIA SAN CHIERLO, 37A
40050 MONTE SAN PIETRO [BO]
TEL. 0516768324
www.bonzara.it

ANNUAL PRODUCTION	70,000 bottles
HECTARES UNDER VINE	16
VITICULTURE METHOD	Conventional

Francesco Lambertini, whose work as a university professor takes precedence over that of wine producer, is fortunate to enjoy the assistance of legendary cellarmaster Mario Carboni and of Lorenzo Landi, a winemaker of enormous experience. Tenuta Bonzara's vineyards lie at elevations among the highest in the Colli Bolognesi and the significant temperature swings between day and night bring out distinctive aromas in the fruit. The winery's two champions, Cabernet Sauvignon Bonzarone and Merlot Rocca di Bonacciara, both '04s, have been released together. Bonzarone won a place in the final taste-offs. It's robust and heady but brimming with energy and the satiny mouthfeel is terrific. The Merlot is only a step behind, showing expansive, refined and silky smooth. The two second-stringers show similar differences. Cabernet Rosso del Borgo is smooth but crisp while Merlot Rosso del Poggio comes across as somewhat more plush. Sauvignon Le Carrate is its usual subtle, refined self, with varietal faithfulness on the nose. Monte Severo is another well-crafted blend of chardonnay and sauvignon blanc in a 40-40 ratio, with the rest pignoletto. Rich tropical fruit complements a luscious, full palate.

○ Albana di Romagna Passito '04	ΨΨ	4*
● Sangiovese di Romagna Sup. Ris. '04	ΨΨ	4*
● Sangiovese di Romagna Sup. Ris. '03	ΨΨ	4
○ Albana di Romagna Passito '03	ΨΨ	4

● C. B. Cabernet Sauvignon Bonzarone '04	ΨΨ	5
● C. B. Cabernet Sauvignon Rosso del Borgo '05	ΨΨ	4
● C. B. Merlot Rocca di Bonacciara '04	ΨΨ	5
○ C. B. Sauvignon Sup. Le Carrate '06	ΨΨ	3*
○ Monte Severo '05	ΨΨ	4
● C. B. Merlot Rosso del Poggio '05	Ψ	4
○ C. B. Pignoletto Cl. Vigna Antica '06	Ψ	3
○ C. B. Pignoletto Frizzante '06		3
● C. B. Cabernet Sauvignon Bonzarone '96	ΨΨΨ	5
● C. B. Cabernet Sauvignon Bonzarone '97	ΨΨΨ	5
● C. B. Cabernet Sauvignon Bonzarone '03	ΨΨ	5

Tenuta Ca' Lunga

VIA CA' LUNGA BUORE, 5
40026 IMOLA [BO]
TEL. 0542609257
www.tenutacalunga.it

ANNUAL PRODUCTION 90,000 bottles
HECTARES UNDER VINE 12
VITICULTURE METHOD   Conventional

The area around Imola seems to be
bursting with new wineries and impressive
bottles, the fruit of widespread dynamism
and down-to-earth attitudes. Tenuta Ca'
Lunga is an active player on this stage, with
an incredibly effective team composed of
owner Paolo Cassetta, assisted by his
father Angelo and the rest of the family,
along with agronomist Remigio Bordini and
Lorenzo Landi, the winemaker. Landi
contributes expertise and Bordini
brandishes the potent weapon of his
passion and readiness for hard work. A
number of Ca' Lunga's top wines were not
presented for our tasting but there was
certainly nothing wrong with what we tried.
We found Sangiovese Mistero outstanding.
It boasts a plenitude of velvety, ripe fruit
whose aromas continue unabated
throughout the progression while the palate
displays generous volume and nicely
evolved characteristics. The chardonnay
and sauvignon Diadema unfurls an utterly
seductive palate offering pronounced,
velvety tropical fruit. Incantesimo is all
sangiovese. Still youthful, it's a smooth,
seductive charmer.

Calonga

LOC. CASTIGLIONE
VIA CASTEL LEONE, 8
47100 FORLÌ
TEL. 0543753044
www.calonga.it

ANNUAL PRODUCTION 25,000 bottles
HECTARES UNDER VINE 8
VITICULTURE METHOD   Natural

Maurizio Baravelli took home another Three
Glass award in great style, confirming his
status as one of the finest producers in the
entire region. Clay-sandy soils predominate
in this corner of Romagna, in the first band
of hills between Faenza and Forlì. Their
distinctive qualities enable Baravelli, vintage
after vintage, to put out both cabernet
sauvignons and sangioveses of astonishing
quality. Take his Michelangiolo '04. The
nose is gorgeous with judiciously crafted,
crisp fruit that segues seamlessly into
pungent spice. The palate is well driven and
spacious, with well-balanced structure, juicy
acidity and a generous dose of glossy
tannins. Castellione '03 seems to have
shrugged off the torrid 2003 temperatures,
displaying an elegance and depth unusual
for that vintage. Though heavy laden with
fruit, the aromas remain appealing and
crisp-edged while a dense-textured palate
shows succulent and agile. Minerally
aromas appearing in the bouquet inform a
long-lingering finish.

O Colli d'Imola Bianco Sup. Diadema '06	♟♟ 4
● Colli d'Imola Sangiovese Incantesimo '06	♟♟ 3*
● Sangiovese di Romagna Sup. Mistero '05	♟♟ 4
O Colli d'Imola Bianco Euforia '06	♟ 3
● Colli d'Imola Cabernet Sauvignon Elisir '05	♟ 4
● Colli d'Imola Sangiovese Regale Ris. '05	♟ 5
● Colli d'Imola Cabernet Sauvignon Imperius Ris. '04	♟♟ 5
● Colli d'Imola Sangiovese Regale Ris. '04	♟♟ 5
● Sangiovese di Romagna Sup. Mistero '04	♟♟ 4

● Sangiovese di Romagna Sup. Michelangiolo Ris. '04	♟♟♟ 5
● Castellione Cabernet Sauvignon '03	♟♟ 6
O Pagadebit di Romagna '06	♟ 3
● Sangiovese di Romagna Sup. Il Bruno '06	♟ 3
● Balsamino '06	♟ 3
● Ordelaffo Sangiovese '05	♟ 3
● Sangiovese di Romagna Sup. Michelangiolo Ris. '03	♟♟♟ 5
● Sangiovese di Romagna Sup. Michelangiolo Ris. '01	♟♟ 6
● Castellione Cabernet Sauvignon '01	♟♟ 6
● Castellione Cabernet Sauvignon '00	♟♟ 6

Campodelsole

VIA CELLAIMO, 121
47032 BERTINORO [FC]
TEL. 0543444562
www.campodelsole.it

ANNUAL PRODUCTION 350,000 bottles
HECTARES UNDER VINE 65
VITICULTURE METHOD Conventional

Gabriele Isoldi rose to the challenge of
establishing a top-notch winery and has
won plaudits for its fine quality and modern
style. At his side are his mother, Sandra
Santini, and Friulian winemaker Stefano
Salvini, as well as consulting oenologist
Paolo Caciorgna. Overall, the Campodelsole
wines are clean and well made but varietal
characteristics and individual vineyards play
second fiddle to a production style that
privileges uniformity of expression. This
house style constitutes both the limitation
and the distinguishing characteristic of
Campodelsole wines. Two full Glasses go to
the operation's star wine, Vertice '04. Crisp,
lean and dry, it offers a beautiful suite of
tannins, although the aromas seem
somewhat bland, the result of the
trademark note of honey shared by all the
Campodelsole Sangioveses. Crisp-edged
aromas open Palpedrigo '05 and the palate
is supple enough and well smoothed, if a
tad straightforward. San Maglorio '06 is a
fine offering, showing fragrant, rounded and
delicious.

Cardinali

POD. MONTEPASCOLO
29014 CASTELL'ARQUATO [PC]
TEL. 0523803502
www.cardinalidoc.it

ANNUAL PRODUCTION 30,000 bottles
HECTARES UNDER VINE 8
VITICULTURE METHOD Conventional

Ever since this winery was launched in
1973, it has marched unswervingly along
the path of high quality. Laura and Alberto
Cardinali, who now guide it, have kept
tenaciously to that direction, year after year
dedicating painstaking attention to the
management of the vineyards and cellar.
Gutturnio Riserva Torquato keeps its
reputation polished as one of the
benchmarks for its breed. Crisp, balsam-
veined fruit characterizes this '04 release,
and it shows impressive volume and
extraction, plus warm, heady aromatics on
the palate. Dense, glossy fruit at the
pinnacle of ripeness marks Nicchio, a
standard-label Gutturnio. Powerful and rich
on the palate, it builds a savoury, tangy
finale. Solata '06 is a still version of
Monterosso, a style increasingly popular in
the Colli Piacentini. Appealingly crisp
throughout, it leads off with bright citrus and
mineral, and develops good depth. Cardinali
Brut '03, not too complicated but well
structured, is a classic method sparkler
produced from various local grapes. Ripe
peach and apricot introduce Dolce
Montepascolo, a late-harvest moscato. It
shows warm and heady, already nicely
mature and with good weight in the mouth.

● Sangiovese di Romagna Sup. Palpedrigo '05	▼▼ 4
● Sangiovese di Romagna Sup. Vertice Ris. '04	▼▼ 6
● Sangiovese di Romagna Sup. San Maglorio '06	▼▼ 3*
O Albana di Romagna Passito Font'Enea '04	▼ 5
O Albana di Romagna Secco Selva '06	▼ 2*
O Pagadebit di Romagna San Pascasio '06	▼ 3
● Sangiovese di Romagna Durano '06	▼ 2*
● Sangiovese di Romagna Vertice Ris. '03	▽▽ 6
● Sangiovese di Romagna Sup. Palpedrigo '04	▽▽ 4
● Sangiovese di Romagna Sup. San Maglorio '04	▽▽ 3

● C. P. Gutturnio Cl. Nicchio '06	▼▼ 4*
● C. P. Gutturnio Cl. Torquato Ris. '04	▼▼ 5
O C. P. Monterosso Val d'Arda Solata '06	▼ 4
O Dolce Montepascolo '06	▼ 6
O Cardinali Brut M. Cl. '03	▼ 5
● C. P. Gutturnio Cl. Torquato Ris. '03	▽▽ 5
● C. P. Cabernet Sauvignon Ronchello '01	▽▽ 5
● C. P. Gutturnio Cl. Nicchio '05	▽▽ 4
● C. P. Gutturnio Cl. Nicchio '04	▽▽ 4

Carra

LOC. CASATICO
VIA LA NAVE, 10B
43013 LANGHIRANO [PR]
TEL. 0521863510
www.carradicasatico.com

ANNUAL PRODUCTION 100,000 bottles
HECTARES UNDER VINE 15
VITICULTURE METHOD Conventional

One can't help but admire the passion that Bonfiglio Carra exudes. At harvest time, this translates into a carefully meditated attempt to bring to his already first-rate wines those extra nuances of quality that will drive them still further up the ladder. There's nary a wrinkle in the style that distinguishes the Carra line-up, wines with well-crafted fundamentals, easy drinkability and straightforward but admirable varietal faithfulness. The proof is in the pudding, in this case Acuto, a Charmat method sparkler from malvasia grapes that is impeccably made and even elegant, with classy crispness and appealing florality and spice on the nose. In the mouth, it expands and drives through nicely, unfurling a lengthy, classically varietal finish that yields tasty citrus. Cinque Torri, a classic method brut from chardonnay and pinot nero with good heft, shows finesse on the nose, full-fruited fragrance in the mouth and a lengthy, pleasantly lean conclusion. Arcòl is a very impressive blend of merlot, croatina and pinot nero. It's more expansive on the palate than on the nose, but it displays tasty fruit and elegant balance overall.

- ● Arcòl '05 — 🍷🍷 4*
- ○ Cinque Torri Brut M. Cl. — 🍷🍷 5
- ○ Colli di Parma Malvasia Acuto Extra Dry '06 — 🍷🍷 4*
- ○ Colli di Parma Malvasia Frizzante '06 — 🍷 3
- ○ Malvasia & Moscato Frizzante Dolce '06 — 🍷 3
- ● Torcularia Rosso '06 — 🍷 3
- ⊙ Torcularia Rosa '06 — 🍷 3
- ○ Eden Passito '05 — 🍷 5
- ○ Colli di Parma Sauvignon Frizzante '06 — 🍷 3
- ● Arcòl '04 — 🍸🍸 4
- ● Arcòl '03 — 🍸🍸 4

Casetto dei Mandorli

LOC. PREDAPPIO ALTA
VIA UMBERTO I, 21
47010 PREDAPPIO [FC]
TEL. 0543922361
www.vini-nicolucci.it

ANNUAL PRODUCTION 100,000 bottles
HECTARES UNDER VINE 14
VITICULTURE METHOD Conventional

The Nicolucci family winery is an intimate part of Romagna winemaking history. Its survival and growth is due to Giuseppe's stubborn determination to maintain his operation in the Predappio Alta hills, an area with a historical reputation for fine sangiovese but one that over the years had seen a loss of its vineyards and an exodus of its growers. Alessandro took over leadership of Casetto dei Mandorli from his father. He has brought innovation but has stayed largely within the furrow of tradition, thanks in particular to the excellent efforts of consulting oenologist Leonardo Conti. Emblematic of their approach is the superb Vigna del Generale '04, an impeccable, traditional-style sangiovese. Crisp, sound fruit contributes to a clean-edged introduction, the palate is superbly executed, with a close-woven fabric of fine tannins, and it finishes very round and full. Nero di Predappio, from sangiovese with 25 per cent refosco, shows hard and austere while the two standard-label sangioveses display outstanding craftsmanship. Tre Rocche is refreshing and velvet-smooth; I Mandorli fuller and appealingly fleshy.

- ● Sangiovese di Romagna V. del Generale Ris. '04 — 🍷🍷 5
- ● Nero di Predappio '04 — 🍷🍷 5
- ● Sangiovese di Romagna Sup. I Mandorli '06 — 🍷 3
- ● Sangiovese di Romagna Sup. Tre Rocche '06 — 🍷 4
- ● Nero di Predappio '03 — 🍸🍸 5
- ● Sangiovese di Romagna V. del Generale Ris. '01 — 🍸🍸 5
- ● Sangiovese di Romagna V. del Generale Ris. '00 — 🍸🍸 5

Castelluccio

LOC. POGGIOLO
VIA TRAMONTO, 15
47015 MODIGLIANA [FC]
TEL. 0546942486
www.ronchidicastelluccio.it

ANNUAL PRODUCTION 90,000 bottles
HECTARES UNDER VINE 12
VITICULTURE METHOD Conventional

Old and new live side by side at Castelluccio, continuity and abrupt new directions melding in a combined approach that gives its line-up a distinctive cast. The most venerable antecedents are the sangioveses, the legendary Ronchis. Today's versions boast rich fruit, glossy textures, hefty tannins and oak that may be superlative but is often overly emphatic. Fitting into that mould is Ronco delle Ginestre '04, which exhibits great volume and concentration and smooth, seductive mouthfeel, but is hasty on the finish and presents tannins that are somewhat peremptory and drying. Sacrificing even more depth upon the altar of oak is Ronco dei Ciliegi, which is, oddly, a simpler, less complex wine than in the past. The cabernet sauvignon Ronco del Re, on the other hand, emerges from the oak masterfully unscathed, its imposing character and rich minerality in fine view, gaining complexity with every minute in the glass, precisely as it does over the years in the bottle. The modernist of the group is Massicone, comprised of equal parts of sangiovese and cabernet, an attractively assertive, toasty and rounded red.

Cavicchioli U. & Figli

VIA CANALETTO, 52
41030 SAN PROSPERO [MO]
TEL. 059812411
www.cavicchioli.it

ANNUAL PRODUCTION 18,000,000 bottles
HECTARES UNDER VINE 150
VITICULTURE METHOD Conventional

This historic San Prospero operation presented us with a terrific line-up of Lambruscos. Cavicchioli has been striving for some years to achieve good quality and substantial production at the same time, and its success should be credited to the ever-richer experience and brilliant decisions of Sandro Cavicchioli, who personally directs the winery. Our most pleasant surprise was the return to its customary excellence of Vigna del Cristo, which was the first single-vineyard Lambrusco. The '06 is classic Lambrusco di Sorbara, showing real elegance and lovely subtlety. The real surprise though was Rosé del Cristo, a classic-method sparkler from Sorbara grapes from that vineyard, given three years' maturation on the lees. Sandro Cavicchioli's intuitions and the masterful talents of Christian Bellei have combined to produce a rosé of considerable refinement and long-lingering characteristics. Cavicchioli's Tre Medaglie line, largely targeted at supermarkets, has some absolutely outstanding bottles, particularly given their very reasonable price tags.

● Massicone '04	♟♟ 6
○ Ronco del Re '05	♟♟ 6
● Ronco delle Ginestre '04	♟♟ 6
● Ronco dei Ciliegi '04	♟♟ 5
● Sangiovese di Romagna Le More '06	♟ 4
● Ronco dei Ciliegi '02	♟♟♟ 6
● Massicone '01	♟♟♟ 6
● Ronco dei Ciliegi '00	♟♟♟ 6
● Ronco delle Ginestre '90	♟♟♟ 6
● Massicone '03	♟♟ 6
● Ronco dei Ciliegi '03	♟♟ 6
● Ronco delle Ginestre '03	♟♟ 6
● Ronco delle Ginestre '01	♟♟ 6

⊙ Rosé del Cristo Spumante '03	♟♟ 6
● Lambrusco di Sorbara Tre Medaglie	♟♟ 2*
● Reggiano Lambrusco Tre Medaglie	♟♟ 3*
● Lambrusco di Sorbara V. del Cristo '06	♟♟ 4
● Lambrusco Grasparossa di Castelvetro Tre Medaglie	♟♟ 3*
● Lambrusco Grasparossa di Castelvetro Amabile Tre Medaglie	♟ 2
● Lambrusco Salamino di Santa Croce Semisecco Tre Medaglie	♟ 3
● Lambrusco Grasparossa di Castelvetro Contessa Matilde	♟ 3
● Reggiano Lambrusco Amabile Tre Medaglie	♟ 3

Cantine Ceci

VIA PROVINCIALE, 99
43030 TORRILE [PR]
TEL. 0521810252
www.lambrusco.it

ANNUAL PRODUCTION 600,000 bottles
HECTARES UNDER VINE 20
VITICULTURE METHOD Conventional

The motive force within this family winery is without a doubt Alessandro Ceci. With his boundless energy and dedication, Ceci is always on the lookout for promising opportunities for Cantine Ceci and for the premium Lambrusco wine community as well. One might think that his originality pretty much defines itself in the choice of admittedly striking bottle designs but it's what's in the bottle that counts and the winery's quality lift over the last few years is incontrovertible. The highest quality rung reached so far is the participation by Otello NerodiLambrusco in our national final round for Three Glasses. Dark, dense and sturdily built, it is compelling but at the same time well balanced and easy to enjoy. Spumante Extra Dry Tre, targeted at a broad audience, is very well made with lots of ripe fruit on the nose and a cushiony texture. Arturo's is produced from ultra-ripe lambrusco fruit, perfectly calibrated to feature satisfactory tannic structure wedded to a sweetness that stops well short of cloying. The remaining Ceci sparklers are sound and well made.

Chiarli 1860

VIA DANIELE MANIN, 15
41100 MODENA [MO]
TEL. 0593163311
www.chiarli.it

ANNUAL PRODUCTION 24,000,000 bottles
HECTARES UNDER VINE 110
VITICULTURE METHOD Conventional

The Chiarli family has been producing Lambruscos since 1860 and has lived through all of the vicissitudes that this world-famous wine has experienced. With a businessman's ability to see where trends are heading, Anselmo Chiarli realized that now is the moment to direct some of his products at higher quality instead of staying at the mercy of price mechanisms. The crucial element, of course, was to make all of his staff equally aware of that imperative and in this he seems to have been successful. In fact, Sorbara Vecchia Modena Premium went through to our taste-offs for Three Glasses. In appearance it's somewhat light, as befits a lambrusco di Sorbara, but the nose is as clean and elegant as you could wish and the palate is nicely slim and edgy, featuring a tempting, citrus-like acidity that supports a lean finale. Nivola is its usual dark, dense, creamy self while Vigneto Enrico Cialdini displays the textbook crisp austerity of Lambrusco Grasparossa. Finally, Cletò is a fruity, rounded Charmat method sparkler from pignoletto.

- ● Otello NerodiLambrusco '06 🍷🍷 4*
- ● Vino da Uve Stramature Arturo's 🍷🍷 4
- ○ Extra Dry Tre di Terre Verdiane 🍷🍷 4
- ● Otello Lambrusco Et. Nera '06 🍷 3
- ○ Colli di Parma Malvasia
  Frizzante Otello '06 🍷 4
- ○ Colli di Parma Sauvignon
  Frizzante Otello '06 🍷 4
- ● Lambrusco Terre Verdiane 🍷 3
- ☉ Extra Dry Rosé Otello 🍷 4
- ● Fortana Frizzante
  Fortanina La Luna 3

- ● Lambrusco di Sorbara Vecchia
  Modena Premium MH '06 🍷🍷 4
- ● Lambrusco Grasparossa
  di Castelvetro V. Enrico Cialdini '06 🍷🍷 4
- ○ Pignoletto Extra Dry Cletò 🍷🍷 4
- ● Nivola Lambrusco Scuro 🍷🍷 3*
- ● Lambrusco di Sorbara
  del Fondatore 🍷 4
- ☉ Rosè Brut 🍷 4
- ● Lambrusco Grasparossa
  di Castelvetro Villa Cialdini '06 🍷 3
- ● Lambrusco Grasparossa
  di Castelvetro Pruno Nero 🍷 3
- ● Lambrusco di Sorbara
  Vecchia Modena 🍷 3

Floriano Cinti

FRAZ. SAN LORENZO
VIA GAMBERI, 48
40037 SASSO MARCONI [BO]
TEL. 0516751646
www.collibolognesi.com

ANNUAL PRODUCTION 75,000 bottles
HECTARES UNDER VINE 17.5
VITICULTURE METHOD Natural

It is increasingly difficult to find new ways to describe Floriano Cinti's efforts. He tends his vines with diligence and works on winemaking every day, assisted by his friend and oenologist Giovanni Fraulini, all of course tasks that a small grower must perform with care and dedication. What sets Floriano apart is that he does all of this extremely well. The quality of his wines is impressively high, especially the whites. The production process is not elaborate, in fact all are made in steel except for the chardonnay, but they emerge complex and fresh, all very appealing. Sassobacco, a selection from pignoletto grapes, stands out. After elegant floral and citrus notes, the palate expands surprisingly rich and fat but enlivened by a tangy acidity and crisp succulence. The two Sauvignons, both superb, show only slight differences. The standard version is crisply varietal while the Sassobacco version exhibits a more individual bent and livelier flavours. Pinot Bianco is tasty, fragrant and full-bodied. On the red side, Merlot Sassobacco is satisfyingly full fruited and beautifully textured but lacks that extra touch of complexity that would lift it onto the top rung.

Consorzio Produttori di Brisighella

FRAZ. FOGNANO
VIA CAMPIUME, 6
48010 BRISIGHELLA [RA]
TEL. 054680112
www.campiume.it

ANNUAL PRODUCTION 11,000 bottles
HECTARES UNDER VINE N.A.
VITICULTURE METHOD Natural

This modest consortium has a number of members but the three that interest us the most are Andrea Bragagni, Filippo Manetti of Vigne di San Lorenzo and Paolo Babini of Vigne dei Boschi. They are the ones that concentrate most of their efforts in the best viticultural area, the upper Val Lamone, and share a winemaking approach that eschews technical manipulation and allows the wines to emerge more naturally. The results may not always be right on stylistically but their efforts, and their sturdy determination, are a valuable lesson for local producers and could lead to interesting results down the road. Among the many wines we tasted, two stood out. Paolo Babini's Settepievi '05, a blend of malbo and merlot, is a bit awkward on the nose but it shows good depth and concentration and is quite impressive overall. The cabernet and merlot San Lorenzo '05, produced by Filippo Manetti, is smooth textured with lots of tasty fruit but its progression is perhaps a tad hasty.

○ C. B. Pignoletto Cl. Sassobacco '06	♟♟ 4*
● C. B. Merlot Sassobacco '05	♟♟ 4
○ C. B. Pinot Bianco '06	♟♟ 3*
○ C. B. Sauvignon Sassobacco '06	♟♟ 4
○ C. B. Sauvignon '06	♟♟ 3*
● C. B. Cabernet Sauvignon '05	♟ 3
○ C. B. Chardonnay '06	♟ 3
● C. B. Merlot '06	♟ 3
○ C. B. Pignoletto Passito Colline Marconiane '06	♟ 5
○ C. B. Pignoletto Frizzante '06	♟ 3
● C. B. Cabernet Sauvignon Sel. '03	♟♟ 4
○ C. B. Pignoletto Cl. '05	♟♟ 4
● C. B. Merlot Sel. '03	♟♟ 4
● C. B. Merlot Sel. '02	♟♟ 4

● San Lorenzo '05	♟♟ 5
● Settepievi '05	♟♟ 5
● Campiume '05	♟ 5
● Poggio Tura Sangiovese '04	♟ 5
● Nero Selva '04	♟ 5
○ Rigogolo '05	♟ 4
● Campiume '04	♟♟ 5
● San Lorenzo '04	♟♟ 5
● Poggio Tura '03	♟♟ 5
● Campiume '03	♟♟ 5
● San Lorenzo '03	♟♟ 5
● Settepievi '03	♟♟ 5

Leone Conti
LOC. SANTA LUCIA
VIA POZZO, 1
48018 FAENZA [RA]
TEL. 0546642149
www.leoneconti.it

ANNUAL PRODUCTION 75,000 bottles
HECTARES UNDER VINE 18
VITICULTURE METHOD Conventional

Leone Conti enjoys a special relationship with his local territory and this earns him as much affection and esteem as do his wines. His devotion to local native grape varieties and a generous openness to his fellow producers make him a real treasure in the wine world. His creativity and relentless experimentation reveal how he sees the vocation of oenologist. For Conti, the winemaker must first of all search after ever-finer sensitivity. As to the wines we tasted, the level is universally high, particularly so with the albana-based products. Progetto 1 '06 is varietally faithful, displaying refreshing, lively acidity and multi-layered complexity based on citrus and a generous florality. Overripe fruit gives Progetto 2 elegant botrytis-suffused aromas and a rich, velvet-smooth, luscious palate. Nontiscordardime '04 is one of Romagna's few interesting passitos made from albana grapes. Full and rich, and especially fat on the palate, it flaunts appealing fragrances of honey, dried figs and apricots. The all-syrah Rossonero 2006 is quite delicious, showcasing ultra-sweet fruit and developing a no-nonsense directness in the mouth.

Corte d'Aibo
VIA MARZATORE, 15
40050 MONTEVEGLIO [BO]
TEL. 051832583
www.cortedaibo.it

ANNUAL PRODUCTION 70,000 bottles
HECTARES UNDER VINE 17
VITICULTURE METHOD Certified organic

Antonio Capelli and Mario Pirondini are admirably dedicated and consistent as they continue to direct this modest organic operation, Capelli concentrating largely on the vineyards and Pirondini on the winemaking end. The grapes they use are top-flight but it's a shame that oak predominates at times over everything else in the wine, masking the freshness and ripe flavours of that lovely fruit. This is the case with Cabernet Sauvignon Orfeo '04. It boasts abundant fruit and depth but those qualities seem almost buried beneath sweet notes of vanilla and chewing gum. It's an impressive thoroughbred of a wine, though, and a few more years in the bottle will probably bring it more harmony. The Cabernet Sauvignon Le Borre '05 is very full bodied and expansive, showing better integrated and releasing sweet, ripe fruit nicely enriched with smooth notes of vanilla and liquorice. The finish is lean and dry. Pignoletto Montefreddo missed Two Glasses by a hair. Attractively nuanced, its rich, savoury palate effectively complements excellent fruit on the nose.

O Albana di Romagna Passito Nontiscordardime '04	♟♟ 6
O Albana di Romagna Secco Progetto 1 '06	♟♟ 4*
O Albana di Romagna Secco Progetto 2 '06	♟♟ 4
O Colli di Faenza Bianco Le Rive '06	♟♟ 4*
O Vino da Uve Stramature Oro et Laboro	♟♟ 5
● Rossonero '06	♟♟ 5
● Sangiovese di Romagna '06	♟ 3
O Anghingò '06	♟ 3
● Arcolaio '04	♟♟ 5
O Tu Chiamale se Vuoi Emozioni Lato B '03	♟♟ 6
● Colli di Faenza Rosso Le Ghiande '03	♟♟ 4

● C. B. Cabernet Sauvignon Le Borre '05	♟♟ 4*
● C. B. Cabernet Sauvignon Orfeo Ris. '04	♟♟ 6
● C. B. Barbera Cucherla '06	♟ 3
O C. B. Sauvignon Spungola '06	♟ 3
● C. B. Merlot Roncovecchio '05	♟ 4
O C. B. Pignoletto Cl. Montefreddo '06	♟ 3
● C. B. Cabernet Sauvignon Orfeo Ris. '03	♟♟ 6
● C. B. Cabernet Sauvignon Le Borre '04	♟♟ 4
● C. B. Cabernet Sauvignon Orfeo Ris. '01	♟♟ 6
● C. B. Cabernet Sauvignon Orfeo Ris. '00	♟♟ 6

Corte Manzini
LOC. CÀ DI SOLA
VIA MODENA, 131/3
41014 CASTELVETRO DI MODENA [MO]
TEL. 059702658
www.cortemanzini.it

ANNUAL PRODUCTION 80,000 bottles
HECTARES UNDER VINE 10
VITICULTURE METHOD Natural

Open any of the excellent Lambruscos produced by the Manzini family and you'll immediately find that it has a clearly defined house style. A description might run this way: a dense, cushiony, lingering mousse; extremely clean, well-defined aromas that centre on crisp, well-ripened berry fruit; seductive elegance on the palate, where aromas and succulent fruit create a delicate balance; and delicious drinkability, amply demonstrated by your desire to pour another glass. The small but perceptible differences between one wine and another come down to the different characters of the various vineyards, which are Corte Manzini's jewels. They are planted almost exclusively to lambrusco grasparossa, with the younger plantings going to produce Bolla Rossa and the more mature vineyards L'Acino, which for several years has been able to lay claim to being one of the finest Lambruscos in the region. The oldest vineyards, those 40 and more years of age, yield Grasparossa Secco and Amabile.

● Lambrusco Grasparossa di Castelvetro Secco '06 TT 4*
● Lambrusco Grasparossa di Castelvetro Secco L'Acino '06 TT 4*
● Lambrusco Grasparossa di Castelvetro Secco Bolla Rossa '06 TT 3*
● Lambrusco Grasparossa di Castelvetro Amabile '06 TT 3*
○ Il Gherlo Trebbiano di Modena '06 T 2
⊙ Lambrusco Grasparossa di Castelvetro Fior di Lambrusco '06 T 4
⊙ Brut Rosé Bollicine '06 T 3

Drei Donà Tenuta La Palazza
LOC. MASSA DI VECCHIAZZANO
VIA DEL TESORO, 23
47100 FORLÌ [FC]
TEL. 0543769371
www.dreidona.it

ANNUAL PRODUCTION 120,000 bottles
HECTARES UNDER VINE 30
VITICULTURE METHOD Natural

The winery owned by Claudio and Enrico Drei Donà is one of these rarities in Romagna, a truly reliable producer that puts out consistently high quality wines in a style you can count on. Even in difficult times, Tenuta La Palazza never once considered changing its way of doing things to tempt the market with softer wines or more international styles. The Drei Donà family deserves our thanks and respect for their constancy. In this context, Pruno is not only La Palazza's star wine but also the perfect vehicle for anyone who wants to grasp the authentic expression of sangiovese in Romagna. This '04 is a real delight, although the palate outclasses the nose, which remains a tad blurred but nevertheless admirable. The complex, concentrated mouth shows plenty of energy and develops a crisp, lean elegance. Graf Noir, from sangiovese, cabernet franc and Longanesi, emerges in its best version ever in the '01. It begins with impressive, fresh-tasting fruit that grabs your attention, and then develops complex and almost monumental in the mouth, with a rich mouthfeel that dries out a bit on the finish.

● Graf Noir '01 TT 8
● Sangiovese di Romagna Sup. Pruno Ris. '04 TT 5
● Notturno Sangiovese '05 TT 3*
○ Il Tornese Chardonnay '05 T 5
● Sangiovese di Romagna Sup. Pruno Ris. '01 YYY 5
● Sangiovese di Romagna Sup. Pruno Ris. '00 YYY 5
● Magnificat Cabernet Sauvignon '94 YYY 6
● Magnificat Cabernet Sauvignon '03 YY 6
● Sangiovese di Romagna Sup. Pruno Ris. '03 YY 5
● Graf Noir '00 YY 8
● Magnificat Cabernet Sauvignon '01 YY 6

Stefano Ferrucci

VIA CASOLANA, 3045/2
48014 CASTEL BOLOGNESE [RA]
TEL. 0546651068
www.stefanoferrucci.it

ANNUAL PRODUCTION 95,000 bottles
HECTARES UNDER VINE 15
VITICULTURE METHOD Conventional

Ilaria Ferrucci has taken over management of the winery her father launched just a year ago, and her first step has been to entrust winemaking to Federico Giotto, a promising young oenologist. With Giotto's help, she has put together a programme that provides for a radical restructuring operations and very long-range planning. Improvements need time of course but Ilaria Ferrucci has begun the right journey. While we patiently wait for results that vineyard upgrades will surely bring, we can offer some observations on the standard-label offerings, which compared to previous vintages are already better defined, more expressive and aromatic. Stefano Ferrucci's star wine is Domus Caia '04, made from slightly dried sangiovese. Although a bit slender and restrained on the nose, the palate is dense with plenty of succulent fruit and energy that drives impressively to an almost endless conclusion. There are some rough edges but fine, compact tannins contribute to a wine that is quite complex and impressive overall. Centurione '06 also performs well with lots of fragrant fruit and a crisp, graceful palate.

Paolo Francesconi

LOC. SARNA
VIA TULIERO, 154
48018 FAENZA [RA]
TEL. 054643213
pfrancesconi@racine.ra.it

ANNUAL PRODUCTION 12,000 bottles
HECTARES UNDER VINE 14
VITICULTURE METHOD Certified organic

Merely considering the excellent performances of Paolo Francesconi's wines is not enough to evaluate his efforts. Rather, we should look at his overall philosophy as a grower committed to the fascinating challenge of meshing a commitment to natural expression in his wines with the relentless drive for quality. The current status of his winery should be seen as a stage in a process that is challenging but at the same time yields interesting and consistent results. The light stylistic shortcomings in the current wines should be read as evidence of an approach that simply needs further calibration. The nose on Sangiovese Le Iadi '05 is not as clean as it could be, and its crisp fruit suffers somewhat as a consequence, but the palate redeems everything with its great depth, character and an energetic progression. Limbecca '06 is slow off the blocks but it then takes off with a nice explosion of fruit that is both well ripened and refreshingly crisp. Impavido '05 shows a bit slender on the palate but it's tasty and flaunts a silky mouthfeel. Merlot Simposium '06 is less complex but we liked its attractive fruit.

● Sangiovese di Romagna Sup.	
Domus Caia Ris. '04	❷ 6
○ Albana di Romagna Passito	
Domus Aurea '05	❶ 6
● Sangiovese di Romagna Auriga '06	❶ 3
○ Colli di Faenza Bianco	
Chiaro della Serra '06	❶ 3
● Sangiovese di Romagna Sup.	
Centurione '06	❶ 4
● Sangiovese di Romagna Sup.	
Domus Caia Ris. '03	❷❷ 6
● Sangiovese di Romagna Sup.	
Domus Caia Ris. '02	❷❷ 6
● Sangiovese di Romagna	
Domus Caia Ris. '01	❷❷ 6
● Sangiovese di Romagna	
Domus Caia Ris. '00	❷❷ 6

● Impavido Merlot '05	❷ 5
● Sangiovese di Romagna Sup.	
Le Iadi Ris. '05	❷ 5
● Simposium Merlot '06	❷ 4*
● Sangiovese di Romagna Sup.	
Limbecca '06	❷ 4*
● Impavido Merlot '04	❷❷ 5
● Sangiovese di Romagna Sup.	
Le Iadi Ris. '04	❷❷ 5
● Impavido Merlot '03	❷❷ 5
● Sangiovese di Romagna Sup.	
Le Iadi Ris. '03	❷❷ 4
● Impavido Merlot '02	❷❷ 5

Maria Letizia Gaggioli

VIA RAIBOLINI DETTO IL FRANCIA, 55
40069 ZOLA PREDOSA [BO]
TEL. 051753489
www.gaggiolivini.it

Gallegati

VIA ISONZO, 4
48018 FAENZA [RA]
TEL. 0546621149
www.aziendaagricolagallegati.it

ANNUAL PRODUCTION	160,000 bottles
HECTARES UNDER VINE	24
VITICULTURE METHOD	Conventional

All of the construction work concentrated on the gorgeous agriturismo next to their winery obviously didn't distract Maria Letizia Gaggioli and her father Carlo from the important tasks in the vineyard and cellar, where they can rely on the formidably professional Giovanni Fraulini. Looking at all of the 2006 wines, we were more impressed with the whites than the reds but it's also true that the line-up remains solidly in that range of high quality where it has always been. Sauvignon Superiore displays excellent typicity, showing nicely crisp, with good expansion and energy. Fragrant fruit marks Pinot Bianco Crilò, plus a full palate and a lingering, velvet-lined finale. Those who appreciate fat, luscious, silky whites will love Il Francia Bianco, a partnering of sauvignon, chardonnay and pignoletto, particularly for its tempting aromas of fresh ripe peach. Cabernet Sauvignon Il Francia Rosso is clean edged and confident, offering succulent depth and ripe morello cherry.

ANNUAL PRODUCTION	10,000
HECTARES UNDER VINE	6
VITICULTURE METHOD	Natural

Brothers Cesare and Antonio Gallegati are winemakers who enhance their intellectual grasp of wine by actually making wine and growing grapes, with hands in the dirt, as it were, helping the head to understand. They deliberately chose this lifestyle and their commitment to this small operation goes far beyond mere professional requirements. This year, they presented us with Riserva di Sangiovese Corallo Nero '04, a wine that impressed us last year in its Superiore DOC version. The palate is what stands out best in this present version and the wine represents an excellent paradigm for the Romagna style of sangiovese. It's full bodied to the extreme but expands to enormous volume in all directions, including temporal, displaying a subtle balance between austere leanness and soft texture. An extraordinary Regina di Cuori '03 competed in the our national finals for Three Glasses, thanks to a scrumptious array of dry figs, apricots and dried fruit on the nose, spirited progression and a refreshing crispness that seems to belie its considerable residual sugar.

● C. B. Cabernet Sauvignon Il Francia Rosso Ris. '04	♀♀ 4
○ C. B. Pinot Bianco Crilò '06	♀♀ 3*
○ C. B. Sauvignon Sup. '06	♀♀ 3*
○ Il Francia Bianco '06	♀♀ 4
● Bagazzana Rosso '06	♀ 4
○ C. B. Pignoletto Frizzante '06	♀ 3
○ C. B. Pignoletto Sup. '06	♀ 3
● C. B. Merlot '06	♀ 4
○ C. B. Chardonnay Lavinio '06	♀ 3
● C. B. Cabernet Sauvignon Il Francia Rosso Ris. '03	♀♀ 4
● C. B. Merlot '05	♀♀ 4

○ Albana di Romagna Passito Regina di Cuori '03	♀♀ 5
● Sangiovese di Romagna Sup. Corallo Nero Ris. '04	♀♀ 5
○ Colli di Faenza Bianco Corallo Bianco '06	♀ 4
○ Albana di Romagna Passito Regina di Cuori Ris. '04	♀♀ 6
● Sangiovese di Romagna Sup. Corallo Nero '04	♀♀ 5
● Sangiovese di Romagna Sup. Corallo Nero '03	♀♀ 5

Gradizzolo

VIA INVERNATA, 2
40050 MONTEVEGLIO [BO]
TEL. 051830265
www.gradizzolo.it

ANNUAL PRODUCTION 30,000 bottles
HECTARES UNDER VINE 5
VITICULTURE METHOD Conventional

Antonio Ognibene's passion for the barbera grape is well known. Historically, barbera has yielded its best results in this corner of the Colli Bolognesi in the vineyards around Montebudello. Its characteristics here at Gradizzolo are quite distinctive and the wine is made in a style that privileges extractive depth and sturdy body over crisp fruit and easy drinkability. A contributing factor to such traits is lengthy maturation in wood, which at times has the unfortunate effect of drying the wine and imbuing it with excessive smokiness and quasi-sweetness. These observations are pertinent for two of the wines under discussion, the Riserva Garò and the younger Bricco dell'Invernata, yet both display considerable class, the former showing more volume and depth, the latter a bit too dried. Not everything comes up barbera here. Merlot Calastrino showed the best results of any wine this time. It bears the stamp of Ognibene's preferred lean, somewhat rigid, austerity, and it unveils exuberant tannins that are slightly drying, but this is an eminently enjoyable and accessible offering.

Isola

FRAZ. MONGIORGIO
VIA G. BERNARDI, 3
40050 MONTE SAN PIETRO [BO]
TEL. 0516768428
isola1898@interfree.it

ANNUAL PRODUCTION 60,000 bottles
HECTARES UNDER VINE 12.5
VITICULTURE METHOD Natural

If there is a single wine that shows best the Isola style, and more generally the approach of the Franceschinis, Marco and his son Gianluca, Chardonnay '06 answers the call. Vinified solely in steel, it's a straightforward, tasty white, showing complex but without any bells or whistles. Marco and Gianluca are farmers who love their work, and who are comfortable with tradition, but they also keep their eyes on new developments around them. Gianluca in particular has his own unique, increasingly natural and sustainable, methods in the vineyard. But far from running after the latest fashion, the Franceschinis are simply striving to make the best, most distinctive, wines they can. The silky textured Cabernet Sauvignon Monte Gorgii is masterfully executed, as is the vivacious, cask-aged Barbera Monte Gorgii, like its Chardonnay cousin in the same line. Collaboration between the Franceschinis and their friend Maurizio Vallona resulted in Spumante Essè, made from pignoletto. Though graceful and elegant, the body is satisfying full and the finale smooth and cushiony.

● C. B. Barbera Garò Ris. '04	♟♟ 4*
● Calastrino Merlot '05	♟♟ 4*
● C. B. Barbera Bricco dell'Invernata '05	♟ 3
● Rovo Nero Cabernet '05	♟ 4
O Il Rebbio Pinot '06	♟ 3
● C. B. Barbera Bricco dell'Invernata '04	♟♟ 3
● C. B. Barbera Garò Ris. '03	♟♟ 5
● C. B. Barbera Bricco dell'Invernata '03	♟♟ 3
● C. B. Merlot Calastrino '03	♟♟ 4
● C. B. Barbera Ris. '01	♟♟ 4
● C. B. Merlot Calastrino '02	♟♟ 4

● C. B. Cabernet Sauvignon Monte Gorgii '05	♟♟ 4
● C. B. Barbera Monte Gorgii '05	♟♟ 4
O Essè Brut Spumante	♟♟ 4
O C. B. Chardonnay '06	♟♟ 3*
● C. B. Cabernet Sauvignon '06	♟ 3
O C. B. Chardonnay Monte Gorgii '06	♟ 4
O C. B. Pignoletto Sup. '06	♟ 3
O C. B. Pignoletto Frizzante '06	♟ 3
● C. B. Cabernet Sauvignon Monte Gorgii '04	♟♟ 4
O C. B. Chardonnay Monte Gorgii '05	♟♟ 4
● Barbera Monte Gorgii '03	♟♟ 4

Tenuta La Viola

VIA COLOMBARONE, 888
47032 BERTINORO [FC]
TEL. 0543445496
www.tenutalaviola.it

ANNUAL PRODUCTION 30,000 bottles
HECTARES UNDER VINE 5
VITICULTURE METHOD Natural

Tenuta La Viola is one of the promising new players on the well-peopled stage of Bertinoro winemaking, an area that has been demonstrating its considerable gifts for sangiovese. The youthful Stefano Gabellini directs this operation and has just begun a relationship with Romagna oenologist Franco Calini. The vineyards are the bailiwick of Stefano's mother, Lidia, whose efforts are unremitting and well focused, her watchful eye on every detail. While we wait for Sangiovese Riserva Petra Honorii '05 to reach optimum maturity, we can more than console ourselves with Il Colombarone '05, La Viola's second-tier Sangiovese. Still a little closed on the nose, it builds complexity and depth in the mouth, with a dense charge of tannins that tend to dry its lengthy, dynamic finish. Particella 25, a blend of cabernet and merlot with ten per cent sangiovese, is more impressive. Heady aromas with more than a hint of fresh grass open on the nose before the palate shows imposing concentration, good length and all components nicely in place. Oddone may be the winery's most uncomplicated wine, but it's crisp and fragrant, and wins One Glass.

Luretta

LOC. CASTELLO DI MOMELIANO
29010 GAZZOLA [PC]
TEL. 0523971070
www.luretta.com

ANNUAL PRODUCTION 250,000 bottles
HECTARES UNDER VINE 43
VITICULTURE METHOD Natural

Lucio Salamini has chosen the non-interventionist approach to management of Luretta's vineyards, as well as low yields. Together with unrelenting research and painstaking attention to winemaking, these practices are his keys to producing wines that we have seen assuming positions of importance in markets that are ever more bewilderingly complex. No wonder then that Luretta has become, in just a few years, one of the fastest growing wineries in the region. Although we weren't able to taste some of Luretta's stars, this year's line-up is nonetheless impressive. Brut Rosé On Attend les Invités enters very smoothly and displays a nicely tart edge. A crisp vegetal nuance opens Sauvignon I Nani e Le Ballerine, which offers a dry, wonderfully refreshing palate. Malvasia Boccadirosa releases a decent bouquet, smooth texture and a pleasantly bitterish finale. Among the reds, Gutturnio L'Ala del Drago masterfully balances ripe fruit and acidity in the mouth with a steady, well-driven progression. Luretta's blend of barbera, bonarda and cabernet sauvignon, usually referred to as Pantera, opens to smooth, rounded impressions of dark berry fruit and spice.

● Particella 25 '05	▼▼ 6
● Sangiovese di Romagna Sup. Il Colombarone '05	▼▼ 4*
● Sangiovese di Romagna Oddone '06	▼ 3
● Sangiovese di Romagna Petra Honorii Sup. Ris. '04	▽▽ 5
● Sangiovese di Romagna Sup. La Badia Ris. '03	▽▽ 5
● Sangiovese di Romagna Sup. Il Colombarone '04	▽▽ 4
● Sangiovese di Romagna Sup. Il Colombarone '03	▽▽ 3
● Sangiovese di Romagna Sup. La Badia Ris. '01	▽▽ 4

☉ C. P. Brut Rosé On Attend les Invités '02	▼▼ 5
○ C. P. Malvasia Boccadirosa '06	▼▼ 4*
● Come La Pantera e I Lupi nella Sera '04	▼▼ 5
● C. P. Gutturnio Sup. L'Ala del Drago '04	▼▼ 4*
● C. P. Gutturnio Sup. '05	▼▼ 4*
○ C. P. Sauvignon I Nani e Le Ballerine '06	▼ 4
○ Principessa Brut	▼ 4
● C. P. Cabernet Sauvignon Corbeau '00	▽▽▽ 6
● C. P. Cabernet Sauvignon Corbeau '04	▽▽ 7
● C. P. Pinot Nero Achab '04	▽▽ 6
● C. P. Cabernet Sauvignon Corbeau '03	▽▽ 6

Gaetano Lusenti

LOC. CASE PICCIONI, 57
29010 ZIANO PIACENTINO [PC]
TEL. 0523868479
www.lusentivini.it

ANNUAL PRODUCTION 100,000 bottles
HECTARES UNDER VINE 17
VITICULTURE METHOD Conventional

Of all the wineries in the Piacenza area, Lodovica Lusenti's is one of the most successful in communicating the considerable qualities of the local terroir. She shows a sturdy attachment to local traditions but at the same time does not close her eyes to new developments in the wine world. Regina Bianca, a Malvasia that is given a brief maceration on the skins, offers a well-calibrated balance between fresh varietal fragrances and refined development on the palate. Gutturnio Cresta al Sole shows somewhat reduced on the nose but splendidly ripe fruit follows in the mouth and it closes on pungent notes of spice. The well-matured bonarda vineyards over 30 years old that yield La Picciona contribute to a heady, spice-filled palate and robust tannins, which do however seem to dry its finish. Cabernet Villante is solidly built and well balanced, with a rich tannic weave and an aromatic medley of bright wild berry, spice and subtle fresh greens. A delicate onion-skin hue announces Pinot Nero Spumante, which then opens to heady, youthful fragrances, a dense, smooth mousse and good length.

Giovanna Madonia

LOC. VILLA MADONIA
VIA DE' CAPPUCCINI, 130
47032 BERTINORO [FC]
TEL. 0543444361
www.giovannamadonia.it

ANNUAL PRODUCTION 45,000 bottles
HECTARES UNDER VINE 12
VITICULTURE METHOD Conventional

The area around Bertinoro may be quite limited in extent but it boasts a number of quite distinctive subzones that may yield very different wines in the same vintage. Giovanna Madonia's vineyards are located in the section that faces south, an area that is a bit out of the way but with ideal exposures. The qualities of these terroirs are on display in the wines that Giovanna crafts with valiant help from oenologist Attilio Pagli. Generally powerful and austere, they rely on a tannic structure that requires years of ageing to mellow out. We found the winery's two Sangioveses at their usual high level of quality. Ombroso '04 may not display the opulent fruit and class of previous vintages but there is no denying its fine body and smooth texture or with its supple progression and dense supporting tannins. Fermavento '05, on the other hand, offers lovely nuances of spice that lift well-ripened fruit. The palate is defined by extractive power and crisp, succulent fruit well bolstered by lively acidity, signing off with the right degree of dryness on the finish.

○ C. P. Malvasia V. T.	
Regina Bianca '05	▼▼ 4*
⊙ C. P. Pinot Nero	
Spumante Rosé '00	▼▼ 5
● C. P. Cabernet Sauvignon	
Villante '04	▼▼ 4*
● C. P. Bonarda La Picciona '04	▼ 4
● C. P. Gutturnio Frizzante '06	▼ 3
● C. P. Gutturnio Sup.	
Cresta al Sole '05	▼ 4
○ C. P. Ortrugo Frizzante '06	▼ 3
● C. P. Cabernet Sauvignon	
Villante '03	▼▼ 4
● C. P. Gutturnio Sup.	
Cresta al Sole '04	▼▼ 4
● C. P. Bonarda La Picciona '03	▼▼ 4
● C. P. Cabernet Sauvignon	
Villante '02	▼▼ 5

● Sangiovese di Romagna Sup.	
Fermavento '05	▼▼ 4*
● Sangiovese di Romagna Sup.	
Ombroso Ris. '04	▼▼ 5
○ Albana di Romagna Passito	
Chimera '04	▼ 5
● Sterpigno Merlot '04	▼ 6
● Sangiovese di Romagna Sup.	
Ombroso Ris. '01	▼▼▼ 5
● Sangiovese di Romagna Sup.	
Ombroso Ris. '03	▼▼ 5
○ Albana di Romagna Passito	
Chimera '03	▼▼ 5
● Sterpigno Merlot '03	▼▼ 6
● Sterpigno Merlot '00	▼▼ 6
● Sangiovese di Romagna Sup.	
Ombroso Ris. '00	▼▼ 5

La Mancina

FRAZ. MONTEBUDELLO
VIA MOTTA, 8
40050 MONTEVEGLIO [BO]
TEL. 051832691
www.lamancina.it

ANNUAL PRODUCTION 120,000 bottles
HECTARES UNDER VINE 40
VITICULTURE METHOD Conventional

La Mancina's lengthy journey over recent years has reached, and completed, its final stage. The new winemaking facility is now finished so the production staff, which of course includes talented consultant Giandomenico Negro, now enjoys excellent control over vinification. The vineyards too have been very carefully restructured. Finally, and perhaps less significantly but crucially for marketing, the labels have been made over to bring them up to date and give them more visual impact. All this in fact reflects the character of the young owner, Francesca Zanetti. We expect that these efforts will bring a leap to the kind of quality that La Mancina deserves. For now, we're pleased at the usual good performance from Merlot Lanciotto, which exhibits crisp, tasty fruit, a nicely sculpted body and excellent progression that make if an easy-drinking delight. Rosato Frizzante Chiosa is both intriguing and well executed. A bright fruit nose presents cherry, raspberry and fresh wild strawberries that return on the finish and the palate has refreshing liveliness and impressive savouriness. No less crisp is Barbera Il Foriere, which shows nice suppleness and is ready to enjoy right now.

Ermete Medici & Figli

LOC. GAIDA
VIA NEWTON, 13A
42040 REGGIO EMILIA
TEL. 0522942135
www.medici.it

ANNUAL PRODUCTION 800,000 bottles
HECTARES UNDER VINE 60
VITICULTURE METHOD Conventional

The very experienced Medici family has for many years demonstrated its familiarity with the recipe for producing outstanding Lambruscos. The secret is meticulous vineyard management, sound fruit and cellar equipment for careful vinification while avoiding excessive procedures. It seems pretty obvious but this is after all the secret of making good wine anywhere in the world and it's a shame that some in Emilia often lose sight of it. This year, we found it difficult to decide among wines that are all excellent and well made but the laurels went once again to Assolo. It's dark in tone, with just the right degree of dryness, and although not exactly fizzy, the mousse is quite dense and fascinating. Nicely delineated red berry fruit creates a complex, ripe nose, the weight is well calibrated and the texture silky. A companion in quality is the terrific I Quercioli, exuding rich cherry and showing off a creamy but not facile palate. We expected Concerto to be good and it is, showing generous, multi-layered and glossy. Antica Osteria is judiciously balanced and lays out plenty of fruit. A delight.

● C. B. Barbera Il Foriere '06	♼♼ 3*
● C. B. Merlot Lanciotto '06	♼♼ 3*
● C. B. Cabernet Sauvignon '06	♼ 3
● C. B. Cabernet Sauvignon Comandante della Guardia '05	♼ 4
⊙ Chiosa Rosato Frizzante '06	♼ 3
○ C. B. Pignoletto Terre di Montebudello '05	♼ 3
○ C. B. Pignoletto Frizzante '06	3
● C. B. Cabernet Sauvignon Comandante della Guardia '04	♼♼ 4
● C. B. Merlot Lanciotto '05	♼♼ 3
● C. B. Barbera Il Foriere '03	♼♼ 3
● C. B. Cabernet Sauvignon Comandante della Guardia '03	♼♼ 4

● Reggiano Assolo '06	♼♼ 3*
● Reggiano Lambrusco Secco I Quercioli '06	♼♼ 3*
● Antica Osteria Lambrusco	♼♼ 2*
● Reggiano Lambrusco Secco Concerto '06	♼♼ 3
⊙ Brut Rosé M. Cl. Unique '05	♼ 4
● Reggiano Lambrusco Dolce I Quercioli	♼ 3
● Reggiano Lambrusco Secco	♼ 2
○ Colli di Scandiano e di Canossa Malvasia Daphne '06	♼ 3
● Colli di Scandiano e di Canossa Grasparossa Bocciolo '06	♼ 3
○ Nebbie d'Autunno Dolce '06	3

Monte delle Vigne
LOC. OZZANO TARO
VIA MONTICELLO, 13
43046 COLLECCHIO [PR]
TEL. 0521309704
www.montedellevigne.it

ANNUAL PRODUCTION 250,000 bottles
HECTARES UNDER VINE 30
VITICULTURE METHOD Conventional

Monte delle Vigne's enlargement project is drawing to a close, much to the satisfaction of Andrea Ferrari and his partner Paolo Pizzarotti. Their initial seven hectares of vineyard have now grown to 30, all in production, a total that will double over the next few years. Following the advice of agronomist Federico Curtaz, the traditional local barbera and bonarda grapes were planted in the west and to the east went the white malvasia, which in the local terroir develops lovely aromatics. Consulting oenologist Attilio Pagli will be able to reach new levels of quality, since a new cellar rises in the midst of the vines. It's functional but also an impressive piece of architecture. At our tastings, we very much liked the dense, fine-grained tannins and pulpy fruit of Nabucco, from 70 per cent barbera and 30 per cent merlot. Malvasia Callas is on the same level, with ample aromas and sterling balance. Colli di Parma Rosso Frizzante also stands out for its appealing fragrances and accessibility while the still Rosso is smooth and uncomplicated.

Fattoria del Monticino Rosso
VIA MONTECATONE, 7
40026 IMOLA [BO]
TEL. 054240577
www.fattoriadelmonticinorosso.it

ANNUAL PRODUCTION 65,000 bottles
HECTARES UNDER VINE 16
VITICULTURE METHOD Conventional

Consistency is a difficult challenge to meet for such a winery as small as that of the Zeoli siblings, particularly for a cellar that has been operating for such a short time. Only recently has Fattoria del Monticino Rosso left pretty much behind its old model of bulk wine in demijohns and switched to bottles. The favourable results reported in this year's Guide are a big step up and also reflect the good work of oenologist Giancarlo Soverchia, even if here and there some wines seem to reflect more of the past than the future. Emblematic is Codronchio, an Albana Secco made with late-harvested fruit allowed to contract botrytis. The bouquet is appealingly sweet, exhibiting honey and candied fruit, but the palate is not as smooth and unctuous as it could be, creating a discontinuity with respect to the nose. Malvasia Passito on the other hand is rich and dense, with a leisurely, luscious sweetness. Albana Secco is refreshing and appreciably full bodied, showcasing tasty citrus in the mouth.

O Callas Malvasia '06	▼▼	5
● Colli di Parma Rosso Frizzante '06	▼▼	3*
● Nabucco '05	▼▼	5
● Monte delle Vigne Rosso '06	▼	4
● Lambrusco '06	▼	3
O Colli di Parma Malvasia Secco '06	▼	3
O Malvasia Dolce Frizzante '06	▼	4
● Nabucco '04	♈♈	5
● Nabucco '03	♈♈	5
● Nabucco '02	♈♈	5
● Nabucco '01	♈♈	5
O Callas Malvasia '05	♈♈	5

O Albana di Romagna Secco '06	▼▼	3*
O Albana di Romagna Secco Codronchio '05	▼▼	4
O Malvasia Passito '03	▼▼	5
O Albana di Romagna Passito '04	▼	5
O Colli d'Imola Pignoletto '06	▼	2
● Sangiovese di Romagna Sup. '05		3
O Albana di Romagna Secco Codronchio '04	♈♈	4
O Albana di Romagna Passito '03	♈♈	5

Poderi Morini

LOC. ORIOLO DEI FICHI
VIA GESUITA
48018 FAENZA [RA]
TEL. 0546634257
info@poderimorini.com

ANNUAL PRODUCTION 100,000
HECTARES UNDER VINE 40
VITICULTURE METHOD Conventional

Alessandro Morini's vineyards are divided into two separate sections. One lies on the eastern slope of Torre di Oriolo, a growing area traditionally recognized for high quality, while the other is located in the first band of hills at Forlì, near the border with Faenza. Morini has made considerable investments in the past in these vineyards but he has not yet been able to transfer their potential into his wines. All too often, the wines seem to be struggling to find their true stylistic groove. He has the equipment at hand and all he needs to push Poderi Morini into new growth that will allow the natural qualities of the local terroirs to shine. There is no doubt that the potential is there and that Morini is worth watching, even in a year such as the present one, when we were given only the simpler wines. The one exception was Riserva di Albana Passito, redolent of luscious peach marmalade and zabaglione, followed by a nice medicinal note. The palate shows just the right level of sweetness, well this side of cloying.

Perinelli

LOC. I PERINELLI
29028 PONTE DELL'OLIO [PC]
TEL. 0523877185
www.perinelli.it

ANNUAL PRODUCTION 60,000 bottles
HECTARES UNDER VINE 17
VITICULTURE METHOD Conventional

Perinelli is a relatively new operation in Val Nure but it is making brisk progress in commitment to quality and reliability, and its stylistic features are becoming clearer with time. Its no-nonsense, traditional qualities are making it one of the benchmark wineries in the Colli Piacentini. Perinelli's Malvasia Torre della Ghiacciaia '06 is a fine effort and continues its consistent evolution, in general displaying citrus and rose petals on the nose and then lively freshness in the mouth with steady development from start to finish. Gutturnio Costa dei Salina is on a par, opening to captivating floral and fruit essences, with a palate notable for its velvety suppleness and good breadth. It closes on a succulent vein of acidity that crowns its delicious drinkability. We thought Vigna Vecchia was just a pace off its usual performance. A blend of pinot nero, cabernet and barbera, it weaves a soft texture in the mouth but seems somewhat tight on the nose and sluggish in progression. Finally, Anno Quattro, a partnership of malvasia, sémillon and viognier, is delightfully lively and very fluid.

O Albana di Romagna Passito Cuore Matto Ris. '04	♟♟ 5
O Colli di Faenza Bianco Alba di Luna '06	♟ 3
● Sangiovese di Romagna Sup. Beccafico '06	♟ 3
O Trebbiano di Romagna Brivido '06	♟ 3
O Albana di Romagna Secco Sette Note per Dani '05	3
● Rubacuori da Uve Stramature '04	♟♟ 5
● Sangiovese di Romagna Sup. Nonno Rico Ris. '03	♟♟ 5
● Traicolli '03	♟♟ 5
● Sangiovese di Romagna Sup. Torre di Oriolo '03	♟♟ 4
● Nadèl '01	♟♟ 5

O Anno Quattro '04	♟♟ 4*
● C. P. Gutturnio Costa dei Salina '06	♟♟ 4*
O C. P. Malvasia Torre della Ghiacciaia '06	♟♟ 4*
● C. P. Gutturnio Vivace '06	♟ 4
● Vigna Vecchia '05	♟ 4
O Anno Tre '03	♟♟ 4
● C. P. Gutturnio Costa dei Salina '05	♟♟ 4
● Vigna Vecchia '04	♟♟ 4
O Anno Due '02	♟♟ 4
● Vigna Vecchia '03	♟♟ 4

Poderi dal Nespoli

LOC. NESPOLI
VILLA ROSSI, 50
47012 CIVITELLA DI ROMAGNA [FC]
TEL. 0543989637
www.poderidalnespoli.com

ANNUAL PRODUCTION 300,000 bottles
HECTARES UNDER VINE 41
VITICULTURE METHOD Conventional

Poderi dal Nespoli is one of Romagna's soundest and most capable operations. It sources from vineyards in the Bidente valley at elevations ranging from 120 to 250 metres, on soils of different configurations, clayey at the lower elevations, mixed sandstone and clays higher up. The house style emphasizes elegance over power, a more difficult road perhaps but one that is interesting and appealing to consumers. We found Sangiovese Prugneto '06 outstanding. The nose presents sound, clean-edged fruit in a rather sober fashion, with no flashy gloss. Stellar acidity keeps a super-rich palate under control, and the admirably lean finish ends with a dynamic flourish. Chardonnay Damaggio '06 also showed well with even-handed fruitiness and satisfactory weight in the mouth, although a bitterish note of wood tends to mar the finish. We waited for Borgo dei Guidi '04 while it was undergoing lengthy bottle ageing. It has emerged a trifle weak but overall it's still generous and ready to enjoy.

Il Poggiarello

LOC. SCRIVELLANO DI STATTO
29020 TRAVO [PC]
TEL. 0523957241
www.ilpoggiarellovini.it

ANNUAL PRODUCTION 100,000 bottles
HECTARES UNDER VINE 18
VITICULTURE METHOD Conventional

The wines from Poggiarello have for some time now been stylistically distinctive, thanks to a well-designed programme put together by the Perini family. Over the last few years, it has been yielding increasingly positive results. Gutturnio Riserva La Barbona's well-calibrated tannins and multi-layered aromatics do a terrific job of supporting its rich, full body. Barbera 'L Piston, released only in magnums, turned in a surprisingly impressive performance. Powerful expression both lifts its suite of aromatics and effectively restrains the acidity. Although Cabernet Perticato Novarei is somewhat slow to open on the nose, the palate shows good varietal characteristics and expressive tannins. Among the standard-label whites, Malvasia Beatrice Quadri releases elegant notes of citrus and blossoms while Sauvignon Perticato Il Quadri shows refined typicity on the nose and a complex but lively palate with a base of generously aromatic fruit. The oak has not yet found its balance in Chardonnay La Piana, drying the mouth and allowing the alcohol too much of a role at the moment.

● Borgo dei Guidi '04	ŸŸ 6
● Sangiovese di Romagna Prugneto '06	ŸŸ 4*
O Damaggio Chardonnay '06	ŸŸ 3*
● Sangiovese di Romagna Sup. Santodeno '06	Ÿ 3
● Il Nespoli Sangiovese '04	ŸŸ 5
● Borgo dei Guidi '03	ŸŸ 6
● Il Nespoli Sangiovese '03	ŸŸ 5
● Borgo dei Guidi '01	ŸŸ 6
● Borgo dei Guidi '00	ŸŸ 6
● Borgo dei Guidi '99	ŸŸ 6

● C. P. Barbera 'L Piston '06	ŸŸ 4*
● C. P. Gutturnio La Barbona Ris. '05	ŸŸ 5
O C. P. Malvasia Perticato Beatrice Quadri '06	ŸŸ 4*
● C. P. Cabernet Sauvignon Perticato del Novarei '05	ŸŸ 5
● C. P. Gutturnio Perticato Valandrea '06	Ÿ 4
O C. P. Chardonnay Perticato La Piana '06	Ÿ 4
O C. P. Sauvignon Perticato Il Quadri '06	Ÿ 4
● C. P. Gutturnio La Barbona Ris. '04	ŸŸ 5
● C. P. Cabernet Sauvignon Perticato del Novarei '04	ŸŸ 5
● C. P. Gutturnio La Barbona Ris. '03	ŸŸ 5
● C. P. Gutturnio La Barbona Ris. '01	ŸŸ 5

Tenuta Poggio Pollino
VIA MONTE MELDOLA, 2T
40026 IMOLA [BO]
TEL. 0522942135
www.agriturismotenutapoggiopollino.it

ANNUAL PRODUCTION 46,000 bottles
HECTARES UNDER VINE 16
VITICULTURE METHOD Conventional

The galaxy of properties owned by Ermete Medici of Reggio Emilia includes the Tenuta Poggio Pollino in Romagna. The Manzi family founded this small-scale operation and later formed a fruitful relationship with the Medici, whose contributions are evident everywhere. The determination to achieve top-notch results is visible in every step of the production cycle, from the choice of hillslope vineyards, with their perfectly marshalled rows of spur-cordoned vines, to the manual picking of the grapes, and to the use of small oak casks. All of this seems carefully designed to ensure respect for both tradition and innovation in equal measures. Progress towards this goal is nicely on display in Sangiovese Vigna di Cambro, whose subtle fragrances give way to pulpy, ready to enjoy fruit on the palate and a supple, utterly delicious finish. On the other hand, Terre di Maestrale '05, a partnership of sangiovese, cabernet and merlot, is soft textured and austere at the same time, with a finish somewhat dried by the cask ageing.

Podere Riosto
VIA DI RIOSTO, 12
40065 PIANORO [BO]
TEL. 051777109
www.podereriosto.it

ANNUAL PRODUCTION 80,000 bottles
HECTARES UNDER VINE 16
VITICULTURE METHOD Conventional

The Galletti family continues to amaze us, since they seem to invent new wines with every harvest, adding to their already very ambitious line-up. The number of hectares in full production is getting impressive and the different varieties are planted in full respect of the various site conditions. We acknowledge that a young operation must, as it were, test it wings. Still, Podere Riosto is approaching maturity, and the solid achievements might well suggest cutting down the number of wines produced. Two new reds emerged this year, Grifone and Aquilante. The former is a Cabernet Sauvignon with crisp, succulent fruit, a rich, energy-laden palate and lovely, lean finale. But Aquilante, a blend of barbera, cabernet sauvignon and merlot, disappointed a little, being lighter and not as dynamic, and showing a touch too much acid on the finish. But we were very impressed by Sauvignon '06. It shows refined typicity in its aromatics while the palate is as fat and savoury as you could want, but crisp throughout, and development is exemplary. The '05 versions of Cabernet Sauvignon and Merlot are uncomplicated but sound and fruity, and Barbera Podere Riosto shows light and refreshing.

● Terre di Maestrale '05	¶¶ 4
● Sangiovese di Romagna Sup. V. di Cambro '05	¶¶ 3*
○ Albana di Romagna Secco Monte di Cambro '06	¶ 3
● Sangiovese di Romagna Campo Rosso Ris. '04	¶ 4
● Sangiovese di Romagna Sup. Campo Rosso Ris. '02	¶¶ 4

● C. B. Cabernet Sauvignon Grifone '04	¶¶ 5
○ C. B. Sauvignon V. del Pino '06	¶¶ 4*
● Aquilante '04	¶ 4
● C. B. Cabernet Sauvignon V. Bel Poggio '05	¶ 4
○ C. B. Pignoletto Sup. V. della Torre '06	¶ 3
● C. B. Merlot V. della Valle '05	¶ 5
● C. B. Barbera V. della Valle '05	¶ 4
○ C. B. Pignoletto Frizzante V. della Torre '06	3
● C. B. Barbera Sel. V. della Valle '03	¶¶ 4

San Patrignano
VIA SAN PATRIGNANO, 53
47852 CORIANO [RN]
TEL. 0541362362
www.sanpatrignano.org

ANNUAL PRODUCTION 500,000 bottles
HECTARES UNDER VINE 110
VITICULTURE METHOD Conventional

San Patrignano boasts a spacious cellar with up-to-date technology and plenty of winemaking know-how. It has shown that it is not afraid to take difficult decisions and make investments, paying close attention to the markets and responding intelligently, but at the same time complying with a philosophy of planning long term and maintaining a spirit of passionate commitment. In addition, it always turns out top-notch wines. What this list makes clear is that San Patrignano is a great winery. Its masterpieces share common characteristics. They are always elegant, made with optimally ripe fruit and restrained use of oak. Montepirolo '04 is a perfect Three Glass gem. It is silk smooth, supple and seductive but at the same time almost electric in its power, with a nearly endless finish and platonically perfect finesse. The sangiovese Avi is rounder and fuller bodied, showing dense-packed, sturdy tannins with fabulous fruit and a precious texture. Vie, a new Sauvignon, is a varietal treat. Noi, 60 per cent sangiovese, 20 per cent cabernet and merlot, is slightly gamey and vegetal but exhibits tremendous structure and depth.

San Valentino
FRAZ. SAN MARTINO IN VENTI
VIA TOMASETTA, 13
47900 RIMINI
TEL. 0541752231
www.vinisanvalentino.com

ANNUAL PRODUCTION 140,000 bottles
HECTARES UNDER VINE 28
VITICULTURE METHOD Conventional

Colli di Rimini's wines always display a lovely softness and a mouthfilling allure, somewhat crisper and more complex in the Bordeaux varieties and a bit warmer and more forthright in the sangioveses. Roberto Mascarin and his oenologist Fabrizio Moltard are now striving to express this natural style in such a way as to develop even further the wines' elegance and to tone down the power. San Valentino's philosophy is in a state of change, portending wines that look set to be impressive in the future. Actually, the results are already visible in this year's offerings. Luna Nuova '04, a classic Bordeaux blend, does show a good bit of oak but it's rich, spicy stuff with a superbly crisp, dynamic palate that seems to drive forever into an extraordinarily complex finish. In Terra di Covignano '04, the elegance and expression of the sangiovese are better delineated than in previous versions and this vintage shows more stylish and better nuanced. This is the debut of Montepulciano, the only monovarietal Montepulciano in Romagna. There is abundant varietal fruit on the nose and the palate is heavy and rich but relieved by appreciably crisp acidity.

Wine	Rating
● Colli di Rimini Cabernet Montepirolo '04	▼▼▼ 6
● Sangiovese di Romagna Sup. Avi Ris. '04	▼▼ 6
● Colli di Rimini Rosso Noi '05	▼▼ 5
○ Vie '06	▼▼ 5
○ Aulente Bianco '06	▼ 4
● Aulente Sangiovese '06	▼ 4
● Colli di Rimini Rosso Noi '04	♆♆♆ 5
● Colli di Rimini Cabernet Montepirolo '01	♆♆♆ 6
● Sangiovese di Romagna Sup. Avi Ris. '01	♆♆♆ 6
● Sangiovese di Romagna Sup. Avi Ris. '00	♆♆♆ 6
● Sangiovese di Romagna Sup. Avi Ris. '99	♆♆♆ 6
● Montepirolo '99	♆♆♆ 6

Wine	Rating
● Sangiovese di Romagna Sup. Terra di Covignano Ris. '04	▼▼ 5
● Montepulciano '04	▼▼ 8
● Luna Nuova '04	▼▼ 6
● Eclissi di Sole '06	▼▼ 5
● Sangiovese di Romagna Sup. Scabi '06	▼ 4
● Sangiovese di Romagna Sup. Terra di Covignano Ris. '03	♆♆♆ 5
● Sangiovese di Romagna Sup. Terra di Covignano Ris. '02	♆♆♆ 5
● Sangiovese di Romagna Sup. Terra di Covignano Ris. '01	♆♆♆ 5
● Luna Nuova '03	♆♆ 6
● Colli di Rimini Cabernet Sauvignon Luna Nuova '02	♆♆ 5

Santarosa

FRAZ. SAN MARTINO IN CASOLA
VIA SAN MARTINO, 82
40050 MONTE SAN PIETRO [BO]
TEL. 051969203
www.santarosavini.com

ANNUAL PRODUCTION 30,000 bottles
HECTARES UNDER VINE 10
VITICULTURE METHOD Conventional

The three international varieties merlot, cabernet sauvignon and chardonnay have a deep-rooted tradition in the Colli Bolognesi. They also are the foundation of Santarosa, Giovanna della Valentina's operation. The choice, some years ago, of a style for Santarosa's wines was understandably more oriented to the global market than to local traditions. These are rich, creamy creations where well-ripened fruit comes to the fore, always laced with cask-driven essences of vanilla and spice, and of tropical fruit in the whites. That is what we found in the wine we liked the most, Merlot Giòtondo '05. Rich, heady scents of ripe red berry fruit precede a velvety rich palate that manages to show tasty verve. In much the same style is Giòrosso '05, which is a little too hard and dried out. Santarosa Rosso '06, though, is a terrific everyday quaffer. This youthful, heady Bordeaux blend is crisp edged and shows lots of energy, its rich fruit and smooth mouthfeel giving it great appeal.

Tenuta Santini

FRAZ. PASSANO
VIA CAMPO, 33
47853 CORIANO [RN]
TEL. 0541656527
www.tenutasantini.com

ANNUAL PRODUCTION 25,000 bottles
HECTARES UNDER VINE 22
VITICULTURE METHOD Conventional

Sandro Santini enjoys a reputation for expertise and realistic goals, and he has quickly turned Tenuta Santini into a serious, reliable producer. His winery is the southernmost of those in Romagna reviewed in our Guide, with vineyards practically on the Adriatic itself planted on gently rolling hills among olive groves and expanses of wheat. This is relevant information, since the warm conditions of the Colli di Rimini area are increasingly being recognized as ideal for growing of Bordeaux varieties. Local vineyards yield crisp-edged, elegant wines that meld together appeal, depth and significant complexity. The cabernet sauvignon and merlot Battarreo '05, though recognizably a wine of breed, struggles against a generally unfavourable year. The nose shows a tad harsh and blurred, and the finish is slightly dried, although the mouth shows rich enough and the texture is nicely rounded. Beato Enrico '06 merits serious attention. Opening with well-ripened, fleshy sangiovese fruit, it develops warm and filling in the mouth, with dense, ripe tannins and an overall expression that is refreshing and elegant.

● C. B. Merlot Giòtondo '05	♟♟	4*
● C. B. Cabernet Sauvignon Giòrosso '05	♟♟	5
● Santarosa Rosso '06	♟♟	3*
○ Giòcoliere Chardonnay '06	♟	4
○ Pignoletto '06	♟	3
● C. B. Merlot Giòtondo '00	♟♟♟	4
● C. B. Merlot Giòtondo '04	♟♟	4
● C. B. Cabernet Sauvignon Giòrosso '04	♟♟	4
● C. B. Cabernet Sauvignon Giòrosso '03	♟♟	4
● C. B. Merlot Giòtondo '03	♟♟	4
● C. B. Merlot Giòtondo '01	♟♟	4

● Sangiovese di Romagna Sup. Beato Enrico '06	♟♟	4*
● Battarreo '05	♟♟	4*
● Battarreo '04	♟♟	4
● Sangiovese di Romagna Sup. Cornelianum Ris. '04	♟♟	5
● Battarreo '03	♟♟	4
● Sangiovese di Romagna Sup. Cornelianum Ris. '03	♟♟	5
● Sangiovese di Romagna Sup. Beato Enrico '04	♟♟	3

Cantine Spalletti - Colonna

LOC. CASTELLO DI RIBANO
VIA SOGLIANO, 104
47039 SAVIGNANO SUL RUBICONE [FC]
TEL. 0541945111
www.spalletticolonnadipaliano.com

ANNUAL PRODUCTION 500,000 bottles
HECTARES UNDER VINE 75
VITICULTURE METHOD Conventional

Last year's Guide mentioned the new developments at this long-established cellar. As we know, good seed bears fine fruit and we are now seeing the results: excellent showings across almost the entire line. A common thread runs though all of Spalletti-Colonna's wines and links their good performances. It is a healthy respect for fine fruit and the good sense to allow it to unfold its innate qualities, without recourse to excessive technical acrobatics in the cellar. These are fruit-forward wines, with a refreshing tastiness and an admirable coherence of nose and progression in the mouth. Kudos goes to winemaker Leonardo Conti. We were bowled over by the velvety softness of Cabernet Monaco di Ribano, which has a fleshy, alluringly crisp mouthfeel. Merlot Gianello is more complex and riper, and Cabernet Sabinio gives off fine, elegant fragrances. Villa Rasponi is a first-rate old-style sangiovese, with appreciable acidic grip. Albana Duchessa di Montemar is flawless and eschews fluffy pretensions. Albana Passito Carpe Diem unfurls a scrumptious parade of apricot, fig and peach fruit and beautifully calibrated sweetness.

La Stoppa

LOC. ANCARANO
29029 RIVERGARO [PC]
TEL. 0523958159
www.lastoppa.it

ANNUAL PRODUCTION 150,000 bottles
HECTARES UNDER VINE 32
VITICULTURE METHOD Natural

Respect the natural expression of your local corner of the earth is the essence of the credo shared by Elena Pantaleoni and Giulio Armani. They live that approach in Val Trebbiola, teasing out long-lived wines, rich in character and extractive power. Macchiona '03, a mix of barbera and bonarda, demonstrates La Stoppa's philosophy to perfection. It is currently starting to show warmer expression, with reductive characteristics now yielding to impressions of ripe red fruit and to an expansive, bracing, acid-etched palate. The standard-label Gutturnio exhibits terrific overall complexity and a palate that is markedly assertive and nervy. Ageno is made with malvasia that receives a lengthy maceration on the skins, which yields good complexity on the nose and a tannic, fairly imposing palate. Turning to the two sweet wines, Vigna del Volta is not its usual outrageous self on the nose and the palate, while powerful and fat, reveals tannins that tend to dry its mouth. The rare Buca delle Canne, produced from botrytis-infected sémillon, offers up candied fruit followed by luscious opulence and a fine balance of all components.

O Albana di Romagna	
Duchessa di Montemar '06	♟♟ 3*
O Albana di Romagna Passito	
Carpe Diem '05	♟♟ 7
● Sabinio Cabernet '05	♟♟ 4
● Sangiovese di Romagna Sup.	
Villa Rasponi Ris. '04	♟♟ 4
● Monaco di Ribano Cabernet '04	♟♟ 5
● Gianello Merlot '05	♟♟ 4
O Principessa Ghika '06	♟ 4
● Sangiovese di Romagna	
Castelvecchio di Ribano '06	♟ 3
● Sangiovese di Romagna Sup.	
Rocca di Ribano '04	♟ 4
● Sangiovese di Romagna Sup.	
Principe di Ribano '06	♟ 3
● Sangiovese di Romagna Sup.	
Villa Rasponi Ris. '03	♟♟ 4

O C. P. Malvasia Passito	
V. del Volta '05	♟♟ 5
O Ageno '05	♟♟ 4
● C. P. Gutturnio '06	♟♟ 3*
O Buca delle Canne '05	♟♟ 7
● Macchiona '03	♟♟ 5
O C. P. Malvasia Passito	
V. del Volta '04	♟♟♟ 6
O C. P. Malvasia Passito	
V. del Volta '03	♟♟♟ 5
O C. P. Malvasia Passito	
V. del Volta '97	♟♟♟ 5
O Ageno '04	♟♟ 5
● I Padri '04	♟♟ 5
● C. P. Cabernet Sauvignon	
Stoppa '03	♟♟ 5
● C. P. Barbera della Stoppa '00	♟♟ 4
● Macchiona '01	♟♟ 5

Tizzano

via Marescalchi, 13
40033 Casalecchio di Reno [BO]
tel. 051571208
visconti@tizzano.191.it

ANNUAL PRODUCTION 140,000 bottles
HECTARES UNDER VINE 35
VITICULTURE METHOD Conventional

You have to wonder at times whether one of the requirements for success of a winery isn't the trotting out of a series of amazing new wines with every vintage. Tizzano is a case in point for the other side, for continuity, that is, in results, in style, in image and in consistency that the consumer can appreciate and expect. This is not to imply that Luca Visconti di Modrone's operation suffers from immobility. Actually, its good showings are due to the expertise and curiosity of Gabriele Forni, who manages Tizzano and knows how to weave together ancient rural lore and the latest technological advances for continuity of results. Both of his '05 reds are very fine. The Merlot proffers outstanding fruit, exemplary body and a nicely tannic finale while the Cabernet Sauvignon '05 is less complex but still effective on the palate and crisply fruity on the nose. Pignoletto is produced in three versions, all delightful as usual. The Spumante offers fragrant green apple, the drier Frizzante comes off nicely floral and the bright Superiore expands to generous volume.

● C. B. Cabernet Sauvignon '05	🍷🍷 4*
● C. B. Merlot '05	🍷🍷 4*
○ C. B. Pignoletto Frizzante '06	🍷 3
○ C. B. Pignoletto Spumante Brut	🍷 4
○ C. B. Sauvignon '06	🍷 3
○ C. B. Pignoletto Sup. '06	🍷 3
● C. B. Merlot '04	♀♀ 4
● C. B. Cabernet Sauvignon Ris. '01	♀♀ 5
● C. B. Cabernet Sauvignon '02	♀♀ 4

Torre Fornello

loc. Fornello
29010 Ziano Piacentino [PC]
tel. 0523861001
www.torrefornello.it

ANNUAL PRODUCTION 450,000 bottles
HECTARES UNDER VINE 60
VITICULTURE METHOD Conventional

Nine years from its launch, Torre Fornello is taking a new direction intended, says owner Enrico Sgorbati, "to ensure that the wines display a more personal style and that they offer a more faithful expression of their terroir". The 2006 whites reveal less intrusive use of the cask and increased aromatic expression. The crisp fragrances emanating from Sauvignon Cà del Rio are in fact pleasantly herbaceous, with a lengthy palate that echoes them faithfully. The aroma-rich, supple Sauvignon Frizzante is an utter delight and La Malvasia Donna Luigia is equally fragrant, but with good typicity and an impressively long, clean-edged finish. Hints of toasty oak and candied citrus introduce Chardonnay La Jara, which segue into a clean, refreshing mouth and a lean finish. Pratobianco is a blend of malvasia, chardonnay and sauvignon that unfolds very expressive aromatics and a nicely balanced, spirited palate. Gutturnio Diacono Gerardo is both ready and ripe on the mouth but excessive oak cramps its development. The robust, powerful Bonarda Latitudo 45 abounds in acid, alcohol and tannin but they find it difficult to fuse together.

○ C. P. Malvasia Donna Luigia '06	🍷🍷 4*
○ C. P. Sauvignon Cà del Rio '06	🍷🍷 4*
○ Pratobianco '06	🍷🍷 4*
● C. P. Bonarda Latitudo 45 '03	🍷 5
○ C. P. Sauvignon Frizzante '06	🍷 3
○ C. P. Malvasia Frizzante '06	🍷 3
● C. P. Gutturnio Diacono Gerardo 1028 Ris. '03	🍷 5
○ C. P. Chardonnay La Jara '06	🍷 4
● C. P. Gutturnio Sup. Sinsäl '05	♀♀ 4
● C. P. Cabernet Sauvignon Ca' Bernesca '03	♀♀ 5

La Tosa

LOC. LA TOSA
29020 VIGOLZONE [PC]
TEL. 0523870727
www.latosa.it

ANNUAL PRODUCTION 120,000 bottles
HECTARES UNDER VINE 13
VITICULTURE METHOD Natural

Utter ripeness of fruit, veneration for balance and aromatic integration and meticulously calibrated oak are some of the principles that Stefano Pizzamiglio has been following, with Calvinistic rigour, for quite some time now, flanked by his wife Augusta and his brother Ferruccio. The results are wines that offer delight tonight but which can also develop unexpected complexity and longevity. Sauvignon '06 surprised us with its distinctiveness, displaying intense varietal fruit and a self-confident palate packed with crisp, pulpy fruit. Malvasia Sorriso di Cielo exudes superb harmony, building a flawless medley of aromas and a supple palate, not in the least hindered by its considerable residual sugar. Turning to the reds, Gutturnio Vignamorello shows fruit and spice, and a judicious roundedness. The difficult 2005 vintage hampers Cabernet Luna Selvatica, which is less rich and complex than the '04. Still, it is fresh and well balanced, finishing long. Lovely peach and candied citrus open L'Ora Felice, which then displays a consistent, well-balanced palate as tasty as you could wish.

Tre Monti

LOC. BERGULLO
VIA LOLA, 3
40026 IMOLA [BO]
TEL. 0542657116
www.tremonti.it

ANNUAL PRODUCTION 160,000
HECTARES UNDER VINE 55
VITICULTURE METHOD Conventional

Tre Monti is one of Romagna's longest-standing wineries and the overall high quality of the range is good testimony to its reliability. Vittorio Navacchia, who oversees both vineyards and winemaking, ensures that the local terroir is properly reflected in the wines. Local conditions tend to yield elegant, subtle wines with a mineral edge and a unique characteristic: a note of sea-brine that is just hinted at but there. It's possible that this has something to do with the mud volcanoes of Bergullo, known as "buldur" in the local dialect, which pour out their clayey mud not far from the back of the vineyards. Sangiovese Thea '05 reveals a sweet whiff of oak but not enough to mar the refined delicacy of the fruit. The palate is dense and close knit, if a tad dry perhaps, showing austere but excellent. Sangiovese Petrignone '04 shows finesse on the nose, with only a slight hint of grassiness, and that elegance carries over to the nicely subtle, complex palate, which does show a bit tight and rough. Fragrant citrus characterizes Ciardo '06, which offers impressive weight in the mouth without suffocating its considerable energy and suppleness. That signature salty note enlivens the progression.

O C. P. Sauvignon '06	▼▼ 4*
● C. P. Cabernet Sauvignon Luna Selvatica '05	▼▼ 6
O C. P. Malvasia Sorriso di Cielo '06	▼▼ 4
O C. P. Malvasia Passito L'Ora Felice '06	▼▼ 5
● C. P. Gutturnio Vignamorello '06	▼▼ 5
● C. P. Gutturnio '06	▼ 3
O C. P. Valnure Frizzante '06	▼ 3
● C. P. Cabernet Sauvignon Luna Selvatica '04	▼▼▼ 6
● C. P. Cabernet Sauvignon Luna Selvatica '97	▼▼▼ 5
● C. P. Gutturnio Vignamorello '05	▼▼ 5
● C. P. Gutturnio Vignamorello '04	▼▼ 4
● C. P. Cabernet Sauvignon Luna Selvatica '03	▼▼ 5

● Sangiovese di Romagna Sup. Thea Ris. '05	▼▼ 5
● Sangiovese di Romagna Sup. Petrignone Ris. '04	▼▼ 4*
O Colli d'Imola Chardonnay Ciardo '06	▼▼ 4*
● Sangiovese di Romagna Sup. Campo di Mezzo '06	▼ 3
O Albana di Romagna Passito Casa Lola '05	▼ 5
O Albana di Romagna Secco V. Rocca '06	▼ 4
O Colli d'Imola Salcerella '06	▼ 5
O Trebbiano di Romagna V. Rio '06	4
● Sangiovese di Romagna Sup. Thea '04	▼▼ 5
● Sangiovese di Romagna Sup. Thea '03	▼▼ 5

Trerè

LOC. MONTICORALLI
VIA CASALE, 19
48018 FAENZA [RA]
TEL. 054647034
www.trere.com

ANNUAL PRODUCTION 200,000 bottles
HECTARES UNDER VINE 35
VITICULTURE METHOD Conventional

This spot fairly exudes elegance, from the warm hues of the winery complex, which includes an agriturismo, to the vineyard-patterned countryside and on to the design of the wine labels. It might seem gratuitous or worse to impute all of this to a woman's touch but femininity and elegance are so characteristic of Morena Trerè that it is difficult to miss these qualities in whatever falls under her influence. The Trerè production philosophy strives for finesse and a subtle but exemplary style that expresses modernity while wisely preserving the best of tradition. It is no mere coincidence that Amarcord d'un Ross, a Sangiovese Riserva and the winery's favoured offspring, sparks memories of remoter times, with aromas of fruit and cream, and a palate that opens smoothly to impressions of chocolate and perky acidity that enlivens the development. An equally impressive palate marks Montecorallo, from cabernet and merlot with a dollop of sangiovese. Smooth, sweet fruit dominates until the finish, which is rather marked by tannin. The sauvignon and chardonnay Rebianco lays out plenty of crisp-edged, succulent fruit.

Uccellaia

LOC. ALBAROLA DI VIGOLZONE
29028 VIGOLZONE [PC]
TEL. 0523870298
www.vinipiacentini.net

ANNUAL PRODUCTION 20,000 bottles
HECTARES UNDER VINE 7
VITICULTURE METHOD Natural

This small, organically farmed winery debuts in our Guide this year. Uccellaia is located in the woodlands of Albarola, in a part of Val Nure that was formerly a game reserve, hence its name, which refers to wildfowl. Ably managed by Chicca and Lali Nicoletti, Uccellaia produces only still wines. The standard-label Gutturnio is very impressive, self-confident and well-balanced, figuring among the best in the denomination. Forward and appealing, it flaunts a nose of rich florality and wonderful pulpy fruit, which then spreads out tasty and sweet on the palate. The Merlot also turned in a fine performance, showing quite dense but with a dynamic progression that contributes substantially to its appreciable balance. Rosso dell'Uccellaia, a blend of merlot and barbera, comes across as more austere and nervy. There's no lack of power or character but it's still fairly closed up. Finally, Cerasuolo, from barbera, croatina and cabernet sauvignon, is delightfully refreshing and supple, offering clean-edged fragrances of wild berry fruit and more than decent weight on the palate.

O Colli di Faenza Rebianco '06	♍♍ 3*
● Sangiovese di Romagna Amarcord d'un Ross Ris. '05	♍♍ 4
● Colli di Faenza Rosso Montecorallo Ris. '05	♍♍ 4
O Albana di Romagna Passito '04	♍ 5
● Sangiovese di Romagna Sup. Sperone '06	♍ 3
O Albana di Romagna Secco '06	♍ 3
● Sangiovese di Romagna V. del Monte '06	♍ 2*
● Colli di Faenza Rosso Montecorallo Ris. '04	♍♍ 4
● Sangiovese di Romagna Amarcord d'un Ross Ris. '04	♍♍ 4
● Sangiovese di Romagna Amarcord d'un Ross Ris. '03	♍♍ 4

● Colli Piacentini Gutturnio Gutturnium '06	♍♍ 4*
● Merlot '05	♍♍ 5
● Rosso dell'Uccellaia '04	♍♍ 5
⊙ Cerasuolo dell'Uccellaia '06	♍ 4

Tenuta Valli

LOC. RAVALDINO IN MONTE
VIA DELLE CAMINATE, 38
47100 FORLÌ [FC]
TEL. 054524393
www.tenutavalli.it

ANNUAL PRODUCTION 100,000 bottles
HECTARES UNDER VINE 30
VITICULTURE METHOD Conventional

Emilio Polgrossi's business interests often keep him away from the winery but Tenuta Valli can fortunately rely on the dedicated professionalism of Roberto Donati, who personally directs all aspects of production. The sun-blessed vineyards are almost enclosed in a magnificent, curved hillside facing the Adriatic, near the road that rises from Forlì to Rocca delle Caminate. The winery itself remains in its historic location, just outside Lugo di Romagna. The bottles that leave these premises follow a solid tradition of well-executed, uncomplicated wines that are never flashy or faddish. Two wines stand out from all of the rest. Sangiovese Riserva della Beccaccia shows a nose that is a touch country-style but nicely floral and builds good energy, fuelling a spacious, smooth palate with good balance. Cabernet Sauvignon Borgo Rosso opens with ultra-generous fruit and follows rich and velvety on the palate. Finally, Trebbiano Capomaggio is a new project that we're sure will give fascinating results in the future. Right now, this '05 shows lashings of volume and abundant fruit.

Vallona

FRAZ. FAGNANO
VIA SANT'ANDREA, 203
40050 CASTELLO DI SERRAVALLE [BO]
TEL. 0516703058

ANNUAL PRODUCTION 90,000 bottles
HECTARES UNDER VINE 28
VITICULTURE METHOD Conventional

The 2005 growing year may not have been very favourable but Maurizio Vallona enjoys an intimate daily rapport with his vines and boasts expertise to spare in the cellar. He was able to produce two solid '05 reds in his usual straightforward, no-frills style but with performances so outstanding that both easily jumped into our national finals. Cabernet Diggioanni is huge, rich and focused, not to say absolutely impressive to the last drop. The second red, Merlot Affederico, flaunts a typically Bordeaux nose and develops a superb, finely-balanced palate marked by juicy, succulent fruit. Given the admirable consistency for which Vallona is known, there is no shifting down in quality with the whites. Quite the reverse for the Pignoletto is a magisterial wine, showing fresh and delicious, with great finesse on the nose, while the Sauvignon is savoury and splendidly varietal, with satisfying progression. Spumante Essè is the fruit of a collaborative project between Vallona and the Franceschinis of Isola. Largely pignoletto, it enters subtle and refined, concluding with a soft, generous flourish.

● Borgo Rosso Cabernet Sauvignon '05	♟♟ 4*
● Sangiovese di Romagna Sup. Riserva della Beccaccia Ris. '04	♟♟ 4*
○ Albana di Romagna Passito Mythos '04	♟ 5
● Sangiovese di Romagna Sup. Il Tibano '06	♟ 3
○ Trebbiano di Romagna Capomaggio Sel. Vecchie Vigne '05	♟ 4
○ Albana di Romagna Secco I Vinchi '06	♟ 4
○ Trebbiano di Romagna La Battilana '06	3
● Sangiovese di Romagna Sup. Riserva della Beccaccia Ris. '03	♟♟ 4

● Diggioanni Cabernet Sauvignon '05	♟♟ 5
● Affederico Merlot '05	♟♟ 5
○ C. B. Pignoletto '06	♟♟ 4*
○ C. B. Sauvignon '06	♟♟ 4*
○ Essè Brut	♟♟ 4*
● C. B. Cabernet Sauvignon '06	♟ 4
○ C. B. Pignoletto Vivace '06	♟ 3
○ Primedizione Cuvée 2007 '06	♟ 4
● Diggioanni Cabernet Sauvignon '04	♟♟♟ 5
● C. B. Merlot Affederico '01	♟♟♟ 5
● C. B. Cabernet Sauvignon Sel. '99	♟♟♟ 5
● C. B. Cabernet Sauvignon Sel. '97	♟♟♟ 5
● Affederico Merlot '04	♟♟ 5
● Diggioanni Cabernet Sauvignon '03	♟♟ 5

Podere Vecciano
VIA VECCIANO, 23
47852 CORIANO [RN]
TEL. 0541658388
www.poderevecciano.it

ANNUAL PRODUCTION 50,000 bottles
HECTARES UNDER VINE 10
VITICULTURE METHOD Conventional

Podere Vecciano's constant growth in quality has brought it into the top ranks of producers in Colli di Rimini, and these good performances have induced Davide Bigucci to attempt even greater challenges. His wines represent a fascinating angle of vision for assessing the qualities of the area, so intimately affected by the nearby Adriatic, which brings moderate temperatures, abundant light and good ventilation. Bigucci is looking for balance in the vineyard and in the cellar, and our tastings reveal a deep-rooted respect for the natural expression of the vine and a winemaking approach that eschews excessive power and heat. Riserva D'Enio '04 offers a luminous, fully finished expression of sangiovese, with a low-key but eloquent nose with brightness and spice. The palate is assertive and sturdily structured, but crisp, full and dynamic as well, with a conclusion that is flawless in every respect. Sangiovese VignalMonte '05 benefited from the decision not to produce a Riserva in 2005. It opens appealingly fresh and the palate is supple, smooth and tight knit, with succulent fruit throughout.

Villa di Corlo
LOC. BAGGIOVARA
S.DA CAVEZZO, 200
41100 MODENA [MO]
TEL. 059510736
www.villadicorlo.com

ANNUAL PRODUCTION 95,000 bottles
HECTARES UNDER VINE 32
VITICULTURE METHOD Natural

Maria Antonia Munari Giacobazzi, a warm, market-savvy wine professional, manages a winery based on two separate estates. Villa di Corlo, the original property, lies around a modern wine facility and the superb estate residence located on the Baggiovara lowlands just outside Modena. Lambrusco is the only variety grown here and it goes into the full-bodied Grasparossa, the elegant Sorbara and Corleto, as well as the massive, energy-laden Lambrusco that is the winery's iconic product. Newer, organically farmed vineyards have recently come into production on the hills above Reggio at elevations between 300 and 500 metres. These vineyards yield the cabernet sauvignon, cabernet franc and merlot grapes that make up Giaco di Viano and Gelsomoro di Viano. The first develops considerable depth with expansive, well-ripened fruit. Although the attack is rounded, it develops some dryness on the finish. Its younger brother, Gelsomoro di Viano, is more straightforward.

● Sangiovese di Romagna Sup. D'Enio Ris. '04	♛♛ 5
● Sangiovese di Romagna Sup. VignalMonte '05	♛♛ 4*
O Colli di Rimini Rebola Vigna la Ginestra '06	♛ 4
● Sangiovese di Romagna Sup. D'Enio Ris. '03	♟♟ 5

● Corleto Lambrusco '06	♛♛ 3*
● Giaco di Viano '05	♛♛ 4
● Gelsomoro di Viano '05	♛ 4
● Rosso Estella Lambrusco '06	♛ 3
● Lambrusco Grasparossa di Castelvetro '06	3
● Lambrusco di Sorbara '06	3
● Corleto Lambrusco '05	♟♟ 3

Villa Liverzano
VIA VALLONI, 47
48013 BRISIGHELLA [RA]
TEL. 054680565
www.liverzano.it

ANNUAL PRODUCTION 6,600 bottles
HECTARES UNDER VINE 2.8
VITICULTURE METHOD Conventional

It is difficult to find a wine producer who can talk as lucidly as Marco Montanari on the style that his wines should display. If you add to this the fact that he works in the Vena dei Gessi Romagnoli, an area of unique chalk seams, then you start to understand how Villa Liverzano wines can offer such unusual characteristics, with their elegant, silk-smooth mouthfeel that seems to come straight from the terroir. Montanari makes an emphatic contribution to these discussions of Romagna wines, with a lack of preconceptions. Sometimes, he makes use of varieties not often seen in Romagna but which find an essential role within his overall approach. Rebello '05 is a totally delicious sangiovese and merlot blend that is elegant, crisp and ably balanced, with a dense, vivacious palate yet showing spacious and lengthy. The carmenère and cabernet franc Don '05 displays a spirited but refined grassiness on the nose, while the palate is refined, bright and well balanced.

Villa Papiano
VIA IBOLA, 24
47015 MODIGLIANA [FC]
TEL. 0546941790
www.villapapiano.it

ANNUAL PRODUCTION 25,000 bottles
HECTARES UNDER VINE 10
VITICULTURE METHOD Conventional

The Bordini family powers an interesting collaborative project that gathers its resources and ideas from various other Romagna producers, showing ever more interesting outcomes every year. Remigio Bordini, a talented, highly respected agronomist, supplies fertile ideas that complement the ability of his winemaker son Francesco, and the result is an innovative interaction that draws on a rich heritage of viticultural tradition. Villa Papiano's vineyards are among the highest in Romagna and flourish in an area of high biodiversity. This uniqueness is on display in the wines. Papiano di Papiano took our Three Glass trophy for the first time with this '04 edition. A partnership of merlot, centesimino and other local native grapes, it is anything but a powerhouse, showing a fine complexity throughout, crisp and fluid in the mouth, tight-knit and concentrated, and with a magisterially lengthy development. I Probi di Papiano '04 is uniquely sangiovese, expanding flawlessly on the palate, while Le Papesse di Papiano '05 is generous and fleshy, with an impressively spicy nose. The '06 Sauvignon, Le Tresche di Papiano, is quite distinctive, flaunting intense minerality.

● Rebello '05	🍷🍷 6
● Don '05	🍷🍷 6
● Don '04	🍷🍷 6
● Rebello '04	🍷🍷 6
● Rebello '03	🍷🍷 5

● Papiano di Papiano '04	🍷🍷🍷 5
● Sangiovese di Romagna I Probi di Papiano Ris. '04	🍷🍷 4*
○ Le Tresche di Papiano '06	🍷🍷 4*
● Sangiovese di Romagna Le Papesse di Papiano '05	🍷🍷 4*
● Sangiovese di Romagna I Probi di Papiano Ris. '03	🍷🍷 4
● Papiano di Papiano '03	🍷🍷 6
● Sangiovese di Romagna I Probi di Papiano Ris. '02	🍷🍷 4
● Papiano di Papiano '02	🍷🍷 6
● Papiano di Papiano '01	🍷🍷 6

Villa Trentola

LOC. CAPOCOLLE DI BERTINORO
VIA MOLINO BRATTI, 1305
47032 BERTINORO [FC]
TEL. 0543741389
www.villatrentola.it

ANNUAL PRODUCTION	12,000 bottles
HECTARES UNDER VINE	20
VITICULTURE METHOD	Conventional

Although it lies fairly close to Cesena, Villa Trentola by all rights should be considered within the orbit of Bertinoro. It's on a slope that faces the Adriatic, where the sangiovese grape tends to yield dense wines with copious, tight tannins. The winemaking staff has changed recently, and production is now in the hands of Tuscan consulting oenologist Fabrizio Moltard, who is beginning to make his mark in Romagna. This change was dictated by the need to achieve greater growth, following restructuring of the operation, which is managed in person by Federica Prugnoli. Moltard oversaw the blends for the 2005 vintage, and the result is a great Sangiovese Il Moro. Tightly-knit and austere, and showing impressive weight and density, it develops dynamic volume in the mouth. The acidity is perfect, and dense-packed tannins do tend to dry the finish, but this is part and parcel of this wine's distinctive expression.

★ Fattoria Zerbina

FRAZ. MARZENO
VIA VICCHIO, 11
48018 FAENZA [RA]
TEL. 054640022
www.zerbina.com

ANNUAL PRODUCTION	220,000 bottles
HECTARES UNDER VINE	31
VITICULTURE METHOD	Conventional

We have sung the praises of this winery at considerable length on other occasions, and we do so willingly once again. It is to Cristina Geminiani's credit that Zerbina adds another Three Glass award to its rich history, for the accomplishments of this winery have become an integral part of the heritage of so many emerging Romagna producers in recent years. As usual, the overall quality of the wines is extremely high. Pietramora, a thoroughbred Sangiovese, leads here with exquisitely ripe fruit and extractive power that does nothing to lessen the wine's flawless elegance. Torre di Ceparano, Zerbina's second-tier Sangiovese, impressed us with a richness and concentration superior to all past vintages. Scacco Matto offers its expected touch of botrytis delicately caressing voluptuous fruit, plus a crisp-edged palate with ultra-delicious sweetness and perfect balance. Its younger sibling Arrocco is only slightly less rich and sweet. We are not reviewing here Albana Passito Riserva '04 because of its production run of only 250 half bottles, but it is one of the finest sweet wines ever produced in Italy. We leave tasting comments to those privileged few who will be able to purchase it.

● Sangiovese di Romagna Sup. Il Moro di Villa Trentola '05		5
● Sangiovese di Romagna Sup. Il Prugnolo di Villa Trentola '05		4
● Sangiovese di Romagna Sup. Placidio '04		8
● Sangiovese di Romagna Sup. Il Moro di Villa Trentola '04		5
● Sangiovese di Romagna Sup. Il Moro di Villa Trentola '03		6
● Sangiovese di Romagna Sup. Il Moro di Villa Trentola '02		5

● Sangiovese di Romagna Sup. Pietramora Ris. '04		6
○ Albana di Romagna Passito Scacco Matto '05		7
● Sangiovese di Romagna Sup. Torre di Ceparano '05		4*
○ Albana di Romagna Passito Arrocco '05		6
● Sangiovese di Romagna Ceregio '06		3
● Marziено '03		6
● Sangiovese di Romagna Sup. Pietramora Ris. '03		7
● Marziено '01		6
● Marziено '00		6
● Marziено '99		6
● Marziено '97		6
● Marziено '98		6

OTHER WINERIES

Aldrovandi
VIA MARZATORE, 36
40050 MONTEVEGLIO [BO]
TEL. 0516810296

Federico Aldrovandi's small winery turned in an excellent performance, particularly given the unfavourable 2005 vintage. Merlot, the only wine produced, is strikingly full bodied. With a lean, confident nose, it is solidly structured in the mouth, although the tannic support may be a bit too expansive.

● C. B. Merlot Alto Vanto '05	♀♀	5
● C. B. Merlot Alto Vanto '04	♀♀	5

Tenuta Amalia
FRAZ. DIEGARO
VIA EMILIA PONENTE, 2619
47023 CESENA [FC]
TEL. 0547347037
www.cantinacesena.it

We were unable to taste the two winery stars, Sangiovese Riserva Pergami and Case Rosse, since they weren't ready. Albana di Romagna '06 is light and delicate, and Sangiovese Barone Bartolomeo '06 exuberant. It has sweet, ripe fruit, but is somewhat drying in the mouth.

○ Albana di Romagna Secco '06	♀	3
● Sangiovese di Romagna		
Barone Bartolomeo '06	♀	3

Balìa di Zola
VIA CASALE, 11
47015 MODIGLIANA [FC]
TEL. 0546948654
bzola@libero.it

Veruska Eluci continues to do well. She used to be involved at Castelluccio with her husband. Her two Sangioveses show clear stylistic differences. Redinoce displays well-ripened fruit and toasty oak, fine tannins and an expansive, dynamic development, while Balitore is lighter and more restrained.

● Redinoce '05	♀♀	5
● Sangiovese di Romagna		
Balitore '06	♀	4

La Berta
VIA BERTA, 13
48013 BRISIGHELLA [RA]
TEL. 054684998
azienda@laberta.it

Costantino Giovannini's wines showed less well than usual, perhaps because of poor growing years. The Sangiovese Olmatello is fruity but cramped and unilinear in the mouth, and the finish is drying. Sangiovese Solano displays riper fruit and is a crisp, delicious quaffer.

● Sangiovese di Romagna		
Olmatello Ris. '05	♀	5
● Ca' di Berta '04	♀	5
● Sangiovese di Romagna Sup.		
Solano '06	♀	4

Ca' de' Medici
LOC. CADÈ
VIA DELLA STAZIONE, 32
42040 REGGIO EMILIA
TEL. 0522942141
www.cademedici.it

Marica Medici's operation is solid and its wines impressively distinctive. The most interesting is Terra Calda, a dark-hued Lambrusco with intense fruit, then creamy and dense in the mouth. San Giacomo Maggiore is simpler and lighter, and Malvasia Rubigalia shows subtly sweet.

● Terra Calda Frizzante	♀♀	3*
○ Malvasia Dolce Rubigalia	♀	2
● Reggiano Lambrusco Chiaro		
San Giacomo Maggiore	♀	2

Fattoria Ca' Rossa
VIA CELLAIMO, 735
47032 BERTINORO [FC]
TEL. 0543445130
www.fattoriacarossa.it

Massimo Masotti is a benchmark in the Bertinoro area. The well-executed albana-based passito AAA shows a fine botrytis-touched nose, a fat, well-balanced palate and a finish with a citrus and pineapple edge. Barbera Cavalcaonte is crisp and tasty as usual, displaying scents of ripe dark cherry.

○ Vino da Uve Stramature AAA	♀♀	5
● Cavalcaonte Barbera '05	♀	3
● Sangiovese di Romagna Sup.		
Costa del Sole Ris. '03	♀♀	4

OTHER WINERIES

Fattoria Camerone

LOC. BIANCANIGO
VIA BIANCANIGO, 1485
48014 CASTEL BOLOGNESE [RA]
TEL. 054650434
www.fattoriacamerone.it

The historic Fattoria Camerone has a solid series of Sangioveses. The traditional-style Riserva Millennium is nicely austere. Rosso del Camerone is similar but shows more fruit, with a smooth, elegant finish, while the younger Marafò is fruity, crisp edged and ultra-fragrant in the mouth.

● Sangiovese di Romagna Sup.	
Millennium Ris. '03	🍷🍷 4
● Sangiovese di Romagna Sup.	
Rosso del Camerone Ris. '03	🍷🍷 4
● Sangiovese di Romagna Sup. Marafò '06	🍷 2

Podere Casale

LOC. VICO BARONE
VIA CRETA
29010 ZIANO PIACENTINO [PC]
TEL. 0523868302
www.poderecasale.it

Nicolas Rigamonti keeps his standards high, as is evident from Ortrugo '06, where scents of oak yield to flowers, followed by a rounded, soft palate. Gutturnio '05 enters tight and lean, ending pleasantly bitterish. The dark, purplish hue of Gutturnio Frizzante '06 complements a heady, spicy palate.

● C. P. Gutturnio '05	🍷🍷 4*
○ C. P. Ortrugo '06	🍷🍷 4*
● C. P. Gutturnio Frizzante '06	🍷 3

Celli

VIA CARDUCCI, 5
47032 BERTINORO [FC]
TEL. 0543445183
www.celli-vini.com

This historic cellar could have turned in a better performance. Sangiovese Le Grillaie Riserva shows lovely, sound fruit and good development, and the sweet sparkler La Talandina is citrus-scented and well balanced. But Chardonnay Bron & Rusèval is held down by an excess of oak.

○ Albana di Romagna Spumante	
La Talandina	🍷🍷 3*
○ Bron & Rusèval Chardonnay '06	🍷 4
● Sangiovese di Romagna Sup.	
Le Grillaie Ris. '04	🍷 3

Costa Archi

LOC. SERRA
VIA RINFOSCO, 1690
48014 CASTEL BOLOGNESE [RA]
TEL. 3384818346

Gabriele Succi has put out two terrific wines. The nicely crisp Sangiovese Il Beneficio releases vanilla and liquorice, building a fine texture. Prima Luce, from cabernet and ten per cent sangiovese, offers a generous, rich nose, with crisp fruit and a touch of grass, plus a smooth, complex palate.

● Prima Luce '05	🍷🍷 4*
● Sangiovese di Romagna Sup.	
Il Beneficio '05	🍷🍷 4*
● Sangiovese di Romagna Sup.	
Assiolo '06	🍷 3

Lamoretti

LOC. CASATICO
S.DA DELLA NAVE, 6
43013 LANGHIRANO [PR]
TEL. 0521863590
www.lamorettivini.com

The always reliable Isidoro Lamoretti is a long-time Guide regular. His classic Malvasia Frizzante is intensely aromatic. From his reds, we liked the austere, lean barbera and cabernet Serbato and Vinnalunga 71, a grassy Bordeaux blend with delicious, succulent fruit.

○ Colli di Parma Malvasia	
Frizzante '06	🍷 3
● Vinnalunga 71 '05	🍷 4
● Serbato '05	🍷 4

Rocca Le Caminate

S.DA ROCCA DELLE CAMINATE
47014 MELDOLA [FC]
TEL. 0545493482
www.roccalecaminate.it

Michele Fabbri is turning out increasingly fine offerings. The steel-fermented Sangiovese Sbargoleto features admirable fresh fruit with an energetic, appealing palate. The cask-aged Vitignano unveils spice-enriched red berry fruit and a soft-textured mouth but the finish is a tad dry.

● Sangiovese di Romagna Sup.	
Sbargoleto '05	🍷🍷 3*
● Sangiovese di Romagna Sup.	
Vitignano '05	🍷🍷 4

OTHER WINERIES

Lini 1910
VIA VECCHIA CANOLO, 7
42015 CORREGGIO [RE]
TEL. 0522690162
www.vinilini.it

The Lini family has many generations of experience with classic method sparklers. We very much liked the elegant Brut Rosso, from lambrusco salamino. Brut '00 is fragrant and vivacious, with good expansion, and the full-bodied Lambrusco Scuro finishes tasty and lean.

- In Correggio Brut Rosso M. Cl. '03 ⚑⚑ 5
- In Correggio Brut M. Cl. '00 ⚑⚑ 5
- In Correggio Lambrusco Scuro '06 ⚑ 3

Enrico Loschi
FRAZ. BACEDASCO ALTO
VIA RIVA, 10
29010 CASTELL'ARQUATO [PC]
TEL. 0523895560
www.loschivini.it

This Val d'Arda cellar made a fine Guide debut. Gutturnio Le Rivette shines with ripe fruit and the palate is smooth, lively and complex. La Brighella shows citrussy, with fine volume and alcohol, while the late-harvest Monterosso Terre di Guccio is full-bodied but lacks complete balance.

- C. P. Gutturnio Le Rivette '05 ⚑⚑ 4*
- C. P. Malvasia La Brighella '06 ⚑⚑ 4*
- C. P. Monterosso Val d'Arda
  Terre di Guccio '05 ⚑ 4

Alberto Lusignani
LOC. VIGOLENO
VIA CASE ORSI, 9
29010 VERNASCA [PC]
TEL. 0523895178
lusignani@agonet.it

Marco Lusignani makes some 1,000 bottles each year of the traditional Vin Santo di Vigoleno. The '99 shows a countryish nose of tamarind and zabaglione leading to an ample, pulpy palate, although the development is less impressive than usual. Gutturnio '05 has ripe fruit and a heady, expansive palate.

- C. P. Vin Santo di Vigoleno '99 ⚑⚑ 6
- C. P. Gutturnio Sup. '05 ⚑ 4

Manara
FRAZ. VICOMARINO
29010 ZIANO PIACENTINO [PC]
TEL. 0523860209
manara@netline.it

This up-to-date operation offers a broad, reliable line-up. Ortrugo Frizzante '06 is a supple, fine quaffer while the ortrugo and sauvignon Fralica '06 opens with pear and pineapple, showing savoury and balanced in the mouth. Gutturnio Superiore '04 is ripe and ready, with excellent progression.

- C. P. Gutturnio Sup. '04 ⚑⚑ 4
- C. P. Ortrugo Frizzante '06 ⚑ 3
- Fralica '06 ⚑ 3

Silvio, Lino e Flavio Marengoni
LOC. CASA BIANCA
29028 PONTE DELL'OLIO [PC]
TEL. 0523877229
www.vitivinicolamarengoni.it

The Marengonis debut in the Guide, thanks largely to their new merlot and cabernet sauvignon Rosso della Casa Bianca. It opens spicy and varietal, then displays confident, succulent fruit. Gutturnio Riserva '04 is a tad light, but dynamic and crisp, while Valnure '06 is fragrant and lively.

- Rosso della Casa Bianca '05 ⚑⚑ 4
- C. P. Gutturnio Ris. '04 ⚑ 4
- C. P. Valnure Frizzante '06 ⚑ 3

Massina
VIA MASSINA, 1
29010 VERNASCA [PC]
TEL. 0523895384
www.vitivinicolamassina.it

Paolo Loschi's very rare Vin Santo di Vigoleno did well again. From dried santa Maria and melara grapes, and cask-aged for five years, the '01 is well evolved, opulent and almost viscous, but not at all cloying. The intriguing Gutturnio Frizzante is bottle fermented, and shows supple and sturdy.

- C. P. Vin Santo di Vigoleno '01 ⚑⚑ 6
- C. P. Gutturnio Frizzante '06 ⚑ 3

OTHER WINERIES

Mattarelli
VIA MARCONI, 35
44049 VIGARANO MAINARDA [FE]
TEL. 053243123
www.mattarelli-vini.it

The Mattarellis have long been making fine Fortanas, sourced from sandy soils at Bosco Eliceo, near the Adriatic. Two are sparkling. Crisp cherry opens the drier version, which has an aromatic palate, while the sweeter has tasty fruit and fine balance. The Sauvignon shows good weight and subtle typicity.

● Bosco Eliceo Fortana Frizzante Dolce '06		🍷 3
● Bosco Eliceo Fortana Frizzante '06		🍷 3
○ Bosco Eliceo Sauvignon Palina '06		🍷 4

Molinelli
V.LE DEI MILLE, 21
29010 ZIANO PIACENTINO [PC]
TEL. 0523863230
www.molinelli.it

Ginetto Molinelli always has a lot of irons in the fire. His new line, La Celata, boasts the aroma-rich, nicely tropical Malvasia Route 212 and the late-harvest Scriptorium, a sweet, fat blend of molinelli and picolit. La Polveriera '06 is a nice ripe, heady barbera that shows a tad warm in the finish.

○ C. P. Malvasia Route 212 '05		🍷🍷 3*
○ Vendemmia Tardiva Scriptorium '04		🍷🍷 3*
● C. P. Barbera La Polveriera '06		🍷 4

Il Monticino
VIA PREDOSA, 72
40069 ZOLA PREDOSA [BO]
TEL. 051755260
www.ilmonticino.it

The Morandi family's young winery debuts in the Guide with a complex, sturdy Cabernet Sauvignon with good balance and development, and a mineral-edged finish. Pignoletto '06 releases appealing fruit and a juicy, crisp, delicious palate, while the sparkling version is expansive with a gorgeous mousse.

○ C. B. Pignoletto '06		🍷🍷 4*
● C. B. Cabernet Sauvignon '05		🍷🍷 4*
○ C. B. Pignoletto Frizzante '06		🍷 4

Moro - Rinaldini
FRAZ. CALERNO
VIA ANDREA RIVASI, 27
42049 SANT'ILARIO D'ENZA [RE]
TEL. 0522679190
www.rinaldinivini.it

Paola Rinaldini's Cabernet Sauvignon Riserva '04 is austere and impressively full in the mouth, if a bit too pungently balsamic and vanillaed on the nose. Vecchio Moro shows what Moro-Rinaldini can do with lambrusco. Traditionally ripe and rustic, its hefty extraction gives huge volume in the mouth.

● Colli di Scandiano e di Canossa Cabernet Sauvignon Ris. '04		🍷🍷 4*
● Colli di Scandiano e di Canossa Lambrusco Grasparossa Vecchio Moro '06		🍷 4

Il Negrese
LOC. IL NEGRESE
29010 ZIANO PIACENTINO [PC]
TEL. 0523864804

Matteo Braga only began bottling in 2001 but his Malvasia Passito quickly became one of the local benchmarks. The '05 again charms with its rich aromatic complex and a dense, sunny opulence in the mouth. Gutturnio '05 is bracing and brawny while the Rosso shows ripe fruit and lovely earthy notes.

○ C. P. Malvasia Passito '05		🍷🍷 5
● Rosso '06		🍷 4
● C. P. Gutturnio '05		🍷 4

Tenuta Pandolfa
FRAZ. FIUMANA
VIA PANDOLFA, 35
47010 PREDAPPIO [FC]
TEL. 0543940073
www.pandolfa.it

Pandolfa's two signature reds are very good again. Sangiovese Villa degli Spiriti opens with liquorice-infused, crisp fruit and then develops fine weight and a rounded, vanilla-laced finish. Cabernet Sauvignon Pezzolo is subtly herbaceous, appealingly lean and very well calibrated throughout.

● Pezzolo Cabernet Sauvignon '05		🍷🍷 4
● Sangiovese di Romagna Sup. Villa degli Spiriti Ris. '05		🍷🍷 4

OTHER WINERIES

Fattoria Paradiso
LOC. CAPOCOLLE
VIA PALMEGGIANA, 285
47032 BERTINORO [FC]
TEL. 0543445044
www.fattoriaparadiso.com

The 2005 vintage was not kind to this historic winery. Still, Mito impressed with subtle but savoury character and steady development. The sound fruit of Sangiovese Maestri di Vigna '06 is a little overlaid with oak but the albana Gradisca shows plenty of sweet pineapple and candied fruit.

● Mito '05	🍷🍷 6
● Sangiovese di Romagna Sup. Maestri di Vigna '06	🍷 4
○ Gradisca '06	🍷 4

Pavolini
FRAZ. BACEDASCO ALTO
LOC. PAOLINI, 3
29010 VERNASCA [PC]
TEL. 0523895407

Graziano Terzoni continues his good work with local Piacenza varieties. The malvasia Aquapazza '06 releases bright fragrances of elderberry and tropical fruit but closes a bit cramped. Terre di Bigarola '06 is a cask-fermented Ortrugo that shows supple and refreshing, developing steadily.

○ C. P. Ortrugo Terre di Bigarola '06	🍷🍷 4*
○ C. P. Malvasia Aquapazza '06	🍷🍷 4*

Tenuta Pennita
LOC. TERRA DEL SOLE
VIA PIANELLO, 34
47011 CASTROCARO TERME [FC]
TEL. 0543767451
www.lapennita.it

After his good results with olive oil, Gianluca Tumidei is doing well with wine production. We liked two reds. Sangiovese Riserva TerreDelsol releases fresh fruit aromas, with a rather lean, dry palate. Edmeo, sangiovese with 25 per cent each of cabernet and merlot, is dense, long lingering and very fruity.

● Sangiovese di Romagna TerreDelsol '04	🍷🍷 4*
● Edmeo '04	🍷🍷 4
● Sangiovese di Romagna La Pennita '05	🍷 3

Tenimenti San Martino in Monte
VIA SAN MARTINO IN MONTE
47015 MODIGLIANA [FC]
TEL. 3292984507

Four friends are doing well indeed at this Faenza cellar. A well cared-for sangiovese vineyard planted to the bush style in 1922 yields Vigna 1922, a wine of immense depth and appeal. The nose presents terrific complexity and the palate has dense but well balanced concentration.

● Sangiovese di Romagna Vigna 1922 '04	🍷 7
● Sangiovese di Romagna Vigna 1922 '03	🍷🍷 7

Tenuta Santa Croce
VIA ABÈ, 33
40050 MONTEVEGLIO [BO]
TEL. 0516702069
tenutasantacroce@chiarli.it

We were impressed by three wines in particular from the vast range of this Chiarli di Modena property. Cabernet Sauvignon Sermedo '03 is attractively lean, while the smoother standard-label '04 shows more vanilla. Pignoletto Frizzante is lovely, with rich fragrances and lots of fruit.

● C. B. Cabernet Sauvignon Sermedo Ris. '03	🍷🍷 3*
○ C. B. Pignoletto Frizzante '06	🍷 3
● C. B. Cabernet Sauvignon '04	🍷 4

Tenuta Volpe
P.ZZA BYRON, 19
47020 RONCOFREDDO [FC]
TEL. 0541949183
www.tenutavolpe.it

Cecilia Fanfani, located in the charming village of Monteleone in the upper Rubicone valley, has released her first wines. They're uncomplicated but well executed. Fedro is very traditional in style, with good breadth and velvety mouthfeel, while Bevitaliano is lighter but offers a succulent enough palate.

● Sangiovese di Romagna Sup. Fedro '05	🍷🍷 4
● Sangiovese di Romagna Bevitaliano '06	🍷 3

OTHER WINERIES

TerraGens
VIA PROVINCIALE FAENTINA, 46
47015 MODIGLIANA [FC]
TEL. 0546675611
www.terragens.com

TerraGens is an ambitious, long-term project of the Caviro group, with input from oenologist Attilio Pagli. It produces only three Sangioveses, all modern in style but with a nod to tradition. Rubio is the most impressive, showing subtle notes of vanilla and eucalyptus, pulpy fruit and dynamic progression.

● Rubio '05	♟♟ 5
● Sangiovese di Romagna Sup.	
TerraGens Ris. '04	♟ 5
● Sangiovese di Romagna Sup.	
TerraGens '06	♟ 4

Torricella
VIA SAMOGGIA, 534G
40060 SAVIGNO [BO]
TEL. 0516708552
www.vinitorricella.it

Alessandro Bartolini spends more time in the vineyards than he does at his day job in the building trade. His wines are very well crafted. Cabernet Sauvignon Narciso is velvety, full-bodied and energetic while Sauvignon Mastronicola displays elegant, intense varietal character and impressive volume.

● C. B. Cabernet Sauvignon	
Narciso '05	♟♟ 4
O C. B. Sauvignon Mastronicola '06	♟♟ 4
● C. B. Merlot Lanselmo '05	♟ 4

Tenuta Uccellina
VIA GARIBALDI, 51
48026 RUSSI [RA]
TEL. 0544580144

Alberto Rusticali's long-standing expertise with the Longanesi grape gives us a magisterially smooth, well-balanced Bursôn Etichetta Nera '03. Etichetta Blu '05 is simpler and lighter bodied, but refreshing. The Albana Passito Dorotea 2004 is heady and generously sweet, showing caramel and vanilla on the nose.

● Bursôn Et. Nera '03	♟♟ 4*
O Albana di Romagna Passito	
Dorotea Ris. '04	♟ 5
● Bursôn Et. Blu '05	♟ 4

Cantina Sociale Valtidone
VIA MORETTA, 58
29011 BORGONOVO VAL TIDONE [PC]
TEL. 0523862168
www.cantinavaltidone.it

The best of the few still wines from this Colli Piacentini winery was Gutturnio Flerido. The nose is rich with red berry fruit, and it shows powerful, self-confident and fairly energetic in the mouth. Gutturnio Bollo Rosso is fruity and supple while Ortrugo Frizzante Armonia is its usual refreshing self.

● C. P. Gutturnio Sup.	
Borgo del Conte Flerido '04	♟♟ 4
● C. P. Gutturnio Sup. Bollo Rosso '04	♟ 3
O C. P. Ortrugo Armonia Frizzante '06	♟ 3

Vigneto delle Terre Rosse
VIA PREDOSA, 83
40069 ZOLA PREDOSA [BO]
TEL. 051755845
www.terrerosse.com

We noticed what we hope is only a temporary blip in quality from the Vallania family's operation. But Cabernet Sauvignon Cuvée '01 was elegant, refined and just slightly herbaceous. The traditional-style Merlot Petroso '04 we found ripe, spacious and just a bit rustic on the finish.

● C. B. Cabernet Sauvignon Cuvée '01	♟♟ 6
● Petroso Merlot '04	♟ 5
● C. B. Cabernet Sauvignon Cuvée '00	♟♟ 6

Villa Bagnolo
LOC. BAGNOLO
VIA BAGNOLO, 160
47011 CASTROCARO TERME [FC]
TEL. 0543769047
www.villabagnolo.it

The emerging Ballarati winery in the Castrocaro Terme hills displays an admirably clear philosophy. The standard-label Sassetto '06 offers crisp, fresh, sound fruit and a lovely palate that is rounded and well balanced. Riserva Bagnolo is velvety, with sweet oak, while Alloro is lean but smooth.

● Sangiovese di Romagna Sup.	
Sassetto '06	♟♟ 3*
● Sangiovese di Romagna Sup.	
Bagnolo Ris. '05	♟ 4
● Alloro '05	♟ 4

TUSCANY

Once again, Tuscany is Italy's top region in the Three Glass stakes with 65 prize-winners. It could hardly have been any other way, given the vintages that were on show. Montalcino is again one of the region's strongholds, thanks to the average level of quality achieved by the zone's wines. But the '02 Brunello di Montalcinos, which underline the limitations of the vintage, are an exception, above all because their variety – they come from sangiovese only – performed poorly and the wines lack depth. It's a completely different story with the '01 Selezione and Riserva wines. A seriously good vintage has endowed them with structure, cut and oodles of personality. Proof comes from the total of 16 Three Glass awards, including the Decennale '01 from Poggio di Sotto, which, inexplicably, was rejected by the DOCG tasting committee but for us is a Riserva by any standards. Chianti Classico is another zone that did well, both for its DOCG wines and the humbler but very Chianti-esque IGTs, winning a creditable 26 top awards. Here it was 2004, a vintage that lived up to expectations, that did the trick. The wines are complex, mouthfilling and superbly defined in their acidity and tannins. It was tannicity that stood out most clearly in many of the 2003 wines tasted last year, which were generally lacking in balance because the tannins had not matured. It's a vintage to buy and lay down because it has a long future in the cellar ahead of it. Montepulciano held no particular surprises as regards Three Glass wines although we should note that we perceived greater self-awareness and sense of purpose at many of the wineries. Bolgheri and neighbouring areas again showed that they know how to make the most of a good growing year. The fantastic '04s picked up 11 top prizes. Complex and very sun-ripe with an intriguing range of nuances, they describe their territory with a precision few others can match and flaunt consistent class. This is the zone, at a winery near Lucca to be precise, that won this year's Award for Sustainable Viticulture. The estate in question is Valgiano and the man in the frame is Saverio Petrilli, an agronomist, oenologist and vibrantly practical star of the biodynamic movement. There was positive news from the Arezzo area, where this year the usual Galatrona, from '05 this time, was joined in the Three Glass club by Caberlot '04, Oreno '05 and Cortona Syrah Il Bosco '04. Less well-known zones also did well with Monteregio, Montecucco and Rufina showing the results of a quality focus that intensifies with each growing year. Generally, however, we should point out that Tuscany seems to want to go back to being Tuscany, putting the accent on territory focus through wine type. This time, perhaps, it will eschew the smoke and mirrors that premium-quality wine can frankly do without.

Agricoltori del Chianti Geografico

LOC. MULINACCIO
VIA MULINACCIO, 10
53013 GAIOLE IN CHIANTI [SI]
TEL. 0577749489
www.chiantigeografico.it

ANNUAL PRODUCTION 2,000,000 bottles
HECTARES UNDER VINE 580
VITICULTURE METHOD Conventional

Overall results confirm the good work going on at this Gaiole-based winery whose products continue to be attractively priced. Credit must go the estate manage, Carlo Salvadori, currently also chair of the Chianti Classico DOP olive oil producers' consortium. He has focused relations with member growers on grape quality, the key to effective vineyard management. Nor should we forget consultant oenologist Lorenzo Landi, who has managed to communicate his ideas to those in charge of day-to-day cellar work. This year, the top bottle was the sangiovese and cabernet sauvignon Ferraiolo '04, which went through to the finals thanks to a complex range of aromatics, elegant structure and good balance. But the workhorses are still the Chianti Classico wines. The Riserva Montegiachi '04 is powerful and savoury while the Contessa di Radda '05 is outstandingly drinkable. The base Chianto Classico '05 is a fine everyday wine and the merlot-only Pulleraia '05 is temptingly soft.

Castello d'Albola

LOC. PIAN D'ALBOLA, 31
53017 RADDA IN CHIANTI [SI]
TEL. 0577738019
www.albola.it

ANNUAL PRODUCTION 800,000 bottles
HECTARES UNDER VINE 157
VITICULTURE METHOD Conventional

Castello d'Albola is the Chianti outpost of the Zonin family. Again this year, it showed just how well made its wines are. There was a particularly gratifying result for Acciaiolo '04 put on a splendid show to earn Three Glasses at our final tastings. This sangiovese and cabernet sauvignon blend is slow to open on the nose, starting with blackberry and raspberry fruit that gives way to spice refreshed by balsam. The solid entry on the palate is nicely gauged, offering admirable balance and a long, sweet finish. The rest of the range is little more than well made, including the wines from the Rocca di Montemassi estate. Based at Roccastrada in the province of Grosseto, its style looks more towards the countryside of Siena than the Maremma. But what these wines, including the Chiantis, lack is a more fully rounded sense of the territory from which they come. For now, the watchword is simplicity because the potential for greater complexity and sophisticated appeal is very much there.

● Ferraiolo '04	♟♟ 6
● Chianti Cl. Contessa di Radda '05	♟♟ 4
● Pulleraia '05	♟♟ 6
● Chianti Cl. Montegiachi Ris. '04	♟♟ 5
● Chianti Cl. '05	♟ 4
O Vernaccia di S. Gimignano Pietravalle '06	♟ 4
O Vin Santo del Chianti Cl. '03	♟ 6
● Chianti Cl. Contessa di Radda '04	♟♟ 4
● Pulleraia '03	♟♟ 5
● Pulleraia '01	♟♟ 6

● Acciaiolo '04	♟♟♟ 7
O Chardonnay '06	♟ 4
● Chianti Cl. Le Ellere '04	♟ 4
● Le Focaie '06	♟ 4
O Vin Santo del Chianti Classico '99	♟ 7
O Vermentino Rocca di Montemassi '06	♟ 4
● Monteregio di Massa Marittima Sassabruna '05	♟ 4
● Acciaiolo '01	♟♟♟ 7
● Acciaiolo '95	♟♟♟ 6

★★ Castello di Ama
FRAZ. LECCHI IN CHIANTI
LOC. AMA
53013 GAIOLE IN CHIANTI [SI]
TEL. 0577746031
www.castellodiama.com

ANNUAL PRODUCTION 350,000 bottles
HECTARES UNDER VINE 85
VITICULTURE METHOD Conventional

Castello di Ama is one of the most dependable and influential wineries in all Chianti Classico. Every year, it releases marvellously characterful wines that reflect the territory they come from and the people who created them. Lorenza Sebasti and Marco Pallanti, a well-matched couple at home and in the cellar, are behind this success story, in addition to Ama, of course, and its land. Chianti Classico in standard and vineyard selection versions has long been the estate's workhorse and this year we tasted Castello di Ama and La Casuccia, one of the two selections. Both are '04s and both are big hitters, requiring time to open and give their best. We thought the selection was the more complete wine and awarded Three Glasses for its density, weight, surefootedness and impressive tannic weave. Castello di Ama was a touch dumber but we are confident it will repay our patience if we wait for it to evolve. L'Apparita '03, a single-variety Merlot with a Chianti accent, has yet to develop but its structure is impressive.

Fattoria Ambra
VIA LOMBARDA, 85
59015 CARMIGNANO [PO]
TEL. 3358282552
www.fattoriaambra.it

ANNUAL PRODUCTION 80,000 bottles
HECTARES UNDER VINE 19
VITICULTURE METHOD Conventional

Fattoria di Ambra is back on course and regained a full profile with a fine performance across the range. The crucial difference in comparison to last year may have come from the beautifully balanced '04 vintage, which that admirable winemaker Beppe Rigoli interpreted to perfection. Confirmation of his excellent work comes from the Carmignano Le Vigne Alte di Montalbiolo Riserva '04, a wine with great personality that went through to our finals. Its intriguing, austere nose ushers in a close-knit palate that unfolds assertively, backed up by attractive acidity and savoury tannins, to a delightful lifting finish. Only a shade less exciting is the Riserva Elzana '04 with its exquisitely handled texture, a juicy, vibrantly coherent wine that is a pleasure to drink. The more expressive on nose and palate of the two base Carmignanos is the Santa Cristina in Pilli '05, which has good structure, nice acid-tannin balance and seamless progression. The warm, ripe Montefortini '05 has velvety tannins. It's shy on the nose, warm on the palate and shortish in the finish. We were pleasantly surprised by the sweet, distinctly elegant Vin Santo di Carmignano '00.

● Chianti Cl. La Casuccia '04	♛♛♛ 8
● Chianti Cl. Castello di Ama '04	♛♛ 8
● V. l'Apparita Merlot '03	♛♛ 8
☉ Rosato '06	♛ 4
● Chianti Cl. Bellavista '01	♛♛♛ 8
● Chianti Cl. Bellavista '95	♛♛♛ 6
● Chianti Cl. Bellavista '99	♛♛♛ 8
● Chianti Cl. Castello di Ama '00	♛♛♛ 6
● Chianti Cl. Castello di Ama '99	♛♛♛ 5
● Chianti Cl. Bellavista '90	♛♛♛ 8
● Chianti Cl. La Casuccia '97	♛♛♛ 8
● V. l'Apparita Merlot '92	♛♛♛ 8
● V. l'Apparita Merlot '01	♛♛♛ 8
● V. l'Apparita Merlot '00	♛♛♛ 8
● Chianti Cl. La Casuccia '01	♛♛♛ 8
● Chianti Cl. Castello di Ama '03	♛♛♛ 6
● Chianti Cl. Castello di Ama '01	♛♛♛ 6

● Carmignano Le Vigne Alte di Montalbiolo Ris. '04	♛♛ 5
● Carmignano Elzana Ris. '04	♛♛ 5
○ Vin Santo di Carmignano '00	♛♛ 6
● Carmignano V. S. Cristina in Pilli '05	♛♛ 4
● Carmignano V. di Montefortini '05	♛ 4
● Carmignano Elzana Ris. '01	♛♛ 5
● Carmignano V. S. Cristina in Pilli '03	♛♛ 4
● Carmignano Elzana Ris. '99	♛♛ 5
● Carmignano V. S. Cristina in Pilli '01	♛♛ 4
● Carmignano Le Vigne Alte di Montalbiolo Ris. '00	♛♛ 5
○ Vin Santo di Carmignano '99	♛♛ 6
● Carmignano Le Vigne Alte di Montalbiolo Ris. '01	♛♛ 5

★ Marchesi Antinori

P.ZZA DEGLI ANTINORI, 3
50123 FIRENZE [FI]
TEL. 05523595
www.antinori.it

ANNUAL PRODUCTION 18,000,000 bottles
HECTARES UNDER VINE 1.400
VITICULTURE METHOD Conventional

It has been 11 years since Tignanello, the wine that wrought the great quality revolution in Chianti Classico, earned Three Glasses. We cannot deny that it was with some emotion that we tasted the latest release, which is as superb as it ever was. Over the years, Tignanello seemed to have lost a little of its character as Solaia year by year acquired more of that self-same quality. It must be the winery's internal alchemy. But back to the '04 Tignanello with its complex, whistle-clean red fruits, briar, rain-soaked earth and hints of smokiness. In the mouth, the keynote comes from sangiovese's acidity, which draws out the satisfying, fresh-tasting finish. Solaia '04 has a very different style, Full-bodied and muscular, with serious tannins, it offers a powerful counterpoint to the Tignanello's elegance. Solaia will evolve, beyond any doubt. It's only a question of time. Chianti Classico Badia a Passignano Riserva '04 is a wine to bank on. Cherries, dried roses and spices introduce a succulent, vigorously expansive palate. Finally, the Chianti Classico Pèppoli '05 is very good but quality is sound right down the list.

Argentiera

LOC. DONORATICO
VIA AURELIA, 410
57024 CASTAGNETO CARDUCCI [LI]
TEL. 0565773176
www.argentiera.eu

ANNUAL PRODUCTION 400,000 bottles
HECTARES UNDER VINE 60
VITICULTURE METHOD Conventional

Last year, Argentiera earned a place in the Guide. It was a modest place in the Other Wineries section but it reflected the cellar's solid quality, which only needed the right growing year to make its mark. The year arrived in 2004 and with it came a well-deserved Three Glass award. Bolgheri Superiore Argentiera, the flagship wine, is from equal proportions of cabernet sauvignon and merlot with a little cabernet franc. Prominent, pleasingly fresh vegetal notes and liquorice on the nose precede taut acidity and impeccable extract, making this one of the most convincingly gracious, elegant wines on the coast. Also exceptionally good is Villa Donoratico '04, from a cabernet sauvignon-heavy blend with merlot and cabernet franc. It, too, is persuasive and beautifully poised. Syrah replaces cabernet franc with the usual 50 per cent cabernet sauvignon and 25 per cent merlot in Poggio ai Ginepri '05, which may be a shade less complex but is nonetheless well worth uncorking.

● Tignanello '04	￮￮￮	8
● Solaia '04	￮￮	8
● Chianti Cl. Pèppoli '05	￮￮	4
● Chianti Cl. Badia a Passignano Ris. '04	￮￮	6
● Villa Antinori Rosso '04	￮	4
● Chianti Cl. Badia a Passignano Ris. '01	￯￯￯	6
● Solaia '01	￯￯￯	8
● Solaia '03	￯￯￯	8
● Solaia '98	￯￯￯	8
● Solaia '94	￯￯￯	6
● Solaia '96	￯￯￯	6
● Solaia '95	￯￯￯	8
● Chianti Cl. Badia a Passignano Ris. '97	￯￯￯	5
● Solaia '99	￯￯￯	8
● Solaia '97	￯￯￯	8
● Solaia '00	￯￯￯	8

● Bolgheri Sup. Argentiera '04	￮￮￮	8
● Bolgheri Villa Donoratico '04	￮￮	5
● Bolgheri Poggio ai Ginepri '05	￮￮	4*
● Bolgheri Sup. Argentiera '03	￯￯	8

★ Avignonesi

FRAZ. VALIANO DI MONTEPULCIANO
VIA COLONICA, 1
53040 MONTEPULCIANO [SI]
TEL. 0578724304
www.avignonesi.it

ANNUAL PRODUCTION	700,000 bottles
HECTARES UNDER VINE	119
VITICULTURE METHOD	Conventional

After a difficult year last year, the long-established Avignonesi winery is back punching its full weight, picking up a top award as usual. The Falvo estate is managed today by Alberto, brother of Ettore, who has left the family business after leading it successfully for many years. The Three Glasses went to the '95 Vin Santo, a wine almost aromatic in the intensity of its iodine-laced nose and whose density and exuberant sweetness are tempered by well-gauged acidity. Occhio di Pernice '95 is as intriguing as ever; indeed it's an extreme wine with a unique sensory profile. The Avignonesi reds were also on top form. As its name implies, 50 & 50 is an equal blend of sangiovese from the Capannelle estate in Chianti and Avignonesi's merlot. Now as in the past, it is a wine of breeding. The outstandingly well-balanced Nobile '04 and the muscular, richly extracted Cortona Desiderio '04 from merlot only are seriously good wines. But Grandi Annate Riserva '03, with its vigorous palate and rather muzzy aromas, was not on top form. The rest of the range is reliable.

Badia a Coltibuono

LOC. BADIA A COLTIBUONO
53013 GAIOLE IN CHIÁNTI [SI]
TEL. 0577746110
www.coltibuono.com

ANNUAL PRODUCTION	1,000,000 bottles
HECTARES UNDER VINE	72
VITICULTURE METHOD	Certified organic

Emanuela Stucchi Prinetti has done it. After many years of trying, she wrested Three Glasses from our tasters for her excellent Riserva '04, the wine that more than any other embodies the estate's territorial character and production philosophy. The award came at the end of a period of restructuring that absorbed much of Emanuela's time and energy for she was its guiding spirit. A former chair of the Black Rooster consortium, she opted for radical changes in the estate's winemaking that culminated in the decision to convert the entire vine stock to organic viticulture. It was not an easy path to take but encouraging results are arriving. Now we look forward to rest of the range achieving the same high standards of quality. We were pleasantly surprised by the chardonnay and sauvignon Trappoline '06 but the rest of the reds lack a little definition on the nose. Sangioveto '03, from sangiovese only, was probably showing the effects of the growing year in its over-assertive tannins.

O Vin Santo '95	♈♈♈	8
● Vin Santo Occhio di Pernice '95	♈♈	8
● 50 & 50 Avignonesi e Capannelle '03	♈♈	8
● Cortona Desiderio '04	♈♈	7
● Nobile di Montepulciano '04	♈♈	5
● Nobile di Montepulciano Grandi Annate Ris. '03	♈	8
● Rosso Avignonesi '05	♈	4
O Cortona Sauvignon Blanc '06	♈	4
● Rosso di Montepulciano '06	♈	4
O Vin Santo '88	♈♈♈	6
O Vin Santo '93	♈♈♈	8
● 50 & 50 Avignonesi e Capannelle '99	♈♈♈	8
● 50 & 50 Avignonesi e Capannelle '97	♈♈♈	8
● Vin Santo Occhio di Pernice '93	♈♈♈	8
O Vin Santo Occhio di Pernice '90	♈♈♈	8
O Vin Santo Occhio di Pernice '89	♈♈♈	8
O Vin Santo '89	♈♈♈	8

● Chianti Cl. Ris. '04	♈♈♈	6
O Trappoline '06	♈♈	4
● Chianti Cl. '05	♈	5
● Chianti Cl. Cultus Boni '04	♈	5
● Sangioveto '03	♈	7
● Chianti Cl. R. S. '05	♈	4
● Sangioveto '95	♈♈♈	6
● Sangioveto '01	♈♈	7
● Chianti Cl. Cultus Boni '03	♈♈	5
● Chianti Cl. Cultus Boni '01	♈♈	5

Badia di Morrona
VIA DI BADIA, 8
56030 TERRICCIOLA [PI]
TEL. 0587658505
www.badiadimorrona.it

ANNUAL PRODUCTION 180,000 bottles
HECTARES UNDER VINE 80
VITICULTURE METHOD Conventional

There's good news at Badia di Morrona. After a year's absence from the Guide, the Gaslini Alberti family's wines are back to tell us all about their splendid territory of origin with 500 hectares of unspoiled countryside, 80 of which are under vine. The estate team under Filippo Gaslini Alberti comprises oenologist Giorgio Marone and agronomist Valerio Barbieri. Together, they have brought production back up to the standard that has made Badia di Morrona one of the beacons of premium-quality wine on the Tuscan coast. When we uncorked Vigna Alta '04, we found ourselves looking at a no-nonsense Sangiovese. Intense red fruits and sweet spice interweave with restrained toastiness that is gauged to perfection. A juicy, dynamic palate complements the young, but very well-crafted, tannic weave. The strong suit of N'Antia '04, from cabernet sauvignon, cabernet franc and merlot grapes, is balance. The initial grassiness is lifted by a rich note of blackberries then the surefooted palate reveals elegance and power in surprisingly equal measure. Finally, the Vin Santo is extremely enjoyable.

Fattoria di Bagnolo
LOC. BAGNOLO-CANTAGALLO
VIA IMPRUNETANA PER TAVARNUZZE, 48
50023 IMPRUNETA [FI]
TEL. 0552313403
www.bartolinibaldelli.it

ANNUAL PRODUCTION 25,000 bottles
HECTARES UNDER VINE 10
VITICULTURE METHOD Conventional

Marco Bartolini Baldelli's winery powers on like a diesel engine, regularly picking up fine results at our tastings. It's indicative of the work Marco put in several years ago replanting vineyards and rationalizing the cellar. The buildings here date from the 16th century, and in fact the main villa once belonged to Nicolò Machiavelli, and the estate embraces the vineyards of the Fattoria di Scaletta in the municipality of San Miniato in the province of Pisa. At this year's tastings, we very much liked the two versions of Chianti Colli Fiorentini. The '05 has fresh fruit mingling with attractive aromatic herbs before the supple palate reveals bright tannins well tucked in and a lovely savoury finish. The aromatics of the Riserva '04 are more complex, with clove-led spice complementing mixed fruit jam. In the mouth, good body and juicy fruit take you through to a lingering finish.

● N'Antia '04	♟♟	5
○ Vin Santo '03	♟♟	6
● Vigna Alta '04	♟♟	6
● N'Antia '01	♟♟	6
● Vigna Alta '01	♟♟	6
● N'Antia '98	♟♟	6
● N'Antia '02	♟♟	6
● Vigna Alta '98	♟♟	6
● Vigna Alta '99	♟♟	6
● N'Antia '97	♟♟	6

● Chianti Colli Fiorentini '05	♟♟	3*
● Chianti Colli Fiorentini Ris. '04	♟♟	5
● Capro Rosso '04	♟♟	5
● Chianti Colli Fiorentini '04	♟♟	3
● Chianti Colli Fiorentini Ris. '03	♟♟	5
● Chianti dei Colli Fiorentini '03	♟♟	3

Tenuta di Bagnolo
FRAZ. BAGNOLO
VIA MONTALESE, 156
50045 MONTEMURLO [PO]
TEL. 0574652439
www.pancrazi.it

ANNUAL PRODUCTION 30,000 bottles
HECTARES UNDER VINE 17
VITICULTURE METHOD Conventional

Never before has Tenuta di Bagnolo presented us with a range of wines so focused on Burgundy. With the exception of San Donato, produced at the other estate holding, all the wines are pinot nero-based. The choice was a good one because the wines are well made, very moreish and flaunt their origin with pride. The intriguingly varietal '04 Villa di Bagnolo is a fine example. Its flowers, red berry fruit and earthy notes introduce a palate of weight and structure, savoury tannins and a lively vein of acidity leading to a dry, restrained and very attractive finish. Vigna Baragazza '04 is complex, its ripe fruit aromas lifted by spice and incense. The palate is chewy and well extracted, progressing into appreciable length and a finish that for now is austere but bodes well for the future. Equally convincing is the quality of the base wines. Villa di Bagnolo Rosato '06 is delicately fragranced, supple on the palate, fresh-tasting and delightfully drinkable. The gamay and pinot nero San Donato '06 unveils delicious fruit aromas and an intriguing palate.

I Balzini
LOC. PASTINE, 19
50021 BARBERINO VAL D'ELSA [FI]
TEL. 0558075503
www.ibalzini.it

ANNUAL PRODUCTION 40,000 bottles
HECTARES UNDER VINE 5.4
VITICULTURE METHOD Conventional

There were fine results for the two labels released by Vincenzo and Antonella D'Isanto. Quality is reliably good and the winery is a fixture in the Guide. Despite the drought-plagued '03 vintage, the D'Isantos managed to make two very satisfying wines, thanks in part to their well-aspected plots and in part to shrewd vineyard management. We thought the merlot and cabernet sauvignon Black Label emerged just ahead. Its garnet-flecked ruby ushers in a warm nose of spice-laced ripe fruit and forest floor. Power melds with softness on the palate, which holds up well to a lingering, attractively balanced finish. White Label, from sangiovese and cabernet sauvignon, is in the same league, its well-rounded nose presenting red fruits and aromatic herbs. Its silky, juicy palate, braced by vibrant acidity, hangs together well, signing off with finish that is a whisper too dry and a tad clenched.

● Pinot Nero V. Baragazza '04	▼▼ 8
● Pinot Nero Villa di Bagnolo '04	▼▼ 7
⊙ Pinot Nero Villa di Bagnolo Rosato '06	▼ 4
● San Donato '06	▼ 4
● Casaglia '02	♀♀ 5
● Casaglia '03	♀♀ 5
● Casaglia '00	♀♀ 4*
● Casaglia '01	♀♀ 5
● Casaglia '04	♀♀ 6
● Pinot Nero V. Baragazza '01	♀♀ 8
● San Donato '04	♀♀ 3*
● San Donato '03	♀♀ 3*
● Pinot Nero Villa di Bagnolo '01	♀♀ 6
● Pinot Nero Villa di Bagnolo '00	♀♀ 6
● Pinot Nero V. Baragazza '03	♀♀ 8

● I Balzini Black Label '03	▼▼ 6
● I Balzini White Label '03	▼▼ 5
● I Balzini Black Label '01	♀♀ 6
● I Balzini Black Label '00	♀♀ 7
● I Balzini White Label '02	♀♀ 5
● I Balzini White Label '01	♀♀ 5
● I Balzini White Label '00	♀♀ 6
● I Balzini Black Label '99	♀♀ 7

★ Castello Banfi
LOC. SANT'ANGELO SCALO
CASTELLO DI POGGIO ALLE MURA
53024 MONTALCINO [SI]
TEL. 0577840111
www.castellobanfi.com

ANNUAL PRODUCTION 11,500,000 bottles
HECTARES UNDER VINE 850
VITICULTURE METHOD Conventional

As ever, Montalcino's American winery and its quintessentially Italian manager Enrico Viglierchio put on a good show. All the wines performed well in their various price bands, hinting at great dependability and careful winemaking. Again this year, there is a Three Glass wine. The thoroughbred is Sant'Antimo Mandrielle '04, a single-variety merlot with a fresh nose of black fruits and grassiness, a well-sustained palate with acidity and extract complementing each other, and a long finish. We liked the Brunello '02. A deep, intense nose with prominent fruit and restrained oak precedes a successful marriage of acidity and tannins with caressing glycerine richness, to end with a close-knit, rich-textured finish. This year, the cellar's impressively structured wines are a little held back by the wood, for example the cabernet sauvignon, sangiovese and syrah Sant'Antimo Summus, the cabernet sauvignon and merlot Sant'Antimo Excelsus and the Sant'Antimo Cum Laude, from cabernet sauvignon, merlot, sangiovese and syrah. All are '04s. Also reliable are Moscadello Florus '05, the cabernet sauvignon-only Tavernelle '04 and Centine '06 from sangiovese, cabernet sauvignon and merlot. The '05 Rosso di Montalcino is nice.

Riccardo Baracchi
LOC. CAMUCIA
VIA CEGLIOLO, 21
52042 CORTONA [AR]
TEL. 0575612679
www.baracchiwinery.com

ANNUAL PRODUCTION 45,000 bottles
HECTARES UNDER VINE 20
VITICULTURE METHOD Conventional

Riccardo Baracchi's winery is new but already it has achieved a truly remarkable standard of quality. Situated in the hills of Cortona, not far from the family's Il Falconiere country hotel and restaurant, the cellar turns out a range of whistle-clean wines, from international and native vines, impeccably made in the modern idiom. Top of the range is the cabernet and syrah Ardito. Usually dense and richly extracted, in the '04 version it foregrounds dark notes lifted by minerality and savoury hints. Slow to open, it does however offer good depth. We really liked the two Cortona Smeriglio '05 reds. The Merlot is muscular, mature and attractively grassy, the oak perceptible but nicely gauged and the overall balance good. Precise is the word for the juicy Sangiovese, a fresh-tasting wine that progresses effortlessly to a satisfying reprise of the fruit on the back palate. Always interesting is the nicely savoury Astore '06, obtained from trebbiano meticulously vinified with skin contact to emerge full flavoured and faintly oxidative.

● Sant'Antimo Mandrielle '04	▼▼▼	5
● Brunello di Montalcino '02	▼▼	7
● Sant'Antimo Cum Laude '04	▼▼	4
● Sant'Antimo Tavernelle '04	▼▼	5
● Sant'Antimo Summus '04	▼▼	7
● Sant'Antimo Excelsus '04	▼▼	7
● Centine '06	▼▼	3*
○ Moscadello di Montalcino Florus '05	▼▼	5
● Rosso di Montalcino '05	▼	4
● Brunello di Montalcino Poggio alle Mura '98	♈♈♈	8
● Brunello di Montalcino Poggio all'Oro Ris. '90	♈♈♈	6
● Brunello di Montalcino Poggio all'Oro Ris. '95	♈♈♈	8
● Sant'Antimo Summus '97	♈♈♈	6
● Sant'Antimo Excelsus '99	♈♈♈	8
● Sant'Antimo Excelsus '03	♈♈♈	7
● Brunello di Montalcino Poggio all'Oro Ris. '99	♈♈♈	8
● Brunello di Montalcino Poggio all'Oro Ris. '93	♈♈♈	6
● Brunello di Montalcino Poggio alle Mura '99	♈♈♈	8

● Ardito '04	▼▼	6
● Cortona Smeriglio Merlot '05	▼▼	5
● Cortona Smeriglio Sangiovese '05	▼▼	5
○ Astore '06	▼	4
● Ardito '02	♈♈	6
● Cortona Smeriglio Merlot '03	♈♈	5
● Cortona Smeriglio Sangiovese '04	♈♈	5
● Cortona Smeriglio Merlot '04	♈♈	5
● Ardito '03	♈♈	6

Fattoria dei Barbi
LOC. PODERNOVI, 170
53024 MONTALCINO [SI]
TEL. 0577841111
www.fattoriadeibarbi.it

ANNUAL PRODUCTION 800,000 bottles
HECTARES UNDER VINE 90
VITICULTURE METHOD Conventional

Stefano Cinelli Colombini's cellar is one of the best-known Montalcino wineries in the world. The reasons for that are well-established market visibility and the shrewd pricing that has always been a feature of Fattoria dei Barbi wines. Every bottle reflects respect for and awareness of tradition, particularly in the selection of wood for the Brunellos. Indicative of that respect is the decision to set up a Brunello museum on the premises. From this year's range, we were particularly impressed by the Brunello di Montalcino Vigna del Fiore '01. Its textbook ruby accompanies attractive sweet tobacco aromas that meld with Brunello's signature ripe cherry while the well-integrated extract fuses satisfyingly into the structure of the elegant, eminently drinkable palate. The rest of the range performed well, pointing to all-round progress. We especially liked the clean aromatics and very moreish palate of the Brunello Riserva '01.

Baroncini
LOC. CASALE, 43
53037 SAN GIMIGNANO [SI]
TEL. 0577940600
www.baroncini.it

ANNUAL PRODUCTION 2,500,000 bottles
HECTARES UNDER VINE 120
VITICULTURE METHOD Conventional

Bruna and Stefano Baroncini's plans are gradually becoming reality. No longer is the Baroncini label restricted to San Gimignano: they have taken it into other Tuscan wine zones, Montalcino and Maremma, where results are proving they were right to do so. As usual, the outstanding wines on the well-furnished list are the Vernaccia Dometaia Riserva '05 and the La Faina '05 white from slightly overripe trebbiano grapes. Dometaia is bright straw, unveiling a spice-lifted spectrum of ripe fruit aromatics. Its full palate is perked up by vigorous acidity and the savoury finish lingers. La Faina's complex nose hints are florality and citrus mingling with honey. The good progression of the juicy palate is well supported by acidity and the sweet finish reveals a touch of minerality. The freshness and balance of the Vernaccia Poggio ai Cannicci '06 also impressed. Baroncini's Maremma wines scored well. Morellino Rinaldone dell'Osa '05 follows a fruit and earth nose with a bright, savoury palate while Il Fulgente '04's dark fruit aromatics are complemented by juicy sweetness in the mouth. The rest of the range is reliable.

● Brunello di Montalcino Ris. '01	♟♟ 8
● Brunello di Montalcino V. del Fiore '01	♟♟ 7
● Brunello di Montalcino '02	♟ 6
● Birbone Toscano '04	♟ 5
● Rosso di Montalcino '05	♟ 4
● Brunello di Montalcino '00	♛♛ 6
● Brunello di Montalcino '01	♛♛ 6
● Brunello di Montalcino Ris. '00	♛♛ 8
● Brunello di Montalcino Ris. '99	♛♛ 8

● Il Fulgente '04	♟♟ 5
O La Faina '05	♟♟ 4
● Morellino di Scansano Rinaldone dell'Osa '05	♟♟ 4*
O Vernaccia di S. Gimignano Dometaia Ris. '05	♟♟ 4*
● Chianti Colli Senesi Sup. V. S. Domenico Sovestro '06	♟ 3
O Vernaccia di S. Gimignano Poggio ai Cannici Sovestro '06	♟ 3*
● Mercuzio '06	♟ 3*
O Vernaccia di S. Gimignano Dometaia Ris. '04	♛♛ 4

★ Barone Ricasoli

LOC. CASTELLO DI BROLIO
53013 GAIOLE IN CHIANTI [SI]
TEL. 05777301
www.ricasoli.it

ANNUAL PRODUCTION 2,000,000 bottles
HECTARES UNDER VINE 250
VITICULTURE METHOD Conventional

Castello di Brolio symbolizes Chianti Classico. The role was thrust upon it by history and by its 250-hectare vineyard holding, all now replanted to modern criteria at high densities with clones of sangiovese in particular that ensure the best possible quality for the crop. Francesco Ricasoli can be happy with what he has achieved since the early 1990s, when he decided to take the estate back to the heights it had occupied until the 1960s. This time, the Chianti Classico Castello di Brolio '04 had our tasters nodding in approval. A modern wine, it reveals, at least now in its youth, the small wood used for ageing. It has loads of texture and the character that comes from Brolio, which shines through brilliantly, so we gave it the traditional Three Glasses. Casalferro '04, a 70-30 blend of sangiovese with merlot, lagged a little behind this year. It's spicy on the nose, beefy, close-knit and very well extracted. Finally, the Riserva Rocca Guicciarda '04 is good and the rest of the list well made.

Fattoria di Basciano

V.LE DUCA DELLA VITTORIA, 159
50068 RUFINA [FI]
TEL. 0558397034
www.renzomasibasciano.it

ANNUAL PRODUCTION 200,000 bottles
HECTARES UNDER VINE 35
VITICULTURE METHOD Conventional

As we pen the Masi family's profile, we can't help thinking that there should be many more wineries like this. Year after year, the Masis maintain impeccable quality across the range yet never lose sight of value for money. The wines are invariably good and gradually they are acquiring greater territory focus. Excellence shines though here and there, such as the '01 Vin Santo tasted this time. A delicious range of aromas from citrus to honey via nuts greets the nose before a rich, velvet-smooth, caressing entry on the palate and a long, sweet finish. Other distinctly good wines are the soft, modern Erta e China '05, a moreish 50-50 blend of sangiovese and cabernet; I Pini '05, from equal proportions of syrah, cabernet and merlot; Corto '05, from sangiovese with a dash of cabernet, which is more austere and structured; and the characterful '05 Chianti Rufina, redolent of spice and balsam, with a close-knit tannic weave. The Chianti Riserva '04 and Rosato '06 are enjoyably well made.

● Chianti Cl. Castello di Brolio '04	♟♟♟	8
● Casalferro '04	♟♟	8
● Chianti Cl. Rocca Guicciarda Ris. '04	♟♟	6
● Chianti Cl. Brolio '05	♟	5
○ Torricella '06	♟	6
● Casalferro '03	♟♟♟	6
● Casalferro '98	♟♟♟	6
● Chianti Cl. Castello di Brolio '00	♟♟♟	7
● Chianti Cl. Castello di Brolio '99	♟♟♟	7
● Chianti Cl. Castello di Brolio '98	♟♟♟	6
● Chianti Cl. Castello di Brolio '97	♟♟♟	6
● Chianti Cl. Castello di Brolio '03	♟♟♟	7
● Chianti Cl. Castello di Brolio '01	♟♟♟	7
● Casalferro '99	♟♟♟	6

● Chianti Rufina '05	♟♟	3*
● I Pini '05	♟♟	5
○ Vin Santo Rufina '01	♟♟	4
● Il Corto '05	♟♟	5
● Erta e China '05	♟♟	3*
● Chianti Ris. '04	♟	3
⊙ Rosato '06	♟	2
● Chianti Rufina Ris. '04	♟	5
● Chianti Rufina '03	♟♟	3
● I Pini '04	♟♟	5
● Erta e China '04	♟♟	3*
● Il Corto '03	♟♟	5
● Il Corto '04	♟♟	5
● I Pini '03	♟♟	5
● Erta e China '03	♟♟	3
● Chianti Rufina Ris. '03	♟♟	5

Tenuta Belguardo

LOC. MONTEBOTTIGLI - VII ZONA
58100 GROSSETO [GR]
TEL. 057773571
www.belguardo.it

Belriguardo

VIA BELRIGUARDO, 107
53100 SIENA [SI]
TEL. 0258313436
info@gngmusica.com

ANNUAL PRODUCTION	215,000 bottles
HECTARES UNDER VINE	34
VITICULTURE METHOD	Conventional

ANNUAL PRODUCTION	7,000 bottles
HECTARES UNDER VINE	8
VITICULTURE METHOD	Conventional

The Maremma branch of the Mazzei family's holding makes superb wines with richly extracted palates and an abundance of fruit. In fact, they are some of Maremma's best wines and amply live up to the standards of one of Italy's most reliable labels. Overall, the range is unfailingly solid, lacking perhaps only a pinch of personality. Generous fruit laced with subtle minerals and spices marks out the aromatics of Tenuta di Belguardo '04, a blend of cabernet sauvignon and cabernet franc that has compact structure, polished tannins and depth in the mouth and a lingering finish. Serrata di Belguardo '05, from sangiovese and alicante, intrigues with its bright, youthful aromas, here and there giving way to toastiness, but the palate comes into its own with lovely fresh acidity set off against fat, fruity tannins. Over-assertive oak on nose and palate detracts slightly from the marvellous texture of the Morellino Bronzone '05.

Back in the Guide is the winery owned by Gianna Nannini, the celebrated Siena-born rock singer, which came to our attention a few years ago with some excellent early results. After falling into oenological oblivion for a while, Belriguardo is in the spotlight again, thanks to wines that now have finesse and elegance, as well as attitude. The consultant oenologist is Renzo Cotarella, a name to bank on, and Renzo has now got things in the vineyard and cellar organized to his satisfaction. Both the sangiovese and merlot Rosso di Clausura '04, intensely fruity with a supple yet complex structure, and the Chiostro di Venere '04, from cabernet sauvignon with a dash of sangiovese, did well. Spice and balsam laced with cinnamon usher in a smooth, expansive palate, well-defined extract and a savoury finish. The best-known wine is certainly Baccano, which commemorates one of Ms Nannini's greatest hits. In the '04 version, the blend is sangiovese with syrah and merlot. A tempting nose precedes a palate that has yet to open up.

● Serrata di Belguardo '05	♟♟	4
● Tenuta Belguardo '04	♟♟	7
● Morellino di Scansano		
Bronzone '05	♟	5
● Serrata di Belguardo '01	♟♟	5
● Tenuta Belguardo '01	♟♟	8
● Tenuta Belguardo '03	♟♟	7
● Tenuta Belguardo '02	♟♟	8
● Tenuta Belguardo '00	♟♟	6
● Serrata di Belguardo '03	♟♟	5
● Serrata di Belguardo '02	♟♟	5
● Serrata di Belguardo '04	♟♟	4

● Chiostro di Venere '04	♟♟	4
● Rosso di Clausura '04	♟♟	5
● Baccano '04	♟	6
● Rosso di Clausura '04	♟♟	5
● Il Chiostro '00	♟♟	4
● Baccano '00	♟♟	5

Podere Le Berne
LOC. CERVOGNANO
VIA POGGIO GOLO, 7
53040 MONTEPULCIANO [SI]
TEL. 0578767328
www.leberne.it

ANNUAL PRODUCTION 25,000 bottles
HECTARES UNDER VINE 6
VITICULTURE METHOD Conventional

The high road to reliable quality is all
downhill now for Andrea Natalini's cellar and
he has carved himself a niche in the front
ranks of Montepulciano winemaking.
Andrea crafts his wines from excellent raw
material that manages to preserve a
convincing harmony with its territory of
origin. A fine example of this is the Nobile
Riserva '03. It has shaken off the effects of
the growing year's torrid heat to take full
advantage of the Montepulciano terroir,
which is generally cooler than other parts of
Tuscany, particularly in the superb subzone
of Cervognano. What has come out of the
cellar is a wine that puts the accent on
freshness. The fruit is crystal clear and the
follow through on the palate unfolds
delightfully, the savoury tannins and bright
acidity falling into place with poised
elegance. The full-flavoured Nobile '04
offers well-defined aromatics and fruit that is
still attractively crunchy. Finally, the Rosso di
Montepulciano '06 is one of the best, a
fruit-forward easy drinker with a light touch.

Bibi Graetz
VIA DI VINCIGLIATA, 19
50014 FIESOLE [FI]
TEL. 055597289
www.bibigraetz.com

ANNUAL PRODUCTION N.A.
HECTARES UNDER VINE 37
VITICULTURE METHOD Conventional

Bibi Graetz has a season ticket to our finals:
every year he comes up with a couple of
seriously good labels. This time, we noticed
progress in the winery's style. Wines are
now less international and increasingly
bound up with their territory of provenance.
Of no wine is this truer than Bugia '05, a
white obtained from ansonica grapes grown
on Isola del Giglio, which shows the way
forward for cellar-worthy whites in a zone
that until recently was considered of
secondary importance. Nonetheless,
Testamatta is still the flagship wine, a blend
of sangiovese, colorino, canaiolo and
moscato nero in proportions that vary from
year to year. The '05 has a broad suite of
fragrances ranging from spicy pepper and
cinnamon to ripe red fruits. There's a fine
tannic weave on the expansive, full-bodied
palate, which ends on a sweet note. As
ever, the colorino-based '05 Colore is
fascinating. Its fresh fruit mingles balsam
and aromatic herbs on the nose before the
juicy palate unveils restrained tannins well
tucked in and plenty of vitality. The Grilli di
Testamatta '05 is temptingly delicious.

● Nobile di Montepulciano '04	♙♙	4
● Nobile di Montepulciano Ris. '03	♙♙	6
● Rosso di Montepulciano '06	♙♙	4
● Nobile di Montepulciano Ris. '01	♙♙	6
● Nobile di Montepulciano '03	♙♙	4
● Nobile di Montepulciano Ris. '00	♙♙	6
● Nobile di Montepulciano '98	♙♙	4

● Colore '05	♙♙	8
● Testamatta '05	♙♙	8
○ Bugia '05	♙♙	7
● Grilli del Testamatta '05	♙♙	6
○ Bugia '04	♙♙	7
● Colore '03	♙♙	8
● Testamatta '04	♙♙	8
● Testamatta '03	♙♙	8
● Testamatta '02	♙♙	8
● Testamatta '01	♙♙	8
● Testamatta '00	♙♙	8
○ Bugia '02	♙♙	6
○ Bugia '03	♙♙	7
● Canaiolo '03	♙♙	8
● Canaiolo '04	♙♙	8
● Colore '04	♙♙	8

Bindella

FRAZ. ACQUAVIVA
VIA DELLE TRE BERTE, 10A
53040 MONTEPULCIANO [SI]
TEL. 0578767777
www.bindella.it

ANNUAL PRODUCTION   120,000 bottles
HECTARES UNDER VINE 30
VITICULTURE METHOD   Conventional

Deaf to the siren song of oenological fads, the long-established Bindella winery at Montepulciano prefers to develop its own style for its own wines. This consistency-focused strategy has certainly paid off, given the level of quality achieved by production these days at this cellar based in the subzone of Argiano. In general, the wines display good personality and on some occasions they are excellent, as was the case at our tastings this year. The '04 version of the Nobile di Montepulciano I Quadri could well be one of the best with its fresh, rain-soaked earth, liquorice and flowery fragrances. Tight, taut tannins unfold elegantly on the deep palate, powering you through to an attractively savoury finish. Equally good and stylistically comparable is the Vallocaia '04, from prugnolo gentile, cabernet sauvignon and syrah. The non-native grapes lift the overall roundness of the wine, which is still bright and vibrant thanks to attractive acidity and self-assured savouriness. The '03 Vallocaia is warmer and less agile while the Nobile '04 still has a few rough edges to smooth out. The rest of the range is enjoyable.

Bindi Sergardi

LOC. POGGIOLO
FATTORIA I COLLI, 2
53035 MONTERIGGIONI [SI]
TEL. 0577309309
www.bindisergardi.it

ANNUAL PRODUCTION   40,000 bottles
HECTARES UNDER VINE 100
VITICULTURE METHOD   Conventional

This is the first Guide profile for Nicolò Casini, who owns a number of farms in various areas and produces olive oil and cereal crops, as well as wine. The Casinis are one of those families, of whom there are many in Tuscany, that have passed their property down from generation to generation since the 15th century, although it is the current owner who has focused energy on winemaking. The Chianti Classico comes from the 70 hectares under vine at Tenuta di Mocenni while a further 20 hectares have been planted on Tenuta di Marcianella at Chiusi. At Tenuta i Colli, the nerve centre of the enterprise, olive oil plays a major role alongside wine. This year, the Chianti Classico Riserva '04 was on top form, showing minerality and balsamic tones, solid body and nice length in the finish. The merlot and cabernet sauvignon Climax '04 was equally attractive, its fruit-led nose introducing a gentle, balanced structure. Also nice, if less complex, is the Chianti Classico '05.

● Nobile di Montepulciano		
I Quadri '04	♟♟	5
● Vallocaia '04	♟♟	6
● Vallocaia '03	♟♟	6
● Nobile di Montepulciano '04	♟	5
● Rosso di Montepulciano		
Fosso Lupaio '06	♟	4
O Vin Santo Dolce Sinfonia '03	♟	6
● Nobile di Montepulciano		
I Quadri '01	♟♟	5
● Nobile di Montepulciano		
I Quadri '03	♟♟	5
● Nobile di Montepulciano		
I Quadri '00	♟♟	5

● Climax '04	♟♟	6
● Chianti Cl. Ris. '04	♟♟	5
● Chianti Cl. '05	♟	4

Biondi Santi - Tenuta Il Greppo
LOC. VILLA GREPPO, 183
53024 MONTALCINO [SI]
TEL. 0577848087
www.biondisanti.it

Le Bocce
VIA CASE SPARSE, 76
50020 PANZANO [FI]
TEL. 055852153
www.stefanofarinavini.it

ANNUAL PRODUCTION 70,000 bottles
HECTARES UNDER VINE 25.7
VITICULTURE METHOD Conventional

ANNUAL PRODUCTION 300,000 bottles
HECTARES UNDER VINE 46
VITICULTURE METHOD Conventional

Not for the first time, we take off our hats to Franco Biondi Santi this year. After last time's superb Brunello '01, the Riserva from the same vintage is simply fantastic. It goes to show that at Il Greppo, a Riserva label means exactly what it says. We would also point out that since 1995, the cellar has been introducing one or two almost imperceptible adjustments to its wines. Colours are richer, fragrances are more complex and better defined, there is a focus on sangiovese's keynote fruit, acidity is more restrained and the extract is more gracious. All this contributes to making Il Greppo's Brunellos even more distinctive. The Riserva is intense ruby and the nose unveils an array of cherries that hint at jammy notes, as well as spice and tobacco. Entry is nicely supported by alcohol and heralds a steady crescendo into a broad, mouthfilling finish with great length. The Rosso di Montalcino '04 is nice with balance on the palate and sustained, acidity-driven freshness.

The Farina family's oenological universe embraces Piedmont, Puglia and Tuscany but the winery that gives them greatest satisfaction is Le Bocce at Panzano, although the estate at Subbiano in the province of Arezzo is increasingly reliable in its results. Sangiovese is the mainstay, not just for Chianti Classico but also in the various Supertuscans that provide variations on the same theme, as if to show how much potential there is in a grape considered by many to be less than versatile. This year, the top wine seems to be the '05 Il Paladino. A single-variety Sangiovese, it gives crisp mineral fragrances tinged with florality, nice structure, gutsy tannins and a lingering finish. The Riserva '04 is also good, showing intense flavour and vibrant structure, but the other two Supertuscans, the '05 San Leonino and the Subbiano-sourced Sassaia di Albereto '05, were slightly disappointing.

● Brunello di Montalcino Ris. '01	♛♛♛	8
● Rosso di Montalcino '04	♛	6
● Brunello di Montalcino '01	♛♛♛	8
● Brunello di Montalcino Ris. '99	♛♛♛	8
● Brunello di Montalcino Ris. '95	♛♛♛	6
● Brunello di Montalcino '97	♛♛	8
● Brunello di Montalcino '99	♛♛	8
● Brunello di Montalcino '00	♛♛	8
● Rosso di Montalcino '03	♛♛	6
● Brunello di Montalcino Ris. '97	♛♛	8

● Chianti Cl. Ris. '04	♛♛	5
● Il Paladino '05	♛♛	5
● San Leonino '05	♛	5
● Sassaia di Albereto '05	♛	5
● Il Paladino '04	♛♛	5
● San Leonino '04	♛♛	5
● Sassaia di Albereto '04	♛♛	5

Il Borghetto

LOC. MONTEFIRIDOLFI
VIA COLLINA SANT'ANGELO, 21
50026 SAN CASCIANO IN VAL DI PESA [FI]
TEL. 0558244491
www.borghetto.org

ANNUAL PRODUCTION 16,000 bottles
HECTARES UNDER VINE 6
VITICULTURE METHOD Conventional

This compact San Casciano cellar earned a first small profile last year and a full one this time. It is set in a historic location for on the estate is the seventh-century B.C. Etruscan Tomb of the Archer and the farm itself and cellars were created from the remains of the medieval settlement. Olive oil from a range of Tuscan cultivars is a major product, as well as wine, and the owner, Antonio Cavallini, personally looks after the vineyard and cellar while Tim Manning consults on vineyard management and winemaking. Only two wines were submitted for tasting but both are excellent. The Riserva '04 comes in a curious Burgundy bottle. It gives subtle aromatic herbs followed by cherry-led red berry fruits. The impressively structured palate flaunts lovely balance shot through with good acidity. The tannins are silky and the lingering finish is a delight. Rosie '04, a merlot-led blend with a little cabernet sauvignon, gives spice on the nose then a soft, creamy body and long length on the palate.

Il Borro

FRAZ. SAN GIUSTINO VALDARNO
LOC. IL BORRO, 1
52020 LORO CIUFFENNA [AR]
TEL. 0559772921
www.ilborro.it

ANNUAL PRODUCTION 150,000 bottles
HECTARES UNDER VINE 40
VITICULTURE METHOD Conventional

The 2005 wines from the Ferragamo family estate performed well both for consistency and quality across the whole of the range. The house style continues to be that laid down from the first release, which means well-made, technically impeccable wines that put the accent on fruit and balsam with good structure and a tendency towards softness and drinkability on release. Almost entirely absent are the rough edges so typical of Tuscan wines. Il Borro wines are less terroir-oriented and more approachable for an international clientele. Il Borro '05, from merlot, cabernet, syrah and petit verdot, is a particularly successful example, giving intense black fruit with spice and balsam before revealing its impressive structure, rich extract and decent depth. The '05 version of the syrah and sangiovese base Pian di Nova is juicy, approachably fruity, fresh-tasting and follows through well on the palate. Finally, Polissena '05, a dark, oak-scarred Sangiovese, is slow to open for the time being.

● Chianti Cl. Ris. '04	7
● Rosie '04	6
● Collina 21 '03	5

● Il Borro '05	7
● Pian di Nova '05	4
● Polissena '05	6
● Il Borro '00	8
● Il Borro '03	7
● Il Borro '02	8
● Il Borro '01	8
● Il Borro '04	7
● Pian di Nova '01	4
● Pian di Nova '03	6
● Polissena '02	6

Poderi Boscarelli

FRAZ. CERVOGNANO
VIA DI MONTENERO, 28
53040 MONTEPULCIANO [SI]
TEL. 0578767277
www.poderiboscarelli.com

ANNUAL PRODUCTION 80,000 bottles
HECTARES UNDER VINE 13.5
VITICULTURE METHOD Conventional

In the past, we have raised the occasional eyebrow at Boscarelli wines where there were worrying blips on the quality radar but nowadays the De Ferrari family turn out solidly dependable products that put them in the front rank of Tuscan winemaking. Sobriety of style is their watchword. This year, the cellar uncorked two superb bottles for our tasters. Nobile Nocio dei Boscarelli '04 picked up Three effortless Glasses, confirming its superior status. Pencil lead and sweet spice on the nose tell you the oak has yet to be absorbed but this in no way detracts from the wonderfully fresh fruit or the teasing hints of minerality. But this is a wine that is stunning on the palate for balance, rich, pulpy fruit and complexity. Also excellent is the Nobile Riserva '03, another finalist, whose nose of tobacco, liquorice, red berry fruit and earthiness finds a lovely foil in the vibrantly savoury palate. The Nobile '04 is fresh-tasting and consistent with good depth while the De Ferrari '05, from sangiovese with a little merlot, is very tasty. Finally, the '05 Rosso di Montalcino Prugnolo is upfront and uncomplicated.

Castello di Bossi

LOC. BOSSI IN CHIANTI
53019 CASTELNUOVO BERARDENGA [SI]
TEL. 0577359330
www.castellodibossi.it

ANNUAL PRODUCTION 400,000 bottles
HECTARES UNDER VINE 124
VITICULTURE METHOD Conventional

The Baccis sent two wines to our finals, a fine result that was backed up by good scores from the wines made on the Maremma estate. The passionate enthusiasm that Marco and Maurizio lavish on their work is truly admirable. Their attention to detail at every stage from vineyard to cellar is almost obsessive. Proof of this emerges in their ability to interpret the various growing environments in Chianti Classico and Maremma but neither should we forget Montalcino, which will see its first release next year. Every wine has its own distinct identity and is a treat for the taste buds. The merlot-only Girolamo '04 gives elegant liquorice and spice before the subtly elegant palate develops, its tannins just a little assertive, to a savoury finish. Equally attractive is the Riserva Berardo '04, a medley of spice on the nose, which leads into a broad, soft-textured palate. The sangiovese and cabernet Corbaia '04, showing slightly below par, offers balsam fragrances and beefy structure. All the Maremma wines are delicious.

● Nobile di Montepulciano Nocio dei Boscarelli '04	♟♟♟ 7
● Nobile di Montepulciano Ris. '03	♟♟ 6
● De Ferrari '05	♟♟ 4
● Nobile di Montepulciano '04	♟♟ 5
● Rosso di Montepulciano Prugnolo '05	♟ 4
● Nobile di Montepulciano Nocio dei Boscarelli '01	♟♟♟ 7
● Nobile di Montepulciano V. del Nocio Ris. '91	♟♟♟ 7
● Nobile di Montepulciano Nocio dei Boscarelli '03	♟♟♟ 7
● Nobile di Montepulciano V. del Nocio '99	♟♟ 7
● Nobile di Montepulciano V. del Nocio '00	♟♟ 7

● Chianti Cl. Berardo Ris. '04	♟♟ 6
● Girolamo '04	♟♟ 7
● Corbaia '04	♟♟ 7
● Morellino di Scansano Tempo Terra di Talamo '06	♟♟ 4
○ Vento Vermentino '06	♟♟ 4
● Chianti Cl. '05	♟ 5
⊙ Piano...Piano '06	♟ 4
● Corbaia '03	♟♟♟ 7
● Corbaia '99	♟♟♟ 8
● Chianti Cl. Berardo Ris. '03	♟♟ 6
● Girolamo '03	♟♟ 7

Tenuta Bossi

LOC. BOSSI
VIA DELLO STRACCHINO, 32
50065 PONTASSIEVE [FI]
TEL. 0558317830
www.gondi.com

ANNUAL PRODUCTION 30,000 bottles
HECTARES UNDER VINE 18.6
VITICULTURE METHOD Conventional

Bonaccorso and Bernardo Gondi's Tenuta Bossi claims its full profile, testifying to significant progress that is affecting the whole of Chianti Rufina. The Gondis are an old family and Tenuta Bossi, built in the 15th century, was purchased in 1592 from the Tolomei family. In all, the estate has 18 hectares under vine and 32 planted to olives. Tenuta Bossi wines are territory-focused, reflecting and expressing the characteristics of their origins. We thought the best this time was the fruit and balsam Chianti Rufina San Giuliano '04. It has elegant body, subtle tannic weave and assertive acidity, making it quite deliciously drinkable. The Vin Santo Riserva '02 also impressed with its signature oxidative notes, dried fruit and nut aromas and soft mouthfeel well supported by acidity through to a long, sweet finale. Pian dei Sorbi and Villa Bossi, both '03 Riservas, are good, although over-enthusiastic extract tends to hold back development on the palate.

Fattoria La Braccesca

FRAZ. GRACCIANO
VIA STELLA DI VALIANO, 10
53040 MONTEPULCIANO [SI]
TEL. 0578724252
www.antinori.it

ANNUAL PRODUCTION 600,000 bottles
HECTARES UNDER VINE 220
VITICULTURE METHOD Conventional

Year after year, Antinori's wines from Montepulciano and the new neighbouring designated zone of Cortona are technically faultless and supremely drinkable, in line with the centuries-long oenological experience of this influential label. A wine from Tenuta La Braccesca is a wine to bank on. All that is missing is the touch of extra personality that would take the range into the stratosphere. The best of this year's offerings was the Nobile di Montepulciano '04, a wine with satisfyingly deep fruit aromas and an elegantly restrained palate. We also like the syrah-based Cortona Bramasole '04, which is balanced and enviably well extracted. The Nobile Santa Pia '04 is succulent but slightly over-oaked while there's a newcomer, the malbech-only Vie Cave '05, from the 90 hectares of vineyard at Fattoria Aldobrandesca in Maremma at Sovana. Coffee powder mingles with well-defined fruit aromas before the attractively relaxed palate unfolds, despite a little too much oak. Aleatico '06 is fresh and subtly sweet.

● Chianti Rufina San Giuliano '04	▼▼ 3
○ Vin Santo del Chianti Rufina Ris. '02	▼▼ 5
● Chianti Rufina Pian dei Sorbi Ris. '03	▼ 4
● Chianti Rufina Villa di Bossi Ris. '03	▼ 4

● Cortona Bramasole '04	▼▼ 5
● Vie Cave '05	▼▼ 5
● Nobile di Montepulciano '04	▼▼ 5
● Aleatico '06	▼ 5
● Nobile di Montepulciano Santa Pia '04	▼ 6
● Cortona Bramasole '00	▼▼ 6
● Cortona Bramasole '01	▼▼ 6
● Nobile di Montepulciano '03	▼▼ 5
● Nobile di Montepulciano Santa Pia '03	▼▼ 6
● Nobile di Montepulciano '98	▼▼ 5
● Nobile di Montepulciano '97	▼▼ 5
● Nobile di Montepulciano Santa Pia '01	▼▼ 6

Brancaia
LOC. POPPI, 42
53017 RADDA IN CHIANTI [SI]
TEL. 0577742007
www.brancaia.it

Brunelli - Le Chiuse di Sotto
LOC. PODERNOVONE
53024 MONTALCINO [SI]
TEL. 0577849337
www.giannibrunelli.it

ANNUAL PRODUCTION 30,000 bottles
HECTARES UNDER VINE 25
VITICULTURE METHOD Conventional

ANNUAL PRODUCTION 30,000 bottles
HECTARES UNDER VINE 6.3
VITICULTURE METHOD Conventional

This year's haul takes the Widmer family's Three Glass total to nine since they purchased Brancaia in 1981. In the intervening period, they have kept the cellar well up to speed with regard to quality. As usual, the top estate wine is Il Blu '05, a blend of sangiovese, merlot and cabernet sauvignon with a whistle-clean nose that foregrounds balsam and forest fruits. Soft and beautifully rounded, the palate melds its extract perfectly with the alcohol, sweeping through to a sweet, lingering finish. Ilatraia '05 is also delightful. It hails from Maremma, where there are 45 hectares planted to vine, purchased in 1998. Cabernet sauvignon and sangiovese go into the blend with a splash of petit verdot. It's a wine that impeccably embodies its territory, drinking slightly rustic but with a very full flavour. Tre '05, from sangiovese with some cabernet sauvignon and merlot, is again a delicious wine that combines elegance with drinkability. Finally, the '05 Chianti Classico was punching below its weight, unveiling decent aromatics and a certain lack of structure.

All of Gianni Brunelli's volcanic energy is channelled into his Montalcino winery. His appearances at the "osteria" in Siena that has made his name known round the world are increasingly infrequent. But in the cellar, things are going like clockwork. Even so, there is a real need to expand the winemaking facilities as space is insufficient for current requirements. The '02 Brunello was not released because the vintage was not considered up to Gianni's strict standards. On the other hand, the '01 Riserva is the best the cellar has ever released. The style is classic Brunelli: elegant and rather reminiscent of Burgundy. The classic entry on the nose has depth as well as faintly jammy briary fruit, cherry and morello cherry. The oak is kept well in check. The very delicate palate offers elegant polymerized tannins that meld beautifully with the acidity that is typical of local wines. Finally, a fresh back palate, which follows through well, lingers longer than you might expect. It's a very classy Brunello absolutely true to its origins. Finally, both the Rosso '05 and the '04 Amor Costante are somewhat clenched.

● Brancaia Il Blu '05	￥￥￥ 7
● Brancaia Tre '05	￥￥ 5
● Ilatraia '05	￥￥ 7
● Chianti Cl. '05	￥ 6
● Brancaia '97	￥￥￥ 6
● Brancaia '94	￥￥￥ 6
● Brancaia '99	￥￥￥ 8
● Brancaia Il Blu '04	￥￥￥ 7
● Brancaia Il Blu '03	￥￥￥ 7
● Brancaia Il Blu '01	￥￥￥ 7
● Brancaia Il Blu '00	￥￥￥ 7
● Brancaia '98	￥￥￥ 6

● Brunello di Montalcino Ris. '01	￥￥ 8
● Amor Costante '04	￥ 6
● Rosso di Montalcino '05	￥ 5
● Amor Costante '03	￥￥ 6
● Brunello di Montalcino '01	￥￥ 7
● Brunello di Montalcino '99	￥￥ 8
● Brunello di Montalcino '00	￥￥ 7

Fattoria del Buonamico

LOC. CERCATOIA
VIA PROVINCIALE DI MONTECARLO, 43
55015 MONTECARLO [LU]
TEL. 058322038
www.buonamico.it

ANNUAL PRODUCTION   120,000 bottles
HECTARES UNDER VINE 23
VITICULTURE METHOD   Conventional

The story of wine is intimately bound up with people, places and landscapes. This has always been true for great wines and it is equally valid for smaller wineries whose heritage is special, or even extraordinary. Fattoria del Buonamico is a very good example. Year after year, the cellars in Montecarlo have filled with wonderful wines and a heritage whose leading witness today is the manager, Vasco Grassi. A chat with Vasco will take you through the history of a cellar and indeed of Italian wine. Since Turin's celebrated Gatto Nero restaurant first ordered the Fattoria di Buonamico wines that are now a fixture in our Guide, they have been emblematic of drinkability, quality and sense of place. Cercatoja Rosso is one of our favourite wines and the '04 edition was well up to snuff, its liqueur cherries shading into minerality and rain-soaked earth backed up by nicely extracted tannins and nimble yet fleshy fruit. The syrah-only Il Fortino still needs to absorb its oak but the base Montecarlo wines are as persuasive as ever.

Ca' Marcanda

LOC. SANTA TERESA, 272
57022 CASTAGNETO CARDUCCI [LI]
TEL. 0173635158
camarcanda@virgilio.it

ANNUAL PRODUCTION   390,000 bottles
HECTARES UNDER VINE 100
VITICULTURE METHOD   Conventional

The winery that Angelo Gaja created more than ten years ago near Bolgheri faithfully reflects its founder's personality and the attention to detail that has always been his hallmark. The vineyards make a stupendous setting for the equally stupendous cellar, a perfect fusion of functionality, thanks to its size, and aesthetic appeal, deriving from materials that echo the colours of the land round about. There were three labels on offer: Bolgheri Camarcanda '04, from 50 per cent merlot, cabernet sauvignon and a touch of cabernet franc; Magari '05, again 50 per cent merlot with equal portions of cabernet sauvignon and cabernet franc; and Promis '05, a blend of 55 per cent merlot, 35 per cent syrah and ten per cent sangiovese. Our favourite, even if it isn't the flagship wine, was Magari, which has a complex nose of black fruits and balsam, attractive thrust on the well-integrated, close-knit palate and a perfect pinch of invigorating acidity. Camarcanda has warm jammy notes and tannins that are a tad too drying while the Promis is masked by oak on nose and palate.

● Cercatoja Rosso '04	♟♟	5
● Il Fortino Syrah '04	♟	7
○ Montecarlo Bianco '06	♟	3
● Montecarlo Rosso '06	♟	4
● Cercatoja Rosso '99	♟♟	6
● Il Fortino Syrah '00	♟♟	7
● Il Fortino Syrah '98	♟♟	7
● Cercatoja Rosso '97	♟♟	6
● Cercatoja Rosso '98	♟♟	6
● Cercatoja Rosso '00	♟♟	6
● Cercatoja Rosso '03	♟♟	5
● Il Fortino Syrah '03	♟♟	7

● Magari '05	♟♟	8
● Promis '05	♟♟	8
● Bolgheri Camarcanda '04	♟♟	8
● Bolgheri Camarcanda '01	♟♟♟	8
● Magari '03	♟♟♟	7
● Magari '01	♟♟	8
● Magari '02	♟♟	8
● Magari '04	♟♟	8

Tenuta Le Calcinaie

LOC. SANTA LUCIA, 36
53037 SAN GIMIGNANO [SI]
TEL. 0577943007
www.tenutalecalcinaie.it

ANNUAL PRODUCTION 60,000 bottles
HECTARES UNDER VINE 10
VITICULTURE METHOD Certified organic

There are no adjectives that can describe
how good Simone Santini is. This young
winemaker turns out characterful wines that
do more than their share to uphold the
reputation of Vernaccia. Year after year, his
convincing products are among the best in
the designated area. Vernaccia Vigna ai
Sassi '05 is beautifully made. From the first
sniff, its florality and fruit enthral before the
palate's structure and irresistible
progression win your heart thanks to
restrained minerality and a long-lingering,
savoury finish. The '06 Vernaccia is lovely,
proffering spring flowers and apricot-led fruit
aromas. On the palate, its full body is
tempered with a perky freshness that
makes this a very moreish wine. The finish is
moderately long. We noted red berry fruits
and spicy notes on the nose of the Chianti
Colli Senesi '06 leading into a fresh-tasting,
nicely tannic palate with a lovely morello
cherry finish. Finally, the Teodoro '04 had yet
to go into bottle when we were tasting.

O Vernaccia di S. Gimignano		
V. ai Sassi '05	♈♈	4
O Vernaccia di S. Gimignano '06	♈♈	4*
● Chianti Colli Senesi '06	♈	4
O Vernaccia di S. Gimignano		
V. ai Sassi '03	♉♉	4
O Vernaccia di S. Gimignano		
V. ai Sassi '04	♉♉	4
● Teodoro '99	♉♉	5
O Vernaccia di S. Gimignano '05	♉♉	3
O Vernaccia di S. Gimignano		
V. ai Sassi '02	♉♉	4
O Vernaccia di S. Gimignano '04	♉♉	3

Camigliano

LOC. CAMIGLIANO
VIA D'INGRESSO, 2
53024 MONTALCINO [SI]
TEL. 0577816061
www.camigliano.it

ANNUAL PRODUCTION 300,000 bottles
HECTARES UNDER VINE 90
VITICULTURE METHOD Conventional

The likeable Ghezzis tenaciously dedicate
their efforts to promoting the village of
Camigliano in an admirable spirit of
philanthropy. In the meantime, work on the
new larger and more rational cellar has been
completed, in perfect harmony with their
ambitious project of restoring the
Camigliano area to its medieval glory. More
space was needed because the new
plantings, and replantings, are now on
stream and there is more wine to be made.
The barrel stock has also been expanded
and a substantial number of new tonneaux
and barriques have been brought in to join
the traditional medium-sized Slavonian oak
barrels. Overall, the wines are good,
although there are no high notes. The
Brunello Gualto Riserva '01 needs time to
aerate but then unveils attractive red and
black fruit jam, offsetting the juicy fruit on
the palate with lively acidity and robust
extract. We liked the '02 Brunello for its
intense, well-defined briary fruit and cherry
leading in to a satisfyingly tasty palate.
Finally, the Rosso di Montalcino and the
cabernet sauvignon-only Sant'Antimo
Poderuccio, both '05s, are very impressive.

● Brunello di Montalcino '02	♈♈	6
● Brunello di Montalcino		
Gualto Ris. '01	♈♈	8
● Poderuccio '05	♈	4
● Rosso di Montalcino '05	♈	4
● Brunello di Montalcino '98	♉♉	6
● Brunello di Montalcino '99	♉♉	6
● Poderuccio '02	♉♉	4
● Brunello di Montalcino Gualto '99	♉♉	8
● Brunello di Montalcino '00	♉♉	6
● Brunello di Montalcino '01	♉♉	6

Campo alla Sughera
LOC. CACCIA AL PIANO, 280
57020 BOLGHERI [LI]
TEL. 0565766936
www.campoallasughera.com

Canalicchio di Sopra
LOC. CASACCIA, 73
53024 MONTALCINO [SI]
TEL. 0577848316
www.canalicchiodisopra.com

ANNUAL PRODUCTION 90,000 bottles
HECTARES UNDER VINE 16.3
VITICULTURE METHOD Conventional

ANNUAL PRODUCTION 40,000 bottles
HECTARES UNDER VINE 15
VITICULTURE METHOD Conventional

This year, the Knauf winery confirmed that its high standards of quality are a given. Set up ten or so years ago, Campo alla Sughera has all its vine stock in the Bolgheri zone, where the warm but well-ventilated climate ripens the grapes to perfection. The varieties planted are the classic Bolgheri cabernet sauvignon, merlot, cabernet franc and petit verdot. And these are the grapes involved in the '04 Bolgheri Superiore Arnione, which again went through to the finals. Wonderful balance is the keynote of wines from this vintage and this is no exception. Vegetal and fresh dark berry fruit on the nose precede taut, beautifully handled acidity that drives the attractive palate through to the finish. The youthfully boisterous tannins will mellow with the passage of time. Also delicious is the Bolgheri Rosso Adeo '05, a fine wine from a vintage that lacked concentration. Finally, the sauvignon and viognier Arioso is one of the best in the designated area, showing typical aromatics and bright acidity.

As you climb to Montalcino from Buonconvento, you pass the Canalicchi subzone. It is easily recognizable from the changing soil, which is less clayey and has more stones and pebbles. Here, the growing environment is one of the finest on the north-facing slope. The Ripaccioli family has been tending vines for many years and their wines are benchmarks for their ability to communicate a sense of place. The new generation has been working hard on quality, focusing their efforts on improving the clarity and definition of the aromas. The Brunello Riserva '01 shows just how far they have come and cruised to a Three Glass award at our finals. If allowed to breathe in the glass for a short while, it releases elegantly traditional aromas of tobacco-laced cherry. That provenance from the northern part of the DOCG zone is apparent on the palate, which has grip enough to tell you that this is a wine for the cellar. The tannins are vigorous but very fine grained and the finish is endless. The Brunello '02, from an indifferent vintage, is below par but the Rosso '05 is very nice.

● Bolgheri Superiore Arnione '04	♟♟ 7
○ Arioso '06	♟♟ 4
● Bolgheri Rosso Adeo '05	♟ 5
● Arnione '01	♟♟ 7
● Bolgheri Superiore Arnione '03	♟♟ 7
● Arnione '02	♟♟ 6

● Brunello di Montalcino Ris. '01	♟♟♟ 8
● Brunello di Montalcino '02	♟ 6
● Rosso di Montalcino '05	♟ 4
● Brunello di Montalcino '01	♟♟ 6
● Brunello di Montalcino Ris. '97	♟♟ 8
● Brunello di Montalcino Ris. '99	♟♟ 7
● Brunello di Montalcino '00	♟♟ 6
● Brunello di Montalcino '99	♟♟ 8

Candialle

via San Leolino, 71
50020 Panzano [FI]
tel. 055852201
www.candialle.com

ANNUAL PRODUCTION 15,000 bottles
HECTARES UNDER VINE 5.8
VITICULTURE METHOD Conventional

Tuscany is still the favourite destination for many non-Italians. In fact, some are so in love with the region that they opt to settle and work here. Two such immigrants are German-born Josephin Cramer and Jarkko Peranen from Finland. They took the advice of two experienced wine men like Remigio Bordini and Vittorio Fiore and headed for the Conca d'Oro at the very south of Panzano, where they found a farm that suited their requirements. Over the years, scrupulous integrated vineyard management and meticulous cellar work have done the rest. This time, the best wine was the sangiovese-only Pli '04. Fragrances that range from forest floor to fruit introduce a full-bodied but well-balanced palate, good length and delicious savouriness. The Chianti Classico '05 is another winner, its fascinating aromatic herb and forest fruits nose complementing balanced structure and soft tannins. But the Ciclope '05, from merlot and sangiovese with a modest amount of syrah, is soft and lacks depth.

● Chianti Cl. '05	ΨΨ 4
● Ciclope '05	Ψ 5
● Pli '04	Ψ 7
● Ciclope '04	ΨΨ 5

Canonica a Cerreto

loc. Canonica a Cerreto
53019 Castelnuovo Berardenga [SI]
tel. 0577363261
www.canonicacerreto.it

ANNUAL PRODUCTION 50,000 bottles
HECTARES UNDER VINE 20
VITICULTURE METHOD Conventional

The Lorenzi family's cellar put on another sterling performance, again sending the Chianti Classico Riserva to our finals. The '04 edition has a tempting nose of spice and red fruits-led aromatics before the palate progresses delightfully to an admirably flavourful finish. This all-round improvement in quality is hardly surprising, given the superbly sited vines in the southern part of Chianti Classico, the Herculean efforts that have gone into replanting and the construction of a new cellar. The '04 Sandiavolo is as good as ever. The blend of equal parts of sangiovese, cabernet sauvignon and merlot has lent it intriguing aromatics, mouthfilling body and lovely balance while the Chianti Classico '05 puts the accent on elegance, albeit with slightly rugged tannins that are not quite offset by the structure.

● Chianti Cl. Ris. '04	ΨΨ 5
● Sandiavolo '04	ΨΨ 5
● Chianti Cl. '05	Ψ 4
● Chianti Cl. Ris. '03	ΨΨ 5
● Sandiavolo '00	ΨΨ 5
● Sandiavolo '03	ΨΨ 5

Tenuta Cantagallo
VIA VALICARDA, 35
50056 CAPRAIA E LIMITE [FI]
TEL. 0571910078
www.enricopierazzuoli.com

ANNUAL PRODUCTION 112.600 bottles
HECTARES UNDER VINE 29.5
VITICULTURE METHOD Conventional

Encouraging signals are arriving from Enrico Pierazzuoli's winery. In a short time, two new plantings will come onstream at estate vineyards located on Montalbano. This fruit will further improve wines that are already good and made to a modern style that aims for rich fruit and concentration. Emblematic of this approach is the Carmignano Le Farnete Riserva '04. A complex swath of aromatics ranges from red berry fruit to grassy hints, with distinct hints of toastiness. Concentration, a close-knit tannic weave and decent progression are all there on the palate but it does lack a little depth. There was another good performance from the Chianti Montalbano Riserva '04 whose black fruits and dark chocolate nose accompany a dense, well-structured palate. Millarium '01, which has moved into the Vin Santo del Chianti Montalbano designated area, has made an impressive quality leap with its opulent mouthfeel, pastryshop sensations and dried fig aromas. Crunchy fruit and a close-textured palate sum up the Chianti Montalbano '06, the Carnmignano '06 is a juicy mid weight wine and the Gioveto '04 is robust but lacks oomph. Barco Real '06 has intense fruit flavours.

Tenuta di Capezzana
LOC. SEANO
VIA CAPEZZANA, 100
59015 CARMIGNANO [PO]
TEL. 0558706005
www.capezzana.it

ANNUAL PRODUCTION 600,000 bottles
HECTARES UNDER VINE 140
VITICULTURE METHOD Conventional

If the territorial identity of Carmignano has survived, it is thanks in large part to the Contini Bonaccossi family. This close-knit family is gifted with ability and entrepreneurial skills, thanks to which the designated zone's superior wine quality has kept the national and international credibility of Carmignano buoyant. This time, the cellar's flagship Carmignano Villa di Capezzana was missing from the list. Instead, our tasters were happy to note a fine team effort that saw three wines go through to the national finals. The cabernet sauvignon and merlot Ghiae della Furba '03 is beefy and seriously structured, which is perhaps why it takes time to open. The extremely fine Vin Santo Riserva '01 is fat but not cloying, offering aromas of dried fruit and nuts and lacking only the hint of acidity that would bolster its wealth of pulpy fruit. There was a fine performance from the golden Trebbiano '04. It has a complex, oak-tinged nose and a bright palate perfectly poised between fullness and freshness. Equally impressive was the Carmignano Villa di Trefiano '04 whose juicy, well-modulated palate puts drinkability first. Finally, the Barco Reale '05 is fruit forward and dependable.

● Carmignano Le Farnete Ris. '04	🍷🍷 6
○ Vin Santo del Chianti Millarium '01	🍷🍷 6
● Chianti Montalbano Ris. '04	🍷🍷 4
● Barco Reale '06	🍷 4*
● Gioveto '04	🍷 5
● Chianti Montalbano '06	🍷 3*
● Carmignano Le Farnete '04	🍷 4
● Carmignano Le Farnete Ris. '97	🍷🍷🍷 5
● Carmignano Le Farnete Ris. '00	🍷🍷 7
● Carmignano Le Farnete Ris. '03	🍷🍷 7
● Carmignano Le Farnete Ris. '01	🍷🍷 7
● Chianti Montalbano Ris. '03	🍷🍷 4
● Gioveto '03	🍷🍷 5
● Gioveto '01	🍷🍷 5
● Chianti Montalbano '04	🍷🍷 3*

● Ghiaie della Furba '03	🍷 6
○ Trebbiano '04	🍷 5
○ Vin Santo di Carmignano Ris. '01	🍷🍷 6
● Carmignano Villa di Trefiano '04	🍷🍷 6
● Barco Reale '05	🍷 4
● Carmignano Villa di Capezzana '99	🍷🍷🍷 5
● Ghiaie della Furba '98	🍷🍷🍷 5
● Ghiaie della Furba '01	🍷🍷🍷 6
● Carmignano Villa di Capezzana '04	🍷🍷 5
○ Vin Santo di Carmignano Ris. '98	🍷🍷 6
○ Vin Santo di Carmignano Ris. '96	🍷🍷 5*
○ Trebbiano '03	🍷🍷 6
● Ghiaie della Furba '99	🍷🍷 6
● Ghiaie della Furba '00	🍷🍷 6
● Carmignano Villa di Trefiano '00	🍷🍷 6
● Ghiaie della Furba '97	🍷🍷 5

Podere La Cappella

FRAZ. SAN DONATO IN POGGIO
S.DA CERBAIA, 10
50020 TAVARNELLE VAL DI PESA [FI]
TEL. 0558072727
www.poderelacappella.it

ANNUAL PRODUCTION	20,000 bottles
HECTARES UNDER VINE	10
VITICULTURE METHOD	Conventional

Not for the first time, the Rossini family's estate was on good form. Bruno, the father, looks after the vineyards and cellar, and his daughter Natascia, is in charge of distribution. Together, they make an excellent team. There was no Cantico, the single-variety Merlot we liked so much last year, but the estate has adopted the shrewd strategy of releasing its Supertuscans in alternate years. This year it was the turn of Corbezzolo '03, an undeniably good sangiovese-heavy red. Ripe, mainly jammy, notes on the notes introduce a palate that is juicy, if not as succulent as other versions we recall. Still, the growing year was a difficult one because of very high temperatures. Riserva Querciolo '04 is better balanced and more dynamic, its broad, red fruits, aromatic herbs and spices unfolding nicely. The tannins are austere but well tucked in and the finish shows enjoyable thrust. Finally, the '05 Chianti Classico is a tad stiff and dumb on the nose. Its tannins have a slightly rough edge, although they are nicely absorbed into the generous body.

Podere Il Carnasciale

LOC. PODERE IL CARNASCIALE
52020 MONTEVARCHI [AR]
TEL. 0559911142

ANNUAL PRODUCTION	2,500 bottles
HECTARES UNDER VINE	2
VITICULTURE METHOD	Conventional

Last year, we ended our profile with a note about Caberlot '04, which we tasted while it was still ageing and were thoroughly impressed with. We predicted it would be a great vintage for the wine. In the event, our sensation was borne out at the official tastings, where Caberlot '04 earned Three well-deserved Glasses. It is obtained from a special variety, which has given its name to the wine and which appears to be a genetic mutation of cabernet. Cosseted and cuddled like a newborn child by Bettina Rogosky on her tiny estate, it is released in magnums. Only 2,000 units are available, adding rarity value to the organoleptic qualities that wine enthusiasts prize so much. But what makes this wine so unique among premium products is its one-of-a-kind sensory profile, which reaches a peak with the '04. The dark fruit is crisp and clean, fusing magnificently with a fresh, pungent profusion of pepper-led spice. Depth and elegance in the mouth are exalted by superb extract while the sheer power is kept well on track by substantial sinewy acidity.

● Chianti Cl. Querciolo Ris. '04	🍷🍷 5		● Caberlot '04	🍷🍷🍷 8
● Corbezzolo '03	🍷🍷 5		● Caberlot '00	🍷🍷🍷 8
● Chianti Cl. '05	🍷 4		● Caberlot '01	🍷🍷 8
● Corbezzolo '00	🍷🍷 7		● Caberlot '03	🍷🍷 8
● Corbezzolo '01	🍷🍷 7		● Caberlot '99	🍷🍷 8
● Chianti Cl. '03	🍷🍷 4		● Caberlot '98	🍷🍷 6
			● Caberlot '02	🍷🍷 8
			● Caberlot '96	🍷🍷 6
			● Caberlot '97	🍷🍷 6

Carobbio

VIA SAN MARTINO IN CECIONE, 26
50020 PANZANO [FI]
TEL. 0558560133
info@carobbiowine.com

ANNUAL PRODUCTION 45,000 bottles
HECTARES UNDER VINE 10
VITICULTURE METHOD Conventional

The fine standards here were confirmed this year by excellent results from the wines of the Novarese family. This was not unexpected as recent vintages have yielded some great wines. Two wines went forward to the finals, the sangiovese-only Leone di Carobbio '03 and the '04 Riserva version of Chianti Classico. Carobbio is a long-established estate. The earliest document that bears the place name dates from the 12th century but the current owners actually arrived from Lombardy in the late 1980s. The farm is far more than a weekend retreat in the country. When Carlo saw Carobbio, he realized it was the ideal setting in which to make characterful wines. That is a fair description of the '04 Riserva, whose rich, slightly minerally nose precedes a soft, expansive palate. The Leone '03 has tertiary aromas on the nose and a very solid structure with tannins that are still clenched. Finally, the base Chianti Classico is well executed with crisp, clean aromas but lacks a little body.

Fattoria Carpineta Fontalpino

FRAZ. MONTEAPERTI
LOC. CARPINETA
53019 CASTELNUOVO BERARDENGA [SI]
TEL. 0577369219
www.carpinetafontalpino.it

ANNUAL PRODUCTION 70,000 bottles
HECTARES UNDER VINE 16
VITICULTURE METHOD Natural

This year, Carpineta Fontalpino doubled its success by sending the new Dofana through to the finals with Do ut Des, a long-standing contender at the Three Glass taste-offs. Wines from this Castelnuovo Berardenga estate have long flaunted a reliable, distinctive style, good typicity and a very natural personality but now they are just a step away from absolute excellence. We believe that Gioia Cresti, a very competent oenologist, is aware of this and continues to work in her vineyards and cellar in the knowledge that a top prize is sure to arrive soon. The merlot-only Dofana '04 has outstandingly ripe aromas with sophisticated, beautifully poised balance. The juicy, elegant palate powers on attractively, held back only slightly by a hint of intrusive oak. The Do ut Des '05 is every bit as good. From equal parts of sangiovese, cabernet sauvignon and merlot, its temptingly well-defined fragrances precede serious weight that unfolds confidently on the palate flanked by docile tannins and bright acid freshness. Finally, the sangiovese, gamay and alicante Montaperto '06 is full bodied if a tad rustic.

● Chianti Cl. Ris. '04	▼▼ 5
● Leone di Carobbio '03	▼▼ 6
● Chianti Cl. '05	▼ 4
● Chianti Cl. Ris. '01	♈♈ 5
● Leone di Carobbio '01	♈♈ 6

● Do Ut Des '05	▼▼ 6
● Dofana '04	▼▼ 8
● Montaperto '06	▼ 4
● Do Ut Des '00	♈♈ 6
● Do Ut Des '01	♈♈ 6
● Do Ut Des '03	♈♈ 6
● Do Ut Des '99	♈♈ 6
● Do Ut Des '04	♈♈ 6
● Do Ut Des '02	♈♈ 6
● Do Ut Des '97	♈♈ 6
● Do Ut Des '98	♈♈ 6

Casa alle Vacche

FRAZ. PANCOLE
LOC. LUCIGNANO, 73A
53037 SAN GIMIGNANO [SI]
TEL. 0577955103
www.casaallevacche.it

ANNUAL PRODUCTION 120,000 bottles
HECTARES UNDER VINE 21.5
VITICULTURE METHOD Conventional

For some time now, the Ciappi family's wines have been crafted to a style that puts the accent on proportion. The Vernaccia Crocus Riserva '05 is a well-made product with an intense nose that fuses spices with florality and fruit. Savoury on the palate, it has enough body to progress confidently with good length and complexity. We liked the I Macchioni '06 selection. Classic tropical fruit and spring flowers greet the nose then the full, fresh-tasting body displays poise and a bitterish twist in the finish. The reds, too, performed well. Aglieno '05, from sangiovese and merlot, has full fruit aromas and a close-knit, fresh-tasting palate that holds up well. San Gimignano Acantho '04 is from sangiovese, cabernet and colorino and unveils elegant balsamic aromas and a full, well-calibrated palate with nice savouriness. The well-executed Chianti Colli Senesi Cinabro Riserva '04 is a fruity, coherent wine and the rest of the range offers value for money.

Casa Emma

LOC. CORTINE
S.P. DI CASTELLINA IN CHIANTI, 3
50021 BARBERINO VAL D'ELSA [FI]
TEL. 0558072239
www.casaemma.com

ANNUAL PRODUCTION 85,000 bottles
HECTARES UNDER VINE 21
VITICULTURE METHOD Conventional

The Bucalossi family have got their full profile back thanks to an excellent all-round performance led by the merlot-only Supertuscan Soloìo '04. Their estate's name comes from the previous owner, the Florentine aristocrat Emma Bizzarri, from whom the Bucalossis purchased the property in the early 1970s. They liked the name and decided to keep it. Casa Emma's vines are about 400 metres above sea level and have a territorial note that comes through in the minerally nuances of the aromas. Soloìo is in fact rather Chiantified and manages to express its sense of place more fully than the profile of its variety. The Riserva '04 has juicy body, breadth on the palate and remarkable length. Perhaps it was the growing year but the Chianti Classico '05's tannins are a tad stiff, if well supported by alcohol. Apart from olive oil and wine, the Bucalossi family also makes specialty products like wine jellies, rose syrup and "vino cotto" (cooked, fermented and aged must).

Wine	Rating
● Aglieno '05	🍷🍷 4
● S. Gimignano Rosso Acantho '04	🍷🍷 4
O Vernaccia di S. Gimignano Crocus Ris. '05	🍷🍷 4
O Vernaccia di S. Gimignano I Macchioni '06	🍷🍷 3*
● Chianti Colli Senesi Cinabro Ris. '04	🍷 4
● Aglieno '04	🏆🏆 4
O Vernaccia di S. Gimignano Crocus Ris. '02	🏆🏆 4
● Chianti Colli Senesi Cinabro Ris. '02	🏆🏆 4
O Vernaccia di S. Gimignano Crocus '00	🏆🏆 4
● S. Gimignano Rosso Acantho '01	🏆🏆 6
O Vernaccia di S. Gimignano Crocus '01	🏆🏆 4

Wine	Rating
● Chianti Cl. Ris. '04	🍷🍷 6
● Soloìo '04	🍷🍷 7
● Chianti Cl. '05	🍷 4
● Chianti Cl. Ris. '93	🏆🏆🏆 4
● Chianti Cl. Ris. '95	🏆🏆🏆 4
● Soloìo '94	🏆🏆🏆 5
● Chianti Cl. '96	🏆🏆 3
● Chianti Cl. Ris. '99	🏆🏆 6
● Chianti Cl. '97	🏆🏆 4
● Chianti Cl. Ris. '03	🏆🏆 6
● Chianti Cl. Ris. '00	🏆🏆 6
● Soloìo '00	🏆🏆 6
● Soloìo '03	🏆🏆 7
● Soloìo '01	🏆🏆 8

Fattoria Casaloste
VIA MONTAGLIARI, 32
50020 PANZANO [FI]
TEL. 055852725
www.casaloste.com

ANNUAL PRODUCTION 55,000 bottles
HECTARES UNDER VINE 10.5
VITICULTURE METHOD Certified organic

After years of unflaggingly high quality, this time the wines of Giovan Battista and Emilia D'Orsi's estate were a little below par. Admittedly, it was not a great vintage for the winery's flagship, Chianti Classico Riserva Don Vincenzo, and this is reflected in the '03 version, which is full and flavoursome but lacks balance. The nose proffers hints of ripe berries, plum jam, tobacco and herbaceousness. On the palate, the alcohol tends to dilute the finish, which is held back by tannins that have not integrated. Riserva '04 is more relaxed and pleasant, reflecting its vintage. On the nose, it throws well-defined aromas of ripe fruit with balsamic hints and vegetal notes while the firmly structured palate has assertive but fine-grained tannins and a long, nicely acidic finish. Chianti Classico '05 is pleasant but rather held back by tannins from both fruit and oak. We await next year's wines, confident that the estate will return to its usual high quality.

Fattoria Le Casalte
FRAZ. SANT'ALBINO
VIA DEL TERMINE, 2
53045 MONTEPULCIANO [SI]
TEL. 0578798246
lecasalte@libero.it

ANNUAL PRODUCTION 45,000 bottles
HECTARES UNDER VINE 13
VITICULTURE METHOD Conventional

In recent years, Chiara Barioffi's winery has been one of the cellars that have made the biggest and most consistent gains in quality in the entire Vino Nobile di Montepulciano DOCG zone. Credit goes to painstaking, uncompromising work that gives pride of place expressing the territory. The result is a range of wines with a distinctive character, capable of redeeming themselves from the odd hesitation on the nose and occasionally over-enthusiastic oak that once marked them down. Nobile Quercetonda '04 made it into our finals with a complex, well-balanced spectrum of aromatics, in which the fruit notes are complemented by hints of minerality and smokiness. On the palate, it shows seamlessly well sustained into a clean, lip-smacking finish. Nobile '04 is a wine with well-defined aromas and an invigoratingly bright palate. The greatest attraction of the stylish and highly drinkable Rosso di Montepulciano '05 is its freshness. Rosso Toscano '05, from sangiovese and canaiolo grapes grown in the estate's youngest vineyards, is equally drinkable.

● Chianti Cl. Ris. '04	🍷🍷 6
● Chianti Cl. '05	🍷 5
● Chianti Cl. Don Vincenzo Ris. '03	🍷 7
● Chianti Cl. Don Vincenzo Ris. '01	🍷🍷🍷 7
● Chianti Cl. Don Vincenzo Ris. '00	🍷🍷 8
● Chianti Cl. Don Vincenzo Ris. '97	🍷🍷 8
● Chianti Cl. Don Vincenzo Ris. '96	🍷🍷 5
● Chianti Cl. Don Vincenzo Ris. '99	🍷🍷 8

● Nobile di Montepulciano Quercetonda '04	🍷🍷 6
● Nobile di Montepulciano '04	🍷🍷 5
● Rosso di Montepulciano '05	🍷 4
● Rosso Toscano '05	🍷 2
● Nobile di Montepulciano Quercetonda '03	🍷🍷 5
● Nobile di Montepulciano Quercetonda '01	🍷🍷 6
○ Vin Santo '97	🍷🍷 5

★ Casanova di Neri

POD. FIESOLE
53024 MONTALCINO [SI]
TEL. 0577834455
www.casanovadineri.com

ANNUAL PRODUCTION 185,000 bottles
HECTARES UNDER VINE 48
VITICULTURE METHOD Conventional

Giacomo Neri has finished moving winemaking and maturation facilities to the new cellar, a functional building almost invisible from the town and the road from Torrenieri. The vine stock has also been made over, with new vineyards at the winery embodying the estate's philosophy: high density plantings at about 6,000 vines per hectare and clones and rootstock that build on past experience. The wines did superbly at our tastings. As usual, the celebrated Brunello Cerretalto '01 was in a class of its own, notching up yet another Three Glass triumph. It's a wine that faithfully reflects its terroir and lovely red soil. A deep colour ushers in a nose that requires a few moments to release its full complexity, commencing with fruity notes of wild and morello cherries before progressing to medicinal herbs. In the mouth, there is concentration and impressive depth, with close-knit but well-integrated tannins, the full body nicely supported by acidity. The finish is exceptionally long and the cellar prospects are excellent. Rosso di Montalcino '05 is a nice wine while Pietradonice '04, from cabernet sauvignon, is held back by oak-derived tannins.

Casanuova delle Cerbaie

LOC. CASANOVA DELLE CERBAIE, 335
53024 MONTALCINO [SI]
TEL. 0577849284
www.casanuovadellecerbaie.com

ANNUAL PRODUCTION 40,000 bottles
HECTARES UNDER VINE 16
VITICULTURE METHOD Conventional

This handsome estate in southern Montalcino maintains high quality standards year after year. Meticulous attention is paid to the smallest detail and each aspect of production is part of a project aimed at achieving excellence. The vines are fairly densely planted in exceptional wine country and include several vineyards in Montosoli in the western part of the district. Overall performance was good, particularly considering the difficulties of the 2002 and 2005 growing years. It's no coincidence that the star of the show was Brunello Riserva '01 from a truly wonderful vintage. Deep ruby in hue, it has a nose that requires slight aeration to give its best, with classic morello cherry notes and hints of cinchona and coffee. The austere palate is slightly stiff, mainly from a lack of acid-tannin balance, but time will help it to unbend. The lustrous Rosso '05 is first-rate, displaying fresh cherry and bramble aromas and a spirited palate with good length. Brunello '02 is merely pleasant.

● Brunello di Montalcino Cerretalto '01	￥￥￥ 8
● Sant'Antimo Pietradonice '04	￥￥ 8
● Rosso di Montalcino '05	￥ 5
● Brunello di Montalcino '00	￥￥￥ 6
● Brunello di Montalcino Cerretalto '95	￥￥￥ 8
● Brunello di Montalcino Cerretalto '99	￥￥￥ 8
● Brunello di Montalcino Cerretalto '00	￥￥￥ 8
● Brunello di Montalcino Cerretalto Ris. '88	￥￥￥ 8
● Brunello di Montalcino Tenuta Nuova '97	￥￥￥ 7
● Sant'Antimo Pietradonice '01	￥￥￥ 8
● Sant'Antimo Pietradonice '00	￥￥￥ 8
● Brunello di Montalcino Tenuta Nuova '99	￥￥￥ 7
● Brunello di Montalcino Tenuta Nuova '01	￥￥￥ 7
● Brunello di Montalcino '99	￥￥ 6
● Brunello di Montalcino Cerretalto '96	￥￥ 8
● Brunello di Montalcino Cerretalto '97	￥￥ 8

● Brunello di Montalcino Ris. '01	￥￥ 8
● Rosso di Montalcino '05	￥￥ 5
● Brunello di Montalcino '02	￥ 6
● Brunello di Montalcino Ris. '97	￥￥￥ 7
● Brunello di Montalcino Ris. '99	￥￥￥ 8
● Brunello di Montalcino '00	￥￥ 6
● Cerbaione '04	￥￥ 6
● Brunello di Montalcino '97	￥￥ 7
● Brunello di Montalcino '01	￥￥ 6
● Brunello di Montalcino '99	￥￥ 7

Podere Casina

FRAZ. ISTIA D'OMBRONE
PIAGGE DEL MAIANO
58040 GROSSETO [GR]
TEL. 0564408210
www.poderecasina.com

ANNUAL PRODUCTION 60,000 bottles
HECTARES UNDER VINE 11
VITICULTURE METHOD Conventional

Podere Casina is one of the estates on the busy Maremma wine scene that most deserves to be monitored. Although still characterized by obvious oak that partly penalizes their potential, the wines crafted by Rahel Kimmich and Marcello Pirisi have plenty of character. Part of the merit for this is due the excellent raw material used in their production. Morellino '06 is a very attractive, upfront wine that still manages to show complexity, particularly on the nose, where the intense fruit-led entry is nicely complemented by minty notes. The palate is less exciting. It's sinewy and flavoursome but not very deep. Morellino Marchele '06 is an exceptionally well-crafted wine, with fresh blackberry aromas and spicy hints, albeit weighed down by rather invasive toasty notes. The full, concentrated palate echoes the nose, right down to the slightly excessive oak that slows its development. Finally, the monovarietal sangiovese Aione '05 throws a blackberry, black cherry and spice nose followed by a deep, dynamic palate.

Castagnoli

LOC. CASTAGNOLI
53011 CASTELLINA IN CHIANTI [SI]
TEL. 0577740446
castagnoli@valdelsa.net

ANNUAL PRODUCTION 30,000 bottles
HECTARES UNDER VINE 9
VITICULTURE METHOD Conventional

Following several years' absence from the Guide, Hans Joachim Dobbelin's estate returns to the Guide. Its vineyards are situated at Castellina, about 400 metres above sea level. The winery has been following the dictates of organic farming as rigorously and consistently as possible for many years, as is demonstrated by the choice not to present its wines when quality is considered inadequate, as was the case last year with the 2003 vintage. This year's wines seemed very well made, with a well-defined, balsam-led nose in the case of the Merlot and spicy nuances in the Syrah. These two wines both boast wonderfully balanced structure in which the acidity fuses nicely with the alcohol. The Merlot is more caressing and rounded but the Syrah is spirited and full-flavoured. Both have a more than decently long finish. Chianti Classico '05 impressed with a generous aromatic nose, nicely gauged if not massive body and pleasing length.

● Aione '05	▼▼ 5
● Morellino di Scansano Marchele '06	▼▼ 4
● Morellino di Scansano '06	▼▼ 4
● Aione '03	♀♀ 5
● Morellino di Scansano '04	♀♀ 3*
● Morellino di Scansano Marchele '04	♀♀ 4
● Morellino di Scansano '05	♀♀ 4

● Syrah '04	▼▼ 6
● Merlot '04	▼▼ 6
● Chianti Cl. '05	▼ 5
● Syrah '04	♀♀ 6

Castelgiocondo
LOC. CASTELGIOCONDO
53024 MONTALCINO [SI]
TEL. 057784191
www.frescobaldi.it

Castellare di Castellina
LOC. CASTELLARE
53011 CASTELLINA IN CHIANTI [SI]
TEL. 0577742903
www.castellare.it

ANNUAL PRODUCTION 600,000 bottles
HECTARES UNDER VINE 130
VITICULTURE METHOD Conventional

ANNUAL PRODUCTION 180,000 bottles
HECTARES UNDER VINE 24
VITICULTURE METHOD Conventional

The Montalcino colossus owned by the Frescobaldi family made a good overall show. After all, it boasts first-rate technical staff, headed by Niccolo D'Afflitto, and over 130 hectares of well-aspected vineyards in prime locations. The only possible criticism we could make would be the lack of a true superstar. Among the best of the vintage, the Brunello di Montalcino '02 has a nose with an attractive streak of orange peel that mingles well with hints of chocolate and wild cherry. This is followed by an attractively relaxed palate with good length in a broad, silk-smooth finish. Brunello Ripa del Convento Riserva '01 is utterly different, with a nose that focuses on warm blackcurrant jam and pencil lead. The powerfully extracted palate offers slightly stiff tannins that detract from drinkability. Rosso di Montalcino '05 is very convincing, with warm notes of ripe fruit and a rich palate, characteristics that are shared by Luce '04, a merlot-heavy blend with a touch of sangiovese.

Again this year, Paolo Panerai and his estate manager Alessandro Cellai have received our top accolade. They achieved the feat with a masterly version of I Sodi di San Niccolò '03, one of the most intriguing and charismatic sangiovese-based Supertuscans. The vintage was not a straightforward one for the summer was one of the hottest in recent years and has resulted in very unbalanced wines, particularly in terms of tannins. However, I Sodi has emerged unscathed. The nose immediately yields ripe fruit, broom and rain-soaked earth while the full-bodied palate is perfectly complemented by fine-grained tannins and austere yet lively acidity, finishing long and promising excellent longevity. The two '05 wines submitted, Chianti Classico and the pure merlot Poggio ai Merli, are both outstanding. The first is very true to type, with well-defined berry aromas, a juicy, supple palate and nice tannins, while the latter is still young and consequently a little oaky. The other wines are good.

Wine	Rating
● Brunello di Montalcino '02	♟♟ 7
● Rosso di Montalcino Campo ai Sassi '05	♟♟ 4
● Luce '04	♟♟ 8
● Brunello di Montalcino Ripa al Convento Ris. '01	♟♟ 8
● Brunello di Montalcino '00	♟♟♟ 7
● Luce '94	♟♟♟ 8
● Brunello di Montalcino '98	♟♟ 7
● Brunello di Montalcino '99	♟♟ 7
● Brunello di Montalcino Ripa al Convento '99	♟♟ 8
● Brunello di Montalcino Ris. '95	♟♟ 8

Wine	Rating
● I Sodi di San Niccolò '03	♟♟♟ 8
● Chianti Cl. '05	♟♟ 4
● Poggio ai Merli '05	♟♟ 8
● Coniale '03	♟♟ 7
● Chianti Cl. Ris. '04	♟ 5
● Chianti Cl. V. il Poggiale Ris. '04	♟ 6
● Chianti Cl. V. il Poggiale Ris. '00	♟♟♟ 6
● Chianti Cl. V. il Poggiale Ris. '97	♟♟♟ 6
● I Sodi di San Niccolò '98	♟♟♟ 8
● I Sodi di San Niccolò '97	♟♟♟ 8
● I Sodi di San Niccolò '95	♟♟♟ 8
● I Sodi di San Niccolò '02	♟♟♟ 8
● I Sodi di San Niccolò '01	♟♟♟ 8
● Chianti Cl. V. il Poggiale Ris. '01	♟♟♟ 6

Castelvecchio

LOC. SAN PANCRAZIO
VIA CERTALDESE, 30
50026 SAN CASCIANO IN VAL DI PESA [FI]
TEL. 0558248032
www.castelvecchio.it

ANNUAL PRODUCTION 100,000 bottles
HECTARES UNDER VINE 30
VITICULTURE METHOD Conventional

This year, it was time for the Rocchi family's estate to go into our finals with the Supertuscan Brecciolino '04, based on sangiovese with petit verdot and merlot. This is a sure sign of the progress made in recent years through the unstinting passion invested in the estate by brother-and-sister team Filippo and Stefania, who share the work equally, Filippo looking after the vineyards and cellar operations while Stefania oversees the commercial side. Their achievement is no mean feat for the estate was originally designed for the production of unbottled wine. Then came the turnaround, starting in the vineyards where the vines were ripped out and replaced with the best-suited varieties and clones. After that, it was the cellar's turn. Those efforts are now starting to be repaid with comforting results. Chianti Colli Fiorentini '05 is great, with an inviting, refreshing nose and a well-balanced, juicy body. Numero Otto '06, from pure canaiolo, is singular and intriguing, its alluring nose offering minty notes before a flavoursome, dynamic palate takes you into a nice long finish.

● Il Brecciolino '04	🍷🍷 6
● Numero Otto '06	🍷🍷 5
● Chianti Colli Fiorentini Il Castelvecchio '05	🍷🍷 4
● Chianti Santa Caterina '05	🍷 3
● Il Brecciolino '02	🍷🍷 6
● Il Brecciolino '03	🍷🍷 6

Tenuta Castiglioni

FRAZ. MONTAGNANA VAL DI PESA
VIA MONTEGUFONI, 35
50020 MONTESPERTOLI [FI]
TEL. 0571671387
www.frescobaldi.it

ANNUAL PRODUCTION 1,000,000 bottles
HECTARES UNDER VINE 148
VITICULTURE METHOD Conventional

Tenuta Castiglioni, in the heart of the Florentine hills, represents the beginnings of the Marchesi Frescobaldi story. While not as famous as the family's other estates, it has still made a name for itself in over the past few years for its very sound, well-crafted wines. Giramonte, a merlot and sangiovese blend, stole the limelight, demonstrating a class that had lately become a little tarnished, but thankfully the '05 is back up to standard. The fruit of the elegant, intense nose is well balanced with oak and balsamic notes. Entry on the palate is gutsy, with rich fruit and a very fine tannic texture, before it signs off with a lingering if not particularly deep finish. The '05 Cabernet Sauvignon is also nice, alternating concentrated berry aromas with vegetal and sweet spicy tones. The weighty palate reveals smooth, well-behaved tannins and a very attractive fruity after-aroma. The Chianti '06 has a compact nose and pepper and spice notes layered over a fruity background. On the palate there is complex, well-balanced structure, followed by an appealing full-flavoured finish.

● Chianti '06	🍷🍷 3*
● Cabernet Sauvignon '05	🍷🍷 5
● Giramonte '05	🍷🍷 8
● Giramonte '00	🍷🍷🍷 8
● Giramonte '01	🍷🍷 8
● Giramonte '02	🍷🍷 8
● Cabernet Sauvignon '01	🍷🍷 5
● Giramonte '99	🍷🍷 6
● Giramonte '04	🍷🍷 8
● Giramonte '03	🍷🍷 8
● Cabernet Sauvignon '04	🍷🍷 5
● Cabernet Sauvignon '02	🍷🍷 5
● Cabernet Sauvignon '03	🍷🍷 5

Famiglia Cecchi

LOC. CASINA DEI PONTI, 56
53011 CASTELLINA IN CHIANTI [SI]
TEL. 057754311
www.cecchi.net

ANNUAL PRODUCTION 7,200,000 bottles
HECTARES UNDER VINE 299
VITICULTURE METHOD Certified organic

The Cecchi brothers have achieved consistent results over the past few years by releasing pleasant wines at very reasonable prices. That said, we think the time is ripe for Cesare and Andrea to be a little more daring and offer wines with a bit more personality and character. This is the route that seems to have been taken, with no little success, at the family's Villa Cerna estate, where consistency of results combines with the increasing quest for territory focus, which comes through directly in the wines. We liked the Riserva '04, which offers a bouquet of mineral and fruit aromas that precedes a pleasantly dynamic palate graced by firm but well-integrated tannins and a long finish. Spargolo '04, from pure sangiovese, is also good, with a spicy nose and soft, juicy structure. The rest of the list is well styled, the Chianti Classico Villa Cerna '05 being worthy of special mention.

Centolani

LOC. FRIGGIALI
S.DA MAREMMANA
53024 MONTALCINO [SI]
TEL. 0577849454
info@tenutafriggialiepietranera.it

ANNUAL PRODUCTION 250,000 bottles
HECTARES UNDER VINE 43
VITICULTURE METHOD Conventional

The Centolani winery is split into estates situated at Friggiali, on the western side of Montalcino, and Pietranera, near Castello della Velona, in the Castelnuovo dell'Abate district. The soil types and site climates of the two properties are significantly different so the vinification of their grapes and bottling of their wines are carried out separately. We were captivated by the Brunello Riserva '01, which has a dark hue and pronounced fruit aromas. The fine, close-knit tannins and acidity give focus to the exceptionally deep palate, which powers on purposefully to culminate in a succulent, full finish. Our favourite from the two '02 Brunellos was the Pietranera, which has a more complex nose, with white cherry and spices, and a well-defined, solid palate, with ripe tannins well tucked in. The reverse is true for the '05 Rosso di Montalcino wines: the Friggiali has better balance and an attractive, well-rounded palate.

- Chianti Cl. Villa Cerna Ris. '04 ▼▼ 5
- Spargolo '04 ▼▼ 7
- Chianti Cl.
  Messer Pietro di Teuzzo '05 ▼ 5
- Chianti Cl. Villa Cerna '05 ▼ 4

- Brunello di Montalcino
  Tenuta Friggiali Ris. '01 ▼▼ 8
- Brunello di Montalcino Pietranera '02 ▼▼ 7
- Rosso di Montalcino
  Tenuta Friggiali '05 ▼▼ 4
- Brunello di Montalcino
  Tenuta Friggiali '02 ▼ 6
- Rosso di Montalcino Pietranera '05 ▼ 4
- Brunello di Montalcino
  Tenuta Friggiali Ris. '99 ▼▼▼ 8
- Brunello di Montalcino Pietranera '01 ▼▼ 7
- Brunello di Montalcino Pietranera '99 ▼▼ 7
- Brunello di Montalcino
  Tenuta Friggiali '00 ▼▼ 6
- Brunello di Montalcino Pietranera '97 ▼▼ 7
- Brunello di Montalcino Pietranera '00 ▼▼ 7
- Brunello di Montalcino
  Tenuta Friggiali '01 ▼▼ 6

La Cerbaiola
P.ZZA CAVOUR, 19
53024 MONTALCINO [SI]
TEL. 0577848499

Cerbaiona
LOC. CERBAIONA
53024 MONTALCINO [SI]
TEL. 0577848660

ANNUAL PRODUCTION 15,000 bottles
HECTARES UNDER VINE 4
VITICULTURE METHOD Conventional

Giulio and Mirella Salvioni's winery has not
released a '02 Brunello. The decision was
dictated by the vintage, which the estate did
not consider sufficiently good for the
production of a Brunello worthy of the
name. This major decision in the first place
protects the consumer and consequently
safeguards the winery's image. We will
certainly be left wondering about this 2002
that never saw the light and that could,
perhaps, in the future have given the same
satisfaction offered by minor vintages such
as '87, '89 and '91 when tasted several
years after release. Growth at the estate
continues and the recently extended
vineyards now surround the Salvioni family's
house. The vat cellar is still separate from
the areas used for ageing, which remains in
the original premises in Piazza del
Municipio. All this means that this year, the
sole consolation for the winery's many fans
is the Rosso '05. It, too, comes from a
difficult vintage and the fruit aromas are
somewhat marked by hints of oak. The
palate is dominated by acidity and tannins
that have yet to achieve a perfect balance.

ANNUAL PRODUCTION 15,000 bottles
HECTARES UNDER VINE 3.2
VITICULTURE METHOD Conventional

Diego Molinari surprises you with something
new when you're least expecting it. This
year, it's the return of the winery's Rosso
Montalcino, in the '05 version, following
several years of absence. The winery style is
clearly evident, making it a far from
predictable bottle. It shows a classic deep
ruby, while the nose is dominated by notes
of fruit and autumn leaves. Entry on the
palate is good, carried by alcohol that only
just manages to control the close-knit
tannins. The finish is nicely orchestrated and
lingers, with a finale marked by liquorice
sensations. Brunello di Montalcino '02 is
good, with very clean, well-defined aromas
reminiscent of white cherry and dried
flowers. It is very appealing on the palate,
thanks to a well-gauged balance of
exceptionally elegant tannins and acidity,
and the finish is emphatic, in keeping with
tradition. But the Cerbaiona '04 has little
focus and a sensation of slight dilution on
the finish.

● Rosso di Montalcino '05	♥ 6
● Brunello di Montalcino '00	♥♥♥ 8
● Brunello di Montalcino '85	♥♥♥ 8
● Brunello di Montalcino '97	♥♥♥ 8
● Brunello di Montalcino '99	♥♥♥ 8
● Brunello di Montalcino '98	♥♥ 8
● Rosso di Montalcino '04	♥♥ 6

● Brunello di Montalcino '02	♥♥ 8
● Rosso di Montalcino '05	♥♥ 5
● Cerbaiona '04	♥ 6
● Brunello di Montalcino '01	♥♥♥ 8
● Brunello di Montalcino '99	♥♥♥ 8
● Brunello di Montalcino '90	♥♥♥ 8
● Brunello di Montalcino '97	♥♥♥ 8
● Brunello di Montalcino '98	♥♥ 8
● Brunello di Montalcino '00	♥♥ 8
● Brunello di Montalcino '94	♥♥ 6
● Brunello di Montalcino '93	♥♥ 8

Cerreto Libri

VIA ARETINA, 90
50065 PONTASSIEVE [FI]
TEL. 0558314528
www.cerretolibri.it

ANNUAL PRODUCTION 20,000 bottles
HECTARES UNDER VINE 10
VITICULTURE METHOD Certified biodynamic

This year saw the debut of Cerreto Libri in our Guide. Long present in the Rufina zone, the family-owned winery presented us with an interesting range of well-styled wines. The territory has a long history, having been inhabited since the days of the Etruscans. During the Middle Ages, Rufina had great strategic importance, as is clear from the number of watchtowers that dot the area. The current configuration of the Cerreto Libri estate began with extensive remodelling in the late 1700s, which continued throughout the following century. The agricultural side of the business is carefully monitored by Andrea Zanfei, who decided to switch to biodynamic cultivation methods ten years ago. The two vintages of Chianti Rufina Riserva presented, '03 and '04, are interesting if very different. Gamey notes of leather and fur are evident in the first, which boasts firm body with powerful but well-controlled tannins and a full-flavoured finish. In contrast, the '04 has a subtler, balsam-edged nose, an elegant, well-orchestrated structure and long flavour. Chianti Rufina '05 is also attractive, with a fruity nose and a supple, lively palate. Podernovo '05, a blend of sangiovese and canaiolo, is an upfront pleaser.

Fattoria del Cerro

FRAZ. ACQUAVIVA
VIA GRAZIANELLA, 5
53040 MONTEPULCIANO [SI]
TEL. 0578767722
www.saiagricola.it

ANNUAL PRODUCTION 800,000 bottles
HECTARES UNDER VINE 170
VITICULTURE METHOD Conventional

Fattoria del Cerro's current strategy now focuses exclusively on Montepulciano, marking an end to the production of the Manero and Poggio Golo IGT reds. The seriousness of the estate's commitment and its respect for the hierarchy of the range is confirmed by the excellent results of its Montepulciano wines, starting with the Nobile Antica Chiusina, which retains its historic status as standard-bearer of this winery owned by the Saiagricola group. The '04 vintage effortlessly reached our finals with a complex spectrum of aromatics alternating red and black berry fruit, spices, smoky notes and mineral hints. In the mouth, the attack is restrained, set off by lively tannins and a solid acid backbone, and the fullness is held back only by a tad too much oak at times. Nobile '04 is solid and well balanced, while Nobile Riserva '03 displays a ripe nose and lively flavour. Poggio a Tramontana '06, from pure chardonnay, is a surprising wine, with fresh-tasting, well-coordinated aromas and a rich palate. Corte d'Oro Vendemmia Tardiva '05, from sauvignon, boasts alluring aromas of candied orange and peaches in syrup but is a little lacking in density. The other wines are sound.

Wine	Rating
● Chianti Rufina '05	♈♈ 3*
● Chianti Rufina Ris. '04	♈♈ 5
● Chianti Rufina Ris. '03	♈♈ 5
● Podernovo '05	♈ 5

Wine	Rating
● Nobile di Montepulciano Vign. Antica Chiusina '04	♈♈ 7
○ Corte d'Oro V.T. '05	♈♈ 6
● Nobile di Montepulciano Ris. '03	♈♈ 5
● Nobile di Montepulciano '04	♈♈ 4
○ Braviolo '06	♈ 2
○ Poggio a Tramontana '06	♈ 4
● Rosso di Montepulciano '06	♈ 4
● Chianti Colli Senesi '06	♈ 3
● Nobile di Montepulciano '90	♈♈♈ 4*
● Nobile di Montepulciano Vign. Antica Chiusina '99	♈♈♈ 7
● Nobile di Montepulciano Vign. Antica Chiusina '98	♈♈♈ 7
● Nobile di Montepulciano Vign. Antica Chiusina '00	♈♈♈ 7
● Nobile di Montepulciano Ris. '01	♈♈ 5

Vincenzo Cesani

FRAZ. PANCOLE
VIA PIAZZETTA, 82D
53037 SAN GIMIGNANO [SI]
TEL. 0577955084
www.agriturismo-cesani.com

ANNUAL PRODUCTION   100,000 bottles
HECTARES UNDER VINE 19
VITICULTURE METHOD   Conventional

Vincenzo Cesani is a genuine grower. A frank, proud man, he lets his wines do the talking. His attitude is laudable for his great humility and hard work have earned him the respect of wine lovers and colleagues. Vincenzo's wines continue to charm us, too. Luenzo '04, from sangiovese and colorino, performed well at our tasting finals, confirming its status as the estate's jewel. While not the best version ever, it is nonetheless a wine of great character. It shows spice and ripe fruit on the nose and has a good tannic weave and reasonable complexity, even though it lacks a little depth and length on the finish. Vernaccia Sanice '05 is a confidently executed wine, its nose offering hints of spring flowers, fruit and spices. On the palate, it's not terribly deep but there is softness with occasional mineral hints. The leisurely finish has a slightly tannic aftertaste. The attractive Chianti Colli Senesi '06 is gutsy, fruity and flavoursome while the quality of the well-balanced, pleasant Vernaccia '06 is always dependable.

Ciacci Piccolomini D'Aragona

FRAZ. CASTELNUOVO DELL'ABATE
LOC. MOLINELLO
53024 MONTALCINO [SI]
TEL. 0577835616
www.ciaccipiccolomini.com

ANNUAL PRODUCTION   200,000 bottles
HECTARES UNDER VINE 40
VITICULTURE METHOD   Conventional

Towards the end of the 1980s, this cellar was the first to reveal the potential of the Castelnuovo dell'Abate subzone in the extensive Montalcino district. It continues to be one of the most representative of the entire area, successfully combining a distinctive winery style with the constant improvement of its wines. The latest investments have renewed the barrel stock. This year, the joint efforts of owner Paolo Bianchini and oenologist Paolo Vagaggini have earned Three Glasses for Brunello Pianrosso Riserva '01. A very deep ruby wine, its nose reveals clear and often jammy hints of blackberry and morello cherry before the palate progresses confidently with a richness that emerges in a well-developed crescendo of emotions, followed by a very long, liquorice-lifted finish. The '02 Brunello is another well-crafted offering, with an interesting nose of peaches and florality. While the palate is not sensational, as you would expect from this vintage, it is nonetheless elegant and dynamic, with an intriguingly fresh flavour. Fabius '04 and Rosso '05 are pleasant.

● Luenzo '04	♥♥ 5
○ Vernaccia di S. Gimignano Sanice '05	♥♥ 4
● Chianti Colli Senesi '06	♥ 3*
○ Vernaccia di S. Gimignano '06	♥ 3
● Luenzo '97	♥♥♥ 5
● Luenzo '99	♥♥♥ 5
● Luenzo '00	♥♥ 6
● Luenzo '01	♥♥ 6
● Luenzo '02	♥♥ 6
● Chianti Colli Senesi '05	♥♥ 3*
○ Vernaccia di S. Gimignano Sanice '04	♥♥ 4
● San Gimignano Rosso Cellori '02	♥♥ 6
○ Vernaccia di S. Gimignano Sanice '02	♥♥ 4
● San Gimignano Rosso Cellori '03	♥♥ 6

● Brunello di Montalcino V. di Pianrosso Ris. '01	♥♥♥ 8
● Brunello di Montalcino V. di Pianrosso '02	♥♥ 8
● Sant'Antimo Ateo '04	♥♥ 5
● Rosso di Montalcino '05	♥ 5
● Sant'Antimo Fabius '04	♥ 6
● Brunello di Montalcino V. di Pianrosso '90	♥♥♥ 8
● Brunello di Montalcino V. di Pianrosso Ris. '95	♥♥♥ 6
● Brunello di Montalcino V. di Pianrosso Ris. '99	♥♥♥ 8
● Brunello di Montalcino V. di Pianrosso '98	♥♥♥ 7
● Brunello di Montalcino Ris. '97	♥♥ 8
● Brunello di Montalcino V. di Pianrosso '00	♥♥ 7
● Brunello di Montalcino V. di Pianrosso '01	♥♥ 8
● Brunello di Montalcino V. di Pianrosso '99	♥♥ 7
● Brunello di Montalcino V. di Pianrosso '97	♥♥ 8
● Sant'Antimo Fabius '03	♥♥ 7

Le Cinciole

VIA CASE SPARSE, 83
50020 PANZANO [FI]
TEL. 055852636
www.lecinciole.it

ANNUAL PRODUCTION 43,000 bottles
HECTARES UNDER VINE 11
VITICULTURE METHOD Conventional

Knowing Luca Orsini and his partner in life and business, Valeria Viganò, as well as we do, we are quite sure that the Three Glass award for Camalaione '04, their only sangiovese-free wine, will bring a smile to their faces. Actually, they are both passionate about sangiovese, a difficult vine to understand, work with and express to best effect. In Camalaione, however, it is above all the unique soil and climate of Panzano's Conca d'Oro that shine through. This winner of our top award is a blend of cabernet sauvignon, syrah and merlot, whose nose opens with notes of berry fruit and mixed spice. Entry on the palate is warm and creamy, revealing firm structure and good balance. The finish is sweet and lingers delightfully on the back palate. Riserva Petresco '03 is in good form, although it suffers a little from unbalanced, edgy tannins that tend to curb the finish, despite its awesome backbone. Chianti Classico '05 is well styled and attractive.

Col di Bacche

S.DA DI CUPI
58010 MAGLIANO IN TOSCANA [GR]
TEL. 0577738526
www.coldibacche.com

ANNUAL PRODUCTION 65,000 bottles
HECTARES UNDER VINE 11
VITICULTURE METHOD Conventional

There's no denying it. A Three Glass award from the Guide is source of great satisfaction for any grower. This year, it was the first time for Col di Bacche's Morellino Rovente and the sense of gratification is sure to be felt even more keenly. That said, little has changed as far as we are concerned, for our overall opinion of the work of Alberto Carnasciali in his vineyards in Magliano has always been very high. We would have continued to respect his work even if his wines had missed our highest accolade, as they have done before in the past. The top award not only pays tribute to the cellar's unwavering quality but also to the enhanced fullness of this wine. After finding complete expression of character, elegance, power and fully ripe fruit, it has gone on to acquire those additional elements of complexity that the '05 vintage has drawn directly from the terroir. The rest of the list is very good. Morellino di Scansano '06 is a minor masterpiece of balance and appeal. Bright, crystal-clear aromatics introduce a succulent, well-flavoured palate with sweet hints of crisp fruit. Cupinero '05 has a fine nose and a supple palate.

● Camalaione '04	♟♟♟	8
● Chianti Cl. Petresco Ris. '03	♟♟	6
● Chianti Cl. '05	♟	5
● Chianti Cl. Petresco Ris. '01	♟♟♟	6
● Camalaione '03	♟♟	7
● Chianti Cl. '04	♟♟	5
● Chianti Cl. '01	♟♟	4

● Morellino di Scansano Rovente '05	♟♟♟	5
● Cupinero '05	♟♟	6
● Morellino di Scansano '06	♟♟	4
● Cupinero '02	♟♟	6
● Morellino di Scansano Rovente '03	♟♟	5
● Morellino di Scansano Rovente '04	♟♟	5
● Cupinero '01	♟♟	5
● Morellino di Scansano Rovente '02	♟♟	5
● Cupinero '03	♟♟	6
● Cupinero '04	♟♟	6

★ Tenuta Col d'Orcia
LOC. SANT'ANGELO IN COLLE
53020 MONTALCINO [SI]
TEL. 057780891
www.coldorcia.it

ANNUAL PRODUCTION 800,000 bottles
HECTARES UNDER VINE 142
VITICULTURE METHOD Conventional

This year, Tenuta Col d'Orcia earned two coveted awards. The first was bestowed by the Montepulciano winegrowers, who elected its owner Marone Cinzano president of the Consorzio, while the second was our Three Glasses for the newly released Brunello di Montalcino Poggio al Vento '99. Never was a long wait so justly rewarded, for the wine has achieved truly extraordinary balance and perfection. The classic hue has slightly garnet highlights, while its nose flaunts very ripe cherry notes and more developed hints of tobacco and medicinal herbs with remarkably attractive aromatic complexity. On the palate, the elegant, strikingly well tucked in tannins accompany a fullness worthy of a truly superlative wine. All of this is supported by exemplary acidity, which will sustain the wine throughout its long life. Rosso di Montalcino Banditella '04 is very good, with a complex nose of spices, blackberry and cherries, and a rich, juicy palate. We were also impressed by Sant'Antimo Nearco '03, a merlot, cabernet sauvignon and syrah blend. Brunello '02, Rosso degli Spezieri '06, from sangiovese, cabernet and ciliegiolo, and Rosso '05 are all pleasing.

Colle Massari
LOC. POGGI DEL SASSO
58044 CINIGIANO [GR]
TEL. 0564990496
www.collemassari.it

ANNUAL PRODUCTION 250,000 bottles
HECTARES UNDER VINE 66
VITICULTURE METHOD Certified organic

Claudio Tipa and his sister Maria Iris Tipa Bertarelli have created one of Tuscany's finest wineries. Set in a wild, incredibly beautiful area in the heart of the huge Montecucco zone, Colle Massari extends over 66 hectares of vineyards that produce different types of wines and includes a very modern cellar that blends modestly into the local surroundings. The '04 Montecucco Rosso Colle Massari Riserva, from sangiovese, ciliegiolo and cabernet sauvignon, is the best version to date. This complex wine, with a mineral nose and a full, powerful palate, is in a class of its own. Montecucco Rosso Rigoleto '05, from sangiovese, ciliegiolo and montepulciano, is simpler and more approachable. The fragrant, easy-drinking Grottolo '06 and Montecucco Vermentino Le Melacce '06 are both pleasant. Irisse '05, the estate's other Montecucco Vermentino, which is briefly aged in small oak casks, is firmer and a little more ambitious.

● Brunello di Montalcino Poggio al Vento Ris. '99	♈♈♈ 8
● Rosso di Montalcino Banditella '04	♈♈ 5
● Sant'Antimo Nearco '03	♈♈ 6
● Brunello di Montalcino '02	♈ 6
● Rosso degli Spezieri '06	♈ 3*
● Rosso di Montalcino '05	♈ 4
● Brunello di Montalcino Poggio al Vento Ris. '90	♈♈♈ 8
● Brunello di Montalcino Poggio al Vento Ris. '95	♈♈♈ 8
● Brunello di Montalcino Poggio al Vento Ris. '97	♈♈♈ 8
● Olmaia '94	♈♈♈ 7
● Olmaia '01	♈♈♈ 7
● Olmaia '00	♈♈♈ 7
● Brunello di Montalcino '01	♈♈ 6
● Nearco '00	♈♈ 7

● Montecucco Rosso Colle Massari Ris. '04	♈♈ 6
● Montecucco Rosso Rigoleto '05	♈♈ 4
● Grottolo '06	♈ 3
O Montecucco Vermentino Le Melacce '06	♈ 3
O Montecucco Vermentino Irisse '05	♈ 4
● Montecucco Rosso Colle Massari Ris. '03	♈♈ 6

Collelungo

LOC. COLLELUNGO
53011 CASTELLINA IN CHIANTI [SI]
TEL. 0577740489
www.collelungo.com

ANNUAL PRODUCTION 30,000 bottles
HECTARES UNDER VINE 20
VITICULTURE METHOD Conventional

The estate owned by the Cattelans, husband and wife, forges steadily ahead. This year, the wines performed well, with the first-rate Chianti Classico '05 deserving a special mention because of the challenges of the vintage. Over the past few years, we have observed a gradual change in the style of the wines submitted, with a move from massively concentrated products that gave rise to rich, velvety sensations to more relaxed, approachably enjoyable structure. There is still much room for improvement on the nose, which is short on finesse and elegance, but that will be the next objective. We liked the Riserva '04, which gives balsam and forest fruits, such as blackberries and currants, followed by fullness in the mouth and well-integrated tannins that lead into a sweet, lingering finish. Riserva Campo Cerchi '03 is less convincing. It has plenty of structure but lacks balance. The dependable Merlot '05 is rather untypical on nose and palate with its fresh-tasting minerality. Vin Santo Invidia '04 is pleasant but somewhat lacking in unctuousness and sweetness.

● Chianti Cl. '05	▼▼	4
● Chianti Cl. Ris. '04	▼▼	5
● Chianti Cl. Campo Cerchi Ris. '03	▼	8
● Merlot '05	▼	5
○ Vin Santo del Chianti Cl. Invidia '04	▼	6
● Chianti Cl. Ris. '03	▽▽	5
● Chianti Cl. Campo Cerchi Ris. '00	▽▽	8

Collemattoni

LOC. SANT'ANGELO IN COLLE
POD. COLLEMATTONI, 100
53020 MONTALCINO [SI]
TEL. 0577844127
www.collemattoni.it

ANNUAL PRODUCTION 35,000 bottles
HECTARES UNDER VINE 6.7
VITICULTURE METHOD Conventional

Marcello Bucci continues to produce great wines in his cellar facing the village of Sant'Angelo in Colle. Brunello Fontelontano Riserva '01 repeated the triumph of the '99 version and picked up our highest honour. We were more than happy to award Three Glasses to this wine, which is a tribute to the area's Brunello tradition. The name Collemattoni comes from the winery's proximity to a spring in a sunny location, which was used by the local population until the 1940s. Vinification is in the classic manner, without excessive maceration, and the wine ages in medium-sized Slavonian oak barrels. A deep ruby hue introduces an intense, well-rounded nose offering well-defined aromas with distinct notes of peach and berries against a pleasantly balsamic backdrop. The attractive acid-tannic structure and rich, intense finish hint at excellent cellarability. In short, this is a wine that combines weight and elegance, not least because of its bell-clear nose-palate consistency. We also liked the Rosso '05, which was one of the best tasted this year, and were intrigued by the pleasant, reasonably priced Adone '06.

● Brunello di Montalcino Fontelontano Ris. '01	▼▼▼	7
● Rosso di Montalcino '05	▼▼	4*
● Adone '06	▼	3
● Brunello di Montalcino '02	▼	6
● Brunello di Montalcino '01	▽▽▽	6
● Brunello di Montalcino '00	▽▽	6
● Brunello di Montalcino Fontelontano Ris. '99	▽▽	7
● Brunello di Montalcino '99	▽▽	6
● Rosso di Montalcino '04	▽▽	4

Colognole

LOC. COLOGNOLE
VIA DEL PALAGIO, 15
50068 RUFINA [FI]
TEL. 0558319870
www.colognole.it

ANNUAL PRODUCTION   100,000 bottles
HECTARES UNDER VINE 27
VITICULTURE METHOD   Conventional

Following its return to the Guide last year, the estate owned by the Spalletti Trivelli family has now won our ultimate honour with an excellent performance by its Chianti Rufina Riserva del Don '04. Brothers Mario and Cesare Coda Nunziante form a winning team, with the former managing agricultural and cellar operations and the latter the commercial side. The arrival of Andrea Giovannini as consultant oenologist has coincided with a change in the style of the wines, which are still territory-dedicated but now display considerably more finesse on the nose and more balanced structure. The estate's history is fairly recent. It was purchased by Venceslao Spalletti Trivelli, a forebear of current owner Gabriella, mother of Cesare and Mario, at the end of the 19th century after he had been appointed senator. The Riserva has a rich nose that focuses on tertiary notes of fur and leather, firm body, good structure, crisp tannins and a very flavoursome finish. Chianti Rufina '05 is extremely drinkable while Quattro Chiacchere '04, from chardonnay, is pleasant in the mouth but slightly overripe on the nose.

Il Colombaio di Cencio

LOC. CORNIA
53013 GAIOLE IN CHIANTI [SI]
TEL. 0577747178
colombaiodicencio@tin.it

ANNUAL PRODUCTION   100,000 bottles
HECTARES UNDER VINE 25
VITICULTURE METHOD   Conventional

While last year we were mistaken in saying that Il Colombaio di Cencio did not hit a high note when in fact its Riserva won the Three Glass award, this is sadly not the case this year. Indeed, the high note was missing altogether this time. Despite punching its full weight again, the finalist – this time Futuro '04, a blend of sangiovese, cabernet sauvignon and merlot – did not manage to go the full distance and pick up a top honour. Elegant aromas laced with intriguing spiciness combine with nice hints of fruit and a soft, silky body but then the palate reveals a bit of a hole in the middle, before recovering backbone in the finish. Riserva I Massi '04 is also pleasant, with an elegant, powerful nose. Entry on the palate is tasty and there is a nice roundness to the body and pleasant length. Still, these results confirm that Il Colombaio di Cencio is on the right track with Riserva I Massi. The wine is always of the highest quality, with the exception of those vintages with less favourable weather. We also liked two other products: the Monticello '04, a sort of "second vin" to Futuro, given that it is made from the same blend; and the pure chardonnay Sassobianco '06.

● Chianti Rufina Ris. del Don '04	♟♟	5
● Chianti Rufina '05	♟	4
○ Quattro Chiacchere '04	♟	5
● Chianti Rufina '01	♟♟	3
● Chianti Rufina '02	♟♟	4
● Chianti Rufina Ris. del Don '03	♟♟	5

● Il Futuro '04	♟♟	7
● Chianti Cl. I Massi Ris. '04	♟♟	6
● Monticello '04	♟	4
○ Sassobianco '06	♟	4

Il Colombaio di Santa Chiara
LOC. SAN DONATO, 1
53037 SAN GIMIGNANO [SI]
TEL. 0577942004
www.colombaiosantachiara.it

ANNUAL PRODUCTION 25,000 bottles
HECTARES UNDER VINE 3.5
VITICULTURE METHOD Conventional

Following last year's achievement, the Logi brothers have confirmed their presence in our Guide with a fine performance that derives directly from their passion for viticulture and the skills accumulated by their father Mario during his long career as a grower-producer. The aim has always been to produce genuine, true-to-type wines at reasonable prices. Vernaccia Selvabianca '06 is very expressive, with a floral nose, full, piquant flavour and a typical almondy finish. Vernaccia Albereta '06 is splendidly crafted, its oak tones never overpowering the fruit. It's soft, well balanced and displays good progression. San Gimignano Colombaio '04, from sangiovese, canaiolo and colorino, has made a great leap forwards and now boasts an intense, elegant, spicy nose and dense, fleshy flavour braced by succulent, fine-grained tannins. Il Priore '05, a blend of sangiovese and canaiolo, is charming. The character of the sangiovese is fully discernible on the palate, although the nose is rather blurred. The rest of the list is well styled and goodish.

Fattoria Le Corti
LOC. LE CORTI
VIA SAN PIERO DI SOTTO, 1
50026 SAN CASCIANO IN VAL DI PESA [FI]
TEL. 055829301
www.principecorsini.com

ANNUAL PRODUCTION 230,000 bottles
HECTARES UNDER VINE 50
VITICULTURE METHOD Conventional

Two of the wines produced by Duccio Corsini's estate reached our finals. Although neither netted the Three Glass award, the winery can be satisfied with the overall result. Interesting growth can be seen across the range and the wines display character and personality. Products from the Maremma estate have reached maturity, managing to stand out and assert their territorial provenance. Chianti Classico Don Tommaso '04 is perhaps a little short on cleanliness on the nose, which reveals vegetal tones and ripe fruit such as plum, but tightens up on the austere palate with a long and convincing finish. Marsiliana '04, from cabernet sauvignon, merlot and sangiovese, presents an aromatic spectrum dominated by animal notes and autumn leaves. Entry on the palate is very nice, full and pervasive but it falls down a little on the finish, which is slightly cropped. The two basic wines, Chianti Classico '05 and Birillo '05, a pure Maremma sangiovese, are very pleasant. We were also impressed by Riserva Cortevecchia '04, with clear berry fruit and floral aromas, attractive body, smooth tannins and a lip-smacking finish.

O Vernaccia di San Gimignano Selvabianca '06	♟♟ 3*
● S. Gimignano Rosso Colombaio '04	♟♟ 5
O Vernaccia di S. Gimignano Albereta '06	♟♟ 4
● Il Priore '05	♟ 4
● Il Priore '04	♟♟ 4
O Vernaccia di S. Gimignano Albereta '05	♟♟ 4
O Vernaccia di San Gimignano Selvabianca '05	♟♟ 3*

● Chianti Cl. Don Tommaso '04	♟♟ 6
● Marsiliana '04	♟♟ 6
● Chianti Cl. Cortevecchia Ris. '04	♟♟ 5
● Birillo '05	♟ 4
● Chianti Cl. '05	♟ 4
● Marsiliana '01	♟♟ 6
● Marsiliana '02	♟♟ 6
● Marsiliana '03	♟♟ 6
● Chianti Cl. '04	♟♟ 4
● Chianti Cl. Don Tommaso '03	♟♟ 6

Fattoria Corzano e Paterno

FRAZ. SAN PRANCAZIO
VIA PATERNO, 8
50020 SAN CASCIANO IN VAL DI PESA [FI]
TEL. 0558248179
www.corzanoepaterno.it

ANNUAL PRODUCTION 75,000 bottles
HECTARES UNDER VINE 16
VITICULTURE METHOD Conventional

Fattoria di Corzano e Paterno, expertly directed by Alioscia Goldschmidt, once again confirmed its consistent high quality with a very interesting range of wines. Corzano '04, from sangiovese, cabernet and merlot, is in a class of its own and strolled straight into our national finals. It is a wine of great typicity that reveals its naturalness, forthrightness and territorial provenance during tasting. On the palate, it appealingly combines the rugged fullness typical of sangiovese with the softness and elegance of the Bordeaux varieties. The finish is long and flavoursome. Chianti I Tre Borri Riserva '03 is almost as impressive. Long ageing has smoothed out the edginess of the tannins and the palate presents warm and silky, with harmonious progression, rich flavour and a long finish. Passito '98 is a sensorial treat for the nose while the palate has striking finesse and well-calibrated sweetness, leading into a deep, lingering finish. The forthright, approachable Chianti Terre di Corzano '05 is well coordinated, flavoursome and an early drinker.

Cupano

LOC. CAMIGLIANO
PODERE CENTINE, 31
53024 MONTALCINO [SI]
TEL. 0577816055
cupano@cupano.it

ANNUAL PRODUCTION 11,000 bottles
HECTARES UNDER VINE 3.1
VITICULTURE METHOD Certified organic

The estate is located on the far south-west side of Montalcino, near the village of Camigliano. It was founded several years ago and has always offered innovative, modern, territory-focused wines. In the cellar, small wooden casks are the norm while the vineyards have always been organically managed. The subzone faces towards Maremma and so is the warmest and sunniest of the entire district. Indeed, in the past the grapes have sometimes been overripe, which has held back the aromas in particular. But there is no trace of any of this in the wines submitted this year, which are the products of fairly cool vintages. Brunello di Montalcino '02 is very attractive, with a nose still displaying slight notes of toast, coffee and chocolate from the oak while the assertive palate is very attractive. Rosso '04 is excellent, with a fruity, floral nose that unveils very subtle, almost imperceptible hints of oak. The supple, juicy palate is extremely convincing.

● Il Corzano '04	▼▼ 6
● Chianti I Tre Borri Ris. '03	▼▼ 6
○ Passito di Corzano '98	▼▼ 7
● Chianti Terre di Corzano '05	▼ 4
● Il Corzano '97	♟♟♟ 5
● Chianti I Tre Borri '99	♟♟ 6
○ Vin Santo '94	♟♟ 6
○ Passito di Corzano '97	♟♟ 7
○ Passito di Corzano '96	♟♟ 7
● Il Corzano '99	♟♟ 6
● Chianti Terre di Corzano '03	♟♟ 4
● Il Corzano '00	♟♟ 7
● Il Corzano '02	♟♟ 5
● Il Corzano '03	♟♟ 6
● Il Corzano '01	♟♟ 6
○ Passito di Corzano '95	♟♟ 6

● Rosso di Montalcino '04	▼▼ 6
● Brunello di Montalcino '02	▼▼ 8

La Cura

LOC. CURA NUOVA, 12
58024 MASSA MARITTIMA [GR]
TEL. 0566918094
lacuramonteregio@email.it

ANNUAL PRODUCTION 30,000 bottles
HECTARES UNDER VINE 5
VITICULTURE METHOD Conventional

It seems as though the way to truly consistent quality is now completely clear for the estate owned by the skilful Enrico Corsi, who every year continues to present a range of well-made wines with plenty of personality. The elegant, well-styled La Cura, from merlot only, is perhaps still the cellar's best wine. The '05 version expresses fresh, well-honed aromas and a lively palate marked by attractive acid vein and disturbed only by a touch too much oak. Monteregio Breccerosse '06 is firm with a fine Mediterranean character, deep, concentrated aromas and a supple, juicy palate. Predicatore '06 is a very interesting sweet wine made mainly from late-harvested merlot with a small addition of aleatico. It is the fruit of a joint venture with the University of Pisa, which attractively combines the softness of the Bordeaux grape with the fragrance of the variety grown on the Tuscan coast. The results are original and very pleasing. Trinus '06 is a fragrant, flavoursome blend of chardonnay, trebbiano and malvasia. Valdemàr '06, from malvasia and trebbiano, is uncomplicated and coherent.

Tenimenti Luigi D'Alessandro

VIA DI MANZANO, 15
52042 CORTONA [AR]
TEL. 0575618667
www.tenimentidalessandro.it

ANNUAL PRODUCTION 150,000 bottles
HECTARES UNDER VINE 50
VITICULTURE METHOD Conventional

We'll start by mentioning an important new feature in the ownership of the winery: Francesco D'Alessandro has been replaced by Giuseppe Calabresi, an old friend of Massimo D'Alessandro. The change should not result in any dramatic differences in the range or the dynamics that have allowed the estate to become a leading force in promoting the image of the recently created Cortona DOC zone over the past few years. Il Bosco is one of the first names that come to mind, in terms of quality and consistency, when you're talking about syrah in Italy today. The decision to delay the release and presentation of the '04 vintage to allow longer ageing was wise one, as our tasting revealed. This Syrah comes from a hot subzone, where it acquires plenty of colour, structure and weight. Not that all this holds it back for the nose is fresh and full with dark fruit that merges well with intriguing spicy, balsamic notes. On the palate, it is deep, balanced, full flavoured and consistent. Already, it fully deserves our Three Glass award but it will certainly acquire further complexity as the years go by. Syrah '05 is more approachable while Fontarca '05 is pleasant.

● La Cura Merlot '05	▼▼ 5
○ Predicatore '06	▼▼ 5
○ Trinus '06	▼▼ 4
● Monteregio di Massa Marittima Rosso Breccerosse '06	▼ 4
○ Valdemàr '06	▼ 3
● La Cura Merlot '04	♟♟ 5
● La Cura Merlot '02	♟♟ 5
○ Trinus '05	♟♟ 4
● La Cura Merlot '03	♟♟ 5

● Cortona Il Bosco '04	▼▼▼ 7
○ Fontarca '05	▼ 5
● Cortona Syrah '05	▼ 4
● Cortona Il Bosco '01	♟♟♟ 7
● Cortona Il Bosco '03	♟♟♟ 7
● Podere Il Bosco '97	♟♟♟ 5
● Podere Il Bosco '95	♟♟♟ 5
● Podere Il Bosco '99	♟♟ 6
○ Vin Santo '94	♟♟ 6
● Cortona Il Bosco '00	♟♟ 6

Maria Caterina Dei
VIA DI MARTIENA, 35
53045 MONTEPULCIANO [SI]
TEL. 0578716878
www.cantinedei.com

Tenuta Di Sesta
FRAZ. CASTELNUOVO DELL'ABATE
LOC. SESTA
53020 MONTALCINO [SI]
TEL. 0577835612
www.tenutadisesta.it

ANNUAL PRODUCTION 140,000 bottles
HECTARES UNDER VINE 44
VITICULTURE METHOD Conventional

ANNUAL PRODUCTION 120,000 bottles
HECTARES UNDER VINE 30
VITICULTURE METHOD Conventional

There was a prominent absentee among Maria Caterina Dei's wines this year. There was no '05 version of the Sancta Catharina as the cellar considered the quality of the grapes from this vintage inadequate for such an important wine. Although this decision was undoubtedly difficult, it is further proof that the Villa Martiena estate is one of the Montepulciano wineries that keep their eye firmly on quality. Of the wines we did taste, Nobile di Montepulciano Bossona Riserva emerged head and shoulders above the rest to make it into our finals. The '03 version has an elegant nose with fine cohesion between the plentiful fruit and smoky notes, lifted by tantalizing hints of pencil lead. Tight-knit and full-bodied on the palate, honed by vibrant, well-sustained acidity and tasty tannins. Although still very young, this Nobile has enormous potential for ageing, as indeed is typical of Caterina Dei's wines. Nobile '04 is very well styled, with subtle and clean aromas and a deep, dynamic palate. The approachable and extremely tasty Rosso di Montepulciano '06 is delightful and in no way banal.

Giovanni Ciacci's estate presented a very convincing range of wines, revealing that the modernization of the winery commenced a few years ago is bearing its fruits. The entire section used for ageing the wines is brand new, featuring medium and large Slavonian oak barrels but no barriques, which Giovanni does not consider suitable for the sangiovese of this area. Replanting of the vineyards has also been completed and almost the entire area under vine is now productive. Brunello Riserva '01 is excellent. Wild cherry jam, blackberry and Mediterranean herbs define the nose, evoking the wonderful subzone of Sesta. The superior tannins are well coordinated and alcohol gets the upper hand towards the end but without diluting the finish. Brunello '02 is also very good, with aromas reminiscent of peach and cherry. The palate is pleasant and well calibrated, supported by fresh acidity that lengthens the finish. Poggio d'Arna '05 is held back by rather excessive extract.

Wine	Rating
● Nobile di Montepulciano Bossona Ris. '03	▼▼ 6
● Nobile di Montepulciano '04	▼▼ 5
● Rosso di Montepulciano '06	▼▼ 4
● Nobile di Montepulciano Bossona Ris. '01	♀♀ 6
● Nobile di Montepulciano Ris. '97	♀♀ 5
● Nobile di Montepulciano Bossona Ris. '99	♀♀ 6
● Nobile di Montepulciano Ris. '98	♀♀ 5
● Sancta Catharina '03	♀♀ 6
● Sancta Catharina '01	♀♀ 6
● Sancta Catharina '00	♀♀ 6
● Sancta Catharina '04	♀♀ 6

Wine	Rating
● Brunello di Montalcino Ris. '01	▼▼ 8
● Brunello di Montalcino '02	▼▼ 6
● Poggio d'Arna '05	▼ 4
● Brunello di Montalcino '01	♀♀ 7
● Brunello di Montalcino Ris. '95	♀♀ 8
● Brunello di Montalcino '00	♀♀ 6
● Brunello di Montalcino Ris. '97	♀♀ 8
● Brunello di Montalcino '99	♀♀ 7
● Brunello di Montalcino Ris. '99	♀♀ 8

Fattoria di Dievole

VIA DIEVOLE, 6
53010 CASTELNUOVO BERARDENGA [SI]
TEL. 0577322613
www.dievole.it

ANNUAL PRODUCTION 550,000 bottles
HECTARES UNDER VINE 90
VITICULTURE METHOD Conventional

This year's performance is further confirmation of the success of the Schwenn family, which is continuing along the path it has taken in recent years: greater precision in cellar operations combined with increasingly meticulous care of the vineyards, which stand in excellent wine country near Castelnuovo Berardenga. We would go as far as to say that, unlike the past when the winery invested heavily in advertising, it now pays more attention to substance than to form. Our favourite wines were the two Chianti Classico Riservas. Novecento '04 boasts ripe-fruit aromas and is more austere on the palate, with rich, full body and firm, well-integrated tannins, while Dielulele '04 has a fresher nose with notes of aromatic herbs and a bright, juicy palate. The easy-drinking Chianti Classico La Vendemmia '05 is lively and refreshing, with fruit and flower notes and a spirited palate. We were less impressed by Broccato '03, a sangiovese-heavy blend, which is stiffened by edgy tannins, despite its attractively full body.

Casato Prime Donne
Donatella Cinelli Colombini

LOC. CASATO
53024 MONTALCINO [SI]
TEL. 0577849421
www.cinellicolombini.it

ANNUAL PRODUCTION 160,000 bottles
HECTARES UNDER VINE 37
VITICULTURE METHOD Conventional

Donatella Cinelli Colombini manages to run her estate despite her countless other activities. We applaud the dynamism of a woman who again sent a wine to our finals this year, the delectable Brunello Riserva '01. The fruity nose displays intriguing hints of pencil lead and cinchona. Entry on the palate is more leisurely and the close-knit tannic weave is perfectly contrasted by the alcohol, ending with a lingering finish. For the first time, the winery submitted its Montalcino Prime Donne '02, which closely resembles many of the best Brunellos of the same vintage. This is because Donatella was unconvinced by the Brunello '02 and downgraded it to Rosso, with a price to match despite the long ageing. The oak can be perceived in the notes of cocoa and vanilla that mingle with fruity sensations of white cherry. On the palate, the wine is marked out by its elegance, balance and pleasant drinkability that lead to a succulent, satisfying finish. Rosso di Montalcino '05 is more straightforward.

● Chianti Cl. Novecento Ris. '04	▼▼	6
● Chianti Cl. Dieulele Ris. '04	▼▼	6
● Broccato '03	▼	6
● Chianti Cl. La Vendemmia '05	▼	5
● Chianti Cl. Dieulele Ris. '01	♈♈	5

● Brunello di Montalcino Ris. '01	▼▼	7
● Rosso di Montalcino Prime Donne '02	▼▼	5
● Rosso di Montalcino '05	▼	5
● Brunello di Montalcino Prime Donne '01	♈♈♈	7
● Brunello di Montalcino Ris. '00	♈♈	7
● Brunello di Montalcino Ris. '98	♈♈	7
● Brunello di Montalcino '00	♈♈	6
● Brunello di Montalcino Prime Donne '00	♈♈	7
● Brunello di Montalcino Ris. '99	♈♈	7
● Brunello di Montalcino '99	♈♈	6
● Brunello di Montalcino Prime Donne '99	♈♈	7

Donna Olga

LOC. FRIGGIALI
S.DA MAREMMANA
53024 MONTALCINO [SI]
TEL. 0577849454
www.donnaolga.com

ANNUAL PRODUCTION 27,000 bottles
HECTARES UNDER VINE 4
VITICULTURE METHOD Conventional

Olga Peluso, the go-getting owner of this estate, continues to present wines that are paragons of solidity and territory focus. After a little stylistic indecision during the early years of production, they now elegantly embody their Montalcino terroir. Olga's flair for patronage has prompted her to fund the shows of up-and-coming Italian artists who will be able to display their works in special areas of the winery during the summer. Each year, one of them will design a label that will be applied to a limited number of bottles. This year, the estate presented a single, great wine: Brunello Riserva '01. It's a wine of substance, which took our Three Glass award hands down. The nose is rich, with evident notes of morello cherry, along with other red berries and a charming streak of aromatic herbs. Perfectly ripened grapes ensure an excellent initial impact on the palate, which develops elegantly and assuredly, largely due to the perfectly balanced acidity. The finish has great character, with superlative, mellow tannins.

Il Faggeto

FRAZ. SANT'ALBINO
VIA FONTELELLERA
53045 MONTEPULCIANO [SI]
TEL. 3343986357
www.baroncini.it

ANNUAL PRODUCTION 180,000 bottles
HECTARES UNDER VINE 7.5
VITICULTURE METHOD Conventional

Il Faggeto put on a very respectable performance this year. The range of wines presented by the Montalcino estate of the Baroncini family, long-established Tuscan winemakers based in San Gimignano, combined impressive quality with personality and its star touched absolute excellence. We're talking about the Nobile Pietra Nera Riserva '03, which steamed into our finals. It flaunts an attractive complex nose, distinguished by concentrated, clean berry aromas with elegantly integrated hints of sweet spices and vanilla. Development in the mouth is full, continuous and well defined, with just a touch of dryness on the finish. The Nobile '04 has a balanced, basically elegant nose and is firm and full, although not particularly complex. Rosso di Montepulciano Lupaio '06 is also very good and indeed among the best of its type, showing a fresh, fruity nose and lively contrasting palate. We also liked the pleasantly drinkable Chianti Colli Senesi Fortilizio '06, which has an uncomplicated nose and palate. Fontanile '06, a blend of malvasia and sauvignon blanc, is refreshing and zesty.

● Brunello di Montalcino Ris. '01	▼▼▼ 8
● Brunello di Montalcino Donna Olga '01	♀♀♀ 7
● Brunello di Montalcino Donna Olga '98	♀♀ 8
● Brunello di Montalcino Donna Olga '97	♀♀ 7
● Rosso di Montalcino '04	♀♀ 4
● Brunello di Montalcino Donna Olga '99	♀♀ 7

● Nobile di Montepulciano Pietra Nera Ris. '03	♀♀ 6
● Nobile di Montepulciano Pietra del Diavolo '04	♀♀ 4
● Rosso di Montepulciano Lupaio '06	♀♀ 3
● Chianti Colli Senesi Governato Fortilizio '06	♀ 3
○ Fontanile '06	♀ 4
● Nobile di Montepulciano Pietra del Diavolo '02	♀♀ 4
● Nobile di Montepulciano Pietra del Diavolo '03	♀♀ 5

Fanti - San Filippo

FRAZ. CASTELNUOVO DELL'ABATE
POD. PALAZZO
53020 MONTALCINO [SI]
TEL. 0577835795
balfanti@tin.it

ANNUAL PRODUCTION 150,000 bottles
HECTARES UNDER VINE 50
VITICULTURE METHOD Conventional

Baldassarre Filippo Fanti, known as Sarrino, has completed his long term as president of the Consorzio del Brunello after ten years, a record performance, especially considering that it was only the statute that prevented his re-election for the umpteenth time! During his tenure, Fanti has contributed to elevating Brunello to cult status, making it an emblem of Italian quality worldwide. In the meantime, he has not been neglecting his estate, as is demonstrated by the fame it has achieved. Renovation has included the construction of a huge, well-camouflaged new cellar and major expansion of the area under vine. This year, the cellar released its Brunello '02, a pleasant wine overall, with a nose marked by a little greenness and underripe fruit, and a juicy but slightly lightweight palate. Sant'Antimo Rosso '05 performed better, with lightly toasted caramel notes on a fruit background with herbaceous and balsamic tones. The palate is stylish and full, with sweet tannins offering an elegant finish.

Farnetella

S.DA SIENA-BETTOLLE, KM 37
53048 SINALUNGA [SI]
TEL. 0577355117
www.felsina.it

ANNUAL PRODUCTION 236,000 bottles
HECTARES UNDER VINE 60
VITICULTURE METHOD Conventional

This estate, owned by Fattoria di Felsina, is back in our Guide and its standard-bearer, Poggio Granoni '04, a sangiovese, cabernet sauvignon, merlot and syrah blend, confidently reached our finals. Farnetella's entire range is sound and would benefit from greater distinctiveness. These well-styled wines lack the elegant note that so impressed us in the beginning. Nonetheless, they still express their provenance well, albeit in a more rustic and less clearly defined manner. The finalist's nose is characterized by vegetal aromas and notes of bell pepper. Entry on the palate is warm and fresh, if not overly powerful, and the finish is sweet but not enormously long. We also liked Lucilla '05, a blend based largely on sangiovese and cabernet sauvignon, which can point to attractive balsamic notes on the nose and pleasing juiciness on the palate. The remaining wines in the range are reliably sound, with the Nero di Nubi '03 a cut above the rest.

● Sant'Antimo Rosso '05	♀♀ 4
● Brunello di Montalcino '02	♀ 7
● Rosso di Montalcino '05	♀ 4
● Brunello di Montalcino '00	♀♀♀ 7
● Brunello di Montalcino '97	♀♀♀ 7
● Brunello di Montalcino '01	♀♀ 7
● Brunello di Montalcino '98	♀♀ 7

● Poggio Granoni '04	♀♀ 8
● Lucilla '05	♀♀ 4
● Chianti Colli Senesi '05	♀ 4
● Nero di Nubi '03	♀ 5
○ Sauvignon '05	♀ 4
● Poggio Granoni '01	♀♀ 6
● Lucilla '03	♀♀ 4
● Nero di Nubi '01	♀♀ 5

Fassati

FRAZ. GRACCIANO
VIA DI GRACCIANELLO, 3A
53040 MONTEPULCIANO [SI]
TEL. 0578708708
www.fazibattaglia.com

ANNUAL PRODUCTION 800,000 bottles
HECTARES UNDER VINE 85
VITICULTURE METHOD Conventional

Fassati, the Montepulciano estate owned by
Fazi Battaglia, gave a comfortingly solid
performance confirming the high quality of
its wines, although this year the usually well-
calibrated oak conditioning seems to have
increased across the entire range. The best
wines were the three Nobiles: Pasiteo '04,
which has a well-adjusted nose and
flavoursome palate, despite having lost a
little of its usual personality; Gersemi '04,
with fine structure and generous tannins,
although the oak support still intrudes; and
Salarco Riserva '03, with a warm, pervasive
nose and a relaxed, tasty palate. Rosso di
Montepulciano Selciaia '06 is supple and
well rounded but we also enjoyed the lower-
key sangiovese rosé Spigo '06. The
Maremma wines produced by the Greto
delle Fate estate are new to the Guide this
year. Situated in the Tuscan town of
Magliano, the property currently has 11
hectares under vine. Morellino '06 already
has good character, with an intense nose
and flavoursome palate. Our tasters also
liked Vermentino '06, which is very simple
but has nice freshness and tanginess.

Fattoi

LOC. SANTA RESTITUTA
POD. CAPANNA, 101
53024 MONTALCINO [SI]
TEL. 0577848613
www.fattoi.it

ANNUAL PRODUCTION 45,000 bottles
HECTARES UNDER VINE 9
VITICULTURE METHOD Conventional

Fattoi performed very well this year. Credit
must go to the solidly consistent range of
wines presented, which managed to
embody all the cellar's true potential. None
of this, though, is down to chance. The
wines that we tasted are the fruit of massive
investment over time in the general
renovation of the winery, particularly the
barrel stock, and greater attention to the
selection of raw materials. Fattoi's vineyards
are located in one of the best zones on the
western side of Montalcino, near the church
of Santa Restituta, where the clay gives way
to more stony soil. The Brunello Riserva '01
is very traditional. After a little aeration, the
wine discloses aromas of tobacco, leather
and medicinal herbs, while the palate has
good body supported by perfectly gauged
acidity, which supports development
through to a lingering finish. The '02
Brunello is also good and fruit-led on the
nose. The juicy, eminently drinkable Rosso
'05 is among the best from the vintage.

● Nobile di Montepulciano Gersemi '04	💯 6
● Nobile di Montepulciano Salarco Ris. '03	💯 6
● Nobile di Montepulciano Pasiteo '04	💯 5
● Morellino di Scansano Greto delle Fate '06	💯 4
● Rosso di Montepulciano Selciaia '06	💯 4
○ Vermentino Greto delle Fate '06	💯 4
☉ Spigo '06	💯 4
● Nobile di Montepulciano Gersemi '00	💯 6
● Nobile di Montepulciano Pasiteo '03	💯 5
● Nobile di Montepulciano Pasiteo '02	💯 5
● Nobile di Montepulciano Gersemi '01	💯 6
● Nobile di Montepulciano Salarco Ris. '01	💯 6
● Nobile di Montepulciano Gersemi '03	💯 6

● Brunello di Montalcino '02	💯 6
● Rosso di Montalcino '05	💯 4
● Brunello di Montalcino Ris. '01	💯 7
● Brunello di Montalcino Ris. '98	💯 7
● Brunello di Montalcino '01	💯 6
● Brunello di Montalcino Ris. '97	💯 8

★★ Fattoria di Felsina

VIA DEL CHIANTI, 101
53019 CASTELNUOVO BERARDENGA [SI]
TEL. 0577355117
www.felsina.it

ANNUAL PRODUCTION   400,000 bottles
HECTARES UNDER VINE 62
VITICULTURE METHOD   Conventional

Giuseppe Mazzocolin is a regular winner of
our Three Glass award and again this year,
our top honour went to his Chianti Classico
Rancia Riserva. The '04 boasts a deliciously
heady bouquet that parades a well-
orchestrated medley of berry notes and
mixed spice. The caressing, full-bodied
palate shows good generosity, subtle, well-
distributed tannins and an extremely long
finish. This excellent showing somewhat
overshadows the nonetheless admirable
result achieved by Fontalloro '04, the
winery's classic all-sangiovese Supertuscan.
This wine reached our finals on the strength
of its complex nose, rounded, well-balanced
body and long finish. It should nonetheless
be noted that quality is high across the
entire range, with the sole exception of
Maestro Raro '03, from cabernet sauvignon
only, which was a little too grassy on the
nose and stemmy on the palate. But the Vin
Santo '99 cheered us up with its citrus
aromas and soft, velvety body.

Le Filigare

LOC. LE FILIGARE
VIA SICELLE, 35
50020 BARBERINO VAL D'ELSA [FI]
TEL. 0558072796
www.lefiligare.it

ANNUAL PRODUCTION   40,000 bottles
HECTARES UNDER VINE 10
VITICULTURE METHOD   Conventional

Carlo Burchi's estate is back with a full
profile this year after a good overall
performance from its wines. The only
criticism we would offer regards the focus
on concentration, which is sometimes
excessive and hinders drinkability and
balance. Le Filigare's vineyards are located
in excellent wine country, as testified by the
writings of Francesco Datini, which reveal
that viticulture was already practised in the
area in the 15th century. The village that
grew up on Poggio delle Filigare was
subsequently included in the zone delimited
by the Grand Duke of Tuscany in 1716 as a
production area of quality wines, in practice
laying down the earliest boundaries of
Chianti. Riserva '04 Maria Vittoria performed
well in this year's tastings, its spicy nose
accompanied by a soft, caressing palate, a
prominent vein of acidity and a rising finish.
The two Chianti Classicos from the same
vintage are both well executed. We also
retasted Podere le Rocce '03, which is still
in excellent form.

● Chianti Cl. Rancia Ris. '04	♟♟♟	6
● Fontalloro '04	♟♟	6
○ Vin Santo del Chianti Cl. '99	♟♟	5
● Chianti Cl. Ris. '04	♟♟	5
● Chianti Cl. '05	♟	4
○ I Sistri '05	♟	4
● Maestro Raro '03	♟	6
● Chianti Cl. Rancia Ris. '00	♟♟♟	6
● Fontalloro '86	♟♟♟	5
● Fontalloro '99	♟♟♟	6
● Fontalloro '98	♟♟♟	6
● Fontalloro '97	♟♟♟	6
● Fontalloro '95	♟♟♟	6
● Fontalloro '93	♟♟♟	6
● Fontalloro '85	♟♟♟	5
● Fontalloro '01	♟♟♟	6
● Chianti Cl. Rancia Ris. '03	♟♟♟	6
● Chianti Cl. Rancia Ris. '93	♟♟♟	5

● Chianti Cl. Maria Vittoria Ris. '04	♟♟	6
● Podere Le Rocce '03	♟♟	7
● Chianti Cl. '05	♟	5
● Chianti Cl. Lorenzo '05	♟	5
● Podere Le Rocce '00	♟♟♟	7
● Podere Le Rocce '01	♟♟	7
● Chianti Cl. Lorenzo '04	♟♟	5

Tenute Ambrogio e Giovanni Folonari

LOC. PASSO DEI PECORAI
VIA DI NOZZOLE, 12
50022 GREVE IN CHIANTI [FI]
TEL. 055859811
www.tenutefolonari.com

ANNUAL PRODUCTION 150,000 bottles
HECTARES UNDER VINE 60
VITICULTURE METHOD Conventional

This year, Ambrogio and Giovanni Folonari have taken our top honour with Il Pareto '04, a pure cabernet sauvignon, and their sangiovese and cabernet sauvignon Cabreo Il Borgo '04 also reached our finals. That said, the entire range performed well, testifying to the fact that meticulous, passionate work will always yield excellent results. The history of this operation is fairly recent. It was founded in 2000 by the above-mentioned father-and-son team and is organized in an unusual manner. Instead of a single brand covering many wines, there are various small properties situated in outstanding wine areas – almost all in Tuscany – with different names, guaranteeing that the grapes used in production are solely from the estates. Nozzole is the original core of the group. On the nose, Il Pareto offers toasty notes, elegant fruit nuances and a slight hint of spice. The palate is full and rounded, with subtle, well-distributed tannins and a lingering, tasty finish. Cabreo Il Borgo has a fruity nose and tempting supple body but the finish is slightly lacking in depth. Riserva '04 shows juicy and powerful, while the all-chardonnay Cabreo La Pietra '05 is elegant and piquant.

★★ Castello di Fonterutoli

LOC. FONTERUTOLI
VIA OTTONE III DI SASSONIA, 5
53011 CASTELLINA IN CHIANTI [SI]
TEL. 057773571
www.fonterutoli.it

ANNUAL PRODUCTION 710,000 bottles
HECTARES UNDER VINE 117
VITICULTURE METHOD Conventional

There's big news from the Mazzei family estate: the awesome new cellar has finally been completed. It's built on three storeys, most of it underground. Designed by Agnese Mazzei, sister of Filippo and Francesco, it will enable an entirely gravity-fed vinification process, avoiding the shock to the wine caused by the use of pumps. In short, it's quality, quality, quality at Castello di Fonterutoli, where, after concentrating on the vineyards with the replanting and purchases of the past few years, attention has now shifted to the facilities. But there's nothing new about the results of our tastings. We again awarded Three Glasses to Chianti Classico Castello di Fonterutoli '04, which has spearheaded the estate's wines for many years, together with Siepi. It's a modern wine in conception and style and is not afraid to show it. The use of small oak is evident on both nose and the palate, which is dominated by luxuriant close-knit tannins. This is a wine that deserves cellar time. Siepi '04, a 50-50 blend of merlot and sangiovese, is impressively built and only a step behind. Chianti Classico '05 is pleasant but lacks depth while Poggio alla Badiola '05, from sangiovese with the addition of merlot, is juicy.

● Il Pareto '04	♈♈♈	8
● Cabreo Il Borgo '04	♈♈	6
○ Cabreo La Pietra '05	♈♈	6
● Chianti Cl. La Forra Ris. '04	♈♈	5
● Cabreo Il Borgo '00	♈♈	6
● Cabreo Il Borgo '01	♈♈	6

● Chianti Cl. Castello di Fonterutoli '04	♈♈♈	7
● Siepi '04	♈♈	8
● Chianti Cl. '05	♈	5
● Poggio alla Badiola '05	♈	4
● Chianti Cl. Castello di Fonterutoli '00	♈♈♈	8
● Chianti Cl. Castello di Fonterutoli '01	♈♈♈	7
● Chianti Cl. Castello di Fonterutoli '03	♈♈♈	7
● Chianti Cl. Castello di Fonterutoli '97	♈♈♈	8
● Chianti Cl. Castello di Fonterutoli '95	♈♈♈	5
● Siepi '99	♈♈♈	8
● Siepi '98	♈♈♈	8
● Siepi '97	♈♈♈	8
● Siepi '96	♈♈♈	8
● Siepi '95	♈♈♈	8
● Siepi '03	♈♈♈	8
● Siepi '01	♈♈♈	8
● Siepi '00	♈♈♈	8
● Chianti Cl. Castello di Fonterutoli '99	♈♈♈	8

Fattoria Le Fonti

LOC. LE FONTI
50020 PANZANO [FI]
TEL. 055852194
www.fattorialefonti.it

ANNUAL PRODUCTION 40,000 bottles
HECTARES UNDER VINE 8.6
VITICULTURE METHOD Conventional

The Schmitt-Vitali estate achieved good results but didn't quite reach the heights to which it had accustomed us a few years ago. Nonetheless, there is no lack of commitment or desire to make good wines, not to mention the fact that the subzone is one of the most interesting in the whole of Chianti Classico. The estate's history is fairly recent. In 1993, Konrad Schmitt was a successful businessman in the field of publishing in Germany. He didn't think twice when he received a good offer for his company, selling everything and moving to Italy to make wine. Schmitt chose the territory of Panzano, where he found the estate of his dreams. There was much work to do and many changes to make, both in the vineyards and in the cellar, but he had plenty of enthusiasm and the results were reassuring. Chianti Classico Riserva '04 performed best at our tastings this year. It proffers generous notes of fruit preserve, crisply focused body, crunchy tannins and a rising finish. The other wines shone less brilliantly. The Chianti Classico '05 and Rosato '06 are both decent while the tight, roughish Fontissimo '03, from sangiovese and cabernet sauvignon, shows the adverse effects of the vintage.

Le Fonti

LOC. SAN GIORGIO
53036 POGGIBONSI [SI]
TEL. 0577935690
fattoria.lefonti@libero.it

ANNUAL PRODUCTION 95,000 bottles
HECTARES UNDER VINE 23
VITICULTURE METHOD Conventional

This year, the estate owned by the Imbeni family regained its full profile, following several years in the Other Wineries section. The improvement in quality stems from a range of factors but the crucial improvement is in the sharper definition of the style. In recent years, bottles were often over-extracted and focused on abundant ripe fruit combined with excessive oak. This year, the results were different, showing well-calibrated oak and greater overall balance, with better control of the tannins. The main beneficiaries of this move forward are the estate's two flagships: Vito Arturo '04, from sangiovese, and Chianti Classico Riserva '04. They remain modern-style wines but with a leaner, juicier structure. The Riserva in particular offers attractive full-flavoured body. The less ambitious wines have also come on, like the fresh Chianti Classico '05, with its fruity nose and flavoursome palate, and the highly drinkable Sangiovese '05.

● Chianti Cl. Ris. '04	▼▼ 5
● Chianti Cl. '05	▼ 4
● Fontissimo '03	▼ 6
◉ Sangiovese Rosato '06	▼ 2
● Fontissimo '01	▽▽ 6

● Chianti Cl. Ris. '04	▼▼ 6
● Vito Arturo '04	▼▼ 6
● Chianti Cl. '05	▼ 4
● Sangiovese '05	▼ 3
● Chianti Cl. Ris. '99	▽▽ 5
○ Vin Santo del Chianti Cl. '99	▽▽ 5
● Vito Arturo '00	▽▽ 6
● Vito Arturo '01	▽▽ 6

★ Tenuta Fontodi

FRAZ. GREVE IN CHIANTI
VIA SAN LEOLINO, 89
50020 PANZANO [FI]
TEL. 055852005
www.fontodi.com

La Fornace

POD. FORNACE, 154A
53024 MONTALCINO [SI]
TEL. 0577848465
www.agricola-lafornace.it

ANNUAL PRODUCTION 300,000 bottles
HECTARES UNDER VINE 70
VITICULTURE METHOD Conventional

ANNUAL PRODUCTION 17,000 bottles
HECTARES UNDER VINE 4.5
VITICULTURE METHOD Conventional

Fontodi failed to achieve our Three Glass award this year but Giovanni Manetti needn't worry: we're confident that he will make up for lost time next year. The jewel in the estate's crown, Flaccianello delle Pieve '04, a monovarietal sangiovese with extraordinary personality, was not ready in time for our tastings so we'll have to wait. By way of compensation, Syrah Case Via '04 was very convincing, with a complex nose of pepper, spices, ripe berries and animal aromas. On the palate, there is character and pleasantness from a perfect balance of tannins, silkiness and acidity. Pinot Nero Case Via '04 is agreeable, juicy and fresh, with a delicately tempting nose of red berry fruit. Chianti Classico '05 is uncomplicated but by no means to be looked down on and well reflects its vintage. Aromas of cherry and smoky notes are accompanied by a tight dry palate and an attractive clean finish. Vin Santo '99 is charming, with a pervasive nose of dry fruit, dates, apricot and acacia honey, disclosing a concentrated palate with just the right amount of sweetness and good acidity. The monovarietal pinot blanc Meriggio '06 is pleasant and refreshing.

This small estate, with around five hectares under vine entirely planted to Brunello, is situated on the eastern side of Montalcino in one of the best wine areas in the district. Once he had realized the territory's potential, Fabio Giannetti was able to transfer it to the wine, a passage that is anything but a foregone conclusion. The improvements in the estate's wines are now evident, thanks to Giannetti's commitment and the invaluable input of agronomist Silvia Cenni. After ensuring a supply of first-rate fruit from the vines, the Giannetti turned his attention to the cellar, where he invested in improving the barrel stock. The two Brunellos presented this year are very well made. Riserva '01 has a clean, concentrated nose, with notes of bramble, cherry jam and spices. Full on the palate, it reveals good acidity and a satisfying finish. The Brunello '02 is almost as good. The nose has fresh notes of peach and blackberry before the development on the palate is nicely supported by crisp tannins. Rosso '05 is pleasant and fruity if a tad lacking in weight.

● Chianti Cl. V. del Sorbo Ris. '03	♀♀ 7
○ Vin Santo '99	♀♀ 6
● Syrah Case Via '04	♀♀ 7
● Chianti Cl. '05	♀ 5
● Pinot Nero Case Via '04	♀ 7
○ Meriggio '06	♀ 5
● Chianti Cl. V. del Sorbo Ris. '01	♀♀♀ 7
● Syrah Case Via '98	♀♀♀ 7
● Chianti Cl. V. del Sorbo Ris. '90	♀♀♀ 7
● Chianti Cl. V. del Sorbo Ris. '94	♀♀♀ 7
● Flaccianello della Pieve '90	♀♀♀ 7
● Flaccianello della Pieve '91	♀♀♀ 7
● Flaccianello della Pieve '01	♀♀♀ 7
● Flaccianello della Pieve '97	♀♀♀ 7
● Flaccianello della Pieve '03	♀♀♀ 7
● Flaccianello della Pieve '00	♀♀♀ 7

● Brunello di Montalcino '02	♀♀ 6
● Brunello di Montalcino Ris. '01	♀♀ 8
● Rosso di Montalcino '05	♀ 4
● Brunello di Montalcino '01	♀♀ 7
● Brunello di Montalcino Ris. '95	♀♀ 6
● Brunello di Montalcino Ris. '97	♀♀ 8

Podere La Fortuna

LOC. LA FORTUNA, 83
53024 MONTALCINO [SI]
TEL. 0577848308
www.tenutalafortuna.it

ANNUAL PRODUCTION 60,000 bottles
HECTARES UNDER VINE 13
VITICULTURE METHOD Conventional

Owner Gioberto Zannoni is celebrating La
Fortuna's 100th anniversary this year. The
winery, which he manages with the help of
his entire family, has grown in recent times.
It has purchased vineyards in areas away
from the long-standing winery complex,
which is located in the northeast quadrant
of the Montalcino zone. The cellar, too, has
been enlarged and is now almost a self-
contained village that is most attractive and
blends perfectly into the surrounding
landscape. Brunello Riserva '01 did not,
unfortunately, repeat the performance of last
year's standard 2001, stopping just a step
short of the top rung. The nose initially
offers impressive complexity, with classic
sour cherry nicely melding into pungent
spice but oak still wields the whip-hand
there and on the palate, and the tannins are
still biting hard. The right stuff is in there,
obviously, and it would be a shame to see
oak masking all of that. A little more bottle
ageing will smooth at least some of the
rough edges. The 2002 growing year was
not deemed propitious for producing
Brunello. Sant'Antimo La Fortuna '04 is
first-rate, releasing a generous swath of wild
berry fruit and building equal complexity in
the mouth before it ends with good length.

Frascole

LOC. FRASCOLE, 27A
50062 DICOMANO [FI]
TEL. 0558386340
www.frascole.it

ANNUAL PRODUCTION 55,000 bottles
HECTARES UNDER VINE 15
VITICULTURE METHOD Certified organic

Vin Santo is again the team leader from the
wines produced by Elisa Santoni and Enrico
Lippi and competed as usual in the national
finals. Theirs is a distinctive style,
exuberantly rich on the nose, flaunting
dates, figs and other dried fruits, but lifted
by intriguing notes of cinchona and orange
zest, and brandishing a delicious finish that
just keeps going. The only quibble is that
the alcohol raises its head a bit much. The
rest of the line-up performed well but the
aromas could perhaps be better defined.
Some muddled bouquets do no favours to
fruit that is out of the top drawer. We liked
Venia '04 best, composed of sangiovese
with a small helping of merlot. Plenty of ripe
cherry fruit adorns the nose while the palate
is crisp and vivacious. Well-integrated
tannins provide good tensile support and
the palate concludes with an impressive
fanfare. The tannins in Chianti Rufina
Riserva '04 still betray some rough edges
and tend to muffle what the wine could do
on the palate. Chianti Rufina '05 is
uncomplicated but tasty in every way.

● Brunello di Montalcino Ris. '01	▼▼	7
● Sant'Antimo La Fortuna '04	▼▼	6
● Rosso di Montalcino '05	▼	5
● Brunello di Montalcino '01	♀♀♀	7
● Brunello di Montalcino Ris. '97	♀♀	7
● Sant'Antimo La Fortuna '01	♀♀	6
● Brunello di Montalcino '00	♀♀	6
● Sant'Antimo La Fortuna '02	♀♀	5
● Brunello di Montalcino '99	♀♀	6
● Brunello di Montalcino Ris. '99	♀♀	7

○ Vin Santo del Chianti Rufina '97	▼▼	8
● Vènia '04	▼▼	5
● Chianti Rufina '05	▼	4
● Chianti Rufina Ris. '04	▼	5
○ Vin Santo del Chianti Rufina '95	♀♀	8
○ Vin Santo del Chianti Rufina '96	♀♀	8
● Chianti Rufina Ris. '01	♀♀	5
● Chianti Rufina Ris. '03	♀♀	5

Tenuta La Fuga

LOC. CAMIGLIANO
53024 MONTALCINO [SI]
TEL. 055859811
www.tenutefolonari.com

ANNUAL PRODUCTION 50,000 bottles
HECTARES UNDER VINE 10
VITICULTURE METHOD Conventional

Tenuta La Fuga, which forms part of the Tenute Ambrogio e Giovanni Folonari, is located near the village of Camigliano on the slopes of Montalcino that face the Maremma, which means that the area that is sunnier and warmer than other subzones. Giovanni Folonari's able viticultural hand in the vineyard steers these wines in the direction of brawn and rich alcohol. In line with this philosophy is Brunello di Montalcino Le Due Sorelle Riserva '01, dedicated to Giovanni's mother and to aunt. The nose is rich, dark and compelling, giving an amalgam of wild cherry, roasted espresso beans and chocolate. Bright acidity and admirably judicious tannins encourage steady development, capped by a satisfying, solid finish. The unfavourable 2002 season led to the laudable decision to skip Brunello for that vintage. Rosso di Montalcino '05 is spot-on, showing lovely fresh-picked plum and raspberry, and fruit of matching quality on the palate. Tannins that are still a bit crunchy fail to detract from overall drinkability.

● Brunello di Montalcino La Due Sorelle Ris. '01	♟♟ 8
● Rosso di Montalcino '05	♟♟ 5
● Brunello di Montalcino '01	♟♟ 7
● Brunello di Montalcino '99	♟♟ 7
● Brunello di Montalcino '97	♟♟ 7
● Brunello di Montalcino La Due Sorelle Ris. '99	♟♟ 8
● Brunello di Montalcino '00	♟♟ 7
● Rosso di Montalcino '04	♟♟ 5

Eredi Fuligni

VIA SALONI, 33
53024 MONTALCINO [SI]
TEL. 0577848039
brunellofuligni@virgilio.it

ANNUAL PRODUCTION 50,000 bottles
HECTARES UNDER VINE 12
VITICULTURE METHOD Conventional

Presenting our trophy to Roberto Guerrini is a true pleasure. Despite multifarious responsibilities, above all his job as university professor, Roberto carves out the time necessary to direct his wine operation with great competence. Passion will always find a way. His wines demonstrate a quite distinctive style, made up of equal parts of austerity and finesse. Brunello Riserva '01 is the perfect mirror of his approach. This glorious wine unveils delicate notes of roasted coffee and morello cherry over a base of ripe white cherry, infused with an appealingly sweet nuance of fresh leather, in a very rich, cleanly defined bouquet. The palate is every bit as complex but adds an elegant, clean-edged definition, thanks to velvety tannins and the juicy acidity of the best sangioveses. Exemplary progression concludes with as much length as you could wish. Rosso di Montalcino Ginestreto '05 is not quite its usual self, seeming somewhat awkward overall, and the same has to be said for SJ '05, marked by still obstreperous tannins. No Brunello '02, since the growing year was judged below par.

● Brunello di Montalcino Ris. '01	♟♟♟ 8
● Rosso di Montalcino Ginestreto '05	♟ 5
● S. J. '05	♟ 4
● Brunello di Montalcino Ris. '97	♟♟♟ 8
● Brunello di Montalcino '01	♟♟ 7
● Brunello di Montalcino Vigneti dei Cottimelli '97	♟♟ 7
● S. J. '01	♟♟ 5
● Brunello di Montalcino '99	♟♟ 7
● Brunello di Montalcino Ris. '99	♟♟ 8
● Rosso di Montalcino Ginestreto '04	♟♟ 5
● S. J. '04	♟♟ 4

Castello di Gabbiano

FRAZ. MERCATALE VAL DI PESA
VIA GABBIANO, 22
50024 SAN CASCIANO IN VAL DI PESA [FI]
TEL. 055821053
www.castellogabbiano.it

ANNUAL PRODUCTION 420,000 bottles
HECTARES UNDER VINE 68
VITICULTURE METHOD Conventional

Beringer Blass's Italian operation turned in another good performance. We are impressed by the fact that, year after year, the wines achieve a consistency of quality that ensures that at least one of them goes into our final tasting round. They retained their Italian winemaking staff, flanking the team with an American oenologist, Ed Sbragia, and it seems synergies pay off sometimes. Although the lion's share of production is directed to North America, the wines are still deeply rooted in their local territories and display none of the facile roundedness or over-extracted body that would rob them of their identity. This year, Alleanza '04 reached the national finals. Merlot and cabernet sauvignon, with some help from sangiovese, contribute to form a variegated mosaic of tanned leather, animal and dark ripe fruit. The palate shows impressive integration and breadth, with well tucked-in tannins and silky texture, even though it finishes a tad abruptly. The sangiovese-only Bellezza '04 comes across a little too stiff in the mouth, although it opens to very nice floral notes and ripe fruit. Riserva '04 is a finely built Chianti Classico, ending on a crisp note of juicy acidity.

Gattavecchi

LOC. SANTA MARIA
VIA DI COLLAZZI, 74
53045 MONTEPULCIANO [SI]
TEL. 0578757110
www.gattavecchi.it

ANNUAL PRODUCTION 280,000 bottles
HECTARES UNDER VINE 40
VITICULTURE METHOD Conventional

Gattavecchi made a stellar debut in our Guide. Luca Gattavecchi, newly installed president of the Consorzio del Vino Nobile, runs this estate with his brother Gionata and sister Daniela. The winery actually has two distinct, complementary facilities. The first is the original Gattavecchi cellar founded right in Montepulciano's historic centre by their father Valente after the war, which puts out wines pretty much exclusively for the domestic market. The more modern Poggio alla Sala is their operation in the outstanding subzone of Argiano, where they make their more impressive wines. Both lines show a signature style with distinct character well reflecting their terroir, which derives from lengthy restructuring of vineyard and cellar operations at both facilities. We thought the two Vino Nobiles, Gattavecchi and Poggio alla Sala, were first-rate. The '03 Riservas are firmly structured with well-delineated aromatics while the '04 Nobiles are marked by crisp, lean fragrances and energetic, supple palates. The rest of the wines performed well.

● Alleanza '04	♟♟ 6
● Bellezza '04	♟♟ 6
● Chianti Cl. Ris. '04	♟♟ 5
● Alleanza '01	♟♟ 7
● Bellezza '01	♟♟ 7
● Chianti Cl. Ris. '01	♟♟ 5

● Nobile di Montepulciano '04	♟♟ 5
● Nobile di Montepulciano Riserva dei Padri Serviti '03	♟♟ 5
● Nobile di Montepulciano Poggio alla Sala Ris. '03	♟♟ 5
● Nobile di Montepulciano Poggio alla Sala '04	♟♟ 5
● Rosso di Montepulciano '06	♟ 4
○ Vin Santo di Montepulciano Poggio alla Sala '97	♟ 7
○ Vin Santo di Montepulciano '99	♟ 7
● Rosso di Montepulciano Poggio alla Sala '06	♟ 4

Tenuta di Ghizzano

FRAZ. GHIZZANO
VIA DELLA CHIESA, 19
56030 PECCIOLI [PI]
TEL. 0587630096
www.tenutadighizzano.com

ANNUAL PRODUCTION 70,000 bottles
HECTARES UNDER VINE 20
VITICULTURE METHOD Natural

Ginevra Venerosi Pesciolini seems to have decided that her wines should amaze us a bit more each year. Every release seems to be not just the best she has ever produced but difficult to outdo at all. Then the following year, she comes up trumps again. After last year's superb Nambrot '04, this year's Veneroso '04 is simply extraordinary. We find ourselves uncorking a wine that is perfect, impeccable and utterly complete, a creation that, as always, draws its dynamism and its personality from the woman who shaped and cherished it with maternal care. But the wine began in the earth, its origins respected and treated with an intimacy that seems to grow ever deeper. We gave this glorious '04 Three resounding Glasses. The nose lays out a banquet of full, ripe, rich cherry fruit, rounded off by intriguing pencil lead and moist earth. The palate is flawless, every component where it belongs, each one drawing energy from the other elements and contributing in turn. Acidity supports the fruit and tannins, which in turn act as its foil, creating a masterful intaglio. The oak has already been absorbed, so enjoy this wonder wine now, or put it away for many years. We must wait until next year for Nambrot.

I Giusti e Zanza

VIA DEI PUNTONI, 9
56043 FAUGLIA [PI]
TEL. 058544354
www.igiustiezanza.it

ANNUAL PRODUCTION 80,000 bottles
HECTARES UNDER VINE 18
VITICULTURE METHOD Conventional

The ability to produce wines that are modern in style, but at the same balanced, appealing and not merely fashionable seems to have become the specialty of I Giusti e Zanza. Two factors that make this possible are the growing maturity of their new vineyards, which means lower crop yields, and the ever more sapient use of the large oak tonneaux in which their reds mature. Together with the talent of Paolo Giusti, these factors have brought to the fore wines that display a contemporary sheen but which maintain an intimate relationship with their origins. Take for example PerBruno '05. All syrah, it displays an opulent, full body but exuberant tannins provide a jolt of energy and it exudes pungent Mediterranean scrub, juniper berry and red pepper. Dulcamara '04, from cabernet and merlot, evinces similar power and dynamism. A complex, intriguing nose leads into an ultra-savoury palate marked by a vibrant progression. The sangiovese and merlot Belcore '05 is well crafted and a delight to drink.

● Veneroso '04	▼▼▼	6
● il Ghizzano '06	▼	4
● Nambrot '00	♀♀♀	8
● Nambrot '01	♀♀♀	8
● Nambrot '03	♀♀♀	7
● Veneroso '01	♀♀♀	6
● Nambrot '04	♀♀♀	7
● Veneroso '03	♀♀	6
● Veneroso '00	♀♀	7

● PerBruno '05	▼▼	5
● Dulcamara '04	▼▼	6
● Belcore '05	▼	4
● Dulcamara '00	♀♀	6
● PerBruno '04	♀♀	5
● Dulcamara '01	♀♀	6
● Dulcamara '03	♀♀	5
● PerBruno '03	♀♀	6
● Dulcamara '99	♀♀	6
● Dulcamara '97	♀♀	5
● Dulcamara '98	♀♀	6

Grattamacco

LOC. PODERE GRATTAMACCO
57022 CASTAGNETO CARDUCCI [LI]
TEL. 0565765069
www.collemassari.it

ANNUAL PRODUCTION 250,000 bottles
HECTARES UNDER VINE 66.6
VITICULTURE METHOD Conventional

Yet again Claudio Tipa brings the Three Glass trophy home to the Bolgheri zone. His Grattamacco '04 is truly magisterial, demonstrating exemplary style and a sober elegance. The classic Bolgheri mix of cabernet sauvignon and merlot, here 65-20, is given an additional 15 per cent sangiovese, which makes all the difference. Red berry fruit and pungent fresh greens make up a rich olfactory experience and a taut, well-delineated palate offers relaxed, spacious tannins, capped by a succulent finish. This is a wine of significant stature now but it will travel on for many years. Equally extraordinary is the other Bolgheri Superiore, L'Alberello '04, a partnership of cabernet sauvignon, cabernet franc and petit verdot. Right at its first appearance it zoomed into the national finals, where it was a stand-out. That was understandable, given its fragrant nose crisply veined with an elegant herbaceousness, and similar characteristics on its well-defined palate, where tannins and acidity play a gorgeous duet. Bolgheri Rosso '05 is well made and pleasurable.

Castelli del Grevepesa

FRAZ. MERCATALE IN VAL DI PESA
VIA GREVIGIANA, 34
50024 SAN CASCIANO IN VAL DI PESA [FI]
TEL. 055821911
www.castellidelgrevepesa.it

ANNUAL PRODUCTION 5,800,000 bottles
HECTARES UNDER VINE 1.000
VITICULTURE METHOD Conventional

This co-operative winery marches steadily on without any substantial change in direction. Castelli del Grevepesa's 185 grower-members are mostly in the Chianti Classico, and 650 of their overall 1,000 hectares of vineyard are located within that zone. They do their job surprisingly well, always striving to do justice to the various growing areas. They have always done a good job of highlighting Lamole and Panzano. Nor have they neglected emerging areas, such as Maremma. We do wish, though, that they would show a bit more daring and take the extra steps that would allow their more noble grape varieties to turn in even better performances. The sangiovese Coltifredi '03, for example, shows significant power but excessive tannins have too tight a grip. Riserva Clemente VII '04 is much better, with pleasurable aromas of spice over a base of bright fruit, a rich, velvety palate and a notably lengthy finale. The other offerings are all extremely well executed, with their common trait privileging easy-drinking approachability over complexity.

● Bolgheri Rosso Sup. Grattamacco '04	TTT 8
● Bolgheri Rosso Sup. L'Alberello '04	TT 7
● Bolgheri Rosso '05	T 5
● Bolgheri Rosso Sup. Grattamacco '01	TTT 8
● Grattamacco '85	TTT 8
● Bolgheri Rosso Sup. Grattamacco '03	TTT 8
● Bolgheri Rosso Sup. Grattamacco '99	TTT 8

● Chianti Cl. Clemente VII Ris. '04	TT 5
● Chianti Cl. Castelgreve L?essenziale '05	T 4
● Merlot Aprile '06	T 3
● Coltifredi '03	T 6
● Chianti Cl. Clemente VII '05	T 4
● Syrah '05	T 5
● Chianti Cl. Clemente VII Ris. '00	TT 5
● Coltifredi '01	TT 6
● Coltifredi '00	TT 6
● Chianti Cl. Clemente VII '04	TT 4
● Syrah '00	TT 5
● Chianti Cl. Clemente VII Ris. '99	TT 5
● Chianti Cl. Clemente VII Ris. '03	TT 5
● Chianti Cl. Clemente VII Ris. '01	TT 5

Grignano

FRAZ. GRIGNANO
VIA DI GRIGNANO, 22
50065 PONTASSIEVE [FI]
TEL. 0558398490
www.fattoriadigrignano.com

ANNUAL PRODUCTION 160,000 bottles
HECTARES UNDER VINE 49
VITICULTURE METHOD Conventional

The Inghirami family's wines put on another fine show overall, with Grignano as reliable as always. The range does an excellent job of bringing out the special qualities of the Rufina area, one of the Chianti zones that has made most progress towards even higher quality. Grignano's origins date as far back as the 15th century and it has a long tradition of farming fruit and cereals, as well as grapes and olives. The agricultural estate is divided into 47 parcels, each with its own well-mapped characteristics, a convincing example of the Inghiramis' determination to understand every aspect of the estate. Salicaria '04 was the wine that most impressed us this year. Composed of sangiovese and merlot, it is unabashedly modern, redolent of toasty oak and smooth spice, notably rounded in the mouth, with fine-grained tannins and just the right amount of length. Chianti Rufina Riserva '04 boasts a gorgeous nose revealing nicely evolved nuances of pungent leather and tobacco leaf, and a lean, energy-laden palate with expansive tannins and a full-flavoured conclusion. The remaining wines easily passed muster.

Tenuta Guado al Tasso

LOC. BELVEDERE, 140
57020 BOLGHERI [LI]
TEL. 0565749735
www.antinori.it

ANNUAL PRODUCTION 660,000 bottles
HECTARES UNDER VINE 300
VITICULTURE METHOD Conventional

Antinori's Bolgheri estate is among the largest in the area and has succeeded for some time now in maintaining high standards that at times are among the best. This year's tastings confirmed that position. Best of the four wines tasted, we thought, was the winery's standard-bearer, the admirable Guado al Tasso '04, largely cabernet sauvignon with some help from merlot and syrah. We liked it for the ripeness of its fruit, still caressed by some impressions of spicy oak, and for the lively tension on the palate, the result of youthful, exuberant tannins that will relax over time. Bruciato '05 is an almost equal partnership of cabernet sauvignon and merlot with five per cent of syrah. Fragrances of red berry fruit emerge in profusion, yielding slowly to tangy baked bell pepper, while the palate manages to be tightly knit without becoming over-muscled. With its nicely succulent fruit, it is a terrific, well-balanced pleaser. The crisp, tasty Vermentino '06 and Scalabrone '06 are outstanding representatives of their respective categories and in fact Scalabrone is one of the finest rosés along the Tuscan coast.

● Chianti Rufina Ris. '04	▼▼ 4
● Salicaria '04	▼▼ 6
● Chianti Rufina '05	▼ 3
○ Pietramaggio Bianco '06	▼ 4
○ Vin Santo del Chianti Capsula Oro '00	▼ 5
● Chianti Rufina '03	▼▼ 3
● Salicaria '03	▼▼ 6
● Chianti Cl. Poggio Gualtieri Ris. '00	▼▼ 5

● Bolgheri Rosso Sup. Guado al Tasso '04	▼▼ 8
⊙ Bolgheri Rosato Scalabrone '06	▼ 4
○ Bolgheri Vermentino '06	▼ 4
● Bolgheri Rosso Bruciato '05	▼ 5
● Bolgheri Rosso Sup. Guado al Tasso '01	▼▼▼ 8
● Bolgheri Rosso Sup. Guado al Tasso '90	▼▼▼ 8
● Bolgheri Rosso Sup. Guado al Tasso '00	▼▼ 8

Gualdo del Re
LOC. NOTRI, 77
57028 SUVERETO [LI]
TEL. 0565829888
www.gualdodelre.it

Guicciardini Strozzi
Fattoria Cusona
LOC. CUSONA, 5
53037 SAN GIMIGNANO [SI]
TEL. 0577950028
www.guicciardinistrozzi.it

ANNUAL PRODUCTION 100,000 bottles
HECTARES UNDER VINE 20
VITICULTURE METHOD Conventional

ANNUAL PRODUCTION 650,000 bottles
HECTARES UNDER VINE 70
VITICULTURE METHOD Conventional

Nico Rossi has done a fantastic job of turning around last year's "only good" performance. This time, his wines are hitting the ball out of the park, amply reflecting their terroirs as well as demonstrating the considerable potential that Gualdo del Re still has. The champion hitter is Rennero '05 and it captured our Three Glasses. An all-merlot varietal, it succeeds in marrying depth and concentration to wonderful drinkability. Spice-edged, well-ripened fruit is gloriously abundant on the nose before a vibrant palate shows off a well-crafted complex of good extraction, tannins and crisp acidity, all contributing to a lingering finale. The all-cabernet sauvignon Federico Primo '05 is hardly less distinctive, showing full-bodied, expansive and complex, with an energy-laden progression that gives every sign of lasting far into the future. Eliseo Rosso '05 is well worth uncorking. Largely sangiovese with 20 per cent canaiolo, it throws a nuanced, intriguing medley of smoke, spice and earth. The whites – Eliseo '06, mostly trebbiano, Strale '05, from pinot bianco, and Vermentino Valentina '06 – are all recommended. Ripe cherry fruit and a tannic yet velvety palate characterize Aleatico Amansio '06.

Principe Guicciardini Strozzi launched a long-range development programme, acquiring new properties in Bolgheri, in Maremma and on the island of Pantelleria. The result seems to be quality levels that are close to those of the original winery. Bolgheri Rosso Vignarè '04 is admirable now and may continue to do so in the future. Fruit at the height of its maturity is matched by a silky textured, spacious palate marked by warm alcohol and good progression. Bolgheri Rosso Ocra '05 is still showing young and without much interest. But an intriguing earthiness, silky tannins and decent depth propelled the sangiovese-only Sodole into the national taste-offs. Millanni '04 is equally fine. Its cabernet-merlot blend builds fine structure and power but it will have to wait for complexity to emerge. Lovely fruit fragrances help Morellino Poggio Moreto '05 turn in a good performance, as did the crisp and delicious Morellino Titolato '06 and Monteregio Guidoriccio '06, with its pungent aromas and vibrant, toothsome flavours. Vernaccia Cusona 1933 '06 debuts with minerally crispness in a new version of the traditional style. Vernaccia Riserva '05 remains fairly straightforward while Vermentino Arabesque '06 is pleasing.

● Val di Cornia Rosso l'Rennero '05	🍷🍷🍷 7
● Federico Primo '05	🍷🍷 6
○ Strale '05	🍷 5
○ Val di Cornia Vermentino Valentina '06	🍷 4
● Val di Cornia Rosso Eliseo '05	🍷 3
● Val di Cornia Aleatico Amansio '06	🍷 5
○ Val di Cornia Bianco Eliseo '06	🍷 3
● Val di Cornia Rosso l'Rennero '01	🍷🍷🍷 8
● Val di Cornia Gualdo del Re '01	🍷🍷 6
● Federico Primo '00	🍷🍷 6
● Federico Primo '04	🍷🍷 6
● Val di Cornia Gualdo del Re '04	🍷🍷 6
● Val di Cornia Rosso l'Rennero '04	🍷🍷 6
● Val di Cornia Rosso l'Rennero '00	🍷🍷 8

● Sodole '04	🍷🍷 6
● Millanni '04	🍷🍷 7
● Bolgheri Vignarè '04	🍷🍷 7
○ Vernaccia di S. Gimignano Cusona 1933 '06	🍷🍷 5
○ Arabesque '06	🍷 4
● Morellino di Scansano Titolato '06	🍷 4
● Morellino di Scansano Poggio Moreto '05	🍷 5
○ Vernaccia di S. Gimignano Ris. '05	🍷 4
● Monteregio di Massa Marittima Guidoriccio '06	🍷 4
● Bolgheri Ocra '05	🍷 4
● Millanni '99	🍷🍷🍷 7
● Millanni '00	🍷🍷 7
● Sodole '03	🍷🍷 6
○ Vernaccia di S. Gimignano Titolato '05	🍷🍷 3

I Veroni

VIA TIFARITI, 5
50065 PONTASSIEVE [FI]
TEL. 0558368886
www.iveroni.it

ANNUAL PRODUCTION 60,000 bottles
HECTARES UNDER VINE 15
VITICULTURE METHOD Conventional

Following a few up and down years in the Guide, I Veroni unleashed some true star power this year and won a place among the major profiles. The winery dates back to the Middle Ages and once belonged to the Conti Guidi. It takes its name from special terraces at the edges of the threshing floor, which were used to dry tobacco and grain. The Maleschi family has owned I Veroni since the 19th century, and Lorenzo Mariani now manages the operation, assisted by wine consultant Emilio Monechi. But back to that star power: two of the wines won a spot in the final taste-offs, Chianti Rufina Riserva '04 and Vin Santo '99. The Riserva is redolent of wild red berry fruit with a subtle pungency throughout. On entry, it immediately shows a kind of sober elegance, and then lays out a beautiful suite of smooth tannins and an energetic finale. Vin Santo flaunts compelling hazelnut and honey fragrances edged with hints of citrus and one marvels at the allure of its velvety smooth depth in the mouth and at its sweet, yet vibrant finish. Chianti Rufina '05 shows complex and finely structured while Terre del Pelacane '05, a mix of merlot, petit verdot and syrah, is pleasant enough but still stiffish.

Innocenti

FRAZ. TORRENIERI
LOC. CITILLE DI SOTTO, 45
53028 MONTALCINO [SI]
TEL. 0577834227
www.innocentivini.com

ANNUAL PRODUCTION 25,000 bottles
HECTARES UNDER VINE 4.8
VITICULTURE METHOD Conventional

After its laudable showing last year, Innocenti has now outdone itself, bringing home Three Glasses with a fantastic Brunello Riserva '01. Classical to its fingertips, it offers an aromatic amalgam of ripe black cherry cosseted by those nuances of medicinal herbs, tanned leather and tobacco leaf that are the very essence of a Brunello. The attack shows good grip and the progression is impressively lean, its superb texture supported by tannins and acidity that although generous are impeccably crafted. The finish is almost endless and mirrors beautifully all of the preceding olfactory richness. Brunello '02 defies an unfavourable growing year to put on a fine show of sound fruit, superlative tannins and a full, satisfying finale. Also impressive is Rosso di Montalcino '05, as is Vignalsole '04. Fruit comes from the Vignalsole vineyard in the nearby Torrenieri area. Winery operations are carried out in a 1980s style country residence where the ground floor hosts classic 30-litre Slavonian oak casks.

● Chianti Rufina Ris. '04	♈♈	4
○ Vin Santo del Chianti Rufina '99	♈♈	5
● Chianti Rufina '05	♈♈	3*
● Terre del Pelacane '05	♈	4
○ Vin Santo del Chianti Rufina '97	♈♈	5

● Brunello di Montalcino Ris. '01	♈♈♈	8
● Brunello di Montalcino '02	♈♈	6
● Rosso di Montalcino '05	♈♈	4
● Vignalsole '04	♈♈	4
● Brunello di Montalcino '01	♈♈	6
● Brunello di Montalcino '00	♈♈	6
● Brunello di Montalcino '99	♈♈	7
● Brunello di Montalcino Ris. '99	♈♈	7

★ Isole e Olena
LOC. ISOLE, 1
50021 BARBERINO VAL D'ELSA [FI]
TEL. 0558072763
www.isoleolena.it

Lanciola
LOC. POZZOLATICO
VIA IMPRUNETANA, 210
50023 IMPRUNETA [FI]
TEL. 055208324
www.lanciola.net

ANNUAL PRODUCTION 220,000 bottles
HECTARES UNDER VINE 50
VITICULTURE METHOD Conventional

ANNUAL PRODUCTION 250,000 bottles
HECTARES UNDER VINE 40
VITICULTURE METHOD Conventional

As often happens with stars in any field, Paolo De Marchi, owner of Isole e Olena, makes more news when his wines miss our prestigious Three Glass award than when they take it home. This year, regrettably, his all-sangiovese Cepparello '04 missed out by a whisker. The nose displays all of the ultra-luscious attractiveness that we have come to expect, giving lively fruit and subtle herbal impressions, and the finish amounts to a delicious sensory masterpiece, but the palate, despite its elegance and delicacy, falters somewhat in mid course. Syrah '04 performed well, as did the Chardonnay '05. The latter belongs to the Collezione De Marchi, a line Paolo developed to showcase what Chianti-grown international varieties can do. In fact, these wines do communicate the qualities of their terroir far more than most, with varietal characteristics playing second fiddle. Paolo has met his challenge: a Piedmontese who has become a consummate ambassador for Tuscan wine.

After a brief hiatus last year, the Guarneri family is back in the Guide with a full profile, thanks largely to a good showing by Terricci '03. But Lanciola still lacks the flair that so impressed us in past years, almost as if the winery is going through a period of transition. The commitment is certainly there, and the will to achieve, but the full potential is not, for the moment, being exploited. Some wines were not presented for our tasting, such the Chianti Classico estate's products, so it is reasonable to expect that next year will see a comeback. Returning to Terricci, it is a partnership of sangiovese and cabernet sauvignon. We appreciated the integrated medley of evolved notes of leather and tobacco, which complement the prominent acidity and tannins on the full-bodied palate, which leads into a delectable lingering conclusion. Vin Santo '02 releases classic oxidative characteristics along with scents of dried fig and almond and subtle hints of spice. Warm and expansive in the mouth, it signs off with a crisp flourish. Chianti Colli Fiorentini '04 is delicious and accessible.

● Cepparello '04	♀♀	8
○ Chardonnay Collezione De Marchi '05	♀♀	7
● Syrah Collezione De Marchi '04	♀♀	8
● Chianti Cl. '05	♀	5
● Cepparello '00	♀♀♀	7
● Cepparello '97	♀♀♀	5
● Cabernet Sauvignon '88	♀♀♀	6
● Syrah '99	♀♀♀	7
● Cepparello '88	♀♀♀	6
● Cepparello '86	♀♀♀	6
● Cabernet Sauvignon '96	♀♀♀	6
● Cabernet Sauvignon '95	♀♀♀	6
● Cabernet Sauvignon '90	♀♀♀	6
● Cabernet Sauvignon '97	♀♀♀	8
● Cepparello '99	♀♀♀	6
● Cepparello '98	♀♀♀	6
● Cepparello '03	♀♀♀	8
● Cepparello '01	♀♀♀	7

● Terricci '03	♀♀	6
○ Vin Santo del Chianti '02	♀♀	6
● Chianti Colli Fiorentini '04	♀	3
● Terricci '01	♀♀	6
● Riccionero '02	♀♀	5
● Riccionero '03	♀♀	7
● Terricci '00	♀♀	5
● Riccionero '04	♀♀	7
● Terricci '99	♀♀	6
○ Vin Santo Colli Fiorentini '00	♀♀	6
● Chianti Cl. Le Masse di Greve '02	♀♀	4

La Lastra

FRAZ. SANTA LUCIA
VIA R. DE GRADA, 9
53037 SAN GIMIGNANO [SI]
TEL. 0577941781
www.lalastra.it

ANNUAL PRODUCTION 53,600 bottles
HECTARES UNDER VINE 7
VITICULTURE METHOD Conventional

It was to be expected that La Lastra would quickly rise to the challenge of making up for its absence from last year's edition of our Guide. This year's array of wines showed a very high standard that is shared by all the labels. Vernaccia di San Gimignano Riserva '05 had no trouble in qualifying for the national finals. Almond, floral essences and citrus compose a fine suite of aromas, and the elegant progression shows off lively acidity, concluding with a touch of earthy mineral in the background. The Rovaio '05, from sangiovese, cabernet sauvignon and merlot, turned in another stand-out performance, foregrounding rich spice and earthy tones over well-ripened fruit, followed by judicious extraction, supple, tasty tannins and bright flavours. Overall, this is a consistent, elegantly styled wine. Chianti Colli Senesi '05 is pleasurable and fruit-forward while Vernaccia di San Gimignano '06, showing crisp and attractively bitterish with a lovely vein of acidity, is pleasant enough.

Lavacchio

VIA DI MONTEFIESOLE, 55
50065 PONTASSIEVE [FI]
TEL. 0558317472
www.fattorialavacchio.com

ANNUAL PRODUCTION 100,000 bottles
HECTARES UNDER VINE 20
VITICULTURE METHOD Certified organic

The Lottero family scored high marks right across the board this year, an obvious sign that the efforts of Faye Lottero and her husband are paying off handsomely. All of Lavacchio's wines touched heights of quality, with Vin Santo '01 emerging as the champion. Many factors have contributed to bring about this leap in quality: the choice to go totally organic; unrelenting commitment and dedication; and a desire to make Lavacchio a benchmark for everything it produced. At one time, the winery was known in particular for Oro del Cedro, a late-harvest Traminer Aromatico; now it is the reds that are making everyone take notice. The modern-styled Fontegalli '04, for instance, from merlot, sangiovese and cabernet sauvignon, is infused with toasty oak and pungent spice, rolling out viscous and full-bodied with a lovely, long-lingering ending. The Riserva is leaner, opening on lively menthol and then building a rich, multi-layered palate that concludes with a burst of flavour. Viognier, chardonnay and sauvignon go into the fine Pachar '05, a mineral-charged and very savoury bottle. But Vin Santo '01 merits special mention for its lush opulence, hedonistic nose and lengthy finish.

O Vernaccia di S. Gimignano Ris. '05	♟♟	4*
● Rovaio '05	♟♟	5
● Chianti Colli Senesi '05	♟	3
O Vernaccia di S. Gimignano '06	♟	3
● Rovaio '01	♟♟	5
● Rovaio '00	♟♟	5
O Vernaccia di S. Gimignano '04	♟♟	4
O Vernaccia di S. Gimignano Ris. '02	♟♟	4
O Vernaccia di S. Gimignano Ris. '03	♟♟	4
O Vernaccia di S. Gimignano Ris. '01	♟♟	4

O Vin Santo del Chianti Rufina '01	♟♟	5
● Fontegalli '04	♟♟	6
O Oro del Cedro '06	♟♟	6
O Pachar '05	♟♟	4
● Chianti Rufina Cedro Ris. '04	♟♟	5
● Fontegalli '03	♟♟	6
O Oro del Cedro V. T. '01	♟♟	5
● Cortigiano '00	♟♟	6
O Oro del Cedro '98	♟♟	3

Cantine Leonardo da Vinci
VIA PROVINCIALE MERCATALE, 291
50059 VINCI [FI]
TEL. 0571902444
www.cantineleonardo.it

ANNUAL PRODUCTION 3,500,000 bottles
HECTARES UNDER VINE 520
VITICULTURE METHOD Conventional

Cantine Leonardo da Vinci is a large, highly respected co-operative in the province of Florence that produces an extensive range of generally well executed and reliable wines from almost every Tuscan denomination. Among the most memorable that we tasted was Merlot degli Artisti '04, mistakenly reviewed last year, which boasts a sumptuous body and generous fruit flanked by supple tannins. Sadly, the finish lacks the expected complexity. Morellino di Scansano '06 lays out plenty of black pepper-led spice and ripe fruit. The mouth develops significant depth but manages to remain crisp and enormously palatable. Rosso di Montalcino '05 is finely crafted, releasing a rich complex of ripe fruit followed by an energy-filled, crisp palate with just the right dose of tannins. Equally rewarding is the all-sangiovese San Zio '05. Full and concentrated throughout, it also has nicely complementary acid zest and tannic grip that provide good energy against a finish somewhat constricted by too much oak. Chianti Leonardo '06, Chianti Leonardo Riserva '04, the syrah-merlot Sant'Ippolito '05, and Brunello di Montalcino '02 are all sound and deserve attention.

Tenuta di Lilliano
LOC. LILLIANO, 8
53011 CASTELLINA IN CHIANTI [SI]
TEL. 0577743070
www.lilliano.com

ANNUAL PRODUCTION 250,000 bottles
HECTARES UNDER VINE 50
VITICULTURE METHOD Conventional

The Ruspoli family did well again, even though they obviously have the stuff for even more stellar results. Tenuta di Lilliano lies in an exceptional terroir in Chianti Classico, one of the areas renowned for the qualities that it can coax from sangiovese. Winemaking at Lilliano goes back to the 19th century, although production only took off only in the early 20th century, when the property was acquired by the Berlingieri family. The winery's golden age began in the 1960s, thanks to the hard work of Eleonora Berlingieri Ruspoli, who took over the reins of the winery. One of the first women in Italy to be involved in winemaking, she turned out superb vintages that won widespread esteem. Anagallis '04, a sangiovese, merlot and colorino blend, performed well, its mineral-edged aromas and zesty flavours complementing a powerful palate and lengthy conclusion. Equally fine is Chianti Classico Riserva '04. No less dense, its strong points are a pungent balsam on the nose and lively, spacious tannins. Chianti Classico '05 is uncomplicated but enjoyable.

Wine	Rating
● Merlot degli Artisti '04	♀♀ 6
● Morellino di Scansano '06	♀♀ 3*
● San Zio '05	♀♀ 4
● Rosso di Montalcino '05	♀♀ 4*
● Brunello di Montalcino '02	♀ 7
● Chianti Da Vinci '06	♀ 3*
● Sant'Ippolito '05	♀ 5
● Chianti Leonardo Ris. '04	♀ 4
● Chianti Leonardo '06	♀ 3*
● San Zio '03	♀♀ 4
● Chianti Leonardo Ris. '01	♀♀ 4
● Sant'Ippolito '04	♀♀ 5
● Merlot degli Artisti '01	♀♀ 6
● Merlot degli Artisti '02	♀♀ 6
● San Zio '02	♀♀ 4
● Sant'Ippolito '03	♀♀ 5
● San Zio '04	♀♀ 4

Wine	Rating
● Anagallis '04	♀♀ 6
● Chianti Cl. Ris. '04	♀♀ 5
● Chianti Cl. '05	♀ 4
● Chianti Cl. E. Ruspoli Berlingieri Ris. '85	♀♀♀ 6
● Chianti Cl. '04	♀♀ 4
● Chianti Cl. Ris. '03	♀♀ 5
● Anagallis '99	♀♀ 6

Lisini

LOC. SANT'ANGELO IN COLLE
53020 MONTALCINO [SI]
TEL. 0577844040
www.lisini.com

ANNUAL PRODUCTION 100,000 bottles
HECTARES UNDER VINE 18
VITICULTURE METHOD Conventional

There can be no doubt that Lisini has all of its takes to produce truly exceptional wines. Familiarity with the land here goes back generations while the vineyards in Sesta occupy one of the area's most envied locations, boasting mature vines that yield beautifully well-balanced fruit. Finally, the cellar has top-notch production staff, with talented winemaker Filippo Paoletti in charge. All this comes together in the magnificent Brunello Ugolaia '01. It would probably have won Three Glass for its nose alone, a masterpiece of complexity, introducing morello and sour cherry that slowly meld into richer impressions of moist earth and tanned leather. The palate conveys extraordinary harmony and intensity. The fine quality of the tannins renders them dense but quite supple, perfectly underpinned by measured acidity that powers on to a nearly endless finish of pure sensory eloquence. No Brunello '02, for a vintage that was not of the best for Montalcino's iconic wine. We gave a warm welcome to Rosso '05, one of the best we tasted. Balsam-laced fragrances of wild red and black berry fruit, and an expansive, juicy palate, make it exceptionally delicious.

Livernano

LOC. LIVERNANO, 67A
53017 RADDA IN CHIANTI [SI]
TEL. 0577738353
www.livernano.it

ANNUAL PRODUCTION 35,000 bottles
HECTARES UNDER VINE 12.5
VITICULTURE METHOD Conventional

One good sip invites another and after Robert Cuillo walked off with our Three Glasses on his personal debut last year, he has now encored that performance with his Chianti Classico Riserva '04. Despite the absence of the two Livernano standard-bearers, Livernano and Purosangue, the careful labours of the past have borne magnificent fruit and augur a bright future. Respect for the terroir, very evident in the several versions of Chianti Classico produced, very able production staff and attention to the winery image are the most obvious elements of the Livernano philosophy. The Riserva offers lovely ripe fruit along with subtle floral and menthol notes, then opens full and rich in the mouth, its velvet-smooth tannins well integrated into all of the other components, before closing sweet and lengthy. The other wines are good, too. Janus '04 is a new Cabernet Sauvignon that shows unbelievable depth and balance. Anima '05, an assemblage of chardonnay, traminer, viognier and sauvignon, is elegant and substantial.

Wine	Rating
● Brunello di Montalcino Ugolaia '01	▼▼▼ 8
● Rosso di Montalcino '05	▼▼ 5
● Brunello di Montalcino '90	♀♀♀ 6
● Brunello di Montalcino '88	♀♀♀ 6
● Brunello di Montalcino Ugolaia '00	♀♀♀ 8
● Brunello di Montalcino Ugolaia '91	♀♀♀ 8
● Brunello di Montalcino '01	♀♀ 7
● Brunello di Montalcino Ugolaia '99	♀♀ 8
● Brunello di Montalcino '99	♀♀ 7

Wine	Rating
● Chianti Cl. Ris. '04	▼▼▼ 5
O Anima '05	▼▼ 6
● Chianti Cl. '05	▼▼ 4
● Janus '04	▼▼ 8
● Livernano '03	♀♀♀ 8
● Livernano '97	♀♀♀ 8
● Livernano '99	♀♀♀ 8
● Livernano '98	♀♀♀ 8

Fattoria Lornano

LOC. LORNANO, 11
53035 MONTERIGGIONI [SI]
TEL. 0577309059
www.fattorialornano.it

ANNUAL PRODUCTION 100,000 bottles
HECTARES UNDER VINE 48
VITICULTURE METHOD Conventional

More good results from the Taddei family brought them back into the Guide but Fattoria Lornano has the potential for even greater exploits. The estate lies near the border of the Chianti Classico zone, an area that can look back on many centuries of history. The mild climate and beauty of the countryside made this the favourite summer retreat of the canons of Siena cathedral. Documents dating from the days of Innocent III attest to agricultural lands next to the church and other buildings. A late 18th-century restructuring is responsible for the current appearance of the complex. In our tastings this year, we especially liked the '01 Vin Santo. A fragrant bouquet presents irresistibly appealing dates, honey and mixed spices, and the palate's luscious, creamy texture is nicely enlivened by crisp acidity. The conclusion is lengthy and satisfying. Commendator Enrico '04, a partnership of sangiovese and merlot, performed equally well. Toasty oak and hints of wild berry and smooth vanilla serve as a satisfying foil to a full body and nicely tucked-in tannins, and the finish is as delectable as one could wish. Chianti Classico '05 and Chianti Colli Senesi '06 are both sound offerings.

Lunadoro

FRAZ. VALIANO DI MONTEPULCIANO
LOC. TERRAROSSA PAGLIERETO
53040 MONTEPULCIANO [SI]
TEL. 0578748154
www.lunadoro.com

ANNUAL PRODUCTION 40,000 bottles
HECTARES UNDER VINE 12
VITICULTURE METHOD Conventional

Dario Cappelli and Gigliola Cardinali couldn't have engineered a better debut in our Guide. Lunadoro lies on the Valiano ridge, one of the most exceptional growing areas in Montepulciano, and their wines seem already to have found a stylistic niche, exhibiting flawless technical craftsmanship joined with an easy naturalness and faithfulness to terroir. These qualities propelled Nobile Quercione '04 into the national finals. The nose is more than winning, with subtle oak toast masterfully woven into an expanse of crisp-edged fruit. That balance carries over to a palate revealing decent complexity and featuring a satisfying duet of eloquent tannins and zesty acidity that contributes to depth and progression. Nobile '04 tends to be leaner and more austere but it is beautifully balanced, offering a forthright, no-frills earthiness on the nose and a dynamic, savoury palate. Rosso di Montepulciano '05 is well crafted and ready to enjoy while the trebbiano and malvasia Pagliareto '06 is fragrant and straightforward.

O Vin Santo del Chianti Cl. '01	�	6
● Commendator Enrico '04	�	5
● Chianti Cl. '05	♔	4
● Chianti Colli Senesi '06	♔	3
● Commendator Enrico '01	♕♕	5
● Chianti Cl. '03	♕♕	4
● Chianti Cl. Ris. '01	♕♕	5

● Nobile di Montepulciano		
Quercione '04	♔♔	5
● Nobile di Montepulciano '04	♔♔	5
● Pagliareto '06	♔	4
● Rosso di Montepulciano '05	♔	4

★ Le Macchiole
VIA BOLGHERESE, 189A
57020 BOLGHERI [LI]
TEL. 0565766092
www.lemacchiole.it

ANNUAL PRODUCTION 90,000 bottles
HECTARES UNDER VINE 21
VITICULTURE METHOD Conventional

Sadly, none of Cinzia Campolmi's highly respected wines was able to bring home our Three Glasses. This is a shame, since in a vintage year like 2004 we had high expectations from a winery that stands out at Bolgheri for its admirable style and solid direction. We found all the wines heavily influenced by oak, showing hard, drying tannins. Perhaps time will temper them but they are nevertheless currently preventing the wines from showing as they should. Still, Paleo was head and shoulders above the others. All cabernet franc, it first offers a fine mosaic of well-ripened dark berry fruit foregrounding spice, black pepper, clove and pencil lead. Full and concentrated on the palate, it delivers good supporting acidity, which will stand it in good stead through many years. But those tannins are still much too stiff. Messorio is a dark, brooding all-varietal merlot that is grained by oak throughout. On the nose, oak tones vitiate the fruit and tannins hold too much sway on the palate. The all-syrah Scrio repeats the same script but Bolgheri Rosso '05 is refreshing and delicious.

● Messorio '04	**YY**	8
● Paleo Rosso '04	**YY**	8
● Bolgheri Rosso '05	**Y**	5
● Scrio '04	**Y**	8
● Bolgheri Rosso Sup. Paleo '96	YYY	8
● Messorio '01	YYY	8
● Messorio '99	YYY	8
● Bolgheri Rosso Sup. Paleo '97	YYY	8
● Paleo Rosso '03	YYY	8
● Scrio '01	YYY	8
● Paleo Rosso '01	YYY	8
● Messorio '98	YYY	8
● Messorio '97	YYY	8
● Bolgheri Rosso Sup. Paleo '95	YYY	8
● Bolgheri Rosso Sup. Paleo '00	YY	8
● Messorio '03	YY	8
● Scrio '03	YY	8
● Messorio '00	YY	8

Machiavelli
LOC. SANT'ANDREA IN PERCUSSINA
50026 SAN CASCIANO IN VAL DI PESA [FI]
TEL. 055828471
www.giv.it

ANNUAL PRODUCTION 200,000 bottles
HECTARES UNDER VINE 26.6
VITICULTURE METHOD Conventional

Back with a full profile is one the most important wineries belonging to Gruppo Italiano Vini. In fact, Machiavelli is the classic line of the group, whose headquarters is just a few metres away from the Consorzio del Chianti Classico. The origin of the winery's name is fairly obvious. It was to Sant'Andrea in Percussina that Nicolò Machiavelli was exiled and in between his sessions writing The Prince, he enjoyed playing cards in the local osteria. Winemaking was carried out on the estate under the ownership of the Conti Seristori, and then the Gruppo Italiano Vini acquired the entire property in the 1980s. Turning now to this year's tastings, we liked Chianti Classico Riserva Vigna di Fontalle '04, which has notably evolved tones of fragrant tanned leather and tobacco leaf over a base of ripe blackberry preserves. In the mouth, it is as rich and succulent as you could wish, the tannins lively but under control, and it closes with a fanfare. Chianti Classico Solatio del Tani '05 has a more modern slant, with plenty of fruit and spice on the nose, and a rounded but bright palate. The all-pinot noir Il Principe '04 is likeable enough.

● Chianti Cl. Solatìo del Tani '05	**YY**	6
● Chianti Cl. V. di Fontalle Ris. '04	**YY**	6
● Il Principe '04	**Y**	6
● Chianti Cl. V. di Fontalle Ris. '95	YYY	5
● Il Principe '95	YYY	4
● Chianti Cl. V. di Fontalle Ris. '97	YYY	5
● Ser Niccolò Solatio del Tani '88	YYY	4
● Chianti Cl. V. di Fontalle Ris. '01	YY	5
● Ser Niccolò Solatio del Tani '01	YY	7
● Chianti Cl. V. di Fontalle Ris. '00	YY	5
● Chianti Cl. V. di Fontalle Ris. '98	YY	5
● Chianti Cl. V. di Fontalle Ris. '03	YY	7
● Ser Niccolò Solatio del Tani '99	YY	6

La Madonnina - Triacca

LOC. STRADA IN CHIANTI
VIA PALAIA, 39
50027 GREVE IN CHIANTI [FI]
TEL. 055858003
www.triacca.com

ANNUAL PRODUCTION 600,000 bottles
HECTARES UNDER VINE 100
VITICULTURE METHOD Conventional

In the Triacca family profile last year, we mentioned that they seemed to be taking a reflective pause. That seems to have been beneficial for this year the Chianti Classico Riserva '04 won Three Glasses. Wild berry fruit is appealingly freshened with pungent herbs and slaty mineral on the nose, and the palate is pure seduction, with an energy-laden progression, tannins and alcohol mutually complementary, and crisp acidity infusing all the components. The energy continues to propel the finish, which is intensely savoury. It is certainly not easy to read and interpret a particular local terroir when your own roots are elsewhere but the Triaccas, a wine family from Valtellina, manage to do just that. They leave nothing to chance, closely following vineyard replantings and relying on an expert in the area, Vittorio Fiore. Considering the substantial size of their vineyard holdings, it is to their further credit that they can put out wines of such outstanding quality. Among the Chianti Classicos, La Palaia '04 is the best with a pungent, herbaceous nose, good complexity on the palate and solid backbone. Il Mandorlo '04, a cabernet sauvignon-sangiovese partnership, lacked balance and was not up to snuff.

Fattoria di Magliano

LOC. STERPETI, 10
58051 MAGLIANO IN TOSCANA [GR]
TEL. 0564593040
www.fattoriadimagliano.it

ANNUAL PRODUCTION 200,000 bottles
HECTARES UNDER VINE 47
VITICULTURE METHOD Conventional

Agostino Lenci's operation is already one of the wineries to watch in the Maremma. His wines are consistently impressive and often superb. Poggio Bestiale '05, for instance, from equal parts cabernet sauvignon and merlot, went through again to our final round of tastings. It greets the nose with a concentrated, clean-edged array of dark fruit nicely lifted by suggestions of graphite and peppery balsam, following this with a spacious, even progression in the mouth characterized by dense, silky tannins and fine, tart grip. The all-vermentino Pagliatura '06 is a delight and one of the best versions that Fattoria di Magliano has put out. Lime blossom and pungent scrub give the wine its distinctive character, ably matched by fine weight on the palate and zesty acidity. This is just the third release for Perenzo '05, a monovarietal Syrah, and it has yet to find its stylistic groove. It shows a tad too extracted and the oak is laid on fairly thick. Morellino Heba '06 exhibits admirably clean aromas of bright morello cherry and a warm, rounded palate.

● Chianti Cl. Ris. '04	🍷🍷🍷 4	
● Chianti Cl. V. La Palaia '04	🍷🍷 4*	
● Chianti Cl. Bello Stento '05	🍷 4	
● Il Mandorlo '04	🍷 4	
● Chianti Cl. Bello Stento '03	🍷🍷 4	
● Il Mandorlo '01	🍷🍷 5	
● Chianti Cl. Ris. '03	🍷🍷 4	
● Il Mandorlo '03	🍷🍷 5	
● Chianti Cl. V. La Palaia '03	🍷🍷 5	
● Chianti Cl. V. La Palaia '01	🍷🍷 5	

● Poggio Bestiale '05	🍷🍷 6	
O Pagliatura '06	🍷🍷 4	
● Morellino di Scansano Heba '06	🍷 4	
● Perenzo '05	🍷 6	
● Perenzo '03	🍷🍷 7	
● Poggio Bestiale '02	🍷🍷 6	
● Poggio Bestiale '04	🍷🍷 6	
● Poggio Bestiale '01	🍷🍷 6	
● Perenzo '04	🍷🍷 6	

Mannucci Droandi

FRAZ. MERCATALE VALDARNO
VIA CAPOSELVI, 61
52020 MONTEVARCHI [AR]
TEL. 0559707276
www.chianticlassico.com

ANNUAL PRODUCTION 36,000 bottles
HECTARES UNDER VINE 31
VITICULTURE METHOD Conventional

Roberto Droandi operates on two fronts. One area of production is in the Colli Aretini area, between Valdarno and the Chianti hills, while the other lies not very far away in Chianti Classico. In recent years, this has been a producer to watch. One reason is that the quality of the wines is uniformly high and all are clearly territory-focused. But Roberto also deserves kudos for his lengthy efforts, in collaboration with the experimental viticulture institute in Arezzo, to bring back and explore the potential of some grape varieties long-established in the Arezzo area but now threatened with extinction. We will soon see the first concrete results since the winery will be releasing its first modest amounts of the barsaglina and foglia tonda-based wines. Campolucci and Riserva di Chianti Classico weren't presented at our tastings this year but Chianti Classico Ceppeto '04 did the honours nicely. We found it well matured, savoury and complex, with just the right measure of earthiness and youthful burr. Chianti '05 is pure pleasure, its bright, no-nonsense fruit the perfect foil to overall classic austerity. The delightful sangiovese rosé, Rossinello '06, flaunts the crisp, heady fragrances of fresh-made wine.

● Chianti Cl. Ceppeto '04	🍷🍷	4*
● Chianti Colli Aretini '05	🍷🍷	3*
⊙ Rossinello '06	🍷	3
● Campolucci '00	♡♡	5
● Campolucci '01	♡♡	5
● Chianti Colli Aretini '04	♡♡	3*
● Chianti Cl. Ceppeto Ris. '01	♡♡	5
● Campolucci '03	♡♡	5

Mantellassi

LOC. BANDITACCIA, 26
58051 MAGLIANO IN TOSCANA [GR]
TEL. 0564592037
www.fatt-mantellassi.it

ANNUAL PRODUCTION 550,000 bottles
HECTARES UNDER VINE 60
VITICULTURE METHOD Conventional

Aleardo and Giuseppe Mantellassi refuse to yield an inch to the newer oenological fashions that have taken hold lately in Maremma. The wines of Mantellassi in fact are a good mirror in which to catch reflections of classic Morellino di Scansano character, wines with distinctive qualities well rooted in the local terroir. By a quirk of fate, this very role is fittingly conveyed in the name of the wine that best embodies these qualities, Morellino Le Sentinelle Riserva '04. It is indeed a "sentinel", safeguarding this traditional wine type with a lean, well-defined suite of aromatics and a rich palate that displays solid structure and the expected earthiness. The winery flagship is Querciolaia, a traditionally styled Alicante, a variety cultivated for centuries in the Maremma. Last year's Guide mistakenly referred to the '04, instead of the '03. The nose is spot on varietally and exuberant acidity infuses the progression with admirable liveliness. Lovely fragrances and flavours grace Morellino San Giuseppe '06 while the remaining wines are linear and well executed.

● Morellino di Scansano Le Sentinelle Ris. '04	🍷🍷	5
● Morellino di Scansano San Giuseppe '06	🍷🍷	4
● Querciolaia '04	🍷🍷	5
● Morellino di Scansano Mentore '06	🍷	4
○ Vermentino Scalandrino '06	🍷	4
● Morellino di Scansano San Giuseppe '02	♡♡	4
● Querciolaia '01	♡♡	5
● Morellino di Scansano Le Sentinelle Ris. '01	♡♡	5
● Morellino di Scansano Le Sentinelle Ris. '03	♡♡	5
● Querciolaia '03	♡♡	5
● Querciolaia '04	♡♡	5
● Morellino di Scansano San Giuseppe '04	♡♡	4*
● Morellino di Scansano San Giuseppe '05	♡♡	4
● Morellino di Scansano San Giuseppe '03	♡♡	4

La Marcellina

VIA CASE SPARSE, 74
50020 PANZANO [FI]
TEL. 055852126
www.lamarcellina.it

ANNUAL PRODUCTION 70,000 bottles
HECTARES UNDER VINE 13
VITICULTURE METHOD Conventional

The Castellacci family seems to enjoy playing blind man's buff. They didn't bring out any wines for last year's tasting whereas this year they rolled out such a line-up of fine offerings that La Marcellina went straight to a full profile. Luca, the winery owner, loves to tell the story of the property's name. The legend goes back more than a thousand years, to the days when the Firidolfi family ruled the settlement of Panzano. The property where the winery now stands is said to have been given by the Firidolfi to a Florentine named Marcello, who had helped kill someone who had assassinated one of the Firidolfis. Passing on to the wines, Comignole '04 received a lengthy maceration on the skins and at least 18 months' cask ageing. The results are outstanding, complex, evolved sensations on the nose heralding succulent fruit and elegant tannins, and signing off with an expansive flourish on the finish. Riserva Sassocupo '04 is equally fine. Camporosso '04, on the other hand, did not quite meet expectations. A blend of sangiovese and cabernet sauvignon, it is well executed but somewhat thin and lacking in presence.

Marchesi de' Frescobaldi

VIA SANTO SPIRITO, 11
50125 FIRENZE [FI]
TEL. 05527141
www.frescobaldi.it

ANNUAL PRODUCTION 9,000,000 bottles
HECTARES UNDER VINE 1,200
VITICULTURE METHOD Conventional

Chianti Rufina Montesodi has taken out a season ticket to our national finals. Although the '05 missed the ultimate prize, Montesodi remains one of the finest benchmarks in the area. Another accomplishment by Frescobaldi is the ability to produce literally millions of bottles every year at a very high overall level of quality. Led by Vittorio Frescobaldi, the winery took the crucial step of focusing attention on each of its estates as individual viticultural entities, taking into account the climates and conditions peculiar to each. This has enabled them to create a more intimate relationship between wines and territory. Castello di Nipozzano remains the epicentre of production but their activities in Pomino, one of Italy's smallest DOCs, and in the Maremma testify to their renewed vigour. Chianti Rufina Nipozzano Riserva '04, one of the Frescobaldi icons, is beautifully balanced and delicious, quite a feat considering that its production is over a million bottles. The chardonnay-based Pomino whites were impressive, the '06 showing lively and full flavoured while the fuller-bodied Il Benefizio '05 is nicely sculpted. Among the Supertuscans, Mormoreto '04, an assemblage of cabernet sauvignon, merlot and cabernet franc, is its usual stirring self.

Wine		Rating
● Chianti Cl. Comignole '04	♟♟	5
● Chianti Cl. Sassocupo Ris. '04	♟♟	5
● Camporosso '04	♟	5
● Chianti Cl. Sassocupo '05	♟	4
● Chianti Cl. Comignole '03	♟♟	5

Wine		Rating
● Chianti Rufina Montesodi '05	♟♟	7
● Chianti Rufina Nipozzano Ris. '04	♟♟	4
● Mormoreto '04	♟♟	7
O Pomino Bianco '06	♟♟	4
● Pomino Rosso '04	♟♟	5
O Pomino Il Benefizio '05	♟♟	6
● Morellino di Scansano Santa Maria '06	♟♟	4
O Albizzia '06	♟	3
O Castello di Pomino Vin Santo '02	♟	6
⊙ Rosa di Corte '06	♟	3
● Chianti Rufina Montesodi '01	♟♟♟	7
● Chianti Rufina Montesodi '99	♟♟♟	7
● Mormoreto '01	♟♟♟	7
● Chianti Rufina Montesodi '97	♟♟♟	7
● Chianti Rufina Montesodi Ris. '88	♟♟♟	7
● Chianti Rufina Montesodi Ris. '96	♟♟♟	7
● Mormoreto '97	♟♟♟	6
● Chianti Rufina Montesodi Ris. '90	♟♟♟	7

Renzo Marinai
VIA CASE SPARSE, 6
50020 GREVE IN CHIANTI [FI]
TEL. 0558560237
www.renzomarinai.it

★ La Massa
VIA CASE SPARSE, 9
50020 PANZANO [FI]
TEL. 055852722
info@fattorialamassa.com

ANNUAL PRODUCTION 30,000 bottles
HECTARES UNDER VINE 5.5
VITICULTURE METHOD Certified organic

ANNUAL PRODUCTION 110,000 bottles
HECTARES UNDER VINE 25
VITICULTURE METHOD Conventional

Renzo Marinai's operation continues to grow apace, with his Chianti Classico Riserva '04 gaining a place this year in the finals. Marinai seems almost to have torn a page from a utopian manual, for he sees his role as viticulturist extending far beyond the mere production of high-quality wines. His is a philosophy of life shaped by respect for nature and Renzo's decision to embrace organic grape-growing, to recover local farming practices, to raise wheat that is low yielding but nutritionally rich, and to recycle in an ecologically responsible manner all his organic residues. He also puts on a harvest festival in the summer, derives other valuable products, such as soap, from his olive oil, and bakes wood-fired bread that lasts an entire week. Renzo's wines are constantly improving. The Riserva offers generous ripe fruit and smooth impressions of spice, then a rounded palate with a great tannic weave and an enchanting, tasty finish. The cabernet sauvignon-based Guerrante '04 stands out as well, with pungent mint and balsam leading into a powerful, well-structured palate of compelling energy. Chianti Classico '05 is a charmer.

It happens sometimes, to paraphrase a popular song, although in the case of La Massa, perhaps "rarely" would be more appropriate. For rarely has La Massa's owner Giampaolo Motta failed to walk away with Three Glasses, courtesy of his flagship wine, Giorgio Primo, a partnership of sangiovese and merlot. But the '04 left us not entirely convinced. The nose is appealingly herbaceous over a generous base of very ripe fruit, with a dark gaminess in the background. The palate is rich and complex but too affected by drying tannins that considerably slow its development. Perhaps the vintage influenced the overall performance. Motta is always striving for perfection and sometimes that drive can lead to excess when you lose sight of harmony and overall pleasure. His second wine, La Massa '05, is a fine effort. Nuances of menthol nicely vein the dark fruit that develops slowly on the nose while the palate shows satisfying heft and judicious tannins.

● Chianti Cl. Ris. '04	♈♈ 5
● Guerrante '04	♈♈ 5
● Chianti Cl. '05	♈ 4
● Chianti Cl. Ris. '03	♈♈ 5

● Giorgio Primo '04	♈♈ 8
● La Massa '05	♈♈ 6
● Chianti Cl. Giorgio Primo '00	♈♈♈ 7
● Chianti Cl. Giorgio Primo '99	♈♈♈ 7
● Chianti Cl. Giorgio Primo '98	♈♈♈ 7
● Chianti Cl. Giorgio Primo '97	♈♈♈ 7
● Chianti Cl. Giorgio Primo '96	♈♈♈ 7
● Chianti Cl. Giorgio Primo '95	♈♈♈ 7
● Chianti Cl. Giorgio Primo '94	♈♈♈ 7
● Chianti Cl. Giorgio Primo '93	♈♈♈ 7
● Giorgio Primo '03	♈♈♈ 8
● Chianti Cl. Giorgio Primo '01	♈♈♈ 8
● La Massa '01	♈♈♈ 5

Massanera
FRAZ. CHIESANUOVA
VIA FALTIGNANO, 76
50020 SAN CASCIANO IN VAL DI PESA [FI]
TEL. 0558242222
www.massanera.com

ANNUAL PRODUCTION 35,000 bottles
HECTARES UNDER VINE 7
VITICULTURE METHOD Conventional

Carlo Cattaneo's winery seems at last well on the way to consistent high quality and returns to the Guide with a full profile. His collaboration with Andrea Paoletti has paid off handsomely. Massanera's wines have thrown off the excessively ripe edge that characterized them for many years, reacquiring fragrance and character. The name Massanera derives from a dense wood of holm-oaks on the property and the present winery building served as a hunting lodge for the Medicis. It was then restructured in the 18th century into a noble residence. Today, Massanera not only produces wine and olive oil but is well known for raising the distinctive cinta senese breed of pigs. Prelato '04, largely sangiovese, is outstanding, a lovely, mineral-infused bouquet with plenty of well-ripened fruit preceding a supple mouthfeel and a luscious finale. Per Me '04, made from international varieties, turned in an equally fine performance. After emphatic oak on the nose, fine-grained tannins contribute to a pliant palate and the finish is long. Chianti Classico '05 is appealing.

Mastrojanni
FRAZ. CASTELNUOVO DELL'ABATE
POD. LORETO SAN PIO
53024 MONTALCINO [SI]
TEL. 0577835681
www.mastrojanni.com

ANNUAL PRODUCTION 80,000 bottles
HECTARES UNDER VINE 23.7
VITICULTURE METHOD Conventional

Mastrojanni is one of the longest-established Montalcino producers, a winery that has contributed greatly, since the 1970s, to the respect that the Castelnuovo dell'Abate area enjoys today. The family relies on oenologist Andrea Machetti, who has long managed the operation with passionate commitment. This year, Mastrojanni presented the '01 version of the Brunello Schiena d'Asino selection, a long-time Montalcino-area classic that has demonstrated fantastic cellarability over the decades. This edition has that traditional character in spades. After a textbook ruby hue, it offers red berry, morello cherry and yellow peach melding into the expected sweet tobacco and dried hay. It lays out impressive extractive weight but beguiling acidity and masterful tannins provide a perfect foil, and it weaves everything together with a harmonious, aromatic finish. In short, a wine of great distinction with no frills or excesses. It simply needs a bit of cellar time to be at its best. No Brunello was made in 2002 because of unfavourable conditions and Rosso '05 is still showing fairly rough edged and tartish.

● Per Me '04	▼▼ 5
● Prelato di Massanera '04	▼▼ 6
● Chianti Cl. '05	▼ 4
● Prelato di Massanera '03	♀♀ 6

● Brunello di Montalcino V. Schiena d'Asino '01	▼▼ 8
● Rosso di Montalcino '05	▼ 5
● Brunello di Montalcino '90	♀♀♀ 7
● Brunello di Montalcino Schiena d'Asino '90	♀♀♀ 7
● Brunello di Montalcino '97	♀♀♀ 7
● Brunello di Montalcino Schiena d'Asino '93	♀♀♀ 7
● Brunello di Montalcino '00	♀♀ 7
● Brunello di Montalcino '01	♀♀ 7
● Brunello di Montalcino V. Schiena d'Asino '99	♀♀ 8
● Rosso di Montalcino '04	♀♀ 5

Castello di Meleto
LOC. MELETO
53013 GAIOLE IN CHIANTI [SI]
TEL. 0577749217
www.castellomeleto.it

Melini
LOC. GAGGIANO
53036 POGGIBONSI [SI]
TEL. 0577998511
www.cantinemelini.it

ANNUAL PRODUCTION 575,000 bottles
HECTARES UNDER VINE 180
VITICULTURE METHOD Conventional

ANNUAL PRODUCTION 5,000,000 bottles
HECTARES UNDER VINE 145
VITICULTURE METHOD Conventional

This winery had a peculiar birth, to say the least. Today, you would not expect to run into a newspaper advert that offers interested parties shares in a winery. Yet Castello di Meleto began life as what we would call today a publicly-held company. In this case, a host of individuals became co-owners and bound their fortunes, in the event more emotionally than in financial terms, to this respected Chianti-area operation. Top management currently resides in Switzerland but the winery staff, directed by Roberto Garcea, couldn't have stronger bonds with their local area and the style of the wines shows it. Rainero '04 stood out as the best wine presented this year. A blend in equal parts of sangiovese, merlot and cabernet sauvignon, it boasts clean, admirably focused fruit on the nose and medium weight in the mouth. We liked Chianti Classico Vigna Casi Riserva '04 for its tasty vein of acidity and overall savouriness. The sangiovese-merlot Fiore '03, on the other hand, betrays fruit that is overripe, even though the wine is solidly built and nicely defined on the palate.

This year brings more high marks for Melini and its owner, Gruppo Italiano Vini. Their iconic Chianti, La Selvanella Riserva Classico, is a magnificent cru in Radda in Chianti, and it competed as usual in our national finals. Initial fragrances are slightly blurred in the '04 but it quickly recovers, showing a fleshy mouthfeel and abundant energy in the mouth, along with powerful tannins, exuberant acidity and a finish that could perhaps be a tad more expansive. The beginnings of the winery, located at Pontassieve in the heart of the Chianti Rufina zone, go back to the early 19th century. Laborel, a young member of the Melini dynasty, developed an idea proposed by a glassmaker, Paolo Carrai, and began using the rounded fiasco as a wine bottle. The rest, of course, is history, and sales success on a worldwide scale. The Melinis prospered until the early 20th century, when the winery and label passed through various ownerships until finding its current proprietor. Returning to the wines, the newest creation, Vin Santo Occhio di Pernice '95, is terrific, releasing heady fragrances of sweet dried fruit and then unrolling a luscious, fat palate that just goes on and on. The rest of the wines are equally excellent.

● Chianti Cl. V. Casi Ris. '04	♟♟ 5
● Rainero '04	♟♟ 7
● Chianti Cl. '05	♟ 4
● Fiore '03	♟ 6
● Chianti Cl. Ris. '03	♟♟♟ 5
● Rainero '03	♟♟ 7

● Chianti Cl. La Selvanella Ris. '04	♟♟ 7
○ Vin Santo del Chianti Occhio di Pernice '95	♟♟ 6
● Chianti '06	♟ 3
○ Vernaccia di S. Gimignano Le Grillaie '06	♟ 4
● Chianti Cl. Granaio '05	♟ 4
● Chianti Cl. La Selvanella Ris. '00	♟♟♟ 5
● Chianti Cl. La Selvanella Ris. '01	♟♟♟ 5
● Chianti Cl. La Selvanella Ris. '99	♟♟♟ 6
● Chianti Cl. La Selvanella Ris. '03	♟♟♟ 5

Mocali

LOC. MOCALI
53024 MONTALCINO [SI]
TEL. 0577849485
azmocali@tiscali.it

ANNUAL PRODUCTION 80,000 bottles
HECTARES UNDER VINE 9
VITICULTURE METHOD Conventional

Tiziano Ciacci, once an accomplished motocross rider, has learned to accept competition results with equanimity. This year, they were very good indeed. Not only did Mocali's Brunello Riserva '01 go through to the national finals but the entire line-up of wines performed at laudably high levels. The vineyards enjoy the advantage of a stupendous location, a well-ventilated site on what amounts to a terrace at 350-400 metres' elevation, overlooking the entire area of the church of Santa Restituta. This gives them fruit that is optimally ripe and in superb condition. We preferred the standard version of the two Brunello Riservas we tasted. Blackberry and redcurrant fruit are beautifully framed with nuances of smoke and roasted espresso beans, and we were delighted by the elegance of the palate, where the considerable extractive richness is balanced by nervy acidity. Fine, dense-textured tannins did nothing to slow the good finish. Brunello Vigna delle Raunate is richer and denser but every bit as good, although it needs some time to sand down a few rough edges. I Piaggioni '05 is a pleasant wine.

Il Molino di Grace

LOC. IL VOLANO LUCARELLI
50022 PANZANO [FI]
TEL. 0558561010
www.ilmolinodigrace.com

ANNUAL PRODUCTION 150,000 bottles
HECTARES UNDER VINE 45
VITICULTURE METHOD Conventional

With each successive year, Frank Grace's winery shows that it is no flash in the pan of Chianti wine. The nomination by our Guide of Il Molino di Grace as Up-and-Coming Winery of the Year took some by surprise but succeeding years have confirmed the solidity of his foundations, both in vineyard and in cellar, as is amply attested by the steady stream of subsequent awards. Once again, Frank walked away with Three Glasses, this time courtesy of Chianti Classico Il Margone Riserva '04. Draughts of pungent herbs and bright red berry fruit precede serious power and volume in the mouth, tannins are nicely integrated and a terrific, long-lingering finale is aromatic to a fault. Chianti Classico Riserva '04 also merited a place in the national finals, sterling in its typicity and distinctiveness. But there were a good number of wines in the same class, proof that Il Molino is perfectly capable of working small-lot magic on wines produced in large runs. The all-sangiovese Gratius '05, for example, is an admirable offering with a spicy nose and a lacquered palate. Finally, both versions of Chianti Classico '05 are delicious, well-executed quaffers.

● Brunello di Montalcino Ris. '01	▼▼ 7
● Brunello di Montalcino V. delle Raunate Ris. '01	▼▼ 8
● I Piaggioni '05	▼▼ 4*
● Rosso di Montalcino '05	▼ 4
● Brunello di Montalcino Ris. '98	♀♀ 7
● Brunello di Montalcino '01	♀♀ 6
● Brunello di Montalcino V. delle Raunate '98	♀♀ 7
● Brunello di Montalcino V. delle Raunate '01	♀♀ 7
● Brunello di Montalcino '99	♀♀ 6

● Chianti Cl. Il Margone Ris. '04	▼▼▼ 7
● Chianti Cl. Ris. '04	▼▼ 6
● Gratius '05	▼▼ 7
● Le Falcole '05	▼ 7
● Il Volano '05	▼ 4
● Chianti Cl. Ris. '01	♀♀♀ 5
● Gratius '04	♀♀♀ 7
● Gratius '00	♀♀♀ 7
● Chianti Cl. Il Margone Ris. '01	♀♀ 6
● Chianti Cl. Il Margone Ris. '99	♀♀ 5

Castello di Monsanto

FRAZ. MONSANTO
VIA MONSANTO, 8
50021 BARBERINO VAL D'ELSA [FI]
TEL. 0558059000
www.castellodimonsanto.it

ANNUAL PRODUCTION 400,000 bottles
HECTARES UNDER VINE 72
VITICULTURE METHOD Conventional

Fabrizio Bianchi put on his usual good performance, even though we expected a tad more. True, Il Poggio, the Chianti Classico selection, was missing but the rest of the wines, particularly Riserva '04, just missed that next step up. We believe that Castello di Monsanto has the potential to produce truly remarkable wines. Fabrizio Bianchi was among the first to produce Chianti Classico exclusively with red grapes and one of the few producers, if not the only one, to hold back a significant stock of each good vintage, demonstrating a truly long-term vision. When he put in international varieties, he was also one of the few to keep those wines distinct from his Chianti Classicos, which continued to be made from native grapes only. All of this gives us confidence that we will witness a return to the quality levels that we were used to. This year, the cabernet sauvignon-only Nemo '04 was the best of the wines we tasted. The nose has a lovely pungency and notes of slaty mineral while the palate is rounded, dense and quite savoury. Chianti Classico '05 and Riserva '04 are powerful but they struck us as awkward, with immature tannins that preclude any kind of development. Chardonnay '05 is also below par, lacking its usual flair.

Fattoria di Montecchio

FRAZ. SAN DONATO IN POGGIO
VIA MONTECCHIO, 4
50020 TAVARNELLE VAL DI PESA [FI]
TEL. 0558072235
www.fattoriamontecchio.it

ANNUAL PRODUCTION 113,000 bottles
HECTARES UNDER VINE 33
VITICULTURE METHOD Conventional

Ivo Nuti's winery is back in the Guide after several years' absence, since the wines are finally back up to the quality levels we had come to expect. Fattoria di Montecchio is located in one of the most venerable areas of the Chianti Fiorentino zone. The villa residence, ennobled by the spacious garden surrounding it, belonged to the Marchesi Torrigiani. Nuti purchased it in the 1950s and then in the 1990s began the gradual replanting of the vineyards, renewing the estate's olive groves as well. We liked best Pietracupa '04, Montecchio's sangiovese and cabernet sauvignon Supertuscan. There is abundant ripe fruit leading a medley of other fragrances and then vibrant energy on the palate, although the finish is straitened a little by tannins. Chianti Classico '04 is spirited and imposing, with lovely floral notes and plenty of fruit. Riserva '04 is too unyielding while La Papessa '04, all merlot, seems blurred and out of kilter.

● Nemo '04	♟♟ 7
● Chianti Cl. '05	♟ 4
● Chianti Cl. Ris. '04	♟ 5
O Fabrizio Bianchi Chardonnay '05	♟ 5
● Nemo '01	♟♟♟ 7
● Nemo '00	♟♟ 7
● Chianti Cl. '03	♟♟ 4
● Chianti Cl. Ris. '01	♟♟ 5

● Chianti Cl. '04	♟♟ 4
● Pietracupa '04	♟♟ 6
● Chianti Cl. Ris. '04	♟ 5
● La Papessa '04	♟ 6

Fattoria Montellori

VIA PISTOIESE, 1
50054 FUCECCHIO [FI]
TEL. 0571260641
www.fattoriamontellori.it

ANNUAL PRODUCTION   300,000 bottles
HECTARES UNDER VINE 53
VITICULTURE METHOD   Conventional

Montellori is one of the most prestigious wineries in the area around Florence and it exudes an air of passion, hard work, confidence and high expectations. The results of this year's tastings confirmed that Alessandro Neri knows how to channel these sentiments for he continues to create a series of wines that are outstandingly good. The two thoroughbreds of the stable, Salamartano, a cabernet sauvignon-merlot blend, and the all-sangiovese Dicatum, will from now on alternate release dates to make room for longer bottle ageing. This year, it's the turn of Dicatum '04, which conveys varietal fidelity nicely enriched with subtle spice and earth. The mouth is all about judicious balance and it concludes medium long with welcome complexity. On pretty much the same high level is Moro '05, an easy-drinking mix of sangiovese, malvasia nera and cabernet that reveals a supple structure, glossy tannins and decent elegance. In Chianti Le Caselle '06, good acid and fruit bolster a nice fabric of tannins. Chianti '06 shows bright, appealing flavours while Mandorlo '06, an assemblage of viognier, clairette, marsanne and roussanne, is crisp and linear. The remaining wines are well executed.

Montenidoli

LOC. MONTENIDOLI
53037 SAN GIMIGNANO [SI]
TEL. 0577941565
www.montenidoli.com

ANNUAL PRODUCTION   N.A.
HECTARES UNDER VINE N.A.
VITICULTURE METHOD   Conventional

Elisabetta Fagiuoli describes her Vernaccia as "a red in white's clothing". For her, the first term conveys the wine's body and serious ageing potential, the second its appearance and delicious approachability. To prove it, Elisabetta has brought out a series of strikingly distinctive wines. Vernaccia Carato '03 is vibrant and well defined all the way through, its heady alcohol reflecting the hot vintage, but at the same time showing succulent and juicy with a fine finish to round things off. Both vintages of Il Templare, composed of vernaccia, trebbiano and malvasia, are sublimely expressive. The '03 has great depth and volume, as well as a smooth, savoury palate while the '99, produced in only 2,000 bottles, shows glossy and supple but with no lack of assertive self-confidence, and the finish is nicely mineral edged. Freshness and crisp acidity are the calling cards of Vernaccia Fiore '05 but it has a fine complex foundation, too. Sono Montenidoli '01, all sangiovese, merits attention. Youthful and still fairly homogeneous, it flaunts significant tannic structure. Both the rosé Canaiuolo '06 and Chianti Colli Senesi '04 are lovely, fruit-filled wines and Vernaccia Tradizionale '05 is first-rate.

● Chianti Fattoria Le Caselle '06	♈♈ 3*
● Moro '05	♈♈ 4
● Dicatum '04	♈♈ 6
● Chianti '06	♈ 3
○ Montellori Brut '03	♈ 5
○ Mandorlo '06	♈ 3
● Salamartano '04	♈♈ 6
● Chianti Fattoria Le Caselle '05	♈♈ 3
● Salamartano '01	♈♈ 6
● Tuttosole '04	♈♈ 5
● Salamartano '03	♈♈ 6
● Salamartano '00	♈♈ 6
○ Montellori Brut '01	♈♈ 5
● Dicatum '02	♈♈ 5
● Dicatum '03	♈♈ 5
● Dicatum '01	♈♈ 6

○ Vernaccia di S. Gimignano Carato '03	♈♈ 6
○ Il Templare '03	♈♈ 4
○ Vernaccia di S. Gimignano Tradizionale '05	♈♈ 3*
○ Vernaccia di S. Gimignano Fiore '05	♈♈ 4
● Sono Montenidoli '01	♈♈ 5
○ Il Templare '99	♈♈ 4
☉ Canaiuolo '06	♈ 4
● Chianti Colli Senesi '04	♈ 4
○ Vernaccia di S. Gimignano Carato '02	♈♈♈ 6
○ Vernaccia di S. Gimignano Carato '01	♈♈ 5
○ Vernaccia di S. Gimignano Fiore '01	♈♈ 4
○ Vernaccia di S. Gimignano Fiore '04	♈♈ 4

Monteraponi

LOC. MONTERAPONI
53017 RADDA IN CHIANTI [SI]
TEL. 055352601
www.monteraponi.it

ANNUAL PRODUCTION 30,000 bottles
HECTARES UNDER VINE 9.5
VITICULTURE METHOD Conventional

The Braganti family debuted two years ago
in the Guide, with a wine in the finals, but
last year was a pause of sorts. This time,
they're back with a full profile. Monteraponi
sits on its the hill it is named after where
once was a medieval hamlet belonging to
Conte Ugo, Marchese and ruler of Tuscany
in the late tenth century. He later transferred
it to the monastery he founded at Poggio
Martori, today the upper part of Poggibonsi.
The Monteraponi cellars, right under the
tower, probably date back to the 12th
century, when the main structure was built.
Today, they house the binning cellars. The
Braganti philosophy is to focus as closely as
possible on the expression of terroir. In
terms of sangiovese, this means an elegant
wine that eschews excessive power and
whose forte is an interplay of nuances. This
is precisely what we find in Il Campitello '04,
a wine that went to the national finals. The
flavours on the palate are full without being
overwhelming and the finale is long and
utterly delicious. In contrast, the tannins
seem a tad clenched in the Chianti Classico
'05, and the nose blurred, but the palate is
appealing and savoury enough.
Monteraponi also enjoys an enviable
reputation for its extravirgin olive oil.

★ Montevertine

LOC. MONTEVERTINE
53017 RADDA IN CHIANTI [SI]
TEL. 0577738009
www.montevertine.it

ANNUAL PRODUCTION 75,000 bottles
HECTARES UNDER VINE 15
VITICULTURE METHOD Conventional

For Montevertine, the difference between a
great year and a so-so year is measured in
Three Glass awards. In vintages of middling
quality, Pergole Torte comes to the fore, its
characteristic elegance and confident,
stately progression always managing to
eclipse its fellows. In exceptional vintages,
another wine – Montevertine – joins it,
striding along at the same majestic pace.
The 2004 vintage was great, of course, and
both wines earned Three Glasses. It is
difficult to find new descriptors for wines
that for the last 20 years have been thrilling
wine lovers, remaining so consistently
faithful to themselves and at the same time
so uncannily in touch with what is needed
to retain contemporary appeal. The all-
sangiovese Pergole Torte shows more
backbone and support from its various
components. We relish, amidst its clean-
edged fruit, the expected note of rain-
soaked earth and subtle, faded flower petal.
It unfurls self-confident vitality in the mouth,
empowered by acidity that is exquisitely
magisterial. Equally vibrant, albeit in a
different way, is Montevertine, from
sangiovese, canaiolo and colorino.
Radiantly elegant, it knows it has few peers.
Pian del Ciampolo '05 is a slender wine
from a slender year.

● Chianti Cl. Ris. Il Campitello '04	♟♟	5
● Chianti Cl. '05	♟	4
● Chianti Cl. '03	♟♟	4

● Le Pergole Torte '04	♟♟♟	8
● Montevertine '04	♟♟♟	6
● Pian del Ciampolo '05	♟	4
● Le Pergole Torte '01	♟♟♟	8
● Le Pergole Torte '90	♟♟♟	8
● Le Pergole Torte '92	♟♟♟	8
● Le Pergole Torte '88	♟♟♟	8
● Montevertine Ris. '85	♟♟♟	5
● Le Pergole Torte '83	♟♟♟	8
● Montevertine '01	♟♟♟	6
● Le Pergole Torte '99	♟♟♟	8
● Le Pergole Torte '03	♟♟♟	8
● Le Pergole Torte '86	♟♟♟	8

Moris Farms
LOC. CURA NUOVA
FATTORIA POGGETTI
58024 MASSA MARITTIMA [GR]
TEL. 0566919135
www.morisfarms.it

ANNUAL PRODUCTION 450,000 bottles
HECTARES UNDER VINE 70
VITICULTURE METHOD Conventional

Adolfo Parentin directs Moris Farms, increasingly assisted by his son Giulio. Their profile this year is unfortunately marked by a lacuna where Avvoltore should be. In 2005 a sudden hailstorm so damaged the fruit from that vineyard that the staff could not produce the wine that year. Despite this significant setback, the other wines all showed well, demonstrating again the solid stature of this major Maremma-based producer. It comes as no surprise then that Morellino Riserva '04 was among our finalists. It parades its own personality right from the start with an elegant medley of luxuriant fruit lifted by spice and hints of smoke. Heft in the mouth provides an excellent foil, along with scrumptious tannins and an athletic thrust, plus almost cutting acidity. Intriguing scents of earth infuse Morellino '06, which is overall crisp and ultra-supple. Monteregio '05 is still a bit closed on the nose but its racy, vivacious palate makes it a real pleaser. Vermentino '06 is straightforward and not too exciting.

La Mormoraia
LOC. SANT'ANDREA, 15
53037 SAN GIMIGNANO [SI]
TEL. 0577940096
www.mormoraia.it

ANNUAL PRODUCTION N.A.
HECTARES UNDER VINE 27
VITICULTURE METHOD Conventional

Years ago, Pino and Franca Passoni decided to add a winery to a property that had been just a real estate investment. But the Tuscan landscape exercised such a fascination that they ended up creating a model operation and very nearly moved here permanently from Milan. Today, Mormoraia comprises 90 hectares, with almost 30 under vine, and the wines run from Vernaccia DOCG to full-bodied reds. The '05 Riserva again ranked among the best from the Vernaccia di San Gimignano DOCG. After an intense, luminous straw yellow, it develops rich fragrances of well-ripened fruit, cakes, toasty oak and pungent herbs. The palate shows similar character, masterfully built up and balanced, well fruited throughout, and drives into a captivating, mineral-laced finish. From the other bottles, we liked the superb, succulent and crisp San Gimignano Merlot '05 with its glossy tannins. The cask-aged Mytilus '04 is from sangiovese, merlot and syrah. We found it full-bodied, velvet smooth and attractively spicy. Ostrea Grigia '05, a medley of chardonnay, pinot bianco and sauvignon, is well structured, but we would have liked to see a tad more acid edge. The other wines are more than satisfactory.

● Morellino di Scansano Ris. '04	♟♟ 5
● Morellino di Scansano '06	♟♟ 4
● Monteregio di Massa Marittima Rosso '05	♟ 4
○ Vermentino '06	♟ 4
● Avvoltore '00	♟♟♟ 6
● Avvoltore '04	♟♟♟ 6
● Avvoltore '01	♟♟♟ 6
● Avvoltore '99	♟♟♟ 6
● Avvoltore '02	♟♟ 6
● Avvoltore '03	♟♟ 6
● Morellino di Scansano Ris. '00	♟♟ 5
● Morellino di Scansano Ris. '01	♟♟ 5
● Morellino di Scansano Ris. '97	♟♟ 4
● Morellino di Scansano Ris. '98	♟♟ 4
● Morellino di Scansano Ris. '99	♟♟ 5

○ Vernaccia di S. Gimignano Ris. '05	♟♟ 5*
● Mitylus '04	♟♟ 6
○ Vernaccia di S. Gimignano '06	♟♟ 4*
● San Gimignano Merlot '05	♟♟ 5*
○ Ostrea Grigia '05	♟♟ 5
● Neitea '05	♟♟ 5
● Chianti Colli Senesi '06	♟ 4
○ Vernaccia di S. Gimignano Passoni '06	♟ 4
○ Vernaccia di S. Gimignano Ris. '03	♟♟ 4
○ Vernaccia di S. Gimignano Ris. '04	♟♟ 4
● San Gimignano Merlot '04	♟♟ 5
● Neitea '04	♟♟ 4
● Neitea '03	♟♟ 4

Niccolai - Palagetto
VIA MONTEOLIVETO, 46
53037 SAN GIMIGNANO [SI]
TEL. 0577943090
www.tenuteniccolai.it

ANNUAL PRODUCTION 350,000 bottles
HECTARES UNDER VINE 100
VITICULTURE METHOD Conventional

Around San Gimignano, the name Palagetto carries a certain weight. But at our last tastings, we were expecting more from these wines, especially considering their potential and renown, despite a generally commendable standard of quality. Actually, we did notice some changes, like the reorganization of the range of products and more care over release to market, but they did not have the desired effect. We were particularly impressed with the Vernaccia Riserva '04, with its subtle notes of spring flowers and aromatic herbs on the nose, and generous, harmonious palate with minerally finesse, measured use of oak and fairly long finish. The Vernaccia Santa Chiara '06 is equally good, showing nice fruit and flowers on the nose, alongside hints of vanilla, followed by a palate with good dynamic acidity. The Vin Santo di San Gimignano '01 is a pleasant new addition while the San Gimignano Sottobosco '03 is well focused, soft and succulent with smooth tannins and nice complexity. There were less impressive performances from the San Gimignano Syrah Uno di Quattro '04, with a supple flavour, and the white Niccolò '06, made from vermentino, chardonnay and sauvignon.

Fattoria Nittardi
LOC. NITTARDI
53011 CASTELLINA IN CHIANTI [SI]
TEL. 0577740269
www.chianticlassico.com

ANNUAL PRODUCTION 90,000 bottles
HECTARES UNDER VINE 21
VITICULTURE METHOD Conventional

The overall result from Peter Fenfert and Stefania Canali's winery was good, with two wines through to the final. We expected no less from this property, which has shown remarkably consistent results over the years. There was an interesting performance from Nectar Dei '05, produced in Maremma from mainly merlot and cabernet sauvignon. Despite considerable structure, partly because of over-generous use of oak, the wine dips mid palate but the aromas, which include fruit and aromatic herbs, are very generous. Some of the bottles of Riserva di Chianti Classico '04 have labels designed by famous artists and the latest is by John Lennon's widow, Yoko Ono. This wine has a clearly defined nose with fruity, subtly spicy aromas and a rounded, fleshy body with nicely blended tannins and a good lingering finish. The Chianti Classico '05 is fresh-tasting, characterful and appetizing.

● San Gimignano Sottobosco '03	⟡⟡ 5
○ Vernaccia di S. Gimignano Ris. '04	⟡⟡ 4
○ Vernaccia di S. Gimignano V. Santa Chiara '06	⟡⟡ 4*
○ Vin Santo di San Gimignano '01	⟡⟡ 6
● Chianti Colli Senesi '05	⟡ 3
○ Vernaccia di S. Gimignano '06	⟡ 3
○ l'Niccolò '06	⟡ 4
● San Gimignano Syrah Uno di Quattro '04	⟡ 7
○ Vernaccia di S. Gimignano Ris. '01	♟♟ 4
○ Vernaccia di S. Gimignano Ris. '02	♟♟ 4
○ l'Niccolò '04	♟♟ 4
● San Gimignano Uno di Quattro '03	♟♟ 8
○ Vernaccia di S. Gimignano V. Santa Chiara '05	♟♟ 4
○ l'Niccolò '05	♟♟ 5

● Chianti Cl. Ris. '04	⟡⟡ 7
● Nectar Dei '05	⟡⟡ 7
● Chianti Cl. Casanuova di Nittardi '05	⟡ 5
● Chianti Cl. Ris. '98	♟♟♟ 7
● Chianti Cl. Ris. '99	♟♟ 7
● Nectar Dei '03	♟♟ 6
● Chianti Cl. Ris. '00	♟♟ 7
● Chianti Cl. Casanuova di Nittardi '04	♟♟ 5

★ Tenuta dell'Ornellaia

VIA BOLGHERESE, 191
57022 BOLGHERI [LI]
TEL. 056571811
www.ornellaia.it

Siro Pacenti

LOC. PELAGRILLI, 1
53024 MONTALCINO [SI]
TEL. 0577848662
pacentisiro@libero.it

ANNUAL PRODUCTION 730,000 bottles
HECTARES UNDER VINE 97
VITICULTURE METHOD Conventional

ANNUAL PRODUCTION 80,000 bottles
HECTARES UNDER VINE 20
VITICULTURE METHOD Conventional

With the release of the '04 vintage of the leading wines, Ornellaia and Masseto, Tenuta dell'Ornellaia recovers from last year's lean pickings. Both wines won Three Glasses, demonstrating, if there any need, that this is one of the best wineries in Italy. Elegance is, as usual, the most apposite word for the '04 Bolgheri Superiore Ornellaia. Cherry jam, liquorice, hints of balsam on the nose precede a wonderfully balanced, harmonious palate thanks to the perfect pairing of tannin and acidity that both supports and defines the very lingering finish. A fruitier, more pervasive wine than the '01, this is another version of an acknowledged masterpiece. The other jewel in the winery's crown is the mouthfilling Masseto, a monovarietal Merlot, which has more impact and texture. Side by side on the nose are the classic plum and blackberry jam aromas of the grape and the minerally, fumé sensations of the superb territory. Explosive on entry, the palate unfolds with supple, well-defined tannins. The growing year was a little less generous with Le Volte and Le Serre Nuove, both '05.

Giancarlo Pacenti has always been one of Montalcino's leading producers. He was the first to start using barriques for Montalcino wines, both the Rosso and the Brunello, and asked for help from famous external consultants to fully understand the possible synergies of ageing Brunello is smaller oak barrels, in the process acquiring extensive knowledge of the subject. He was also the first to really believe in Rosso di Montalcino, a wine that had not, historically, been given much consideration. In Giancarlo's view, the Rosso should also be treated as an important wine that can represent the local area and its potential, albeit in a less complex and more accessible way than Brunello. This year, we only tasted the Rosso '05, since the Brunello was not produced in '02, which was reckoned to be a substandard vintage. Vibrant cherry and red berry fruit on the nose lead into a palate nicely supported by acidity, with lively, rigid tannins and an intense finish.

● Bolgheri Sup. Ornellaia '04	♟♟♟	8
● Masseto '04	♟♟♟	8
● Bolgheri Rosso Le Serre Nuove '05	♟	7
● Le Volte '05	♟	4
● Bolgheri Sup. Ornellaia '01	♟♟♟	8
● Bolgheri Sup. Ornellaia '97	♟♟♟	8
● Masseto '00	♟♟♟	8
● Masseto '98	♟♟♟	8
● Masseto '94	♟♟♟	8
● Masseto '93	♟♟♟	8
● Ornellaia '93	♟♟♟	8
● Masseto '95	♟♟♟	8
● Masseto '99	♟♟♟	8
● Masseto '97	♟♟♟	8
● Masseto '01	♟♟♟	8
● Bolgheri Sup. Ornellaia '99	♟♟♟	8
● Bolgheri Sup. Ornellaia '98	♟♟♟	8
● Bolgheri Sup. Ornellaia '02	♟♟♟	8

● Rosso di Montalcino '05	♟♟	6
● Brunello di Montalcino '88	♟♟♟	8
● Brunello di Montalcino '95	♟♟♟	8
● Brunello di Montalcino '97	♟♟♟	8
● Brunello di Montalcino '96	♟♟♟	8
● Rosso di Montalcino '01	♟♟	6
● Brunello di Montalcino '01	♟♟	8
● Brunello di Montalcino '99	♟♟	8
● Rosso di Montalcino '99	♟♟	5
● Brunello di Montalcino '00	♟♟	8

Podere Il Palazzino

FRAZ. MONTI IN CHIANTI
POD. IL PALAZZINO
53013 GAIOLE IN CHIANTI [SI]
TEL. 0577747008
www.podereilpalazzino.it

ANNUAL PRODUCTION 60,000 bottles
HECTARES UNDER VINE 20
VITICULTURE METHOD Conventional

Our tasting of the Sderci family's wines this time left us feeling a little let down. For many wineries two wines achieving Two Glasses would be more than flattering but this is not the case with Podere Il Palazzino. Over the years, they have astounded us with their sound, stylistically flawless wines. Their passion and care is almost unique, as is shown by the fact that the grapes from the various vineyard selections are fermented separately to bring out the features of their provenance. Only native grape varieties are used: sangiovese, canaiolo, malvasia nera. The Chianti Classicos, the local wine par excellence, reveal a style that owes more to elegance than strength. Yet all this was not enough this year. The Grosso Sanese '04 struggles to find expression on the nose, although the palate is rounded and characterful, with a tangy, flavoursome finish. The Argenina '05 is also confused initially, opening out into minerally, fruity aromas and strong tannins on the palate, which signs off unhurriedly. La Pieve '04 is less impressive, showing ruffled and poorly balanced. Casina Girasole '05, from sangiovese with malvasia nera and canaiolo, and Vin Santo '98 are pleasant and uncomplicated.

● Chianti Cl. Argenina '05	🍷🍷	4
● Chianti Cl. Grosso Sanese '04	🍷🍷	6
● Casina Girasole '05	🍷	3
● Chianti Cl. La Pieve '04	🍷	5
O Vin Santo del Chianti Cl. '98	🍷	6
● Chianti Cl. Grosso Sanese '00	🍷🍷🍷	8
● Chianti Cl. Grosso Sanese '01	🍷🍷🍷	8
● Chianti Cl. Grosso Sanese '03	🍷🍷	6

Il Palazzone

LOC. DUE PORTE, 245
53024 MONTALCINO [SI]
TEL. 0577835764
www.ilpalazzone.com

ANNUAL PRODUCTION 20,000 bottles
HECTARES UNDER VINE 10
VITICULTURE METHOD Conventional

We report good results as usual for Il Palazzone, the Montalcino estate owned by Dick Parsons. The vineyards are situated in two different but somehow complementary parts of the area: some near the winery centre, at 500 metres above sea level, and the others to the east towards Val d'Orcia. The wines are classic in style, like new arrival Lorenzo e Isabella '05, named after the owner's parents. Although produced from international grape varieties, this wine has a certain austerity, black berry fruit on the nose with hints of toasty aromas heralding a characterful palate free of any excess. The Brunello Riserva '01 is wonderful. A vibrant, generous nose layers clear morello and wild cherries over stylish boisé and cocoa powder, hints of spice, cinnamon and vanilla, classic leaf tobacco and a sweet veining of leather. The palate is confident and austere with well-defined acidity and tannin and a complex, very lingering finish. The Brunello '02 is below par, showing rather too predictable and lacking personality.

● Brunello di Montalcino Ris. '01	🍷🍷🍷	7
● Lorenzo e Isabella '05	🍷🍷	5
● Brunello di Montalcino '02	🍷	7
● Brunello di Montalcino '01	🍷🍷🍷	7
● Brunello di Montalcino Ris. '99	🍷🍷🍷	7
● Brunello di Montalcino '00	🍷🍷	7
● Brunello di Montalcino '99	🍷🍷	7
● Brunello di Montalcino Ris. '97	🍷🍷	8

Castello della Paneretta

LOC. MONSANTO
S.DA DELLA PANERETTA, 35
50021 BARBERINO VAL D'ELSA [FI]
TEL. 0558059003
stefano.paneretta@tin.it

ANNUAL PRODUCTION 120,000 bottles
HECTARES UNDER VINE 22.5
VITICULTURE METHOD Conventional

Fewer wines were presented than usual this year by Castello della Paneretta but enough to guarantee the long profile, given the results they achieved. The area has an ancient vocation for wine, as we can tell from the castle's four centuries of activity and the character of the area is clear in the ageing potential of the wines. It would be difficult to call these bottles easy-going or accessibly seductive. They need time to express themselves, hence the decision to extend the maturation period of Le Terrine '03. This blend of sangiovese and canaiolo has striking mineral and black berry fruit aromas, powerful structure, firm tannins and freshness that make it a beautifully drinkable wine. The Riserva Torre a Destra '04 tends to open reluctantly on the nose but then unveils a range of prevalently fruity aromas. The palate is tangy and very lingering. The Chianti Classico '05 has fresher aromas than the others, with hints of aromatic herbs, but the finish is held back somewhat by rigid tannin on the palate.

Giovanni Panizzi

FRAZ. SANTA MARGHERITA
LOC. RACCIANO, 34
53037 SAN GIMIGNANO [SI]
TEL. 0577941576
www.panizzi.it

ANNUAL PRODUCTION 200,000 bottles
HECTARES UNDER VINE 30
VITICULTURE METHOD Conventional

In an increasingly standardized world, where even wines seem to be all the same, there is a refreshing exception in Giovanni Panizzi's Vernaccia. Giovanni's style has become known and admired around the world, achieving national and international recognition, and consolidating his reputation as an excellent exponent of the art of white winemaking. The Vernaccia Riserva '03, which came close to winning Three Glasses, is not only one of the best versions ever made. It also impressively argues the case for the wine's cellarability. Bright in colour, with greenish highlights, it throws an enchanting fruit and flower nose lifted by the spiciness of the oak. In the mouth, it is fresh, tangy and well sustained with a lingering finish. The Vigna Santa Margherita '06 is a fine bottle. Fragrant oak-laced fruit on the nose precedes a lively, well-coordinated palate. The Bianco di Gianni '04, from chardonnay, surprised us, showing buttery, invigorating and well sustained. The Vernaccia '06 is impeccably enjoyable, with good concentration and depth. The Chianti Colli Senesi Vertunno '04 and Ceraso '06 are sound.

● Chianti Cl. Torre a Destra Ris. '04	▼▼	5
● Le Terrine '03	▼▼	5
● Chianti Cl. '05	▼	4
● Le Terrine '01	♀♀	6
● Chianti Cl. Torre a Destra Ris. '03	♀♀	6

O Vernaccia di S. Gimignano Ris. '03	▼▼	6
O Bianco di Gianni '04	▼▼	4
O Vernaccia di San Gimignano V. Santa Margherita '06	▼▼	4
O Vernaccia di S. Gimignano '06	▼▼	4
● Ceraso '06	▼	4
● Chianti Colli Senesi Vertunno '04	▼	4
O Vernaccia di S. Gimignano Ris. '98	♀♀♀	6
O Vernaccia di S. Gimignano Ris. '02	♀♀	5
O Vernaccia di San Gimignano V. Santa Margherita '05	♀♀	4
O Vernaccia di San Gimignano V. Santa Margherita '04	♀♀	4
O Vernaccia di S. Gimignano Ris. '99	♀♀	6
O Vernaccia di San Gimignano V. Santa Margherita '03	♀♀	4
O Vernaccia di S. Gimignano '05	♀♀	4

Panzanello

VIA CASE SPARSE, 86
50022 PANZANO [FI]
TEL. 055852470
www.panzanello.it

ANNUAL PRODUCTION 70,000 bottles
HECTARES UNDER VINE 22
VITICULTURE METHOD Certified organic

The Sommaruga family winery did well this
year, although we might add that the area's
full potential has not yet been tapped.
Documents preserved in the Florence land
register show that this estate, which is
traditionally part of the Chianti Classico
zone, has grown grapes and olives since
the 15th century. On top of that, the
vineyards have been certified organic for
almost ten years, and care of the vineyards
and winemaking are entrusted to the widely
respected Gioia Cresti. This year, the most
impressive wine was Il Manuzio '03, a
monovarietal Sangiovese with a generous
nose that marries blackberry jam aromas
with hints of cinnamon and cloves. The
palate is austere, with very fine-grained
tannins and an echo of fruit in the finish. The
surprising Tregaio '06, made from malvasia
and trebbiano, has fresh, appetizing
aromas, with lively, complex florality, and a
lean but tangy palate with an enjoyable
finish. The Chianti Classico '05 is less
successful. The nose is closed and the
structure stiffish.

Il Paradiso

LOC. STRADA, 21A
53037 SAN GIMIGNANO [SI]
TEL. 0577941500
www.telematicaitalia.it/ilparadiso

ANNUAL PRODUCTION 150,000 bottles
HECTARES UNDER VINE 27.8
VITICULTURE METHOD Conventional

The quality of Poderi del Paradiso wines is
always high. The winery established itself in
the front rank of local and Italian
winemaking some years ago, thanks both
to repeated critical recognition and to the
enviable market success of the wines. The
way to win the market's heart, according to
Vasco Cetti, is through adequate bottle
ageing. Which is why this year he presented
us with a reduced number of wines,
postponing until next year the release of the
sangiovese Paterno II and the merlot-only A
Filippo. Meanwhile, the cabernet and merlot
Saxa Calida '04 and the '04 Mangiafoco,
from cabernet sauvignon, both went
through to the final selections. The former
has earthy, vegetal aromas on a spicy
background and a succulently dynamic,
fairly deep palate with a tangy finish. The
Mangiafoco has an intriguing nose with
hints of pepper and spice alternating with
black berry fruit. The palate is fruity with
sweet, close-knit tannins and the finish
lingers. The Vernaccia '06 and the
Biscondola '05 are both nice while the
Bottaccio '03 is below par.

● Il Manuzio '03	♟♟	7
○ Tregaio '06	♟♟	4
● Chianti Cl. Panzanello '05	♟	4
● Il Manuzio '01	♟♟	6
● Chianti Cl. Panzanello '04	♟♟	4
● Il Manuzio '00	♟♟	6
● Chianti Cl. Panzanello Ris. '03	♟♟	6

● Mangiafoco '04	♟♟	6
● Saxa Calida '04	♟♟	7
○ Vernaccia di S. Gimignano '06	♟♟	3*
○ Vernaccia di S. Gimignano Biscondola '05	♟♟	4
● Bottaccio '03	♟	5
● A Filippo '02	♟♟♟	5
● Saxa Calida '00	♟♟♟	6
● Saxa Calida '99	♟♟♟	5
● Mangiafoco '03	♟♟	5
● Paterno II '99	♟♟	6
● Saxa Calida '03	♟♟	7
● Saxa Calida '02	♟♟	7

Petra

LOC. S. LORENZO ALTO, 131
57028 SUVERETO [LI]
TEL. 0565845308
www.petrawine.it

Villa Petriolo

VIA DI PETRIOLO, 7
50050 CERRETO GUIDI [FI]
TEL. 057155284
www.villapetriolo.com

ANNUAL PRODUCTION 250,000 bottles
HECTARES UNDER VINE 95
VITICULTURE METHOD Conventional

ANNUAL PRODUCTION 55,500 bottles
HECTARES UNDER VINE 14
VITICULTURE METHOD Conventional

This year Petra, the Tuscan arm of the Moretti group, won Three Glasses for the magnificent '04 version of the wine of the same name. At last, it expresses the potential we had seen for years. The futuristic cellar, very extensive vineyards and enormous commitment poured into every aspect of the operation were waiting for their just reward. No sooner said than done. This year, the wines are much more clearly defined and show the typical elegance of this area. The cabernet sauvignon and merlot Petra '04 reveals all the qualities of a thoroughbred. A stylish, intriguing range of aromas complements a palate that impresses for its finesse and long, intense finish. The Petra '03, one of the best wines from that inauspicious year, combines fruity softness and sweetness with slightly austere tannin and a well-sustained, tangy finish. Val di Cornia Ebo '04 has a spicy, vegetal nose and a sweet, nicely harmonious flavour. The Zingari '05, from merlot, syrah, petit verdot and sangiovese, is unpretentious and well made.

Silvia Maestrelli certainly doesn't lack ideas or energy. Last year, she reclaimed a place in the Guide and this year she has consolidated it, as well as dreaming up a new way to enhance her cellar's visibility in Tuscan winemaking. She has launched a wine-related literary competition that has enjoyed remarkable success, and rounded things off with the debut of a new red. This latest addition is the Chianti Rosae Mnemosis '06, a single vineyard selection with a contemporary style and lovely personality. Youthful, almost heady, fruit with aromatic herbs on the nose usher in a deliciously succulent palate with sweet, flavoursome tannins and a consistent finish. Golpaja '05, from sangiovese, cabernet and merlot, is equally good and very appealing. The palate shows concentration, good progression and structure, never missing a beat through to the lingering finish. The '06 Chianti is a good wine with a vibrant ripe fruit flavour, offset by a generously caressing mouthfeel. The Vin Santo '02 has aromas of chestnut jam, dried figs and vanilla, then well-gauged sweetness on the palate.

● Petra Rosso '04	￦￦￦ 8
● Petra Rosso '03	￦￦ 8
● Val di Cornia Ebo '04	￦ 4
● Zingari '05	￦ 4
● Petra Rosso '97	￦￦ 5
● Petra Rosso '98	￦￦ 6

● Golpaja '05	￦￦ 5
● Chianti Rosae Mnemosis '06	￦￦ 5
● Chianti Villa Petriolo '06	￦ 4*
O Vin Santo del Chianti '02	￦ 6
● Golpaja '00	￦￦ 4
O Vin Santo del Chianti '00	￦￦ 5
O Vin Santo del Chianti '98	￦￦ 5
● Golpaja '99	￦￦ 4
● Golpaja '04	￦￦ 5
● Golpaja '01	￦￦ 5
● Golpaja '03	￦￦ 5

Fattoria Petrolo

FRAZ. MERCATALE VALDARNO
LOC. GALATRONA
VIA PETROLO, 30
52021 BUCINE [AR]
TEL. 0559911322
www.petrolo.it

ANNUAL PRODUCTION 55,000 bottles
HECTARES UNDER VINE 31
VITICULTURE METHOD Conventional

One of the keys to the consistently excellent quality of the wines from Fattoria di Petrolo is the unique combination of viticulture-friendly factors. These include the local Colli Aretini area, the hills flanking the Chianti mountains, which has for centuries been recognized as outstanding wine country; shrewd, highly selective vineyard management; and a skill in the cellar that produces wines that are generally modern in colour, density, and extract without limiting themselves to such basic parameters. Petrolo wines have a very strong sense of place. A magnificent example of this is the Galatrona, a Merlot of depth that generally requires cellar time to achieve its best expression and always maintains its signature Chianti-style acid grip and backbone. These features are particularly evident in the gutsy, sturdy '05 version, which swept up Three Glasses. The sangiovese Torrione '05 is not quite as successful as the '04, not least because of the growing year, and is only very good, as is the Vin Santo '99.

Piaggia

LOC. POGGETTO
VIA CEGOLI, 47
59016 POGGIO A CAIANO [PO]
TEL. 0558705401
aziendapiaggia@virgilio.it

ANNUAL PRODUCTION 65,000 bottles
HECTARES UNDER VINE 15
VITICULTURE METHOD Conventional

A producer's professionalism can be inferred above all from consistently high quality. In this sense Mauro Vannucci is every inch a professional. Every year, he guarantees constancy, overcoming the problems of the various vintage years thanks above all to his scrupulous hard work in the vineyards. From '04 and '05 come wines that are more balanced with greater finesse, shrewd use of oak and extract that is as remarkable as ever. It is no coincidence that the Carmignano Sasso '05 has a juicy, dense, fruit-led palate and a slim body that adds impetus to the flavour as it progresses into an intense, fruity, lingering finish. The Carmignano Riserva '04 is equally good with complex, profound aromas and a very dense, firm, fruit-rich palate and good length, as well as powerful tannic structure that still requires a little softening. The Poggio de' Colli, a monovarietal Cabernet Franc is growing. In the '05 edition, it is dark, with hints of balsam and spice on the nose. There is remarkable impact and structure on the palate, which is a little cropped by slightly over-assertive tannins.

● Galatrona '05	♟♟♟	8
● Torrione '05	♟♟	5
○ Vin Santo del Chianti '99	♟♟	6
● Galatrona '00	♟♟♟	8
● Galatrona '97	♟♟♟	7
● Galatrona '99	♟♟♟	7
● Galatrona '98	♟♟♟	7
● Galatrona '04	♟♟♟	7
● Galatrona '01	♟♟♟	8
● Galatrona '02	♟♟	8
● Torrione '04	♟♟	5
● Galatrona '03	♟♟	8

● Carmignano Ris. '04	♟♟	6
● Carmignano Sasso '05	♟♟	5
● Poggio de' Colli '05	♟♟	7
● Carmignano Ris. '97	♟♟♟	5
● Il Sasso '01	♟♟♟	5
● Carmignano Ris. '98	♟♟♟	6
● Carmignano Ris. '99	♟♟♟	6
● Carmignano Ris. '00	♟♟	6
● Carmignano Ris. '01	♟♟	6
● Il Sasso '03	♟♟	5
● Il Sasso '00	♟♟	5
● Carmignano Ris. '03	♟♟	6
● Carmignano Ris. '02	♟♟	6
● Poggio de' Colli '04	♟♟	8

Piancornello

LOC. PIANCORNELLO
53024 MONTALCINO [SI]
TEL. 0577844105
piancorello@libero.it

ANNUAL PRODUCTION 50,000 bottles
HECTARES UNDER VINE 10
VITICULTURE METHOD Conventional

Piancornello is situated in the deep south of Montalcino near Val d'Orcia, an area that produces rich, powerful wines. Former doctor Roberto Monaci runs the family winery with serious commitment, as is shown by his continuous vinification tests to improve the already excellent products. Monaci did not release a '02 Brunello, choosing to skip that very tricky year because the wine would not have been up to the cellar's standard. But the Brunello Riserva '01 is a more than adequate consolation, and made it to the finals, as it so often does. It is held back only by slightly excessive oak, especially on the nose, where the toasted coffee aromas overwhelm the fruit. The generous palate makes a good impact, although the development is hindered by over-generous tannin, toasty sensations returning on the intense finish. The Rosso di Montalcino '05 is one of the year's best. Balanced toasted oak aromas blend well with lovely ripe cherries on the nose and the palate is dynamic and appealing, with well-judged acidity.

Piazzano

VIA DI PIAZZANO, 5
50053 EMPOLI [FI]
TEL. 0571994032
www.fattoriadipiazzano.it

ANNUAL PRODUCTION 60,000 bottles
HECTARES UNDER VINE 34
VITICULTURE METHOD Conventional

There was confident confirmation for the Guide profile earned by the Bettarini brothers' winery. The ambitious, determined pair have drawn on their father's experience while exploring news ideas and objectives, which highlight the huge potential that was only occasionally revealed by the previous management. We had already noted their desire to do well and experiment last year and the modern, nicely put-together wines are presented in the new vintage with a new label. The Sangiovese '05 is good, presenting a rounded, sweet palate with well-judged tannin and a lingering fruity finish. The spicy Syrah '05 impresses with supple, well-sustained progression on the generous, mouthfilling palate. The Chianti Camerata Riserva '04 is not bad, showing gutsy, tannic and flavoursome with good follow-through. The debut of the Merlot '05, though, was not very exciting. It's firm and generous but less than satisfying as the tannins are still rigid in the finish. The heady, smooth Chianti, the fruity, balanced Chianti Rio Camerata '06 and the weighty, tannic Ventoso, from sangiovese and canaiolo, are all well made.

● Brunello di Montalcino Ris. '01	▼▼	7
● Rosso di Montalcino '05	▼▼	4
● Brunello di Montalcino '99	♀♀♀	7
● Brunello di Montalcino '01	♀♀	7
● Brunello di Montalcino '96	♀♀	6
● Brunello di Montalcino '97	♀♀	7
● Brunello di Montalcino '00	♀♀	7

● Chianti Rio Camerata Ris. '04	▼▼	5
● Piazzano Syrah '05	▼▼	5
● Piazzano Sangiovese '05	▼▼	5
● Chianti '06	▼	3*
● Ventoso '06	▼	3
● Merlot '05	▼	5
● Chianti Rio Camerata '06	▼	4
● Chianti '05	♀♀	3*
● Piazzano Syrah '04	♀♀	5
● Piazzano Sangiovese '04	♀♀	6

Il Pinino
LOC. PININO, 327
53024 MONTALCINO [SI]
TEL. 0577849381
www.pinino.com

ANNUAL PRODUCTION 20,000 bottles
HECTARES UNDER VINE 13
VITICULTURE METHOD Conventional

Montalcino is now one of Italy's most international wine-producing areas. It's not so much because of the many tourists who visit the town but because so many foreigners fall in love with the beauties of the area, decide to buy estates and set out to make Brunello. In the wake of all the Americans, Germans and French, here is a pleasant Spanish couple, the Hernandez, who own Pinino. The range is good quality and the Brunello '02 towers above the rest, with intense ruby red colour and a generously fruity nose that hints at white and wild cherries blending harmoniously with the smoky wood aromas. The well-balanced palate with its extremely appealing mouthfeel and follow-through leads to a generous, lingering finish. Particular attention is paid to extract so it is no surprise to find such balance already. Of the two Rosso di Montalcinos, we found the standard-label more impressive than the Clandestino. The former has generous black berry aromas and a subtle, relaxed palate culminating in a generously fruity finish, while the Clandestino shows still rather biting if not actually bitter tannin, which shortens the finish. Why not withhold release for another year?

Podere Brizio
LOC. PODERE BRIZIO, 67
53024 MONTALCINO [SI]
TEL. 0577846004
www.poderebrizio.it

ANNUAL PRODUCTION 50,000 bottles
HECTARES UNDER VINE 17
VITICULTURE METHOD Conventional

Roberto Bellini has been making wine in Montalcino for several years, first with the Chiesa di Santa Restituta winery, which was sold to Angelo Gaja, and then, after taking a break from wine for a few years, with his current estate, Podere Brizio. After a couple of close calls, with wines through to the finals, Roberto finally hit the bull's-eye with his Brunello Riserva '01, a perfect synthesis of the traditional and the contemporary. Confident wild cherry aromas on the nose and a hint of sweet tobacco blend with sensations of balsam and sweet spices from the wood. The palate is generous and nicely balanced, with no excess, so the tannins are relaxed and enjoyably sweet, creating plentiful support for a structure that does not hold back the rounded, weighty finish. The Rosso di Montalcino '04, reviewed in error last year, is also well made, with enjoyable apple and pear fruit on the nose and a good weighty palate. The Pupà Pepu '04 is succulent but the tannins are a tad clenched.

● Brunello di Montalcino '02	♀♀ 7
● Rosso di Montalcino '05	♀♀ 4
● Rosso di Montalcino Clandestino '05	♀ 5
● Brunello di Montalcino '01	♀♀ 7
● Rosso di Montalcino '04	♀♀ 4

● Brunello di Montalcino Ris. '01	♀♀♀ 8
● Rosso di Montalcino '04	♀♀ 4
● Pupà Pepu '04	♀ 8
● Brunello di Montalcino '01	♀♀ 7
● Brunello di Montalcino '99	♀♀ 7
● Podere Brizio '03	♀♀ 5
● Pupà Pepu '03	♀♀ 8

Podere Ciona

LOC. MONTEGROSSI
53013 GAIOLE IN CHIANTI [SI]
TEL. 0577749127
www.podereciona.com

ANNUAL PRODUCTION	20,000 bottles
HECTARES UNDER VINE	4
VITICULTURE METHOD	Conventional

We report a good debut in the Guide for Franco Gatteschi's winery. The Chianti Classico Riserva '04 made it to the finals while the new merlot-heavy Supertuscan Le Viaccie '04 also performed well. The current owner bought the estate in 1990 and immediately began replanting the vineyards and equipping a modern cellar. The soil derives originally from sandstone and is excellent for the production of wines with a distinctive territory focus. Stefano Chioccioli takes care of both winemaking and vineyard management. The finalist has minerally, pencil lead aromas followed by minty, balsam sensations while the entry on the palate is rounded and subtle with nicely measured acidity and silky tannins taking you into a dynamic, savoury finish. Le Viaccie has forward, fruity aromas of wild berries and cinnamon-like spice on the nose and a generous, mouthfilling palate. It is held back a little in the finish by rather excessively mouth-drying tannin.

Poggerino

LOC. POGGERINO
53017 RADDA IN CHIANTI [SI]
TEL. 0577738958
www.poggerino.com

ANNUAL PRODUCTION	60,000 bottles
HECTARES UNDER VINE	10
VITICULTURE METHOD	Conventional

The winery owned by Piero and Benedetta Lanza earned a full profile, thanks above all to the excellent performance of the Chianti Classico '04, which deservedly made it to our final taste-offs. This little farm is rich in history, and inside is a church dating back to the 12th century. It was originally part of a huge estate own by the Ginori Contis, one of the oldest noble Florentine families. One member of the family, Floriana Ginori Conti, inherited this estate from her father in the 1970s, and began bottling Chianti Classico under the current label in 1980. In 1999, ownership passed to her children, who had already been running the farm since the late 1980s. The finalist impressed us, alternating the wild berries on the nose with fresh, minty aromas, and its delicious soft sweet tannins on the palate, although it is slightly held back on the finish. The less well-made Riserva '03 has ripe jammy aromas on the nose and a powerful but rigid, poorly balanced body, although the finish is compelling.

● Chianti Cl. Ris. '04	♈♈	5
● Le Viaccie '04	♈♈	6

● Chianti Cl. '04	♈♈	4
● Chianti Cl. Ris. '03	♈	5
● Primamateria '01	♈♈♈	6
● Chianti Cl. '01	♈♈	4
● Primamateria '99	♈♈	5
● Primamateria '00	♈♈	6

Poggio al Sole
LOC. BADIA A PASSIGNANO
S.DA RIGNANA, 2
50028 TAVARNELLE VAL DI PESA [FI]
TEL. 0558071850
www.poggioalsole.com

ANNUAL PRODUCTION 65,000 bottles
HECTARES UNDER VINE 18
VITICULTURE METHOD Conventional

We had seen it coming and were happy when it arrived, we thought as we looked over the results for Giovanni Davaz's cellar, with a wine back in the finals in the shape of his Syrah '05. We had been hoping for some time for a return to the appealing standard of quality we so appreciated a few years ago. This is well back on track, for the wines avoid what athletes would call overtraining, which for wines means excessive extract. Instead, Giovanni strives for good balance of the various components. The wine that made it to the finals has spicy aromas with hints of freshly ground pepper and animal skins, while the palate is perky with good acidity, nicely put together structure and a sweet, enjoyable finish. The Chianti Classico Casasilia '04 is also very appealing thanks to the mineral and balsam aromas on the nose and structure defined by crunchy tannins, well-balanced alcohol and a rising finish. The Chianti Classico '05 is less enthralling with a tighter range of aromas and a light, stiffish body.

Poggio Antico
LOC. POGGIO ANTICO
53024 MONTALCINO [SI]
TEL. 0577848044
www.poggioantico.com

ANNUAL PRODUCTION 120,000 bottles
HECTARES UNDER VINE 32.5
VITICULTURE METHOD Natural

In just a few years, Paola Gloder has finished renovation at the winery, which has involved replanting most of the vineyards and rebuilding the cellar. The new plantings are very attractive indeed, with a high density of plants per hectare. This is an excellent choice, given the area where the vineyards are situated. The cellar has been totally renovated and the spaces reorganized in a more functional manner. The Brunello Riserva '01 is completely free of the excessive oak that held back the Brunello Altero last year. There's good balance on the nose, with its charming combination of yellow-fleshed fruit and eucalyptus blending well with the hints of vanilla. The acidity typical of the sangiovese grape is noticeable on the palate, and is the reason for the long lifespan this wine will almost certainly enjoy. The stylish subtle tannins are perfectly integrated in the structure of the wine and the finish is deep and well developed, with a reprise of the fruit sensations. The Brunello '02 was not made because the growing year was not up to snuff. The reliably good Madre '04 has fresh, vegetal aromas.

● Syrah '05	7
● Chianti Cl. Casasilia '04	7
● Chianti Cl. '05	5
● Chianti Cl. Casasilia '99	7
● Syrah '99	7
● Syrah '01	7
● Chianti Cl. '03	5
● Chianti Cl. '04	5
● Syrah '03	7
● Chianti Cl. Casasilia '01	7

● Brunello di Montalcino Ris. '01	8
● Madre '04	6
● Rosso di Montalcino '05	5
● Brunello di Montalcino Altero '99	7
● Brunello di Montalcino '99	7
● Madre '01	7
● Brunello di Montalcino '00	7
● Brunello di Montalcino '01	7
● Brunello di Montalcino Ris. '00	7
● Brunello di Montalcino Altero '01	7
● Brunello di Montalcino Ris. '99	7

Poggio Argentiera

LOC. BANDITELLA DI ALBERESE
58010 GROSSETO [GR]
TEL. 0564405099
www.poggioargentiera.com

Poggio Bonelli

LOC. POGGIO BONELLI
53019 CASTELNUOVO BERARDENGA [SI]
TEL. 0577355382
www.poggiobonelli.it

ANNUAL PRODUCTION 200,000 bottles
HECTARES UNDER VINE 32
VITICULTURE METHOD Conventional

ANNUAL PRODUCTION 250,000 bottles
HECTARES UNDER VINE 80
VITICULTURE METHOD Conventional

The winery owned by the skilled, dedicated Giampaolo Paglia has earned a thoroughly respectable position in the front rank of Maremma estates. While Giampaolo's wines tend to express ripe fruit with good oak-derived sensations and powerful structure, they never lack the necessary freshness for a fluid, relaxed mouthfeel. This year, the '05 Morellino Capatosta again made it to our final tastings, consolidating its position as one of the best wines of its type. With its fresh, powerful nose and, contrastingly, fruit-forward, profound palate, flavour is its strong suit from the first sip. The alicante and syrah Finisterre '05 is as gutsy and bright on the palate as it is spicy and balsamic on the nose. The Morellino Bellamarsilia '06 is also good and impressed us with its fresh cherry aromas and savoury flavour. The Lalicante is a very original monovarietal alicante-based dried-grape wine with clear hints of olives. The chardonnay and fiano Fonte_40 and the Guazza, from ansonica and vermentino, are both simple, well-made whites. The '06 Maremmante, from alicante and syrah, is moreish.

As of this year, the two wineries owned by Monte dei Paschi di Siena will unite under the Poggio Bonelli brand. Chigi Saracini is therefore no more but the wines remain. The feather in the cap of this range is the Tramonto d'Oca '04, a blend of sangiovese and merlot, which got through to the finals. This historic location has produced wine and wheat since the 16th century, thanks originally to the efforts of the Bonelli family, who owned the property until the 17th century. Subsequently, the estate passed into the hands of the Piccolomini and Landucci families. When the Siena-based MPS bank bought the estate, the vineyards were extensively renovated and the cellar reorganized. Our finalist has berries and layers of spice on the nose, and a smooth impact on the palate. It's appealing and not too muscular, with an enjoyably sweet finish. Poggiassai '05, from sangiovese and cabernet sauvignon, has a less expressive nose but a nice firm palate with flavoursome acidity and a savoury finish. The Chianti Classico '05 and Chianti '06 are both very nice.

● Finisterre '05	▼▼	7
● Morellino di Scansano Capatosta '05	▼▼	6
● Morellino di Scansano Bellamarsilia '06	▼▼	4
● Lalicante	▼▼	6
○ Fonte_40 '06	▼	5
○ Guazza '06	▼	3
● Maremmante '06	▼	3
● Morellino di Scansano Capatosta '00	♀♀♀	6*
● Finisterre '01	♀♀	7
● Finisterre '02	♀♀	7
● Morellino di Scansano Capatosta '04	♀♀	6
● Morellino di Scansano Capatosta '03	♀♀	6
● Morellino di Scansano Capatosta '01	♀♀	6
● Finisterre '03	♀♀	7
● Finisterre '04	♀♀	7
● Morellino di Scansano Bellamarsilia '03	♀♀	4
● Morellino di Scansano Bellamarsilia '05	♀♀	4

● Tramonto d'Oca '04	▼▼	6
● Poggiassai '05	▼▼	6
● Chianti Cl. '05	▼	4
● Chianti Villa Chigi Saracini '06	▼	3
● Tramonto d'Oca '01	♀♀	6
● Tramonto d'Oca '03	♀♀	6
● Chianti Cl. '04	♀♀	4
● Chianti Cl. Ris. '03	♀♀	6

Poggio Brigante

VIA COLLE DI LUPO, 13
58051 MAGLIANO IN TOSCANA [GR]
TEL. 0564592507
www.poggiobrigante.it

ANNUAL PRODUCTION 100,000 bottles
HECTARES UNDER VINE 16
VITICULTURE METHOD Conventional

On the increasingly varied Maremma wine scene, it is getting complicated to find products that stand out for their originality. But you can't say that about Leonardo Rossi's wines, which have strikingly individual personalities, intriguing aromas and flavours and very respectable quality. The Morellino Arsura '05 is very interesting with its remarkably complex aromas of spices, red berries, and hints of earth and scrubland. Entry on the palate is good, with rich, well-coordinated structure nicely backed up by tangily fresh acidity. The Morellino '06 shows a sweeter, more accessible tone with aromas of oriental spices and black berry fruit ahead of the enjoyably uncomplicated, relaxed palate. After a moment's hesitation, with slightly rustic aromas, the Syrah '05 opens out into a fruity nose with balsamic and gamy hints. This vibrant, full-bodied wine is more intriguing on the palate, where tasty tannins take you into a fruity finish. The Vermentino '06 is very subtle and restrained.

Poggio di Sotto

FRAZ. CASTELNUOVO DELL'ABATE
LOC. POGGIO DI SOTTO
53024 MONTALCINO [SI]
TEL. 0577835502
www.poggiodisotto.com

ANNUAL PRODUCTION 25,000 bottles
HECTARES UNDER VINE 12
VITICULTURE METHOD Certified organic

We have always liked Piero Palmucci's Brunello Riservas and that tradition continues this year with Three Glasses for his Il Decennale '01, the Riserva, although it doesn't say so in the name. The DOCG boards, inexplicably, did not consider this quintessentially typical Montalcino wine to be true enough to type. Not everyone, it seems, is able to understand the local and the great wines that originate there. This wine presents a textbook hue and makes a big impact on the nose with aromas of fruit, tobacco, medicinal herbs, floral hints and refreshing balsam. The palate is elegant in style and exceedingly well balanced, with everything in place and no flaws or forcing. The tannins are already resolved and perfectly complement the acidity, taking the wine through to a very stylish finish. There is no Brunello '02 because Piero did not feel the year was up to standard. The Rosso di Montalcino '04 is good, with classic aromas of yellow peaches and morello cherries, and a mouth-watering palate with nice fresh acidity.

● Morellino di Scansano Arsura '05	♟♟	5
● Morellino di Scansano '06	♟♟	4
● Syrah '05	♟♟	4
O Vermentino '06	♟	4
● Morellino di Scansano '04	♟♟	4
● Morellino di Scansano Arsura '04	♟♟	5
● Morellino di Scansano '05	♟♟	4
● Morellino di Scansano Arsura '03	♟♟	6

● Il Decennale '01	♟♟♟	8
● Rosso di Montalcino '04	♟♟	6
● Brunello di Montalcino '99	♟♟♟	8
● Brunello di Montalcino Ris. '99	♟♟♟	8
● Brunello di Montalcino Ris. '95	♟♟♟	8
● Brunello di Montalcino '01	♟♟	8
● Brunello di Montalcino '00	♟♟	8
● Brunello di Montalcino '97	♟♟	8

Poggio Molina

LOC. POGGIO MOLINA
52021 BUCINE [AR]
TEL. 0559789402
www.poggiomolina.it

ANNUAL PRODUCTION 60,000 bottles
HECTARES UNDER VINE 16
VITICULTURE METHOD Conventional

Poggio Molina is situated in a lovely position on the Valdambra hills near the Arezzo end of the Arno valley. This young winery was founded by the enthusiastic Claudio Bossini, who threw himself into this great adventure just a few years ago with his wife Alba. Claudio is an ebullient character but also very well aware of the extent of his knowledge of wine, so he immediately placed himself in the hands of consultant Stefano Chioccioli. Together, they traced the guidelines for the layout of the winery and the vineyards, replanting new ones according to modern criteria and recovering the best of the older vineyards. The wines tend to reflect quite a technical approach with a nice balance of parameters like rich colour, extract, weight and softness. Le Caldie '04m from merlot with some cabernet and sangiovese, is the winery's leading product and an excellent wine that presents dark and ripe, with balsamic hints, good balance and thrust. In the absence of the '05 Scopaio, which has not been released yet, we very much liked the sangiovese-only Vinobono '05. It's a particularly good version with rich red berries and spices on the nose and a pleasantly fresh-tasting, well put together palate.

Podere Poggio Scalette

LOC. RUFFOLI
VIA BARBIANO, 7
50022 GREVE IN CHIANTI [FI]
TEL. 0558546108
www.poggioscalette.it

ANNUAL PRODUCTION 35,000 bottles
HECTARES UNDER VINE 15
VITICULTURE METHOD Natural

The prize-winning team formed by longstanding winemaker Vittorio Fiore and his son Jurij continues to produce excellent wines with distinctive local character that surprise us more when they do not win Three Glasses than when they do. This year, they didn't manage it, although the monovarietal sangiovese Il Carbonaione '04 and the Piantonaia '04 from merlot both made it through to the finals. We are pleased to note the shared sense of purpose that unites the Fiore family: Vittorio's other son, Claudio, owns the Castelluccio winery in Romagna. Working together closely as a family may not always be successful but in this case it works beautifully. Moving on to the wines that made it to the finals, Il Carbonaione has mainly wild berries and assorted spices on the nose with still rather upfront oak. The palate is firm-bodied, stylish and soft with a complex finish, toastiness returning on the back palate. The Piantonaia struggles to open out on the nose, with forward vegetal aromas alongside animal skins and leather, but is more dynamic on the succulent palate, which offers fine-grained tannins and an appetizing finish.

● Le Caldie '04	♥♥ 6
● Vinobono '05	♥♥ 4*
● Le Caldie '01	♥♥ 6
● Lo Scopaio '02	♥♥ 4
● Lo Scopaio '03	♥♥ 5
● Le Caldie '03	♥♥ 6
● Le Caldie '02	♥♥ 6

● Il Carbonaione '04	♥♥ 7
● Piantonaia '04	♥ 8
● Il Carbonaione '00	♥♥♥ 8
● Il Carbonaione '03	♥♥♥ 8
● Il Carbonaione '98	♥♥♥ 8
● Il Carbonaione '96	♥♥♥ 8
● Piantonaia '03	♥♥ 8

Poggio Torselli
VIA SCOPETI, 10
50026 SAN CASCIANO IN VAL DI PESA [FI]
TEL. 0558290241
www.poggiotorselli.it

ANNUAL PRODUCTION   50,000 bottles
HECTARES UNDER VINE 25
VITICULTURE METHOD   Conventional

This San Casciano winery now has a full profile, having succeeded in just a few years in carving itself a thoroughly respectable niche in the Chianti area. It has done so by devoting special attention to vineyard management. The vine stock has been subdivided according to the features of the land, and the type of soil has determined the choice of grape planted. While native grape varieties account for the bulk of the vines – sangiovese for reds and trebbiano and malvasia for whites – some plots have been planted with international varieties like cabernet sauvignon and merlot, which are fermented and bottled separately. Once again, the best this year was the cabernet-only Tieri del Fula '05, which has sweet spicy aromas, a soft, well-rounded body and a good lingering finish. The Monna Aldola '06, from trebbiano and malvasia, has surprising fruit and flower aromas and a lively, fresh-tasting, beautifully tangy palate. Of the two Chianti Classicos from the '04 vintage, the basic version is better than the Riserva, showing more accessible on the nose and unveiling a sweet, expansive palate.

Tenuta Il Poggione
FRAZ. SANT'ANGELO IN COLLE
LOC. MONTEANO
53024 MONTALCINO [SI]
TEL. 0577844029
www.tenutailpoggione.it

ANNUAL PRODUCTION   500,000 bottles
HECTARES UNDER VINE 118
VITICULTURE METHOD   Conventional

This long-established operation at Sant'Angelo in Colle continues to turn out good wines at more than fair prices. The new winery is particularly attractive and well-organized, reflecting the style of its owners. who eschew excess and special effects. Tenuta Il Poggione's reliability was again confirmed at this year's tastings. The Brunello '02 is very good while the Brunello Riserva '01 fell a little short of our expectations. Although the nose is clean, with morello cherry aromas and light hints of balsam, the acidity and tannin on the palate are still unresolved. Appropriate bottle ageing should help soften those sharp edges. The Brunello '02 is very enjoyable and beautifully drinkable, with subtle balance from a vintage year that has been nicely interpreted by the cellar staff. The wine is succulent and attractively deep with austere aromas of cherries and blackberries. The Rosso di Montalcino and Il Poggione, both '05, are very attractive and expansive while the San Leopoldo '04 is a little clenched.

● Chianti Cl. '04	♟♟ 4
● Tieri del Fula '05	♟♟ 5
O Monna Aldola '06	♟♟ 4
● Chianti Cl. Ris. '04	♟ 5
● Tieri del Fula '03	♟♟ 5
● Tieri del Fula '04	♟♟ 5

● Brunello di Montalcino '02	♟♟ 6
● Brunello di Montalcino Ris. '01	♟♟ 7
● Il Poggione '05	♟ 3*
● San Leopoldo '04	♟ 5
● Rosso di Montalcino '05	♟ 4
● Brunello di Montalcino Ris. '97	♟♟♟ 8
● Brunello di Montalcino Ris. '99	♟♟ 7
● Brunello di Montalcino '99	♟♟ 6
● San Leopoldo '03	♟♟ 5
● Il Poggione '04	♟♟ 3*

Fattoria Poggiopiano
VIA DI PISIGNANO, 28/30
50026 SAN CASCIANO IN VAL DI PESA [FI]
TEL. 0558229629
www.fattoriapoggiopiano.it

★ Poliziano
LOC. MONTEPULCIANO STAZIONE
VIA FONTAGO, 1
53040 MONTEPULCIANO [SI]
TEL. 0578738171
www.carlettipoliziano.com

ANNUAL PRODUCTION   100,000 bottles
HECTARES UNDER VINE 9
VITICULTURE METHOD   Conventional

ANNUAL PRODUCTION   600,000 bottles
HECTARES UNDER VINE 140
VITICULTURE METHOD   Conventional

The Rosso di Sera '05 missed the highest accolade by a hair's breadth, although the fact that it was selected for the finals yet again – and has made regular appearances there practically since its first release – speaks volumes for its reliability. This is thanks to scrupulous care in both vineyard and cellar. Since the estate has a very limited area under vine, it has chosen to focus on a few grape varieties and just two wines, which are cosseted in every possible way. The Rosso di Sera is a blend of sangiovese and colorino, with a good intense colour and a generous swath of aromas combining wild berries, cinnamon-led spice and faint whiffs of mint. The palate shows rich, well-sustained texture with fine-grained tannins and a lingering finish. The Chianti Classico '05 is also good. Florality and toastiness on the nose precede an elegant structure that marries tannins and alcohol taking you into a good, flavoursome finish.

Poliziano wines, like few others in Italy, have long represented a benchmark for consumers. This is the most important achievement of a winery that today is seriously committed to welcoming the world, with a special reception area in the winery for enthusiasts. The objective closest to Federico Carletti's heart, and incidentally achieved with incredible continuity, is to guarantee to anyone uncorking one of his wines, whether at the top or bottom of the range, superbly satisfactory quality in relation to the price paid. This is apparently an easy, indeed obvious, goal but in the increasingly competitive world of wine, it is not something that very many estates actually deliver. Confirmation that Poliziano can do the business again comes in the shape of Glasses. The Nobile di Montepulciano Asinone '04 won its 11th Three Glass award. The Nobile '04, the cabernet sauvignon and merlot Le Stanze '04 and Mandrone di Lhosa '04, based on cabernet sauvignon, alicante and petit verdot from Maremma, all made it to the final tastings. The wines from the basic end of the range are never a disappointment and the Morellino '06 stands out in particular.

● Rosso di Sera '05	♟♟ 7
● Chianti Cl. '05	♟♟ 4
● Rosso di Sera '03	♟♟♟ 7
● Rosso di Sera '04	♟♟♟ 7
● Rosso di Sera '00	♟♟ 8
● Rosso di Sera '01	♟♟ 8
● Chianti Cl. '03	♟♟ 4
● Chianti Cl. '04	♟♟ 4

● Nobile di Montepulciano Asinone '04	♟♟♟ 7
● Le Stanze '05	♟♟ 8
● Mandrone di Lohsa '05	♟♟ 6
● Nobile di Montepulciano '04	♟♟ 5
● Morellino di Scansano '06	♟♟ 4
● Cortona Merlot In Violas '05	♟ 6
● Rosso di Montepulciano '06	♟ 4
● Le Stanze '00	♟♟♟ 7
● Le Stanze '03	♟♟♟ 7
● Nobile di Montepulciano Asinone '00	♟♟♟ 7
● Le Stanze '98	♟♟♟ 7
● Nobile di Montepulciano Asinone '01	♟♟♟ 7
● Nobile di Montepulciano Asinone '97	♟♟♟ 6
● Nobile di Montepulciano Asinone '99	♟♟♟ 6
● Nobile di Montepulciano Vigna dell'Asinone '95	♟♟♟ 5
● Nobile di Montepulciano Vigna dell'Asinone '93	♟♟♟ 5
● Nobile di Montepulciano Asinone '98	♟♟♟ 6
● Nobile di Montepulciano Asinone '03	♟♟♟ 7

Castello di Poppiano

FRAZ. POPPIANO
VIA DI FEZZANA, 45
50025 MONTESPERTOLI [FI]
TEL. 05582315
www.conteguicciardini.it

ANNUAL PRODUCTION 600,000 bottles
HECTARES UNDER VINE 130
VITICULTURE METHOD Conventional

Conte Ferdinando Guicciardini's winery forges ahead with a range that offers particularly good value for money, despite lacking the touch of personality and character necessary to scale the heights of quality. This is probably the direction to take in the future. In recent years, the Colli Fiorentini DOC has demonstrated a remarkable ability to set itself apart from the rest of Chianti, indicating that real potential exists and has yet to be fully exploited. The wine that most impressed us this year was the Syrah '05, which has a small dollop of sangiovese. Fresh, spicy sensations, mainly of pepper and cinnamon, a stylish well-rounded body and a good lingering flavour are all there. The Chianti Colli Fiorentini Riserva '04 is more austere, with ripe fruit aromas, firm structure braced by tannins and a good finish. The Tricorno '04, from sangiovese, cabernet and merlot, has a modern nose on which toasted oak sensations emerge, and a concentrated, mouthfilling palate. The rest of the range is well typed.

● Chianti Colli Fiorentini Ris. '04	🍷🍷 5
● Tricorno '04	🍷🍷 6
● Syrah '05	🍷🍷 4
● Chianti Colli Fiorentini Il Cortile '05	🍷 4
● Toscoforte '05	🍷 4
○ Vin Santo della Torre Grande del Chianti '99	🍷 5
● Tricorno '00	🍷🍷 6
● Chianti Colli Fiorentini Ris. '00	🍷🍷 5
● Tricorno '03	🍷🍷 6
● Tricorno '01	🍷🍷 6
● Toscoforte '03	🍷🍷 4
● Syrah '04	🍷🍷 4
● Syrah '03	🍷🍷 4

Fattoria di Presciano

LOC. PIEVE A PRESCIANO
VIA GIOVANNI XXIII, 2
52020 PERGINE VALDARNO [AR]
TEL. 0575897160
www.fattoriadipresciano.it

ANNUAL PRODUCTION 100,000 bottles
HECTARES UNDER VINE 24
VITICULTURE METHOD Conventional

The wines presented by Fattoria di Presciano grow in number every year. For the first time, energetic owner Pasquale Cometti, who is a firm believer in the new Pietraviva DOC, presented us with monovarietal wines from this DOC, following the winery's recent work to promote and recover traditional local varieties. For the moment. the results are encouraging and in line with the usual standard of quality of a winery that produces clean, well-typed, reliable wines that may sometimes lack a little personality. But that is not the case with the Rosso Veleno, mainly sangiovese with some merlot, which was produced from '01 on under the name of Cometti's wife, Marina Mouritch. The '04 version is excellent, showing robust, spicy, mouthfilling and with good depth. The Sangiovese I Greti '03 has good staying power, considering the hot year, and is sound and healthy with a nice vein of acidity balancing the warmth and perking up the massive extract. From the many other wines, we picked out the appealing Rosé Brut, made from pinot noir grapes using the long Charmat method and sold only in magnums.

● I Greti '03	🍷🍷 6
● Rosso Veleno Vigneti di Marina Mouritch '04	🍷🍷 6
● Chianti Ris. '03	🍷 5
● Pietraviva Rosso '06	🍷 4
● Pietraviva Ciliegiolo '05	🍷 5
⊙ Rosé Brut	🍷 7
○ Pietraviva Bianco '06	🍷 4
● Pietraviva Canaiolo '05	🍷 5
● Rosso Veleno Vigneti di Marina Mouritch '01	🍷🍷 6
● Primadonna Vigneti di Marina Mouritch '03	🍷🍷 5
● Rosso Veleno Vigneti di Marina Mouritch '03	🍷🍷 6
● Priscus '03	🍷🍷 5
● Priscus '01	🍷🍷 5

Provveditore

LOC. SALAIOLO, 174
58054 SCANSANO [GR]
TEL. 0564599237
www.provveditore.it

ANNUAL PRODUCTION 200,000 bottles
HECTARES UNDER VINE 30
VITICULTURE METHOD Conventional

There was a valid performance from the wines presented by Alessandro Bargagli, chairman of the Consorzio di Tutela del Morellino di Scansano, which from the 2007 vintage onwards will be able to boast DOCG status. The range produced by the Provveditore estate consists almost entirely of Maremma's most famous wine type, and stylistically all the products are firmly rooted in tradition with a strong sense of place. During our tastings, we were especially impressed by the Morellino Provveditore '05, which went on to the finals. Its fresh aromas have a nice earthy character, reflected on the palate with its well-defined, dynamic and tangy flavour. The Morellino Sassato '06 is also very good, showing more approachable but with well-defined, vibrant fruit on the nose and a flavoursome and well-balanced, if not especially deep, palate. The Morellino Primo Riserva '03 also has an excellent sensory profile, giving warm, complex aromas on the nose and an enjoyably mouthfilling palate. The Bianco di Pitigliano Bargaglio '06 is uncomplicated, with a subtle nose and low-key palate.

★ Fattoria Le Pupille

LOC. PIAGGE DEL MAIANO
58040 GROSSETO [GR]
TEL. 0564409518
www.elisabettageppetti.com

ANNUAL PRODUCTION 450,000 bottles
HECTARES UNDER VINE 66
VITICULTURE METHOD Conventional

In the last edition of the Guide, we noted a significant absence from this profile: release of the '04 Saffredi had been postponed. The gap has been filled this year and an extra year's bottle ageing seems to have benefited the wine, which is in dazzling form. Saffredi '04 walked away with Three Glasses in one of its best-ever versions. This stylish blend of cabernet sauvignon, merlot and alicante has crystal clear aromas and beautifully gauged oak. The palate is soft and sophisticated with very subtle tannins and delightful progression. The Solalto '05, a blend of late-harvested traminer, sauvignon and sémillon, gives appealingly fresh candied orange peel and apricot aromas and a subtle, perfectly sweet palate. The Morellino Poggio Valente '05 has very balsamic aromas and a vibrant, succulent palate. Morellino '06 is a reliably good, well-sustained wine and the Poggio Argentato '06, from traminer and sauvignon, is less ambitious but far from ordinary.

● Morellino di Scansano '05	♏♏	4
● Morellino di Scansano Primo Ris. '03	♏♏	5
● Morellino di Scansano Sassato '06	♏♏	4
○ Bianco di Pitigliano Bargaglino '06	♏	3
● Campo La Chiesa '00	♟♟	6
● Campo La Chiesa '01	♟♟	5
● Morellino di Scansano '03	♟♟	4
● Campo La Chiesa '05	♟♟	4

● Saffredi '04	♏♏♏	8
● Morellino di Scansano Poggio Valente '05	♏♏	6
● Morellino di Scansano '06	♏	4
○ Solalto '05	♏	4
○ Poggio Argentato '06	♏	4
● Morellino di Scansano Poggio Valente '04	♟♟♟	6
● Saffredi '00	♟♟♟	8
● Saffredi '02	♟♟♟	8
● Saffredi '97	♟♟♟	8
● Saffredi '90	♟♟♟	8
● Saffredi '03	♟♟♟	8
● Saffredi '01	♟♟♟	8
● Morellino di Scansano Poggio Valente '99	♟♟♟	6
● Morellino di Scansano Poggio Valente '98	♟♟♟	6
● Morellino di Scansano Poggio Valente '01	♟♟	6
● Morellino di Scansano Poggio Valente '03	♟♟	6
● Morellino di Scansano Poggio Valente '02	♟♟	6

La Querce
VIA IMPRUNETANA PER TAVARNUZZE, 41
50023 IMPRUNETA [FI]
TEL. 0552011380
www.laquerce.com

ANNUAL PRODUCTION 22,000 bottles
HECTARES UNDER VINE 8
VITICULTURE METHOD Conventional

We can report an identical result to last year, and indeed to two years ago, for Massimo Marchi's winery, indicating that production has achieved a really excellent level of reliability. This is also thanks to the winery manager, Marco Ferretti, who since the 1990s has been wholeheartedly involved in the renovation of first the vineyards and then the cellar. We can now legitimately expect another little step forward, especially in terms of land-rootedness. The wines seem to hint at a very contemporary idea of style with their fruit-oak aromas, which makes them sensorially impeccable but detracts a little from personality. The '05 La Querce, a blend of sangiovese and colorino, reached the finals with its fresh, balsamic aromas, ripe, spicy fruit and dense, soft, lively body. The Chianti Colli Fiorentini '05 has appetizing cherry aromas and lively structure with nice grip. The whole range is very fairly priced and good value for money.

Castello di Querceto
FRAZ. LUCOLENA
LOC. QUERCETO
VIA DUDDA, 61
50020 GREVE IN CHIANTI [FI]
TEL. 05585921
www.castellodiquerceto.it

ANNUAL PRODUCTION 600,000 bottles
HECTARES UNDER VINE 78
VITICULTURE METHOD Conventional

This traditional Greve winery continues to make progress at a steady pace, every year presenting wines that are basically well typed with some peaks among the most popular wines like the Chianti Classicos. This year, perhaps, the standard is not the highest ever but it does not invalidate the enthusiastic efforts of the owners, the husband and wife François team. Although the winery does not produce many wine types, they all faithfully reflect the range of site climates offered by the vineyards. It is interesting to see how long these wines will age, as we have noted at vertical tastings. The leading wines demonstrate excellent staying power although a little more care could be taken with the tannins, since they tend to overburden and tighten the palate. The Riserva '04 got through to the finals with its very ripe fruit and nice grip. The characterful Riserva Il Picchio '04 is also good while the rest of the range is are merely decent, from the cabernet and merlot Cignale '04 to the '03 Querciolaia '03, from sangiovese and cabernet, the cabernet-only Il Sole di Alessandro '04 and La Corte '03, from sangiovese.

● La Querce '05	♉ 5
● Chianti Colli Fiorentini La Torretta '05	♉♉ 4
● Chianti Sorrettole '06	♉ 3
● La Querce '03	♉♉ 5
● La Querce '04	♉♉ 5
● Chianti Colli Fiorentini La Torretta '02	♉♉ 4
● Chianti Colli Fiorentini La Torretta '03	♉♉ 4*
● Chianti Colli Fiorentini La Torretta '04	♉♉ 4

● Chianti Cl. Ris. '04	♉♉ 5
● Chianti Cl. Il Picchio Ris. '04	♉♉ 6
● Chianti Cl. '05	♉ 4
● Cignale '04	♉ 8
● Il Sole di Alessandro '04	♉ 8
● La Corte '03	♉ 6
● Querciolaia '03	♉ 7
○ Vin Santo del Chianti Cl. '03	♉ 5
● Chianti Cl. Il Picchio Ris. '03	♉♉ 6
● Chianti Cl. Il Picchio Ris. '98	♉♉ 6
● Chianti Cl. Ris. '01	♉♉ 5
● Chianti Cl. Ris. '03	♉♉ 5
● Chianti Cl. Il Picchio Ris. '01	♉♉ 6
● Cignale '03	♉♉ 7
● Cignale '01	♉♉ 7
● Il Sole di Alessandro '01	♉♉ 8

★ Querciabella

VIA BARBIANO, 17
50022 GREVE IN CHIANTI [FI]
TEL. 05585927777
www.querciabella.com

ANNUAL PRODUCTION 200,000 bottles
HECTARES UNDER VINE 76.5
VITICULTURE METHOD Natural

As tradition requires, there was another Three Glass prize for the Cossia Castiglionis' winery. How could it be otherwise, given that the vintage year – '04 – was one of the most impressive in recent memory? The Camartina, from mainly cabernet sauvignon with sangiovese, opens out to aromas of red berries, earth, and vegetal and minerally sensations. The palate has well-defined, austere structure as well as good acidity that bolsters and sustains the long finish. The tannins are still a little edgy but time will smooth them down. While a great Camartina is no longer a surprise to anyone, it is quite different for the Chianti Classico '05. Something is changing and it shows. This version of the area's signature wine seems to be more carefully thought-out and deeply felt, as if the winery wanted to focus more on the wine type. The result offers red berries and dried violets on the nose and a fresh, silky, characterful palate. And this wasn't even one of the better growing years. The impressive chardonnay and pinot bianco Bàtar '05 is a little too sweet from oak-derived buttery, vanilla-like sensations.

★ Castello dei Rampolla

VIA CASE SPARSE, 22
50020 PANZANO [FI]
TEL. 055852001
castellodeirampolla.cast@tin.it

ANNUAL PRODUCTION 90,000 bottles
HECTARES UNDER VINE 42
VITICULTURE METHOD Natural

It was worth a year's wait for these results from the Di Napoli family's wines. The top wine on the list is once again the d'Alceo, a blend of cabernet sauvignon and petit verdot, that soared to our Three Glass podium. Dense colour introduces a broad swath of fruity aromas enhanced by hints of spice on the convincing nose. The soft, rounded entry on the palate builds good progression right through to the tangy, lingering finish. That said, the whole range of wines confirms the validity of decisions made over the years, like the one ten years ago to adopt biodynamic methods in the vineyards. The '04 Sammarco, a classic Chianti blend of sangiovese and cabernet sauvignon, is excellent, showing subtle but assertive on the nose, then rich and flavoursome on the palate. The Chianti Classico '04 is a fine example of a wine that is both well-made and extremely drinkable while the Trebianco '04, from late-harvested traminer aromatico, chardonnay, malvasia and sauvignon blanc, has captivatingly delicate aromas and an alluring palate.

● Camartina '04	⊽⊽⊽ 8
● Chianti Cl. '05	⊽⊽ 5
○ Bàtar '05	⊽⊽ 7
● Camartina '00	⊽⊽⊽ 8
● Camartina '01	⊽⊽⊽ 8
● Camartina '88	⊽⊽⊽ 8
● Camartina '94	⊽⊽⊽ 8
● Camartina '97	⊽⊽⊽ 8
● Camartina '99	⊽⊽⊽ 8
● Camartina '95	⊽⊽⊽ 8
● Camartina '90	⊽⊽⊽ 8
● Camartina '03	⊽⊽⊽ 8

● d'Alceo '04	⊽⊽⊽ 8
● Chianti Cl. '04	⊽⊽ 5
● Sammarco '04	⊽⊽ 8
○ Trebianco V. T. '04	⊽⊽ 5
● d'Alceo '00	⊽⊽⊽ 8
● Sammarco '94	⊽⊽⊽ 8
● La Vigna di Alceo '96	⊽⊽⊽ 8
● La Vigna di Alceo '98	⊽⊽⊽ 8
● La Vigna di Alceo '99	⊽⊽⊽ 8
● La Vigna di Alceo '97	⊽⊽⊽ 8
● d'Alceo '03	⊽⊽⊽ 8
● d'Alceo '01	⊽⊽⊽ 8
● Sammarco '98	⊽⊽ 8
● Sammarco '99	⊽⊽ 8
● Sammarco '03	⊽⊽ 8

Rasa - Laserena

PODERE RASA I, 133
53024 MONTALCINO [SI]
TEL. 0577848659
la_serena@virgilio.it

ANNUAL PRODUCTION 23.500 bottles
HECTARES UNDER VINE 8.5
VITICULTURE METHOD Conventional

Great steps have been taken at this winery, which has markedly improved the quality of the wines in just a few years while boosting quantity at the same time. Congratulations to Andrea Mantengoli, who oversees operations from the new, well-organized winery designed by his brother Marcello, an architect. The vineyards are situated at altitudes between 290 and 400 metres above sea level on different types of soil. The very good Brunello Gemini '01 comes from a special selection, aged entirely in barriques and only released to market six years after the harvest. It presents an intense ruby red, giving black and red berries on the nose alongside hints of balsam and sweet spices and a confident entry on the weighty, dynamic palate, well sustained by unassertive alcohol. Good acidity gives the palate suppleness and fruity aromas return on the finish. The Brunello'02 is enjoyable if uncomplicated with fresh fruit on the nose, forward acidity and decent extract.

Riecine

LOC. RIECINE
53013 GAIOLE IN CHIANTI [SI]
TEL. 0577749098
www.riecine.com

ANNUAL PRODUCTION 45,000 bottles
HECTARES UNDER VINE 11
VITICULTURE METHOD Certified organic

And that makes seven. With the Three Glasses awarded this year to the '04 La Gioia, a monovarietal sangiovese, Gary Baumann's winery is striding confidently towards a Star. Until now the awards were divided equally between the Supertuscan and the Chianti Classico Riserva, proof that terroir is a trump card along with the work of Riecine's secret weapon, Sean O'Callaghan. The vineyard manager and winemaker has long first-hand knowledge of the vineyards where he has worked since 1992, when winery founder John Dunkley called him in. This explains the alchemy that yields these results. The winning wine is on dazzling form thanks to the fruity, vegetal sand medicinal herb aromas that usher in a beautifully crafted palate with very fine-grained tannins and long, flavoursome finish. The Chianti Classico Riserva '04 is also very good, with spicy sensations and a dynamic, well-balanced palate. A special mention goes to the Rosato '06, with its appetizing aromas and fragrant flavour.

● Brunello di Montalcino Gemini '01	♟♟ 7
● Brunello di Montalcino '02	♟ 7

● La Gioia '04	♟♟♟ 7
● Chianti Cl. Ris. '04	♟♟ 6
☉ Rosé '06	♟ 4
● La Gioia '01	♟♟♟ 7
● La Gioia '98	♟♟♟ 8
● Chianti Cl. Ris. '99	♟♟♟ 8
● La Gioia '95	♟♟♟ 8
● La Gioia '00	♟♟ 8
● La Gioia '03	♟♟ 7
● Chianti Cl. Ris. '98	♟♟ 5
● Chianti Cl. Ris. '01	♟♟ 6
● Chianti Cl. Ris. '03	♟♟ 7

Rietine

LOC. RIETINE, 27
53013 GAIOLE IN CHIANTI [SI]
TEL. 0577731110
www.rietine.com

ANNUAL PRODUCTION 65,000 bottles
HECTARES UNDER VINE 13
VITICULTURE METHOD Conventional

The winery owned by Mario Gaffuri and Galina Lazarides gave us a lovely surprise as the Chianti Classico Riserva '04 picked up a well-deserved Three Glass prize without fuss or fanfares. All the work has paid off, we might say, for the fact is that the winery has always managed to release good products at a fair price. The vineyards surround the hamlet after which the small estate is named and the view is picture postcard stuff. The village comprises a handful of houses surrounding the old church, which is the main building. The award-winning wine has vibrant ripe fruit aromas of plums and cherries on the nose and a rounded, profound entry on the palate, succulent tannins and a savoury, rising finish. Also good is the Tiziano '03, a blend of cabernet sauvignon and merlot. By the way, last year we reviewed the '01 vintage although in fact it was the '00. The '03 has some hints of oak on nose and plate, with confident mouth-drying tannins and a savoury finish. The Chianti Classico '05 is well typed and enjoyable.

Rocca delle Macìe

LOC. MACÌE, 45
53011 CASTELLINA IN CHIANTI [SI]
TEL. 05777321
www.roccadellemacie.com

ANNUAL PRODUCTION 4,500,000 bottles
HECTARES UNDER VINE 200
VITICULTURE METHOD Conventional

We are quite frankly disappointed by the performance of Sergio Zingarelli's winery this year. Although he presented the usual long list of wines, none of them showed great character. This may be acceptable for the basic wines but a below par performance from the selections is astonishing. Only the Roccato '04 stands out. This blend of sangiovese and cabernet sauvignon gives an aromatic nose including ripe, plum-like fruit and sweet cinnamon and cloves spice before a rounded entry takes you into a vibrant palate. We thought the Vermentino Occhio al Vento '06 from the Maremma estate was very good. Citrus, pear and apple fruit on the nose precede a slender but lively palate braced by acidity and a nice savoury finish. The sangiovese-heavy Ser Gioveto '04 is rather austere and inexpressive on the nose and the powerful palate fails to expand sufficiently. The rest of the range was in danger of becoming much of muchness although we believe this is an isolated episode linked to the growing year. Rocca delle Macìe has always been able to manage quality despite the millions of bottles produced.

● Chianti Cl. Ris. '04	♟♟♟ 5
● Chianti Cl. '05	♟ 4
● Tiziano '03	♟ 6
● Chianti Cl. '03	♟♟ 4

● Roccato '04	♟♟ 6
○ Vermentino Occhio a Vento '06	♟♟ 4
● Chianti Cl. Fizzano Ris. '04	♟ 6
● Chianti Cl. Tenuta S. Alfonso '05	♟ 5
● Chianti dei Colli Senesi Rubizzo '06	♟ 4*
○ Vernaccia di S. Gimignano '06	♟ 3
● Ser Gioveto '04	♟ 6
● Morellino di Scansano Campomaccione '06	♟ 4
● Roccato '03	♟♟ 7
● Morellino di Scansano Campomaccione '05	♟♟ 4

Rocca di Castagnoli

LOC. CASTAGNOLI
53013 GAIOLE IN CHIANTI [SI]
TEL. 0577731004
www.roccadicastagnoli.com

ANNUAL PRODUCTION 300,000 bottles
HECTARES UNDER VINE 132
VITICULTURE METHOD Conventional

At last, lawyer Calogero Calì is reaping the fruits of the renovation and reconstruction work carried out at all his wineries over the last few years, from Rocca di Castagnoli to Capraia, from which he has recently disengaged, and San Sano. Much investment has been poured into improving the quality of the wines, starting with the vineyards, and it shows. Quite apart from the outstanding performance of the Chianti Classico Poggio ai Frati Riserva '04 – Three Glasses for a wine that embodies the soul of Chianti, something we encounter increasingly rarely – the entire range shows surprising quality, definition and character. The prize-winner, a hymn to the sangiovese grape, has subtle red berries, dried flowers and aromatic herbs on the nose and a taut, succulent palate whereas the great Chianti Classico Tenuta Capraia Riserva '04 is rounded and austere. The '03 Buriano, a monovarietal Cabernet Sauvignon, suffers a little from a poor vintage. The full-bodied Chianti Classico Tenuta Capraia '05 is very impressive, as is the Stielle '04, which is just a little too young to be appreciated.

Rocca di Frassinello

LOC. GIUNCARICO
58040 GAVORRANO [GR]
TEL. 0577742903

ANNUAL PRODUCTION 120,000 bottles
HECTARES UNDER VINE 150
VITICULTURE METHOD Conventional

It did not take Rocca di Frassinello long to hit the heights after a very flattering debut in the last edition of the Guide. Quality here is underwritten by two of the leading names in European and world winemaking: the French Lafite-Rothschild group and Chianti-based Castellare di Castellina, who have formed a joint venture in this Maremma estate. The wines are already flawless in style, the superb raw material being handled with absolute elegance. All this is supremely well expressed in the Rocca di Frassinello '05, which we gave Three Glasses. A breath-takingly broad swath of deep, complex aromatics introduces an equally powerful, stylish tannic structure, nicely supported by magnificently assimilated oak. The other wines on the list are all very good. The '05 Sughere di Frassinello has generous, concentrated aromas and expands over the palate with vibrant energy and progression. The Poggio alla Guardia '05 is pleasantly fresh and spicy. All three wines are a blend of sangiovese, cabernet sauvignon and merlot in different percentages.

● Chianti Cl. Poggio ai Frati Ris. '04	♈♈♈ 5
● Buriano '03	♈♈ 7
● Chianti Cl. Tenuta di Capraia Ris. '04	♈♈ 5
● Chianti Cl. Tenuta di Capraia '05	♈♈♈ 4
○ Molino delle Balze '05	♈♈♈ 5
● Stielle '04	♈♈ 5
● Chianti Cl. '05	♈ 4
○ Vin Santo del Chianti Cl. '99	♈ 8
● Stielle '00	♈♈♈ 8
● Stielle '01	♈♈ 8
● Le Pratola '00	♈♈ 8
● Le Pratola '01	♈♈ 8
● Chianti Cl. Capraia Ris. '03	♈♈ 5
● Chianti Cl. Capraia Ris. '00	♈♈ 6
● Chianti Cl. Capraia Ris. '01	♈♈ 6

● Rocca di Frassinello '05	♈♈♈ 7
● Le Sughere di Frassinello '05	♈♈ 6
● Poggio alla Guardia '05	♈♈ 5
● Rocca di Frassinello '04	♈♈ 7
● Le Sughere di Frassinello '04	♈♈ 6
● Poggio alla Guardia '04	♈♈ 5

Rocca di Montegrossi

FRAZ. MONTI IN CHIANTI
53010 GAIOLE IN CHIANTI [SI]
TEL. 0577747977

ANNUAL PRODUCTION 80,000 bottles
HECTARES UNDER VINE 18
VITICULTURE METHOD Conventional

We want to extend our compliments to Marco Ricasoli Firidolfi, the owner of this winery, now that our tastings are over. Of course, the ultimate prize of Three Glasses is missing but it is also true that it is hard to find at one winery so many high quality wines that so triumphantly maintain their own distinctive sensory profiles. Credit goes to the owner, who is in love with the land and profoundly convinced that wines should showcase territory without losing sight of tradition. We found proof of this in his Vin Santo '00, acknowledged to be one of the best in Chianti. The appealing nose with citrus and dried fruit aromas, particularly hazelnuts, introduces velvet-smooth, buttery, mellow palate that both fills the mouth and lingers endlessly. The other finalist is, once again, the Chianti Classico Vigneto San Marcellino Riserva. The '04 has a very subtle nose that mingles pencil lead blends with hints of blueberries and blackberries. The tasty follow-through on the palate reveals stylish body and silky tannins that balance the other elements. The Geremia '04, a blend of cabernet and merlot, is vibrant and generous while the Chianti Classico '05 is also very satisfying.

★ Tenimenti Ruffino

P.LE RUFFINO, 1
50065 PONTASSIEVE [FI]
TEL. 05583605
www.ruffino.it

ANNUAL PRODUCTION 14,500,000 bottles
HECTARES UNDER VINE 600
VITICULTURE METHOD Conventional

It was just a question of waiting for the right vintage to see Ruffino earn another Three Glasses. This year, the winner is the very subtle, elegant Modus '04, from sangiovese and cabernet sauvignon. The nose opens with clean, well-defined aromas of red berries and aromatic herbs before the offers excellent balance and a long, succulent finish. This is very fine wine that epitomizes a style and a character. The Romitorio di Santedame '04 is only a step behind with its deep, complex nose, aromas of black berry fruit, damp earth and vegetal sensations. The palate is vibrant, full and confident, marked out by prominent tannins and good acidity, although the finish is very slightly evanescent. The Chianti Classico Santedame '05 impressed us, especially considering the growing year. It may not be able to count on fullness and rich extract but it plays the card of elegance and appeal very shrewdly. The same applies to the Riserva Ducale Oro '03, a classic among classics that suffers a little from a less than perfect vintage. The monovarietal pinot noir Nero al Tondo '04, Libaio '06 and La Solatia Chardonnay '06 – the last two both from chardonnay – are all good and the rest of the range is reliably good.

● Chianti Cl. Vigneto S. Marcellino Ris. '04	ҮҮ	6
○ Vin Santo del Chianti Cl. '00	ҮҮ	8
● Chianti Cl. '05	ҮҮ	4*
● Geremia '04	ҮҮ	6
● Chianti Cl. Vigneto S. Marcellino Ris. '99	ҮҮҮ	5
● Geremia '03	ҮҮ	6
● Geremia '99	ҮҮ	6
○ Vin Santo del Chianti Cl. '97	ҮҮ	8
○ Vin Santo del Chianti Cl. '98	ҮҮ	8
● Chianti Cl. '03	ҮҮ	4
● Geremia '01	ҮҮ	6
● Chianti Cl. Vigneto S. Marcellino Ris. '01	ҮҮ	6

● Modus '04	ҮҮҮ	6
● Romitorio di Santedame '04	ҮҮ	7
● Chianti Cl. Santedame '05	ҮҮ	4*
○ La Solatia Chardonnay '06	ҮҮ	5
● Nero al Tondo '04	ҮҮ	6
● Chianti Cl. Ris. Ducale Oro '03	ҮҮ	6
○ Libaio '06	ҮҮ	3*
○ La Solatia Pinot Grigio '06	Ү	3
● Torgaio '06	Ү	3
● Chianti Cl. Ris. Ducale Oro '00	ҮҮҮ	6
● Romitorio di Santedame '00	ҮҮҮ	8
● Chianti Cl. Ris. Ducale Oro '88	ҮҮҮ	5
● Chianti Cl. Ris. Ducale Oro '90	ҮҮҮ	5
● Chianti Cl. Ris. Ducale Oro '01	ҮҮҮ	6

Russo

LOC. PODERE LA METOCCHINA
VIA FORNI, 71
57028 SUVERETO [LI]
TEL. 0565845105
az.ag.russo@katamail.com

ANNUAL PRODUCTION 60,000 bottles
HECTARES UNDER VINE 12
VITICULTURE METHOD Conventional

The Russo brothers' winery is now one of the most highly regarded around Suvereto. The brothers' secret is an ability to interpret the territory, the cycle of nature and the various growing seasons. This is how they manage to maintain the steady quality that we again saw this year. The house champion was Barbicone '05, from sangiovese, colorino, canaiolo, ciliegiolo and giacomino, which follows a complex, well-knit nose with good texture on the full-bodied, well-structured palate. Sadly, the finish is a tad held back by over-extracted tannins. The '06 Sassobucato from merlot and cabernet sauvignon is less precise. Its dark colour introduces a generously deep nose with vegetal, spice and balsamic hints. On the warm, full-bodied palate, the alcohol tends to overwhelm the sweet, shortish finish. The Val di Cornia Ceppitaio '06 is simple but not ordinary, presenting fresh-tasting, succulent, fruit-rich and savoury. The approachable Vermentino Pietrasca '06 is refreshing and varietal.

Salcheto

LOC. SANT'ALBINO
VIA DI VILLA BIANCA, 15
53045 MONTEPULCIANO [SI]
TEL. 0578799031
www.salcheto.it

ANNUAL PRODUCTION 130,000 bottles
HECTARES UNDER VINE 32
VITICULTURE METHOD Conventional

We welcome the prompt, confident return to a full profile for the winery run by Michele Manelli. Not only did he give us a series of beautifully made wines, he also walked away with Three Glasses for Nobile Salco Evoluzione '01. The wine, destined for release to market after six years' ageing, partly in barriques and partly in large barrels, derives from meticulous research in the vineyards, where the cellar identified an estate clone of prugnolo gentile called salco, and painstaking care in the cellar. In fact, the wine is a combination of batches fermented in stainless steel and in wooden vats. The '01 edition is extraordinary, starting from its sound sensory profile. Remarkably well-coordinated, prevalently minerally, aromas are the prelude to a wonderful, extremely complex palate. As we said the rest of the range is also very good. The impressive Nobile '04 has a clean nose and nicely balanced follow-through on the palate. The Rosso di Montepulciano '06 and Chianti Colli Senesi '06 are both approachable and appealing, the latter showing particularly fresh and dynamic.

● Barbicone '05	♟ 5
● Pietrasca '06	♟ 3*
● Val di Cornia Rosso Ceppitaio '06	♟ 4
● Sassobucato '06	♟ 5
● Val di Cornia Rosso Barbicone '00	♟♟♟ 5*
● Sassobucato '00	♟♟ 6
● Sassobucato '02	♟♟ 6
● Sassobucato '04	♟♟ 5
● Sassobucato '03	♟♟ 5
● Val di Cornia Rosso Barbicone '01	♟♟ 5
● Barbicone '04	♟♟ 5
● Val di Cornia Rosso Ceppitaio '04	♟♟ 4
● Sassobucato '01	♟♟ 5

● Nobile di Montepulciano Salco Evoluzione '01	♟♟♟ 7
● Nobile di Montepulciano '04	♟♟ 5
● Chianti Colli Senesi '06	♟ 4
● Rosso di Montepulciano '06	♟ 4
● Nobile di Montepulciano Salco '00	♟♟ 6
● Nobile di Montepulciano '03	♟♟ 5
● Nobile di Montepulciano '98	♟♟ 5
● Nobile di Montepulciano '02	♟♟ 5
● Nobile di Montepulciano Salco Evoluzione '99	♟♟ 7
● Nobile di Montepulciano Salco '99	♟♟ 6
● Nobile di Montepulciano Salco '01	♟♟ 6
● Nobile di Montepulciano '99	♟♟ 5

Fattoria San Fabiano - Borghini Baldovinetti

LOC. SAN FABIANO, 33
52100 AREZZO [AR]
TEL. 057524566
www.fattoriasanfabiano.it

San Fabiano Calcinaia

LOC. CELLOLE
53011 CASTELLINA IN CHIANTI [SI]
TEL. 0577979232
www.sanfabianocalcinaia.com

ANNUAL PRODUCTION 700,000 bottles
HECTARES UNDER VINE 170
VITICULTURE METHOD Natural

ANNUAL PRODUCTION 160,000 bottles
HECTARES UNDER VINE 42
VITICULTURE METHOD Conventional

Fattoria San Fabiano, owned by the noble Borghini Baldovinetti family, is a big estate for the Arezzo zone and its history has deep roots. To the original holding, set just on the edge of the city of Arezzo, have now been added Tenuta di Campriano, lying a little further afield, and Tenuta Poggio Uliveto in Montepulciano. A recent consolidation of production processes has enabled the quality of the wines to rise to match quantity. This year's entry might appear somewhat slim. This is because the top wine, Armaiolo, was not submitted for tasting, and neither was the new vintage of the straight Chianti, which will appear next year. The most impressive wine in this year's range is Nobile Poggio Uliveto '04, a clean, sound, generous glassful of good depth with well-judged oaking and good flavour on the finish. Piocaia '04, from sangiovese, merlot and cabernet, is rich, ripe, broad, succulent and mouthfilling, although it's a touch static and there are suggestions of over-evolution. The new Chianti Etichetta Nera '05 is most attractive and has great typicity, even though it has deliberately been made softer, darker and fruitier than the standard Etichetta Bianca (White Label).

It's as if Guido Serio had season tickets to the red Glasses arena for his two top wines, Cerviolo Rosso, from sangiovese, merlot and cabernet, and Chianti Classico Riserva. This year's '04s performed exactly like last year's. So even though top honours have not yet arrived, Guido confirms his remarkable ability to attain consistently high quality year after year. An additional factor of significance is that the wines hold up perfectly over time. Proof comes at vertical tastings, where the older vintages still reveal plenty of drive and vitality. This year, Cerviolo Bianco '05, from 100 per cent chardonnay, was another high flier. The nose is mineral and floral; the palate vigorous and vibrant, and there is good balance and flavour on the finish. The two finalists both struggle a little initially to express themselves on the nose but both have good texture. The Cerviolo is more reactive, pervasive and assertive on the palate, the Riserva showing greater complexity and flavour separation. The other two wines submitted showed well, too, an easy-drinking '05 Casa Boschino, made from the same grapes as Cerviolo, and the '05 Chianti Classico.

● Nobile di Montepulciano Poggio Uliveto '04	♥♥ 4*
● Chianti Et. Nera '05	♥ 3*
● Piocaia '04	♥ 4
● Armaiolo '03	♥♥ 5
● Armaiolo '00	♥♥ 6
● Armaiolo '97	♥♥ 5
● Armaiolo '98	♥♥ 5
● Piocaia '03	♥♥ 4
● Piocaia '01	♥♥ 4*
● Nobile di Montepulciano Poggio Uliveto '03	♥♥ 4
● Armaiolo '99	♥♥ 6

● Cerviolo Rosso '04	♥♥ 7
● Chianti Cl. Cellole Ris. '04	♥♥ 6
O Cerviolo Bianco '05	♥♥ 5
● Casa Boschino '05	♥ 4
● Chianti Cl. '05	♥ 4
● Cerviolo Rosso '00	♥♥♥ 7
● Cerviolo Rosso '98	♥♥♥ 6
● Cerviolo Rosso '99	♥♥♥ 6
● Chianti Cl. Cellole Ris. '00	♥♥♥ 6
● Cerviolo Rosso '97	♥♥♥ 6
● Cerviolo Rosso '96	♥♥♥ 6
● Cerviolo Rosso '01	♥♥ 7
● Chianti Cl. Cellole Ris. '03	♥♥ 6
● Chianti Cl. Cellole Ris. '01	♥♥ 6
● Cerviolo Rosso '03	♥♥ 7
● Casa Boschino '04	♥♥ 4

San Felice

LOC. SAN FELICE
53019 CASTELNUOVO BERARDENGA [SI]
TEL. 05773991
www.agricolasanfelice.it

ANNUAL PRODUCTION 1,000,000 bottles
HECTARES UNDER VINE 210
VITICULTURE METHOD Conventional

Agricola San Felice took home a brand new set of Three Glasses, thanks to a highly successful Chianti Classico Poggio Rosso Riserva '03. Despite the vintage, which was not one of the easiest to manage, it's a wine of distinction with deep, sound fruit and an open, accessible palate. There is red and black berry fruit on the nose plus gaminess and smokiness, and the palate is shaped to perfection by good acidity. The tannin – and this is the vital point – has nothing to do with what we have come to expect of the '03s. Instead, it's ripe, fine-grained and already well integrated. All this is down to the highly skilled team of Leonardo Bellaccini in the cellar and Carlo Salvinelli in the vineyards, while Fabrizio Nencioni takes care of sales. The vigorous, well-structured Vigorello '03, from sangiovese, cabernet sauvignon and merlot, is also impressive. The nose has preserved fruit with balsamic and vegetal notes, and the intense palate doesn't disappoint, even though it is still possibly too youthful. Chianti Classico '05 is as juicy and attractive as the vintage would suggest but the '04 Riserva Il Grigio doesn't quite match expectations.

San Giusto a Rentennano

FRAZ. MONTI IN CHIANTI
LOC. SAN GIUSTO, 20
53013 GAIOLE IN CHIANTI [SI]
TEL. 0577747121
www.fattoriasangiusto.it

ANNUAL PRODUCTION 85,000 bottles
HECTARES UNDER VINE 29
VITICULTURE METHOD Natural

Two wines from the Martini di Cigala siblings reached the finals: Percarlo '04, from 100 per cent sangiovese, and La Ricolma '04, from merlot. The estate always takes extreme care, paying great attention to detail, plus there's an integrity of approach that ensures all the wines are fine ambassadors for their homeland. True, the use of oak has recently become more pronounced. It's also true that vintages have their influence, generating more powerful or more elegant wines. Percarlo is a full-bodied, well-defined wine with a balsamic, minty nose, its only failing being a little too much oak tannin. There is more intensity of aroma on the rounded, mouthfilling La Ricolma, and plenty of fruit alongside the oak, although it too remains reined in by tannin. Chianti Classico Riserva Le Baroncole '04 is a little disappointing, its aromas indistinct and balance eluding it. Chianti Classico '05 is more expressive on the nose but here again too much tannin holds it back.

● Chianti Cl. Poggio Rosso Ris. '03	♚♚♚	6
● Vigorello '03	♚♚	7
● Perolla Poggibano '05	♚♚	5
● Chianti Cl. '05	♚	4
● Chianti Cl. Il Grigio Ris. '04	♚	5
● Chianti Cl. Poggio Rosso Ris. '00	♚♚♚	6
● Vigorello '97	♚♚♚	5
● Chianti Cl. Poggio Rosso Ris. '95	♚♚♚	5
● Chianti Cl. Poggio Rosso Ris. '90	♚♚♚	6
● Vigorello '98	♚♚	6
● Vigorello '99	♚♚	7
● Vigorello '01	♚♚	7

● La Ricolma '04	♚♚	7
● Percarlo '04	♚♚	8
● Chianti Cl. '05	♚	5
● Chianti Cl. Le Baroncole '04	♚	6
● Percarlo '95	♚♚♚	8
● Percarlo '97	♚♚♚	8
● Percarlo '99	♚♚♚	8
● Percarlo '01	♚♚	8
● Percarlo '03	♚♚	8
● Chianti Cl. '03	♚♚	5
● La Ricolma '98	♚♚	8
● Chianti Cl. Ris. '99	♚♚	6
● La Ricolma '03	♚♚	7
● Chianti Cl. '04	♚♚	5
● La Ricolma '01	♚♚	7

★ Tenuta San Guido
LOC. CAPANNE, 27
57020 BOLGHERI [LI]
TEL. 0565762003
www.sassicaia.com

San Luciano
LOC. SAN LUCIANO, 90
52048 MONTE SAN SAVINO [AR]
TEL. 0575848518
www.sanlucianovini.it

ANNUAL PRODUCTION 430,000 bottles
HECTARES UNDER VINE 90
VITICULTURE METHOD Conventional

ANNUAL PRODUCTION 350,000 bottles
HECTARES UNDER VINE 63
VITICULTURE METHOD Conventional

The '04 release of Bolgheri Sassicaia is quite simply majestic, one of the best ever. This surprises no-one, of course. We're talking about one of Italy's greatest wines here, and a vintage which has given superb results, especially in the coastal areas. Even so, it's difficult not to get excited when faced with such stylistic precision, such character, such personality. The nose has intense red berry fruits followed by damp earth, leather, sandalwood and even dried flowers. The palate is overwhelming, so perfect is the relationship between the beautifully defined tannin and the taut, vibrant acidity. The finish simply never ends. This magnificent bottle will give great pleasure if drunk now, and will continue to do so for who knows how many more years. The estate's second-label wine, Guidalberto '05, made mainly from merlot and cabernet sauvignon with a little sangiovese, is also very good indeed. The vintage is a lesser one, not so perfect, and the high points of the wine are its drinkability, its attractiveness and its caressing mouthfeel. Similar comments apply but on a slightly lesser scale to the juicy, lively, yet laid-back Le Difese '05, from cabernet sauvignon with some sangiovese.

There's a touch of regret this year in our review of the San Luciano wines, which derive from the determination and passion of the entire Ziantoni family. It's not because the results are less than impressive nor because the estate has strayed from its well-established quality standards, but simply because, after the glorious '03 release of D'Ovidio, which made it to the finals for the first time, we had very high hopes for the '04. Mainly from sangiovese and montepulciano, with some merlot and cabernet, it reflects the high quality of these grapes but its profile is overridden by dark, toasty, bitter and astringent notes stemming from the oak used in its ageing. We really hope that, given a suitable maturation period, these will attenuate. So let us pass on quickly to highlight the earthy, spicy, balsamic Boschi Salviati '05, from sangiovese, montepulciano and cabernet, and the highly attractive '05 Colle Carpito, from sangiovese and montepulciano, a textbook example of how to provide great drinking at a fair price. The whites, as ever, are reliably fresh and zesty, with Resico '06, from chardonnay, grechetto and trebbiano, a neck ahead for structure.

● Bolgheri Sassicaia '04	▼▼▼	8
● Guidalberto '05	▼▼	7
● Le Difese '05	▼▼	5
● Bolgheri Sassicaia '00	♈♈♈	8
● Bolgheri Sassicaia '01	♈♈♈	8
● Bolgheri Sassicaia '02	♈♈♈	8
● Bolgheri Sassicaia '96	♈♈♈	8
● Sassicaia '84	♈♈♈	8
● Sassicaia '93	♈♈♈	6
● Sassicaia '92	♈♈♈	8
● Sassicaia '90	♈♈♈	8
● Sassicaia '88	♈♈♈	8
● Sassicaia '85	♈♈♈	8
● Bolgheri Sassicaia '99	♈♈♈	8
● Bolgheri Sassicaia '98	♈♈♈	8
● Bolgheri Sassicaia '97	♈♈♈	8
● Bolgheri Sassicaia '95	♈♈♈	8
● Bolgheri Sassicaia '03	♈♈♈	8

● Boschi Salviati '05	▼▼	4*
● D'Ovidio '04	▼▼	6
● Colle Carpito '05	▼	3*
O Valdichiana Luna di Monte '06	▼	3
O Resico '06	▼	3
● D'Ovidio '03	♈♈	6
● D'Ovidio '99	♈♈	5
● Colle Carpito '04	♈♈	4*
● D'Ovidio '01	♈♈	6
O Vin Santo Savinus '00	♈♈	6

Castello di San Sano

LOC. SAN SANO
53013 GAIOLE IN CHIANTI [SI]
TEL. 0577746056
www.castellosansano.com

ANNUAL PRODUCTION 200,000 bottles
HECTARES UNDER VINE 87
VITICULTURE METHOD Conventional

This is Castello di San Sano's first full entry in the Guide. The winery is owned by Calogero Calì, who owns Rocca di Castagnoli and Capraia, also in Gaiole. Cali's policy is to diversify the production of each holding so that each develops a distinct style and this has led him to separate all three into independent entities. It requires assiduous work and time for things to fall into place but it is beginning to bear fruit. Hence the San Sano wines never echo the others: as well as delivering excellent quality they have more clear-cut personalities. The best this year is Borro al Fumo '04, made from sangiovese and cabernet sauvignon. It is a good bright ruby, the aromas revolve around tones of balsam, the palate is balanced and the wine grows through the mouth, but not too much. Riserva Guarnellotto '04 is also very good. This is a modern, fruit-forward style of wine, the nose gaining class from fresh spiciness, and good impetus marking out the dynamic palate. Given the vintage, the '05 Chianti Classico is really rather successful, with welcome freshness.

San Vincenti

LOC. SAN VINCENTI
POD. DI STIGNANO, 27
53013 GAIOLE IN CHIANTI [SI]
TEL. 0577734047
www.sanvincenti.it

ANNUAL PRODUCTION 40,000 bottles
HECTARES UNDER VINE 8
VITICULTURE METHOD Conventional

The Pucci family's wines may not be as exciting as they were some years back but the overall impression is one of soundness. All they need for real excellence is a bit of spark. Of course, there are a thousand variables in winemaking but it's also true that once you've reached the top you have a model to live up to. You also know you have the potential to get there: the only problem is managing to achieve a repeat performance. So we continue to hope. Stignano, a sangiovese-based Supertuscan, showed very well. It is rather reticent on the nose before opening to give fresh notes of aromatic herbs and black berry fruits. There is good substance on the palate, although the tannins are a bit edgy, but it finishes full of flavour. Chianti Classico Riserva '04, is also successful. This has clearer defined, forest fruits aromas, a lively, well-structured palate with good backbone and an attractive finish. The distinctly short Chianti Classico '05 is less impressive.

● Borro al Fumo '04	▼▼ 6
● Chianti Cl. Guarnellotto Ris. '04	▼▼ 5
● Chianti Cl. '05	▼ 4
● Chianti Cl. '04	♀♀ 4

● Chianti Cl. Ris. '04	▼▼ 6
● Stignano '04	▼▼ 6
● Chianti Cl. '05	▼ 5
● Chianti Cl. Ris. '01	♀♀♀ 6
● Stignano '00	♀♀♀ 7
● Stignano '01	♀♀ 7
● Chianti Cl. '04	♀♀ 5
● Chianti Cl. Ris. '03	♀♀ 6
● Stignano '03	♀♀ 6

Tenuta San Vito
VIA SAN VITO, 59
50056 MONTELUPO FIORENTINO [FI]
TEL. 057151411
www.san-vito.com

Sassotondo
LOC. SOVANA
PIAN DI CONATI, 52
58010 SORANO [GR]
TEL. 0564614218
www.sassotondo.it

ANNUAL PRODUCTION 170,000 bottles
HECTARES UNDER VINE 30
VITICULTURE METHOD Certified organic

Tenuta San Vito, one of the earliest Tuscan estates to turn to organic viticulture, has retained its place in the Guide, confirming that last year's wines really were the result of the new approach carefully set in place by owner Roberto Drighi. It wasn't just a matter of luck. Our preferences from the range this year remain the same too, with Colle dei Mandorli, made solely from merlot, in top place. This has an intense, youthful nose with ripe fruit melded into oak spiciness. It's full on the palate, with lively tannins and a balancing acidic backbone leading to a long, tangy finish. Madiere '05, from sangiovese and cabernet, is also a high flyer. The nose and palate are equally concentrated, while balanced tannin brings dynamism throughout the mouth, leading to a savoury, flavoursome finish. Chianti Darno '06 is a good wine, showing even and fruity, with a lively, full finish. The '06 Chianti has a delicate nose and very nice balance. Vin Santo Malmantico '00 is less successful, though, lacking weight in the mouth.

ANNUAL PRODUCTION 50,000 bottles
HECTARES UNDER VINE 12
VITICULTURE METHOD Certified organic

Edoardo Ventimiglia from Rome, previously a documentary maker, and his wife, agronomist Carla Benini, started producing wine in this corner of the Maremma around the mid 1990s. They have achieved what they set out to do: the estate soon became successful and has remained so, to the extent that it is now a beacon on the Maremma wine scene. They have also freed the ciliegiolo variety from an oblivion it did not deserve. The wines are highly dependable, both qualitatively and stylistically, especially for those looking for bottles of individual, refined character. They are miles away from the over-muscular styles so popular recently. The '04 release of San Lorenzo, made from 100 per cent ciliegiolo, is again a wine of great elegance and reached the finals. The cool year has given its nose a delicate fruitiness enhanced by hints of pepper and balsam. The vigorous palate is exuberant, held back only by its tannins, some of them from oak. Sovana Riserva Franze '04 also showed very well, with an earthy nose and a long, lively palate. All the other wines are attractive easy drinkers with good character.

● Chianti dei Colli Fiorentini Darno '06	♟♟ 4*
● Colle dei Mandorli '05	♟♟ 6
● Madiere '05	♟♟ 5
● Chianti '06	♟ 3*
O Vin Santo del Chianti Malmantico '00	♟ 5
O Amantiglio '05	♟♟ 4
● Madiere '04	♟♟ 5
● Colle dei Mandorli '04	♟♟ 6
● Chianti dei Colli Fiorentini Darno '05	♟♟ 4*

● San Lorenzo '04	♟♟ 6
● Sovana Sangiovese Franze Ris. '04	♟♟ 6
O Bianco di Pitigliano '06	♟ 4
● Ciliegiolo '05	♟ 6
● Sovana Rosso '05	♟ 4
● San Lorenzo '00	♟♟ 6
● San Lorenzo '03	♟♟ 6
● San Lorenzo '99	♟♟ 5
● San Lorenzo '02	♟♟ 6
● San Lorenzo '01	♟♟ 6
● San Lorenzo '98	♟♟ 5
● San Lorenzo '97	♟♟ 4

Michele Satta

LOC. CASONE UGOLINO, 23
57022 CASTAGNETO CARDUCCI [LI]
TEL. 0565773041
www.michelesatta.com

ANNUAL PRODUCTION 160,000 bottles
HECTARES UNDER VINE 28
VITICULTURE METHOD Conventional

Although Michele Satta's wines are always very good indeed, nothing was truly outstanding this year. Now, given the meticulous vineyard work that distinguishes the estate, it is not unreasonable to for us to expect something special, especially when the vintage is as starry as that of '04. But then it also has to be said that Cavaliere was absent from our tastings since, probably, it had been left to gain more bottle age before release. Bolgheri Superiore I Castagni '04, from cabernet sauvignon, syrah and teroldego, is a really good wine. Still youthful, it has a broad, deep, complex nose with gamey notes, leather and tobacco. The palate is full and tight knit, needing only the tannins to settle and allow it to expand. Diambra Rosso '05, made mainly from sangiovese, with some colorino, malvasia and ciliegiolo, is extremely attractive, the nose brimming with black berry fruit and hints of balsam, and the palate full and tannic with a juicy finish. Bolgheri Rosso '05 is a good reflection of the vintage: inviting, not overly large, ripely fruited on the nose and abundantly acidic on the palate.

Savignola Paolina

VIA PETRIOLO, 58
50022 GREVE IN CHIANTI [FI]
TEL. 0558546036
www.savignolapaolina.it

ANNUAL PRODUCTION 35,000 bottles
HECTARES UNDER VINE 7
VITICULTURE METHOD Conventional

For our report on the Fabbri family's wines this year we could quite easily just repeat last year's: the results are the same, as is the way they have been working to achieve quality. The Chianti Classico Riserva, this year the '04, again reached the finals and while it didn't manage to breach the Three Glass barrier, it is again a perfect example of how fine wines can be coaxed, year after year, even from small vineyard areas. This is not as easy as it might seem. You need to keep a watch on your vineyard almost as if it were a garden. Even the slightest error can cost you dear. The upside of all this effort, though, is the satisfaction of making wines that always have a recognizable style. And this year, it is again the overall elegance and finesse of the Riserva that is so striking. The nose is classy and refined, the oak is well tempered, the palate is supple and full but not over-full, there's good length and it makes for enjoyable drinking. The Chianti Classico '05 is simpler, with a lesser array of aromas and a straightforward, but well balanced, palate.

● Bolgheri Rosso Diambra '05	♟♟ 4	
● Bolgheri Rosso Sup. I Castagni '04	♟♟ 8	
⊙ Bolgheri Rosato '06	♟ 4	
● Bolgheri Rosso '05	♟ 5	
● Bolgheri Rosso Piastraia '01	♟♟♟ 7	
● Bolgheri Rosso Piastraia '02	♟♟♟ 7	
● Bolgheri Rosso Piastraia '00	♟♟ 7	
● Bolgheri Rosso Sup. I Castagni '00	♟♟ 8	
● Bolgheri Rosso Sup. I Castagni '01	♟♟ 8	
● Bolgheri Rosso Sup. I Castagni '03	♟♟ 8	
● Cavaliere '01	♟♟ 8	
● Cavaliere '00	♟♟ 7	
● Cavaliere '99	♟♟ 7	

● Chianti Cl. Ris. '04	♟♟ 5	
● Chianti Cl. '05	♟ 4	
● Chianti Cl. Ris. '03	♟♟ 5	
● Granaio '01	♟♟ 6	
● Chianti Cl. '03	♟♟ 4	
● Granaio '02	♟♟ 6	
● Granaio '03	♟♟ 5	

La Selva

FRAZ. SAN DONATO - ALBINIA
LOC. LA SELVA
58010 ORBETELLO [GR]
TEL. 0564885799
www.bioselva.it

ANNUAL PRODUCTION 200,000 bottles
HECTARES UNDER VINE 19
VITICULTURE METHOD Certified organic

Karl Egger's estate hasn't been going long, and his new cellars were only finished in 2000, yet he has taken no time at all to find a way of achieving reliably high quality. He is only a step away from hitting real peaks. His exploit is driven by a clearly defined production philosophy of not forcing his wines into any direction but letting them express themselves naturally. Two wines reached the finals this year: Prima Causa '05, from cabernet sauvignon and merlot, and Morellino Colli dell'Uccellina '06. The former has aromas of dark-skinned fruit, pencil lead and sweet spices, leading to a succulent, almost fat yet gentle palate with a relaxed feel. The Morellino has a more elegant aromatic profile and a fresh, lively palate with silky tannins and good flavour. The '05 Ciliegiolo is also most successful and has fruit-driven aromas and peppery, balsamic notes bringing liveliness. The palate is understated yet nicely savoury and develops evenly. Morellino '06 is slightly untogether, especially on the nose, but tasty and racy on the palate. Vermentino La Selva '06 is fresh yet slender, showing best on its lively, easy-drinking palate.

● Morellino di Scansano Colli dell'Uccellina '06	🍷🍷	4*
● Prima Causa '05	🍷🍷	6
● Ciliegiolo '05	🍷🍷	5
● Morellino di Scansano '06	🍷	3
○ Vermentino La Selva '06	🍷	3
● Morellino di Scansano '05	ΥΥ	3
● Prima Causa '01	ΥΥ	5
● Prima Causa '04	ΥΥ	6
● Morellino di Scansano Colli dell'Uccellina '03	ΥΥ	4

Fattoria Selvapiana

LOC. SELVAPIANA, 43
50068 RUFINA [FI]
TEL. 0558369848
www.selvapiana.it

ANNUAL PRODUCTION 220,000 bottles
HECTARES UNDER VINE 59.7
VITICULTURE METHOD Conventional

Francesco Giuntini's Selvapiana has a long history and, crucially, epitomizes the traditional concept of the Rufina zone, having been one of the first estates to take the wine to drinkers abroad. Chianti Rufina Bucerchiale, from the Bucerchiale vineyard, is the most characteristic of its wines and this year's '03 reached the finals. The nose is invigorating and still youthful, with aromas of preserved fruit. It is succulent and full of drive as it hits the palate, there's balanced tannicity, a refreshing acid backbone and a savoury finish with good follow-through. Longevity is a classic characteristic of Rufina wines and recent vertical tastings have demonstrated just how well Bucerchiale can age. The Supertuscan La Fornace '04, based on merlot, cabernet sauvignon and sangiovese, also showed well. There's fruit and elegant spiciness on the nose, and softness and refinement on the palate, which has a subtle tannic weave and a clean finish. Vin Santo '01 is simply delicious, with vanilla, honey and hazelnut aromas, a creamy, dense structure, and a long finish with an orange-like aftertaste. Chianti Rufina '05 is simple but well made.

● Chianti Rufina Bucerchiale Ris. '03	🍷🍷	6
● La Fornace '04	🍷🍷	6
● Chianti Rufina '05	🍷	4
● La Fornace '00	ΥΥ	7
● Chianti Rufina Bucerchiale Ris. '00	ΥΥ	5
○ Vin Santo della Rufina '97	ΥΥ	5
○ Vin Santo della Rufina '99	ΥΥ	6
○ Chianti Rufina Vin Santo '98	ΥΥ	6
● La Fornace '01	ΥΥ	7
● La Fornace '03	ΥΥ	6
● Chianti Rufina Bucerchiale Ris. '01	ΥΥ	6

Serraiola

FRAZ. FRASSINE
LOC. SERRAIOLA
58025 MONTEROTONDO MARITTIMO [GR]
TEL. 0566910026
www.serraiola.it

ANNUAL PRODUCTION 50,000 bottles
HECTARES UNDER VINE 10
VITICULTURE METHOD Conventional

Fiorella Lenzi's Serraiola, situated on the provincial border where Grosseto meets Livorno, forms, as it were, the last bastion of the Monteregio di Massa Marittima denomination. Although the estate's whites are good, its real vocation seems to be with the reds, at least judging by this year's results. Campo Montecristo '05, made from merlot, sangiovese and syrah, reached the finals. The nose is powerful and intense, dark-skinned fruit underlies quinine, oriental spices and coffee powder. The palate is succulent, very deep and full of richness. The flavoursome Shyraz '05 is tauter and more restrained in style. Its refined fruitiness is well-defined and enlivened by notes of balsam and spice; its palate is tangy, almost edgy. Monteregio Lentisco '05 is another fine red, with aromas cleanly focused towards great liveliness, and a slim palate full of flavour. Monteregio Cervone '06 is nicely made. Both Monteregio Bianco Violina '06 and Vermentino '06 are uncomplicated, the latter showing a touch better.

Sesti - Castello di Argiano

FRAZ. SANT'ANGELO IN COLLE
LOC. CASTELLO DI ARGIANO
53024 MONTALCINO [SI]
TEL. 0577843921
giuseppesesti@sesti.net

ANNUAL PRODUCTION 62,000 bottles
HECTARES UNDER VINE 8.5
VITICULTURE METHOD Conventional

Sesti is based in the awe-inspiring Castello di Argiano, which was once part of the medieval fortifications of the small village of Camigliano. The estate has always aimed for high quality in its wines. Indeed, the last two vintages of the classy Brunello Phenomena Riserva came within a hair of Three Glasses. Naturally, there was huge interest in this year's '01 release and, as predicted, it made the grade. The label is highly individual, representing an eclipse that occurred during the vintage. The wine itself is less idiosyncratic. The nose has the classic blackberry fruit, spices, leather and tobacco, leading to a palate that is soft and powerful. Mellow tannins together with perfectly balanced supporting acidity give it amazing thrust, leading to a long, deep finish. Grangiovese '05 is well made, with a fruity, balsamic nose and an intense palate. Brunello '02 is succulent but lacks a bit of size. The '05 Rosso is fairly structured. Sauvignon '06, with its typical, varietal, tomato leaf aromas, is the most notable of the other wines submitted.

● Campo Montecristo '05	♈♈ 6
● Shyraz '05	♈♈ 5
● Monteregio di Massa Marittima Rosso Lentisco '05	♈♈ 5
○ Monteregio di Massa Marittima Bianco Violina '06	♈ 4
○ Vermentino '06	♈ 4
● Monteregio di Massa Marittima Cervone '06	♈ 4
● Campo Montecristo '00	♈♈ 6
● Shyraz '04	♈♈ 5
● Campo Montecristo '04	♈♈ 6
● Campo Montecristo '99	♈♈ 5
● Campo Montecristo '02	♈♈ 6
● Campo Montecristo '01	♈♈ 6

● Brunello di Montalcino Phenomena Ris. '01	♈♈♈ 8
● Grangiovese '05	♈♈ 4
● Brunello di Montalcino '02	♈ 7
☉ Rosato '06	♈ 4
○ Sauvignon '06	♈ 4
● Rosso di Montalcino '05	♈ 5
● Brunello di Montalcino '01	♈♈ 7
● Brunello di Montalcino Phenomena Ris. '00	♈♈ 8
● Brunello di Montalcino '97	♈♈ 8
● Brunello di Montalcino Phenomena Ris. '99	♈♈ 8
● Brunello di Montalcino '99	♈♈ 8
● Grangiovese '04	♈♈ 4

Tenuta Sette Ponti
LOC. VIGNA DI PALLINO
VIA SETTE PONTI, 71
52029 CASTIGLION FIBOCCHI [AR]
TEL. 055477857
www.tenutasetteponti.it

ANNUAL PRODUCTION 200,000 bottles
HECTARES UNDER VINE 50
VITICULTURE METHOD Conventional

There's little to say about this year's impeccable range of wines from Tenuta Sette Ponti. Never before have overall quality levels across the two holdings, Sette Ponti in the province of Arezzo and Poggio al Lupo in Maremma, been so high. This stems from the skilful handling of the '05 vintage by the estate's winemaking team, and compliments are in order. The established estate style is fully recognizable, meaning emphasis on intensity of colour, concentration and depth of extract. This has been achieved with great technical aplomb, bringing praiseworthy balance. There's even the icing on the cake this year of a new set of Three Glasses for Oreno, made from merlot, cabernet and sangiovese. The '05 marries ripeness, dark-skinned fruitiness, spiciness, refined tannicity and depth of expression. Crognolo '05, from sangiovese and merlot, is also excellent, full of fruit tempered by aromatic herbs, open and elegantly calibrated. Poggio al Lupo '05, from cabernet, alicante and petit verdot, is full, flavoursome, sweetly fruity and has balsamic freshness. Morellino Poggio al Lupo '06, while still quite taut, is clean and deep. It has good body and avoids an excess of oak.

Solaria - Cencioni
POD. CAPANNA, 102
53024 MONTALCINO [SI]
TEL. 0577849426
www.solariacencioni.com

ANNUAL PRODUCTION 35,000 bottles
HECTARES UNDER VINE 9
VITICULTURE METHOD Conventional

Firm resolve and attention to detail have been the main prongs of Patrizia Cencioni's approach to running her estate, and the result has justifiably been widespread acclaim. Her meticulous care in the vineyards and her ferociously severe selection of the grapes at harvest time led to good results even in '02, a difficult vintage to say the least, allowing her to come up with one of the year's most impressive Brunello di Montalcino bottles. The nose is generous, floral and fruity, with peach alongside the more typical red berry fruit, and the oaking is delicate and balanced, enhancing rather than dampening the aromas. The palate is attractive, elegant and has good cadence. So this is no monster of a wine. Actually, it represents Barolo in its lightest-bodied incarnation, that of the poorest vintages, and does so with great dignity. There's nothing to complain about with the '05 Rosso either, which is one of the best in its class, sporting clean, intense aromas centred on red berry fruits, and an attractive, open, flavour-filled palate with a good finish.

● Oreno '05	♟♟♟ 8
● Crognolo '05	♟♟ 5
● Morellino di Scansano Poggio al Lupo '06	♟♟ 4*
● Poggio al Lupo '05	♟♟ 6
● Oreno '00	♟♟♟ 6
● Oreno '01	♟♟ 6
● Poggio al Lupo '03	♟♟ 6
● Poggio al Lupo '01	♟♟ 6
● Oreno '03	♟♟ 7
● Oreno '99	♟♟ 6
● Crognolo '04	♟♟ 5
● Crognolo '03	♟♟ 5

● Brunello di Montalcino '02	♟♟ 7
● Rosso di Montalcino '05	♟♟ 5
● Brunello di Montalcino '97	♟♟♟ 7
● Brunello di Montalcino '00	♟♟ 6
● Brunello di Montalcino '98	♟♟ 8
● Brunello di Montalcino '99	♟♟ 7
● Brunello di Montalcino '01	♟♟ 7

Solatione

FRAZ. MERCATALE VAL DI PESA
VIA VALIGONDOLI, 53A
50024 SAN CASCIANO
IN VAL DI PESA [FI]
TEL. 055821623
www.solatione.it

ANNUAL PRODUCTION   10,000 bottles
HECTARES UNDER VINE 5
VITICULTURE METHOD   Conventional

The last few years have seen a fluctuating presence in the Guide for this estate, owned by the Giachi family. This time, it's a full entry, the wines having generally shown well. The estate was founded in 1972, the aim at that time being to produce wine and oil to sell in bulk, but the quality that emerged prompted them to start bottling in 1992. The Giachis decided right from the start to concentrate on indigenous varieties, meaning sangiovese and canaiolo for the reds, and trebbiano and malvasia for the whites. They have additionally always paid particular attention to producing Vin Santo, and this includes the Occhio di Pernice version made using red grapes. We adjudged both '04 Chianti Classicos, the standard version and the Riserva, to be of equivalent worth. The former is, if anything, more ebullient, showing fruit-led, supple and balanced, with an appealingly zesty finish. The Riserva has greater power and fuller structure, with an incisive nose and meaty tannins, and grows towards its finish.

Le Sorgenti

LOC. VALLINA
VIA DI DOCCIOLA, 8
50012 BAGNO A RIPOLI [FI]
TEL. 055696004
www.fattoria-lesorgenti.com

ANNUAL PRODUCTION   40,000 bottles
HECTARES UNDER VINE 16
VITICULTURE METHOD   Conventional

The Ferrari family's wines showed well this year. The excellent Scirus, based on cabernet sauvignon and merlot, made its first appearance in the finals with the '04. The inviting nose is all wild berry jam, vanilla and spices. The palate is soft and even, gains polish from a fresh swathe of acidity, and has silky tannins and a good, long finish. But the whole range seems to have found greater stability, consistent with the estate's stated objective of achieving wines of character that stand out from the crowd but are never obvious. Now that Filippo, the owners' son, is in sole charge of grape-growing and winemaking, things will certainly get even more interesting, given his conflict with his father Gabriele, who has always been dedicated to the vineyards. Gaiaccia '05, from sangiovese and merlot, performed well. There's pencil lead and leather on the nose, and evident yet not oppressive tannin on the succulent palate, which has a good, savoury finish. Sghiras '05 – last year it was the '04 we tasted – from chardonnay and sauvignon, is another success story, with a lively lemon-like nose and a taut, tasty palate. Chianti Fiorentini '05 has good style.

● Chianti Cl. '04	♟♟ 4
● Chianti Cl. Ris. '04	♟♟ 5
● Chianti Cl. Ris. '01	♟♟ 5

● Scirus '04	♟ 6
● Gaiaccia '05	♟♟ 4
● Chianti Colli Fiorentini Respiro '05	♟ 4
○ Sghiras '05	♟ 4
● Scirus '01	♟♟ 6
● Gaiaccia '04	♟♟ 4
● Scirus '00	♟♟ 6
○ Vin Santo '97	♟♟ 6
● Scirus '99	♟♟ 5
● Gaiaccia '02	♟♟ 4
● Scirus '03	♟♟ 6

Talenti

FRAZ. SANT'ANGELO IN COLLE
LOC. PIAN DI CONTE
53020 MONTALCINO [SI]
TEL. 0577844064
www.talentimontalcino.it

ANNUAL PRODUCTION 80,000 bottles
HECTARES UNDER VINE 21
VITICULTURE METHOD Conventional

This is an excellent year for Riccardo Talenti, who picked up Three more Glasses for the trophy cupboard. The winner was Brunello di Montalcino Vigna del Paretaio Riserva '01, made from selected grapes from a vineyard planted by his father, Pierluigi, just outside Sant'Angelo in Colle. The nose is very intense, led by blackberry and cherry fruit, and supported by light notes of spice and cocoa powder. There is good impact on the palate, its alcohol firmly sustained by an even, high-quality mesh of acid and tannin, resulting in great balance. It develops, taut and well-defined, to finish supremely long. Rosso di Montalcino '05 is also excellent. In fact, it is one of the best of the whole denomination. The lively nose offers red berry fruit, coffee and vanilla, and the beautifully balanced palate is easy-going yet has plenty of intensity and zip. Pian di Conte '05 is another well-made wine with attractive aromas of pencil lead and blueberries. Brunello di Montalcino '02 is succulent and attractive but needs to be bigger.

Tenimenti Angelini

LOC. VAL DI CAVA
53024 MONTALCINO [SI]
TEL. 057780411
www.tenimentiangelini.it

ANNUAL PRODUCTION 890,000 bottles
HECTARES UNDER VINE 173
VITICULTURE METHOD Conventional

If the two Tenimenti Angelini estates, Tre Rose from Montepulciano and Val di Suga from Montalcino, were in competition, this year the former would be the winner. Nobile di Montepulciano La Villa '03 impresses with a pervasive, blackcurrant and cherry nose enhanced by toastiness and cocoa powder. On the palate, the tannins are close-woven but not too drying, which is rare for the vintage, the acidity is well balanced and the finish is long. Another fine showing came from Nobile di Montepulciano Simposio '03, made solely from selected prugnolo gentile. Plum jam marks out the nose and the palate is firm. The '04 Nobile is attractive. Best of the Val di Suga range is the '01 Brunello Vigneto Spuntali, one of the most impressive of recent years. Both the Brunello '02 and the Rosso '05 are nice enough, but no more. Refurbishment at the estate, which has involved the more northerly vineyards as well as the cellar, is almost complete and we keenly await the improvements they will no doubt bring to the wines.

● Brunello di Montalcino Ris. Vigna del Paretaio '01	▼▼▼ 7
● Rosso di Montalcino '05	▼▼ 4*
● Pian di Conte '05	▼▼ 5
● Brunello di Montalcino '02	▼ 6
● Brunello di Montalcino Ris. '99	♀♀♀ 7
● Brunello di Montalcino '00	♀♀ 6
● Brunello di Montalcino '01	♀♀ 6
● Brunello di Montalcino '98	♀♀ 7

● Brunello di Montalcino V. Spuntali '01	▼▼ 8
● Nobile di Montepulciano La Villa '03	▼▼ 6
● Nobile di Montepulciano Simposio '03	▼▼ 6
● Brunello di Montalcino '02	▼ 6
● Nobile di Montepulciano Trerose '04	▼ 5
● Rosso di Montalcino '05	▼ 4
● Brunello di Montalcino V. del Lago '95	♀♀♀ 8
● Brunello di Montalcino V. Spuntali '95	♀♀♀ 8
● Brunello di Montalcino V. Spuntali '93	♀♀♀ 8
● Brunello di Montalcino V. del Lago '90	♀♀♀ 8
● Brunello di Montalcino V. del Lago '93	♀♀♀ 8
● Brunello di Montalcino '01	♀♀ 6
● Nobile di Montepulciano Simposio '01	♀♀ 6
● Nobile di Montepulciano Simposio '00	♀♀ 6
● Brunello di Montalcino '99	♀♀ 6

Terrabianca

LOC. SAN FEDELE A PATERNO
53017 RADDA IN CHIANTI [SI]
TEL. 057754029
www.terrabianca.com

ANNUAL PRODUCTION 360,000 bottles
HECTARES UNDER VINE 52
VITICULTURE METHOD Conventional

Roberto Guldener's is an important estate, both in terms of the quantities produced and the reliability of its more everyday wines. Yet there remain ups and downs. What we can't fathom is how his top wines rarely manage to get past "well made". The land does not lack potential and every detail of cellar and vineyard work is organized with care and attention. Guldener's approach is reassuringly open-minded. All this would suggest significantly higher quality from the wines. The best of the range this year is Chianti Classico Croce Riserva '04. The nose marries vegetal tones with ripe scents of blackberry jam and the palate is warm and full, with meaty tannins that are well knit into the alcohol. The finish is relaxed. Campaccio '04, from sangiovese and cabernet sauvignon; Cipresso '04, from 100 per cent sangiovese; Ceppate '04, from merlot and cabernet sauvignon; and Tesoro '04, solely from merlot, are all attractive.

● Chianti Cl. Croce Ris. '04	♟♟	6
● Campaccio '04	♟	6
● Il Tesoro '04	♟	6
● Cipresso '04	♟	6
● Chianti Cl. Scassino '05	♟	5
● Ceppate '04	♟	7
● Campaccio '00	♟♟	5
● Ceppate '01	♟♟	7
● Ceppate '99	♟♟	7
● Campaccio '01	♟♟	5
● Ceppate '03	♟♟	7
● Piano del Cipresso '01	♟♟	5
● Chianti Cl. Scassino '04	♟♟	4

Terralsole

VILLA COLLINA D'ORO
53024 MONTALCINO [SI]
TEL. 0577835678
www.terralsole.com

ANNUAL PRODUCTION 45,000 bottles
HECTARES UNDER VINE 12
VITICULTURE METHOD Conventional

Quality at Mario Bollag's estate continues to rise. With Paolo Vagaggini looking after winemaking, the estate has forged ahead, taking a remarkably short time to emerge with wines of great personality, favoured by a well organized, rational estate plan. The set-up is very attractive with a modern cellar, both in terms of its equipment and the use of small oak. The real interest this year comes from the release of three new wines produced from new plantings of cabernet sauvignon and merlot: Pasticcio, Col d'Oro and Solista, all '05. Nevertheless, the star of the range is Brunello Riserva '01, thereby confirming that it is not just barrel size that determines a style. The nose goes beyond ripe cherry to reveal floral notes and medicinal herbs. The palate is a triumph of elegance from dense, compact tannins that are already well integrated into the wine's soft weave. The effort of careful grape selection is repaid by the well-crafted Brunello '02. It has an intensely fruity, white cherry nose, with good eucalyptus-like balsam, and a very close-knit palate, bearing in mind the vintage. The finish reveals good personality.

● Brunello di Montalcino Ris. '01	♟	8
● Brunello di Montalcino '02	♟♟	7
● Pasticcio '05	♟♟	5
● Rosso di Montalcino '05	♟	4
● Solista '05	♟	4
● Col d'Oro '05	♟	4
● Brunello di Montalcino '01	♟♟	7

★ Castello del Terriccio

LOC. TERRICCIO
56040 CASTELLINA MARITTIMA [PI]
TEL. 050699709
www.terriccio.it

ANNUAL PRODUCTION 320,000 bottles
HECTARES UNDER VINE 53
VITICULTURE METHOD Conventional

This has been a fabulous year for Gian Annibale Medelana Ferri and his Castello del Terriccio with so much having been written about the estate, about the deep ties between the grapes and their origin, the uniqueness of its wines and, especially, the amazing qualitative consistency that has long marked them out. So all that is left for us to do is describe the two wines that gained the highest of honours, thanks to a perfect handling of the '04 vintage. Castello del Terriccio is full of texture and acidic drive. The innate balsamic note of the nose integrates sublimely with its aromas of blackberry and vanilla. There's real alchemy in the marriage of grounded elements deriving from the terroir and the spiritual joy it provides when drunk. Lupicaia is a classic, an archetype of balance and personality. Here, too, there is balsam, this time united with earthiness and pencil lead, and enhanced by vegetal nuances. The sumptuous, highly attractive palate is well supported by a wealth of tannin. Tassinaia, again '04, is very successful with its tobacco and black berry fruit preceding a palate of great attractiveness.

Tolaini

S. P. 9 DI PIEVASCIATA, 28
53019 CASTELNUOVO BERARDENGA [SI]
TEL. 0577356972
www.tolaini.it

ANNUAL PRODUCTION 100,000 bottles
HECTARES UNDER VINE 50
VITICULTURE METHOD Conventional

After Pierluigi Tolaini's full entry last year, he has taken his most prestigious wine, the petit verdot-laced merlot and cabernet sauvignon Picconero, into the finals at its first release, '04. But the excellent impression is more widespread, with quality across the board. It is evident that the vines are more mature and that the style of each wine type is ever more specific. At this point, Tolaini must feel that he has fulfilled the dream he's had since a young lad: to make a great wine in his homeland. He emigrated from the Lucca area to Canada when he was 20 years old, "out of hunger", as he says, and there built up the country's largest fresh and frozen food distribution company. The fruit and spice aromas on Picconero are in perfect balance. The mouthfilling palate is broad, deep and well modulated, and comes to a long, flavoursome finish. The other wines, the rounded, dynamic Due Santi '04, from cabernet sauvignon, merlot and cabernet franc, and the lively, succulent Al Passo '04, from sangiovese and merlot, are both good.

● Castello del Terriccio '04	♟♟♟	8
● Lupicaia '04	♟♟♟	8
● Tassinaia '04	♟♟	7
○ Con Vento '06	♟♟	5
○ Rondinaia '06	♟	5
● Castello del Terriccio '00	♟♟♟	8
● Lupicaia '99	♟♟♟	8
● Lupicaia '98	♟♟♟	8
● Lupicaia '97	♟♟♟	8
● Lupicaia '96	♟♟♟	8
● Lupicaia '95	♟♟♟	8
● Castello del Terriccio '01	♟♟♟	8
● Castello del Terriccio '03	♟♟♟	8
● Lupicaia '00	♟♟♟	8
● Lupicaia '93	♟♟♟	8
● Lupicaia '01	♟♟♟	8

● Picconero '04	♟♟	8
● Al Passo '04	♟♟	5
● Due Santi '04	♟♟	6
● Al Passo '03	♟♟	5
● Due Santi '03	♟♟	6

Torraccia di Presura

LOC. STRADA IN CHIANTI
VIA DELLA MONTAGNOLA, 130
50027 GREVE IN CHIANTI [FI]
TEL. 0558588656
www.torracciadipresura.it

ANNUAL PRODUCTION   180,000 bottles
HECTARES UNDER VINE 33
VITICULTURE METHOD   Conventional

The Osti family's wines have been on the market for over 20 years and although the family didn't send a wine to the finals this year, as they did last time, the overall consistency of quality has done them proud. In years past, there had been a certain homogeneity in the range, as if the concentration on modernity in the styling came at the expense of a sense of place. But things seem to have changed. A case in point is the greater prominence now given to canaiolo. Chianti Classico Riserva Il Tarocco '04 was the most impressive wine of the wines submitted, with toasty, spicy aromas, breadth and depth on the palate, followed by good length. Lucciolaio '03, from sangiovese and cabernet sauvignon, is full of stuffing but lacks balance and is weighed down by too much tannin. Chianti Classico Il Tarocco '05 is attractive even though a touch stalky. Arcante '03, from equal parts of cabernet sauvignon, merlot and sangiovese, has a good array of aromas although the palate is struggling to find harmony.

La Torraccia

LOC. TORRACCIA
53024 MONTALCINO [SI]
TEL. 0577848156
www.latorracciamontalcino.com

ANNUAL PRODUCTION   N.A.
HECTARES UNDER VINE N.A.
VITICULTURE METHOD   Conventional

This small, serious-minded estate is one of the Roman colonizers who settled in Montalcino in the 1990s. It continues to ride high, the main strength being well-focused wines deriving from the great care taken in both vineyard and cellar. They can also manage lesser vintages with ease thanks to a degree of flexibility in the barrels they can use. This is probably why the '02 Brunello is so successful. A classic, not too deep, ruby colour, it needs some aeration before its nicely intense, typical aromas of morello cherry and sweet tobacco emerge, while elegance and great balance mark out the palate, which finishes deep and long. It's certainly not a big, full wine, more one that homes in on attractiveness and lively drinkability. Bricco della Torre '06 scored a touch higher. There's wild cherry, medicinal herbs and cinnamon spiciness on the nose. The palate is full, supported by good acidity and assertive but not bitter tannins, and has a deep, long finish. Canalone '06 is uncomplicatedly attractive.

● Chianti Cl. Il Tarocco Ris. '04	▼▼ 5
● Chianti Cl. Il Tarocco '05	▼ 4
● Lucciolaio '03	▼ 6
● Arcante '03	▼ 6
● Chianti Cl. Il Tarocco Ris. '01	♀♀ 5
● Chianti Cl. Il Tarocco Ris. '03	♀♀ 5
● Lucciolaio '00	♀♀ 6
● Lucciolaio '01	♀♀ 6

● Brunello di Montalcino '02	▼▼ 7
● Bricco della Torre '06	▼▼ 5
● Canalone '06	▼ 4
● Brunello di Montalcino '01	♀♀ 7
● Canalone '04	♀♀ 4
● Rosso di Montalcino '04	♀♀ 5

Fattoria Torre a Cona
LOC. SAN DONATO IN COLLINA
50010 RIGNANO SULL'ARNO [FI]
TEL. 055699000
www.villatorreacona.com

ANNUAL PRODUCTION 30,000 bottles
HECTARES UNDER VINE 14
VITICULTURE METHOD Conventional

This is the first entry for the Rossi di
Montelera family's Tuscan estate. It's had a
long presence in the area but until this
year, when quality has been ramped up,
the wines were ordinary. The property lies
south-east of Florence. The central
building is a large villa easily seen from the
main road. Its origins date back to the 18th
century when the Marchesi Rinuccini
created it by converting a 14th-century
castle. The current owners bought the
property at the start of the 1900s. The best
wine is the lively, fruity Terre di Cino '04,
made solely from sangiovese, which has
aromatic herbs on the nose and an
elegant, succulent palate with a good
savoury finish. Vin Santo '01 is also good.
A quinine and dried fruits nose with
oxidative notes is followed by a soft,
mouthfilling palate that offers an intriguing
vein of acidity and good length. The fruity,
savoury Chianti Colli Fiorentini '05 is
attractive.

Travignoli
VIA TRAVIGNOLI, 78
50060 PELAGO [FI]
TEL. 0558361098
www.travignoli.com

ANNUAL PRODUCTION 250,000 bottles
HECTARES UNDER VINE 70
VITICULTURE METHOD Conventional

Giovanni Busi's estate regained its full entry
this year, which ties in perfectly with his new
presidency of the Consorzio del Chianti
Rufina. But the spirit of revival that is in the
air in Rufina is also apparent in the corridors
of power. There's a fresh lease of life on the
consortium board, too, probably stimulated
by the ever better reviews the wines are
receiving. Over the past few years, the
policy at Travignoli has been to produce
wines of standing while keeping prices fair,
to pay greater attention to details, and to up
overall quality levels. Top of the tree this
year is Chianti Rufina Riserva '04, which has
an earthy, ripe fruit nose and a characterful
palate with crisp tannins and a good, long
finish. Tegolaia '04, from sangiovese and
cabernet sauvignon, also showed well, its
wild berry fruit melding into nuances of
mintiness and its juicy, dynamic palate
coming to a strong finish. Calice del Conte
'04, based on merlot and cabernet, is
another good wine, showing developed and
round with a savoury finish. Everything else
is straightforward but well made.

● Terre di Cino '04	▼▼	4
○ Vin Santo del Chianti Merlaia '01	▼▼	5
● Chianti dei Colli Fiorentini '05	▼	2

● Calice del Conte '04	▼▼	6
● Tegolaia '04	▼▼	5
● Chianti Rufina Ris. '04	▼▼	5
● Chianti Rufina '05	▼	3
○ Vin Santo del Chianti '99	▼	6
○ Gavignano '06	▼	3
● Chianti Rufina Ris. '03	♀♀	5
● Chianti Rufina Ris. '01	♀♀	4

Castello del Trebbio

via S. Brigida, 9
50060 Pontassieve [FI]
tel. 0558304900
www.vinoturismo.it

ANNUAL PRODUCTION 340,000 bottles
HECTARES UNDER VINE 52
VITICULTURE METHOD Conventional

Anna Baj-Macario and Stefano Casadei's estate is back in the Guide, the wines having performed excellently this year. The duo's philosophy is simple and unambiguous: provenance is central. Without this, how could the wines ever develop precise definition and personality? The property has a long history. It was the Pazzi family from Florence who built the castle, probably adding to a fortification that already existed. Legend has it that the famous plot that led to the assassination of Giuliano de' Medici, Lorenzo's brother, was hatched here. The most impressive of the wines is Chianti Rufina Riserva Lasticato '03. The nose is balsamic, the structure full, the tannins overt but integrated and the finish punchy. Pazzesco '03, from sangiovese, merlot and syrah, is also admirable, with a spicy nose, a firm, balanced palate and a lip-smacking finish. The merlot-only Rosso della Congiura '03 has a lively yet gamey nose, plentiful dynamism and structure, and an attractive finish. Bianco di Castignano '05, based on chardonnay, is minerally and full of zest. Everything else is attractive and enjoyable.

● Chianti Rufina Lastricato Ris. '03	🍷🍷	5
● Pazzesco '03	🍷🍷	6
● Rosso della Congiura '03	🍷🍷	7
○ Bianco della Congiura '06	🍷	5
○ Bianco di Castignano '06	🍷	5
● Chianti '06	🍷	2
● Pazzesco '99	YY	6

Tenuta di Trinoro

via Val d'Orcia, 15
53047 Sarteano [SI]
tel. 0578267110
www.trinoro.it

ANNUAL PRODUCTION 78,000 bottles
HECTARES UNDER VINE 29
VITICULTURE METHOD Natural

Half measures don't exist for Andrea Franchetti: his aim is absolute quality. The vineyards are strictly biodynamic and picking is delayed until as late as possible. No technological wizardry is permitted in the cellars, fermentation takes place in concrete vats, the yeasts are exclusively indigenous and ageing takes place in carefully chosen barriques. This no-compromise approach has resulted in a lost corner of the province of Siena being transformed into a mini Bordeaux and, needless to say, the results tally with the maniacal effort put in. Tenuta di Trinoro '05, from merlot, cabernet franc, cabernet sauvignon and petit verdot, has impressive power and fruit ripeness but also a complexity that could only come from the soil. Le Cupole '05, from cabernet franc, merlot, cabernet sauvignon, petit verdot, cesanese and uva di Troia, is the estate's second wine, produced from younger vines, and it shows ripe and rounded. Cincinnato is made only in particularly hot years so there was no release this time round.

● Tenuta di Trinoro '05	🍷🍷	8
● Le Cupole di Trinoro '05	🍷🍷	6
● Tenuta di Trinoro '03	YYY	8
● Tenuta di Trinoro '04	YYY	8
● Le Cupole di Trinoro '02	YY	6
● Tenuta di Trinoro '01	YY	8
● Le Cupole di Trinoro '04	YY	6
● Le Cupole di Trinoro '03	YY	6

★ Tua Rita
LOC. NOTRI, 81
57028 SUVERETO [LI]
TEL. 0565829237
www.tuarita.it

Uccelliera
FRAZ. CASTELNUOVO DELL'ABATE
POD. UCCELLIERA, 45
53020 MONTALCINO [SI]
TEL. 0577835729
www.uccelliera-montalcino.it

ANNUAL PRODUCTION 8,000 bottles
HECTARES UNDER VINE 25
VITICULTURE METHOD Conventional

ANNUAL PRODUCTION 36,000 bottles
HECTARES UNDER VINE 6
VITICULTURE METHOD Conventional

Sometimes even champions don't win. And that was the case this year at Tua Rita, one of Italy's cult estates, and one whose wines are sought after like few others. It's Redigaffi, from 100 per cent merlot, and the Syrah that are the most coveted but neither of these clinched Three Glasses this year. Of course the vintage, '05, can't be considered one of the best of recent years but the scores had more to do with the fact that the wines had only been bottled a few days before we tasted them. Maybe it's time to consider delaying release of these top wines, perhaps by a year, as they do in Bolgheri. The Redigaffi is very oaky on both nose and palate. Its blackberry and balsamic aromas lead to an intense but still very taut palate that needs to open out. Similar considerations apply to the highly peppery Syrah. For now, Giusto di Nostri '05, from cabernet sauvignon and merlot, is more accessible. Rosso dei Notri '06 is balanced, lively and very attractive. Perlato del Bosco '05 is straightforward and Lodano '05 is too oaky.

The cordial, affable, extremely down-to-earth Andrea Cortonesi has finally completed the Herculean renovation of his estate, which has absorbed his attentions for several years. The vineyards are close to an old onyx cave, a location which enabled him to produce a Brunello di Montalcino in '02, although it proved an impossible task in other parts of the zone with different site climates. The estate style is apparent in the wine. The nose is traditional, with medicinal herbs, tobacco and leather, and has great intensity, especially after some aeration. There is good stuffing on the palate, sustained by its acidity, which also lengthens the finish. Brunello di Montalcino Riserva '01 also has much to offer. There's a complex nose, with florality, citrus fruit, bramble berries and soft leather, and a well-defined palate with crisp tannin which, once the wine gains some bottle age, will without doubt become perfectly integrated. Rosso di Montalcino '05 is succulent, lively and attractive.

● Redigaffi '05	♟♟	8
● Syrah '05	♟♟	8
● Giusto di Nostri '05	♟♟	8
● Rosso dei Notri '06	♟♟	6
○ Lodano '05	♟	5
● Perlato del Bosco Rosso '05	♟	6
● Redigaffi '00	♟♟♟	8
● Redigaffi '99	♟♟♟	8
● Redigaffi '98	♟♟♟	8
● Redigaffi '96	♟♟♟	8
● Redigaffi '04	♟♟♟	8
● Redigaffi '01	♟♟♟	8
● Redigaffi '03	♟♟♟	8
● Redigaffi '02	♟♟♟	8
● Syrah '03	♟♟	8
● Syrah '04	♟♟	8

● Brunello di Montalcino Ris. '01	♟♟	8
● Brunello di Montalcino '02	♟♟	7
● Rosso di Montalcino '05	♟	5
● Brunello di Montalcino Ris. '97	♟♟♟	8
● Brunello di Montalcino '00	♟♟	7
● Brunello di Montalcino '01	♟♟	7
● Brunello di Montalcino '98	♟♟	7
● Brunello di Montalcino Ris. '99	♟♟	8
● Brunello di Montalcino '99	♟♟	7

F.lli Vagnoni

LOC. PANCOLE, 82
53037 SAN GIMIGNANO [SI]
TEL. 0577955077
www.fratellivagnoni.com

Tenuta Val di Cava

LOC. VAL DI CAVA
53024 MONTALCINO [SI]
TEL. 0577848261

ANNUAL PRODUCTION 120,000 bottles
HECTARES UNDER VINE 20
VITICULTURE METHOD Conventional

The significant shift towards the production of high quality Vernaccia when few believed in its potential was due to a small group of producers, Fratelli Vagnoni among them. As time has moved on, the siblings' wines have helped bring the denomination the visibility it deserves, throughout the region and the rest of Italy, while bringing prestige to their estate. Vernaccia Riserva Mocali '05 matches its lofty reputation. Oakiness on the nose does not compromise the aromas of fruit and aromatic herbs. The palate is full and soft, with an enlivening swath of acidity, and finishes on a good almondy aftertaste. Vernaccia Fontabuccio '06 has textbook typicity. I Sodi Lunghi, from sangiovese and colorino, is a wine on the up. The '04 has intriguing aromas of forest fruits and earthiness; the palate is juicy, with a good tannic weave, and eases to a sweetly long finish. Vernaccia '06 puts the accent on freshness and balance. The profile of San Biagio '03 is smooth and soft. Everything else is highly dependable.

ANNUAL PRODUCTION 57,000 bottles
HECTARES UNDER VINE 19
VITICULTURE METHOD Conventional

Vincenzo Abbruzzese's wines continue to receive worldwide acclaim. Yet we are a little concerned about the differences in style apparent on the '01s. Brunello Madonna del Piano Riserva '01 is an example. Appearance, nose and palate are all intense. There's a wide spectrum of aromas, with wild cherry, blackberry and other red and black berry fruits, plus well integrated spiciness, followed by exuberance on the palate, with a wealth of decidedly astringent tannin that time should help to soften. The finish is broad, long and well supported by good acidity. So technically it has it all. But it lacks the fillip of Montalcino character that was so evident in the '99. Rosso di Montalcino '05 is similarly well made. Cherry and vanilla on the nose are followed by a decisive palate with enlivening acidity. There is no '02 Brunello, the vintage having been particularly poor in this northern part of Montalcino.

● I Sodi Lunghi '04	♀♀ 4
O Vernaccia di S. Gimignano Mocali Ris. '05	♀♀ 5
O Vernaccia di S. Gimignano V. Fontabuccio '06	♀♀ 4*
⊙ Il Pancolino '06	♀ 3
● Toscana Rosso '05	♀ 2
● San Gimignano Rosso San Biagio '03	♀ 4
O Vernaccia di S. Gimignano '06	♀ 2
O Vinbrusco '06	♀ 2
O Vernaccia di S. Gimignano Mocali Ris. '01	♀♀ 5
O Vernaccia di S. Gimignano Mocali Ris. '02	♀♀ 5
O Vernaccia di S. Gimignano Mocali Ris. '04	♀♀ 4
O Vernaccia di S. Gimignano V. Fontabuccio '04	♀♀ 3

● Brunello di Montalcino Madonna del Piano Ris. '01	♀♀ 8
● Rosso di Montalcino '05	♀♀ 4
● Brunello di Montalcino '99	♀♀ 8
● Brunello di Montalcino Madonna del Piano Ris. '96	♀♀ 8
● Brunello di Montalcino Madonna del Piano Ris. '99	♀♀ 3
● Brunello di Montalcino '00	♀♀ 7
● Rosso di Montalcino '01	♀♀ 4
● Brunello di Montalcino '01	♀♀ 7

Cooperativa Agricola Valdarnese

LOC. PATERNA, 96
52028 TERRANUOVA BRACCIOLINI [AR]
TEL. 055977052
www.paterna.it

ANNUAL PRODUCTION 40,000 bottles
HECTARES UNDER VINE 5
VITICULTURE METHOD Certified organic

After a real high-flier of a wine last year, this
year's submissions from Marco Noferi's
Cooperativa Agricola Valdarnese Paterna
are again good but with no peaks. We feel
that this is only to be expected and in line
with the policy of respecting nature and
keeping treatments to a minimum, views
that have always guided all decisions at the
winery: it has been completely organic for
over 20 years. After all, a corollary of such a
policy has to be that vintages can, indeed
must, vary significantly. And in this fairly cool
area, on the slopes of Pratomagno on the
right bank of the river Arno, it was hardly
likely that the '04 vintage would be as big as
the '03. That's exactly what comes through
on Vignanova '04, made solely from
sangiovese. It's fairly forward, nicely open
and savoury with good aroma, but the
structure is lightish and the oaking is a little
too apparent. Chianti '05 is lightweight,
fruity, immediate, lively and hugely drinkable.

Tenuta Valdipiatta

VIA DELLA CIARLIANA, 25A
53040 MONTEPULCIANO [SI]
TEL. 0578757930
www.valdipiatta.it

ANNUAL PRODUCTION 120,000 bottles
HECTARES UNDER VINE 34
VITICULTURE METHOD Conventional

Tenuta Valdipiatta has set in place a
programme of rigorous stylistic fine-tuning in
its wines, creating a clear distinction
between those conceived as provenance-
led and those designed to be estate-led.
The former comprises the zone's traditional
wines, which age well, have a well-defined
character and incline more to elegance than
opulence. Leading them is a highly
successful '04 release of Nobile Vigna
d'Alfiero. A floral, earthy nose of personality
leads to a very youthful, dynamic palate with
good grip, ensuring a fine ageing profile.
The '04 straight Nobile is also good, its
nose tending to the austere but the palate
lively and racy, making for attractive
drinking. The first release of the Vin Santo,
the '03, has a traditional stamp. There are
dried and candied fruit aromas, and a full-
bodied, very sweet palate that never cloys.
The estate-led wines include Trincerone,
which was not available for tasting this year,
and the monovarietal Pinot Nero, from '05.
This is made from vines that are still very
young so the wine displays only the most
superficial characteristics of this complex
variety.

● Vignanova '04	▼▼ 5
● Chianti Colli Aretini Paterna '05	▼ 3*
● Vignanova '03	▼▼▼ 5
● Vignanova '00	▼▼ 4
● Vignanova '01	▼▼ 5
● Vignanova '99	▼▼ 4
● Vignanova '98	▼▼ 4

● Nobile di Montepulciano V. d'Alfiero '04	▼▼ 7
● Nobile di Montepulciano '04	▼▼ 5
O Vin Santo di Montepulciano '03	▼▼ 7
● Pinot Nero '05	▼ 7
● Nobile di Montepulciano V. d'Alfiero '99	▼▼▼ 6
● Nobile di Montepulciano V. d'Alfiero '01	▼▼ 6
● Nobile di Montepulciano '03	▼▼ 5
● Nobile di Montepulciano '98	▼▼ 5
● Nobile di Montepulciano V. d'Alfiero '03	▼▼ 6
● Nobile di Montepulciano '99	▼▼ 5

Tenuta di Valgiano
FRAZ. VALGIANO
VIA DI VALGIANO, 7
55018 LUCCA [LU]
TEL. 0583402271
www.tenutadivalgiano.it

ANNUAL PRODUCTION 60,000 bottles
HECTARES UNDER VINE 25
VITICULTURE METHOD Natural

"Without 'terra' (land) you can't even talk about terroir. The essence of terroir is, and always will be, la 'terra'". We are happy to quote oenologist Saverio Petrilli of Tenuta di Valgiano, the winner of the Award for Sustainable Viticulture this year, to get across how much the environment and the life it supports influences the estate's philosophy, which again earned owners Moreno Petrini and Laura di Collobiano Three Glasses. It's not just the one superlative wine that we salute but the profound, complex nature of the way this estate works, allowing decisions to be driven solely by what the land can give. Back to that superlative wine, Tenuta di Valgiano '04. It's a true reflection of a wonderful vintage. The nose initially gives penetrating aromas of blackberry and plum, before more complex sensations of tobacco, wet earth and black pepper emerge. Its passage through the palate hangs on the textbook elegance of its tannic extraction and its natural, unwavering concentration, which underpins finely judged succulence. The final refreshing note of balsam is endless. The '05 Palistorti is less impressive than usual but still attractive.

Vecchie Terre di Montefili
VIA SAN CRESCI, 45
50022 PANZANO [FI]
TEL. 055853739
www.vecchieterredimontefili.com

ANNUAL PRODUCTION 50,000 bottles
HECTARES UNDER VINE 13.5
VITICULTURE METHOD Conventional

Even though there are no Three Glass awards for Roccaldo Acuti's estate this year, the wines performed wonderfully at our tastings. The most prestigious, Bruno di Rocca '04, made from cabernet sauvignon and sangiovese, went through to the finals. The feeling from the estate is rather as if it were enjoying a second spurt of youth. It's been around for almost 30 years and has seen fashions and styles in wine come and go but it has remained faithful to the philosophy that the more natural a wine is, the better. Hence provenance-based rather than variety-based characteristics are always to the fore. That's easy to say but far less easy to put into practice, even though being close to Panzano helps things along. Leather and wet dog dominate the nose of our finalist, followed by forest fruits. The initial impact on the palate is of succulence, followed by overt, lively tannins, refreshing acidity and then a lip-smacking finish. Anfiteatro '04, from 100 per cent sangiovese, is elegant and taut, yet dynamic and broad. Chianti Classico '04 has alluring floral and cherry aromas and a long, vibrant palate.

● Colline Lucchesi Tenuta di Valgiano '04	♟♟♟ 7
● Colline Lucchesi Palistorti '05	♟ 5
● Colline Lucchesi Tenuta di Valgiano '01	♟♟♟ 8
● Colline Lucchesi Tenuta di Valgiano '03	♟♟♟ 7
● Colline Lucchesi Tenuta di Valgiano '00	♟♟ 8
● Colline Lucchesi Tenuta di Valgiano '99	♟♟ 8
● Colline Lucchesi Tenuta di Valgiano '02	♟♟ 7

● Bruno di Rocca '04	♟♟ 8
● Anfiteatro '04	♟♟ 8
● Chianti Cl. '04	♟♟ 5
● Anfiteatro '03	♟♟♟ 8
● Anfiteatro '94	♟♟♟ 8
● Anfiteatro '01	♟♟ 8
● Bruno di Rocca '01	♟♟ 8
● Bruno di Rocca '03	♟♟ 8
● Bruno di Rocca '02	♟♟ 8

La Velona

LOC. CASTELNUOVO DELL'ABATE
POD. PIETRANERA, 30
53024 MONTALCINO [SI]
TEL. 0577835525
www.lavelona.com

ANNUAL PRODUCTION 60,000 bottles
HECTARES UNDER VINE 12
VITICULTURE METHOD Conventional

As usual, the wines here showed well. The estate is situated below the beautiful castle of Velona, where it is protected from most weather systems by Mount Amiata, and lies on sandy, rather loose-grained soils. As a result, even in a year like '02, selective picking ensured fairly healthy grapes. So Brunello '02 has a ruby colour before a fruit-forward nose of cherry and blackberry, which meld into unassertive vegetal notes. The palate gives good weight with nice acid-tannin balance as it passes through the mouth taking you to fairly long finish without rough edges. The '05 Rosso di Montalcino scored similarly. Here too there are vegetal aromas. Arbutus and not overly ripe blackberry precede the more classic white cherry. The palate is spirited thanks to refreshing acidity meshed with smooth, ripe tannin. Sant'Antimo Mefysto '05 is less successful, the nose showing rather overripe and the palate over-tannic.

Ventolaio

LOC. VENTOLAIO, 51
53024 MONTALCINO [SI]
TEL. 0577835779

ANNUAL PRODUCTION 70,000 bottles
HECTARES UNDER VINE 13
VITICULTURE METHOD Conventional

Luigi Fanti's estate is situated in a rather unusual, and fascinating, part of Montalcino, on a plateau 450 to 500 metres high between the roads leading to Sant'Angelo in Colle and Castenuovo dell'Abate. It's therefore very "ventoso" (windy), hence the name of the estate, and in some ways wild. Unfortunately, a serious accident prevented Luigi from letting us have his Brunello '01 for tasting last year. But it's a fine wine which we're happy to recommend now, even at a distance of 12 months. This time round we have the '02, an unfortunate vintage, but one that is ideal for demonstrating the qualitative consistency of the estate's wines. The Brunello is distinctive and has a cleanly defined, complex nose with wild cherry, blackberry and a little liquorice. These bring personality and elegance that also come through on the supple, long palate with its refined tannicity. Rosso di Montalcino '05 also showed well. The oaking is discreet and doesn't overwhelm the white cherry fruit and lively vegetal tones, acidity giving the palate a stylish, spirited style that is nicely gauged.

● Brunello di Montalcino '02	▼▼	8
● Rosso di Montalcino '05	▼▼	6
● Sant'Antimo Rosso Mefysto '05	▼	7
● Brunello di Montalcino '01	♀♀	8
● Brunello di Montalcino '99	♀♀	8
● Brunello di Montalcino '00	♀♀	8
● Sant'Antimo Rosso Mefysto '03	♀♀	7
● Rosso di Montalcino '04	♀♀	6
● Rosso di Montalcino '03	♀♀	6
● Rosso di Montalcino '01	♀♀	4

● Brunello di Montalcino '02	▼▼	6
● Rosso di Montalcino '05	▼▼	4*

Castello di Verrazzano

LOC. SAN MARTINO IN VALLE, 12
50022 GREVE IN CHIANTI [FI]
TEL. 055854243
www.verrazzano.com

ANNUAL PRODUCTION 265,000 bottles
HECTARES UNDER VINE 44
VITICULTURE METHOD Conventional

Luigi Cappellini's long-standing estate is back with its full entry in the Guide, as generally there was good style throughout the range this year. Even so, the impression from tasting the wines is that there is huge potential in the vineyards that still remains to be harnessed. The wines are certainly not without structure or backbone, and they have clear-cut character, suggesting that they come from a specific territory with a proclivity for viticulture, but they lack attractiveness and balance. Instead, they are dominated by hardness-related elements that leave everything else in the shadows. The best of the range is Bottiglia Particolare '04, from sangiovese and cabernet sauvignon. Aromatic herbs and forest fruits aromas bring liveliness. The palate has good grip and the alcohol manages to calm down the wine's tannic thrust, leading to a savoury, attractively long finish. Sassello '04 is simpler and a touch rustic, Chianti Classico '05 is more multi-faceted and inviting, and Verrazzano Rosso '05 is little more than pleasant.

● Bottiglia Particolare '04	▼▼ 6
● Chianti Cl. '05	▼ 4
● Verrazzano Rosso '05	▼ 3
● Sassello '04	▼ 7
● Sassello '97	▼▼▼ 6
● Chianti Cl. Ris. '90	▼▼▼ 5
● Bottiglia Particolare '01	▼▼ 6

Castello di Vicchiomaggio

LOC. LE BOLLE
VIA VICCHIOMAGGIO, 4
50022 GREVE IN CHIANTI [FI]
TEL. 055854079
www.vicchiomaggio.it

ANNUAL PRODUCTION 300,000 bottles
HECTARES UNDER VINE 33
VITICULTURE METHOD Conventional

There is absolutely no doubt that John Matta is now devoting considerable attention to achieving provenance-related style in his wines. Their performance was fantastic this year, to say the least, with a gaggle of wines in the finals. Even better than that was the exceptional FSM '04, from 100 per cent merlot, which shot to a triumphal Three Glasses for its amazing precision and wealth of flavours. The nose of red berry fruits and spices is elegant and inviting. The palate impressively marries firmness and roundness, its tannins perfectly melded into the whole and the finish complex and long. The '04 Riserva Agostino Petri is again very fine with a lively, small berry fruits nose and a dynamic, rounded palate. Riserva La Prima '04 shares its limelight, the fascination here deriving from greater austerity and powerful structure. Ripa delle More '04, from 100 per cent sangiovese, is also excellent but almost eclipsed by its stablemates. The two attractive non-Riserva Chiantis and Ripa delle Mandorle '05, made from sangiovese and cabernet, have good style but Riserva Gustavo Petri '01 is vegetal and a touch tired.

● FSM '04	▼▼▼ 8
● Chianti Cl. La Prima Ris. '04	▼▼ 7
● Chianti Cl. Agostino Petri Ris. '04	▼▼ 6
● Ripa delle More '04	▼▼ 7
● Chianti Cl. San Jacopo '05	▼ 5
● Ripa delle Mandorle '05	▼ 5
● Chianti Cl. Montevasco '05	▼ 5
● Chianti Cl. Gustavo Petri Ris. '01	▼ 7
● Ripa delle More '97	▼▼▼ 6
● Ripa delle Mandorle '04	▼▼ 5
● Chianti Cl. Petri Ris. '03	▼▼ 6

Villa a Sesta
LOC. VILLA A SESTA
P.ZZA DEL POPOLO, 1
53019 CASTELNUOVO BERARDENGA [SI]
TEL. 0577359014
www.villasesta.com

ANNUAL PRODUCTION 100,000 bottles
HECTARES UNDER VINE 47
VITICULTURE METHOD Conventional

Riccardo Tattoni's wines did not shine as
bright this year as they did last but still
showed well. Riccardo goes for modern,
attractive wines and takes particular care
over value for money. The estate takes its
name from its location, a village lying half
way between San Gusmé and Brolio. There
has been massive work on the property,
which stretches over 1,000 hectares, giving
the ancient centre, of Etruscan origins, a
complete overhaul and breathing new life
into the church, the manor house, an old oil
mill and the farmhouses. The wine that
most impressed us was Vas '05, made from
sangiovese, merlot and colorino. The nose
combines forest fruits such as raspberries
and blueberries with spiciness and toasty
notes from the oak then the palate shows
soft and round with well formed tannins and
a flavour that grows strongly to the finish.
The fine Chianti Classico Riserva '04 is
earthier and gamier, with an austere
structure but a relaxed finish. Chianti
Classico '05 is simple but balanced. Chianti
Colli Aretini Ripaltella '06 is a little slim.

Villa Branca
LOC. MERCATALE IN VAL DI PESA
VIA NOVOLI, 10
50024 SAN CASCIANO
IN VAL DI PESA [FI]
TEL. 055821033
www.villabranca.it

ANNUAL PRODUCTION 180,000 bottles
HECTARES UNDER VINE 52
VITICULTURE METHOD Conventional

After a number of years in the Other
Wineries section, the Branca family, who
have owned this property for over 50 years,
earned a full entry. Villa Branca's history is
documented from at least 1348. But it
was 1950 when Pierluigi Branca fell in love
with the place, then comprising a villa and a
series of plots, and bought it, gradually
turning it into a modern wine estate.
Pierluigi produces only Chianti Classico so
sangiovese remains the main variety
planted but there are also some cabernet
and merlot vines in the vineyards. The best
wine this year is Chianti Classico Riserva
'04. Wet fur and leather dominate the nose.
The palate is firm and well structured with
an overt acid backbone and an attractively
long finish. Chianti Classico Alef is an
intriguing wine, produced under the
supervision of the chief rabbi of Florence so
as to be kosher. Intense fruit melded with
fresh, almost minty notes marks out the
nose and the palate is supple, with good
weight and a flavoursome finish. Everything
else is well made.

● Chianti Cl. Ris. '04	▼▼ 4
● Vas '05	▼▼ 5
● Chianti Cl. Il Palei '05	▼ 4
● Chianti Colli Aretini Ripaltella '05	▼ 4
● Chianti Cl. Il Palei '03	♀♀ 4
● Chianti Cl. Ris. '03	♀♀ 4
● Chianti Cl. Ris. '01	♀♀ 4
● Vas '03	♀♀ 5
● Vas '04	♀♀ 5

● Chianti Cl. Kosher Alef '03	▼▼ 5
● Chianti Cl. Ris. '04	▼▼ 5
● Chianti Cl. Bellarco '05	▼ 3
O Vin Santo del Chianti Cl. Ris. '00	▼ 7
● Chianti Cl. Ris. '01	♀♀ 6

Villa Cafaggio

via San Martino a Cecione, 5
50020 Panzano [FI]
tel. 0558549094
www.villacafaggio.it

ANNUAL PRODUCTION 400,000 bottles
HECTARES UNDER VINE 31
VITICULTURE METHOD Conventional

The Villa Cafaggio wines performed well this year, but not exceptionally so. The best wine is San Martino '03, made solely from sangiovese. Ripe fruit melds with spicy hints; the palate is fleshy, with overt but integrated tannins, a balanced swath of acidity and a flavoursome finish. The locality has ancient winemaking traditions and the estate ownership has changed often throughout the centuries, even involving at some time Benedictine monks from Siena. Now it is the turn of the Lavis group, which took over two years ago. Major renovation work was undertaken by Stefano Farkas, who started to replant the vineyards at the end of the 1960s, concentrating mainly on sangiovese. In the 1980s, cabernet sauvignon made its appearance and goes into the Supertuscan Cortaccio, which wasn't submitted this year. The '04 Chianti Classico Riserva '04 is lovely. The nose is lively with small berry fruit and aromatic herbs followed by a weighty but balanced palate with a long finish. Chianti Classico '05 is an honest, well-made wine.

● Chianti Cl. Ris. '04	🍷🍷	6
● San Martino '03	🍷🍷	8
● Chianti Cl. '05	🍷	4
● Chianti Cl. Ris. '03	🍷🍷🍷	6
● San Martino '99	🍷🍷🍷	7
● San Martino '98	🍷🍷🍷	6
● Cortaccio '01	🍷🍷🍷	8
● San Martino '00	🍷🍷🍷	8
● San Martino '97	🍷🍷🍷	5
● Cortaccio '00	🍷🍷	8
● San Martino '01	🍷🍷	8
● Chianti Cl. Ris. '00	🍷🍷	6
● Cortaccio '03	🍷🍷	8

Villa Mangiacane

via Faltignano, 4
50026 San Casciano
in Val di Pesa [FI]
tel. 0558290123
www.mangiacane.it

ANNUAL PRODUCTION N.A.
HECTARES UNDER VINE 46
VITICULTURE METHOD Conventional

This estate, owned by South African businessman Glynn David Cohen, regains a full entry thanks to a fine showing by this year's wines, especially the new merlot-only Aleah '04. The eye-catching villa is situated opposite the offices of the Chianti Classico consortium. Alongside the wine and oil, Glynn has created a luxurious country hotel with a high quality restaurant adjoining it. The wines are in a distinctly modern style with one eye on overseas markets. There's plentiful use of new oak and much effort is devoted to achieving roundness. Aleah is rich and powerful with overt toasty notes but what really comes over is its softness, which leads to an intense, long finish. The '04 Chianti Classico Riserva is more dynamic. There's predominantly ripe fruit on the nose and it has racy structure with evident tannin and acidity before coming to a nicely ongoing finish. Chianti Classico '05 is attractive but maybe the structure is a touch slim.

● Chianti Cl. Ris. '04	🍷🍷	5
● Aleah '04	🍷🍷	6
● Chianti Cl. '05	🍷	4
● Chianti Cl. '02	🍷🍷	5
● Chianti Cl. '03	🍷🍷	5
● Chianti Cl. Ris. '01	🍷🍷	5

Villa Pillo
VIA VOLTERRANA, 24
50050 GAMBASSI TERME [FI]
TEL. 0571680212
www.villapillo.com

ANNUAL PRODUCTION 200,000 bottles
HECTARES UNDER VINE 36
VITICULTURE METHOD Conventional

The Villa Pillo wines are back on excellent
form. With the '05, the Syrah has brushed
up its credentials as a wine of class and
returned to the finals. The nose has well-
defined varietal characteristics,
complemented by dark-skinned fruit,
spiciness and excellently judged oak. The
palate is ripe, racy and surefooted,
sustained by balanced acidity and well-
modulated tannins that lead to a spicy,
attractive finish. The '05 release of Vivaldaia,
from cabernet franc, is terrific. An elegant,
well-delineated nose of ripe fruit, balsamic
notes and spices leads to a succulent,
crisp, multi-layered palate with a tight, well-
integrated tannic weave and a flavoursome
finish that is a little short only because the
wine is still young. The impressive Merlot
Sant'Adele '05 has clean-cut aromas of
blackberry, cherry and black pepper, and a
concentrated but nicely dynamic palate
finishing firm and dry. The slim, lively,
savoury, complex Borgoforte '05, from
sangiovese, cabernet and merlot, has good
style.

Villa Poggio Salvi
LOC. POGGIO SALVI
53024 MONTALCINO [SI]
TEL. 0577848486
www.biondisantispa.com

ANNUAL PRODUCTION 200,000 bottles
HECTARES UNDER VINE 40
VITICULTURE METHOD Conventional

Engineer Tagliabue continues to strive for
outstanding great quality and, after years
stuck at the same level, his wines are now
improving by leaps and bounds. Getting to
this point has involved taking numerous
decisions, many of them involving hefty
expenditure. Tagliabue didn't produce a
Brunello di Montalcino in '02 since he didn't
consider the grapes good enough, but he
did produce a Brunello Riserva '01. It was
distinctive enough to reach the finals. It has
a traditional stamp, the nose centred on
tobacco, leather, medicinal herbs and red
berry fruit, and the palate dependent on
well-honed acidity and tannin to bring it
strength and character. As a result, it's a
wine that wins you over with its finesse and
elegance rather than its muscle. We also
tasted a new wine, Tosco '05, from 100 per
cent sangiovese, which seems a little too
oaky on both nose and palate. Rosso di
Montalcino '04 is a little too vegetal.

● Syrah '05	▼▼ 6
● Borgoforte '05	▼▼ 4
● Merlot Sant'Adele '05	▼▼ 6
● Vivaldaia '05	▼▼ 6
● Syrah '97	▼▼▼ 5
● Syrah '99	♈♈ 5
● Borgoforte '04	♈♈ 4
● Merlot Sant'Adele '01	♈♈ 6
● Syrah '00	♈♈ 6
● Syrah '03	♈♈ 6
● Vivaldaia '04	♈♈ 6
● Vivaldaia '03	♈♈ 6
● Syrah '01	♈♈ 6
● Merlot Sant'Adele '04	♈♈ 6
● Merlot Sant'Adele '03	♈♈ 6
● Merlot Sant'Adele '00	♈♈ 6

● Brunello di Montalcino Ris. '01	▼▼ 8
● Rosso di Montalcino '04	▼ 6
● Il Tosco '05	▼ 6
● Brunello di Montalcino '01	♈♈ 7
● Brunello di Montalcino '99	♈♈ 7
● Brunello di Montalcino Ris. '99	♈♈ 8

Villa Vignamaggio

VIA DI PETRIOLO, 5
50022 GREVE IN CHIANTI [FI]
TEL. 055854661
www.vignamaggio.com

ANNUAL PRODUCTION 230,000 bottles
HECTARES UNDER VINE 52
VITICULTURE METHOD Conventional

We were truly delighted to be able to award Three Glasses to a wine from Giovanni Nunziante's estate once more. It went to one of the best releases ever of Vignamaggio, the '04, made from 100 per cent cabernet franc. Underlying all aspects of the work carried out at Vignamaggio is the owner's huge passion for the enterprise and the way he manages to convey this to his staff, motivating them to ever greater achievements. Riserva Monna Lisa '04 is another wine of distinction. The lively, mineral nose has aromatic herbs plus a little finely judged oak leading to a palate that is balanced, substantial and attractively long. The two '05 Chianti Classicos are uncomplicated but stylish. On the other hand, Obsession '04, from merlot, syrah and cabernet sauvignon, has a rather indistinct nose and a soft structure which is slightly lacking balance, especially in terms of tannin. Vin Santo '02 has an appealing range of aromas, including honey and nuts, but doesn't really fill the mouth.

Tenuta Vitereta

VIA CASA NUOVA, 108
52020 LATERINA [AR]
TEL. 057589058
www.tenutavitereta.com

ANNUAL PRODUCTION 80,000 bottles
HECTARES UNDER VINE 45
VITICULTURE METHOD Natural

This estate, lying in the Pratomagno foothills on the right bank of the river Arno, was acquired by the Del Tongo and Bidini families in 1973. In the 1980s, the Casarossa holding which, it seems, had once produced wine for the royal house of Savoy, was also taken over, this time by Duca Amedeo di Savoia. By the end of the 1990s, all the prerequisites for producing high quality grapes were already in place. It was then that Marcello Bidini, the current owner, decided to direct his energies to the marketplace. The wines, made both from traditional and international varieties, have shown admirable consistency of late. Their quality is high and their conception more technique-led than territory-focused. The wine that usually stands out from the pack is Cabernet Villa Bernetti and the '04 follows the trend, being taut, austere and restrained, with dark-skinned fruit and mineral hints. The second Cabernet, Capitoni '05, is more openly soft, fruity, immediate and enjoyable. The whites also show character. Donna Aurora '05 is a full-bodied, nicely savoury Chardonnay and Trebbiano '05, made partly with semi-dried grapes, is a powerful, warm, individual wine.

● Vignamaggio '04	￥￥￥ 7
● Chianti Cl. Monna Lisa Ris. '04	￥￥ 6
● Chianti Cl. '05	￥ 5
● Chianti Cl. Terre di Prenzano '05	￥ 4
● Obsession '04	￥ 7
O Vin Santo del Chianti Cl. '02	￥ 6
● Chianti Cl. Monna Lisa Ris. '99	￥￥￥ 6
● Vignamaggio '00	￥￥￥ 7
● Vignamaggio '01	￥￥￥ 7
● Obsession '00	￥￥ 7
● Obsession '01	￥￥ 7
● Vignamaggio '99	￥￥ 7
● Vignamaggio '03	￥￥ 7
● Obsession '99	￥￥ 7
● Chianti Cl. '04	￥￥ 5
O Vin Santo del Chianti Cl. '01	￥￥ 6

● Capitoni '05	￥￥ 4*
● Villa Bernetti '04	￥￥ 5
O Donna Aurora '05	￥
● Ripa della Mozza '05	￥ 5
O Trebbiano di Toscana '05	￥ 5
● Ripa della Mozza '03	￥￥ 5
● Villa Bernetti '03	￥￥ 5
● Villa Bernetti '01	￥￥ 5

Viticcio

VIA SAN CRESCI, 12A
50022 GREVE IN CHIANTI [FI]
TEL. 055854210
www.fattoriaviticcio.com

ANNUAL PRODUCTION 200,000 bottles
HECTARES UNDER VINE 35
VITICULTURE METHOD Conventional

The encouraging results from this estate owned by Alessandro Landini are just like last year's, only with different wines. We can't help feeling, though, that there is further potential here which is not being fully realized and that Landini's efforts to achieve the concentration that marks out his soft, very oaky wines, is achieved at the expense of drinkability. If there were more emphasis on balance, the fine characteristics the wines already possess would probably be greatly enhanced. Chianti Classico Riserva '04 is the most impressive of the range, with a spicy oakiness and a warm, full, tannic palate well supported by an attractive swath of acidity. Prunaio '04, from 100 per cent sangiovese, is also accomplished, homing in on a forest fruits nose, and proffering an austere palate with a savoury finish. Chianti Classico '05 is well made and appealing, its delicious nose all aromatic herbs and red berry fruits, the palate dynamic and long. Monile '04, from cabernet and merlot, though, seems a little too firm and reined in by its tannin, although it has good fleshiness. Neither does Chianti Classico Riserva Beatrice '04 open out well, which limits its appeal.

● Chianti Cl. '05	♟♟	4
● Prunaio '04	♟♟	7
● Chianti Cl. Ris. '04	♟♟	5
● Chianti Cl. Beatrice Ris. '04	♟	6
● Monile '04	♟	6
● Prunaio '99	♟♟♟	7
● Prunaio '01	♟♟	8
● Chianti Cl. '03	♟♟	5
● Chianti Cl. Ris. '01	♟♟	6
● Prunaio '03	♟♟	7
● Monile '03	♟♟	6
● Chianti Cl. Beatrice Ris. '01	♟♟	6
● Chianti Cl. '04	♟♟	4

Castello di Volpaia

LOC. VOLPAIA
P.ZZA DELLA CISTERNA, 1
53017 RADDA IN CHIANTI [SI]
TEL. 0577738066
www.volpaia.com

ANNUAL PRODUCTION 250,000 bottles
HECTARES UNDER VINE 45
VITICULTURE METHOD Certified organic

The Mascheroni family are back in the big time, clinching Three Glasses for there Chianti Classico Coltassala Riserva '04. It was no accident, given the consistently excellent quality wines they have been producing in the past few years. Indeed, we are more than positive about their recent stylistic change of heart as this has led to wines that are much more rounded and attractive but retain their firm provenance-based roots. Volpaia is almost a unique entity in Chianti, partly due to its geographical position but also thanks to the acumen of the Mascheronis, who prefer to continue using the ancient buildings in the hamlet where they work as cellars rather than tear out its soul to work in more rational spaces. They have preserved a considerable architectural heritage intact at the expense of daily inconvenience, an admirable decision, we feel. Coltassala '04 has sweetly spicy aromas, a soft, silky palate and good length. The basic Riserva is also first-rate. Balifico '04, from sangiovese and cabernet, is powerful and austere. Chianti Classico '05 and Vin Santo '00 are both well made and attractive.

● Chianti Cl. Coltassala Ris. '04	♟♟♟	7
● Balifico '04	♟♟	8
● Chianti Cl. Ris. '04	♟♟	6
● Chianti Cl. '05	♟	4
○ Vin Santo del Chianti Cl. '00	♟	6
● Balifico '00	♟♟♟	7
● Chianti Cl. Coltassala Ris. '01	♟♟♟	7
● Chianti Cl. Coltassala Ris. '03	♟♟	7
● Balifico '03	♟♟	7
● Chianti Cl. Ris. '03	♟♟	6
● Chianti Cl. '04	♟♟	4

OTHER WINERIES

Agricola Alberese
FRAZ. ALBERESE
LOC. SPERGOLAIA
58010 GROSSETO
TEL. 0564407180
www.alberese.com

This new entry, owned by the Tuscan regional authority, extends over 50 hectares in the Uccellino national park. The two Morellinos are good. The '05 has intriguing notes of Mediterranean scrub and a characterful palate while Barbicato '04 is fresh and tasty. The '06 Vermentino Castelmarino is predictable.

● Morellino di Scansano '05	▼▼	4
● Morellino di Scansano Barbicato '04	▼▼	4
O Vermentino Castelmarino '06	▼	4

Fattoria dell'Aiola
FRAZ. VAGLIAGLI
53010 CASTELNUOVO BERARDENGA [SI]
TEL. 0577322615
www.aiola.net

Maria Grazia Malagodi's estate had a low-key year. Rosso del Senatore '04 from cabernet sauvignon, merlot and sangiovese offers satisfying ripe fruit, tertiary aromas of leather and animal skins and nice thrust. The Riserva '04 is less successful and the simple, fresh Chianti Classico '05 is pleasant.

● Rosso del Senatore '04	▼▼	6
● Chianti Cl. '05	▼	4
● Chianti Cl. Ris. '04	▼	5

Altura
LOC. MULINACCIO
58012 GIGLIO [GR]
TEL. 0564806106

Francesco Carfagna produces around 4,000 bottles of Ansonica on the Isola del Giglio. His three hectares of vines planted on terraces suspended over the sea are a triumph over nature. This wine is spontaneously biodynamic, showing complex on the nose and then warm, potent and minerally on the palate.

O Ansonica dell'Isola del Giglio '06	▼▼	5

Lorella Ambrosini
LOC. TABARÒ, 96
57028 SUVERETO [LI]
TEL. 0565829301
loreambrowine@katamail.com

Riflesso Antico is conspicuous by its absence and the other two house labels, Subertum and Tabarò, are only well made. That's why the Ambrosini estate is in the Other Wineries section this time. The young, intensely fruity Subertum '05 lacks harmony on the palate and Tabarò '06 is coherent and agreeable.

● Val di Cornia Rosso Tabarò '06	▼	4
● Val di Cornia Subertum '05	▼	6

Ampeleia
LOC. MELETA
58036 ROCCASTRADA [GR]
TEL. 0564567155
www.ampeleia.it

Elisabetta Foradori's Maremma estate is coming along nicely. Ampeleia '05, a blend of cabernet franc, sangiovese and merlot, is the only wine in production at the moment but it's a classy one. An excess of oak rather reins in the nose but on the palate it is elegant and full of personality.

● Ampeleia '05	▼▼	6
● Ampeleia '04	♀♀	6

Tenuta di Arceno
FRAZ. SAN GUSMÉ
LOC. ARCENO
53010 CASTELNUOVO BERARDENGA [SI]
TEL. 0577359346
www.tenutadiarceno.com

Instead of its traditional wide range of labels, Kendall Jackson's estate presented just two Chianti Classicos this year. We liked the Riserva '04 for its spicy nose and velvety body with elegant tannins and a finish that develops well. The Chianti Classico '05 is modern in style but light in structure.

● Chianti Cl. Ris. '04	▼▼	6
● Chianti Cl. '05	▼	5

OTHER WINERIES

Argiano
FRAZ. SANT'ANGELO IN COLLE
53024 MONTALCINO [SI]
TEL. 0577844037
www.argiano.net

This lovely, historic estate showed well. The nice Brunello '02 displays classic morello cherry notes on the nose and a mid-weight palate whose tannins are still rather aggressive. The pure sangiovese Suolo '04 is well styled and has mature aromas on the nose. The Rosso '05 is a bit clenched.

● Brunello di Montalcino '02	♀♀	8
● Non Confunditur '05	♀	5
● Rosso di Montalcino '05	♀	5
● Suolo '04	♀	8

Artimino
FRAZ. ARTIMINO
V.LE PAPA GIOVANNI XXIII, 1
59015 CARMIGNANO [PO]
TEL. 0558751423
www.artimino.com

This year, the Artimino estate was punching its weight. Villa Medicea Riserva '04 shows well with its no-nonsense, tannic palate. The Carmignano '05 combines a spicy, peppery nose with density and superb follow-through on the palate. The Chianti Montalbano '06 and Rosato di Carmignano '06 are pleasant.

● Carmignano Villa Medicea Ris. '04	♀♀	5
● Carmignano Villa Artimino '05	♀	4
● Chianti Montalbano '06	♀	3*
☉ Carmignano Villa Artimino Rosato '06	♀	3*

Erik Banti
LOC. FOSSO DEI MOLINI
58054 SCANSANO [GR]
TEL. 0564508006
www.erikbanti.com

Erik Banti's wines are rooted solidly in their territory of origin, not least the Morellino di Scansanos. The Morellino '05 is a tad rustic on the nose but wonderfully fresh and tangy on the palate. The Morellino Ciabatta Riserva '05 has a similar style but tends to be rather clenched on the palate.

● Morellino di Scansano Carato '05	♀♀	4
● Morellino di Scansano Ciabatta Ris. '05	♀	5
● Poggio Maestrino Anno Sesto '04	♀♀	5
● Morellino di Scansano Ciabatta Ris. '04	♀♀	5

Batzella
LOC. BADIA
VIA DEI CAMPI AL MARE, 227
57024 CASTAGNETO CARDUCCI [LI]
TEL. 3393975888
www.batzella.com

Franco and Khanh Batzella's estate is back with two fine wines, Bolgheri Superiore Tam '04 and Bolgheri Bianco Mezzodì '06. The first, cabernet sauvignon with a little cabernet franc, has a vegetal nose and a smooth, elegant palate while the second, mainly viognier, has a flowery nose and fruity palate.

○ Bolgheri Mezzodì '06	♀♀	4
● Bolgheri Superiore Tam '04	♀♀	5

Tenuta di Bibbiano
VIA BIBBIANO, 76
53011 CASTELLINA IN CHIANTI [SI]
TEL. 0577743065
www.tenutadibibbiano.com

The Marzi Morrocchesi family estate produced some good results this year. The Riserva Vigna del Capannino '04 did well thanks to its well-balanced palate and attractive nose profile. The Chianti Classico '05 is easy, fresh-tasting and very drinkable, but the Montornello '05 selection is a tad rigid.

● Chianti Cl. V. del Capannino Ris. '04	♀♀	5
● Chianti Cl. Montornello '05	♀	4
● Chianti Cl. '05	♀	4

Tenuta Bonomonte
VIA SAN FILIPPO, 27
50021 BARBERINO VAL D'ELSA [FI]
TEL. 0558079131
www.bonomonte.com

We have an interesting new entry from the Formichi family estate. It grows local varieties only and its production is dominated by the Camp'albracco '05, a pure sangiovese with mineral tones and notes of pencil lead, a very well-defined palate and a tasty finish. The rest of the range is nice enough.

● Camp'albracco '05	♀♀	5
● Campodoro '06	♀	5
● Chianti Cl. Formichi '05	♀	4

OTHER WINERIES

Borgo Scopeto
LOC. VAGLIAGLI
53010 CASTELNUOVO BERARDENGA [SI]
TEL. 0577322729
www.borgoscopeto.com

The wines presented by Elisabetta Gnudi Angelini's estate are below par this year. There are no major fiascos but we expected something more. From sangiovese, syrah and cabernet sauvignon, the Borgonero '03 has great backbone but fails to express itself fully. The two Chianti Classicos are well managed.

● Borgonero '03	♟ 6
● Chianti Cl. '05	♟ 4
● Chianti Cl. Misciano Ris. '04	♟ 5

Bruni
FRAZ. FONTEBLANDA
LOC. LA MARTA, 6
58010 ORBETELLO [GR]
TEL. 0564885445
www.aziendabruni.it

Brothers Marco and Moreno Bruni produce distinctive wines. The Morellino Marteto '06 is fruity and pleasant. The very interesting Perlaia '06 from pure vermentino offers crisp lime blossom and cedar notes and a big, racy palate of reasonable complexity. Capalbio Bianco Plinio '05 is fresh and tasty.

● Morellino di Scansano Marteto '06	♟♟ 4
O Vermentino Perlaia '06	♟♟ 4
O Capalbio Bianco Vermentino Plinio '06	♟ 4
● Morellino di Scansano Laire '04	♟♟ 5

Buccianera
LOC. CAMPRIANO, 10
52100 AREZZO [AR]
TEL. 0575361040
www.buccianera.it

There was a fine show from this estate in a lovely, well-positioned zone just outside Arezzo. The two good-value reds are nice. The subtle, tasty Il Camprianese '05 derives mainly from sangiovese while Amadio '04, from sangiovese, cabernet and merlot, is long and complex. Donna Patrizia '06 is pleasant.

● Amadio '04	♟♟ 5
● Il Camprianese '05	♟♟ 3*
O Donna Patrizia '06	♟ 3

Bulichella
LOC. BULICHELLA, 131
57028 SUVERETO [LI]
TEL. 0565829892
www.bulichella.it

Bulichella's wines made scant impression this year. Val di Cornia Tuscanio '04 has red fruit aromas and faint vegetal tones on the nose but the agreeable palate dries on the finish. Rubino '06 is coherent on the palate but green tannins upset its balance. The Aleatico '06 is sweet, lively and tannic.

● Val di Cornia Aleatico '06	♟ 6
● Val di Cornia Rosso Tuscanio '04	♟ 5
● Val di Cornia Rosso Rubino '06	♟ 3

Castello di Cacchiano
FRAZ. MONTI IN CHIANTI
LOC. CACCHIANO
53010 GAIOLE IN CHIANTI [SI]
TEL. 0577747018
www.chianticlassico.com

It was an up and down year for Giovanni Ricasoli Firidolfi's estate. Top of the range is the big, enveloping Vin Santo '00 with its delicious dry fruit and spice nose. The reds faltered. The Riserva '03 has coarse tannins, the Rosso '04 is rather simple and the Chianti Classico '04 is very fresh.

O Vin Santo '00	♟♟ 6
● Chianti Cl. Ris. '03	♟ 5
● Chianti Cl. '04	♟ 5

La Calonica
FRAZ. VALIANO DI MONTEPULCIANO
VIA DELLA STELLA, 27
53040 MONTEPULCIANO [SI]
TEL. 0578724119
www.lacalonica.com

The Nobile '04 is very good, its powerful notes of black berry fruit the prelude to a sweet, juicy palate. Cortona Girifalco '05 is similar in style, and also has strong character, but fruit freshness is the keynote. The Nobile Riserva '03 is flavoursome but not particularly smooth.

● Cortona Girifalco '05	♟♟ 5
● Nobile di Montepulciano '04	♟♟ 5
● Nobile di Montepulciano Ris. '03	♟ 6
● Nobile di Montepulciano '03	♟♟ 5

OTHER WINERIES

Camposilio di Rustioni

LOC. PRATOLINO
VIA BASCIANO, 805
50036 VAGLIA [FI]
TEL. 055696456
www.camposilio.it

Alessandro Rustioni's estate is in the obscure but high-potential zone north of Florence. After a promising debut, it rather lost the plot but this year it's back in the Guide. Camposilio '04, a blend of cabernet sauvignon, merlot and sangiovese, is good and I Venti di Camposilio '05, from sangiovese, is nice.

● Camposilio '04	♥♥	6
● I Venti di Camposilio '05	♥	4

Canneto

VIA DEI CANNETI, 14
53045 MONTEPULCIANO [SI]
TEL. 0578757737
www.canneto.com

These are fine results from the estate run by Ottorino De Angelis. Nobile Riserva '03 has rather rustic notes but is nicely challenging on the palate while the new Filippone '04, from prugnolo gentile and merlot, offers generous aromas and a full palate. Nobile '04 is rather grassy on both nose and palate.

● Filippone '04	♥♥	6
● Nobile di Montepulciano Ris '03	♥♥	5
● Nobile di Montepulciano '04	♥	5
● Nobile di Montepulciano '03	♥♥	4

Capanna di Cencioni

LOC. CAPANNA, 333
53024 MONTALCINO [SI]
TEL. 0577848298

Patrizio Cencioni's estate offered us a classic Brunello Riserva '01 with nice oaky notes leading into classic tobacco and sweet leather. The palate flaunts young, gutsy tannins that bolster the firm backbone all the way to the finish. The traditionally vinified Moscadello '05 is interesting.

● Brunello di Montalcino Ris. '01	♥♥	8
● Brunello di Montalcino '02	♥	6
○ Moscadello di Montalcino '05	♥	3
● Rosso di Montalcino '05	♥	4

Capanne Ricci

FRAZ. SANT'ANGELO IN COLLE
LOC. CASELLO
53024 MONTALCINO [SI]
TEL. 0577844095
www.tenimentiricci.it

In a few short years, this estate has changed its style, orienting itself towards more structured wines and increased use of small barrels. Its Brunello '02 is one of this year's best. The clearly defined nose mingles notes of wild cherry jam with smoky nuances and vanilla tones. The palate is weighty.

● Brunello di Montalcino '02	♥♥	6
● Rosso di Montalcino '05	♥	4
● Brunello di Montalcino '99	♥♥	7

Capannelle

LOC. CAPANNELLE, 13
53013 GAIOLE IN CHIANTI [SI]
TEL. 057774511
www.capannelle.com

The only red this year was Solare '03. This sangiovese and malvasia nera blend is a bit muddled because of overripe, not very clean aromas. In contrast, the Chardonnay '05 is very fine, offering delicious notes of spice and aromatic herbs and a palate with backbone and excellent tanginess.

● 50 & 50 Avignonesi e Capannelle '03	♥♥	8
○ Chardonnay '05	♥♥	8
● Solare '03	♥	8
● 50 & 50 Avignonesi e Capannelle '99	♥♥♥	8

Caparsa

LOC. CAPARSINO, 48
53017 RADDA IN CHIANTI [SI]
TEL. 0577738174
www.caparsa.it

There's nothing particularly earth-shattering to report from Paolo Cianferoni's estate. Riserva Doccio a Matteo '04 stands out for its complex aromas and powerful if rather taut body. The well-typed Riserva Caparsino '04 has a fascinating nose of red berry fruit but the palate is a bit taut.

● Chianti Cl. Doccio a Matteo Ris. '04	♥♥	6
● Chianti Cl. Caparsino Ris. '04	♥	4
● Chianti Cl. Doccio a Matteo Ris. '00	♥♥♥	6

OTHER WINERIES

Tenuta Caparzo

LOC. CAPARZO
S.P. DEL BRUNELLO
53024 MONTALCINO [SI]
TEL. 0577848390
www.caparzo.com

Following the steady renovation undertaken by the new owners over the last few years, this estate gave us with a very convincing Brunello Riserva '01. Cherry-like and faintly smoky sensations fill the nose while the palate is well-balanced but lacks grip. The rest of the range is decent.

- Brunello di Montalcino Ris. '01   ♈♈ 8
- Rosso di Montalcino La Caduta '04   ♈ 5
- Rosso di Montalcino '05   ♈ 4
- Caparzo Sangiovese '05   ♈ 4

Tenuta Carlina

LOC. TAVERNELLE
S.DA DI ARGIANO - POD. PODERUCCIO
53024 MONTALCINO [SI]
TEL. 0668803000
www.brunellolatogata.com

This estate has grown exponentially with the acquisition of plots in various zones across the area but in terms of quality, it has taken a step or two back. The Brunello Riserva '01 is the best of the bunch with rather overripe fruit and spice aromas and firm structure. The finish is still a bit edgy, though.

- Brunello di Montalcino La Togata Ris. '01 ♈♈ 8
- Brunello di Montalcino La Togata '02 ♈ 7
- Rosso di Montalcino La Togata '05   ♈ 5
- Brunello di Montalcino
  Sel. La Togata dei Togati '02   ♈ 8

Casa Sola

S.DA DI CORTINE, 5
50021 BARBERINO VAL D'ELSA [FI]
TEL. 0558075028
www.fattoriacasasola.com

In the absence of the Supertuscan Montarsiccio, the rest of the range steps into the breach. The Riserva '04 is particularly good, showing complex, fascinating aromas and solid body with a big, tasty finish. The Chianti Classico '05 is a bit stiff while the sangiovese-based Per gli Amici '05 is agreeable.

- Chianti Cl. Ris. '04   ♈♈ 6
- Chianti Cl. '05   ♈ 4
- Per gli Amici '05   ♈ 3

Fattoria Casabianca

FRAZ. CASCIANO
LOC. MONTE PESCINI
53010 MURLO [SI]
TEL. 0577811026
www.fattoriacasabianca.it

This Murlo estate put on a fine show starting with the stylishly drinkable, aroma-rich sangiovese, cabernet sauvignon and merlot Tenuta Casabianca '04. The Chianti Colli Senesi Riserva '04 is flavoursome while the Colli Senesi '06 and Poggio Gonfienti, from sangiovese, canaiolo and colorino, are simpler.

- Tenuta Casabianca '04   ♈♈ 5
- Chianti dei Colli Senesi '06   ♈ 3
- Chianti dei Colli Senesi
  Poggio Cenni Ris. '04   ♈ 4
- ☉ Poggio Gonfienti '06   ♈ 2

Fattoria Casisano Colombaio

LOC. COLLINA POD. COLOMBAIO, 336
53024 MONTALCINO [SI]
TEL. 0577835540
www.brunello.org

The lovely Fattoria Casisano Colombaio sits on rather a cool, windy plateau. This year, the Brunello Riserva '01 is on excellent form, presenting a complex nose with aromas of jam, red berry fruit, spices and aniseed, a robust, layered palate and a very generous finish. The '02 Brunello is a bit evanescent.

- Brunello di Montalcino Ris. '01   ♈♈ 8
- Brunello di Montalcino '02   ♈ 6
- Brunello di Montalcino '01   ♈♈ 6

Podere Il Castagno

LOC. IL CASTAGNO
52040 CORTONA [AR]
TEL. 063223541
fabdio@tin.it

Fabrizio Dionisio, a Rome-based lawyer, has his feet firmly planted on the ground. In just a few years, this passionate convert to viticulture has carved out a respectable niche in the Cortona wine world. His '05 Syrah is rich and spicy with nice tension. It's still closed so keep it in the cellar for now.

- Cortona Syrah '05   ♈♈ 5
- Cortona Syrah '03   ♈♈ 5
- Cortona Syrah '04   ♈♈ 5

OTHER WINERIES

Castiglion del Bosco

LOC. CASTIGLION DEL BOSCO
53024 MONTALCINO [SI]
TEL. 0577807078
www.castigliondelbosco.it

This lovely estate is part of the Ferragamo family's project to rebuild an entire village. The wines this year are rather interesting, first and foremost the Brunello Campo del Drago '01 with its flowery nose and a powerful palate held back by rigid tannins. A bit more time in the bottle should do the trick.

● Brunello di Montalcino Campo del Drago '01	♈♈ 8
● Brunello di Montalcino '02	♈ 6
● Dainero '05	♈ 4

Giovanni Chiappini

LOC. LE PRESELLE
POD. FELCIAINO, 189B
57020 BOLGHERI [LI]
TEL. 0565749665
www.giovannichiappini.it

We tasted three stunning wines from Giovanni Chiappini. They share the same name and year, differing only in their variety. The Merlot's vegetal and gamey aromas precede good pressure and body; the Cabernet Sauvignon is vegetal and tight-knit; and the Franc has long thrust. It's a pity production is limited.

● Lienà Cabernet Sauvignon '04	♈♈ 8
● Lienà Merlot '04	♈♈ 8
● Lienà Cabernet Franc '04	♈♈ 8

La Ciarliana

FRAZ. GRACCIANO
VIA CIARLIANA, 31
53040 MONTEPULCIANO [SI]
TEL. 0578758423
www.laciarliana.it

Luigi Frangiosa's estate always presents well-defined wines. The Nobile '04 convinces with its dynamic palate and floral, smoky sensations. Santo Pellegrino '03, from cabernet sauvignon, is solid and tasty. Vigna Scianello '04 has yet to balance out and shows too much oak on nose and palate.

● Nobile di Montepulciano '04	♈♈ 5
● Santo Pellegrino '03	♈♈ 6
● Nobile di Montepulciano V. Scianello '04	♈ 6

Cima

FRAZ. ROMAGNANO
VIA DEL FAGIANO, 1
54100 MASSA [MS]
TEL. 0585831617
www.aziendagricolacima.it

Another convincing line-up from the Cima farm offers well-managed, stylistically coherent wines. Our preference is for the pure sangiovese Anchigi '05, which has quite an impact on the nose and impressive depth on the palate. A special mention goes to the fresh, pleasant Massaretta '05, from a local variety.

● Anchigi '05	♈♈ 5
● Massaretta '05	♈ 6
● Romalbo '05	♈ 6
○ Candia dei Colli Apuani '06	♈ 4

La Cipriana

LOC. CAMPASTRELLO 176B
57022 CASTAGNETO CARDUCCI [LI]
TEL. 0565775568
www.lacipriana.it

The Fabiani brothers offer further proof of the potential of their small estate. Their Bolgheri Superiore San Martino '04 is very good indeed, unveiling blackberry, tobacco and balsam and a smooth, silky palate. Scopaio '04 is a bit too oaky and this renders the tannins mouth-drying and bitterish.

● Bolgheri Sup. San Martino '04	♈♈ 6
● Bolgheri Rosso Scopaio '04	♈ 5

Colle Bereto

LOC. COLLE BERETO
53017 RADDA IN CHIANTI [SI]
TEL. 0554299330
www.collebereto.it

In the absence of the two house crus, Tocco and Cenno, the Pinzauti family estate earned no more than a short profile. From the Chianti Classicos, we preferred the Riserva '04 for its fascinating cornucopia of aromas and soft, thick body. The '05 is rather held back by tannins.

● Chianti Cl. Ris. '04	♈♈ 5
● Chianti Cl. '05	♈ 4

OTHER WINERIES

Colle di Bordocheo
LOC. SEGROMIGNO IN MONTE
VIA DI PIAGGIORI BASSO, 107
55018 CAPANNORI [LU]
TEL. 0583929821
dchelini@tin.it

Led by a very successful Bianco dell'Oca '06, Colle di Bordocheo wines have made a comeback to the Guide. This blend of sauvignon and chardonnay is pleasanter than ever with its country herbs and tropical fruit preceding well-gauged acidity that adds zap to its balance. Picchio '05 also showed well.

O Colline Lucchesi Bianco dell'Oca '06	♟♟	5
O Colline Lucchesi Bordocheo '06	♟	4
● Colline Lucchesi Picchio '05	♟	5

Il Colle
LOC. IL COLLE 102B
53024 MONTALCINO [SI]
TEL. 0577848295
ilcolledicarli@katamail.com

Caterina Carli is doing a fine job running this estate. The Brunello '02 bears witness to the skilful way the cellar deals with challenging growing years. A fruity nose reveals notes of white cherry, dried chestnuts and refreshing balsam. The palate is soft but buttressed by good acidity.

● Brunello di Montalcino '02	♟♟	6
● Rosso di Montalcino '05	♟	4
● Brunello di Montalcino '01	♟♟	6

Fattoria Colle Verde
FRAZ. MATRAIA
LOC. CASTELLO
55010 LUCCA [LU]
TEL. 0583402310
www.colleverde.it

In a sangiovese and syrah '04 version, Brania delle Ghiandaie again earned Fattoria Colle Verde a place in our Guide. This very well-made wine has enormous extractive weight yet is also supple and stylish. Hints of ripe morello cherry and sweet spices lead into a palate that foregrounds tight-knit tannins.

● Colline Lucchesi Rosso Brania delle Ghiandaie '04	♟♟	5
O Brania del Cancello '05	♟	5

Tenuta di Collosorbo
FRAZ. CASTELNUOVO DELL'ABATE
LOC. VILLA A SESTA, 25
53020 MONTALCINO [SI]
TEL. 0577835534
www.collosorbo.com

This Montalcino estate is in the beautiful subzone of Sesta. The interesting Brunello Riserva '01 has attractive aromas of yellow peach, morello cherry and cherry, and a complex, full palate that is already well balanced with a nice finish. The fruity Rosso di Montalcino '05 is well styled and pleasant.

● Brunello di Montalcino Ris. '01	♟♟	8
● Rosso di Montalcino '05	♟	5

La Colombina
VIA DEL LUOGO NUOVO, 1
53024 MONTALCINO [SI]
TEL. 0577849231
www.lacolombinavini.it

We have a new entry in this Castelnuovo dell'Abate estate. The wines presented for tasting were very good, starting with the Brunello '02, which combines a complex nose of vanilla-led spice, morello cherry and faint smoky nuances, then nice density supported by well-balanced acidity and very ripe tannins.

● Brunello di Montalcino '02	♟♟	6
● Rosso di Montalcino '05	♟♟	4
● Brunello di Montalcino Ris. '01	♟	7

Contucci
VIA DEL TEATRO, 1
53045 MONTEPULCIANO [SI]
TEL. 0578757006
www.contucci.it

Alamanno Contucci's historic cellar in the centre of Montepulciano makes wines of great character. Pietra Rossa '03 offers a powerful, lip-smacking palate and well-defined warm, deep aromas. The lighter weight Mulinvecchio '03 has tempting aromas while the Nobile '04 has an earthy, almost salty nose.

● Nobile di Montepulciano Pietra Rossa '03	♟♟	5
● Nobile di Montepulciano '04	♟	5
● Nobile di Montepulciano Mulinvecchio '03	♟	5

OTHER WINERIES

Il Conventino
VIA DELLA CIARLIANA, 25B
53040 MONTEPULCIANO [SI]
TEL. 0578715371
www.ilconventino.it

What a fine personality this Nobile Riserva
'03 has. Although the nose tends to the
rustic, the palate flaunts energy and depth.
Nobile '04 is readier and more
approachable in its aromas but its tannins
have yet to smooth out. The grapes on this
estate are cultivated organically.

- Nobile di Montepulciano Ris. '03   ▼▼ 6
- Nobile di Montepulciano '04   ▼ 5
- Nobile di Montepulciano Ris. '01   ♀♀ 6

Tenuta Il Corno
FRAZ. SAN PANCRAZIO
VIA MALAFRASCA, 64
50026 SAN CASCIANO IN VAL DI PESA [FI]
TEL. 0558248009
www.tenutailcorno.com

We welcome back Maria Teresa Frova's
estate, located at the edge of the Chianti
Classico area. The best wine is the Colorino
'03 with fresh aromas, solid body, tight-knit
tannins and nice acidity. Minna e Moro '05,
from sangiovese and colorino, is pleasant and
the Chianti Colli Fiorentini '05 is well typed.

- Colorino del Corno '03   ▼▼ 6
- Chianti Colli Fiorentini '05   ▼ 3
- Minna e Moro '05   ▼ 4

Corte Pavone
LOC. CORTE PAVONE
53024 MONTALCINO [SI]
TEL. 0577848110
www.loacker.net

The Montalcino branch of the Loacker
winery in Alto Adige gave us some good
quality wines but we expected better. The
best of the bunch is Brunello Riserva '01. Its
austere nose is still marked by oak and the
fruit is a tad overripe. The Rosso di
Montalcino '05 is fresh and complex.

- Brunello di Montalcino Ris. '01   ▼▼ 8
- Rosso di Montalcino '05   ▼ 5
- Brunello di Montalcino '99   ♀♀ 7

Andrea Costanti
LOC. COLLE AL MATRICHESE
53024 MONTALCINO [SI]
TEL. 0577848195
www.costanti.it

This historic Montalcino estate continues to
make characterful wines. We liked the
Brunello Riserva '01 for its complex floral
nose enhanced by sweet tobacco, liquorice
and leather. The tannins have already found
a measure of balance on the palate, which
has good supporting acidity and a nice long
finish.

- Brunello di Montalcino Ris. '01   ▼▼ 8
- Brunello di Montalcino Calbello '99   ♀♀ 7

Tenuta degli Dei
LOC. SAN LEOLINO
VIA SAN LEOLINO, 56
50020 PANZANO [FI]
TEL. 055852593
www.deglidei.com

Tommaso Cavalli's estate debuts in the
Guide in its first year of production.
Obtained from cabernet franc and
sauvignon, merlot, petit verdot and a little
alicante, the '04 Cavalli's modern style
combines spicy aromas with wild berries.
The tannic palate is rather cramped by the
decisive use of oak.

- Cavalli '04   ▼▼ 6

I Fabbri
LOC. LAMOLE
VIA CASALE, 52
50022 GREVE IN CHIANTI [FI]
TEL. 0552345719
www.agricolaifabbri.it

The symphony of Susanna Grassi's estate is
in a minor key for this year. The Riserva was
missing and the '05 growing year was not
kind: witness the reduced quantity of wine
bottled. The two versions of Chianti
Classico performed well, especially on the
nose, but the palates are lightish.

- Chianti Cl. '05   ▼ 4
- Chianti Cl. Terra di Lamole '05   ▼ 4

OTHER WINERIES

Cantine Faralli
LOC. FASCIANO, 4
52040 CORTONA [AR]
TEL. 0575613128
www.cantinefaralli.com

The wines from this Cortona cellar are a tad rustic but very flavoursome. The full, poised and powerful Sorbo '04 from merlot and sangiovese has nice tertiary notes, character and solid backbone. The nose of the sangiovese and merlot Novantadieci '04 is muddled but it has good depth.

● Il Sorbo '04	♀♀	5
● Cortona Novantadieci '04	♀	4

Ferrero
FRAZ. SANT'ANGELO IN COLLE
LOC. PASCENA
53024 MONTALCINO [SI]
TEL. 0577844170
claudia.ferrero@gmail.it

Now here's a very interesting new estate. Located in the south of the Montalcino area, it gave us a captivating Brunello '02. The fruity nose reveals aromas of herbs, coffee and caramel while the palate displays good weight and ripe tannins that elegantly refrain from curbing the lovely long finish.

● Brunello di Montalcino '02	♀♀	7
● Rosso di Montalcino '05	♀	5
● Brunello di Montalcino '00	♀♀	7

Fertuna
LOC. GRILLI
VIA AURELIA VECCHIA KM 205
58040 GAVORRANO [GR]
TEL. 056688138
www.fertuna.it

Ezio Rivella's wines never fail to impress with their class and impeccable style. The fresher, more approachable Lodai '05 has a flowing, tasty palate. Messiio '05 is still very young but more complex. Both are obtained from sangiovese, cabernet sauvignon and merlot, blended in differing proportions.

● Lodai '05	♀♀	5
● Messiio '05	♀♀	6
● Lodai '04	♀♀	5
● Messiio '03	♀♀	6

Ficomontanino
LOC. FICOMONTANINO
53043 CHIUSI [SI]
TEL. 0578821180
www.agricolaficomontanino.it

A normal, generally cool growing year like '04 brings out the far from dull characteristics of the all-cabernet sauvignon Lucumone, enhancing the freshness of its grassy nose and the agreeably edgy, lip-smacking palate. The '05 Chianti Colli Senesi Tutulus is nicely managed.

● Lucumone '04	♀♀	6
● Chianti Colli Senesi Tutulus '05	♀	5
● Lucumone '03	♀♀	6
● Lucumone '02	♀♀	5

La Fiorita
FRAZ. CASTELNUOVO DELL'ABATE
PIAGGIA DELLA PORTA, 3
53020 MONTALCINO [SI]
TEL. 0577835657
www.fattorialafiorita.it

This small Castelnuovo dell'Abate cellar is run by well-known oenologist Roberto Cipresso. This year's range performed well across the board, with the Brunello Riserva '01 outstanding. Eloquent on the nose, it gives oleander and fruit before flaunting personality on the palate. Laurus '04 also showed well.

● Brunello di Montalcino Ris. '01	♀♀	7
● Laurus '04	♀♀	4
● Brunello di Montalcino '02	♀	7

Fontaleoni
LOC. SANTA MARIA, 39A
53037 SAN GIMIGNANO [SI]
TEL. 0577950193
www.fontaleoni.com

The Fontaleoni range performed well. The excellent Vernaccia Vigna Casanuova '06 is fresh and concentrated with a lovely long finish. The Vernaccia Notte di Luna '06, the standard-label '06 and the pleasant, great-value Chianti Tramonto '06 are every bit as good.

● Chianti Tramonto '06	♀♀	3*
○ Vernaccia di S. Gimignano Notte di Luna '06	♀♀	3*
○ Vernaccia di S. Gimignano V. Casanuova '06	♀♀	4*
○ Vernaccia di S. Gimignano '06	♀♀	4*

OTHER WINERIES

Fornacelle

LOC. FORNACELLE, 232A
57022 CASTAGNETO CARDUCCI [LI]
TEL. 0565775575
info@fornacelle.it

A fine overall performance from Fornacelle saw it debut in our Guide. We particularly like the pure cabernet franc Foglio 38 '04, with its very vegetal nose and firm palate with good acidity and slightly mouth-drying tannins. The two '06 Zizzolos, Bianco and Rosso, are simple and agreeable.

● Foglio 38 '04	▼▼	7
○ Zizzolo Bianco '06	▼	4
● Zizzolo Rosso '06	▼	4

Fornacina

POD. FORNACINA, 153
53024 MONTALCINO [SI]
TEL. 0577848464
www.cantinafornacina.it

This organic Montalcino-based estate that owns vineyards in several zones gave us a first-class Riserva '01. It has dense colour and a generous fruity nose that reveals delicate notes of vanilla and caramel when left to breathe. Ripe, fine-grained tannins give the palate nice body and balance.

● Brunello di Montalcino Ris. '01	▼▼	7
● Rosso di Montalcino '05	▼	4

Podere Forte

LOC. PETRUCCI, 13
53023 CASTIGLIONE D'ORCIA [SI]
TEL. 05778885100
www.podereforte.it

In the absence of its top wines, granted an extra year in the bottle, Podere Forte has a short profile this year. We tasted just one bottle, Petruccino '05, a simple but technically irreproachable easy drinker with dark berry fruit, flowers and spices lifted by a well-gauged dose of oak.

● Orcia Petruccino '05	▼▼	5
● Orcia Guardiavigna '01	▼▼▼	8
● Orcia Guardiavigna '03	▼▼	8
● Orcia Petrucci '02	▼▼	8

Gagliole

LOC. GAGLIOLE, 42
53011 CASTELLINA IN CHIANTI [SI]
TEL. 0577740369
www.gagliole.com

Gagliole's flagship wine, Pecchia, was missing from our tasting table this year. The best results went to the '05 Chianti Classico Rubiolo, which displays mineral, fruity aromas and solid body with nice weighty tannins and a flavoursome finish. The sangiovese-based Gagliole '05 is not quite up to snuff.

● Chianti Cl. Rubiolo '05	▼▼	4
● Gagliole Rosso '05	▼	6

Giannoni Fabbri

LOC. SAN MARCO, 2
52044 CORTONA [AR]
TEL. 0575630502
marco.giannoni@libero.it

We welcome back to the Guide a Cortona estate that in years past impressed us mainly with the quality of its old Vin Santos. The Cabernet '04 we tasted this time round stands out for its well-defined profile of dark berry fruit but it is also attractively savoury, dry, austere and smooth.

● Cortona Cabernet '04	▼▼	4
○ Vin Santo '92	▼▼	6

Azienda Agricola Godiolo

VIA DELL'ACQUAPUZZOLA, 13
53045 MONTEPULCIANO [SI]
TEL. 0578757251
www.godiolo.it

Franco Fiorini's estate produces wines with lots of character. The interesting Nobile Riserva '03 makes quite an impact with well-balanced aromatics on the nose and rich, full-flavoured, gutsy palate. The agreeably drinkable Nobile '04 puts the accent on very sweet tones.

● Nobile di Montepulciano Ris. '03	▼▼	6
● Nobile di Montepulciano '04	▼	5
● Nobile di Montepulciano '03	▼▼	5

OTHER WINERIES

Fattoria di Gracciano
FRAZ. GRACCIANO
VIA UMBRIA, 63
53040 MONTEPULCIANO [SI]
TEL. 055859811
www.tenutefolonari.com

The wines from Ambrogio and Giovanni Folonari's Montepulciano estate show solid quality and a well-defined style. The fine, elegantly balanced Nobile '04 is well supported by refined, whistle-clean aromas. The '03 Nobile Riserva is more robust on the slightly tart palate and the nose is a tad grassy.

- Nobile di Montepulciano Torcalvano '04 ♀♀ 4
- Nobile di Montepulciano
  Torcalvano Ris. '03 ♀ 5
- Nobile di Montepulciano Torcalvano '03 ♀♀ 4

I Greppi
LOC. I GREPPI
57022 CASTAGNETO CARDUCCI [LI]
TEL. 055854210
www.fattoriaviticcio.com

This Castagneto Carducci estate, established in 2001, is a new entry. Credit goes to the excellent performance from both of the wines presented, Bolgheri Superiore Greppicaia '04 and Bolgheri Greppicante '05. The first is round and dense, if rather oak-dominated, while the second is simpler and juicy.

- Bolgheri Greppicante '05 ♀♀ 4
- Bolgheri Sup. Greppicaia '04 ♀ 6

Greppone Mazzi
Tenimenti Ruffino
LOC. GREPPONE
53024 MONTALCINO [SI]
TEL. 05583605
info@ruffino.it

This estate, a member of the Ruffino group, offered us a very decent Brunello Riserva '01 this year. The intense colour and generous black cherry-led aromas are followed by citrus fruit and a faint grassy sensation. The concentrated palate displays balanced, mature tannins and perfect supporting acidity.

- Brunello di Montalcino Ris. '01 ♀♀ 6
- Brunello di Montalcino '99 ♀♀♀ 8
- Brunello di Montalcino Ris. '99 ♀♀♀ 6

Icario
VIA DELLE PIETROSE, 2
53045 MONTEPULCIANO [SI]
TEL. 0578758845
www.icario.it

The elegant Nobile '04 offers great drinkability, lifted by a very tasty attack and extremely refreshing progression. The Vitaroccia '04 is a tad oak-dominated but has a very sweet nose profile and a soft if rather flabby palate. Rubì delle Pietrose, '05 from sangiovese, teroldego and merlot, is well made.

- Nobile di Montepulciano '04 ♀♀ 5
- Nobile di Montepulciano Vitaroccia '04 ♀ 5
- Rubì delle Pietrose '05 ♀ 3
- Nobile di Montepulciano Vitaroccia '03 ♀♀ 5

Ispoli
FRAZ. MERCATALE VAL DI PESA
VIA SANTA LUCIA, 2
50024 SAN CASCIANO IN VAL DI PESA [FI]
TEL. 055821613
ispoli@tin.it

The Mattheis estate alternates full profiles with short ones, as its limited size makes it highly susceptible to the vagaries of the growing year. The sangiovese and merlot Ispolaia '05 is first-rate. It has a lovely fruity nose and a solid palate with fresh acidity and a long, savoury finish.

- Ispolaia Rosso '05 ♀♀ 6

Fattoria La Striscia
VIA DEI CAPPUCCINI, 3
52100 AREZZO [AR]
TEL. 057526740
fattorialastrisc@hotmail.com

Fattoria La Striscia in Arezzo, owned by the Conti Occhini, maintains high standards. The '05 Occhini, from sangiovese with merlot, offers warm, ripe fruit with hints of spice and a flavoursome, earthy palate with nice character. The Chianti Bernardino '05 is pleasantly rustic and traditional.

- Occhini '05 ♀♀ 4
- Chianti Berardino '05 ♀ 3
- Occhini '04 ♀♀ 4
- Occhini '04 ♀♀ 4*

OTHER WINERIES

Villa Le Prata

LOC. LE PRATA, 261
53024 MONTALCINO [SI]
TEL. 0577848325
www.villaleprata.com

Villa Le Prata always presents a valid range of wines. Rosso di Montalcino Tirso takes pride of place this year and is among the best in its category. The generous nose offers notes of blackberry, blueberry and wild cherry well integrated with the oak, excellent depth and nice length.

● Rosso di Montalcino Tirso '05	ᵀᵀ 5
● Brunello di Montalcino '02	ᵀ 6
● Le Prata '04	ᵀ 5

Il Lebbio

LOC. SAN BENEDETTO, 11c
53037 SAN GIMIGNANO [SI]
TEL. 0577944725
www.illebbio.it

Il Lebbio has taken a big step up in quality. Vernaccia Tropìe '06 is very nice, presenting edgy, balanced and flavoursome. Polito '04 is solid, soft and complex, the fruit-rich I Grottoni '06 is well focused and the attractively priced Chianti '06 has a fragrant palate.

● Polito '04	ᵀᵀ 6
O Vernaccia di S. Gimignano Tropìe '06	ᵀᵀ 4*
● Chianti '06	ᵀ 3
● I Grottoni '06	ᵀ 4

Castello La Leccia

LOC. LA LECCIA
53011 CASTELLINA IN CHIANTI [SI]
TEL. 0577743148
www.castellolaleccia.com

Francesco Daddi's wines performed well, even if we think that the Chianti Classico Bruciagna has yet to realize its full potential. The '04 version has an agreeable nose of intense fruity sensations and a dynamic, juicy palate. The Chianti Classico '05's palate is impeccable.

● Chianti Cl. Bruciagna '04	ᵀᵀ 5
● Chianti Cl. '05	ᵀ 4
● Chianti Cl. Bruciagna '01	ᵀᵀᵀ 6

La Lecciaia

LOC. VALLAFRICO
53024 MONTALCINO [SI]
TEL. 0583928366
www.lecciaia.it

This cellar in eastern Montalcino continues to grow. The excellent Brunello Riserva '01 has a fruity nose setting black and wild cherry aromas off against vanilla. Acidity sustains the palate's wonderful texture. The two '02 Brunellos, the standard label and the Vigna Manapietra, are well typed and pleasant.

● Brunello di Montalcino Ris. '01	ᵀᵀ 8
● Brunello di Montalcino Manapetra '02	ᵀ 6
● Rosso di Montalcino '05	ᵀ 4
● Brunello di Montalcino '02	ᵀ 6

Lodola Nuova - Tenimenti Ruffino

FRAZ. VALIANO
VIA LODOLA, 1
53045 MONTEPULCIANO [SI]
TEL. 0578724032
www.ruffino.com

We can always count on Lodola Nuova to produce wines of quality. The aromas of the '03 Nobile Riserva are muddled as yet but the palate is well rounded and complex. The simple but bright Nobile '04 is very drinkable. The Rosso '06 is approachable, fresh-tasting and well sustained.

● Nobile di Montepulciano Ris. '03	ᵀᵀ 5
● Nobile di Montepulciano '04	ᵀ 5
● Rosso di Montepulciano '06	ᵀ 4
● Nobile di Montepulciano '03	ᵀᵀ 5

Castello di Lucignano

LOC. LUCIGNANO
53013 GAIOLE IN CHIANTI [SI]
TEL. 0577747810
www.castellodilucignano.com

Gerd Schué is back in the Guide with an exciting '04 version of Il Sommo. Obtained from merlot only, it has an unusual range of mineral-led aromatics. The other wines on offer are less inspiring. They're well styled but stiff tannins tend to hold back progression.

● Il Sommo '04	ᵀᵀ 5
● Chianti Cl. '04	ᵀ 4
● Solissimo '03	ᵀ 7

OTHER WINERIES

Luiano
LOC. MERCATALE VAL DI PESA
VIA DI LUIANO, 32
50024 SAN CASCIANO IN VAL DI PESA [FI]
TEL. 0558211039
www.luiano.it

This estate in Mercatale Val di Pesa makes its first appearance in the Guide with a very attractive Lui '04 from cabernet sauvignon, merlot and colorino. Spice and jam on the nose precede a well-rounded, supple body that ends in a sweet finish. Sangiò '05 from sangiovese and merlot is pleasant.

● Lui '04	♟♟	5
● Sangiò '05	♟	5

Le Macioche
S.P. 55 DI SANT'ANTIMO, KM 4,85
53024 MONTALCINO [SI]
TEL. 0577849168
lemacioche@tiscali.it

Brunello Riserva '01 was the only wine presented for tasting this year by Le Macioche but what a wine it is, earning a place in our finals. The complex peach and morello cherry nose is lifted by nuances of medicinal herbs and leather, then fine tannins lend elegance to a palate with a lingering finale.

● Brunello di Montalcino Ris. '01	♟♟	7
● Brunello di Montalcino '99	♟♟	6
● Brunello di Montalcino Ris. '97	♟♟	7

La Magia
LOC. LA MAGIA
53024 MONTALCINO [SI]
TEL. 0577835667
fattorialamagia@tiscali.it

La Magia sits on a stunning terrace overlooking the abbey of Sant'Antimo. This year, we enjoyed a first-rate Brunello Riserva '01 with intense fruit mingling with flowers on the nose. The convincing palate is well sustained by tannins and shows substantial extractive weight.

● Brunello di Montalcino Ris. '01	♟♟	8

Fattoria Maionchi
LOC. TOFORI
VIA DI TOFORI, 81
55012 LUCCA [LU]
TEL. 0583978194
www.fattoriamaionchi.it

Fattoria Maionchi is located in the charming amphitheatre of hills that rises above the Lucca plain. This year's good performance was mainly down to Cintello '03, from sangiovese with a little canaiolo. It develops subtly and seamlessly on the palate, parading balanced tannins.

● Cintello '03	♟♟	5
● Colline Lucchesi Rosso '06	♟	4

Malenchini
LOC. GRASSINA
VIA LILLIANO E MEOLI, 82
50015 BAGNO A RIPOLI [FI]
TEL. 055642602
www.malenchini.it

The Malenchini family's estate repeated last year's performance but we believe it can do even better. The sangiovese and cabernet sauvignon Bruzzico '04 is particularly good, giving fresh aromatic herbs and black berry fruit, solid but balanced body and a finish that builds up nicely.

● Bruzzico '04	♟♟	5
● Chianti Colli Fiorentini '05	♟	4

La Mannella
LOC. LA MANNELLA, 322
53024 MONTALCINO [SI]
TEL. 0577848268
www.lamannella.it

Marco Cortonesi presented two fine wines from a vintage that was particularly challenging. The Brunello '02 has a complex nose with concentrated notes of blackberry and cherry and follows through full and tasty in the mouth, supported by sweet tannins. The finish is amazingly intense for the growing year.

● Brunello di Montalcino '02	♟♟	6
● Rosso di Montalcino '02	♟♟	4*

OTHER WINERIES

Il Marroneto
LOC. MADONNA DELLE GRAZIE, 307
53024 MONTALCINO [SI]
TEL. 0577849382
www.ilmarroneto.it

Coming from two cool growing years – and 2002 also had copious rainfall – the two wines offered by Il Marroneto this year were not really up to snuff. Although technically faultless, both the Brunello '02 and the Rosso '05 lack the complexity on the palate that would have earned another Glass.

● Brunello di Montalcino '02	▼	7
● Rosso di Montalcino Ignaccio '05	▼	5
● Brunello di Montalcino '01	▼▼	7

Martoccia
POD. MARTOCCIA
53024 MONTALCINO [SI]
TEL. 0577848540
www.tenutabrunelli.it

Luca Brunelli's estate showed well on the back of its two Brunellos. The '02's warm nose melds clear red berry and blackberry aromas with attractively balanced oaky notes. The ripe tannins are close-knit and the finish is harmonious. The well-made Riserva '01 is compact in structure.

● Brunello di Montalcino '02	▼▼	6
● Brunello di Montalcino Ris. '01	▼▼	7
● Rosso di Montalcino '05	▼	4

Cosimo Maria Masini
VIA POGGIO AL PINO, 16
56028 SAN MINIATO [PI]
TEL. 3488660042
www.cosimomariamasini.it

There's clear improvement in the wines produced by this small San Miniato cellar. The very attractive chardonnay and sauvignon Annick '06 offers a subtle, crisp nose of peaches and aromatic herbs. The reds also showed well, having lost their over-concentration and acquired a nice territory focus.

O Annick '06	▼▼	4
● Nicole '05	▼	4
● Nicolò '04	▼	5

Giorgio Meletti Cavallari
57022 CASTAGNETO CARDUCCI [LI]
TEL. 0565775620
www.vini-meletticavallari.com

Giorgio Meletti Cavallari founded his estate in 2002 with ten hectares planted to vine in various zones. Bolgheri Rosso Borgeri '06 from cabernet sauvignon, syrah and merlot is admirable. Its full, complex nose offers vegetal, black berry fruit aromas but the young palate is rather curbed by its tannins.

● Bolgheri Rosso Borgeri '06	▼▼	4
● Bolgheri Rosso Impronte '04	▼▼	6

Fattoria Migliarina
LOC. MIGLIARINA, 84
52021 BUCINE [AR]
TEL. 0559788243
www.migliarina.it

This estate in the Colli Aretini next to Valdarno and Valdambra debuts in the Guide with some interesting wines. Obtained from sangiovese, merlot and cabernet, the Cavasonno '05 has all the style, density, power and depth of the noblest Supertuscans. All this and value for money. The Chianti '04 is pleasant.

● Cavasonno '05	▼▼	3*
● Chianti Sup. '04	▼	3

Poderi di Miscianello
LOC. PONTE A BOZZONE
S.S. CHIANTIGIANA, 408
53010 SIENA [SI]
TEL. 0577356840
www.miscianello.it

Miscianello is a pretty little village transformed into an agriturismo complex. Wine production is limited. The '04 version of the Riserva del Chianti Classico is very successful, offering lovely fruit and flower sensations then a solid, edgy palate with a long, satisfying finish. The Petti Rosso '04 is nice.

● Chianti Classico Regio Ris. '04	▼▼	5
● Petti Rosso '04	▼	4

OTHER WINERIES

Monte Bernardi
VIA CHIANTIGIANA
50020 PANZANO [FI]
TEL. 055852400
www.montebernardi.com

The wines produced by Michael Schmelzer's estate put on a so-so performance this time. The nose of the Tzingana '05 has yet to absorb the oak while the dynamic palate has depth of flavour and a fascinating finish. The Chianti Classico '05 is elegant and fresh-tasting.

● Tzingana '05	♟♟ 7
● Chianti Cl. '05	♟ 5
● Tzingana '97	♟♟♟ 6

Montecalvi
VIA CITILLE, 85
50022 GREVE IN CHIANTI [FI]
TEL. 0558544665
www.montecalvi.com

Jacqueline Bolli and Daniel O'Byrne's wines were below par this year. Montecalvi VV '04, from sangiovese, cabernet sauvignon and other varieties, is good. It's rather closed on the nose but shows well in the mouth, where it tends to elegance rather than power. The Chianti Classico '05 is nice if light-bodied.

● Montecalvi Vieille Vigne '04	♟♟ 7
● Chianti Cl. '05	♟ 5

Montecucco
LOC. MONTECUCCO
58044 CINIGIANO [GR]
TEL. 0564999029
www.tenutadimontecucco.it

Known as the territory's emblematic cellar, this is the estate that put Montecucco on the map. It offers a series of very interesting reds with the Montecucco Sangiovese Le Coste '04 in fine fettle. Rigomoro, its flagship wine, pays the price for a poor growing year.

● Montecucco Le Coste '04	♟♟ 5
● Canaiolo '06	♟ 3
● Montecucco Passonaia '05	♟ 4
● Montecucco Rigomoro Ris. '03	♟ 5

Tenuta Monteti
S.DA DELLA SGRILLA, 6
58011 CAPALBIO [GR]
TEL. 0564896160
www.tenutamonteti.it

Derived from cabernet sauvignon, alicante and merlot, the '05 Caburnio is deliciously fresh and drinkable. Monteti '05, from cabernet sauvignon, petit verdot and cabernet franc with a little alicante and merlot, is more complex and richly textured, but has still to integrate the oak of the barriques.

● Caburnio '05	♟♟ 4
● Monteti '05	♟♟ 6
● Monteti '04	♟♟ 6
● Caburnio '04	♟♟ 4

Tenute Silvio Nardi
LOC. CASALE DEL BOSCO
53024 MONTALCINO [SI]
TEL. 0577808269
www.tenutenardi.com

Two challenging years in northern Montalcino have not prevented Emilia Nardi from presenting a Brunello '02 and a Rosso '05 that may not be huge but are well styled. The very fine Merlot '05 has well-defined raspberry and currants offset against toasty sensations and a smooth, captivating palate.

● Rosso di Montalcino '05	♟ 5
● Brunello di Montalcino '02	♟ 6
● Sant'Antimo Tùran '05	♟ 4
● Sant'Antimo Merlot '05	♟ 4

Nottola
FRAZ. GRACCIANO
VIA BIVIO DI NOTTOLA, 9A
53040 MONTEPULCIANO [SI]
TEL. 0578707060
www.cantinanottola.it

There was a low-key performance from Giomarelli family's wines. The Nobile '04 is complex on the palate but the nose is muddled and hangs mainly on toastiness from barrique ageing. Meanwhile, the Vigna del Fattore '03 offers an attractive nose but the stiffish palate has difficulty unbending.

● Nobile di Montepulciano '04	♟ 5
● Nobile di Montepulciano V. del Fattore '03	♟ 6
● Nobile di Montepulciano '03	♟♟ 5
● Nobile di Montepulciano V. del Fattore '02	♟♟ 5

OTHER WINERIES

No,vo'li'

LOC. SANT'ALBINO
VIA FONTECORNINO
53045 MONTEPULCIANO [SI]
TEL. 0578799166
www.no-vo-li.it

Giuseppe Putzulu's range did well, with all the virtues and vices of wines from young vines. The cabernet sauvignon and merlot-based Tavernaia '05 and La Scudiscia '05, from sangiovese, syrah and merlot, are well made. Cavernano '05, from sangiovese, cabernet sauvignon, merlot and syrah, lacks definition.

● Tavernaia '05	🍷🍷	5
● La Scudiscia '05	🍷🍷	5
● Cavernano '05	🍷	4

Podere Orma

VIA BOLGHERESE
57022 CASTAGNETO CARDUCCI [LI]
TEL. 0575477857
www.tenutasetteponti.it

It was a good Guide debut for Antonio Moretti's Bolgheri winery, stablemate of his Arezzo-based Tenuta Sette Ponti. The first vintage, Orma '05, a creditable, equal parts blend of cabernet franc and merlot, integrated with cabernet sauvignon, had a deep-toned, balsamic nose and a taut, full, tannic palate.

● Orma '05	🍷🍷	8

Pakravan-Papi

LOC. ORTACAVOLI - NOCOLINO
56046 RIPARBELLA [PI]
TEL. 0586786076
www.pakravan-papi.it

At long last Pakravan Papi's wines made it into the Guide, thanks to a monovarietal merlot, Beccacciaia '05, making a good show with good aromatic intensity and a dynamic palate. We liked the very drinkable monovarietal sangiovese, Gabbriccio '05.

● Beccacciaia '05	🍷🍷	6
○ Serra dei Cocci '06	🍷	4
● Montescudaio Gabbriccio '05	🍷	4

Castello Il Palagio

FRAZ. CAMPOLI
VIA CAMPOLI, 140
50024 SAN CASCIANO IN VAL DI PESA [FI]
TEL. 055821630
www.palagio.net

Il Palagio is back in the Guide, thanks mainly to a positive Chianti Classico '04 with appealing fruity notes and a compact body, nice tannic weave and a tasty finish. The rest of the range is more run-of-the-mill, like the Riserva '03, whose complex structure lacks symmetry. The Vin Santo '99 is well styled.

● Chianti Cl. '04	🍷🍷	4
● Chianti Cl. Ris. '03	🍷	4
○ Vin Santo del Chianti Cl. '99	🍷	7

Fattoria Il Palagio

FRAZ. CASTEL SAN GIMIGNANO
LOC. IL PALAGIO
53030 COLLE DI VAL D'ELSA [SI]
TEL. 0577953004
www.ilpalagio.com

Sauvignon, here an '06, continues to be a winner for this winery. The intense nose reveals fruit, tomato and elder leaves, then the full palate has supple freshness and pleasing finish. The Chardonnay '06 has a brisk, balanced palate but little depth. Vernaccia '06 has a dry palate and floral fragrances.

○ Il Palagio Sauvignon '06	🍷🍷	4
● Chianti Colli Senesi '06	🍷	3
○ Il Palagio Chardonnay '06	🍷	4
○ Vernaccia di S. Gimignano '06	🍷	4

Il Palagione

VIA PER CASTEL SAN GIMIGNANO, 36
53037 SAN GIMIGNANO [SI]
TEL. 0577953134
www.ilpalagione.com

Il Palagione's Vernaccias are preferable to its reds. The lively Vernaccia Hydra '06 is well balanced and the new Vernaccia Ori '04 is full, zesty and deep. Antajr, a sangiovese, cabernet sauvignon and merlot blend, lacks acidic drive. The Chianti Riserva Draco '04 is worth trying.

○ Vernaccia di S. Gimignano Hydra '06	🍷🍷	3*
○ Vernaccia di S. Gimignano Ori '04	🍷🍷	5
● Chianti Colli Senesi Draco Ris. '04	🍷	4
● Antajr '04	🍷	6

OTHER WINERIES

Palazzo
LOC. PALAZZO, 144
53024 MONTALCINO [SI]
TEL. 0577848479
www.aziendapalazzo.it

Le Cerbaie is one of the best areas on Montalcino's eastern slope, and this winery is a good example. A well-typed Brunello Riserva '01 presents a fruity, balsamic nose, nuanced with incense, then a weighty palate had a touch too much bite in the tannin. The Brunello '02 is satisfying.

- Brunello di Montalcino Ris. '01   ♟♟ 8
- Brunello di Montalcino '02   ♟ 7
- Rosso di Montalcino '05   ♟ 5

Palazzo Vecchio
FRAZ. VALIANO
VIA TERRAROSSA, 5
53040 MONTEPULCIANO [SI]
TEL. 0578724170
www.vinonobile.it

Palazzo Vecchio's owners, Marco Sbernadori and Maria Alessandra Zorzi, presented attractive wines. The lively Nobile '04, with its subtle, nuanced fragrances, has an easy, full-flavoured palate. Nobile Terrarossa '03 was more succulent, showing character but tripping on the tannins. The Rosso '05 is a good effort.

- Nobile di Montepulciano '04   ♟♟ 5
- Nobile di Montepulciano Terrarossa '03 ♟♟ 6
- Rosso Montepulciano '05   ♟ 4

Parmoleto
LOC. MONTENERO D'ORCIA
POD. PARMOLETONE, 44
58040 CASTEL DEL PIANO [GR]
TEL. 0564954131
www.parmoleto.it

This small winery produces just 20,000 bottles from less than five hectares of estate. The top wine is the '05 Sormonno, a splendid sangiovese base with touches of cabernet sauvignon and montepulciano. We also liked the Montecucco Rosso '05, Montecucco Sangiovese Riserva '04 and Carabatto Bianco '06.

- Sormonno '05   ♟♟ 5
- O Carabatto '06   ♟♟ 3
- Montecucco Rosso '05   ♟♟ 4
- Montecucco Sangiovese Ris. '04   ♟ 5

Tenuta La Parrina
S.DA VICINALE DELLA PARRINA
58010 ALBINIA [GR]
TEL. 0564862636
www.parrina.it

We thought Franca Spinola's wines were below par. The expansive Parrina Riserva '05 is broad juicy. Parrina Muraccio '05 is unexciting but even and flavoursome. Radaia '05 is a little over-evolved on the nose, but better on the palate, which is refreshing, lively and well sustained.

- Parrina Rosso Ris. '05   ♟♟ 5
- Parrina Rosso Muraccio '05   ♟ 4
- Radaia '05   ♟ 7
- Radaia '04   ♟♟ 7

Perazzeta
LOC. MONTENERO D'ORCIA
VIA DELL'AIA, 14
58040 CASTEL DEL PIANO [GR]
TEL. 0564954158
www.perazzeta.it

A mere eight hectares under vine here yield just over 50,000 bottles. Our favourite is the Merlot '05, which gives a faultless rendering of the grape. The other reds aren't bad at all and the Alfeno '06, a white from chardonnay, trebbiano, malvasia and sauvignon, is also agreeable.

- Merlot '05   ♟♟ 6
- O Alfeno Bianco '06   ♟ 3
- Montecucco Alfeno Rosso '05   ♟ 4
- Montecucco Terre dei Bocci '04   ♟ 4

Fattoria La Peschiera
LOC. LA PESCHIERA
58050 SATURNIA [GR]
TEL. 0564601019
www.fattorialapeschiera.com

A good Morellino di Scansano '05 surprised us with its complex balsamic notes, which give some edge to the distinctly intense fruit. Well orchestrated on the palate, it gives sturdy flesh underpinned by lively acidity. The Morellino Vivius '04 is tasty and complex but the finish is a little mouth-drying.

- Morellino di Scansano '05   ♟♟ 4
- Morellino di Scansano Vivius '04   ♟♟ 4
- Morellino di Scansano '03   ♟♟ 4

OTHER WINERIES

Fattoria di Petroio

LOC. QUERCEGROSSA
VIA DI MOCENNI, 7
53010 CASTELNUOVO BERARDENGA [SI]
TEL. 0577328045
www.chianticlassico.com

The Lenzi winery seems to be struggling to repeat the excellent achievements of past years. A good Riserva '04 has ripe fruit hints and just a bit too much tannin. The Chianti Classico '05 is less balanced but the Poggio al Mandorlo '06, from sangiovese and merlot, is enjoyable.

● Chianti Cl. Ris. '04	♥♥ 5
● Chianti Cl. '05	♥ 4
● Poggio al Mandorlo '06	♥ 3

Pian del Pino

P.ZZA ANDROMEDA, 10
52100 AREZZO [AR]
TEL. 057522092
giovannibatacchi@virgilio.it

This winery, with vines beneath Pratomagno, at Campogialli, made it Guide debut with two interesting wines. The expansive Sangiovese Jubilus '05 is nuanced with flowers and aromatic herbs. The savoury Pian del Pino '05, from sangiovese, colorino and canaiolo, is more closed, earthy and still edgy.

● Jubilus '05	♥♥ 4
● Pian del Pino '05	♥ 4

Agostina Pieri

FRAZ. SANT'ANGELO SCALO
LOC. PIANCORNELLO
53026 MONTALCINO [SI]
TEL. 0577844163
pieriagostina@libero.it

There are good bottles from this winery, one of the best-known on Montalcino's southern boundary. The Brunello '02 has a classic nose, with medicinal herbs, warm hide and floral touches. We'd say it's mouthfilling, agile and lingering, buoyed by its acid backbone. The Rosso '05 also did well.

● Brunello di Montalcino '02	♥♥ 6
● Rosso di Montalcino '05	♥♥ 5
● Rosso di Montalcino '95	♥♥♥ 5
● Brunello di Montalcino '97	♥♥ 7

Pieve di Campoli

VIA CAMPOLI, 123
50026 SAN CASCIANO
IN VAL DI PESA [FI]
TEL. 055821043

The winery owned by the diocese of Florence made it into the Guide for a second year, thanks to a good show from the Chianti Classico Riserva '04. This sturdy wine with minerals and fruit on the nose has a plush but symmetrical body and a lip-smacking finish. The Chianti Classico '05 is agreeable but thinnish.

● Chianti Cl. Ris. '04	♥♥ 5
● Chianti Cl. '05	♥ 4

La Pieve

LOC. LA PIEVE
VIA SANTO STEFANO
50050 MONTAIONE [FI]
TEL. 0571697764
simonetognetti@virgilio.it

Simone Tognetti did well again this year with a good, solid Rosso del Pievano '05, from sangiovese and cabernet sauvignon, showing deep spice on the nose and developing with promise. The Chianti '06 has a concentrated, approachable palate. The austere, tannin-rich Chianti Fortebraccio '05 finishes crisp.

● Chianti Cl. La Pieve '06	♥♥ 3*
● Rosso del Pievano '05	♥♥ 4
● Chianti Fortebraccio '05	♥ 3*

Tenuta Podernovo

LOC. TERRICCIOLA
VIA PODERNUOVO, 13
56030 PISA [PI]
TEL. 0587655173
www.tenutapodernovo.it

Corrado Dalpiaz's skilled vineyard and cellar management produce some attractively well-defined wines, as you might expect when Tuscan warmth meets the Lunelli family's northern thoroughness. The Aliotto '05 is still maturing but shows promise but the '04 Teuto is not as good as last year's.

● Aliotto '05	♥♥ 4
● Teuto '04	♥ 5

OTHER WINERIES

Poggio al Tesoro
LOC. FELCIAINO
VIA BOLGHERESE, 189B
57020 BOLGHERI [LI]
TEL. 0565765245
info@poggioaltesoro.it

The winery was founded by the Allegrini family, from Valpolicella, in partnership with Leonardo Lo Cascio, a US wine distributor. This year, we tried two excellent wines: Sondraia '04, mainly cabernet sauvignon, with merlot and cabernet franc; and Dedicato a Walter '04, a monovarietal cabernet franc.

● Sondraia '04	¶¶	6
● Dedicato a Walter '04	¶¶	6
● Sondraia '03	¶¶	6

Poggio Amorelli
LOC. POGGIO AMORELLI
53011 CASTELLINA IN CHIANTI [SI]
TEL. 0571668733
poggioamorelli@libero.it

Marco Mazzarrini's winery is under par this year after the '05 harvest. We were unexcited by the Chianti Classico or the sangiovese-based Gode II. The former has more texture and the latter is thinner, so despite being decent wines, they aren't up to the usual standards. We're sure this is a temporary setback.

● Gode II '05	¶	4
● Chianti Cl. '05	¶	4

Poggio Capponi
LOC. SAN DONATO A LIVIZZANO
VIA MONTELUPO, 184
50025 MONTESPERTOLI [FI]
TEL. 0571671914
www.poggiocapponi.it

Poggio Capponi wines get better and better. We like the Tinorso '05, a merlot and syrah blend with an intense, intriguing nose, a full, developing palate and sweet tannins. A zesty monovarietal chardonnay, Sovente '06, has a lush, substantial flavour, with acidic backbone. The Chianti '06 is smooth and tidy.

O Sovente '06	¶¶	4
● Tinorso '05	¶¶	5
● Chianti Poggio Capponi '06	¶	3*

Poggio Foco
LOC. POGGIO FUOCO
58014 MANCIANO [GR]
TEL. 0564620537
www.poggiofoco.com

An exquisite Sesà '04 from cabernet sauvignon and merlot is the key wine from the Kovarich cellar. The aromatics are well defined and the palate impresses with stylish tannic weave and a lingering finish. The flavoursome Sovana Secondo '05 is a little predictable but has texture and is juicy and drinkable.

● Sesà '04	¶¶	6
● Sovana Rosso Sup. Secondo '05	¶¶	5
● Sesà '02	¶¶	6
● Sesà '03	¶¶	6

Poggio Lungo
LOC. VII ZONA GRANCIA
58100 GROSSETO [GR]
TEL. 0564409268

The Poggio Lungo winery, owned by the Fornaseri family, is a welcome new entry with three very intriguing Morellinos. The well-balanced '05 has intense aromas and a flavoursome palate. The Riserva '01 is full flavoured, with a healthy nose and an austere palate. We enjoyed the Riserva '03.

● Morellino di Scansano '05	¶¶	4
● Morellino di Scansano Ris. '01	¶¶	4
● Morellino di Scansano Ris. '03	¶	4

Tenuta Poggio Verrano
S.DA PROVINCIALE N° 9 - KM 4
58051 MAGLIANO IN TOSCANA [GR]
TEL. 0564589943
www.poggioverrano.it

Dròmos '05 – the name refers to Etruscan tomb architecture – is the only wine made by Francesco Bolla. This distinctive blend of sangiovese, cabernet sauvignon, cabernet franc and alicante went into the taste-offs again this year, thanks to a successful mix of layered structure, elegance and symmetry.

● Dròmos '05	¶¶	8
● Dròmos '04	¶¶	8
● Dròmos '03	¶¶	8

OTHER WINERIES

Il Poggiolo
LOC. POGGIOLO, 259
53024 MONTALCINO [SI]
TEL. 0577848412
www.ilpoggiolomontalcino.com

Rudy Cosimi presented various wines this year but we opted for the excellent poise of the very appealing Rosso di Montalcino Quello Buono '05. The Rosso '05, clenched by over-the-top tannins, didn't quite hit the spot. The Brunello '02 is typical of the vintage, showing slightly thin.

● Rosso di Montalcino Quello Buono '05	♟♟ 4
● Brunello di Montalcino '02	♟ 7
● Rosso di Montalcino '05	♟ 4

Poggiopaoli
LOC. POMONTE
V.LE RAGNAIE, 64
58054 SCANSANO [GR]
TEL. 0564599408
poggiopaoli@infinito.it

Paolo Fiorani and Paola Emanuelli's 20-hectare estate produces about 30,000 bottles a year, most of them Morellino. The tasty Lorenzolo '06 shows nice flesh and intense aromas. The spirited '06 Pomonte's refreshing nose is nicely set off by a taut palate.

● Morellino di Scansano Lorenzolo '06	♟♟ 4
● Morellino di Scansano Pomonte '06	♟♟ 4
● Morellino di Scansano Lorenzolo '05	♟♟ 4
● Morellino di Scansano Pomonte '04	♟♟ 4

Il Pozzo
VIA PIAVE, 1
50068 RUFINA [FI]
TEL. 0558399102
gianfranco.caselli@tin.it

The Bellini family purchased this estate in 1998 and its well-styled Chianti Rufina Riserva '04 justifies this Guide entry with a cool, pleasing nose and plush, symmetrical body, accompanied by a juicy finish. The Chianti Rufina '05 is agreeable but somewhat thin.

● Chianti Rufina Ris. '04	♟♟ 4
● Chianti Rufina '05	♟ 3

Querceto di Castellina
LOC. QUERCETO, 9
53011 CASTELLINA IN CHIANTI [SI]
TEL. 0577733590
www.querceto.com

The '05 harvest affected Jacopo Di Battista's winery. We picked out the Podalirio '05, a sangiovese and merlot blend with aromas of spice and toasty oak notes. The velvety body fades mid palate but has a juicy finish. The Chianti Classico '05 is a tad unbending on the palate.

● Podalirio '05	♟♟ 6
● Chianti Cl. L'Aura '05	♟ 4
● Podalirio '01	♟♟♟ 6

Quercia al Poggio
FRAZ. MONSANTO
S.DA QUERCIA AL POGGIO, 4
50021 BARBERINO VAL D'ELSA [FI]
TEL. 0558075278
www.quercialpoggio.com

This winery is guaranteed to come up with attractive products every year. This time, we found the Chianti Classico '04 to be delicious and complex, with a well-developed bouquet, mineral tang and racy structure with a nice follow-through. The Riserva '03 was less appealing, flagging on the back palate.

● Chianti Cl. '04	♟♟ 4
● Chianti Cl. Ris. '03	♟ 5

Rampa di Fugnano
FRAZ. CELLOLE
LOC. FUGNANO
53037 SAN GIMIGNANO [SI]
TEL. 0577941655
www.rampadifugnano.it

We were disappointed with Rampa di Fugnano's performance this year. Vernaccia Privato '05 stands out for its dense, cool, ripe palate. The viognier-only Vi ogni è '05 has a round, ripe palate but not much grip. The Merlot Gisèle '05 has little complexity or depth. The flowery Vernaccia Alata '06 is nice.

O Vernaccia di S. Gimignano Privato '05	♟♟ 4
● Gisèle '05	♟ 6
O Vernaccia di S. Gimignano Alata '06	♟ 4
O Vi ogni è '05	♟ 4

OTHER WINERIES

La Rasina
LOC. RASINA, 132
53024 MONTALCINO [SI]
TEL. 0577848536
www.larasina.it

Last year's revelation winery did not produce a Brunello '02, feeling the vintage was not up to its standards. The only wine presented was a Rosso di Montalcino '05, which weaves nuances of fruit, flowers and tobacco on the nose. It's pleasant, if a little predictable, in the mouth, with nice tannins.

● Rosso di Montalcino '05	♟	5
● Brunello di Montalcino '00	♟♟♟	6
● Brunello di Montalcino '01	♟♟♟	7
● Brunello di Montalcino Il Divasco '01	♟♟♟	7

Redi
VIA DI COLLAZZI, 5
53045 MONTEPULCIANO [SI]
TEL. 0578716092
www.cantinadelredi.com

We enjoyed a very good Orbaio '04, from sangiovese, merlot and cabernet sauvignon, with good black berry and graphite aromas and a flavoursome, vibrant palate. Mild fruitiness distinguishes the Vecchia Cantina Nobile '04, which is full bodied and uncomplicated on the palate.

● Orbaio '04	♟♟	5
● Nobile di Montepulciano Vecchia Cantina '04	♟	4

La Regola
VIA A. GRAMSCI, 1
56046 RIPARBELLA [PI]
TEL. 0586698145
www.laregola.com

The Nuti brothers just made the grade this year. Their best effort was the sangiovese and cabernet sauvignon Vallino '05, which is sound and fresh, showing personality and a lavish nose of red fruits and spices, unfolding attractively on the palate. The Steccaia '06 is clean and consistent.

● Montescudaio Rosso Vallino '05	♟♟	5
● Montescudaio Rosso La Regola '04	♟	6
● Montescudaio Rosso Ligustro '06	♟	4
O Montescudaio Bianco Steccaia '06	♟	4

Renieri
LOC RENIERI
53024 MONTALCINO [SI]
TEL. 0577359330
www.renierimontalcino.com

Chianti-based Castello di Bossi's Montalcino winery gave us well-typed wines again. We liked the Regina di Renieri '04 this year, for the spice and mineral notes on a nose nuanced with jam and a hint of grass. The dense palate is a touch too tannic. We're waiting to see how the first Brunello turns out.

● Re di Renieri '05	♟	6
● Rosso di Montalcino '05	♟	5
● Regina di Renieri '04	♟	6

Rignana
LOC. RIGNANA, 15
50022 GREVE IN CHIANTI [FI]
TEL. 055852065
www.rignana.it

Cosimo Gericke's winery comes and goes in our Guide with its small quantities of distinctively feisty, well-styled wines. This time, we preferred the Chianti Classico '04, with complex aromatic nuances, an expansive body and firm tannins. The Riserva '03 wasn't quite so relaxed.

● Chianti Cl. '04	♟♟	4
● Chianti Cl. Ris. '03	♟	5

Rigoloccio
VIA PROVINCIALE, 82
58023 GAVORRANO [GR]
TEL. 056645464
www.rigoloccio.it

The Abati and Puggelli families, with cellarman Fabrizio Moltard, make their Guide debut. Il Sorvegliante '05, from cabernet sauvignon, cabernet franc and alicante, has a solid palate and stylish nose. The savoury Chardonnay Fiano '06 is fresh-tasting. The less complex '05 Merlot and Cabernet Alicante are OK.

O Chardonnay Fiano '06	♟♟	4
● Il Sorvegliante '05	♟♟	5
● Cabernet Alicante '05	♟	4
● Merlot '05	♟	4

OTHER WINERIES

Il Rio
VIA DI PADULE, 131
50039 VICCHIO [FI]
TEL. 0558407904

Il Rio is a niche winery. We liked the monovarietal pinot nero Ventisei '05, aged in barrique for 12 months, for its delicate aromas on the nose and balanced, well-sustained palate, with gentle, close-woven tannins and fruity finish. The fleshy Annita '06, from chardonnay and pinot nero, has good grip.

● Ventisei '05	♟♟	5
O Annita '06	♟	4

Fattoria La Ripa
FRAZ. SAN DONATO IN POGGIO
S.P. PER CASTELLINA IN CHIANTI, 27
50021 BARBERINO VAL D'ELSA [FI]
TEL. 0558072948
www.laripa.it

The best of the range is the Santa Brigida '03, a sangiovese and cabernet sauvignon blend with ripe fruits-led aromatics and a well-structured, compact body with a lengthy, full-flavoured finish. The rest of the range is acceptable.

● Santa Brigida '03	♟♟	5
● Chianti Cl. '05	♟	4
● Chianti Cl. Ris. '03	♟	5
● Le Terre di Monna Lisa '04	♟	3

Massimo Romeo
FRAZ. GRACCIANO
LOC. NOTTOLA, S.S. 326, 25
53040 MONTEPULCIANO [SI]
TEL. 0578708599
www.massimoromeo.it

Nobile Lipitiresco – '04 this time – again emerged as the flagship from Massimo Romeo. The fragrance is rich and upfront, with ripe fruit and hints of spice to round off. The compact, solidly built palate has a sweet finish. The Nobile '04 is subtle and understated while the fresh Rosso '06 is nice.

● Nobile di Montepulciano Lipitiresco '04	♟♟	6
● Nobile di Montepulciano '04	♟	5
● Rosso di Montepulciano '06	♟	4
● Nobile di Montepulciano Lipitiresco '03	♟♟	5

Castello Romitorio
LOC. ROMITORIO, 279
53024 MONTALCINO [SI]
TEL. 0577897220
www.castelloromitorio.com

Sandro Chia's admirable winery is back to its usual standards after a slight setback. The Brunello '02 is solid, with marked balsam on the nose backing up the intense florality. The palate is nicely balanced thanks to restrained extraction and appealingly discreet acidity.

● Brunello di Montalcino '02	♟♟	8
● Sant'Antimo Rosso Romito del Romitorio '04	♟♟	6
● Rosso di Montalcino '05	♟	5
● Brunello di Montalcino Ris. '97	♟♟♟	8

La Sala
LOC. PONTEROTTO
VIA SORRIPA, 34
50026 SAN CASCIANO IN VAL DI PESA [FI]
TEL. 055828111
www.lasala.it

Laura Baronti's wines were a bit of a let-down. We picked out a Chianti Classico Riserva '04 for its wide-ranging aromatic profile, where ripe fruit fuses pleasantly with stylish spice. The dense, full-bodied palate offers a nicely co-ordinated finish. The other wines lack balance.

● Chianti Cl. Ris. '04	♟♟	6
● Campo all'Albero '04	♟	6
● Chianti Cl. '05	♟	4

Podere Salicutti
POD. SALICUTTI, 174
53024 MONTALCINO [SI]
TEL. 0577847003
www.poderesalicutti.it

This was a transition year for this winery, owned by Francesco Leanza, a Sicilian who moved to Montalcino years ago. He was one of the first to opt for organic methods. This year, Francesco gave us a range of well-typed wines. Our favourite was Dopoteatro '05, for its personality and sound tannins.

● Brunello di Montalcino '02	♟	8
● Dopoteatro '05	♟	6
● Rosso di Montalcino '05	♟	5
● Brunello di Montalcino '97	♟♟♟	8

OTHER WINERIES

Fattoria San Donato
Loc. San Donato, 6
53037 San Gimignano [SI]
TEL. 0577941616
www.sandonato.it

This year, Fattoria San Donato presented interesting wines. The Vernaccia Angelica '05 has a full, fresh palate that holds together well and lingers nicely. We thought the feisty, aromatic Chianti Fiamma '05 was tasty, as was the appealingly unfussy Chianti Riserva Fede '04, which has spice and structure.

● Chianti Colli Senesi Fiamma '05	♟♟	4*
● Chianti Colli Senesi Fede Ris. '04	♟♟	4*
O Vernaccia di S. Gimignano Angelica '05	♟♟	4*

Castello di San Donato in Perano
Loc. San Donato in Perano
53013 Gaiole in Chianti [SI]
TEL. 0577738012
www.castellosandonato.it

After some intensive replanting, the first results are now starting to come through. We liked the Chianti Classico '04 best, for its clean, crisp fruit fragrance and vibrant, well-defined body. The other wines are still seeking their true identity.

● Chianti Cl. '04	♟♟	4*
● Chianti Cl. Ris. '04	♟	5
O Il Dolce del Castello '06	♟	4

San Filippo
Loc. San Filippo
53024 Montalcino [SI]
TEL. 0577847176
www.sanfilippomontalcino.com

This winery, acquired by the Giannelli family, is now showing what it can do. The Brunello Le Coste Riserva '01 was excellent, with red fruits, hints of incense and smoky nuances on the nose. The palate was generous and lingered well. The Brunello '02 is pleasant but rather thin.

● Brunello di Montalcino		
Le Coste Ris. '01	♟♟	7
● Brunello di Montalcino '02	♟	7
● Sant'Antimo Staffato '05	♟	4

Tenuta San Jacopo
Loc. Castiglioncelli, 151
52022 Cavriglia [AR]
TEL. 055966003
info@tenutasanjacopo.it

This is the Guide debut for a winery located near Cavriglia, between Valdarno and Chianti Classico. We were favourably impressed by Orma del Diavolo '04, a merlot and cabernet blend with a well-rounded, flowers and balsam profile, relaxed, nicely honed tannins and good depth.

● Orma del Diavolo '04	♟♟	4*
● Chianti Classico Poggio ai Grilli '04	♟	3*

San Michele a Torri
Via San Michele, 36
50020 Scandicci [FI]
TEL. 055769111
www.fattoriasanmichele.it

The San Michele a Torri winery is stable. We liked the Chianti Classico Riserva '04, with its classic fruit fragrance, even body and evident but well-controlled tannins. The rest of the range only just made the grade, including Murtas '04, from sangiovese, colorino and cabernet sauvignon, which was below par.

● Chianti Cl. La Gabbiola Ris. '04	♟♟	5
● Chianti Colli Fiorentini '05	♟	4
● Murtas '04	♟	6
● San Giovanni Novantasette '04	♟	6

San Polino
Loc. San Polino
53024 Montalcino [SI]
TEL. 0577835775

This organic winery, on the eastern side of Montalcino, makes some distinctive wines. The Brunello Riserva '01 has a nose layered with liquorice and blackberry, smoky nuances and, of course, wild cherry. The palate has a good weight, although the tannins hold it back a little.

● Brunello di Montalcino Ris. '01	♟♟	7
● Brunello di Montalcino '02	♟	7
● Rosso di Montalcino '05	♟	5

OTHER WINERIES

Sangervasio
LOC. SAN GERVASIO
56036 PALAIA [PI]
TEL. 0587483360
www.sangervasio.com

Sadly, we found Sangervasio's vineyard selection for this year to be over-extracted, with too much oak. Which is a shame, because the raw material is top class, as is shown by the clean nose and appeal of the Sangervasio Rosso and Bianco '06, aged in glass-lined cement.

- O Sangervasio Bianco '06 ▼▼ 4
- ● Sangervasio Rosso '05 ▼▼ 4
- ● A Sirio '03 ▼ 5

Santa Lucia
FRAZ. FONTEBLANDA
VIA AURELIA NORD, 66
58010 ORBETELLO [GR]
TEL. 0564885474
www.azsantalucia.it

Luciano Scotto's wines tend to be well orchestrated, despite heavy extraction. Betto '05, a blend of sangiovese, cabernet sauvignon and merlot, with its lush aromas and juicy palate, has real Mediterranean appeal. The Capalbio Cabernet Sauvignon '05 is also good, with a supple, relaxing palate.

- ● Betto '05 ▼▼ 4
- ● Capalbio Cabernet Sauvignon '05 ▼▼ 4
- ● Cabernet Sauvignon '04 ▽▽ 5

Fattoria Santa Vittoria
LOC. POZZO
VIA PIANA, 43
52042 FOIANO DELLA CHIANA [AR]
TEL. 0575661807
www.fattoriasantavittoria.com

The wines presented by the Santa Vittoria winery included not only the usual suspect, a reliable, austere and well-typed Vin Santo '02, but also a typically territorial Poggio al Tempio '05, from sangiovese, foglia tonda and pugnitello. It's edgy, husky and savoury with strong acid backbone.

- ● Poggio del Tempio '05 ▼▼ 2*
- O Valdichiana Vin Santo '02 ▼▼ 5
- O Valdichiana Vin Santo '01 ▽▽ 5

Sante Marie
LOC. VIGNONI ALTO
PODERE SANTA MARIA
53027 SAN QUIRICO D'ORCIA [SI]
TEL. 0577898141
studiogenerali@virgilio.it

More than anything, Franco Generali wants his wines to be a natural expression of the growing year's best traits. The coolly aromatic Curzio and Adone '04 have earthiness, with the latter a tad more rounded. Sunto '04, from sangiovese, cabernet sauvignon, merlot and syrah, is pleasant but predictable.

- ● Orcia Rosso Adone '04 ▼▼ 4
- ● Orcia Rosso Curzio '04 ▼▼ 4
- ● Sunto '04 ▼ 4

Enrico Santini
LOC. CAMPO ALLA CASA, 74
57022 CASTAGNETO CARDUCCI [LI]
TEL. 0565774375
enricosantini@interfree.it

Enrico Santini's winery has got back into the Guide thanks to the Bolgheri Rosso Montepergoli '04. This very tannic, round, compact wine shows distinct oak on nose and palate. We could say the same for the Bolgheri Rosso Poggio al Moro '06, although the texture is less close knit.

- ● Bolgheri Rosso Montepergoli '04 ▽▽ 7
- ● Bolgheri Rosso Poggio al Moro '06 ▼ 4
- ● Bolgheri Rosso Sup. Montepergoli '01 ▽▽▽ 7

Podere Sapaio
LOC. LO SCOPAIO, 212
57022 CASTAGNETO CARDUCCI [LI]
TEL. 0565765187
www.sapaio.com

It's a great Guide debut for Podere Sapaio, a young winery at Castagneto Carducci. Both wines made here are Bordeaux blends. Volpolo '05 is still not ready and rather in thrall to the oak. The elegant Sapaio '04 is compact, lively and tannic, with a leisurely finish.

- ● Bolgheri Sup. Sapaio '04 ▽▽ 7
- ● Bolgheri Volpolo '05 ▼ 5

OTHER WINERIES

Sasso di Sole

FRAZ. TORRENIERI
LOC. PODERE SANTA GIULIA I, 48A
53028 MONTALCINO [SI]
TEL. 0577844238

The Tezuoli Bindi partnership continues to turn out well-made wines at Torrenieri, hitting the jackpot with the Brunello '02. Despite the ill-fated vintage, the Brunello's well-developed nose proffers a classic fruit note but also has toastiness and vanilla. The palate is still taut and weighty; the finish leisurely.

● Brunello di Montalcino '02	♟♟	7
● Brunello di Montalcino '01	♟♟	7

Scopetani

VIA FIORENTINA, 33
50068 RUFINA [FI]
TEL. 0558397032
www.scopetani.it

The Scopetani family winery is back in the Guide with an encouraging performance. The labels on offer are many, with a definite prevalence of Chianti Rufina, the best version this year being the Riserva Stellario '03. The other wines are well managed and Quarta Luna '06 Chardonnay is worth uncorking.

● Chianti Rufina Stellario Ris. '03	♟♟	4*
● Chianti Rufina V. Macereto Ris. '03	♟	4
O Quarta Luna '06	♟	3
● Chianti Rufina 813 Ris. '03	♟	4

Podere Sesta di Sopra

LOC. CASTELNUOVO DELL'ABATE
53020 MONTALCINO [SI]
TEL. 0577835698
www.sestadisopra.it

This family-run winery produces wines with a precise sense of place from vineyards in the upper Sesta area. We were taken with the Brunello '02, which has a good, red berry-led nose. On the palate, it foregrounds cool acidity and then a crisp, lingering finish.

● Brunello di Montalcino '02	♟♟	8
● Rosso di Montalcino '05	♟	5
● Brunello di Montalcino '00	♟♟	7

Setriolo

LOC. SETRIOLO, 61
53011 CASTELLINA IN CHIANTI [SI]
TEL. 0577743079

For many years, the Soderi family business was selling grapes. The family's first wines have made it to the Guide and deservedly so, if the well-extracted Memores '05 is anything to go by. A 50-50 sangiovese and merlot blend, it has delightful fragrances and juicy body. The Chianti Classico '05 is enjoyable.

● Memores '05	♟♟	5
● Chianti Classico '05	♟	4

Sonnino

VIA VOLTERRANA NORD, 6A
50025 MONTESPERTOLI [FI]
TEL. 0571609198
www.castellosonnino.it

Quality at Castello di Sonnino is a given. The pleasing, juicy Sanleone '04, a merlot and sangiovese blend, is spicy, balanced and well structured. Cantinino '05, a monovarietal Sangiovese, has a confident palate softly permeated with tannin. Leone Rosso '06 is balanced and finishes sweet.

● Cantinino '05	♟♟	5
● Sanleone '04	♟♟	7
● Leone Rosso '06	♟	3

Spadaio e Piecorto

VIA SAN SILVESTRO, 1
50021 BARBERINO VAL D'ELSA [FI]
TEL. 0558072915
spadaiopiecorto@tiscali.it

The Stefanelli family is back in the Guide thanks to a good show from Pietra Rossa '04, a sangiovese and cabernet sauvignon blend with balsamic aromas, lush structure and a fresh, tasty finish that lingers nicely. The two Chianti Classico '05s are juicy, if lean and edgy.

● Pietra Rossa '04	♟♟	4
● Chianti Cl. Piecorto '05	♟	4
● Chianti Cl. '05	♟	4

OTHER WINERIES

Stomennano
LOC. STOMENNANO
53035 MONTERIGGIONI [SI]
TEL. 0577304033
www.stomennano.it

Matteo Lupi's winery made its Guide debut with three wines from native vines. We noted the Chianti Classico '04, with its poise and solid body but we had doubts about the Rosso Toscano '05, a blend of sangiovese, canaiolo and colorino. The Bianco Toscano '06, from trebbiano and Malvasia, is predictable.

● Chianti Cl. '04	♥♥ 4*
○ Bianco Toscano '06	♥ 3
● Rosso Toscano '05	♥ 3

Podere Terreno alla Via della Volpaia
VIA DELLA VOLPAIA
53017 RADDA IN CHIANTI [SI]
TEL. 0577738312
www.podereterreno.it

Marie Sylvie Haniez's small, respected winery at Radda is back in the Guide. A good Chianti Classico Riserva '04 has mineral and fruit aromas, a streamlined but well-balanced body and a very drinkable finish. The Supertuscan Pierfrancesco '04, a sangiovese and cabernet sauvignon blend, is less successful.

● Chianti Cl. Ris. '04	♥♥ 5
● Pierfrancesco '04	♥ 6

Giuliano Tiberi
FRAZ. CASALGUIDI
VIA CASTEL BIAGINI, 23
51034 SERRAVALLE PISTOIESE [PT]
TEL. 0573527589
www.giulianotiberi.it

Giuliano Tiberi's commitment to his small winery continues. He presented two new wines, I Merli '05, a Merlot with a soft palate and an easy-drinking balance of extract and acidity and the appealing, fruity, full-flavoured Chianti Imbricci '06. There's also a fresh Sangiovese Le Vespe '04.

● I Merli '05	♥♥ 5
● Chainti Montalbano Imbricci '06	♥ 3
● Le Vespe '04	♥ 4

Podere Terenzuola
VIA VERCALDA, 14
54035 FOSDINOVO [MS]
TEL. 0187680030
www.terenzuola.com

Lunigiana and vermentino have always been an item. This year the Podere Terenzuola winery rendered the concept perfectly. Two '06 vineyard selections, Montesagna and Fosso di Corsano, show individuality and intensity, the former with surefooted, pulpy fruit, and the latter with scrubland aromas.

○ Colli di Luni Vermentino Fosso di Corsano '06	♥♥ 4
○ Colli di Luni Vermentino Montesagna '06	♥♥ 4
● Merla della Miniera '04	♥ 5

Teruzzi & Puthod
LOC. CASALE, 19
53037 SAN GIMIGNANO [SI]
TEL. 0577940143
www.teruzzieputhod.it

This established winery is about to undergo some radical reorganization. Founder Enrico Teruzzi has sold to the Campari group. There is a vast range on offer but we liked the mineral nuances of the fragrant, zesty Vernaccia Vigna a Rondolino '06 and the red Peperino '05, a sangiovese and merlot mix.

● Peperino '05	♥♥ 4
○ Vernaccia di S. Gimignano V. Rondolino '06	♥♥ 4
○ Terre di Tufi '06	♥ 5
○ Vernaccia di S. Gimignano '06	♥ 4

Tornesi
LOC. LE BENDUCCE, 207
53024 MONTALCINO [SI]
TEL. 0577848689

Tornesi is small but has potential so it was a shame that there were so few bottles of the excellent Riserva '01, with its aromas of classic red fruits laced with liquorice and sweet spice. The stylish, balanced palate has a very tempting finish. The other wines are well styled and pleasing.

● Brunello di Montalcino Ris. '01	♥♥ 7
● Brunello di Montalcino '02	♥ 6
● Rosso di Montalcino '05	♥ 4

OTHER WINERIES

Torre
LOC. VICO D'ELSA
P.ZZA TORRIGIANI, 15
50021 BARBERINO VAL D'ELSA [FI]
TEL. 0558073001
www.marchesitorrigiani.it

Marchese Torrigiani wines are becoming increasingly dependable. Guidaccio '04, from merlot, cabernet sauvignon and sangiovese, has an earthy, spicy nose, and mouthfilling weight, with smooth tannins and plenty of zest. Torre di Ciardo '04, from sangiovese, merlot and canaiolo, is soft and balanced.

● Guidaccio '04	🍷🍷 5
● Torre di Ciardo '04	🍷🍷 4

Torre a Cenaia
LOC. CENAIA
VIA DELLE COLLINE
56040 CRESPINA [PI]
TEL. 050643739
www.torreacenaia.it

The Torre a Cenaia estate performed well again this year. Vajo '04, a sangiovese, cabernet and syrah blend, may be a tad husky but it's still feisty and persuasive. The winery whites are well-made, including a Pitti Vermentino '06 with impressive aromatic breadth.

● Vajo '04	🍷🍷 5
O Pitti Bianco '06	🍷 4
O Pitti Vermentino '06	🍷 4

Le Torri
VIA SAN LORENZO A VIGLIANO, 31
50021 BARBERINO VAL D'ELSA [FI]
TEL. 0558076161
www.letorri.net

This young winery, on the edge of Chianti Classico, confirms its guide profile. The territory can make distinctive, vigorous wines and we liked the Vigliano '04, a single-variety Cabernet Sauvignon, for its balsamic notes on the nose and appealing body with a tasty finish. The other wines are also good.

● Vigliano '04	🍷🍷 6
● Chianti Colli Fiorentini '05	🍷 4
● Chianti Colli Fiorentini Ris. '04	🍷 5

Fattoria La Traiana
LOC. TRAIANA, 16
52028 TERRANUOVA BRACCIOLINI [AR]
TEL. 0559179004
fatt.latraiana@libero.it

Fattoria La Traiana, in the Pratomagno foothills, makes some interesting wines. The '03 vintages are sound, with sound density, especially the Cabernet Pian del Pazzo, which is remarkable for its balance and aromatic span. The lush Campo Arsiccio Sangiovese is warm and ripe.

● Pian del Pazzo '03	🍷🍷 6
● Campo Arsiccio '03	🍷 6
● Chianti Sup. '05	🍷 4

Fattoria di Travalda
LOC. SANTA LUCIA, 1
56025 PONTEDERA [PI]
TEL. 0587292900
www.castelwine.it

Fattoria di Travalda is part of the Castellani SPA group and releases just one wine, named after the cellar. The '04 has a good attack on the palate impetus, preceded by a spectrum of aromatics that focuses on black berries and with a mild hint of chocolate. The finish is intense and long.

● Fattoria di Travalda '04	🍷🍷 5

Le Tre Stelle
LOC. SAN BENEDETTO
VIA FONTE DI CAMPAINO,17B
53037 SAN GIMIGNANO [SI]
TEL. 0577944406
www.letrestelle.com

Tre Stelle is a steady producer and performs consistently well. Again, the best of the range is the Ciliegiolo. The pervasive '05 has good tannic weave, fruit and length. The palatable Vernaccia '06 is balanced and flowery. San Gimignano Doanto '05 is soft and straightforward. The fruity Chianti '06 has nice flavour.

● Ciliegiolo '05	🍷🍷 5
● Chianti dei Colli Senesi '06	🍷 3*
O Vernaccia di San Gimignano '06	🍷 3*
● San Gimignano Doanto '05	🍷 4

OTHER WINERIES

Val delle Corti

LOC. LA CROCE
CASE SPARSE VAL DELLE CORTI, 144
53017 RADDA IN CHIANTI [SI]
TEL. 0577738215
www.valledellecorti.it

This small vineyard gives Roberto Bianchi appealing, very distinctive wines that he obtains from native vines. Sadly, the Chianti Classico Riserva '04 lacks symmetry and is less persuasive than the tastier, more relaxed standard version.

● Chianti Cl. '04	♟♟ 4*
● Chianti Cl. Ris. '04	♟ 5

Val delle Rose

LOC. POGGIO LA MOZZA
58100 GROSSETO [GR]
TEL. 0564409062
www.valdellerose.it

The Maremma winery owned by the Cecchi family duplicated last year's results with mathematical precision. The Morellino '06 was a tad hard to pin down on the nose but is an easy drinker. The Morellino Riserva '04 aromas has grassy aromas and a good, layered mouthfeel. The Vermentino Litorale '06 is fresh.

● Morellino di Scansano Ris. '04	♟♟ 5
● Morellino di Scansano '06	♟ 3
O Litorale '06	♟ 3
● Morellino di Scansano '05	♟♟ 4

La Valle

VIA SANMINIATESE, 8
50050 MONTAIONE [FI]
TEL. 0571698059
www.agricolalavalle.it

The Bigazzi winery underscored the good impression made on its debut. Mandragola, from sangiovese, cabernet sauvignon and colorino, with hints of black fruits and spice, revealed a distinct tannic weave and follow through. The new, tonneau-aged Chianti Becconero '05 has a spice nose and close-knit tannins.

● Mandragola '05	♟♟ 4*
● Chianti Becconero '05	♟ 4

Verbena

LOC. VERBENA, 100
53024 MONTALCINO [SI]
TEL. 0577848432
aziendaverbena@tiscali.it

The established local winery has made a quality leap. The Brunello '02 was one of the best in the category, its layered nose of fresh blackberry, white cherry has tempting florality. The palate shows style with a perfect balance of tannins and acidity melding into the underlying texture.

● Brunello di Montalcino '02	♟♟ 7
● Rosso di Montalcino '05	♟ 5

Vescine

LOC. VESCINE
53017 RADDA IN CHIANTI [SI]
TEL. 0422768167
www.paladin.it

The Paladin family winery has earned a Guide place. We were especially impressed with the very drinkable Chianti Classico Lodolaio Riserva '04 with its fresh aromatic herbs and violets, and juicy body. The other two wines are uncomplicated and very palatable.

● Chianti Classico Lodolaio Ris. '04	♟♟ 5
● Chianti Classico '05	♟ 4
● Chianti Colli Senesi '06	♟ 3

Vigliano

LOC. SAN MARTINO ALLA PALMA
VIA CARCHERI, 309
50018 SCANDICCI [FI]
TEL. 0558727040
www.vigliano.com

We are happy to see Vigliano back in the Guide. There are two versions of Erta '05. One is a Sangiovese Cabernet, with rich alcohol and a lively, substantial flavour. The other is Sangiovese and shows fresh and coherent, with decent length. The harmonious Vigliano Rosso '05 is very moreish.

● L'Erta Sangiovese '05	♟♟ 5
● L'Erta Sangiovese Cabernet '05	♟♟ 5
● Rosso Vigliano '05	♟♟ 4*

OTHER WINERIES

Podere La Vigna
LOC. TORRENIERI
53028 MONTALCINO [SI]
TEL. 0577834252
www.poderelavigna.it

Alvaro Rubegni's Torrenieri winery put on a fine show. Careful selection produced a well-made Brunello '02 with flowers, sweet tobacco and medicinal herbs on the nose, and a palate of balanced acidity, tannins and extract, then a lingering, flavoursome finish. We also liked the Rosso '05.

● Brunello di Montalcino '02	♥♥ 7
● Rosso di Montalcino '05	♥♥ 4*

Cantina Cooperativa Vignaioli del Morellino di Scansano
LOC. SARAGIOLO
58054 SCANSANO [GR]
TEL. 0564507288
www.cantinadelmorellino.it

The Morellino di Scansano co-operative was below par, only one wine making any impact. That was the Morellino Vignabenefizio '06, which has well-defined aromas and a sweet, tasty palate. The Morellino Roggiano '06, with its expansive, consistent palate, lacks depth and has a slightly mouth-drying finish.

● Morellino di Scansano Vignabenefizio '06	♥♥ 4*
● Morellino di Scansano Roggiano '06	♥ 4
● Morellino di Scansano Vignabenefizio '04	♥♥ 4

Vignavecchia
SDRUCCIOLO DI PIAZZA, 7
53017 RADDA IN CHIANTI [SI]
TEL. 0577738090
www.vignavecchia.com

The Beccari family winery is struggling to recover the pace and polish of the past. The red wines we tasted all revealed overripeness and over-assertive tannins. Titanum '06, a monovarietal Chardonnay, is better, proffering fresh nuances of aromatic herbs.

O Titanum '06	♥♥ 6
● Chianti Cl. Ris. '03	♥ 5
● Chianti Cl. '05	♥ 4

Villa Calcinaia
FRAZ. GRETI
VIA CITILLE, 84
50022 GREVE IN CHIANTI [FI]
TEL. 055854008
www.villacalcinaia.it

Capponi family wines are a true expression of their territory of origin. We hope the Capponis will succeed in focusing the balance of the range because all the wines suffer from slightly intrusive tannins that tend to hold them back. The best on the list is the solid Riserva '04, with its rising finish.

● Chianti Cl. Ris. '04	♥♥ 6
● Casarsa '04	♥ 7
● Chianti Cl. '05	♥ 4

Villa Cilnia
FRAZ. BAGNORO
LOC. MONTONCELLO, 27
52040 AREZZO [AR]
TEL. 0575365017
www.villacilnia.com

Villa Cilnia is a well-known Arezzo winery and while it rarely produces superstars, its wines do not disappoint. This year, we liked the dark, pondered Vocato '04, a vibrant sangiovese and cabernet blend, and the tight-knit Cign'Oro '04, from sangiovese, cabernet and merlot, which is savoury and still closed.

● Vocato '04	♥♥ 5
● Cign'Oro '04	♥♥ 5
● Chianti Colli Aretini '05	♥ 3
● Chianti Colli Aretini Ris. '04	♥ 4

Villa di Geggiano
LOC. PIANELLA
VIA DI GEGGIANO, 1
53010 CASTELNUOVO BERARDENGA [SI]
TEL. 0577356879
www.villadigeggiano.com

The Bianchi Bandinelli family have made it into the Guide. Their villa, famous as a film location and for its gardens, has been producing wine since the 1700s. We really liked the Chianti Classico Riserva '04, with its lengthy finish. The Chianti Classico '05 is more predictable.

● Chianti Classico Ris. '04	♥♥ 5
● Chianti Classico '05	♥ 4

OTHER WINERIES

Villa La Ripa
LOC. ANTRIA, 38
52100 AREZZO [AR]
TEL. 0575315118
www.villalaripa.it

Villa La Ripa left its Tiratari '05 to age a little
longer and presented an interesting new
wine instead. Apart from the offbeat name,
the full-flavoured Psyco '04, from equal
parts of sangiovese and cabernet,
impressed with its relaxed, mature profile,
veined with earthiness and minerals, and
good depth.

● Psyco '04	♥♥ 4*
● Tiratari '02	♀♀ 5
● Tiratari '03	♀♀ 5
● Tiratari '04	♀♀ 5

Villa Sant'Andrea
LOC. MONTEFIRIDOLFI
VIA DI FABBRICA, 63
50020 SAN CASCIANO IN VAL DI PESA [FI]
TEL. 0558244254
www.villas-andrea.it

This winery's key product is still its Vin
Santo. The '01's nose is dominated by
honey and hazelnuts, the dense, creamy
body preceding a sweet, well-sustained
finish. The reds are promising and well
managed, giving distinctive, fruit-led aromas
and relying more on elegance than power
on the palate.

○ Vin Santo Chianti Cl. '01	♥♥ 6
● Chianti Cl. Borgo Conda '05	♀ 4
● Citille '05	♀ 5
● Chianti Cl. Borgo Conda Ris. '04	♀ 4

Villa Sant'Anna
FRAZ. ABBADIA DI MONTEPULCIANO
53045 MONTEPULCIANO [SI]
TEL. 0578708017
www.villasantanna.it

The winery is owned by Simona, Anna and
Margherita Frabroni. The Vin Santo '99 is
sweet but never cloys and has a good,
intense aromatic profile layered with dried
fruit and nuts, walnutskin, and iodine. The
Nobile '04 is still a tad stiff but full and the
Rosso '05 is very drinkable.

○ Vin Santo '99	♥♥ 8
● Nobile di Montepulciano '04	♀ 5
● Rosso di Montepulciano '05	♀ 4
● Nobile di Montepulciano Poldo '03	♀♀ 6

Tenuta Vitanza
FRAZ. TORRENIERI
POD. BELVEDERE, S.P. 71 DI COSONA KM 250
53028 MONTALCINO [SI]
TEL. 0577832882
www.tenutavitanza.it

This very nice Torrenieri winery presented
just two wines. The Brunello Riserva '01
made it to our taste-offs for its well-
developed vegetality with some caramel
and vanilla, as well as the classic touch of
red and black cherries. The palate strains at
the leash with crunchy tannins and well-
integrated acidity.

● Brunello di Montalcino Ris. '01	♥♥ 8
● Rosso di Montalcino '05	♀ 4
● Brunello di Montalcino '00	♀♀♀ 7
● Brunello di Montalcino '01	♀♀ 7

La Poderina
FRAZ. CASTELNUOVO DELL'ABATE
LOC. PODERINA
53022 MONTALCINO [SI]
TEL. 0577835737
www.saiagricola.it

La Poderina wines are rich and intense on
nose and palate. This year, two went
through to the finals. Moscadello, this time
the '05, is a regular, showing citrus and a
fresh, well-gauged palate. The vibrant,
tannic Brunello Poggio Banale '01 also went
to the taste-offs. The rest of the range is
reliable.

● Brunello di Montalcino Poggio Banale '01	♥♥ 8
○ Moscadello di Montalcino V.T.	♥♥ 6
● Rosso di Montalcino '05	♥♥ 5
● Brunello di Montalcino '02	♀ 7

MARCHE

We started last year's notes by saying that 2005 was a poor harvest, particularly for Verdicchio. This time round, we can confirm that opinion, particularly after our first tastings from the following vintage, which revealed that 2006 was a truly excellent year. No less than four young Verdicchios won Three Glasses: Santa Barbara's Le Vaglie, Tenuta di Tavignano's Misco and Sparapani's Il Priore, all in the Jesi area, and Collestefano's Verdicchio di Matelica. Oddly enough, on many estates the basic Verdicchios, in other words the more reasonably priced versions, performed better than selections from the preceding year. Not that the selections were bad; they just didn't live up to their pedigree with the exception of one magnificent white, Villa Bucci, which displays majestic elegance even in a lesser vintage. One reason why the 2006 whites performed so well overall is because they were readier and more polished than in earlier vintages when we came to taste them. We anxiously look forward to the selections that will be released over the next few years. Meanwhile, we were bowled over by several stupendous bottles from 2004, an underrated year that produced extraordinary quality. Pietrone from Bonci, to our minds the best Marche wine we tasted this year, and Plenio from Umani Ronchi stand out. The results earned by these two wines only go to show yet again that verdicchio is extremely well adapted to ageing and can be made in a range of styles, depending on interpretation and area of origin. In fact, we believe it is high time that Verdicchio territories were classified so that the consumer can identify the different characteristics of each subzone, as is the case in the world's best wine areas. Given the region's potential, very few Marche reds were awarded high marks and not because of any prejudice on the part of our judges. It's probably because most of the estates were established fairly recently and have only started to produced high-quality bottled wine in the last few years. Velenosi's Roggio del Filare and the Sassi Neri from the Fattoria Le Terrazze are the only two wines that represent the historic Marche DOCs, Rosso Piceno Superiore and Conero Riserva, the name of the new DOCG that became effective with wines from the 2004 harvest; Rosso Conero remains a DOC wine. We also have a superb Vespro from Fausti that blends montepulciano, used on its own in the two previous versions, with syrah. The last wine to wine Three Glasses is Fattoria Dezi's Solo, a marvellous Sangiovese that merely confirms what we have thought for some time. This aristocratic variety responds very well across the entire region when cultivated inland, towards the mountains, unlike montepulciano, which tends to perform better on the coast.

Aurora

LOC. SANTA MARIA IN CARRO
C.DA CIAFONE, 98
63035 OFFIDA [AP]
TEL. 0736810007
www.viniaurora.it

ANNUAL PRODUCTION 45,000 bottles
HECTARES UNDER VINE 9
VITICULTURE METHOD Certified organic

Aurora's partners have taken their failure to
net their fifth consecutive Three Glasses on
the chin. It's no surprise, as 2005 was just
not the right year: too much rain, erratic
bursts of hot weather and a difficult harvest.
Producers who are rigorously organic in
their methods are more prey to the vagaries
of the climate. Nevertheless, the
Barricadiero did well and displayed all of its
customary feisty character. Dark liquorice
sensations are refined by hints of balsam
and the palate is at once generous and
austere, if a little more closed than usual
and tinged by the odd vegetal nuance. Its
contemporary, the Rosso Piceno Superiore,
could almost be said to give the same
impression of rather rugged tannins if the
quest for a more generous and enveloping
fruit hadn't produced dense aromas of
morello cherry on both nose and palate
leading to a stiffish finish. The freshness of
the vintage lends the Pecorino Fiobbo a
certain elegance. It is dense and complex,
with leisurely, wonderfully lip-smacking
length. Meanwhile, the Rosso Piceno '06 is
eminently drinkable and dynamic,
underlining that a new year can bring a
change of gear.

Belisario

VIA ARISTIDE MERLONI, 12
62024 MATELICA [MC]
TEL. 0737787247
www.belisario.it

ANNUAL PRODUCTION 800,000 bottles
HECTARES UNDER VINE 300
VITICULTURE METHOD Conventional

Simple, substantial and strongly territorial
are the words that best describe the style
and identity of the wines produced by this
big co-operative cellar in Matelica. Belisario
has become a solid point of reference for all
the growers in the district. The three
adjectives could also be applied to Roberto
Potentini, the manager of the winery and its
heart and soul. The various Verdicchios
presented for tasting this year were all up to
their usual high standards. Cream of the
crop is a lovely version of Cambrugiano.
Fresh-tasting, ripe aromas of sweet fruit are
enhanced by notes of citrus fruit and
botrytis, while the palate is warm, generous
and supple. The Vigneti del Cerro is an
archetypal Verdicchio di Matelica.
Impeccable in its varietal expression, it
conquers the palate with the fresh juiciness
of its fruit and its wonderful drinkability.
Obtained from organic grapes, Vigneti
Belisario is just as agreeable, although more
powerful and deeper. Its edgy acidity and
elegant minerality prolong a finish that
echoes the notes of flowers and apple on
the nose.

● Barricadiero '05	ΨΨ 5
○ Offida Pecorino Fiobbo '05	ΨΨ 4*
● Rosso Piceno Sup. '05	ΨΨ 4*
● Rosso Piceno '06	Ψ 3
● Barricadiero '01	ΨΨΨ 5
● Barricadiero '02	ΨΨΨ 5
● Barricadiero '04	ΨΨΨ 5
● Barricadiero '03	ΨΨΨ 5
● Barricadiero '00	ΨΨ 5
○ Offida Pecorino Fiobbo '04	ΨΨ 4

○ Verdicchio di Matelica Cambrugiano Ris. '04	ΨΨ 4*
○ Verdicchio di Matelica Vign. del Cerro '06	ΨΨ 3*
○ Verdicchio di Matelica Vign. Belisario '06	ΨΨ 4*
● Colli Maceratesi Rosso San Leopardo Ris. '04	Ψ 4
● Esino Rosso Colferraio '06	Ψ 2
○ Verdicchio di Matelica Terre di Valbona '06	Ψ 2
● Colli Maceratesi Rosso Coll'Amato '06	3
○ Esino Bianco Ferrante '06	2
○ Verdicchio di Matelica Cambrugiano Ris. '02	ΨΨΨ 4
○ Verdicchio di Matelica Cambrugiano Ris. '03	ΨΨ 4

Boccadigabbia

LOC. FONTESPINA
C.DA CASTELLETTA, 56
62012 CIVITANOVA MARCHE [MC]
TEL. 073370728
www.boccadigabbia.com

ANNUAL PRODUCTION 150,000 bottles
HECTARES UNDER VINE 25
VITICULTURE METHOD Conventional

For years we have been under the spell of two enchanting wines from Elvio Alessandri's estate, Cabernet Akronte and Merlot Pix. The Cabernet charms with its austere elegance and the Merlot with its round appeal. Unfortunately, we were unable to taste either of them this year as Elvio has wisely decided to leave his '04s to age longer than usual. But the wines we did taste made quite an impression. Some are obtained from local varieties and others from French grape types, which have been grown at Boccadigabbia since Napoleonic times. Character and aromatic density are the hallmark of the Rosso Piceno. Aromas of black cherry and currants announce a generously fragrant, well-integrated palate. The Pinot Nero Girone mingles juicy notes of fruit with hints of sweet spice, and offers a deep, fluent palate. On the white front, the Mont'Anello has a fruity, flowery nose and a robust if rather static palate. The Chardonnay Montalperti shows good balance on the palate and a skilful use of oak in blending in the fruity sensations. Last but not least, the Pinot Grigio La Castelletta put on a fine performance. Clear fruity and vegetal notes fill the nose and the palate has well-gauged structure and a lovely fresh finish.

Bucci

FRAZ. PONGELLI
VIA CONA, 30
60010 OSTRA VETERE [AN]
TEL. 071964179
www.villabucci.com

ANNUAL PRODUCTION 120,000 bottles
HECTARES UNDER VINE 26
VITICULTURE METHOD Natural

Obtained from selected grapes and matured in large barrels, Verdicchio Riserva Villa Bucci treated us to an aristocratic sequence of dried fruit, straw and spring flowers. Entry on the palate is leisurely, almost a whisper, and it maintains this elegant moderation right through the lingering finish that is flawless in its consistency. The full palate has long, refined minerality. It doesn't matter whether you taste the 2005, the latest release, the balanced 2001 or even the torrid 2003, the result is always the same, with minimal variations, showing that the wine has a life of its own. Hats off to Ampelio Bucci's blending skills and the expertise of oenologist Giorgio Grai for this stunning Three Glass champion. This year's Verdicchio shows all the same qualities but expresses them with greater freshness and a more direct approachability that is equally fascinating. One or two of the reds bear comparison with their French relations: light extraction, carefully gauged alcohol and layered complexity. Our tastings of the watercolour-soft Villa Bucci Rosso and of the subtle Pongelli reveal a style that is hard to reproduce, at least this far south.

● Girone Pinot Nero '04	♟♟ 6
○ Montalperti Chardonnay '04	♟♟ 5
○ La Castelletta Pinot Grigio '06	♟♟ 4
● Rosso Piceno Boccadigabbia '05	♟♟ 4*
○ Colli Maceratesi Ribona Mont'Anello '06	♟ 3
● Saltapicchio Sangiovese '04	♟ 5
● Akronte '93	♟♟♟ 7
● Akronte '95	♟♟♟ 7
● Akronte '97	♟♟♟ 7
● Akronte '94	♟♟♟ 7
● Akronte '98	♟♟♟ 7
● Akronte '01	♟♟ 7
● Akronte '03	♟♟ 8
● Pix Merlot '01	♟♟ 7
● Pix Merlot '03	♟♟ 7

○ Verdicchio dei Castelli di Jesi Cl. Villa Bucci Ris. '05	♟♟♟ 6
○ Verdicchio dei Castelli di Jesi Cl. Sup. '06	♟♟ 4*
● Rosso Piceno Villa Bucci '04	♟♟ 5
● Rosso Piceno Tenuta Pongelli '05	♟♟ 4
○ Verdicchio dei Castelli di Jesi Cl. Villa Bucci Ris. '00	♟♟♟ 6
○ Verdicchio dei Castelli di Jesi Cl. Villa Bucci Ris. '98	♟♟♟ 6
○ Verdicchio dei Castelli di Jesi Cl. Villa Bucci Ris. '99	♟♟♟ 6
○ Verdicchio dei Castelli di Jesi Cl. Villa Bucci Ris. '04	♟♟♟ 6
○ Verdicchio dei Castelli di Jesi Cl. Villa Bucci Ris. '03	♟♟♟ 6
○ Verdicchio dei Castelli di Jesi Cl. Villa Bucci Ris. '01	♟♟♟ 6

Le Caniette

C.DA CANALI, 23
63038 RIPATRANSONE [AP]
TEL. 07359200
www.lecaniette.it

ANNUAL PRODUCTION 60,000 bottles
HECTARES UNDER VINE 16
VITICULTURE METHOD Natural

We could talk for hours about the style of red wines produced by the Vagnoni family, and indeed we often have with Giovanni, who is in charge of public relations for the estate. In the end, we have always agreed that, irrespective of personal taste, Le Caniette produces a very unusual interpretation of montepulciano that favours rich extraction, robust tannins and ripe fruit over approachable fruity fragrance and easy drinkability. The Morellone and Rosso Bello exhibit all of these characteristics plus, obviously, a few individual traits. Morellone is more mature and weighty while Rosso Bello is younger and lighter. The estate's approach to pecorino is also quite atypical, and the Iosonogaia non sono Lucrezia has a very successful oxidized style. The complex palate is enhanced by vibrant acidity with attractive oaky notes and dairy sensations following on from citrus fruit and aromatic herbs. The new version of the traditional Vino Santo is obtained from passerina only and its alcoholic warmth invigorates the well-defined aromas of dried fruit.

La Canosa

C.DA SAN PIETRO, 6
63030 ROTELLA [AP]
TEL. 0736374556

ANNUAL PRODUCTION 250,000 bottles
HECTARES UNDER VINE 25
VITICULTURE METHOD Conventional

Building a large winery at the foot of a mountain may seem rather an odd thing to do. But if Etna is yielding excellent results, why not Monte dell'Ascensione, which is 1,000 metres high but not so far from the sea? The brave heart who has placed his faith in the quality of this territory is not some small entrepreneur with pioneering tendencies, but Riccardo Reina, whose family owns the beverage giant, Illva Saronno. Despite the significant investment required, everything on this estate happens one calm, prudent step at a time. Wines and vineyards have all the time they need to mature. Our first tastings bode well. Servator, a white from 100 per cent passerina, takes advantage of elevation and the temperature range to enhance its intense citrus freshness and distinctive backbone. The Rosso Piceno Nummaria is elegance incarnate. Crystal clear aromas of red berry fruit are the prelude to an elegant, tidy palate on which the full, juicy profile reveals its weight in a very long, deep finish. The estate's full range of wines is due to be released next year.

O Offida Pecorino Iosonogaia non sono Lucrezia '05	♀♀	5
O Offida Passerina Vino Santo Sibilla '03	♀♀	5
● Rosso Piceno Morellone '04	♀	5
● Rosso Piceno Rosso Bello '05	♀	4
O Offida Passerina Lucrezia '06		4
● Rosso Piceno Morellone '02	♀♀	5
● Rosso Piceno Nero di Vite '01	♀♀	7
● Rosso Piceno Morellone '03	♀♀	5
● Rosso Piceno Morellone '00	♀♀	5
● Rosso Piceno Nero di Vite '00	♀♀	7
● Rosso Piceno Nero di Vite '02	♀♀	7
● Rosso Piceno Morellone '99	♀♀	5
● Rosso Piceno Nero di Vite '03	♀♀	7
● Rosso Piceno Morellone '01	♀♀	5

● Rosso Piceno Sup. Nummaria '05	♀♀	4*
O Servator '06	♀♀	2*

Carminucci

VIA SAN LEONARDO, 39
63013 GROTTAMMARE [AP]
TEL. 0735735869
www.carminucci.com

ANNUAL PRODUCTION 200,000 bottles
HECTARES UNDER VINE 46
VITICULTURE METHOD Conventional

The Carminuccis' wines get better and better with every passing harvest. Father and son team Piero and Giovanni have quite a history in the world of wine as they are the heirs to a family tradition that spans almost a century. They originally dealt in unbottled wine but to their credit they changed direction and made major financial investments to bottle their products. The jewel in the estate crown is Paccaosso, a Montepulciano whose modern slant is evident in its toasty, spicy aromas. The palate is full and expansive but slightly cowed by the oak. The other house gem is the Rosso Piceno Naumachos, a more direct wine, showing dark and dense yet refreshing in its balsamic notes. It has the trademark montepulciano muscle that produces a concentrated, reactive palate while maintaining its tannic bite. By way of contrast to this bountiful structure, we have the dynamic succulence of the Rosso Piceno Grotte sul Mare, which is led by its outstanding backbone. From the Naumachos whites, we particularly liked the big, tropical fruits Chardonnay and the green Falerio with its sage and citrus fruit nose.

Casalfarneto

VIA FARNETO, 16
60030 SERRA DE' CONTI [AN]
TEL. 0731889001
www.casalfarneto.it

ANNUAL PRODUCTION 380,000 bottles
HECTARES UNDER VINE 25
VITICULTURE METHOD Conventional

Since its acquisition by the Togni group, Casalfarneto has seen some major changes. First and foremost, there's a modern new cellar, thoughtfully designed to blend into the landscape of the Serra de' Conti hills. The cellar was built to accommodate growing production as the new vineyards planted under the direction of estate manager, Danilo Solustri, and oenologist, Roberto Potentini, come onstream. The Verdicchios we were offered for tasting vary in style but they all made quite an impression. We'll start our notes with the Riserva Grancasale, which proffers generous notes of sweet tropical fruit and a dynamic, tangy palate. The nose of the Fontevecchia reveals subtle aromas of apple-like and citrus fruit that combine on the palate with the wonderful chorus of freshness, ripe flesh and rich minerality. The Solustro has fragrant flowery nuances and a soft palate whereas Cimaio is obtained from verdicchio grapes harvested when overripe and has a very mature, evolved, almost sweet palate. Up last was Rosso Piceno Pitulum, which reveals crisp notes of blackberry and black cherry and a palate given weight and concentration by tight-knit, velvety tannins.

● Paccaosso '04	♟♟ 8
● Rosso Piceno Sup. Naumachos '04	♟♟ 4*
● Rosso Piceno Grotte sul Mare '06	♟♟ 3*
○ Falerio dei Colli Ascolani Naumachos '06	♟♟ 3*
○ Chardonnay Naumachos '06	♟♟ 4
○ Falerio dei Colli Ascolani Grotte sul Mare '06	♟ 2
● Paccaosso '01	♟♟ 7
● Paccaosso '02	♟♟ 7
● Paccaosso '03	♟♟ 8
● Rosso Piceno Sup. Naumachos '03	♟♟ 4

● Rosso Piceno Pitulum '05	♟♟ 4
○ Verdicchio dei Castelli di Jesi Cl. Solustro '06	♟♟ 3*
○ Verdicchio dei Castelli di Jesi Cl. Grancasale Ris. '05	♟♟ 4
○ Verdicchio dei Castelli di Jesi Cl. Sup. Fontevecchia '06	♟♟ 3*
○ Cimaio '04	♟ 5
● Rosso Conero Tonos '05	♟ 4
○ Verdicchio dei Castelli di Jesi Cl. Sup. Cimaio '03	♟♟ 4
● Rosso Piceno Pitulum '04	♟♟ 4
○ Verdicchio dei Castelli di Jesi Cl. Sup. Grancasale '05	♟♟ 4
○ Verdicchio dei Castelli di Jesi Cl. Sup. Cimaio '01	♟♟ 4
○ Verdicchio dei Castelli di Jesi Cl. Sup. Grancasale '04	♟♟ 4

Maria Pia Castelli

C.DA S. ISIDORO, 22
63015 MONTE URANO [AP]
TEL. 0734841774
www.mariapiacastelli.it

ANNUAL PRODUCTION 20,000 bottles
HECTARES UNDER VINE 8
VITICULTURE METHOD Natural

Just reading these notes on Maria Pia Castelli's wines may not do her justice. Maria Pia and her husband Enrico Bartoletti aspire to imbue their bottles with originality, character and accents that denote a unique style far removed from the norm. A perfect example is Stella Flora, a white obtained from pecorino, passerina, trebbiano and malvasia fermented on the skins then aged for 18 months in barriques. The barely discernible hint of oak, nuances of citrus peel and bitter herbs, and the neat final sensation of dried fruit would look, on paper, to be utterly distinct from one another but on tasting this wine proves to be very well integrated. The estate's flagship red, Erasmo Castelli, also displays the fine balance that distinguishes structure from weight, youthful severity from roughness, and power from alcohol. More time in the cellar will undoubtedly give it substance that translates into complexity. The Sangiovese Orano is more coherent but no less tasty for that. Sant'Isidoro, an oak-matured rosé, may prompt contrasting opinions but no one can deny that it is unique for the thrust and intensity it displays on the palate.

Cantine di Castignano

C.DA SAN VENANZO, 31
63032 CASTIGNANO [AP]
TEL. 0736822216
www.cantinedicastignano.com

ANNUAL PRODUCTION 300,000 bottles
HECTARES UNDER VINE 550
VITICULTURE METHOD Conventional

Montemisio, a tiny sanctuary situated between Castignano and Rotella, has given its name to the most prestigious wine produced by the local producers' co-operative. Offida Pecorino has a palate with very pleasant notes of pineapple and spring flowers. The cellar's propensity for interesting whites is further confirmed by Falerio Destriero, with its full palate and aromas of golden delicious apples, and the soft Gramelot obtained from a mix of whites, trebbiano, verdicchio and passerina, picked when slightly overripe to enhance the fruit. From the reds on offer, it was the ripe, spicy Offida Gran Maestro that stood out, its well-behaved acidity buttressed by mature, well-rounded tannins. The merlot and sangiovese Templaria offers similar sensations in a simpler key. The rest of the range is well managed, clean and very reasonably priced and there are two new recruits to the ranks. The organic Sangiovese is uncomplicated and Offida Passerina has subtle florality and a fluent, fragrant palate.

● Erasmo Castelli '05	❦❦	6
● Orano '06	❦❦	4*
○ Stella Flora '05	❦❦	4
☉ Sant'Isidoro '06		3
● Erasmo Castelli '02	❦❦	6
● Erasmo Castelli '03	❦❦	6
● Erasmo Castelli '04	❦❦	6
● Orano '03	❦❦	4
○ Stella Flora '04	❦❦	4
○ Stella Flora '04	❦❦	4
● Orano '04	❦❦	4
● Orano '05	❦	4

● Offida Rosso Gran Maestro '03	❦❦	4
○ Offida Pecorino Montemisio '06	❦❦	3*
○ Gramelot '05	❦❦	3*
○ Falerio dei Colli Ascolani Destriero '06	❦❦	3*
● Templaria '05	❦❦	3*
● Rosso Piceno '06	❦	2
● Rosso Piceno Sup. Destriero '05	❦	3
● Sangiovese '05	❦	2
○ Falerio dei Colli Ascolani '06	❦	2
○ Offida Passerina '06	❦	3
● Offida Rosso Gran Maestro '02	❦❦	4

Ciù Ciù

LOC. SANTA MARIA IN CARRO
C.DA CIAFONE, 106
63035 OFFIDA [AP]
TEL. 0736810001
info@ciuciu.com

ANNUAL PRODUCTION 330,000 bottles
HECTARES UNDER VINE 98
VITICULTURE METHOD Natural

Tano Belloni was an extraordinary cyclist who notched up no less than 100 second places in the course of his career. Given all of the wines that they have sent to our finals over the years without a Three Glass trophy to show for their efforts, we would hate the Bartolomei brothers to fall victim to the same eternal runner-up syndrome. But that doesn't look likely. Indeed, we are pleased to note that Ciù Ciù's wines are increasingly well made thanks to the solid experience amassed by their makers. Oppidum is obtained from late-harvest montepulciano and flaunts sumptuous fruitiness, which is clearly mirrored on a palate that progresses impressively checked only by a hint of astringency in the finish. The same power and energy are evident in the round, balsamic Gotico and the elegant Esperanto, a smooth, supple Offida Rosso. Pecorino Le Merlettaie is well rounded, its clear aromas of ripe fruit announcing a deep, broad palate. We'll end our notes here but not before saying that Belloni did finally win the Giro d'Italia!

Cocci Grifoni

LOC. SAN SAVINO
C.DA MESSIERI, 12
63038 RIPATRANSONE [AP]
TEL. 073590143
www.tenutacoccigrifoni.it

ANNUAL PRODUCTION 400,000 bottles
HECTARES UNDER VINE 45
VITICULTURE METHOD Conventional

Guido Cocci Grifoni has kept a firm hand on the reins of this estate over the years. He still pulls the strings but now he has been joined by his two daughters. Marilena takes care of the commercial side of things while Paola, an oenologist, runs the cellar with the support of consultant Roberto Potentini. The one thing that hasn't changed with the advent of the new generation is the solid, reliable style of the wines, particularly what has become the estate's most representative product, the Pecorino Colle Vecchio. Its very traditional nose proffers lovely ripe, evolved notes with more flowers than fruit. Similarly, the palate favours freshness and tanginess over richness of texture. The Rosso Piceno Le Torri shows nice density and refreshing fruit while the Tellus, from montepulciano, cabernet and merlot, gives sensations of crushed fruit on the nose and a simple, coherent palate with a faintly aromatic note in the finish. The Falerio Vigneti San Basso is lightweight and fruity with good acidity and the classic Falerio is uncomplicated.

● Offida Rosso Esperanto '04	🍷🍷 5
○ Offida Pecorino Le Merlettaie '06	🍷🍷 4*
● Oppidum '03	🍷🍷 5
● Rosso Piceno Sup. Gotico '05	🍷🍷 4*
● Rosso Piceno Sup. Orum '05	🍷🍷 3*
● Saggio Sangiovese '05	🍷🍷 5
○ Gaudio Chardonnay '06	🍷🍷 3*
○ Evoè Passerina '06	🍷 3
○ Falerio dei Colli Ascolani Oris '06	🍷 3
● Rosso Piceno Bacchus '06	🍷 3
● Offida Rosso Esperanto '01	🍷🍷 5
● Offida Rosso Esperanto '02	🍷🍷 6
● Oppidum '02	🍷🍷 5
● Oppidum '01	🍷🍷 5
● Oppidum '00	🍷🍷 3
● Saggio Sangiovese '04	🍷🍷 5

○ Offida Pecorino Podere Colle Vecchio '06	🍷🍷 4
● Rosso Piceno Sup. Le Torri '04	🍷🍷 3*
● Tellus '06	🍷 3
○ Falerio dei Colli Ascolani '06	🍷 3
○ Offida Passerina Gaudio Magno Brut	🍷 4
○ Falerio dei Colli Ascolani Vign. San Basso '06	🍷 3
● Rosso Piceno Sup. V. Messieri '02	🍷🍷 4
● Rosso Piceno Sup. V. Messieri '03	🍷🍷 4
● Offida Rosso Il Grifone '02	🍷🍷 5
● Rosso Piceno Sup. Le Torri '03	🍷🍷 3

Collestefano

LOC. COLLE STEFANO, 3
62022 CASTELRAIMONDO [MC]
TEL. 0737640439
www.collestefano.com

ANNUAL PRODUCTION	60,000 bottles
HECTARES UNDER VINE	10
VITICULTURE METHOD	Certified organic

Fabio Marchionni comes from a family that has always worked for the local co-operative winery. After completing his studies in agriculture and several jobs in Germany and Alsace, he realized just how much potential the verdicchio variety actually has. Fabio releases just one fabulously drinkable wine, a deep, delicate, extremely savoury white, It's a wine that refuses to rely on glycerine-driven power or sheer alcohol. Its astonishing fragrances combine the freshness of citrus fruits with gentler notes of hawthorn and complex mineral sensations that emerge to dominate the nose as they unfold. This white is sourced from the few vineyards around the house, vineyards caressed by the whispers of Apennine woods at night, vineyards that live side by side with olives ripening on the trees in a pristine environment. No chemicals are used on the vines, in accordance with the organic discipline that Fabio's love for his territory demands. We have always known that this crisp, elegant white was capable of great things and its time has finally come. We gave it Three resounding Glasses in tribute to the humility and tenacity of a great wine man.

La Cantina dei Colli Ripani

VIA TOSCIANO, 28
63038 RIPATRANSONE [AP]
TEL. 07359505
www.colliripani.it

ANNUAL PRODUCTION	600,000 bottles
HECTARES UNDER VINE	1,100
VITICULTURE METHOD	Conventional

The Cantina dei Colli Ripani is a point of reference for many small producers around Ripatransone and Offida. Over the years, it has pursued a strategy of offering good quality bottled wines at a reasonable price. Its products, even the cheapest, are always well typed and well made. Vinified traditionally, they set out to express the characteristics of the various local varieties as simply and approachably as possible. The Pecorino Rugaro presents clear, clean notes of pear, citrus fruit and flowers before unveiling a deep, leisurely palate with lovely savoury length. We liked Brezzolino not just for its nice fruity nose but also for its wonderfully long, fresh and fragrant palate. And we appreciated it all the more because it is a Falerio, a DOC that many producers seem to have neglected entirely. On the red side of the equation, the Khorakhanè from equal parts of cabernet and montepulciano tends to conceal its fruit at first but opens on the palate to end in a lovely finish of sweet spice. This year, however, the Leo Ripanus disappointed. It is a little lacklustre with a palate encumbered by over-evolved notes.

O Verdicchio di Matelica Collestefano '06	¶¶¶	4*
O Verdicchio di Matelica Collestefano '02	¶¶	4
O Verdicchio di Matelica Collestefano '04	¶¶	4
O Verdicchio di Matelica Collestefano '03	¶¶	4
O Verdicchio di Matelica Collestefano '05	¶¶	4
O Verdicchio di Matelica Collestefano '01	¶¶	4

O Falerio dei Colli Ascolani Brezzolino '06	¶¶	3*
O Offida Pecorino Rugaro '06	¶¶	4
● Khorakhanè '03	¶¶	6
● Offida Rosso Leo Ripanus '04	¶	4
● Rosso Piceno Transone '06	¶	2
O Offida Passerina Ninfa Ripana '06	¶	2
● Offida Rosso Leo Ripanus '02	¶¶	4
● Offida Rosso Leo Ripanus '03	¶¶	4
● Khorakhanè '02	¶¶	6

Cantina Cològnola

LOC. COLÒGNOLA
62011 CINGOLI [MC]
TEL. 0733616438
www.agrarialombardi.it

Conti di Buscareto

VIA SAN S. APOLLINARE, 126
60011 ARCEVIA [AN]
TEL. 0717988020
www.contidibuscareto.com

ANNUAL PRODUCTION 50,000 bottles
HECTARES UNDER VINE 21.5
VITICULTURE METHOD Conventional

For several years now, Antonietta
Lombardi's estate has been vinifying
verdicchio and several red varieties growing
in the vineyards it owns just outside Cingoli.
Each year, Cantina Cològnola continues to
improve and its wines are beginning to
acquire a definite personality, even if in
some cases they still tend to lack fragrance.
A case in point is Riserva di Verdicchio
Labieno. It has pleasing flowers and fruit
aromas, and nice tanginess, but the buttery,
vanillaed notes are a little too evident. As for
the other whites, Ghiffa is the most
interesting. Almondy aromas combine with
vegetal nuances and florality, introducing a
mid-weight palate that shows fresh-tasting
and supple. The San Michele della Ghiffa is
round on both nose and palate with fruit
and tanginess that struggle to find a
balance in the mouth. The reds on offer
include Sestiere with aromas of sweet fruit
and spice, powerful backbone and fine-
grained tannins that dry out a bit in the
finish. Finally, the heady Buraco is bursting
with youthful exuberance.

ANNUAL PRODUCTION 80,000 bottles
HECTARES UNDER VINE 65
VITICULTURE METHOD Conventional

Lacrima and verdicchio are the classic
varieties on these slopes rising up behind
Senigallia. The Conti di Buscareto estate
adheres to this tradition but obtains its
wines from several different territories. The
entire white production comes from the
municipality of Arcevia, towards the
Apennines, and all of the Verdicchios offer
more than decent quality. The
Ammazzaconte selection is first-rate.
Varietal and elegant in its aromas of apple-
like fruit and almond, it maintains its poise
on the deep, very complex palate. What the
basic version loses in elegance it gains in
force thanks to vibrant backbone and a
confident, tangy finish. Finally, the Passito is
a warm wine with a voluptuous palate that
discloses lingering sensations of dried
apricots and macaroons. The Lacrimas
come from plots at Morro d'Alba.
Compagnia della Rosa and Nicolò di
Buscareto both reveal a faint hint of dried
roses and morello cherries followed by a
concentrated, chewy palate. The first of
these two selections is fresher and more
enjoyable. Also decent is the '06 Lacrima.

O Verdicchio dei Castelli di Jesi Cl. Labieno Ris. '05	♟♟ 4
O Verdicchio dei Castelli di Jesi Ghiffa '06	♟♟ 3*
● Sestiere '04	♟♟ 4
● Buraco '06	♟ 4
O Verdicchio dei Castelli di Jesi Cl. Sup. S. Michele della Ghiffa '05	♟ 4
O Verdicchio dei Castelli di Jesi Passito Cingulum '05	5
● Buraco '04	♟♟ 4
O Verdicchio dei Castelli di Jesi Cl. Sup. S. Michele della Ghiffa '04	♟♟ 4

O Verdicchio dei Castelli di Jesi '06	♟♟ 3*
O Verdicchio dei Castelli di Jesi Ammazzaconte '06	♟♟ 3*
O Verdicchio dei Castelli di Jesi Passito '04	♟♟ 5
● Lacrima di Morro d'Alba Nicolò di Buscareto '04	♟♟ 6
● Lacrima di Morro d'Alba Compagnia della Rosa '04	♟♟ 5
● Lacrima di Morro d'Alba '06	♟ 4
● Crimà '06	♟ 3
● Rosso Piceno '06	♟ 3
O Verdicchio dei Castelli di Jesi Passito '03	♟♟ 5
● Lacrima di Morro d'Alba Compagnia della Rosa '03	♟♟ 5

Contrada Tenna
C.DA TENNA
VIA TENNA
63025 RAPAGNANO [AP]
TEL. 048162166

ANNUAL PRODUCTION 20,000 bottles
HECTARES UNDER VINE 8
VITICULTURE METHOD Conventional

In spring 2000, Nicola Manferrari, owner of the Borgo del Tiglio estate in Friuli, was on his way to Piceno. During the journey, he came across an abandoned farm and experienced a sort of epiphany. He fell under the property's spell and bought it on the spot, excited not only by the sheer beauty of the place but also by the idea of working with montepulciano and sangiovese. The eight hectares of vineyards had been planted 40 years earlier and were in a wretched state. With the help of the old farm workers who had originally planted the plots, Nicola brought the estate back to life. In 2002, he made his first experimental harvest and the following year he started work in earnest, vinifying the fruit at his cellar in Cormons. The Nereo is obtained from montepulciano only and this very elegant interpretation of the grape displays whistle-clean, ripe fruit on the palate. The excellence of the Sangiovese, with notes of jam and spice on the nose, then silky and aristocratic on the palate, highlights the great potential of the variety in this territory. Obtained from montepulciano and sangiovese, the Milleuve has intense, fresh wild berries and a soft, warm, elegant palate.

Coroncino
C.DA CORONCINO, 7
60039 STAFFOLO [AN]
TEL. 0731779494
coroncino@libero.it

ANNUAL PRODUCTION 45,000 bottles
HECTARES UNDER VINE 9.5
VITICULTURE METHOD Conventional

The lovely Staffolo hills look out over swaths of unspoiled countryside and views of a boundless sea. In this environment, the verdicchio grape expresses itself in a completely original way, different not just to fruit grown on the opposite bank of the Esino but also to grapes from nearby Cupramontana. Lucio Canestrari's wines are a good reflection of the land: powerful, weighty and austere but never over the top. They are always buoyed by elegant balance and rich savouriness. A vivid acid vein enlivens the Coroncino and makes its presence felt even more clearly in the Gaiospino, a sure guarantee of the cellarability and growth that these wines will demonstrate over the next few years. The differences between the two Verdicchios owe more to the ways in which they are harvested and vinified than anything else. Refined oaky notes hint at impeccable technique with small wood in the Gaiospino while the Coroncino offers more in the way of softness and fruit. The Bacco selection is simpler but far from ordinary, showing fragrant and very drinkable.

● Sangiovese '03	♥♥ 5
● Nereo '03	♥♥ 5
● Milleuve Rosso '04	♥♥ 4*

○ Verdicchio dei Castelli di Jesi Cl. Sup. Coroncino '05	♥♥ 4*
○ Verdicchio dei Castelli di Jesi Cl. Sup. Gaiospino '05	♥♥ 5
○ Verdicchio dei Castelli di Jesi Cl. Sup. Il Bacco '06	♥♥ 3*
○ Verdicchio dei Castelli di Jesi Cl. Sup. Gaiospino '03	♥♥♥ 5
○ Verdicchio dei Castelli di Jesi Cl. Sup. Gaiospino '97	♥♥♥ 5
○ Verdicchio dei Castelli di Jesi Cl. Sup. Coroncino '04	♥♥ 4
○ Verdicchio dei Castelli di Jesi Cl. Sup. Gaiospino '04	♥♥ 5
○ Verdicchio dei Castelli di Jesi Cl. Sup. Gaiospino '02	♥♥ 5
○ Verdicchio dei Castelli di Jesi Cl. Sup. Gaiospino Fumé '03	♥♥ 6

Costadoro

via Monte Aquilino, 2
63039 San Benedetto
del Tronto [AP]
tel. 073581781
www.vinicostadoro.com

ANNUAL PRODUCTION 1,500,000 bottles
HECTARES UNDER VINE 87
VITICULTURE METHOD Conventional

Although its most prestigious wines were unavailable for tasting this year, the estate belonging to the Costantini Brancadoro family still presented some quite admirable products. The range pays tribute to the solid effort over the years that enables the cellar to release such a large number of bottles to market. Costadoro is living proof that big volumes do not always preclude quality when work in the vineyard and cellar is carried out competently and carefully. A perfect example of value for money is the Rosso Piceno Superiore La Rocca. Although not particularly powerful, it shows fresh-tasting and fragrant with bags of red berry fruit on the nose and a soft palate rendered even more interesting by an impressively savoury finish. The Pecorino is vinified in stainless steel and offers lovely fruit and flower sensations, good body, delightful softness and a fabulously long finish lifted by elegant minerality. The Passerina has a simple nose and a no-nonsense palate.

● Rosso Piceno Sup. La Rocca '05	🍷🍷 3*
○ Offida Pecorino '06	🍷🍷 3*
○ Offida Passerina '06	🍷 2
○ Falerio dei Colli Ascolani '06	2
● Offida Rosso Diciottoquarantotto '01	YY 5
● Il Crinale Merlot '02	YY 5
● Rosso Piceno Sup. La Rocca '04	YY 4
● Rosso Piceno Sup. La Rocca '03	YY 4
● Offida Rosso Diciottoquarantotto '02	YY 4

Tenuta De Angelis

via San Francesco, 10
63030 Castel di Lama [AP]
tel. 073687429
www.tenutadeangelis.it

ANNUAL PRODUCTION 500,000 bottles
HECTARES UNDER VINE 50
VITICULTURE METHOD Conventional

Anghelos, obtained from montepulciano with a small amount of cabernet, came very close to winning our top award again this year. It's all a question of nuance in a wine that is indisputably great, combining elegance, freshness and fruit complexity – its notes of cassis, blackberry and black cherry are intense and exhilarating – with juicy, velvety flesh. But Anghelos is merely the jewel in the crown of an extremely reliable estate that has earned a reputation for the typicity and approachable appeal of its wines. We have long been aware of Quinto Fausti's knack with good reds, which he produces with the help of experienced oenologist Roberto Potentini in the cellar. Yet again, it is two superb Rosso Piceno Superiores that keep the De Angelis flag flying high. The basic version offers gorgeous aromas of fresh and candied fruit followed by a soft, fragrant, tempting palate with good progression. The Oro selection is fuller and richer, despite its more rigid, austere style, and is enhanced by lovely notes of balsam.

● Anghelos '05	🍷🍷 5
● Rosso Piceno Sup. Oro '05	🍷🍷 4
● Rosso Piceno Sup. '05	🍷🍷 3*
● Rosso Piceno '06	🍷 2
○ Falerio dei Colli Ascolani '06	🍷 2
○ Prato Grande Chardonnay '06	🍷 2
● Anghelos '01	YYY 5
● Anghelos '99	YYY 5
● Anghelos '00	YY 5
● Anghelos '02	YY 5
● Anghelos '03	YY 5
● Anghelos '04	YY 5
● Rosso Piceno Sup. Oro '03	YY 5
● Rosso Piceno Sup. Oro '04	YY 4

Degli Azzoni Avogadro Carradori

c.so CARRADORI, 13
62010 MONTEFANO [MC]
TEL. 0733850002
www.degliazzoni.it

ANNUAL PRODUCTION 100,000 bottles
HECTARES UNDER VINE 130
VITICULTURE METHOD Conventional

The combination of Filippo degli Azzoni's clear ideas and prudent management with the expertise and steady hand of young cellarman Lorenzo Gigli, supported by oenologist Salvatore Lovo, ensure consistent production at this well-known estate in the Macerata hinterland. The fact that Lorenzo can select the best batches of grapes from 130 hectares of vineyards is certainly beneficial to the limited production of bottled wines, although it must be said that the unbottled wine sold through the cellar is actually very decent. The Rosso Cantalupo, a blend of 50 per cent montepulciano, 40 per cent merlot and ten per cent sangiovese, and the Passatempo, obtained mainly from montepulciano with a little merlot and cabernet, are both excellent. The first impresses with its simplicity and coherence, its soft, harmonious palate displaying agreeable ripe fruit. The second has a rounder, almost sweet profile, with good alcoholic presence and a substantial finish. From the whites, we liked the Sauvignon for its vegetal, aniseed-laced notes and the Bianco Cantalupo, a blend of verdicchio with some sauvignon and viognier that has aromas of almond and acacia blossom, good backbone and fluency on the palate.

Fattoria Dezi

VIA FONTE MAGGIO, 14
63029 SERVIGLIANO [AP]
TEL. 0734710090
fattoriadezi@hotmail.com

ANNUAL PRODUCTION 50,000 bottles
HECTARES UNDER VINE 15
VITICULTURE METHOD Natural

In previous editions, we have told the story of the Dezi family and the efforts of young brothers Stefano and Davide who divide their time between their vineyards, cellar and public relations. With his energy and curiosity, Stefano is the mastermind behind the estate's PR, charming clients with his frank charm and attractive Marche accent. The wines produced at Fattoria Dezi reflect the qualities of the family for they, too, are genuine, solid and uncompromising. This year the Solo, an exemplary interpretation of sangiovese – full-bodied, flowery, dense and mouthfilling – romped home to win a Three Glass trophy. This magnificent wine has a great future ahead of it. Regina del Bosco '04 is a Montepulciano with a refined, balsamic nose and a creamy, elegant palate. The Dezio plays the part of a rather prestigious second wine, a succulent offering with concentrated development on the palate. Last but not least, the Dezis presented us with a surprise: 3,500 bottles of a Regina del Bosco '00 selection that has spent two extra years in the cellar. Its concentrated fruit is perfectly mature and comes through powerfully without the slightest hint of overripeness. To the contrary, it is compact, fresh and austere.

● Passatempo '05	♟♟ 5
● Rosso Cantalupo '05	♟♟ 4*
○ Colli Maceratesi Bianco '06	♟ 2
○ Bianco Cantalupo '06	♟ 3
○ Sauvignon Blanc '06	♟ 4
● Rosso Piceno '05	♟ 3
○ Grechetto '06	♟ 3
● Passatempo '02	♟♟ 5
● Passatempo '03	♟♟ 5
● Passatempo '04	♟♟ 5
● Rosso Cantalupo '04	♟♟ 4
● Rosso Cantalupo '03	♟♟ 4

● Solo Sangiovese '05	♟♟♟ 7
● Regina del Bosco '04	♟♟ 7
● Regina del Bosco '00	♟♟ 8
● Dezio Vign. Beccaccia '05	♟♟ 5
○ Le Solagne '06	♟ 4
● Regina del Bosco '03	♟♟♟ 6
● Solo Sangiovese '00	♟♟♟ 6
● Solo Sangiovese '01	♟♟♟ 6
● Regina del Bosco '01	♟♟ 6
● Solo Sangiovese '03	♟♟ 7
● Solo Sangiovese '02	♟♟ 6
● Regina del Bosco '02	♟♟ 6
● Solo Sangiovese '04	♟♟ 6

La Distesa
VIA ROMITA, 28
60034 CUPRAMONTANA [AN]
TEL. 0731781230
www.ladistesa.it

ANNUAL PRODUCTION   10,000 bottles
HECTARES UNDER VINE 3
VITICULTURE METHOD   Natural

Corrado Dottori is stubborn, determined and strong-willed. He refuses to use chemicals and has little time for elaborate processes and procedures in the cellar. He believes in his palate and the experience he has acquired day after day, step after step, as he tramps up and down his rows. And his wines reflect the restless, solid character of their maker, showing personality and scant respect for convention and reactivity. The Terre Silvate is an archetypal Verdicchio. The acid vein is well supported by impressive salty extract that integrates with well-gauged alcohol, the assertive aromas roundly proclaiming aniseed, almond and roasted hazelnut-like notes. Gli Eremi is even less biddable. Part of the must ferments in barrique, emerging with buttery sensations that lead on the nose but do not overwhelm the fine, wilful palate. Obtained from sangiovese and montepulciano with a dash of cabernet, the Nocenzio still has room to grow. Its earthy notes and rather unruly, roughish tannins are edgy as yet.

Fausti
C.DA CASTELLETTA, 16
63023 FERMO [AP]
TEL. 0734620492

ANNUAL PRODUCTION   70,000 bottles
HECTARES UNDER VINE 11
VITICULTURE METHOD   Conventional

The die is cast: Domenico D'Angelo has crossed his metaphorical Rubicon. He has made the big decision not to go down the sangiovese route, as the river in Romagna would suggest, but has opted instead to terminate all consultancy and third-party work. This will allow him to dedicate himself exclusively to the estate he owns in partnership with his companion Cristina Fausti. Domenico realized that to maintain the standard that won him our top prize two years ago and almost netted another last year, he would have to devote every moment of his day to his vineyards and cellar. That total commitment has been repaid by the Three Glass trophy awarded this year to the apple of his eye, Vespro. Obtained from 70 per cent montepulciano with a little syrah, it weds power with elegance, developing firmly on the palate with rare coherence to suggest a perfect blend of red berry fruit and black pepper aromas with a hint of cocoa powder in the finish. The pure syrah Perdomenico exhibits the same spicy, concentrated character but is a little less balanced. The '06 Rosso Piceno Fausto is a decent wine with a soft, enveloping style while the Falerio Vispo shows nice typicity but little more.

O Verdicchio dei Castelli di Jesi Cl.	
Sup. Terre Silvate '06	♥♥ 3*
O Verdicchio dei Castelli di Jesi Cl.	
Sup. Gli Eremi Ris. '05	♥♥ 4
● Nocenzio '04	♥ 5
O Verdicchio dei Castelli di Jesi Cl.	
Sup. Gli Eremi Ris. '04	♥♥ 4
O Verdicchio dei Castelli di Jesi Cl.	
Sup. Terre Silvate '05	♥♥ 3
● Nocenzio '03	♥♥ 4

● Vespro '05	♥♥♥ 5
● Perdomenico Syrah '05	♥♥ 5
● Rosso Piceno Fausto '06	♥♥ 3*
O Falerio dei Colli Ascolani	
Vispo '06	♥ 3
● Vespro '03	♥♥♥ 4
● Vespro '01	♥♥ 4
● Vespro '02	♥♥ 4
● Vespro '04	♥♥ 5

Fazi Battaglia

via Roma, 117
60032 Castelplanio [AN]
tel. 073181591
www.fazibattaglia.it

ANNUAL PRODUCTION 3,000,000 bottles
HECTARES UNDER VINE 300
VITICULTURE METHOD Conventional

With understandable emotion, Fazi Battaglia presented a restyled version of the cellar's best-known wine, Verdicchio Titulus. We applaud this courage, as it is not easy to change a label that is known worldwide, thanks to an annual output of 2,800,000 bottles. For obvious reasons, the amphora-shaped bottle and the quality of its contents also remain unchanged: this is an upfront wine that has to cater for everyone's palate. Turning to the rest of the Verdicchios, the Massaccio from overripe grapes has honeyed, fruity aromas and ends in an almost resinous finish that is both unusual and rather pleasant. The San Sisto shows more adept use of small barrels, throwing peachy fruit aromas with a hint of camphor that are picked up in the finish of the mid-weight palate. The edgy, tangy Le Moie is very varietal while Arkezia, from sun-dried grapes, starts out on concentrated notes of peach then moves on to reveal sweetness on the fairly long palate. The Conero Riserva Passo del Lupo is substantial with just the right degree of dryness in the finish.

● Conero Passo del Lupo Ris. '04	ΨΨ	5
○ Verdicchio dei Castelli di Jesi Cl. Sup. Massaccio '05	ΨΨ	5
○ Verdicchio dei Castelli di Jesi Cl. San Sisto Ris. '04	ΨΨ	5
○ Arkezia Muffo di S. Sisto '04	Ψ	6
○ Verdicchio dei Castelli di Jesi Cl. Sup. Le Moie '06	Ψ	4
● Rosso Conero '06		4
○ Verdicchio dei Castelli di Jesi Cl. Titulus '06		4
○ Verdicchio dei Castelli di Jesi Cl. Sup. Massaccio '03	YYY	4
○ Verdicchio dei Castelli di Jesi Cl. Sup. Massaccio '01	YYY	4
○ Verdicchio dei Castelli di Jesi Cl. Sup. Massaccio '04	YY	4

Fiorini

via Giardino Campioli, 5
61040 Barchi [PU]
tel. 072197151
www.fioriniwines.it

ANNUAL PRODUCTION 160,000 bottles
HECTARES UNDER VINE 44
VITICULTURE METHOD Conventional

As you come to Barchi, stop for a moment on the edge of town to admire the view of the Fiorini estate with its neat rows of ordered vines. It is clear, even to those of us who are not green-fingered, that this small valley was made for the cultivation of vines. The estate was founded by Luigi Fiorini, passed to Valentino, and is run today by his daughter Carla, an oenologist, with the support of her mother, Silvana. They grow mainly bianchello, otherwise known as biancame, along with montepulciano and sangiovese. Sangiovese is the base of a standard label wine, Sirio, that offers fragrant notes of fresh fruit. The white grapes go into two Bianchellos: Tenuta Campioli is one of the best of its category, offering ripe fruit aromas, a full palate and a long, tangy finish, while Vigna Sant'Ilario is fresh-tasting and lighter in style. Obtained from 60 per cent montepulciano and 40 per cent cabernet sauvignon, Bartis has lovely hints of ripe, raspberry and blueberry-led fruit. The refreshing palate shows just the right amount of concentration and good development, with smooth tannins rounding out the finish.

● Colli Pesaresi Rosso Bartis '04	ΨΨ	4
○ Bianchello del Metauro Tenuta Campioli '06	ΨΨ	3*
● Colli Pesaresi Sangiovese Sirio '06	Ψ	3
○ Bianchello del Metauro V. Sant'Ilario '06	Ψ	2*
○ Bianchello del Metauro Tenuta Campioli '05	YY	3

Cantine Fontezoppa
C.DA SAN DOMENICO, 24
CIVITANOVA MARCHE [MC]
TEL. 0733790504
www.cantinefontezoppa.it

★ Gioacchino Garofoli
P.LE G. GAROFOLI, 1
60022 CASTELFIDARDO [AN]
TEL. 0717820162
www.garofolivini.it

ANNUAL PRODUCTION 50,000 bottles
HECTARES UNDER VINE 40
VITICULTURE METHOD Conventional

ANNUAL PRODUCTION 2,000,000 bottles
HECTARES UNDER VINE 50
VITICULTURE METHOD Conventional

Although Fontezoppa grows varieties such as cabernet sauvignon and merlot, its roots are firmly planted in Macerata. We mention this because the cellar aims to imbue its wines with the spirit of a territory that extends from vineyards on the coast at one end of the province to Serrapetrona, a few twisting kilometres from the Apennines, at the other. Almost all of the wines are blends except those produced with vernaccia nera, such as the robust Morò, which has a varietal green note with a hint of pepper followed by an austere, close-knit palate. The well-styled Cascià is a surprising sipping wine. A partridge eye pale red introduces dried figs, white chocolate and walnut that spill over onto the velvety, extremely long palate. The Falcotto, from vernaccia and sangiovese, is also very good, showing elegantly rustic on the incisive palate and powering through to an assertive finish. We liked the Piccinì, a supple, fruity rosé, above all for its irresistible drinkability.

Garofoli's wines are thoroughly reliable. That reliability has deep roots in this long-standing, recently expanded and modernized estate that has always been a family-run affair, and owes much to the acknowledged savoir faire of Carlo Garofoli, and it comes through in the quality of the wines that appear on our tasting table each year. Podium fell below the dizzying standards it has set in previous editions but then again 2005 was a challenging harvest across the board. But we did taste a very attractive Verdicchio with intense notes of sweet, ripe fruit, rich flesh and a lovely, elegantly tangy finish. The 2006 growing year was an altogether different kettle of fish and the recently released Macrina shows this in its fragrance and balance, flowing flawlessly across the palate to reveal sweet sensations of white-fleshed fruit. Serra Fiorese is a little curbed by oak ageing but it still manages to captivate with delicate notes of aniseed and broom leading into juiciness and minerality on the palate. Grosso Agontano is a full, elegant wine with a generous, attractive palate but a faintly jarring note is discernible on the nose.

● Morò '04	▼▼ 6
● Cascià Passito '02	▼▼ 6
● Serrapetrona Falcotto '05	▼▼ 5
☉ Piccinì '06	▼ 4
● Colli Maceratesi Rosso Carapetto Sel. Goduriose '04	▼ 5
● Colli Maceratesi Rosso Vardò '05	▼ 3
● Morò '03	♀♀ 6
● Colli Maceratesi Rosso Carapetto '04	♀♀ 5
● Serrapetrona Falcotto '04	♀♀ 5

○ Verdicchio dei Castelli di Jesi Cl. Serra Fiorese Ris. '04	▼▼ 5
○ Verdicchio dei Castelli di Jesi Cl. Sup. Podium '05	▼▼ 4*
● Conero Grosso Agontano Ris. '04	▼▼ 5
○ Brut Riserva M. Cl. '02	▼▼ 5
○ Verdicchio dei Castelli di Jesi Cl. Sup. Macrina '06	▼▼ 3*
○ Brut Charmat	▼ 3
○ Verdicchio dei Castelli di Jesi Cl. Serra del Conte '06	▼ 2
● Rosso Conero Piancarda '04	▼ 4
● Rosso Piceno Colle Ambro '04	▼ 3
● Rosso Conero Grosso Agontano Ris. '01	♀♀♀ 5
○ Verdicchio dei Castelli di Jesi Cl. Sup. Podium '04	♀♀♀ 4

Piergiovanni Giusti

LOC. MONTIGNANO
VIA CASTELLARO, 97
60019 SENIGALLIA [AN]
TEL. 071918031
www.lacrimagiusti.it

ANNUAL PRODUCTION 40,000 bottles
HECTARES UNDER VINE 12
VITICULTURE METHOD Conventional

The time and energy dedicated to the construction of new premises designed to rationalize Piergiovanni Giusti's cellar have had no effect whatsoever on the quality of the wines presented. True, the Lacrima failed to make it to the Three Glass finals this year but 2005 was not a good growing year. The weather prevented the grapes from reaching that perfect pitch of phenolic ripeness that is so critical to the elegance, power and balance of this particular variety. Nevertheless, the Rubbjano was the best we tasted from the DOC: black cherry juice, dried rose petals and faint attractive oaky sensations combine on the nose to echo perfectly across the palate, well-supported by the mouthfilling texture. The Luigino selection is not quite so well defined but it's still young. Although flavoursome and well-sustained, it needs to find the right balance between alcohol and boisterous, biting tannins. The '06 Lacrima is an absolute gem of a wine with typical flowery notes nicely buttressed by a palate of crunchy tannicity. The Rose di Settembre is a fragrant rosé whose irresistible palate is redolent of flowers and fresh almonds.

Esther Hauser

C.DA CORONCINO, 1A
60039 STAFFOLO [AN]
TEL. 0731770203
esther.hauser@virgilio.it

ANNUAL PRODUCTION 6,000 bottles
HECTARES UNDER VINE 1
VITICULTURE METHOD Natural

Esther Hauser left her native Switzerland to settle in Staffolo, inspired by the idea of living in surroundings of stunning natural beauty. She lives in the midst of her rows of vines and the sturdy olive trees from which she obtains a very prestigious oil. When she first arrived, Esther was not ashamed to admit her naive approach to country life or to communicate it in her first, broken words of Italian stiffened by her German-speaker's accent. Fifteen years have passed since then and little has changed. The cramped buildings struggle to contain the estate's few barriques, Esther's accent has barely softened and the wines produced here are as excellent and extraordinary as they were back then. Cupo is a splendid Montepulciano whose enveloping mouthfeel derives from the interweaving of very tight-knit tannins, alcoholic fullness and dynamic acid backbone. Its sole defect is the limited number of bottled produced: just over 3,000 a year. Ceppo is produced from the same variety and numbers are more generous. It lacks something in terms of overall harmony but offers plenty of sound fruit aromatics and an impressive entry on the palate.

● Lacrima di Morro d'Alba Luigino '05	🍷🍷 5
● Lacrima di Morro d'Alba Rubbjano '05	🍷🍷 4
● Lacrima di Morro d'Alba '06	🍷🍷 3*
☉ Le Rose di Settembre '06	🍷🍷 3*
● Lacrima di Morro d'Alba Rubbjano '04	🍷🍷 4
● Lacrima di Morro d'Alba Luigino '04	🍷🍷 5
● Lacrima di Morro d'Alba Luigino '03	🍷🍷 4
● Lacrima di Morro d'Alba Rubbjano '03	🍷🍷 4

● Il Cupo '05	🍷🍷 6
● Il Ceppo '05	🍷🍷 5
● Il Cupo '04	🍷🍷 6
● Il Cupo '03	🍷🍷 6
● Il Cupo Vecchie Vigne '02	🍷🍷 6
● Il Ceppo '04	🍷🍷 5

Fattoria Laila
VIA S. FILIPPO SUL CESANO, 27
61040 MONDAVIO [PU]
TEL. 0721979353
www.fattorialaila.it

ANNUAL PRODUCTION 100,000 bottles
HECTARES UNDER VINE 40
VITICULTURE METHOD Conventional

Andrea Crocenzi took over this estate in 1990 and with great enthusiasm has continued to build upon the foundations laid by its creator Aristide Licenzi. The winery has its headquarters in Mondavio in the municipality of Pesaro. Next to the existing vineyards that extend along the valley of Cesano at the foot of the Corinaldo hills, Andrea has planted new plots mainly to verdicchio and montepulciano. The estate has taken a significant step forward over the last few years and its wines acquire greater character and personality with each passing harvest. Rosso Piceno Lailum possesses compact fruit, clear notes of jam, spice and chocolate, a full palate with marked tannins and a leisurely finish. The '06 label Rosso Piceno offers simpler aromas of raspberry and blueberry with the odd trace of youthful asperity on the palate. Turning to the Verdicchios, Eklektikos reveals flowery nuances with hints of tropical and citrus fruit on both nose and palate and distinct savouriness that enhances its fragrance. The Riserva Lailum has a well-rounded style, sweet aromas of peachy fruit and a sensuous profile with a very soft, and perhaps too soft, finish.

Lanari
FRAZ. VARANO
VIA POZZO, 142
60029 ANCONA
TEL. 0712861343
www.lanarivini.it

ANNUAL PRODUCTION 50,000 bottles
HECTARES UNDER VINE 12
VITICULTURE METHOD Conventional

Over the years, Luca Lanari has imprinted his estate with that familiar, almost artisan style characteristic of a true grower-producer. He plays an active role in each step of the winemaking process, supported by Giancarlo Soverchia, who offers advice in both the vineyard and cellar. The standard-label Rosso Conero accounts for the lion's share of production. Solid in its tannic density and concentrated aromas of plum and black cherry, it pays the price for its full extraction in a stiffish finish. These sensations are even more evident in the Clivio selection, whose unresolved roughness tightens the palate in hints of bitter herbs and liquorice. A few more months' ageing will enable this firmly structured wine to realize its full potential. Riserva Aretè Ben is an altogether different proposition. The complex dark nuances discernible in the initial hint of tar quickly give way to notes of morello cherry, cocoa powder and spice. Entry on the palate is confident and pressure is maintained right through to the finish, whose only defect lies in a tad too much alcohol. The simple, upfront Lanari Rosa is released in a limited number of bottles and is ready for drinking now.

○ Verdicchio dei Castelli di Jesi Cl. Sup. Eklektikos '06	♟♟ 4*
○ Verdicchio dei Castelli di Jesi Cl. Lailum Ris. '05	♟♟ 5
● Rosso Piceno Lailum '04	♟♟ 5
● Rosso Piceno Fattoria Laila '06	♟ 3
○ Verdicchio dei Castelli di Jesi Cl. Sup. Fattoria Laila '06	♟ 3
○ Verdicchio dei Castelli di Jesi Cl. Lailum Ris. '04	♟♟ 4
● Rosso Piceno Lailum '03	♟♟ 5
● Lailum '01	♟♟ 5
● Lailum '02	♟♟ 5
● Lailum '00	♟♟ 5

● Rosso Conero Aretè Ris. '03	♟♟ 6
● Rosso Conero Clivio '05	♟♟ 5
● Rosso Conero '06	♟ 4
☉ Lanari Rosa '06	♟ 3
● Rosso Conero Fibbio '99	♟♟♟ 6
● Rosso Conero Fibbio '01	♟♟ 6
● Rosso Conero Fibbio '03	♟♟ 6
● Rosso Conero Fibbio '04	♟♟ 7
● Rosso Conero Clivio '04	♟♟ 5
● Rosso Conero Aretè '01	♟♟ 5

Luciano Landi
VIA GAVIGLIANO, 16
60030 BELVEDERE OSTRENSE [AN]
TEL. 073162353
www.aziendalandi.it

ANNUAL PRODUCTION 100,000 bottles
HECTARES UNDER VINE 18
VITICULTURE METHOD Conventional

Luciano Landi's estate was originally founded in 1950 when his grandfather Sergio acquired the first plots of land and decided to cultivate lacrima, a variety widely planted in the zone. Luciano's work is impressive for the care and attention that he dedicates to this challenging grape type. The maturation and cellar processes are designed to produce wines with plenty of fruit to express all of lacrima's aromatic properties. A perfect example is the Gavigliano. Its ripe fruit aromas of cherry and blackberry are sweetened by a hint of vanilla, and the full, powerful, supple palate ends in a fruity finish that echoes the spicy sensations. The basic Lacrima offers fresh, varietal aromatics and a simple, fragrant palate that cleanly mirrors the fruit. Obtained from montepulciano with a little merlot and cabernet, Goliardo has an intense fruity nose and a potent palate but tannins dry the finish and limit its complexity. The well-balanced Lacrima Passito is sweet and tannic to just the right degree, while the '06 Verdicchio has a delicate flowery nose and a firmly structured, fruity palate that is pleasantly tangy. Ragosto, from montepulciano with 20 per cent syrah, has yet to find the perfect balance.

Conte Leopardi Dittajuti
VIA MARINA II, 24
60026 NUMANA [AN]
TEL. 0717390116
www.leopardiwines.com

ANNUAL PRODUCTION 220,000 bottles
HECTARES UNDER VINE 52
VITICULTURE METHOD Natural

On Piervittorio Leopardi Dittajuti's estate, harvesting starts early and ends late. At the end of August, sometimes even earlier, the sauvignon cultivated at Sirolo just a stone's throw from the sea already shows its lovely golden hue. It is the range of temperatures created by continuous breezes that give the Bianco del Coppo its pressure and green aromatics. But the estate's best fruit goes to make the Calcare, whose vivid sensations of sage are the prelude to a palate offering wonderful drinkability sharpened by marked acidity. Next to ripen is the verdicchio destined for the simple but typical and almondy Castelverde. Early October sees the harvest of the first bunches of montepulciano that form the basis of the various Rosso Coneros. While they all possess full fruitiness and just the right amount of softness, the Pigmento is the best of the bunch. Gorgeous aromas of chocolate, red berry fruit and liquorice announce rather an austere, full-bodied palate, but it has excellent growth prospects. Casirano is the only Rosso Conero to blend montepulciano with 15 per cent cabernet and syrah, as permitted by the production protocol. The fruit is chewy and its austerity a little edgy.

● Lacrima di Morro d'Alba Gavigliano '05	♥♥	4*
● Goliardo '04	♥♥	5
○ Verdicchio dei Castelli di Jesi Cl. '06	♥♥	3*
● Lacrima di Morro d'Alba Passito '05	♥♥	6
● Lacrima di Morro d'Alba '06	♥	3
● Ragosto '04	♥	4
● Goliardo '03	♥♥	6
● Torre di Re '02	♥♥	4
● Lacrima di Morro d'Alba Gavigliano '04	♥♥	4

● Conero Pigmento Ris. '04	♥♥	6
○ Calcare Sauvignon '06	♥♥	4
○ Verdicchio dei Castelli di Jesi Cl. Castelverde '06	♥♥	4*
● Rosso Conero Casirano '05	♥♥	5
● Rosso Conero Vigneti del Coppo '05	♥♥	5
● Rosso Conero Fructus '06	♥♥	4
○ Bianco del Coppo Sauvignon '06		3
● Rosso Conero Casirano '04	♥♥	4
● Rosso Conero Pigmento '03	♥♥	5
● Rosso Conero Pigmento '01	♥♥	5
● Rosso Conero Vigneti del Coppo '03	♥♥	4

Roberto Lucarelli
LOC. RIPALTA
VIA PIANA, 20
61030 CARTOCETO [PU]
TEL. 0721893019
www.laripe.com

ANNUAL PRODUCTION 90,000 bottles
HECTARES UNDER VINE 18
VITICULTURE METHOD Conventional

When we reviewed Roberto Lucarelli's estate two years ago, we paid tribute to the progress made by this small producer located in Cartoceto, an area particularly well known for the production of excellent extravirgin olive oil. There have been some changes since then, including the advent of a skilled new young oenologist, Aroldo Belelli, who takes over from Giancarlo Soverchia. All this meant that Roberto was not able to dedicate the necessary care and attention to his estate and the steady pace of advancement slowed. Now things seemed to have settled down and the rhythm has picked up again. This year, we were offered two superb Bianchello del Metauros to taste. The Rocho has a richly fruity nose revealing lovely notes of banana and pear, preceding a full, dynamic palate that makes up in taste what it lacks in length. Ripe has subtle, elegant aromas and a palate that is just as full but fresher. The reds are all sangiovese-based. We particularly liked the notes of brandied fruit and firm body displayed by Goccione, the full ripeness of Insieme's fruit, and the vanillaed sweetness of La Ripe, whose oak-ageing has left it rather rigid and inhibited.

Stefano Mancinelli
VIA ROMA, 62
60030 MORRO D'ALBA [AN]
TEL. 073163021
www.mancinelli-wine.com

ANNUAL PRODUCTION 150,000 bottles
HECTARES UNDER VINE 25
VITICULTURE METHOD Conventional

Mention Lacrima and the name Stefano Mancinelli automatically springs to mind. His label can be found in many restaurants and wine bars and it's easy to understand why. Stefano has spent years championing this variety, putting all his faith in it and convincing many of the zone's producers that it was worth their while to invest in it. Today, Stefano's efforts have produced results in the form of wines that are rich in fruit and pleasant on the palate. One is the Lacrima Santa Maria del Fiore, which presents cherry and blackberry aromas on the nose and a fresh, clean, fragrant palate. Lacrima Superiore, a wine type introduced into the DOC in 2005, is very interesting, giving intense notes of rose and lavender, cherry and black cherry. The palate is substantial, fresh-tasting and balanced before it signs off with an agreeably fruity finish. Finally, the Verdicchio Santa Maria del Fiore possesses ripe peachy fruit aromas, nice backbone on the palate, refreshing tanginess and measured aromatics.

O Bianchello del Metauro Rocho '06	¶¶ 3
O Bianchello del Metauro La Ripe '06	¶¶ 2*
● Colli Pesaresi Sangiovese Goccione '04	¶ 5
● Colli Pesaresi Sangiovese La Ripe '05	¶ 3
● Colli Pesaresi Sangiovese Insieme Ris. '04	¶ 5
● Colli Pesaresi Sangiovese Goccione Sur Lies '02	¶¶ 5

● Lacrima di Morro d'Alba Sup. '05	¶¶ 4*
● Lacrima di Morro d'Alba S. Maria del Fiore '06	¶¶ 4*
● Lacrima di Morro d'Alba Sensazioni di Frutto '06	¶ 4
O Verdicchio dei Castelli di Jesi Cl. '06	¶ 2
O Verdicchio dei Castelli di Jesi Cl. Sup. S. Maria del Fiore '06	¶ 3
● Lacrima di Morro d'Alba Passito Re Sole '03	¶¶ 6
● Lacrima di Morro d'Alba Passito Re Sole '00	¶¶ 5
● Rubrum '03	¶¶ 3
● Terre dei Goti '01	¶¶ 6

Fattoria Mancini
S.DA DEI COLLI, 35
61100 PESARO [PU]
TEL. 072151828
www.fattoriamancini.com

Marchetti
FRAZ. PINOCCHIO
VIA DI PONTELUNGO, 166
60131 ANCONA [AN]
TEL. 071897386
www.marchettiwines.it

ANNUAL PRODUCTION 75,000 bottles
HECTARES UNDER VINE 31
VITICULTURE METHOD Conventional

ANNUAL PRODUCTION 80,000 bottles
HECTARES UNDER VINE 20
VITICULTURE METHOD Conventional

Only a burning passion could have driven Luigi Mancini to plant pinot nero – notoriously the world's most difficult variety – in his vineyard in the San Bartolo Park on an inaccessible slope that looks as if it's about to slide into the Adriatic sea. Luigi's mission is to use these grapes to create a wine that embodies his territory with all the elegance, allure and measured, wonderfully deep assertiveness that this Burgundy grape can muster. Luigi's Impero does not disappoint: delicate smoky nuances are integrated into a broader cornucopia of red berry fruit aromas whose expression expands on the dynamic, concentrated palate with its hints of austerity. The version vinified off the skins is less successful. The nose is still oak-dominated and doesn't have the strength to overcome the prevailing vanilla, although the palate does have poise and backbone. The citrus-laced florality of the Roncaglia, restrained on the nose but full and convincing on the palate, and the fruity, firmly structured Sangiovese both show well.

The Marchetti estate boasts a long winemaking tradition that goes back to last century. As early as the 1970s, the late lamented Mario, using methods different to those currently employed, was winning international acclaim for bottles that are still attractive today and show few signs of decline. Mario's son, Maurizio, now runs the estate with equal aplomb and the support of oenologist Lorenzo Landi. Maurizio has successfully combined modern technologies with traditional vinification techniques to produce wines whose fruit and balance is their major strength. In the absence of the Riserva Villa Bonomi, the only Montepulciano we tasted was the Rosso Conero '05. Its sweet, fleshy red berry fruit aromas are softened by faint vegetal notes while body and extract integrate perfectly on the palate to ensure balance and appeal. Verdicchio Tenuta del Cavaliere is also interesting for its flowery nose and aromas of tropical fruit, followed by a fresh, savouring, long-lingering palate. The Verdicchio Classico presents citrus fruit sensations, subtle freshness and a lip-smacking palate.

● Colli Pesaresi Sangiovese '05	♟♟ 4*
● Colli Pesaresi Focara Pinot Nero Impero '05	♟♟ 6
○ Colli Pesaresi Roncaglia '06	♟♟ 4*
○ Impero Blanc de Pinot Noir '05	♟ 6
● Blu '00	♟♟ 6
● Blu '01	♟♟ 6
● Colli Pesaresi Focara Pinot Nero Impero Ris. '01	♟♟ 6
● Colli Pesaresi Focara Pinot Nero Impero '01	♟♟ 6
● Colli Pesaresi Focara Pinot Nero Impero '03	♟♟ 6
● Colli Pesaresi Focara Pinot Nero Impero '04	♟♟ 6
● Colli Pesaresi Sangiovese '05	♟♟ 4

● Rosso Conero '05	♟♟ 4*
○ Verdicchio dei Castelli di Jesi Cl. Sup. Tenuta del Cavaliere '06	♟♟ 4*
○ Verdicchio dei Castelli di Jesi Cl. '06	♟ 3
● Rosso Conero Villa Bonomi Ris. '02	♟♟♟ 5
● Rosso Conero Villa Bonomi Ris. '03	♟♟ 5
● Rosso Conero Villa Bonomi Ris. '04	♟♟ 5
● Rosso Conero Villa Bonomi Ris. '01	♟♟ 5

Marotti Campi

VIA S. AMICO, 14
60030 MORRO D'ALBA [AN]
TEL. 0731618027
www.marotticampi.it

ANNUAL PRODUCTION 160,000 bottles
HECTARES UNDER VINE 56
VITICULTURE METHOD Conventional

Donderè is the only Campi wine to be obtained from a blend of several varieties: 50 per cent petit verdot with equal parts of montepulciano and cabernet sauvignon. Charming in its spicy sensations of cloves and black pepper, it offers firm body, soft tannins and a finish redolent of dried rose petals. Regarding the rest of the range, the youthful, go-getting Lorenzo Marotti Campi travels the world proudly promoting the two local varieties he vinifies on their own, verdicchio and lacrima. From the Verdicchios, we particularly liked the crispness of the citrus-like sensations offered by the unassuming Albiano. We were even more impressed by the clean fruity vein nicely integrated with typical varietal savouriness of the Luzano. Salmariano is always very convincing and has appeared on our final tasting table more than once. This year, however, it feels the effects of a vintage in which the overripeness of the grapes seems to have weighed down the generous aromatics rather than giving it complexity, so that the overall impression is one of excessive warmth and glycerine. Turning to the lacrima-based wines, we preferred the Orgiolo, soft and embracing in its hints of flowers and candied fruit, to the younger, vegetal Rùbico.

La Monacesca

C.DA MONACESCA
62024 MATELICA [MC]
TEL. 0733812602
www.monacesca.it

ANNUAL PRODUCTION 150,000 bottles
HECTARES UNDER VINE 27
VITICULTURE METHOD Conventional

Solidity, elegance and cellarability are the characteristics that set Ado Cifola's wines apart. The Verdicchio Mirum usually expresses these qualities in a defined, limpid manner but this year the estate opted to forgo this wine in the challenging growing year that was 2005. Stricter selection of the grapes would no doubt have enabled the Mirum to achieve its customary quality but the number of bottles produced would have been very low and insufficient to keep the market happy. All told, it was a wise decision not to release the wine, even if the financial impact for Cifola has been significant. On the other hand, the estate's already sound reputation for reliability has grown and we greatly look forward to tasting the 2006 version. If the magnificent Verdicchio La Monacesca is anything to go by, it will be a stunner. This is the standard version but is so good we thought it was one of the best Verdicchios we tasted. We were very pleased to retaste the Camerte, obtained from two-thirds sangiovese and one-third merlot. This delicate, decently structured red has a soft attack and shows just the right amount of tannins on the back palate.

● Donderè '05	♟♟ 5
○ Verdicchio dei Castelli di Jesi Cl. Sup. Luzano '06	♟♟ 3*
● Lacrima di Morro d'Alba Orgiolo '05	♟♟ 4*
○ Verdicchio dei Castelli di Jesi Cl. Albiano '06	♟ 2
○ Verdicchio dei Castelli di Jesi Cl. Salmariano Ris. '04	♟ 4
○ Verdicchio dei Castelli di Jesi Passito Onyr '04	♟ 4
● Lacrima di Morro d'Alba Rùbico '06	♟ 4
○ Verdicchio dei Castelli di Jesi Cl. Salmariano Ris. '03	♟♟ 4
● Donderè '04	♟♟ 5
● Donderè '03	♟♟ 5

○ Verdicchio di Matelica La Monacesca '06	♟♟ 4*
● Camerte '04	♟♟ 5
○ Mirum '94	♟♟♟ 5
○ Mirus '91	♟♟♟ 5
○ Verdicchio di Matelica Mirum Ris. '02	♟♟♟ 5
○ Verdicchio di Matelica Mirum Ris. '04	♟♟♟ 5
○ Verdicchio di Matelica La Monacesca '94	♟♟♟ 4
● Camerte '99	♟♟♟ 5
● Camerte '98	♟♟ 5
○ Ecclesia '05	♟♟ 4
○ Verdicchio di Matelica Mirum Ris. '03	♟♟ 5

Monte Schiavo

FRAZ. MONTESCHIAVO
VIA VIVAIO
60030 MAIOLATI SPONTINI [AN]
TEL. 0731700385
www.monteschiavo.it

ANNUAL PRODUCTION 1,800,000 bottles
HECTARES UNDER VINE 115
VITICULTURE METHOD Conventional

This estate belonging to the Pieralisi family is a solid point of reference in the Marche wine world. Its well-tended vineyards lie in the heart of the classic Verdicchio zone and the skills of oenologist Pier Luigi Lorenzetti produce wines that manage to combine large volume with reliable quality. The series of Verdicchios is very decent. Riserva Le Giuncare has a very sweet fruit and flower nose while the palate balances out its manifest roundness with freshness and savouriness. The Pallio di San Floriano is interesting for its pleasant flower and citrus notes, as well as the vividness and richness of flavour it shows on the palate. Coste del Molino is more delicate but extremely elegant and minerally. The Bando presents peach and tropical fruit aromas and a soft, full palate. From the reds, we liked Pieralisi For Friends, a new recruit to the ranks obtained from sangiovese and merlot. Notes of red berry fruit and jam are followed by a full-bodied, free-flowing palate and a dry finish that recalls spices and balsam. The Esio from cabernet, montepulciano and merlot alternates fruity sensations with vegetal nuances on the nose and offers a generous, well-made palate.

Montecappone

VIA COLLE OLIVO, 2
60035 JESI [AN]
TEL. 0731205761
www.montecappone.com

ANNUAL PRODUCTION 120,000 bottles
HECTARES UNDER VINE 70
VITICULTURE METHOD Conventional

All of Montecappone's wines have one thing in common: immediate appeal. It could be said that they sacrifice a certain level of complexity to achieve this but when you uncork a bottle produced by the Mirizzi brothers you know it will be drunk to the last drop. So what is their secret? We think it's the fruity fullness and well-defined varietal characterization in the glass and the attention dedicated to eliminating every hint of asperity without resorting to shortcuts. Sauvignon La Breccia offers clear, heady aromas of elderflower blossom, tropical fruit, grapefruit and peach enveloped in enormous roundness that is smoothed out by generous alcohol. The same precision is evident in the Chardonnay Colle Onorato, which is less potent yet also very drinkable. Monovarietal Verdicchio is as its best in the generous fruit and refreshing hints of citrus offered by the Montesecco and in the lip-smacking fullness of the Tabano Bianco's golden delicious aromas. A notch or two below comes the Riserva Utopia, weighed down by its oaky aromas and glycerine sensations, and the pleasant Akinos from moscato.

● Esino Pieralisi For Friends '04	▼▼ 6
○ Verdicchio dei Castelli di Jesi Cl. Sup. Pallio di S. Floriano '06	▼▼ 4
○ Verdicchio dei Castelli di Jesi Cl. Il Bando '03	▼▼ 4
○ Verdicchio dei Castelli di Jesi Cl. Coste del Molino '06	▼▼ 3*
● Esio '04	▼▼ 5
○ Verdicchio dei Castelli di Jesi Cl. Le Giuncare Ris. '05	▼▼ 4
○ Verdicchio Castelli di Jesi Cl. Passito Arché '05	▼ 5
○ Verdicchio dei Castelli di Jesi Cl. Ruviano '06	▼ 3
● Rosso Conero Adeodato '00	▼▼▼ 6
○ Verdicchio dei Castelli di Jesi Cl. Le Giuncare Ris. '04	♈♈ 4
● Rosso Conero Adeodato '04	♈♈ 6

○ La Breccia Sauvignon '06	▼▼ 4*
○ Verdicchio dei Castelli di Jesi Cl. Sup. Montesecco '06	▼▼ 4*
○ Esino Bianco Tabano '06	▼▼ 5
○ Colle Onorato Chardonnay '06	▼▼ 4
○ Akinos '06	▼ 4
○ Verdicchio dei Castelli di Jesi Cl. Utopia Ris. '05	▼ 5
● Rosso Piceno Montesecco '06	▼ 4
● Colle Paradiso '06	▼ 4
○ Verdicchio dei Castelli di Jesi Cl. Utopia Ris. '04	♈♈ 5
○ Esino Bianco Tabano '05	♈♈ 5
○ Esino Rosso Tabano '04	♈♈ 5
○ Esino Rosso Tabano '03	♈♈ 5
○ Esino Rosso Tabano '02	♈♈ 5

Alessandro Moroder

LOC. MONTACUTO
VIA MONTACUTO, 112
60029 ANCONA
TEL. 071898232
www.moroder-vini.it

ANNUAL PRODUCTION   140,000 bottles
HECTARES UNDER VINE 32
VITICULTURE METHOD   Conventional

Alessandro Moroder belongs to that small group of entrepreneurs who are also wine men, unafraid to dirty their hands in vineyard and cellar while maintaining a clear head and a certain sophistication of approach. For evidence, look at the indisputable elegance of his rationally set out estate and the appeal that every bottle of Conero bearing the Moroder brand has for the consumer. Alessandro's basic Rosso Conero is reasonably priced and has a well-sustained fruity vein that makes it easy and satisfying to drink. Add to this the fact that it is easy to find on the market and you have a winning consumer strategy. For the more demanding drinker, there is Dorico, an elegantly varietal wine, complex and layered, that is already at well advanced along its development curve while promising to mature even further in the bottle. We'll end our notes with the simple, agreeable Rosa di Montacuto and two dessert wines. The BianConero, a sweet filtrate, or partially fermented must, of moscato and white-vinified alicante, is fragrant and not very alcoholic. Oro is a moscato passito with tempting nuances of thyme and basil-led aromatic herbs and a big, velvety palate that echoes the sensations of the nose.

Oasi degli Angeli

C.DA SANT'EGIDIO, 50
63012 CUPRA MARITTIMA [AP]
TEL. 0735778569
www.kurni.it

ANNUAL PRODUCTION   5,000 bottles
HECTARES UNDER VINE 7
VITICULTURE METHOD   Natural

Marco Casolanetti and Eleonora Rossi have added a second wine to their range: Kupra, available in just a few hundred bottles. It is the result of the painstaking work carried out over years by Marco after he discovered not far from the house a vineyard that had been more or less abandoned. He coaxed the old vines back to life and propagated the first rooted cuttings himself, realizing at once that this was not montepulciano but an old variety that the local farmers called bordò. Studies conducted by ASSAM have identified it as a unique biotype of grenache. The wine has a very unusual nose that mingles spice, cinchona and rhubarb. The palate is full-bodied but harmonious with gutsy tannins that lift the finish. Exemplary fruity fullness and velvety creaminess are all present as usual in the Kurni, a very individual interpretation of montepulciano, as we have come to expect from Oasi degli Angeli. In this wine, Eleonora and Marco have reconciled extremes. Balanced as only Kurni can be, it is emblematic of a project to push the winemaking envelope that is perhaps unique in Italy and deserves to be followed with passionate interest.

● Rosso Conero Dorico Ris. '03	▼▼ 6
● Rosso Conero '05	▼▼ 4*
○ Oro '03	▼▼ 5
○ BianConero Filtrato Dolce '06	▼ 4
◉ Rosa di Montacuto '06	▼ 3
● Rosso Conero Dorico '88	▼▼▼ 5
● Rosso Conero Dorico '90	▼▼▼ 5
● Rosso Conero Dorico '93	▼▼▼ 5
● Rosso Conero Dorico Ris. '01	▼▼ 6
● Rosso Conero Dorico '00	▼▼ 5
● Rosso Conero Dorico '98	▼▼ 5
● Ankon '03	▼▼ 6
● Ankon '00	▼▼ 6

● Kupra '05	▼▼ 8
● Kurni '05	▼▼ 8
● Kurni '00	▼▼▼ 8
● Kurni '03	▼▼▼ 8
● Kurni '04	▼▼▼ 8
● Kurni '97	▼▼▼ 8
● Kurni '98	▼▼▼ 8
● Kurni '02	▼▼▼ 8
● Kurni '01	▼▼▼ 8
● Kurni '99	▼▼ 8

Pievalta

VIA MONTESCHIAVO, 18
60030 MAIOLATI SPONTINI [AN]
TEL. 0309848311
www.baronepizzini.it

ANNUAL PRODUCTION 53,000 bottles
HECTARES UNDER VINE 27
VITICULTURE METHOD Natural

Pievalta is the Marche estate belonging to Barone Pizzini, which is headquartered in Franciacorta. A quick glance at the results below seems to indicate that the impressive progress made in the space of a few short years seems to have slowed down. On closer inspection, however, you can see that this is not the case. True, the two '05 Verdicchios – the Dominè and the Passito Curina – failed to repeat the great showings they have made in the past but this particular harvest posed problems across the entire Jesi territory. On the other hand, the estate's basic product, Verdicchio Pievalta, put on a very fine show. A year younger and produced from organic grapes, it throws a fresh, clean nose of crisp peach and fresh flowers. The palate is complex and full flavoured with wonderful, refreshing drinkability. The Verdicchio Riserva is missing from the line-up this year, as it was decided to give it more ageing and defer released. Having retasted the 2004 and found it greatly improved after an extra year in bottle, we can only applaud this decision.

Poderi Capecci - San Savino

LOC. SAN SAVINO
VIA SANTA MARIA IN CARRO, 13
63038 RIPATRANSONE [AP]
TEL. 073590107
www.sansavino.com

ANNUAL PRODUCTION 120,000 bottles
HECTARES UNDER VINE 32
VITICULTURE METHOD Natural

A producer can push ripening on the vine to the limit or attempt audacious extraction of tannins during vinification. The more technologically inclined can take shortcuts using must concentrators. But on the San Savino estate, they put their faith in the old vineyards situated in perfect, sunny positions and steer vinification along the well-tried lines of ancient rituals that Simone Capecci has revamped with great sensitivity. It is no surprise, then, that the montepulciano-based Quinta Regio has delightfully intense notes of peach and morello cherry on the nose that are mirrored on the crunchily fresh palate. In the Fedus, the same characteristics are filtered through sangiovese's stronger acid grip and more elegant style. The Rosso Piceno Picus is explosive but this is only youthful exuberance and it will calm down if left to age in the bottle, further smoothing a character that is already velvety. In a range that flexes such big muscles, the Pecorino Ciprea stands out in a subtly refined version that is one of the best ever. Grapefruit and sage aromas spill over from the nose onto the palate and then into the deep, fascinating finish.

○ Verdicchio dei Castelli di Jesi Cl. Sup. Pievalta '06	�♛ 3*
○ Verdicchio dei Castelli di Jesi Passito Curina '05	♛ 5
○ Verdicchio dei Castelli di Jesi Cl. Sup. Dominè '05	♛ 4
○ Verdicchio dei Castelli di Jesi Cl. San Paolo Ris. '04	♛♛ 4
○ Verdicchio dei Castelli di Jesi Cl. Sup. Dominè '04	♛♛ 4
○ Verdicchio dei Castelli di Jesi Passito Curina '04	♛♛ 5

○ Offida Pecorino Ciprea '06	♛♛ 4*
● Quinta Regio '03	♛♛ 6
● Fedus Sangiovese '05	♛♛ 5
● Rosso Piceno Sup. Picus '05	♛♛ 4*
● Rosso Piceno Collemura '06	♛ 3
○ Falerio dei Colli Ascolani Collemura '06	♛ 3
● Quinta Regio '00	♛♛♛ 6
● Quinta Regio '01	♛♛♛ 6
● Moggio Sangiovese '98	♛♛♛ 6
○ Offida Pecorino Ciprea '05	♛♛ 4
● Ver Sacrum '03	♛♛ 6
● Ver Sacrum '05	♛♛ 4
● Rosso Piceno Sup. Picus '03	♛♛ 5
● Rosso Piceno Sup. Picus '01	♛♛ 4
● Fedus Sangiovese '03	♛♛ 6
● Fedus Sangiovese '01	♛♛ 6
● Quinta Regio '02	♛♛ 6

Il Pollenza
VIA CASONE, 4
62029 TOLENTINO [MC]
TEL. 0733961989
www.ilpollenza.it

Rio Maggio
C.DA VALLONE, 41
63014 MONTEGRANARO [AP]
TEL. 0734889587
www.riomaggio.it

ANNUAL PRODUCTION 80,000 bottles
HECTARES UNDER VINE 50
VITICULTURE METHOD Conventional

ANNUAL PRODUCTION 100,000 bottles
HECTARES UNDER VINE 18
VITICULTURE METHOD Conventional

The invaluable skills of a first-class staff headed by Giacomo Tachis and Umberto Trombelli made the difference in the hot, notoriously difficult growing year that was 2003. The team managed to fuse fruit freshness and perfectly integrated tannins with austere profiles and very refined aromas for both the Pollenza 2003 and the Cosmino 2003 gave very convincing performances. In the first, obtained from cabernet sauvignon, cabernet franc and merlot, notes of cedar wood, sweet spice and delicate hints of ripe bell pepper announce a palate of stunning breadth and depth that exhibits all the elegance of a Bordeaux. Based on merlot and cabernet sauvignon, the Cosmino has little to envy its senior sibling and shows sounder fruit, although it lacks the Pollenza's austere fascination. The Pius IX Mastai is always delightful. This blend of sun-dried traminer and sauvignon is available in a limited number of bottles only. A honeyed note of botrytis is the prelude to more Mediterranean aromas of dried fig and apricot on a very sweet, tempting palate.

Montegranaro is better known for its shoe manufacturing industry than for the ancient farming tradition that inspired its name. Simone Santucci and his wife Tiziana are two of the precious few who still farm these hills. They cultivate local and international varieties to produce characterful, cellarable wines. The Sauvignon Collemonteverde earned a place on our final Three Glass tasting table for its alluring nose of tomato leaf, sage and citrus fruit, enhanced by iodine notes. This is followed by an elegant, very long palate that combines volume and fullness of flavour with balance. The Chardonnay from the same line offers notes of ripe peachy fruit and a well-rounded palate while the Falerio Telusiano shows interesting fresh hints of flowers and fruit and a mineral, firmly structured palate that promises to develop well. The two Rosso Picenos are also very well made. The GrAnarijS gives notes of jam and sweet spice introducing a robust palate with assertive tannins. The Rubeo has rather overripe fruit and unbends on the palate to sign off with a toasty, chocolate finish.

● Cosmino '03	♟♟ 5
● Il Pollenza '03	♟♟ 8
○ Pius IX Mastai '05	♟♟ 6
○ Briano '06	♟ 4
○ Pius IX Mastai '03	♟♟ 6
○ Pius IX Mastai '04	♟♟ 6
● Il Pollenza '02	♟♟ 7
● Il Pollenza '01	♟♟ 7
● Porpora '04	♟♟ 4

○ Collemonteverde Sauvignon '06	♟♟ 4*
○ Collemonteverde Chardonnay '06	♟♟ 4
○ Falerio dei Colli Ascolani Telusiano '06	♟♟ 4
● Rosso Piceno Rubeo '04	♟♟ 5
● Rosso Piceno GrAnarijS '05	♟♟ 5
○ Falerio dei Colli Ascolani Monte del Grano '06	♟ 2*
● Collemonteverde Pinot Nero '03	♟ 5
● Artias Pinot Nero '01	♟♟ 5
● Rosso Piceno GrAnarijS '03	♟♟ 5
● Rosso Piceno GrAnarijS '04	♟♟ 5

Saladini Pilastri

VIA SALADINI, 5
63030 SPINETOLI [AP]
TEL. 0736899534
www.saladinipilastri.it

ANNUAL PRODUCTION 760,000 bottles
HECTARES UNDER VINE 160
VITICULTURE METHOD Certified organic

The pergola training system is widely despised. This ancient technique is in fact used with the aim of producing the largest possible quantity of grapes. Yet if skilfully employed, in combination with short pruning and a watchful eye on the ripening of the fruit, it can produce excellent results. It is no coincidence that Saladini Pilastri, an estate with a 300-year-old history, adopts this method for its most prestigious wine, Vigna Monteprandone. Dark in appearance, its ripe fruitiness is perfectly integrated with notes of coffee and chocolate announcing a palate with impressive backbone bolstering soft tannins. The Pregio del Conte is also very attractive. Derived from an unusual blend of montepulciano and aglianico, it is absolutely ripe and remarkably vigorous. The other Rosso Picenos all offer good value for money and cater to every taste. You can choose from the full body of the Montetinello, the flavoursome palate of the Piediprato, or the fresh fruitiness of the Parnaso. Rounding off the range there was a fine performance from the subtle but rather elegant Falerio Palazzi and the uncomplicated Falerio.

San Filippo

C.DA CIAFONE, 17A
63035 OFFIDA [AP]
TEL. 0736889828
www.vinisanfilippo.it

ANNUAL PRODUCTION 15,000 bottles
HECTARES UNDER VINE 28
VITICULTURE METHOD Natural

"It is not being first to see something new but seeing as new the ancient, that which was already known in ancient times and is seen and disregarded by all…" Thus spake Frederick Nietzsche and the Stracci brothers, who have chosen to put the quote on their web site. For the Straccis, who were born in the country, respect for tradition – albeit filtered through a modern vision – is sacred. And their wines reflect this perspective. Obtained from montepulciano with 30 per cent cabernet, Lupo del Ciafone has all the intensity and generosity of the best Piceno wines combined with the elegance bestowed by the noble tannins of its Bordeaux grape. The Rosso Piceno Katharsis offers lingering balsamic aromas and invigorating roundness on the palate. The white DOCs are also here in force, including a well-styled, flowery Falerio and an Offida Pecorino whose palate is invigorated by the lively acid backbone that sustains the progression and imbues the nose with vivid citrus-like sensations. The Rubino Ventoso, the estate's '06 Merlot, offers fragrant vegetal sensations.

● Rosso Piceno Sup. V. Monteprandone '04	♟♟ 5
○ Falerio dei Colli Ascolani '06	♟♟ 2*
○ Falerio dei Colli Ascolani V. Palazzi '06	♟♟ 3*
● Rosso Piceno Piediprato '05	♟♟ 4*
● Rosso Piceno Sup. V. Montetinello '05	♟♟ 4*
● Rosso Piceno Parnaso '05	♟♟ 4*
● Pregio del Conte '04	♟♟ 5
● Rosso Piceno '06	♟ 3
● Rosso Piceno Sup. V. Monteprandone '00	♟♟♟ 4
● Rosso Piceno Sup. V. Monteprandone '03	♟♟ 3
● Rosso Piceno Sup. V. Montetinello '04	♟♟ 4

● Lupo del Ciafone '04	♟♟ 5
● Rosso Piceno Sup. Katharsis '05	♟♟ 4*
○ Offida Pecorino '06	♟♟ 4*
○ Falerio dei Colli Ascolani Archè '06	♟ 3
● Rubino Ventoso Merlot '06	♟ 3
● Lupo del Ciafone '03	♟♟ 5
○ Offida Pecorino '05	♟♟ 4

San Giovanni
C.DA CIAFONE, 41
63035 OFFIDA [AP]
TEL. 0736889032
www.vinisangiovanni.it

ANNUAL PRODUCTION   100,000 bottles
HECTARES UNDER VINE 28
VITICULTURE METHOD   Natural

Gianni Di Lorenzo has reorganized production in three moves. He eliminated all superfluous processes; he produces DOC wines only; and he has extended ageing for his flagship reds, Offida Rosso Zeii and Rosso Piceno Superiore Leo Guelfus. In the absence of these two champions, the Axeé stepped magnificently into the breach as standard bearer for the house reds. Intense, restrained notes of liquorice and toastiness mingle on the nose with more delicate florality while the palate shows length and assertiveness without falling into the traps of muddle or over-extraction. The white range is, as usual, highly satisfactory. Kiara is a pure Pecorino that flaunts admirable elegance in aniseed and almond tones followed by nice energy on the palate. The Falerio Leo Guelfus is the choice of those who seek balance between fruit and length of palate in this wine type. In addition, we have a new release in the shape of Marta, which many of our readers will remember as a late-harvested Falerio. It has been transformed into an Offida Passerina and in terms of charm and drinkability is the best of the versions obtained exclusively from this indigenous Marche grape.

Poderi San Lazzaro
C.DA SAN LAZZARO, 65/67
63035 OFFIDA [AP]
TEL. 0736889189
www.poderisanlazzaro.it

ANNUAL PRODUCTION   30,000 bottles
HECTARES UNDER VINE 15
VITICULTURE METHOD   Natural

Poderi San Lazzaro had a challenging start to life. Space was limited in the old house, the vineyards demanded lots of tender loving care, equipment was sparse and experience was virtually non-existent. Only the steadfast determination to carry out their joint project and the conviction that they had all the right elements to bottle quality kept Pino Ottavi and Paolo Capriotti going. Today, Poderi San Lazzaro has a firm base and the partners tackle each logistical problem one at a time. This year's tastings confirmed that Pino and Paolo are still driven by a burning desire to do well. We particularly liked the fruity compactness of Grifola, a pure montepulciano of enormous power. Although not particularly elegant, it is dynamic, varietal and sure to impress. The Rosso Piceno Podere 72 lags a step or two behind. It has aromas of aromatic herbs and liquorice and an austere, well-sustained palate that is still developing. The Polesio is simple by design, a standard Sangiovese whose strong suit is its flowery fragrance. Up last was Pistillo, an interesting Pecorino matured partly in oak. It is juicy and savoury but still a but muddled on the nose.

O Offida Pecorino Kiara '06	♀♀	4*
O Falerio dei Colli Ascolani		
Leo Guelfus '06	♀♀	3*
O Offida Passerina Marta '06	♀♀	3*
● Rosso Piceno Sup. Axeé '04	♀♀	5
● Offida Rosso Zeii '01	♀♀	5
● Offida Rosso Zeii '02	♀♀	5
● Offida Rosso Zeii '03	♀♀	5
● Rosso Piceno Sup.		
Leo Guelfus '04	♀♀	4
O Marta '05	♀♀	4
O Offida Pecorino Kiara '05	♀♀	4
● Rosso Piceno Sup. Axeé '03	♀♀	5

● Grifola '05	♀♀	5
● Rosso Piceno Sup. Podere 72 '05	♀♀	4*
O Pistillo Pecorino '06	♀	4
● Polesio Sangiovese '06	♀	2
● Grifola '04	♀♀	5
● Podere 72 '04	♀♀	4

Fattoria San Lorenzo

VIA SAN LORENZO, 6
60036 MONTECAROTTO [AN]
TEL. 073189656
az-crognaletti@libero.it

ANNUAL PRODUCTION 100,000 bottles
HECTARES UNDER VINE 36
VITICULTURE METHOD Natural

A quick glance would seem to suggest that little has changed at Natalino Crognaletti's place. The estate continues to produce superb, convincing wines with a prevalence of whites over reds. But it's not as simple as that. Natalino is always experimenting with new approaches to give his wines greater complexity, originality and cellarability. Different ageing periods, long fermentations, lees contact: no stone is left unturned and this year's tastings pay tribute to his efforts. The Verdicchio Riserva Vigna delle Oche has an alluring nose with notes of orange peel, a mineral hint and an elegant trace of botrytis before the palate opens out confidently to reveal generous, enveloping sensations. The Superiore has a more direct, deep approach. It offers aromas of dried fruit and a solid, full-bodied character that brooks no compromise. The concentrated almondy aromas of Vigna di Gino put the accent on varietal shades. The Solleone was missing from the red line-up this year but in compensation the Rosso Conero shows a lovely fruity tone, outstripping the Vigna Burello, which is a bit short on freshness.

Santa Barbara

B.GO MAZZINI, 35
60010 BARBARA [AN]
TEL. 0719674249
www.vinisantabarbara.it

ANNUAL PRODUCTION 650,000 bottles
HECTARES UNDER VINE 40
VITICULTURE METHOD Conventional

Last year's reference to St Barbara, the patron saint of artillery, has a sequel for this year we have a real live bomb in our midst! We're talking about the Verdicchio Le Vaglie, a very reasonably priced wine that earned an explosive Three Glasses for its graceful elegance. Notes of flowers, apple-like fruit and almond unfold into very complex nuances of tropical and citrus fruit. Perfectly balanced between weight and fullness of flavour, the palate is enhanced by an intriguing finish of aniseed and mint. The Riserva Stefano Antonucci also has excellent fruity, honeyed and delicately toasty aromas, a supple, harmonious palate and a perfect savoury finish. Turning to the reds, the pure montepulciano Il Maschio da Monte offers black cherry and cassis sensations on the nose, a well-rounded profile and confident tannins on the palate. Pathos, from merlot, cabernet and syrah, weds well-integrated notes of aromatic herbs and fruit with a palate full of fruity fragrance and delicate tannins. The merlot, cabernet and montepulciano blend, Stefano Antonucci Rosso, has appeal and substantial pulp, grassiness getting the better of aromas of black berry fruit.

O Verdicchio dei Castelli di Jesi Cl.	
Vigna delle Oche Ris. '04	♈♈ 5
● Rosso Conero '04	♈♈ 4
O Verdicchio dei Castelli di Jesi Cl.	
Sup. Vigna delle Oche '05	♈♈ 4*
O Verdicchio dei Castelli di Jesi Cl.	
Vigna di Gino '06	♈♈ 3*
● Rosso Piceno Vigna Burello '04	♈ 4
O Verdicchio dei Castelli di Jesi Cl.	
Vigna delle Oche Ris. '01	♈♈♈ 5
● Vigneto del Solleone '02	♈♈ 6
O Verdicchio dei Castelli di Jesi Cl.	
Vigna delle Oche Ris. '03	♈♈ 5
● Vigneto del Solleone '01	♈♈ 6
O Verdicchio dei Castelli di Jesi Cl.	
Sup. Vigna delle Oche '04	♈♈ 4

O Verdicchio dei Castelli di Jesi Cl.	
Le Vaglie '06	♈♈♈ 4*
O Verdicchio dei Castelli di Jesi Cl.	
Stefano Antonucci Ris. '05	♈♈ 4*
● Rosso Piceno	
Il Maschio da Monte '05	♈♈ 6
● Pathos '05	♈♈ 7
● Stefano Antonucci Rosso '05	♈♈ 4
O Verdicchio dei Castelli di Jesi Cl.	
Tardivo ma non Tardo '04	♈♈ 6
O Verdicchio dei Castelli di Jesi '06	♈ 3
O Verdicchio dei Castelli di Jesi	
Pignocco '06	♈ 3
● Vigna San Bartolo '05	♈ 4
● Pathos '01	♈♈♈ 7
● Rosso Piceno	
Il Maschio da Monte '04	♈♈♈ 5

Sartarelli
VIA COSTE DEL MOLINO, 24
60030 POGGIO SAN MARCELLO [AN]
TEL. 073189732
www.sartarelli.it

Sparapani - Frati Bianchi
VIA BARCHIO, 12
60034 CUPRAMONTANA [AN]
TEL. 0731781216
www.fratibianchi.it

ANNUAL PRODUCTION   300,000 bottles
HECTARES UNDER VINE 66
VITICULTURE METHOD   Conventional

ANNUAL PRODUCTION   40,000 bottles
HECTARES UNDER VINE 12
VITICULTURE METHOD   Conventional

In recent years, a Verdicchio named Balciana has stunned tasters and consumers with the enormous potential of the variety's complexity and versatility, convincing all-comers with the appeal and elegance that each new harvest has brought. We are unable to review the 2005 version, as the year failed to produce the climatic conditions essential to such a unique wine and Donatella Sartarelli and Patrizio Chiacchiarini opted not to produce it. We applaud their professionalism. It is with great pleasure, however, that we present two Verdicchios peerless for their elegance and complexity: Classico and Tralivio. The Tralivio shows all the elegance of a cool growing year in a cornucopia of flower, fruit, almond and mint aromas. Fullness and richness of flavour combine perfectly on the palate to ensure balance, continuity and an elegant, lingering finish. The Classico offers very clean notes of flowers and white-fleshed fruit. It has all the energy of the 2006 vintage on the palate but adds taste and wonderful savouriness that guarantee appeal and drinkability.

Awarding Three Glasses to a Sparapani wine is not just a tribute to a truly outstanding product. It is also an acknowledgement of all the years of brilliant behind-the-scenes work that Settimio and his sons have put in. They have been aided and abetted in their endeavour by oenologist Sergio Paolucci, that great Verdicchio expert, particularly well-known for wines from Cupramontana and the surrounding area. Unfortunately, the number of bottles available is limited and they are all sold by word of mouth, an effective strategy that works only for wines of the highest pedigree. The Priore is a Verdicchio that bears comparison with the very best in the category and thoroughly deserves our top prize. Generous notes of peach and apricot are the most prominent of the aromas offered on the wide-ranging, fruit-led nose. The same fullness returns on the long, wonderfully lip-smacking finish, the climax of a palate that manages to be caressing and full at the same time. As is often the case in the Jesi area, the estate's second wine has more backbone and minerality: the Salerna's forthright, delicious almond aromas are irresistible.

O Verdicchio dei Castelli di Jesi Cl. Sup. Tralivio '05	♙♙	4*
O Verdicchio dei Castelli di Jesi Cl. '06	♙	3*
O Verdicchio dei Castelli di Jesi Cl. Sup. Contrada Balciana '97	♙♙♙	6
O Verdicchio dei Castelli di Jesi Cl. Sup. Balciana '04	♙♙♙	6
O Verdicchio dei Castelli di Jesi Cl. Sup. Contrada Balciana '98	♙♙♙	6
O Verdicchio dei Castelli di Jesi Cl. Sup. Contrada Balciana '01	♙♙	6
O Verdicchio dei Castelli di Jesi Cl. Sup. Tralivio '04	♙♙	4
O Verdicchio dei Castelli di Jesi Cl. Sup. Contrada Balciana '03	♙♙	6

O Verdicchio dei Castelli di Jesi Cl. Sup. Il Priore '06	♙♙♙	4*
O Verdicchio dei Castelli di Jesi Cl. Salerna '06	♙♙	3*
O Verdicchio dei Castelli di Jesi Cl. Sup. Il Priore '05	♙♙	4

Spinsanti
VIA FONTE INFERNO, 11
60021 CAMERANO [AN]
TEL. 071731797
cspisanti@alice.it

ANNUAL PRODUCTION 26,000 bottles
HECTARES UNDER VINE 7.5
VITICULTURE METHOD Natural

The introduction of a new process – using cement vats instead of stainless steel tanks to age the wine – has delayed maturation of the Rosso Conero Camars. As a result, the wine was not presented for tasting and its absence has had quite an impact on Spinsanti's scorecard. The other standard-label Rosso Conero, Adino, was presented but it too was not as ready as in previous years. Nevertheless, a series of retastings revealed how the more leisurely aromatic development can actually enhance the fullness of structure that the wine reveals in its soft entry and tannins-invigorated finale. The estate's flagship wine, Sassòne, is obtained from 90 per cent montepulciano grown in the oldest vineyards plus a selection of top-quality fruit from a small plot of merlot. Elegant and confident, it comes across rather edgy because of slightly rigid tannins that bottle time should remedy. A little patience will produce a glass that offers the fruitiest, most varietal essence of the montepulciano grape combined with a flavoursome palate showing compact fruit and a big personality.

Silvano Strologo
VIA OSIMANA, 89
60021 CAMERANO [AN]
TEL. 071731104
www.vinorossoconero.com

ANNUAL PRODUCTION 57,000 bottles
HECTARES UNDER VINE 15
VITICULTURE METHOD Conventional

Silvano Strologo embarked on winemaking route ten years ago. Following the death of his father, Giulio, he decided to abandon the production of unbottled wine in favour of a bottled Rosso Conero. At this point, he switched his priorities to careful vineyard management and selective harvesting of the grapes. A production style started to emerge based on very ripe grapes, concentrated fruit and powerful extraction. You may or may not agree, but Silvano believes 100 per cent in this approach. At this year's tastings, the wines revealed greater fragrance than those offered in recent years. We'll start our notes with Traiano, which offers ripe red berry fruit aromas, continuity on the palate, lively but smooth tannins and a fruity finish with subtle spice. Decebalo's nose is still a bit closed, but gives spice, tobacco and forest floor before giving way to the fruit. The palate is very interesting, showing creamy and firmly structured with nice persistence of its morello cherry and blackberry aromas. The standard label Rosso Conero Julius has tasty fruit that is still rather muddled and a fresh-tasting, juicy palate.

● Sassòne '05	⬤⬤ 6
● Rosso Conero Adino '06	⬤⬤ 3*
● Sassòne '01	⬤⬤ 5
● Sassòne '00	⬤⬤ 5
● Sassòne '02	⬤⬤ 5
● Sassòne '03	⬤⬤ 5
● Sassòne '04	⬤⬤ 5
● Rosso Conero Camars '05	⬤⬤ 4
● Rosso Conero Camars '04	⬤⬤ 4
● Rosso Conero Adino '05	⬤⬤ 3
● Rosso Conero Adino '04	⬤⬤ 3

● Conero Decebalo Ris. '04	⬤⬤ 5
● Rosso Conero Traiano '05	⬤⬤ 5
● Rosso Conero Julius '06	⬤⬤ 4*
☉ Rosa Rosae '06	3
● Rosso Conero Traiano '00	⬤⬤⬤ 5
● Rosso Conero Traiano '01	⬤⬤ 5
● Rosso Conero Traiano '02	⬤⬤ 5
● Rosso Conero Traiano '03	⬤⬤ 5
● Rosso Conero Traiano '04	⬤⬤ 5
● Rosso Conero Decebalo Ris. '02	⬤⬤ 5
● Rosso Conero Decebalo Ris. '03	⬤⬤ 6

Tenuta di Tavignano

LOC. TAVIGNANO
62011 CINGOLI [MC]
TEL. 0733617303
tavignano@libero.it

ANNUAL PRODUCTION 120,000 bottles
HECTARES UNDER VINE 28
VITICULTURE METHOD Conventional

Quality will out, whatever limits are set by man. Take the verdicchio variety, which has chosen this strip of land on which to produce absolutely first-class grapes. The estate belonging to the Lucangeli Aymerich di Laconi family lies in the province of Macerata but the hill on which it sits overlooks the city of Jesi. Revelling in a well-paced, formidable growing year, the Misco '06 impressed us with the precision of its intense dried fruit and acacia blossom aromas. The palate echoes these notes in an understated yet inexorable follow-through and a wonderfully tangy finish. We are very happy to award its first Three Glasses to this worthy wine. The Misco Riserva '04 is a step or two behind, offering greater aromatic complexity and evolution on both the nose and the elegantly long palate. Another two superb versions of this great Marche variety, Tavignano and Vigna Verde, show how this estate is capable of producing fullness on the palate and also freshness, energy and easy drinkability. Hats off to oenologist Pierluigi Lorenzetti. A soft, chewy Rosso Piceno adds a touch of red to this otherwise white panorama.

Fattoria Le Terrazze

VIA MUSONE, 4
60026 NUMANA [AN]
TEL. 0717390352
www.fattorialeterrazze.it

ANNUAL PRODUCTION 90,000 bottles
HECTARES UNDER VINE 21
VITICULTURE METHOD Conventional

Any team that relies on a single player to score the winning goal is going to come a cropper sooner or later. Antonio Terni's estate manages to maintain its impressive level of quality precisely because it produces more than one champion a year. Chaos, that magnificent blend of montepulciano, merlot and syrah, is missing from the line-up this year so Conero Sassi Neri steps up to take its place. The nose is intense and full of those morello cherry sensations so typical of montepulciano, mingling with alluring smoky and spicy nuances. The palate's nicely balanced contrast carries the progression through to the captivating finish. Visions of J, an unusual montepulciano selection produced only in better vintages, would also have taken home Three Glasses if it hadn't been for a tad too much structure. Nothing that cellar time won't fix, though. Obtained from montepulciano with 25 per cent merlot, the very smooth, enveloping Planet Waves is quite good but a little predictable. We also noted a fine showing by the Rosso Conero, a soft, substantial wine that is ideal for everyday drinking.

O Verdicchio dei Castelli di Jesi Cl. Sup. Misco '06	♟♟♟	4*
O Verdicchio dei Castelli di Jesi Cl. Misco Ris. '04	♟♟	5
O Verdicchio dei Castelli di Jesi Cl. Sup. Tavignano '06	♟♟	3*
● Rosso Piceno Castel Rosino '06	♟	2
O Verdicchio dei Castelli di Jesi Cl. Vigna Verde '06	♟	2
● Rosso Piceno Libenter '03	♟♟	4
O Verdicchio dei Castelli di Jesi Cl. Sup. Misco '03	♟♟	4
O Verdicchio dei Castelli di Jesi Cl. Sup. Misco '04	♟♟	4
O Verdicchio dei Castelli di Jesi Cl. Sup. Misco '05	♟♟	4

● Conero Sassi Neri Ris. '04	♟♟♟	6
● Conero Visions of J Ris. '04	♟♟	8
● Planet Waves '04	♟♟	7
● Rosso Conero '05	♟♟	4*
O Le Cave Chardonnay '06	♟	4
● Chaos '04	♟♟♟	7
● Chaos '01	♟♟♟	7
● Chaos '97	♟♟♟	7
● Rosso Conero Visions of J '97	♟♟♟	8
● Rosso Conero Visions of J '01	♟♟♟	8
● Rosso Conero Sassi Neri '02	♟♟♟	6
● Rosso Conero Sassi Neri '99	♟♟♟	6
● Rosso Conero Sassi Neri '98	♟♟♟	6
● Chaos '03	♟♟	6
● Rosso Conero Sassi Neri '03	♟♟	6
● Planet Waves '03	♟♟	6

Terre Cortesi Moncaro
VIA PIANDOLE, 7A
60036 MONTECAROTTO [AN]
TEL. 073189245
www.moncaro.com

ANNUAL PRODUCTION 7,500,000 bottles
HECTARES UNDER VINE 1.618
VITICULTURE METHOD Conventional

Moncaro's wines are distinctive, thanks to the cellar's deliberate quest for style. This big co-operative has made an art of that soft balance and appealing fullness that so fascinates the consumer. Attracting the interest of the market is important when you produce seven and a half million bottles a year. This cellar ensures that all of the Marche's characteristic wine types are properly represented. The list of Verdicchios is diverse and includes Passito Tordiruta, obtained from a vineyard selection of botrytis-infected grapes, which has earned a reputation as the best sipping wine in the region. Some may prefer the fresh nose and consistency of the Verde Ca' Ruptae or the unusual aromatic development and concentrated savouriness of Le Vele to the complex, intense Vigna Novali. A touch of aniseed lifts the generous flowery notes of the Passerina Ofithe while the Pecorino is solid and firmly structured. The reds all share an explosive fruity fullness that is more effective when accompanied by the lovely soft, dynamic body of the Conero Cimerio, the Rosso Piceno Campo delle Mura and the Barocco, a 50-50 blend of montepulciano and cabernet.

Umani Ronchi
S.S.16 KM 310,400, 74
60027 OSIMO [AN]
TEL. 0717108019
www.umanironchi.com

ANNUAL PRODUCTION 4,000,000 bottles
HECTARES UNDER VINE 230
VITICULTURE METHOD Conventional

Michele Bernetti has taken over the management of this estate from his father, Massimo. In a very short time, Michele and brilliant Piedmont oenologist Beppe Caviola have managed to lift the quality of Umani Ronchi's wines to even greater heights, stamping them with a distinct, well-defined style. This is most evident in the reds, where they have produced an interpretation of montepulciano that highlights the elegance and freshness of the variety rather than its beefy concentration. Just try tasting the fabulous Cùmaro, whose perfect nose and deep, gratifying palate took it to within a hair's breadth of Three Glasses, or the softly assertive, dynamic San Lorenzo for proof. The Pelago, from cabernet, montepulciano and a little merlot, is rather hesitant on the nose but has good weight and soft elegance on the palate. Results from Verdicchio are even more interesting and we rewarded them with Three Glasses. Once again the proud winner is the sophisticated Plenio, a flowing dignified wine rendered truly outstanding by impeccable use of oak. Casal di Serra is extremely dense and never before so complex on a nose that precedes a juicy palate of explosive energy.

○ Verdicchio dei Castelli di Jesi Cl. Vigna Novali Ris. '03	🍷🍷	4*
● Conero Cimerio Ris. '04	🍷🍷	4*
● Barocco '04	🍷🍷	4
● Rosso Piceno Sup. Campo delle Mura '04	🍷🍷	5
○ Verdicchio dei Castelli di Jesi Cl. Sup. Verde Ca' Ruptae '06	🍷🍷	4
○ Verdicchio dei Castelli di Jesi Passito Tordiruta '04	🍷🍷	7
○ Verdicchio dei Castelli di Jesi Cl. Le Vele '06	🍷🍷	3*
○ Offida Pecorino Ofithe '06	🍷	4
○ Offida Passerina Ofithe '06	🍷	4
● Conero Vigneti del Parco Ris. '04	🍷	5
● Rosso Piceno Sup. Roccaviva '04	🍷	4
○ Verdicchio dei Castelli di Jesi Cl. Vigna Novali Ris. '02	🍷🍷	4

○ Verdicchio dei Castelli di Jesi Cl. Plenio Ris. '04	🍷🍷🍷	5
○ Verdicchio dei Castelli di Jesi Cl. Sup. Casal di Serra '06	🍷🍷	4*
● Pelago '04	🍷🍷	6
● Conero Cùmaro Ris. '04	🍷🍷	5
○ Maximo Botrytis Cinerea '04	🍷🍷	5
○ Verdicchio dei Castelli di Jesi Cl. Sup. Casal di Serra V. V. '05	🍷🍷	5
○ Verdicchio dei Castelli di Jesi Cl. Sup. Villa Bianchi '06	🍷🍷	3*
● Rosso Conero S. Lorenzo '04	🍷🍷	4
○ Le Busche '05	🍷	5
● Rosso Conero Serrano '06	🍷	3
○ Verdicchio dei Castelli di Jesi Cl. Plenio Ris. '02	🍷🍷🍷	4
○ Verdicchio dei Castelli di Jesi Cl. Plenio Ris. '03	🍷🍷🍷	5

Vallerosa Bonci
VIA TORRE, 13
60034 CUPRAMONTANA [AN]
TEL. 0731789129
www.vallerosa-bonci.com

Velenosi
LOC. MONTICELLI
VIA DEI BIANCOSPINI, 11
63100 ASCOLI PICENO
TEL. 0736341218
www.velenosivini.com

ANNUAL PRODUCTION 250,000 bottles
HECTARES UNDER VINE 35
VITICULTURE METHOD Conventional

ANNUAL PRODUCTION 1,100,000 bottles
HECTARES UNDER VINE 105
VITICULTURE METHOD Conventional

Cupramontana is one of the best-known wine territories in the Castelli di Jesi area, and it is here that the Bonci family has been producing Verdicchio for three generations. With fruit from his splendid vineyards, Giuseppe Bonci brings out the full potential and different characteristics of the variety. His wines are always characterful, elegant and eminently drinkable. This year, the Riserva Pietrone picked up Three effortless Glasses. The magnificently sophisticated nose alternates botrytis aromas with fruit, citrus and minerality. Dense, balanced and weighty on the palate, it becomes captivating in the finish with quite sumptuous aromatic progression and subtle savouriness. The Le Case selection is not quite up to the same standards. Generous aromas of fruit, honey and aniseed are the prelude to an elegant, substantial and well-balanced palate. San Michele offers clear notes of ripe fruit and yeast while the Viatorre has sweet nuances of peachy fruit and restrained freshness. Casanostra, a red from montepulciano and ten per cent sangiovese, also performed well with ripe red berry fruit and spice aromas accompanying a fresh-tasting, fragrant palate.

No surprises here. Three Glasses go to Roggio del Filare, an austerely complex wine that marries suppleness and balance with fine fleshy fruit and plush, round tannins. We were unsurprised because we know that Angela Velenosi has a set purpose in everything she does and believes that the only way to produce quality is to plan determinedly and work with skill. The first edition of her Pecorino is particularly successful, its well-marshalled weight moving smoothly into a savoury finish lifted by refined notes of aniseed and grapefruit. The Ludi was a no show this year but the reds include a newcomer, Il Brecciarolo Gold, a selection in the style of the Il Brecciarolo. Both display lovely fruity compactness, good follow-through on the palate and a soft, lip-smacking finish. We preferred Il Brecciarolo at our tastings. In the friendly rivalry involving the two Metodo Classico Spumantes, The Rose came out on top. It has more fragrance and elegant depth whereas the Velenosi Brut is fuller and more firmly bodied. Finally, Chardonnay Villa Angela is rich in ripe, tangy fruit and Falerio Vigna Solaria is soft with pleasant nuances of tropical fruit.

○ Verdicchio dei Castelli di Jesi Cl. Pietrone Ris. '04	♛♛♛ 5	
○ Verdicchio dei Castelli di Jesi Cl. Sup. Le Case '05	♛♛ 4*	
● Casanostra '05	♛♛ 4	
○ Verdicchio dei Castelli di Jesi Cl. Viatorre '06	♛♛ 3*	
○ Verdicchio dei Castelli di Jesi Cl. Sup. S. Michele '05	♛♛ 4	
○ Verdicchio dei Castelli di Jesi Cl. Spumante Brut Bonci	♛ 4	
○ Verdicchio dei Castelli di Jesi Passito Rojano '05	♛ 5	
○ Verdicchio dei Castelli di Jesi Cl. Sup. S. Michele '00	♛♛♛ 4	
○ Verdicchio dei Castelli di Jesi Cl. Sup. Le Case '04	♛♛♛ 4	

● Rosso Piceno Sup. Roggio del Filare '04	♛♛♛ 6	
☉ The Rose Brut Rosé '04	♛♛ 6	
○ Villa Angela Pecorino '06	♛♛ 4*	
○ Velenosi Brut M. Cl.	♛♛ 5	
○ Verdicchio dei Castelli di Jesi Cl. '06	♛♛ 4	
○ Villa Angela Chardonnay '06	♛♛ 4	
○ Falerio dei Colli Ascolani V. Solaria '06	♛♛ 3*	
● Rosso Piceno Sup. Il Brecciarolo '04	♛♛ 3	
● Rosso Piceno Sup. Il Brecciarolo Gold '05	♛ 5	
● Rosso Piceno Sup. Roggio del Filare '03	♛♛♛ 6	
● Rosso Piceno Sup. Roggio del Filare '02	♛♛♛ 6	
● Rosso Piceno Sup. Roggio del Filare '01	♛♛♛ 6	

Vignamato

VIA BATTINEBBIA, 4
60038 SAN PAOLO DI JESI [AN]
TEL. 0731779197
www.vignamato.com

ANNUAL PRODUCTION 55,000 bottles
HECTARES UNDER VINE 14
VITICULTURE METHOD Conventional

After the slight downturn in quality of last year's wines, we are pleased to note that Maurizio and Serenella Ceci's range has returned to its usual high standards. We would have been surprised if it had been otherwise, given two major contributing factors. First, the excellent harvest, particularly for the Verdicchio '06, and second, the serious day-by-day work in the vineyards and cellar carried out with passion by Maurizio, Serenella and their three young children. The three Verdicchios produced are all extremely well made but Versiano has qualities that raise it above the rest. Gorgeous notes of fresh flowers, citrus fruit and aniseed are the prelude to a full, lip-smackingly supple palate with a full, elegantly savoury finish. Valle delle Lame Più is coherent and uncomplicated, showing fragrant and wonderfully pleasant on the palate. The basic Verdicchio is lightweight but convinces with subtle flowery nuances. We were able to taste the Rosso Piceno Campalliano again after it had completed a suitable period of ageing. Its lovely mature notes are still fruity, the extract packs a punch and the palate is soft and lingering.

Villa Pigna

C.DA CIAFONE, 63
63035 OFFIDA [AP]
TEL. 073687525
www.villapigna.com

ANNUAL PRODUCTION 600,000 bottles
HECTARES UNDER VINE 100
VITICULTURE METHOD Conventional

Annamaria Rozzi is the daughter of the late lamented Costantino, who founded this estate in deepest Ascoli Piceno. Since she decided to revamp the management style at Villa Pigna several years ago, with the help of consultant oenologist Riccardo Cotarella, a lot has changed on the estate. First and foremost, the style of the wines produced here has become increasingly well defined. All have a modern slant based on chewy, fruity weight and velvet-smooth tannic softness. Montepulciano, a variety that goes to make many of the wines in this broad range, is the perfect ally in this quest. A case in point is the montepulciano-only Rozzano with its pervasive aromas of morello cherry and warm, rounded palate. The Cabernasco is just as generous in its fruity notes but slightly more rigid and dry on the palate, perhaps because of the presence of 30 per cent cabernet sauvignon and 20 per cent merlot. But it was not only the reds that impressed us. Majia, a passerina-heavy blend with small additions of chardonnay and sauvignon, showed very well indeed. This white has a highly confident personality that comes out in fascinating citrus fruit and limpid freshness on the palate.

○ Verdicchio dei Castelli di Jesi Cl. Sup. Versiano '06	▾▾ 4
● Rosso Piceno Campalliano '04	▾▾ 4
○ Verdicchio dei Castelli di Jesi Cl. '06	▾▾ 2*
○ Verdicchio dei Castelli di Jesi Cl. Valle delle Lame '06	▾▾ 3*
● Rosso '06	▾ 2
● Esino Rosso Rosolaccio '05	3
○ Verdicchio dei Castelli di Jesi Cl. Sup. Versiano '05	♈♈ 4

● Rozzano '05	▾▾ 5
○ Offida Passerina Majia '06	▾▾ 4*
● Offida Rosso Cabernasco '04	▾▾ 5
○ Falerio dei Colli Ascolani Pliniano '06	▾ 3
● Rosso Piceno Sup. Vergaio '05	▾ 4
● Rosso Piceno Eliano '06	▾ 3
○ Offida Pecorino Rugiasco '06	▾ 4
● Rozzano '03	♈♈♈ 5
● Rozzano '01	♈♈ 5
● Rozzano '04	♈♈ 5
● Briccaio '04	♈♈ 4
● Rozzano '00	♈♈ 5
● Rosso Piceno Sup. Vergaio '04	♈♈ 4
● Offida Rosso Cabernasco '03	♈♈ 5

OTHER WINERIES

Accadia

FRAZ. CASTELLARO
VIA AMMORTO, 19
60048 SERRA SAN QUIRICO [AN]
TEL. 0731859007
az.accadia@tiscali.it

Talented Verdicchio producer Angelo Accadia presented Consono from his mountain terrain. Its charming nose of apple and pear is the prelude to a palate that follows through nicely to a dry finish. Conscio has sugary, almost aromatic notes, a big if not overly full palate and a slightly bitterish finish.

O Verdicchio dei Castelli di Jesi Cl.		
Sup. Conscio '06	♟♟	4
O Verdicchio dei Castelli di Jesi Cl.		
Consono '06	♟♟	3*

Mario Basilissi

LOC. PIANDELBELGIO, 471
62024 MATELICA [MC]
TEL. 3355297166
marebas@libero.it

Mario Basilissi has long been active in the wine world but had never released his own range. With oenologist Aroldo Belelli, he gave us two impeccably made, very varietal Verdicchios. The '05 selection shows rich notes of apple-like fruit, aniseed and almond while the standard white is a pleaser.

O Verdicchio di Matelica		
Sussi Biri Bissi '05	♟♟	4*
O Verdicchio di Matelica Basilissi '06	♟♟	4*

Mario & Giorgio Brunori

V.LE DELLA VITTORIA, 103
60035 JESI [AN]
TEL. 0731207213
www.brunori.it

Carlo Brunori and his son Giorgio are famous around Jesi for producing first-class versions of Verdicchio San Nicolò year after year. The '06 has citrus fruit, aromatic herbs and aniseed, followed by a palate with good backbone, freshness and tanginess. The florality-led Le Gemme is simpler.

O Verdicchio dei Castelli di Jesi Cl.		
Sup. San Nicolò '06	♟♟	4*
O Verdicchio dei Castelli di Jesi Cl.		
Le Gemme '06	♟	3

Capinera

C.DA CROCETTE, 12
62010 MORROVALLE [MC]
TEL. 0733222444
www.capinera.com

The Capinera brothers offered us their usual range of fine wines, starting with the pure merlot Cardinal Minio. It has good concentration, subtly pleasant vegetal notes and a dry, austere finish. The '06 Chardonnay is fresh, young and agreeable while the Beato Masseo is simple, tannic and alcohol-rich.

● Cardinal Minio '05	♟♟	5
● Colli Maceratesi Rosso		
Beato Masseo Ris. '04	♟	5
O La Capinera Chardonnay '06	♟	4

Enrico Ceci

VIA SANTA MARIA D'ARCO, 7
60038 SAN PAOLO DI JESI [AN]
TEL. 0731779033
www.verdicchiomarche.it/ceci

Every year, Enrico Ceci gives us solid versions of his two unique wines. The Verdicchio has a lovely nose of chamomile, white peach and wild herbs before the palate expands, showing fine balance and well-gauged structure with a nice tangy finish. The Rosso Piceno is enjoyably fresh-tasting and fruit-rich.

O Verdicchio dei Castelli di Jesi Cl.		
Sup. Santa Maria d'Arco '06	♟♟	4*
● Rosso Piceno		
Santa Maria d'Arco '05	♟♟	4*

Colli di Serrapetrona

VIA COLLI, 7/8
62020 SERRAPETRONA [MC]
TEL. 0733908329
www.collidiserrapetrona.it

A fine showing from an estate that focuses on various interpretations of the territory's main variety, vernaccia nera. Obtained from overripe fruit, the Robbione has notes of spice, pepper and stewed prunes and a warm, sustained palate. Collequanto has a soft palate and the sweet Sommo has breadth.

● Sommo '05	♟♟	5
● Serrapetrona Robbione '05	♟♟	5
● Serrapetrona Collequanto '05	♟	3

OTHER WINERIES

Colonnara
VIA MANDRIOLE, 6
60034 CUPRAMONTANA [AN]
TEL. 0731780273
www.colonnara.it

Overall, wines from this long-established co-operative were below par but there were two very decent Verdicchios. The Cuprese is the more inspiring, with young, fresh fruit and fragrantly elegant notes of pears and fresh flowers preceding a soft, delicious palate. The Tùfico is a tad unbending.

O Verdicchio dei Castelli di Jesi Cl.		
Sup. Cuprese '06	￥￥ 4*	
O Verdicchio dei Castelli di Jesi Cl.		
Sup. Tùfico V. T. '04	￥ 4	

Il Conte
VIA COLLE NAVICCHIO, 28
63030 MONTEPRANDONE [AP]
TEL. 073562593
www.ilcontevini.it

The De Angelis family gave us an unusual Passerina this year. From late-harvest fruit, it offers intense sweet ripe fruit and is well sustained on the palate by perfect freshness. Zipolo, a dense, firmly structured montepulciano, merlot and sangiovese blend, alternates ripe fruit and vegetal notes.

● Zipolo '04	￥￥ 6	
O L'Estro del Mastro Passerina '05	￥￥ 5	
O Falerio dei Colli Ascolani Aurato '06	￥ 3	

Del Carmine
LOC. TORRETTE DI ANCONA
VIA DEL CARMINE, 51
60020 ANCONA
TEL. 071889403
www.aziendadelcarmine.it

This Matelica zone winery with headquarters in Ancona wasn't quite up to par. Colli Maceratesi Rosso Petrara has generous aromas of fresh red berry fruit, nice energy and acidity on the palate and a dry, tangy finish. San Vicino is slightly aromatic and Verdicchio Aja Lunga has a mature, evolved style.

● Colli Maceratesi Rosso Petrara '06	￥￥ 3*	
O Verdicchio di Matelica		
Aja Lunga '06	￥ 4	
● San Vicino '06	￥ 4	

Domodimonti
VIA MENOCCHIA, 195
63010 MONTEFIORE DELL'ASO [AP]
TEL. 0734938764

We liked the first wines from Francesco Bellini, an entrepreneur from Ascoli who made his pile in Canada. Solo per Te is a montepulciano with sweet, ripe fruit, a confident palate and a soft, balanced finish. By way of contrast, Messia, an equal blend of montepulciano and merlot, is dry and robust.

● Il Messia '05	￥￥ 6	
● Solo per Te '05	￥￥ 8	
● Picens '06	￥ 4	

Castello Fageto
VIA VALDASO, 52
63016 PEDASO [AP]
TEL. 0734931784
www.castellofageto.it

Rusus is a fine Rosso Piceno that gives rich fruit lifted by balsamic notes and a full, harmonious palate backed up by well-rounded tannins. Claudio Di Ruscio also produces a Pecorino Fenèsia that has a soft style and lots of fruit. Serrone from cabernet sauvignon and merlot is a bit flabby and evolved.

O Offida Pecorino Fenèsia '06	￥￥ 4*	
● Rosso Piceno Rusus '05	￥￥ 5	
● Serrone '05	￥ 5	

Fiorano
C.DA FIORANO, 19
63030 COSSIGNANO [AP]
TEL. 073598446
www.agrifiorano.it

Originally from Lombardy, Paolo Beretta moved to the Marche to pursue his dream of making good organic wine. The dream has come true in Terre di Giobbe, an intensely fruity Rosso Piceno with depth in the mouth. Pecorino Donna Orgilla has a fresh, tangy finish while Sangiovese Fiorano is warmly fragrant.

O Donna Orgilla Pecorino '06	￥￥ 4*	
● Rosso Piceno Sup.		
Terre di Giobbe '05	￥￥ 4*	
● Fiorano Sangiovese '06	￥ 3	

OTHER WINERIES

Laurentina
VIA SAN PIETRO 19A
60036 MONTECAROTTO [AN]
TEL. 073189435
www.laurentinavini.com

The Perticarolis presented just a few wines from their long list but they showed well. Verdicchio Il Vigneto di Tobia's evolved, mature style is enhanced by buttery notes while the '06 Verdicchio is fresher and more approachable. The Rosso Piceno is dry and vanillaed, if a bit held back by the oak.

○ Verdicchio dei Castelli di Jesi Cl.		
Il Vigneto di Tobia '06	♆♆	3*
○ Verdicchio dei Castelli di Jesi Cl. '06	♆	2
● Rosso Piceno '05	♆	3

Malacari
VIA ENRICO MALACARI, 6
60020 OFFAGNA [AN]
TEL. 0717207606
malacari@tin.it

Alessandro Starabba sent us just one wine this year but what a wine it is. You'd be happy to have this reasonably priced Rosso Conero on your table every day. Fresh, crisp aromas of morello cherry are the prelude to a firm, fragrant palate with a leisurely finish of red berry fruit and spice.

● Rosso Conero '05	♆♆	4*
● Rosso Conero '04	♆♆	4
● Rosso Conero Grigiano '03	♆♆	5

Claudio Morelli
V.LE ROMAGNA, 47B
61032 FANO [PU]
TEL. 0721823352
www.claudiomorelli.it

True to form, Claudio Morelli offers his usual two pleasant but very differently styled Bianchellos. Borgo Torre has a soft, velvety profile supported by ripe, sweet fruit. Lovely fresh, almost tropical, fruit is the keynote of La Vigna delle Terrazze's personality.

○ Bianchello del Metauro		
Borgo Torre '06	♆♆	4*
○ Bianchello del Metauro		
La Vigna delle Terrazze '06	♆	3

Filippo Panichi
VIA SCIROLA, 37
63031 CASTEL DI LAMA [AP]
TEL. 0736815339
www.filippopanichi.it

Filippo Panichi's cellar is making its debut in the Guide. The montepulciano-only Rubens, the estate's flagship product, gives ripe, fragrant fruit nicely integrated with the oak and tight-knit tannins on the full, agreeable palate. Falerio Polittico has a sweet fruity nose and a soft full palate.

○ Falerio dei Colli Ascolani		
Polittico '06	♆♆	3*
● Rubens '05	♆♆	4
● Rosso Piceno Sup. Polittico '05	♆	4

Piantate Lunghe
FRAZ. CANDIA
VIA PIANTATE LUNGHE, 91
63131 ANCONA
TEL. 07136464
www.piantatelunghe.it

The wines from this young estate making its first appearance in the Guide are very good. The rich, austere Conero Riserva is characterful, elegant and highly agreeable. The Rosso Conero has a soft, velvety style and restrained notes of black cherry that are mirrored on the fresh, juicy palate.

● Conero Ris. '04	♆♆	6
● Rosso Conero '05	♆♆	4*
● Il Grosso '05	♆	3

Poggio Montali
VIA FONTE ESTATE, 6
60030 MONTE ROBERTO [AN]
TEL. 0731702825
www.poggiomontali.it

No stranger to quality, Carla Panicucci's estate keeps the flag flying with two excellent wines. The Rosso Conero Poggio al Cerro is a bit closed and dusty on the nose but expands vigorously on the palate where solid tannins dry the finish. The '06 Verdicchio is coherent, rich and warmly alcoholic.

○ Verdicchio		
dei Castelli di Jesi Cl. Sup. '06	♆♆	4*
● Rosso Conero		
Poggio al Cerro Ris. '03	♆♆	5

OTHER WINERIES

Alberto Quacquarini
VIA COLLI, 1
62020 SERRAPETRONA [MC]
TEL. 0733908180
www.quacquarini.it

We tasted very decent Dolce and Secco versions of Vernaccia di Serrapetrona, the spumante produced by brothers Luca and Mauro Quacquarini, champions of this lovely, traditional Marche wine. From vernaccia left to dry for several weeks, Petronio '02 has an elegant spicy nose, good backbone and ripe fruit.

● Petronio '02		▼▼ 5
● Vernaccia di Serrapetrona Dolce '06		▼ 3
● Vernaccia di Serrapetrona Secco '06		▼ 3

Sabbionare
LOC. MONTECAROTTO
VIA SABBIONARE, 10
60036 MONTECAROTTO [AN]
TEL. 0731889004
sabbionare@libero.it

Flanked by oenologist Sergio Paolucci, Donatella Paoloni has interpreted the excellent 2006 growing year skilfully to present two great Verdicchios. The Superiore Sabbionare is very tangy, lively, full and dynamic. The cheaper but equally tangy and full-bodied I Pratelli is not as deep but has good fruit.

○ Verdicchio dei Castelli di Jesi Cl. Sup. Sabbionare '06		▼▼ 4
○ Verdicchio dei Castelli di Jesi Cl. I Pratelli '06		▼▼ 3*

Santa Cassella
C.DA SANTA CASSELLA, 7
62018 POTENZA PICENA [MC]
TEL. 0733671507
www.santacassella.it

The Conte Leopoldo, from cabernet with some montepulciano, throws a fruity, vegetal nose followed by a full palate with nice length. The sweet, almost aromatic, Colli Maceratesi Bianco has generous fresh tropical fruit while the Chardonnay Donna Eleonora is big and concentrated on the palate.

● Conte Leopoldo '05		▼▼ 4
○ Donna Eleonora Chardonnay '06		▼▼ 3*
○ Colli Maceratesi Bianco '06		▼ 3

Fattoria Serra San Martino
VIA SAN MARTINO, 1
60030 SERRA DE' CONTI [AN]
TEL. 0731878025
www.serrasanmartino.com

Germans Kirsten and Thomas Weydemann's hillside winery made a great Guide debut. The easy-drinking Merlot Costa dei Zoppi is dense, balanced, elegant and balsamic. The Roccuccio from two thirds montepulciano and the rest merlot has ripe fruit and a rather rugged palate. The Paonazzo Syrah is rustic.

● Costa dei Zoppi Merlot '04		▼▼ 5
● Il Roccuccio '03		▼▼ 4
● Il Paonazzo Syrah '04		▼ 6

Tenuta dell'Ugolino
LOC. MACINE
VIA COPPARONI, 32
60031 CASTELPLANIO [AN]
TEL. 360487114
www.tenutaugolino.it

Andrea Petrini dedicates himself heart and soul to his four hectares of verdicchio. He presented two wines this year. The elegant, flavoursome Vigneto del Balluccio selection has intense notes of peach and citrus fruit while the very fragrant '06 wine offers fresh flowers and aniseed, and nice thrust.

○ Verdicchio dei Castelli di Jesi Cl. Sup. Vigneto del Balluccio '06		▼▼ 4
○ Verdicchio dei Castelli di Jesi Cl. '06		▼▼ 3*

Zaccagnini
VIA SALMÀGINA, 9/10
60039 STAFFOLO [AN]
TEL. 0731779892
www.zaccagnini.it

In the absence of several labels, two Verdicchios kept Rosella Zaccagnini's estate flag flying. The historic Salmàgina selection has faint flowery notes and a nice palate held back by sweet sensations that tend to muffle its progression and tanginess. The simpler Superiore Zaccagnini is light but good.

○ Verdicchio dei Castelli di Jesi Cl. Sup. Zaccagnini '06		▼ 3
○ Verdicchio dei Castelli di Jesi Cl. Sup. Salmàgina '06		▼ 4

UMBRIA

Our profile of Umbrian wine has often opened with an indisputable observation about quantity. This modest-sized region produces fewer than 1,000,000 hectolitres a year. That fact remains unchanged but it needs to be put in perspective. Umbrian wines are less nondescript these days. Just look at the boom in new wineries and the huge number of new launchings. Over the last three or four years, wine samples for our tastings have shot up by 30 per cent and the total is now pushing 500. The region also boasts 11 DOCs and two DOCGs, which all explains why current wine quality has pushed Umbria up the Italian wine ladder. The Superumbrians, IGT wines often containing a generous dollop of international varieties, have of course been playing an influential role in this cultural revolution over the last 20 years and no doubt will continue to do so. But increasingly, the tastes of growers, wine aficionados and simple consumers have restored the appeal of the denominations and traditional varieties. Two areas, Torgiano and Montefalco, stand out in this regard. Another, Orvieto, is coming forward while a fourth, Trasimeno, is consolidating its gains. Now to the details. Torgiano was back in the spotlight, thanks to Cantine Lungarotti's Rubesco Riserva Vigna Monticchio 2003, a wine so well executed, intriguing and representative of its prestigious history that it will thrill the most jaded drinker. Montefalco emerged from the furnace of 2003 to offer up very impressive 2004s, proving that cooler years, which can tamp down vegetative exuberance, bring out the best in the category. This great sagrantino vintage, which took a raft of wines into the national taste-offs, gave the area three top awards. As expected, Còlpetrone was a monster of balance and finesse; the star of Marco Caprai's 25 Anni is back in the firmament; and Sagrantino '04 from Perticaia, Guido Guardagli's operation, is extraordinarily complex and refined. But the region has many more than three stars, as we said. Never before has the overall level of the wines been so good and at least two or three other wineries came close to the top prize, which is sign of things to come. Orvieto brought us a new, exhilarating Cervaro della Sala '05, the iconic Antinori wine crafted by Renzo Cotarella that defies time and fashions. No less finely honed is the sangiovese-cabernet Calanco '03, from Le Velette, a cellar that is now a member of the exclusive club of the region's best houses. Other members for many years now are the Nodaris, husband and wife responsible for the exploits of Castello delle Regine, whose Merlot '05 was again superb. Speaking of merlot, the Cotarella brothers' Falesco has jumped the border into Umbria to send a stellar Montiano '05 into the record books. Finally, with eight Three Glasses to its credit, Umbria turned in one of its best performances ever

Adanti

LOC. ARQUATA
06031 BEVAGNA [PG]
TEL. 0742360295
www.cantineadanti.com

ANNUAL PRODUCTION 150,000 bottles
HECTARES UNDER VINE 30
VITICULTURE METHOD Conventional

Adanti is one of the most exciting wineries in the entire Sagrantino DOCG. With a history going back to the 1960s, it has witnessed a whole series of charismatic figures, all of whom made significant contributions to its current prestige. Alvaro Palini stands out as the legendary cellarmaster who from beginnings as a tailor in Paris, where he acquired a taste for fine wines, became a respected jack-of-all-trades in the wine world, largely thanks to his links with this very winery. The new century finds him still there, always quick with an anecdote or sage advice. His son Daniele is following in his footsteps, patiently and in his own style. Their aim has always been to propose Sagratinos that are not fashion driven but instead reflect the best in local Sagrantino tradition. The Palinis respect for the characteristics of each growing year means that they have produced 2003s with all the virtues and drawbacks of that problematic vintage. Although 2003 doesn't mirror the happy results of vintages such as the upcoming 2004, Adanti's offerings are evidence of fine winemaking. Both Rosso Arquata '03 and Montefalco Rosso '05 are excellent, as is Passito '04.

Antonelli - San Marco

LOC. SAN MARCO, 59
06036 MONTEFALCO [PG]
TEL. 0742379158
www.antonellisanmarco.it

ANNUAL PRODUCTION 250,000 bottles
HECTARES UNDER VINE 40
VITICULTURE METHOD Conventional

This long-standing winery produces its own interpretation of sagrantino and this year's 2004 is a truly fine version. Antonelli is one of those producers who have devoted significant efforts, over many years, to coaxing the best out of this intriguing but refractory variety. The winemaking philosophy has always privileged elegance over extraction and density, an approach not without its challenges since subtle differences can result in thin, rather simple wines. The 2004, however, silences all quibbles for this Sagratino not only hews to Antonelli's philosophy but also displays energy and depth that are far from common. Generous wild red berry fruit, particularly raspberry, adorns the nose while a remarkably refined palate shows well-integrated acidity and supple tannins, subtly enlivened by lively, earthy minerality. The qualities of 2004 also come through in Passito '04, which exudes tasty strawberry preserves, and in Rosso Riserva '04, a style in which Antonelli is a past master.

● Montefalco Sagrantino Arquata '03	♆♆	6
● Montefalco Sagrantino Passito Arquata '04	♆♆	7
● Montefalco Rosso Arquata '05	♆♆	4
● Rosso d'Arquata '03	♆♆	5
● Montefalco Sagrantino Arquata '01	♉♉	6
● Montefalco Sagrantino Arquata '02	♉♉	6
● Rosso d'Arquata '03	♉♉	5
● Montefalco Sagrantino Passito Arquata '03	♉♉	7
● Montefalco Sagrantino Passito '99	♉♉	7
● Montefalco Sagrantino Passito '01	♉♉	6
● Montefalco Sagrantino Arquata '00	♉♉	6

● Montefalco Sagrantino '04	♆♆	6
● Montefalco Rosso Ris. '04	♆♆	5
● Montefalco Sagrantino Passito '04	♆♆	6
● Baiocco '05	♆	3
● Montefalco Rosso '05	♆	4
O Colli Martani Grechetto '06	♆	3
● Montefalco Sagrantino '00	♉♉	7
● Montefalco Sagrantino '01	♉♉	7
● Montefalco Sagrantino '02	♉♉	6
● Montefalco Rosso Ris. '01	♉♉	5
● Montefalco Rosso Ris. '03	♉♉	5
● Montefalco Sagrantino '03	♉♉	6

Barberani - Vallesanta

LOC. CERRETO
05023 BASCHI [TR]
TEL. 0763341820
www.barberani.it

ANNUAL PRODUCTION 350,000 bottles
HECTARES UNDER VINE 55
VITICULTURE METHOD Conventional

Barberani may be one of the oldest wineries in the area but it is perfectly able to refocus to take full advantage of any changes in the wine world at large. Which is not to say that the cellar is not faithful to a carefully defined production philosophy. But a new generation is now participating in management, with Bernardo concentrating on marketing and Niccolò on viticulture and winemaking. The result is a breath of fresh air, which was obvious in the styles of the wines we tasted this year. The whites in particular showed new verve and distinctiveness. Calcaia went to the national taste-offs again with an impressive 2004 marked by impressions of tropical fruit and sea salt that segue onto a supple, smooth-flowing palate of impressive depth and complexity. Villa Monticelli Rosso '03 displays notes of fruit preserves and herbaceous, almost smoky, nuances, a stalwart effort from a torrid vintage. Foresco '05 is an extraordinary, multifarious blend of reds that achieves a level of harmony not reached in the past. Grechetto and Castagnolo, both 2006, stand out among the whites.

Bigi

LOC. PONTE GIULIO
05018 ORVIETO [TR]
TEL. 0763315888
www.giv.it

ANNUAL PRODUCTION 3,900,000 bottles
HECTARES UNDER VINE 193
VITICULTURE METHOD Conventional

The name Bigi has conjured up quality in the Orvieto area for a good number of years now. In fact it was as far back as 1880 that Luigi Bigi launched his winery in Ponte Giulio, in the tufa-rich countryside gazing up to the city on its rocky peak. The Gruppo Italiano Vini has owned Bigi for some time, focusing its energy on patiently consolidating and improving the venerable winemaking heritage of the winery and its immediate area. Our tasting this year revealed a delicious Tamante '06, largely merlot with some sangiovese and montepulciano, which is excellent value for money. We were also impressed with Sartiano '05, the flagship red, a blend of sangiovese, merlot and pinot nero. With its notes of smoky-edged bell pepper and still youthful tannins, it needs a tad more time to find its balance. The whites turned in good performances. Orvieto Classico Torricella '06, redolent of lime blossom and smooth vanilla, is reliable as always while the grechetto Strozza Volpe '06 is stylishly appealing, despite an over-sweet mid palate.

O Orvieto Cl. Sup. Calcaia '04	ŸŸ 6
O Grechetto '06	ŸŸ 4
O Orvieto Cl. Sup. Castagnolo '06	ŸŸ 4
● Lago di Corbara Foresco '05	ŸŸ 4
● Lago di Corbara Rosso Villa Monticelli '03	ŸŸ 5
O Moscato Passito Villa Monticelli '05	Ÿ 6
● Sangiovese '06	Ÿ 3
⊙ Vallesanta Rosato '06	Ÿ 2
● Lago di Corbara Rosso Villa Monticelli '01	♀♀ 5
O Orvieto Cl. Sup. Calcaia '03	♀♀ 6
O Orvieto Cl. Sup. Calcaia '00	♀♀ 6
O Orvieto Cl. Sup. Calcaia '95	♀♀ 5
O Orvieto Cl. Sup. Calcaia '97	♀♀ 5

O Orvieto Cl. Vigneto Torricella '06	ŸŸ 3
● Sartiano '05	ŸŸ 4
● Tamante '06	ŸŸ 3
O Strozza Volpe Grechetto '06	Ÿ 3
● Sartiano '01	♀♀ 4
● Tamante '04	♀♀ 3*
● Tamante '05	♀♀ 3*

★ Arnaldo Caprai

LOC. TORRE
06036 MONTEFALCO [PG]
TEL. 0742378802
www.arnaldocaprai.it

ANNUAL PRODUCTION 750,000 bottles
HECTARES UNDER VINE 137
VITICULTURE METHOD Conventional

Caprai's 25 Anni is back! Last year's performance brought, alas, no trophy, with the national finals featuring a 2003 that simply showed too rich and opulent for a wine from which one expects elegance and complexity, and the difficult 2002 growing year was an understandable lacuna. But 2004, with its kinder, more classic weather patterns, has again served up to 25 Anni fans a fabulous edition of the wine that, despite ever more intense competition, still sets the benchmark for Sagrantino di Montefalco. Truly monumental, ever fascinating, it flaunts dense fragrances of wild blackberry, leather and tobacco leaf, which flow seamlessly onto a massive but cleanly etched palate. Vibrant depth, powerful tannins and superb finesse combine to ensure that yet another year will be laid down among the numerous earlier vintages to flaunt its formidable qualities for years to come. The remaining three wines, all impressive, risk being overshadowed, which should in fact be enough to indicate the overall quality level of everything produced here. Only iconoclastic petulance would foolishly seek to tarnish such accomplishments.

Cardeto

FRAZ. SFERRACAVALLO
LOC. CARDETO
05018 ORVIETO [TR]
TEL. 0763341286
www.cardeto.com

ANNUAL PRODUCTION 3,000,000 bottles
HECTARES UNDER VINE 880
VITICULTURE METHOD Conventional

Cardeto's annual production of 3,000,000 bottles puts it in the spotlight of consumer expectations for the overall quality levels of Orvieto-area wines. Our own judgement, based at least on the general quality of Cardeto wines in our tastings, is that they are rising to that challenge very well. In general terms, this translates into fine quality over an extensive line of wines, ranging from the local classics to more pioneering reds in recent years, all with appealing price tags. Turning to our tastings, the all-sangiovese Nero della Greca '05 again turned in a thoroughbred performance. Its overall depth is presaged by intense ruby and offers boiled sweets and toasty oak over an impressive gamut of wild berry fruit, plus fair depth and a very nice overall balance of all its components. The Bordeaux blend Arciato '05 runs at the same pace, exhibiting rose-water and cocoa powder, with Rupestro '06, a standard Orvieto that often shows flashes of a finer pedigree, perhaps a nose ahead. From the whites, we liked the tropics-edged Febeo '06 and the superb Colbadia '06, all citrus and balsam, with succulent fruit and multi-layered depth.

● Montefalco Sagrantino 25 Anni '04	♟♟♟	8
● Montefalco Sagrantino Passito '04	♟♟	8
● Montefalco Sagrantino Collepiano '04	♟♟	7
● Rosso Outsider '05	♟♟	7
○ Colli Martani Grechetto Grecante '06	♟♟	4
● Montefalco Rosso '05	♟♟	5
● Montefalco Sagrantino Collepiano '02	♟♟♟	7
● Montefalco Sagrantino 25 Anni '99	♟♟♟	8
● Montefalco Sagrantino 25 Anni '98	♟♟♟	8
● Montefalco Sagrantino 25 Anni '97	♟♟♟	8
● Montefalco Sagrantino 25 Anni '94	♟♟♟	8
● Montefalco Sagrantino 25 Anni '01	♟♟♟	8
● Montefalco Sagrantino 25 Anni '00	♟♟♟	8
● Montefalco Sagrantino 25 Anni '96	♟♟♟	8
● Montefalco Sagrantino 25 Anni '95	♟♟♟	8
● Montefalco Sagrantino Collepiano '03	♟♟♟	7

● Arciato '05	♟♟	4
● Nero della Greca '05	♟♟	5
● Rupestro '06	♟♟	2*
○ Orvieto Cl. Sup. Febeo '06	♟♟	4
○ Colbadia '06	♟♟	4
● Alborato '06	♟	3
○ Orvieto Cl. Pierleone '06	♟	3
○ Grechetto '06	♟	2
● Nero della Greca '01	♟♟	5
● Rupestro '04	♟♟	3*
● Nero della Greca '04	♟♟	4*
● Arciato '04	♟♟	4

Carini

FRAZ. COLLE UMBERTO
S.DA DEL TEGOLARO
06070 PERUGIA [PG]
TEL. 0755829102
www.agrariacarini.it

ANNUAL PRODUCTION   40,000 bottles
HECTARES UNDER VINE 10
VITICULTURE METHOD   Conventional

Amidst hot debates over the increasing uniformity of wine styles, even those coming out of different vintage years, Carini merits consideration as a model. The winery's iconic Tegolaro, a masterful blend of merlot, cabernet and sangiovese, clearly exhibits a common thread that runs through its various editions. Yet it also faithfully reflects weather variations occurring in different growing years, a characteristic considerably assisted by significant improvements in vineyard management and finely calibrated cellar practices. The 2002 release, though elegant, was somewhat slender, the 2003 lush and almost overripe, while the magisterial 2004 showed unmatched depth and vibrancy. The 2005 is a true child of its vintage. It opens to an earthy, intriguingly unique, aromatic palette enlivened by generous impressions of fruit and balsam, then develops a lithe, supple palate, fine, vivacious acidity and a finish infused with a refreshing bouquet of medicinal herbs. Scarcely less fine is Poggio Canneto '06, a chardonnay, pinot bianco and grechetto blend that shows a tasty, iodide-edged sapidity, as well as Òscano '06, a wonderfully delicious standard red.

La Carraia

LOC. TORDIMONTE, 56
05018 ORVIETO [TR]
TEL. 0763304013
info@lacarraia.it

ANNUAL PRODUCTION   500,000 bottles
HECTARES UNDER VINE 119
VITICULTURE METHOD   Conventional

La Carraia boasts one of the best-organized operations in the Orvieto area, with vineyards in exceptional terroirs, a spanking new winemaking cellar and, most impressive of all, an unmatched resource in the two families that launched the winery in 1988. The Giallettis have worked local vineyards for decades, and the Cotarellas have formidable expertise in the cellar. Fobiano '05, a classic Bordeaux blend, is still their standard-bearer. This year's version showcases muscular structure, incredible depth and concentration, and a rich aromatic spectrum that ranges from redcurrant and fresh-sliced morello cherries to subtle hints of pungent balsam and new-mown grass. No less impressive is the all-montepulciano Giro di Vite '05, which has taken very few vintages to command respect: here, a deep purplish hue is matched by textbook varietal characteristics and plush mouthfeel. Tizzonero '05, a 50-50 blend of sangiovese and montepulciano, is every bit its equal, exuding lovely notes of cherry and caramel. Sangiovese '06 is a fine offering, which we can also say for the reliable Orvieto Classico Poggio Calvelli '06 and the simpler Orvieto Classico '06.

● Tegolaro '05	♈♈ 6
● O'Scano '06	♈♈ 4
○ Poggio Canneto '06	♈♈ 4
● Tegolaro '04	♉♉ 6
● Tegolaro '01	♉♉ 6
● Tegolaro '02	♉♉ 6
● Tegolaro '03	♉♉ 6

● Fobiano '05	♈♈ 5
● Giro di Vite '05	♈♈ 5
● Tizzonero '05	♈♈ 4
○ Orvieto Cl. Poggio Calvelli '06	♈♈ 3*
● Sangiovese '06	♈♈ 3*
○ Orvieto Cl. '06	♈ 2
● Fobiano '03	♉♉♉ 5
● Fobiano '99	♉♉♉ 6
● Fobiano '98	♉♉♉ 5
● Fobiano '04	♉♉ 5
● Giro di Vite '04	♉♉ 5
● Sangiovese '05	♉♉ 3*
● Tizzonero '04	♉♉ 4

Fattoria Colle Allodole

LOC. COLLE ALLODOLE
06031 BEVAGNA [PG]
TEL. 0742361897

ANNUAL PRODUCTION N.A.
HECTARES UNDER VINE 10
VITICULTURE METHOD Conventional

Francesco Antano is a rock-solid, passionate grower who obsessively follows every step of his wine from vineyard to cellar to market. When he succeeds in personally supervising even the tiniest detail during that long journey into the wine-lover's glass not only shall we have an extraordinary winemaker at our service but Sagrantino will finally be able to flaunt one of its finest expressions. Francesco's jealously guarded artisanal flair, which we hope he will maintain, has won him a growing troop of aficionados but these are wines that could aspire to even greater heights. That said, the vintage has been a terrific one for this modest operation, although it could have gone even higher. Three wines, all of the Sagrantinos released, jumped into our finals. Colle delle Allodole '04, cask-matured in Slavonian oak, was the standout. Powerful and broad-shouldered, it has a mineral-edged savouriness compounded of fruit that is supple and luscious yet well under control, and concludes with a lovely citrusy fanfare. Equally outstanding are the standard Sagrantino '04, aged in larger barrels and a bit shy yet, and Passito '04, showing cassis and chocolate.

Cantina dei Colli Amerini

LOC. FORNOLE
ZONA INDUSTRIALE
05022 AMELIA [TR]
TEL. 0744989721
www.colliamerini.it

ANNUAL PRODUCTION 1,000,000 bottles
HECTARES UNDER VINE 400
VITICULTURE METHOD Conventional

This is a transitional year for Colli Amerini, which is involved in a fairly significant makeover. After years of relatively few changes, cellar and vineyard practices are being improved, which is a major step. We should eschew any firm judgments in this time of flux, which does in fact betray, inevitably, some unevenness in the wines presented. Carbio '05, perhaps the co-operative's most representative wine, seems to suffer from a general tiredness, perceptible above all in the aromas but on the palate as well. True, there is some good fruit but the palate is too thin and the finish comes across rough. Cilegiolo is a variety that is under some experimentation. Cilegiolo di Narni '06 showed fairly well, with medium ruby, decent balance and crisp notes of fresh plum and citron. We also liked Olmeto '06, a Merlot that is lively, heady and discloses a subtle but appealing herbaceousness. Rocca Nerina '06, from chardonnay and malvasia, is fine, offering delicious tropical fragrances.

● Montefalco Sagrantino Colle delle Allodole '04	♥♥ 7
● Montefalco Sagrantino Passito '04	♥♥ 5
● Montefalco Sagrantino '04	♥♥ 6
● Montefalco Rosso '05	♥♥ 5
● Montefalco Rosso Ris. '04	♥♥ 6
● Montefalco Rosso Colle Allodole '04	♥♥ 5
● Montefalco Sagrantino Colle delle Allodole '03	♀♀ 7
● Montefalco Rosso Ris. '03	♀♀ 6
● Montefalco Sagrantino Colle delle Allodole '98	♀♀ 6
● Montefalco Sagrantino '98	♀♀ 5
● Montefalco Sagrantino '01	♀♀ 6

● C. Amerini Rosso Sup. Carbio '05	♀ 5
○ Rocca Nerina '06	♀ 4
● Ciliegiolo 30 Anni '06	♀ 6
● Olmeto '06	♀ 4
● C. Amerini Rosso Sup. Carbio '04	♀♀ 5
● C. Amerini Rosso Sup. Carbio '00	♀♀ 5
● C. Amerini Rosso Sup. Carbio '01	♀♀ 5
● C. Amerini Rosso Sup. Carbio '03	♀♀ 5
● Ciliegiolo di Narni 30 Anni '05	♀♀ 4*
● C. Amerini Rosso Sup. Carbio '99	♀♀ 5

Còlpetrone

LOC. MARCELLANO
VIA PONTE LA MANDRIA, 8/1
06035 GUALDO CATTANEO [PG]
TEL. 057899827
www.saiagricola.it

ANNUAL PRODUCTION 115,880 bottles
HECTARES UNDER VINE 63
VITICULTURE METHOD Conventional

The energy and size of the Saiagricola group are well known but the tenacity that has brought such achievements to Còlpetrone must be applauded. Confining our comments for the moment just to the wine front, it is the Sagrantino programme that seems to us to show the best results so far. A new, well-organized cellar, beautifully sited amid the gentle profiles of the hills at Gualdo Cattaneo, has contributed mightily to this success. Turning to the Sagrantinos, the 2004 may show a tad less exuberant than the previous vintage, which seemed more forward at this point, but the current edition may very well edge ahead in the long run, thanks to its crisp, lively profile, considerable complexity and almost endless progression. Dark red berry fruit melds admirably into pungent balsam and the conclusion is ennobled by a truly elegant tannic weave. We were also impressed too by Passito '04, heady and showing abundant menthol, as well as by the concentrated but well-rounded Rosso di Montefalco '05.

Castello di Corbara

LOC. CORBARA, 7
05018 ORVIETO [TR]
TEL. 0763304035
www.castellodicorbara.it

ANNUAL PRODUCTION 160,000 bottles
HECTARES UNDER VINE 140
VITICULTURE METHOD Certified organic

Castello di Corbara received another string of high marks, which simply go to confirm that the winery is firmly on the right track, although you might have expected even higher quality following two years of growth. In fact, leaving scores aside, our tastings seemed to indicate a slight regression, particularly in the overall style of the wines. Too often, they betray a heavy hand on the oak, quite in contrast to the aromatic characteristics that we had come to expect. This means we can't say any longer that our favourites among the reds include Merlot De Coronis, The '04 edition is but a pale version of its former self, with fairly invasive wood and an astringent palate, while the estery, caramel-laced Cabernet Sauvignon '05 also disappoints. Lago di Corbara Rosso '05 is a definite improvement, showing nicely balsamic and perked up by a vein of zesty acidity. Also improved are Calistri '04, a bold sangiovese with supple fruit, and Podere Il Caio Rosso '06, simpler but with all its cards in order. From the whites, we were impressed by Grechetto '06, which releases aniseed and toasty almond over crisp citrus.

● Montefalco Sagrantino '04	♟♟♟ 6		● Lago di Corbara Rosso '05	♟♟ 5
● Montefalco Sagrantino Passito '04	♟♟ 6		● Calistri '04	♟♟ 5
● Montefalco Rosso '05	♟♟ 4		○ Grechetto Podere Il Caio '06	♟♟ 3
● Montefalco Sagrantino '00	♟♟♟ 6		● Podere Il Caio Rosso '06	♟♟ 4
● Montefalco Sagrantino '99	♟♟♟ 6		○ Orvieto Cl. Sup. Podere Il Caio '06	♟ 3
● Montefalco Sagrantino '98	♟♟♟ 5		● Lago di Corbara Merlot De Coronis '04	♟ 5
● Montefalco Sagrantino '97	♟♟♟ 5		● Lago di Corbara Cabernet Sauvignon '05	♟ 5
● Montefalco Sagrantino '01	♟♟♟ 6		● Lago di Corbara De Coronis '03	♟♟ 5
● Montefalco Sagrantino '96	♟♟♟ 4		● Calistri '03	♟♟ 5
● Montefalco Sagrantino '03	♟♟♟ 6		● Lago di Corbara Cabernet Sauvignon '04	♟♟ 5

Tenuta Corini
VOC. CASINO, 53
05010 MONTEGABBIONE [TR]
TEL. 0763837535
www.tenutacorini.it

ANNUAL PRODUCTION 24,000 bottles
HECTARES UNDER VINE 10
VITICULTURE METHOD Conventional

After doing quite well abroad, the Corini family returned to their home soil and some years ago got it into their heads to grow wine in an area that had been rather overlooked until their start-up. Come off the autostrada at Fabro and you are in gorgeous countryside, set between Orvieto and Lake Trasimeno. The winery is not far, near the village of Montegabbione. Set amidst vineyards is the splendid villa that welcomes visitors from all corners of the globe. The Corinis went largely for the international varieties, although they do also nod to long-time local denizens. From this mixture emerge three wines, which express eloquently the winery's production philosophy. Frabusco '05 is a dense-hued blend of sangiovese, montepulciano and merlot whose heady bouquet proffers ultra-rich fruit. A well-balanced palate is nicely defined and appealingly complex, although it lacks that extra touch of excitement. The all-pinot nero Camerti '05 is a more than decent effort, already showing appreciable evolution, and equally well made is Casteldifiori '06, a fragrantly citrus-themed sauvignon.

Duca della Corgna
VIA ROMA, 236
06061 CASTIGLIONE DEL LAGO [PG]
TEL. 0759652493
www.ducadellacorgna.it

ANNUAL PRODUCTION 280,000 bottles
HECTARES UNDER VINE 55
VITICULTURE METHOD Conventional

The line-up of this year's tasting differed from the past, since the house thoroughbred, Corniolo, which has often contended in the final taste-offs, will be stabled a few more months in the cellars. Our attention shifted to two wines that speak in the softer tones of Trasimeno, particularly because of their grape variety, gamay perugino, also known appropriately here as gamay del Trasimeno. Capable of fine results similar to grenache, it has grown seemingly forever on the hills around the lake and may with justice be called a local native. We found both of these wines, under the Divina Villa label, to be particularly fine this year. Etichetta Nera '05 shows crisp, refreshing and nicely layered while the Etichetta Bianca '06, which is not put into cask, boasts tasty wild cherry highlighted by a subtle rose-petal and violets florality. All the other wines are admirably well made, and enviable bargains as well. Plaudits go to this future-focused co-operative so ably directed by dynamic notary Paolo Biavati.

● Frabusco '05	▼▼ 6
○ Casteldifiori '06	▼ 4
● Pinot Nero Camerti '05	▼ 6
● Frabusco '01	▼▼ 6
○ Casteldifiori '05	▼▼ 4
● Pinot Nero Camerti '04	▼▼ 6
● Pinot Nero Camerti '01	▼▼ 6
● Frabusco '04	▼▼ 6

○ C. del Trasimeno Baccio del Bianco '06	▼▼ 2
● C. del Trasimeno Gamay Divina Villa Et. Bianca '06	▼▼ 4
○ C. del Trasimeno Grechetto Nuricante '06	▼▼ 3
● C. del Trasimeno Gamay Divina Villa Et. Nera '05	▼▼ 4
● C. del Trasimeno Baccio del Rosso '06	▼▼ 3
● C. del Trasimeno Rosso Corniolo '03	▼▼ 4
● C. del Trasimeno Gamay Divina Villa Et. Nera '04	▼▼ 4
● C. del Trasimeno Gamay Divina Villa Et. Bianca '04	▼▼ 4*
● C. del Trasimeno Rosso Corniolo '04	▼▼ 4

★ Falesco

LOC. SAN PIETRO
05020 MONTECCHIO [TR]
TEL. 07449556
www.falesco.it

ANNUAL PRODUCTION   2,900,000 bottles
HECTARES UNDER VINE 370
VITICULTURE METHOD   Conventional

The Cotarella brothers, Renzo and Riccardo, have moved Falesco into Umbria but its transcendent quality has not suffered at all. Their new cellar, an extraordinary blend of spaciousness, functionality and technology, is now located in Montecchio, not far from Orvieto, and our Guide takes this change of address into account. With regard to our tasting results, after last year's '04 Marciliano gained the top trophy, along came an extraordinary Montiano '05 that just nosed out the other winery contenders. A 100 per cent merlot, Montiano absolutely enraptures, laying out a range of fragrances that range from wild berry fruit and rich spices to tanned leather and tobacco leaf, with a depth and complexity that few wines from this variety can equal. Marciliano '05 remains the heavy hitter it has always been. After an incisive nose that delivers dark cherry and chocolate, the palate is concentrated and tight through to a superb finale lined with masterful tannins. The other wines are very, very good indeed, with plaudits for price tags as well. The powerful Ferentano '06, a roscetto with lively fruit and notes of toasty oak, shows lovely depth.

Goretti

LOC. PILA
S.DA DEL PINO, 4
06132 PERUGIA [PG]
TEL. 075607316
www.vinigoretti.com

ANNUAL PRODUCTION   400,000 bottles
HECTARES UNDER VINE 60
VITICULTURE METHOD   Conventional

Goretti is at its usual position near the top of the class. Year after year, consistency, reliability and enviable overall quality are the highlights of their Guide profile. But consistency is not at the cost of movement since this Perugia operation has seen a number of developments over the last few years. We note the new cellar in Montefalco, just now ramping up, renovation of the historic tower at the main winery, a new winemaking staff, and just this year the arrival at the firm of Sara Goretti, daughter of one of the owners. She seems to be bringing a breath of fresh, breezy air to the cellar. From this year's wines, we liked L'Arringatore '04, a sangiovese, merlot and ciliegiolo mix. Its dense, multi-layered palate is reflected on the nose in an amalgam of wild berry fruits, upfront notes of spice and chocolate, toasty oak, and subtle hints of balsam. The whites are equally alluring. Moggio '06 is a grechetto with a few months in barrel and Colli Perugini Grechetto '06 is one of the finest interpretations of the variety. On the Montefalco front, we were thoroughly impressed with the deep, concentrated Sagrantino '03 and Rosso di Montefalco '05, a tad more slender but vibrantly powerful.

● Montiano '05	♟♟♟	6
○ Ferentano '05	♟♟	4
● Marciliano '05	♟♟	6
○ Est Est Est di Montefiascone Poggio dei Gelsi '06	♟♟	3
● Tellus '06	♟♟	4
● Vitiano '06	♟♟	3
○ Est Est Est di Montefiascone Falesco '06	♟	2
○ Passirò '05	♟	5
● Pesano '06	♟	4
● Marciliano '04	♟♟♟	6
● Montiano '00	♟♟♟	6
● Montiano '03	♟♟♟	6
● Montiano '01	♟♟♟	6
● Montiano '04	♟♟	6
● Marciliano '01	♟♟	6
● Marciliano '03	♟♟	6

○ Colli Perugini Grechetto '06	♟♟	3
● Montefalco Sagrantino Le Mure Saracene '03	♟♟	6
● Montefalco Rosso Le Mure Saracene '05	♟♟	4
○ Il Moggio '06	♟♟	4
● Colli Perugini Rosso L'Arringatore '04	♟♟	5
○ Colli Perugini Chardonnay '06	♟	3
● Fontanella Rosso '06	♟	3
○ Colli Perugini Grechetto '05	♟♟	3*
● Colli Perugini Rosso L'Arringatore '00	♟♟	5
● Colli Perugini Rosso L'Arringatore '01	♟♟	5
● Montefalco Sagrantino Le Mure Saracene '99	♟♟	6
● Colli Perugini Rosso L'Arringatore '03	♟♟	5

Lamborghini
LOC. SODERI, 1
06064 PANICALE [PG]
TEL. 0758350029
www.lamborghinionline.it

Lungarotti
VIA MARIO ANGELONI, 16
06089 TORGIANO [PG]
TEL. 075988661
www.lungarotti.it

ANNUAL PRODUCTION 127,000 bottles
HECTARES UNDER VINE 32
VITICULTURE METHOD Conventional

ANNUAL PRODUCTION 2,900,000 bottles
HECTARES UNDER VINE 310
VITICULTURE METHOD Conventional

A final seven hectares, planted to sangiovese, bring the winery's replantings to 19 of its total 32 hectares. Begun in 1997, this crowns a remarkable programme of renovation of Lamborghini's vineyard and production resources. Such dedication speaks eloquently of the masterful attention to winemaking that distinguishes Lamborghini, as well as its entire history, from the moment in the early 1970s when Ferruccio fell in love with this area and decided to revive his family's agricultural heritage by growing grapes. Today, Patrizia carries that work forward, producing three wines that exemplify the local area's potential for great reds. The merlot and sangiovese Campoleone '05 missed Three Glasses by a hair's breadth. The nose offers fruit that is fully ripe, and perhaps even a shade beyond, plus aromas of sliced morello cherry, rose water and cassis, then the palate opens spacious and impressively textured, supported by well-crafted tannins. Torami '05, a grassy-edged blend of cabernet, sangiovese and montepulciano, is a winner while Trescone '05, from sangiovese, ciliegiolo and merlot, is somewhat simpler.

Chiara Lungarotti, who manages this long-established cellar with her sister Teresa, carries out her responsibilities with a firm hand and clear vision. But our first thoughts this year go to her handsome new baby, Giovanni, hoping that this new generation will contribute, over time, to a family tradition that has few peers in the world of Italian wine. That perennial fascination is rekindled each time a cork is pulled from a bottle from this noble house in Torgiano. But now new wines have been flanking the classics, at least in the last few years, bringing with them a whole new cornucopia of pleasures. Torgiano Rosso Rubesco Vigna Monticchio Riserva scored big in 2001, was out of the ring in the unfortunate 2002 year and with the '03 roars back to recapture Three glasses, and effortlessly to boot. Simply put, this is a fantastic red that bewitches with its stylish wild berry notes magisterially integrated with delicate toast and a thread of earthy mineral. Just as stylish on the palate, it exhibits incredible breadth and depth, infused throughout with medicinal herbs and subtle tar. All the other wines are top drawer, with special kudos for Aurente '05, an ultra-rich chardonnay.

● Campoleone '05	♟♟ 6
● Torami '05	♟ 5
● Trescone '05	♟ 4
● Campoleone '00	♟♟♟ 6
● Campoleone '99	♟♟♟ 6
● Campoleone '04	♟♟♟ 7
● Campoleone '01	♟♟♟ 6
● Campoleone '02	♟♟ 6
● Campoleone '03	♟♟ 6

● Torgiano Rosso Vigna Monticchio Ris. '03	♟♟♟ 6
O Aurente '05	♟♟ 5
● Montefalco Sagrantino '04	♟♟ 5
● Montefalco '05	♟♟ 4
● Torgiano Rosso Rubesco '04	♟♟ 4
O Torgiano Bianco Torre di Giano '06	♟♟ 3
O Torgiano Bianco Torre di Giano V. il Pino Ris. '05	♟ 4
● Torgiano Rosso Vigna Monticchio Ris. '01	♟♟♟ 7
● Torgiano Rosso Vigna Monticchio Ris. '88	♟♟♟ 5
● Torgiano Rosso Vigna Monticchio Ris. '00	♟♟ 6

Madonna Alta

via Piceni, 14
06036 Montefalco [PG]
tel. 0742378568
www.madonnalta.it

ANNUAL PRODUCTION 130,000 bottles
HECTARES UNDER VINE 16
VITICULTURE METHOD Conventional

A love affair with this corner of earth led the Ferraro family, originally from Campania, to dedicate themselves to the area's most prized resource, sagrantino. A few years after purchasing their first vineyards, replanting them, and then building their cellar, everything seems to be well set and performance levels are excellent. There were very high marks this year for Montefalco Sagrantino '04, a delicious offering that infuses dark berry fruit with intriguing hints of cinchona root, followed by an appealing fruity succulence in the mouth that is masked slightly by a dab too much oak. Equally fine is Passito '04, in which leather and tobacco act as an interesting foil to the customary fruit preserves. Nor could anyone cavil with the predominantly sangiovese Falconero Rosso '05, which is gutsy and pleasantly herbaceous. Just One Glass went to the '05 Rosso di Montefalco, balsamic but still too tight, and Grechetto '06, nicely fat but a tad bitterish on the finish.

● Falconero Rosso '06	🍷🍷 3
● Montefalco Sagrantino '04	🍷🍷 6
● Montefalco Sagrantino Passito '04	🍷🍷 6
○ Colli Martani Grechetto '06	🍷 4
● Montefalco Rosso '05	🍷 4
● Montefalco Rosso '04	🍷🍷 4
● Montefalco Sagrantino '02	🍷🍷 6
● Montefalco Sagrantino Passito '03	🍷🍷 6

Castello di Magione

via dei Cavalieri di Malta, 31
06063 Magione [PG]
tel. 075843547
www.castellodimagione.it

ANNUAL PRODUCTION 90,000 bottles
HECTARES UNDER VINE 30
VITICULTURE METHOD Conventional

"We'd still like to see a step-up in quality with the reds" was our parting shot for Castello di Magione in last year's Guide. And so it came to pass. Colli del Trasimeno Rosso Morcinaia '04 is a fascinating wine that needs further watching in the years ahead of course, but this vintage impressed us mightily. Its fragrances practically erupt from the glass, intense and complex, a panoply of essences ranging from black berry fruit to suggestions of petrol and tar, followed by an attack so laden with smooth, succulent fruit as to seem to hail from the left bank of the Garonne. The grechetto Monterone, on the other hand, no longer surprises, merely confirming its expected quality, and the '06 is no exception. Luxurious citrus and floral notes intermingle beautifully, perfectly complemented by a crispness and mineral-driven liveliness that render this grechetto the regional benchmark. Even the standard Grechetto '06 is irresistible and delicious, demonstrating Castello di Magione's fine hand with a variety that is anything but biddable. But Grechetto has long been, and continues to be, the keystone of white winemaking in Umbria.

● Colli del Trasimeno Rosso Morcinaia '04	🍷🍷 5
○ Grechetto '06	🍷🍷 2
○ Colli del Trasimeno Grechetto Monterone '05	🍷🍷 3*
○ Colli del Trasimeno Grechetto Monterone '04	🍷🍷 2*
○ Grechetto '05	🍷🍷 2*

Cantina Monrubio
FRAZ. MONTERUBIAGLIO
LOC. LE PRESE, 22
05010 CASTEL VISCARDO [TR]
TEL. 0763626064
cantina.monrubio@tiscali.it

La Palazzola
LOC. VASCIGLIANO
05039 STRONCONE [TR]
TEL. 0744609091
info@lapalazzola.it

ANNUAL PRODUCTION 800,000 bottles
HECTARES UNDER VINE 700
VITICULTURE METHOD Conventional

ANNUAL PRODUCTION 150,000 bottles
HECTARES UNDER VINE 36
VITICULTURE METHOD Conventional

The debate over the role of co-operatives in Umbria not only has yet to be resolved but remains full of intriguing questions and heated polemics. On the other hand, it would be hard to dismiss the co-operative model if the quality-price relationship of the wines were that achieved by Monrubio di Castel Viscardo, an operation on the doorstep of Orvieto. This year's tastings revealed another terrific edition of its flagship, Palaia '05. A merlot, pinot nero and cabernet sauvignon blend, it throws a nose laden with sweet, smooth, ripe fruit and lifted by alluring notes of toasty oak and cigar leaf, which segues into a hefty palate with well-built tannins but full of energy and complexity. Both Monrubio Rosso '06 and Orvieto Classico Superiore Soana '06 turned in performances that were more than laudable. The former, from sangiovese, ciliegiolo, montepulciano and merlot, offers an experience far superior to its price range and the Soana struck us as one the year's best efforts anywhere: rich and full-bodied, with strikingly stylish citrus on the nose. The two remaining whites are well made, a fairly straightforward Le Coste '06 and a more complex Salceto '06.

Stefano Grilli is without a doubt one of Umbria's most independent and imaginative figures, shunning conformity, innovating relentlessly and hard to fit into any pre-conceived category. His wines too are protean, embodying new developments and creative experimentation, albeit always within the bounds of a well-defined style that many, including ourselves, appreciate. All of the wines we tasted this year exhibit something to admire, as expected. The '04 version of the largely cabernet sauvignon Rubino is a compelling, utterly self-confident wine: a crisp vein of balsam enlivens rich chocolate and candied fruit on the nose, and it concludes with perfectly measured tannins. On the same high rung is Syrah '05, with its spicy mosaic of black pepper and clove. Grilli's special wines are always just that. The crisp, ripe fruit of Gran Cuvée '04 melds into a creamy elegance, and the latest arrival, Brut Rosé '04, is worthy of attention. While Riesling Brut '02 may show a tad less brio than usual, Vin Santo '03 is as superb as ever, as is Vendemmia Tardiva '06. The sangiovese Vin Santo Bacca Rossa '03 debuts to more than polite applause.

● Palaia '05	♟♟ 5
○ Orvieto Cl. Sup. Soana '06	♟♟ 3
● Monrubio '06	♟♟ 3*
○ Orvieto Cl. Salceto '06	♟ 3
○ Le Coste '06	♟ 1*
● Palaia '03	♟♟ 5
● Palaia '04	♟♟ 5
● Monrubio '05	♟♟ 3*
● Monrubio '04	♟♟ 3*

○ Vin Santo '03	♟♟ 5
● Syrah '05	♟♟ 4
⊙ Brut Rosé '04	♟♟ 5
○ V. T. da Uve Muffate '06	♟♟ 4
○ Gran Cuvée Brut '04	♟♟ 5
● Rubino '04	♟♟ 5
○ Riesling Brut M. Cl. '02	♟ 5
● Vin Santo Bacca Rossa '03	♟ 5
● Merlot '97	♟♟♟ 5
○ Vin Santo '00	♟♟ 5
● Merlot '04	♟♟ 5
○ Vin Santo '01	♟♟ 5
○ Gran Cuvée Brut '01	♟♟ 5
○ V. T. da Uve Muffate '04	♟♟ 4
○ Riesling Brut M. Cl. '01	♟♟ 5

Palazzone

LOC. ROCCA RIPESENA, 68
05018 ORVIETO [TR]
TEL. 0763344921
www.palazzone.com

ANNUAL PRODUCTION 100,000 bottles
HECTARES UNDER VINE 24
VITICULTURE METHOD Conventional

Giovanni Dubini is a boots-in-the-dirt grower, fiercely proud of his work and of the winemaking traditions of an area as historically prominent as Orvieto. It is to be expected then that his winemaking approach should be unambiguous, centred on clearly defined principles and little inclined to compromise. Giovanni produces distinctive wines with characteristics that will enable them to stand up over time. As with good marathon runners, there is a price to pay in the short run. These performers are certainly not at their best at release, revealing their qualities and breeding only with the passage of the years. That means we should project Campo del Guardiano '04 into a felicitous future, and as such it is quite impressive, going through to the national finals. Complex and still tight, it demonstrates all of the pent-up energy and richly faceted aromatics of a white with great cellaring potential. Fruit and floral expressions intertwine with intriguing minerally nuances and a pungent vein of balsam and fresh greens, matched by a savoury thread of acidity supporting the palate. The cabernet sauvignon-heavy Armaleo '05 is equally magisterial, with endless finesse and elegance, as are Terre Vineate '06 and Muffa Nobilis '05.

● Armaleo '05	🍷🍷	8
○ Orvieto Cl. Campo del Guardiano '04	🍷🍷	5
○ Muffa Nobilis '05	🍷🍷	6
○ Orvieto Cl. Sup. Terre Vineate '06	🍷🍷	4
○ Grechetto '06	🍷	4
○ L'Ultima Spiaggia '06	🍷	5
● Piviere San Donato '06	🍷	5
● Rubbio '06	🍷	4
● Armaleo '00	🍷🍷🍷	6
● Armaleo '95	🍷🍷🍷	6
● Armaleo '97	🍷🍷🍷	6
● Armaleo '98	🍷🍷🍷	6
○ Muffa Nobilis '03	🍷🍷	6
○ Orvieto Cl. Campo del Guardiano '03	🍷🍷	5

F.lli Pardi

VIA GIOVANNI PASCOLI, 7/9
06036 MONTEFALCO [PG]
TEL. 0742379023
www.cantinapardi.it

ANNUAL PRODUCTION 40,000 bottles
HECTARES UNDER VINE 11
VITICULTURE METHOD Conventional

We were not mistaken. After an impressive debut last year, which won the Pardis their first full profile in the Guide, this year brings further, and even more convincing, progress. The family name is well known in Montefalco, since the winery is located right at the city walls, but even more so for its production of fine textiles and for winemaking traditions that go back to the mid 1900s. That family heritage inspired Francesco, Gianluca Rio and Alberto Mario Pardi to dust off those historical traces and refresh the family's venerable winemaking reputation. And probably to surpass it, given the quality of their Sagrantino '04. After lily of the valley and violets play about with dark berry fruit on the nose, the wine develops with total self-confidence and suppleness, the mid palate marked by sustained sapidity and a long-lingering finale yielding a lovely aromatic collection of wildflowers, blackberry and cinnamon. The alluring Montefalco Rosso '05 is generous and full flavoured to a fault, even displaying an almost salt-edged mineral tang. The Pardis are certainly on the right track.

● Montefalco Sagrantino '04	🍷🍷	6
● Rosso di Montefalco '05	🍷🍷	4
● Montefalco Sagrantino '03	🍷🍷	6
● Rosso di Montefalco '03	🍷🍷	4*
● Rosso di Montefalco '04	🍷🍷	4
● Montefalco Sagrantino Passito '03	🍷🍷	6

Perticaia

VIA E. CATTANEO, 39
06035 GUALDO CATTANEO [PG]
TEL. 0742379014
www.perticaia.it

ANNUAL PRODUCTION 90,000 bottles
HECTARES UNDER VINE 15
VITICULTURE METHOD Conventional

Guido Guardigli has pulled it off. He has been equal to the challenge. He got himself talked about, built a winery from scratch and refused to enjoy a peaceful retirement to write a few influential pages in the recent history of Italian wine. Perhaps he needed a happy ending. Perhaps he needed Perticaia, the winery that now stands out at Montefalco, in Umbria and indeed in Italy. His operation has become a model. Perticaia has succeeded in growing exponentially in a very short time and in creating one of the most successful interpretations of sagrantino. That's right, the very wine that struck him so forcefully the first time, years ago, when he began to investigate the characteristics of the local terroir. Guido's 2004 carried off Three Glasses with a marvellous interpretation of the variety that is almost stunning for its bouquet, packed with blackberry tightly wrapped in pungent, balsam-like medicinal herbs and lush spices. The palate fulfils that promise: spacious and deep, dense-packed yet dynamic, with an ultra-luxe skein of tannins. Still young, of course, it will reveal its true soul down the years. As to the other wines, they are more than up to snuff, in particular the Rosso di Montefalco '05.

Poggio Bertaio

FRAZ. CASAMAGGIORE
VIA FRATTAVECCHIA, 29
06061 CASTIGLIONE DEL LAGO [PG]
TEL. 075956921
poggiobertaio@libero.it

ANNUAL PRODUCTION 76,000 bottles
HECTARES UNDER VINE 20
VITICULTURE METHOD Conventional

Only by visiting Poggio Bertaio can one gain a true idea of the obsessive attention that characterizes Fabrizio and Ugo Ciufoli's growing. The two brothers have tended their vineyards like gardens for years and now process the fruit in a brand-new cellar. Building on the tradition begun by their father, Fabrizio, a winemaker of considerable renown, and Ugo, the agronomist, have added the professionalism and market know-how that have made Poggio Bertaio a highly respected producer of fine wines. There are three of them, produced in a modern key, cask aged and very distinctive. The merlot and cabernet sauvignon Crovello '04, matured for two years in barriques, shows its makers' skills: nearly opaque ruby, then caramel, roasted coffee and chocolate backgrounding ripe berry fruit introduce a remarkably full, spacious body and a finish well supported by judicious extract. Cimbolo '05 will make its appearance in the next edition of the Guide so we conclude with the newest arrival. Stucchio '04 is a standard-version sangiovese. It's got less heft than its cousins and deserves a somewhat lighter dose of oak.

● Montefalco Sagrantino '04	♀♀♀	6
● Montefalco Rosso '05	♀♀	4
● Montefalco Sagrantino Passito '04	♀	6
● Umbria Rosso '06	♀	3
● Montefalco Sagrantino '01	♀♀	6
● Montefalco Sagrantino '03	♀♀	6
● Montefalco Sagrantino '00	♀♀	6

● Crovello '04	♀♀	7
● Stucchio '04	♀	4
● Crovello '01	♀♀♀	8
● Crovello '02	♀♀	8
● Crovello '03	♀♀	7
● Cimbolo '01	♀♀	6
● Cimbolo '04	♀♀	6
● Cimbolo '03	♀♀	6

Tenuta Poggio del Lupo

VOC. BUZZAGHETTO, 100
05011 ALLERONA [TR]
TEL. 0763628350
www.tenutapoggiodellupo.it

ANNUAL PRODUCTION 80,000 bottles
HECTARES UNDER VINE 42
VITICULTURE METHOD Conventional

The Polato family faced a considerable challenge in transforming a rather traditional winery, with the qualities but more importantly the drawbacks associated with such operations, at least within the parameters of what used to be mainstream oenology in Umbria. But after some five years, we feel we can say that they have risen to the challenge and turned Poggio del Lupo into one of the stars in the Umbrian firmament, a thoroughly modern, reliable maker of premium-quality wines. The all-montepulciano Silentis '05 is again a superlative offering, with all that variety's condensed exuberance. A contributory factor could be the terroir, marl laced with limestone sediments and marine fossils. The price tag would not lead you to expect a performance like this from Lupiano '06, a blend of merlot, cabernet sauvignon and ciliegiolo that merits applause for its balance, sapidity and rounded fruit. Up there with it is Orvieto Novilunio '06, an exemplary Orvieto that follows up acacia blossom and subtle fruit with a lithe palate and a refreshing line of acidity.

● Rosso Silentis '05	🍷🍷 5
● Rosso Orvietano Lupiano '06	🍷🍷 3
○ Orvieto Novilunio '06	🍷 3
● Rosso Silentis '03	🍷🍷 5
● Rosso Silentis '04	🍷🍷 6
○ Màrneo '05	🍷🍷 5
● Rosso Silentis '02	🍷🍷 5

Pucciarella

LOC. VILLA DI MAGIONE
06063 MAGIONE [PG]
TEL. 0758409147
azienda.pucciarella@virgilio.it

ANNUAL PRODUCTION N.A.
HECTARES UNDER VINE 200
VITICULTURE METHOD Conventional

Although Pucciarella's first vineyards date back to 1977, it was in the early 1990s that they launched an ambitious upgrade programme that would focus on top-quality wines from the Lake Trasimeno area. Owned by Fondo Pensioni Cariplo, this attractive winery boasts in excess of 200 hectares overall, many of them planted to vines and olive trees, as is the local custom. They actually turned the corner, oenologically speaking, in 2005, with a reshuffling of their winemaking staff that brought them into the limelight in the Umbrian wine world, and into the pages of our Guide. The superb Empireo is back in a fine '05 edition. Its merlot, sagrantino and cabernet sauvignon blend produces a deep hue and fragrances of blueberry and eucalyptus; in the mouth, it is admirably compact, with just the right dose of oak. Equally impressive is the Colli del Trasimeno Rosso Berlingero '05, a sangiovese, gamay, ciliegiolo and merlot quartet that offers up pungent tones of scrubland and peppercorns. Arsiccio '06, a full-flavoured chardonnay showing good acidic grip, returned to enthusiastic reviews.

○ Chardonnay Arsiccio '06	🍷🍷 4
● Empireo '05	🍷🍷 4
● C. del Trasimeno Rosso Berlingero '05	🍷🍷 4
○ C. del Trasimeno Vin Santo Eletto '03	🍷 4
○ C. del Trasimeno Bianco Agnolo '06	🍷 4
○ C. del Trasimeno Vin Santo Eletto '01	🍷🍷 4
● Empireo '04	🍷🍷 4

Castello delle Regine

LOC. LE REGINE
VIA DI CASTELLUCCIO
05022 AMELIA [TR]
TEL. 0744702005
www.castellodelleregine.com

ANNUAL PRODUCTION 350,000 bottles
HECTARES UNDER VINE 87
VITICULTURE METHOD Conventional

It is probably misleading to refer to Castello delle Regine as a fast-growing operation since this recently established winery has demonstrated star quality practically from its birth. Yet the wines we tasted this year, without exception, impressed us even more than usual, with quite obvious styles, character and energy. But let's begin with the magnificent Merlot '05, which has by now gained legendary status in the region. A wide range of wild berry fruits leads into a palate that is both expansive and impressively deep, with dense, concentrated fruit, enlivened throughout by glorious acidity that makes this thoroughbred a truly graceful wine. Very close behind is Sangiovese Selezione del Fondatore, which shrugs off the unfavourable 2002 weather. Princeps '04, from cabernet, merlot and sangiovese, shows lots of savoury length and Podernovo '04, largely sangiovese with some help from montepulciano and syrah, is redolent of raspberry and wild fennel. Both are terrific, and amply demonstrate that full-bodied wines can indeed show an elegant ankle as well. We found the aromatic, uncomplicated Bianco delle Regine 2006 to be quite sound.

Rocca di Fabbri

LOC. FABBRI
06036 MONTEFALCO [PG]
TEL. 0742399379
www.roccadifabbri.com

ANNUAL PRODUCTION 230,000 bottles
HECTARES UNDER VINE 64.5
VITICULTURE METHOD Conventional

Roberta and Simona Vitali now share responsibility for ensuring continuity at one of the longest-established wineries at Montefalco. Gracing the lovely hillslopes around the eponymous fortress, the Rocca di Fabbri, both the vineyards and the cellar are run in exemplary fashion, with the latter housing both large and small oak. The result is wines that are not only impressive but also extremely individual, in line with the history and traditions of the winery and its local area. Sagrantino '04 still displays some youthful awkwardness but there's no doubt it will throw that off and attain impressive maturity in a few years. At the moment, raspberry and crisp balsamic notes mingle nicely and a supple palate displays a fine tannic fabric and acidic verve. Passito '04 is well crafted, very smooth and already evolved but with tannins that are still a shade too assertive. The cabernet-sagrantino Faroaldo '04 is just as well executed, in the international style of course but with an elegant, savoury edge. The overly slender, rather intractable Rosso di Montefalco '05 falls off a step but the Chardonnay '06 hit the bull's-eye, as usual.

● Merlot '05	♈♈♈	7
● Sangiovese Sel. del Fondatore '02	♈♈	6
● Princeps '04	♈♈	6
● Rosso di Podernovo '04	♈♈	4
○ Bianco delle Regine '06	♈	4
● Merlot '01	♟♟♟	7
● Merlot '03	♟♟♟	7
● Merlot '04	♟♟♟	7
● Merlot '02	♟♟♟	6
● Sangiovese Sel. del Fondatore '00	♟♟	6
● Sangiovese Sel. del Fondatore '01	♟♟	6

○ Chardonnay '06	♈♈	3
● Montefalco Sagrantino '04	♈♈	7
● Montefalco Sagrantino Passito '04	♈♈	6
● Faroaldo '04	♈♈	6
● Montefalco Rosso '05	♈	5
○ Colli Martani Grechetto '06	♈	4
● Montefalco Sagrantino '02	♟♟	7
● Montefalco Sagrantino '03	♟♟	7
● Faroaldo '03	♟♟	6
● Montefalco Sagrantino '01	♟♟	7

★ Castello della Sala

LOC. SALA
05016 FICULLE [TR]
TEL. 076386051
www.antinori.it

Scacciadiavoli

LOC. CANTINONE, 31
06036 MONTEFALCO [PG]
TEL. 0742371210
scacciadiavoli@tin.it

ANNUAL PRODUCTION 1,500,000 bottles
HECTARES UNDER VINE 160
VITICULTURE METHOD Conventional

ANNUAL PRODUCTION 200,000 bottles
HECTARES UNDER VINE 32
VITICULTURE METHOD Conventional

In 1940, Piero's father Marchese Niccolò Antinori decided to purchase an estate in Umbria, convinced that the Orvieto terroir was ideal for adding a world-class white to the family portfolio. It is all too easy now, after all those years, to laud the unerring intuition and extraordinary efforts that were devoted to bringing to Umbria, and to all of Italy, that giant of a white, Cervaro della Sala. A combination of chardonnay and a bit of grechetto, it is a masterpiece both for its fine breeding and for longevity that has racked up an impressive series of outstanding vintages and today is grander than ever. In fact, Cervaro della Sala is perhaps the best vehicle for the history of Castello della Sala. We are convinced that the '05 version will be one of tomorrow's classics, adding further lustre and authority to lineage. The bouquet magisterially melds notes of toast and subtle spice with peach and lime, intriguingly edged with medicinal herbs that complete the aromatic complex and provide an almost bracing crispness. In the mouth, the wine builds a stunningly complex, energy-laden monumentality exuding a sea-salt, minerally tang.

Scacciadiavoli's owner, Amilcare Pambuffetti, is both charismatic and decisive. He showed no hesitation in taking radical action when his winery seemed to be floundering in relative anonymity. This was regrettable, since the winery complex itself is probably the most architecturally fascinating in all of Umbria with a history that stretches back to the late 19th century. Now, some years after the sea change and the consequent investments took effect, Pambuffetti's convictions and actions have proved correct. The result is an '04 ultra-Sagrantino that proffers rich, ripe fruit foregrounding appealing, almost petrolly essences, in addition to floral notes of violets and rose petals. A beautifully crafted palate expands in the mouth to reveal multi-faceted depth and velvet-smooth tannins. The Passito is a faithful mirror of the great 2004 growing year, releasing delicious roasted coffee and preserves. Montefalco Rosso '05 is good but relies too much on toasty oak-derived coconut.

O Cervaro della Sala '05	▼▼▼	7
O Bramito del Cervo '06	▼▼	4
O Muffato della Sala '05	▼▼	6
O Orvieto Cl. Sup. San Giovanni della Sala '06	▼▼	4
O Conte della Vipera '05	▼	5
O Cervaro della Sala '90	▽▽▽	6
O Cervaro della Sala '04	▽▽▽	7
O Cervaro della Sala '94	▽▽▽	6
O Cervaro della Sala '96	▽▽▽	6
O Cervaro della Sala '95	▽▽▽	6
O Cervaro della Sala '93	▽▽▽	6
O Cervaro della Sala '01	▽▽▽	6
O Cervaro della Sala '00	▽▽▽	6

● Montefalco Sagrantino '04	▼▼	6
● Montefalco Sagrantino Passito '04	▼▼	6
● Montefalco Rosso '05	▼▼	4
● Montefalco Sagrantino '00	▽▽	6
● Montefalco Sagrantino '01	▽▽	6
● Montefalco Sagrantino '03	▽▽	6
● Montefalco Sagrantino Passito '01	▽▽	6

Sportoletti

LOC. CAPITAN LORETO
VIA LOMBARDIA, 1
06038 SPELLO [PG]
TEL. 0742651461
www.sportoletti.com

ANNUAL PRODUCTION   220,000 bottles
HECTARES UNDER VINE 30
VITICULTURE METHOD   Conventional

True, our top trophy has eluded Sportoletti for a while now but its well-founded reliability over the years, as witnessed by excellent wines that are consistently faultless, serve to keep this operation high up in the ranks of Umbrian producers. Credit goes to brothers Remo and Ernesto, who, with help from the entire family, carefully watch every step in the production process. That includes manicured vineyards in the hills between Spello and Assisi and a brand-new cellar that is spacious and well laid out. More than average finesse is the hallmark of Villa Fidelia Rosso '05, from merlot, cabernet sauvignon and cabernet franc. It may show a tad overripe on the nose, and the tannins may be somewhat stiff as yet, but overall we have here a complex, luscious and very well-made red. Villa Fidelia Bianco '05 is more delicious than ever. A combination of grechetto and chardonnay, it exudes a delicate scent of plane-tree blossoms, an elegance that carries over to a palate of appealing finesse, marked by zesty fruit and a vibrant, lip-smacking acidity. Extraordinary as ever, particularly considering the price tag, are the Assisi Rosso '06, a blend of sangiovese, merlot and cabernet, and Assisi Grechetto '06.

Tabarrini

FRAZ. TURRITA
06036 MONTEFALCO [PG]
TEL. 0742379351
www.tabarrini.com

ANNUAL PRODUCTION   700,000 bottles
HECTARES UNDER VINE 11
VITICULTURE METHOD   Conventional

Whether a winery receives Three Glasses or not can be a question of nuances, as well as the condition of the wine at the moment of tasting, which are difficult to reduce to mere numbers. Take, for example, Giampaolo Tabarrini's Sagrantino Colle Grimaldesco '04. We could say that those Two full Glasses are not really two and a half, as in other cases, but at least two and three quarters! It's a wine that missed the bull's-eye by the merest of whiskers. It is a wine of immense appeal, showing remarkable depth and finesse. Having manage brilliantly to weave together a complex of wild blackberry with nuanced impressions of cumin and spice, tobacco leaf and smoky oak, it matches this with a finely structured palate of absolute elegance. One small cavil is that it could have been given a few more months in the bottle before release. Montefalco Rosso '05 is its usual fine self but Passito '04 is punching below its weight. Bocca di Rosa '06, a slightly tannic sagrantino rosé, is a fun quaffer. Next year's tastings will feature Adarmando '06, a trebbiano spoletino that amazed us in an early tasting.

● Villa Fidelia Rosso '05	♟♟ 6
○ Villa Fidelia Bianco '05	♟♟ 4
● Assisi Rosso '06	♟♟ 4
○ Assisi Grechetto '06	♟♟ 3
● Villa Fidelia Rosso '98	♟♟♟ 6
● Villa Fidelia Rosso '99	♟♟ 6
● Villa Fidelia Rosso '04	♟♟ 6
● Villa Fidelia Rosso '03	♟♟ 6
● Villa Fidelia Rosso '00	♟♟ 7
● Villa Fidelia Rosso '97	♟♟ 4
● Villa Fidelia Rosso '01	♟♟ 7
● Villa Fidelia Rosso '02	♟♟ 6

● Montefalco Sagrantino	
Colle Grimaldesco '04	♟♟ 6
⊙ Bocca di Rosa '06	♟♟ 4
● Il Padrone delle Vigne '06	♟♟ 3
● Montefalco Rosso '05	♟♟ 4
● Montefalco Sagrantino Passito '04	♟ 7
● Montefalco Sagrantino	
Colle Grimaldesco '01	♟♟♟ 6
● Montefalco Sagrantino	
Colle Grimaldesco '02	♟♟ 6
● Montefalco Sagrantino	
Colle Grimaldesco '03	♟♟ 6
● Montefalco Sagrantino Passito '03	♟♟ 7

Terre de La Custodia
LOC. PALOMBARA
06035 GUALDO CATTANEO [PG]
TEL. 0742929595

Todini
FRAZ. COLLEVALENZA
06050 TODI [PG]
TEL. 075887122
www.cantinafrancotodini.com

ANNUAL PRODUCTION N.A.
HECTARES UNDER VINE N.A.
VITICULTURE METHOD Conventional

ANNUAL PRODUCTION 200,000 bottles
HECTARES UNDER VINE 70
VITICULTURE METHOD Conventional

Terre de La Custodia turned in a performance that signals several steps forward. It is a very new operation, owned by the Farchioni group, which also owns one of the largest olive oil firms in Umbria and Italy. Investment money was therefore available and has produced a gorgeous cellar surrounded by vineyards planted to sagrantino and other reds traditional to the area. The whites are predominantly grechetto and trebbiano, sourced from the Todi area. Montefalco Sagrantino '04 quickly put the preceding vintage in the shade. The ripest of fruit builds stunning aromatic depth on the nose, attractively offset by pungent notes of spice. That same depth is amply evident on the palate, which achieves considerable volume from the attack and evidences smooth, rounded tannins that continue seamlessly into a lengthy finale. The compelling Montefalco Sagrantino Exubera '04 exhibits incredible body but needs more time to knit everything together. We liked the heady, subtly rustic Rosso di Montefalco '05, as well as the rich Grechetto Plentis '05 and Collezione '05, a mix of sangiovese, montepulciano, merlot and sagrantino.

For the first time, a Todini wine made it to the national tasting finals for Three Glasses. Nero della Cervara was the talented contestant, a masterful 50-50 partnership of cabernet sauvignon and merlot that has never been quite so impressive as this '05. The aromas take their time to open but then blossom out, foregrounding blackberry and raspberry, bell pepper and hints of pink pepper. Deep and magnificently extracted, it lays out sweet, velvety fruit with impressions of clove. The citrus-edged and nimble Colli Martani Sangiovese Rubro '05 seems to have won for itself a distinctive niche within the denomination. Colli Martani Grechetto di Todi Bianco della Cervara '06 deserves its by now customary plaudits. A wine of considerable substance, it summons up initial luscious ripe fruit and closes with toasty almond on the finish, a terrific performance, perhaps the best ever, from a winery that knows how to get the best out of its investments. Todini shows every sign of being firmly on the right track, one that leads into the top ranks of Umbrian producers.

● Montefalco Sagrantino '04	▼▼	8
● Collezione '05	▼▼	3*
O Colli Martani Grechetto Plentis '05	▼▼	3*
● Montefalco Sagrantino Exubera '04	▼▼	7
● Montefalco Rosso '05	▼▼	4*
● Montefalco Sagrantino Passito Melanto '03	▼	7
● Montefalco Sagrantino Exubera '03	♈♈	7

● Nero della Cervara '05	▼▼	6
O Colli Martani Grechetto di Todi Bianco della Cervara '06	▼▼	4*
● Colli Martani Sangiovese Rubro '05	▼▼	5
O Colli Martani Grechetto di Todi '05	♈♈	4*
● Colli Martani Sangiovese Rubro '04	♈♈	5
● Nero della Cervara '03	♈♈	6
● Nero della Cervara '04	♈♈	6

Tordimaro
LOC. TORDIMONTE, 37
05019 ORVIETO [TR]
TEL. 0763304227
www.tordimaro.com

Tudernum
PIAN DI PORTO, 146
06059 TODI [PG]
TEL. 0758989403
www.tudernum.it

ANNUAL PRODUCTION   30,000 bottles
HECTARES UNDER VINE 11
VITICULTURE METHOD   Conventional

Who hasn't ever been tempted, at least once, to throw over the traces, move to another country, and begin afresh? Reinmar and Caterina Fülleman left their successful professions in Switzerland and made their dream reality. For several years now, they have been managing this modest but lovely farm they purchased in the Orvieto area, personally managing the vineyards and all of the steps in production, including marketing and sales. The results have been impressive, turning round in almost record time an operation that seemed stuck in the doldrums. At our tastings, we thought Rosso Orvietano Sangiovese '05 was again the stand-out. Marked by good varietal characteristics on the nose, it unwinds self-confident and spacious in the mouth, with succulent, zesty fruit and signs off with a hint of liquorice. Torello '06 may be simpler but this mix of sangiovese, barbera and montepulciano is a super-delicious quaffer that is anything but banal, drawing you in with lashings of wild berries and bright acidity. We liked the well-crafted Orvieto Classico '06 but the surprise of the year was Passito '03, an all sauvignon pouring out pineapple and tropical fruit, a wine of great verve and sapient balance.

ANNUAL PRODUCTION   3,000,000 bottles
HECTARES UNDER VINE 7
VITICULTURE METHOD   Conventional

True, the history of this co-operative stretches as far back as 1958 but it is also true that its wines began to attract the attention of critics and local wine lovers only in the last few years. The reason is simple: Tudernum has undergone a revolution. The wines have gone from being rather characterless, forgettable products to some of the best-performing wines in Umbria. And a number of them are truly iconic for affordability, a quality that seems to be part of the winemaking and marketing credo in these parts. Tudernum's recipe for success has been a well thought-out programme, generous investments, capable professionals and tons of enthusiasm. Among their numerous offerings, we liked the complex, smoky-edged Sagrantino '04, and Rojano '04, from sangiovese and merlot with a small bit of sagrantino, was decent, giving off spice and some meaty nuances. We noted the usual good performances from the two varietals, Merlot '06 and Cabernet Sauvignon '06. The Grechettos merit separate attention: the very fine Colle Nobile '06 shows sturdy and lightly tannic, with nice yeastiness and an impression of ripe wheat but the standard Grechetto '06 disappointed, being somewhat too fat and one-dimensional.

O Passito '03	🍷🍷 5
● Rosso Orvietano Sangiovese '05	🍷🍷 4*
O Orvieto Cl. '06	🍷 2
● Torrello '06	🍷 3
● Rosso Orvietano Cabernet '03	🍷🍷 5
● Rosso Orvietano Cabernet '04	🍷🍷 5
● Rosso Orvietano Sangiovese '04	🍷🍷 5
● Torrello '04	🍷🍷 3*

● Montefalco Sagrantino Tudernum '04	🍷🍷 6
● Cabernet Sauvignon '06	🍷🍷 3*
● Merlot '06	🍷🍷 3*
● Rojano '04	🍷🍷 4*
O Colli Martani Grechetto di Todi Colle Nobile '06	🍷🍷 4*
O Colli Martani Grechetto di Todi '06	🍷 2
● Colli Martani Sangiovese '06	🍷 2
● Montefalco Sagrantino Tudernum '01	🍷🍷 5
● Rojano '03	🍷🍷 4*
● Merlot '05	🍷🍷 3*

Tenuta Le Velette

FRAZ. CANALE DI ORVIETO
LOC. LE VELETTE, 23
05019 ORVIETO [TR]
TEL. 076329090
www.levelette.it

ANNUAL PRODUCTION 400,000 bottles
HECTARES UNDER VINE 109
VITICULTURE METHOD Conventional

The quality curve of many wineries is easily to predict if you look carefully at all of the various indicators. That is certainly true of Le Velette. If, however, a couple of years ago they had suggested they might achieve their present performances, even taking in to account that they were a healthily growing operation, we probably wouldn't have believed it. Corrado and Cecilia Bottai are not just producing exceptional wines; they make extraordinary interpretations of the qualities of their local terroir, a superb natural amphitheatre that gazes proudly towards Orvieto's massif. These are wines that go far beyond the parameters of the traditions and denominations of their zone. Last year's Three Glasses went to the all-merlot Gaudio but this year the laurels go to a fantastic Calanco '03, a blend of sangiovese and cabernet sauvignon. Its fragrances jump from the glass in a richly nuanced amalgam of wild red berry fruit and laurel leaf that almost explodes in exuberant balsam-led pungency. There's no pause between the attack and a progression marked by ultra-tasty fruit with mineral-edged succulence, hedonistic tannic textures, compelling acidic support and a complexity that just drives on and on.

Villa Mongalli

LOC. CAPPUCCINI
06031 BEVAGNA [PG]
TEL. 3485110506

ANNUAL PRODUCTION N.A.
HECTARES UNDER VINE N.A.
VITICULTURE METHOD Conventional

Villa Mongalli makes its first entrance in the Guide through the main gate. This very new winery, owned by the Menghini family, will be featuring in wine pages in the future. Lying in the hills between Bevagna and Montefalco, in an area that grows outstanding sagrantino, the vineyards are superb, planted in gravel-rich, clayey soils that are warm and fairly loose. These are conditions that yield wines that are perhaps less powerful than others but which make up for it in elegance and complexity, which our tastings seemed to confirm. Its striking nose sent Sagrantino Pozzo del Curato '04 straight through to the national taste-offs. Leading off with a dark, smoky nuance, it opens up alluringly to wild dark berry, pungent cigar tobacco and nutmeg. The palate is extremely well crafted, and develops with a definite elegance, despite tannins that are still awkward and incisive. Of the two vintages of Rosso di Montefalco, we preferred the more generous and pulpy 2004, although there's no denying the breeding of Col Cimino '05, a 50-50 partnership of sagrantino and cabernet.

● Calanco '03	▼▼▼	5
● Gaudio '04	▼▼	5
○ Orvieto Cl. Sup. Lunato '06	▼▼	4*
○ Orvieto Cl. Berganorio '06	▼▼	3*
● Rosso Orvietano		
Rosso di Spicca '06	▼▼	3*
○ Solo '06	▼▼	4*
○ Traluce '06	▼	4
● Gaudio '03	♈♈♈	5
● Calanco '01	♈♈	5
● Gaudio '98	♈♈	5
● Gaudio '00	♈♈	5
● Gaudio '99	♈♈	5

● Montefalco Sagrantino		
Pozzo del Curato '04	▼▼	5
● Montefalco Rosso Le Grazie '04	▼▼	4*
● Col Cimino '05	▼▼	4*
● Montefalco Rosso Le Grazie '05	▼	4
● Umbria Rosso '06	▼	3

OTHER WINERIES

Tenuta Alzatura
LOC. FRATTA - ALZATURA, 108
06036 MONTEFALCO [PG]
TEL. 0742399435
www.tenuta-alzatura.it

We welcome impressive results from the Cecchi family's Umbrian operation. The elegant Sagrantino Uno di Sette '04 shows spice and green notes over ripe fruit, good extract and a bergamot-edged finale. Montefalco '05 is an excellent red with notes of bright cherry and pungent clove.

● Montefalco Rosso '05	🍷🍷 4*
● Montefalco Sagrantino Uno di Sette '04	🍷🍷 6

Benincasa
LOC. CAPRO, 99
06031 BEVAGNA [PG]
TEL. 0742361307
www.aziendabenincasa.com

Once again, a fantastic Montefalco Rosso is the high note of the Benincasa siblings' growing year. One of the longest-established small-scale Sagrantino wineries, Benincasa released a 2005 edition with wonderful aromatic complexity, where medicinal herbs, spices and plant roots lift smooth, generous fruit.

● Montefalco Rosso '05	🍷🍷 4*
● Montefalco Sagrantino '03	🍷 6
● Vincastro '06	🍷 2
● Montefalco Sagrantino '01	♀♀ 6

Brogal Vini
LOC. BASTIA UMBRA
VIA DEGLI OLMI, 9
06083 PERUGIA [PG]
TEL. 0758001501
www.brogalvini.com

Antigniano's headquarters are at Bastia Umbra. Results were uneven but among the best wines are Torgiano Rosso '04 and Torgiano Rosso Riserva Santa Caterina '03, with a heady bouquet and notes of smoky oak and earthy roots.

● Torgiano Rosso Antigniano '04	🍷🍷 4*
● Torgiano Rosso Santa Caterina Ris. '03	🍷🍷 6
● Montefalco Sagrantino Antigniano '04	🍷 7
○ Torgiano Bianco Antigniano '06	🍷 4

Flavio Busti
FRAZ. SANT' ELENA
06052 MARSCIANO [PG]
TEL. 075879458
www.cantinebusti.it

Flavio Busti is a young, talented winemaker with a cellar and vineyards right next to the charming village of Sant'Elena near Marsciano. Now he has found a length, his wines have acquired a distinctive style and are always well crafted. Flavio's Grechetto is outstanding again in this 2006 version.

● Castel Sant'Elena '06	🍷🍷 4*
○ Grechetto '06	🍷🍷 3*
● Sangiovese '06	🍷 3

Tenuta Castelbuono
LOC. BEVAGNA
VOC. FOSSATO, 54
PERUGIA [PG]
TEL. 0742362060
www.ferrarispumante.it

Tenuta Castelbuono is the Umbrian cellar of the Lunelli family, celebrated for their high-quality Trentino bubbly. Many hectares of their estate are planted to sagrantino. The 2003 version is an especially fine one, thanks to intriguing mineral and charcoal notes.

● Montefalco Sagrantino '03	🍷🍷 6
● Montefalco Rosso '05	🍷 4

Chiorri
LOC. SANT'ENEA
VIA TODI, 100
06132 PERUGIA [PG]
TEL. 075607141
www.chiorri.it

With help from his daughter, enthusiastic grower Tito Mariotti manages a beautiful cellar set into the high ridge of Perugia's hills. It is now fully operative and his wines this year seem to have a new brilliance and sheen, although they haven't lost any of their artisanal character.

○ Colli Perugini Bianco '06	🍷🍷 2*
● Cabernet Sel. Antonio Chiorri '05	🍷🍷 5
○ Grechetto '06	🍷🍷 3*
⊙ Colli Perugini Rosato '06	🍷 3

OTHER WINERIES

Decugnano dei Barbi

LOC. FOSSATELLO, 50
05019 ORVIETO [TR]
TEL. 0763308255
www.decugnanodeibarbi.com

Sadly, we have to report the present hardly thrilling state of one of the region's finest wineries. We hope for a speedy return to form and look forward to more of the masterpieces Decugnano dei Barbi has produced in the past. But Lago di Corbara Rosso '05 is attractively fruit-led and subtly herbaceous.

● Lago di Corbara Decugnano Rosso '05	▼▼ 4 *
● Lago di Corbara Pinot Nero '04	▼ 6
○ Decugnano Brut '03	▼ 5
○ Orvieto Cl. Sup. Decugnano Bianco '06	▼ 4

Cantina La Spina

FRAZ. SPINA
VIA EMILIO ALESSANDRINI, 1
06050 MARSCIANO [PG]
TEL. 0758738120
www.cantinalaspina.it

Moreno Peccia lavishes loving care on his modest operation, carefully attending to every step from vineyard to marketplace. His are genuine garage wines, each quite different from the others but all with a common thread. We thought Rosso Spina '05, a blend of montepulciano, merlot and gamay, was the best.

● Merlato '06	▼▼ 4 *
● Rosso Spina '05	▼▼ 5
● Polimante '05	▼ 5
● Rosso Spina '04	♈♈ 5

Martinelli

LOC. SASSO, 12A
06031 BEVAGNA [PG]
TEL. 0742362124
www.cantinemartinelli.com

Martinelli's wines are very good and we were delighted by their two versions of the area's iconic red wine, Sagrantino. The standard Sagrantino '04 is superb, enviably complementing body with finesse, ripe fruit and zesty crispness. Soranna '04 is still very young.

● Montefalco Sagrantino '04	▼▼ 5
● Montefalco Sagrantino Sel. Soranna '04	▼▼ 7
○ Bianco dell'Umbria '06	▼ 4

Cantine Novelli

LOC. PERDELLE
VIA MOLINO CAPALDINI
06036 MONTEFALCO [PG]
TEL. 0744803301
www.cantinanovelli.it

This brand-new cellar, owned by the Novelli family of Spoleto, makes its Guide debut. We tasted a Sagrantino di Montefalco '04 that was right on the money, a dense, characterful Rosso '05 and a slightly unusual Trebbiano Spoletino '06 redolent of rose petals and tomato leaf.

● Montefalco Rosso '05	▼▼ 5
● Montefalco Sagrantino '04	▼▼ 6
○ Trebbiano Spoletino '06	▼ 4

Ruggeri

VIA MONTEPENNINO, 5
06036 MONTEFALCO [PG]
TEL. 0742379294

Giuliano Ruggeri owns one of the smallest operations around Montefalco but it you look at his wines, which are delightfully crafted, it's a different story. Ruggeri is well up the quality ladder and Giuliano's Rosso di Montefalco '05, with nuances of dried plum and liquorice, blew us away.

● Montefalco Sagrantino '04	▼▼ 6
● Montefalco Rosso '05	▼▼ 4 *
● Montefalco Sagrantino Passito '04	▼ 6
● Montefalco Sagrantino '03	♈♈ 6

Tenuta di Salviano

LOC. CIVITELLA DEL LAGO
VOC. SALVIANO, 44
05020 BASCHI [TR]
TEL. 0744950459

Tenuta di Salviano is set in a landscape of rare beauty. Although the wines are enviably reliable, there were ups and downs this year. We felt that the best of those presented was Lago di Corbara Turlò '05, a partnership of sangiovese, cabernet and merlot.

● Lago di Corbara Turlò '05	▼▼ 4 *
● Lago di Corbara Solideo '04	▼ 4
● Lago di Corbara Solideo '03	♈♈ 4
● Lago di Corbara Turlò '04	♈♈ 4

OTHER WINERIES

Spoletoducale
LOC. PETROGNANO, 54
06049 SPOLETO [PG]
TEL. 074356224
www.spoletoducale.it

Casale Triocco is the premium line from
Spoletoducale. Standing out at our tastings
was Trebbiano Spoletino, a wine that
shows great potential and is definitely one
to watch. The 2006 shows a succulent
pear and apple nose before unveiling a
bright, juicy palate with plenty of oomph.

O Trebbiano Spoletino '06	🍷🍷	2*
● Montefalco Sagrantino Casale Triocco '04	🍷	5
● Montefalco Rosso Casale Triocco '05	🍷	4
O Colli Martani Grechetto Arcato '06	🍷	3

Terre de' Trinci
VIA FIAMENGA, 57
06034 FOLIGNO [PG]
TEL. 0742320165
www.terredetrinci.com

The Terre dei Trinci co-operative produces
about half a million bottles a year, which
makes it one of the largest producers of
Sagrantino and other wines in the area. The
best performance came from the flagship
Sagrantino di Montefalco Ugolino '04,
which has appealing fragrances of
blackberry and redcurrant.

● Montefalco Sagrantino Ugolino '04	🍷	7
● Montefalco Sagrantino '04	🍷	6
● Cajo '06	🍷	4

Tiburzi
ZONA ARTIGIANA PIETRAUTA
06036 MONTEFALCO [PG]
TEL. 0742379864
www.tiburzicantine.com

Tiburzi is located just three kilometres from
historic Montefalco but its vineyards, all
planted to red varieties, are about 450 metres
above sea level. Montefalco Sagrantino
Taccalite '04 is nice, with a fine attack and
good varietal definition, as well as tasty sour
cherry and rounded tannins.

● Montefalco Sagrantino Taccalite '04	🍷🍷	6
● Rosso Colle Scancellato '06	🍷🍷	3*
● Montefalco Santambrà '05	🍷	4

Tenuta Vitalonga
LOC. MONTIANO
05016 FICULLE [TR]
TEL. 0763836722
www.vitalonga.it

This is the Maravalle family's second year of
production and the second good
performance from their very distinctive
wines. The cellar, located in Montiano near
Orvieto, has turned out a fine Elcione '05
from merlot and cabernet sauvignon.
Equally good is the montepulciano and
merlot Terra di Confine '05.

● Elcione '05	🍷🍷	4*
● Terra di Confine '05	🍷🍷	5
● Elcione '04	🍷🍷	4
● Terra di Confine '04	🍷🍷	5

LAZIO

Slow but sure is Lazio's motto. The region continues to progress in small but steady steps, gradually consolidating its gains. Those who hoped to see great leaps in quality and a case full of Three Glass trophies will be disappointed. Only two estates captured the coveted award, although the transfer of the Falesco cellars to Umbria means that Lazio could reasonably lay claim to an extra winner. We're more than satisfied, though. For the first time since 2001, Lazio managed to make the most of a good harvest in 2006. Wineries produced a series of bottles that are much superior to those we've seen in recent years and in net contrast to results in 2004, for example. For those who, like us, take a global view of Lazio production, tasting as we do more than 500 wines every year, this represents real progress and is much more significant than the odd new big hitter. It means that the entire Lazio winemaking sector is growing and has acquired the technology that enables it to fully exploit opportunities that come its way. The region's production is still largely based on white wine, which even more than red requires appropriate cellar procedures. Another positive aspect is that this growth is finally a bit more even across the region's various zones. We have seen great progress not only in the province of Latina – where there has been an impressive growth in quality over the last three or four years – but also in the province of Viterbo and the Castelli Romani zone. This year, Castelli Romani emerges as a quite a force, increasingly confident is its own resources and the directions it is taking in its quest for quality. Meanwhile, Frosinone, which produces mainly reds and therefore benefited less from the 2006 growing year, presented a range of passerina-based wines the like of which we have never seen before. And this takes us to another point in favour of Lazio this year: most of the progress we have seen is in the DOC wine category, and just when we were beginning to think that IGT was the only route to improving quality. Every single DOC, from big names like Frascati, Cori and Montecompatri to zones such as Zagarolo that have almost disappeared off the map, has produced astonishing quantities of high-quality wine. In short, this has been a great year and we hope that it is just the beginning. If Lazio continues like this, it will be taking home more of those long-awaited Three Glasses. We close with a tribute to this year's winners. No surprises here, as they have topped the roll of honour in previous years. The champs are Sergio Mottura's Grechetto Latour a Civitella '05, one of Italy's best whites in terms of character and cellarability, and the '05 Il Vassallo, from Paola di Mauro's Colle Picchioni estate, a great Lazio classic that is back on superb form.

Marco Carpineti

LOC. CAPO LE MOLE
S.P. VELLETRI-ANZIO, KM 14,300
04010 CORI [LT]
TEL. 069679860
www.marcocarpineti.it

ANNUAL PRODUCTION 65,000 bottles
HECTARES UNDER VINE 19
VITICULTURE METHOD Certified organic

Over the years, Marco Carpineti has given us ample proof of his skills. This year's fine performance, the best so far from this estate, comes as no great surprise, even if sending two whites to the finals is quite an achievement. While we rather expected the greco-based Moro '06, with its generous tropical fruitiness and nose-palate complexity, to go through, the '06 Cori Bianco Capolemole is the best ever to come out of this DOC: elegant on the nose, then lingering and consistent on the palate. The triumph of the whites is further highlighted by Collesanti '06 and Ludum '05, both obtained from arciprete. The first shows gorgeous notes of peach and banana whereas Ludum is a passito that we expect to develop further. In this impressive line-up, the Dithyrambus '04 strikes a slightly discordant note and fails to repeat the performance of the 2003 version, perhaps penalized by a complexity and fullness that need time to find their balance. By contrast, the Tufaliccio '06, from montepulciano with a small amount of cesanese, offers agreeable body with violet, strawberry and cherry aromas. The Cori Rosso Capolemole '05 is, as ever, well-managed.

Casale del Giglio

LOC. LE FERRIERE
S.DA CISTERNA-NETTUNO KM 13
04010 APRILIA [LT]
TEL. 0692902530
www.casaledelgiglio.it

ANNUAL PRODUCTION 750,000 bottles
HECTARES UNDER VINE 138
VITICULTURE METHOD Conventional

The wines of Latina province are positively exploding onto the scene and at the forefront of the area's growth is Antonio Santarelli's estate. Antonio was one of the first to embark on this adventure and over the last 20 years he has carved out a well-deserved and unrivalled position as one of the area's top producers. Witness this year's impressive range. The wines on offer run from good to excellent and it is not just the top performers that excel. Mater Matuta '04 is a splendid version of this shiraz and petit verdot blend, and the elegant, harmonious Antinoo '05 from chardonnay and viognier claimed its usual place in the finals. But it was the medium-range wines that really impressed us. From the reds, we particularly liked the '05 Shiraz, perhaps the estate's best so far, the Cabernet Sauvignon '04 with its generous, mouthfilling fruit, and the agreeable, balanced Madreselva '04. The whites did well, too. The '06 Satrico is easy-drinking but never dull; the Chardonnay '06 is generous on the nose and flowery, fruity palate; and the Aphrodisum '06, from a late harvest, is ready to make that final leap in quality. A mention also goes to the Albiola '06, which has emerged as one of the region's best rosés.

O Cori Bianco Capolemole '06	♟♟ 4*
O Moro '06	♟♟ 4*
O Collesanti '06	♟♟ 4
● Rosso Tufaliccio '06	♟♟ 4
● Cori Rosso Capolemole '05	♟ 4
● Dithyrambus '04	♟ 6
O Ludum '05	♟ 6
● Dithyrambus '03	♟♟ 6
● Dithyrambus '00	♟♟ 5
O Moro '04	♟♟ 3*
O Moro '05	♟♟ 4*
● Dithyrambus '01	♟♟ 5

O Antinoo '05	♟♟ 4*
● Mater Matuta '04	♟♟ 6
O Aphrodisium '06	♟♟ 6
● Madreselva '04	♟♟ 5
O Chardonnay '06	♟♟ 3*
● Shiraz '05	♟♟ 4
O Satrico '06	♟♟ 2*
● Cabernet Sauvignon '04	♟♟ 5
⊙ Albiola '06	♟ 4
O Sauvignon '06	♟ 3
● Petit Verdot '05	♟ 4
● Merlot '05	♟ 4
O Antinoo '03	♟♟ 4*
● Mater Matuta '01	♟♟ 6
● Mater Matuta '99	♟♟ 6
● Mater Matuta '03	♟♟ 6
O Antinoo '04	♟♟ 4*
● Mater Matuta '00	♟♟ 6

Casale Marchese

VIA DI VERMICINO, 68
00044 FRASCATI [RM]
TEL. 069408932
www.casalemarchese.it

ANNUAL PRODUCTION 200,000 bottles
HECTARES UNDER VINE 40
VITICULTURE METHOD Conventional

The Carletti family continues to forge ahead with sagacity and determination, pursuing the solid growth they have always had as their goal. Work on the new cellar is complete and the new visitors' area is almost finished. Meanwhile, the family continues to dedicate its usual care and attention to the vineyards, aspiring to produce a well-balanced range. Paolo Peira's skilled hand is clearly evident in the character of the whites, which are obtained from fruit that offers both quality and potential. There was a good showing from the '06 Clemens, a splendid fusion of malvasia puntinata and chardonnay that makes an immediate impression with its confident flowery tone, fragrant tropical fruit palate and the refined, vivacious harmony of its almondy finish. The Frascati Superiore '06 is also superb, showing fresh aromas and a balanced palate that is pleasantly tasty and leisurely. By contrast, the reds didn't really cut the mustard. Although they confirm the high quality of the fruit, they fail to reach the standards we have come to expect.

Castel de Paolis

VIA VAL DE PAOLIS
00046 GROTTAFERRATA [RM]
TEL. 069413648
www.casteldepaolis.it

ANNUAL PRODUCTION 90,000 bottles
HECTARES UNDER VINE 14
VITICULTURE METHOD Certified organic

Castel de Paolis is a point of reference for the Castelli Romani territory and its image of quality. Fabrizio Santarelli has taken his estate to the very peak of organic production and plays a leading role in the Strada dei Vini dei Castelli Romani, the key organization promoting the territory's wine country. Fabrizio has expanded and made over the reception area to accommodate more visitors. Yet even the mighty stumble every now and then and this year's performance was not as inspiring as we have seen in previous ranges. The Frascati Superiore '06 is on top form, offering concentrated notes of summer flowers and a fragrant if rather aggressive long finish. By contrast, the '06 Donna Adriana, which comes from a more elegant blend of 50 per cent viognier, 40 per cent malvasia puntinata and a splash of sauvignon, is less convincing in its aromas than earlier versions. The extended cellar time given to Quattro Mori '04, obtained from 60 per cent syrah with merlot, cabernet sauvignon and petit verdot, has failed to give it the intended boost in quality that is certainly within its reach. The rest of the range is well-balanced and agreeable.

O Clemens '06	♟♟ 4*
O Frascati Sup. '06	♟♟ 3*
● Marchese dei Cavalieri '04	♟ 4
● Rosso di Casale Marchese '06	♟ 3
O Clemens '05	♟♟ 5

O Frascati Sup. '06	♟♟ 4
O Campo Vecchio Bianco '06	♟ 4
● Quattro Mori '04	♟ 6
O Donna Adriana '06	♟ 5
O Muffa Nobile '06	♟ 6
O Muffa Nobile '05	♟♟ 6
● Quattro Mori '00	♟♟ 6
O Vigna Adriana '05	♟♟ 5
O Vigna Adriana '02	♟♟ 5
● Quattro Mori '01	♟♟ 6
● Quattro Mori '03	♟♟ 6
O Vigna Adriana '03	♟♟ 5
O Vigna Adriana '04	♟♟ 5

Cantina Agricola Cincinnato

VIA CORI-CISTERNA KM 2
04010 CORI [LT]
TEL. 069679380
www.cantinacincinnato.it

ANNUAL PRODUCTION 300,000 bottles
HECTARES UNDER VINE 400
VITICULTURE METHOD Certified organic

Cincinnato is a big volume co-operative that has managed to combine numbers with quality, thanks largely to the leadership of chairman Nazareno Milita and oenologist Carlo Morettini. This year as never before, nero buono di Cori, a highly valued but often overlooked local variety, expressed its full potential in three superb wines. Nero Buono '04, well sustained by the oak, and Rosso dei Dioscuri '05, whose stainless steel conditioning brings out its cleanliness and pleasantness, are both based 100 per cent on this variety, while it is blended with montepulciano and cesanese to make the highly complex and balanced Cori Raverosse '04. The bellone grape is just as successful in its first pure version, Bellone '05, aged in 900-litre casks to produce a warm, fruity, varietal wine. The same goes for the refreshingly approachable Bianco dei Dioscuri '06, matured in stainless steel. As ever, the '06 Cori Illirio is pleasant on the palate, where the malvasia's aromas are clearly in evidence. We also liked the unusual Brut Cincinnato Spumante, a 100 per cent bellone-based Charmat that is flowery and agreeable.

Colacicchi

VIA ROMAGNANO, 2
03012 ANAGNI [FR]
TEL. 064469661
info@trimani.com

ANNUAL PRODUCTION 25,000 bottles
HECTARES UNDER VINE 6
VITICULTURE METHOD Conventional

The historical tradition of a prestigious estate and the winemaking skills of a family like the Trimanis, who have run it for years, make for a winning combination. This year, Colacicchi celebrates the return to top form of Torre Ercolana in '04 with a version that could well be the best we've ever tasted. The tried and tested blend of cabernet, merlot and cesanese comes together harmoniously to create a wine that is complex, full and mouthfilling, yet at the same time rounded and not over the top. We were particularly impressed by the sweetness of the very long finish. We have high hopes that the other two Bordeaux and cesanese blends produced by the estate may be able to emulate this extraordinary performance in the future. Of the two, we preferred the Schiaffo '06, which is approachable in its fruit – no oak-ageing here – and pleasantly drinkable. The Romagnano Rosso '05, however, has yet to develop and find its identity. The Romagnano Bianco '06 has no problems on this score, showing the typical aromatics of Lazio malvasia and a convincing acid vein in the finish.

O Bellone '05	▼▼	4
● Nero Buono '04	▼▼	4
● Cori Rosso Raverosse '04	▼▼	3*
● Rosso dei Dioscuri '05	▼▼	2*
O Bianco dei Dioscuri '06	▼	2*
O Cori Bianco Illirio '06	▼	3
O Brut Cincinnato Spumante	▼	2
O Bellone '03	♈♈	3*
● Cori Rosso Raverosse '02	♈♈	3*
● Nero Buono '03	♈♈	4

● Torre Ercolana '04	▼▼	7
O Romagnano Bianco '06	▼	5
● Romagnano Rosso '05	▼	5
● Schiaffo '06	▼	5
● Torre Ercolana '01	♈♈	6
● Torre Ercolana '03	♈♈	7
● Torre Ercolana '97	♈♈	6
● Torre Ercolana '98	♈♈	6

Antonello Coletti Conti
VIA VITTORIO EMANUELE, 116
03012 ANAGNI [FR]
TEL. 0775728610
www.coletticonti.it

Colle Picchioni - Paola Di Mauro
LOC. FRATTOCCHIE
VIA COLLE PICCHIONE, 46
00040 MARINO [RM]
TEL. 0693546329
www.collepicchioni.it

ANNUAL PRODUCTION 20,000 bottles
HECTARES UNDER VINE 20
VITICULTURE METHOD Conventional

ANNUAL PRODUCTION 120,000 bottles
HECTARES UNDER VINE 13
VITICULTURE METHOD Conventional

Antonello Coletti Conti – congratulations on his recent marriage! – manages to transfer to his wines the class and style that distinguish his own demeanour. The wines favour elegance over strength, and balance over showiness. Fine examples are his two Cesanese del Piglios, the Hernicus '06, which put on a fine show to win a place on our final tasting table, and the Romanico '05, which failed to make it to the finals by a mere whisker. Obtained from the most prestigious clone, cesanese d'Affile, they both made quite an impression. Hernicus exhibits red berry fruit aromas and a palate that already seems to have balanced out. The barrique is still working to smooth the tannins and high alcoholic content in the second but it shows huge growth potential. The '05 Arcadia, a wine derived from incrocio Manzoni, impressed us with its originality but Antonello did not deem this year's version ready for tasting. It was left to the third red, Cosmato '05, to round off the list. Obtained from cesanese with Bordeaux varieties and syrah, it is a blend that has yet to find a happy balance.

Anyone who doesn't know Paola Di Mauro may be forgiven for thinking that at the ripe old age of 84, she would be content to take a comfortable backseat role. She could be an oenological icon, hosting the hordes of friends that gather at "Colle" from all over to enjoy one of her sublime spaghettis. Not so. She is still going strong and her drive is evident in the solid management style of her son, Armando, and the energy of her young grandson, Valerio. Again, this family-run estate presented us with its jewel of a red, Il Vassallo '05, derived from 60 per cent merlot, 30 per cent cabernet sauvignon and cabernet franc. The name may have changed but the wine continues to charm with its unique character, combining enormous elegance with expression in a bouquet of lingering intensity. Three undisputed Glasses. The rest of the range is also superb. Marino Donna Paola '06 is refined and Le Vignole '05, from 60 per cent malvasia, 25 per cent trebbiano and sauvignon, is full and concentrated. There was a fine showing from the '06 Perlaia, from 35 per cent each of merlot and sangiovese with cabernet sauvignon, a fabulous wine that, with the Marino Coste Rotonde '06, highlights a style that is obvious throughout the range.

- Cesanese del Piglio Hernicus '06 ▼▼ 4*
- Cesanese del Piglio Romanico '05 ▼▼ 6
- Cosmato '05 ▼ 6
- Cesanese del Piglio Hernicus '05 ♀♀ 4
- Arcadia '05 ♀♀ 4
- Cesanese del Piglio Hernicus '04 ♀♀ 4
- Cosmato '03 ♀♀ 6

- Il Vassallo '05 ▼▼▼ 6
- Le Vignole '05 ▼▼ 4
- Perlaia '06 ▼▼ 4
- Marino Donna Paola '06 ▼▼ 4
- Marino Coste Rotonde '06 ▼ 3
- Vigna del Vassallo '00 ♀♀♀ 6
- Vigna del Vassallo '01 ♀♀♀ 6
- Vigna del Vassallo '02 ♀♀ 6
- Vigna del Vassallo '04 ♀♀ 6
- Vigna del Vassallo '03 ♀♀ 6

Paolo e Noemia D'Amico

FRAZ. VAIANO
LOC. PALOMBARO
01024 CASTIGLIONE IN TEVERINA [VT]
TEL. 0761948034
www.paoloenoemiadamico.it

ANNUAL PRODUCTION 90,000 bottles
HECTARES UNDER VINE 20
VITICULTURE METHOD Conventional

A wind of positive and promising change is
blowing through the production of this lovely
estate, which occupies a breathtaking
position in the upper Tiber valley
overlooking a beautiful landscape of ravines.
Tasting the wines, you can detect renewed
energy and a more refined oenological style
that emerges in its elegant, restrained
character, pointing firmly towards the future.
Credit for this goes to the D'Amicos'
passion but also to the solid, close-knit,
team that runs the estate with style and
composure. Based on this stable
foundation, the estate is evolving and has a
new range of labels lined up for a small but
carefully made range that reflects the
extraordinary richness of its vineyards. Hats
off to the delightful Calanchi di Vaiano '06,
obtained from 100 per cent chardonnay
matured in stainless steel, which earned a
place in our finals with its extraordinarily
elegant fruit and very pleasant finish. Falesia
'05 is a fragrant, harmonious, eloquently full
wine; Orvieto Noe '06 exhibits agreeable
character; and the Villa Tirrena '04, a
merlot-based red, is back on good form.
The basic Seiano line, both red and white, is
pleasant and very drinkable.

Fontana Candida

VIA FONTANA CANDIDA, 11
00040 MONTE PORZIO CATONE [RM]
TEL. 069401881
www.giv.it

ANNUAL PRODUCTION 6,000,000 bottles
HECTARES UNDER VINE 97
VITICULTURE METHOD Conventional

What a year for the whites produced by this
famous Castelli Romani estate! The results
achieved pay tribute to the bountiful 2006
harvest, which yielded grapes bursting with
character. When you consider that
production amounts to several million
bottles, you can appreciate just how
impressive these results are. Fontana
Candida's range is one of the best in the
region in terms of quality and it remains one
of the Gruppo Italiano Vini's most
representative brands. We noted a fine
showing from the refined Frascati Santa
Teresa '06, an object of passion for all those
who love its elegant, lip-smacking, enfolding
structure. The Malvasia Terre dei Grifi '06 is
equally fine, showing powerful, leisurely,
varietally aromatic and pleasantly fragrant
overall. Our compliments also go to the
flowery Graeco '06, a dynamic wine with a
pleasantly dry finish. The rest of the range is
very expressive and appealing, although the
reds lack some of that fascination and
conviction that we have enjoyed in previous
versions.

O Calanchi di Vaiano '06	♼♼	4*
O Falesia '05	♼♼	5
O Orvieto Noe '06	♼	3
● Villa Tirrena '04	♼	4
● Seiano Rosso '06	♼	3
O Seiano Bianco '06	♼	3
O Calanchi di Vaiano '00	♼♼	4
O Calanchi di Vaiano '05	♼♼	4*
O Falesia '04	♼♼	5

O Frascati Sup. Santa Teresa '06	♼♼	5
O Graeco '06	♼♼	4
O Malvasia del Lazio Terre dei Grifi '06	♼♼	4*
O Frascati Sup. Terre dei Grifi '06	♼	3
● Kron '05	♼	5
● Siroe '06	♼	4
● Kron '01	♼♼	6
O Frascati Sup. Santa Teresa '05	♼♼	5
● Kron '02	♼♼	5
● Kron '04	♼♼	6

Marcella Giuliani
LOC. VICO
VIA ANTICOLANA KM 5
03012 ANAGNI [FR]
TEL. 0644235908
matolu@tiscalinet.it

ANNUAL PRODUCTION 28,000 bottles
HECTARES UNDER VINE 10.5
VITICULTURE METHOD Conventional

Marcella Giuliani has always approached her work with passion and professionalism. Her efforts are paying off. Flanked by expert consultant Riccardo Cotarella, she is certainly not resting on her laurels, however well-deserved those laurels are, given that Dives is one of the best wines in the Cesanese del Piglio DOC. The cellar releases nine wines, including Sum, a blend of cesanese with international varieties that is still under preparation, while Il Graffio '06 is already a winner, combining the charm of its youth with complexity and backbone. As for the Cesanese del Piglio Dives, the '05 shows slightly less body than the magnificent 2004 version. Still in thrall to the oak, it does proffer a background hint of spiciness and weighty tannins are beginning to emerge. Rounding off the range we have the Cesanese Alagna '06 with its violet and cherry aromas set in measured astringency, and an almost aromatic Alagna Bianco '06 obtained from pure passerina that is fresh and fairly well-balanced. Marcella Giuliani can be proud of these results.

Sergio Mottura
LOC. POGGIO DELLA COSTA, 1
01020 CIVITELLA D'AGLIANO [VT]
TEL. 0761914533
www.motturasergio.it

ANNUAL PRODUCTION 95,000 bottles
HECTARES UNDER VINE 37
VITICULTURE METHOD Certified organic

Joking apart, Sergio Mottura could be defined as the most skilled interpreter of grechetto in the world. When you talk to him it's easy to see why. Like every man with a passion, he tends to wax lyrical, dwelling on the more fascinating details of his subject as he smiles in pleasure and delight. It would be hard to find a man more in love with his grapes. New vineyards densely planted with rooted cuttings obtained from ongoing estate selection are meticulously tended and ensure that the highest quality fruit is always available. This is the inspiration behind the new Latour a Civitella '05, which took home a Three Glass trophy for the third time. This glorious archetype of elegance and aromatic length exhibits breadth and complexity without sacrificing any of its body or harmony. This, too, is the strength of finalist Poggio della Costa '06, a stunning example of elegance and structure combined with great balance and uninterrupted eloquence. As in all the best years, the '06 Orvieto Classico Vigna Tragugnano and the '04 Nenfro, a red from 60 per cent merlot with montepulciano, are generous and compelling, a fitting tribute to a family that aims for distinction in every bottle it produces.

● Cesanese del Piglio Dives '05	♈♈ 5
● Il Graffio '06	♈♈ 4
○ Alagna Bianco '06	♈ 3
● Cesanese del Piglio Alagna '06	♈ 3
● Cesanese del Piglio Dives '04	♈♈ 5
● Cesanese del Piglio Dives '02	♈♈ 5
● Cesanese del Piglio Dives '03	♈♈ 5

○ Grechetto Latour a Civitella '05	♈♈♈ 5*
○ Grechetto Poggio della Costa '06	♈♈ 4*
● Nenfro '04	♈♈ 5
○ Orvieto Cl. Vigna Tragugnano '06	♈♈ 4
○ Orvieto '06	♈ 4
○ Grechetto Latour a Civitella '01	♈♈♈ 4
○ Grechetto Latour a Civitella '04	♈♈♈ 5*
○ Grechetto Latour a Civitella '02	♈♈ 5
○ Grechetto Latour a Civitella '00	♈♈ 5
○ Grechetto Poggio della Costa '05	♈♈ 4
○ Grechetto Latour a Civitella '03	♈♈ 5
○ Muffo '01	♈♈ 5
○ Grechetto Latour a Civitella '96	♈♈ 4
● Magone '04	♈♈ 5
○ Grechetto Latour a Civitella '02	♈♈ 5
○ Grechetto Latour a Civitella '99	♈♈ 4

Principe Pallavicini
VIA CASILINA KM 25,500
00043 COLONNA [RM]
TEL. 069438816
www.vinipallavicini.com

ANNUAL PRODUCTION 600,000 bottles
HECTARES UNDER VINE 84
VITICULTURE METHOD Conventional

In today's wine world, continuously proving your worth as a reliable producer can mean more than a single, one-off exploit. And that is exactly what the indefatigable team in charge of this hard-working Castelli Romani cellar has managed to do. The estate, created and supported by the aristocratic Pallavicini family, produces a very interesting range of wines. There are big plans for the future based on the great potential of its vineyards in the zone of Cerveteri, a project to launch new labels and the development of initiatives for the crowds of wine lovers who pass through the Castelli Romani area. The estate's excellent Frascati Sup. Poggio Verde '06 possesses typical fruity aromas and a delicious profile. The generous, harmonious Moroello '04, a sangiovese grosso and merlot blend, is also very expressive, as is the soft, lingering Pagello '06, whose greco base gives it a clear, citrus-like tonality. The rest of the wines on offer present a range of characteristics designed to satisfy all preferences with their sound personality, such as the sweet, complex Stillato '06, from malvasia puntinata.

Pietra Pinta
S.P. PASTINE KM. 20.300
04010 CORI [LT]
TEL. 069678001
www.pietrapinta.it

ANNUAL PRODUCTION 250,000 bottles
HECTARES UNDER VINE 115
VITICULTURE METHOD Certified organic

Thanks to the good overall quality of its performance, this estate belonging to brothers Cesare and Francesco Ferretti returned to the levels we have come to expect. Pietra Pinta continues to attract attention in the Monti Lepini wine world, which is coming on in leaps and bounds. As testimony to its versatility, both reds and whites, and local and international varieties, showed similarly well at our tastings. The Petit Verdot '05 offers a well-developed, well-typed interpretation bursting with red berry fruit aromas; the Costa Vecchia '05 is a successful blend of several varieties, including 50 per cent nero buono di Cori, 35 per cent montepulciano, ten per cent merlot and petit verdot; and the surprisingly agreeable Falanghina '06 seems to have come through its experimental phase. But the rest of the range also did the estate proud. The long-standing Colle Amato '04, a cabernet sauvignon with an addition of shiraz, regains the fruit-barrique balance that it had lost in previous versions. The Shiraz '04 is a lovely expression of pepper and vanilla aromas. Finally, the Chardonnay '06 is fresh-tasting and agreeable.

O Frascati Sup. Poggio Verde '06	▼▼	4*
O Pagello '06	▼▼	4
● Moroello '04	▼▼	6
● Amarasco '05	▼	5
● Soleggio '04	▼	4
O Stillato '06	▼	5
● La Cavata '04	▼	3
O La Giara '06	▼	3
● Amarasco '03	♀♀	4
O Stillato '05	♀♀	5
O Stillato '03	♀♀	4
● Moroello '03	♀♀	6

● Costa Vecchia '05	▼▼	4
● Petit Verdot '05	▼▼	4
O Falanghina '06	▼▼	4
O Chardonnay '06	▼	4
● Colle Amato '04	▼	5
● Shiraz '04	▼	4
● Merlot '05	▼	4
● Colle Amato '99	♀♀	5
● Colle Amato '00	♀♀	5
● Colle Amato '98	♀♀	3

Poggio Le Volpi

VIA COLLE PISANO, 27
00040 MONTE PORZIO CATONE [RM]
TEL. 069426980
www.poggiolevolpi.it

ANNUAL PRODUCTION 200,000 bottles
HECTARES UNDER VINE 30
VITICULTURE METHOD Conventional

Producer Felice Mergè's credo is rooted
firmly in hard work, dedication to his
vineyards, strict management of all
production processes, and involving and
training of his entire team, from cellar
technicians to labourers and vineyard
managers. He is also a passionate advocate
of local varieties and a persevering
experimenter of new wine trends that allow
his grapes to express their full potential. All
of this is reflected in the gratifying results
obtained by Poggio Le Volpi and the
unusual personality of its wines, which bear
an extremely strong varietal stamp. First we
have two wines that are different in
character but similar in their stylistic and
challenging approach. The Baccarossa '05
from 100 per cent nero buono di Cori offers
generous aromas and elegant, eloquent
fullness, and the Frascati Superiore Epos
'06 displays enveloping aromas with a long,
taut, elegant finish. We also liked the dried-
grape Odos '05, an equal blend of malvasia
del Lazio and sauvignon, which has
complex notes of ripe fruit, and the intense
Donnaluce '06, from 60 per cent malvasia
del Lazio, 30 per cent greco and
chardonnay, with its delightful mouthfeel
and flavour.

Il Quadrifoglio

LOC. DOGANELLA DI NINFA
VIA ALESSANDRO III, 5
04012 CISTERNA DI LATINA [LT]
TEL. 069601530
ilquadrifoglio.ss@libero.it

ANNUAL PRODUCTION 60,000 bottles
HECTARES UNDER VINE 30
VITICULTURE METHOD Conventional

This year, the estate belonging to Andrea
and Francesco De Gregorio gave a stunning
overall performance that merits a full profile.
The De Gregorios manage their vineyards,
cellar and agriturismo near the beautiful
Gardens of Ninfa with consummate skill and
Il Quadrifoglio is emerging as one of the
leading estates in the zone. The vineyards
all lie on the slopes of Cori and their grapes
– including international varieties – benefit
from the position and subsoil. It is difficult to
choose between the reds vinified in
stainless steel, Muro Pecoraro '06 and
Perazzeto '06. The first weds
montepulciano and cabernet giving notes of
cherry and bell pepper while the Perazzeto
combines merlot and syrah with wild berry
fruit and pepper nuances. Both are firmly
structured with clean tannins. The '04
Ottavione is different in approach. Obtained
from montepulciano and petit verdot aged
for a year in barriques, it offers rich tertiary
and leather aromas but the fruit and oak
have yet to find their balance. The Pezze di
Ninfa '06, a pleasing, well-managed
chardonnay, is matured in stainless steel
and presents notes of fruit and summer
flowers together with a refreshing, leisurely
palate.

● Baccarossa '05	🍷🍷	6
○ Frascati Sup. Epos '06	🍷🍷	5
○ Donnaluce '06	🍷🍷	5
○ Passito Odôs '05	🍷🍷	4*
● Baccarossa '04	🍷🍷	6
○ Donnaluce '05	🍷🍷	5
● Bacca Rossa '01	🍷🍷	5
● Bacca Rossa '02	🍷🍷	5
● Baccarossa '03	🍷🍷	5
○ Frascati Sup. Epos '05	🍷🍷	5

● Muro Pecoraro '06	🍷🍷	4*
● Perazzeto '06	🍷🍷	3*
● Ottavione '04	🍷🍷	5
○ Pezze di Ninfa '06	🍷🍷	3*
● Muro Pecoraro '05	🍷🍷	4*
● Perazzeto '05	🍷🍷	3*

Sant'Andrea

LOC. BORGO VODICE
VIA RENIBBIO, 1720
04010 TERRACINA [LT]
TEL. 0773755028
www.cantinasantandrea.it

ANNUAL PRODUCTION 200,000 bottles
HECTARES UNDER VINE 70
VITICULTURE METHOD Conventional

Gabriele and Andrea Pandolfo will be justifiably proud of the DOC obtained in 2007 as a tribute to the success of moscato di Terracina. They were the first to promote this variety and in celebration have added two sparkling Moscatos to their range, one dry and one slightly sweet. Actually, they are still in the experimentation phase. Meanwhile, the dry version of Oppidum '06 returned to pole position, bringing out moscato's aromas and taste-palate complexity. This variety is also nicely interpreted in the slightly sweet version of the Templum '06, and in the Passito Capitolium '05. We have two fine repeat performances and a surprise from the Circeo DOC, which also owes a great deal to Sant'Andrea. The first confirmation came from the Dune '05, obtained from malvasia and trebbiano nicely merged by well-gauged oak, and the second was the Sogno '04, a rich, complex blend of merlot and cesanese. The surprise came in the form of the Circeo Bianco Riflessi '06 that has never been so easy-drinking yet complex and fascinating. Finally, the other two Circeo Rossos are well styled, particularly the Preludio alla Notte '05 with its aromas of red berry and spice.

Terra delle Ginestre

LOC. CAMPOLUNGO
VIA FORNELLO, 94
04020 SPIGNO SATURNIA [LT]
TEL. 0771700297
http://member.xoom.it/ginestravini

ANNUAL PRODUCTION 10,000 bottles
HECTARES UNDER VINE 2
VITICULTURE METHOD Conventional

The passion of a group of friends and the skill of oenologist Maurizio De Simone are the driving forces behind the continuous development of this young estate which, this year in particular, is proving itself to be a serious producer of whites. The moscato di Terracina grapes that form the basis of both the Invito '06 and the Stellaria '06 come from the zone of Vallemarina. The former is obtained from ungrafted rootstock that is over 50 years old, and is varietal in its aromas and almondy finish. The Stellaria seems to have succeeded in the difficult task of combining an aromatic grape type with the barrique. We also liked the Lentisco '05, which is derived from pure bellone. It is fermented in 300-litre casks made of chestnut and this gives it a pleasant rusticity, nice minerality and tanginess. The Generale '04 is less convincing but nevertheless worthy of note for its use of local varieties that are not particularly appreciated in these zones, such as primitivo and aglianico. The estate has a project to add even more obscure varieties, including metolano, uva vipera and abbuoto. We'll be keeping a watchful eye on this.

O Circeo Bianco Riflessi '06	♟♟ 2*
O Circeo Bianco Dune '05	♟♟ 4
● Circeo Rosso Il Sogno '04	♟♟ 4
O Moscato di Terracina Secco Oppidum '06	♟♟ 3*
● Circeo Rosso Preludio alla Notte '05	♟ 3
● Circeo Rosso Riflessi '06	♟ 2
O Moscato di Terracina Passito Capitolium '05	♟ 3
O Moscato di Terracina Amabile Templum '06	♟ 3
O Circeo Bianco Dune '03	♟♟ 4*
● Circeo Rosso Il Sogno '03	♟♟ 4*
O Moscato di Terracina Passito Capitolium '04	♟♟ 3*
O Circeo Bianco Dune '04	♟♟ 4
O Moscato di Terracina Secco Oppidum '05	♟♟ 3*

O Invito '06	♟♟ 2*
O Lentisco '05	♟♟ 3*
O Stellaria '06	♟♟ 4
● Il Generale '04	♟ 4
O Invito '05	♟♟ 2*
O Lentisco '04	♟♟ 3*

Trappolini
VIA DEL RIVELLINO, 65
01024 CASTIGLIONE IN TEVERINA [VT]
TEL. 0761948381
trappolini@wooow.it

ANNUAL PRODUCTION 150,000 bottles
HECTARES UNDER VINE 24
VITICULTURE METHOD Conventional

Roberto and Paolo Trappolini's estate is a leading light in the oenological renaissance of the province of Viterbo. Since starting out in the winemaking business, the Trappolinis have had some very interesting results and those in the know reckon the have a bright future ahead of them. The Trappolinis have gone from strength to strength over the years, overcoming a series of challenges to create a style that is eloquently forthright and impressively consistent. The 2006 growing year was a good one for white grapes, here as elsewhere. Proof positive comes in the form of the excellent Brecceto, an equal blend of chardonnay and grechetto showing admirable balance between its structure and generous bouquet, and the classic Orvieto whose green notes give a certain gutsiness to the lovely long finish. The Paterno '05, obtained from pure sangiovese, enhanced its reputation with a fine performance. It displays grip, austerity and measured tannins in the body that will smooth out with cellaring. The rest of the wines on offer have considerable personality and are good value for money.

Villa Simone
VIA FRASCATI COLONNA, 29
00040 MONTE PORZIO CATONE [RM]
TEL. 069449717
www.pierocostantini.it

ANNUAL PRODUCTION 200,000 bottles
HECTARES UNDER VINE 20
VITICULTURE METHOD Conventional

Piero Costantini's love affair with Frascati has endured over the years and this is the wine that has come to represent him in the oenological world. He has also had some very successful results with his reds, proposing products of quality and weight, such as this year's splendid Torraccia '06. Obtained from an equal blend of cesanese and sangiovese, it astonishes with its balance and robust, expressive profile and possesses a generously agreeable finish. But it is the three Frascatis that lovers of this category await on tenterhooks each year. Once again, Vigneto Filonardi dominates the line-up, showing invigorating and caressing in its typical, firm texture and with a pleasant, long-lingering finish. Hot on its heels come the tangy, fruity Villa dei Preti and the Villa Simone, an extremely reliable evergreen. This cellar is a benchmark for Frascati and thanks to Piero's extensive experience, it has earned a reputation for quality and consistency. A word of warning, though. These days tastes can change very quickly and an injection of energy could soon prove useful, if not crucial.

○ Brecceto '06	♟♟ 4*
○ Orvieto '06	♟♟ 2*
● Paterno '05	♟♟ 4
● Cenereto '06	♟ 2*
○ Est Est Est di Montefiascone '06	♟ 2*
○ Sartei '06	♟ 2*
● Paterno '03	♟♟ 4*
○ Brecceto '05	♟♟ 4*
● Idea '02	♟♟ 4
● Paterno '04	♟♟ 4
● Paterno '01	♟♟ 4

○ Frascati Sup. Vign. Filonardi '06	♟♟ 4
● Torraccia '06	♟♟ 4
○ Frascati Sup. Villa dei Preti '06	♟ 4
○ Frascati Sup. Villa Simone '06	♟ 3
● Ferro e Seta '00	♟♟ 6
● Ferro e Seta '01	♟♟ 6
● Ferro e Seta '03	♟♟ 6
● Torraccia '05	♟♟ 4
● Torraccia '04	♟♟ 4
● Ferro e Seta '04	♟♟ 6

OTHER WINERIES

Alcioni
LOC. SAN PIETRO
04010 CORI [LT]
TEL. 0668801137
www.alcioni.it

This Cori-based new entry has clear ideas.
The Neleo '05, from steel-aged
montepulciano, nero buono and
sangiovese, showed well with cherry and
red berry fruit aromas and good nose-palate
consistency. The bellone, arciprete and
greco moro Fauno '05 has a tropical fruit
nose and a fresh, tangy palate.

● Neleo '05	▼▼ 4*
○ Fauno '05	▼ 4

Flavio Buttarelli
VIA MAREMMANA SUPERIORE KM 1,100
00035 OLEVANO ROMANO [RM]
TEL. 069564570
www.vinibuttarelli.it

Flavio Buttarelli's estate makes its Guide
debut with some quality wines. The best is
Clivus '06, citrussy in its aromas and fresh
on the palate with lots of body. We also liked
the two Cesanese di Olevano Romanos, the
soft, fruity Vignalibus '06 and the more
austere, tannic Colline Morra Roscia '04.

○ Clivus '06	▼▼ 3*
● Cesanese di Olevano Romano Colline della Morra Roscia '04	▼ 4
● Cesanese di Olevano Romano Vignalibus '06	▼ 3

Camponeschi
VIA PIASTRARELLE, 14
00040 LANUVIO [RM]
TEL. 069374390
www.collilanuvini.it

Camponeschi is a solid family-run estate
based on fine traditions. Today, this
dynamic, growing winery makes particularly
good whites, including a well-typed,
coherent interpretation of Colli Lanuvini
Superiore '06 and a generous Malvasia '06.
The soft Carato Rosso '04 is also attractive.

● Carato Rosso '04	▼ 5
○ Colli Lanuvini Sup. '06	▼ 2
○ Malvasia '06	▼ 3

Casale Cento Corvi
VIA AURELIA KM 45,500
00052 CERVETERI [RM]
TEL. 069903902
www.casalecentocorvi.com

Casale Cento Corvi did well this year, a
tribute to the energy of this hospitable cellar,
open to both visitors and clients. The
Giacché '05 is again the estate's flagship, a
happy marriage of the character of its
ancient variety and a skilled hand in the
cellar. The other labels are also very
enjoyable.

● Giacché '05	▼▼ 7
● Kantharos Rosso '05	▼ 4
○ Kottabos Bianco '06	▼ 4
● Kottabos Rosso '05	▼ 4

Casale della Ioria
P.ZZA REGINA MARGHERITA, 1
03010 ACUTO [FR]
TEL. 0775744282
www.casaledellaioria.com

Paolo Perinelli has partly reorganized his
estate. This year, Cesanese del Piglio Torre
del Piano '05 is back on good form and the
Passerina del Frusinate Colle Bianco is
perhaps the best interpretation of the type
from 2006. The other Cesanese is well
styled but the new Tres '05 is a bit
muddled.

● Cesanese del Piglio Torre del Piano '05	▼▼ 5
● Cesanese del Piglio '06	▼ 4
○ Passerina del Frusinate Colle Bianco '06	▼ 3
● Tres '06	▼ 4

Casale Mattia
LOC. COLLE MATTIA
VIA MONTE MELLONE, 19
00040 MONTECOMPATRI [RM]
TEL. 069426249
www.casalemattia.it

This highly regarded Castelli Romani estate
stays true to its philosophy of producing
reliable wines at reasonable prices. There is
little to choose between the reds and
whites. The Frascati Terre del Casale '06 is
fragrantly aromatic and soft; the Merlot
Linea Storica '05 is generous and lingering.

○ Frascati Sup. Terre del Casale '06	▼ 4
● Millesoli '05	▼ 4
● Merlot Linea Storica '05	▼ 5
○ Nemesis '06	▼ 3

OTHER WINERIES

Cavalieri
VIA MONTECAGNOLO, 16
00045 GENZANO DI ROMA [RM]
TEL. 069375807
www.cavalieri.it

There was a triumphant Guide debut for this
family-run estate in the heart of the Castelli
Romani, where it has been making wine
since 1879. Of the wines on offer, two stand
out. The red Rutilo '04 offers enveloping,
richly fruity sensations and the fresh white
Infiorata '06 has a long finish. The rest of the
range is very decent.

O Infiorata '06	♟♟ 3*
● Rutilo '04	♟♟ 5
● Facesole '05	♟ 4
O Teresa '06	♟ 3

Cantina Cerquetta
VIA DI FONTANA CANDIDA, 20
00040 MONTE PORZIO CATONE [RM]
TEL. 069424147
www.cantinacerquetta.it

The Ciuffa family's estate releases a wide
range of reds and whites, all consistently
good and well typed. This year the
Montecompatri Superiore '06 dominated
the line-up, highlighting a small but
interesting DOC that deserves more
attention. The other wines on offer are all up
to snuff.

O Montecompatri Colonna Sup. '06	♟♟ 2*
O Frascati Sup. Antico Cenacolo '06	♟ 4
● Grotta del Cenacolo '05	♟ 4
● Fulgor '05	♟ 2*

Cantina Cerveteri
VIA AURELIA KM 42,700
00052 CERVETERI [RM]
TEL. 06994441
www.cantinacerveteri.it

Cantina Cerveteri has 700 members, 1,200
hectares under vine and an annual
production of around 4,000,000 bottles.
This is the year of the whites, notably the
malvasia-based Novae '06, which offers
citrus and balsam aromas and a clean,
aromatic palate. The Cerveteri Viniae
Grande '06 is upfront and agreeable.

O Cerveteri Bianco Viniae Grande '06	♟ 4
O Novae '06	♟ 3

Cantine Ciolli
VIA DEL CORSO
00035 OLEVANO ROMANO [RM]
TEL. 069564547
cantineciolli@alice.it

Damiano Ciolli has opted to give his top
wine, Cirsium, an extra year in glass and we
cannot but applaud his decision. In its
absence, the only wine presented this year
was Silene '05. It is, as usual, pleasant with
balsamic, spicy aromas and good fruit.

● Cesanese di Olevano Silene '05	♟ 4
● Cesanese di Olevano Cirsium '01	♟♟ 6
● Cesanese di Olevano Cirsium '04	♟♟ 5

Colle di Maggio
VIA PASSO DEI CORESI, 25
00049 VELLETRI [RM]
TEL. 0696453072
www.colledimaggio.com

This estate continues to develop but its
efforts have yet to bear fruit. Results pay
tribute to solid winemaking but there is still
room for improvement. Both the white and
red versions of Porticato and Velitrae reveal
sinew on the palate, approachability,
versatility at table and attractive pricing.

O Porticato Bianco '06	♟ 4
O Velitrae Bianco '06	♟ 4
● Velitrae Rosso '06	♟ 4
● Porticato Rosso '05	♟ 4

Colletonno
LOC. COLLETONNO
03012 ANAGNI [FR]
TEL. 0775769271
www.colletonno.it

The Di Cosimo family estate made a fine
debut with its Colle Sape Corte dei Papi
'06, a successful blend of malvasia,
chardonnay and trebbiano, and Cesanese
del Piglio Colle Ticchio '05, with ripe red
berry fruit aromas and velvety tannins. The
San Magno '05 is ambitious but lags a step
or two behind.

● Cesanese del Piglio Colle Ticchio '05	♟♟ 4*
O Colle Sape Corte dei Papi '06	♟♟ 3*
● Cesanese del Piglio San Magno '05	♟ 5

OTHER WINERIES

Compagnia di Ermes
VIA SAN FRANCESCO D'ASSISI, 95
00035 OLEVANO ROMANO [RM]
TEL. 069564025

This estate run by a group of friends has everything it takes to become a major force around Olevano. Its two traditional Cesanese di Olevano Romanos flaunt tobacco and leather, the Attis '05 being fuller and more structured while Cibele '06 from ottonese bianco and bellone is pleasantly rustic.

● Cesanese di Olevano Romano '05	♀	3
○ Cibele '06	♀	3
● Cesanese di Olevano Romano Attis '05	♀	4

Federici
VIA SANTA APOLLARIA VECCHIA, 30
00039 ZAGAROLO [RM]
TEL. 0695461022
www.vinifederici.com

"The best Zagarolo ever" was our panel's opinion after tasting Federici's Zagarolo Superiore '06. Complex on the nose, where almond, pear and citrus fruit emerge, it presents a pleasant, consistent palate with good body and length. We also liked the fresh, fruity Le Ripe Rosso '05.

○ Zagarolo Sup. '06	♀♀	2*
● Le Ripe Rosso '05	♀	5

Gotto d'Oro
LOC. FRATTOCCHIE
VIA DEL DIVINO AMORE, 115
00040 MARINO [RM]
TEL. 0693022211
www.gottodoro.it

This Castelli Romani estate is experiencing a moment of renewal and redirection. This year's line-up includes the classic labels, the dry, solidly built Marino '06 and the pleasant Frascati '06. Sol '05 from the experimental Mitreo line showed well, as did the agreeably eloquent reds.

○ Frascati Sup. '06	♀	2
● Merlot del Lazio '05	♀	3
○ Marino Sup. '06	♀	2*
○ Mitreo Sol '05	♀	4

Mazziotti
LOC. MELONA BONVINO
VIA CASSIA, KM 110
01023 BOLSENA [VT]
TEL. 0644291377
www.mazziottiwines.com

Valeria Mazziotti's estate is back on form with a Canuleio '06 that almost made it to the finals. From 60 per cent chardonnay with sauvignon and malvasia, this rich, complex wine offers lovely citrus and mineral notes. Volgente '05, from 50 per cent merlot with cabernet sauvignon and sangiovese, is also good.

○ Canuleio '06	♀♀	4
● Volgente Rosso '05	♀	5

Isabella Mottura
LOC. RIO CHIARO, 1
01020 CIVITELLA D'AGLIANO [VT]
TEL. 3357077931
isabellamottura@libero.it

An excellent '05 edition of Amadis saw this estate in Viterbo's Tuscia area return to the Guide in style. From pure montepulciano, it melds spicy aromas with hints of plum; the nice fleshy palate is long and fragrant. We also liked Akemi '06 for its quinine and cherry. The palate is fruity, if rather simple.

● Amadis '05	♀♀	6
● Akemi '06	♀	4

L'Olivella
VIA DI COLLE PISANO, 5
00044 FRASCATI [RM]
TEL. 069424527
www.racemo.it

Once again, it is Racemo Rosso '04 that stands out from the range at this well-regarded organic cellar. Like the other Racemo, the Frascati '06, it has freshness and firm backbone. Tre Grome '06 offers typicity and the 40/60 '06 is a velvety blend of syrah and cesanese.

○ Frascati Sup. Racemo '06	♀♀	4
● Racemo Rosso '04	♀♀	5
○ Tre Grome '06	♀	5
● 40/60 '05	♀	4

OTHER WINERIES

Cantine Palombo
LOC. PONTE MELFA
C.SO MUNANZIO PLANCO
03042 ATINA [FR]
TEL. 0776610200
www.vinipalombo.it

Unexpectedly, Cantine Palombo's simplest and cheapest wine, the Merlot '06, was the best. We preferred its coherence and easy-drinking qualities to the two still unbalanced Atina Cabernets, although the Duca Cantelmi '04 shows backbone and well-matured tannins. The sauvignon-only Somigliò '06 is nice.

● Merlot '06	♥♥	4*
● Atina Cabernet '05	♥	4
○ Somigliò '06	♥	4
● Atina Cabernet Duca Cantelmi Ris. '04	♥	6

Puri Charlotte
VIA CASSIA, KM 119,7
01020 SAN LORENZO NUOVO [VT]
TEL. 0763727160
charlotte.puri@tin.it

Charlotte Puri's estate did well thanks to a series of solidly made wines. We particularly liked the Calenne '06 for its tropical fruit-laced citrus and long, minerally palate with good backbone. The pleasant, spicy Pontone '06 and the simple, fruity Montemoro '05 are also very decent.

○ Calenne '06	♥♥	4*
● Montemoro '05	♥	5
● Pontone '06	♥	4

Tenuta Le Quinte
VIA DELLE MARMORELLE, 71
00040 MONTECOMPATRI [RM]
TEL. 069438756

Tenuta Le Quinte, owned by the Papi family, is the Montecompatri DOC's standard bearer. We loved the Montecompatri Superiore Virtù Romane '06, which has sage and tropical fruit aromas and a soft yet refreshing palate. The Malvasia Orchidea '06 and the Rasa di Marmorata '05, a red, are also well made.

○ Montecompatri Colonna Sup.		
Virtù Romane '06	♥♥	3*
○ Malvasia Orchidea '06	♥	3
● Rasa di Marmorata '05	♥	3

Riserva della Cascina
LOC. FIORANO
VIA APPIA ANTICA
00043 ROMA [RM]
TEL. 067917221
riservadellacascina@inwind.it

The Branettis – husband and wife – know just how much dedication a family wine business requires. Quality matches previous vintages despite the recent distractions of work on their new cellar. We preferred the more balanced, deeper-tasting red Castelli Romani '06 to the agreeable, heady Marino '06.

● Castelli Romani Rosso '06	♥♥	3*
○ Marino Sup. '06	♥	2

Cantine San Marco
LOC. VERMICINO
VIA DI MOLA CAVONA, 26/28
00044 FRASCATI [RM]
TEL. 069409403
www.sanmarcofrascati.it

Cantine San Marco is run by the Violo and Notarnicola families, and the best thing to come out of their broad range this year was Soloshiraz '05, which is back in fine fettle. The whites are good, particularly the '06 Frascatis, which vary in character and approach. Solomalvasia '06 is agreeable.

● Soloshiraz '05	♥♥	4*
○ Frascati Sup. De Notari '06	♥	4
○ Frascati Sup. Crio 8 '06	♥	3
○ Solomalvasia '06	♥	4

Tenuta Santa Lucia
LOC. SANTA LUCIA
02047 POGGIO MIRTETO [RI]
TEL. 076524616
www.tenutasantalucia.com

A short profile this time round but results at Tenuta Santa Lucia were far from disappointing. The reds showed very well, notably the Collis Pollionis Rosso '06 with fruity aromas and a fresh, firmly structured palate. Otio '05 is full but rather unbalanced. From the whites, We liked the clean, citrus Collis Pollionis '06.

● Colli della Sabina		
Collis Pollionis Rosso '06	♥♥	5
○ Colli della Sabina		
Collis Pollionis Bianco '06	♥	5
● Otio '05	♥	7

OTHER WINERIES

Sant'Isidoro
LOC. PORTACCIA
01016 TARQUINIA [VT]
TEL. 0766869716
www.santisidoro.net

Situated near Tarquinia just ten kilometres from the coast, Sant'Isidoro is a quality-focused estate. The splendid Soremidio '05, a montepulciano-based red, offers tobacco and black berry fruit-laced spice and a full, consistent palate. The fresh, fruity Corithus '06 is good and the Forca di Palma '06 well typed.

● Soremidio '05	🍷🍷	6
○ Forca di Palma '06	🍷	4
● Corithus '06	🍷	5

Giovanni Terenzi
LOC. LA FORMA
VIA PRENESTINA, 140
03010 SERRONE [FR]
TEL. 0775594286
www.viniterenzi.com

In the absence of the cesanese-based Velobra, Cesanese del Piglio Colle Forma '05, a firmly structured wine with good nose-palate consistency, and the simpler but well-styled Cesanese di Olevano Romano Colle San Quirico '05 stood in. Passerina del Frusinate Villa Santa '06 has flowers and apple-like fruit.

● Cesanese del Piglio Colle Forma '05	🍷🍷	5
● Cesanese di Olevano Romano Colle S. Quirico '05	🍷	3
○ Passerina Villa Santa '06	🍷	3

Castello Torre in Pietra
VIA DI TORRIMPIETRA, 247
00050 FIUMICINO [RM]
TEL. 0661697070
www.castelloditorreinpietra.it

A full, pleasant '06 version of Tarquinia Bianco turns the spotlight on this small but interesting DOC on the coast of Lazio. The rest of the range is very good, including a fragrant Chardonnay '06 and a forthright Syrah '05 that confirm the territory's potential.

○ Tarquinia Bianco '06	🍷🍷	2*
○ Chardonnay '06	🍷	3
● Syrah '05	🍷	4

Villa Gianna
LOC. B.GO SAN DONATO
S.DA MAREMMANA
04010 SABAUDIA [LT]
TEL. 077350757
www.villagianna.it

The Giannini family estate continues to improve its Vigne del Borgo line. A varietal Sauvignon '06 shows yellow-fleshed fruit while the Cabernet '05 is clean with well-gauged tannins. To our surprise, the simple but balanced Rudestro '05 outstripped the ambitious Barriano '04, which needs more cellar time.

● Rudèstro '05	🍷🍷	3*
● Vigne del Borgo Cabernet Sauvignon '05	🍷🍷	4
○ Vigne del Borgo Sauvignon '06	🍷🍷	4*
● Barriano '04	🍷	4

Villafranca
VIA VILLAFRANCA, 14
00040 ALBANO LAZIALE [RM]
TEL. 069344277
www.cantinavillafranca.com

Villafranca again marshalled an impressive line-up to underline the high quality of this interesting Castelli Romani estate. The Castelli Romani Rosso Tenuta Gasperini '04 stands head and shoulders above the rest for its no-nonsense character and deep, full palate. The other wines are well managed.

● Castelli Romani Rosso Tenuta Gasperini '04	🍷🍷	3*
○ Frascati Sup. Couvage '06	🍷	3
● Cabernet Sauvignon Villa Chigi '05	🍷	4

Conte Zandotti
VIA VIGNE COLLE MATTIA, 8
00132 ROMA [RM]
TEL. 0620609000
www.cantinecontezandotti.it

This year, Malvasia Rumon '06 is back on form. It's an elegantly complex, full-bodied wine from the estate's historic vineyards. There's also an exciting new line, Aurora, for wines with a more relaxed personality. The Frascati Superiore '06's solid personality is in the estate's distinctive style.

○ Malvasia del Lazio Rumon '06	🍷🍷	4
○ Frascati Sup. '06	🍷	4
○ Conte Enrico Bianco Aurora '06	🍷	3
● Conte Enrico Rosso Aurora '05	🍷	3

ABRUZZO

That breath of revival we mentioned last year in these pages has gained strength – and, as tends to happen to breezes that come up against our Majella mountain, it has naturally become fuller and more blustery. A while ago, a new wave of committed young producers appeared in Abruzzo's winemaking sector. The newcomers respected the well-ploughed furrow of tradition and paid heed to the teachings of the local gurus, bringing their own enthusiasm and verve to traditional wineries and founding new ones. The results are right before our eyes: over 30 wines in the final, ten of which deservedly picked up Three Glasses. An in-depth look at the list of these outstanding wines shows us a cross-section of the region. There are gurus, aspiring gurus and finally those young lions. What unites them is their focus on typical varieties, their love for old-fashioned vinification techniques that are mindful of tradition, their knowledge of modern techniques, and a shared striving to interpret native grapes, each according to his or her particular talents. These are the wines that represent the reality of this region. A synthesis of history and modernity is the glue holding today's Abruzzo together. The standard-bearer, as usual, is Francesco Paolo Valentini with his extraordinarily fine, rustic-style wines followed by Gianni Masciarelli and his outstanding Trebbiano del Castello di Semivicoli, aged in stainless steel, and the classic Villa Gemma, a fine, mouthfilling Montepulciano. Next is Dino Illuminati, a true pillar of the Colline Teramane, and Luigi Cataldi Madonna, the professor, finally doing full justice to his love for the pecorino grape, which displays all its potential in the '05 vintage. The young lions continue to enjoy success: Leonardo Pizzolo's Valle Reale and Federica Morricone's Villa Medoro are now a certainty, not a surprise. Closing the parade is Nicodemi's Neromoro, a big robust wine with extraordinary texture. Behind them, a crowd of eager wineries a stone's throw from the summit – Barba, La Quercia, Torre dei Beati, Cantina Tollo and Centorame. These cellars unite to represent the excellent quality of a region that produces almost 4,000,000 hectolitres of wine every year and takes fifth place on the list of Italian regions.

Agriverde

LOC. CALDARI
VIA STORTINI, 32A
66020 ORTONA [CH]
TEL. 0859032101
www.agriverde.it

ANNUAL PRODUCTION 600,000 bottles
HECTARES UNDER VINE 65
VITICULTURE METHOD Certified organic

This winery, situated on the sunny hills of Ortona overlooking the sea, has become a regional model for modern, dynamic management: beautiful vineyards, a cellar built to the tenets of bioarchitecture, a modern, sophisticated hotel and a focus on organic farming and wine therapy. But what matters most of all to us is the excellent line-up of fine quality wines. The Montepulciano d'Abruzzo Plateo, now a banker, will not be released to market until the end of next year, so we'll postpone tasting until the 2009 edition of the Guide. The uncomplicated, agreeable Montepulciano d'Abruzzo Piane di Maggio '06 won us over with its sweet, almost date-like aromas and well-judged oak. It unfolds nicely on the palate showing lovely varietal character and tanginess. The Montepulciano d'Abruzzo Solàrea '02 is mouthfilling and fruity with a generous, concentrated and slightly tannic palate. Among the whites, the Chardonnay Riseis '06 stands out as a lovely interpretation of the variety, fragrant and pleasantly rustic with delicious acidity on the palate.

F.lli Barba

LOC. SCERNE DI PINETO
S.DA ROTABILE PER CASOLI
64025 PINETO [TE]
TEL. 0859461020
www.fratellibarba.it

ANNUAL PRODUCTION 300,000 bottles
HECTARES UNDER VINE 68
VITICULTURE METHOD Conventional

The Barba brothers continue their hard work to renew and improve the range of products from this traditional leading winery in the province of Teramo. This year, their lovely Pineto winery presented a significant series of wines with peaks of outstanding quality. The Montepulciano d'Abruzzo Vignafranca '04 came close to a top award for its subtle, typical aromas and sweet, fruity, pleasantly tangy palate. Its only flaw, as it were, is that it is too young for a traditional wine destined to last a long time. But the entire range is impressive: sound wines with extraordinary texture, in line with local tradition. The simplest is the Montepulciano d'Abruzzo Colle Morino, which has concentrated, enfolding aromas and substantial but beautifully handled texture. Turning to the whites, we are pleased to include the clean, uncomplicated Trebbiano d'Abruzzo Colle Morino '05, with its generous, tangy palate, and the ambitious Trebbiano d'Abruzzo Vignafranca '05, which gives stylish toastiness and chamomile aromas followed by a weighty but soft body. All the wines are excellent value for money.

O Chardonnay Riseis di Recastro '06	♟♟ 3*
● Montepulciano d'Abruzzo Piane di Maggio '06	♟♟ 2*
● Montepulciano d'Abruzzo Riseis di Recastro '05	♟ 4
O Pecorino Riseis di Recastro '06	♟ 3
O Trebbiano d'Abruzzo Piane di Maggio '06	♟ 2*
● Montepulciano d'Abruzzo Solàrea '02	♟ 5
● Montepulciano d'Abruzzo Plateo '00	♟♟♟ 7
● Montepulciano d'Abruzzo Plateo '01	♟♟♟ 7
● Montepulciano d'Abruzzo Plateo '98	♟♟♟ 6
● Montepulciano d'Abruzzo Solàrea '01	♟♟ 5
O Pecorino Riseis di Recastro '05	♟♟ 3*
● Montepulciano d'Abruzzo Riseis di Recastro '04	♟♟ 4*

● Montepulciano d'Abruzzo Vignafranca '04	♟♟ 4
⊙ Montepulciano d'Abruzzo Cerasuolo Colle Morino '05	♟♟ 2*
O Trebbiano d'Abruzzo Vignafranca '05	♟♟ 4
O Trebbiano d'Abruzzo Colle Morino '06	♟ 2*
● Montepulciano d'Abruzzo Vignafranca '01	♟♟ 4*
● Montepulciano d'Abruzzo Vignafranca '03	♟♟ 4*
● Montepulciano d'Abruzzo Vignafranca '00	♟♟ 4

Barone Cornacchia
C.DA TORRI, 20
64010 TORANO NUOVO [TE]
TEL. 0861887412
www.baronecornacchia.it

Luigi Cataldi Madonna
LOC. PIANO
67025 OFENA [AQ]
TEL. 0862954252
cataldimadonna@virgilio.it

ANNUAL PRODUCTION 312,000 bottles
HECTARES UNDER VINE 42
VITICULTURE METHOD Certified organic

Last year, we gave this classic Torano Nuovo winery its full profile back, an act of justice to what some consider to be the region's most beautiful estate and certainly one of the oldest and most traditional around Teramo. The wines lined up for us this year are all interesting, fragrant and varietal, especially the standard-label products. Paradoxically, the top of the range wines are the least successful. The Montepulciano d'Abruzzo '05 is very typical; although slightly veiled by wood, the palate is pleasant and engaging. The ambitious Vigna Le Coste '04 is much more evolved. The new Montepulciano d'Abruzzo Colline Teramane Vizzarro '03 has stylish balsam aromas and a dynamic, savoury palate with a slightly bitterish finish from the aggressive tannins. The Poggio Varano '04 impressed with its pleasantly rustic, intensely fruity nose and juicy flavour with lovely acidity supporting the palate.

ANNUAL PRODUCTION 250,000 bottles
HECTARES UNDER VINE 27
VITICULTURE METHOD Conventional

In this edition of the Guide, Luigi Cataldi Madonna confirms last year's winning brace: two Three Glasses, four out of six wines in the national final, and the other two earning Two Glasses. That this grower-philosopher continues to reap success is due to a number of factors: the magnificent, challenging uplands of Ofena and Capestrano, the ancient traditions of a historic winery and Luigi's own character, as a man of culture and an extraordinary wine enthusiast. All this produces wines that are both traditional and modern in style. Perhaps the biggest surprise was the excellent Pecorino '05 – mistakenly included in the Guide last year instead of the '04 actually tasted – an astonishingly generous, tangy and minerally white that does full justice to the variety. The Montepulciano d'Abruzzo Tonì '04 has strikingly rich, complex, smoky aromas and a stylish, juicy palate. The Malandrino '05 has a subtle nose, lightly veiled by oak, with a full, richly extracted palate. The Piè delle Vigne '05 is quite simply the region's best rosé – complex, austere and minerally. The Trebbiano '06 is a little gem of simplicity and fragrance, as is the standard-label Montepulciano '05.

● Montepulciano d'Abruzzo Poggio Varano '04	🍷🍷 4
● Controguerra Rosso Villa Torri '03	🍷 4
● Montepulciano d'Abruzzo '05	🍷 3*
● Montepulciano d'Abruzzo Colline Teramane Vizzarro '03	🍷 5
● Montepulciano d'Abruzzo V. Le Coste '04	🍷 4
● Montepulciano d'Abruzzo '03	🍷🍷 3*
● Montepulciano d'Abruzzo Poggio Varano '03	🍷🍷 4
● Montepulciano d'Abruzzo V. Le Coste '03	🍷🍷 4
● Montepulciano d'Abruzzo Poggio Varano '01	🍷🍷 4

● Montepulciano d'Abruzzo Tonì '04	🍷🍷🍷 6
○ Pecorino '05	🍷🍷🍷 6
⊙ Montepulciano d'Abruzzo Cerasuolo Piè delle Vigne '05	🍷🍷 5
● Montepulciano d'Abruzzo Malandrino '05	🍷🍷 5
● Montepulciano d'Abruzzo '05	🍷🍷 4*
○ Trebbiano d'Abruzzo '06	🍷🍷 3*
● Montepulciano d'Abruzzo Malandrino '03	🍷🍷🍷 5
● Montepulciano d'Abruzzo Malandrino '04	🍷🍷🍷 5*
● Montepulciano d'Abruzzo Tonì '03	🍷🍷🍷 6
⊙ Montepulciano d'Abruzzo Cerasuolo Piè delle Vigne '04	🍷🍷 4*
○ Pecorino '04	🍷🍷 6
○ Trebbiano d'Abruzzo '05	🍷🍷 3*

Centorame

LOC. CASOLI DI ATRI
VIA DELLE FORNACI, 15
64030 ATRI [TE]
TEL. 0858709115
www.centorame.it

ANNUAL PRODUCTION 50,000 bottles
HECTARES UNDER VINE 7
VITICULTURE METHOD Conventional

Continuing its positive trend, this lovely Teramo winery has found for itself a prestigious role in the area in just a few years, thanks to the industrious Lamberto Vannucci and the absolute quality of his wines. Since our very first tastings, we have greatly appreciated these wines over the years for their strong focus on provenance, balanced handling of oak and importance of texture. The same applies this year. The '05 version of the ambitious Colline Teramane Castellum Vetus made it to the national finals again, thanks to its typical, healthy aromas, concentrated, full-bodied palate and rich, subtle texture. The less complicated San Michele '05 is a juicy, varietal Montepulciano with impressively stylish, concentrated aromas and an agreeably tangy palate. From the whites, we'd like to mention the fragrant, well-typed Trebbiano d'Abruzzo San Michele, with its fresh, flavoursome palate. Closing the range is the excellent Trebbiano d'Abruzzo Castellum Vetus, with outstanding weight and richly extracted texture. It's a pity about the excessive wood that slightly masks the nose but this may be just a youthful flaw.

● Montepulciano d'Abruzzo Colline Teramane Castellum Vetus '05	🍷🍷 5
● Montepulciano d'Abruzzo San Michele '05	🍷🍷 3*
○ Trebbiano d'Abruzzo Castellum Vetus '05	🍷 4
○ Trebbiano d'Abruzzo San Michele '06	🍷 3
● Montepulciano d'Abruzzo Colline Teramane Castellum Vetus '03	🍷🍷 5
○ Trebbiano d'Abruzzo Castellum Vetus '04	🍷🍷 4
● Montepulciano d'Abruzzo Colline Teramane Castellum Vetus '04	🍷🍷 5
● Montepulciano d'Abruzzo San Michele '03	🍷🍷 5
● Montepulciano d'Abruzzo San Michele '04	🍷🍷 3*

Cerulli Irelli Spinozzi

LOC. CASALE 26
S.S. 150 DEL VOMANO KM 17,600
64020 CANZANO [TE]
TEL. 086157193
www.cerullispinozzi.it

ANNUAL PRODUCTION 130,000 bottles
HECTARES UNDER VINE 60
VITICULTURE METHOD Certified organic

The Cerulli Irelli Spinozzi winery, passionately managed by the enthusiastic Enrico Cerulli Irelli, makes its debut in this year's Guide with four wines. We were most impressed by the simpler wines, which are varietal and enjoyable, while we believe the more exclusive wines require further fine-tuning. The Montepulciano d'Abruzzo '05 is true to type and fragrant with fruity, secondary aromas and a savoury, full-bodied and reasonably concentrated palate. The Cortalto '06 is a fresh, agreeable expression of the currently fashionable and greatly appreciated pecorino grape, showing forward citrus aromas on the nose and a varietally bitterish aftertaste. The Ambitious Torre Migliori '04 is a Montepulciano with intense, enfolding aromas but the palate is slightly diluted by the hint of alcohol. The Montepulciano Cerasuolo '06 is a coherent, varietal rosé that shows soft and enchanting.

○ Cortalto '06	🍷🍷 3*
● Montepulciano d'Abruzzo '05	🍷🍷 4*
● Montepulciano d'Abruzzo Colline Teramane Torre Migliori '04	🍷 5
⊙ Montepulciano d'Abruzzo Cerasuolo '06	🍷 3

Chiarieri

VIA SANT'ANGELO, 20
65019 PIANELLA [PE]
TEL. 085971365
www.chiarieri.com

ANNUAL PRODUCTION 180,000 bottles
HECTARES UNDER VINE 35
VITICULTURE METHOD Conventional

We like this Pianella winery, which is run with a sure hand by father and son team Giovanni and Ciriaco Chiarieri, and we like their wines, too, which come from a noble rural heritage. The reds are traditional with a very personal style. The 2003 Hannibal, a Montepulciano with a seriously ambitious name, impressed us with its nicely varietal, concentrated aromas and coherent flavour, although the palate is also a shade too forward and slightly weighed down by a rather too bitterish finish. The new Invidia '06, another Montepulciano d'Abruzzo, is a gutsy red with no-nonsense, varietal aromas that pave the way for a savoury, dynamic palate.

Citra

C.DA CUCULLO
66026 ORTONA [CH]
TEL. 0859031342
www.citra.it

ANNUAL PRODUCTION 18,000,000 bottles
HECTARES UNDER VINE 8000
VITICULTURE METHOD Conventional

A huge number of grape-supplying members, an impressive array of wines, hectare upon hectare of vineyards, a mind-boggling total of bottles released, widespread market presence – these are the ingredients in Citra's winning recipe. We were sent plenty of wines to taste so let's take a look at the ones we found most impressive. The first of these was the Caroso '04, an ambitious Montepulciano with substantial texture, rich aromas and a confident, still slightly tannic palate. The Montepulciano d'Abruzzo Palio '05, an old acquaintance of the Guide, is an interestingly priced red with subtle, pervasive aromas and a savoury, richly extracted palate. Laus Vitae '02 is another big, ambitious Montepulciano with fruity, complex aromas and a full, stylish – if still a little tight – palate, which we tasted and gave good marks to last year. The well-typed, uncomplicated Montepulciano '06, has subtle, varietal aromas and a savoury, juicy palate. Turning to the whites, the Sistina line Pecorino '06 is fresh-tasting, tangy and crisp while the Trebbiano d'Abruzzo '06 is a clean, uncomplicated expression of the grape.

● Montepulciano d'Abruzzo Hannibal '03		♥♥ 5
● Montepulciano d'Abruzzo Invidia '06		♥ 3
● Montepulciano d'Abruzzo Hannibal '97		♀♀ 4
● Montepulciano d'Abruzzo Granaro '04		♀♀ 3*
● Montepulciano d'Abruzzo Hannibal '01		♀♀ 5
● Montepulciano d'Abruzzo Hannibal '99		♀♀ 5
● Montepulciano d'Abruzzo Hannibal '02		♀♀ 5

● Montepulciano d'Abruzzo Caroso '04		♥♥ 5
● Montepulciano d'Abruzzo Citra '06	♥♥ 2*
● Montepulciano d'Abruzzo Palio '05	♥♥ 4*
● Montepulciano d'Abruzzo Sistina '05		♀ 4
O Pecorino Sistina '06		♀ 4
O Trebbiano d'Abruzzo Palio '06		♀ 3
O Trebbiano d'Abruzzo Sistina '06		♀ 4
● Montepulciano d'Abruzzo Palio '03	♀♀ 3*
● Montepulciano d'Abruzzo Palio '04	♀♀ 3*

Contesa

C.DA CAPARRONE, 65
65010 COLLECORVINO [PE]
TEL. 0858205078
www.contesa.it

ANNUAL PRODUCTION 150,000 bottles
HECTARES UNDER VINE 25
VITICULTURE METHOD Conventional

Contesa, meaning dispute, the name of this winery near Pesacara, is indicative of the determination that went into its creation. Now that the cellar is finally completed, owner and winemaker Rocco Pasetti has presented us with the first wines to undergo the entire vinification process here and the results speak for themselves. The Montepulciano d'Abruzzo '03 has seductive, stylish aromas, with hints of fruit and light sweet oak sensations. The palate is subtle, juicy and agreeably tangy. Vigna Corvino '05 is a fragrant, uncomplicated Montepulciano with clearly defined varietal aromas and a winningly typical, appealing palate. The ambitious red Lady P. '06, from montepulciano with about one third sangiovese, is a modern, mouthfilling wine that also offers minerality and savouriness wine. Turning to the whites, we were very impressed with the Trebbiano '04 we had already tasted last year. It combines subtle citrus aromas and a confident, typical flavour. The Pecorino '06, an exemplary interpretation of the grape, is one of the most popular in the region with an outstandingly delectable palate.

De Angelis Corvi

C.DA PIGNOTTO
64010 CONTROGUERRA [TE]
TEL. 086189475
www.deangeliscorvi.it

ANNUAL PRODUCTION 30,000 bottles
HECTARES UNDER VINE 9
VITICULTURE METHOD Certified organic

This emerging Controguerra-based winery, situated in the heart of the Teramo hills, is a very pleasant surprise. Love for the local area takes the form here of organic winegrowing, traditional vinification methods and scrupulous interpretation of traditional Abruzzo varieties and these are the elements that produced the impressive series of wines we tasted. The Montepulciano d'Abruzzo '05 breezed through to the finals. A fragrant, coherent red with seductively subtle and varietal aromas, it follows this with a full-bodied, dynamic palate of style lengthened by delicious acidity. Also very good is the Fonte Raviliano, the winery's second Montepulciano. This '05 version is clearly defined and stylish on the nose with a strikingly crisp and coherent palate. The Montepulciano Cerasuolo '06 is also impressive, with an attractively complex structure on the palate culminating in a nice hint of liquorice.

● Montepulciano d'Abruzzo '03	♟♟ 5
○ Pecorino '06	♟♟ 4
○ Trebbiano d'Abruzzo '04	♟♟ 4
● Lady P. '06	♟ 4
● Montepulciano d'Abruzzo V. Corvino '05	♟ 3

● Montepulciano d'Abruzzo '05	♟♟ 4*
● Montepulciano d'Abruzzo Fonte Raviliano '05	♟♟ 3*
⊙ Montepulciano d'Abruzzo Cerasuolo '06	♟ 3

Farnese

LOC. CASTELLO CALDORA
VIA DEI BASTIONI
66026 ORTONA [CH]
TEL. 0859067388
www.farnese-vini.com

ANNUAL PRODUCTION 11,000,000 bottles
HECTARES UNDER VINE 180
VITICULTURE METHOD Conventional

This year, Farnese and Caldora, which are part of the same group, presented a broad range of wines. Numbers at Farnese are particularly impressive for the winery makes millions of bottles with widespread distribution on Italian and non-domestic markets. In consequence, the winemaking style caters for the tastes of consumers worldwide. Let's review the best of these wines. The Montepulciano Farnese '06 has good fruity aromas and a savoury, weighty palate while the well-known Montepulciano d'Abruzzo Colline Teramane '04 is a well-made, coherent red. The ambitious Montepulciano d'Abruzzo Colline Teramane Opi Riserva '04 is well-defined and pervasive on the nose with a nice savouriness on the dense palate. Yume '04, from the Caldora line and obtained from montepulciano grapes, is close-knit, vigorous, rich and mature with well-gauged oak. From the whites, we liked the modern, opulently rich Chardonnay Opi '06. The sensations of banana and oak are slightly predictable but the texture concentrated and the length good. The Chardonnay '06 from the Caldora line is agreeably fruity and fragrant.

Cantina Frentana

VIA PERAZZA, 32
66020 ROCCA SAN GIOVANNI [CH]
TEL. 087260152
www.cantinafrentana.it

ANNUAL PRODUCTION 400,000 bottles
HECTARES UNDER VINE N.A.
VITICULTURE METHOD Conventional

Frenta is an attractive feature of Chieti's varied co-operative panorama and has been pursuing quality for several years, and with increasing confidence. The wines are interesting and often seriously good, as well as excellent value for money. The feather in the winery's cap is still Panarda, a substantial, generous Montepulciano d'Abruzzo just like the traditional banquet after which it is named. The '04 vintage has lovely toasty, pervasive aromas and a savoury, tannic flavour although it is slightly marred by the light veiling of bitterness in the finish. The simpler Montepulciano d'Abruzzo Frentano '06 is remarkably well typed and enjoyable with a seamless, savoury flavour. Rubesto '05, another Montepulciano d'Abruzzo, is an ambitious red with concentrated aromas and evolved, slightly fuzzy texture. Turning to the whites, the Trebbiano d'Abruzzo '06 deserves a mention for its fresh, attractive varietal aromas and nice gutsy palate, beautifully supported by good acidity. We thought they were much better than the more ambitious, expensive whites, some from exotic grape varieties.

- Montepulciano d'Abruzzo Farnese '06 ¶¶ 3*
- Montepulciano d'Abruzzo Colline Teramane Opi Ris. '04 ¶¶ 6
- Montepulciano d'Abruzzo Yume Caldora '04 ¶¶ 4
- Montepulciano d'Abruzzo Colline Teramane '04 ¶¶ 5
- O Chardonnay Opi '06 ¶ 5
- O Chardonnay Caldora '06 ¶ 3*
- Sangiovese Caldora '06 ¶ 3*
- Montepulciano d'Abruzzo Colle dei Venti Caldora '05 ¶ 3
- Montepulciano d'Abruzzo Caldora '06 ¶ 3
- Edizione 5 Autoctoni '03 ¶¶ 6
- Montepulciano d'Abruzzo Opi Ris. '03 ¶¶ 6
- Montepulciano d'Abruzzo Casale Vecchio '05 ¶¶ 4*
- Montepulciano d'Abruzzo Colline Teramane '03 ¶¶ 5

- Montepulciano d'Abruzzo Panarda '04 ¶¶ 4
- Montepulciano d'Abruzzo Frentano '06 ¶ 1*
- O Trebbiano d'Abruzzo Frentano '06 ¶ 1*
- O Trebbiano d'Abruzzo '06 ¶ 1*
- Montepulciano d'Abruzzo Rubesto '05 ¶ 3
- Montepulciano d'Abruzzo Panarda '01 ¶¶ 4
- Montepulciano d'Abruzzo Panarda '03 ¶¶ 4

Dino Illuminati

C.DA SAN BIAGIO, 18
64010 CONTROGUERRA [TE]
TEL. 0861808008
www.illuminativini.it

ANNUAL PRODUCTION 1,200,000 bottles
HECTARES UNDER VINE 120
VITICULTURE METHOD Conventional

These are important years for Illuminati. The younger generations are working with increasing dedication alongside Cavaliere Dino, now over 70 but young in spirit and passion. The winery produces seriously ambitious, land-rooted wines like Zanna, a traditional Montepulciano d'Abruzzo Colline Teramane Riserva we like very much. The '03 earned Three Glasses, just like the '01, thanks to typical, concentrated aromas and a stylish, full-bodied, subtly rustic palate. The Pieluni '03, another Montepulciano d'Abruzzo Colline Teramane, sailed through to the final thanks to its more contemporary aromatics, stylish, pervasive hints of balsam and a full-bodied, potent palate. The Montepulciano Riparosso swept all before it. It's exactly what it sets out to be: a clean, crisply defined red with an appealing, rich, fresh-tasting palate. The new Ilico '05 has an impressively fruity, pervasive nose and a tangy, close-knit palate. The Brut '04 is a rather nice citrus-laced sparkling wine with a winning flavour. Turning to the whites, the simple Controguerra Costalupo 2006 is clean and coherent but by no means dull.

★ Masciarelli

VIA GAMBERALE, 1
66010 SAN MARTINO
SULLA MARRUCINA [CH]
TEL. 087185241
www.masciarelli.it

ANNUAL PRODUCTION 1,200,000 bottles
HECTARES UNDER VINE 195
VITICULTURE METHOD Conventional

It is some time since Gianni Masciarelli and Marina Cvetic opened a small winery beneath the Majella, where they produce wines that made Italian winemaking history. But this couple are devoted wine entrepreneurs with increasingly varied interests ranging from distribution of leading quality wines to the creation of new wineries in the region. The range they presented was extensive and the results were remarkable, with seven wines in the final and two Three Glasses. Let's begin with the latest wine, the Trebbiano Castello di Semivicoli '05, a great white aged in stainless steel. It impressed with its complex, varietal aromas and minerality preceding a very appealing palate, despite the considerable structure. Villa Gemma '04 is a worthy heir to the noble line of Montepulcianos. Richly extracted with lovely smoky aromas, it proffers a rounded, juicy palate lifted by generous but fairly well-balanced oak. The Iskra '04, from the vineyards in the Teramo area, is a well-typed, consistent Montepulciano with a palate that stays fresh despite the structure. If anything, it is perhaps just a little youthful. Next come the ambitious wines from the Marina Cvetic line: Montepulciano, Chardonnay, Trebbiano and Cabernet, and the stunning Cerasuolo Villa Gemma '06.

● Montepulciano d'Abruzzo Colline Teramane Zanna Ris. '03	🍷🍷🍷 6
● Montepulciano d'Abruzzo Colline Teramane Pieluni Ris. '03	🍷🍷 7
○ Illuminati Brut '04	🍷🍷 5
● Montepulciano d'Abruzzo Ilico '05	🍷🍷 4*
● Montepulciano d'Abruzzo Riparosso '06	🍷🍷 3*
○ Controguerra Bianco Costalupo '06	🍷 2*
○ Controguerra Bianco Pligia '06	🍷 3
● Controguerra Rosso Lumen '97	🍷🍷🍷 6
● Montepulciano d'Abruzzo Colline Teramane Zanna Ris. '01	🍷🍷🍷 5
● Montepulciano d'Abruzzo Colline Teramane Pieluni Ris. '00	🍷🍷🍷 7
● Montepulciano d'Abruzzo Colline Teramane Pieluni Ris. '01	🍷🍷🍷 7
● Controguerra Rosso Lumen '01	🍷🍷 6
● Controguerra Rosso Lumen '03	🍷🍷 6

● Montepulciano d'Abruzzo Villa Gemma '04	🍷🍷🍷 8
○ Trebbiano d'Abruzzo Castello di Semivicoli '05	🍷🍷🍷 6
● Cabernet Sauvignon Marina Cvetic '03	🍷🍷 8
● Montepulciano d'Abruzzo Marina Cvetic '04	🍷🍷 5*
⊙ Montepulciano d'Abruzzo Cerasuolo Villa Gemma '06	🍷🍷 4*
○ Chardonnay Marina Cvetic '05	🍷🍷 6
○ Trebbiano d'Abruzzo Marina Cvetic '05	🍷🍷 6
● Iskra '04	🍷🍷 5
● Montepulciano d'Abruzzo '05	🍷🍷 3*
● Montepulciano d'Abruzzo Marina Cvetic '03	🍷🍷🍷 5*
● Montepulciano d'Abruzzo Villa Gemma '00	🍷🍷🍷 8
● Montepulciano d'Abruzzo Villa Gemma '03	🍷🍷🍷 8
● Montepulciano d'Abruzzo Villa Gemma '97	🍷🍷🍷 6
● Montepulciano d'Abruzzo Villa Gemma '99	🍷🍷🍷 8
● Montepulciano d'Abruzzo Villa Gemma '98	🍷🍷🍷 7
● Montepulciano d'Abruzzo Villa Gemma '95	🍷🍷🍷 6
● Montepulciano d'Abruzzo Villa Gemma '01	🍷🍷🍷 8

Antonio e Elio Monti
VIA PIGNOTTO, 62
64010 CONTROGUERRA [TE]
TEL. 086189042
www.vinimonti.it

Bruno Nicodemi
C.DA VENIGLIO
64024 NOTARESCO [TE]
TEL. 085895493
www.nicodemi.com

ANNUAL PRODUCTION 80,000 bottles
HECTARES UNDER VINE 12
VITICULTURE METHOD Conventional

ANNUAL PRODUCTION 200,000 bottles
HECTARES UNDER VINE 30
VITICULTURE METHOD Certified organic

We applauded a wonderful performance at the tastings by the wines from Antonio and Elio Monti, a traditional winery located on one of the sunniest and most favourably positioned slopes at Controguerra. Yet again they come close to Three Glasses with Pignotto, a Montepulciano d'Abruzzo Colline Teramane, whose potent varietal aromas impressed us greatly. The subtle, juicy palate has marvellously sound texture and this really is a thoroughbred of a wine. But we were impressed by the whole range, from the solidly traditional Montepulciano d'Abruzzo Senior with its lovely roasted coffee aromas and vibrant flavour, to the more contemporary Voluptas, slightly masked by oak but with astonishing texture. And lastly to the Controguerra Rio Moro Riserva '05, from merlot, cabernet and sangiovese grapes aged in small oak barrels. An unabashedly international blend with concentrated, very modern aromas, it reveals a lovely tangy note on the palate. It's a pity about the slightly bitter, over-tannic finish.

We were saying last year how passionately the Nicodemis were setting about their work. Today, the results are there for all to see because the Montepulciano d'Abruzzo Colline Teramane Neromoro Riserva '03 won Three Glasses, the tenth Abruzzo wine to scale the heights at our national taste-offs this year. This extreme Montepulciano comes from the old pergola-trained vineyards next to the beautiful winery at Notaresco. Extraordinary concentration, smoky aromas, substantial but well-judged oak and generously powerful texture with plenty of extract. We were less impressed by the wines from the ambitious Notari line. Despite their seriously rich texture, they still don't seem focused. As usual, though, the standard-label wines are excellent. The fragrant, well-typed Montepulciano '05 is only slightly veiled by oakiness and the Trebbiano '06 flaunts stylish minerally aromas and a tangy, appealing palate.

- Montepulciano d'Abruzzo Colline Teramane Pignotto Ris. '04 — ♀♀ 5
- Montepulciano d'Abruzzo Senior '04 — ♀♀ 4
- Montepulciano d'Abruzzo Voluptas '06 — ♀♀ 3*
- Controguerra Rosso Rio Moro Ris. '05 — ♀ 5
- Montepulciano d'Abruzzo Colline Teramane Pignotto Ris. '03 — ♀♀ 5
- Montepulciano d'Abruzzo Senior '03 — ♀♀ 4*
- Montepulciano d'Abruzzo Colline Teramane Pignotto '03 — ♀♀ 6

- Montepulciano d'Abruzzo Colline Teramane Neromoro Ris. '03 — ♀♀♀ 6
- Montepulciano d'Abruzzo '05 — ♀♀ 4*
- Trebbiano d'Abruzzo '06 — ♀♀ 3*
- Montepulciano d'Abruzzo Colline Teramane Notari '04 — ♀ 5
- Trebbiano d'Abruzzo Notàri '06 — ♀ 4
- Montepulciano d'Abruzzo Colline Teramane Ris. '00 — ♀♀ 5
- Montepulciano d'Abruzzo '03 — ♀♀ 4*
- Montepulciano d'Abruzzo Colline Teramane Neromoro Ris. '02 — ♀♀ 5
- Trebbiano d'Abruzzo '05 — ♀♀ 3*
- Trebbiano d'Abruzzo Notàri '05 — ♀♀ 4
- Montepulciano d'Abruzzo '04 — ♀♀ 4*

Orlandi Contucci Ponno

LOC. PIANA DEGLI ULIVI, 1
64026 ROSETO DEGLI ABRUZZI [TE]
TEL. 0858944049
www.orlandicontucci.com

ANNUAL PRODUCTION 180,000 bottles
HECTARES UNDER VINE 31
VITICULTURE METHOD Conventional

This lovely Roseto winery was one of the first to join the revival in the 1990s. Its wines are ambitious, often international in style, but almost always nicely put-together. Sometimes they have impressed us mightily, and on other occasions not so much, but we think the range presented for this edition of the Guide is the most interesting of recent years. The best of the crop is Colle Funaro '04, a red from cabernet, with distinctively fragrant varietal aromas, just slightly obscured by woody notes, and a fresh, savoury, beautifully lingering palate. The Montepulciano d'Abruzzo Colline Teramane Riserva '04, after an excellent growing year, is very enjoyable, as are the other wines made from international grape varieties, especially the Ghiaiolo, a subtle Sauvignon, and the Roccesco, made from chardonnay grapes. Lastly, the Liburnio, is one of the winery's most famous reds, made from cabernet sauvignon grapes with small proportions of sangiovese and malbec.

Franco Pasetti

LOC. C.DA PRETARO
VIA SAN PAOLO, 21
66023 FRANCAVILLA AL MARE [CH]
TEL. 08561875
www.pasettivini.it

ANNUAL PRODUCTION 420,000 bottles
HECTARES UNDER VINE 40
VITICULTURE METHOD Conventional

Last year, we predicted that big results were not far off for this lovely winery at Francavilla al Mare, thanks to the hard work of life and business partners Franco and Mimma Pasetti. And we were right. Harimann '02, the most prestigious Montepulciano d'Abruzzo, got through to the final, although all the wines presented this year are particularly high in quality. But to return to that characterful red, obtained from an unusually late harvest. The '02 version is incredibly focused and savoury with substantial but beautifully handled texture. The basic Montepulciano is only apparently a simple red: it has a forward fruity note and a savoury, richly extracted palate. The '03 version of Tenuta di Testarossa, a traditional-style Montepulciano, is weighty and dense with good texture slightly masked by the oak but stylish toasted coffee aromas. The Pecorino '06 stands out from the other whites for its well-typed, distinctly minerally aromas and a flavour profile nicely supported by acidity.

● Cabernet Sauvignon	
Colle Funaro '04	♟♟ 5
● Liburnio '04	♟ 6
● Montepulciano d'Abruzzo Colline	
Teramane Ris. '04	♟ 6
○ Chardonnay Roccesco '05	♟ 4
○ Sauvignon Ghiaiolo '06	♟ 4
● Liburnio '99	♟♟ 7
● Cabernet Sauvignon	
Colle Funaro '03	♟♟ 5
● Montepulciano d'Abruzzo Colline	
Teramane Ris. '98	♟♟ 6
● Liburnio '97	♟♟ 7
● Montepulciano d'Abruzzo	
La Regia Specula '00	♟♟ 4
● Liburnio '98	♟♟ 7

● Montepulciano d'Abruzzo Harimann '02	♟♟ 7
● Montepulciano d'Abruzzo	
Fattoria Pasetti '05	♟♟ 4*
● Montepulciano d'Abruzzo	
Tenuta di Testarossa '03	♟♟ 5
○ Pecorino Pasetti '06	♟♟ 4
● Montepulciano d'Abruzzo Harimann '00	♟♟ 7
● Montepulciano d'Abruzzo	
Fattoria Pasetti '04	♟♟ 4*
● Montepulciano d'Abruzzo	
Tenuta di Testarossa '99	♟♟ 5
● Montepulciano d'Abruzzo	
Tenuta di Testarossa '02	♟♟ 5
● Montepulciano d'Abruzzo	
Tenuta di Testarossa '01	♟♟ 5
● Montepulciano d'Abruzzo Harimann '01	♟♟ 7
● Montepulciano d'Abruzzo	
Tenuta di Testarossa '00	♟♟ 5

Emidio Pepe

LOC. TORANO NUOVO
VIA CHIESI, 10
64010 TERAMO [TE]
TEL. 0861856493
www.emidiopepe.com

ANNUAL PRODUCTION 70,000 bottles
HECTARES UNDER VINE 12
VITICULTURE METHOD Certified organic

Most people either love or hate Emidio
Pepe's wines. Whatever your opinion, these
are bottles that deserve respect for their
contribution to Abruzzo's winemaking
history. That said, we did not send the
Trebbiano '01 and the Montepulciano '03 to
the national finals out of mere respect: they
genuinely impressed us. For many years,
the beautiful cellar at Torano Nuova in the
Teramo area has been turning out highly
distinctive wines that are often over-
assertive to the point of aggression but
reflect scrupulous if perhaps extreme
choices. In more recent years, they have
surprised us by acquiring more grace, while
remaining undeniably rustic, and we like to
attribute this to the arrival of a new
generation on the winery team in the person
of Sofia Pepe. The Montepulciano '03
impressed us with vibrant aromas that start
out fruity but then shade into minerality and
smokiness. The palate unbends well with
roughish tannins but a sweet, juicy finish.
The classic Trebbiano d'Abruzzo '01 has
stylish floral aromas and an impressively
continuous array of sensations on the
palate, from elderflower to star anise.

● Montepulciano d'Abruzzo '03	🍷🍷	5
○ Trebbiano d'Abruzzo '01	🍷🍷	6
● Montepulciano d'Abruzzo '04	🍷🍷	5
● Montepulciano d'Abruzzo Colline Teramane '03	🍷🍷	7
● Montepulciano d'Abruzzo '01	🍷🍷	6
○ Trebbiano d'Abruzzo '02	🍷🍷	5

La Quercia

C.DA COLLE CROCE
64020 MORRO D'ORO [TE]
TEL. 0858959110
www.vinilaquercia.it

ANNUAL PRODUCTION 100,000 bottles
HECTARES UNDER VINE 12.5
VITICULTURE METHOD Certified organic

After the sparks of last year, this winery
confirmed its status as an emerging
presence in the Colline Teramane. We like
these authentic, typical wines with their
distinctively effective, rural style. Scrupulous
vineyard selection, large oak only, traditional
grape varieties and a good dose of passion
are the key features. The most prestigious
wine in the fairly limited range is the
Montepulciano d'Abruzzo Colline Teramane
Primamadre '04, which breezed through to
the national finals thanks to its subtle,
crisply defined aromas, appealing flavour,
rounded, powerful body and acidity that will
enable it to evolve further for some time. All
in all, it's a lovely relaxed and enjoyable red,
despite the substantial body. The basic
Montepulciano d'Abruzzo '04 is a sturdy yet
subtle red with good austere, concentrated
aromas and a savoury, lingering palate. The
Trebbiano d'Abruzzo '06 is a clean,
uncomplicated white but far from
uninteresting. It intrigues with a fresh palate
and some perhaps excessively rustic notes
on the nose. The new Pecorino '06, on the
other hand, is a simpler and more
approachable proposition, indifferent to the
trends that threaten to alter the
characteristics of the wine type.

● Montepulciano d'Abruzzo Colline Teramane Priamadre '04	🍷🍷	5
● Montepulciano d'Abruzzo '04	🍷🍷	4 *
○ Santapupa Pecorino '06	🍷	4
○ Trebbiano d'Abruzzo '06	🍷	3
● Montepulciano d'Abruzzo Colline Teramane La Quercia Ris. '02	🍷🍷	5
● Montepulciano d'Abruzzo '03	🍷🍷	4 *

San Lorenzo
C.DA PLAVIGNANO, 2
64035 CASTILENTI [TE]
TEL. 0861999325
www.sanlorenzovini.com

Terra d'Aligi
LOC. PIAZZANO
VIA PIANA LA FARA, 90
66041 ATESSA [CH]
TEL. 0872897916
www.terradaligi.it

ANNUAL PRODUCTION N.A.
HECTARES UNDER VINE 150
VITICULTURE METHOD Conventional

This is quite a famous winery, situated on the border of the provinces of Teramo and Pescara, and run with aplomb by Gianluca Galasso, who is meticulous about every detail. So we are sorry that the range of wines did not shine at the tasting this year as we had hoped. There were plenty of wines on show, from the simpler Trebbianos to the weightier reds. The most impressive of all was Escol Riserva '04, a full-bodied, ambitious Montepulciano with vibrant black cherry and oak aromas. The palate is rounded and well-typed, showing lovely texture just slightly covered by tannins from the oak barrels. The Colline Teramane Oinos '04 is almost impenetrable in hue, throwing fruit and vanilla aromas and a dense, richly extracted palate with lively, slightly excessive, acidity that has yet to integrate. Montepulciano Antares '04 is simpler but with enfolding minerally aromas and a richly extracted, mouthfilling savouriness. Outstanding among the whites are the well-typed, varietal Trebbiano d'Abruzzo Sirio '06, which has quite an enjoyably soft palate, and the fresh, fragrantly juicy Chardonnay Chioma di Berenice '06.

ANNUAL PRODUCTION 535,000 bottles
HECTARES UNDER VINE 50
VITICULTURE METHOD Conventional

Situated in the Frentano hills in the province of Chieti, Terra d'Aligi is run with dynamic energy by the Spinelli brothers. Every year, it turns out enjoyable, well-made and occasionally ambitious wines so it was no surprise to receive a good quality range this time. Let's begin with the mouthfilling Montepulciano d'Abruzzo Tolos '04, which got as far as Two Glasses this year. It has a nice intense ruby red colour, aromas initially obscured by the new oak but then more concentrated and varietal, and substantial, juicy texture on the palate, although the finish is slightly bitterish. The Montepulciano d'Abruzzo '04 Tatone is a subtle, stylish red with slightly over-evolved aromas and a rounded palate perked up by nice fresh acidity. The basic Montepulciano d'Abruzzo is also evolved on the nose and slightly tight on the appealingly savoury palate. From the whites, the Trebbiano d'Abruzzo '06 has a strikingly fresh, well-typed palate and the Pecorino '06 is fragrant, varietal and unpretentious.

● Montepulciano d'Abruzzo Antares '04	🍷🍷 3*
● Montepulciano d'Abruzzo Colline Teramane Escol Ris. '04	🍷🍷 5
O Chardonnay Chioma di Berenice '06	🍷 4
O Trebbiano d'Abruzzo Sirio '06	🍷 2*
● Montepulciano d'Abruzzo Colline Teramane '04	🍷 5
● Montepulciano d'Abruzzo Colline Teramane '03	🍷🍷 5
● Montepulciano d'Abruzzo Colline Teramane Escol Ris. '01	🍷🍷 6
● Montepulciano d'Abruzzo Colline Teramane Escol Ris. '02	🍷🍷 5
● Montepulciano d'Abruzzo Colline Teramane Escol Ris. '03	🍷🍷 5

● Montepulciano d'Abruzzo Tatone '04	🍷🍷 4
● Montepulciano d'Abruzzo Tolos '04	🍷🍷 6
● Montepulciano d'Abruzzo '05	🍷 3
O Pecorino '06	🍷 3
O Trebbiano d'Abruzzo Terra d'Aligi '06	🍷 3
● Montepulciano d'Abruzzo Tolos '01	🍷🍷 5
● Montepulciano d'Abruzzo Tolos '03	🍷🍷 5
● Montepulciano d'Abruzzo '04	🍷🍷 3*
● Montepulciano d'Abruzzo Tatone '00	🍷🍷 4
● Montepulciano d'Abruzzo Tolos '00	🍷🍷 5
● Montepulciano d'Abruzzo Tatone '01	🍷🍷 4
● Montepulciano d'Abruzzo Tolos '02	🍷🍷 4

Tiberio
C.DA LA VOTA
65020 CUGNOLI [PE]
TEL. 0858576744
www.tiberio.it

ANNUAL PRODUCTION 70,000 bottles
HECTARES UNDER VINE 27
VITICULTURE METHOD Conventional

This winery has begun an interesting project to make fine-quality wine in the hills of the province of Pescara. The wines we tasted were in fact very impressive, presenting modern, clean and well defined but bearing the clear stamp of tradition and respect for the local area. The ambitious Althea '05 is an impressive Montepulciano that unveils subtle, stylish aromas and well-judged oak before the rounded, nicely tannic palate shows still slightly clenched after too little time in bottle. The fragrant Montepulciano d'Abruzzo '06 is a mouthfilling, richly extracted red with a generous, juicy palate. Trebbiano d'Abruzzo '06 is an interesting interpretation of the variety with typical, coherent aromas and a very drinkable fresh, tangy palate. The Pecorino '06 is an appealingly well-made white that may not be very varietal but is still very well defined and moreishly drinkable.

Cantina Tollo
VIA GARIBALDI, 68
66010 TOLLO [CH]
TEL. 087196251
www.cantinatollo.it

ANNUAL PRODUCTION 12,000,000 bottles
HECTARES UNDER VINE 3,500
VITICULTURE METHOD Conventional

Again this year, the Cantina at Tollo showed that it is an influential co-operative on the Abruzzo wine scene. This time, the range of wines presented was genuinely outstanding and we were impressed by the high overall quality. The most striking wine was the classic Cagiòlo '04, one of the best known Montepulciano d'Abruzzos in the region. Its stylish, concentrated nose has a lovely, distinctive note of balsam and a dense, opulent palate. Next were the excellent, traditional Trebbiano and Montepulciano from the Aldiano line. These are extraordinarily well-typed wines and excellent value for money. The Pecorino '06 has always been one of the most varietal in the region while the impressive, delicious Passito '04, made from moscato grapes, is rustic and aromatic. The wines of the Colle Secco line deserve a special mention. Production numbers are very impressive and prices very affordable but the wines themselves are also well made and disarmingly enjoyable.

● Montepulciano d'Abruzzo '06	▼▼ 3*
○ Trebbiano d'Abruzzo '06	▼▼ 3*
● Montepulciano d'Abruzzo Althea '05	▼▼ 5
○ Pecorino '06	▼ 4

● Montepulciano d'Abruzzo Cagiòlo '04	▼ 5
● Montepulciano d'Abruzzo Aldiano '05	▼▼ 4*
○ Trebbiano d'Abruzzo Aldiano '06	▼▼ 4*
● Montepulciano d'Abruzzo Colle Secco '04	▼ 3
○ Trebbiano d'Abruzzo Menir '05	▼ 5
○ Trebbiano d'Abruzzo Colle Secco '06	▼ 3
● Montepulciano d'Abruzzo Colle Secco Rubino '04	▼ 3
○ Pecorino '06	▼ 4
○ Passito '04	▼ 5
● Montepulciano d'Abruzzo Aldiano '00	▼▼ 5
● Montepulciano d'Abruzzo Aldiano '03	▼▼ 4*
○ Trebbiano d'Abruzzo Aldiano '05	▼▼ 4*
○ Pecorino '05	▼▼ 4
○ Trebbiano d'Abruzzo Menir '04	▼▼ 5
○ Trebbiano d'Abruzzo Colle Secco '05	▼▼ 3*

Torre dei Beati

C.DA POGGIORAGONE, 56
65014 LORETO APRUTINO [PE]
TEL. 3333832344
adgalas@tin.it

ANNUAL PRODUCTION 60,000 bottles
HECTARES UNDER VINE 17
VITICULTURE METHOD Certified organic

After a flying start last year, this young Loreto Aprutino winery, passionately and energetically run by life and business partners Adriana Galasso and Fausto Albanesi, swept through to the finals with a magnificent '04 version of Montepulciano d'Abruzzo Mazzamurello. Traditional, low-impact agriculture, rigorous selection, fanatical care of the montepulciano grape and commitment to organic farming all contribute go into the making of these special, very distinctive wines. That '04 Mazzamurello is an ambitious, individual Montepulciano with complex, toasty aromas and well-judged oak. The palate is rounded and crisp with a dynamic, mouthfilling flavour. The Montepulciano d'Abruzzo Cocciapazza '04, on the other hand, has varietal, attractively rustic aromas leading into a well-rounded flavour with a slightly bitterish finish. The Montepulciano d'Abruzzo '05 is very interesting, with a pleasantly balsamic, fragrant nose and austere palate. Rosa-ae '06 is an unusual, intriguing Cerasuolo with vibrant minerality.

Torre Zambra

V.LE REGINA MARGHERITA, 18
66010 VILLAMAGNA [CH]
TEL. 0871300121
www.torrezambra.it

ANNUAL PRODUCTION 445,000 bottles
HECTARES UNDER VINE 40
VITICULTURE METHOD Conventional

The winery's vineyards at Villamagna and Miglianico produce interesting, territory-focused wines that are remarkably good value for money. This preamble is by way of saying that this year's range from Torre Zambra is again deserving of close attention. The Montepulciano d'Abruzzo Colle Maggio '04 has complex, minerally aromas and a distinctively gutsy, savoury flavour. The fresh-tasting Montepulciano d'Abruzzo '05 stands out for its pleasant red berry fruit aromas and an impressive palate with a rounded, well-typed, savouriness. Among the whites, the Trebbiano d'Abruzzo '06 from the Colle Maggio line is clean and simple with typical, fragrant aromas and a fresh tangy palate thanks to lovely acidity. The Pecorino '06, also from the Colle Maggio line, is a well-defined, varietal white with healthy, lively fruit. The ambitious Trebbiano d'Abruzzo Diogene '04 is mouthfilling and complex but has slightly over-evolved aromas. All the other wines presented were at least well made.

● Montepulciano d'Abruzzo Mazzamurello '04	♟♟ 5
● Montepulciano d'Abruzzo '05	♟♟ 4*
☉ Montepulciano d'Abruzzo Cerasuolo Rosa-ae '06	♟♟ 3*
● Montepulciano d'Abruzzo Cocciapazza '04	♟♟ 5
● Montepulciano d'Abruzzo Cocciapazza '03	♟♟ 5
● Montepulciano d'Abruzzo '04	♟♟ 4*

● Montepulciano d'Abruzzo Colle Maggio '04	♟♟ 4*
● Montepulciano d'Abruzzo '05	♟ 1*
○ Pecorino Colle Maggio '06	♟ 3
○ Trebbiano d'Abruzzo Colle Maggio '06	♟ 2*
○ Trebbiano d'Abruzzo Diogene '04	♟ 4
● Montepulciano d'Abruzzo Diomede '06	♟ 3
● Montepulciano d'Abruzzo Brume Rosse '97	♟♟ 5
● Montepulciano d'Abruzzo Colle Maggio '01	♟♟ 4*
○ Trebbiano d'Abruzzo Diogene '03	♟♟ 4
● Montepulciano d'Abruzzo Brune Rosse '00	♟♟ 5
● Montepulciano d'Abruzzo Colle Maggio '03	♟♟ 4*

Fattoria La Valentina
VIA TORRETTA, 52
65010 SPOLTORE [PE]
TEL. 0854478158
www.fattorialavalentina.it

★★ Valentini
VIA DEL BAIO, 2
65014 LORETO APRUTINO [PE]
TEL. 0858291138

ANNUAL PRODUCTION 330,000 bottles
HECTARES UNDER VINE 40
VITICULTURE METHOD Conventional

ANNUAL PRODUCTION 40,000 bottles
HECTARES UNDER VINE 64
VITICULTURE METHOD Conventional

This lovely winery in the Pescara hills makes special, distinctive wines. The reason is the Di Properzio family's genuine love for this sun-kissed land with its seaside smells and fresh breezes that arrive from the Majella massif. Whether these wines are appreciated or criticized, it's impossible not to acknowledge their well-knit texture, deriving from grapes grown in beautiful vineyards managed with sincere affection and passion. We tasted several different types, with only the Binomio missing as it was not released this year. The Montepulciano d'Abruzzo '05 has concentrated blackberry aromas and a juicy, well-typed palate with nice savouriness and great drinkability. Montepulciano d'Abruzzo Bellovedere '04 is ambitious and mouthfilling with a seductive toasty, fruity nose, perhaps a little veiled by wood, and considerable texture on its assertively tannic palate. The evolved, overripe aromas of the Montepulciano d'Abruzzo Spelt '03 are also due to the vintage year. The palate reveals significant alcohol but also a richly extracted, tannin-heavy texture. The Trebbiano d'Abruzzo '06 is a lovely fresh white with remarkable, almost salty, tanginess.

Although Edoardo Valentini left a huge gap in our hearts, we must say his son Francesco Paolo carries on his father's work and regularly presents us with unforgettable wines. The Montepulciano d'Abruzzo '02 is from a growing year that was nowhere near as poor here as it was in other regions, and this wine is a true monument to tradition and typicity. Vibrant, enfolding, complex aromas with minerally, smoky notes and precise hints of wild cherries introduce a palate that is rounded, potent yet stylish with fairly well-integrated tannins. Next is the Trebbiano d'Abruzzo '04. The aromas are less closed than in other versions, with hints of yeast joining the yellow plums and almonds. The wonderfully generous palate is close-knit and delightfully braced by refreshing acidity. Last in line is the Montepulciano d'Abruzzo Cerasuolo '05, which is perhaps simpler and fruitier than past versions. With this year's two Three Glasses the winery reaches a total of 20, which means a double star. Welcome to Italy's winemaking elite.

Wine	Glasses
● Montepulciano d'Abruzzo '05	♟♟ 3*
● Montepulciano d'Abruzzo Bellovedere '04	♟♟ 7
● Montepulciano d'Abruzzo Spelt '03	♟ 5
○ Trebbiano d'Abruzzo '06	♟ 3*
● Montepulciano d'Abruzzo Bellovedere '00	♟♟ 7
● Montepulciano d'Abruzzo Bellovedere '01	♟♟ 7
● Montepulciano d'Abruzzo Spelt '98	♟♟ 5
● Montepulciano d'Abruzzo Spelt '99	♟♟ 5
● Montepulciano d'Abruzzo Spelt '97	♟♟ 4
● Montepulciano d'Abruzzo '03	♟♟ 3*
○ Trebbiano d'Abruzzo '05	♟♟ 3
● Montepulciano d'Abruzzo '04	♟♟ 3*
● Montepulciano d'Abruzzo Spelt '01	♟♟ 5

Wine	Glasses
● Montepulciano d'Abruzzo '02	♟♟♟ 8
○ Trebbiano d'Abruzzo '04	♟♟♟ 7
☉ Montepulciano d'Abruzzo Cerasuolo '05	♟♟ 7
● Montepulciano d'Abruzzo '00	♟♟♟ 8
● Montepulciano d'Abruzzo '90	♟♟♟ 6
● Montepulciano d'Abruzzo '95	♟♟♟ 6
● Montepulciano d'Abruzzo '88	♟♟♟ 6
● Montepulciano d'Abruzzo '85	♟♟♟ 6
○ Trebbiano d'Abruzzo '99	♟♟♟ 8
○ Trebbiano d'Abruzzo '96	♟♟♟ 5
○ Trebbiano d'Abruzzo '95	♟♟♟ 5
○ Trebbiano d'Abruzzo '92	♟♟♟ 5
○ Trebbiano d'Abruzzo '02	♟♟♟ 7
○ Trebbiano d'Abruzzo '01	♟♟♟ 6
○ Trebbiano d'Abruzzo '00	♟♟♟ 6
● Montepulciano d'Abruzzo '97	♟♟♟ 7
● Montepulciano d'Abruzzo '92	♟♟♟ 6
● Montepulciano d'Abruzzo '01	♟♟♟ 8

Valle Reale

LOC. SAN CALISTO
65026 POPOLI [PE]
TEL. 0859871039
www.vallereale.it

ANNUAL PRODUCTION 570,000 bottles
HECTARES UNDER VINE 60
VITICULTURE METHOD Conventional

This Popoli winery, with its high altitude vineyards and the elegant, rugged style of its wines, is a beautiful addition to Abruzzo's wine scene. In its young life, Valle Reale has enjoyed increasing success with critics and consumers alike. This year, we were impressed by the elegance and complexity of San Calisto '05, the winery's leading Montepulciano. The ruby red colour is not too intense and the nose is vibrantly fruity with blackberry and wild cherry aromas. We liked the austere texture and the acidity that will guarantee this wine a long lifespan. The Montepulciano d'Abruzzo Valle Reale '05 has distinctively concentrated and pervasive, albeit less stylish, aromas while the palate is firmer and more approachable. The enjoyable Montepulciano d'Abruzzo Vigne Nuove '06 is astonishingly good value for money, showing well-defined with pleasant acidity on the palate. The Montepulciano d'Abruzzo Cerasuolo Vigne Nuove '06 is quite simply one of the best of its type while Trebbiano d'Abruzzo Vigne Nuove '06 is a clean, fresh white with subtle, stylish aromas.

Valori

VIA TORQUATO AL SALINELLO, 8
64027 SANT'OMERO [TE]
TEL. 086188461
vinivalori@tin.it

ANNUAL PRODUCTION 30,000 bottles
HECTARES UNDER VINE 16
VITICULTURE METHOD Conventional

Valori has established itself as a benchmark for the lovely Colline Teramane zone. The wines produced on the two estates at Sant'Omero and Controguerra are significant in both quality and quantity and also bear the name of one of today's top Italian wine men, Gianni Masciarelli, who went into business with the Valori family a few years ago. The Vigna Sant'Angelo '05 is an ambitious, robust Montepulciano with vibrant wild cherry and vanilla aromas and weighty, juicy texture. The standard-label Montepulciano d'Abruzzo, produced in increasingly large numbers, is no longer a surprise, presenting rounded, varietal aromas and stylish flavour on a light, savoury palate. Turning to the whites, the Trebbiano d'Abruzzo '06, another big numbers bottle, is exactly what it should be: clean and upfront, with lovely fresh aromas and an even, undemanding palate.

● Montepulciano d'Abruzzo San Calisto '05	♙♙♙ 6
☉ Montepulciano d'Abruzzo Cerasuolo Vigne Nuove '06	♙♙ 2*
● Montepulciano d'Abruzzo Vigne Nuove '06	♙♙ 2*
● Montepulciano d'Abruzzo Valle Reale '05	♙♙ 4
○ Trebbiano d'Abruzzo Vigne Nuove '06	♙ 2*
● Montepulciano d'Abruzzo San Calisto '04	♟♟♟ 6
● Montepulciano d'Abruzzo San Calisto '03	♟♟ 5
● Montepulciano d'Abruzzo Valle Reale '04	♟♟ 4
● Montepulciano d'Abruzzo Valle Reale '03	♟♟ 4
● Montepulciano d'Abruzzo San Calisto '00	♟♟ 5
● Montepulciano d'Abruzzo Vigne Nuove '04	♟♟ 2*
● Montepulciano d'Abruzzo San Calisto '01	♟♟ 5

● Montepulciano d'Abruzzo Vigna S. Angelo '05	♙♙ 5
● Montepulciano d'Abruzzo '06	♙♙ 3*
○ Trebbiano d'Abruzzo '06	♙ 3
● Montepulciano d'Abruzzo Vigna S. Angelo '03	♟♟♟ 5
● Montepulciano d'Abruzzo '05	♟♟ 3*
● Montepulciano d'Abruzzo Vigna S. Angelo '04	♟♟ 5
● Montepulciano d'Abruzzo Vigna S. Angelo '01	♟♟ 5

Villa Medoro

FRAZ. FONTANELLE
64030 ATRI [TE]
TEL. 0858708142
www.villamedoro.it

ANNUAL PRODUCTION 300,000 bottles
HECTARES UNDER VINE 92
VITICULTURE METHOD Conventional

Villa Medoro, owned by the explosive Federica Morricone, earned its third Three Glass prize in a row for the increasingly renowned Adrano, a Montepulciano d'Abruzzo Colline Teramane, and sashayed into the final with its second wine, the Montepulciano d'Abruzzo Rosso del Duca. But we were impressed by the entire range of wines tasted, the products of the winery's relentless pursuit of quality throughout the range and not only just in the high-visibility bottles. Adrano '05 is once again a very powerful, generous, juicy Montepulciano with well-measured oak and sound, close-knit texture. The Rosso del Duca '05 has smokier, more rustic aromas but an impressively savoury, richly extracted palate. The uncomplicated Montepulciano Villa Medoro '05 easily earned itself Two Glasses for its varietal aromas and substantial but well-managed texture. The traditional Trebbiano d'Abruzzo '06 is clean and coherent, offering freshness and good structure. The lovely, moreish Montepulciano d'Abruzzo Cerasuolo '06 quite simply stands out as one of the best in its category.

Ciccio Zaccagnini

C.DA POZZO
65020 BOLOGNANO [PE]
TEL. 0858880195
www.cantinazaccagnini.it

ANNUAL PRODUCTION 800,000 bottles
HECTARES UNDER VINE 128
VITICULTURE METHOD Conventional

This year, Marcello Zaccagnini presented a remarkable range of wines for tasting, both in terms of quality and of quantity. The line-up includes many wine types, from the more traditional to ambitious interpretations of international grape varieties, but it never loses sight of the tricky balance of quality, varietal characterization and the demands of the market. For reasons of space, we will mention only the ones we liked the best. The San Clemente is a thoroughbred Montepulciano d'Abruzzo and a regular visitor to our final tastings. We always enjoy its power on the palate and distinctive minerality, slightly obscured by intrusive oak. The '05 version of the Montepulciano Vini del Tralcetto, released at competitive prices in seriously large numbers, has good minerally aromas and delicious acidity. It's a big wine for a modest price. Then there's Chronicon '04, a savoury, close-knit Montepulciano, Cuvée dell'Abate '05, another Montepulciano but more stylish and subtle, and the Trebbiano San Clemente Montepulciano06, an interesting white with well-typed, fragrant aromas, although the oak is over-assertive. The Chardonnay San Clemente '06 is an international-style wine with a fragrant, tangy texture.

Wine	Rating
● Montepulciano d'Abruzzo Colline Teramane Adrano '05	𝟙𝟙𝟙 6
● Montepulciano d'Abruzzo Rosso del Duca '05	𝟙𝟙 4*
● Montepulciano d'Abruzzo '05	𝟙𝟙 3*
☉ Montepulciano d'Abruzzo Cerasuolo '06	𝟙𝟙 3*
○ Trebbiano d'Abruzzo '06	𝟙𝟙 3*
○ Chimera Bianco '06	𝟙 4
● Montepulciano d'Abruzzo Colline Teramane Adrano '03	𝟙𝟙𝟙 6
● Montepulciano d'Abruzzo Colline Teramane Adrano '04	𝟙𝟙𝟙 6
● Montepulciano d'Abruzzo '03	𝟙𝟙 3*
● Montepulciano d'Abruzzo Rosso del Duca '03	𝟙𝟙 4
● Montepulciano d'Abruzzo Colline Teramane Adrano '98	𝟙𝟙 5
● Montepulciano d'Abruzzo Colline Teramane Adrano '01	𝟙𝟙 6
● Montepulciano d'Abruzzo Rosso del Duca '04	𝟙𝟙 4*

Wine	Rating
● Montepulciano d'Abruzzo S. Clemente '05	𝟙𝟙 6
○ Chardonnay S. Clemente '06	𝟙𝟙 5
● Montepulciano d'Abruzzo Cuvée dell'Abate '05	𝟙𝟙 3*
● Montepulciano d'Abruzzo Tralcetto '05	𝟙𝟙 3*
● Montepulciano d'Abruzzo Chronicon '04	𝟙𝟙 4
● Capsico Rosso '03	𝟙 5
○ Yamada '06	𝟙 4
○ Trebbiano d'Abruzzo S. Clemente '06	𝟙 5
○ Plaisir Bianco '06	𝟙 5
○ Ibisco Bianco '06	𝟙 4
● Montepulciano d'Abruzzo Abbazia S. Clemente '02	𝟙𝟙 6
● Montepulciano d'Abruzzo S. Clemente '04	𝟙𝟙 6
● Montepulciano d'Abruzzo S. Clemente '03	𝟙𝟙 6
● Montepulciano d'Abruzzo Cuvée dell'Abate '04	𝟙𝟙 3*
● Montepulciano d'Abruzzo Tralcetto '04	𝟙𝟙 3*
○ Trebbiano d'Abruzzo S. Clemente '05	𝟙𝟙 5

OTHER WINERIES

Nestore Bosco
C.DA CASALI, 147
65010 NOCCIANO [PE]
TEL. 085847345
www.nestorebosco.com

This major traditional winery did not present its best 2004 wines, the two Montepulciano d'Abruzzos, Don Bosco and Pan. The good basic Montepulciano '05 is impressive, though, offering dark, minerally aromas and a savoury rounded flavour. The Pecorino '06 is well-typed but slightly masked by wood.

● Linfa '03   🍷 4
● Montepulciano d'Abruzzo '05   🍷 3*
○ Pecorino '06   🍷 4

Bove
VIA ROMA, 216
67051 AVEZZANO [AQ]
TEL. 086333133
bovevini@virgilio.it

This small winery presented simple, well-typed wines that offer excellent value for money. The impressive Indio '04 Montepulciano has good ripe, varietal aromas while the simpler Avegiano '05 is clean and coherent with an enjoyably fresh flavour.

● Montepulciano d'Abruzzo Indio '04   🍷🍷 4*
● Montepulciano d'Abruzzo
   Avegiano '05   🍷 2*

Podere Castorani
VIA CASTORANI, 5
65020 ALANNO [PE]
TEL. 3355312961
www.poderecastorani.it

Podere Castorani is owned by Formula One driver Jarno Trulli. We thought the simpler wines were more successful. The Costa delle Plaie '06 is a fragrant, well-typed Montepulciano, not huge but lovely and juicy on the palate. The Amorino '05, from montepulciano, syrah, cabernet and merlot, is a weighty, tangy red.

● Amorino Rosso '05   🍷🍷 4
● Montepulciano d'Abruzzo
   Costa delle Plaie '06   🍷🍷 4*

Col Del Mondo
C.DA CAMPOTINO, 35C
65010 COLLECORVINO [PE]
TEL. 0858207831
www.coldelmondo.com

A Montepulciano '04 with full, pervasive aromas and a rounded, gutsy palate. The ambitious Kerrias '03 has a generous, concentrated nose and an impressively powerful, flavoursome palate. The Trebbiano and Montepulciano from the Sunnae line are decent.

● Montepulciano d'Abruzzo Kerrias '03   🍷🍷 5
● Montepulciano d'Abruzzo '04   🍷🍷 4*
● Montepulciano d'Abruzzo Sunnae '05   🍷 3
○ Trebbiano d'Abruzzo Sunnae '06   🍷 2*

Collefrisio
LOC. PIANE DI MAGGIO
66030 FRISA [CH]
TEL. 0859039074
www.collefrisio.it

This new winery at Frisa, not far from Ortona, makes well-styled wines with good, often weighty, texture. The well-typed, fragrant wines of the unpretentious Zero line are focused than bottles from their more ambitious fellows. The clean, linear Pecorino '06 and the Montepulciano '05 are particularly fine.

● Montepulciano d'Abruzzo Zero '05   🍷🍷 3*
○ Pecorino '06   🍷 4
○ Trebbiano d'Abruzzo Zero '06   🍷 3

Filomusi Guelfi
VIA F. FILOMUSI GUELFI, 11
65028 TOCCO DA CASAURIA [PE]
TEL. 085986908
elleffegi@tiscali.it

In less favourable years, this famous Popoli winery has the courage not to bottle its wines. We had to make do with the fragrant Montepulciano '05 and the imaginative sweet white, Le Scuderie del Cielo, made from sauvignon and malvasia toscana, with small additions of chardonnay and cococciola.

○ Le Scuderie del Cielo '06   🍷 4
● Montepulciano d'Abruzzo '05   🍷 4

OTHER WINERIES

Gentile

VIA DEL GIARDINO, 7
67025 OFENA [AQ]
TEL. 0862956618
www.gentilevini.it

It was an indifferent year for this small Ofena winery. After last year's success, the wines we tasted this time were not as impressive as we had hoped. The only one we really liked was the new Zeus '04, a well-typed, beefy Montepulciano, slightly masked by wood but with rich concentrated texture.

● Montepulciano d'Abruzzo Zeus '04 ▼▼ 5
● Montepulciano d'Abruzzo Zefiro '03 ▼ 4
● Montepulciano d'Abruzzo Orfeo '04 ♀♀ 3*
● Montepulciano d'Abruzzo Zefiro '01 ♀♀ 4

Lepore

C.DA CIVITA, 29
64010 COLONNELLA [TE]
TEL. 086170860
www.vinilepore.it

The anxiously awaited return from this classic Teramo winery was only partly forthcoming. The Montepulciano Colline Teramane Re '05 has stylish varietal aromas and a subtle, richly extracted palate. The standard-label Montepulciano d'Abruzzo, also '05, is not bad.

● Montepulciano d'Abruzzo
   Colline Teramane Re '05 ▼▼ 5
● Montepulciano d'Abruzzo '05 ▼ 4

Montipagano

C.DA CASAL THAULERO
64026 ROSETO DEGLI ABRUZZI [TE]
TEL. 0717201210
www.montipagano.com

This estate is part of the famous Marche-based Umani Ronchi winery. Costamorro '04 is an ambitious, richly extracted, well-typed Montepulciano Colline Teramane. The Trebbiano '06 is an enjoyable, uncomplicated interpretation of the grape, showing very well defined and drinkable.

● Montepulciano d'Abruzzo
   Colline Teramane Costamorro '04 ▼▼ 5
○ Trebbiano d'Abruzzo '06 ▼ 4

Camillo Montori

LOC. PIANE TRONTO
64010 CONTROGUERRA [TE]
TEL. 0861809900
www.montorivini.it

We were less impressed with the wines presented by Montori this year. The Fonte Cupa '03, a mouthfilling, traditional Montepulciano, paid the price for an unfortunate growing year. The Montepulciano '05 has vegetal aromas and a subtle, drying palate. The Pecorino '06 was no more than decent.

● Montepulciano d'Abruzzo Colline
   Teramane Fonte Cupa '03 ▼ 6
● Montepulciano d'Abruzzo '05 ▼ 3
○ Pecorino '06 ▼ 4

Peperoncino

LOC. PIANO
67025 OFENA [AQ]
TEL. 0862954252
peperoncino.srl@virgilio.it

This winery operates under the prestigious name of Cataldi Madonna and turns out simple, fragrant wines that are excellent value for money. The Montepulciano '05 has fruity, varietal aromas and a rounded, pleasantly tangy palate. The Pecorino '06 is a rustic white with considerable body and structure.

● Montepulciano d'Abruzzo
   Capestrano '05 ▼▼ 1*
○ Pecorino '06 ▼ 3*

Pietrantonj

VIA SAN SEBASTIANO, 38
67030 VITTORITO [AQ]
TEL. 0864727102
www.vinipietrantonj.it

Pietrantonj has been making wines traditionally since the 19th century in the lovely Valle Peligna. These are mountain wines, with a characteristic, intrinsically traditional style and marked acidity. The Montepulciano Arboreo '04 has ripe, varietal aromas and a gutsy palate. The Trebbiano Arboreo '06 is subtle and well typed.

○ Trebbiano d'Abruzzo Arboreo '06 ▼ 2
● Montepulciano d'Abruzzo Arboreo '04 ▼ 2

OTHER WINERIES

Cantina Sangro
VIA PER SANTA MARIA IMBARO, 1
66022 FOSSACESIA [CH]
TEL. 087257412
www.cantinasangro.it

The short profile this year for this old co-operative in the Ortona hills is a result of the very few wines that were presented. In fact, we only tasted two: the '04 version of the ever-decent Terra Regia, an austere and typical Montepulciano, and the Pecorino Kaleo '06, which is not bad.

● Montepulciano d'Abruzzo Terra Regia '04 ꙳꙳ 4
○ Pecorino Kaleo '06 ꙳ 2

Strappelli
LOC. TORRI
VIA TORRI, 15
64010 TORANO NUOVO [TE]
TEL. 0861887402
www.cantinastrappelli.it

There's a short profile this year for Strappelli but only because too few wines were presented. We were only given two whites to taste but both performed well. The Trebbiano '06 has a fragrant, varietal nose and a good fresh, tangy palate. Soprano '06 is a clean, uncomplicated Pecorino.

○ Trebbiano d'Abruzzo '06 ꙳꙳ 3*
○ Pecorino Soprano '06 ꙳ 4
● Montepulciano d'Abruzzo Colline Teramane Celibe Ris. '03 ꙳꙳ 6

Cantine Talamonti
C.DA PALAZZO
65014 LORETO APRUTINO [PE]
TEL. 0858289039
www.cantinetalamonti.it

This new Loreto Aprutino cellar is doing good work. Only a few wines were presented but they were all impressive. Modà '05 is a fragrant, well-typed Montepulciano. Kudos '03, from montepulciano with 30 per cent merlot, is a mature red with a slightly astringent finish.

● Montepulciano d'Abruzzo Modà '05 ꙳ 3*
● Kudos '03 ꙳ 5

Valle Martello
C.DA VALLE MARTELLO, 10
66010 VILLAMAGNA [CH]
TEL. 0871300330
www.vallemartello.net

This solid, very traditional, farming estate is located in the Chieti hill country and run with dedicated hard work by the Masci family. Primaterra '05 is an austere, mouthfilling Montepulciano with a savoury, tannic palate. Brado '06 is clean and uncomplicated.

● Montepulciano d'Abruzzo Primaterra '05 ꙳꙳ 5
● Montepulciano d'Abruzzo Brado '06 ꙳ 4

Villa Bizzarri
LOC. VILLA BIZZARRI
64010 TORANO NUOVO [TE]
TEL. 0861856933
www.villabizzarri.com

We were very taken with the Colle Creta '03: subtle, stylish, almost Burgundy aromas, and a traditional elegant palate with a distinctive, mouthfilling palate and sophisticated tannins. Unfortunately, the other wines presented for tasting were not up to the standard of this little gem.

● Montepulciano d'Abruzzo Colle Creta '03 ꙳꙳ 4

MOLISE

A few years ago, we decided to devote a separate section of the Guide to this lovely little region, which has long been associated with Abruzzo, thanks to the Royal House of Bourbon. We were impressed by the confident steps forward being taken in the region's winemaking sector. Viticulture in Molise is expanding and developing significantly as growers strive for quality. New wineries are being opened, and old ones renovated, as the revival respectfully follows tradition and remains faithful to local history and origins, which is the true Molise way. Grapes have always been an essential part of Molise's agricultural economy, wine production is significant at over 250,000 hectolitres and average quality standards are very respectable. But now we are witnessing upheaval in a region that slopes gently down from the Apennines to the Adriatic, where the climate is less harsh, the temperatures more manageable and the land rich and fertile. We are now seeing sound, dynamic wineries offering good wines at competitive prices, in a well-tried market strategy. The most widely grown varieties are montepulciano, which has very distinctive features in this area, and a fresher, simpler version of the aglianico grape than we are used to. Among white varieties, the most commonly grown are trebbiano and falanghina. The native tintilia variety deserves a separate mention. As the name suggests, this grape yields very strikingly coloured red wines with typical minerally aromas. After some initial hesitation, these wine types are becoming very ambitious and are well worth keeping an eye on. What about the best producers? Another very welcome Three Glasses went to a classic local wine, Molise Rosso Riserva Don Luigi from Di Majo Norante. The 2005 edition of this classy red is particularly sound and mouthwateringly juicy, a wine that does full justice to its maker's reputation. Then there is the recently established Borgo Colloredo, Cipressi, newcomer D'Uva and its traditional wines, Masserie Flocco, with its delightful Tintilia, and finally Catabbo. So keep an eye on wines from Molise. It may be a small regional but it is increasingly prestigious.

Borgo di Colloredo

LOC. NUOVA CLITERNIA
86042 CAMPOMARINO [CB]
TEL. 087557453
www.borgodicolloredo.com

ANNUAL PRODUCTION 300,000 bottles
HECTARES UNDER VINE 60
VITICULTURE METHOD Conventional

This lovely Campomarino winery presented a very interesting range of clean, uncomplicated wines that are enjoyable to drink and easy on the pocket. This is down to the fruit from the estate's vineyards and the commitment of Enrico and Pasquale Di Giulio, pioneers of Molise winemaking. The Molise Rosso '04, from montepulciano grapes, is remarkable. The aromas are coherently varietal and the palate is rounded, moreish, soft and mouthfilling. The Biferno Rosso Gironia '01, from montepulciano with a little aglianico, is a red with fairly pervasive aromas and a pleasant, if not huge, palate. The Rosato '06 is slightly sweetish and as drinkable as you could wish. The three types of white wine are fresh, agreeable and essentially well made. The '06 Falanghina didn't disappoint, showing lovely, savoury minerality with a nicely rustic flavour. The Greco '06 is soft and mouthfilling with a very pleasing palate while the '06 Gironia, Biferno Bianco, from trebbiano, bombino and malvasia, has floral aromas and a straightforward, no-nonsense palate.

Cipressi

C.DA MONTAGNA
86030 SAN FELICE DEL MOLISE [CB]
TEL. 0874874535
www.cantinecipressi.it

ANNUAL PRODUCTION 51,000 bottles
HECTARES UNDER VINE 25
VITICULTURE METHOD Certified organic

This winery, owned by Claudio Cipressi and Ernesto Travaglini, has about 25 hectares of vineyards in the San Felice del Molise and Guglionesi areas and is a well-established feature on the region's winemaking scene. Wines are made both from traditional and more exotic international grape varieties and are invariably ambitious, well made and excellent value for money. The range presented for tasting this year gave a slightly less exciting performance than in previous years. First in line is Rumen '05, a Molise Rosso with crisply varietal aromas and a subtle, consistent palate with pleasantly savoury palate. The '05 Mekan, another red, has marked aromas of peaches and flowers on the nose and a soft, evolved palate. Lastly, the ace up the winery's sleeve is Molise Tintilia Macchiarossa '05, which may well be the best monovarietal interpretation of this grape. Its spicy, pervasive aromas and rounded gutsy flavour more than compensate for the less than impressive performance of the whites.

● Molise Rosso '04	▼▼ 3*	
○ Biferno Bianco Gironia '06	▼ 3	
● Biferno Rosso Gironia '01	▼ 4	
○ Greco '06	▼ 3	
○ Molise Falanghina '06	▼ 4	
⊙ Biferno Rosato Gironia '06	▼ 3	
● Biferno Rosso Gironia '98	▼▼ 4	
● Biferno Rosso Gironia '00	▼▼ 4	

● Molise Tintilia Macchiarossa '05	▼▼ 6	
● Molise Rosso Mekan '05	▼ 4	
● Molise Rosso Rumen '05	▼ 4	
● Molise Rosso Rumen '03	▼▼ 3*	

Di Majo Norante
FRAZ. NUOVA CLITERNIA
VIA RAMITELLI, 4
86042 CAMPOMARINO [CB]
TEL. 087557208
www.dimajonorante.com

ANNUAL PRODUCTION 800,000 bottles
HECTARES UNDER VINE 85
VITICULTURE METHOD Natural

The traditional Di Majo Norante winery is synonymous with fine quality wines and has profoundly influenced the winemaking revival in Molise. Thanks to the family's hard work and investments – Alessio Di Majo above all – the estate's beautiful vineyards produce ambitious, technically flawless wines in the modern idiom. We were thrilled to be able to give the '05 Don Luigi, the prestigious Di Majo Norante flagship, yet another Three Glass award. This great red, made from montepulciano with some tintilia, is extraordinarily sound with marked aromas of blackcurrants and cocoa powder on the complex, concentrated nose and a big, rock-solid yet beautifully poised palate. But we like all the products presented for tasting, from the simpler and more quaffable bottles to the really ambitious wines. Contado '04 is a thoroughbred. This very reasonably priced Aglianico has complex, fruity aromas slightly obscured by wood and a generous, rounded palate with wonderful texture. The Ramitello '04 from montepulciano with a splash of aglianico is a coherent, well-styled red with a fresh, enjoyable palate. Outstanding among the whites was the uncomplicated Molì '06, which proffers lovely minerality.

D'Uva
C.DA RICUPO, 13
86035 LARINO [CB]
TEL. 0874822320
www.cantineduva.com

ANNUAL PRODUCTION 100,000 bottles
HECTARES UNDER VINE 15
VITICULTURE METHOD Conventional

This important Molise winery played a major role in the renaissance of the tintilia grape, which is believed to be the region's only true native variety. The winery is developing all its wine types confidently and we particularly liked the traditional rusticity of the range. The '06 Tintilia is an exemplary interpretation of the grape, presenting evolved, pervasive, heady aromas and hints of black cherry on the nose, while the rounded palate has rich extract with the merest suggestion of tannins. The ambitious Molise Rosso Console Vibio '04 is a dangerously ripe Montepulciano with evolved, slightly oxidized aromas and lovely texture on the palate which earned it a comfortable One Glass. The Ricupo '05 is even more striking. Generous and pervasive on the nose, it unveils a juicy, pleasantly tannic palate. Flying the flag for the whites is Kantharos '06, a simple but by no means dull Trebbiano with lovely subtle, minerally aromas and a soft, rounded palate.

● Molise Don Luigi '05	♔♔♔ 6
● Molise Aglianico Contado '04	♔♔ 4*
● Biferno Rosso Ramitello '04	♔ 4
○ Molì Bianco '06	♔ 2*
● Molise Aglianico Contado '03	♔♔♔ 4*
● Molise Aglianico Contado '99	♔♔♔ 4*
● Molise Don Luigi '99	♔♔♔ 5
● Molise Aglianico Contado '00	♔♔ 4*
● Molise Don Luigi '04	♔♔ 6
● Molise Don Luigi '02	♔♔ 6
● Molise Aglianico Contado '02	♔♔ 4*

● Molise Tintilia '06	♔♔ 6
○ Molise Trebbiano Kantharos '06	♔ 5
● Molise Rosso Ricupo '05	♔ 5
● Molise Rosso Console Vibio '04	♔ 6

OTHER WINERIES

I.A.C. - Catabbo
C.DA PETRIERA
86046 SAN MARTINO IN PENSILIS [CB]
TEL. 0875604945
www.catabbo.it

Catabbo presented an interesting range that performed well. The '05 Tintilia stands out for its even, smoky aromas and rounded, dense palate while the whites include Xaatuis 05 is a buttery, mouthfilling Falanghina. The Molise Rosso '05 is rather good.

○ Falanghina Xaatuis '05	▼	3
● Molise Rosso '05	▼	4
● Molise Tintilia '05	▼	4

Masserie Flocco
C.DA DIFENSOLA
86045 PORTOCANNONE [CB]
TEL. 0875590032
www.masserieflocco.com

This winery produces enjoyable, well-made wines from both traditional and non-native grape varieties. Again this year, we liked the Molise Tintilia Kuq '06 and the Trebbiano Podere del Canneto, also '06, with its savoury, almost salty, palate. The Falanghina '06 is also good.

○ Falanghina '06	▼	3
● Molise Tintilia Kuq '06	▼	4
○ Trebbiano Podere del Canneto '06	▼	3

CAMPANIA

Often, numbers don't tell the whole story, especially with wine, where they hide an infinity of perhaps minuscule variables and nuances. This is even truer in a region like Campania which remains in a state of flux. If the headline figure, the ten Three Glass wines, is down from last year's plethora of laurels, this should not be allowed to hide other, equally important, points. Witness the many wines reaching the finals and the growing number of estates submitting bottles, a constant trend. Some of the newcomers are from emerging zones but others come from longstanding denominations that have survived periods in the doldrums and are now finding new lustre. The province of Benevento is the most contradictory of areas in this respect: it still has no truly superlative wines or any outstanding estates that can drive the rest forward, yet there are far more Sannio estates in the Guide, and there is plenty of promise from Solopaca and Guardia Sanframondi. There is ambivalence in the province of Salerno, too. In Cilento and thereabouts there seems little beyond the ever-bright estates of Maffini and De Conciliis, and Montevetrano continues to shine with a fabulous '05, but few doubt the excellence now coming from Costa d'Amalfi. It's a small district where growers make wines of outstanding style and personality as well as quality. The prime example is Marisa Cuomo, whose Fiorduva earned its third Three Glasses with the '06, but also Giuseppe Apicella, Fattoria San Francesco and, especially, Ettore Sammarco. The province of Naples is showing some timid signs of revival. Things are also moving forward in the multi-faceted province of Caserta, where Terre del Principe and Alois bring out the strengths of pallagrello and casavecchia, Adolfo Spada in Galluccio does likewise for aglianico, Galardi took his fourth consecutive Three Glasses for the chameleon-like Terra di Lavoro '05 and Villa Matilde won its second for Falerno del Massico Bianco Caracci '05. The scene in Irpinia needs careful reading. The aspirations of several great classic estates and other determined newcomers have been reined in by the poor vintages of 2003 for Taurasi and 2006 for Fiano di Avellino but overall quality is rising and the wines that won through are real pearls. Mastroberardino won yet another double for a vibrant Greco di Tufo Novaserra '06 and an inspiring Taurasi Radici Riserva '01, both classy and elegant. Neither is it a novelty for Feudi di San Gregorio to pick up two Three Glass awards, this year for a powerful Serpico '05 and a surprisingly good Greco di Tufo Cutizzi '06. Pietracupa's fabulous '06 Greco di Tufo '06 is a release to remember while Antonio Caggiano is back at the top with Taurasi Vigna Macchia dei Goti '04, an exciting forerunner of a vintage that is set to be one of the best ever for this prince of red wines.

Alois
LOC. AUDELINO
VIA REGAZZANO
81040 PONTELATONE [CE]
TEL. 0823876710
www.vinialois.it

Aminea
VIA SANTA LUCIA
83040 CASTELVETERE SUL CALORE [AV]
TEL. 082765787
www.aminea.com

ANNUAL PRODUCTION 82,000 bottles
HECTARES UNDER VINE 14
VITICULTURE METHOD   Conventional

ANNUAL PRODUCTION 500,000 bottles
HECTARES UNDER VINE 22
VITICULTURE METHOD   Conventional

Caserta's up-and-coming wine scene needs estates like this. The Alois family's recent work with Riccardo Cotarella has led to the inevitable conclusion that the area has the potential to produce serious long-lived wines yet can also satisfy needs in the mid-range sector by providing considerable quantities of attractive, easily understood wines. This concept is fully supported by the wines we tasted for this year's Guide. The '06 Campole is, as usual, one of the few examples of a young Aglianico that is easy-going yet has character. Pallagrello Nero '06 is a new wine of great promise. It's fruit-forward, with blackberry and blackcurrant interwoven with balsamic and slightly earthy notes, but hits the limits of its youth on the palate. Here the initial impact is of a mouthfilling wine with good stuffing but the follow-through is held back by the amount of oak and by the tannins which, in typical Caserta style, are rather unyielding. Pallagrello Bianco Caiatì '06 and Falanghina Caulino '06 follow the style of previous releases but Casavecchia Trebulanum '05 is a little disappointing.

Glass by glass, tasting score by tasting score, this newish winery belonging to Mimì Mongiello and partners is rising through the ranks of Campania's wines. Their style eschews making a big bang for the sake of it, favouring quiet, ongoing work behind the scenes. The results are even more impressive when you take into account the quantities involved: Aminea is certainly no garage estate. Great attention has been focused on developing some fine new wines, like Quindici, a dried-grape passito from fiano, and Uno, an aglianico, piedirosso and sangiovese blend that has aspirations to being a Supercampanian, but it's the classics that continue to lead the group and provide its highest scores. Top of the tree is Fiano di Avellino '06, an individual wine of substance, which has aromas of white peach, ivy and olive twigs, held together by a sweetly firm palate. Greco di Tufo '06 is not far behind. This is more timid on the nose and initially slimmer on the palate but gains punch and density as it opens out and finishes strongly with white melon and citron. Taurasi Baiardo '02 shows remarkably well, considering the vintage, being lively and minerally despite rather too much oak. Macerone '06 is more than adequate.

● Campole '06	♟♟	4*
● Pallagrello Nero '06	♟♟	4*
○ Pallagrello Bianco Caiatì '06	♟	4
● Trebulanum '05	♟	5
○ Caulino '06	♟	4
● Campole '03	♟♟	3*
● Trebulanum '03	♟♟	5
● Campole '04	♟♟	4
● Campole '05	♟♟	4

○ Fiano di Avellino '06	♟♟	4*
○ Greco di Tufo '06	♟♟	4*
● Taurasi Baiardo '02	♟♟	5
○ Quindici '06	♟♟	6
● Macerone '06	♟	3
● Uno '05	♟	5

Antonio Caggiano
C.DA SALA
83030 TAURASI [AV]
TEL. 082774723
www.cantinecaggiano.it

Colli di Castelfranci
C.DA BRAUDIANO
83040 CASTELFRANCI [AV]
TEL. 082772392
www.collidicastelfranci.com

ANNUAL PRODUCTION 132,000 bottles
HECTARES UNDER VINE 16
VITICULTURE METHOD Conventional

Take one globe-trotting photographer with an overweening passion for wine and a friendship with a professor of aglianico, one of the best vineyards in Irpinia, and a vintage to die for, and you have Taurasi Vigna Macchia dei Goti '04, a Three Glass wine to cherish and remember. It's deep ruby in hue. The nose initially gives black pepper and liquorice, followed by new oak which does not mask a fruit-led profile of rare vitality and depth. Its citrus hints also come through on the tight, flavour-packed palate, which is completed by classy tannins. This superb year for the Caggiano-Moio partnership doesn't end there though. Their Greco di Tufo Devon has never been as good. The '06 steamed through the finals, its full, elegant profile embracing modernity without overdoing the tropical fruits, and its yeastier notes well melded into more subtle mint and citron. The '03 release of Mel, a dried-grape wine from late-harvested fiano, is back up to speed. The only slight disappointment comes from Salae Domini '05. Although it has plentiful concentration we prefer the calm fullness of the deep, earthy, vigorous Taurì '05.

ANNUAL PRODUCTION 120,000 bottles
HECTARES UNDER VINE 20
VITICULTURE METHOD Conventional

If Colli di Castelfranci were a football team, it would be one that opponents fear. The defence is difficult to penetrate, the midfield solid and the attack is always poised to strike. Indeed, Giuseppe Gregorio and Gerardo Colucci's squad is one of the best organized in the region. Based on humility and consistency, it doesn't set out to blast you with fancy footwork but sooner or later it scores the decisive goal. And this year they again played a great match with an array of very fine wines scoring well above the Two Glass threshold. First comes the nicely open Greco di Tufo Grotte '06, which evokes Sicilian pastries with its nose of elderflower, pistachio and almond plus enlivening incursions of basil. The palate is initially slightly sweetish then broadens out decisively at mid palate, its finish giving just a touch excess acidity. Fiano di Avellino Pendino '06 is more compact but the structure is a little less sustained. The pervasive, sharp nose sways between lime blossom and lemon peel, leading to a taut, edgy palate. The '06 Paladino, from late-harvested fiano, is sweeter than usual with more tertiary characteristics but has plenty of vigour and drive.

● Taurasi V. Macchia dei Goti '04	♟♟♟ 6
○ Greco di Tufo Devon '06	♟♟ 4*
○ Fiano di Avellino Béchar '06	♟♟ 4*
● Taurì '05	♟♟ 4*
● Salae Domini '05	♟ 6
○ Mel '03	♟ 6
● Taurasi V. Macchia dei Goti '99	♟♟♟ 7
● Taurasi V. Macchia dei Goti '00	♟♟ 7
● Taurasi V. Macchia dei Goti '01	♟♟ 7
● Taurasi V. Macchia dei Goti '03	♟♟ 6
● Salae Domini '00	♟♟ 6

○ Fiano di Avellino Pendino '06	♟♟ 4
○ Greco di Tufo Grotte '06	♟♟ 4
○ Paladino V.T. '06	♟♟ 4
● Candriano '05	♟ 4
○ Paladino V.T. '04	♟♟ 4
○ Fiano di Avellino Pendino '05	♟♟ 4*
○ Fiano di Avellino Pendino '04	♟♟ 4
○ Paladino V.T. '05	♟♟ 5
○ Greco di Tufo Grotte '04	♟♟ 4
○ Greco di Tufo Grotte '05	♟♟ 4

Colli di Lapio

VIA ARIANIELLO
83030 LAPIO [AV]
TEL. 0825982184
collidilapio@libero.it

ANNUAL PRODUCTION	50,000 bottles
HECTARES UNDER VINE	5
VITICULTURE METHOD	Conventional

At a time when it's cool to confess, we too should come out and declare our frailty. It's called fiano fever and it attacks those who believe that the "vitis apiana" lauded by Plinio and Columella is one of the most complete Italian varieties, one of those best able to reflect the nuances of terroir and inspire emotion as years go by. We became infected while wandering around Arianiello near Lapio, where Clelia Romano and her family are based, an area where Fiano di Avellino adopts its most northern style, giving amazing levels of firmness and aromatic complexity. Clelia's '06 is no exception and has a deep, multi-faceted nose recalling moss, rocks and grapefruit, and giving intense underlying smokiness. The only thing it seems to need is a touch more texture and depth on the palate but only time will tell. Taurasi Vigna Andrea '03 is the result of intelligent handling of a very warm year. The palate is racy and the nose a little less so, being shadowed by vanilla, coffee and walnutskin. The '05 Irpinia Aglianico Donnachiara is along the lines of previous releases.

Contrade di Taurasi

VIA MUNICIPIO, 39
83030 TAURASI [AV]
TEL. 0815442457
www.contradeditaurasi.it

ANNUAL PRODUCTION	20,000 bottles
HECTARES UNDER VINE	5
VITICULTURE METHOD	Conventional

Enza Lonardo's Taurasi is one to watch. First of all, it's a Taurasi from Taurasi itself, that small location in Irpinia where the volcanic soils are lighter and sandier than elsewhere. It has an uncommon stylistic slant, angled more towards grace and sobriety than concentration, and the tannins are well under control. The '03 vintage was certainly not the best for these characteristics but the result is nonetheless admirable. The nose initially wavers between toastiness, black pepper and leather but the palate has power and a laid-back liveliness, and although it lacks a touch of dynamism, the finish is warm and relaxed. Keeping it company is a fascinating, long-lived Taurasi '99, from an austere year. It is initially rather reduced but then emerges to frame rare spicy elegance with aromas of pipe tobacco, candied citron peel and antique wood. The palate is also clearly defined but possibly just a touch too firm, and the tannins are still rather dominant. Despite a slight lack of polish, the pleasant, straight-down-the-line yet not pedestrian Aglianico '05 shows very well.

O Fiano di Avellino '06	🍷	5
● Taurasi Vigna Andrea '03	🍷🍷	6
● Irpinia Aglianico Donna Chiara '05	🍷	5
O Fiano di Avellino '04	🍷🍷🍷	5
O Fiano di Avellino '05	🍷🍷🍷	5
O Fiano di Avellino '03	🍷🍷	5
● Taurasi Vigna Andrea '01	🍷🍷	6
O Fiano di Avellino '00	🍷🍷	4*
O Fiano di Avellino '01	🍷🍷	5
O Fiano di Avellino '02	🍷🍷	5

● Taurasi '03	🍷🍷	6
● Aglianico '05	🍷🍷	4
● Taurasi '99	🍷🍷	7
● Taurasi Ris. '01	🍷🍷	7
● Taurasi '00	🍷🍷	6
● Taurasi '01	🍷🍷	6

D'Ambra Vini d'Ischia

FRAZ. PANZA
VIA MARIO D'AMBRA, 16
80075 FORIO [NA]
TEL. 081907210
www.dambravini.it

ANNUAL PRODUCTION 500,000 bottles
HECTARES UNDER VINE 18
VITICULTURE METHOD Conventional

If these are island wines, then three cheers for islands. For once let's forget about "heroic viticulture", the monorail and the vintage festival when talking about the Frassitelli brothers' estate and simply look at a brilliant range of wines, both old and new, that is better than we've seen for years. The old wine is Tenuta Frassitelli. The '06 release is a stand-out and seems to have captured the entire aromatic spectrum of its birthplace. There's sage, broom, Mediterranean scrubland and a very classy iodine undercurrent. The palate doesn't explode with flavour but does give continuous flow and movement. To be perfect, it would have to have a touch more texture and final zip but it's hard to ask perfection of a Biancolella. New is represented by the '05 Kyme. It's back to the splendours of previous releases, giving a potpourri of floral sensations, from lime blossom to magnolia, and adding vitality to the tertiary characteristics of its varieties, which Andrea D'Ambra brought to Ischia from the Aegean. The palate has no great peaks but it's a coastal wine from head to toe. The basic Ischia Biancolella '06 is satisfying. Ischia Forastera Euposia '06's strong suits are flesh and grip.

D'Antiche Terre - Vega

C.DA LO PIANO - S.S. 7 BIS
83030 MANOCALZATI [AV]
TEL. 0825675689
www.danticheterre.it

ANNUAL PRODUCTION 360,000 bottles
HECTARES UNDER VINE 40
VITICULTURE METHOD Conventional

After losing its Guide profile, Gaetano Ciccarella's estate has shot straight back. All earlier small disappointments have now been swept aside by this year's utterly convincing range. To tell the truth, we're not terribly surprised that it has bounced back because D'Antiche Terre is one of the longest-standing wineries in Avellino province, it owns vineyards in top sites in Irpinia's denominated zones and its wines have scored highly more than once before. So let's hope they now maintain such quality levels. We'll start by declaring our enthusiasm for Fiano di Avellino '06. The profile is strongly minerally, releasing delicate sensations of lime blossom and pineapple, buttressed by hints of balsam. The palate is taut and elegant, almost salty and a touch alcoholic on the finish. It's a great wine and perfectly partnered by the – literally – bubbly, Irpinia Coda di Volpe '06 with its greater weight and mobility. Irpinia Aglianico '05 is exemplary in its calibration and attractiveness; Aglianico Coriliano '04 is more conventional; and Greco di Tufo '06 is only good, needing a touch more attack and roundness of fruit.

O Ischia Bianco Kyme '05	♟♟ 5
O Ischia Biancolella Tenuta Frassitelli '06	♟♟ 5
O Ischia Biancolella '06	♟♟ 4*
O Ischia Forastera Euposia '06	♟♟ 4*
O Ischia Biancolella Tenuta Frassitelli '90	♟♟♟ 4
O Ischia Biancolella Tenuta Frassitelli '01	♟♟ 5*
O Ischia Bianco Kyme '02	♟♟ 5
O Ischia Biancolella Tenuta Frassitelli '04	♟♟ 5
O Ischia Forastera Euposia '05	♟♟ 4
O Ischia Biancolella Tenuta Frassitelli '05	♟♟ 5
O Ischia Bianco Kyme '04	♟♟ 5

O Fiano di Avellino '06	♟♟ 4*
O Coda di Volpe '06	♟♟ 3*
● Irpinia Aglianico '05	♟♟ 4*
● Coriliano '04	♟ 3
O Greco di Tufo '06	♟ 4
O Eliseo di Serra '06	♟ 3
O Greco di Tufo '03	♟♟ 4*
● Taurasi '00	♟♟ 5

Viticoltori De Conciliis

LOC. QUERCE, 1
84060 PRIGNANO CILENTO [SA]
TEL. 0974831090
www.viticoltorideconciliis.it

ANNUAL PRODUCTION 160,000 bottles
HECTARES UNDER VINE 25
VITICULTURE METHOD Conventional

Too much. There is no other way to describe the wines of Bruno De Conciliis, once at Bologna university's drama, arts and music department and now a grower-winemaker in Cilento. His wines are pushed to limit by relentless work in vineyard and cellar, bearing the distinctive traits of a zone where aglianico is anything but a "nebbiolo of the south". The archetype of his philosophy is Naima, or at least it was until the '04 release, which seems to be heading towards greater openness and drinkability. Its classic notes of liqueur cherries and hot spices have gained refinement from florality. The initial impact on the palate is of sweetness and succulence, development is then measured, and the finish tight and a little dusty. The style of Zero, from aglianico, has remained unaltered. Its extractive and glycerine-rich power seems modelled on Amarone and this, added to its notable tannic input, takes it almost over the top. Delicious red berry fruit leads the way with the Aglianico Decimo Anno '06, a wine that worthily commemorates ten years of success for the estate, a decade of major challenges and ideas brought to fruition with reassuring simplicity.

Di Meo

C.DA COCCOVONI, 1
83050 SALZA IRPINA [AV]
TEL. 0825981419
www.dimeo.it

ANNUAL PRODUCTION 500,000 bottles
HECTARES UNDER VINE 50
VITICULTURE METHOD Conventional

If Three Glasses represent supreme excellence, the string of Two Glass wines listed below denotes solidity and credibility, which is increasingly what we find at Roberto, Erminia and Generoso Di Meo's fine winery. Theirs is no small achievement for an estate that regularly produces over 500,000 bottles, a considerable number for Irpinia. But what we are now looking for is a further move towards wines that can vie with the region's best. Don't get us wrong. Di Meo wines display a rare confidence of approach. Some, most notably Greco di Tufo '06 and Irpinia Aglianico '05, seem to fly on automatic pilot, and in the lower price band the Coda di Volpe '06 and the '05 Isso, an earlydrinking Aglianico of fair substance, shine like never before. But we wanted something more from the '05 Don Generoso, even though there's been an improvement on previous vintages, and especially we wanted more from Taurasi Riserva '01. This is a bit too firm and squashed down, and still needs further time to acquire the open fullness we like. Sannio Falanghina '06 is typically acidulous and Fiano di Avellino '06 deserves a second look.

● Naima '04	♟♟ 7
● Decimo Anno Aglianico '06	♟♟ 4
● Zero '04	♟♟ 8
○ Donnaluna Fiano '06	♟ 4
○ Selim Brut	♟ 4
● Zero '04	8
● Naima '01	♟♟♟ 6
● Naima '00	♟♟ 6
● Naima '02	♟♟ 7
● Naima '99	♟♟ 6
● Naima '03	♟♟ 7

○ Coda di Volpe '06	♟♟ 4*
● Isso '05	♟♟ 4*
● Taurasi Ris. '01	♟♟ 6
○ Greco di Tufo '06	♟♟ 4*
● Aglianico '05	♟♟ 4*
● Don Generoso '05	♟♟ 8
○ Fiano di Avellino '06	♟ 4
○ Sannio Falanghina '06	♟ 4
○ Fiano di Avellino Alessandra '03	♟♟ 5
○ Fiano di Avellino Alessandra '04	♟♟ 5
● Taurasi Ris. '00	♟♟ 6
● Taurasi Ris. '97	♟♟ 6
● Taurasi Ris. '98	♟♟ 6

Di Prisco
C.DA ROTOLE, 27
83040 FONTANAROSA [AV]
TEL. 0825475738
www.cantinadiprisco.it

I Favati
P.ZZA DI DONATO
83020 CESINALI [AV]
TEL. 0825666898
www.cantineifavati.it

ANNUAL PRODUCTION   100,000 bottles
HECTARES UNDER VINE 10
VITICULTURE METHOD   Conventional

ANNUAL PRODUCTION   50,000 bottles
HECTARES UNDER VINE 10
VITICULTURE METHOD   Conventional

Fontanarosa is a small location in the mid Calore valley, known locally for stone working, fabulous soppressata salami and, more recently, the wines of Pasqualino di Prisco. Di Prisco is a placid yet tenacious grape-grower and, for many, this area is to Taurasi as La Morra is to Barolo. The zone's typical volcanic, clayey soils are lighter here, with more sand and limestone, which helps to explain the more tapered, assertive styles of the estate's reds, notably the excellent Taurasi. The hot vintage of '03 yielded a wine with a more expressive, succulently fruity nose than usual and a palate of marvellous cohesion and taut power. Its flavours range from orange zest to ginger and violet but lacking just a touch of structure and length. This prompted the happy thought that in a more classic vintage it could become a real marker. Pietrarosa '05, made from selected grapes aged without oak, is already just that for Greco di Tufo. It has an almond milk character and a slightly loose finish but striking definition and power.

This small gem of an estate, set in a landscape where fiano grapes grow next to hazelnut trees, has been chafing at the bit for some time. Its fiano is not the pointed, almost riesling-ish type that comes from the north side of Lapio, nor the smoky, chameleon-like version growing on the Montefredane hill, nor even the fruit-packed style from Summonte. Here, in the mid Sabato valley, the loose-grained, slightly sandy soils are tailor-made for producing wines of intense varietal character, wines which show their best if handled with restraint rather than pushed to the limit. Many try but few succeed here, which is even more to the credit of I Favati's first-rate '06 Fiano di Avellino. It has an individual stamp of musk and wet rocks, partnering shy but sturdy fruit that is felt evenly throughout the palate. The estate's other wines are also distinguished, with an apparently withdrawn, reserved character that doesn't prevent them opening vigorously in the glass. Taurasi Terzo Tratto '03 happily overcomes the limits of the year; Greco di Tufo Terrantica '06 may well prove a pleasant surprise in a few months. Both easily won Two Glasses, as did Aglianico Cretarossa '05.

● Taurasi '03	▼▼ 6
○ Greco di Tufo Pietrarosa '05	▼▼ 4*
○ Coda di Volpe '06	▼ 3
● Aglianico '03	▽▽ 4
○ Greco di Tufo Pietrarosa '04	▽▽ 4
○ Greco di Tufo '03	▽▽ 4*
● Taurasi '01	▽▽ 6
○ Fiano di Avellino '05	▽▽ 4

○ Fiano di Avellino Pietramara '06	▼▼ 4
○ Greco di Tufo Terrantica '06	▼▼ 4
● Aglianico Cretarossa '05	▼▼ 4
● Taurasi Terzo Tratto '03	▼▼ 5
○ Fiano di Avellino Pietramara '05	▽▽ 4
○ Greco di Tufo Terrantica '05	▽▽ 4

Benito Ferrara

FRAZ. SAN PAOLO, 14A
83010 TUFO [AV]
TEL. 0825998194
www.benitoferrara.it

ANNUAL PRODUCTION 42,000 bottles
HECTARES UNDER VINE 8
VITICULTURE METHOD Conventional

If you ever climb up from Tufo's main square to the tiny outlying area of San Paolo, you soon realize you are in the heart of Greco di Tufo country. There's an isolated, rugged hill, with clay and sulphur-rich soils that give unique character to the wines of Gabriella Ferrara and her husband Sergio, a wine couple if ever there was one. For years, their bottles have been a draw for everyone who admires the powerful, slightly tertiary style of Greco and the '06s are no exception. Both the basic Greco and the Vigna Cicogna cru are intense and opulent with a golden yellow colour, a nose full of honey and dried fruits, and a richly fruited palate. These are distinctive wines but, we think, they could be even better if such powerful material could be handled to bring greater harmony and cohesion, avoiding that hint of overripeness. It ends up compromising the more idiosyncratic mineral components and leaving the alcohol and extractive sweetness to dominate. The smoky Fiano di Avellino '06, with its almost tannic finish, is along the same lines and, in some respects, more successful.

★ Feudi di San Gregorio

LOC. CERZA GROSSA
83050 SORBO SERPICO [AV]
TEL. 0825986611
www.feudi.it

ANNUAL PRODUCTION 3,400,000 bottles
HECTARES UNDER VINE 290
VITICULTURE METHOD Conventional

If we were simply to look at the list of wines below, it would seem that nothing had changed: the amazing array of red and black Glasses, the Three Glass duo, the second star on its way. Yet in fact a lot has changed this year for this juggernaut of a winery. There's new management, a new organizational structure and, for us the most important thing, a complete change of style with a deliberate revolution in intent and results. Emblematic of this new direction is a fabulous '06 Greco di Tufo Cutizzi. It is pervasive and deep, with iodine and citrus aromas topped by classy spicy touches. The palate is direct and salty, and there isn't a trace of that slightly fermentative opulence which tended to be the main trait of previous releases when young. The restyling has, though, left Serpico unaffected and the '05 earned its sixth consecutive top award. It's still edgy and unyielding, still slightly dominated by new oak, but is already revealing now it will develop, with intense body and penetrating aromas of blackberry, cocoa powder and tar, these given a lift by flashes of balsam.

O Greco di Tufo Vigna Cicogna '06	🍷🍷	5
O Fiano di Avellino '06	🍷🍷	5
O Greco di Tufo '06	🍷🍷	4*
● Aglianico V. 4 Confini '05	🍷	4
O Greco di Tufo Vigna Cicogna '04	🍷🍷	5
O Greco di Tufo Vigna Cicogna '01	🍷🍷	5
O Greco di Tufo Vigna Cicogna '02	🍷🍷	5
O Greco di Tufo Vigna Cicogna '03	🍷🍷	5
O Greco di Tufo Vigna Cicogna '05	🍷🍷	5

O Greco di Tufo Cutizzi '06	🍷🍷🍷	4*
● Irpinia Serpico '05	🍷🍷🍷	8
O Fiano di Avellino Pietracalda '06	🍷🍷	4*
● Taurasi '04	🍷🍷	6
O Campanaro '06	🍷🍷	5
O Fiano di Avellino '06	🍷🍷	4
O Greco di Tufo '06	🍷🍷	4*
● Rubrato '05	🍷🍷	4*
☉ Irpinia Rosato '06	🍷	4
O Sannio Falanghina '06	🍷	4
O Fiano di Avellino Pietracalda '04	🍷🍷🍷	5
O Greco di Tufo Cutizzi '03	🍷🍷🍷	5*
● Serpico '03	🍷🍷🍷	8
● Serpico '04	🍷🍷🍷	8
● Pàtrimo '04	🍷🍷🍷	8
● Pàtrimo '02	🍷🍷🍷	8

Galardi

FRAZ. SAN CARLO
S.P. SESSA-MIGNANO
81030 SESSA AURUNCA [CE]
TEL. 0823708900
galardi@napoli.com

ANNUAL PRODUCTION   25,000 bottles
HECTARES UNDER VINE 10
VITICULTURE METHOD   Certified organic

Opaque ruby with purple highlights; a strongly smoky base underlying intense aromas of forest fruits, hot spices and cocoa powder; a palate of impressive volume, depth and balsamic freshness: it might look like a description of any number of heavyweight bottles but anyone who has tasted Terra di Lavoro knows that this cannot be confused with any other wine. And this is not just because of its almost unique aromatic profile. It has more to do with amazing ability to provide easy drinkability while retaining explosive energy, showing that power isn't everything. The wine is from aglianico with a little piedirosso and reveals the unmistakable characteristics of its provenance, one whose excellent viticultural potential was discovered only in the mid 1990s when Fontana Galardi started to achieve international success. The hot, humid '05 vintage has imbued it with an atypical style where the usual fruit and smokiness are camouflaged by an elegant vegetal veil. There isn't the massive fullness of the monumental '04 but this is another wine to cellar with care and await with patience.

Cantine Gran Furor Divina Costiera

VIA G. B. LAMA, 16/18
84010 FURORE [SA]
TEL. 089830348
www.granfuror.it

ANNUAL PRODUCTION   97,000 bottles
HECTARES UNDER VINE 14.5
VITICULTURE METHOD   Natural

Sports champions say that not all victories have the same flavour. The first time it's a pure rush of joy, the second time involves more anxiety and then with the third win comes the sense of truly having made it. It's less of an adrenalin rush and more a feeling of lasting satisfaction. Marisa Cuomo and Andrea Ferraioli must be experiencing these emotions as they pick up their third successive Three Glasses for Fiorduva, an outstanding wine which acquires greater maturity at each release. The '06 possibly has less of the mind-blowing hit about it but has a greater sense of completeness. It's as if it had another engine alongside its customary horsepower, not to give added oomph but just to keep its trajectory ramrod-straight. The usual combination of botrytis, ripe citrus fruit and exuberant tropical fruit gains almost candied peel-like sensations, channelling the palate into a sequence of flavours to die for, between even streams of glycerine-rich glory and impressive slaloms of precision and vigour. Furore Bianco '06 is far more than a simple second wine and also scored high. Furore Rosso '06 has exemplary personality and drinkability and Costa d'Amalfi Rosato '06 made an excellent debut.

● Terra di Lavoro '05	▼▼▼ 8
● Terra di Lavoro '02	♀♀♀ 7
● Terra di Lavoro '03	♀♀♀ 7
● Terra di Lavoro '99	♀♀♀ 7
● Terra di Lavoro '04	♀♀♀ 8
● Terra di Lavoro '00	♀♀ 7
● Terra di Lavoro '01	♀♀ 7
● Terra di Lavoro '97	♀♀ 7
● Terra di Lavoro '98	♀♀ 7

O Costa d'Amalfi Furore Bianco Fiorduva '06	▼▼▼ 7
O Costa d'Amalfi Furore Bianco '06	▼▼ 5
● Costa d'Amalfi Furore Rosso '06	▼▼ 5
☉ Costa d'Amalfi Rosato '06	▼ 5
O Costa d'Amalfi Ravello Bianco '06	▼ 5
O Costa d'Amalfi Furore Bianco Fiorduva '04	♀♀♀ 7
O Costa d'Amalfi Furore Bianco Fiorduva '05	♀♀♀ 7
O Costa d'Amalfi Furore Bianco '05	♀♀ 5
● Costa d'Amalfi Furore Rosso Ris. '02	♀♀ 7
● Costa d'Amalfi Furore Rosso Ris. '03	♀♀ 7
O Costa d'Amalfi Furore Bianco Fiorduva '00	♀♀ 7
O Costa d'Amalfi Furore Bianco Fiorduva '01	♀♀ 7
● Costa d'Amalfi Furore Rosso Ris. '01	♀♀ 7
O Costa d'Amalfi Furore Bianco Fiorduva '03	♀♀ 7

Cantine Grotta del Sole

VIA SPINELLI, 2
80010 QUARTO [NA]
TEL. 0818762566
www.grottadelsole.it

ANNUAL PRODUCTION 850,000 bottles
HECTARES UNDER VINE 35
VITICULTURE METHOD Conventional

Forget superstition about numbers: what counts is their real significance. Although 17 is an unlucky number in Italy, and Neapolitans are more superstitious than most, Grotta del Sole has 17 wines this year with One Glass or more. That's more than ever before, which can't be bad news, or bad luck. The winery is the most important in the Campi Flegrei and these results are even more astounding when you consider that its leading wines come from zones which have certainly not received the kiss of Bacchus. There's Lacryma Christi in all shapes and sizes, from a voluptuous '06 Rosso to a chaste Spumante Dolce; there are the irresistible red sparklers from the Penisola Sorrentina, led by Gragnano; there's an '06 Falanghina dei Campi Flegrei of exemplary aroma, proportions and personality. Indeed, there are too many to mention. But it's clear to all that the better the terroir, the better the Martusciello family does. Quarto di Luna, now under the Greco di Tufo denomination, is spot-on: a synthesis of edges and curves, the sharp acidity of the variety offset by ripe, expressive fruit. The other top wine, Quarto di Sole '05, also punches its weight, offering a sure touch and a rising finish.

La Guardiense

LOC. SANTA LUCIA, 104-105
82034 GUARDIA SANFRAMONDI [BN]
TEL. 0824864034
www.laguardiense.it

ANNUAL PRODUCTION 4,000,000 bottles
HECTARES UNDER VINE 1,850
VITICULTURE METHOD Conventional

The La Guardiense co-operative has never been a no-hoper but, quite honestly, it was hard to imagine that there could be such quality increases here in such a short time. With its 3,000,000-unit output and over 1,000 members, it has traditionally provided a sea of bottles that were decent but little more. Then in September 2006, Riccardo Cotarella took control of winemaking, making an immediate difference in the Selezione and Janare lines. Guardiolo Aglianico '06, for example, is the best red ever produced in this small DOC set in the Valle Telesina. In a frame of uncommon cleanliness and definition comes succulent blackcurrant on the nose, complemented by hints of smoke and balsam, and a wisp of cinnamon, which is reprised on the long finish. The fine impression is enhanced by an almost unbelievably low price and the wine took Two red Glasses. Everything else also seems to be spinning skywards, from an '06 Sannio Greco that looks as if it's challenging its Irpinia cousins for fullness, freshness and flavour, to a strongly pervasive '04 Guardiolo Rosso Riserva that is full of fruit. Nothing else is less than good.

O Greco di Tufo Quarto di Luna '05	♟♟	5
● Quarto di Sole '05	♟♟	5
● Vesuvio Lacryma Christi Rosso '06	♟♟	4
● Penisola Sorrentina Gragnano '06	♟♟	4*
● Aglianico '06	♟	4
O Vesuvio Lacryma Christi Dolce	♟	4
O Vesuvio Lacryma Christi Bianco '06	♟	4
● Penisola Sorrentina Lettere '06	♟	4
O Greco di Tufo '06	♟	4
O Fiano di Avellino '06	♟	4
O Coda di Volpe '06	♟	3
● Campi Flegrei Piedirosso Montegauro Ris. '04	♟	4
● Campi Flegrei Piedirosso '06	♟	4
O Campi Flegrei Falanghina '06	♟	4
O Asprinio d'Aversa '06	♟	4
O Asprinio d'Aversa Brut	♟	4

● Guardiolo Aglianico Sel. '06	♟♟	3*
● Guardiolo Aglianico Lucchero '05	♟♟	4*
● Guardiolo Rosso Ris. '04	♟♟	3*
O Sannio Greco Sel. '06	♟♟	3
O Sannio Greco Pietralata '06	♟♟	4*
O Guardiolo Falanghina Senete '06	♟	4
O Sannio Fiano Colle di Tilio '06	♟	4
● Guardiolo Aglianico Cantari Ris. '04	♟	5
O Sannio Fiano Sel. '06	♟	3*

Macchialupa

FRAZ. SAN PIETRO IRPINO
VIA FONTANA
83020 CHIANCHE [AV]
TEL. 0825996396
www.macchialupa.it

Luigi Maffini

FRAZ. SAN MARCO
LOC. CENITO
84071 CASTELLABATE [SA]
TEL. 0974966345
www.maffini-vini.com

ANNUAL PRODUCTION 130,000 bottles
HECTARES UNDER VINE 15
VITICULTURE METHOD Conventional

ANNUAL PRODUCTION 100,000 bottles
HECTARES UNDER VINE 14
VITICULTURE METHOD Conventional

In a few years, we will know more about the particular characteristics of the small Greco di Tufo subzone that stretches from the sulphur mines to the tiny municipality of Chianche. And that knowledge will come thanks to the work of Angelo Valentino, a gentleman winemaker who was involved with the success of many of the Irpinian wines that came to the fore in the 1990s. For some time now he has been concentrating his efforts on his Macchialupa estate and the wines justify his dedication. All of them easily passed the Two Glass threshold and even though there none actually went through to the finals, they all had a distinct style in the modern idiom. The Greco di Tufo and Fiano di Avellino are notable for a structured creaminess that tempers the less comforting aspects of the varieties. Both have good impact and notable concentration but greater depth and a more convincing lift on the finish would have been welcome. The reds are easier to interpret and are definitely not old style, especially Taurasi Le Surte '03, but they are much more than just softness and oakiness cushioning a firm framework that needs oxygenation and bottle ageing.

Luigi Maffini likes to throw down a nonchalant gauntlet with his wines, which are always textbook examples of Cilento excellence. In some ways, he walks a tightrope with his top wines as he pursues harmonious elegance without skimping on concentration or new oak. In fact, he sometimes places too much emphasis on impact. This year, his two top wines, both '05, Pietraincatenata from fiano and Aglianico Cenito, were just a step short of their third triumph because of subtle elements that emerged when we tasted. The former has a wonderful level of rich fruitiness but seems to lack the definition of the previous vintage and has a little too much vanilla and butter, which weigh down both nose and palate. The '06 release of its younger brother, Kratos, always a good One Glass everyday wine, seems to have more style, if less complexity, as it leaps from the glass with a wealth of citrus and delicately herbaceous notes. Cenito '05 remains the top red in Cilento although the fruit is a bit too forward and the tannins a tad dusty.

● Aglianico '05	♀♀ 4*
● Taurasi Le Surte '03	♀♀ 6
○ Greco di Tufo '06	♀♀ 4*
○ Fiano di Avellino '06	♀♀ 4*
○ Fiano di Avellino '04	♀♀ 4
● Taurasi Le Surte '01	♀♀ 5
○ Fiano di Avellino '05	♀♀ 4
● Taurasi Le Surte '02	♀♀ 6
○ Greco di Tufo '05	♀♀ 4

● Cilento Aglianico Cenito '05	♀♀ 6
○ Pietraincatenata '05	♀♀ 5
○ Kràtos '06	♀♀ 4*
● Cilento Aglianico Cenito '03	♀♀♀ 6
○ Pietraincatenata '04	♀♀♀ 5
● Cenito '00	♀♀ 7
● Cenito '01	♀♀ 7
● Cilento Aglianico Cenito '04	♀♀ 6
● Cenito '99	♀♀ 7
○ Pietraincatenata '03	♀♀ 5

★ Mastroberardino

VIA MANFREDI, 75/81
83042 ATRIPALDA [AV]
TEL. 0825614111
www.mastroberardino.com

ANNUAL PRODUCTION 2,400,000 bottles
HECTARES UNDER VINE 300
VITICULTURE METHOD Conventional

Two sets of Three Glasses for
Mastroberardino is news of the "dog bites
man" variety. And why should we be
amazed by fabulous quality from a Taurasi
Radici Riserva that comes from a five-star
vintage like '01? Truth to tell, a top award is
almost a formality for a wine whose
charisma and disarming depth of flavour
speak more eloquently than its single
components, touches of chalk and cigars
enhancing aristocratic fruit that is only
apparently understated. Nor is chance in
any way involved in the repeat Three
Glasses for Novaserra, a textbook example
of Greco di Tufo from a remarkable year,
'06. Typical, rather odd, rusticity seems to
dissolve like magic into an easy-going wine
with a sure touch, full of peach and aniseed,
and a well-sustained, unwavering palate.
When it comes the group of wines that went
through to the finals, it's not quite "man
bites dog" news but they did make a huge
impression, the highlighter pen coming out
in particular for a scrumptious straight
Greco di Tufo '06, a Taurasi Radici '04
oozing youth and a Falanghina d'Irpinia '06
soaring to levels hitherto unknown to the
variety.

Salvatore Molettieri

C.DA MUSANNI, 19B
83040 MONTEMARANO [AV]
TEL. 082763424
www.salvatoremolettieri.it

ANNUAL PRODUCTION 50,000 bottles
HECTARES UNDER VINE 11
VITICULTURE METHOD Conventional

In today's modern era, when picking times
are determined by meteorological stations
and flow diagrams, it's nice to know that at
Montemarano they stick to the tried and
tested method of placing a lookout in front
of Vigna Cinque Querce. When Salvatore
Molettieri and his family give the OK,
complete frenzy explodes in the hills of the
upper Calore valley. Few can match
Salvatore's grapes, though, and his huge
hands are right there, every single year, to
shape the most powerful, masculine and
sanguine face of Taurasi. At times,
Salvatore's wines can be almost too much,
as with Vigna Cinque Querce '03, where the
boiling hot year didn't detract from the
wine's personality, fruit freshness or
minerality but it did shift the balance a little
too much in the direction of alcohol and
extraction. It earned Two red Glasses but
we'll be following its development. Salvatore
produced a Taurasi Riserva in '02, despite
the rainy vintage, and we can't fault his
decision. Its tannins are still unsettled but,
that aside, it's a classic. Aglianico Cinque
Querce '05 is also looking good.

○ Greco di Tufo Novaserra '06	♈♈♈	4*
● Taurasi Radici Ris. '01	♈♈♈	6
○ Greco di Tufo '06	♈♈	4*
○ Irpinia Falanghina '06	♈♈	4*
● Taurasi Radici '04	♈♈	5
● Aglianico '05	♈♈	4*
○ Irpinia Fiano Passito Melizie '05	♈♈	5
● Taurasi Naturalis Historia '03	♈♈	7
○ Fiano di Avellino '06	♈♈	4*
○ Fiano di Avellino Radici '06	♈♈	4*
○ Fiano di Avellino More Maiorum '05	♈♈	5
☉ Lacrimarosa '06	♈	4
○ Vesuvio Lacryma Christi Bianco '06	♈	4
○ Fiano di Avellino Radici '05	♉♉♉	4*
● Taurasi Radici Ris. '99	♉♉♉	7
● Taurasi Radici Ris. '00	♉♉♉	6

● Taurasi Vigna Cinque Querce '03	♈♈	8
● Taurasi Vigna Cinque Querce Ris. '02	♈♈	8
● Aglianico Cinque Querce '05	♈	5
○ Fiano di Avellino Apianum '06	♈	5
● Ischia Piana '05	♈	5
● Taurasi Vigna Cinque Querce '01	♉♉♉	6
● Taurasi Vigna Cinque Querce Ris. '01	♉♉♉	8
● Taurasi Vigna Cinque Querce '00	♉♉	6
● Taurasi Vigna Cinque Querce Ris. '00	♉♉	7
● Taurasi Vigna Cinque Querce '98	♉♉	7
● Taurasi Vigna Cinque Querce Ris. '97	♉♉	8

★ Montevetrano

LOC. NIDO
VIA MONTEVETRANO, 3
84099 SAN CIPRIANO PICENTINO [SA]
TEL. 089882285
www.montevetrano.it

ANNUAL PRODUCTION 30,000 bottles
HECTARES UNDER VINE 5
VITICULTURE METHOD Conventional

An old southern Italian adage states that no-one is born "imparato" (knowing it). That's not quite true. Just ask the most famous Silvia on the Italian wine scene, Silvia Imparato no less, whose name seems to presage a life of nothing but success. She makes it seem the easiest thing in the world to rustle up a wine like Montevetrano, an elegant red from cabernet sauvignon, merlot and a little aglianico. Montevetrano gained legendary status in no time at all and now is not so much a wine as an icon before which you stand in awe, like a Mozart sonata, a Monet canvas or an Antonioni film. And all you need do to pay it homage is reach for the corkscrew. The 12th Three Glass award from 13 releases goes to a marvellous '05 which, despite the tetchy vintage, has uncompromising thrust and clarity. In some ways, it recalls the powerful but linearly focused '99: graceful nuances of liquorice, cedar wood and white pepper ease perfectly into a fleshy mix of blackberry and raspberry; a breeze of balsam crosses the spicy palate and drives the fruit to even greater depth.

Perillo

C.DA VALLE, 19
83040 CASTELFRANCI [AV]
TEL. 082772252

ANNUAL PRODUCTION 20,000 bottles
HECTARES UNDER VINE 4
VITICULTURE METHOD Conventional

Taurasi has been produced for over a century but in some ways, it is too new for a systematic classification of its crus, which could provide a scientific understanding of its style. For decades, the wine was almost always blended across different vineyards. It was only in the mid 1990s, as more and more growers began to vinify and bottle their own fruit, that we began to understand a little more about the influence of site. One of these new producers was a former manual worker with a passion for grapes and wine, Michele Perillo. He is now the authoritative voice of the unique subzone comprising the areas of Montemarano, Castelfranci and Paternopoli. Reaching 600 metres, it's the highest part of the zone, characterized by savage day-night temperature swings, giving grapes of high potential alcohol and extract that are often picked as late as November. This means that the challenge is always to harness the power and restless impetuosity that aglianico develops here. Perillo's '03 Taurasi demonstrates this perfectly. Aromas of plum, nutmeg and macerated herbs lead to a close-knit, confident but a little too firm palate. Irpinia Coda di Volpe '06, Perillo's first white, made a fine impression.

● Montevetrano '05	♟♟♟	8
● Montevetrano '00	♟♟♟	8
● Montevetrano '01	♟♟♟	8
● Montevetrano '02	♟♟♟	8
● Montevetrano '03	♟♟♟	8
● Montevetrano '95	♟♟♟	8
● Montevetrano '99	♟♟♟	8
● Montevetrano '98	♟♟♟	8
● Montevetrano '97	♟♟♟	8
● Montevetrano '96	♟♟♟	8
● Montevetrano '93	♟♟♟	8
● Montevetrano '04	♟♟♟	8

● Taurasi '03	♟♟	6
○ Coda di Volpe '06	♟♟	4*
● Taurasi Ris. '02	♟	6
● Taurasi '00	♟♟	6
● Taurasi '01	♟♟	6
● Taurasi Ris. '01	♟♟	6
● Taurasi '99	♟♟	6
● Taurasi Ris. '00	♟♟	6

Pietracupa
C.DA VADIAPERTI, 17
83030 MONTEFREDANE [AV]
TEL. 0825607418
pietracupa@email.it

Tenuta Ponte
VIA CARAZITA, 1
83040 LUOGOSANO [AV]
TEL. 082773564
www.tenutaponte.it

ANNUAL PRODUCTION 35,000 bottles
HECTARES UNDER VINE 3.5
VITICULTURE METHOD Conventional

You never forget that first time. Just ask Sabino Loffredo, alias Pietracupa, for whom it's always the first time for something. His was the Up-and-Coming Winery in the 2005 Guide, the first time the award went to Campania; his was the first Fiano to be crowned White of the Year; now this ex-sports instructor can glory in his third Three Glass award for Greco di Tufo, the first time a standard, non-oaked Greco has scaled such heights. The '06 is a stunner with a slim, finely targeted, very youthful profile and a comforting approach. It's for wines like this that that over-used term minerality really makes sense. The nose gives wet rocks, accompanied by nuances of white peach and oregano, and the palate is full of thrust as an iodine-like flavour accompanies its interminable length. It holds together as tightly as a hedgehog expecting trouble yet has an utterly distinctive luminosity. Fiano di Avellino '06 scored just a few points less. The nose is gently aromatic, and the palate is taut, but the wine just lacks the final drive of the best releases. Taurasi '03 is 100 per cent Pietracupa in style. Aglianico Quirico '05 is light, almost understated and as appetizing as ever.

ANNUAL PRODUCTION 180,000 bottles
HECTARES UNDER VINE 35
VITICULTURE METHOD Conventional

In a league table of Campania's wines, based on the Glasses awarded in recent Guides, Tenuta Ponte would be right up there in the Champions League zone. And that's no small achievement. After all, the property is anything but a boutique operation. Nevertheless, it consistently manages to turn out a range of wines of notable substance and identity, and does so with determination and no great fuss. This year, Taurasi again leads the line-up. It's from the hot '03 vintage and the year's effects seem most pronounced on the nose, which starts off strangely reduced and almost gassy. Once aerated, though, an attractive balsamic, mineral character emerges. This also comes through on the flavourful, upfront palate which grows gradually to a sound finish. Taurasi might lead the team but Fiano di Avellino '06 deserves to be vice captain. It has a soft yet exuberant aromatic spectrum ranging from bergamot to gooseberry; the palate has complexity and not quite enough length. Greco di Tufo '06 runs it close for style and quality. Cossano '04, from 100 per cent merlot, can hold its own against the more famous names. Everything else is very good, too.

O Greco di Tufo '06	♟♟♟ 4*
O Fiano di Avellino '06	♟♟ 4*
● Quirico '05	♟♟ 5
● Taurasi '03	♟♟ 6
O Cupo '03	♟♟♟ 4*
O Cupo '05	♟♟♟ 5
O Fiano di Avellino '04	♟♟ 4
O Fiano di Avellino '05	♟♟ 4*
O Greco di Tufo "G" '03	♟♟ 4
O Greco di Tufo '05	♟♟ 4*
O Greco di Tufo '04	♟♟ 4
● Taurasi '00	♟♟ 6

O Fiano di Avellino '06	♟♟ 4*
● Taurasi '03	♟♟ 5
O Coda di Volpe '06	♟♟ 3
● Cossano '04	♟♟ 6
O Greco di Tufo '06	♟♟ 4*
O Falanghina '06	♟♟ 3*
● Irpinia Campi Taurasini '05	♟ 3
O Fiano di Avellino '04	♟♟ 4*
● Taurasi '01	♟♟ 6
● Taurasi '00	♟♟ 5*
● Cossano '03	♟♟ 6
O Fiano di Avellino '05	♟♟ 4
O Greco di Tufo '05	♟♟ 4*

Fattoria La Rivolta

C.DA RIVOLTA
82030 TORRECUSO [BN]
TEL. 0824872921
www.fattorialarivolta.com

Ettore Sammarco

VIA CIVITA, 9
84010 RAVELLO [SA]
TEL. 089872774
www.ettoresammarco.it

ANNUAL PRODUCTION 120,000 bottles
HECTARES UNDER VINE 25
VITICULTURE METHOD Certified organic

ANNUAL PRODUCTION 72,000 bottles
HECTARES UNDER VINE 10
VITICULTURE METHOD Conventional

We don't know what the revolts were that led to the name of this small area, which Paolo Cotroneo has borrowed for his winery. But we do find a sort of combative restlessness in his wines that we can't help linking to the name. We're pretty sure, though, that there won't be any rebellion surrounding the excellent impressions they made this year. The whole range was again full of verve, from the supple, long Aglianico del Taburno '05 to the fascinatingly contradictory Sogno di Rivolta '06. The latter is from falanghina, greco and fiano, showing baroque and rarefied at the same time. Equally good is Terra di Rivolta Riserva. Following the '03 that had fired our imaginations, the '04, from a more normal, productive year, is quintessential in outline and lacks absolutely nothing. The impression is that of a wine in evolution, with a highly promising combination on the nose of smoky, forest floor notes and sweet spiciness, followed by firm tannins that will soften in time.

If there were a prize for the revelation of the year, the candidate from Campania would surely be Sammarco. The surprise comes not so much from the quality of the individual wines, since they have been the best not just of the Ravello subzone but of the entire Costa d'Amalfi for a number of years now. No, what really knocked us sideways about this family-run estate was the impression of a huge upswing, a sharp gear change bringing really exciting style. "Pinot Nero," we exclaimed spontaneously while tasting the delicious Ravello Rosso Selva delle Monache Riserva '03, a wine that whispers more than shouts its notes of water melon and blood orange, its highly refined spicy tone and, underlying that, its stamp of pencil lead. The succulent, racy palate has perhaps even more personality and if it lacks just a touch of stuffing that's not a mortal sin. The standard '05 is in similar style and is equally impressive, with the same light touch yet plentiful flavour. The zone's great classic whites also showed excellently. The Terre Saracene Bianco '06 is broader and spicier while Selva delle Monache Bianco '06 is lighter but more incisive.

● Aglianico del Taburno Terra di Rivolta Ris. '04	♟♟ 6
● Aglianico del Taburno '05	♟♟ 4*
O Sogno di Rivolta '06	♟♟ 4*
O Taburno Falanghina '06	♟♟ 4*
● Piedirosso '06	♟ 4
O Taburno Coda di Volpe '06	♟ 4
O Sannio Fiano '06	♟ 4
● Aglianico del Taburno Terra di Rivolta Ris. '03	♟♟ 6
● Aglianico del Taburno '04	♟♟ 4*
● Aglianico del Taburno Terra di Rivolta Ris. '00	♟♟ 6

● Costa d'Amalfi Ravello Rosso Selva delle Monache Ris. '03	♟♟ 5
● Costa d'Amalfi Ravello Rosso Selva delle Monache '05	♟♟ 4*
O Costa d'Amalfi Terre Sarecene Bianco '06	♟♟ 4
O Costa d'Amalfi Ravello Bianco Selva delle Monache '06	♟♟ 4*
● Costa d'Amalfi Terre Saracene Rosso '05	♟ 4*
O Costa d'Amalfi Ravello Bianco V. Grotta Piana '06	♟ 5
⊙ Costa d'Amalfi Ravello Rosato Selva delle Monache '06	♟ 4
● Costa d'Amalfi Ravello Rosso Selva delle Monache '04	♟♟ 4
O Costa d'Amalfi Ravello Bianco Selva delle Monache '05	♟♟ 4

Tenuta Adolfo Spada

FRAZ. VAGLIE
LOC. FONTANA DI TEANO
81045 GALLUCCIO [CE]
TEL. 0823925709
www.tenutaspada.it

ANNUAL PRODUCTION N.A.
HECTARES UNDER VINE N.A.
VITICULTURE METHOD Conventional

The star of Adolfo Spada is rising. His is the voice of modernity and ambition in Galluccio, a controversial area on the Lazio border with great, but not yet fully realized, potential. Gladius '05, from 100 per cent aglianico, has all the minerality and elegant generosity that the grape should have here, along with fullness and cohesiveness. It's still a fairly new wine but already recognized as a Supercampanian. Riccardo Cotarella is consultant oenologist and his touch is mainly apparent in the precision of the fruit. The nose gives blackcurrant and black cherry shot through with balsam and spice, then the palate seems completely unrestrained, its firm sweetness fully melded into a powerful tannic structure. If any doubts remained about this youngish estate's standing, Spada's second and third wines dispel them. Gallicius '06, from 100 per cent aglianico, is a delightful compromise between austerity and softness, with an attractive tobacco, black pepper and marjoram nose, and a tight-knit, complex palate. The price is surprisingly good, too. Sabus '06, from aglianico, piedirosso and montepulciano, is more straightforward.

Cantina del Taburno

VIA SALA
82030 FOGLIANISE [BN]
TEL. 0824871338
www.cantinadeltaburno.it

ANNUAL PRODUCTION 1,800,000 bottles
HECTARES UNDER VINE 550
VITICULTURE METHOD Conventional

After last year's gratifying results, this year the wines from this large co-operative are again good, but nothing really hit the heights. Of course the top wine, Bue Apis, was absent this year making it harder to achieve something exceptional. We've tasted a cask sample of the '04 but we're waiting till next year to assess it properly. That aside, our desire for something more from the next release of wines is justified because Cantina del Taburno's real strengths come from its across-the-board quality and its historic ability to drive change in a zone where progress is otherwise only timid. Falanghina del Taburno '06 and Fidelis '04 are both wines of surprisingly good definition and attractiveness and their bargain-basement pricing is an additional plus. Delius '04 is more demonstrative and baroque. It's a sort of second-string Bue Apis, both in terms of intent and, often, the final result. Filippo Colandrea brings a sure touch to Torlicoso '06, a good-value, inexpensive blend of aglianico and piedirosso but the barrique-aged Folius '05, from falanghina, shows less confidence. The other wines are fair.

● Gladius '05	♟♟ 5
● Gallicius Rosso '06	♟♟ 3*
● Sabus '06	♟ 4
● Gladius '03	♟♟ 5
● Gladius '02	♟♟ 4*
● Gladius '04	♟♟ 5

● Taburno Aglianico Fidelis '04	♟♟ 4*
○ Taburno Falanghina '06	♟♟ 4*
● Taburno Aglianico Delius '04	♟♟ 6
○ Taburno Falanghina Folius '05	♟ 5
○ Fiano '06	♟ 4
○ Coda di Volpe Amineo '06	♟ 4
● Torlicoso '06	♟ 3
● Bue Apis '00	♟♟♟ 7
● Bue Apis '99	♟♟♟ 7
● Delius '00	♟♟ 6
● Bue Apis '01	♟♟ 8

Terre del Principe
FRAZ. SQUILLE
VIA SS. GIOVANNI E PAOLO, 30
81010 CASTEL CAMPAGNANO [CE]
TEL. 0823867126
www.terredelprincipe.com

ANNUAL PRODUCTION 50,000 bottles
HECTARES UNDER VINE 11
VITICULTURE METHOD Conventional

Describing the performance of Giuseppe Mancini's and Manuela Piancastelli's wines this year is a bit like deciding whether a glass is half full or half empty. If the quantity or quality of the wines we tasted were the criterion, we'd say it was definitely more than half full but when we consider that once again Vigna Piancastelli missed Three Glasses by a whisker, we veer towards half empty. It's hard to say what the '04 lacks. A single-vineyard, 50-50 blend of pallagrello and casavecchia, it has finesse and breadth too from its earthy, tertiary scents of undergrowth. There's also mouthfilling fleshiness, balsamic tautness and good tannic bracing. Yet there's a sweet stamp to the finish that stands slightly apart and leaves a niggle of doubt about longevity. The estate has also produced some excellent wines from '05, despite it not being the best of vintages. Elegance and pace help Castello delle Femmine to rise above the rest but were it not for a tad too much oak, the smoky Casavecchia Centomoggia would match it. The '06 Pallagrello Bianco Fontantavigna is again far and away the best of its type.

Terredora
VIA SERRA
83030 MONTEFUSCO [AV]
TEL. 0825968215
www.terredora.com

ANNUAL PRODUCTION 1,200,000 bottles
HECTARES UNDER VINE 180
VITICULTURE METHOD Conventional

Once more Terredora, the complete antithesis of all smoke and no fire, won a raft of Glasses and value-for-money stars. Following a couple of vintages when the lead was taken by the two Greco di Tufos, this time it was Fiano di Avellino Terre di Dora '06 which made it to the finals. But it didn't quite win top honours, for the same reasons that have held previous releases back. Despite a wealth of exuberant, clearly defined aromas, with apricot, celery stalks and roasted hazelnuts, the palate loses out on balance, butteriness and softness overwhelming the touch of minerality that would give it the edge. Of the two Greco di Tufos, we prefer Loggia della Serra '06, despite its slightly excessive fermentative note, but Terra degli Angeli '06 showed well too and has a good citrus timbre. Although the almost too modern, fruit-forward style that typifies Terredora sometimes gets the better of the more classic denominations, the exuberance often brings out the best in humbler wines, like Coda di Volpe, Falanghina d'Irpinia and Aglianico, all '06. All easily earned Two Glasses and awards for good value.

● Vigna Piancastelli '04	♟♟ 7
● Castello delle Femmine '05	♟♟ 4
● Centomoggia '05	♟♟ 6
○ Fontanavigna Pallagrello Bianco '06	♟♟ 5
● Ambruco '05	♟ 6
● Centomoggia '04	♟♟ 6
○ Le Serole Pallagrello Bianco '03	♟♟ 5
● Ambruco '04	♟♟ 6
● Vigna Piancastelli '03	♟♟ 7
○ Fontanavigna Pallagrello Bianco '05	♟♟ 4

○ Fiano di Avellino Terre di Dora '06	♟♟ 4*
● Aglianico '06	♟♟ 4*
○ Greco di Tufo Loggia della Serra '06	♟♟ 4*
○ Greco di Tufo Terra degli Angeli '06	♟♟ 4*
○ Falanghina d'Irpinia '06	♟♟ 4*
○ Coda di Volpe '06	♟♟ 3*
● Aglianico Il Principio '05	♟ 5
○ Falanghina '06	♟ 4
○ Fiano di Avellino Campo Re '05	♟ 5
● Vesuvio Lacryma Christi Rosso '05	♟ 4
○ Fiano di Avellino Terre di Dora '04	♟♟ 4*
○ Greco di Tufo Loggia della Serra '05	♟♟ 4*
○ Greco di Tufo Terra degli Angeli '05	♟♟ 4*
○ Greco di Tufo Terra degli Angeli '04	♟♟ 4*
○ Greco di Tufo Loggia della Serra '04	♟♟ 4*

Torricino

LOC. TORRICINO, 5
83010 TUFO [AV]
TEL. 0825998119
www.torricino.com

ANNUAL PRODUCTION 30,000 bottles
HECTARES UNDER VINE N.A.
VITICULTURE METHOD Conventional

The competent Stefano Di Marzo did not take an easy route to finding a niche in the heterogeneous Irpinian wine scene. His ideas on what Greco di Tufo should be like are quite uncompromising. For him, it's a wine that has the extraction of traditional small-scale production, that is golden yellow, that has pastryshop aromas, and that has enough opulence on the palate to counter the variety's considerable acidity. And that's exactly how his wines are, Fiano di Avellino included. But, for us, they still need a bit of work. There is fascination in the rich nuances of wood resin, grape skins and toasted almond on the '06 Greco di Tufo but its alcoholic, slightly phenolic and rather over-evolved finish leaves it stuck in the water. Paradoxically, Greco di Tufo Raone '05 has a clearer profile. The vintage is not of the best, the tertiary honey and wax aromas are still rather overwhelmed by oak, but an unexpected citrus and balsamic thrust marks its passage through the mouth and a slightly tannic, medicinal herbs finish gives a strong sense of solidity.

Urciuolo

FRAZ. CELZI
VIA DUE PRINCIPATI, 9
83020 FORINO [AV]
TEL. 0825761649
www.fratelliurciuolo.it

ANNUAL PRODUCTION 100,000 bottles
HECTARES UNDER VINE 25
VITICULTURE METHOD Conventional

If we were bookmakers and decided to take bets on who were to be the future stars of Taurasi, we would think very carefully before giving odds on the Urciuolos. Because the two brothers, Antonello and Cirò, supported by skilled winemaker Carmine Valentino, know what they're on about with aglianico and the quality of their reds improves exponentially year by year. Having come up with an exciting wine from the rainy '02 vintage, they've handled the scorching '03 even better. There's not a trace of overripeness. Instead, elegant hints of balsam enliven a weighty, characterful succulence and pencil lead minerality melds along and across the palate into sweet sensations of cinnamon and black cherry leaves. It came within an inch of the Three Glass threshold, and it surely can't be long before those brilliant brothers bridge the gap. But it's not just the Taurasi that's flying high. The two '06 whites have again distinguished themselves with excellent weight and backbone. If only they had a little more mineral intrigue, especially the highly assertive Fiano di Avellino Faliesi, they would really fly. Aglianico '05 is tight yet meaty.

O Greco di Tufo '06	♟♟	4*
O Greco di Tufo Raone '05	♟♟	4*
O Fiano di Avellino '06	♟♟	4*
● Aglianico '05	♟♟	4*
O Fiano di Avellino '05	♟♟	4*
O Greco di Tufo '04	♟♟	4*
O Greco di Tufo '05	♟♟	4*
O Greco di Tufo Raone '04	♟♟	4

● Taurasi '03	♟♟	6
● Aglianico '05	♟♟	3*
O Fiano di Avellino Faliesi '06	♟♟	4*
O Greco di Tufo '06	♟♟	4*
O Fiano di Avellino '06	♟♟	4*
O Fiano di Avellino Faliesi '04	♟♟	4*
● Taurasi '02	♟♟	6
O Fiano di Avellino Faliesi '05	♟♟	4*
O Greco di Tufo '05	♟♟	4*
● Taurasi '01	♟♟	5
O Fiano di Avellino '04	♟♟	4*
O Fiano di Avellino '05	♟♟	4*
● Taurasi '99	♟♟	6

Vadiaperti
C.DA VADIAPERTI
83030 MONTEFREDANE [AV]
TEL. 0825607270
www.vadiaperti.it

ANNUAL PRODUCTION 50,000 bottles
HECTARES UNDER VINE 8
VITICULTURE METHOD Conventional

The nicest and most difficult part of judging wines for the Guide is finding the right balance between the weight given to the characteristics of a wine as tasted and marks for how we feel it will turn out in the future. It's a double conundrum with wines like those of Raffaele Troisi. His are inscrutable, tightly wound wines that evolve remarkably slowly – this year's more than most – but which can give fabulous sensations to those who have the patience to wait. Fiano di Avellino '05 may well be one of these. It's still tasting very young and currently there are contradictory elements on the nose, a sweetly lactic tenor fighting with rawer, more incisive elements. The palate too contrasts apparent subtlety with a firmness typical of the estate. We shall watch how this develops with great interest. Greco di Tufo Tornante '05 is a notch further down. The two young whites, Greco di Tufo '06 and Fiano di Avellino '06, are difficult to fathom. For now, our preference is for the more powerful, close-knit Greco. Coda di Volpe '06 is not much more than fair.

Villa Diamante
VIA TOPPOLE, 16
83030 MONTEFREDANE [AV]
TEL. 0825670014
villadiamante@tiscali.it

ANNUAL PRODUCTION 10,000 bottles
HECTARES UNDER VINE 2.5
VITICULTURE METHOD Certified organic

There are few estates in the region with such determined, enthusiastic supporters as Villa Diamante's. Its fans love the real passion in the approach of husband-and-wife team Antoione Gaita and Diamante Renna; they adore the fact that the wine is a true cru, from a south-east facing site on the Montefredane hill; and they revere the artisan-like winemaking, in the best sense of the word. Some releases of Fiano di Avellino Vigna della Congregazione have absolutely wowed us but our enthusiasm does not blind us to its lack of consistency. Apart from bottle variation, the wine seems to prefer even-numbered vintages. The highly mineral '04 clinched Three Glasses but it has been followed by a rather ordinary '05 whose ageing potential has raised concerns. It's a deep golden yellow; the nose has some yeasty pungency but is somewhat weighed down with honey and dried fruit; there is breadth and substance on the palate but also a decided whack of acidity that compromises its balance and depth. Still, the '06 is on its way and should, we hope, help us to forget our disappointment.

O Fiano di Avellino Aipierti '05	♀♀	4*
O Fiano di Avellino '06	♀♀	4*
O Greco di Tufo Tornante '05	♀♀	4*
O Greco di Tufo '06	♀♀	4*
● Aglianico '03	♀	4
O Irpinia Coda di Volpe '06	♀	2*
O Irpinia Coda di Volpe '05	♀♀	2*
O Greco di Tufo '05	♀♀	4*
O Greco di Tufo '04	♀♀	4*
O Fiano di Avellino '05	♀♀	4
O Fiano di Avellino '04	♀♀	4
O Fiano di Avellino '93	♀♀	4
O Fiano di Avellino '94	♀♀	4
O Fiano di Avellino '95	♀♀	4
O Fiano di Avellino '96	♀♀	4

O Fiano di Avellino Vigna della Congregazione '05	♀♀	5
O Fiano di Avellino Vigna della Congregazione '04	♀♀♀	5
O Fiano di Avellino Vigna della Congregazione '02	♀♀	5

Villa Matilde

S.S. DOMITIANA, 18 KM. 4,700
81030 CELLOLE [CE]
TEL. 0823932088
www.villamatilde.it

Villa Raiano

LOC. SAN MICHELE DI SERINO
VIA NOCELLETTO, 28B
83020 SERINO [AV]
TEL. 0825595663
www.villaraiano.it

ANNUAL PRODUCTION 700,000 bottles
HECTARES UNDER VINE 120
VITICULTURE METHOD Conventional

ANNUAL PRODUCTION 200,000 bottles
HECTARES UNDER VINE 17
VITICULTURE METHOD Conventional

Is Villa Matilde synonymous with Falerno? Or vice versa? For since the 1960s when Francesco Avallone, then a young lawyer, discovered his vocation as a wine man, the destiny of the estate has been inextricably bound up with this legendary wine of antiquity. His children, Maria Ida and Salvatore, have long trod the path he mapped out, with support from Riccardo Cotarella. The red Camarato '04 is on hold, to benefit from further bottle age before release, leaving the field free for white Caracci to take centre stage. And the '05 repeated the achievement of the '04, bringing home Three Glasses. Its profile is even more racy and direct than last year's version, with a crisp nose full of mandarin, lemon verbena, apples and wafts of other aromas. These sensations also come through on the sweetly fruity but restrained, supple and very long palate. Yet Tenute d'Altavilla '06 is even more amazing and definitely one of the best Greco di Tufos ever. The nose is citrus-like and smoky, with just a slight fermentative hint, and the weighty, long palate is a delight. Cecubo '05 is elegant, minerally and has an attractive incense-like finish. We gave it Two red Glasses.

Some years ago, the Villa Raiano team would probably have died for the string of black and red Glasses they are now picking up year after year. Even so, we don't think that Simone and Sabino Basso, Paolo Sibillo and Luigi Moio can remain happy as things stand. This year, Three Glasses were again at their fingertips, and again slipped through them, for reasons not dissimilar to those that have seen them just miss top honours before. Greco di Tufo sailed into the finals as usual, the '06 shining for cleanliness, precision, fruity exuberance and roundness. But the wine hangs too heavily on butteriness and tropicality and lacks that extra touch of spark and depth that would allow it to soar. Fiano di Avellino '06 has more character on the nose but less cohesiveness and length on the palate. Taurasi Cretanera Riserva '03, another finalist, is modern in style, and has sweet but not cloying ripe cherry fruit on the nose, interwoven with slightly ethery notes of wood resin, myrtle leaves and wet earth; the palate is fleshy and full of extract, favouring breadth over depth.

O Falerno del Massico Bianco Vigna Caracci '05	♟♟♟	5
● Cecubo '05	♟♟	5
O Greco di Tufo Tenute di Altavilla '06	♟♟	4*
● Falerno del Massico Rosso '05	♟♟	4*
● Aglianico Rocca dei Leoni '06	♟	3
O Falanghina Rocca dei Leoni '06	♟	3
O Fiano di Avellino Tenute di Altavilla '06	♟	4
O Falerno del Massico Bianco '06	♟	4
O Falerno del Massico Bianco Vigna Caracci '04	♟♟♟	4*
● Falerno del Massico Rosso Vigna Camarato '98	♟♟♟	6
● Falerno del Massico Rosso Vigna Camarato '97	♟♟♟	6
● Falerno del Massico Rosso Vigna Camarato '00	♟♟♟	6
● Falerno del Massico Camarato '01	♟♟♟	6

O Greco di Tufo '06	♟♟	4*
● Taurasi Cretanera Ris. '03	♟♟	6
O Falanghina Beneventano '06	♟♟	4*
● Taurasi '04	♟♟	6
O Fiano di Avellino Ripa Alta '06	♟♟	5
O Fiano di Avellino '06	♟♟	4*
O Aedon Fiano Passito '05	♟	7
☉ Orano '06	♟	4
O Fiano di Avellino '03	♟♟	4*
O Fiano di Avellino '04	♟♟	4
O Fiano di Avellino '05	♟♟	4*
O Greco di Tufo '03	♟♟	4
O Greco di Tufo '04	♟♟	4
O Greco di Tufo '05	♟♟	4
● Taurasi '01	♟♟	6
● Taurasi Ris. '01	♟♟	7

OTHER WINERIES

Aia dei Colombi
C.DA SAPENZE
82034 GUARDIA SANFRAMONDI [BN]
TEL. 0824817384
www.aiadeicolombi.it

The Pascale brothers' estate is one of those attracting most interest in the zone and now their wines are back in great style. Sannio Fiano '06 is quite simply one of the best Fianos we've ever tasted from outside Irpinia's classic zones. Guardiolo Falanghina '06 is racy and immediate.

O Guardiolo Falanghina '06	￥￥	3*
O Sannio Fiano '06	￥￥	3*
● Colle dell'Aia '04	￥	5

Antica Hirpinia
C.DA LENZE, 10
83030 TAURASI [AV]
TEL. 082774730
www.anticahirpinia.it

This was once just the Taurasi co-operative, the collection point for the grapes of the zone's hundreds of small growers. Now it's a modern, functional concern with the fixed aim of producing good wines at sensible prices. The best of this year's bunch is the excellent Irpinia Aglianico '05.

● Irpinia Aglianico '05	￥￥	3*
O Fiano di Avellino '06	￥	4
O Greco di Tufo '06	￥	4
● Taurasi Ris. '01	￥	5

Giuseppe Apicella
FRAZ. CAPITIGNANO
VIA CASTELLO SANTA MARIA, 1
84010 TRAMONTI [SA]
TEL. 089876075
www.giuseppeapicella.it

Quality growth continues at this small estate in Costa d'Amalfi's Tramonti subzone, which produces some of the finest reds in the whole DOC. The '04 Riserva 'A Scippata is again excellent and the standard '05 is even better with modest structure but lots of flesh and flavour. Tramonti Bianco '06 is fair.

● Costa d'Amalfi Tramonti Rosso A' Scippata Ris. '04	￥￥	6
● Costa d'Amalfi Tramonti Rosso '05	￥￥	4*
O Costa d'Amalfi Tramonti Bianco '06	￥	4

Cantine degli Astroni
VIA SARTANIA, 48
80126 NAPOLI [NA]
TEL. 0815884182
www.cantineastroni.com

This emerging winery often manages to make really good wines in the lower price bracket so the good scores it achieved this year over a wide range don't surprise us. Falanghina dei Campi Flegrei '06 and Lacryma Christi Rosato '06 both earned a red circle.

O Campi Flegrei Falanghina '06	￥	3
☉ Vesuvio Lacryma Christi Rosato '06	￥	3
● Campi Flegrei Piedirosso '06	￥	3
O Astro Falanghina Brut	￥	4

Boccella
VIA S. EUSTACHIO
83040 CASTELFRANCI [AV]
TEL. 082772574

You can be sure we'll be keeping our eye on this brand new estate. At its first release Rasott, from aglianico, leapt into the limelight as the best Irpinia Campi Taurasini, and that's not just because it's full of stuffing. The '06 Irpinia Fiano Casa Fatte is again a wine of breeding.

● Irpinia Aglianico Rasott '05	￥￥	4*
O Irpinia Fiano '06	￥￥	4*

Cà Stelle
VIA NAZIONALE SANNITICA, 48
CASTELVENERE [BN]
TEL. 0824940232
www.castelle.it

There are encouraging signs from Cà Stelle, owned by the skilled yet modest Raffaele and Mariano Assini, and set in the most densely planted municipality in Campania. Sannio Falanghina '06 is clean and precise while the Kydonia '05 selection has more character and complexity. Sannio Rosato '06 is perfumed and juicy.

O Sannio Falanghina Kydonia '05	￥￥	3*
☉ Rosato d'Aglianico '06	￥	4
O Sannio Falanghina '06	￥	3

OTHER WINERIES

I Capitani

VIA BOSCO FAIANO, 15
83030 TORRE LE NOCELLE [AV]
TEL. 0825969182
www.icapitani.com

"The Captains", one of Irpinia's loveliest estates, takes the lead from its name and guides its wines securely along their course, compass safely in hand. Greco di Tufo Serum '06 displays great vitality within a solid structure. Taurasi Bosco Faiano '03 is fleshy and juicy, despite the hot vintage.

○ Greco di Tufo Serum '06	🍷🍷 4*
● Taurasi Bosco Faiano '03	🍷🍷 6
○ Fiano di Avellino Gaudium '06	🍷 4
● Ermè '04	🍷 5

Caputo

VIA CONSORTILE
81032 CARINARO [CE]
TEL. 0815033955
www.caputo.it

It's probably an isolated incident but this year Caputo has been downgraded to economy class. While awaiting the return of its customary quality levels, we can recommend an excellent Greco di Tufo Vigna dei Lupi '06 and a fair, if slightly too sweet, Sannio Aglianico Clanius '06.

○ Greco di Tufo Vigne dei Lupi '06	🍷🍷 4*
● Casavecchia '05	🍷 5
● Sannio Aglianico Clanius '06	🍷 4

La Casa dell'Orco

FRAZ. SAN MICHELE
VIA LIMATURO, 50
83039 PRATOLA SERRA [AV]
TEL. 0825967038
www.lacasadellorco.it

We'd hate to have to answer to the legendary "orco" (ogre), from which the Musto family's estate takes its name but this year it has to lose its full entry. Let's be clear, the wines are still substantial and attractive but they haven't quite the character of those that performed so well in the past.

● Taurasi '03	🍷🍷 6
○ Sannio Falanghina Incontri '06	🍷🍷 4*
● Irpinia Aglianico Campi Taurasini '05	🍷 4
○ Fiano di Avellino Incontri '06	🍷 4

Viticoltori del Casavecchia

VIA MADONNA DELLE GRAZIE, 28
81040 PONTELATONE [CE]
TEL. 0823659198
coopcasavecchia@virglilio.it

No wine was ever better named than Sfizio (whim), which indulged a whim of its own and outscored a lot of other rosés. Success derives from the assured touch at this property, which moulds local grapes into numerous styles without ever losing sight of definition and overall balance.

● Erta dei Ciliegi '06	🍷🍷 3*
⊙ Sfizio Rosa '06	🍷🍷 3*
○ Futo '05	🍷 5
● Corte Rosa '05	🍷 4

Castel dei Franci

VIA VALLE
83040 CASTELFRANCI [AV]
TEL. 082772722
www.casteldeifranci.com

The location is one of Irpinia's best for red wines but it is the whites that really stand out. Fiano di Avellino '06, with its citrus-like fullness and attractive salty seam, came within a hair of the finals. Irpinia Coda di Volpe '06 makes for satisfying drinking.

○ Fiano di Avellino '06	🍷🍷 5
○ Irpinia Coda di Volpe '06	🍷 4
● Taurasi '03	🍷 6

Tenuta del Cavalier Pepe

VIA SANTA VARA
83040 LUOGOSANO [AV]
TEL. 082773766
www.tenutacavalierpepe.it

There is no doubt that this newish estate is aiming high. Milena Pepe is skilled, enthusiastic and ambitious and her first releases, especially Irpinia Aglianico Terra del Varo '05, are seriously good. A minerally, citrus-like Greco di Tufo '06 also made a fine debut.

○ Fiano di Avellino Refiano '06	🍷🍷 4*
● Irpinia Aglianico Terra del Varo '05	🍷🍷 4*
○ Greco di Tufo Nestor '06	🍷 4
● Irpinia Aglianico Santo Stefano '05	🍷 4

OTHER WINERIES

Colli Irpini
LOC. SERRA DI MONTEFUSCO
VIA SERRA (ZONA P.I.P.)
83030 MONTEFUSCO [AV]
TEL. 0825963972
www.montesole.it

The dependability and consistency of the wines from this, one of the largest wineries in Irpinia, is exemplary. We can't list them all for reasons of space but be assured that many of them have impressive substance and attractiveness. Taurasi Riserva '00 showed particularly well.

O Sannio Falanghina Simposium '06	🍷🍷	5
● Taurasi Montesolae Kirios Ris. '00	🍷🍷	5
● Taurasi Montesolae '01	🍷🍷	5
O Sussurro Bianco '06	🍷	4

Michele Contrada
C.DA TAVERNA, 31
83040 CANDIDA [AV]
TEL. 0825988434
www.vinicontrada.it

We were keen to taste the wines of Gerardo Contrada, an enthusiastic grower from the good Candida subzone of Fiano di Avellino. Both the '06 and the '03 Fiano embody the characteristics of their variety and origin but they are outpaced by Greco Gaudioso '06. Taurasi Hirpus '03 is also successful.

O Greco di Tufo Gaudioso '06	🍷🍷	4
O Fiano di Avellino Selvecorte '06	🍷	4
O Fiano di Avellino Selvecorte '03	🍷	4
● Taurasi Hirpus '03	🍷	6

Corte Normanna
LOC. SAPENZIE, 20
82034 GUARDIA SANFRAMONDI [BN]
TEL. 0824817004
www.cortenormanna.it

This winery was originally known for its fine Aglianico del Sannio but recently it's come to the fore for its intriguing whites. The exuberant, intense Sannio Falanghina '06 with its taut, expressive palate took Two Glasses. There is good character on Sannio Rosso Guiscardo '05 and Sannio Fiano '06 is fair.

O Sannio Falanghina '06	🍷🍷	3*
● Sannio Aglianico Tre Pietre '02	🍷	4
O Sannio Fiano '06	🍷	4
● Sannio Rosso Guiscardo '05	🍷	3

De Falco
VIA FIGLIOLA
80040 SAN SEBASTIANO AL VESUVIO [NA]
TEL. 0817713755
www.defalco.it

We thought that the expert team here was ready to blossom but here they are in the Other Wineries. The wines are good but not exceptional. The succulent Gragnano della Penisola Sorrentina again leads the range, this year with the '06, followed by Fiano di Avellino, also '06.

● Penisola Sorrentina Gragnano '06	🍷🍷	4*
O Falanghina del Beneventano '06	🍷	3
O Fiano di Avellino '06	🍷	4
● Taurasi '02	🍷	6

Fontanavecchia
VIA FONTANAVECCHIA
82030 TORRECUSO [BN]
TEL. 0824876275
www.fontanavecchia.info

With the more prestigious labels absent this year, it's the standard wines that show what this winery has to give. Falanghina del Taburno '06 has good typicity and is simply delicious. Aglianico del Taburno '05 is equally nice. The first impact is edgy but it gains grace as it develops in the glass.

● Aglianico del Taburno '05	🍷🍷	4*
O Taburno Falanghina '06	🍷🍷	3*
● Aglianico del Taburno V. Cataratte Ris. '03	🍷	5

Cantina Giardino
VIA PETRARA, 21B
83031 ARIANO IRPINO [AV]
TEL. 0825873084
www.cantinagiardino.com

Irpinia, too, has its natural estate with organically run vineyards and no clarification or filtration during winemaking. But production philosophies aside, Antonio and Daniela De Gruttola's small estate turns out wines of indisputable personality that need only to find a little more harmony.

● Drogone '04	🍷🍷	6
● Le Fole '05	🍷	4

OTHER WINERIES

Lunarossa
VIA ANDREA MEO, 1
84096 MONTECORVINO ROVELLA [SA]
TEL. 0898021016
www.viniepassione.it

The '04 release of the lively top wine Combination, from aglianico and cabernet, is the best ever, and the two new basic wines have such depth that they are basic only in price. That's certainly not bad news. Indeed there is continuous improvement in all the wines here.

● Combination '04	♥♥	4*
○ Costacielo Bianco '06	♥♥	3*
● Costacielo Rosso '06	♥	3*

Manimurci
VIA CASALE, 9BIS
83052 PATERNOPOLI [AV]
TEL. 0827771012
www.cantinemanimurci.com

Here's a fine example of consistency bringing strength. The wines have been hovering around Guide level for some time and a good performance this year keeps them in the running. Best of the bunch is Irpinia Campi Taurasini Rossocupo '05, a modern-style aglianico with good texture. Calore '05 impresses, too.

● Rossocupo '05	♥♥	4*
● Taurasi Poema '03	♥	6
☉ Irpinia Ebe '06	♥	4
● Calore '05	♥	3

Raffaele Marino
FRAZ. CIDA MOIO
VIA FONTANA SARACENA, 9
84043 AGROPOLI [SA]
TEL. 0974821719
www.vinimarino.com

In an area like this, where potential is high but few estates compete for the limelight, wines like Marino's are as necessary as daily bread. Fiano '06 is particularly distinguished. It has great breadth of fruit but no sense of this being forced. The palate has taut body yet is wonderfully easy-going.

○ Fiano '06	♥♥	4*
● Cilento Aglianico '05	♥	4

Guido Marsella
VIA MARONE, 2
83010 SUMMONTE [AV]
TEL. 0825626555

Guido Marsella's great, individualistic Fiano is its usual self in '05 despite the vintage's unusual characteristics. The nose is an expansive mix of mango and pineapple, overlaying an intense smokiness with hints of petrol. The palate is imposingly, perhaps slightly excessively, full and rich.

○ Fiano di Avellino '05	♥♥	4*
○ Fiano di Avellino '03	♥♥	4
○ Fiano di Avellino '04	♥♥	4

Masseria Frattasi
VIA TORRE VARANI, 15
82016 MONTESARCHIO [BN]
TEL. 0824834392
www.masseriafrattasi.it

These Masseria Frattasi wines are cheerful, outgoing bottles that never lose their typical Sannio character. The reds lead the range. Aglianico di Caudium '05 is juicy and lively. Aglianico Riserva '04 is earthier and more complex. There are no complaints with the two Falanghinas, either.

● Taburno Aglianico Ris. '04	♥♥	4
● Taburno Aglianico di Caudium '05	♥♥	4*
○ Taburno Falanghina '06	♥	4
○ Taburno Falanghina Donna Laura '05	♥	4

Michele Moio
V.LE REGINA MARGHERITA, 8
81034 MONDRAGONE [CE]
TEL. 0823978017
www.cantinemoio.it

We hope Michele Moio won't be upset to find himself in Other Wineries this year. It's certainly no comment on the overall standing of his wines. But despite their high quality, Moio 57 in particular, competition is growing. We can't wait to see some more great releases from Campania's king of Primitivo.

● Moio 57 '05	♥♥	4*
○ Falerno del Massico Alaora '05	♥	5
● Falerno del Massico Maiatico '04	♥	6
○ Falerno del Massico Bianco '06	♥	4

OTHER WINERIES

La Molara
C.DA PESCO
83040 LUOGOSANO [AV]
TEL. 082778017
www.lamolara.com

This is another sound new estate making its mark on the busy Irpinian scene. Based in the Taurasi zone, it sources its most impressive wines from this prestigious denomination. Taurasi Santa Vara '03 earned Two Glasses, as did the '06 Greco di Tufo Dioniso.

○ Greco di Tufo Dionisio '06 🍷🍷 4*
● Taurasi Santa Vara '03 🍷🍷 6
● Vigna Claudia '05 🍷 4

Cantina dei Monaci
FRAZ. SANTA LUCIA, 206
83030 SANTA PAOLINA [AV]
TEL. 0825964350
www.cantinadeimonaci.it

Angelo Carpenito and Maria Coppola released a first-rate, very varietal Greco di Tufo from the splendid '06 vintage. The nose starts slightly reduced then opens to give fresh almond and green apple before the vibrant, assertive palate ends on a bitterish note. Fiano di Avellino '06 still shows very young.

○ Greco di Tufo '06 🍷🍷 4*
○ Fiano di Avellino '06 🍷🍷 4*

Montevergine
VIA VALLE PONTICELLI
83100 AVELLINO [AV]
TEL. 0825624655

This small estate shies away from the limelight. It avoids mainstream communication channels yet continues to produce one of the most characterful Fiano di Avellinos in circulation. The '06, which has plenty of grip – in fact almost too much – and smokiness on the palate, again reached the finals.

○ Fiano di Avellino '06 🍷🍷 4*
○ Fiano di Avellino '04 🍷🍷 4*

Lorenzo Nifo Sarrapochiello
VIA PIANA
82030 PONTE [BN]
TEL. 0824876450
www.nifo.eu

Last year, we were astounded by a pair of Falanghinas that were miles away from tradition in style. This time, we found a trio of reds which are all substance and fascination. Sarrapochiello managed to tame the scorching '03 with great success in an easy-going, fragrant Taburno Aglianico D'Erasmo Riserva.

● Taburno Aglianico D'Erasmo Ris. '03 🍷🍷 5
● Taburno Aglianico '06 🍷 3
⊙ Taburno Aglianico Màrosa '06 🍷 3
● Taburno Rosso Serrone '06 🍷 3

Gennaro Papa
P.ZZA LIMATA, 2
81030 FALCIANO DEL MASSICO [CE]
TEL. 0823931267
cantinapapa@libero.it

Campania has a wealth of fascinating wines. Often they are fragile and tend to lack body; others have the opposite problem. One of the latter is Papa's Falerno del Massico Campantuono. The '05 has impressive stuffing but needs more poise.

● Falerno del Massico Primitivo Campantuono '05 🍷🍷 6

Petilia
FRAZ. PINCERA
LOC. CAMPO FIORITO
83011 ALTAVILLA IRPINA [AV]
TEL. 0825991696
petilia@interfree.it

Teresa and Roberto Bruno's splendid '06 Greco di Tufo can hardly be described as a novelty. They have a very soft spot for Greco, they know what making wines of typicity is all about and this wine proves it. It's highly mineral, almost sulphury, and has a citrus attack that tails off only on the finish.

○ Greco di Tufo '06 🍷🍷 4*
○ Fiano di Avellino '06 🍷 4

OTHER WINERIES

Ciro Picariello
C.DA ACQUA FESTA
83010 SUMMONTE [AV]
TEL. 0825702516
www.ciropicariello.com

We're sure this isn't a one-off appearance. A full entry could even be in the offing because the wines impressed us with their quality. The austere Fiano di Avellino '05 in particular has huge character, a slight uncertainty on its stony nose doing nothing to obstruct its confident progress.

O Fiano di Avellino '05	🍷🍷	4*

Azienda Agricola La Pietra di Tommasone
VIA PROVINCIALE FANGO, 98
80076 LACCO AMENO [NA]
TEL. 0813330330
tommasonevini@ischia.it

There's ambition aplenty at this newish estate, which makes modern-style wines from Ischia's traditional grapes. We're waiting to see whether there's continuity. Biancolella and fiano combine beautifully in Pithecusa Bianco '06. Aglianico and montepulciano give Pignanera Rosso '04 its thrust.

● Pignanera '04	🍷🍷	7
● Pithecusa Rosso '05	🍷🍷	5
O Pithecusa Bianco '06	🍷🍷	4*
O Terradei '06	🍷	4

Il Poggio
VIA DEFENZE, 4
82030 TORRECUSO [BN]
TEL. 0824874068
www.ilpoggiovini.it

This newcomer is a good example of the encouraging developments in Campania's most productive province. Two wines immediately sail over the Two Glasses threshold, the chameleon-like Aglianico Mirabilis '05 and the unusual Falanghina del Taburno '06.

● Mirabilis '05	🍷🍷	4*
O Taburno Falanghina '06	🍷🍷	3*
O Coda di Volpe '06	🍷	2*

Quintodecimo
VIA SAN LEONARDO
83036 MIRABELLA ECLANO [AV]
TEL. 0825449321
www.quintodecimo.it

Professor and wine man Luigi Moio will release his first Taurasi next year but for now Aglianico Terra d'Eclano '05 stands proudly on its own. Dense and mouthfilling, it's slightly held back by oak. It will take time to come round but the Quintodecimo style is apparent from the start.

● Terra d'Eclano '05	🍷🍷	7
● Terra d'Eclano '04	🍷🍷	6

Rocca del Principe
LOC. ARIANIELLO
VIA ARIANIELLO, 9
83030 LAPIO [AV]
TEL. 0825982435
aurelia65@tele2.it

We don't often see a debut like this in Campania with Two red Glasses. But the Fabrizio family's Fiano di Avellino '06 doesn't spring from nowhere. The makers are one of Lapio's grape-growing dynasties. The area is ideal for fiano, and the aromatic breadth, minerality and thrust of this wine promise well.

O Fiano di Avellino '06	🍷🍷	4*

San Francesco
VIA SOFILCIANO, 18
84010 TRAMONTI [SA]
TEL. 089876748
aziendasanfrancesco@libero.it

San Francesco is yet another fine new estate emerging from the exciting Costa d'Amalfi. The wines are already nudging excellence. Tramonti Rosso '05 is attractive and sound despite some curious butteriness. Pereva Bianco '06 has the iodine tones typical of the style.

O Costa d'Amalfi Bianco Pereva '06	🍷🍷	4*
● Costa d'Amalfi Tramonti Rosso '05	🍷🍷	4*
O Costa d'Amalfi Tramonti Bianco '06	🍷	4
⊙ Costa d'Amalfi Tramonti Rosato '06	🍷	4

OTHER WINERIES

Sanpaolo
VIA FERROVIA, 42
ATRIPALDA [AV]
TEL. 0825610307
info@cantineemera.com

This is one of the few wineries in Irpinia that can marry quality with quantity, as this year's results have shown. The best seems to be the Greco di Tufo, a cheerful incarnation of the often stalky Avellino variety. But Falanghina del Beneventano '06 also shines and Irpinia Aglianico '06 is sound.

O Greco di Tufo '06	♈♈	4*
O Falanghina del Beneventano '06	♈♈	3*
● Irpinia Aglianico '06	♈	4
O Suavemente Bianco '06	♈	4

Santimartini
VIA BEBIANA, 107A
82036 SOLOPACA [BN]
TEL. 0824971254
www.santimartini.it

Only time will tell if this is a happy combination of events or the start of something big. Our guess is the latter because Santimartini blew us away with the lesser known wine types. We had a new insight into Solpaca and the cellar maintains high quality throughout the entire range.

● Sannio Aglianico Kyathos '04	♈♈	4*
● Solopaca Rosso Cl. Pietre Sparse '04	♈♈	4*
O Sannio Bianco '06	♈♈	2*
O Solopaca Bianco Cl. Pietre Sparse '06	♈	4

Telaro
LOC. CALABRITTO
VIA CINQUE PIETRE, 2
81045 GALLUCCIO [CE]
TEL. 0823925841
www.vinitelaro.it

Would the Guide be complete without the wines from the fine Telaro estate? We don't think so because they are always attractive, well-priced options for those who enjoy drinking more than tasting. Falanghina Tefrite Brut gets better every year. Falanghina Ripabianca '06 is simply delicious.

O Falanghina Tefrite Brut	♈♈	4*
● Calivierno '05	♈	5
O Galluccio Falanghina Ripabianca '06	♈	3
● Galluccio Ara Mundi Ris. '04	♈	5

Terranera
VIA SANDRO PERTINI, 13
83010 GROTTOLELLA [AV]
TEL. 0825671455
www.cantineterranera.it

In Avellino, where properties are highly fragmented, 250,000 bottles a year is a lot. And three wines out of three with Two Glasses is a lot, too, especially for a new estate. The trio share fruity richness, density and verve. Not bad for a first outing.

O Fiano di Avellino V. della Sabina '06	♈♈	4*
O Greco di Tufo V. di Tora '06	♈♈	4*
O Irpinia Coda di Volpe '06	♈♈	4*

Terre Stregate
VIA MUNICIPIO, 105
82034 GUARDIA SANFRAMONDI [BN]
TEL. 0824864312
www.terrestregate.it

There are some things that can't be explained by counting Glasses. Some wines have a soul that is more than the sum of their individual components. They communicate a potential that goes way beyond numbers. Terre Stregate wines excel for honesty and lightness.

O Sannio Aurora '06	♈	4
● Manent '05	♈	4
O Sannio Falanghina Svelato '06	♈	4
O Sannio Fiano Genius Loci '06	♈	4

Torre del Pagus
VIA CIRASIELLO
82030 PAUPISI [BN]
TEL. 0824886084
www.torredelpagus.it

The tragic loss of Luigi Rapuano was a huge blow, even to those who did not know him well. In the face of this, any comment risks seeming rhetorical but we are sincerely convinced that he will live on through his Torre del Pagus wines. We wish his family well.

● Sannio Aglianico '04	♈♈	4*
● Impeto '03	♈	5
O Taburno Falanghina '06	♈	4

OTHER WINERIES

Torre Gaia
VIA BOSCO CUPO, 11
82030 DUGENTA [BN]
TEL. 0824978172
www.torregaia.net

The 14 wines from Torre Gaia prove that this fine estate has not been sitting on its laurels since the brilliant scores of a few years ago. From Sannio Falanghina Opera '06, through Sannio Fiano Gradualis '06 to Sannio Rosso Aia Vecchia '03, this is a range to frame.

O Sannio Falanghina Opera '06	♥♥	4*
O Sannio Fiano Gradualis '06	♥	4
● Sannio Rosso Aia Vecchia '03	♥	6

Antica Masseria Venditti
VIA SANNITICA, 120/122
82037 CASTELVENERE [BN]
TEL. 0824940306
www.venditti.it

You certainly can't take Nicola Venditti's wines for granted. This passionate grape grower makes wines that are difficult and demand patience but those who make the effort can gain new insight from them. Our preference from a fine range goes to Aglianico Marraioli '05.

● Sannio Aglianico Marraioli '05	♥♥	4*
● Sannio Barbera Barbetta '06	♥♥	4*
O Solopaca Bianco Vigna Bacalàt '06	♥	4
● Solopaca Rosso Bosco Caldaia '03	♥	5

Vesevo
C.DA RAPONE
83020 FORINO [AV]
TEL. 0859067388
www.vesevo.it

Add the local experience of Mario Ercolino to the aspirations Farnese team and you have a combination that produces one of the most promising ranges around. Numerous wines scored well and there are some notable peaks, especially the powerful Taurasi '03 and the vibrant Greco di Tufo '06.

● Beneventano Aglianico '05	♥♥	4*
O Fiano di Avellino '06	♥♥	4*
● Taurasi '03	♥♥	6
O Greco di Tufo '06	♥♥	4*

Vestini - Campagnano
FRAZ. SS. GIOVANNI E PAOLO
VIA BARRACCONE, 5
81013 CAIAZZO [CE]
TEL. 0823679087
www.vestinicampagnano.it

Glasses clink in celebration as Vestini Campagnano comes back to the Guide. We reckon it will soon move on to a full entry since lawyer Alberto Barletta is putting everything into the relaunch of his estate, where pallagrello-casavecchia blends give the best results.

O Pallagrello Bianco '06	♥♥	5
● Concarosso '04	♥♥	5
● Connubio '03	♥♥	8
● Casa Vecchia '04	♥	6

BASILICATA

This year Basilicata has proved itself one of the most interesting, dynamic regions on the Italian wine scene. There were an impressive four Three Glass awards for some of its leading producers but considering that several important estates have decided to postpone release of their wines for a year, the haul could have been even bigger. Indeed, Paternoster, Tenuta le Querce and Cantina del Vulture are not featured in this year's Guide. The honours this time go to Michele Cutolo with his Aglianico del Vulture Basilisco '04, the Fucci family with their Aglianico del Vulture Titolo '05, Mario Bisceglia with Aglianico del Vulture Gudarrà '04, a first-time winner of the award, and Gruppo Italiano Vini-owned Terre degli Svevi, which submitted an excellent Aglianico del Vulture Vigneto Serpara '03. Yet the list of winners and that of the producers who have not yet released their wines should not induce us to underrate the other entrants. A remarkable number of wines reached our finals this year and we can confidently say that the average level of Basilicata's production is growing rapidly. Vulture is one of the brightest stars in the Italian wine firmament and the province of Matera, the home of Matera DOC wines and the soon-to-be-released wines from Terre dell'Alta Val d'Agri DOC, is laying the foundations for future success. In the meantime, it's Aglianico all the way, with the four Three Glass-winning wines and at least a dozen more that can rival their expressiveness and immaculate style. Traditional producers – two examples are D'Angelo and Paternoster – have shown they can keep pace with the times and they have been joined by fast-developing, small, family-run wineries and targeted investments by wine-focused enterprises, such as GIV and Feudi di San Gregorio, or businesses from other sectors, like Bisceglia and Di Palma. The panorama is completed by a thriving co-operative sector, with well-run wineries that release a fine range of territory-dedicated bottles at very interesting prices.

Basilisco

VIA UMBERTO I, 129
85028 RIONERO IN VULTURE [PZ]
TEL. 0972725477
basilisco@interfree.it

Winers Basilium

C.DA PIPOLI
85011 ACERENZA [PZ]
TEL. 0971741449
www.basilium.it

ANNUAL PRODUCTION 30,000 bottles
HECTARES UNDER VINE 10
VITICULTURE METHOD Conventional

Michele Cutolo and his wife Nunzia have
once again proved themselves worthy of the
praise that we have lavished on their estate
in past editions with an excellent Aglianico
del Vulture Basilisco '04. The Cutolos first
tasted success with an exemplary '01
vintage and repeated the feat three years
later. A husband-and-wife team assisted by
oenologist Lorenzo Landi, they vinify only
the grapes from their ten hectares of fine
vineyards in Barile and Rionero. The annual
production of 30,000 bottles is divided
equally between two wines, of which
Basilisco is the "grand vin". The '04 vintage
is an inky-dark ruby with an intense bouquet
of red and black berry fruit, oak and
aniseed, mingling with delicate tobacco and
aromatic herbs. Dense, well structured and
tangy in the mouth, without being too heavy
or over-extracted, and caressing, warm and
fruit-filled on the palate, where it displays
excellent tannins and superb aromatic
length. Unusually, the estate's second wine
is almost as good. The Teodosio '05
exhibits an appealingly fresh, well-defined
fullness, exuberant fruit and intense aromas
of red fruits and printer's ink.

ANNUAL PRODUCTION 1,000,000 bottles
HECTARES UNDER VINE 350
VITICULTURE METHOD Conventional

With a production run of around 1,000,000
bottles a year and 100 members tending
approximately 350 hectares of vineyards,
Basilium is one of Basilicata's leading wine
co-operatives. Acerenza forms the
southernmost strip of the Vulture zone and
the co-operative's modern cellar is set in this
majestic landscape. Basilium, headed by
Nicola Bonelli and run by oenologist Angelo
Valentino, offers a wide selection of territory-
focused wines. This year, our favourite was
Aglianico Sicone '04, from the prestigious
Le Gastaldìe range. It's a deep ruby colour,
flaunting concentrated aromas of cherry and
blackberry then solid body on the palate,
smooth tannins and a lingering finish lifted
by chocolate and coffee. Aglianico Riserva
'01 is equally good, with a rich, more
traditional-style character displaying
pleasing earthy and balsamic nuances.
Aglianico Pipoli '04 is sound and good value
for money but we felt that the sweet red
Origini '05 from late-harvest aglianico, with
aromas of rose and hibiscus, still needs
some work. Whites worthy of mention
include Pipoli Chiaro Aglianico vinified off the
skins and the full-flavoured Gastaldie Albula
'05, again from aglianico.

● Aglianico del Vulture Basilisco '04 ♟♟♟ 6	
● Aglianico del Vulture Teodosio '05 ♟♟ 4*	
● Aglianico del Vulture Basilisco '01 ♟♟♟ 6	
● Aglianico del Vulture Basilisco '00 ♟♟ 6	
● Aglianico del Vulture Basilisco '02 ♟♟ 6	
● Aglianico del Vulture Basilisco '99 ♟♟ 5	
● Aglianico del Vulture Basilisco '03 ♟♟ 6	
● Aglianico del Vulture Basilisco '98 ♟♟ 5	
● Aglianico del Vulture Teodosio '04 ♟♟ 4	

● Aglianico del Vulture Le Gastaldie Sicone '04	♟♟ 4*
● Aglianico del Vulture Ris. '01	♟♟ 6
● Aglianico del Vulture Pipoli '04	♟ 3*
● Origini V. T. '05	♟ 5
O Pipoli Chiaro '06	♟ 3
O Le Gastaldie Albula '05	♟ 4
O Greco I Portali '06	♟ 3
● Aglianico del Vulture Valle del Trono '01	♟♟ 5
● Aglianico del Vulture Valle del Trono '03	♟♟ 5

Bisceglia

C.DA FINOCCHIARO
85024 LAVELLO [PZ]
TEL. 097288409
www.agricolabisceglia.com

ANNUAL PRODUCTION 300,000 bottles
HECTARES UNDER VINE 55
VITICULTURE METHOD Certified organic

Mario Bisceglia only set up his cellar in 2001 and in the space of a few short vintages, he has established himself as one of the names to watch in southern Italian winemaking. He now has 55 hectares under vine and his annual production is impressive in terms of quantity and quality. Even more remarkably, his vines are managed to the dictates of organic farming. Bisceglia's most impressive wine, which has earned him his first-ever Three Glass award, is Aglianico del Vulture Gudarrà '04, a superb southern Italian red. Rich, robust and elegant, it boasts a deep dark ruby hue that introduces intense, clean-cut aromas of ripe red and black berry fruit laced with more complex new oak, alluring balsam and toasted coffee notes. The nose is echoed on a solid, well-coordinated palate with juicy, compact fruit, elegant soft tannins and a very long, toast and mineral-enhanced finish. Tréje '05 is a convincing blend of aglianico, syrah and merlot. A big, full-bodied wine, it still manages to be taut and well balanced. The intriguing Armille '06 is spicy with notes of currants and cherries while the rest of the list is sound and remarkably good value.

D'Angelo

VIA PROVINCIALE, 8
85028 RIONERO IN VULTURE [PZ]
TEL. 0972721517
www.dangelowine.com

ANNUAL PRODUCTION 350,000 bottles
HECTARES UNDER VINE 50
VITICULTURE METHOD Conventional

A long-standing Basilicata winery founded in 1930, D'Angelo has always been at the forefront of viticulture in Vulture. Unfortunately, Lucio D'Angelo, one of the two owners, passed away this year but his oenologist brother Donato continues to create a thoughtful range of wines with the same passion. While Vigna Caselle Riserva '03 was unable to repeat the exploits of the '01 vintage, it is one of the most interesting products of what was a rather poor year, showing structure and balance but also a hint of dryness on the back palate. Valle del Noce '05 missed our top accolade by a hair's breadth but did charm the panel with its elegant structure, rich fruitiness, smooth tannins and refined notes of liquorice and printer's ink, which linger on the long finish. Canneto '05 is a close-knit, well-structured, tannic Aglianico IGT aged in new oak and bursting with ripe fruit. The basic Aglianico del Vulture '05 and the white Villa dei Pini '06, from chardonnay, pinot bianco and incrocio Manzoni, are as well made as ever.

Wine	Rating
● Aglianico del Vulture Gudarrà '04	♈♈♈ 5*
● Aglianico del Vulture Terra di Vulcano '05	♈♈ 3*
● Armille '06	♈♈ 4*
○ Terre di Vulcano Fiano di Avellino '06	♈♈ 4*
● Tréje '05	♈♈ 4*
○ Chardonnay '06	♈ 4
○ Fiano di Basilicata '06	♈ 4
○ Terra di Vulcano Falanghina '06	♈ 3
● Aglianico del Vulture Ris. '01	♈♈ 6
● Aglianico del Vulture Terra di Vulcano '03	♈♈ 4
● Aglianico del Vulture '03	♈♈ 6

Wine	Rating
● Aglianico del Vulture V. Caselle Ris. '03	♈♈ 5*
● Aglianico del Vulture Valle del Noce '05	♈♈ 6
● Canneto '05	♈♈ 5
● Aglianico del Vulture '05	♈ 4
○ Vigna dei Pini '06	♈ 4
● Aglianico del Vulture V. Caselle Ris. '01	♈♈♈ 4*
● Aglianico del Vulture Donato D'Angelo '01	♈♈ 5
● Aglianico del Vulture Valle del Noce '03	♈♈ 4
● Aglianico del Vulture Donato D'Angelo '04	♈♈ 5
● Canneto '04	♈♈ 5

Cantine Di Palma

C.DA SCAVONI
85028 RIONERO IN VULTURE [PZ]
TEL. 0972722891
www.cantinedipalma.com

ANNUAL PRODUCTION 130,000 bottles
HECTARES UNDER VINE 15.5
VITICULTURE METHOD Certified organic

After setting up his business a decade ago, Antonio Di Palma has built up a handsome winery, which now boasts impressive figures. There are over 15 hectares under vine, some of which are cultivated organically and some are being converted; a new state-of-the-art cellar; and an annual production of around 130,000 bottles. Last year, Nibbio Grigio '03 was crowned as one of the region's top wines and the '04 is equally rich, full-bodied, complex and engaging. It belies an excellent mix of traditional wine and modern cellar techniques but lacks the touch of length and the hint of softness that would have enabled it to reprise its triumph. Still, it's one of the most representative wines from the territory and it does full justice to the commitment of Antonio and his family. The easy-drinking Aglianico Tenute Piano Regio '04 is agreeable and juicy, with slightly more evolved notes, and we look forward to the Nibbio Grigio '05.

Eubea

VIA ROMA, 209
85028 RIONERO IN VULTURE [PZ]
TEL. 0972723574
www.sacavid.it

ANNUAL PRODUCTION 40,000 bottles
HECTARES UNDER VINE 15
VITICULTURE METHOD Certified organic

Eugenia Sasso is heir to a long winemaking tradition. She puts body and soul into running her Vulture estate, founded about ten years ago and boasting 15 hectares of well-aspected, organically cultivated vineyards in Rionero. Eugenia produces two Aglianicos: Covo dei Briganti and the top-of-the range Ròinos. Covo dei Briganti distinguished itself in our finals again this year, with the deep, close-knit, firmly structured '04 vintage, which throws rich aromas of ripe cherries and wild cherries, smooth, caressing tannins and impressively lingering aromatics. Ròinos '05 is highly concentrated and brims with fruit that we thought was a tad too ripe. It is still has a little way to go but unfolds rich and well structured in the mouth, with elegant tannins, good balance, plenty of flesh and nice length. A touch more harmony would have enabled it to repeat the success of the excellent '01 vintage but that goal has merely been postponed.

● Aglianico del Vulture	
Il Nibbio Grigio Et. Nera '04	♟♟ 6
● Aglianico del Vulture	
Tenuta Piano Regio '04	♟♟ 4*
● Aglianico del Vulture	
Il Nibbio Grigio Et. Nera '03	♟♟♟ 6
● Aglianico del Vulture	
Il Nibbio Grigio '00	♟♟ 6
● Aglianico del Vulture	
Tenuta Piano Regio '03	♟♟ 4
● Aglianico del Vulture	
Il Nibbio Grigio '98	♟♟ 4
● Aglianico del Vulture	
Il Nibbio Grigio '02	♟♟ 6

● Aglianico del Vulture	
Il Covo dei Briganti '04	♟♟ 6
● Aglianico del Vulture Ròinos '04	♟♟ 8
● Aglianico del Vulture Ròinos '01	♟♟♟ 8
● Aglianico del Vulture	
Il Covo dei Briganti '03	♟♟ 6
● Aglianico del Vulture Ròinos '02	♟♟ 8
● Aglianico del Vulture Ròinos '03	♟♟ 8
● Aglianico del Vulture	
Il Covo dei Briganti '00	♟♟ 6
● Aglianico del Vulture	
Il Covo dei Briganti '01	♟♟ 7

Elena Fucci

C.DA SOLAGNA DEL TITOLO
85022 BARILE [PZ]
TEL. 0972770736
az.elenafucci@tiscali.it

ANNUAL PRODUCTION 16,000 bottles
HECTARES UNDER VINE 6.15
VITICULTURE METHOD Conventional

Although the cellar owned by the Fucci family has little more than six hectares of vineyards, the high quality of its wines makes it one of the leading producers in Basilicata and its fame has long transcended its limited annual output of less than 20,000 bottles. One of Salvatore Fucci's great assets is his daughter Elena, an oenology graduate. The rest is taken care of by the well-aspected vineyards in the Solagna del Titolo district of Barile and the loving care that the family lavishes on them. It was no great surprise to see the Titolo '05 come out a winner at our finals. An attractive dark ruby with purple highlights, it throws a rich nose of ripe red berry fruit that develops floral and oaky notes with a delicate hint of spice. The well-balanced, silkily caressing palate is full and elegant, holding up well and revealing well-defined hints of wild cherries and blackberries supported by velvety tannins and signing off with a finish of exceptional length.

Macarico

P.ZZA CARACCIOLO, 7
85022 BARILE [PZ]
TEL. 0972771051
www.macaricovini.it

ANNUAL PRODUCTION 18,000 bottles
HECTARES UNDER VINE 5
VITICULTURE METHOD Conventional

Rino Botte's Macarico is one of the estates to watch on Basilicata's crowded, busy wine scene. Founded in 2001, the estate now covers an area of around ten hectares, five of which are under vine and in production. The vineyards are located chiefly in the Macarico district of Barile, a veritable "premier cru" of the Aglianico DOC. Cellar operations are in the hands of oenologist Gianpaolo Chiettini, who submitted two very convincing wines for tasting. Macarico '04 strode purposefully through to the finals, distinguishing itself with fine concentration heralded by a dense, deep ruby and balsam and spice aromas that mingle with ripe red and black berry fruit and segue into elegant oak. Full-bodied on the palate, although with some way still to go, it flaunts superbly elegant structure underscored by tannins of great finesse. The '05 Macarì is irresistibly alluring thanks to rich, well-defined fruit hovers on the edge of overripeness, elegant hints of oriental spices and aniseed, perfectly calibrated oak and impressive length.

● Aglianico del Vulture Titolo '05	♟♟♟	6
● Aglianico del Vulture Titolo '02	♟♟♟	6
● Aglianico del Vulture Titolo '00	♟♟	5
● Aglianico del Vulture Titolo '03	♟♟	6
● Aglianico del Vulture Titolo '04	♟♟	6
● Aglianico del Vulture Titolo '01	♟♟	6

● Aglianico del Vulture Macarico '04	♟♟	6
● Aglianico del Vulture Macarì '05	♟♟	5
● Aglianico del Vulture Macarico '03	♟♟	6
● Aglianico del Vulture Macarì '03	♟♟	5
● Aglianico del Vulture Macarì '04	♟♟	5

Cantine del Notaio

VIA ROMA, 159
85028 RIONERO IN VULTURE [PZ]
TEL. 0972723689
www.cantinedelnotaio.com

ANNUAL PRODUCTION 110,000 bottles
HECTARES UNDER VINE 27
VITICULTURE METHOD Certified biodynamic

Founded less than ten years ago, Gerardo Giuratrabocchetti's winery is now one of the best in the region. Unfortunately, the past few vintages have not yielded the results merited by the owner's commitment and the quality of his vineyards but we are ready to put money on future performance. In the absence of La Firma, the flagship wine, this year's list is spearheaded by Aglianico Il Sigillo, which debuted with the '03 vintage. It is a deep, opulent red aged in new oak, which unveils impressive structure and concentration. The hot growing year has, however, taken its toll and it the muscle is a tad overdone. But this is nonetheless a very complex wine that still needs a few years to find its balance. Less imposing, but perhaps more convincing, is Repertorio '05, a spicy, tannic wine with plenty of fruit and attractive notes of toast and oak. Autentica '05, an appealing sweet wine based on moscato and malvasia bianca, is truly excellent and we also liked Rogito '05, a satisfying, well-flavoured rosé from aglianico.

Terra dei Re

VIA MONTICCHIO S. S. 167 KM 2,700
85028 RIONERO IN VULTURE [PZ]
TEL. 0972725116
www.terradeire.com

ANNUAL PRODUCTION 70,000 bottles
HECTARES UNDER VINE 31
VITICULTURE METHOD Certified organic

Terra dei Re was founded at the turn of the millennium by the Leone and De Sio families, who have recently been joined by the Rabascos. The ultra-modern winery has an area of 3,000 square metres, largely underground, and the estate's own vineyards taken with those leased now exceed 30 hectares. They are all certified organic and located in well-aspected sites in Barile, Rionero and Melfi. Our favourite wine, crafted with the aid of consultant Sergio Paternoster, was Aglianico Divinus '04, with fine aromas of violet, cherry and spices. It has firm structure, depth and harmony on the palate, where the fruit is compact and juicy, giving way to notes of spice and oak, balanced out by refreshing acidity and elegant tannins. This is a wine that fully deserved to feature in our finals. Aglianico Nocte made an excellent debut. Obtained from grapes harvested at night, it is a close-knit, complex wine that unveils close-knit fruit notes with delicate vegetal hints and a touch of printer's ink. We also liked Pacus '05, based mainly on aglianico, an appealing IGT characterized by black berry fruit, chocolate and tobacco, and the fine Fiano di Avellino Claris '06 made from bought-in grapes.

● Aglianico del Vulture Il Sigillo '03	♈♈ 7
● Aglianico del Vulture Il Repertorio '05	♈♈ 5
○ L'Autentica '05	♈♈ 6
⊙ Il Rogito '05	♈♈ 5
● Aglianico del Vulture La Firma '00	♈♈♈ 6
● Aglianico del Vulture La Firma '01	♈♈ 6
● Aglianico del Vulture La Firma '03	♈♈ 6
● Aglianico del Vulture La Firma '04	♈♈ 7
● Aglianico del Vulture La Firma '02	♈♈ 6

● Aglianico del Vulture Divinus '04	♈♈ 5*
● Aglianico del Vulture Nocte '04	♈♈ 6
● Pacus '05	♈♈ 4*
○ Fiano di Avellino Claris '06	♈ 4
● Aglianico del Vulture Divinus '01	♈♈ 5
● Aglianico del Vulture Divinus '03	♈♈ 5
● Aglianico del Vulture Vultur '01	♈♈ 4

Terre degli Svevi

LOC. PIAN DI CAMERA
85029 VENOSA [PZ]
TEL. 097231263
www.giv.it

ANNUAL PRODUCTION 240,000 bottles
HECTARES UNDER VINE 120
VITICULTURE METHOD Conventional

In 1998, Gruppo Italiano Vini decided to invest heavily in the Vulture zone, founding Terre degli Svevi. It entrusted management of the 120 hectares of excellent vineyards at Venosa to renowned oenologist Nunzio Capurso, head of the group's Tuscan estates and president of the Consorzio del Chianti. This year, the winery has chalked up another Three Glass triumph with an excellent interpretation of the '03 vintage in its Aglianico del Vigneto Serpara. The traditionally styled red vaunts succulent, flavoursome fruit, elegant tannins and remarkable balance and depth. Unfolding with compelling richness on the palate, it signs off with a lingering compact finish of layered wild cherry jam, tobacco and liquorice. Re Manfredi '04 is velvet-smooth and almost as good, with supple tannins and good structure, although slightly over-evolved for its age. The range is completed by the refreshing, inviting Re Manfredi Rosato '06 and two attractive whites, Fonte Luna '05 and Re Manfredi Bianco '06, from müller thurgau and traminer.

Cantina di Venosa

LOC. VIGNALI
VIA APPIA
85029 VENOSA [PZ]
TEL. 097236702
www.cantinadivenosa.it

ANNUAL PRODUCTION 700,000 bottles
HECTARES UNDER VINE 900
VITICULTURE METHOD Conventional

Cantina di Venosa, under the assured management of Teodoro Palermo, has been a landmark winery in Basilicata viticulture since the 1950s. With 450 members and over 800 hectares of vineyards on some of the best sites in the zone, this co-operative winery turns out a vast, well thought-out range of territory-dedicated wines where the Aglianico DOC zone takes centre stage. We were impressed by the crisp, fruity Bali'Aggio '04, whose sturdy palate boasts an elegant tannic weave. Vignali '05 reveals shrewdly calibrated new oak with complex aromatic notes and an overall impression of depth. Madrigale di Gesualdo '04 has a more approachable, impetuous character but nonetheless offers plenty of cherry-led fruit and well-balanced structure. We were less impressed by two of the winery's classics, the over-evolved Carato Venusio '04 and the rather predictable Terre d'Orazio '04. The Dry Muscat '06 and the Malvasia d'Avalos di Gesualdo from the same vintage are both excellent.

● Aglianico del Vulture Vign. Serpara '03	ΨΨΨ 5*
● Aglianico del Vulture Re Manfredi '04	ΨΨ 5
○ Fonte Luna '06	Ψ 4
⊙ Re Manfredi Rosato '06	Ψ 4
○ Re Manfredi Bianco '06	Ψ 4
● Aglianico del Vulture Re Manfredi '99	ΨΨΨ 5*
● Aglianico del Vulture Re Manfredi '00	ΨΨ 5
● Aglianico del Vulture Vign. Serpara '01	ΨΨ 7
● Aglianico del Vulture Re Manfredi '03	ΨΨ 7
● Aglianico del Vulture Re Manfredi '01	ΨΨ 5

● Aglianico del Vulture Bali'Aggio '04	ΨΨ 3*
● Aglianico del Vulture Il Madrigale di Gesualdo '04	ΨΨ 4*
○ D'Avalos di Gesualdo '06	ΨΨ 4*
● Aglianico del Vulture Vignali '05	ΨΨ 3*
○ Dry Muscat Terre di Orazio '06	ΨΨ 3*
● Aglianico del Vulture Carato Venusio '04	Ψ 5
⊙ Terre di Orazio Rosé '06	Ψ 3
● Aglianico del Vulture Terre di Orazio '04	Ψ 4
● Aglianico del Vulture Carato Venusio '01	ΨΨ 5
● Aglianico del Vulture Carato Venusio '03	ΨΨ 5
● Aglianico del Vulture Carato Venusio Ris. '01	ΨΨ 6

OTHER WINERIES

Alovini
VIA GRAMSCI, 30
85013 GENZANO DI LUCANIA [PZ]
TEL. 0971776372
www.alovini.it

Oenologist Oronzo Alò uses estate-grown and purchased grapes to produce good wines at his cellar in Genzano di Lucania. The full, well-balanced Aglianico Le Ralle '05 is interesting and Greco '06 and Rosato '06 are highly drinkable.

● Aglianico del Vulture Le Ralle '05	♀ 3
○ Le Ralle Greco '06	♀ 3
☉ Le Ralle Rosato '06	♀ 3

Camerlengo
VIA T. TASSO, 3
85027 RAPOLLA [PZ]
TEL. 0972760738
www.camerlengodoc.com

Biagio Cristofaro releases two interesting reds made with grapes from the vineyards on his fast-improving estate. Aglianico Camerlengo '05 is intense and velvety, while the fruity Anthelio from the same vintage is more approachable but certainly not banal.

● Aglianico del Vulture Camerlengo '05	♀♀ 5
● Aglianico del Vulture Antelio '05	♀♀ 4*

Cantine Cerrolongo
LOC. C.DA CERROLONGO, 1
75020 NOVA SIRI [MT]
TEL. 0835536174
www.cerrolongo.it

The Battifarano family has farmed this estate in Nova Siri for centuries. We picked out the firm, generous Cerrolongo Rosso '06, from cabernet, aglianico and syrah, and the refreshing Chardonnay Toccaciclo '06, with its pleasant hints of tropical fruit.

● Cerrolongo Rosso '06	♀♀ 4*
○ Chardonnay Toccaciclo '06	♀ 4

Carbone
P.ZZA D'ADDEZIO, 9
85025 MELFI [PZ]
TEL. 0972237866
carbonevini@fastwebnet.it

Luca and Sara Carbone produce two excellent Aglianicos from their 18 hectares of vines. Stupor Mundi '05 is deep, structured and well-orchestrated while Terra dei Fuochi '05 is well styled, tangy and supple. The expert Sergio Paternoster consults.

● Aglianico del Vulture Stupor Mundi '05	♀♀ 4*
● Aglianico del Vulture Terra dei Fuochi '05	♀ 4

Colli Cerentino
TRAV. VIA SANREMO, 26
85025 MELFI [PZ]
TEL. 0972237587
www.collicerentino.com

Sandro Calabrese's estate produces two Aglianicos from its eight hectares of vines. The excellent Masquito, named after the location of the vineyard, shows elegant tannins and plentiful fruit while the Cerentino from the same vintage is equally interesting.

● Aglianico del Vulture Cerentino '05	♀♀ 5
● Aglianico del Vulture Masquito '05	♀♀ 6

Dragone
LOC. PIETRAPENTA
P.ZZA DEGLI OLMI, 66
75100 MATERA [MT]
TEL. 0835261740
www.dragonevini.it

Michele and Cataldo Dragone produce wines and classic method sparklers on their handsome 30-hectare estate. The primitivo-based Ego Sum Rosé is simply excellent and Dragone Silver, from malvasia bianca di Basilicata, is also good.

☉ Ego Sum Rosé	♀♀ 4*
○ Dragone Silver Demi Sec	♀ 3

OTHER WINERIES

Eleano
C.DA PIAZZOLLA
85028 RIONERO IN VULTURE [PZ]
TEL. 0972722273
www.eleano.it

Alfredo Cordisco and Francesca Greco tend
five hectares of fine vineyards in the Pian
dell'Altare district of Rionero. The wines we
liked best were the polished, nicely
balanced Pian dell'Altare '03, the sweet,
aromatic Ambra Moscato '06 and the
pleasant Dioniso '04.

● Aglianico del Vulture	
Pian dell'Altare '03	♥♥ 6
O Ambra Moscato '06	♥♥ 4*
● Aglianico del Vulture Dioniso '04	♥ 4

Giannattasio
P.ZZA ANGELO BOZZA, 5
85022 BARILE [PZ]
TEL. 0972770571
www.giannattasio.net

Last year, we were impressed by barrel
samples of Arcangelo Giannattasio's
Aglianico del Vulture '04. The release of the
wine this year has confirmed our judgement
for it displays firm structure, elegance,
depth, cleanliness and complexity.

● Aglianico del Vulture Arcà '04	♥♥ 5
● Aglianico del Vulture Arcà '03	♀♀ 5

Viticoltori in Vulture Lagala
C.DA LA MADDALENA
85029 VENOSA [PZ]
TEL. 0972375007
www.lagala.it

Antonio Lagala tends seven hectares of
vineyard planted entirely to aglianico at
Venosa. The deep red Aquila del Vulture '04
is excellent, with an abundance of fruit and
beautiful balance. Rosso del Balzo '06, also
from aglianico, is nicely styled.

● Aglianico del Vulture	
Aquila del Vulture '04	♥♥ 6
● Rosso del Balzo '06	♥ 3

Michele Laluce
VIA ROMA, 21
85020 GINESTRA [PZ]
TEL. 0972646145
www.vinilaluce.it

Michele Laluce produces several interesting
territory-dedicated wines on his six hectares
of vines at Ginestra, an excellent grape-
growing area of Vulture. Our choices this
year were the firm, juicy, chamois-soft
Aglianico S'Adatt and the slim-bodied
Zimberno, an Aglianico DOC with fresh fruit
overtones.

● Aglianico del Vulture Zimberno '05	♥ 4
● S'Adatt '06	♥ 4

Lelusi Viticoltori
VIA CROCE, 3
85022 BARILE [PZ]
TEL. 024043805
vinilelusi@libero.it

The team made up of Milanese siblings
Luca, Letizia and Simona Labarbuta
passionately tends six hectares of vines at
Barile. We liked the excellent Aglianico
Letizia '04, which is concentrated, elegant
and lingering, although the clean, fresh-
tasting Aglianico del Vulture Shesh '05 is
juicy and almost as good.

● Aglianico del Vulture Letizia '04	♥♥ 6
● Aglianico del Vulture Shesh '05	♥♥ 4*

Lucania
VIA ALDO MORO, 5
85025 MELFI [PZ]
TEL. 0578717256
grifalcodellalucania@email.it

Fabrizio Piccin and Cecilia Naldoni's passion
for winemaking has not been dampened by
their move from Montepulciano to Melfi, as
you can tell from their dense, juicy,
mouthfilling Grifalco '05, with its nicely
calibrated oak.

● Aglianico del Vulture Grifalco '05	♥♥ 4*
● Aglianico del Vulture Grifalco '04	♀♀ 4*

OTHER WINERIES

Cantine Madonna delle Grazie
LOC. C.DA VIGNALI
VIA APPIA
85029 VENOSA [PZ]
TEL. 097235704
www.cantinemadonnadellegrazie.it

The Latorraca family tends six hectares of vines at Venosa and their cellar releases two Aglianicos. We preferred the firm Bauccio '03, which is brimming with red fruit and balsam, although the less concentrated Aglianico Liscone '05 is also interesting.

● Aglianico del Vulture Bauccio '03	▼▼ 5
● Aglianico del Vulture Liscone '05	▼ 3

Tenuta del Portale
LOC. LE QUERCE
85022 BARILE [PZ]
TEL. 0972724691
tenutadelportale@tiscali.it

Filena Ruppi throws herself heart and soul into her Barile estate with its 20 hectares under vine, which she runs with her oenologist husband Donato D'Angelo. The solidly built Aglianico '05 is deep, with enticing ripe cherry aromas. We also liked the Riserva '03, which has elegant but more evolved notes.

● Aglianico del Vulture Ris. '03	▼▼ 5
● Aglianico del Vulture '05	▼▼ 4*
● Aglianico del Vulture Pian del Carro '05	▼ 5

Agricola Regio
LOC. PIANO REGIO
85029 VENOSA [PZ]
TEL. 0824381021
www.agricolaregio.com

Paolo Zamparelli owns this handsome estate, whose vineyards in the Piano Regio area of Venosa yield an annual production of around 80,000 bottles. Our favourite from the three Aglianicos was the splendid Donpà '04 with its intense fruit-forward nose.

● Aglianico del Vulture Donpà '04	▼▼ 5
● Aglianico del Vulture Genesi '05	▼ 4
● Aglianico del Vulture Solagna '05	▼ 3

Taverna
C.DA TAVERNA, 15
75020 NOVA SIRI [MT]
TEL. 0835877083
www.aataverna.com

Pasquale Angelo Lunati makes wines with fruit from his own vineyards, located in various parts of the region. We particularly liked the round, full-flavoured Lagarino di Dioniso '05, from merlot and cabernet with a touch of aglianico. Greco '06 and Merlot Cabernet '04 are also pleasant.

● Lagarino di Dioniso '05	▼▼ 3*
O Greco '06	▼ 2*
● Merlot Cabernet '04	▼ 3*

Vigne di Mezzo
P.ZZA CARACCIOLO, 7
85022 BARILE [PZ]
TEL. 0972771051
www.feudi.it

Founded in 2001, the Basilicata branch of Irpinia's Feudi di San Gregorio is coming on fast with 32 hectares of lovely vineyards and a prestigious new winery. The sinewy, fruit-led Aglianico '05 is very good with its chocolate and spice notes but we thought Efesto '05 was a tad over-evolved.

● Aglianico del Vulture '05	▼▼ 5
● Aglianico del Vulture Efesto '04	▼▼ 7

Cantina del Vulture
VIA SAN FRANCESCO
85028 RIONERO IN VULTURE [PZ]
TEL. 0972721062

The co-operative headed by Michele Caputo was set up in 1954 and now has 60 members with 100 hectares of DOC vineyards. The wines are well structured and good value. Top of the range is the firm-bodied, fruity Aglianico Carteggio '05 although Aglianico Il Toppo '04 and Malvasia Novalba '05 are also good.

● Aglianico del Vulture Carteggio '05	▼▼ 4*
● Aglianico del Vulture Il Toppo '04	▼ 3
O Novalba Malvasia '05	▼ 2*

PUGLIA

Puglia continues to develop and prosper. The number of Three Glass wines has risen from five to seven, the highest ever. The number of the region's estates in the Guide has also grown, to 70, although the increase has primarily been in the Other Wineries section, the number of full profiles having dropped. Then we have the changes that follow developments in Italian winemaking in general.

There is the ongoing movement towards the use of indigenous varieties, and this is fertile territory for Puglia. There is the more technical approach to cellar operations and vineyard replanting, which is becoming more widespread and more thoughtfully applied. Investment in developing new wineries is growing, too, a strategy that would appear to pay off, given the success of estates like Castello Monaci, Albea, Due Palme, Longo and Emèra. Hence things are looking good overall, the numbers and the quality of the wines fully vindicating the stance we have taken on the region's potential. But all that glisters is not gold. There are less positive aspects to the situation, the most serious one being overproduction. There's still far too much wine, much of it poor quality, some sold in bulk, some in bottle. We're also witnessing an alarming and, we feel, unjustified rise in prices, at least for many wineries. In fact, we are beginning to wonder if what we have always said about Puglia being one of the best places for good value wines is now history. Moving on to the prize winners, Albea gained its first Three Glasses, for Lui '05, a monovarietal Nero di Troia. Two large, important wineries also took home Three Glasses for the first time: Torrevento, for Castel del Monte Rosso Vigna Pedale Riserva '04, and Due Palme, for Salice Salentino Rosso Selvarossa Riserva '04. It is surely no coincidence that both these wines are DOC and are from indigenous varieties. Indeed all this year's Three Glass wines come from traditional grapes, proving once again that Puglia's real strength lies in its fabulous wealth of grape material. We have another Three Glasses debutante in Primitivo di Manduria Dunico Masseria Pepe '05, another DOC wine. This time, the producer isn't new to the honour. It's Accademia dei Racemi, which pioneered the return to bush-trained vines and championed the increasingly esteemed concept of authenticity. Repeat honours go to Masseria Maime '05, from Tormaresca, Artas '05, from Castello Monaci, and the famous Graticciaia, this year the '03, from Agricole Vallone.

Accademia dei Racemi
VIA SANTO STASI PRIMO - Z. I.
74024 MANDURIA [TA]
TEL. 0999711660
www.accademiadeiracemi.it

ANNUAL PRODUCTION 1,200,000 bottles
HECTARES UNDER VINE 150
VITICULTURE METHOD Certified organic

This must have been a very satisfying year for Gregory Perrucci and his agronomist Salvatore Mero. As well as the continuous pleasure he must feel in seeing how right it was to restore the traditional method of bush-training for the primitivo vines and to concentrate on all aspects of authenticity and provenance in his winemaking, there is now the joy of having a new Three Glass award. It wasn't for the '06 release of Zinfandel Sinfarosa, which was still ageing at the time of our tastings. The winner was the '05 Dunico from Masseria Pepe. It meshes attractive drinkability, depth and technical cleanliness into a traditional framework, enhanced by a fresh, clean, fragrant nose, all spices and black berry fruit for an extremely fine Primitivo di Manduria indeed. We would love to see wines like this around more often, rather than the rather extreme, or extremist, types that are so fashionable these days. The soft, rounded, crisp, floral Primitivo di Manduria Giravolta Tenuta Pozzopalo '06 is also impeccable, as is the complex, surprisingly deep Sum '06, made from 100 per cent sussumaniello. The well-made, lively, easy drinking Anarkos '06 and Gioia del Colle Joya '06 round off the range.

Azienda Vinicola Albano Carrisi
C.DA BOSCO
72020 CELLINO SAN MARCO [BR]
TEL. 0831619211
www.albanocarrisi.com

ANNUAL PRODUCTION 425,000 bottles
HECTARES UNDER VINE 65
VITICULTURE METHOD Conventional

We're not sure how much time Albano Carrisi spends at his winery or how hands-on he is, given his fame as a singer and his many artistic commitments, but we do know that his staff have the skills to produce good quality wines. They haven't come up with anything truly exceptional over the last few years but the estate is still one to trust. Platone '04, from negroamaro and primitivo, is a distinguished wine, even though not quite as good as in its best vintages. There are deep aromas of printer's ink, tar and tobacco, and it's sweetly fruited on the tight-knit, well-textured palate. The only failing is a little too much residual sugar. Nostalgia '05, from 100 per cent negroamaro, also impresses, showing taut and fruity with a long, lively finish. Don Carmelo Rosso '05, from negroamaro with 15 per cent primitivo, its nose recalling Mediterranean scrubland, is very decent. The traditionally styled Taras '05, from warm, slightly overripened primitivo, is uncomplicatedly attractive, as is Salice Salentino Rosso '05, which is full of red berry fruit and toasty coffee notes.

● Primitivo di Manduria Dunico Masseria Pepe '05	♈♈♈ 5*
● Primitivo di Manduria Giravolta Tenuta Pozzopalo '06	♈♈ 5
● Susumaniello Sum Torre Guaceto '05	♈♈ 5
● Anarkos '06	♈ 3
● Gioia del Colle Joya '06	♈ 3
● Primitivo di Manduria Zinfandel Sinfarosa '03	♈♈ 5
● Primitivo di Manduria Zinfandel Sinfarosa '05	♈♈ 5
● Primitivo di Manduria Giravolta Tenuta Pozzopalo '05	♈♈ 5
● Primitivo di Manduria Zinfandel Sinfarosa '04	♈♈ 5

● Nostalgia '05	♈♈ 5
● Platone '04	♈♈ 8
● Don Carmelo Rosso '05	♈ 4
● Salice Salentino Rosso '05	♈ 3
● Taras '05	♈ 6
● Platone '98	♈♈♈ 8
● Platone '03	♈♈ 8
● Taras '02	♈♈ 7
● Platone '02	♈♈ 8
● Taras '04	♈♈ 6

Cantina Albea

VIA DUE MACELLI, 8
70011 ALBEROBELLO [BA]
TEL. 0804323548
www.albeavini.com

ANNUAL PRODUCTION 300,000 bottles
HECTARES UNDER VINE 40
VITICULTURE METHOD Conventional

We didn't have to wait long to see this fine winery scale the peaks of Puglian wine. And we knew that this would be the case given the professionalism of its approach and the quality improvements we were seeing year on year. So, with just two releases behind it, both reaching the finals, the '05 Lui clinched Three Glasses, to the joy of Luigi Lippolis and his entire team. It's made solely from nero di Troia aged ten months in barrique. A wine of purple-ruby hue, it proffers intense black berry fruits, followed by scents of balsam. The beautifully clean, close-knit palate echoes these sensations and has assertive but soft, ripe tannins. In short, it's another magnificent Nero di Troia which once again underlines the potential of the variety. Petranera '05 and Petrarosa '06 are both from 100 per cent primitivo and both are wines of class. The former has aromas of small black berry fruits and tobacco, and a nicely composed, lively palate with soft tannins. The Petrarosa is floral on the nose and dynamic on its savoury, spicy palate.

Francesco Candido

VIA A. DIAZ, 46
72025 SAN DONACI [BR]
TEL. 0831635674
www.candidowines.it

ANNUAL PRODUCTION 2,000,000 bottles
HECTARES UNDER VINE 21
VITICULTURE METHOD Conventional

Alessandro Candido runs this long-standing winery with a safe hand and it remains one of the soundest operations in the entire region. The well-known, tried and tested names return to take centre stage this year, traditional wines that Candido releases only when they are properly aged and ready for drinking. Cappello di Prete, made solely from negroamaro, stands out not just for its quality but also for its superb value for money. The '03 is a pale ruby. Floral, balsamic aromas are followed by scents of antique wood and hints of wax. The palate is expansive, and not particularly close-knit, but clean and fragrant. In short, it's a beautifully crafted wine. The '00 release of the estate's flagship, Duca d'Aragona, also scored highly, a clean, elegant, floral, slightly balsamic wine. Salice Salentino Rosso La Finestra '05 is an attractive, soft wine of good texture with aromas of tobacco, tar and red berry fruits, and great drinkability. The '05 release of Immensum, though, is less successful than usual as it remains closed and difficult to fathom.

● Lui '05	▼▼▼ 6
● Petranera '05	▼▼ 4*
● Petrarosa '06	▼▼ 4*
○ Locorotondo Il Selva '06	▼ 3
● Lui '03	♈♈ 6
● Lui '04	♈♈ 6
● Petranera '04	♈♈ 4
● Raro '03	♈♈ 5
● Raro '05	♈♈ 5

● Cappello di Prete '03	▼▼ 4*
● Duca d'Aragona '00	▼▼ 5
● Immensum '05	▼ 5
⊙ Piccoli Passi '06	▼ 3
● Salice Salentino La Finestra '05	▼ 3*
● Primitivo De Vinis '05	▼ 3
● Duca d'Aragona '96	♈♈ 5
● Immensum '04	♈♈ 5*
● Cappello di Prete '00	♈♈ 4*
● Cappello di Prete '01	♈♈ 4*
● Duca d'Aragona '98	♈♈ 5

Cantele

S.P. SALICE SALENTINO
SAN DONACI KM 35,600
73010 GUAGNANO [LE]
TEL. 0832705010
www.cantele.it

ANNUAL PRODUCTION 2,000,000 bottles
HECTARES UNDER VINE 80
VITICULTURE METHOD Conventional

Bearing in mind the characteristics of the region's vineyards, the path that Cantele has taken epitomizes that of many of Puglia's top estates. The aim has been to combine quality and quantity, releasing both top-class niche products and everyday drinking wines that are still well styled and competitive. Their success is borne out by Amativo again being voted into the finals, where it's almost a fixture. There are further improvements in Varius and the superb quality in the Teresa Manara line continues without a break. So much good news can go a long way to softening any disappointment that nothing gained Three Glasses this year. As in the past, Amativo '05, from the classic blend of primitivo and negroamaro, marries finesse with softness. There is balsam, black berry fruit and spiciness on the nose. The clean-cut palate is deep, broad, elegant and long. Varius was a surprise presence in the finals but the '05 is the best ever. It's elegant, lively, well-textured and balanced. Indeed it comes very close to Amativo in terms of both style and quality. The only difference is that it's more supple and forward. The Negroamaro and Chardonnay Teresa Manara are both as fruity and attractive as ever.

Tenuta Coppadoro

S.DA PROVINCIALE, 35
71016 SAN SEVERO [FG]
TEL. 0882242301
www.tenutacoppadoro.it

ANNUAL PRODUCTION 525,000 bottles
HECTARES UNDER VINE 120
VITICULTURE METHOD Conventional

The overall consistency of quality in the wines and the high points that have been achieved over the past three years make Luigi Albano's one of Puglia's gold standard estates. Even when, like this year, nothing wins Three Glasses, the wines made by Giuseppe Pisante and Riccardo Cotarella still have class and personality, reflecting the precision of the winemaking and a diligent approach to viticulture. Cotinone '06, from equal parts of aglianico, montepulciano and cabernet sauvignon, has a pervasive, complex nose foregrounding Cuban cigar tobacco and black berry fruits. The palate is clean, elegant, supple and tight-knit but also multi-faceted, making for very good drinking. This year, like last, it just pipped Radicosa, which is considered the estate's flagship. A monovarietal Montepulciano, the '05 has an intense nose of black berry fruits, quinine and printers' ink. The palate is nicely cohesive if a touch vegetal and the tannins have not yet bedded down. Ratino '06, from bombino with 15 per cent of each of chardonnay and sauvignon, and ten per cent moscato, is another fine wine. Aromas of citrus and white-fleshed fruit lead to a fresh, balanced palate with a long, attractive finish.

Wine	Rating
● Amativo '05	⦿⦿ 5*
● Varius '05	⦿⦿ 4*
○ Teresa Manara Chardonnay '06	⦿⦿ 4*
● Teresa Manara Negroamaro '04	⦿⦿ 4
○ Alticelli '06	⦿ 3
● Primitivo '05	⦿ 3
● Amativo '03	⦿⦿⦿ 5*
● Amativo '00	⦿⦿ 4*
● Amativo '04	⦿⦿ 5*
● Amativo '02	⦿⦿ 5
● Amativo '99	⦿⦿ 6
● Amativo '01	⦿⦿ 5*
○ Teresa Manara Chardonnay '05	⦿⦿ 4
● Varius '04	⦿⦿ 4*
● Teresa Manara Negroamaro '03	⦿⦿ 4

Wine	Rating
● Cotinone '06	⦿⦿ 5
● Radicosa '05	⦿ 7
○ Ratino '06	⦿⦿ 4*
● Pescorosso '06	⦿ 4
⊙ Rosa di Salsola '06	⦿ 4
● Cotinone '05	⦿⦿⦿ 5*
● Radicosa '03	⦿⦿⦿ 7
● Cotinone '03	⦿⦿ 5*
● Radicosa '04	⦿⦿ 7
● Radicosa '02	⦿⦿ 8
● Cotinone '02	⦿⦿ 5
● Pescorosso '04	⦿⦿ 4

D'Alfonso del Sordo

C.DA SANT'ANTONINO
71016 SAN SEVERO [FG]
TEL. 0882221444
www.dalfonsodelsordo.it

ANNUAL PRODUCTION 350,000 bottles
HECTARES UNDER VINE 90
VITICULTURE METHOD Conventional

One of Gianfelice d'Alfonso del Sordo and Luigi Moio's wines easily reached the finals this year while another very nearly made it. What better sign could there be of the estate's overall quality? The finalist was Guado San Leo '05, an old style wine made solely from nero di Troia. The colour is pale ruby; the nose is broad with plum and fig fruitiness; the palate is clean, soft, cohesive, open and attractive, and has a long finish. The near miss was Montero '06, made from montepulciano and cabernet sauvignon, which is similar in style. The varietal characteristics of both varieties are apparent and aromatic herbs further enhance the nose; the palate is clean and cohesive, and has notable finesse, but there's a slight lack of fruit and succulence, and that's what lost it a place in the finals. Everything else is well-made, clean, lively and fruity, from the attractive Catapanus '06, made from bombino bianco, to the San Severo from the Posta Arignano line.

Cantina Due Palme

VIA SAN MARCO, 130
72020 CELLINO SAN MARCO [BR]
TEL. 0831617909
www.cantineduepalme.it

ANNUAL PRODUCTION 4,000,000 bottles
HECTARES UNDER VINE 2,000
VITICULTURE METHOD Conventional

It's been a memorable year for this major co-operative and its 850 or so members, not to mention its president-oenologist-mastermind. The '04 Salice Salentino Selvarossa Riserva, the wine that best encapsulates the winery's essence and the territory's grape-growing potential, gained Three Glasses. It's a wine that has been getting better every year, gaining in precision and cleanliness, and now it has finally thrown off all residual traces of the heaviness and sense of sweetness that once held it back. The nose is complex, with black berry fruits, coffee and chocolate. The palate is highly attractive. Rich, full and juicy, it gives flavours of forest fruits and a long, lively finish. Signs of change are also apparent on the '06 Salice Salentino, which has a bottling run of 400,000 bottles. Plums and smoky hints on the nose are followed by an intense, clean palate that retains some hints of sweetness but is full, cohesive and long, with good backbone. Even though the mellow, cherry-like Brindisi '06 is highly traditional in style, it is still a very good wine, as is the simple, immediate, fruity Ettamiano '04, made solely from primitivo.

● Guado San Leo '05	♟♟ 6
● Montero '06	♟♟ 4*
○ Bombino Bianco Catapanus '06	♟ 3*
● Casteldrione '05	♟ 3
⊙ San Severo Rosato Posta Arignano '06	♟ 2*
● San Severo Rosso Posta Arignano '06	♟ 2
○ San Severo Bianco Posta Arignano '06	♟ 2*
● Cava del Re Cabernet Sauvignon '02	♟♟ 6
● Cava del Re Cabernet Sauvignon '03	♟♟ 6
● Cava del Re Cabernet Sauvignon '05	♟♟ 6
● Doganera Merlot '05	♟♟ 6

● Salice Salentino Rosso Selvarossa Ris. '04	♟♟♟ 4*
● Salice Salentino Rosso '06	♟♟ 4*
● Brindisi Rosso '06	♟ 4
⊙ Due Palme Rosato '06	♟ 3
● Ettamiano '04	♟ 4
● Salice Salentino Rosso Selvarossa Ris. '03	♟♟ 6
● Salice Salentino Rosso Selvarossa Ris. '01	♟♟ 4
● Tenuta Albrizzi '05	♟♟ 4

Felline - Pervini

VIA SANTO STASI PRIMO - Z. I.
74024 MANDURIA [TA]
TEL. 0999711660
www.accademiadeiracemi.it

ANNUAL PRODUCTION 180,000 bottles
HECTARES UNDER VINE 23
VITICULTURE METHOD Conventional

The great success Gregory Perrucci has obtained with his Accademia has not undermined the quality and pace of production on his family properties. Indeed, it was decided to delay the release of Vigna del Feudo '06 by a year to allow it more time in glass. We have long felt that Gregory needed to let his best wines age longer so we are naturally gratified by his decision, even though it means that, for the first time for many years, there is no Felline-Pervini wine in the finals. The best bottles this year were the younger, easy drinkers, the sort where you want to open a second bottle because the first is gone almost before you realize it. Alberello '06 is a perfect example: fragrant, fruity, supple and immediate. Another is Bizantino Rosso '06, all crisp black berry fruit, a real "vin de plaisir". Both are blends of negroamaro and primitivo. Everything else is well made, especially Bizantino Rosato '06, which has gentian aromas and a velvety palate, and the two Primitivo di Mandurias, the richer, more concentrated Archidamo '05, and the soft, clean Segnavento '06.

Fusione

FRAZ. C.DA CACCAMONE
LOC. CASTELLANETA
MASSERIA SIGNORELLA
74011 TARANTO [TA]
TEL. 0998493770
a.mani@amonowine.com

ANNUAL PRODUCTION 180,000 bottles
HECTARES UNDER VINE N.A.
VITICULTURE METHOD Conventional

Elvezia Sbalchiero and Mark Shannon aren't raising the stakes. They've increased their output from 150,000 to 180,000 bottles and also increased the number of old vineyards they control. These are spread practically across the entire region, from Manduria and Sava to San Pietro Vernotico and Putignano, and the couple monitor them through the year to ensure their wines come from high quality grapes. All this means that these grower-producers feel positive about the route they are taking and their operation continues to gain in strength. A Mano Bianco '06, from equal parts of fiano and malvasia, showed very well this year. It's a well-made, attractively fresh, nicely perfumed wine. Promessa '06, from 100 per cent negroamaro, is also very convincing, showing clean, well-structured and with fresh black berry fruitiness, its only failing being a little too much alcoholic warmth on the finish. A Mano Primitivo '05 is another success, a lively, spicy wine with red berry fruitiness well sustained by acidity and an attractive finish. A Mano Rosato '06 is simple and floral but not much more.

● Bizantino Rosso '06	♈♈ 3*
● Alberello '06	♈♈ 3*
● Primitivo di Manduria Archidamo '05	♈ 3
● Primitivo Felline '06	♈ 3
☉ Bizantino Rosato '06	♈ 2*
● Primitivo di Manduria Segnavento '06	♈ 3
● Vigna del Feudo '02	♈♈ 5*
● Vigna del Feudo '04	♈♈ 5
● Vigna del Feudo '05	♈♈ 5
● Primitivo di Manduria Dolce Naturale Primo Amore '05	♈♈ 3*

○ A Mano Bianco '06	♈♈ 3*
● Promessa '06	♈♈ 3*
● A Mano Primitivo '05	♈ 3
☉ A Mano Rosato '06	♈ 3
● Prima Mano '03	♈♈ 5
● Promessa Negroamaro '05	♈♈ 3*

Paolo Leo

via Tuturano, 21
72025 San Donaci [BR]
tel. 0831635073
www.vinagripuglia.it

ANNUAL PRODUCTION 500,000 bottles
HECTARES UNDER VINE 35
VITICULTURE METHOD Conventional

Paolo Leo's estate used to be called Vinagri. He's turned out a range of highly impressive wines this year although we feel that, at 19, there are too many of them. Nevertheless, to maintain such quality levels over such a diverse range of wines is no mean feat. Paolo thoroughly deserves this full profile. Orfeo '05 and Limitone dei Greci Primitivo '05 came within a whisker of the finals. The former, from 100 per cent negroamaro aged a year in barrique, is very modern in style. It looks almost black. The nose has vanilla, black cherry and coffee leading to a palate that is full, deep and succulent but also balanced and lively. The Limitone, on the other hand, sees no oak. It's centred on fruit, elegance and attractiveness and has a more vertical structure. Med '06, made solely from primitivo, is clean and floral with small red berry fruitiness and a clear-cut, cohesive palate. Salice Salentino Riserva '02 is in more traditional style. Clean and full, it has chocolate, spices and black berry fruit on the nose and a long, slightly sweet finish. Negroamaro '06 is rounded and balsamic.

● Limitone dei Greci Primitivo '05	🍷🍷 4*
● Orfeo '05	🍷🍷 5
● Negroamaro '06	🍷🍷 2*
⊙ Med '06	🍷🍷 2*
● Salice Salentino Ris. '02	🍷🍷 4*
● Excubie Rosso '05	🍷 3
○ Falanghina '06	🍷 3
○ Greco '06	🍷 3
● Fiore di Vigna '05	🍷 5
● Primitivo Salento '06	🍷 2
○ Numen '06	🍷 4
● Orfeo '02	YY 4*

Leone de Castris

via Senatore de Castris, 26
73015 Salice Salentino [LE]
tel. 0832731112
www.leonedecastris.com

ANNUAL PRODUCTION 2,500,000 bottles
HECTARES UNDER VINE 250
VITICULTURE METHOD Conventional

There's no resting on laurels at Leone de Castris. Instead, there is experimentation with old varieties which have almost disappeared in the vineyards and there are a couple of promising new sparklers in the cellars to join the rosés and the top-notch Salice Salentinos that typify the estate. And then there is the continuance of soundness, dependability and high quality across the whole range. Salice Salentino Donna Lisa Riserva is once more a finalist, this year with the '03. Aromas of cherry jam and balsam, nuanced with spiciness, are followed by a cohesive, complex, elegant palate with a long, attractive finish. Donna Lisa Bianco '06, made solely from chardonnay, is also admirable. Although it's still slightly oaky, it has good aroma, with scents of spring flowers, and good body sustaining its long, balanced palate. Five Roses is, as usual, one of the top rosés in the country. The straight '06 has an intense nose, full of Mediterranean scrubland, and a clean palate. Anniversario 63° Anno, from 50-year-old vines, has great fullness and complexity on the nose, and a fragrant palate with depth and minerality on the finish.

● Salice Salentino Rosso Donna Lisa Ris. '03	🍷🍷 6
⊙ Donna Lisetta Brut Rosé	🍷🍷 4*
⊙ Five Roses Anniversario 63° Anno '06	🍷🍷 4*
○ Salice Salentino Bianco Donna Lisa '06	🍷🍷 5
⊙ Five Roses '06	🍷🍷 4*
○ Don Piero Brut	🍷 4
● Salice Salentino Rosso Maiana '05	🍷 3
○ Messapia '06	🍷 3
● Primitivo di Manduria Villa Santera '06	🍷 4
● Messere Andrea '04	🍷 5
● Salice Salentino Rosso Donna Lisa Ris. '00	YYY 6
● Salice Salentino Rosso Donna Lisa Ris. '01	YYY 6
● Salice Salentino Rosso Donna Lisa Ris. '02	YY 6

Lomazzi & Sarli

LOC. C.DA PARTEMIO
S.S. 7
72022 LATIANO [BR]
TEL. 0831725898
www.vinilomazzi.it

ANNUAL PRODUCTION 1,000,000 bottles
HECTARES UNDER VINE 108
VITICULTURE METHOD Conventional

The passion, the commitment and the
effort that the Dimastrodonato family, aided
by Marco and Franco Bernabei, put into
winemaking is taking them right to the
heights of the Puglian scene. Nevertheless,
we can't avoid saying that it seems as if the
desire to produce something absolutely
outstanding is taking its toll on the other
wines, all of which were slightly under par.
That "something absolutely outstanding" is
beginning to take shape, though. It's
Nomas, made solely from sussumaniello,
and the '04 got as far as the finals. The
nose is deep, complex and floral but also
still quite oaky, with tobacco and truffle
scents. The close-knit palate is quite
modern and muscular but has a freshly
acidic finish to its chocolate and cherry
flavours. The fine Salice Salentino Rosso
Irenico '05 is also modern in conception.
Fruity aromas of plum and damson lead to
a palate of notable depth and liveliness,
and although the oak isn't yet fully
integrated, there is a good finish with the
merest hint of bitterness. The other wines
are not much more than well styled. Given
the aspirations here we look forward to
seeing better things overall.

Alberto Longo

LOC. C.DA PADULECCHIA
S.P. PIETRAMONTECORVINO KM 4
71036 LUCERA [FG]
TEL. 0881539057
www.albertolongo.it

ANNUAL PRODUCTION 200,000 bottles
HECTARES UNDER VINE 35
VITICULTURE METHOD Conventional

Alberto Longo has achieved his first
objective. Just six years after he planted his
vineyards – using the unusually high
densities, for the region, of 6,000 to 12,000
plants per hectare – and just one year since
he first appeared in the Guide as an Other
Winery, he has a full profile. We're not overly
surprised, given Alberto's character and the
commitment and thoughtfulness he puts
into his work, and we have no doubt that he
is not intending to stop here. The wine we
liked best this year was Calcara Vecchia
'05. This is a Bordeaux blend with aromas
of bell pepper, coffee, oak toast and spices
before a clean, attractive palate gives a
long, fruity finish. The estate's flagship wine,
Le Cruste '05, from 100 per cent nero di
Troia aged in new and second-year
barriques, also showed very well. It's spicy
with mineral and black berry fruits aromas,
and has a close-knit palate, but clearly
needs more bottle age. Next comes
Donnadele '06, an onionskin coloured rosé
made from 100 per cent negroamaro. This
aims more at elegance than power, and is
fresh, clean, elegant and supple. Longo has
a soft spot for Cacc'e Mmitte and his
version is attractive and easy drinking.

● Nomas '04	♟♟ 5
● Salice Salentino Rosso Irenico '05	♟♟ 4*
⊙ Brindisi Rosato Solise '06	♟ 3
● Brindisi Rosso Solise Ris. '04	♟ 4
● Latias '05	♟ 4
○ Imperium '05	♟ 4
● Nomas '03	♟♟ 6

● Calcara Vecchia '05	♟♟ 4*
⊙ Donnadele '06	♟♟ 4*
● Le Cruste '05	♟♟ 5
● Cacc'e Mmitte di Lucera '05	♟ 4
○ Le Fossette '06	♟ 4
● Le Cruste '04	♟♟ 5

Maria Marmo

LOC. C.DA COCEVOLA
S.S. 170 CASTEL DEL MONTE-ANDRIA
KM 9.900
70031 ANDRIA [BA]
TEL. 0883556006
www.tenutacocevola.com

ANNUAL PRODUCTION 36,000 bottles
HECTARES UNDER VINE 6.5
VITICULTURE METHOD Conventional

The Marmo family created Tenuta Cocevola
in 2000, a property on the hills around
Castel del Monte, and set up visitor facilities
as well as olive groves and vineyards. They
planted nero di Troia for their red wines, and
chardonnay and sauvignon for the whites,
and took on Saverio Menga as oenologist
and Luigi Moio as consultant. The repeated
high quality of the wines now confirms the
estate as a leading player in Castel del
Monte. Vandalo again reached the finals this
year, the nose full of lively black berry fruit
nuanced with tobacco and spices, and the
palate clean, close-knit and intense, with a
long, aniseed-like finish. But everything is
startlingly good here. Rosso Cocevola is in
similar style to Vandalo, the only real
differences being a touch less intensity and
greater suppleness. The rosé version is
along similar quality lines, with a spicy,
rosewood nose and a nicely full, attractively
finishing palate which has slight sweetness
but also welcome notes of balsam. A new
wine, Tratto, from sauvignon with a little
chardonnay, is well worthy of consideration.
Aromatic and varietal, it has a touch of
almond on the finish.

Azienda Monaci

LOC. TENUTA MONACI
73043 COPERTINO [LE]
TEL. 0832947512
www.aziendamonaci.com

ANNUAL PRODUCTION 480,000 bottles
HECTARES UNDER VINE 36
VITICULTURE METHOD Conventional

Severino Garofano, one of the most
important players in Puglian winemaking in
the last 40 years, has come out with one of
his best ranges ever – if not the absolute
best – in terms of consistency and overall
quality. All right, nothing won Three Glasses,
Le Braci stopping at the finals, but this has
to be seen in the perspective of the high-
level performance of everything else. And it
leaves little doubt that Monaci is no longer
on the way to becoming the model other
Puglian estates should aspire to: it has
achieved its goal. So let's begin with Le
Braci '04. Made in traditional style from
negroamaro, it has aromas of liqueur
cherries, resin and beeswax, and a clean,
soft, open, evolved palate that is highly
attractive. Joining this flagship in the finals
was Simpotica '03, made from negroamaro
with 15 per cent montepulciano. It has a
balsamic and gently mineral nose followed
by a fragrant, long palate with ripe tannins
and good backbone. Copertino Eloquenzia
'04 and the rosé Girofle '06 are also highly
distinguished wines. On the former the nose
is slightly smoky and clove-like, the palate
clean and supple. Girofle has floral aromas
and blackcurrant-like flavours.

● Castel del Monte	
Nero di Troia Vandalo '05	♈♈ 7
○ Castel del Monte Il Tratto '06	♈♈ 5
● Castel del Monte	
Nero di Troia Rosso Cocevola '05	♈♈ 4*
☉ Castel del Monte Rosato '06	♈♈ 4*
● Castel del Monte	
Nero di Troia Vandalo '04	♈♈ 7
● Castel del Monte	
Nero di Troia Rosso Cocevola '04	♈♈ 4

● Le Braci '04	♈♈ 7
● Simpotica '03	♈♈ 4*
● Copertino Rosso Eloquenzia '04	♈♈ 3*
☉ Girofle '06	♈♈ 3*
● Le Braci '00	♈♈♈ 7
● Le Braci '01	♈♈♈ 7
● Le Braci '03	♈♈ 7
● Sine Pari '04	♈♈ 4*

Castello Monaci

C.DA MONACI
73015 SALICE SALENTINO [LE]
TEL. 0831665700
www.giv.it

ANNUAL PRODUCTION 2,200,000 bottles
HECTARES UNDER VINE 150
VITICULTURE METHOD Conventional

Castello Monaci, owned by Gruppo Italiano Vini, seems now to be cruising along comfortably, as our tasting results confirm. This year's wines and the new labels reflect such a rise in quality, and such an ability to bring out the characteristics of their provenance, that the winery could well be considered a model for Puglian winemaking. Artas gained Three Glasses for the second year running. This year's '05 is a garnet-ruby colour. The nose has a complex array of aromas, led by figs, pomegranate and plum jam. The palate is rich, full and fruity, showing lively and dynamic right through to its long finish. But Artas isn't the only top-notch wine for the '06 vintage has brought new stars into the range. Campure Metrano, from a blend of negroamaro and merlot, gained a place in the finals thanks to its blackcurrant jam aromas and spicy nuances, and its clean, lively, richly elegant palate. Pilùna, made solely from primitivo, is one of the best value wines in Italy. Ripe fruit marks out the nose while the traditionally styled palate is attractively soft and relaxed but certainly not tired. Everything else is well made.

Morella

VIA SAN PIETRO, 65
74024 MANDURIA [TA]
TEL. 0999791482
azag.morella@libero.it

ANNUAL PRODUCTION 14,000 bottles
HECTARES UNDER VINE 7
VITICULTURE METHOD Conventional

All Lisa Gilbee, owner of this estate, now needs is honorary citizenship. The wines this Australian oenologist makes from primitivo are so deeply rooted in the territory and reflect it so profoundly – despite being conceived and made in a very modern mould – that we can only stand in wonder. Indeed, we have little doubt that her wines are among the starriest players on Puglian wine scene. And this year she basks in double glory because two of her wines reached the finals, both made entirely from primitivo. Old Vines was making a repeat appearance, this year with the '05. The colour is deep ruby. The nose is intense with clear scents of red berry fruits, plum jam and tobacco and the palate is rich, full and close-knit, the tannins beautifully integrated and another burst of attractive black berry fruitiness enlivening the finish. The La Signora '05 selection is similarly classy. Aromas of printer's ink and quinine, with nuances of small black berry fruits, lead to a succulent palate of notable structure with silky tannins and a fragrant, fruity finish.

● Artas '05	♈♈♈	5*
● Campure Metrano '06	♈♈	4*
● Pilùna '06	♈♈	3*
☉ Kreos '06	♈	3
● Maru '06	♈	4
● Medos '06	♈	4
● Artas '04	♈♈♈	5*
● Artas '01	♈♈	5*
● Artas '02	♈♈	5
● Artas '03	♈♈	5*

● Primitivo La Signora '05	♈♈	6
● Primitivo Old Vines '05	♈♈	6
● Primitivo Malbek Terre Rosse '05	♈	5
● Old Vines Primitivo '03	♈♈	6
● Primitivo Old Vines '04	♈♈	6
● Primitivo La Signora '04	♈♈	6

Paradiso

VIA MANFREDONIA, 39
71042 CERIGNOLA [FG]
TEL. 0885428720
www.cantineparadiso.it

ANNUAL PRODUCTION   110,000 bottles
HECTARES UNDER VINE 35
VITICULTURE METHOD   Conventional

We think Angelo Paradiso's estate is one of the best in the province of Foggia but for some time now his wines have perplexed us. Paradoxically, this is the case again this year even though one of them made it to the finals for the first time ever. So our doubts certainly don't stem from Angelo Primo '04, made from nero di Troia with 40 per cent negroamaro: it's never been so impressive. The colour is bright ruby. The nose has black berry fruits and aromas along the smoky-tar-iodine-rubber spectrum. A rich, full palate is traditionally styled but has great impact and there is a cohesive, long finish. There's no doubt that this is a first-rate wine. The problem is that an estate can't live on one wine alone, at least when it produces a dozen of them. Our feeling is that Angelo Paradiso has invested so much effort into producing something outstanding in Angelo Primo that he has ignored the more everyday wines that used to be his strength. Indeed, the only other wine that had any real impact was Podere Sant'Andrea Bombino '06, which has attractive white-fleshed fruitiness and good backbone. Naturally, our hope is that all the wines will soon follow Angelo Primo.

Rivera

FRAZ. C.DA RIVERA
S.P. 231 KM 60,500
70031 ANDRIA [BA]
TEL. 0883569501
www.rivera.it

ANNUAL PRODUCTION   1,500,000 bottles
HECTARES UNDER VINE 95
VITICULTURE METHOD   Conventional

Unfortunately, the saying that "good things come in threes" hasn't been proved true here and Puer Apuliae didn't win its third consecutive Three Glass award. That certainly doesn't mean, though, that Rivera didn't submit another scintillating range with numerous wines of impeccable quality. And that's what really counts for consumers, and for us. Indeed the name Rivera practically guarantees quality. The De Corato family and their team have created a series of highly reputable wines that almost never let you down. Puer Apuliae '05 probably still needs a little more bottle age. The nose has plum and oak toast. The palate is long and close-knit, and there is considerable structure, although the tannins are still tight. The two classic Castel del Monte wines are up to their usual standards. The more traditionally styled Cappellaccio, a monovarietal Aglianico, has fruit conserve aromas and a soft, open palate. Falcone, from nero di Troia and montepulciano, is a wine that ages remarkably well and this release is attractive, highly drinkable, cherry-like and long. The clean, fresh, balanced Salice Salentino '06, while not one of Rivera's more typical wines, is worth investigating.

● Angelo Primo '04	▼▼ 5
○ Bombino Podere Sant'Andrea '06	▼ 2*
● Belmantello '03	♀♀ 3*
● Primitivo '04	♀♀ 3*
● Belmantello '04	♀♀ 3*

● Castel del Monte Nero di Troia Puer Apuliae '05	▼▼ 7
● Castel del Monte Cappellaccio '04	▼▼ 4*
● Salice Salentino '06	▼▼ 4*
○ Moscato di Trani Piani di Tufara '06	▼▼ 4*
● Castel del Monte Rosso Violante '06	▼▼ 4*
☉ Castel del Monte Pungirosa '06	▼▼ 3*
● Castel del Monte Rosso Il Falcone Ris. '04	▼▼ 5*
● Castel del Monte Rosso Rupicolo '06	▼ 3
● Triusco '06	▼ 4
● Castel del Monte Nero di Troia Puer Apuliae '03	♀♀♀ 7
● Castel del Monte Nero di Troia Puer Apuliae '04	♀♀♀ 7
● Castel del Monte Nero di Troia Puer Apuliae '01	♀♀ 7
● Castel del Monte Nero di Troia Puer Apuliae '02	♀♀ 7

Rosa del Golfo

VIA GARIBALDI, 56
73011 ALEZIO [LE]
TEL. 0833281045
www.rosadelgolfo.com

Tenute Rubino

VIA E. FERMI, 50
72100 BRINDISI [BR]
TEL. 0831571955
www.tenuterubino.it

ANNUAL PRODUCTION 250,000 bottles
HECTARES UNDER VINE 40
VITICULTURE METHOD   Conventional

This has been an excellent year for Damiano
Calò, who continues to persevere with his
penchant for making high quality rosés. He
now does so in many styles, from the
classic steel-aged types to those aged in
barrique and even sparkling versions. The
'06 Rosa del Golfo, from negroamaro with
ten per cent malvasia nera, is as good as
ever. There's florality, iodine scents, red
berry fruit and Mediterranean scrubland
before richness, cleanliness, good
supporting acidity and a long, cohesive
finish emerge in the mouth. Vigna Mazzì, a
wine Damiano holds particularly dear,
continues to make headway. It is produced
from a barrique-aged blend of negroamaro
with ten per cent malvasia nera di Lecce.
The nose is still a little too oaky but intense
red berry fruit comes through. The full-
bodied palate is tightly knit, finishing soft
and attractive. Brut Rosé, a classic method
sparkler, made from negroamaro with ten
per cent chardonnay, is very decent, the
nose floral and fruity, the palate full yet
elegant. Finally comes Quarantale '03. Last
year, we tasted a cask sample. The
definitive version has ripe black berry fruits
and balsamic aromas, with a long, intense,
refined palate of good texture.

ANNUAL PRODUCTION 700,000 bottles
HECTARES UNDER VINE 200
VITICULTURE METHOD   Conventional

Luigi Rubino is continuing to redefine his
range and has decided to delay the release
of his flagship, Torre Testa, for a year to
allow its style to come through better. This
doesn't mean that there was little of interest
in the wines submitted. After all, Rubino is
known for its enviably consistent quality. So
there's been no break in the habit of a
Rubino wine reaching the finals and this
time it was Primitivo Visellio '05. The wine is
still not ready but can show aromas of
violets, figs and damson. A very close-knit
palate gives evident but ripe tannin and a
lively, plum-like finish. The attractive
Primitivo Punta Aquila '06, all black berry
fruit, spice and resin, also showed brilliantly,
as did Giancola '06. This is a dry Malvasia
which has a citrus nose and a balanced
palate, with good acid backbone and a
fresh, subtly aromatic finish. The rosé
Saturnino '06 is fresh and floral. Marmorelle
Rosso '06, from negroamaro and malvasia
nera, is a well-made, supple, easy-drinking
wine with attractive strawberry and
raspberry fruit.

● Quarantale '03	▼▼ 6
☉ Rosa del Golfo '06	▼▼ 4*
☉ Vigna Mazzì '06	▼▼ 4*
☉ Brut Rosé	▼ 5
● Scaliere '06	▼ 2*
☉ Vigna Mazzì '05	♈♈ 4
● Scaliere '05	♈♈ 2*

● Primitivo Visellio '05	▼▼ 5
○ Giancola '06	▼▼ 4*
● Primitivo Punta Aquila '06	▼▼ 4*
● Marmorelle Rosso '06	▼ 3
☉ Saturnino '06	▼ 3
● Primitivo Visellio '01	♈♈♈ 5*
● Torre Testa '01	♈♈♈ 6
● Torre Testa '02	♈♈♈ 6
● Primitivo Visellio '03	♈♈ 5
● Primitivo Visellio '04	♈♈ 5
● Torre Testa '04	♈♈ 6
● Torre Testa '03	♈♈ 6
● Brindisi Rosso Jaddico '04	♈♈ 5
○ Giancola '05	♈♈ 4

Cosimo Taurino

S.S. 605
73010 Guagnano [LE]
TEL. 0832706490
www.taurinovini.it

Tormaresca

VIA Amendola, 201/9
70055 Bari [BA]
TEL. 0883692631
www.tormaresca.it

ANNUAL PRODUCTION   800,000 bottles
HECTARES UNDER VINE 111
VITICULTURE METHOD   Conventional

ANNUAL PRODUCTION   1,200,000 bottles
HECTARES UNDER VINE 350
VITICULTURE METHOD   certified organic

Maintaining the high quality levels for which this famous estate, a beacon throughout Puglia, is known can't be easy and Francesco and Rosanna Taurino, with their long-standing oenologist Severino Garofano, seem to be hitting some difficulties. It's inevitable. Even the most illustrious wines can sometimes fall below their habitual levels so we've decided to wait another year before assessing their flagship, Patriglione '01. But the cellar banner is kept aloft by A Cosimo Taurino '04 and Scaloti '06. The former is from negroamaro with a little cabernet sauvignon and ages a year in barrique. Aromas of tobacco and liquorice lead to a palate that is long, complex, deep, multi-faceted and evolved. The Scaloti, a rosé produced entirely from negroamaro, has violet and rose floral aromas followed by pastry-shop scents. The palate is fresh, with good backbone, and has a fruity, spicy finish. Notarpanaro '03, all red berry fruit and tobacco, and the soft, rounded Salice Salentino Rosso '04, are also well made.

Masseria Maime strikes again, clinching Three Glasses for the fourth time in six years, and quashing the superstition that it only hits the peaks in even-numbered years. This also makes it one of the Puglian wines gaining the greatest number of Three Glass awards ever. Marchese Piero Antinori was right on beam, as he usually is, when he decided that Puglia had a great deal to offer and decided to buy two properties here, Bocca di Lupo in Murgia and Masseria Maime in the upper Salento, to develop an estate of national standing. The '05 release of Masseria Maime, a monovarietal Negroamaro, has a broad, complex nose, with smokiness and very ripe black berry fruit. The palate is full and very clean, and has more smoky nuances on the finish. The '06 Castel del Monte Chardonnay PietraBianca is also as classy as ever. This "little Cervaro" has clear-cut scents of crusty bread, banana and hazelnut. The palate is full, soft and rounded, and has ripe banana on the finish. The estate's new wine, the well-made, spicy, zesty rosé Calafuria '06, is of similar standing. Everything else showed well.

● A Cosimo Taurino '04	⟁⟁ 5
⊙ Scaloti '06	⟁⟁ 3*
● Notarpanaro '03	⟁ 4
● Salice Salentino Rosso '04	⟁ 4
● Patriglione '85	⟁⟁⟁ 5
● Patriglione '88	⟁⟁⟁ 5
● Patriglione '94	⟁⟁⟁ 8
● A Cosimo Taurino '02	⟁⟁ 5
● A Cosimo Taurino '03	⟁⟁ 5
● Notarpanaro '02	⟁⟁ 5
● Patriglione '99	⟁⟁ 8
● A Cosimo Taurino '02	⟁⟁ 5

● Masseria Maime '05	⟁⟁⟁ 5*
⊙ Calafuria '06	⟁⟁ 4*
○ Castel del Monte	
Chardonnay PietraBianca '06	⟁⟁ 5
● Fichimori '06	⟁ 4
○ Tormaresca Chardonnay '06	⟁ 3
○ Moscato di Trani Kaloro '05	⟁ 5
● Masseria Maime '00	⟁⟁⟁ 5*
● Masseria Maime '04	⟁⟁⟁ 5*
● Masseria Maime '02	⟁⟁⟁ 5
● Castel del Monte	
Rosso Bocca di Lupo '01	⟁⟁ 5
○ Castel del Monte	
Chardonnay PietraBianca '05	⟁⟁ 5

Torrevento

LOC. CASTEL DEL MONTE
S.P. 234 KM 10,600
70033 CORATO [BA]
TEL. 0808980923
www.torrevento.it

ANNUAL PRODUCTION 2,500,000 bottles
HECTARES UNDER VINE 300
VITICULTURE METHOD certified organic

This will be a year to remember for
Torrevento's Francesco Liantonio and for all
his staff, including agronomist Luigi
Tarricone, oenologist Massimo Di Bari and
consultant Pasquale Carparelli. Castel del
Monte Vigna Pedale Riserva, the estate's
flagship wine and the one that most closely
and faithfully reflects its provenance, has
clinched Three Glasses. It's made from
late-picked nero di Troia, grown on a
five-hectare cru and vinified traditionally
before ageing a year in large, old oak botti.
The '04 has a broad, complex nose with red
berry fruits and spices. The palate is
clean-cut and fruity, principally evoking
pomegranate, and has a long, attractive
finish. In a word, it's masterful. But that's not
the end of the story. There's a whole series
of really fine wines. Madrevite Aglianico '04
is well-defined, fresh and clean, with red
berry fruit and oriental spices. Castel del
Monte Bolonero '05 has balance and good
texture, with scents of plum, damson and
tobacco. The rosé Madrevite Bombino Nero
'06 simply bursts with rose, juniper and
caper aromas, and has a full-bodied,
cohesive, balanced palate. Well done.

Agricole Vallone

VIA XXV LUGLIO, 5
73100 LECCE [LE]
TEL. 0832308041
www.agricolevallone.it

ANNUAL PRODUCTION 620,000 bottles
HECTARES UNDER VINE 170
VITICULTURE METHOD certified organic

It seems that sisters Vittoria and Maria
Teresa Vallone have got it sussed.
Graticciaia has now gained Three Glasses
for the second year running. This
exceptional wine is sourced from the oldest
bush-trained negroamaro vines on the
estate and made with grapes left to dry out
until they have lost 50 per cent of their
water content. After last year's triumph, our
tasting panel was again bowled over by the
wine, maybe partly because of the general
change in this type of wine when made with
great care and great precision of style.
Graticciaia '03 has a garnet-tinged ruby
hue. The nose is evolved and pervasive,
with dried fruit, almond-studded figs and
light spiciness. The palate is full, soft and
open, clean and fragrant, slightly sweet,
although less so than other versions, and
has an attractive finish. This superb wine
aside, though, we must advise that the
other wines in the Vallone range are not
really up to speed. Only the floral, well-
structured Brindisi Rosato Vigna Flaminio
'06 is really worthy of mention, which is slim
pickings for such a prestigious estate.

● Castel del Monte Rosso V. Pedale Ris. '04	▼▼▼	4*
● Madrevite Aglianico '04	▼▼	4*
● Castel del Monte Rosso Bolonero '05	▼▼	3*
☉ Madrevite Bombino Nero '06	▼▼	4*
○ Castel del Monte Bianco Pezzapiana '06	▼	3
○ Castel del Monte Bianco Proemio '06	▼	3
☉ Castel del Monte Rosato Primaronda '06	▼	3
● Kebir '02	▼▼	5
● Castel del Monte Rosso V. Pedale Ris. '01	▼▼	4*
● Castel del Monte Rosso V. Pedale Ris. '03	▼▼	4*

● Graticciaia '03	▼▼▼	7
☉ Brindisi Rosato V. Flaminio '06	▼	3*
● Graticciaia '01	▼▼▼	7
● Graticciaia '00	▼▼	7
● Graticciaia '96	▼▼	6
● Graticciaia '98	▼▼	7
● Graticciaia '97	▼▼	7

Vetrere

FRAZ. VETRERE
S.DA PROV. MONTEIASI-MONTEMESOLA
KM 16
74100 TARANTO [TA]
TEL. 0995661054
www.vetrere.it

ANNUAL PRODUCTION 150,000 bottles
HECTARES UNDER VINE 37
VITICULTURE METHOD Conventional

The Bruni sisters, together with oenologists Vincenzo Caragnulo and Vincenzo Laera, usually maintain good quality levels for their wines, although this year they're a little less impressive than usual. The main reason is a hint of sweetness and rather too much oak, especially in the top wines. Still, the rosé Taranta, made from negroamaro with 15 per cent malvasia bianca, seems to have been unaffected by the problem. The palate has achieved a fine balance between attractive drinkability and good body while aromas of capers and spices emerge from a slightly smoky nose. The lively, well-made Livruni '06, a monovarietal Primitivo, is equally admirable, with tobacco and red and black berry fruits, and a clean, supple palate. Laureato '06, from 70 per cent chardonnay with 20 per cent malvasia and a little fiano minutolo, is reasonably good, the nose full of ripe peach and apricot, and the palate soft and juicy, but it suffers from an excess of residual sugar. Barone Pazzo '05, also from primitivo, is even more disappointing, with too much oak and too little freshness. Tempio di Giano '06, from negroamaro, fell short because it's ill-defined, despite being attractively fruity.

Conti Zecca

VIA CESAREA
73045 LEVERANO [LE]
TEL. 0832925613
www.contizecca.it

ANNUAL PRODUCTION 1,800,000 bottles
HECTARES UNDER VINE 320
VITICULTURE METHOD Conventional

Again this year, Nero didn't quite clinch Three Glasses but this certainly doesn't diminish the lustre of the estate because brothers Alcibiade, Francesco, Luciano and Mario Zecca are still successfully combining quality with quantity, and every wine in every line is admirably good or very good. Nero '05, made from negroamaro with 30 per cent cabernet sauvignon, is naturally top of the tree. The nose has bramble jelly, tobacco and oak toast. The palate is deep and mouthfilling, with more black fruits jam on the finish, the only problem being that it's still a bit too oaky. The other leading wines are up to their usual standards. Leverano Rosso Terra Riserva '04 has aromas of black berry fruit, liquorice and oriental spices leading to a palate of good texture with well integrated tannins. Salice Salentino Rosso Cantalupi Riserva '04 has a refined, elegant nose centred on coffee aromas and a lively, supple, cohesive palate. Donna Marzia Rosso '05 is balsamic on the nose, and clean-cut and invigorating on the palate. But practically all 17 of the wines are worthy of mention. Well done!

● Livruni '06	♟♟	3*
☉ Taranta '06	♟♟	3*
● Barone Pazzo '05	♟	4
● Tempio di Giano '06	♟	3
○ Laureato '06	♟	4
● Barone Pazzo '02	♟♟	4
● Barone Pazzo '03	♟♟	4
● Tempio di Giano '05	♟♟	3*
● Barone Pazzo '04	♟♟	4

● Nero '05	♟♟	6
● Donna Marzia Rosso '05	♟♟	2*
● Salice Salentino Rosso Cantalupi Ris. '04	♟♟	4
● Leverano Rosso Terra Ris. '04	♟♟	5
☉ Cantalupi Rosato '06	♟	3
● Donna Marzia Primitivo '05	♟	3
○ Saraceno Malvasia Bianca '06	♟	2*
● Donna Marzia Negramaro '05	♟	2*
● Salice Salentino Rosso Cantalupi '04	♟	3
○ Salice Salentino Bianco Cantalupi '06	♟	3
○ Fiano '06	♟	4
● Nero '00	♟♟♟	6
● Nero '01	♟♟♟	6
● Nero '99	♟♟♟	5
● Nero '98	♟♟♟	5
● Nero '02	♟♟♟	6
● Nero '03	♟♟♟	6

OTHER WINERIES

Masseria Altemura
C.DA PALOMBARA
72028 TORRE SANTA SUSANNA [BR]
TEL. 0831740485
www.masseriaaltemura.it

The Zonin family's Puglian estate, which was founded in 2000 and has around 110 hectares of vineyard, is almost up to speed. Sasseo '05, made solely from primitivo, is very attractive, fresh and fragrant, showing red berry fruits, tobacco and pepper. Fiano '06 is clean, floral and even.

● Sasseo '05	🍷🍷 4*
○ Fiano '06	🍷 4

Antica Enotria
C.DA POSTA UCCELLO
71042 CERIGNOLA [FG]
TEL. 0885418462
www.anticaenotria.it

Antica Enotria is a fine farming estate but could do with a little more quality in its wines. Falanghina '06 is citrus-like and spicy. Rosso di Cerignola '05 is lively and attractive with notable tannin. Aglianico '05 is uncomplicated, giving fruit, hints of smokiness and a slightly sweet finish.

● Aglianico '05	🍷 4
○ Falanghina '06	🍷 4
● Rosso di Cerignola '05	🍷 4

Antica Masseria del Sigillo
VIA PROVINCIALE, 196
73010 GUAGNANO [LE]
TEL. 0832706331
www.vinisigillo.net

The wines here are distinctly low key this year. The only two which are really up their normal standards are the tight-knit, mouthfilling, deeply fruity Terre del Guiscardo, which promises well although still young, and the soft, open Salice Salentino Hilliryos.

● Terre del Guiscardo '05	🍷🍷 5
● Salice Salentino Hilliryos '05	🍷 4

Apollonio
VIA SAN PIETRO IN LAMA, 7
73047 MONTERONI DI LECCE [LE]
TEL. 0832327182
www.apolloniovini.it

Apollonio's wines showed well this year. The clean, tight-knit, spicy Copertino '03 with its tobacco aromas is admirable. The all-chardonnay Laicale '05 is also good, with honey, banana and smoky notes, and a nice, long finish. Squinzano '03 and Salice Salentino '03 are well made, as is everything else.

● Copertino '03	🍷🍷 4
○ Laicale Chardonnay	🍷 4
● Salice Salentino Rosso '03	🍷 4
● Squinzano '03	🍷 4

L'Astore Masseria
LOC. L'ASTORE
73020 CUTROFIANO [LE]
TEL. 0836542020
www.lastoremasseria.it

The Benegiamo family's wines have been improving by leaps and bounds and the estate is now in the Guide. Astore '05, from aglianico and petit verdot, is a spicy, structured complex wine. Krita '06, from chardonnay and malvasia, is similarly good, showing fragrant, aromatic and pervasively citrussy.

○ Krita '06	🍷🍷 4*
● L'Astore '05	🍷🍷 4*
● Argentieri '05	🍷 4
⊙ Il Massaro Rosa '06	🍷 4

Sergio Botrugno
LOC. CASALE
VIA ARCIONE, 1
72100 BRINDISI [BR]
TEL. 0831555587
www.vinisalento.com

Botrugno's wines again did well this year, especially Vigna Lobia '05, a full, barrique-aged, monovarietal Negroamaro with black berry fruit and spiciness. The other Negroamaro, Patrunu Ro' '05, is lighter and attractive drinking while Seno di Ponente '06 is soft and fruity. Both are well made.

● Vigna Lobia Rosso '05	🍷🍷 4*
● Patrunu Ro' '05	🍷 2*
● Seno di Ponente Rosso '06	🍷 3

OTHER WINERIES

Michele Calò & Figli
VIA MASSERIA VECCHIA, 1
73058 TUGLIE [LE]
TEL. 0833596242
www.mjere.it

What more can we say about one of Puglia's most famous estates? Grecàntico '06, from negroamaro with 20 per cent primitivo, is excellent, all cherry and cassis then clean and elegant on the palate. The citrus-fresh, slightly spicy Alezio Rosato Mjère '06 is almost as good. Mjère Rosso '05 is only decent.

● Grecàntico '06	♀♀	4*
☉ Alezio Rosato Mjère '06	♀	4
● Mjère Rosso '05	♀	4

C.a.l.o.s.m.
VIA PIETRO SICILIANI
73058 TUGLIE [LE]
TEL. 0833598051
calosm@libero.it

The C.a.l.o.s.m wines impress more each year. Tisciano '05, from negroamaro with malvasia nera, is clean and balsamic, with red berry fruit and Mediterranean scrubland. Salmace '06 is a fresh, supple, balanced rosé from the same blend. Primitivo Villa Valentino '06 is youthful and fruity with good acidity.

● Tisciano '05	♀♀	4*
☉ Salmace '06	♀	4
● Primitivo Villa Valentino '06	♀	3

Antiche Aziende Canosine
VIA SCONCONCORDIA
70053 CANOSA DI PUGLIA [BA]
TEL. 3289406102

One wine from Canosine, founded in 2004 by Manfred Geier and the Del Vento family, went into the finals. It was Tharen, a complex, fragrant, dried-grape Moscato Passito, with aromas of hazelnut, almond and beeswax, and a fresh palate with citrus peel and dried figs. The rosé Shabin is also very good.

O Tharen '04	♀♀	5
☉ Shabin '06	♀♀	4*
O Halbus '06	♀	4

Cantine Carpentiere
C.DA BAGNOLI
70033 CORATO [BA]
TEL. 0883341104
www.cantinecarpentiere.it

Repeating success is more difficult than achieving it. The Carpentiere family only partly managed to do so but it's enough for them to keep their place in the Guide. Pietra dei Lupi '05 is a nice fruity, supple Nero di Troia. Bianco di Nero, from nero di Troia fermented off its skins, is merely OK.

● Castel del Monte Pietra dei Lupi '05	♀♀	4
☉ Castel del Monte Rosato Esordio '06	♀	4
O Bianco di Nero '06		4

Giancarlo Ceci
C.DA SANT'AGOSTINO
70031 ANDRIA [BA]
TEL. 0883564938

Giancarlo Ceci's wines again maintained their quality. Chardonnay Pozzo Sorgente '05 is richly fruity even though it's a little too oaky. Castel del Monte Rosso Parco Grande '06, from nero di Troia, montepulciano and aglianico, is attractive and well made.

O Pozzo Sorgente '05	♀♀	4*
● Castel del Monte Rosso Parco Grande '06	♀	3
☉ Castel del Monte Rosato '06	♀	3

Cefalicchio
C.SO SAN SABINO, 6
70053 CANOSA DI PUGLIA [BA]
TEL. 0833617601
www.cefalicchio.it

Production at Cefalicchio has been biodynamic since 1992. The wines are good but a little inconsistent and we are still hoping to see a rise in quality. Ponte della Lama '06 is a spicy, well-structured rosé from nero di Troia. Lefkò '05 is a mineral-edged, smoky Chardonnay.

O Lefkò '05	♀	4
☉ Ponte della Lama Rosato '06	♀	4

OTHER WINERIES

d'Aprì
VIA ZANNOTTI, 30
71016 SAN SEVERO [FG]
TEL. 0882227643
www.darapri.it

This is the only estate in south or central
Italy to specialize in classic method
sparklers. Riserva Nobile '02, from bombino
bianco, and Gran Cuvée XXI Secolo '00,
from bombino bianco with 20 per cent pinot
nero, are both complex and mineral. Brut
Rosé, from montepulciano and pinot nero,
is nice and fresh.

O d'Aprì Gran Cuvée XXI Secolo '00	🍷🍷	6
O d'Aprì Nobile Ris. '02	🍷🍷	6
☉ d'Aprì Brut Rosé	🍷	6

De Falco
VIA MILANO, 25
73051 NOVOLI [LE]
TEL. 0832711597
www.cantinedefalco.it

The De Falco family's Salento estate is well
respected. The first-rate Bocca della Verità
'05 is a succulent fruit and spice Primitivo.
Salice Salentino Rosso Falconero Riserva
'03 is clean and lively if not very typical, and
Artiglio '04 is a structured blend of
montepulciano and primitivo. Both are
good.

● Bocca della Verità '05	🍷🍷	4*
● Artiglio '04	🍷	5
● Salice Salentino Rosso Falconero Ris. '03	🍷	4

Emèra
VIA PROVINCIALE, 222
73010 GUAGNANO [LE]
TEL. 0825998977
info@cantineemera.com

Claudio Quarta's estate is new yet the wines
are already of so good that it joins the
Guide. Anima di Niuru Maru '06, a
Negroamaro with tobacco, black berry fruit
and spices then a clean, long, fruity palate,
is excellent. So is the more classic,
mouthfilling Anima di Primitivo '06. Rose '06
is well styled.

● Anima di Niuru Maru '06	🍷🍷	4*
● Anima di Primitivo '06	🍷🍷	4*
☉ Rose '06	🍷	3*

Le Fabriche
LOC. TORRICELLA
C.DA LE FABBRICHE
74020 MANDURIA [TA]
TEL. 0999738284
www.lefabriche.it

Alessia Perrucci, assisted by her oenologist
brother Fabrizio, makes excellent reds from
her 23 hectares. The best of them are the
full-bodied, refined Emmaus '05, from
aglianico and primitivo, and an excellent,
softly spicy Primitivo di Manduria '04.
Negroamaro '05 and Malvasia Nera '05 are
both good, too.

● Emmaus Aglianico '05	🍷🍷	6
● Primitivo di Manduria '04	🍷🍷	5
● Malvasia Nera Le Fabriche '05	🍷	4
● Negroamaro Le Fabriche '05	🍷	4

Gianfranco Fino
LOC. LAMA
VIA FIOR DI SALVIA, 8
74100 TARANTO [TA]
TEL. 0997773970
www.gianfrancofino.it

Gianfranco Fino's 3,000 bottles come from
50-year-old bush-trained vines producing
little more than 500 grams per plant.
Primitivo di Manduria Es '05 ages in new
and second-year French oak barriques and
reaches 15.5 per cent alcohol. It's full and
close-knit with black berry fruit, tobacco
and spices.

● Primitivo di Manduria Es '05	🍷🍷	6

Guttarolo
VIA LAMIE DI FATALONE, KM 2,385
70023 GIOIA DEL COLLE [BA]
TEL. 089236612
www.cantinaguttarolo.it

The good repeat performance from this
small new estate hints at a rosy future. Gioia
del Colle Antello delle Murge reached the
finals. It has well-defined aromas of black
berry fruit, tobacco and spices preceding a
succulently cohesive palate. The standard
Gioia del Colle was less successful this year.

● Gioia del Colle Antello delle Murge '05	🍷🍷	4*
● Gioia del Colle Primitivo '05	🍷	4

OTHER WINERIES

Cantina Locorotondo
VIA MADONNA DELLA CATENA, 99
70010 LOCOROTONDO [BA]
TEL. 0804311644
www.locorotondodoc.com

This co-operative's wines are back in our frame but even so we'd like to see a bit more pizzazz. Best of the bunch this year are the fresh, citrussy Vigneti in Tallinajo and the basic Locorotondo, which has pear and mimosa aromas, and a simple palate of medium body with an attractively almondy finish.

○ Locorotondo '06	♟ 4
○ Locorotondo Vign. in Tallinajo '06	♟ 4

Masseria Li Veli
S.P. CELLINO-CAMPI, KM 1
72020 CELLINO SAN MARCO [BR]
TEL. 0831617906
www.liveli.it

The years go by but the story is always the same here. There's great potential but the wines don't really convince. They're well made but lack flair. Orion '06, a lively Primitivo, is reasonable as is the fruity, attractive Primonero '06, made from negroamaro, primitivo and cabernet sauvignon.

● Orion '06	♟ 3
● Primonero '06	♟ 3

Mille Una
L.GO CHIESA, 11
74020 LIZZANO [TA]
TEL. 0999552638
www.milleuna.it

We remain troubled by the style of wines at Mille Una and by its pricing policy. We did like Capitolo Laureto '04, from negroamaro, which has a balsamic, spicy nose and a nice fruity finish. Maviglia '05, a highly extracted Viognier, and Bacmione '04 are reasonably good.

● Capitolo Laureto '04	♟♟ 8
○ Maviglia '05	♟ 6
● Bacmione '04	♟ 5

Villa Mottura
P.ZZA MELICA, 4
73058 TUGLIE [LE]
TEL. 0833596601
www.motturavini.it

This 170-hectare estate debuts in the Guide. Salice Salentino Rosso '05 is a splendid wine of good length and texture, with aromas of balsam, black berry fruit, tobacco and pepper. The fragrant, fruity Negroamaro '06 and the simple, supple Primitivo di Manduria '05 are also good.

● Salice Salentino Rosso '05	♟♟ 4*
● Negroamaro '06	♟ 4
● Primitivo di Manduria '05	♟ 4

Tenuta Nante's
VIA CAVOUR, 31
72027 SAN PIETRO VERNOTICO [BR]
TEL. 0831671911
www.tenutanantes.it

The Saponaro family's estate owns 35 hectares of vineyard and leases a further ten. Sciarabbà '06, from primitivo, is good, with black berry fruit and spicy aromas, and a lively, well-textured palate. The broad, floral Sirama Rosato '06, and Sirama Rosso '06, a traditional Negroamaro, are both fair.

● Sciarabbà '06	♟♟ 5
⊙ Sirama Rosato '06	♟ 4
● Sirama Rosso '06	♟ 4

Ognissole
VIA LUIGI DI SAVOIA, 3
74026 PULSANO [TA]
TEL. 0825986611
www.ognissole.it

Feudi di San Gregorio's Puglian operation submitted a full, well-made Primitivo di Manduria, Canuddi '05, which has pervasive black berry fruit and spiciness, and an attractive finish. There is also a nice fresh, sage-like Verdeca '06, which expresses the grape's character better than most.

● Primitivo di Manduria Canuddi '05	♟♟ 6
○ Verdeca '06	♟ 5

OTHER WINERIES

Cosimo Palamà
VIA A. DIAZ, 6
73020 CUTROFIANO [LE]
TEL. 0836542865
www.vinicolapalama.com

Mavro '05, from negroamaro with 20 per cent malvasia nera, came to within an inch of the finals. It has an intense nose of black berry fruit, undergrowth and spices. Its full, cohesive palate is nicely fruity and has a fig-like finish. Everything else showed well, too. A full profile is surely on the way.

● Mavro '05	▼▼ 4*
● Albarossa Primitivo '05	▼ 2*
☉ Metiusco Rosato '06	▼ 3*

I Pastini - Carparelli
VIA ITALO BALBO, 22/24
70010 LOCOROTONDO [BA]
TEL. 0804313309
pastini@virgilio.it

The wines here are reliable and good quality. We liked Arpago '05, a rich, concentrated, nicely fruity Primitivo, even though it is still too oaky. The elegant, gently aromatic Rampone '06, from fiano minutolo, is also good. Cupa '06, made solely from bianco d'Alessano is an attractive white.

● Arpago '05	▼▼ 4
○ Cupa '06	▼▼ 4
○ Rampone '06	▼ 5

Giovanni Petrelli
VIA VILLA CONVENTO, 33
73041 CARMIANO [LE]
TEL. 0832603051
www.cantinapetrelli.com

This was a low-key showing by Giovanni Petrelli's wines although they remain well made and attractive. Don Pepé is less successful than usual, showing simple and a bit too sweet. But we liked the fresh, fruity, supple Copertino Tre Archi and Luna Saracena, from 70 per cent fiano with bombino and greco.

● Copertino Tre Archi '04	▼ 4
○ Luna Saracena '06	▼ 3
● Salice Salentino Centopietre '05	▼ 4
● Don Pepè '04	5

Primis
VIA C. COLOMBO, 44
71048 STORNARELLA [FG]
TEL. 0885433333
www.primisvini.com

Word is getting out about Primis. It was founded a few years ago and produces large quantities, although a shorter list wouldn't hurt. Crusta '04, a barrique-aged Montepulciano is excellent. It's concentrated, close-knit, invigorating, fruity and lively on the finish. Nero di Troia '06 and Greco '06 are good.

● Crusta '04	▼▼ 5
○ Greco '06	▼ 3
● Nero di Troia '06	▼ 3

Agricole Rizzello
C.DA RAFI VERDERAME
72020 CELLINO SAN MARCO [BR]
TEL. 0831617847
www.agricolerizzellospa.com

This is a return to the Guide for Rizzello, which is gradually shifting production from bulk to bottle. Solemnis '05, from primitivo, is excellent. Still young, it has spice and chocolate, and notable depth. Verve '05, from negroamaro, is a step behind. It's close-knit and very fleshy but still a bit oaky.

● Solemnis '05	▼▼ 4
● Verve '05	▼ 4
☉ Murex '06	▼ 4

Castel di Salve
FRAZ. DEPRESSA
P.ZZA CASTELLO, 8
73026 TRICASE [LE]
TEL. 0833771041
www.casteldisalve.com

Francesco Marra and Francesco Winspeare submitted an excellent Cento Primitivo '04. Its deep ruby ushers in a close-knit nose and intense, full-bodied palate with good balance. Santi Medici Rosso '06, a warm, structured Negroamaro, and the fruity, supple Santi Medici Bianco '06 are both worth uncorking.

● Cento '04	▼▼ 5
○ Santi Medici Bianco '06	▼ 3*
● Santi Medici Rosso '06	▼ 3*

OTHER WINERIES

Santa Barbara
VIA MATERNITÀ E INFANZIA, 23
72027 SAN PIETRO VERNOTICO [BR]
TEL. 0831652749

The slightly disconcerting, up-and-down results at this major co-operative meant we had to relegate it to the Other Wineries section until consistency returns. The soft, clean, traditional-style Squinzano Rosso '03 and the simple, fruity Salice Salentino Rosso '03 are decent enough.

● Salice Salentino Rosso '03	♟	3
● Squinzano Rosso '03	♟	3

Santa Lucia
S.DA SAN VITTORE, 1
70033 CORATO [BA]
TEL. 0817642888
www.vinisantalucia.com

Recently, more estates have been looking to achieve high quality Castel del Monte DOC. This is one, owned by Perrone Capano. We liked best the floral, highly perfumed Fiano Gazza Ladra '06 but the traditionally styled Vigna del Melograno '05 is also attractive.

○ Gazza Ladra '06	♟♟	4
● Castel del Monte Rosso V. del Melograno '05	♟	4

Santa Maria del Morige
FRAZ. CARPIGNANA
VIA DEL MARE, KM 2
73044 GALATONE [LE]
TEL. 0833864525
www.santamariadelmorige.com

Annalisa Conserva dedicates body and soul to her excellent, traditionally styled wines. Cinabro, a full-bodied wine from 30-year-old, bush-trained negroamaro vines, is again first-rate this year, its nose all black berry fruits and Mediterranean scrubland, the palate structured and full of elegant tannins.

● Cinabro '04	♟♟	4*
● Cinabro '03	♟♟	4*

Santi Dimitri
FRAZ. C.DA SANTI DIMITRI
VIA GUIDANO
73013 GALATINA [LE]
TEL. 0836565866
www.santidimitri.it

Vincenzo Vallone cultivates his 60 hectares with dedication and care for the environment. The succulent, harmonious Fiano Ruah '06 is admirable. Primitivo Sharav '04, the fresh, easy-drinking Margìa '05 from negroamaro, cabernet sauvignon and merlot, and Aruca Rosato '06, from negroamaro, are all good.

○ Ruah '06	♟♟	4*
⊙ Rosato Aruca '06	♟	3*
● Margìa '05	♟	4
● Sharav Primitivo '04	♟	4

Schola Sarmenti
VIA AVV. P. INGUSCI, 45
73048 NARDÒ [LE]
TEL. 0833567247
www.scholasarmenti.it

This newish estate, with just over ten hectares, is back in the Guide with a well-made range. The best wine is Cubardi '04, a complex, spicy, attractive Primitivo. But the lively, supple Nardò Rosso Roccamora '04 and Armentino '06, from negroamaro and primitivo, full of ripe red berry fruitiness, are also nice.

● Cubardi '04	♟	5
● Armentino '06	♟	4
● Nardò Rosso Roccamora '04	♟	4

Soloperto
S.S. 7 TER
74024 MANDURIA [TA]
TEL. 0999794286
www.soloperto.it

Soloperto, which is now renovating its vineyards and cellars, keeps one eye on tradition. It's back in the Guide after several years' absence. We liked the spicy Primitivo di Manduria Centofuochi '05 which is long, with good, close-knit texture and a lively, black berry fruit finish.

● Primitivo di Manduria Centofuochi Tenuta Bagnolo '05	♟♟	5
⊙ Gran Rosé '06	♟	2*
● Primitivo di Manduria Patriarca '04	♟	5

OTHER WINERIES

Torre Quarto
C.DA QUARTO, 5
71042 CERIGNOLA [FG]
TEL. 0885418453
www.torrequartocantine.it

The Torre Quarto wines are well made this year but don't have the qualities that marked them out a couple of years ago. The best is Nina '06, from falanghina, with citrus aromas, good backbone and good texture. Quarto Ducale and Tarabuso are no more than fair. We look forward to a better showing next year.

○ Nina '06	▼▼ 3*
● Quarto Ducale '04	▼ 4
● Tarabuso Primitivo '06	▼ 4

Valle dell'Asso
VIA GUIDANO, 18
73024 GALATINA [LE]
TEL. 0836561470
www.valleasso.it

Gino Vallone is a down-to-earth person who hates compromise and shortcuts, and we are delighted to see his estate back. We liked the Piromàfo '03. There are traditional aromas, with antique wood, liqueur cherries and light oriental spices. The palate is attractive and mature, and has good fragrance.

● Piromàfo '03	▼▼ 5
● Galatina Rosso '03	▼ 3
○ Galatina Bianco '06	▼ 3

Cantina Sociale Cooperativa Vecchia Torre
VIA MARCHE, 1
73045 LEVERANO [LE]
TEL. 0832925053
www.cantinavecchiatorre.it

The wines from this major co-operative are reliable. They showed well, especially Leverano Riserva '04, which has a cherry and chocolate nose, and a well-made, easy-drinking, attractive palate. Best of the rest are the soft, fruity, traditionally styled Primitivo, Arneide '03, and Salice Salentino Rosso '04.

● Leverano Rosso Ris. '04	▼▼ 4*
● Arneide '03	▼ 5
● Salice Salentino Rosso '04	▼ 3*

Vigne & Vini
VIA AMENDOLA, 36
74020 LEPORANO [TA]
TEL. 0995332254
www.vigneevini.it

The absence of the Primitivo di Mandurias meant that the Vigne & Vini range had no big stars this year. Leading it were Moi '06, a Negroamaro with aromas of wild rose and small red berry fruits; the clean, supple Zinfandel '05; and Primadonna '06, from chardonnay, which has a nose of peach and ripe banana.

○ Primadonna '06	▼
☉ Moi '06	▼
● Zinfandel '05	▼

Vigneti Reale
VIA EGIDIO REALE, 55
73100 LECCE [LE]
TEL. 0832248433
www.vignetireale.it

Vigneti Reale debuts in the Guide, mainly thanks to Norie '05, a rich, long, close-knit Negroamaro with ripe black berry fruit. Vivaio '06, a simple, supple rosé; Rudiae '05, a rather old-style Primitivo; and the soft, attractive Santa Croce '03, from negroamaro and primitivo, also showed well.

● Norie '05	▼▼ 4*
● Rudiae '05	▼ 4
● Santa Croce '03	▼ 6
☉ Vivaio '06	▼ 4

Vinicola Mediterranea
VIA MATERNITÀ INFANZIA, 22
72027 SAN PIETRO VERNOTICO [BR]
TEL. 0831676323
www.vinicolamediterranea.it

Once more, the wines here didn't really shine this year. There's nothing particularly wrong with them; they're just not as good as they should be. The best of the bunch is the lively, fruity, long Salice Salentino Rosso Sirio '04. The spicy Squinzano '05 and the supple Brindisi Rosso '05 aren't bad.

● Salice Salentino Rosso Sirio '04	▼▼ 3*
● Brindisi Rosso '05	▼ 3
● Squinzano Rosso '05	▼ 3

CALABRIA

The 2008 edition of the Guide marks an important turn of events for Calabria. For the first time ever, the number of top wines has reached nine: two Three Glass winners and seven finalists. Librandi's Gravello returns to the highest rung of the ladder with the '05 and Scavigna Vigna Garrone from Odoardi joins it with the '04. This sort of result is obviously not completely divorced from the broader context. Indeed, never before has the overall range of wines from Calabria been so impressive. Not only are the following pages peppered with names that are already of high repute in Italy and abroad, such as Librandi, Odoardi, Lento, Statti and Viola, but there are many very exciting newcomers, promising even greater success for the future. More than 30 cellars submitted wines for our tastings, ten of them for the first time. But even more important, we found an upswing in quality everywhere. A wine from one of the newcomers, Feudo dei Sanseverino's outstanding Moscato '01, even shot straight into the finals. Developments in the province of Cosenza we had noted in previous years are now beginning to come to fruition, as can been seen from the fine debuts of the Donnici 99 and Farneto del Principe wineries. In the Cirò zone, we are starting to see the emergence of other producers alongside the long-standing estates. There are the Greco siblings, for example, and two, Scala and Iuzzolini, that show great promise. Luigi Viola is happily no longer on his own in Saracena and now he has some fellow Moscato producers the next move, which we hope won't take long, has to be the granting of a Moscato di Saracena DOC. In Lamezia, the limelight remains on the well-established Lento and Statti. The good news from Reggio Calabria is that there has been a renewed upsurge of interest in Greco di Bianco and the renowned Ceratti is back in the Guide. But there's also the fascination of an up-and-coming, all-female estate, that of the Malaspina sisters. Calabria seems to know where it is going.

Cantine Lento

VIA DEL PROGRESSO, 1
88046 LAMEZIA TERME [CZ]
TEL. 096828028
www.cantinelento.it

ANNUAL PRODUCTION 500,000 bottles
HECTARES UNDER VINE 82
VITICULTURE METHOD Certified organic

The vineyards around Lamezia have always been some of the best in Calabria and the Lento family's wines fully reflect their potential, not to mention the validity of the DOC. There have also been quality rises over the past two years on this sound estate, as our tasting scores reveal. Federico II, from 100 per cent cabernet sauvignon, hasn't been available for a couple of years but is now back in circulation with the '04. It simply flew into the finals and very nearly grabbed a third Glass. The nose has red berry fruits and spiciness leading to a palate with nice flesh and smooth tannins. Lamezia Riserva '02 also showed well. It's a deep ruby, with aromas of red berry fruits and a dense, full, well-structured palate that gains overall balance from soft, close-woven tannins. The fruit-forward Lamezia Dragone '05 worthily earned One Glass. Tisaloro '04, from equal amounts of greco and chardonnay, didn't really shine, though. It's fleshy and well structured but is still oak dominated, probably as a result of the poor vintage.

● Federico II '04	🍷🍷	5
● Lamezia Rosso Ris. '02	🍷🍷	5
● Lamezia Rosso Dragone '05	🍷	4
○ Contessa Emburga Capsula Nera '05	🍷	4
○ Lamezia Bianco Dragone '06	🍷	4
○ Greco Bianco '06	🍷	4
○ Tisaloro '04	🍷	6

Librandi

LOC. SAN GENNARO
S.S. JONICA 106
88811 CIRÒ MARINA [KR]
TEL. 096231518
www.librandi.it

ANNUAL PRODUCTION 2,200,000 bottles
HECTARES UNDER VINE 232
VITICULTURE METHOD Conventional

This has been a fine year for Nicodemo and Antonio Librandi who take home another Three Glasses for a marvellous '05 Gravello, which embodies the effect of the winery's recent stylistic changes. Made from gaglioppo with 30 per cent cabernet sauvignon, it is supremely elegant, yet doesn't lose sight of structure and concentration. The nose is initially tight then opens out to show breadth and range, spanning forest fruits, chocolate and tobacco, and a nicely nuanced balsamic base. It develops well through the full-bodied palate, which is full of close-woven, mellow tannins, to a long coffee-like finish. Magno Megonio '05, from 100 per cent magliocco, reached the finals. It's a fruit-driven, invigorating wine with beautifully integrated soft tannins and great length. The dried-grape passito Le Passule '05, from mantonico, also showed excellently, proffering a broad aromatic spectrum and a palate that's lusciously sweet yet retains freshness. Efeso '06, from 100 per cent mantonico, has a nose of white-fleshed fruit and flowers, good supporting acidity and an attractive mineral finish.

● Gravello '05	🍷🍷🍷	6
● Magno Megonio '05	🍷🍷	5
○ Cirò Bianco '06	🍷🍷	3*
○ Critone '06	🍷🍷	4*
○ Le Passule '05	🍷🍷	5
○ Efeso '06	🍷🍷	5
⊙ Cirò Rosato '06	🍷	3
● Melissa Rosso Asylia '06	🍷	4
○ Melissa Bianco Asylia '06	🍷	4
● Cirò Rosso Cl. '06	🍷	3
● Cirò Rosso Cl. Sup. Duca Sanfelice Ris. '04	🍷	4
⊙ Terre Lontane '06	🍷	4
○ Efeso '05	🍸🍸	6
● Gravello '04	🍸🍸	6
● Magno Megonio '04	🍸🍸	6

G.B. Odoardi

C.DA CAMPODORATO
88047 NOCERA TERINESE [CZ]
TEL. 098429961
odoardi@tin.it

Fattoria San Francesco

LOC. QUATTROMANI
88813 CIRÒ [KR]
TEL. 096232228
www.fattoriasanfrancesco.it

ANNUAL PRODUCTION 300,000 bottles
HECTARES UNDER VINE 95
VITICULTURE METHOD Conventional

Gregorio and Giovan Battista Odoardi's wines are simply excellent this year. To our great delight – and theirs, too, no doubt – Vigna Garrone, from 80 per cent gaglioppo with nerello cappuccino, cabernet franc, cabernet sauvignon and merlot, picked up Three Glasses for the second year running. This time, it's the '04. The nose has red berry fruit, spiciness, balsam, printers' ink, aromatic herbs and even citrus hints. The palate is powerful, concentrated and fleshy, yet elegant, with perfectly ripe, integrated tannins. Vigna Mortilla '04 joined it in the finals. From 50 per cent gaglioppo plus roughly equal quantities of greco nero, magliocco canino, nerello cappuccio and sangiovese, it is a striking wine, right from the first sight of its impenetrable hue, through its deep, elegant nose to its vital, succulent palate. Polpicello '04 is equally admirable, its only fault, if we look for it, being a slight lack of concentration. The distinctive Valeo '06, from late harvested moscato, has a full, elegant nose and a freshly attractive palate.

ANNUAL PRODUCTION 250,000 bottles
HECTARES UNDER VINE 40
VITICULTURE METHOD Conventional

There are mixed messages coming from Francesco Siciliani's fine winery this year. Although most of the wines submitted showed a little better than last time, quality still seems to fall well short of what the estate has achieved in the past. But maybe it's simply that there's no one wine exceptional enough to gain a place in the final. The estate's two selections scored well. Cirò Donna Madda '05 is well made, with red berry fruit supported by coffee and tobacco nicely forward on its complex nose. Close-woven, elegant tannins underpin a similarly complex palate with good initial impact. We found a little less complexity on Cirò Rosso Ronco dei Quattro Venti '05 but it has appreciable structure and concentration. The fresh, zesty, firmly structured Greco Fata Morgana '06 stood out among the whites. Brisi '04, made from greco grapes left to dry at length, vinified and then aged two years in 50-litre oak casks, is attractive and well styled. Pernicolò '06, from greco with a little chardonnay, is appealingly fresh and fruity.

● Scavigna Vigna Garrone '04	♈♈♈ 6
● Savuto Sup. V. Mortilla '04	♈♈ 5
● Scavigna Polpicello '04	♈♈ 7
○ Valeo '06	♈♈ 5
● Savuto '05	♈ 4
○ Scavigna Pian della Corte '06	♈ 4
⊙ Scavigna Rosato '06	♈ 3
● Scavigna Vigna Garrone '03	♈♈♈ 6
● Scavigna Polpicello '03	♈♈ 7
● Savuto Sup. V. Mortilla '03	♈♈ 5

● Cirò Rosso Cl. Donna Madda '05	♈♈ 5
○ Brisi '04	♈ 7
○ Cirò Bianco '06	♈ 4
⊙ Cirò Rosato Cl. Ronco dei Quattroventi '06	♈ 5
○ Pernicolò '06	♈ 4
○ Fata Morgana '06	♈ 5
● Cirò Rosso Cl. Ronco dei Quattro Venti '05	♈ 6
⊙ Cirò Rosato '06	♈ 4

Santa Venere

LOC. TENUTA VOLTAGRANDE
S.P. 04, KM 10,00
88813 CIRÒ [KR]
TEL. 096238519
www.santavenere.com

ANNUAL PRODUCTION 120,000 bottles
HECTARES UNDER VINE 25
VITICULTURE METHOD Certified organic

The Scala family's long-standing estate spreads over 150 hectares in one of the prettiest parts of Cirò, where the hills slope down gently to the Ionian sea. The Santa Venere stream runs right through the middle of the estate, hence its name. Federico Scala moved over to organic farming about ten years ago and in 2004 he decided to sign up with high-ranking oenological consultant Riccardo Cotarella. This year's tastings reveal general improvements throughout the range. Vurgadà '06, from equal quantities of nerello cappuccio, merlot and gaglioppo, is particularly distinctive. There are wild berry aromas overlying spices and tobacco. The palate is assertive and although the tight-knit, fine-grained tannin is not yet completely tamed, the finish is long with a pleasantly fruity aftertaste. The fresh, supple Cirò Bianco '06 has clear-cut sensations of apricot and apple on both nose and palate, the latter overlain by an elegant mineral nuance and preceding a well-defined, savoury finish. It is also excellent value for money. The simple, attractive Cirò Rosso Classico '06 is good, too.

Serracavallo

C.DA SERRACAVALLO
87043 COSENZA [CS]
TEL. 098421144
www.viniserracavallo.it

ANNUAL PRODUCTION 41,000 bottles
HECTARES UNDER VINE 25
VITICULTURE METHOD Conventional

Taking on the role of president of the new Calabria Citra wine consortium has evidently not prevented Demetrio Stancati from keeping on top of his own winery. He has thrown himself 100 per cent into his new task and yet our tastings show that the ongoing improvements at Serracavallo continue. Terraccia '04, from 100 per cent magliocco dolce, does not disappoint. It's a deep, dense ruby. The attractive nose is dominated by red and black berry fruit, with a little balsam adding class, and the palate is vibrant, invigorating and juicy, with a long, cohesive finish. All this presages a good ageing profile. Filì '05, from a savvy blend of pecorello and riesling, the latter grown at high altitude, made a strong debut. It's a well-structured wine with yellow-fleshed fruit aromas, good backbone and impressive length. Sette Chiese '06, from magliocco and cabernet, is a little over-extracted but attractive nonetheless.

O Cirò Bianco '06	ΨΨ	4*
● Vurgadà '06	ΨΨ	4*
⊙ Cirò Rosato '06	Ψ	4
● Cirò Rosso Cl. '06	Ψ	4
● Cirò Rosso Cl. Sup. Federico Scala Ris. '04	Ψ	5
O Vescovado '06	Ψ	4
● Cirò Rosso Cl. Sup. Federico Scala Ris. '01	ΨΨ	5
● Cirò Rosso Cl. Sup. Federico Scala Ris. '02	ΨΨ	5

● Terraccia '04	ΨΨ	5
O Filì '05	ΨΨ	4*
O Besidiae '06	Ψ	3
● Sette Chiese '06	Ψ	4
● Terraccia '03	ΨΨ	5
● Terraccia '02	ΨΨ	5

Statti

C.DA LENTI
88046 LAMEZIA TERME [CZ]
TEL. 0968456138
www.statti.com

ANNUAL PRODUCTION 300,000 bottles
HECTARES UNDER VINE 55
VITICULTURE METHOD Conventional

We can only be pleased that the improvements we've been seeing with Statti wines for some years now are continuing. The wines submitted this year were consistently reliable, all – absolutely all – of them good enough to be listed in this Guide. This reflects the tireless approach of the Statti siblings, who have not stinted on investment in vineyards and cellar. Cauro '05, from magliocco, gaglioppo and cabernet, very nearly reached the finals. Aromas of blackberry, plum and blackcurrant lead to a palate of lively impact, with soft, mellow tannins and a long, attractively fruity finish. Arvino '05, a well-structured wine from gaglioppo and cabernet, showed reasonably well, its style lively and invigorating but not overly deep. The new Mantonico '06 is fruity and zesty, and there is a nice refreshing citrus-like finish. Gaglioppo '06 is enjoyably supple and crisply fruity. Lamezia Greco '06 has a wide array of aromas, good structure and good overall balance. Both of the last pair came close to Two Glasses.

● Arvino '05	🍷🍷	4*
○ Mantonico '06	🍷🍷	4*
● Cauro '05	🍷🍷	5
● Gaglioppo '06	🍷	3
○ Gaglioppo Bianco '06	🍷	3
○ I Gelsi Bianco '06	🍷	2
● I Gelsi Rosso '06	🍷	2
○ Lamezia Greco '06	🍷	4
● Lamezia Rosso '06	🍷	3
⊙ Lamezia Rosato '06	🍷	3
○ Lamezia Bianco '06	🍷	3
○ Nosside '05	🥂🥂	5
● Arvino '04	🥂🥂	3*
● Cauro '04	🥂🥂	5

Luigi Viola

VIA ROMA, 18
87010 SARACENA [CS]
TEL. 098134071
www.cantineviola.it

ANNUAL PRODUCTION 4,500 bottles
HECTARES UNDER VINE 3
VITICULTURE METHOD Certified organic

We don't want to lapse into rhetoric but when we first met Luigi Viola, his drive and generosity made a strong impression. Luigi took on, single handed, the task of restoring life to a wine that was mentioned only in a few history books and which had survived solely for domestic consumption. He didn't do it with the aim of becoming rich or famous but simply because he'd realized that he could set in place a virtuous circle that would bring work and security to the youngsters in this otherwise desolate corner of Calabria. And that is exactly what is happening. Almost miraculously, this year we started to receive samples of other Moscatos produced at Saracena and there are yet more on the way. Naturally, the intervening period has not been burdened by bureaucracy and Luigi, like the rest, cannot use the name Moscato di Saracena on his labels. We can only hope that a DOC will soon be granted, thereby resolving the problem. We are more dismayed than anyone else that Luigi's elegant Moscato '06 missed Three Glasses by a hair. For Luigi, the joy of no longer being the sole producer will surely outweigh any disappointment.

○ Moscato Passito '06	🍷🍷	7
○ Moscato di Saracena '03	🥂🥂	6
○ Moscato di Saracena '05	🥂🥂	7
○ Moscato di Saracena '04	🥂🥂	7
○ Moscato di Saracena '00	🥂🥂	4
○ Moscato di Saracena '01	🥂🥂	4

OTHER WINERIES

Caparra & Siciliani

BIVIO S.S. JONICA 106
88811 CIRÒ MARINA [KR]
TEL. 0962371435
www.caparraesiciliani.it

This winery put on a good overall showing.
Best of the range is Cirò Rosato Le Formelle
'06 with a fruity nose, plus good freshness
giving the palate a lift. The fresh, zesty Cirò
Bianco Curiale '06 also impressed with a
good mineral stamp and a pleasing citrus-
like finish.

⊙ Cirò Rosato Le Formelle '06	🍷🍷 3*
○ Cirò Bianco Curiale '06	🍷 3
● Cirò Rosso Cl. Sup. Ris. '04	🍷 4
● Cirò Rosso Cl. Sup. Ris. Volvito '04	🍷 4

Capo Zefirio

VIA LUNGOFERROVIA, 20
89032 BIANCO [RC]
TEL. 0964911446
www.capozefirio.com

Once Francesco Isola, Giuseppe Vottari and
Cosimo Canturi realized that Greco di
Bianco was disappearing, they immediately
set up the Capo Zefirio winery for the sole
purpose of producing the wine. The '02 has
a complex nose of oven-baked figs, dates
and almonds but also freshness and good
structure.

○ Greco di Bianco '02	🍷🍷 7

Umberto Ceratti

VIA DEGLI UFFIZI, 5
89030 CARAFFA DEL BIANCO [RC]
TEL. 0964956008

We are happy to welcome back one of the
best-known producers of Greco di Bianco,
a wine with ancient origins. The fine '04 has
apricot and white chocolate aromas, and a
cohesive, sweet, full but not overly long
palate. The equally good sweet Mantonico
'04 is full of Mediterranean fragrance.

○ Greco di Bianco '04	🍷🍷 5
○ Mantonico '04	🍷🍷 5

Roberto Ceraudo

LOC. MARINA DI STRONGOLI
C.DA DATTILO
88815 CROTONE [KR]
TEL. 0962865613
www.dattilo.it

After a couple of years of self-imposed
absence, Roberto Ceraudo returns to the
Guide in fine form. His sons are now
involved in running the estate and its farm
holiday centre. The first-rate Petraro '04,
from equal parts of gaglioppo and cabernet,
has an elegant, fruity nose and a tight-knit,
dense palate.

● Petraro '04	🍷🍷 6
⊙ Grayasusi Etichetta Rame '06	🍷 4
○ Imyr '06	🍷 6

Donnici 99

C.DA VERZANO
87100 COSENZA [CS]
TEL. 0984781842
www.donnici99.com

This is a convincing first appearance by a
dynamic young estate. Audace Diverzano
'04, from barbera with 30 per cent merlot, is
the best of the wines submitted. It's intense,
full of red berry and wild berry fruit, and has
a well-defined tannic weave plus a long,
fruity finish.

● Audace Diverzano '04	🍷🍷 4*
● Antico Diverzano '04	🍷 5
● Fugace Diverzano '06	🍷 4
● Ardente Diverzano '05	🍷 5

Cantine Farneto del Principe

C.DA CORVO, 113
87042 ALTOMONTE [CS]
TEL. 0981946208

This winery made a fine debut with Two
well-deserved Glasses for Farneto Rosso
'05, a blend of the indigenous guarnaccia
nera, mantonico nero, lacrima and
magliocco. Balbino '06, from guarnaccia,
greco and malvasia, is fair, giving aromas of
dried roses and white-fleshed fruit, and a
fresh, balanced palate.

● Farneto Rosso '05	🍷🍷 4*
● Ricupo '05	🍷 3
○ Balbino '06	🍷 3

OTHER WINERIES

Feudo dei Sanseverino
VIA VITTORIO EMANUELE, 110
87010 SARACENA [CS]
TEL. 098121461
info@feudodeisanseverino.it

Feudo dei Sanseverino is a small Saracena winery whose first releases sent a wine straight into the finals. It's Moscato al Governo di Saracena '01 and it offers impressive finesse and intensity. Mastro Terenzio, from semi-dried moscato, is a touch less concentrated but still good.

○ Moscato Passito al Governo di Saracena '01	🍷🍷 5
○ Mastro Terenzio	🍷🍷 5
● Gaglioppo '05	🍷 3

Fattorie Greco
VIA MAGENTA, 33
87062 CARIATI [CS]
TEL. 0983969441
www.igreco.it

This is the first appearance in the Guide for the Greco siblings. Their property is huge and already includes 70 hectares of vines but new plantings will soon bring this up to 100. The only wine submitted this year, Cirò Bianco, showed well, with a fruity nose and a fresh, well-structured palate.

○ Cirò Bianco Filù '06	🍷🍷 3*

Ippolito 1845
VIA TIRONE, 118
88811 CIRÒ MARINA [KR]
TEL. 096231106
www.ippolito1845.it

All Ippolito's wines tasted this year are well past satisfactory. The mineral, fresh, zesty, white Cirò Res Dei '06 is better than most. Leading the reds is I Mori '05, from gaglioppo with 30 per cent cabernet. It's fruity, well structured, full of soft tannin and has a long, attractive finish.

● I Mori '05	🍷🍷 4*
○ Cirò Bianco Res Dei '06	🍷 3*
● Cirò Rosso Cl. Sup. Liber Pater '05	🍷 3
● Cirò Rosso Cl. '05	🍷 3

Azienda Vinicola Malaspina
VIA PALLICA, 67
89063 MELITO DI PORTO SALVO [RC]
TEL. 0965781632
www.aziendavinicolamalaspina.com

The Malaspina sisters' all-female winery celebrates its 40th anniversary with its first Guide profile. Almost all the wines are at least decent, especially Palizzi '04 from calabrese, nerello cappuccio and castiglione, which has a floral nose with rose, violet and lavender, and an attractively fruity finish.

⊙ Rosaspina '06	🍷 3
○ Micah '06	🍷 3
● Palizzi '04	🍷 4
● Patros Pietro '04	🍷 4

Malena
LOC. PETRARO
S.S. JONICA 106
88811 CIRÒ MARINA [KR]
TEL. 096231758
www.malena.it

The young Malena siblings are producing wines of good quality across the board but so far nothing truly exceptional. The potential is all there so we will just sit back and wait. Passus '05, a passito from semi-dried greco bianco, has a lavender nose and a succulent, nicely poised palate.

○ Cirò Bianco '06	🍷 3
⊙ Cirò Rosato '06	🍷 3
○ Passus Greco Passito '05	🍷 5
● Cirò Rosso Cl. '05	🍷 3

Luigi Scala
LOC. CASALE SAN VINCENZO
88813 CIRÒ [KR]
TEL. 3388614620
3346316074@tim.it

Luigi Scala's estate was founded over 50 years ago. This year's wines were very interesting, especially Briseo '06, from chardonnay, greco and mantonico, which has an apricot nose and a fresh palate finishing on a nice citrus note. Cirò Classico '05 and Cirò Rosato '06 are well styled.

○ Briseo '06	🍷 4
● Cirò Rosso Cl. '05	🍷 4
⊙ Cirò Rosato '06	🍷 4

OTHER WINERIES

Stelitano
LOC. PALAZZI DI CASIGNANA
C.DA PALAZZI, 1
89030 CASIGNANA [RC]
TEL. 0964913023
stelitano@interfree.it

The Stelitano siblings' Greco di Bianco '05 is truly admirable and possibly the best ever tasted. The nose is elegant and complex, evoking oven-baked figs and dates but also lighter, citrus and lavender tones. The palate melds freshness with structure and flesh, and has good length.

O Greco di Bianco '05	♟♟ 6
O Greco di Bianco '02	♟♟ 7
O Greco di Bianco '04	♟♟ 7

Terre di Balbia
LOC. MONTINO
87042 ALTOMONTE [CS]
TEL. 048161264
www.terredibalbia.it

The wines from the Silvio Caputo-Gianni Venica joint venture showed well overall. SerraMonte '04, from equal quantities of magliocco and sangiovese, has good fruit and notable structure. Montino 101, from 100 per cent magliocco, is full and fruity with attractive spicy nuances.

● Montino 101 '04	♟♟ 5
● SerraMonte '04	♟♟ 7
● Balbium '04	♟ 4
● SerraMonte '02	♟♟ 7

Tenuta Terre Nobili
LOC. MONTALTO UFFUGO
C.DA CARIGLIALTO
87046 COSENZA [CS]
TEL. 0984934005
lidia.matera@libero.it

Lidia Matera's wines are now all consistently good but Cariglio '06, from magliocco with 20 per cent merlot, stands out. It's a lively ruby, the nose is full of blackberry, plum and cherry, and the palate is dense, fleshy and tannic, gaining attractive balance from a fresh swath of acidity.

● Alarico '06	♟ 4
● Cariglio '06	♟ 3
O Santa Chiara '06	♟ 4
⊙ Donna Eleonora '06	♟ 3

Val di Neto
FRAZ. CORAZZO
VIA NAZIONALE
88831 SCANDALE [KR]
TEL. 096254079
www.cantinavaldineto.com

This recently established winery is already acknowledged as one of the region's most dynamic. The wines submitted this year were all sound, especially the attractive, sweet, structured Mutrò '05, from gaglioppo and greco nero. Arkè '05, from aglianico, gaglioppo and greco nero, is intense and long.

● Melissa Rosso Sup. Mutrò '05	♟♟ 4
● Rosso Arkè '05	♟♟ 4

Luigi Vivacqua
C.DA SAN VITO
87040 LUZZI [CS]
TEL. 0984543404
luigivivacqua@libero.it

Filomena Vivacqua's wines continue to be dependably good, which not only cheers us but promises well for the winery's future. All three versions of San Vito di Luzzi – red, white and rosé – are most attractive, as was a retaste of Marinò '03, made from gaglioppo and merlot.

O San Vito di Luzzi Bianco '06	♟ 2
⊙ San Vito di Luzzi Rosato '06	♟ 2
● San Vito di Luzzi Rosso '06	♟ 2

Vinicola Zito
VIA SCALARETTO
88811 CIRÒ MARINA [KR]
TEL. 096231853
www.zito.it

There are mixed messages from Zito. The wines are sound but they still haven't enough style to propel them into the higher quality band that the winery longs for and deserves. Macalla '04, from gaglioppo, is good and a pleasure to drink, but lacks the touch of complexity needed for Two Glasses.

O Cirò Bianco Nosside '06	♟ 3
● Cirò Rosso Cl. Alceo '05	♟ 3
● Cirò Rosso Cl. Krimisa '05	♟ 4
● Macalla '04	♟ 3

SICILY

The 2008 Guide's Red of the Year is the magnificent Faro Palari '05, produced by the Messina-based architect, Salvatore Geraci. But the Best Sweet Wine is also Sicilian, Donnafugata's Passito di Pantelleria Ben Ryè '06, a contender that left all the others at the starting line. What's more, if you glance through last year's Italian Wines, you'll find that the White of the Year was also Sicilian, from Etna to be precise, Benanti's Pietramarina '02. So it doesn't take a genius to put two and two together. Sicily is one of the most vital and brilliant regions flying the Italian flag. For decades, the island's reputation rested on the production of millions of hectolitres – and bottles – of good-value whites and reds while its unbottled wine plumped out those Italian and foreign offerings that lacked structure or alcohol. Things are different these days. Over the years, Sicilian wine entrepreneurs have skilfully laid solid scientific, viticultural and marketing foundations. The last decade was a period of constant product quality enhancement, peaking, as we can see, at the very top of the Italian winemaking scale. Several excellent zones have emerged, including Etna, Pachino, western Sicily and Pantelleria. Each has its own traditional grapes, unique soil and weather conditions, and committed winemakers who have successfully brought local traits to the fore and given the lie to the old story that all wines from hot zones are the same. Even the hot zone concept is imprecise for Sicily has a wide range of very diverse site climates, from Pachino's coastal vineyards to the high hills of the centre and several Etna vineyards at more than 1,000 metres above sea level. Which explains the 15 wines awarded Three Glasses this year. Apart from the wines already mentioned, they include Tenuta Terre Nere's Etna Rosso Feudo di Mezzo '05, Passopisciaro's Franchetti '05 and Benanti's Etna Rosso Serra della Contessa '04, both also from Etna. Benanti was back for an encore with an excellent Drappo '04 from its Pachino vines. Gulfi sent us an outstanding Neromàccarj '04 from the Ragusa vineyards and Donnafugata another high-class red, Milleunanotte '04. Cusumano endorsed its leadership position with Sàgana and Noà '05 while Firriato took Three Glasses with a new label, Quater '05. Three more exemplary wines were Tasca d'Almerita's Rosso del Conte '04, Planeta's Burdese '04 and Santa Anastasia's Litra '04. We'll round off with Paolo Marzotto's Baglio di Pianetto Ramione '04, a fine red blend with real Mediterranean class.

Abbazia Santa Anastasia
C.DA SANTA ANASTASIA
90013 CASTELBUONO [PA]
TEL. 091671959
www.abbaziasantanastasia.it

ANNUAL PRODUCTION 650,000 bottiglie
HECTARES UNDER VINE 62
VITICULTURE METHOD Certified organic

The spotlight is back on Francesco Lena's estate, Abbazia di Santa Anastasia, thanks to Litra '04. We thought it was one of the best vintages so far and it earned another Three Glass prize. This is important for Lena, who has invested steadily in his winery over the years and is now on the threshold of a significant change. With four years of organic viticulture under his belt, Francesco is now converting to biodynamic methods. Litra '04 is austere, intense and minerally, its charm lying in graceful strength and intense fruitiness, with finely polished tannins. But all Santa Anastasia wines are distinctive, fresh and very drinkable, a sure sign that the technical staff are doing their jobs, under the guidance of Riccardo Cotarella, with Professor Anello overseeing organic and biodynamic techniques. The crisply acidic Gemelli '06, from chardonnay grapes, has evident hints of peach in what is an intense, well-balanced wine. We were happy with Montenero '05, a lively blend of nero d'Avola, cabernet sauvignon and merlot, with great convincing tannins. The admirable Contempo Nerello Mascalese '06 is absolutely Mediterranean.

Baglio di Pianetto
VIA FRANCIA
90030 SANTA CRISTINA GELA [PA]
TEL. 0918570002
www.bagliodipianetto.com

ANNUAL PRODUCTION 350,000 bottiglie
HECTARES UNDER VINE 95
VITICULTURE METHOD Conventional

Conte Paolo Marzotto is an amazing man who has given much to the worlds of business and sport. Apart from being a patron of the arts and great wine connoisseur, he also dabbles in winemaking. After years managing the colossal Santa Margherita winery, his passion for wine drew him to Sicily and, enchanted by the island, he set about creating his own estate. In less than a decade, he has built up Baglio di Pianetto, a lovely estate of over 150 hectares at Santa Cristina Gela, near the Piana degli Albanesi lake, 30 kilometres from Palermo. Here he has developed an extensive range of wines, producing about 350,000 bottles a year, and the flagship is Ramione, a nero d'Avola and merlot blend. The succulent '04 is a feisty, concentrated, full-bodied red with more than a hint of spice and soothing tannins. Three Glasses. We might also mention the excellent Viognier Piana del Ginolfo '06 and the plush, elegantly varietal Merlot Piana dei Salici '04. But the entire range is first-class.

● Litra '04	ΨΨΨ	7
○ Gemelli '06	ΨΨ	5
● Montenero '05	ΨΨ	5
● Passomaggio '05	ΨΨ	4*
○ Baccante '06	Ψ	5
○ Contempo Grillo '06	Ψ	3
○ Sinestesia '06	Ψ	4
● Contempo Nero d'Avola '06	Ψ	3*
● Contempo Nerello Mascalese '06	Ψ	3*
○ Contempo Insolia '06	Ψ	3
● Litra '00	ΨΨΨ	7
● Litra '99	ΨΨΨ	7
● Montenero '04	ΨΨΨ	5
● Litra '97	ΨΨΨ	7
● Litra '01	ΨΨΨ	8
● Litra '96	ΨΨΨ	7

● Ramione '04	ΨΨΨ	4*
○ Ficiligno '06	ΨΨ	4
○ Piana del Ginolfo '06	ΨΨ	5
● Shymer '05	ΨΨ	4
● Nero d'Avola '04	ΨΨ	4
● Piana dei Salici '04	ΨΨ	5
○ Moscato di Noto Ra'is '06	Ψ	5
● Piana dei Salici '02	ΨΨ	5
● Piana dei Salici '03	ΨΨ	5
● Ramione '02	ΨΨ	4
● Ramione '03	ΨΨ	4
● Shymer '04	ΨΨ	4*

Benanti
VIA G. GARIBALDI, 475
95029 VIAGRANDE [CT]
TEL. 0957893438
www.vinicolabenanti.it

Vinicola Calatrasi
C.DA PIANO PIRAINO
90040 SAN CIPIRELLO [PA]
TEL. 0918576767
www.calatrasi.it

ANNUAL PRODUCTION 180,000 bottiglie
HECTARES UNDER VINE 44
VITICULTURE METHOD Conventional

Some may have doubted that this famous Sicilian winery, and last season's winner of our Winery of the Year award, could keep up its standards. Thankfully, reassurance comes in two superlative reds released this year by Giuseppe Benanti and his sons Salvino and Antonio, ably assisted by oenologist Salvo Foti. We thoroughly enjoyed the '04 Serra della Contessa, an Etna red using mainly nerello mascalese grapes that give it a lovely deep yet brilliant garnet ruby colour. We found aristocratic aromas of ripe cherry, liquorice and spice, with Mediterranean nuances that lead into a full, balanced palate, supported by strong texture, elegant tannins and long length. The other red is Drappo '04, a hearty, ebullient Nero d'Avola from the Pachino vineyards, bursting with notes of ripe black fruits, smooth tannins and hints of balsam. It is the magnificent, crowning glory of an extensive range of wines, produced mainly from vines on Etna's higher slopes, which includes one of Italy's best whites, the famous Pietramarina from carricante grapes.

ANNUAL PRODUCTION 5,600,000 bottiglie
HECTARES UNDER VINE 2,470
VITICULTURE METHOD Certified organic

In many respects, Calatrasi is a surprising operation, both for its sheer size, comprising three wineries and huge estates in Sicily, Puglia and Tunisia, and for the astonishing annual turnover of more than 15,000,000 euros, from sales of around 10,000,000 bottles of wine. In addition, Calatrasi is flexible in adapting its style and adopts an extremely competent approach to international markets. It has a knack of being one step ahead in sniffing out trends and understanding their logic.
Credit for all this goes to the driving force behind the winery, the polyglot physician Maurizio Miccichè, who is also the president, majority shareholder and sole director. He has surrounded himself with motivated, expert assistants of various nationalities. The D'Istinto Magnifico Shiraz '06 that made the finals this year is an impressively elegant, deliciously fruit-forward monovarietal Syrah with a smooth tannic weave. As always, we noted the accomplished Terre di Ginestra 651 Nero d'Avola/Shiraz '05, for its pure, intense balsamic notes. The spice-led varietal Terre di Ginestra monovarietal '05 Nero d'Avola also showed very well indeed.

● Etna Rosso Serra della Contessa '04	♟♟♟	7
● Il Drappo '04	♟♟♟	6*
O Etna Bianco Sup. Pietramarina '03	♟♟	6
● Etna Rosso Rosso di Verzella '04	♟♟	4*
● Lamorèmio '03	♟♟	6
● Majora '04	♟♟	4
● Nerello Mascalese Il Monovitigno '04	♟♟	6
O Minnella Il Monovitigno '06	♟♟	6
● Etna Rosso Rovittello '03	♟♟	6
O Etna Bianco Bianco di Caselle '06	♟	4
O Etna Bianco Sup. Pietramarina '00	♟♟♟	6
O Etna Bianco Sup. Pietramarina '99	♟♟♟	5
● Etna Rosso Serra della Contessa '03	♟♟♟	7
O Etna Bianco Sup. Pietramarina '02	♟♟♟	6
O Etna Bianco Sup. Pietramarina '01	♟♟♟	6

● D'Istinto Magnifico Shiraz '06	♟♟	5
O D'Istinto Grillo '06	♟♟	4
● Terre di Ginestra 651 '05	♟♟	6
● Terre di Ginestra Nero d'Avola '05	♟♟	5
● Accademia del Sole Cabernet Sauvignon '05	♟	5
● D'Istinto Shiraz '05	♟	4
O Terre di Ginestra 651 Chardonnay '06	♟	5
O Terre di Ginestra Catarratto '06	♟	5
⊙ D'Istinto Rosato '06	♟	4
O D'Istinto Ljetas Bianco '06	♟	4
O Accademia del Sole Viogner '06	♟	5
● D'Istinto Batheos '06	♟	4*
O D'Istinto Chardonnay '06	♟	4
● Accademia del Sole Shiraz '05	♟	5
● D'Istinto Magnifico '04	♟♟	6

Cantina Viticoltori Associati Canicattì
C.DA AQUILATA
92024 CANICATTÌ [AG]
TEL. 0922829371
www.viniaquilae.it

ANNUAL PRODUCTION 550,000 bottiglie
HECTARES UNDER VINE 1,000
VITICULTURE METHOD Conventional

In the tricky world of co-operative wineries, often still trapped in the old mutual support mindset that tends to shy away from change, the Cantina Viticultori di Canicattì's decision to target quality is a shining example of positive winemaking. Judging by the wines we have sampled for the Guide in recent years, the Cantina is well on the way to achieving its aim. A sophisticated programme of vineyard replanting started at the insistence of president Alfonso Lo Sardo seems to be yielding better results than anticipated. The hands-on assistance for member vineyards is implemented by the technical staff of oenologist Angelo Molito and expert winemaking consultant, Tonino Guzzo. The Cantina's thoroughbred is the complex, varietal Aynat '05, sourced from nero d'Avola vines more than 40 years old. We were equally convinced by the well-defined, intense Scialo '05 blend of nero d'Avola and syrah. The other wines on the list are all good and offer excellent value for money.

Ceuso
LOC. SEGESTA
C.DA VIVIGNATO
91013 CALATAFIMI [TP]
TEL. 092422836
www.ceuso.it

ANNUAL PRODUCTION 130,000 bottiglie
HECTARES UNDER VINE 45
VITICULTURE METHOD Conventional

The Melia family winery, with a modern production structure supported by 50 hectares of quality vineyards, is one of the most dependable in Sicily and it's easy to see why. Giuseppe and Vincenzo Melia have spent their entire lives surrounded by vines, cellars and barrels, becoming respectively an oenologist and an agronomist. Although the Ceuso '05, from nero d'Avola with 30 per cent cabernet and 20 per cent merlot, was not a finalist this year, it continues to impress as a complex, superior wine, with a sturdy structure. We liked its gentle fruit bouquet and a well-balanced, lingering flavour. The Fastaia '05, from equal parts of nero d'Avola and merlot grapes with a touch of petit verdot, also had personality and elegance. This hearty wine, with good, spicy fruitiness, enters the palate lively, developing vigorous impetus, revealing a perfect pulpy fusion of structure and tannic weave. We liked the drinkability of the full, delicately varietal Nero d'Avola Scurati '06, which is smooth and well-defined. The tangy Scurati Bianco '06, from grecanico, grillo and chardonnay, is a delight.

● Aquilae Merlot '06	♟♟	3
● Aynat '05	♟♟	5*
● Scialo '05	♟♟	4*
○ Aquilae Catarratto Inzolia '06	♟	2
○ Aquilae Chardonnay '06	♟	3
● Aquilae Nero d'Avola '06	♟	3
● Aquilae Syrah '06	♟	3
● Aynat '04	♟♟	4*
● Aquilae Cabernet Sauvignon '04	♟♟	3*
● Aquilae Cabernet Sauvignon '05	♟♟	3*
● Aquilae Nero d'Avola '04	♟♟	2*

● Ceuso Custera '05	♟♟	6
● Scurati Rosso '06	♟♟	4
● Fastaia '05	♟♟	4*
○ Scurati Bianco '06	♟	4
● Ceuso Custera '01	♟♟♟	6
● Ceuso Custera '03	♟♟	6
● Fastaia '04	♟♟	4
● Ceuso Custera '04	♟♟	6

COS

S. P. 3 AGATE-CHIARAMONTE, KM 14,300
97019 VITTORIA [RG]
TEL. 0932876145
www.cosvittoria.it

ANNUAL PRODUCTION   120,000 bottiglie
HECTARES UNDER VINE 25
VITICULTURE METHOD   Natural

Winemakers in the province of Ragusa are overjoyed at the news that Cerasuolo di Vittoria will be Sicily's first DOCG, seeing it as endorsement of the overall quality of their territory. It comes as no surprise, given the number of years the media had been talking about the stunning architectural and landscape heritage, the excellent cuisine and the lively economy. In the long journey to DOCG, COS was always in the vanguard, thanks to the direct commitment of its owners, Giusto Occhipinti and "Titta" Cilìa, the latter also president of the consortium. The two have established a disciplined approach to business that sets the standard for all those who believe in quality. This year the pair, who as biodynamic farmers march to the rhythms of the land, and not the Guide, sent us a spicy Cerasuolo di Vittoria '05 from nero d'Avola and frappato grapes. There was also a satisfying, elegant-tasting Cerasuolo di Vittoria Pithos '05 that was both minerally and lively. This is another nero d'Avola and frappato blend, fermented in half-buried clay amphoras. Finally, there is fine fruit on the concentrated Pojo di Lupo '05, a monovarietal nero d'Avola.

Cottanera

LOC. IANNAZZO
S.P. 89
95030 CASTIGLIONE DI SICILIA
TEL. 0942963601
www.cottanera.it

ANNUAL PRODUCTION   220,000 bottiglie
HECTARES UNDER VINE 50
VITICULTURE METHOD   Conventional

It took just over five years for brothers Gugliemo and Enzo Cambria to make their admirable winery one of the island's leading producers. They have 50 hectares of vineyards and a modern cellar on the slopes of Etna, set against a backdrop of some very lovely countryside. The '05 vintage is the first to have been completely managed by the skilled Tuscan oenologist, Lorenzo Landi, who is keeping a watchful technical eye on Cottanera. We sampled the structured, lingering Ardenza '05, a worthy finalist that pulled up just short of Three Glasses. It's a truly elegant red from mondeuse grapes with a delightful mineral note. Pure syrah was used for the appealing, intense Sole di Sesta '05 with its fruit and balsam notes. Firm, fruit-rich Merlot Grammonte '05, on the other hand, has solid aromatic structure tinged with tobacco and chocolate. We were more than happy with the quality of the robust Nume '05, from cabernet sauvignon grapes. We noted a well-developed nose on the elegant, dry Fatagione '05, from nerello mascalese grapes with a small percentage of nero d'Avola. All the other wines are good.

● Cerasuolo di Vittoria '05	ŸŸ	4
● Pojo di Lupo '05	ŸŸ	4
● Cerasuolo di Vittoria Pithos '05	ŸŸ	5
● Contrade Labirinto '02	Ÿ	8
O Ramì '06	Ÿ	4
● Frappato '06	Ÿ	4
● Contrade Labirinto '01	ŸŸ	8
● Cerasuolo di Vittoria '03	ŸŸ	4
● Scyri '00	ŸŸ	6
O Ramì '05	ŸŸ	4
● Pojo di Lupo '04	ŸŸ	4
● Pojo di Lupo '03	ŸŸ	4
● Contrade - Dedalo '98	ŸŸ	8
● Cerasuolo di Vittoria Pithos '03	ŸŸ	5
● Cerasuolo di Vittoria Venticinquesima Vendemmia '04	ŸŸ	4

● L'Ardenza '05	ŸŸ	5
● Fatagione '05	ŸŸ	5
● Sole di Sesta '05	ŸŸ	5
● Nume '05	ŸŸ	5
● Grammonte '05	ŸŸ	5
O Barbazzale Bianco '06	Ÿ	3*
● Barbazzale Rosso '06	Ÿ	3*
● Fatagione '04	ŸŸ	5*
● L'Ardenza '04	ŸŸ	6
● Grammonte '04	ŸŸ	6
● Nume '04	ŸŸ	6
● Sole di Sesta '04	ŸŸ	6

Cusumano

C.DA SAN CARLO S.S. 113
90047 PARTINICO [PA]
TEL. 0918903456
www.cusumano.it

ANNUAL PRODUCTION 2,500,000 bottiglie
HECTARES UNDER VINE 450
VITICULTURE METHOD Conventional

A visit to Contrada San Carlo, in Partinico, is crucial for anyone who wants to understand the Cusumano approach. If you wonder how this young company has achieved such astonishing market success, from North America to Russia, you'll find a satisfactory reply to what is quite simply a winemaking and business phenomenon at the estate. Because this is where you'll find visible proof of the mindset and spirit that drive Diego and Alberto Cusumano's Garden of Eden. They have a marvellous state-of-the-art production area and a functional cellar that combines tradition and modernity, embodying the winery's strong suits of simplicity, Mediterranean modernity and elegance. After this year's tastings, we awarded our top accolade to two extraordinary wines, Sàgana '05 and Noà '05. The former is a deep, rich, enchantingly varietal Nero d'Avola while Noà is a nero d'Avola, merlot and cabernet sauvignon blend whose intense, mature red introduces a velvety elegance that is sheer seduction. The other wines are excellent and well worth tasting, especially at these prices.

Donnafugata

VIA SEBASTIANO LIPARI, 18
91025 MARSALA [TP]
TEL. 0923724200
www.donnafugata.it

ANNUAL PRODUCTION 2,650,000 bottiglie
HECTARES UNDER VINE 260
VITICULTURE METHOD Conventional

Giacomo Rallo, whose family has a great winemaking tradition, opened his winery just 25 years ago. The Donnafugata label is now well established internationally thanks to his commitment and the support of Giacomo's wife, Gabriella, and their sons, Antonio and José. Although Donnafugata is a 300-hectare winery that produces more than 2,500,000 bottles of wine a year, it has not lost the family touch that has been its hallmark right from the start.
The range of wines is prestigious to say the least. This year we were again happy to give Three Glasses to an exceptional Milleunanotte '04, a mighty Nero d'Avola aged in new wood. This is a deep, intense wine, verging on overripeness, that develops all its complexity on the palate. Its fruit-rich mouthfilling power is minerally, opulent and tempting. A worthy counterpart is the fabulous Passito di Pantelleria Ben Ryé '06, our top Sweet Wine this year. Its concentration of Mediterranean and fruit aromas is as impressive as its cool drinkability. Don't miss it.

● Noà '05	♥♥♥ 5
● Sàgana '05	♥♥♥ 5
● Benuara '06	♥♥ 4
○ Jalé '06	♥♥ 5
○ Cubìa '06	♥♥ 4
○ Angimbè '06	♥♥ 4*
○ Alcamo '06	♥ 3
○ Inzolia '06	♥ 3
⊙ Rosato '06	♥ 3
● Noà '00	♥♥♥ 5
● Sàgana '03	♥♥♥ 5
● Sàgana '02	♥♥♥ 5
● Sàgana '04	♥♥♥ 5
● Noà '03	♥♥♥ 5
● Noà '04	♥♥♥ 5

● Contessa Entellina Milleunanotte '04	♥♥♥ 7
○ Passito di Pantelleria Ben Ryé '06	♥♥♥ 7
● Contessa Entellina Tancredi '05	♥♥ 5
○ Contessa Entellina Chiarandà '05	♥♥ 6
○ Contessa Entellina Chardonnay La Fuga '06	♥ 4
○ Lighea '06	♥ 4
○ Contessa Entellina V. di Gabri '06	♥ 4
○ Contessa Entellina Chiarandà del Merlo '99	♥♥♥ 5
● Contessa Entellina Milleunanotte '00	♥♥♥ 7
● Contessa Entellina Milleunanotte '03	♥♥♥ 7
● Contessa Entellina Milleunanotte '02	♥♥♥ 7
● Contessa Entellina Milleunanotte '01	♥♥♥ 7
● Contessa Entellina Tancredi '02	♥♥ 5
● Contessa Entellina Tancredi '03	♥♥ 5
● Tancredi '04	♥♥ 5

Duca di Salaparuta - Vini Corvo
VIA NAZIONALE S.S. 113
90014 CASTELDACCIA [PA]
TEL. 091945201
www.vinicorvo.it

ANNUAL PRODUCTION 10,000,000 bottiglie
HECTARES UNDER VINE 139
VITICULTURE METHOD Conventional

The distinguished Casteldaccia winery continues to perform well. Its flagship Nero d'Avola Duca Enrico '04 may not have matched last year's standards but was still a worthy contender in the finals, with pure Mediterranean charm in its distinctive aromas, some fine balsamic notes and the finesse of luscious, vibrant fruit. We also liked the top-of-the-range white, Inzolia Bianca di Valguarnera '05, whose lavish fruity nuances mingle with discreet oak, marked out by fresh acidity on the palate and the faintest hint of sugar. The Risignolo estate at Salemi produced a Kados Risignolo '06 from grillo grapes, with attractive hints of flowers and citrus fruit on the fresh, tangy palate. We were taken with the immediacy of the fruity bouquet and keen acidity of the Megara '05, a frappato and syrah blend. The grecanico and chardonnay Brut Riserva spumante is elegant and well structured, with fresh, fragrant grassy notes and just the right amount of prickle. The traditional aromatized red ALA is delicious, and we recommend the well-styled appeal of the Corvo line, especially the Sciaranera '06, from nero d'Avola and frappato.

Feudo Maccari
LOC. C.DA MACCARI
CASE MACCARI,
S. P. PACHINO-NOTO, KM 13,50
96017 NOTO [SR]
TEL. 0931596894
www.feudomaccari.it

ANNUAL PRODUCTION 145,000 bottiglie
HECTARES UNDER VINE 50
VITICULTURE METHOD Conventional

This year, Antonio Moretti's Sicilian winery has really outdone itself, and we were able to enjoy two of its wines at the taste-offs. For Moretti, Sicily was love at first sight during a holiday spent in the Pachino area, where our man noticed a handsome bush-trained vineyard of about 30 years old was up for sale. It was more or less an impulse buy and the first thing Moretti did was to restore the old farmhouse. In the meantime, he found out that the original estate was actually much bigger so he patiently spent several years restoring it to its former dimensions, buying back land from 70 other owners. He then planted or replanted as necessary, but always to bush-trained vines. The latest good news from the estate is the stunning debut of a weighty, richly extracted and truly elegant Mahâris '05 from nero d'Avola, cabernet and syrah. The fruit-rich, velvety Nero d'Avola Saia '05 has a well-defined bouquet and silky tannins. Finally, the varietal Nero d'Avola ReNoto '06 is very drinkable.

● Duca Enrico '04	🍷🍷	7
○ Bianca di Valguarnera '05	🍷🍷	6
○ Kados '06	🍷🍷	4
● A.L.A. Antico Liquorvino Amarascato	🍷	5
○ Brut Ris.	🍷	4
○ Corvo Colomba Platino '06	🍷	4*
● Corvo Sciaranera '06	🍷	4
● Megara '05	🍷	4
☉ Corvo Rosa '06	🍷	3
● Corvo Rosso '05	🍷	4*
○ Corvo Glicine '06	🍷	3*
○ Corvo Bianco '06	🍷	3
● Duca Enrico '03	🍷🍷🍷	7
● Duca Enrico '01	🍷🍷🍷	7
● Duca Enrico '02	🍷🍷	7

● Mahâris '05	🍷🍷	6
● Saia '05	🍷🍷	5
● ReNoto '06	🍷🍷	4*
☉ ReNoto Rosè '06	🍷🍷	4*
● ReNoto '05	🍷🍷	4*
● Saia '04	🍷🍷	5

Feudo Principi di Butera

C.DA DELIELLA
93011 BUTERA [CL]
TEL. 0934347726
www.feudobutera.it

ANNUAL PRODUCTION 600,000 bottiglie
HECTARES UNDER VINE 180
VITICULTURE METHOD Conventional

From a distance, the Feudo might be mistaken for an oasis in its white desert of limestone and quartz, so typical of the light-coloured soil in this part of Sicily. The ancient village tower forms a backdrop to the estate, which is meticulously organized with vineyards laid out as methodically as a kitchen garden. The extensive modern cellar, with state-of-the-art technology, is spotlessly clean and tidy. The vineyard selections from this Zonin group flagship weren't ready when we were tasting but we actually thought the most gratifying results came from what are considered the Feudo's basic wines. Which was only to be expected, because the technical manager, Franco Giacosa, and his staff are deeply committed to getting the most from Butera's entire range of wines. We found the Syrah '05 and the Nero d'Avola '05 to be very varietal, the former with a nicely marked balsamic note and while the latter showing fruity and nuanced with Mediterranean herbs. Thumbs up, too, for the sweet, intense Riesi '05, a nero d'Avola with a touch of syrah, that finishes on an agreeable note of chocolate. The distinctively cool, minerally Chardonnay '06 and Inzolia '06 are two lovely whites.

○ Chardonnay '06	♟♟	4*
○ Insolia '06	♟♟	4*
● Nero d'Avola '05	♟♟	4
● Syrah '05	♟♟	4
● Riesi '05	♟♟	4*
● Cabernet Sauvignon '05	♟	4
● Merlot '05	♟	4
● Cabernet Sauvignon '00	♟♟♟	7
● Deliella '00	♟♟♟	6
● Deliella '02	♟♟♟	8

Firriato

VIA TRAPANI, 4
91027 PACECO [TP]
TEL. 0923882755
www.firriato.it

ANNUAL PRODUCTION 4,700,000 bottiglie
HECTARES UNDER VINE 200
VITICULTURE METHOD Conventional

If Ribeca, an excellent nero d'Avola and perricone blend, proves that this prestigious winery is back in control of its traditional terroir and vines, then the fascinating Quater Project's practical and conceptual objectives are an open declaration of the deep, multi-faceted significance of being Sicilian. And that Sicilianness is represented by two wines, a white and a red, each from four different native vines that fuse into the very essence of Sicily. Quite rightly, the elegant Quater Rosso '05, from nero d'Avola, perricone, frappato and nerello cappuccino, shot to the top, winning our coveted Three Glasses for its class, intense aromatic profile and stunning vitality. But all Vinzia and Salvatore Di Gaetano's wines, from first to last, are pleasing, stylish and up-to-the-minute, reflecting the winery's dynamic approach. The solid, fruity Harmonium '05, a monovarietal Nero d'Avola, is an example, as is the plush, seductive Camelot '05, a rigorous selection of cabernet sauvignon and merlot.

● Quater Rosso '05	♟♟♟	5
● Camelot '05	♟♟	7
● Harmonium '05	♟♟	5
● Ribeca '05	♟♟	6
● Altavilla della Corte Rosso '05	♟♟	4*
○ Chiaramonte Ansonica '06	♟♟	4
● Chiaramonte Rosso Nero d'Avola '05	♟♟	4*
● Epoca Rosso '05	♟♟	4*
○ Quater Bianco '06	♟♟	5
● Santagostino Rosso Baglio Soria '05	♟♟	5
○ Santagostino Bianco Baglio Soria '06	♟♟	5
● Camelot '01	♟♟♟	7
● Camelot '98	♟♟♟	5
● Harmonium '00	♟♟♟	5
● Harmonium '02	♟♟♟	6
● Harmonium '03	♟♟♟	5

Cantine Florio

VIA VINCENZO FLORIO, 1
91025 MARSALA [TP]
TEL. 0923781111
www.cantineflorio.it

ANNUAL PRODUCTION 3,500,000 bottiglie
HECTARES UNDER VINE N.A.
VITICULTURE METHOD Conventional

The latest product of Marsala's legendary wineries is dedicated to Donna Franca Florio, the belle époque icon and muse of artists like Boldini and D'Annunzio. A luscious, velvety Superiore Riserva, it aged in oak for 15 years. This intense Marsala, layered with spice and dried fruit, is the modern expression of the territory's values and traditions. We voted the Vergine Baglio Florio '94 into our taste-offs for the aristocratic complexity of its bouquet and its finely balanced palate, which signs off with a lingering finish. The warm, convincing Superiore Riserva Targa 1840 '98 was also superb, with well-defined walnutskin and rhubarb aromas. We noted another two Fascia del Sole wines: the Malvasia delle Lipari Passito '06, now a benchmark product for this category, for its splendid consistency, and the flawlessly typed Passito di Pantelleria '05. The Morsi di Luce '05 is a warm, pleasingly overripe, oak-aged Zibibbo and we also enjoyed the temptingly aromatic, fortified Grecale, a blend of zibibbo and moscato bianco grown at Noto.

Cantine Foraci

C.DA SERRONI
91026 MAZARA DEL VALLO [TP]
TEL. 0923934286
www.foraci.it

ANNUAL PRODUCTION 950,000 bottiglie
HECTARES UNDER VINE 75
VITICULTURE METHOD Certified organic

Foraci's decision in 1992 to convert to organic methods, applying eco-friendly cellar protocols, was crucial to the production of serious wines, as was confirmed again this year. The vast vineyards of this winery, founded in 1936 by Pietro Foraci, stretch across Partanna and into the Giudeo Minore district of Mazara. Grapes are also purchased from certified organic sources. The wines are all produced with the crucial assistance of Riccardo Cotarella. The Dorrasita Nero d'Avola '05 flagship wine just missed the podium but it deservedly went into the taste-offs on the strength of its traditional richness and concentration. We enjoyed its fragrant liveliness of red and black berry fruits, nuanced with Mediterranean scrubland. Another equally impressive finalist was the pleasing Tenute Dorrasita Grillo '06, a combination of well-defined bouquet, fresh tang and depth of fruit. Lastly, the dark red Satiro Danzante Nero d'Avola '05 offers morello cherries and closes on a liquorice finish. The rest of the range is good.

O Marsala Vergine Baglio Florio '94	♔♔ 6
O Malvasia delle Lipari Passito '06	♔♔ 6
O Marsala Sup. Targa 1840 Ris. '98	♔♔ 4
O Marsala Sup. Donna Franca Ris.	♔♔ 6
O Passito di Pantelleria '05	♔♔ 6
O Grecale Vino Liquoroso	♔ 4*
O Marsala Sup. Secco Ambra Vecchioflorio	♔ 4
O Morsi di Luce '05	♔ 5
O Malvasia delle Lipari Passito '03	♕♕ 6
O Malvasia delle Lipari Passito '05	♕♕ 7
O Passito di Pantelleria '04	♕♕ 6
O Marsala Vergine Baglio Florio '90	♕♕ 6
O Marsala Vergine Baglio Florio '86	♕♕ 5
O Marsala Terre Arse '98	♕♕ 5
O Marsala Sup. Targa 1840 Ris. '98	♕♕ 4

O Tenute Dorrasita Grillo '06	♔♔ 5
● Tenute Dorrasita Nero d'Avola '05	♔♔ 5
● Nero d'Avola Satiro Danzante '05	♔♔ 4
O Alcamo Conte Ruggero '06	♔ 3*
O Galhasi Inzolia Catarratto '06	♔ 3
● Galhasi Nero d'Avola Syrah '05	♔ 3
● Le Gioie '05	♔ 4
● O' Feo Nero d'Avola '05	♔ 3*
● Galhasi Nero d'Avola '05	♔ 3
● Tenute Dorrasita Nero d'Avola '04	♕♕♕ 5
O Tenute Dorrasita Grillo '05	♕♕ 5
● Tenute Dorrasita Nero d'Avola '03	♕♕ 5
● Nero d'Avola Satiro Danzante '04	♕♕ 5
● Le Gioie '04	♕♕ 5

Gulfi

LOC. ROCCAZZO
VIA MARIA SANTISSIMA DEL ROSARIO, 90
97012 CHIARAMONTE GULFI [RG]
TEL. 0932921654
www.gulfi.it

ANNUAL PRODUCTION 190,000 bottiglie
HECTARES UNDER VINE 70
VITICULTURE METHOD Certified organic

Like many successful entrepreneurs, Vito
Catania couldn't resist the temptation of
starting up a winery, buoyed by the
confidence that comes from being part of a
wine family. In less than ten years, he
acquired vines in the best of Ragusa's wine
territories and built handsome headquarters
at Chiaramonte Gulfi. Now relying on the
support of oenologist Salvo Foti, our hero
produces a range of wines with real
character. Vito Catania's strengths are his
variations on the Nero d'Avola theme but
this year we have to admit that the lavish
Neromàccarj '04 blew us away with its
opulence, its concentrated balsamic and
Mediterranean scrubland notes, its deep,
healthy fruitiness and the sumptuous
finishing touches of cocoa and tobacco. We
liked the upfront Nerobufaleffj '04 and
enjoyed its elegance. The Nerosanlorè is
seductively silky and the Nerojbleo '05
flaunts lovely varietal shading as well as
nuanced Mediterranean scents. Hats off to
the crispy, mineral-edged Carjcanti '05, a
carricante and albarello blend, and one of
the best whites in Sicily.

Marabino

C.DA MARABINO C.P. 19
97014 ISPICA [RG]
TEL. 0932955696
www.marabino.it

ANNUAL PRODUCTION 150,000 bottiglie
HECTARES UNDER VINE 30
VITICULTURE METHOD Conventional

Nello Messina invests any free time from his
many commitments to making wine. An
international figure in the industrial and
energy plants sector, he is a leading
European producer of organic fruit and
vegetables and his latest creation is the
Marabino winery, to which he dedicates
himself heart and soul. Considering the
excellent results achieved again this year,
we're starting to think that it's no
coincidence that the district where most of
the winery's vineyards are located is called,
prophetically, Buonivini, or "good wines".
The Moscato della Torre '06, from fragrant
moscato bianco grapes, went straight into
the taste-offs. This subtle wine shows its
style right from pouring, with a lovely,
brilliant golden hue and shimmering
highlights in the glass. The crisp, well-
developed aromas range from tropical fruit
to aromatic herbs, with good underlying
minerality. The palate is fresh on entry,
reprising the fruit on the nose and
progressing sweet, but not cloying, to close
with a lengthy citrus finish. We appreciated
the attractive Inzolia Violetta '06, with its
flowery nuances and cool, savoury palate.
The Nero d'Avola Archimede '04 also has
nice mineral notes.

● Neromàccarj '04	♟♟♟ 6
○ Carjcanti '05	♟♟ 5*
● Nerobufaleffj '04	♟♟ 6
● Nerojbleo '05	♟♟ 4*
○ Valcanzjria '06	♟♟ 4*
● Nerosanloré '04	♟♟ 6
● Cerasuolo di Vittoria '06	♟ 4
● Rossojbleo '06	♟ 4
● Nerobaronj '03	♟♟ 7
● Nerobufaleffj '02	♟♟ 6
● Neromàccarj '03	♟♟ 6
● Nerobufaleffj '03	♟♟ 6
● Nerojbleo '04	♟♟ 4*

○ Moscato di Noto	
Moscato della Torre '06	♟♟ 6
○ Violetta '06	♟♟ 3*
● Eloro Archimede '04	♟♟ 5
● Carmen '06	♟ 3*
○ Moscato di Noto	
Moscato della Torre '05	♟♟ 6
● Carmen '05	♟♟ 3*
● Eloro Archimede '03	♟♟ 5

Maurigi

C.DA BUDONETTO
94015 PIAZZA ARMERINA [EN]
TEL. 091321788
www.maurigi.it

Morgante

C.DA RACALMARE
92020 GROTTE [AG]
TEL. 0922945579
www.morgantevini.it

ANNUAL PRODUCTION	140,000 bottiglie
HECTARES UNDER VINE	40
VITICULTURE METHOD	Conventional

As the years pass, Francesco Maurigi's dream comes closer to reality. His ambitious project to upgrade the family estate near Piazza Armerina, which had no specific winemaking tradition, by planting mainly international varieties has brought encouraging results. We were very keen on the '06 whites. The Viognier Le Chiare, a Three Glass finalist, has elegant mineral notes on the nose and attractive florality and the palate is cool and approachable with a flawless, lengthy finish. The Sauvignon Coste all'Ombra has intense varietal grapefruit and tropical fruit while Bacca Bianca, a charming inzolia, grecanico and chardonnay blend is uncomplicated and attractive. From the high-end reds that benefit from a courageously far-sighted policy of extended bottle ageing, we preferred the stylish sophistication of the Cabernet Franc Granny '02 with its aristocratic tertiary aromas in full flow and the lingering palate. The Bacca Rossa '06, from nero d'Avola, syrah and cabernet sauvignon, has an appealingly understated style.

ANNUAL PRODUCTION	340,000 bottiglie
HECTARES UNDER VINE	60
VITICULTURE METHOD	Conventional

Antonio Morgante, with sons Carmelo and Giovanni, produces wines in one of the loveliest areas of Sicily, the Grotte countryside not far from the exquisite Valley of the Temples. This hillside estate is at 350 to 550 metres above sea level and sprawls over 200 hectares, with 60 of these dedicated to a huge nero d'Avola vineyard. Riccardo Cotarella, who is no stranger to us, has taken the oenological aspects under his talented wing. Again this year, we confirm the stature of the two Morgante wines. The '05 Don Antonio, an outstanding monovarietal nero d'Avola, is a milestone in modern Sicilian winemaking history. It just missed our top award but that might be because we tasted before it was at its peak. Nonetheless, the intense, richly extracted structure is deeply Mediterranean and in a class all of its own. As always the deliciously drinkable Nero d'Avola '06 was noteworthy, with its brooding ruby colour, refined red fruits and graphite aromas preceding a soft, lively palate. And it's released at a particularly palatable price.

O Le Chiare '06	ŸŸ 4*	● Don Antonio '05	ŸŸ 5
O Coste all'Ombra '06	ŸŸ 5*	● Nero d'Avola '06	ŸŸ 3*
● Granny '02	ŸŸ 6	● Don Antonio '00	ŸŸŸ 6
O Bacca Bianca '06	Ÿ 4	● Don Antonio '03	ŸŸŸ 5
● Bacca Rossa '06	Ÿ 4	● Don Antonio '99	ŸŸŸ 5
O Le Chiare '05	ŸŸ 4*	● Don Antonio '98	ŸŸŸ 5
● Terre di Maria '01	ŸŸ 6	● Don Antonio '02	ŸŸŸ 5
● Terre di Ottavia '02	ŸŸ 6	● Don Antonio '01	ŸŸŸ 5
● Lù '02	ŸŸ 6		
● Saia Grande '04	ŸŸ 5		
● Terre di Maria '02	ŸŸ 6		
● Granny '02	ŸŸ 6		
O Terre di Sofia '04	ŸŸ 5		

Salvatore Murana

C.DA KHAMMA, 276
91017 PANTELLERIA [TP]
TEL. 0923915231
www.salvatoremurana.com

ANNUAL PRODUCTION   30,000 bottiglie
HECTARES UNDER VINE 8
VITICULTURE METHOD   Conventional

There's little more we can say about Salvatore Murana and his passionate campaign to protect the vines and wines of Pantelleria. Salvatore grew up on this tiny sun-scorched, windswept island between Sicily and Tunisia. He has worked among the low, bush-trained vines that huddle behind dry stone walls since he was a child, when he used to help his grandfather in the fields. Over the years, Salvatore has thrilled us with memorable emotions and wines. Of course, wines and grapes are at the mercy of sun, soil and season so it does happen that the labels he presents may be merely extraordinary. As was the case this year. We tasted a round, exuberant Martingana that could have been a tad fresher, a compact Khamma '02, with loads of flesh and Mediterranean aromas rounded off by a gentle, lingering finish, and a varietal Mueggen '05 that mingles apricots, Mediterranean scrubland and dried figs. There's no denying the soundness of the range, completed by the attractively sweet, fresh-tasting Moscato di Pantelleria Turbè '05 with its nuances of rosewater and fig jam.

Palari

LOC. SANTO STEFANO BRIGA
C.DA BARNA
98137 MESSINA [ME]
TEL. 090630194
www.palari.it

ANNUAL PRODUCTION   50,000 bottiglie
HECTARES UNDER VINE 7
VITICULTURE METHOD   Conventional

They say that rain comes after thunder. The wine world has been rumbling for years that the extraordinary Faro Palari created by Salvatore Geraci, ably abetted by Professor Donato Lanati, is the best red in Sicily. Hardliners would go so far as to say it's the best in all Italy since the only reds of comparable elegance and complexity might be a Chambolle Musigny or a Vosne Romanée from the Burgundy heartlands. It was time for us to take a stand and this superb '05 vintage was the perfect opportunity for a unanimous declaration so we voted it the Guide's Red of the Year. You'll soon understand why, even if you aren't professional tasters, so start looking for one of the 25,000 bottles of this fabulous red wine. The luscious, seductive elegance will entrance you as the delicate yet unwavering finesse of the texture casts its spell, unveiling each component in turn. Buy as much as you can of the second wine, the Rosso del Soprano, which is almost as good and is released at an attractive price. No need to thank us.

O Moscato Passito di Pantelleria Khamma '02	♟♟ 7
O Moscato Passito di Pantelleria Martingana '01	♟♟ 8
O Moscato di Pantelleria Turbè '05	♟♟ 5
O Moscato Passito di Pantelleria Mueggen '05	♟♟ 7
O Moscato Passito di Pantelleria Creato '76	♟♟♟ 8
O Moscato Passito di Pantelleria Martingana '96	♟♟♟ 6
O Moscato Passito di Pantelleria Martingana '94	♟♟♟ 6
O Moscato Passito di Pantelleria Martingana '00	♟♟♟ 8
O Moscato Passito di Pantelleria Martingana '98	♟♟♟ 8
O Moscato Passito di Pantelleria Martingana '93	♟♟♟ 6
O Moscato Passito di Pantelleria Martingana '97	♟♟♟ 8
O Moscato Passito di Pantelleria Khamma '01	♟♟ 7

● Faro Palari '05	♟♟♟ 7*
● Rosso del Soprano '05	♟♟ 5
● Faro Palari '00	♟♟♟ 7
● Faro Palari '02	♟♟♟ 7
● Faro Palari '04	♟♟♟ 8
● Faro Palari '96	♟♟♟ 7
● Faro Palari '98	♟♟♟ 7
● Faro Palari '03	♟♟♟ 7
● Faro Palari '01	♟♟♟ 7
● Rosso del Soprano '04	♟♟ 5
● Rosso del Soprano '03	♟♟ 5

Passopisciaro

LOC. LA GUARDIOLA
95030 CASTIGLIONE DI SICILIA [CT]
TEL. 0578267110
www.passopisciaro.com

Carlo Pellegrino

VIA DEL FANTE, 39
91025 MARSALA [TP]
TEL. 0923719911
www.carlopellegrino.it

ANNUAL PRODUCTION 39,000 bottiglie
HECTARES UNDER VINE 29
VITICULTURE METHOD Conventional

ANNUAL PRODUCTION 7,000,000 bottiglie
HECTARES UNDER VINE 300
VITICULTURE METHOD Conventional

Andrea Franchetti's apparent detachment from fads and things material enables him to forge a close bond with various territories and his boundless love of wine reveals their potential. How many of us would have wagered on Sarteano, in Val d'Orcia, where we now find Trinoro and its wines? Yet it became an international label. Something similar occurred about a decade ago, long before the Etna wine revival and rediscovery of this extraordinary territory began, when Andrea decided to start a winery here. His estate covers 30 hectares on Etna's northern slopes, between Castiglione and Randazzo, producing stunning fruit that Andrea transforms into wines of character. Last year, his Passopisciaro '04 was highly acclaimed and this time we are singing the praises of Franchetti '05. The more so as this isn't a classic territorial rendering of a native grape, like nerello mascalese. Andrea followed his intuition and planted petit verdot and cesanese d'Affile at 800 metres. The result? A compact, stylish red heady with the richness of its fruit. It is well balanced, spicy, nuanced with white and black pepper, and topped off with hints of roasted coffee beans.

After the thrilling tasting of last year's two Riserva di Marsala Vergine wines, the '80 and the '62, we turn this year to another heritage-rich territory: the island of Pantelleria. The Passito di Pantelleria Nes '05 had no trouble getting into taste-offs thanks to its sun-drenched intensity woven from resolute, elegant dried apricot and lavender fragrances, and a sweet, filling palate with a lingering aromatic finish. Tripudium '04, a strikingly refined, layered red from a blend of nero d'Avola, cabernet sauvignon and syrah, was on the verge of the finals, too. The Tripudium Bianco '06, a grillo, chardonnay and zibibbo blend, shows deep peach and citrus-like fruit with lively freshness. The new monovarietal Dinari del Duca line features a soft, savoury Chardonnay '06, a Nero d'Avola '05 with strong varietal typicity, as well as a very pleasant, barely mature Syrah '04, and a Grillo '06 with upfront aromas and a cool, uncomplicated palate. The Moscato di Pantelleria Liquoroso '06, and even more so the Passito Liquoroso '06, with their delicious candied orange peel, are charming and inexpensive.

● Franchetti '05	♟♟♟	8
● Passopisciaro '05	♟♟	6
● Passopisciaro '04	♟♟♟	6
● Passopisciaro '01	♟♟	6
● Passopisciaro '03	♟♟	6

O Marsala Sup. Oro Dolce		4
O Passito di Pantelleria Nes '05	♟♟	6
O Duca di Castelmonte Dinari del Duca Chardonnay '06	♟♟	4
O Tripudium Bianco '06	♟♟	5
● Tripudium '04	♟♟	5
O Duca di Castelmonte Dinari del Duca Grillo '06	♟	4*
O Passito di Pantelleria Duca di Castelmonte '06	♟	5
O Moscato di Pantelleria Duca di Castelmonte '06	♟	5
● Duca di Castelmonte Dinari del Duca Nero d'Avola '05	♟	4*
● Duca di Castelmonte Dinari del Duca Syrah '04	♟	4
O Marsala Vergine Ris. del Centenario '80	♟♟	7
O Passito di Pantelleria Nes '05	♟♟	6
● Tripudium '03	♟♟	5
O Marsala Vergine Ris. '62	♟♟	8

★ Planeta
C.DA DISPENSA
92013 MENFI [AG]
TEL. 091327965
www.planeta.it

Cantine Rallo
VIA VINCENZO FLORIO, 2
91025 MARSALA [TP]
TEL. 0923721633
www.cantinerallo.it

ANNUAL PRODUCTION 2,200,000 bottiglie
HECTARES UNDER VINE 350
VITICULTURE METHOD Conventional

ANNUAL PRODUCTION 1,700,000 bottiglie
HECTARES UNDER VINE 77
VITICULTURE METHOD Certified organic

The Planeta family sail determinedly ahead on their odyssey through the world of wine, thanks to the commitment and enthusiasm of cousins Alessio, Francesca and Santi. The winery, founded quite recently in the early 1990s, is now a major player on the Italian wine scene, with four estates – soon to become five, with a new acquisition on Etna – 350 hectares of vines and an annual production in excess of 2,200,000 bottles. But the most important thing is that Planeta standards are high. Sadly, oenologist Carlo Corino, one of the men behind Planeta's success, died prematurely this year. We're in no doubt that Alessio and his cousins will be able to continue Carlo's mission. This year's range of wines was as good as ever. We gave Three Glasses to the tight-knit Burdese '05 for its great depth and elegance, rich minerality and spice aromas that prove Sicily can be a second home for cabernet sauvignon and merlot. We would also recommend the Fiano Cometa '06, the Chardonnay '06, the Nero d'Avola Santa Cecilia '05, the Syrah from the same year and all the other labels. They're all excellent.

Francesco and Andrea Vesco's wine philosophy is to focus on the territory, fostering typicity and protecting the ecosystem. The most recent development in their concept is the Aquamadre project, in partnership with the Whitaker Foundation, which owns the island of Mothia. The island is the source of late-harvest grillo grapes rendered unique by a site climate that puts the vineyards in close contact with the sea. The outcome is surprising. The '06 vintage has intense layered Mediterranean aromatic herbs on the nose and the palate reveals a well-balanced fusion of acidity, sweetness and salty savouriness. We note some excellent results from the established wines: Alcamo Nero d'Avola '06 with its attractive varietal profile; the mature, elegant Vesco Rosso '05, a blend of nero d'Avola and cabernet sauvignon; the delicious Syrah '06 and Merlot '04; and a fragrant, easy-drinking Frappato '06. The whites include the '06 Grillo with its memorable aromas and crunchy fruit; the fresh and flirty Alcamo Bianco Carta d'Oro '06; and the mature, complex grillo-only Gruali '04.

● Burdese '05	♟♟♟ 5*
○ Chardonnay '06	♟♟ 5
○ Cometa '06	♟♟ 5
● Santa Cecilia '05	♟♟ 5*
● Cerasuolo di Vittoria '06	♟♟ 4*
● La Segreta Rosso '06	♟♟ 3*
● Syrah '05	♟♟ 5
○ Moscato di Noto '06	♟♟ 6
● Merlot '05	♟♟ 5
○ Alastro '06	♟ 4
○ La Segreta Bianco '06	♟ 3
● Burdese '03	♟♟♟ 5
○ Cometa '04	♟♟♟ 5
● Santa Cecilia '97	♟♟♟ 5
● Syrah '01	♟♟♟ 5
● Syrah '02	♟♟♟ 5
● Merlot '04	♟♟♟ 5
○ Cometa '05	♟♟♟ 5

● Alcamo Nero d'Avola '06	♟♟ 3*
○ Grillo '06	♟♟ 3
● Merlot '04	♟♟ 4
● Vesco Rosso '05	♟♟ 4
● Syrah '06	♟♟ 3
○ Aquamadre V. T. '06	♟♟ 5
● Alaò '04	♟ 5
○ Gruali '04	♟ 3
○ Muller Thurgau '06	♟ 3
○ Vesco Bianco '06	♟ 3
● Frappato '06	♟ 3
○ Chardonnay '06	♟ 3
○ Alcamo Carta d'Oro '06	♟ 3
● Alcamo Nero d'Avola '05	♟♟ 4*
○ Passito di Pantelleria '04	♟♟ 6

Tenute Rapitalà

c.da Rapitalà
90043 Camporeale [PA]
tel. 092437233
www.rapitala.it

ANNUAL PRODUCTION 3,400,000 bottiglie
HECTARES UNDER VINE 175
VITICULTURE METHOD Conventional

The sudden demise of Conte Hugues Bernard de la Gatinais has deprived the Sicilian wine scenario of one of its great players, an enthusiastic ambassador and, above all, a true gentleman, the sort that is getting scarcer by the minute. His mission will be continued with the same commitment and energy by his widow Gigi and their son, Laurent, working closely with the Gruppo Italiano Vini, which has been involved in running the winery since 1999. We tasted and enjoyed the nicely ripe Hugonis '05, a cabernet sauvignon and nero d'Avola blend with solid fruit and good length, which just missed Three Glasses. The Syrah Solinero '05 is elegant and intense but a little overripe. The '05 vintage was one of the best versions of the chardonnay-based Conte Hugues Bernard de la Gatinais, with just the right touch of oak, a lively, fresh palate and a long, clean finish. We thought the fresh, fleshy Cielo d'Alcamo '05, from a late harvest of sauvignon and catarratto, was equally good, showing rich candied tropical fruit aromas. Our tasters were also intrigued by the Catarratto-Chardonnay Casalj '06, with its citrus tang and appealing acidity. The Nuhar '05, a mix of nero d'Avola and pinot nero, is nicely mature.

- ● Hugonis '05 ▼▼ 6
- ○ Casalj '06 ▼▼ 4
- ○ Conte Hugues Bernard de la Gatinais Grand Cru '05 ▼▼ 5
- ○ Cielo d'Alcamo '05 ▼▼ 6
- ● Solinero '05 ▼▼ 6
- ● Campo Reale Nero d'Avola '06 ▼ 4
- ● Nuhar '05 ▼ 4
- ○ Piano Maltese Bianco '06 ▼ 4
- ● Hugonis '01 ▽▽▽ 7
- ● Solinero '00 ▽▽▽ 6
- ● Solinero '03 ▽▽▽ 6
- ● Solinero '04 ▽▽ 6
- ○ Conte Hugues Bernard de la Gatinais Grand Cru '04 ▽▽ 5

Settesoli

s.s. 115
92013 Menfi [AG]
tel. 092577111
www.mandrarossa.it

ANNUAL PRODUCTION 20,000,000 bottiglie
HECTARES UNDER VINE 6,500
VITICULTURE METHOD Conventional

Cantine Settesoli is Sicily's leading wine co-operative and one of the biggest in Europe. It is also surprisingly successful at combining large-scale production and good quality. We were told that there are about 2,300 contributing members, 6,000 hectares of vineyards, about 20,000,000 bottles sold annually and turnover exceeds 34,000,000 euros. The quality of products is proved by the winery's growing international success and the vast range of wines marketed, all well made with a stylishly modern slant. We're sad to say that Settesoli has lost the input of expert oenologist Carlo Corino, who passed away last summer, but his style is still apparent in all the Mandrarossa wines we tasted this year. The soft, fruity Bonera '04 from nero d'Avola and cabernet was a deserving finalist, with its perfectly integrated tannins. We were also impressed by the Nero d'Avola Chartago '05, which has spice on the nose and a convincingly full palate. The full-flavoured Bendicò '05, from nero d'Avola, syrah and merlot, is richly extracted. Furetta '06, an appealing mix of fiano and chardonnay, is worth investigating but all of the wines are unbeatable value for money.

- ● Bonera Mandrarossa '04 ▼▼ 4*
- ● Bendicò Mandrarossa '05 ▼▼ 5
- ○ Feudo dei Fiori Mandrarossa '06 ▼▼ 4*
- ● Mandrarossa Carthago '05 ▼▼ 5
- ● Syrah Mandrarossa '06 ▼▼ 4*
- ● Merlot Mandrarossa '06 ▼▼ 4*
- ● Cabernet Sauvignon Mandrarossa '06 ▼▼ 4*
- ○ Furetta Mandrarossa '06 ▼▼ 5
- ○ Grecanico Mandrarossa '06 ▼ 4
- ○ Viogner Mandrarossa '06 ▼ 3*
- ● Nero d'Avola Mandrarossa '06 ▼ 4
- ● Mandrarossa Carthago '04 ▽▽ 5
- ● Bendicò Mandrarossa '04 ▽▽ 5

Spadafora

VIA AUSONIA, 90
90144 PALERMO [PA]
TEL. 091514952
www.spadafora.com

ANNUAL PRODUCTION 260,000 bottiglie
HECTARES UNDER VINE 100
VITICULTURE METHOD Conventional

Francesco Spadafora's first-rate winery is at Contrada Virzì, in Monreale, on a lovely, well-ventilated hillside. The 180-hectare estate lies between 250 and 450 metres above sea level and has 100 hectares under vine. The modern, efficient cellar processes only the winery's own grapes, selected to strict quality standards, as is traditional in this ancient family of landed gentry. The stylish, well-extracted Sole dei Padri '04 is an out-of-the-ordinary layered monovarietal Syrah. It reached our taste-offs, where it was pipped at the post for our top award, but its vibrant spice and clean fruit won it many friends. The winery has a long list of other quality wines like Schietto Cabernet Sauvignon '05, a powerful, refined, balsamic wine that conjures up fragrant forest berries, underscored by silky tannins. The two whites, Schietto Chardonnay '06 and Schietto Grillo '06, are both admirable, with well-defined aromatics and healthy, vibrant fruit in evidence. The other wines are irreproachable.

★ Tasca d'Almerita

LOC. C.DA REGALEALI
TENUTA REGALEALI
90020 SCLAFANI BAGNI [PA]
TEL. 0916459711
www.tascadalmerita.it

ANNUAL PRODUCTION 3,000,000 bottiglie
HECTARES UNDER VINE 460
VITICULTURE METHOD Conventional

Lucio Tasca is at the helm of this renowned Sicilian winery, founded in 1830. He is partnered by his sons Giuseppe and Alberto, and supported by skilled, energetic technical staff working with Carlo Ferrini as the consultant oenologist. This goes some way to explaining the continuing success of the Regaleali estate at Sclafani Bagni, in the province of Palermo in the centre of the island. This is a cool area where vines are grown at 400-700 metres above sea level. The 460 hectares of vineyard produce top-quality grapes that go into the extensive range of labels. This year, we gave Three Glasses to the nero d'Avola-heavy Rosso del Conte '04, which again tempted us with its sumptuous weave, its crisp, intense fruits, and its long-lingering finish. These champions are flanked by a series of good, and sometimes excellent, wines including a solidly built, balanced Chardonnay '05; a richly extracted, layered Cabernet Sauvignon '05; Almerita Brut '04, which is fresh, minerally and deep; and an appealing Tenuta Capofaro Malvasia '06, from the lovely island vineyards on Salina.

● Sole dei Padri '04	▼▼ 7
● Schietto Syrah '04	▼▼ 4
● Schietto Syrah '04	▼▼ 5
○ Schietto Grillo '06	▼▼ 4
○ Schietto Chardonnay '06	▼▼ 5
● Schietto Cabernet Sauvignon '05	▼▼ 6
● Don Pietro Rosso '05	▼ 4
● Monreale Syrah '06	▼ 4*
○ Don Pietro Bianco '06	▼ 4
○ Monreale Alhambra '06	▼ 3*
● Schietto Syrah '01	♀♀ 6
● Schietto Syrah '03	♀♀ 6
● Sole dei Padri '01	♀♀ 8
● Sole dei Padri '03	♀♀ 8
● Sole dei Padri '02	♀♀ 8
● Schietto Cabernet Sauvignon '04	♀♀ 6

● Contea di Sclafani Rosso del Conte '04	▼▼▼ 7
● Cabernet Sauvignon '05	▼▼ 6
○ Chardonnay '05	▼▼ 6
⊙ Almerita Rosé Brut '04	▼▼ 6
○ Contea di Sclafani Almerita Brut '04	▼▼ 6
● Cygnus '05	▼▼ 5
○ Diamante d'Almerita '06	▼▼ 6
○ Contea di Sclafani Nozze d'Oro '06	▼▼ 5
● Regaleali Nero d'Avola '06	▼▼ 4*
○ Tenuta Capofaro Malvasia '06	▼▼ 6
⊙ Regaleali Le Rose '06	▼▼ 4*
● Camastra '05	▼▼ 5
● Lamùri '05	▼ 4
○ Regaleali Bianco '06	▼ 4
○ Leone d'Almerita '06	▼ 4
● Contea di Sclafani Rosso del Conte '03	♀♀♀ 6
● Contea di Sclafani Cabernet Sauvignon '02	♀♀♀ 6
● Contea di Sclafani Cabernet Sauvignon '03	♀♀♀ 6

Tenuta delle Terre Nere

C.DA CALDERARA
95036 RANDAZZO [CT]
TEL. 095924002
tenutaterrenere@tiscali.it

ANNUAL PRODUCTION 70,000 bottiglie
HECTARES UNDER VINE 16
VITICULTURE METHOD Natural

Oenologist Marc De Grazia is a cosmopolitan Florentine and terrific talent scout and promoter of Italian wine. He is to be thanked for casting the international spotlight on many of the great small-scale Italian winemakers and their products. For instance, the success achieved by new Italian wines in the 1980s would never have reached the phenomenal levels it did in the States without Marc. If further proof of his intuition is needed, we can look to his achievements on Etna, where he started out only a decade ago. He was one of the first to see the potential of a territory that had been practically forgotten. Now he is presenting labels of outstanding quality and they all come from his 16 hectares of vines, almost all very old and which he selected for the best exposure on the northern slope of the volcanic massif. Marc has three vineyard selections, produced in the fullest respect of the territory and the nerello mascalese and mantellato vines. They are all excellent but we have a soft spot for the Feudo di Mezzo Quadro delle Rose, for its extra complexity and finesse, crisp fruit and medicinal herb aromas, minerality and exquisite tannic weave. Don't miss it.

Valle dell'Acate

C.DA BIDINI
97011 ACATE [RG]
TEL. 0932874166
www.valledellacate.com

ANNUAL PRODUCTION 430,000 bottiglie
HECTARES UNDER VINE 100
VITICULTURE METHOD Conventional

This year, the dynamic Gaetana Jacono produced one of the best reds in Sicily, Tanè '04, a blissful marriage of nero d'Avola and syrah. This fleshy, layered wine, which has oodles of class and surprising elegance, is well coordinated and forceful, and sailed through to the national finals. All of the Bidini wines are good, though. This vast estate is in the valley of the river Dirillo, at Acate, and has been in the Jacono family for six generations. Moro '05, a pure nero d'Avola, is varietal and laced with blueberry, blackberry and graphite, lifted by warmer, more Mediterranean nuances. The Cerasuolo di Vittoria Classico, a nero d'Avola and frappato mix, is a wine to bank on. The stylish, deep '05, is one of the estate's most covetable wines, themed around chocolate and stewed black cherries. We thought the Frappato '06 was fragrance personified, with its intense, seductive nuances of strawberry and cherry. We had few doubts about the '05 Bidis, from chardonnay and insolia, which offers yellow peach and tropical fruit on the nose, followed by a savoury palate with a cool vein of acidity. All the other wines are good.

● Etna Rosso Feudo di Mezzo Quadro delle Rose '05	🍷🍷🍷 7
● Etna Rosso Calderara Sottana '05	🍷🍷 6*
● Etna Rosso Guardiola '05	🍷🍷 7
○ Etna Bianco '06	🍷🍷 4*
● Etna Rosso '06	🍷 4
● Etna Rosso Feudo di Mezzo Quadro delle Rose '04	🍷🍷🍷 6
● Etna Rosso Calderara Sottana '04	🍷🍷 6
● Etna Rosso Guardiola '04	🍷🍷 6
● Etna Rosso Guardiola '03	🍷🍷 6

● Tanè '04	🍷🍷 6
○ Bidis '05	🍷🍷 5
● Il Frappato '06	🍷🍷 4*
● Rusciano '05	🍷🍷 4
● Il Moro '05	🍷🍷 4
● Cerasuolo di Vittoria '05	🍷🍷 4
○ Insolia '06	🍷 3
○ Zagra '06	🍷 4
● Tanè '00	🍷🍷 6
● Tanè '03	🍷🍷 6
● Cerasuolo di Vittoria '02	🍷🍷 4
● Tanè '00	🍷🍷 6
● Cerasuolo di Vittoria '03	🍷🍷 4
● Il Frappato '03	🍷🍷 4
● Il Frappato '04	🍷🍷 4
● Il Frappato '05	🍷🍷 4*
● Il Moro '04	🍷🍷 4

OTHER WINERIES

Tenuta dell'Abate
VIA KENNEDY, 46
93100 CALTANISSETTA [CL]
TEL. 0934584188
tenutadellabate@hotmail.com

Luigi Romano came up with a very drinkable vineyard selection, an intense Monte Palco Nero d'Avola '06, giving red berries and spices. Giffarrò '05, a fine cabernet sauvignon and syrah blend, has distinct blackberries and a velvety palate. The delicate Inzolia Lissandrello '06 is zesty and typically grassy.

● Monte Palco Nero d'Avola '06	▼▼	4*
● Giffarrò '05	▼	4
O Lissandrello '06	▼	3

AgroArgento
C.DA ANGUILLA
92017 SAMBUCA DI SICILIA [AG]
TEL. 0423860930
www.agroargento.it

The new Moretti Polegato and Maggio family winery on Lake Arancio made a promising debut with its Timoleonte '04, a nero d'Avola-based blend that almost edged into our finals for its graceful spice and round harmony. Nero d'Avola Carrivàli '05 is firm and tangy. The fresh Grillo Calancùni '06 pleases.

● Timoleonte '04	▼▼	5
● Carrivàli '05	▼▼	4*
O Calancùni '06	▼	4

Ajello
C.DA GIUDEO
91025 MAZARA DEL VALLO [TP]
TEL. 091309107
www.ajello.info

We recommend Ajello wines, and the flagship Furat '05, from nero d'Avola, cabernet sauvignon, syrah and merlot, confirmed that it is very drinkable, with a fruit-rich, mineral aroma. We were very taken with the elegantly fragrant Shams, from moscato, grillo, inzolia and catarratto.

● Furat '05	▼▼	5
O Shams '06	▼▼	5
O Bizir '06	▼	5
● Majus Nero d'Avola '05	▼	3*

Alessandro di Camporeale
C.DA MANDRANOVA
90043 CAMPOREALE [PA]
TEL. 092437038
www.alessandrodicamporeale.it

The monovarietal syrah Kaid '05 has more than a hint of spices and red berries, and is still this family winery's key product. A lively, very drinkable Nero d'Avola DonnaTà '06 also caught our eye. The well-defined, catarratto-only Benedè '06 is intense and flavoursome.

● DonnaTà '06	▼▼	4*
● Kaid '05	▼▼	5
O Benedè '06	▼	4*

Alto Belice
V.LE ENRICO BERLINGUER, 2
90040 SAN CIPIRELLO [PA]
TEL. 0918573558
www.cantinasocialealtobelice.it

Nino Inzirillo's hard work at the San Cipirello co-operative has paid off. Monreale Nero d'Avola Trerrè '05 is well defined, with a mature, precise bouquet and an austere, stylish palate. The Tre Feudi line includes the well-typed Inzolia '06 and Catarratto '06, both fresh and tangy.

● Monreale Nero d'Avola Trerrè '05	▼▼	4*
O Tre Feudi Catarratto '06	▼	4
O Tre Feudi Inzolia '06	▼	4
● Tre Feudi Nero d'Avola '06	▼	4

Avide
C.DA MASTRELLA, 346
97013 COMISO [RG]
TEL. 0932967456
www.avide.it

The well-made Cerasuolo di Vittoria Barocco '03 has powerful red fruits and on the palate shows mature, firm and lingering. The spicy, fragrant nature of the Cerasuolo di Vittoria Etichetta Nera '05 makes it very drinkable.

● Cerasuolo di Vittoria Barocco '03	▼▼	6
● Cerasuolo di Vittoria Etichetta Nera '05	▼	4*
● Herea Frappato '06	▼	3*
● Herea Syrah '06	▼	4

OTHER WINERIES

Baglio delle Cicale
S.DA PROVINCIALE
PER GRANITOLA, 282
91021 CAMPOBELLO DI MAZARA [TP]
TEL. 092440450
www.bagliodellecicale.it

Since Gianpiero Jelmini and his friends set up this winery nine years ago, it has developed steadily. Their Merlot Baglio delle Cicale '05 is minerally and intensely fruity then smooth on the palate, with a lingering finish. Nero d'Avola and cabernet sauvignon go into the temptingly spirited Uzeda '05.

● Baglio delle Cicale '05	♆♆	5
● Syrah '06	♆	4
○ Iddu '06	♆	4
● Uzeda '05	♆	4

Barone Sergio
VIA CAVOUR, 29
96018 PACHINO [SR]
TEL. 0902927878
www.baronesergio.it

Barone Sergio's top item is the Kalùri dessert wine from white moscato grapes. The '05 vintage appeals for its distinctive aroma and freshness. The Eloro Nero d'Avola Barone Sergio '06 is nicely varietal. Le Mandrie '05, with its rounded, mature fruit, is a blend of nero d'Avola and cabernet sauvignon.

○ Kalùri '05	♆♆	6
● Eloro Nero d'Avola Barone Sergio '06	♆	4
● Le Mandrie '05	♆	4

Capo Croce - Vini Gancia
C.DA CASTELLAZZO
91027 TRAPANI [TP]
TEL. 03489999382
www.gancia.it

Two noteworthy wines, Nero d'Avola Pulpito '05 and Addumari '05, from cabernet sauvignon and syrah, are elegant, appealing and well made, both with interesting ripe fruit. Oenologist Beppe Caviola also did a superb job with Pulvino '06, a grillo-only wine of intense colour and fresh flavour.

● Addumari '05	♆♆	5
● Pulpito '05	♆♆	5
● Nartece '06	♆	4
○ Pulvino '06	♆	4

Barbera
C.DA TORRENOVA, S.P. 79
92013 MENFI [AG]
TEL. 0925570442
www.cantinebarbera.it

The wines produced by this family winery are in the capable hands of oenologist Daniela Barbera. An excellent, richly extracted Coda della Foce '05 from petit verdot, merlot and nero d'Avola was lively enough to get into our finals. The rounded, lingering Riserva La Vota '05 Cabernet Sauvignon is good.

● Coda della Foce '05	♆♆	5
● Menfi La Vota Ris. '05	♆♆	5
○ Piana del Pozzo '06	♆♆	4
○ Inzolia Dietro le Case '06	♆	4*

Barraco
C.DA FONTANELLE, 252
91025 MARSALA [TP]
TEL. 3897955357
vinibarraco@libero.it

Antonino Barraco's unfortified wines coped well with the 2006 heat. The Grillo is elegant and mouthfilling; the Catarratto retains its good mineral overtones; the Zibibbo already shows an intriguing note of hydrocarbons, promising exciting evolution; and the Nero d'Avola '05 will also improve with age.

○ Grillo '06	♆♆	4
○ Zibibbo '06	♆♆	4
○ Catarratto '06	♆	4
● Nero d'Avola '05	♆	4

Castellucci Miano
VIA SICILIA, 1
90029 VALLEDOLMO [PA]
TEL. 0921542385
www.castelluccimiano.it

This Madonie-based winery is coming on under the technical guidance of Tonino Guzzo. The last inzolia harvest yielded La Masa '06, whose delicate mineral notes mingle with pear. Catarratto Shiarà '06, from 40-year-old vines at 700 metres above sea level, has sea breeze and aromatic herb notes.

○ Inzolia La Masa '06	♆♆	4*
○ Shiarà '06	♆♆	4*
○ Catarratto Inzolia '06	♆♆	4*
● Nero d'Avola '05	♆	4

OTHER WINERIES

Tenuta Chiuse del Signore
LOC. ALBORETTO
S.DA PROVINCIALE LINGUAGLOSSA-ZAFFERANA
95015 LINGUAGLOSSA [CT]
TEL. 0942611340
www.gaishotels.com

Sergio De Luca's wines are well-made and well-priced. Serrantico '05, from merlot and syrah, was an elegant, aristocratic finalist. We liked the Rasule Alte Rosso '06, a blend of nerello mascalese and merlot. The inzolia and chardonnay Rasule Alte Bianco '06 is very drinkable.

● Serrantico '05	♟♟	6
● Rasule Alte Rosso '06	♟♟	4*
○ Rasule Alte Bianco '06	♟	4

Cossentino
VIA P.PE UMBERTO, 241
90047 PARTINICO [PA]
TEL. 0918782569
www.cossentino.it

Cossentino, in the province of Trapani, uses organic methods in well-aspected vineyards that enjoy ideal soil and weather conditions. A good Merlot '05 has polished hints of tobacco and coffee. The Cabernet Sauvignon '05 has an intriguing, mature nose. The Nero d'Avola '05 has rustic charm.

● Merlot '05	♟♟	4*
○ Gadì Catarratto '06	♟	3
● Nero d'Avola '05	♟	4
● Cabernet Sauvignon '05	♟	4

Curto
VIA G. GALILEI, 4
97014 ISPICA [RG]
TEL. 0932950161
www.curto.it

We recommend the '04 Nero d'Avola Fontanelle, with a refined nose, Mediterranean and red fruit notes, and a dry, elegant palate. There is also an interesting, lightly spiced Ikano '05 from nero d'Avola, syrah and merlot, with a ripe jam bouquet. We enjoyed the Nero d'Avola Eos '06.

● Eloro Fontanelle '04	♟♟	5
● Curto Ikano '05	♟	4
● Eloro Nero d'Avola Eos '06	♟	3*

Di Giovanna
C.SO UMBERTO I, 137
92017 SAMBUCA DI SICILIA [AG]
TEL. 0925941086
www.digiovanna-vini.it

The Di Giovanna Nero d'Avola G&K '05 reached our taste-offs, thanks to crispy fruit and elegant, silky tannins. The rest of the range is commendable, especially the fresh Grillo '06, with a dash of tropical fruits, and the tangy Gerbino Merlot '05, with its superb nose-palate symmetry.

● G&K Nero d'Avola '05	♟♟	5
● Gerbino Merlot '05	♟♟	3*
○ Grillo '06	♟♟	4
○ Gerbino Chardonnay '06	♟	3*

Gaspare Di Prima
VIA G. GUASTO, 27
92017 SAMBUCA DI SICILIA [AG]
TEL. 0925941201
www.diprimavini.it

Villamaura Syrah '04 is still the cornerstone of this consistent winery in the Sambuca district of Sicily. This bracing wine, buzzing with refined notes of black cherry preserve, chocolate, cinnamon and black pepper, is very drinkable and shows rounded, nicely gauged tannins.

● Villamaura Syrah '04	♟♟	6
● Gibilmoro Nero d'Avola '05	♟	4
● Pepita Rosso '06	♟	4
○ Pepita Bianco '06	♟	4

Disisa
VIA ROMA, 392
90139 PALERMO [PA]
TEL. 091588557
www.vinidisisa.it

The Di Lorenzo winery, with vineyards on the slopes of Monreale, got off to a flying start. Roberto Cipresso orchestrated the complex, mighty Tornamira '04, an excellent, unusually refined cabernet sauvignon, merlot and syrah blend. The Syrah Adhara '05 is fruit-rich.

● Tornamira '04	♟♟	5
● Adhara '05	♟	3
● Nero d'Avola '05	♟	3
○ Charonnay '06	♟	3

OTHER WINERIES

Fatascià

VIA MAZZINI, 40
90139 PALERMO [PA]
TEL. 091332505
www.fatascia.it

Stefania Lena and Giuseppe Natoli's winery has found its feet. An interesting Aliré '05, from syrah and nero d'Avola, is spicy and intense. A laudable fruit-rich Rosso del Presidente '05, from cabernet franc and nero d'Avola, is plump and layered. The varietal Nero d'Avola Almanera '05 has poise.

● Aliré '05	♀♀	4*
● Almanera '05	♀♀	4*
● Rosso del Presidente '05	♀	5
○ Enigma '06	♀	4

Feotto dello Jato

C.DA FEOTTO
90048 SAN GIUSEPPE JATO [PA]
TEL. 0918572650
www.feottodellojato.it

The well-made Rosso Fegotto '05, an intense ruby Nero d'Avola, expresses dominant varietal nuances of plum and spice. But the winery, coordinated by Calogero Todaro, has other strings to its bow, including an attractive late-harvest Zabbia '05, from excellent catarratto grapes.

● Monreale Rosso Fegotto '05	♀♀	4*
○ Iris '06	♀	4
● Monreale V.T. Zabbia '05	♀	6
● Nero d'Avola '06	♀	4

Ferreri

C.DA SALINELLA
91029 SANTA NINFA [TP]
TEL. 092461871
www.ferrerivini.it

The most outstanding Ferreri wine is a fruit-rich, balsamic Nero d'Avola Brasi '05. We were also taken with the other nero d'Avola vineyard selection, the intense, aromatic Al Merat '05, with its well-defined tannic weave. The inviting Karren '05, from cabernet sauvignon, is well styled and poised.

● Al Merat '05	♀♀	5
● Brasi '05	♀♀	5
○ Catarratto '06	♀	4
● Karren '05	♀	5

Feudi del Pisciotto

LOC. PISCIOTTO
93015 NISCEMI [CL]
TEL. 0577742903
www.castellare.it

This new 40-hectare winery, 250 metres above sea level, enjoys cool breezes that blow in from the sea, just six kilometres away. We found all the wines tasted to be excellent, especially the spicy, elegantly varietal Nero d'Avola '05, with its seductively soft, refined tannins.

● Baglio del Sole Nero d'Avola '05	♀♀	3*
○ Baglio del Sole Inzolia '06	♀	3*
○ Baglio del Sole Inzolia Catarratto '06	♀	3*

Feudo Arancio

C.DA PORTELLA MISILBESI
92017 SAMBUCA DI SICILIA [AG]
TEL. 0925579000
www.feudoarancio.it

The Mezzacorona group's Sicilian winery, in Sambuca, produces a value-for-money range of distinctive wines. We were won over by the clean, cool Inzolia '06, a stylish Chardonnay '06, the citrus notes of the Grillo '06, and a persuasive, velvety Hekate '05 dried-grape dessert wine.

○ Hekate Passito '05	♀♀	5
○ Chardonnay '06	♀	4
○ Grillo '06	♀	4
○ Inzolia '06	♀	4

Feudo di Santa Tresa

S.DA COMUNALE MARANGIO, 35
97019 VITTORIA [RG]
TEL. 0932513126
www.santatresa.it

We tasted some good wines from the Maggio family winery, handled by Tuscan oenologist Stefano Chioccioli. The Nero d'Avola Avulisi '04 is intense in all aspects. A successful blend of grillo and viognier grapes underpins a firm, tangy, very aromatic Rina Ianca '06, with tasty acidity.

● Avulisi '04	♀♀	5
○ Rina Ianca '06	♀♀	4*
● Nivuro '04	♀	4

OTHER WINERIES

Feudo Montoni
C.DA MONTONI VECCHI
92022 CAMMARATA [AG]
TEL. 091513106
www.feudomontoni.it

Fabio Sireci has a simple passion: his nero d'Avola grapes for his two top-notch wines. A polished, complex Vrucara '05 made it to the finals for its heady bouquet of spices and black berry fruits. We recommend the elegant, mature Nero d'Avola '05, which is austere and very drinkable.

● Nero d'Avola Sel. Speciale Vrucara '05	🍷🍷	6
● Nero d'Avola '05	🍷🍷	4*

Feudo Zirtari
C.DA PORTELLA MISILIBESI
92017 SAMBUCA DI SICILIA [AG]
TEL. 0421246281
www.feudozirtari.com

The Santa Margherita group's second Sambuca winery offers two excellent value-for-money products, Bianco '06, a fresh, zesty blend of inzolia and chardonnay with fragrant grassy aromas, and a velvety red Rosso '05, with ripe fruit aromas, from 60 per cent nero d'Avola and 40 per cent syrah.

● Feudo Zirtari Rosso '05	🍷	3*
○ Feudo Zirtari Bianco '06	🍷	3*

Geraci
C.DA TARUCCO, S.P. 12 KM 5,3
90032 BISACQUINO [PA]
TEL. 091306503
www.tarucco.com

Stefano and Antonella Geraci have maintained standards at their winery. The nicely intriguing Tarucco Alicante '05 has a fresh, interesting aromatic spectrum, with velvety tannins. Tarucco Colonna Bianco '06 is a well-made chardonnay, grillo and greco dorato blend.

● Tarucco Alicante '05	🍷🍷	4*
○ Tarucco Colonna Bianco '06	🍷	3*

Tenuta Gorghi Tondi
P.ZZA PIEMONTE E LOMBARDO, 27
91025 MARSALA [TP]
TEL. 0923657364
www.tenutagorghitondi.it

This new winery is working with oenologist Tonino Guzzo and the results are well-defined wines with a generous, complex profile. Segreante '05 is a monovarietal Syrah, revealing smooth tannins, and nicely tinged with preserves. We would also mention Kheirè '06, a feisty Grillo.

○ Coste a Preola Bianco '06	🍷🍷	3*
○ Kheirè '06	🍷🍷	4*
● Segreante '05	🍷🍷	4*
● Coste a Preola Rosso '06	🍷	4

Grottarossa
LOC. C.DA GROTTAROSSA
S.S. 640 KM 44,5
93100 CALTANISSETTA [CL]
TEL. 0934939076
www.grottarossavini.it

The winery has its own vineyards in the provinces of Caltanissetta and Agrigento. The intense, intriguingly spicy Nero d'Avola Rosso della Noce '04 is joy for the palate. Makallè '06 is an enjoyable, mature nero d'Avola and merlot blend. We liked the taut fruit in the Nero d'Avola Merlot Eupósion '06.

● Rosso della Noce '04	🍷🍷	4*
● Makallè '06	🍷🍷	4*
● Eupòsion Rosso '06	🍷	3
○ Gemme Inzolia '06	🍷	3

Guccione
S. P. 102 BIS, KM 5,5
90100 MONREALE [PA]
TEL. 3383306583
guccionecerasa@alice.it

The Guccione family runs a biodynamic vineyard whose first wines reflect a commitment to intense local flavour. The Trebbiano Veruzza '05 blends the mineral elegance of clay with rich fruits on the nose and a sun-kissed palate that is fresh and light. The mature Catarratto Girgis '05 is rich and plush.

○ Girgis '05	🍷🍷	4*
○ Veruzza '05	🍷🍷	3*
● Neroli '05	🍷	3*

OTHER WINERIES

Hauner
LOC. SANTA MARIA
VIA UMBERTO I
98050 LIPARI [ME]
TEL. 0909843141

The malvasia and corinto nero Malvasia delle Lipari Carlo Hauner '04 is special. Flaunting nuances of Mediterranean scrubland and delicious echoes of candied citrus, it presents vibrant, elegant and deep. The mighty, fruit-rich Hierà '05 blend of nero d'Avola, alicante and nocera, is worth investigating.

O Malvasia delle Lipari Passito '06	♛♛ 6
O Malvasia Passito Carlo Hauner '04	♛♛ 7
● Hierà '05	♛♛ 4*
● Rosso Antonello '03	♛ 5

Lanzara
VIA E. ALBANESE, 114
90139 PALERMO [PA]
TEL. 0917495042
www.lanzarawines.com

There was a good debut from this young winery with its own vineyards at Menfi and Selinunte, a modern cellar and a newly refurbished 17th-century baglio, or fortified farmstead. The Merlot '05, with mature red plum overtones, and the Bianco San Vincenzo '06, with subtle hints of fruit and flower, are both nice.

O Bianco San Vincenzo '06	♛ 3
O Chardonnay '06	♛ 4
● Cromazio '04	♛ 7
● Merlot '05	♛ 4

Cooperativa Placido Rizzotto Libera Terra
VIA CANEPA, 53
90048 SAN GIUSEPPE JATO [PA]
TEL. 0918577655
www.liberaterra.it

In 2007, two youth co-operatives founded a winery to work impounded Mafia-owned vineyards, with Federico Curtaz and Beppe Caviola taking care of technical issues. Two good wines are dedicated to Placido Rizzotto: a fresh, monovarietal Catarratto, and a fruity, drinkable nero d'Avola and syrah blend.

O Centopassi Placido Rizzotto Bianco '06	♛ 3*
● Centopassi Placido Rizzotto Rosso '06	♛ 3*

Maggio
S.DA C.LE MARANGIO, 35
97019 VITTORIA [RG]
TEL. 0932984771
www.maggiovini.it

Massimo and Barbara Maggio present Amongae '04, a blend of nero d'Avola, cabernet sauvignon and merlot grown at Riesi. The wine has dazzling redcurrants and blueberries on the nose, stylish, meaty nuances and a feisty, lingering palate. The organic Nero d'Avola Rasula '06 has bright varietal notes.

● Amongae '04	♛♛ 4*
● Cerasuolo di Vittoria Vigna di Pettineo '05	♛ 5
● Pithoi Syrah '04	♛ 4
● Rasula Nero d'Avola '06	♛ 4

Masseria Feudo Grottarossa
C.DA GROTTAROSSA
93100 CALTANISSETTA [CL]
TEL. 0934856575
www.masseriadelfeudo.it

Francesco and Carolina Curcurullo produced a complex, concentrated Rosso delle Rose '05 from nero d'Avola and syrah. We liked the fresh, tangy chardonnay Haermosa '06. The delicate, supple Giglio Bianco '06, from grillo and inzolia, and the drinkable, nero d'Avola-only Giglio Rosso '06 are well styled.

● Rosso delle Rose '05	♛♛ 4*
O Haermosa '06	♛ 5
● Il Giglio Rosso '06	♛ 3*
O Il Giglio Bianco '06	♛ 3*

Aziende Vinicole Miceli
C.DA PIANA SCUNCHIPANI, 190
92019 SCIACCA [AG]
TEL. 092580188
www.miceli.net

The best wine this year from Miceli's estates at Sciacca and on Pantelleria is Nia Maro '05, a mature, graceful Merlot with generous, concentrated spice and noteworthy tannins. The delicately scented Miceli Chardonnay '05 is well made and varietal. The rest of the range is impeccable.

● Nia Maro '05	♛♛ 5
● Dama Rovenza '05	♛ 4
O Chardonnay '05	♛ 5
● Nero d'Avola '05	♛ 5

OTHER WINERIES

Cantine Mothia

VIA GIOVANNI FALCONE, 22
91025 MARSALA [TP]
TEL. 0923737295
www.cantine-mothia.com

The Bonomo family winery is evolving. We liked the heady, grillo-based Mulsum '06 dessert wine, with its honey, figs and quince aromas. The elegant Nero d'Avola Mosaikon '05 is fruity and varietal. The Grillo-Chardonnay Vela Latina '06 is fresh and minerally, and we also liked the inzolia Saline '06.

● Mosaikon '05	♆♆	3*
○ Mulsum V. T. '06	♆♆	5
○ Saline '06	♆	2
○ Vela Latina '06	♆	4

Occhipinti

VIA DEI MILLE, 55
97019 VITTORIA [RG]
TEL. 3397383580
info@agricolaocchipinti.it

Oenologist Arianna Occhipinti is committed to organic cultivation. She makes her Guide debut with two commendable wines. The '05 Siccagno, from nero d'Avola, has concentrated aromas, nice acidity and elegant tannins. The fragrant Frappato, also '05, is fresh with a subtle vein of nutmeg.

● Siccagno '05	♆	5
● Frappato '05	♆♆	5

Piana dei Cieli

C.DA BERTOLINO - SCIFITELLI
92013 MENFI [AG]
TEL. 092572060
www.pianadeicieli.com

Siblings Annalisa and Nino Giambalvo come from a wine family. They made a good start, their Syrah '05 showing strong Mediterranean traits and uncomplicated, attractive fruit. The fresh Chardonnay Grecanico '06 has well-defined grassiness and the fragrant, spicy Nero d'Avola '05 is varietal.

○ Chardonnay-Grecanico '06	♆♆	3*
● Syrah '05	♆♆	4*
● Cabernet Sauvignon '05	♆	4
● Nero d'Avola '05	♆	4

Poggio di Bortolone

LOC. ROCCAZZO
C.DA BORTOLONE, 19
97010 CHIARAMONTE GULFI [RG]
TEL. 0932921161
www.poggiodibortolone.it

The Cosenzas are known for their reliability, endorsed by their finalist, Vigna Para Para '04, from nero d'Avola and frappato, and a complex Cerasuolo di Vittoria with ripe cherry and dense, elegant tannins. The Kiron '04, from petit verdot, and the other wines are all well made.

● Cerasuolo di Vittoria V. Para Para '04	♆♆	5
● Cerasuolo di Vittoria Poggio di Bortolone '05	♆♆	4*
● Kiron '04	♆♆	6
● Cerasuolo di Vittoria Contessa Costanza '05	♆	4

Pollara

S.P. 4 BIS, KM 2, C.DA MALVELLO
90046 MONREALE [PA]
TEL. 0918462922
www.principedicorleone.it

Pollara has kept up admirable standards across the range. Monreale Chardonnay Sinedie '05 has a quite complex bouquet and nice nose-palate symmetry. The Monreale Cabernet Sauvignon '03 foregrounds overripe tones while the Chardonnay '06 has fresh, intense florality.

○ Chardonnay Principe di Corleone '06	♆	4
○ Monreale Chardonnay Sinedie Principe di Corleone '05	♆	4
● Narciso Principe di Corleone Rosso '06	♆	3*
● Monreale Cabernet Sauvignon Principe di Corleone '03	♆	4

Pupillo

C.DA LA TARGIA
96100 SIRACUSA [SR]
TEL. 0931494029
www.solacium.it

Nino Pupillo, the man who gave a new lease of life to Moscato di Siracusa, presented fresh, elegant wines with wholesome fruit. A hint of acacia and genteel sweetness in Pollio '06, from moscato bianco, combine with a seductive, brilliant golden hue and luscious aromatic impact.

○ Cyane '06	♆♆	4*
○ Moscato di Siracusa Pollio '06	♆♆	6
○ Moscato di Siracusa Solacium '06	♆♆	6
● Re Federico '06	♆	4

OTHER WINERIES

Riofavara

LOC. C.DA FAVARA
S.P. 49 ISPICA - PACHINO
97014 ISPICA [RG]
TEL. 0932959839
www.riofavara.it

Massimo Padova gave us an elegant Nero d'Avola Sciavè '05 and a delightful Eloro '05 nuanced with mulberry and Mediterranean herbs. The floral, fresh-tasting Nero d'Avola San Basilio '04 has a sense of place while the Marzaiolo '06, a moderately long Inzolia, is well structured.

● Eloro Nero d'Avola Sciavè '05	♟♟	5*
● Eloro Nero d'Avola '05	♟♟	4*
○ Marzaiolo '06	♟	3
● San Basilio '04	♟	3

Rizzuto

C.DA PICONELLO
92011 CATTOLICA ERACLEA [AG]
TEL. 091333081
www.rizzutoguccione.com

The good '04 Ibisco, from nero d'Avola, cabernet and merlot, is austere and well defined. The Piconello Cabernet Sauvignon Chiaro '06 rosé is fresh, well rounded and fruity. The well-made Nero d'Avola Jannicello '06 is supple on the palate and the grassy Piconello Grillo '06 has an almondy finish.

● Ibisco '04	♟♟	5
● Jannicello Nero d'Avola '06	♟	4
⊙ Piconello Cabernet Sauvignon Chiaro '06	♟	4
○ Piconello Grillo '06	♟	4

Sallier de la Tour

C.DA PERNICE
90144 MONREALE [PA]
TEL. 092436797
www.sallierdelatour.it

The outstanding wine this time from Principe Filiberto Sallier de la Tour's recently opened winery is the intense Merlot '04. Elegant and layered, it foregrounds oriental spice and red berry jam, standing out for its balance and gratifying drinkability.

● Syrah '04	♟♟	4*
● Cabernet '04	♟	4
○ Sallier de la Tour Bianco '06	♟	4
● Merlot '04	♟	4

Emanuele Scammacca del Murgo

VIA ZAFFERANA, 13
95010 SANTA VENERINA [CT]
TEL. 095950520
www.murgo.it

This winery has always produced dependable, land-rooted wines, like the fruit-rich, minerally Etna Rosato '06. We liked the smooth tannins of the Cabernet Sauvignon Tenuta San Michele '04. There are some nice nerello mascalese-based sparklers: a cool, zesty Extra Brut '01; and the fragrant Rosé '04.

⊙ Etna Rosato '06	♟♟	3*
● Tenuta San Michele '04	♟	3
○ Murgo Extra Brut '01	♟	4
⊙ Murgo Rosé Brut '04	♟	4

Tenuta di Serramarrocco

LOC. FONTANELLE
C.DA OSPEDALETTO
91100 VALDERICE [TP]
TEL. 063220973
www.serramarrocco.com

Marco and Massimiliano Marrocco Trischitta confirm a Bordeaux-style elegance for their flagship wine, which sailed into the taste-offs. The striking Serramarrocco '05 is a blend of cabernet sauvignon and merlot. A firm wine, it shows stylish, well-defined aromatics and captivating tannins.

● Serramarrocco '05	♟♟	6
● Nero di Serramarrocco '05	♟♟	5
● Baglio di Serramarrocco Nero d'Avola '06	♟	3*
○ Grillo del Barone '06	♟	3*

Solidea

C.DA KADDIUGGIA
91017 PANTELLERIA [TP]
TEL. 0923913016
www.solideavini.it

The three zibibbo, aka moscato d'Alessandria, wines confirm the D'Ancona family as the some of the most exciting producers on Pantelleria. The flagship is an opulent Passito '06 with a vibrant acidic vein. Its two intense, generously fresh-tasting companions are not far behind.

○ Passito di Pantelleria '06	♟♟	6
○ Ilios '06	♟♟	4
○ Moscato di Pantelleria '06	♟♟	5

OTHER WINERIES

Tamburello

C.DA PIETRAGNELLA
90144 MONREALE [PA]
TEL. 0918465272
dagala@libero.it

This year, the '04 Pietragavina Nero d'Avola was the most noteworthy of go-getting Mirella Tamburello's products. Varietal and spicy, it also stands out for its almost austere poise and lingering finish. As usual, the characterful Pietragavina Perricone '04 is good.

| ● Monreale Pietragavina Nero d'Avola '04 | 🍷🍷 4* |
| ● Monreale Pietragavina Perricone '04 | 🍷 4 |

Tenuta Chiarelli Cuffaro Casale Santa Ida

FRAZ. C.DA CONSORTO
95040 SAN MICHELE DI GANZARIA [CT]
TEL. 0916090065
www.tenutachiarellicuffaro.com

Giacoma and Salvatore Cuffaro's winery is located in the breezy San Michele di Ganzaria hills. Donato Lanati was able to produce two interesting wines. Euno '05 is a fruity, minerally monovarietal Nero d'Avola. Pluzia '05, from grillo and chardonnay, tempts with floral nuances.

| ● Euno '05 | 🍷 3* |
| ○ Pluzia '05 | 🍷 3* |

Terrelíade

LOC. SILENE
C.DA PORTELLA MISILBESI
92017 SAMBUCA DI SICILIA [AG]
TEL. 0421246281
www.terreliade.com

This Santa Margherita group winery's top product is (Utti) Majuri. The '05 version of this nero d'Avola and syrah blend was still maturing when we tasted. The grillo-based Timpa Giadda '06 was on form, showing minerality and fresh almonds, with clean, crispy fruitiness. The varietal Shiraz '05 is good.

○ Timpa Giadda '06	🍷🍷 4*
● Musìa '05	🍷 4
● Shiraz '05	🍷 4
● Nirà '05	🍷 4

Vini Biondi

C.SO SICILIA, 20
95039 TRECASTAGNI [CT]
TEL. 0957633933
www.vinibiondi.it

Biondi has been a name in Etna wine since the late 19th century. Ciro Biondi took some time out but is now producing again. His austere, agreeable Outis '04, from nerello cappuccio and nerello mascalese, sourced from one of the loveliest vineyards on Etna, made the finals for its elegance and structure.

| ● Etna Outis '04 | 🍷🍷 6 |
| ● Outis '03 | 🍷🍷 5 |

Zenner

VIA PIETRO MASCAGNI, 72
95131 CATANIA [CT]
TEL. 095530560
www.terradellesirene.com

The Zenner winery produces Nero d'Avola only, from well-established, biodynamically cultivated bush-trained vines, some more than 60 years old. The bright, balanced Terra delle Sirene '05 has an evocative fragrance of red berries, with an extra hint of minerality.

| ● Terra delle Sirene '05 | 🍷 5 |
| ● Terra delle Sirene '04 | 🍷🍷 5 |

Zisola

C.DA ZISOLA
96017 NOTO [SR]
TEL. 057773571
www.zisola.it

Filippo and Francesco Mazzei, with skilled technical support from oenologist Carlo Ferrini, continue to develop their Sicilian winery. We confirm the elegance and layered, varietal character of the intense Zisola Nero d'Avola '05, expressed in scents of Mediterranean scrubland and black berries.

| ● Nero d'Avola '05 | 🍷🍷 4 |

SARDINIA

The broad-scale picture from Sardinia is quite simply that four wines have been awarded Three Glasses, which is really good news. The small-scale picture is more that of four smaller areas of growers, their terrain and its ancient indigenous varieties. Alessandro Dettori has been in the limelight for some years now since he always manages to come up with a terrific range of wines. This year it's Dettori Rosso '04, a fascinating Cannonau, that hit the top spot. The grapes are late-picked and grown to biodynamic tenets, a system that is being increasingly talked about, always positively, among those who know. Antichi Poderi di Jerzu is a co-operative that once seemed destined for oblivion. But then some years ago, its managers woke up to market opportunities, rolled up their sleeves and set to work. They gained the support of their member growers and, with assistance from external consultants, managed to turn the winery round and build up an excellent range of wines. So much so that their Three Glass star, Radames '01, a superb Cannonau, is only the icing on the cake. The story is similar at Cantina di Santadi in Sulcis, although the turnaround started earlier. The latest in a long series of Three Glass wines is Carignano del Sulcis Terre Brune Riserva from the excellent '03 vintage. Both these tales show just how much the co-operative sector has to offer when there is a clear-headed approach and a real desire to achieve quality. The fourth Three Glass wine comes from Contini, a long-standing producer whose name is inextricably linked with that of Vernaccia di Oristano, one of the island's great dessert wines. The stunner is Antico Gregori and it's a classic, with no vintage or age. In fact, it's one of the most genuine dessert wines we've tasted in recent years. So we have four excellent wines from four excellent estates. But the way things are going, there's no reason why this number shouldn't double in the next few years for the island's potential for quality is immeasurable. The real Sardinia is a region of great reds, characterful whites and incredibly fascinating dessert wines. It's not about mass-produced, forgettable Vermentinos, or about wines like those from '06 vintage where, unlike the rest of Italy, they refused to shine. All that's needed is a bit more courage in quality-related decision-making. And that is particularly true when it comes to defining DOC regulations. Otherwise, as some have already done, the island's better wines might anachronistically migrate to IGT, or even straight table wine. Let's hope not.

★ Antonio Argiolas
VIA ROMA, 56/58
09040 SERDIANA [CA]
TEL. 070740606
www.cantine-argiolas.it

Capichera
S.S. ARZACHENA-SANT'ANTONIO, KM. 4
07021 ARZACHENA [SS]
TEL. 078980612
www.capichera.it

ANNUAL PRODUCTION 2,000,000 bottles
HECTARES UNDER VINE 230
VITICULTURE METHOD Conventional

ANNUAL PRODUCTION 250,000 bottles
HECTARES UNDER VINE 50
VITICULTURE METHOD Natural

None of the Argiolas wines managed to clinch Three Glasses this year but the range is still impressive, with two wines reaching the finals and some high-scoring new releases of character. First up is Turriga '03, from cannonau with carignano, bovale sardo and malvasia nera. Aromas of ripe fruit lead to a full, meaty, palate which retains balance and zip right through to the finish. Is Solinas '05, from carignano with a little bovale sardo, is also top rate. The nose is richly fruity and the fullness and acid-tannin balance on the palate are surprisingly good. Antonio Argiolas '03 is a new wine, produced to celebrate the centenary of the estate's founder's birth. It is made from semi-dried cannonau and, in small part, malvasia nera, and has ripe red berry fruitiness and a sweet, lively, balanced palate. Angialis '04, from nasco with a little malvasia, is a wine of incomparable finesse. Everything else showed well, especially the round, full, blackberry and plum Korem '05, from bovaleddu, carignano and cannonau. The fruity, fresh, harmonious Vermentino di Sardegna Is Argiolas '06 and Cerdeña '05, from vermentino and other local varieties, are also good.

The fluctuating presence in the Guide of the Ragnedda brothers' winery isn't only a result of our assessments but also stems from their policy decisions, for which we have great respect. One factor, for example, was their decision to take their Vermentino di Gallura out of the DOCG, leaving Vigna 'Ngena as their only denomination-labelled wine. The '06 has a richly aromatic nose with some minerality, and a soft, balanced palate. Santigaini, from vermentino, sold without vintage, is a new wine, and one that hasn't been over-shaped by high-tech winemaking. The nose is a little veiled, but there's plenty of fruit, and the palate is rich and husky. Capichera '05 is in classic style, fresh and vegetal on both nose and palate. The '04 Vendemmia Tardiva is full and fleshy, but notably oaky. Moving on to the reds, we liked Mantènghja '04, from carignano, which has a pervasive, complex nose and a full and lively yet elegant palate. The '04 Assajè, again from carignano, is not as good as previous vintages but is pleasant enough and decently styled.

● Is Solinas '05	♟♟	4*
● Turriga '03	♟♟	7
○ Angialis '04	♟♟	5
● Cannonau di Sardegna Costera '06	♟♟	4*
● Korem '05	♟♟	5
○ Vermentino di Sardegna Costamolino '06	♟♟	3*
● Antonio Argiolas 100 '03	♟♟	8
○ Vermentino di Sardegna Is Argiolas '06	♟♟	4*
⊙ Serralori Rosato '06	♟♟	2*
○ Nuragus di Cagliari S'Elegas '06	♟♟	2*
● Monica di Sardegna Perdera '06	♟♟	3*
○ Cerdeña '05	♟♟	6
○ Angialis '01	♟♟♟	6
● Turriga '99	♟♟♟	8
● Turriga '98	♟♟♟	8
● Turriga '02	♟♟♟	8
● Turriga '01	♟♟♟	8
● Turriga '00	♟♟♟	8
● Korem '04	♟♟	5

○ Capichera Santigaini	♟♟	8
○ Capichera '05	♟♟	8
● Mantènghja '04	♟♟	8
○ Capichera V.T. '04	♟♟	8
○ Vermentino di Gallura Vigna 'Ngena '06	♟♟	7
● Assajè Rosso '04	♟	7
○ Capichera V.T. '00	♟♟♟	7
○ Capichera V.T. '01	♟♟	8
○ Capichera '03	♟♟	7
○ Capichera V.T. '03	♟♟	8
● Assajè Rosso '02	♟♟	6
● Assajè Rosso '03	♟♟	7
○ Vermentino di Gallura Vigna 'Ngena '04	♟♟	6
○ Capichera '04	♟♟	7

Carpante

VIA GARIBALDI, 151
07049 USINI [SS]
TEL. 079380614
info@carpante.it

ANNUAL PRODUCTION 30,000 bottles
HECTARES UNDER VINE 8
VITICULTURE METHOD Conventional

This can't have been an easy year for this newish estate as shifted from three partners to two. Yet there's been no diminishing of enthusiasm, probably helped by the wines' performance to date. These have also given further signs of the potential of the area for great wines, especially those made from the predominant vermentino and cagnulari. Advice from consultant Dino Addis has been pivotal in shaping winemaking decisions and, as a result, the range continues to gain in character and distinction. There are two Vermentino di Sardegnas: Longhera '06, which is fruity with citrus notes and has an attractive palate, and the more impressive, aromatic Frinas '06, which has vegetal and mineral tones, a round, full palate and a long, clean finish. Moving on to the reds, the top wine, Carpante, was not ready in time for our tastings but we did taste an excellent Lizzos '05, from cagnulari, muristellu, cannonau and girò. It's a complex wine. Plum, morello cherry and spiciness come through on the nose even though it is still a little closed, the palate is rich and concentrated, and there's good acid-tannin balance. Cagnulari '06 is a strategic wine for this estate and remarkably good.

Giovanni Cherchi

LOC. SA PALA E SA CHESSA
07049 USINI [SS]
TEL. 079380273
vinicolacherchi@tiscali.it

ANNUAL PRODUCTION 200,000 bottles
HECTARES UNDER VINE 18
VITICULTURE METHOD Conventional

We don't suppose Giovanni Cerchi realized the effect it would have on his homeland when he started to produce Vermentino and Cagnulari. There are now many following his example, and new plantings are returning the landscape to its old appearance. Increasing his cellar space has enabled Cerchi to diversify his range but he has not taken the international route. This year's wines continue the quality improvements of previous years despite the '06 Vermentino Tuvaoes performing less well than the '05. Nonetheless, the wine has a clean, fresh nose and a crisply acidic, attractive palate. The '06 release of the barrique-aged Vermentino, Boghes, showed well, with an intriguing, slightly vegetal nose and a nicely full palate. Most impressive of the reds are Luzzana '05, from cannonau and cagnulari, its nose fruity, mineral and particularly rich, and its palate soft yet powerful and well-balanced. The soft yet vigorous Cannonau di Sardegna '06 is nice, as is the characterful Cagnulari '06, vegetal and red berry fruits notes dominating a richly cohesive nose. The '06 Vermentino Frinas is as good as ever.

● Cagnulari '06	♈♈ 4
○ Vermentino di Sardegna Longhera '06	♈♈ 4*
● Lizzos '05	♈♈ 5
○ Vermentino di Sardegna Frinas '06	♈♈ 5
● Cagnulari '05	♈♈ 4
● Carpante '03	♈♈ 5
○ Vermentino di Sardegna Frinas '05	♈♈ 5
● Cannonau di Sardegna '05	♈♈ 4

○ Boghes '06	♈♈ 6
● Luzzana '05	♈♈ 6
● Cagnulari '06	♈♈ 5
● Cannonau di Sardegna '06	♈♈ 5
○ Vermentino di Sardegna Pigalva '06	♈ 4
○ Vermentino di Sardegna Tuvaoes '06	♈ 5
● Luzzana '02	♈♈ 6
● Soberanu '03	♈♈ 8
○ Boghes '05	♈♈ 6
● Cagnulari '05	♈♈ 5

Attilio Contini

VIA GENOVA, 48/50
09072 CABRAS [OR]
TEL. 0783290806
www.vinicontini.it

ANNUAL PRODUCTION	600,000 bottles
HECTARES UNDER VINE	70
VITICULTURE METHOD	Conventional

Paolo Contini always produces a fine series of wines but every so often something breaks through the barriers and soars. This time it's Antico Gregori. It's an unusual wine, from a blend of the best vintages from several decades. Its amber hue is seductive but its aromas of toasted almonds are even better. The palate is warm and mouthfilling, and very long. The '05 Nieddera is a very good, soft, balanced wine but not as good as the '04 and still a bit too oaky. Cannonau di Sardegna Inu Riserva '04 has more to offer. There's a ripe fruits nose, a soft, slightly tannic palate and good ageing potential. Rosso di Contini '06, from cannonau, sangiovese and nieddera, is a pleasant surprise, showing youthful and lively on nose and palate. The two Niedderas, the '06 rosé and the '05 red, the '05 Cannonau di Sardegna Tonaghe and Karmis '06, based on vernaccia, are all attractive.

Ferruccio Deiana

VIA GIALETO, 7
09040 SETTIMO SAN PIETRO [CA]
TEL. 070749117
www.ferrucciodeiana.it

ANNUAL PRODUCTION	378,000 bottles
HECTARES UNDER VINE	62
VITICULTURE METHOD	Certified organic

Ferruccio Deiana is a man of vitality but he's also withdrawn and private, sometimes to the extent of being shy to talk about his wines. Yet when you taste them, you know that what goes into them is a professionalism that comes from years of experience and real passion. The '04 Ajana, his flagship, from cannonau, carignano and bovale, again nudged Three Glasses. It has notable intensity on the nose with spiciness, ripe fruit and tobacco. There's powerful structure but underlying it is a full, soft wine that is still evolving. Pluminus '06, from vermentino and nasco, is also highly impressive, with good fruit and a nice citrus streak. Best of the traditional styles are easily Vermentino di Sardegna Arvali '06, which has an attractive nose and a zesty palate, and Cannonau di Sardegna Sileno '05, with blackberry and plum aromas and good balance. The other Vermentino, Donnikalia '06, and the lively, fruity Monica di Sardegna Karel '06 are also good. But the '06 is a rather uncertain release of Oirad, from moscato, malvasia and nasco, as it's pleasant and well styled but a bit weak on the nose.

O Vernaccia di Oristano Antico Gregori	♟♟♟ 7
● Cannonau di Sardegna Inu Ris. '04	♟♟ 5
● Rosso di Contini '06	♟♟ 3*
O Karmis '06	♟♟ 4*
● Nieddera Rosso '05	♟♟ 4*
● Cannonau di Sardegna Tonaghe '05	♟♟ 4*
☉ Nieddera Rosato '06	♟♟ 3*
O Pontis '00	♟♟♟ 5
● Nieddera Rosso '04	♟♟ 4*
● Barrile '03	♟♟ 7
● Cannonau di Sardegna Inu Ris. '03	♟♟ 5
O Pontis '03	♟♟ 6
● Cannonau di Sardegna Inu Ris. '02	♟♟ 5

● Ajana '04	♟♟ 7
● Cannonau di Sardegna Sileno '05	♟♟ 4
O Vermentino di Sardegna	
Donnikalia '06	♟♟ 4*
O Vermentino di Sardegna Arvali '06	♟♟ 4
O Pluminus '06	♟♟ 7
● Monica di Sardegna Karel '06	♟♟ 4*
O Oirad '06	♟ 6
● Ajana '02	♟♟♟ 7
● Ajana '01	♟♟ 7
● Ajana '03	♟♟ 7
● Monica di Sardegna Karel '05	♟♟ 4
O Pluminus '05	♟♟ 7
O Oirad '05	♟♟ 6

Tenute Dettori

LOC. BADDE NIGOLOSU
S.P. 29 KM 10
07036 SENNORI [SS]
TEL. 079514711
www.tenutedettori.it

ANNUAL PRODUCTION 45,000 bottles
HECTARES UNDER VINE 18
VITICULTURE METHOD Natural

Let's start with the new Dettori Bianco '06. What's new about this 100 per cent Vermentino is its vinification: there's now long skin maceration, the use of indigenous yeasts, ageing in concrete vats, no sulphur dioxide and no filtration. The result is a wine that's archaic in the best sense of the word, taken back to its essence, yet set ablaze by the stamp of the amazing Sennori terroir. Its aromas are those of the Mediterranean and of citrus. The palate is mineral, almost tannic, yet lively and expressive. But there's more. We were simply bowled over by the '04 Dettori Rosso, from cannonau grown on a fabulous 100-year-old vineyard overlooking the sea. It could convince even the most sceptical. The nose is fantastically concentrated and warm, as would be expected from an area where Cannonau never dips below 15 per cent alcohol, but also supple with enough acidity to give fragrance and a truly satisfying finish. How could it not take Three Glasses? Then there's the best Moscadeddu that has ever come out of Badde Nigolosu, an excellent Tuderi and two real pearls: Renosu Rosso '05, from cannonau, and Renosu Bianco '06, from vermentino and moscato, sold, only in Sardinia, at an attractive price.

● Dettori Rosso '04	🍷🍷🍷	8
○ Dettori Bianco '06	🍷🍷	6
○ Moscadeddu '05	🍷🍷	6
○ Renosu Bianco '06	🍷🍷	3*
● Tuderi '04	🍷🍷	6
● Renosu Rosso '05	🍷🍷	3*
● Tenores '03	YYY	8
● Chimbanta '03	YY	6
● Tuderi '03	YY	6
● Dettori Rosso '02	YY	8
● Ottomarzo '03	YY	6
● Chimbanta '04	YY	6
○ Moscadeddu '04	YY	5
● Dettori Rosso '01	YY	8
○ Dettori Bianco '04	YY	5

Cantine Dolianova

LOC. SAN'ESU
S.S. 387 KM. 17,150
09041 DOLIANOVA [CA]
TEL. 070744101
www.cantinedolianova.com

ANNUAL PRODUCTION 4,000,000 bottles
HECTARES UNDER VINE 1,200
VITICULTURE METHOD Conventional

This winery was once considered one of the island's many co-operatives that had no future but its perseverance in achieving quality has paid off. Now everything is different, from the scrupulous selections in the vineyards to finely tuned production and sales departments. Results are there for all to see. It's not easy to produce such consistently high quality in such large quantities. Let's start with the most emblematic wine, Falconaro '04, from cannonau, carignano and montepulciano. It is rich and complex, with a fruity, spicy nose and a vigorous, full yet elegant palate, and it reached the finals. The balanced, well-structured Terresicci '04, from 85 per cent barbera sarda plus syrah and montepulciano, all red berry fruit and balsam, is highly successful. The youthful Montesicci '06, from vermentino, nasco and malvasia, is just as impressive, with its generous nose and lively, vegetal palate. Cannonau di Sardegna Blasio Riserva '04 is still a little closed on the nose but the palate is clean and full. Best of the rest – all good – are Cannonau di Sardegna Anzenas '05; the rosé Sibioloa '06, from cannonau, sangiovese and montepulciano, and Moscato di Cagliari '06.

● Falconaro '04	🍷🍷	5
● Cannonau di Sardegna Anzenas '05	🍷🍷	3*
● Terresicci '04	🍷🍷	6
○ Nuragus di Cagliari Perlas '06	🍷🍷	3*
⊙ Sibiola '06	🍷🍷	3*
○ Moscato di Cagliari '06	🍷🍷	4
○ Montesicci '06	🍷🍷	4
● Cannonau di Sardegna Blasio Ris. '04	🍷	4
● Cannonau di Sardegna Blasio Ris. '03	YY	4
● Terresicci '03	YY	6
● Falconaro '01	YY	5
○ Montesicci '05	YY	4
● Falconaro '03	YY	5

Cantina Sociale Dorgali

VIA PIEMONTE, 11
08022 DORGALI [NU]
TEL. 078496143
www.csdorgali.com

ANNUAL PRODUCTION 1,600,000 bottles
HECTARES UNDER VINE 63
VITICULTURE METHOD Conventional

The management of this co-operative is
now convinced of its vineyards' potential
and has decided to go for quality in a big
way. They will be focusing on crus and on
cannonau, the area's leading variety. Giving
them a boost in their endeavours is famed
oenologist and red wine specialist Roberto
Cipresso, whose initial work in the vineyards
has been to lower yields and to programme
picking according to zone and degree of
ripeness. All he has been able to do so far
in the cellars is make the most of the wines
already present, and our first tastings show
that he is making good progress. Vinìola
Riserva '04 is the best of the Cannonau di
Sardegnas. It has an intense, concentrated,
nicely fruity nose and a full, rounded palate.
The Filieri '06 and Vigna di Isalle '06 are
fresher. But Fuìli '04, from cannonau,
merlot, syrah and cabernet, is probably the
most complex of the range, with pervasive
aromas of plum and blackberry, and a long,
rounded palate. Norìolo '05 is lively and
attractive.

Feudi della Medusa

LOC. SANTA MARGHERITA
P.RE SAN LEONARDO, 15
09010 PULA [CA]
TEL. 0709259019
www.feudidellamedusa.it

ANNUAL PRODUCTION 250,000 bottles
HECTARES UNDER VINE 70
VITICULTURE METHOD Conventional

Heide and Francesco Siclari didn't just fall in
love with each other but also with their
corner of Sardinia. They love the good life
and good wine and so make every effort to
ensure that their new estate's range is as
good as possible. Helped by their terroir
and their fine winemaking team, the wines
are indeed surprisingly attractive, showing
great complexity although still young and in
development. Norace '05, from cannonau,
carignano, syrah and cabernet sauvignon,
came within a hair of Three Glasses, its
nose rich, concentrated and redolent of
chocolate, its palate elegant yet full and
structured. Gerione '04, from cagnulari,
cabernet franc and syrah, scored almost as
highly. Biddas '05 is vegetal and spicy with
a broad, satisfying palate. Cannonau di
Sardegna '05 has Mediterranean scrubland
on the nose and is intriguing on the palate.
Arrubias is a full, fruity, soft Carignano made
from ungrafted vines. The lively, mineral,
close-knit, barriqued white Sa Perda '05,
from chardonnay and malvasia, is also of
note. Finally come Aristeo '05, from nasco
and malvasia, Cagnulari '06, and Crisaore
'05, from cagnulari and bovale. All are good.

● Cannonau di Sardegna		
V. di Isalle '06	🍷🍷	4*
● Norìolo '05	🍷🍷	4
● Fuìli '04	🍷🍷	5
● Filieri Rosso '06	🍷🍷	2*
● Cannonau di Sardegna		
Vinìola Ris. '04	🍷🍷	5
● Cannonau di Sardegna		
V. di Isalle '02	🍷🍷	3
● Norìolo '01	🍷🍷	4
● Fuìli '98	🍷🍷	5
● Cannonau di Sardegna		
Vinìola Ris. '02	🍷🍷	5
● Cannonau di Sardegna		
V. di Isalle '04	🍷🍷	4*
● Cannonau di Sardegna		
V. di Isalle '03	🍷🍷	4*
● Fuìli '01	🍷🍷	5

● Norace '05	🍷🍷	7
● Arrubias '05	🍷🍷	7
● Biddas '05	🍷🍷	4*
○ Sa Perda Bianca '05	🍷🍷	5
● Gerione '04	🍷🍷	8
● Cannonau di Sardegna '05	🍷🍷	5
○ Aristeo '05	🍷	6
● Crisaore '05	🍷	7
● Cagnulari '06	🍷	5
○ Alba Nora '04	🍷🍷	6
○ Aristeo '04	🍷🍷	6
● Norace '03	🍷🍷	8
● Gerione '03	🍷🍷	8
● Cagnulari '05	🍷🍷	7
● Cannonau di Sardegna '04	🍷🍷	5

Giuseppe Gabbas

via Trieste, 65
08100 Nuoro [NU]
tel. 078433745
ggabbas@tiscali.it

ANNUAL PRODUCTION 70,000 bottles
HECTARES UNDER VINE 13
VITICULTURE METHOD Conventional

Now that Giuseppe Gabbas can bottle his wines in his own, functional cellar, they have become more reliable. The vineyards are in one of the best areas for cannonau and the variety remains his strength even though he has some non-indigenous grapes planted. The sites rise to 500 metres and soils are deep and granite based. All the wines tasted were very good but some really stood out, most notably Arbeskia '04, from cannonau and cabernet sauvignon, which ages two years in barrique. It's initially closed but then opens to give complex aromas of balsam and vanilla interwoven with fruit. The palate has a fair tannic structure and a soft, long finish. Cannonau di Sardegna Dule Riserva '04 is less complex but anything but simple. Ripe fruit and mineral scents mark out the nose. The palate is well-balanced, with good body, acidity and tannin, and a slightly bitterish finish. The youthful, fruity Cannonau di Sardegna Lillové '06 with its lively, savoury palate is also most pleasing.

● Arbeskia '04	TT	5
● Cannonau di Sardegna Dule Ris. '04	TT	4*
● Cannonau di Sardegna Lillové '06	TT	4*
● Arbeskia '00	YY	5
● Arbeskia '02	YY	5
● Arbeskia '03	YY	5
● Cannonau di Sardegna Dule Ris. '01	YY	4*
● Cannonau di Sardegna Dule Ris. '02	YY	4*
● Cannonau di Sardegna Lillové '05	YY	4*
● Cannonau di Sardegna Lillové '03	YY	4*

Cantina Sociale Gallura

via Val di Cossu, 9
07029 Tempio Pausania [SS]
tel. 079631241
www.cantinagallura.com

ANNUAL PRODUCTION 1,350,000 bottles
HECTARES UNDER VINE 350
VITICULTURE METHOD Conventional

Significant changes in corporate structure led to a difficult year for this winery. That aside, Dino Addis has continued to produce good quality wines at very fair prices. The winery's strength continues to be in Vermentino di Gallura, and Genesi '06 is the most characteristic version, with a wealth of citrus and vegetal aromas and a fresh, piquant palate. But the clean, balanced Piras '06 and the simpler but most attractive Mavriana '06 are both first-rate, too. Only Canayli '06 is a touch disappointing. Gemellae '06 is in more traditional style, showing full and soft, with good body, structure and power. There have also been developments with the reds. Cannonau di Sardegna Templum '06 is excellent. Dolmen '04, from nebbiolo with a little sangiovese, is powerful and concentrated but gains refinement from its fresh, fruity aromas. The '06 Karana, from the same grapes plus a little caricagiola, is, as ever, attractive, lively and easy drinking. The sparkling wines are as good as usual, especially the refined, elegant Moscato.

○ Vermentino di Gallura Sup. Genesi '06	TT	6
● Cannonau di Sardegna Templum '06	TT	4*
● Dolmen '04	TT	5
○ Vermentino di Gallura Piras '06	TT	3*
○ Vermentino di Gallura Gemellae '06	TT	3*
○ Vermentino di Gallura Mavriana '06	TT	3*
○ Moscato di Tempio Pausania '06	TT	4*
● Karana Nebbiolo dei Colli del Limbara '06	TT	3*
⊙ Campos '06	T	3
○ Vermentino di Gallura Sup. Canayli '06	T	4
○ Vermentino di Gallura Sup. Genesi '04	YY	6
● Cannonau di Sardegna Templum '04	YY	4*
○ Vermentino di Gallura Sup. Genesi '05	YY	6
○ Vermentino di Gallura Sup. Canayli '05	YY	4*
○ Vermentino di Gallura Piras '05	YY	3*
● Karana Nebbiolo dei Colli del Limbara '05	YY	3*

Cantina del Giogantinu
VIA MILANO, 30
07022 BERCHIDDA [OT]
TEL. 079704163
www.giogantinu.it

ANNUAL PRODUCTION 1,500,000 bottles
HECTARES UNDER VINE 350
VITICULTURE METHOD Conventional

The Giogantinu co-operative continues to grow, both in terms of quality and quantity. The need to capitalize more fully on viticultural assets has led to major cellar refurbishment. Grapes arrive from 350 hectares of vines, many of them still bush-trained, and planted at varying heights, mostly on granite soils. Traditional varieties still dominate although the newer vineyards include some international varieties. Most interest in the wines comes from the whites, especially Vermentino di Gallura Lughente '06, which has a mineral nose and a complex, rounded palate. Vermentino di Gallura Superiore Karenzia '06, broad on the nose and full on the palate, is also good. The late-harvest Lughente Vendemmia Tardiva '05 has aromas of acacia honey and vanilla. The palate is warm and sweet while retaining good acidity. Vermentino di Gallura Superiore '06 is attractive, with almond tones on both nose and palate. The red Nastarrè '06, from pascale and muristellu, is fair.

Antichi Poderi Jerzu
VIA UMBERTO I, 1
08044 JERZU [NU]
TEL. 078270028
www.jerzuantichipoderi.it

ANNUAL PRODUCTION 1,800,000 bottles
HECTARES UNDER VINE 700
VITICULTURE METHOD Conventional

This winery, which perhaps lost sight of the need to bring out the typicity of its wines, has now changed its look and its philosophy. The set-up is attractive, welcoming and functional, and the cellars have been upgraded to enable the production of wines that are modern yet linked with tradition. The territory and its varieties have been the subject of study and this is beginning to bring exciting results. Last year, we liked Radames, made from 60 per cent cannonau plus carignano and cabernet. But this year's '01 is absolutely stunning and won Three Glasses. Oenologist Bernabei decided to go for longer cask and bottle ageing and this has clearly paid off. The nose is fresh and balsamic. The palate is full and harmonious, and has a long, complex finish. Cannonau di Sardegna Marghìa '05 showed very well too, with fresh, clean aromas of ripe fruit that are well reflected on the palate. Cannonau di Sardegna Josto Miglior Riserva '04 is also full of fruit, and has a succulent palate with soft, elegant tannins. Cannonau di Sardegna Chuerra Riserva '04 and Cannonau di Sardegna Bantu '06 are both pleasing.

○ Lughente V. T. '05	▼▼ 6
○ Vermentino di Gallura Lughente '06	▼▼ 4
○ Vermentino di Gallura Sup. Karenzia '06	▼▼ 5
● Nastarrè '06	▼ 3
○ Vermentino di Gallura Sup. '06	▼ 3*
○ Lughente V. T. '03	♀♀ 5
○ Vermentino di Gallura Sup. Karenzia Vigne Storiche '05	♀♀ 5
○ Vermentino di Gallura Lughente '05	♀♀ 4*
○ Vermentino di Gallura Sup. '05	♀♀ 3*

● Radames '01	▼▼▼ 6
● Cannonau di Sardegna Marghìa '05	▼▼ 4*
● Cannonau di Sardegna Josto Miglior Ris. '04	▼▼ 5
● Cannonau di Sardegna Chuerra Ris. '04	▼ 5
● Cannonau di Sardegna Bantu '06	▼ 4
● Akratos '03	♀♀ 5
● Radames '99	♀♀ 5
● Radames '00	♀♀ 6
● Cannonau di Sardegna Marghìa '04	♀♀ 4
● Cannonau di Sardegna Ris. Chuerra '01	♀♀ 5

Alberto Loi

s.s. 125 km. 124,200
08040 Cardedu [NU]
tel. 070240866
www.cantina.it/albertoloi

Piero Mancini

loc. Cala Saccaia
07026 Olbia [SS]
tel. 078950717
www.pieromancini.it

ANNUAL PRODUCTION 240,000 bottles
HECTARES UNDER VINE 63
VITICULTURE METHOD Conventional

ANNUAL PRODUCTION 1,400,000 bottles
HECTARES UNDER VINE 100
VITICULTURE METHOD Conventional

The Loi siblings have come out with two new wines: an excellent white, Vermentino di Sardegna Theria '06, with a very fresh, fruity, vegetal nose, and a soft, full palate; and a distinctive red, Monica di Sardegna Nibaru '05, which has a youthful, small red berry fruits nose and a pleasing, clean, lively palate. Astangia '04, from cannonau, carignano, bovale and monica, has evolved fruitiness on the nose and similar characteristics on the palate, as does Loi Corona '03, from cannonau, carignano, muristellu and cabernet sauvignon. Better things come from Cannonau Alberto Loi Riserva '03 with its spicy nose and warm, full palate. Cannonau Cardedo Riserva '04 also impresses, giving a ripe fruits nose and mineral palate. There is, though, still some oakiness on Tuvara '03, from cannonau, carignano and muristellu, although it has good acid-tannin balance, bringing it notable structure. Cannonau Sa Mola '05 is simpler, centring on youthful liveliness on both nose and palate. Finally comes the intriguing Leila '05, from cannonau, vermentino and arvesiniadu, a late-harvest wine with aromas of honey, citrus and ripe fruit, and an attractive, warm, rounded, long palate.

Mancini is now up and running. The wines have found their style and their quality is dependable. Three wines are particularly good this year: the warm, spicy, mineral Cannonau di Sardegna '05; the intense, penetrating Vermentino di Sardegna Saraina '06 with its fresh aromas and its soft, mouthfilling, long palate; and the complex Antiche Cussorgie Rosso '05, from cabernet sauvignon, merlot and cannonau. Saccaia, from cabernet sauvignon and cannonau, also retains its appeal, with captivating aromas of blackberry and ripe plum, and good texture, warmth and tannic balance. Vermentino di Gallura Cucaione '06 has almond blossom aromas and a fresh palate. Vermentino di Sardegna '06 is clean with good backbone and the rosé Montepino '06 is fresh and attractive. All three are inviting.

● Cannonau di Sardegna Jerzu Alberto Loi Ris. '03	ŸŸ 5
● Cannonau di Sardegna Jerzu Cardedo Ris. '04	ŸŸ 4
○ Leila V. T. '05	ŸŸ 5
○ Vermentino di Sardegna Theria '06	ŸŸ 3*
● Astangia '04	Ÿ 5
● Cannonau di Sardegna Jerzu Sa Mola '05	Ÿ 4*
● Tuvara '03	Ÿ 6
● Monica di Sardegna Nibaru '05 ●	Ÿ 3
● Loi Corona '03	Ÿ 6
● Tuvara '01	ŸŸ 6
● Astangia '03	ŸŸ 5
● Cannonau di Sardegna Jerzu Alberto Loi Ris. '02	ŸŸ 5
● Loi Corona '01	ŸŸ 6
● Tuvara '02	ŸŸ 6
● Cannonau di Sardegna Jerzu Alberto Loi Ris. '01	ŸŸ 5
● Loi Corona '02	ŸŸ 6

● Cannonau di Sardegna '05	ŸŸ 4*
● Antiche Cussorgie Rosso '05	ŸŸ 6
○ Vermentino di Gallura Saraina '06	ŸŸ 5
⊙ Montepino '06	Ÿ 4
● Saccaia	Ÿ 4
○ Vermentino di Gallura Cucaione '06	Ÿ 4
○ Vermentino di Sardegna '06	Ÿ 3
● Cannonau di Sardegna '04	ŸŸ 4*
● Saccaia '02	ŸŸ 3*
○ Vermentino di Gallura Saraina '05	ŸŸ 5
● Saccaia '02	ŸŸ 3*
● Saccaia '01	ŸŸ 3*
● Antiche Cussorgie '04	ŸŸ 6
● Antiche Cussorgie '03	ŸŸ 6

Masone Mannu

C.SO UMBERTO, 46
07026 OLBIA [SS]
TEL. 078947140
www.masonemannu.com

ANNUAL PRODUCTION 110,000 bottles
HECTARES UNDER VINE 17
VITICULTURE METHOD Conventional

Masone Mannu lies on granite soils just outside Olbia and produces a distinctive range of wines from indigenous and international grape varieties. "Mannu" means grand in the Sardinian dialect and Mannu '05 is a complex blend of traditional varieties – 40 per cent bovale sardo, 30 per cent of each of cannonau and carignano – which still gives an international style wine. It's full of ripe fruit, most notably blackberry, with minerality, pepper and chocolate. The palate is powerful and firmly impressive, yet soft, and finishes on a slightly bitterish note. Ammentu '05, from late-picked, botrytized vermentino and malvasia, some dried on the vine, is another excellent wine. Aromas of toasted almond and dried fig lead to a warm, pervasive palate with great length. Best of the whites is a first-rate Vermentino di Gallura Superiore Costarenas '06. This has a tropical fruits and melon nose with vegetal hints, and a warm palate of good intensity, enlivened by an acid backbone that brings depth to the attractive finish. The other Vermentino di Gallura, Petrizza '06, is in a lower key, showing simple, fruity and easy drinking.

Mesa

LOC. SU BARONI
09010 SANT'ANNA ARRESI [CI]
TEL. 0781689390
info@cantinamesa.it

ANNUAL PRODUCTION N.A.
HECTARES UNDER VINE 50
VITICULTURE METHOD Conventional

After Mesa's exciting debut last year, with two wines in the finals, it is now clear that it is one of the most promising estates in Sardinia. Its strengths are dynamism and professionalism, and the soils and climate are further assets. Although things are still at an early stage, the owners seem already to have learnt how to marry tradition and innovation, and how to raise the profile of indigenous varieties, whether used singly or blended. Two of the wines stand out: Malombra '05, from carignano and syrah, which has a ripe fruits, spices and vanilla nose, and an elegant and soft if rather undeveloped palate; and Buio Buio '05, from 100 per cent carignano, which is still young but a balsamic, mineral, full, satisfying wine with great depth of flavour. Cannonau di Sardegna Moro '06 is also of note, with a youthful, lively nose and an attractive, long palate. Buoi '05, from 100 per cent carignano, has ripe blackberry fragrance and vegetal notes, followed by a firm, well-balanced palate. Best of the whites is the fruitily aromatic Opale Barricato '05, from vermentino and chardonnay, which is full, powerful and rounded. The Vermentinos Opale '06 and Giunco '06 are also good. Rosa Grande '06 is fair.

○ Ammentu '05	♟♟ 6
● Mannu '05	♟♟ 8
○ Vermentino di Gallura Sup. Costarenas '06	♟♟ 5
○ Vermentino di Gallura Petrizza '06	♟ 4
● Entu '04	♟♟ 4
○ Ammentu '04	♟♟ 5
○ Costarenas '05	♟♟ 5
● Mannu '04	♟♟ 7
○ Ammentu '04	♟♟ 5
● Mannu '03	♟♟ 5
● Entu '05	♟♟ 5

● Malombra '05	♟♟ 7
● Buio Buio '05	♟♟ 5
● Cannonau di Sardegna Moro '06	♟♟ 5
○ Opale Barricato '05	♟♟ 5
○ Opale '06	♟ 5
☉ Rosa Grande '06	♟ 4
● Buio '05	♟ 4
○ Giunco '06	♟ 4
● Buio Buio '04	♟♟ 5
● Malombra '04	♟♟ 7
● Cannonau di Sardegna Moro '04	♟♟ 5

F.lli Pala
VIA VERDI, 7
09040 SERDIANA [CA]
TEL. 070740284
www.pala.it

ANNUAL PRODUCTION 400,000 bottles
HECTARES UNDER VINE 58
VITICULTURE METHOD   Natural

There's nothing to complain about in this performance from the Pala siblings' wines. For some time now they have been better known outside the island than on it, not because the siblings turn their noses up at the local market but because they feel the need to compete elsewhere to gain a fuller understanding of the extent of their wines' potential. Results so far have been highly satisfying. Top of the tree is still S'Arai, a blend of cannonau, carignano, barbera sarda and bovale, and the '04 has a wealth of broad, intense aromas of ripe fruit and balsam with well integrated oak. The palate is soft, full and elegant, and has a long, clean finish. The '06 release of Entemari, made from vermentino, chardonnay and malvasia, is also good. The nose is vegetal and fragrant, the palate soft and long. Two more fine '06s are Nuragus Salnico, which has tropical fruits aromas and a fresh, enticing palate, and the savoury, still youthful Monica di Sardegna Elima. The '06 Vermentino di Sardegna Stellato is as inviting as usual. The vegetal, full, still slightly tannic Essentija '05, from 100 per cent bovale, is attractive, as is Assoluto '06, made from nasco and vermentino.

Pedres
Z.I. SETTORE 7
07026 OLBIA [SS]
TEL. 0789595075
www.cantinapedres.it

ANNUAL PRODUCTION 300,000 bottles
HECTARES UNDER VINE 40
VITICULTURE METHOD   Conventional

Pedres is a winery that continues to expand, with new wines being produced each year. Some of the vineyards are planted in the Gallura foothills while others are at higher altitudes further inland. Soils are sandy and so vermentino takes the lion's share of plantings, accounting for 80 per cent of total production. The rest comes from moscato, cannonau and other indigenous and international varieties. The best of the wines submitted were white, most notably Vermentino di Gallura Plebi '06. This has a highly concentrated, floral, citrus nose, and a fleshy, rich palate with good balance between acidity and softness. The other two Vermentino di Galluras, Jaldinu '06 and Superiore Thilibas '06, are simpler but good nonetheless, characterized by cleanliness and drinkability. Maranto '04, from sangiovese, cabernet and syrah, is attractive with a ripe fruits nose and a soft, balanced, slightly tannic palate. Moscato di Sardegna Spumante Dolce is delicious, all elegant fruitiness and inviting drinkability. Lu Gadduresu Spumante Brut is good.

O Entemari '06	▼▼ 5
● Monica di Sardegna Elima '06	▼▼ 3*
● S'Arai '04	▼▼ 6
O Vermentino di Sardegna Stellato '06	▼▼ 4
O Nuragus di Cagliari Sálnico '06	▼▼ 3*
O Assoluto '06	▼ 5
● Cannonau di Sardegna Triente '06	▼ 4
● Essentija '05	▼ 4
O Assoluto '05	♈ 5
O Entemari '05	♈ 5
O Vermentino di Sardegna Stellato '05	♈ 4*
● S'Arai '03	♈ 5
● S'Arai '02	♈ 5

O Moscato di Sardegna Spumante Dolce	▼▼ 5
O Vermentino di Gallura Plebi '06	▼▼ 4
O Lu Gadduresu Spumante Brut	▼ 4
● Maranto '04	▼ 4
O Vermentino di Gallura Jaldinu '06	▼ 4
O Vermentino di Gallura Sup. Thilibas '06	▼ 4
O Vermentino di Gallura Sup. Thilibas '04	♈ 4

Cantina Sociale Santa Maria La Palma

LOC. SANTA MARIA LA PALMA
07041 ALGHERO [SS]
TEL. 079999008
www.santamarialapalma.it

ANNUAL PRODUCTION 3,500,000 bottles
HECTARES UNDER VINE 750
VITICULTURE METHOD Conventional

The Santa Maria La Palma co-operative has been in operation for almost 50 years and it now has over 300 members cultivating more than 700 hectares. This gives a clear idea of potential output but, such figures aside, it is also worth remembering that the flagship wine, Aragosta, is a wine that has been on the market for 45 years. And throughout this entire period it has been one of the most consistent and one of the best-value wines. So it's right it should lead our reviews. The '06 has fresh, vegetal aromas and a palate rendered attractive by balancing acidity. The other Vermentinos, both the lemony, perfumed Papiri '06 and Blu '06, with its fresh nose and soft palate, are nicely made. Yet we found more interest on the reds, in particular Alghero Cagnulari '05, which has eucalyptus-like balsamic aromas and a well-structured, pleasantly soft palate, and the harmonious, balanced, excellently priced Cannonau di Sardegna Le Bombarde '06. Monica di Sardegna '06 is attractively spicy. Cannonau di Sardegna '03 is good.

Cantina Sociale di Santadi

VIA CAGLIARI, 78
09010 SANTADI [CI]
TEL. 0781950127
www.cantinadisantadi.it

ANNUAL PRODUCTION 1,700,000 bottles
HECTARES UNDER VINE 606
VITICULTURE METHOD Conventional

Santadi is one of Sardinia's most noted co-operatives and this has been an important year, as three of its wines reached the finals. Indeed, its most classic red, Carignano del Sulcis Superiore Terre Brune '03, went even further and took Three Glasses. The aromas range across hay, jam and mineral notes. The palate is deep, dense and powerful. The other Carignano, Rocca Rubia Riserva '04, didn't quite breach the Three Glass barrier but is still a very fine wine, with a ripe plum and blackberry nose and a full, savoury palate. Latinia '04 is also superlative, with honeyed, citrus aromas and a soft, elegant palate leading to a long, appealing finish. Shardana '03, from carignano and syrah, is a further wine of note. Dried flowers and coffee lead to a palate with noticeable but well-judged oak and a long finish. The aromas on Araja '05, made from carignano and sangiovese, evoke black berry fruits, preceding a soft, balanced palate. Antigua '06 is one of the most enjoyable Monica di Sardegnas of the year. The '05 releases of Carignano Grotta Rossa and the vegetal, fresh, harmonious Villa di Chiesa, from vermentino and chardonnay, are as good as ever. The rest of the range is OK.

● Alghero Cagnulari '05	♥♥ 5
● Cannonau di Sardegna Le Bombarde '06	♥♥ 4*
○ Vermentino di Sardegna Aragosta '06	♥♥ 3*
● Cannonau di Sardegna '03	♥ 4
○ Vermentino di Sardegna Blu '06	♥ 3
○ Vermentino di Sardegna I Papiri '06	♥ 4
● Monica di Sardegna '06	♥ 3
● Alghero Cagnulari '04	♥♥ 5
● Cannonau di Sardegna Ris. '02	♥♥ 5

● Carignano del Sulcis Sup. Terre Brune '03	♥♥♥ 7
● Carignano del Sulcis Rocca Rubia Ris. '04	♥♥ 5
○ Latinia '04	♥♥ 6
● Araja '05	♥♥ 4
○ Villa di Chiesa '05	♥♥ 6
● Shardana '03	♥♥ 6
● Monica di Sardegna Antigua '06	♥♥ 3*
● Carignano del Sulcis Grotta Rossa '05	♥♥ 3*
○ Nuragus di Cagliari Pedraia '06	♥ 3
○ Vermentino di Sardegna Villa Solais '06	♥ 3*
○ Vermentino di Sardegna Cala Silente '06	♥ 4
● Carignano del Sulcis Sup. Terre Brune '00	♥♥♥ 7
○ Latinia '01	♥♥♥ 5
● Carignano del Sulcis Sup. Terre Brune '98	♥♥♥ 6
● Carignano del Sulcis Sup. Terre Brune '01	♥♥♥ 7
● Araja '04	♥♥ 4*
○ Latinia '02	♥♥ 6

Sardus Pater
VIA RINASCITA, 46
09017 SANT'ANTIOCO [CA]
TEL. 0781800274
www.cantinesarduspater.com

Tenute Sella & Mosca
LOC. I PIANI
07041 ALGHERO [SS]
TEL. 079997700
www.sellaemosca.com

ANNUAL PRODUCTION 500,000 bottles
HECTARES UNDER VINE 300
VITICULTURE METHOD Conventional

ANNUAL PRODUCTION 7,000,000 bottles
HECTARES UNDER VINE 540
VITICULTURE METHOD Conventional

The Sardus Pater co-operative was set up over 50 years ago and now has 300 members scattered across the whole of Sulcis. Together they own more than 300 hectares of vines, many of them bush trained and ungrafted. This provides an excellent source of grapes that are highly concentrated in colour and sugars, and in times past the wines were sold in bulk to markets in Italy and abroad. But now the whole focus of production has changed, to great effect. One of the most compelling examples is Carignano del Sulcis Nur '06, a wine of great structure. The nose has ripe fruit, jam and balsamic notes. The palate is austere but also soft and appealing. The real revelation, though, is another Carignano, Arruga '04, aged ten months in barrique, a new wine which went straight into the finals. There are intense aromas nuanced with mineral and spicy notes and the succulent palate is softly tannic and long. The '06 releases of Monica Insula and Carignano Is Solus are as good as ever but the '05 Carignano Kanai is a little disappointing as the nose seems over-evolved, although the palate is nicely savoury. Lugore '06 and Terre Fenice '06, both Vermentino, showed well.

It was a close run thing but we didn't award Three Glasses to the two wines which reached the finals. We were still very impressed by the entire range. Ownership of the winery changed some years ago but not the highly skilled, established winemaking team. Let's start our review with the two finalists: the classic Anghelu Ruju and Medeus '05. The former is made only in good vintages and is produced from cannonau aged for six years or more in large old oak botti. The '00 is one of the best releases for decades. The nose has remarkable depth and intensity, with spices and walnutskin, and the palate is inviting. Medeus '05 comes from a blend of merlot, carignano, cannonau and cabernet sauvignon. Florality and balsam lead to an intriguing, full palate. The other reds showed well, especially Alghero Tanca Farr‡ '03, which has a vegetal nose and a soft, lively palate. Vanilla from the oak remains on Carignano del Sulcis Terre Rare Riserva '03. Both Raim '04, from carignano and merlot, and Cannonau di Sardegna Riserva '04 are less complex but still well made. There's a little more excitement on Alghero Rosato Oleandro '06 and Alghero Torbato Terre Bianche '06. But nothing was less than successful.

- Carignano del Sulcis Sup.
  Arruga '04 ᵀᵀ 6
- Carignano del Sulcis Is Solus '06 ᵀᵀ 4*
- Vermentino di Sardegna Lugore '06 ᵀᵀ 4
- Monica di Sardegna Insula '06 ᵀᵀ 4*
- Carignano del Sulcis Nur '06 ᵀᵀ 4*
- Carignano del Sulcis Kanai '05 ᵀ 4
- Vermentino di Sardegna
  Terre Fenice '06 ᵀ 3
- Carignano del Sulcis Is Solus '05 ♉ 4
- Carignano del Sulcis
  Kanai Ris. '03 ♉ 4
- Vermentino di Sardegna
  Lugore '05 ♉ 4
- Monica di Sardegna Insula '05 ♉ 3

- Alghero Anghelu Ruju '00 ᵀᵀ 6
- Medeus '05 ᵀᵀ 6
- Alghero Rosato Oleandro '06 ᵀᵀ 4*
- Alghero Torbato Terre Bianche '06 ᵀᵀ 4
- Alghero Tanca Farrà '03 ᵀᵀ 5
- Alghero Le Arenarie '06 ᵀ 4
- Vermentino di Sardegna La Cala '06 ᵀ 4
- Raim '04 ᵀ 4
- Carignano del Sulcis Terre Rare Ris. '03 ᵀ 4
- Cannonau di Sardegna Ris. '04 ᵀ 4
- Alghero Marchese di Villamarina '00 ♉♉ 7
- Alghero Marchese di Villamarina '93 ♉♉ 7
- Alghero Marchese di Villamarina '95 ♉♉ 7
- Alghero Marchese di Villamarina '97 ♉♉ 6
- Alghero Marchese di Villamarina '99 ♉♉ 6
- Alghero Marchese di Villamarina '01 ♉♉ 7

Tenute Soletta

LOC. SIGNOR'ANNA
07040 CODRONGIANOS [SS]
TEL. 079435067
www.tenutesoletta.it

ANNUAL PRODUCTION 100,000 bottles
HECTARES UNDER VINE 15
VITICULTURE METHOD Conventional

Tenute Soletta is a family-run estate which has been active for little more than a decade, its focus firmly set on high quality wines from indigenous varieties. Dolce Valle Moscato Passito again reached the finals, this year with the '04. The grapes are dried before crushing – some on the vine, some on rush mats – and yields are kept very low, not exceeding 50 quintals per hectare. The wine has broad, intense aromas of flowers and Mediterranean plants, curry plant and bay in particular. The fine palate is sweet but not cloying, and elegant and appealing right to the finish. The admirable Cannonau di Sardegna Riserva '04 has a richly fruity nose with mineral tones, and a balanced, harmonious palate. Cannonau di Sardegna Firmadu '05 is along similar lines but shows rather more evolved on the nose and the palate is warmer and softer. Vermentino di Sardegna Prestizu '06 is fresh and citrus-like on both nose and palate. The '05 Kianos, from vermentino, incrocio Manzoni, riesling and pinot bianco, has suffered from the disappointing vintage. The nose is light and the palate a touch over-evolved. The rosé Petalo '06 is a good, fresh, easy-drinking wine.

Cantine Surrau

S.P. ARZACHENA - PORTO CERVO
07021 ARZACHENA [SS]
TEL. 078982933
info@vignesurrau.it

ANNUAL PRODUCTION 120,000 bottles
HECTARES UNDER VINE 20
VITICULTURE METHOD Conventional

This new estate makes its first appearance in the Guide. It was set up by the Demuro family, partly to preserve family traditions but also because they were driven by great enthusiasm. There are about 20 hectares under vine on granite soils not far from the coast, planted with vermentino, cannonau, cabernet sauvignon, carignano and muristellu. The cellars are modern and highly functional, with significant production capacity, and hold a fair number of 900-litre tonneaux. The aim is to produce wines that are modern while retaining the stamp of tradition. The best of the range is Barriu '05, from cannonau, cabernet, carignano and muristellu, which ages about a year in oak. The nose is full, with salty, vegetal notes, but there's more interest on the palate which is soft, well-structured and has good acid-tannin balance. Surrau '06 is a younger, non-oaked version of the same blend, and is appealingly fresh with blackberry aromas. Cannonau di Sardegna Sincaru '06 is a good wine but still closed. Vermentino di Gallura Sciala '06 is a bit too lean compared with the denomination's best wines.

O Dolce Valle Moscato Passito '04	♥♥	4*
● Cannonau di Sardegna Firmadu '05	♥♥	4*
O Kianos '05	♥♥	5
● Cannonau di Sardegna Ris. '04	♥♥	4
⊙ Petalo Rosato '06	♥	3
O Vermentino di Sardegna Prestizu '06	♥	4
O Dolce Valle Moscato Passito '03	♥♥	4*
● Cannonau di Sardegna Firmadu '03	♥♥	4*
● Cannonau di Sardegna Ris. '03	♥♥	4
● Cannonau di Sardegna Firmadu '02	♥♥	4*
O Kianos '04	♥♥	5
O Dolce Valle Moscato Passito '02	♥♥	4
O Dolce Valle Moscato Passito '01	♥♥	4

● Barriu '05	♥♥	6
● Cannonau di Sardegna '06	♥	6
O Vermentino di Gallura Sciala '06	♥	5
● Surrau '06	♥	5

OTHER WINERIES

Agricola Punica
LOC. BARRUA
09010 SANTADI [CI]
TEL. 0781953007
agripunica@tiscali.it

It's early days here but the winery has all it takes to compete with the big boys. The Tachis touch is apparent and Barrua '04, from carignano, merlot and cabernet, is a great little wine. It's still developing but the nose is broad and pervasive. Vegetal and vanilla notes come through on nose and palate.

● Barrua '04	▼▼ 6

Cantina Arvisionadu
VIA LODI, 4
07010 BENETUTTI [SS]
TEL. 079796947
chessadomenico@virgilio.it

The always interesting wines from this small estate are made from rare varieties. Lesitanus '06, soft and stylish on the nose, is from 100 per cent arvisionadu. Labirintu '06 comes from arvisionadu, vermentino and caricagiola while Contraruia '06 is from muristellu, cannonau, cagnulari and carignano.

O Lesitanus '06	▼▼ 4
O Labirintu '06	▼ 4
● Contraruia '06	▼ 4

Cantina di Calasetta
VIA ROMA, 134
09011 CALASETTA [CI]
TEL. 078188413
www.cantinacalasetta.com

We are pleased to see further improvements here that will raise the profile of Carignano del Sulcis. Tupei '06 is a fine wine, with a rich nose of fruit preserve over a balsamic base, and a full, firm palate. Piede Franco '06 is less concentrated but balanced. Moscato di Cagliari In Fundu '06 is attractive.

● Carignano del Sulcis Tupei '06	▼▼ 4
● Carignano del Sulcis Piede Franco '06	▼ 4
O Moscato di Cagliari In Fundu '06	▼ 4

Cantina Sociale di Castiadas
LOC. OLIA SPECIOSA
09040 CASTIADAS [CA]
TEL. 0709949004
www.castiadasonline.it

Two lovely wines reflect the fine potential of the territory here and the winery's quest for high quality. Cannonau di Sardegna Capo Ferrato Rei '03 has a balsamic nose and a pleasant, lively palate. The '03 Riserva is fuller, with more body. It's rounded and redolent of Mediterranean scrubland and ripe fruit.

● Cannonau di Sardegna Capo Ferrato Rei '03	▼▼ 4
● Cannonau di Sardegna Capo Ferrato Ris. '03	▼▼ 4*

Chessa
VIA SAN GIORGIO
07049 USINI [SS]
TEL. 3283747069
www.cantinechessa.it

This is a new estate run by young Giovanna Chessa, who cultivates her family's old vineyards with enthusiasm and passion. Vermentino di Sardegna Mattariga '06 comes from her hillside cru's calcareous soils where it grows with cagnulari and moscato. It's fresh and warm, full of fruit and vegetal notes.

O Vermentino di Sardegna Mattariga '06	▼▼ 4

Columbu
VIA MARCONI, 1
08013 BOSA [NU]
TEL. 0785373380
www.vinibosa.com

What we like about Battista Columbu is the way he produces wine simply with respect for tradition and how he communicates this better than most. The very nice Malvasia di Bosa '04 has an evolved nose and a complex palate with a long finish. The more youthful Planargia Alvarega '06 has great character.

O Malvasia di Bosa '04	▼▼ 7
O Planargia Alvarega '06	▼▼ 6

OTHER WINERIES

Deidda

S.S. 388, KM 7.200
09088 SIMAXIS [OR]
TEL. 0783406142
www.cantinadeidda.it

Giampiero Deidda has added some promising reds to his range but it's the classic method sparklers, notably Marzani Brut, that are his real strength. The soft, balanced Cannonau di Sardegna Mariano IV Riserva '04 is excellent. Simmaco '03, from cannonau and carignano, and Cannonau Arcais '05 are both good.

- Cannonau Mariano IV Ris. '04   ♈♈ 4
- Cannonau Arcais '05   ♈ 3
- Simmaco '03   ♈ 5
- O Marzani Brut M. Cl.   ♈ 5

Paolo Depperu

LOC. SAS RUINAS
07025 LURAS [OT]
TEL. 079647314
azienda.depperu@tiscali.it

There's new lustre from Depperu with a new red, Kabaradis '04, from 100 per cent nebbiolo and aged 12 months in barrique. The complex nose gives red berry fruit, spices and pencil lead. The palate is full and deep with balanced tannin. The '06 Ruinas, made from vermentino only, is as good as ever.

- O Ruinas '06   ♈♈ 5
- Kabaradis '04   ♈♈ 5

Gostolai

VIA FRIULI VENEZIA GIULIA, 24
08025 OLIENA [NU]
TEL. 0784288417
gostolai.arcadu@tiscali.it

The estate is small but its range is large, mostly cannonau-based reds. One of them, Nepente Riserva '03, is the best we tasted this year, with a ripe fruits and vegetal nose, and a balanced palate. Sos Usos De Una la '01 is a little over-evolved. A Medas Annos '05, from moscato, is soft and honeyed.

- Cannonau di Sardegna
  Nepente di Oliena Ris. '03   ♈♈ 5
- O A Medas Annos '05   ♈♈ 4
- Cannonau di Sardegna Nepente
  di Oliena Sos Usos de Una la '01   ♈ 4

Antonella Ledà d'Ittiri

LOC. ARENOSLI, 29
07100 ALGHERO [SS]
TEL. 3292528891
www.margallo.it

This has been an unsettled year for this newish estate, which clearly has the potential for further improvement. Margallò '05, from cabernet, merlot and sangiovese, has restrained aromas of ripe fruit. The palate is pleasant with fair balance.

- Margallò '05   ♈ 4

Li Duni

LOC. LI PARISI
07030 BADESI [SS]
TEL. 079585844
www.cantinaliduni.it

We have never tasted a late-harvest Vermentino di Sardegna like Nozzinnà '05. The grapes come from old, ungrafted, bush-trained vineyards. The nose is concentrated, with citrus, ripe fruit and curry plant. The palate is warm and rich-textured, but not cloying, and finishes long.

- O Vermentino di Sardegna
  Nozzinnà '05   ♈♈ 5

Li Seddi

VIA MARE, 29
07030 BADESI [SS]
TEL. 079683052
www.cantinaliseddi.it

This small winery, with attractive vineyards overlooking the northern coastline, continues to advance. So far, there are two reds. Petra Ruja '06, from cannonau, bovale, monica and girò, is youthful and lively. Lu Ghiali '06, from cannonau and muristellu, has a more concentrated nose but a slimmer palate.

- Petra Ruja '06   ♈♈ 4
- Lu Ghiali '06   ♈ 5

OTHER WINERIES

Cantina Sociale del Mandrolisai
C.SO IV NOVEMBRE, 20
08038 SORGONO [NU]
TEL. 078460113
www.mandrolisai.com

Given the potential of the lands around here, we continue to feel that there's more to be had from this winery. The vineyards grow a miscellany of indigenous grapes. The warm, full Kent'Annos '02, with morello cherry and plum, is top of the bunch. Mandrolisai '04 is well made and easy drinking.

● Kent'Annos '02	♀♀	5
● Mandrolisai Rosso '04	♀	3

Melis
VIA SANTA SUINA, 20
09098 TERRALBA [OR]
TEL. 0783851090
melis.vini@tiscali.it

This is another estate concentrating on indigenous grapes, bovale in particular. It has 27 hectares planted on alluvial plains. Our tastings confirm reasonable quality across the board, led by Vermentino localia '06, Terralba Dominariu '04, a red from bovale, and Malvasia Spumante Dolce.

○ Vermentino di Sardegna localia '06	♀	4
○ Malvasia Spumante	♀	5
● Terralba Dominariu '04	♀	5

Meloni Vini
VIA GALLUS, 79
09047 SELARGIUS [CA]
TEL. 070852822
www.melonivini.com

The Meloni Vini range performed reasonably well again. Vermentino di Sardegna Salike '06 is appealing on both nose and palate. Monica di Sardegna Jaccia '06 is youthfully enticing. Cannonau di Sardegna Terreforru '05 has a fruity nose with mineral notes and a full, broad palate.

● Cannonau di Sardegna Terreforru '05	♀♀	3*
● Monica di Sardegna Jaccia '06	♀	3*
○ Vermentino di Sardegna Salike '06	♀	3*

Maria Giovanna Mulas
VIA G.A. MURA, 16
07011 BONO [SS]
TEL. 0797949077
www.arvesiniadu.com

Mulas, which became known for the indigenous white variety arvesiniadu, returns to the Guide. There are two clean, intense wines: the sweet Avrè '05, with rather delicate aromas and fair nose-palate harmony, and the simpler, less intense, dry Niadu '05.

○ Niadu '05	♀	4
○ Avrè '05	♀	4

Mura
LOC. AZZANIDÒ, 1
07020 LOIRI PORTO SAN PAOLO [OT]
TEL. 078941070
www.vinimura.it

There's good news at Mura. Jara '05, from cannonau, carignano, bovale and cabernet sauvignon, has nice fruit and an enticing palate. Cannonau Cortes '06 is pleasing, although still young. Vermentino di Gallura Cheremi '06 is the best white. The other Vermentino, Sienda '06, is well styled but a little uninspiring.

● Jara '05	♀♀	4*
○ Vermentino di Gallura Cheremi '06	♀♀	4*
● Cannonau di Sardegna Cortes '06	♀	4
○ Vermentino di Gallura Sup. Sienda '06	♀	4

Cantina Sociale Il Nuraghe
S.S. 131 KM 62
09095 MOGORO [OR]
TEL. 0783990285
www.ilnuraghe.it

There's another good performance for this winery this time and the range is decent, focusing on semidano, which goes into the Superiore Puisteris '05. The nose is full but the palate is a touch aggressive. Vermentino di Sardegna Don Giovanni '06 is more balanced. Moscato di Cagliari Capodolce '05 is good.

○ Moscato di Cagliari Capodolce '05	♀	4
○ Vermentino di Sardegna Don Giovanni '06	♀	4
○ Sardegna Semidano Mogoro Sup. Puisteris '05	♀	5

OTHER WINERIES

Tenute Olbios
LOC. VENAFIORITA
VIA LOIRI, 83
07026 OLBIA [SS]
TEL. 0789641003
info@tenuteolbios.com

There have been notable improvements here. But, considering the territory's potential, this is hardly surprising. Vermentino di Sardegna Lupus in Fabula '06 has all the characteristics of a great Gallura white. The palate is warm and rounded but there's fragrance and lemony notes which bring it elegance.

O Vermentino di Sardegna	
Lupus in Fabula '06	♟♟ 5

Cantina Cooperativa di Oliena
VIA NUORO, 112
08025 OLIENA [NU]
TEL. 0784287509
www.cantinasocialeoliena.it

It was Nepente '06, enticingly youthful, lively and full-bodied, which most impressed us from the Cannonau di Sardegnas produced at this co-operative. Corrasi Riserva '04 has an overripe, balsamic nose and a palate that gains warmth and roundness from its high degree of alcohol.

● Cannonau di Sardegna	
Nepente di Oliena '06	♟♟ 4*
● Cannonau di Sardegna Corrasi	
Nepente di Oliena Ris. '04	♟ 5

Pedra Majore
VIA ROMA, 106
07020 MONTI [OT]
TEL. 078943185

This estate has concentrated its efforts on Vermentino di Gallura and, given the results, it looks a good idea. The warm, fragrant, rounded Superiore Hysonj '06 tops the range. Graniti '06 has admirable softness. Le Conche '06 instead stands out for vivacity and freshness.

O Vermentino di Gallura Sup. Hysonj '06	♟♟ 5
O Vermentino di Gallura I Graniti '06	♟♟ 4*
O Vermentino di Sardegna Le Conche '06	♟ 4

Perda Rubia
VIA ASPRONI, 29
08100 NUORO [NU]
TEL. 0782615367
www.perdarubia.it

Perda Rubia is a long-standing Ogliastra estate that has always respected local traditions in its Cannonau production. Two wines were submitted, both Cannonau di Sardegna. The '03 is evolved and overripe but a little too warm on the palate. Mirei '05 is fresher but also more tannic.

● Cannonau di Sardegna Mirei '05	♟ 4
● Cannonau di Sardegna '03	♟ 4

Gigi Picciau
FRAZ. PIRRI
VIA ITALIA, 196
09134 CAGLIARI [CA]
TEL. 070560224
www.picciau.com

Gigi Picciau, who has always concentrated on indigenous varieties, returns to the Guide. The full, round Sardegna Semidano '06 has aromas of broom and is first-rate. The vegetal, savoury Nasco di Cagliari '02 is also sound. Vermentino di Sardegna '06 is floral and vegetal.

O Sardegna Semidano '06	♟♟ 3*
O Nasco di Cagliari '02	♟ 4
O Vermentino di Sardegna '06	♟ 3*

Josto Puddu
VIA SAN LUSSORIO, 1
09070 SAN VERO MILIS [OR]
TEL. 078353329
www.cantinapuddu.it

Tradition is no traitor, and so here we have a great Vernaccia di Oristano Riserva '02. Toasty, almondy notes dominate the intense nose and the palate is warm, rounded and long. Vermentino di Sardegna Maris '06 and Monica Torremora '05 are both well-made easy drinkers.

O Vernaccia di Oristano Ris. '02	♟♟ 4
● Monica di Sardegna Torremora '05	♟ 4
O Vermentino di Sardegna Maris '06	♟ 4

OTHER WINERIES

Giampietro Puggioni
VIA NUORO, 11
08024 MAMOIADA [NU]
TEL. 0784203516
www.cantinagiampietropuggioni.it

Giampiero Puggioni is a Cannonau man. His skills are apparent on Ilisi '04, which has a broad, pervasive nose of red berry fruits, spices, tobacco and mineral notes, and a full, juicy palate. But the fresher Lakana '05, with harmony and body, is also excellent. Mamuthone '05 is nicely fruity and vegetal.

● Cannonau di Sardegna Ilisi '04	ㅇㅇ 6*
● Cannonau di Sardegna Lakana '05	ㅇㅇ 4*
● Cannonau di Sardegna Mamuthone '05	ㅇ 4

Cooperativa Romangia
VIA MARINA, 5
07037 SORSO [SS]
TEL. 079351666
www.vinidellaromangia.it

Romangia is known for Cannonau and Moscato, less for Vermentino. But Romangia Bianco '06, from 100 per cent vermentino, is a distinctively full-bodied wine. Cannonau di Sardegna Noeddu '05 is also successful, with nose and palate balanced. The '06 Moscato di Sorso Sennori Tres Montes is as good as ever.

○ Moscato di Sorso Sennori Tres Montes '06	ㅇㅇ 5
○ Romangia Bianco '06	ㅇ 4
● Cannonau di Sardegna Noeddu '05	ㅇ 4

Tenute Silattari
LOC. SILATTARI
08013 BOSA [NU]
TEL. 3339599741
www.silattari.com

This new estate, run by youngsters determined to make high-quality, high-priced wine, makes its Guide debut. Ofelia '06, from malvasia della Planargia, has delicate aromas and a soft palate. Vendemmia Ottobre '06, also from malvasia, is full of ripe fruit, and is warm and succulent, finishing attractively.

○ Vendemmia Ottobre '06	ㅇㅇ 7
○ Ofelia '06	ㅇ 6

Cantina Tondini
LOC. SAN LEONARDO
07023 CALANGIANUS [OT]
TEL. 079661359
cantinatondini@tiscali.it

Tondini is a new estate still finding its feet. So far the wines are good, like Siddaju '04, from nebbiolo, cannonau and sangiovese aged in large old casks, which has a full nose and good balance. Taroni '06, from nebbiolo and cannonau, is good. Vermentino di Gallura Karagnani '06 is also pleasing on the palate.

● Siddaju '04	ㅇㅇ 7
○ Vermentino di Gallura Karagnani '06	ㅇ 5
● Taroni '06	ㅇ 4

Cantina Trexenta
V.LE PIEMONTE, 40
09040 SENORBÌ [CA]
TEL. 0709808863
www.cantina-trexenta.it

It's been a difficult year. The wines are many but not all are convincing. The warm, full Antigu '03, from cannonau and carignano, is interesting but closed and a bit oaky. The '03 Tanca su Conti, from carignano and cannonau, is better but not as good as in the past. Monica di Sardegna Duca di Mandas '05 is good.

● Altigu '03	ㅇ 5
● Tanca Su Conti '03	ㅇ 5
● Monica di Sardegna Duca di Mandas '05	ㅇ 2

Cantina del Vermentino
VIA SAN PAOLO, 1
07020 MONTI [OT]
TEL. 078944012
www.vermentinomonti.it

The wines here are as attractive as ever. Vermentino di Gallura Superiore Arakena '05 stands out with its nicely fruity nose, good body and length. The lively, balanced Abbaìa '06, from cannonau, monica, pascale and malaga; and Funtanaliras '06, with its stylish aromas, are both good.

○ Vermentino di Gallura Sup. Arakena '05	ㅇㅇ 6
○ Vermentino di Gallura Funtanaliras '06	ㅇ 5
● Abbaìa '06	ㅇ 3*

OTHER WINERIES

Cantina Sociale Cooperativa di Vernaccia

LOC. RIMEDIO - VIA ORISTANO, 149
09170 ORISTANO [OR]
TEL. 078333155
vinovernaccia@tiscali.it

This long-standing co-operative is driving for high quality and has the potential to bring increasing renown to the highly individual Vernaccia di Oristano. The '03 has the characteristic aroma of roasted hazelnuts, and a palate that's warm and soft but also offers good acid backbone.

O Vernaccia di Oristano '03	🍷🍷 3*

Villa di Quartu

VIA G. GARIBALDI, 90
09045 QUARTU SANT'ELENA [CA]
TEL. 070826997
www.villadiquartu.ory.it

Quality grows from enthusiasm. The proof is Yanna '04, from carignano and bovale, one of the year's best reds. It's a well-structured, full-bodied wine, its broad nose strongly led by tobacco and spices. Maripintau '06, all vermentino, and Cepola Rosso '05, from cannonau, monica, bovale and barbera, are good.

● Yanna '04	🍷🍷 6
● Cepola Rosso '05	🍷 4
O Maripintau '06	🍷 5

Virdis

VIA J. F. KENNEDY, 6
07049 USINI [SS]
TEL. 079380133
vitivinicola.virdis@tiscali.it

Quality is on an even keel at this small estate, known for its Cagnulari and Vermentino. Ammentos '04, from bush-trained cagnulari, is warm and ethery with liqueur fruit aromas and a slightly bitter finish. Virdis Bianco '04 has elegant aromas and makes for attractive drinking.

● Virdis Rosso Ammentos Monte Alvanu '04	🍷🍷 6
O Virdis Bianco Su Monte de S'Ulimu '04	🍷 5

Zarelli Vini

VIA VITTORIO EMANUELE, 36
08010 MAGOMADAS [NU]
TEL. 078535311
zarellivinisrl@libero.it

Raimondo Zarelli has decided to call his most important wine Malvasia di Bosa instead of Planargia, and he's no longer producing the sparkling version. The '04 is a warm, soft, long wine with aromas that range from dried fruit to almond blossom.

O Malvasia di Bosa '04	🍷🍷 5

PRODUCERS IN ALPHABETICAL ORDER

PRODUCERS BY REGION

PRODUCERS IN ALPHABETICAL ORDER

PRODUCERS BY REGION